THE DIALOGUES OF PLATO

JOWETT

This book is reprinted by arrangement with the Oxford University Press, and contains the complete text and marginal notes from the Third, and last, Edition of Jowett's translation of THE DIALOGUES OF PLATO

The Dialogues of Plato

TRANSLATED INTO ENGLISH BY

B. JOWETT, M. A.

MASTER OF BALLIOL COLLEGE · REGIUS PROFESSOR OF GREEK IN THE

UNIVERSITY OF OXFORD · DOCTOR IN THEOLOGY OF THE

UNIVERSITY OF LEYDEN

WITH AN INTRODUCTION BY

PROFESSOR RAPHAEL DEMOS

OF HARVARD UNIVERSITY

IN TWO VOLUMES

VOLUME TWO

RANDOM HOUSE · NEW YORK

Fifth Printing

TO MY FORMER PUPILS IN BALLIOL COLLEGE

AND IN THE UNIVERSITY OF OXFORD

WHO DURING FIFTY YEARS HAVE BEEN THE

BEST OF FRIENDS TO ME THESE VOLUMES ARE

INSCRIBED IN GRATEFUL RECOGNITION OF

THEIR NEVER FAILING ATTACHMENT

CONTENTS · VOLUME II

TIMAEUS

TIMAEUS

PERSONS OF THE DIALOGUE

SOCRATES   CRITIAS

TIMAEUS   HERMOCRATES

Socrates. ONE, two, three; but where, my dear Timaeus, is the fourth of those who were yesterday my guests and are to be my entertainers to-day?

Steph.
17
SOCRATES,
TIMAEUS.

Timaeus. He has been taken ill, Socrates; for he would not willingly have been absent from this gathering.

The appointed meeting.

Soc. Then, if he is not coming, you and the two others must supply his place.

Tim. Certainly, and we will do all that we can; having been handsomely entertained by you yesterday, those of us who remain should be only too glad to return your hospitality.

Soc. Do you remember what were the points of which I required you to speak?

The chief points in the Republic:—

Tim. We remember some of them, and you will be here to remind us of anything which we have forgotten: or rather, if we are not troubling you, will you briefly recapitulate the whole, and then the particulars will be more firmly fixed in our memories?

Soc. To be sure I will: the chief theme of my yesterday's discourse was the State—how constituted and of what citizens composed it would seem likely to be most perfect.

Tim. Yes, Socrates; and what you said of it was very much to our mind.

Soc. Did we not begin by separating the husbandmen and the artisans from the class of defenders of the State?

(1) Separation of classes.

Tim. Yes.

Soc. And when we had given to each one that single employment and particular art which was suited to his nature, we spoke of those who were intended to be our warriors, and said that they were to be guardians of the city against attacks from within as well as from without, and to have no other employment; they were to be merciful in judging their subjects, of whom they were by nature

(2) Division of labour.

18

friends, but fierce to their enemies, when they came across them in battle.

Tim. Exactly.

Soc. We said, if I am not mistaken, that the guardians should be gifted with a temperament in a high degree both passionate and philosophical; and that then they would be as they ought to be, gentle to their friends and fierce with their enemies.

Tim. Certainly.

Soc. And what did we say of their education? Were they not to be trained in gymnastic, and music, and all other sorts of knowledge which were proper for them [1]?

Tim. Very true.

Soc. And being thus trained they were not to consider gold or silver or anything else to be their own private property; they were to be like hired troops, receiving pay for keeping guard from those who were protected by them—the pay was to be no more than would suffice for men of simple life; and they were to spend in common, and to live together in the continual practice of virtue, which was to be their sole pursuit.

Tim. That was also said.

Soc. Neither did we forget the women; of whom we declared, that their natures should be assimilated and brought into harmony with those of the men, and that common pursuits should be assigned to them both in time of war and in their ordinary life.

Tim. That, again, was as you say.

Soc. And what about the procreation of children? Or rather was not the proposal too singular to be forgotten? for all wives and children were to be in common, to the intent that no one should ever know his own child, but they were to imagine that they were all one family; those who were within a suitable limit of age were to be brothers and sisters, those who were of an elder generation parents and grandparents, and those of a younger, children and grandchildren.

Tim. Yes, and the proposal is easy to remember, as you say.

Soc. And do you also remember how, with a view of securing as far as we could the best breed, we said that the chief magistrates, male and female, should contrive secretly, by the use of certain lots, so to arrange the nuptial meeting, that the bad of either sex and the good of either sex might pair with their like; and there was to be no quarrelling on this account, for they would imagine that the union was a mere accident, and was to be attributed to the lot?

Tim. I remember.

[1] Or 'which are akin to these;' or τούτοις may be taken with ἐν ἅπασι.

Soc. And you remember how we said that the children of the good parents were to be educated, and the children of the bad secretly dispersed among the inferior citizens; and while they were all growing up the rulers were to be on the look-out, and to bring up from below in their turn those who were worthy, and those among themselves who were unworthy were to take the places of those who came up?

Tim. True.

Soc. Then have I now given you all the heads of our yesterday's discussion? Or is there anything more, my dear Timaeus, which has been omitted?

Tim. Nothing, Socrates; it was just as you have said.

Soc. I should like, before proceeding further, to tell you how I feel about the State which we have described. I might compare myself to a person who, on beholding beautiful animals either created by the painter's art, or, better still, alive but at rest, is seized with a desire of seeing them in motion or engaged in some struggle or conflict to which their forms appear suited; this is my feeling about the State which we have been describing. There are conflicts which all cities undergo, and I should like to hear some one tell of our own city carrying on a struggle against her neighbours, and how she went out to war in a becoming manner, and when at war showed by the greatness of her actions and the magnanimity of her words in dealing with other cities a result worthy of her training and education. Now I, Critias and Hermocrates, am conscious that I myself should never be able to celebrate the city and her citizens in a befitting manner, and I am not surprised at my own incapacity; to me the wonder is rather that the poets present as well as past are no better—not that I mean to depreciate them; but every one can see that they are a tribe of imitators, and will imitate best and most easily the life in which they have been brought up; while that which is beyond the range of a man's education he finds hard to carry out in action, and still harder adequately to represent in language. I am aware that the Sophists have plenty of brave words and fair conceits, but I am afraid that being only wanderers from one city to another, and having never had habitations of their own, they may fail in their conception of philosophers and statesmen, and may not know what they do and say in time of war, when they are fighting or holding parley with their enemies. And thus people of your class are the only ones remaining who are fitted by nature and education to take part at once both in politics and philosophy. Here is Timaeus, of Locris in Italy, a city which has admirable laws, and who is himself in wealth and rank the equal of any of

Timaeus

19
SOCRATES,
TIMAEUS.

(9) Transposition of good and bad citizens.

Socrates desires to breathe life into his state; he would like to describe its infant struggles. But he has not the gift of description himself, and finds the poets equally incapable. The Sophists have no state of their own, and therefore are not politicians.

He turns to Timaeus, Critias and Hermocrates.

20

Timaeus

SOCRATES,
TIMAEUS,
HERMO-
    CRATES,
CRITIAS.

his fellow-citizens; he has held the most important and honourable offices in his own state, and, as I believe, has scaled the heights of all philosophy; and here is Critias, whom every Athenian knows to be no novice in the matters of which we are speaking; and as to Hermocrates, I am assured by many witnesses that his genius and education qualify him to take part in any speculation of the kind. And therefore yesterday when I saw that you wanted me to describe the formation of the State, I readily assented, being very well aware, that, if you only would, none were better qualified to carry the discussion further, and that when you had engaged our city in a suitable war, you of all men living could best exhibit her playing a fitting part. When I had completed my task, I in return imposed this other task upon you. You conferred together and agreed to entertain me to-day, as I had entertained you, with a feast of discourse. Here am I in festive array, and no man can be more ready for the promised banquet.

Hermocrates tells Socrates how Critias had narrated a story which may satisfy his demands.

Her. And we too, Socrates, as Timaeus says, will not be wanting in enthusiasm; and there is no excuse for not complying with your request. As soon as we arrived yesterday at the guest-chamber of Critias, with whom we are staying, or rather on our way thither, we talked the matter over, and he told us an ancient tradition, which I wish, Critias, that you would repeat to Socrates, so that he may help us to judge whether it will satisfy his requirements or not.

Crit. I will, if Timaeus, who is our other partner, approves.

Tim. I quite approve.

Critias consents to repeat it. He had heard the tale from his grand-

[21]

father, who received it from Solon. It told of the glories of ancient Athens.

Crit. Then listen, Socrates, to a tale which, though strange, is certainly true, having been attested by Solon, who was the wisest of the seven sages. He was a relative and a dear friend of my great-grandfather, Dropides, as he himself says in many passages of his poems; and he told the story to Critias, my grandfather, who remembered and repeated it to us. There were of old, he said, great and marvellous actions of the Athenian city, which have passed into oblivion through lapse of time and the destruction of mankind, and one in particular, greater than all the rest. This we will now rehearse. It will be a fitting monument of our gratitude to you, and a hymn of praise true and worthy of the goddess, on this her day of festival.

Soc. Very good. And what is this ancient famous action of the Athenians, [1] which Critias declared, on the authority of Solon, to be not a mere legend, but an actual fact [1]?

[1] Or 'which, though unrecorded in history, Critias declared, on the authority of Solon, to be an actual fact?'

Crit. I will tell an old-world story which I heard from an aged man; for Critias, at the time of telling it, was as he said, nearly ninety years of age, and I was about ten. Now the day was that day of the Apaturia which is called the Registration of Youth, at which, according to custom, our parents gave prizes for recitations, and the poems of several poets were recited by us boys, and many of us sang the poems of Solon, which at that time had not gone out of fashion. One of our tribe, either because he thought so or to please Critias, said that in his judgment Solon was not only the wisest of men, but also the noblest of poets. The old man, as I very well remember, brightened up at hearing this and said, smiling: Yes, Amynander, if Solon had only, like other poets, made poetry the business of his life, and had completed the tale which he brought with him from Egypt, and had not been compelled, by reason of the factions and troubles which he found stirring in his own country when he came home, to attend to other matters, in my opinion he would have been as famous as Homer or Hesiod, or any poet.

And what was the tale about, Critias? said Amynander.

About the greatest action which the Athenians ever did, and which ought to have been the most famous, but, through the lapse of time and the destruction of the actors, it has not come down to us.

Tell us, said the other, the whole story, and how and from whom Solon heard this veritable tradition.

He replied:—In the Egyptian Delta, at the head of which the river Nile divides, there is a certain district which is called the district of Sais, and the great city of the district is also called Sais, and is the city from which King Amasis came. The citizens have a deity for their foundress; she is called in the Egyptian tongue Neith, and is asserted by them to be the same whom the Hellenes call Athene; they are great lovers of the Athenians, and say that they are in some way related to them. To this city came Solon, and was received there with great honour; he asked the priests who were most skilful in such matters, about antiquity, and made the the discovery that neither he nor any other Hellene knew anything worth mentioning about the times of old. On one occasion, wishing to draw them on to speak of antiquity, he began to tell about the most ancient things in our part of the world—about Phoroneus, who is called 'the first man,' and about Niobe; and after the Deluge, of the survival of Deucalion and Pyrrha; and he traced the genealogy of their descendants, and reckoning up the dates, tried to compute how many years ago the events of which he was speaking

Timaeus

CRITIAS.

The priests of Sais declared the traditions of Egypt to be far older than those of Hellas,

23

because Greek history had been frequently interrupted by deluges.

happened. Thereupon one of the priests, who was of a very great age, sa.d: O Solon, Solon, you Hellenes are never anything but children, and there is not an old man among you. Solon in return asked him what he meant. I mean to say, he replied, that in mind you are all young; there is no old opinion handed down among you by ancient tradition, nor any science which is hoary with age. And I will tell you why. There have been, and will be again, many destructions of mankind arising out of many causes; the greatest have been brought about by the agencies of fire and water, and other lesser ones by innumerable other causes. There is a story, which even you have preserved, that once upon a time Phaëthon, the son of Helios, hav:ng yoked the steeds in his father's chariot, because he was not able to drive them in the path of his father, burnt up all that was upon the earth, and was himself destroyed by a thunderbolt. Now this has the form of a myth, but really signifies a declination of the bodies moving in the heavens around the earth, and a great conflagration of things upon the earth, which recurs after long intervals; at such times those who live upon the mountains and in dry and lofty places are more liable to destruction than those who dwell by rivers or on the seashore. And from this calamity the Nile, who is our never-failing saviour, delivers and preserves us. When, on the other hand, the gods purge the earth with a deluge of water, the survivors in your country are herdsmen and shepherds who dwell on the mountains, but those who, like you, live in cities are carried by the rivers into the sea. Whereas in this land, neither then nor at any other time, does the water come down from above on the fields, having always a tendency to come up from below; for which reason the traditions preserved here are the most ancient. The fact is, that wherever the extremity of winter frost or of summer sun does not prevent, mankind exist, sometimes in greater, sometimes in lesser numbers. And whatever happened either in your country or in ours, or in any other region of which we are informed—if there were any actions noble or great or in any other way remarkable, they have all been written down by us of old, and are preserved in our temples. Whereas just when you and other nations are beginning to be provided with letters and the other requisites of civilized life, after the usual interval, the stream from heaven, like a pestilence, comes pouring down, and leaves only those of you who are destitute of letters and education; and so you have to begin all over again like children, and know nothing of what happened in ancient times, either among us or among yourselves. As for those genealogies of yours which you just now recounted to us, Solon, they are no better than the tales of children.

In the first place you remember a single deluge only, but there were many previous ones; in the next place, you do not know that there formerly dwelt in your land the fairest and noblest race of men which ever lived, and that you and your whole city are descended from a small seed or remnant of them which survived. And this was unknown to you, because, for many generations, the survivors of that destruction died, leaving no written word. For there was a time, Solon, before the great deluge of all, when the city which now is Athens was first in war and in every way the best governed of all cities, and is said to have performed the noblest deeds and to have had the fairest constitution of any of which tradition tells, under the face of heaven. Solon marvelled at his words, and earnestly requested the priests to inform him exactly and in order about these former citizens. You are welcome to hear about them, Solon, said the priest, both for your own sake and for that of your city, and above all, for the sake of the goddess who is the common patron and parent and educator of both our cities. She founded your city a thousand years before ours [1], receiving from the Earth and Hephaestus the seed of your race, and afterwards she founded ours, of which the constitution is recorded in our sacred registers to be 8000 years old. As touching your citizens of 9000 years ago, I will briefly inform you of their laws and of their most famous action; the exact particulars of the whole we will hereafter go through at our leisure in the sacred registers themselves. If you compare these very laws with ours you will find that many of ours are the counterpart of yours as they were in the olden time. In the first place, there is the caste of priests, which is separated from all the others; next, there are the artificers, who ply their several crafts by themselves and do not intermix; and also there is the class of shepherds and of hunters [2], as well as that of husbandmen; and you will observe, too, that the warriors in Egypt are distinct from all the other classes, and are commanded by the law to devote themselves solely to military pursuits; moreover, the weapons which they carry are shields and spears, a style of equipment which the goddess taught of Asiatics first to us, as in your part of the world first to you. Then as to wisdom, do you observe how our law from the very first made a study of the whole order of things, extending even to prophecy and medicine which gives health, out of these divine elements deriving what was needful for human life, and adding every sort of knowledge which was akin to them. All this order

Timaeus
CRITIAS.

Athens one thousand years more ancient than Sais. [24] The goddess Athene was the foundress of both: this explains the similarity of their institutions.

---

[1] Observe that Plato gives the same date (9000 years ago) for the foundation of Athens and for the repulse of the invasion from Atlantis. (Crit. 108 E).

[2] Reading τὸ τῶν θηρευτῶν.

Timaeus
CRITIAS.

and arrangement the goddess first imparted to you when establishing your city; and she chose the spot of earth in which you were born, because she saw that the happy temperament of the seasons in that land would produce the wisest of men. Wherefore the goddess, who was a lover both of war and of wisdom, selected and first of all settled that spot which was the most likely to produce men likest herself. And there you dwelt, having such laws as these and still better ones, and excelled all mankind in all virtue, as became the children and disciples of the gods.

The most glorious act of ancient Athens was the deliverance of Europe and Libya [25] from the power of Atlantis.

Many great and wonderful deeds are recorded of your state in our histories. But one of them exceeds all the rest in greatness and valour. For these histories tell of a mighty power which unprovoked made an expedition against the whole of Europe and Asia, and to which your city put an end. This power came forth out of the Atlantic Ocean, for in those days the Atlantic was navigable; and there was an island situated in front of the straits which are by you called the pillars of Heracles; the island was larger than Libya and Asia put together, and was the way to other islands, and from these you might pass to the whole of the opposite continent which surrounded the true ocean; for this sea which is within the Straits of Heracles is only a harbour, having a narrow entrance, but that other is a real sea, and the surrounding land may be most truly called a boundless continent. Now in this island of Atlantis there was a great and wonderful empire which had rule over the whole island and several others, and over parts of the continent, and, furthermore, the men of Atlantis had subjected the parts of Libya within the columns of Heracles as far as Egypt, and of Europe as far as Tyrrhenia. This vast power, gathered into one, endeavoured to sudue at a blow our country and yours and the whole of the region within the straits; and then, Solon, your country shone forth, in the excellence of her virtue and strength, among all mankind. She was pre-eminent in courage and military skill, and was the leader of the Hellenes. And when the rest fell off from her, being compelled to stand alone, after having undergone the very extremity of danger, she defeated and triumphed over the invaders, and preserved from slavery those who were not yet subjugated, and generously liberated all the rest of us who dwell within the pillars.

Soon afterwards both empires disappeared.

But afterwards there occurred violent earthquakes and floods; and in a single day and night of misfortune all your warlike men in a body sank into the earth, and the island of Atlantis in like manner disappeared in the depths of the sea. For which reason the sea in those parts is impassable and impenetrable, because there is a shoal of mud in the way; and this was caused by the subsidence of the island.

I have told you briefly, Socrates, what the aged Critias heard from Solon and related to us. And when you were speaking yesterday about your city and citizens, the tale which I have just been repeating to you came into my mind, and I remarked with astonishment how, by some mysterious coincidence, you agreed in almost every particular with the narrative of Solon; but I did not like to speak at the moment. For a long time had elapsed, and I had forgotten too much; I thought that I must first of all run over the narrative in my own mind, and then I would speak. And so I readily assented to your request yesterday, considering that in all such cases the chief difficulty is to find a tale suitable to our purpose, and that with such a tale we should be fairly well provided.

And therefore, as Hermocrates has told you, on my way home yesterday I at once communicated the tale to my companions as I remembered it; and after I left them, during the night by thinking I recovered nearly the whole of it. Truly, as is often said, the lessons of our childhood make a wonderful impression on our memories; for I am not sure that I could remember all the discourse of yesterday, but I should be much surprised if I forgot any of these things which I have heard very long ago. I listened at the time with childlike interest to the old man's narrative; he was very ready to teach me, and I asked him again and again to repeat his words, so that like an indelible picture they were branded into my mind. As soon as the day broke, I rehearsed them as he spoke them to my companions, that they, as well as myself, might have something to say. And now, Socrates, to make an end of my preface, I am ready to tell you the whole tale. I will give you not only the general heads, but the particulars, as they were told to me. The city and citizens, which you yesterday described to us in fiction, we will now transfer to the world of reality. It shall be the ancient city of Athens, and we will suppose that the citizens whom you imagined, were our veritable ancestors, of whom the priest spoke; they will perfectly harmonize, and there will be no inconsistency in saying that the citizens of your republic are these ancient Athenians. Let us divide the subject among us, and all endeavour according to our ability gracefully to execute the task which you have imposed upon us. Consider then, Socrates, if this narrative is suited to the purpose, or whether we should seek for some other instead.

Soc. And what other, Critias, can we find that will be better than this, which is natural and suitable to the festival of the god-

Timaeus

SOCRATES, CRITIAS.

The arrangements of the ideal state recalled to [26] Critias' mind the narrative of Solon.

Socrates is satisfied that

Timaeus

27

SOCRATES,
TIMAEUS,
CRITIAS.

the re-
hearsal of
this nar-
rative
will be a
suitable
continu-
ation of
the dis-
cussion.

But Ti-
maeus
will begin
the feast
by de-
scribing
the gen-
eration of
the
Universe
down to
the cre-
ation of
man:
Critias
will fol-
low him.

At the
com-
mence-
ment
Timaeus
invokes
the gods.

28

dess, and has the very great advantage of being a fact and not a fiction? How or where shall we find another if we abandon this? We cannot, and therefore you must tell the tale, and good luck to you; and I in return for my yesterday's discourse will now rest and be a listener.

Crit. Let me proceed to explain to you, Socrates, the order in which we have arranged our entertainment. Our intention is, that Timaeus, who is the most of an astronomer amongst us, and has made the nature of the universe his special study, should speak first, beginning with the generation of the world and going down to the creation of man; next, I am to receive the men whom he has created of whom some will have profited by the excellent education which you have given them; and then, in accordance with the tale of Solon, and equally with his law, we will bring them into court and make them citizens, as if they were those very Athenians whom the sacred Egyptian record has recovered from oblivion, and thenceforward we will speak of them as Athenians and fellow-citizens.

Soc. I see that I shall receive in my turn a perfect and splendid feast of reason. And now, Timaeus, you, I suppose, should speak next, after duly calling upon the Gods.

Tim. All men, Socrates, who have any degree of right feeling, at the beginning of every enterprise, whether small or great, always call upon God. And we, too, who are going to discourse of the nature of the universe, how created or how existing without creation, if we be not altogether out of our wits, must invoke the aid of Gods and Goddesses and pray that our words may be acceptable to them and consistent with themselves. Let this, then, be our invocation of the Gods, to which I add an exhortation of myself to speak in such manner as will be most intelligible to you, and will most accord with my own intent.

First then, in my judgment, we must make a distinction and ask, What is that which always is and has no becoming; and what is that which is always becoming and never is? That which is appre-hended by intelligence and reason is always in the same state; but that which is conceived by opinion with the help of sensation and without reason, is always in a process of becoming and perishing and never really is. Now everything that becomes or is created must of necessity be created by some cause, for without a cause nothing can be created. The work of the creator, whenever he looks to the unchangeable and fashions the form and nature of his work after an unchangeable pattern, must necessarily be made fair and perfect; but when he looks to the created only, and uses a created pattern, it is not fair or perfect. Was the heaven then or the world, whether called by this or by any other more appropriate name— assuming the name, I am asking a question which has to be asked at the beginning of an enquiry about anything—was the world, I say, always in existence and without beginning? or created, and had it a beginning? Created, I reply, being visible and tangible and having a body, and therefore sensible; and all sensible things are apprehended by opinion and sense and are in a process of crea- tion and created. Now that which is created must, as we affirm, of necessity be created by a cause. But the father and maker of all this universe is past finding out; and even if we found him, to tell of him to all men would be impossible. And there is still a question to be asked about him: Which of the patterns had the artificer in view when he made the world,—the pattern of the unchangeable, or of that which is created? If the world be indeed fair and the artificer good, it is manifest that he must have looked to that which is eternal; but if what cannot be said without blasphemy is true, then to the created pattern. Every one will see that he must have looked to the eternal; for the world is the fairest of creations and he is the best of causes. And having been created in this way, the world has been framed in the likeness of that which is apprehended by reason and mind and is unchangeable, and must therefore of necessity, if this is admitted, be a copy of something. Now it is all- important that the beginning of everything should be according to nature. And in speaking of the copy and the original we may as- sume that words are akin to the matter which they describe; when they relate to the lasting and permanent and intelligible, they ought to be lasting and unalterable, and, as far as their nature allows, irrefutable and immovable—nothing less. But when they express only the copy or likeness and not the eternal things themselves, they need only be likely and analogous to the real words. As being is to becoming, so is truth to belief. If then, Socrates, amid the many opinions about the gods and the generation of the universe, we are not able to give notions which are altogether and in every respect exact and consistent with one another, do not be surprised. Enough, if we adduce probabilities as likely as any others; for we must remember that I who am the speaker, and you who are the judges, are only mortal men, and we ought to accept the tale which is probable and enquire no further.

Soc. Excellent, Timaeus; and we will do precisely as you bid us. The prelude is charming, and is already accepted by us—may we beg of you to proceed to the strain?

Tim. Let me tell you then why the creator made this world of

Timaeus

SOCRATES,
TIMAEUS.

The world was cre- ated, and is there- fore ap- prehend- ed by sense.

God was the cause of it, and he fashioned [29] it after the eter- nal pat- tern.

The eter- nal pat- tern can be spoken of with certainty; the creat- ed copy can only be de- scribed in the lan- guage of probabil- ity.

God
made the
world
good,
wishing
every-
thing to
be like
himself.
To this
end he
brought
order into
it and
endowed
it with
soul and
intelli-
gence.

The
original
of the
universe
is a per-
fect ani-
mal,
which
compre-
hends all
intelli-
gible ani-
mals, just
as the
copy con-
[31]
tains all
visible
animals.

generation. He was good, and the good can never have any jealousy of anything. And being free from jealousy, he desired that
all things should be as like himself as they could be. This is in
the truest sense the origin of creation and of the world, as we shall
do well in believing on the testimony of wise men: God desired that
all things should be good and nothing bad, so far as this was attainable. Wherefore also finding the whole visible sphere not at
rest, but moving in an irregular and disorderly fashion, out of disorder he brought order, considering that this was in every way
better than the other. Now the deeds of the best could never be or
have been other than the fairest; and the creator, reflecting on the
things which are by nature visible, found that no unintelligent
creature taken as a whole was fairer than the intelligent taken as a
whole; and that intelligence could not be present in anything
which was devoid of soul. For which reason, when he was framing
the universe, he put intelligence in soul, and soul in body, that he
might be the creator of a work which was by nature fairest and
best. Wherefore, using the language of probability, we may say
that the world became a living creature truly endowed with soul
and intelligence by the providence of God.

This being supposed, let us proceed to the next stage: In the
likeness of what animal did the Creator make the world? It would
be an unworthy thing to liken it to any nature which exists as a
part only; for nothing can be beautiful which is like any imperfect
thing; but let us suppose the world to be the very image of that
whole of which all other animals both individually and in their
tribes are portions. For the original of the universe contains in
itself all intelligible beings, just as this world comprehends us and
all other visible creatures. For the Deity, intending to make this
world like the fairest and most perfect of intelligible beings, framed
one visible animal comprehending within itself all other animals of
a kindred nature. Are we right in saying that there is one world, or
that they are many and infinite? There must be one only, if the
created copy is to accord with the original. For that which includes
all other intelligible creatures cannot have a second or companion;
in that case there would be need of another living being which
would include both, and of which they would be parts, and the
likeness would be more truly said to resemble not them, but that
other which included them. In order then that the world might be
solitary, like the perfect animal, the creator made not two worlds
or an infinite number of them; but there is and ever will be one
only-begotten and created heaven.

Now that which is created is of necessity corporeal, and also

visible and tangible. And nothing is visible where there is no fire,
or tangible which has no solidity, and nothing is solid without
earth. Wherefore also God in the beginning of creation made the
body of the universe to consist of fire and earth. But two things
cannot be rightly put together without a third; there must be
some bond of union between them. And the fairest bond is that
which makes the most complete fusion of itself and the things
which it combines; and proportion is best adapted to effect such
a union. For whenever in any three numbers, whether cube or
square, there is a mean, which is to the last term what the first
term is to it; and again, when the mean is to the first term as the
last term is to the mean,—then the mean becoming first and last,
and the first and last both becoming means, they will all of them of
necessity come to be the same, and having become the same with
one another will be all one. If the universal frame had been created
a surface only and having no depth, a single mean would have sufficed to bind together itself and the other terms; but now, as the
world must be solid, and solid bodies are always compacted not
by one mean but by two, God placed water and air in the mean between fire and earth, and made them to have the same proportion
so far as was possible (as fire is to air so is air to water, and as air
is to water so is water to earth); and thus he bound and put together a visible and tangible heaven. And for these reasons, and out
of such elements which are in number four, the body of the world
was created, and it was harmonized by proportion, and therefore
has the spirit of friendship; and having been reconciled to itself,
it was indissoluble by the hand of any other than the framer.

Now the creation took up the whole of each of the four elements;
for the Creator compounded the world out of all the fire and all
the water and all the air and all the earth, leaving no part of any
of them nor any power of them outside. His intention was, in the
first place, that the animal should be as far as possible a perfect
whole and of perfect parts: secondly, that it should be one, leaving
no remnants out of which another such world might be created:
and also that it should be free from old age and unaffected by
disease. Considering that if heat and cold and other powerful
forces which unite bodies surround and attack them from without
when they are unprepared, they decompose them, and by bringing
diseases and old age upon them, make them waste away—for this
cause and on these grounds he made the world one whole, having
every part entire, and being therefore perfect and not liable to old
age and disease. And he gave to the world the figure which was
suitable and also natural. Now to the animal which was to com-

which
could
hurt or
destroy
it.

It re-
ceived a
spherical
form,—
without
eyes, ears,
mouth,
hands,
feet, and
was made
to revolve
in a cir-
cle on the
the same
spot.

34

In the
centre
was
placed the
soul,
which
pervaded
the whole,
and even
surround-
ed it.

Though
posterior
to the

prehend all animals, that figure was suitable which comprehends within itself all other figures. Wherefore he made the world in the form of a globe, round as from a lathe, having its extremes in every direction equidistant from the centre, the most perfect and the most like itself of all figures; for he considered that the like is infinitely fairer than the unlike. This he finished off, making the surface smooth all around for many reasons; in the first place, because the living being had no need of eyes when there was nothing remaining outside him to be seen; nor of ears when there was nothing to be heard; and there was no surrounding atmosphere to be breathed; nor would there have been any use of organs by the help of which he might receive his food or get rid of what he had already digested, since there was nothing which went from him or came into him: for there was nothing beside him. Of design he was created thus, his own waste providing his own food, and all that he did or suffered taking place in and by himself. For the Creator conceived that a being which was self-sufficient would be far more excellent than one which lacked anything; and, as he had no need to take anything or defend himself against any one, the Creator did not think it necessary to bestow upon him hands: nor had he any need of feet, nor of the whole apparatus of walking; but the movement suited to his spherical form was assigned to him, being of all the seven that which is most appropriate to mind and intelligence; and he was made to move in the same manner and on the same spot, within his own limits revolving in a circle. All the other six motions were taken away from him, and he was made not to partake of their deviations. And as this circular movement required no feet, the universe was created without legs and without feet.

Such was the whole plan of the eternal God about the god that was to be, to whom for this reason he gave a body, smooth and even, having a surface in every direction equidistant from the centre, a body entire and perfect, and formed out of perfect bodies. And in the centre he put the soul, which he diffused throughout the body, making it also to be the exterior environment of it; and he made the universe a circle moving in a circle, one and solitary, yet by reason of its excellence able to converse with itself, and needing no other friendship or acquaintance. Having these purposes in view he created the world a blessed god.

Now God did not make the soul after the body, although we are speaking of them in this order; for having brought them together he would never have allowed that the elder should be ruled by the younger; but this is a random manner of speaking which we have, because somehow we ourselves too are very much under the dominion of chance. Whereas he made the soul in origin and excellence prior to and older than the body, to be the ruler and mistress, of whom the body was to be the subject. And he made her out of the following elements and on this wise: Out of the indivisible and unchangeable, and also out of that which is divisible and has to do with material bodies, he compounded a third and intermediate kind of essence, partaking of the nature of the same [1] and of the other, and this compound he placed accordingly in a mean between the indivisible, and the divisible and material. He took the three elements of the same, the other, and the essence, and mingled them into one form, compressing by force the reluctant and unsociable nature of the other into the same. When he had mingled them with the essence and out of three made one, he again divided this whole into as many portions as was fitting, each portion being a compound of the same, the other, and the essence. And he proceeded to divide after this manner:— First of all, he took away one part of the whole [1], and then he separated a second part which was double the first [2], and then he took away a third part which was half as much again as the second and three times as much as the first [3], and then he took a fourth part which was twice as much as the second [4], and a fifth part which was three times the third [9], and a sixth part which was eight times the first [8], and a seventh part which was twenty-seven times the first [27]. After this he filled up the double intervals [i. e. between 1, 2, 4, 8] and the triple [i. e. between 1, 3, 9, 27], cutting off yet other portions from the mixture and placing them in the intervals, so that in each interval there were two kinds of means, the one exceeding and exceeded by equal parts of its extremes [as for example 1, $\frac{4}{3}$, 2, in which the mean $\frac{4}{3}$ is one-third of 1 more than 1, and one-third of 2 less than 2], the other being that kind of mean which exceeds and is exceeded by an equal number [2]. Where there were intervals of $\frac{3}{2}$ and of $\frac{4}{3}$ and of $\frac{9}{8}$, made by the connecting terms in the former intervals, he filled up all the intervals of $\frac{4}{3}$ with the interval of $\frac{9}{8}$, leaving a fraction over; and the interval which this fraction expressed was in the ratio of 256 to 243 [3]. And thus the whole mixture out of which he cut these portions was all exhausted by him. This entire compound he divided lengthways into two parts, which

TIMAEUS.

35
body in the order of our exposition, in the order of creation it is prior to it.

It was created thus. First out of the indivisible (i.e. the Same) and the divisible (i. e. the Other) God made Essence. He then mingled these [36] three elements and divided the whole mixture into parts, according to the proportions of the Pythagorean Tetractys and of the Diatonic scale.

[1] Omitting αὖ πέρι.

[2] e.g. $\overline{1, \frac{4}{3}, \frac{3}{2}, 2}, \frac{8}{3}, 3, \overline{4, \frac{16}{3}}, 6, \overline{8}$; and

$\overline{1, \frac{3}{2}}, 2, \overline{3, \frac{9}{2}}, 6, \overline{9, \frac{27}{2}}, 18, 27$.

[3] e.g. $243 : 256 :: \frac{81}{64} : \frac{4}{3} :: \frac{243}{128} : 2 :: \frac{81}{32} : \frac{8}{3} :: \frac{243}{64} : 4 :: \frac{81}{16} : \frac{16}{3} :: \frac{243}{32} : 8$.

(MARTIN.)

Timaeus

TIMAEUS.

The com-
pound
was cut
into two
strips,
which
were
crossed
and then
bent
round
into an
outer
circle,
revolving
to the
right
(i. e. the
circle of
the
Same),
and an
inner,
revolving
diagon-
ally
to the left
(i.e. the
[37]
circle of
the
Other).
The latter
was sub-
divided
into seven
unequal
circles
(i.e. the
orbits of
the seven
planets).

After
framing
the soul,
God
formed
within
her the
body of
the uni-
verse.

he joined to one another at the centre like the letter X, and bent them into a circular form, connecting them with themselves and each other at the point opposite to their original meeting-point; and, comprehending them in a uniform revolution upon the same axis, he made the one the outer and the other the inner circle. Now the motion of the outer circle he called the motion of the same, and the motion of the inner circle the motion of the other or diverse. The motion of the same he carried round by the side [1] to the right, and the motion of the diverse diagonally [2] to the left. And he gave dominion to the motion of the same and like, for that he left single and undivided; but the inner motion he divided in six places and made seven unequal circles having their intervals in ratios of two and three, three of each, and bade the orbits proceed in a direction opposite to one another; and three [Sun, Mercury, Venus] he made to move with equal swiftness, and the remaining four [Moon, Saturn, Mars, Jupiter] to move with unequal swiftness to the three and to one another, but in due proportion.

Now when the Creator had framed the soul according to his will, he formed within her the corporeal universe, and brought the two together, and united them centre to centre. The soul, interfused everywhere from the centre to the circumference of heaven, of which also she is the external envelopment, herself turning in herself, began a divine beginning of never-ceasing and rational life enduring throughout all time. The body of heaven is visible, but the soul is invisible, and partakes of reason and harmony, and being made by the best of intellectual and everlasting natures, is the best of things created. And because she is composed of the same and of the other and of the essence, these three, and is divided and united in due proportion, and in her revolutions returns upon herself, the soul, when touching anything which has essence, whether dispersed in parts or undivided, is stirred through all her powers, to declare the sameness or difference of that thing and some other; and to what individuals are related, and by what affected, and in what way and how and when, both in the world of generation and in the world of immutable being. And when reason, which works with equal truth, whether she be in the circle of the diverse or of the same—in voiceless silence holding her onward course in the sphere of the self-moved—when reason, I say, is hovering around the sensible world and when the circle of the diverse also moving truly imparts the intimations of sense to the whole soul,

[1] i. e. of the rectangular figure supposed to be inscribed in the circle of the Same.

[2] i. e. across the rectangular figure from corner to corner.

then arise opinions and beliefs sure and certain. But when reason is concerned with the rational, and the circle of the same moving smoothly declares it, then intelligence and knowledge are necessarily perfected. And if any one affirms that in which these two are found to be other than the soul, he will say the very opposite of the truth.

When the father and creator saw the creature which he had made moving and living, the created image of the eternal gods, he rejoiced, and in his joy determined to make the copy still more like the original; and as this was eternal, he sought to make the universe eternal, so far as might be. Now the nature of the ideal being was everlasting, but to bestow this attribute in its fulness upon a creature was impossible. Wherefore he resolved to have a moving image of eternity, and when he set in order the heaven, he made this image eternal but moving according to number, while eternity itself rests in unity; and this image we call time. For there were no days and nights and months and years before the heaven was created, but when he constructed the heaven he created them also. They are all parts of time, and the past and future are created species of time, which we unconsciously but wrongly transfer to the eternal essence; for we say that he 'was,' he 'is,' he 'will be,' but the truth is that 'is' alone is properly attributed to him, and that 'was' and 'will be' are only to be spoken of becoming in time, for they are motions, but that which is immovably the same cannot become older or younger by time, nor ever did or has become, or hereafter will be, older or younger, nor is subject at all to any of those states which affect moving and sensible things and of which generation is the cause. These are the forms of time, which imitates eternity and revolves according to a law of number. Moreover, when we say that what has become *is* become and what becomes *is* becoming, and that what will become *is* about to become and that the non-existent *is* non-existent,—all these are inaccurate modes of expression [1]. But perhaps this whole subject will be more suitably discussed on some other occasion.

Time, then, and the heaven came into being at the same instant in order that, having been created together, if ever there was to be a dissolution of them, they might be dissolved together. It was framed after the pattern of the eternal nature, that it might resemble this as far as was possible; for the pattern exists from eternity, and the created heaven has been, and is, and will be, in all time. Such was the mind and thought of God in the creation of time. The sun and moon and five other stars, which are called the plan-

[1] Cp. Parmen. 141.

Timaeus

TIMAEUS.

which is
immove-
able. The
modes of
time are
not to be
applied
to the
eternal
essence.

The seven
planets
were in-
tended to
preserve
the num-
bers of
time.

The circle
of the
[39]
Same
controls
the circle
of the
Other,
which
moves
diagonal-
ly to it.
Thus the
planets in
their re-
volutions
describe
spirals,
and the
slowest
seem to
overtake
the fast-
est.

The sun
was cre-
ated to
afford a
visible
measure
of the
swiftness
of the
planets.

ets, were created by him in order to distinguish and preserve the numbers of time; and when he had made their several bodies, he placed them in the orbits in which the circle of the other was revolving (cp. 36 D),—in seven orbits seven stars. First, there was the moon in the orbit nearest the earth, and next the sun, in the second orbit above the earth; then came the morning star and the star sacred to Hermes, moving in orbits which have an equal swiftness with the sun, but in an opposite direction; and this is the reason why the sun and Hermes and Lucifer overtake and are overtaken by each other. To enumerate the places which he assigned to the other stars, and to give all the reasons why he assigned them, although a secondary matter, would give more trouble than the primary. These things at some future time, when we are at leisure, may have the consideration which they deserve, but not at present.

Now, when all the stars which were necessary to the creation of time had attained a motion suitable to them, and had become living creatures having bodies fastened by vital chains, and learnt their appointed task, moving in the motion of the diverse, which is diagonal, and passes through and is governed by the motion of the same, they revolved, some in a larger and some in a lesser orbit,—those which had the lesser orbit revolving faster, and those which had the larger more slowly. Now by reason of the motion of the same, those which revolved fastest appeared to be overtaken by those which moved slower although they really overtook them; for the motion of the same made them all turn in a spiral, and, because some went one way and some another, that which receded most slowly from the sphere of the same, which was the swiftest, appeared to follow it most nearly. That there might be some visible measure of their relative swiftness and slowness as they proceeded in their eight courses, God lighted a fire, which we now call the sun, in the second from the earth of these orbits; that it might give light to the whole of heaven, and that the animals, as many as nature intended, might participate in number, learning arithmetic from the revolution of the same and the like. Thus, then, and for this reason the night and the day were created, being the period of the one most intelligent revolution. And the month is accomplished when the moon has completed her orbit and overtaken the sun, and the year when the sun has completed his own orbit. Mankind, with hardly an exception, have not remarked the periods of the other stars, and they have no name for them, and do not measure them against one another by the help of number, and hence they can scarcely be said to know that their wanderings, being infinite in number and admirable for their variety, make up time. And yet there is no difficulty in seeing that the perfect number of time fulfils the perfect year when all the eight revolutions, having their relative degrees of swiftness, are accomplished together and attain their completion at the same time, measured by the rotation of the same and equally moving. After this manner, and for these reasons, came into being such of the stars as in their heavenly progress received reversals of motion, to the end that the created heaven might imitate the eternal nature, and be as like as possible to the perfect and intelligible animal.

Thus far and until the birth of time the created universe was made in the likeness of the original, but inasmuch as all animals were not yet comprehended therein, it was still unlike. What remained, the creator then proceeded to fashion after the nature of the pattern. Now as in the ideal animal the mind perceives ideas or species of a certain nature and number, he thought that this created animal ought to have species of a like nature and number. There are four such; one of them is the heavenly race of the gods; another, the race of birds whose way is in the air; the third, the watery species; and the fourth, the pedestrian and land creatures. Of the heavenly and divine, he created the greater part out of fire, that they might be the brightest of all things and fairest to behold, and he fashioned them after the likeness of the universe in the figure of a circle, and made them follow the intelligent motion of the supreme, distributing them over the whole circumference of heaven, which was to be a true cosmos or glorious world spangled with them all over. And he gave to each of them two movements: the first, a movement on the same spot after the same manner, whereby they ever continue to think consistently the same thoughts about the same things; the second, a forward movement, in which they are controlled by the revolution of the same and the like; but by the other five motions they were unaffected (cp. 43 B), in order that each of them might attain the highest perfection. And for this reason the fixed stars were created, to be divine and eternal animals, ever-abiding and revolving after the same manner and on the same spot; and the other stars which reverse their motion and are subject to deviations of this kind, were created in the manner already described. The earth, which is our nurse, clinging [1] around the pole which is extended through the universe, he framed to be the guardian and artificer of night and day, first and eldest of gods that are in the interior of heaven. Vain would be the attempt to tell all the figures of them circling as in dance, and their juxtaposi-

[1] Or 'circling.'

Timaeus

TIMAEUS.

Night and day.
The month and year.

The cyclic year.

After the creation of time God fashions in the created animal four species [40] like those which exist in the ideal: e.g. the gods of heaven (i.e. fixed stars and planets), birds, sea and land animals.

The fixed stars revolve on their axes and are carried round in the sphere of the Same. The motions of the planets have been already (38 ff.) described. The earth is the im-

Timaeus

TIMAEUS.

move-
able (?)
centre of
the uni-
verse.

tions, and the return of them in their revolutions upon themselves, and their approximations, and to say which of these deities in their conjunctions meet, and which of them are in opposition, and in what order they get behind and before one another, and when they are severally eclipsed to our sight and again reappear, sending terrors and intimations of the future to those who cannot calculate their movements—to attempt to tell of all this without a visible representation of the heavenly system [1] would be labour in vain. Enough on this head; and now let what we have said about the nature of the created and visible gods have an end.

As for
the Gods
of myth-
ology, we
must
accept the
state-
ments of
their chil-
dren
about
them.

To know or tell the origin of the other divinities is beyond us, and we must accept the traditions of the men of old time who affirm themselves to be the offspring of the gods—that is what they say—and they must surely have known their own ancestors. How can we doubt the word of the children of the gods? Although they give no probable or certain proofs, still, as they declare that they are speaking of what took place in their own family, we must conform to custom and believe them. In this manner, then, according to them, the genealogy of these gods is to be received and set forth.

41

Oceanus and Tethys were the children of Earth and Heaven, and from these sprang Phorcys and Cronos and Rhea, and all that generation; and from Cronos and Rhea sprang Zeus and Herè, and all those who are said to be their brethren, and others who were the children of these.

The cre-
ator of
the uni-
verse bids
the creat-
ed gods
fashion
the mor-
tal bodies
of man
and of the
lower
animals:
he himself
will fur-
nish the
immortal
principle
of the
soul.

Now, when all of them, both those who visibly appear in their revolutions as well as those other gods who are of a more retiring nature, had come into being, the creator of the universe addressed them in these words: 'Gods, children of gods, who are my works, and of whom I am the artificer and father, my creations are indissoluble, if so I will. All that is bound may be undone, but only an evil being would wish to undo that which is harmonious and happy. Wherefore, since ye are but creatures, ye are not altogether immortal and indissoluble, but ye shall certainly not be dissolved, nor be liable to the fate of death, having in my will a greater and mightier bond than those with which ye were bound at the time of your birth. And now listen to my instructions:—Three tribes of mortal beings remain to be created—without them the universe will be incomplete, for it will not contain every kind of animal which it ought to contain, if it is to be perfect. On the other hand, if they were created by me and received life at my hands, they would be on an equality with the gods. In order then that they may be mortal, and that this universe may be truly universal, do

[1] Reading τοῖς οὐ δυν. and τούτων αὐτῶν.

ye, according to your natures, betake yourselves to the formation of animals, imitating the power which was shown by me in creating you. The part of them worthy of the name immortal, which is called divine and is the guiding principle of those who are willing to follow justice and you—of that divine part I will myself sow the seed, and having made a beginning, I will hand the work over to you. And do ye then interweave the mortal with the immortal, and make and beget living creatures, and give them food, and make them to grow, and receive them again in death.'

Thus he spake, and once more into the cup in which he had previously mingled the soul of the universe he poured the remains of the elements, and mingled them in much the same manner; they were not, however, pure as before, but diluted to the second and third degree. And having made it he divided the whole mixture into souls equal in number to the stars, and assigned each soul to a star; and having there placed them as in a chariot, he showed them the nature of the universe, and declared to them the laws of destiny, according to which their first birth would be one and the same for all,—no one should suffer a disadvantage at his hands; they were to be sown in the instruments of time severally adapted to them, and to come forth the most religious of animals; and as human nature was of two kinds, the superior race would hereafter be called man. Now, when they should be implanted in bodies by necessity, and be always gaining or losing some part of their bodily substance, then in the first place it would be necessary that they should all have in them one and the same faculty of sensation, arising out of irresistible impressions; in the second place, they must have love, in which pleasure and pain mingle; also fear and anger, and the feelings which are akin or opposite to them; if they conquered these they would live righteously, and if they were conquered by them, unrighteously. He who lived well during his appointed time was to return and dwell in his native star, and there he would have a blessed and congenial existence. But if he failed in attaining this, at the second birth he would pass into a woman, and if, when in that state of being, he did not desist from evil, he would continually be changed into some brute who resembled him in the evil nature which he had acquired, and would not cease from his toils and transformations until he followed the revolution of the same and the like within him, and overcame by the help of reason the turbulent and irrational mob of later accretions, made up of fire and air and water and earth, and returned to the form of his first and better state. Having given all these laws to his creatures, that he might be guiltless of future evil in any of

He makes the human soul of the same elements as the universal; and having distributed it into souls equal in number [42] to the stars, sets one soul in each star and reveals to them their future life on the planets, when they will have mortal bodies.

Those who then live well will return to their original star; those who live badly will take a lower

form at
their next
birth.

them, the creator sowed some of them in the earth, and some in the moon, and some in the other instruments of time; and when he had sown them he committed to the younger gods the fashioning of their mortal bodies, and desired them to furnish what was still lacking to the human soul, and having made all the suitable additions, to rule over them, and to pilot the mortal animal in the best and wisest manner which they could, and avert from him all but self-inflicted evils.

The
created
gods pro-
vide for
the
human
soul

[43]
bodies
com-
pounded
of earth,
air, fire
and
water.

When the creator had made all these ordinances he remained in his own accustomed nature, and his children heard and were obedient to their father's word, and receiving from him the immortal principle of a mortal creature, in imitation of their own creator they borrowed portions of fire, and earth, and water, and air from the world, which were hereafter to be restored—these they took and welded them together, not with the indissoluble chains by which they were themselves bound, but with little pegs too small to be visible, making up out of all the four elements each separate body, and fastening the courses of the immortal soul in a body which was in a state of perpetual influx and efflux. Now these courses, detained as in a vast river, neither overcame nor were overcome; but were hurrying and hurried to and fro, so that the whole animal was moved and progressed, irregularly however and irrationally and anyhow, in all the six directions of motion, wandering backwards and forwards, and right and left, and up and down, and in all the six directions. For great as was the advancing and retiring flood which provided nourishment, the affections produced by external contact caused still greater tumult—when the body of any one met and came into collision with some external fire, or with the solid earth or the gliding waters, or was caught in the tempest borne on the air, and the motions produced by any of these impulses were carried through the body to the soul. All such motions have consequently received the general name of 'sensations,' which they still retain. And they did in fact at that time create a very great and mighty movement; uniting with the everflowing stream in stirring up and violently shaking the courses of the soul, they completely stopped the revolution of the same by their opposing current, and hindered it from predominating and advancing; and they so disturbed the nature of the other or diverse, that the three double intervals [i. e. between 1, 2, 4, 8], and the three triple intervals [i. e. between 1, 3, 9, 27], together with the mean terms and connecting links which are expressed by the ratios of 3 : 2, and 4 : 3, and of 9 : 8,—these, although they cannot be wholly undone except by him who united them, were twisted by them in all sorts

The
courses of
the soul,
when
placed in
them, are
so dis-
turbed
by the
ebbing
and flow-
ing
stream of
nutri-
ment and
by ex-
ternal
sensa-
tions,
that the
revolu-
tion of
the same
is
stopped,

of ways, and the circles were broken and disordered in every possible manner, so that when they moved they were tumbling to pieces, and moved irrationally, at one time in a reverse direction, and then again obliquely, and then upside down, as you might imagine a person who is upside down and has his head leaning upon the ground and his feet up against something in the air; and when he is in such a position, both he and the spectator fancy that the right of either is his left, and left right. If, when powerfully experiencing these and similar effects, the revolutions of the soul come in contact with some external thing, either of the class of the same or of the other, they speak of the same or of the other in a manner the very opposite of the truth; and they become false and foolish, and there is no course or revolution in them which has a guiding or directing power; and if again any sensations enter in violently from without and drag after them the whole vessel of the soul, then the courses of the soul, though they seem to conquer, are really conquered.

And by reason of all these affections, the soul, when encased in a mortal body, now, as in the beginning, is at first without intelligence; but when the flood of growth and nutriment abates, and the courses of the soul, calming down, go their own way and become steadier as time goes on, then the several circles return to their natural form, and their revolutions are corrected, and they call the same and the other by their right names, and make the possessor of them to become a rational being. And if these combine in him with any true nurture or education, he attains the fulness and health of the perfect man, and escapes the worst disease of all; but if he neglects education he walks lame to the end of his life, and returns imperfect and good for nothing to the world below. This, however, is a later stage; at present we must treat more exactly the subject before us, which involves a preliminary enquiry into the generation of the body and its members, and as to how the soul was created,—for what reason and by what providence of the gods; and holding fast to probability, we must pursue our way.

First, then, the gods, imitating the spherical shape of the universe, enclosed the two divine courses in a spherical body, that, namely, which we now term the head, being the most divine part of us and the lord of all that is in us: to this the gods, when they put together the body, gave all the other members to be servants, considering that it partook of every sort of motion. In order then that it might not tumble about among the high and deep places of the earth, but might be able to get over the one and out of the other, they provided the body to be its vehicle and means of loco-

TIMAEUS.

and the mean terms which unite the sphere of the other are disordered. [44] Thus at first the soul does not attain to truth and wisdom.

As the stream of nutriment abates, the courses of the soul regain their proper motions, and the man becomes a rational creature.

True education renders him perfect.

These courses were encased in the head, which, like the universe, is in the form of a sphere. The body,

motion; which consequently had length and was furnished with four limbs extended and flexible; these God contrived to be instruments of locomotion with which it might take hold and find support, and so be able to pass through all places, carrying on high the dwelling-place of the most sacred and divine part of us. Such was the origin of legs and hands, which for this reason were attached to every man; and the gods, deeming the front part of man to be more honourable and more fit to command than the hinder part, made us to move mostly in a forward direction. Wherefore man must needs have his front part unlike and distinguished from the rest of his body. And so in the vessel of the head, they first of all put a face in which they inserted organs to minister in all things to the providence of the soul, and they appointed this part, which has authority, to be by nature the part which is in front. And of the organs they first contrived the eyes to give light, and the principle according to which they were inserted was as follows: So much of fire as would not burn, but gave a gentle light, they formed into a substance akin to the light of every-day life; and the pure fire which is within us and related thereto they made to flow through the eyes in a stream smooth and dense, compressing the whole eye, and especially the centre part, so that it kept out everything of a coarser nature, and allowed to pass only this pure element. When the light of day surrounds the stream of vision, then like falls upon like, and they coalesce, and one body is formed by natural affinity in the line of vision, wherever the light that falls from within meets with an external object. And the whole stream of vision, being similarly affected in virtue of similarity, diffuses the motions of what it touches or what touches it over the whole body, until they reach the soul, causing that perception which we call sight. But when night comes on and the external and kindred fire departs, then the stream of vision is cut off; for going forth to an unlike element it is changed and extinguished, being no longer of one nature with the surrounding atmosphere which is now deprived of fire: and so the eye no longer sees, and we feel disposed to sleep. For when the eyelids, which the gods invented for the preservation of sight, are closed, they keep in the internal fire; and the power of the fire diffuses and equalizes the inward motions; when they are equalized, there is rest, and when the rest is profound, sleep comes over us scarce disturbed by dreams; but where the greater motions still remain, of whatever nature and in whatever locality, they engender corresponding visions in dreams, which are remembered by us when we are awake and in the external world. And now there is no longer any difficulty in understanding the creation of images in mirrors and all smooth and bright surfaces. For from the communion of the internal and external fires, and again from the union of them and their numerous transformations when they meet in the mirror, all these appearances of necessity arise, when the fire from the face coalesces with the fire from the eye on the bright and smooth surface. And right appears left and left right, because the visual rays come into contact with the rays emitted by the object in a manner contrary to the usual mode of meeting; but the right appears right, and the left left, when the position of one of the two concurring lights is reversed; and this happens when the mirror is concave and its smooth surface repels the right stream of vision to the left side, and the left to the right [1]. Or if the mirror be turned vertically, then the concavity makes the countenance appear to be all upside down, and the lower rays are driven upwards and the upper downwards.

All these are to be reckoned among the second and co-operative causes which God, carrying into execution the idea of the best as far as possible, uses as his ministers. They are thought by most men not to be the second, but the prime causes of all things, because they freeze and heat, and contract and dilate, and the like. But they are not so, for they are incapable of reason or intellect; the only being which can properly have mind is the invisible soul, whereas fire and water, and earth and air, are all of them visible bodies. The lover of intellect and knowledge ought to explore causes of intelligent nature first of all, and, secondly, of those things which, being moved by others, are compelled to move others. And this is what we too must do. Both kinds of causes should be acknowledged by us, but a distinction should be made between those which are endowed with mind and are the workers of things fair and good, and those which are deprived of intelligence and always produce chance effects without order or design. Of the second or co-operative causes of sight, which help to give to the eyes the power which they now possess, enough has been said. I will therefore now proceed to speak of the higher use and purpose for which God has given them to us. The sight in my opinion is the source of the greatest benefit to us, for had we never seen the stars, and the sun, and the heaven, none of the words which we have spoken about the universe would ever have been uttered. But now the sight of day and night, and the months and the revolutions of the years, have created number, and have given us a conception of

Timaeus

TIMAEUS

In the case of reflections in plane mirrors, the transposition of right and left is due to the fact that the light from the eye and the object meet in an unusual manner. In a concave mirror, if held horizontally, there is no transposition; but if it be held vertically, the image is inverted.

Enough of the secondary or irrational causes of sight; the first or in-
[47] telligent cause is the purpose for which God gave it.

---

[1] He is speaking of two kinds of mirrors, first the plane, secondly the concave; and the latter is supposed to be placed, first horizontally, and then vertically.

Timaeus

TIMAEUS.

From
sight we
derive
number
and
philoso-
phy;

and the
observa-
tion of
the in-
telligent
motions
of the
heavens
enables
us to cor-
rect the
erring
courses of
our souls.

Speech,
hearing,
harmony,
and
rhythm
have the
same ob-
ject in
view.

So far we
have
spoken
chiefly of
[48]
the works
of mind;
now we
must tell
of the
works of
necessity
and of the
variable
cause.

Thus we
are led to
consider
the na-

time, and the power of enquiring about the nature of the universe; and from this source we have derived philosophy, than which no greater good ever was or will be given by the gods to mortal man. This is the greatest boon of sight: and of the lesser benefits why should I speak? even the ordinary man if he were deprived of them would bewail his loss, but in vain. Thus much let me say however: God invented and gave us sight to the end that we might behold the courses of intelligence in the heaven, and apply them to the courses of our own intelligence which are akin to them, the unperturbed to the perturbed; and that we, learning them and partaking of the natural truth of reason, might imitate the absolutely unerring courses of God and regulate our own vagaries. The same may be affirmed of speech and hearing: they have been given by the gods to the same end and for a like reason. For this is the principal end of speech, whereto it most contributes. Moreover, so much of music as is adapted to the sound of the voice [1] and to the sense of hearing is granted to us for the sake of harmony; and harmony, which has motions akin to the revolutions of our souls, is not regarded by the intelligent votary of the Muses as given by them with a view to irrational pleasure, which is deemed to be the purpose of it in our day, but as meant to correct any discord which may have arisen in the courses of the soul, and to be our ally in bringing her into harmony and agreement with herself; and rhythm too was given by them for the same reason, on account of the irregular and graceless ways which prevail among mankind generally, and to help us against them.

Thus far in what we have been saying, with small exception, the works of intelligence have been set forth; and now we must place by the side of them in our discourse the things which come into being through necessity—for the creation is mixed, being made up of necessity and mind. Mind, the ruling power, persuaded necessity to bring the greater part of created things to perfection, and thus and after this manner in the beginning, when the influence of reason got the better of necessity, the universe was created. But if a person will truly tell of the way in which the work was accomplished, he must include the other influence of the variable cause as well. Wherefore, we must return again and find another suitable beginning, as about the former matters, so also about these. To which end we must consider the nature of fire, and water, and air, and earth, such as they were prior to the creation of the heaven, and what was happening to them in this previous state [2]; for no one has as yet explained the manner of their generation, but we speak of

---

[1] Reading φωνῇ and placing the comma after ἀκοήν.   [2] Cp. *infra*, 53 A.

fire and the rest of them, whatever they mean, as though men knew
their natures, and we maintain them to be the first principles and
letters or elements of the whole, when they cannot reasonably be
compared by a man of any sense even to syllables or first compounds. And let me say thus much: I will not now speak of the first
principle or principles of all things, or by whatever name they are
to be called, for this reason,—because it is difficult to set forth my
opinion according to the method of discussion which we are at present employing. Do not imagine, any more than I can bring myself
to imagine, that I should be right in undertaking so great and difficult a task. Remembering what I said at first about probability, I
will do my best to give as probable an explanation as any other,—
or rather, more probable; and I will first go back to the beginning
and try to speak of each thing and of all [1]. Once more, then, at the
commencement of my discourse, I call upon God, and beg him to be
our saviour out of a strange and unwonted enquiry, and to bring us
to the haven of probability. So now let us begin again.

This new beginning of our discussion of the universe requires a
fuller division than the former; for then we made two classes, now
a third must be revealed. The two sufficed for the former discussion: one, which we assumed, was a pattern intelligible and always
the same; and the second was only the imitation of the pattern,
generated and visible. There is also a third kind which we did not
distinguish at the time, conceiving that the two would be enough.
But now the argument seems to require that we should set forth in
words another kind, which is difficult of explanation and dimly
seen. What nature are we to attribute to this new kind of being?
We reply, that it is the receptacle, and in a manner the nurse, of all
generation. I have spoken the truth; but I must express myself in
clearer language, and this will be an arduous task for many reasons,
and in particular because I must first raise questions concerning fire
and the other elements, and determine what each of them is; for to
say, with any probability or certitude, which of them should be
called water rather than fire, and which should be called any of
them rather than all or some one of them, is a difficult matter. How,
then, shall we settle this point, and what questions about the elements may be fairly raised?

In the first place, we see that what we just now called water, by
condensation, I suppose, becomes stone and earth; and this same
element, when melted and dispersed, passes into vapour and air.

At the
beginning
of our
discourse
we as-
sumed
[49]
two
natures:
(1) an in-
telligible
pattern;
(2) a
created
copy.
Now we
must add
a third—
(3) the
receptacle
of all
genera-
tion, i. e.
space.

Since the
elements
are per-
petually

---

[1] Putting the comma after μᾶλλον δὲ; or, following Stallbaum and omitting
the comma, 'or rather, before entering on this probable discussion, we will
begin again, and try to speak of each thing and of all.'

changing
into and
out of one
another
and have
in them
nothing
perma-
nent, they
should be
called,
not 'this'
or 'that,'
but al-
ways
'such'.
Unchang-
ing space
is the
only
fixed
nature.

50

An illus-
tration.

Space is
that
which,
being
without
form, can
receive
any form,
i.e. the
impress
of any
idea.

Air, again, when inflamed, becomes fire; and again fire, when condensed and extinguished, passes once more into the form of air; and
once more, air, when collected and condensed, produces cloud and
mist; and from these, when still more compressed, comes flowing
water, and from water comes earth and stones once more; and thus
generation appears to be transmitted from one to the other in a circle. Thus, then, as the several elements never present themselves in
the same form, how can any one have the assurance to assert positively that any of them, whatever it may be, is one thing rather than
another? No one can. But much the safest plan is to speak of them
as follows:—Anything which we see to be continually changing, as,
for example, fire, we must not call 'this' or 'that,' but rather say
that it is 'of such a nature;' nor let us speak of water as 'this,' but
always as 'such;' nor must we imply that there is any stability in
any of those things which we indicate by the use of the words 'this'
and 'that,' supposing ourselves to signify something thereby; for
they are too volatile to be detained in any such expressions as 'this,'
or 'that,' or 'relative to this,' or any other mode of speaking which
represents them as permanent. We ought not to apply 'this' to any
of them, but rather the word 'such;' which expresses the similar
principle circulating in each and all of them; for example, that
should be called 'fire' which is of such a nature always, and so of
everything that has generation. That in which the elements severally grow up, and appear, and decay, is alone to be called by the
name 'this' or 'that;' but that which is of a certain nature, hot or
white, or anything which admits of opposite qualities, and all things
that are compounded of them, ought not to be so denominated. Let
me make another attempt to explain my meaning more clearly.
Suppose a person to make all kinds of figures of gold and to be always transmuting one form into all the rest;—somebody points to
one of them and asks what it is. By far the safest and truest answer is, That is gold; and not to call the triangle or any other figures which are formed in the gold 'these,' as though they had existence, since they are in process of change while he is making the
assertion; but if the questioner be willing to take the safe and indefinite expression, 'such,' we should be satisfied. And the same argument applies to the universal nature which receives all bodies—
that must be always called the same; for, while receiving all things,
she never departs at all from her own nature, and never in any way,
or at any time, assumes a form like that of any of the things which
enter into her; she is the natural recipient of all impressions, and is
stirred and informed by them, and appears different from time to
time by reason of them. But the forms which enter into and go out

of her are the likenesses of real existences modelled after their patterns in a wonderful and inexplicable manner, which we will hereafter investigate. For the present we have only to conceive of three natures: first, that which is in process of generation; secondly, that in which the generation takes place; and thirdly, that of which the thing generated is a resemblance. And we may liken the receiving principle to a mother, and the source or spring to a father, and the intermediate nature to a child; and may remark further, that if the model is to take every variety of form, then the matter in which the model is fashioned will not be duly prepared, unless it is formless, and free from the impress of any of those shapes which it is hereafter to receive from without. For if the matter were like any of the supervening forms, then whenever any opposite or entirely different nature was stamped upon its surface, it would take the impression badly, because it would intrude its own shape. Wherefore, that which is to receive all forms should have no form; as in making perfumes they first contrive that the liquid substance which is to receive the scent shall be as inodorous as possible; or as those who wish to impress figures on soft substances do not allow any previous impression to remain, but begin by making the surface as even and smooth as possible. In the same way that which is to receive perpetually and through its whole extent the resemblances of all eternal beings ought to be devoid of any particular form. Wherefore, the mother and receptacle of all created and visible and in any way sensible things, is not to be termed earth, or air, or fire, or water, or any of their compounds or any of the elements from which these are derived, but is an invisible and formless being which receives all things and in some mysterious way partakes of the intelligible, and is most incomprehensible. In saying this we shall not be far wrong; as far, however, as we can attain to a knowledge of her from the previous considerations, we may truly say that fire is that part of her nature which from time to time is inflamed, and water that which is moistened, and that the mother substance becomes earth and air, in so far as she receives the impressions of them.

Let us consider this question more precisely. Is there any self-existent fire? and do all those things which we call self-existent exist? or are only those things which we see, or in some way perceive through the bodily organs, truly existent, and nothing whatever besides them? And is all that which we call an intelligible essence nothing at all, and only a name? Here is a question which we must not leave unexamined or undetermined, nor must we affirm too confidently that there can be no decision; neither must we inter-

Timaeus

TIMAEUS.

The three natures which have been assumed may be likened to a father, child, and mother.

51

The elements are only affections of space, produced by the impression of ideas.

But have ideas any existence?

We must
admit
that they
have, if,
as is the
case,
mind and
true opin-
ion differ;
for corre-
sponding
to the
difference
between
these
mental
states,
there
        [52]
must be
a differ-
ence
between
the ob-
jects
appre-
hended
by them.

Space is
not per-
ceived by
sense, but
by a kind
of spuri-
ous
reason.

polate in our present long discourse a digression equally long, but if it is possible to set forth a great principle in a few words, that is just what we want.

Thus I state my view:—If mind and true opinion are two distinct classes, then I say that there certainly are these self-existent ideas unperceived by sense, and apprehended only by the mind; if, however, as some say, true opinion differs in no respect from mind, then everything that we perceive through the body is to be regarded as most real and certain. But we must affirm them to be distinct, for they have a distinct origin and are of a different nature; the one is implanted in us by instruction, the other by persuasion; the one is always accompanied by true reason, the other is without reason; the one cannot be overcome by persuasion, but the other can: and lastly, every man may be said to share in true opinion, but mind is the attribute of the gods and of very few men. Wherefore also we must acknowledge that there is one kind of being which is always the same, uncreated and indestructible, never receiving anything into itself from without, nor itself going out to any other, but invisible and imperceptible by any sense, and of which the contemplation is granted to intelligence only. And there is another nature of the same name with it, and like to it, perceived by sense, created, always in motion, becoming in place and again vanishing out of place, which is apprehended by opinion and sense. And there is a third nature, which is space, and is eternal, and admits not of destruction and provides a home for all created things, and is apprehended without the help of sense, by a kind of spurious reason, and is hardly real; which we beholding as in a dream, say of all existence that it must of necessity be in some place and occupy a space, but that what is neither in heaven nor in earth has no existence. Of these and other things of the same kind, relating to the true and waking reality of nature, we have only this dream-like sense, and we are unable to cast off sleep and determine the truth about them. For an image, since the reality, after which it is modelled, does not belong to it[1], and it exists ever as the fleeting shadow of some other, must be inferred to be in another [i. e. in space], grasping existence in some way or other, or it could not be at all. But true and exact reason, vindicating the nature of true being, maintains that while two things [i. e. the image and space] are different they cannot exist one of them in the other and so be one and also two at the same time.

Thus have I concisely given the result of my thoughts; and my

---

[1] Or, 'since in its very intention it is not self-existent'—which, though obscure, avoids any inaccuracy of construction.

verdict is that being and space and generation, these three, existed in their three ways before the heaven; and that the nurse of generation, moistened by water and inflamed by fire, and receiving the forms of earth and air, and experiencing all the affections which accompany these, presented a strange variety of appearances; and being full of powers which were neither similar nor equally balanced, was never in any part in a state of equipoise, but swaying unevenly hither and thither, was shaken by them, and by its motion again shook them; and the elements when moved were separated and carried continually, some one way, some another; as, when grain is shaken and winnowed by fans and other instruments used in the threshing of corn, the close and heavy particles are borne away and settle in one direction, and the loose and light particles in another. In this manner, the four kinds or elements were then shaken by the receiving vessel, which, moving like a winnowing machine, scattered far away from one another the elements most unlike, and forced the most similar elements into close contact. Wherefore also the various elements had different places before they were arranged so as to form the universe. At first, they were all without reason and measure. But when the world began to get into order, fire and water and earth and air had only certain faint traces of themselves, and were altogether such as everything might be expected to be in the absence of God; this, I say, was their nature at that time, and God fashioned them by form and number. Let it be consistently maintained by us in all that we say that God made them as far as possible the fairest and best, out of things which were not fair and good. And now I will endeavour to show you the disposition and generation of them by an unaccustomed argument, which I am compelled to use; but I believe that you will be able to follow me, for your education has made you familiar with the methods of science.

In the first place, then, as is evident to all, fire and earth and water and air are bodies. And every sort of body possesses solidity, and every solid must necessarily be contained in planes; and every plane rectilinear figure is composed of triangles; and all triangles are originally of two kinds, both of which are made up of one right and two acute angles; one of them has at either end of the base the half of a divided right angle, having equal sides, while in the other the right angle is divided into unequal parts, having unequal sides. These, then, proceeding by a combination of probability with demonstration, we assume to be the original elements of fire and the other bodies; but the principles which are prior to these God only knows, and he of men who is the friend of God. And next we have

Space, being, and generation existed before the heaven. Space, on taking the forms [53] of the elements was filled with dissimilar forces, which swayed her to and fro. Thus earth, air, fire and water, were sifted into their proper places, while they were yet in a rudimentary state, before God perfected them by form and number.

The manner of their generation was as follows:— The four elements

are solid
bodies,
and all
solids are
made up
of plane
surfaces,
[54]
and all
plane sur-
faces of
triangles.
All tri-
angles
are ulti-
mately
of two
kinds,—
i.e. the
rectangu-
lar isos-
celes, and
rectangu-
lar sca-
lene.

The rec-
tangular
isosceles,
which has
but one
form, and
that one
of the
many
forms of
scalene
which is
half of an
equilate-
ral tri-
angle
were
chosen
for mak-
ing the
elements.

Three of
them are
generated
out of the
latter:
the
fourth

to determine what are the four most beautiful bodies which are unlike one another, and of which some are capable of resolution into
one another; for having discovered thus much, we shall know the
true origin of earth and fire and of the proportionate and intermediate elements. And then we shall not be willing to allow that there
are any distinct kinds of visible bodies fairer than these. Wherefore we must endeavour to construct the four forms of bodies which
excel in beauty, and then we shall be able to say that we have sufficiently apprehended their nature. Now of the two triangles, the
isosceles has one form only; the scalene or unequal-sided has an infinite number. Of the infinite forms we must select the most beautiful, if we are to proceed in due order, and any one who can point
out a more beautiful form than ours for the construction of these
bodies, shall carry off the palm, not as an enemy, but as a friend.
Now, the one which we maintain to be the most beautiful of all the
many triangles (and we need not speak of the others) is that of
which the double forms a third triangle which is equilateral; the
reason of this would be long to tell; he who disproves what we are
saying, and shows that we are mistaken, may claim a friendly victory. Then let us choose two triangles, out of which fire and the
other elements have been constructed, one isosceles, the other having the square of the longer side equal to three times the square of
the lesser side.

Now is the time to explain what was before obscurely said: there
was an error in imagining that all the four elements might be generated by and into one another; this, I say, was an erroneous supposition, for there are generated from the triangles which we have
selected four kinds—three from the one which has the sides unequal; the fourth alone is framed out of the isosceles triangle.
Hence they cannot all be resolved into one another, a great number of small bodies being combined into a few large ones, or the
converse. But three of them can be thus resolved and compounded,
for they all spring from one, and when the greater bodies are
broken up, many small bodies will spring up out of them and take
their own proper figures; or, again, when many small bodies are
dissolved into their triangles, if they become one, they will form
one large mass of another kind. So much for their passage into one
another. I have now to speak of their several kinds, and show out
of what combinations of numbers each of them was formed. The
first will be the simplest and smallest construction, and its element
is that triangle which has its hypothenuse twice the lesser side.
When two such triangles are joined at the diagonal, and this is repeated three times, and the triangles rest their diagonals and shorter

sides on the same point as a centre, a single equilateral triangle is formed out of six triangles; and four equilateral triangles, if put together, make out of every three plane angles one solid angle, being that which is nearest to the most obtuse of plane angles; and out of the combination of these four angles arises the first solid form which distributes into equal and similar parts the whole circle in which it is inscribed. The second species of solid is formed out of the same triangles, which unite as eight equilateral triangles and form one solid angle out of four plane angles, and out of six such angles the second body is completed. And the third body is made up of 120 triangular elements, forming twelve solid angles, each of them included in five plane equilateral triangles, having altogether twenty bases, each of which is an equilateral triangle. The one element [that is, the triangle which has its hypothenuse twice the lesser side] having generated these figures, generated no more; but the isosceles triangle produced the fourth elementary figure, which is compounded of four such triangles, joining their right angles in a centre, and forming one equilateral quadrangle. Six of these united form eight solid angles, each of which is made by the combination of three plane right angles; the figure of the body thus composed is a cube, having six plane quadrangular equilateral bases. There was yet a fifth combination which God used in the delineation of the universe.

Now, he who, duly reflecting on all this, enquires whether the worlds are to be regarded as indefinite or definite in number, will be of opinion that the notion of their indefiniteness is characteristic of a sadly indefinite and ignorant mind. He, however, who raises the question whether they are to be truly regarded as one or five, takes up a more reasonable position. Arguing from probabilities, I am of opinion that they are one; another, regarding the question from another point of view, will be of another mind. But, leaving this enquiry, let us proceed to distribute the elementary forms, which have now been created in idea, among the four elements.

To earth, then, let us assign the cubical form; for earth is the most immoveable of the four and the most plastic of all bodies, and that which has the most stable bases must of necessity be of such a nature. Now, of the triangles which we assumed at first, that which has two equal sides is by nature more firmly based than that which has unequal sides; and of the compound figures which are formed out of either, the plane equilateral quadrangle has necessarily a more stable basis than the equilateral triangle, both in the whole and in the parts. Wherefore, in assigning this figure to earth, we adhere to probability; and to water we assign that one of

Timaeus

TIMAEUS.

55
alone
from the
former.
Therefore
only
three can
pass into
each
other.

The first
and
simplest
solid, the
pyramid,
has four
equilateral tri-
angular
surfaces,
each
formed
by the
union of
six
rectangular
scalene
triangles.

The
second
species,
the octa-
hedron,
has eight
such sur-
faces,
and the
third, the
icosa-
hedron,
twenty.

The
fourth,
the cube,
has six
square
surfaces,
each

56

formed of
four
rectangu-
lar
isosceles
triangles.
There is
also a
fifth
species.
Although
there are
five ele-
mentary
solids,
there is
but one
world.

We have
now to
assign to
the four
elements
their re-
spective
forms,—
to earth,
the cube,
to water
the icosa-
hedron,
to air the
octa-
hedron, to
fire the
pyramid.

Indivi-
dual par-
ticles
cannot be
seen:
masses of
[57]
each kind
are
visible.

Of the
three ele-
ments,
fire, air,
water, a
denser,

the remaining forms which is the least moveable; and the most moveable of them to fire; and to air that which is intermediate. Also we assign the smallest body to fire, and the greatest to water, and the intermediate in size to air; and, again, the acutest body to fire, and the next in acuteness to air, and the third to water. Of all these elements, that which has the fewest bases must necessarily be the most moveable, for it must be the acutest and most penetrating in every way, and also the lightest as being composed of the smallest number of similar particles: and the second body has similar properties in a second degree, and the third body in the third degree. Let it be agreed, then, both according to strict reason and according to probability, that the pyramid is the solid which is the original element and seed of fire; and let us assign the element which was next in the order of generation to air, and the third to water. We must imagine all these to be so small that no single particle of any of the four kinds is seen by us on account of their smallness: but when many of them are collected together their aggregates are seen. And the ratios of their numbers, motions, and other properties, everywhere God, as far as necessity allowed or gave consent, has exactly perfected, and harmonized in due proportion.

From all that we have just been saying about the elements or kinds, the most probable conclusion is as follows:—earth, when meeting with fire and dissolved by its sharpness, whether the dissolution take place in the fire itself or perhaps in some mass of air or water, is borne hither and thither, until its parts, meeting together and mutually harmonizing, again become earth; for they can never take any other form. But water, when divided by fire or by air, on re-forming, may become one part fire and two parts air; and a single volume of air divided becomes two of fire. Again, when a small body of fire is contained in a larger body of air or water or earth, and both are moving, and the fire struggling is overcome and broken up, then two volumes of fire form one volume of air; and when air is overcome and cut up into small pieces, two and a half parts of air are condensed into one part of water. Let us consider the matter in another way. When one of the other elements is fastened upon by fire, and is cut by the sharpness of its angles and sides, it coalesces with the fire, and then ceases to be cut by them any longer. For no element which is one and the same with itself can be changed by or change another of the same kind and in the same state. But so long as in the process of transition the weaker is fighting against the stronger, the dissolution continues. Again, when a few small particles, enclosed in many larger ones, are in process of decomposition and extinction, they only cease from their tendency to extinction when they consent to pass into the conquering nature, and fire becomes air and air water. But if bodies of another kind go and attack them [i. e. the small particles], the latter continue to be dissolved until, being completely forced back and dispersed, they make their escape to their own kindred, or else, being overcome and assimilated to the conquering power, they remain where they are and dwell with their victors, and from being many become one. And owing to these affections, all things are changing their place, for by the motion of the receiving vessel the bulk of each class is distributed into its proper place; but those things which become unlike themselves and like other things, are hurried by the shaking into the place of the things to which they grow like.

Now all unmixed and primary bodies are produced by such causes as these. As to the subordinate species which are included in the greater kinds, they are to be attributed to the varieties in the structure of the two original triangles. For either structure did not originally produce the triangle of one size only, but some larger and some smaller, and there are as many sizes as there are species of the four elements. Hence when they are mingled with themselves and with one another there is an endless variety of them, which those who would arrive at the probable truth of nature ought duly to consider.

Unless a person comes to an understanding about the nature and conditions of rest and motion, he will meet with many difficulties in the discussion which follows. Something has been said of this matter already, and something more remains to be said, which is, that motion never exists in what is uniform. For to conceive that anything can be moved without a mover is hard or indeed impossible, and equally impossible to conceive that there can be a mover unless there be something which can be moved;—motion cannot exist where either of these are wanting, and for these to be uniform is impossible; wherefore we must assign rest to uniformity and motion to the want of uniformity. Now inequality is the cause of the nature which is wanting in uniformity; and of this we have already described the origin. But there still remains the further point —why things when divided after their kinds do not cease to pass through one another and to change their place—which we will now proceed to explain. In the revolution of the universe are comprehended all the four elements, and this being circular and having a tendency to come together, compresses everything and will not allow any place to be left void. Wherefore, also, fire above all things penetrates everywhere, and air next, as being next in rarity of the elements; and the two other elements in like manner penetrate ac-

if over-
powered
by a
rarer, is
forced to
change
into a
rarer, and
*vice
versa*.
Earth,
however,
which is
the dens-
est of all,
cannot
change,
because
its com-
ponent
triangles
are unlike
those of
the other
elements.

Change
of nature
is accom-
panied by
change
of place.

The
varieties
of the
four ele-
ments are
due to
differ-
ences in
[58]
the size
of the
elemen-
tary tri-
angles.

How is it
that the
elements
are per-
petually
mov-
ing?—
i.e. How

Timaeus

TIMAEUS.

is absence of uniformity, the condition of motion, secured for them?

We have seen that there is a continual tendency to produce uniformity, due to the motion of the receiving vessel. There is also a tendency to destroy it, due to the revolution of the universe, which thrusts the elements into each other.

59

Kinds of fire:—
(i) flame;
(ii) light;
(iii) red heat.
Kinds of air:—
(i) æther;
(ii) mist.
There are also other kinds without names.

cording to their degrees of rarity. For those things which are composed of the largest particles have the largest void left in their compositions, and those which are composed of the smallest particles have the least. And the contraction caused by the compression thrusts the smaller particles into the interstices of the larger. And thus, when the small parts are placed side by side with the larger, and the lesser divide the greater and the greater unite the lesser, all the elements are borne up and down and hither and thither towards their own places; for the change in the size of each changes its position in space. And these causes generate an inequality which is always maintained, and is continually creating a perpetual motion of the elements in all time.

In the next place we have to consider that there are divers kinds of fire. There are, for example, first, flame; and secondly, those emanations of flame which do not burn but only give light to the eyes; thirdly, the remains of fire, which are seen in red-hot embers after the flame has been extinguished. There are similar differences in the air; of which the brightest part is called the aether, and the most turbid sort mist and darkness; and there are various other nameless kinds which arise from the inequality of the triangles. Water, again, admits in the first place of a division into two kinds; the one liquid and the other fusile. The liquid kind is composed of the small and unequal particles of water; and moves itself and is moved by other bodies owing to the want of uniformity and the shape of its particles; whereas the fusile kind, being formed of large and uniform particles, is more stable than the other, and is heavy and compact by reason of its uniformity. But when fire gets in and dissolves the particles and destroys the uniformity, it has greater mobility, and becoming fluid is thrust forth by the neighbouring air and spreads upon the earth; and this dissolution of the solid masses is called melting, and their spreading out upon the earth flowing. Again, when the fire goes out of the fusile substance, it does not pass into a vacuum, but into the neighbouring air; and the air which is displaced forces together the liquid and still moveable mass into the place which was occupied by the fire, and unites it with itself. Thus compressed the mass resumes its equability, and is again at unity with itself, because the fire which was the author of the inequality has retreated; and this departure of the fire is called cooling, and the coming together which follows upon it is termed congealment. Of all the kinds termed fusile, that which is the densest and is formed out of the finest and most uniform parts is that most precious possession called gold. which is hardened by filtration through rock; this is unique in kind, and has both a glittering and a yellow colour. A shoot of gold, which is so dense as to be very hard, and takes a black colour, is termed adamant. There is also another kind which has parts nearly like gold, and of which there are several species; it is denser than gold, and it contains a small and fine portion of earth, and is therefore harder, yet also lighter because of the great interstices which it has within itself; and this substance, which is one of the bright and denser kinds of water, when solidified is called copper. There is an alloy of earth mingled with it, which, when the two parts grow old and are disunited, shows itself separately and is called rust. The remaining phenomena of the same kind there will be no difficulty in reasoning out by the method of probabilities. A man may sometimes set aside meditations about eternal thnigs, and for recreation turn to consider the truths of generation which are probable only; he will thus gain a pleasure not to be repented of, and secure for himself while he lives a wise and moderate pastime. Let us grant ourselves this indulgence, and go through the probabilities relating to the same subjects which follow next in order.

Water which is mingled with fire, so much as is fine and liquid (being so called by reason of its motion and the way in which it rolls along the ground), and soft, because its bases give way and are less stable than those of earth, when separated from fire and air and isolated, becomes more uniform, and by their retirement is compressed into itself; and if the condensation be very great, the water above the earth becomes hail, but on the earth, ice; and that which is congealed in a less degree and is only half solid, when above the earth is called snow, and when upon the earth, and condensed from dew, hoar-frost. Then, again, there are the numerous kinds of water which have been mingled with one another, and are distilled through plants which grow in the earth; and this whole class is called by the name of juices or saps. The unequal admixture of these fluids creates a variety of species; most of them are nameless, but four which are of a fiery nature are clearly distinguished and have names. First, there is wine, which warms the soul as well as the body: secondly, there is the oily nature, which is smooth and divides the visual ray, and for this reason is bright and shining and of a glistening appearance, including pitch, the juice of the castor berry, oil itself, and other things of a like kind: thirdly, there is the class of substances which expand the contracted parts[1] of the mouth, until they return to their natural state, and by reason of this property create sweetness;—these are included under the general name of honey: and, lastly, there is a frothy nature, which dif-

[1] Cp. 65 C, 66 C.

Timaeus

TIMAEUS.

Kinds of water:—
(i) liquid;
(ii) fusile. The former is mobile; the latter is solid, but melts when heated,—congealing again as it cools.

Of the fusile kind are

(1) gold,

(2) adamant,

(3) copper.

The phenomenon of rust.

To natural science the student of the eternal may [60] turn for recreation.

From water of the liquid kind are formed

(1) hail or ice,

(2) snow,

(3) hoarfrost,

fers from all juices, having a burning quality which dissolves the flesh; it is called *opos* (a vegetable acid).

As to the kinds of earth, that which is filtered through water passes into stone in the following manner:—The water which mixes with the earth and is broken up in the process changes into air, and taking this form mounts into its own place. But as there is no surrounding vacuum it thrusts away the neighbouring air, and this being rendered heavy, and, when it is displaced, having been poured around the mass of earth, forcibly compresses it and drives it into the vacant space whence the new air had come up; and the earth when compressed by the air into an indissoluble union with water becomes rock. The fairer sort is that which is made up of equal and similar parts and is transparent; that which has the opposite qualities is inferior. But when all the watery part is suddenly drawn out by fire, a more brittle substance is formed, to which we give the name of pottery. Sometimes also moisture may remain, and the earth which has been fused by fire becomes, when cool, a certain stone of a black colour. A like separation of the water which had been copiously mingled with them may occur in two substances composed of finer particles of earth and of a briny nature; out of either of them a half-solid body is then formed, soluble in water— the one, soda, which is used for purging away oil and earth, the other, salt, which harmonizes so well in combinations pleasing to the palate, and is, as the law testifies, a substance dear to the gods. The compounds of earth and water are not soluble by water, but by fire only, and for this reason:—Neither fire nor air melt masses of earth; for their particles, being smaller than the interstices in its structure, have plenty of room to move without forcing their way, and so they leave the earth unmelted and undissolved; but particles of water, which are larger, force a passage, and dissolve and melt the earth. Wherefore earth when not consolidated by force is dissolved by water only; when consolidated, by nothing but fire; for this is the only body which can find an entrance. The cohesion of water again, when very strong, is dissolved by fire only—when weaker, then either by air or fire—the former entering the interstices, and the latter penetrating even the triangles. But nothing can dissolve air, when strongly condensed, which does not reach the elements or triangles; or if not strongly condensed, then only fire can dissolve it. As to bodies composed of earth and water, while the water occupies the vacant interstices of the earth in them which are compressed by force, the particles of water which approach them from without, finding no entrance, flow around the entire mass and leave it undissolved; but the particles of fire, entering into the interstices of the water, do to the water what water does to earth and fire to air[1], and are the sole causes of the compound body of earth and water liquefying and becoming fluid. Now these bodies are of two kinds; some of them, such as glass and the fusible sort of stones, have less water than they have earth; on the other hand, substances of the nature of wax and incense have more of water entering into their composition.

I have thus shown the various classes of bodies as they are diversified by their forms and combinations and changes into one another, and now I must endeavour to set forth their affections and the causes of them. In the first place, the bodies which I have been describing are necessarily objects of sense. But we have not yet considered the origin of flesh, or what belongs to flesh, or of that part of the soul which is mortal. And these things cannot be adequately explained without also explaining the affections which are concerned with sensation, nor the latter without the former: and yet to explain them together is hardly possible; for which reason we must assume first one or the other and afterwards examine the nature of our hypothesis [2]. In order, then, that the affections may follow regularly after the elements, let us presuppose the existence of body and soul.

First, let us enquire what we mean by saying that fire is hot; and about this we may reason from the dividing or cutting power which it exercises on our bodies. We all of us feel that fire is sharp; and we may further consider the fineness of the sides, and the sharpness of the angles, and the smallness of the particles, and the swiftness of the motion;—all this makes the action of fire violent and sharp, so that it cuts whatever it meets. And we must not forget that the original figure of fire [i. e. the pyramid], more than any other form, has a dividing power which cuts our bodies into small pieces (χερματίζει), and thus naturally produces that affection which we call heat; and hence the origin of the name (θερμὸς, χέρμα). Now, the opposite of this is sufficiently manifest; nevertheless we will not fail to describe it. For the larger particles of moisture which surround the body, entering in and driving out the lesser, but not being able to take their places, compress the moist principle in us; and this from being unequal and disturbed, is forced by them into a state of rest, which is due to equability and compression. But things which are contracted contrary to nature are by nature at war, and force themselves apart; and to this war and convulsion the name of shivering and trembling is given; and

---

[1] The text seems to be corrupt.
[2] Omitting ὕστερα.

only, which penetrates the water in them. Earth and water, however, in their natural state are soluble, the former by water only, the latter by fire and air.

From objects of sense we pass on to consider flesh, which perceives sensations, and sensations themselves.

62

i. Sensations common to the whole body:—
(1) Heat, due to the sharpness of fire, which cuts the flesh.

(2) Cold, due to contraction.

the whole affection and the cause of the affection are both termed cold. That is called hard to which our flesh yields, and soft which yields to our flesh; and things are also termed hard and soft relatively to one another. That which yields has a small base; but that which rests on quadrangular bases is firmly posed and belongs to the class which offers the greatest resistance; so too does that which is the most compact and therefore most repellent. The nature of the light and the heavy will be best understood when examined in connexion with our notions of above and below; for it is quite a mistake to suppose that the universe is parted into two regions, separate from and opposite to each other, the one a lower to which all things tend which have any bulk, and an upper to which things only ascend against their will. For as the universe is in the form of a sphere, all the extremities, being equidistant from the centre, are equally extremities, and the centre, which is equidistant from them, is equally to be regarded as the opposite of them all. Such being the nature of the world, when a person says that any of these points is above or below, may he not be justly charged with using an improper expression? For the centre of the world cannot be rightly called either above or below, but is the centre and nothing else; and the circumference is not the centre, and has in no one part of itself a different relation to the centre from what it has in any of the opposite parts. Indeed, when it is in every direction similar, how can one rightly give to it names which imply opposition? For if there were any solid body in equipoise at the centre of the universe, there would be nothing to draw it to this extreme rather than to that, for they are all perfectly similar; and if a person were to go round the world in a circle, he would often, when standing at the antipodes of his former position, speak of the same point as above and below; for, as I was saying just now, to speak of the whole which is in the form of a globe as having one part above and another below is not like a sensible man. The reason why these names are used, and the circumstances under which they are ordinarily applied by us to the division of the heavens, may be elucidated by the following supposition:—If a person were to stand in that part of the universe which is the appointed place of fire, and where there is the great mass of fire to which fiery bodies gather— if, I say, he were to ascend thither, and, having the power to do this, were to abstract particles of fire and put them in scales and weigh them, and then, raising the balance, were to draw the fire by force towards the uncongenial element of the air, it would be very evident that he could compel the smaller mass more readily than the larger; for when two things are simultaneously raised by one and the same power, the smaller body must necessarily yield to the superior power with less reluctance than the larger; and the larger body is called heavy and said to tend downwards, and the smaller body is called light and said to tend upwards. And we may detect ourselves who are upon the earth doing precisely the same thing. For we often separate earthy natures, and sometimes earth itself, and draw them into the uncongenial element of air by force and contrary to nature, both clinging to their kindred elements. But that which is smaller yields to the impulse given by us towards the dissimilar element more easily than the larger; and so we call the former light, and the place towards which it is impelled we call above, and the contrary state and place we call heavy and below respectively. Now the relations of these must necessarily vary, because the principal masses of the different elements hold opposite positions; for that which is light, heavy, below or above in one place will be found to be and become contrary and transverse and every way diverse in relation to that which is light, heavy, below or above in an opposite place. And about all of them this has to be considered:—that the tendency of each towards its kindred element makes the body which is moved heavy, and the place towards which the motion tends below, but things which have an opposite tendency we call by an opposite name. Such are the causes which we assign to these phenomena. As to the smooth and the rough, any one who sees them can explain the reason of them to another. For roughness is hardness mingled with irregularity, and smoothness is produced by the joint effect of uniformity and density.

· The most important of the affections which concern the whole body remains to be considered,—that is, the cause of pleasure and pain in the perceptions of which I have been speaking, and in all other things which are perceived by sense through the parts of the body, and have both pains and pleasures attendant on them. Let us imagine the causes of every affection, whether of sense or not, to be of the following nature, remembering that we have already distinguished between the nature which is easy and which is hard to move; for this is the direction in which we must hunt the prey which we mean to take. A body which is of a nature to be easily moved, on receiving an impression however slight, spreads abroad the motion in a circle, the parts communicating with each other, until at last, reaching the principle of mind, they announce the quality of the agent. But a body of the opposite kind, being immobile, and not extending to the surrounding region, merely receives the impression, and does not stir any of the neighbouring parts; and since the parts do not distribute the original impression to other

Timaeus

TIMAEUS.

are drawn towards the mass of their kindred with a force proportionate to their size. The greater this force, the greater the weight.

(7) Roughness; and 64

(8) Smoothness.

How is it that sensations are accompanied by pleasure and pain? Sensations arise thus. An object comes into contact with an organ of sense. This, if composed of fine parts, it has no effect of motion on the whole animal, and therefore produces no effect on the patient. This is true of the bones and hair and other more earthy parts of the human body; whereas what was said above relates mainly to sight and hearing, because they have in them the greatest amount of fire and air. Now we must conceive of pleasure and pain in this way. An impression produced in us contrary to nature and violent, if sudden, is painful; and, again, the sudden return to nature is pleasant; but a gentle and gradual return is imperceptible and *vice versa*. On the other hand the impression of sense which is most easily produced is most readily felt, but is not accompanied by pleasure or pain; such, for example, are the affections of the sight, which, as we said above, is a body naturally uniting with our body in the day-time (45); for cuttings and burnings and other affections which happen to the sight do not give pain, nor is there pleasure when the sight returns to its natural state; but the sensations are clearest and strongest according to the manner in which the eye is affected by the object, and itself strikes and touches it; there is no violence either in the contraction or dilation of the eye. But bodies formed of larger particles yield to the agent only with a struggle; and then they impart their motions to the whole and cause pleasure and pain—pain when alienated from their natural conditions, and pleasure when restored to them. Things which experience gradual withdrawings and emptyings of their nature, and great and sudden replenishments, fail to perceive the emptying, but are sensible of the replenishment; and so they occasion no pain, but the greatest pleasure, to the mortal part of the soul, as is manifest in the case of perfumes. But things which are changed all of a sudden, and only gradually and with difficulty return to their own nature, have effects in every way opposite to the former, as is evident in the case of burnings and cuttings of the body.

Thus have we discussed the general affections the whole body, and the names of the agents which produce them. And now I will endeavour to speak of the affections of particular parts, and the causes and agents of them, as far as I am able. In the first place let us set forth what was omitted when we were speaking of juices, concerning the affections peculiar to the tongue. These too, like most of the other affections, appear to be caused by certain contractions and dilations, but they have besides more of roughness and smoothness than is found in other affections; for whenever earthy particles enter into the small veins which are the testing instruments of the tongue, reaching to the heart, and fall upon the moist, delicate portions of flesh—when, as they are dissolved, they contract and dry up the little veins, they are astringent if they are rougher, but if not so rough, then only harsh. Those of them which are of an abstergent nature, and purge the whole surface of the tongue, if they do it in excess, and so encroach as to consume some part of the flesh itself, like potash and soda, are all termed bitter. But the particles which are deficient in the alkaline quality, and which cleanse only moderately, are called salt, and having no bitterness or roughness, are regarded as rather agreeable than otherwise. Bodies which share in and are made smooth by the heat of the mouth, and which are inflamed, and again in turn inflame that which heats them, and which are so light that they are carried upwards to the sensations of the head, and cut all that comes in their way, by reason of these qualities in them, are all termed pungent. But when these same particles, refined by putrefaction, enter into the narrow veins, and are duly proportioned to the particles of earth and air which are there, they set them whirling about one another, and while they are in a whirl cause them to dash against and enter into one another, and so form hollows surrounding the particles that enter—which watery vessels of air (for a film of moisture, sometimes earthy, sometimes pure, is spread around the air) are hollow spheres of water; and those of them which are pure, are transparent, and are called bubbles, while those composed of the earthy liquid, which is in a state of general agitation and effervescence, are said to boil or ferment;—of all these affections the cause is termed acid. And there is the opposite affection arising from an opposite cause, when the mass of entering particles, immersed in the moisture of the mouth, is congenial to the tongue, and smooths and oils over the roughness, and relaxes the parts which are unnaturally contracted, and contracts the parts which are relaxed, and disposes them all according to their nature;—that sort of remedy of violent affections is pleasant and agreeable to every man, and has the name sweet. But enough of this.

The faculty of smell does not admit of differences of kind; for all smells are of a half-formed nature, and no element is so proportioned as to have any smell. The veins about the nose are too narrow to admit earth and water, and too wide to detain fire and air; and for this reason no one ever perceives the smell of any of them; but smells always proceed from bodies that are damp, or putrefying, or liquefying, or evaporating, and are perceptible only in the intermediate state, when water is changing into air and air into water; and all of them are either vapor or mist. That which is passing out of air into water is mist, and that which is passing from water into air is vapour; and hence all smells are thinner than

Timaeus

TIMAEUS.

produced by contraction and dilation of the veins. They are as follows

a. Astringency.
[66]
b. Harshness.
c. Bitterness.
d. Saltness.
e. Pungency.
f. Acidity.
g. Sweetness.

(2) Of the nostrils. Smells can only be distinguished as pleasant or the reverse. The substances which emit

them,
vapour
and mist,
are half-
formed,
being in-
termedi-
ate be-
tween
water
and air.

(3) Of
the ear.
Sounds
are
blows
which
pass
through
the ears
to the
soul.
They are
acute and
grave,
smooth
and
harsh, &c.

(4) Of
the eye.
Colours
are
flames
emitted
by ob-
jects.

Simple
colours
are:

a. Trans-
parent.

b. White.

68

c. Black.

d. Bright.

water and thicker than air. The proof of this is, that when there is any obstruction to the respiration, and a man draws in his breath by force, then no smell filters through, but the air without the smell alone penetrates. Wherefore the varieties of smell have no name, and they have not many, or definite and simple kinds; but they are distinguished only as painful and pleasant, the one sort irritating and disturbing the whole cavity which is situated between the head and the navel, the other having a soothing influence, and restoring this same region to an agreeable and natural condition.

In considering the third kind of sense, hearing, we must speak of the causes in which it originates. We may in general assume sound to be a blow which passes through the ears, and is transmitted by means of the air, the brain, and the blood, to the soul, and that hearing is the vibration of this blow, which begins in the head and ends in the region of the liver. The sound which moves swiftly is acute, and the sound which moves slowly is grave, and that which is regular is equable and smooth, and the reverse is harsh. A great body of sound is loud, and a small body of sound the reverse. Respecting the harmonies of sound I must hereafter speak.

There is a fourth class of sensible things, having many intricate varieties, which must now be distinguished. They are called by the general name of colours, and are a flame which emanates from every sort of body, and has particles corresponding to the sense of sight. I have spoken already, in what has preceded, of the causes which generate sight, and in this place it will be natural and suitable to give a rational theory of colours.

Of the particles coming from other bodies which fall upon the sight, some are smaller and some are larger, and some are equal to the parts of the sight itself. Those which are equal are imperceptible, and we call them transparent. The larger produce contraction, the smaller dilation, in the sight, exercising a power akin to that of hot and cold bodies on the flesh, or of astringent bodies on the tongue, or of those heating bodies which we termed pungent. White and black are similar effects of contraction and dilation in another sphere, and for this reason have a different appearance. Wherefore, we ought to term white that which dilates the visual ray, and the opposite of this is black. There is also a swifter motion of a different sort of fire which strikes and dilates the ray of sight until it reaches the eyes, forcing a way through their passages and melting them, and eliciting from them a union of fire and water which we call tears, being itself an opposite fire which comes to them from an opposite direction—the inner fire flashes forth like lightning, and the outer finds a way in and is extinguished in the moisture, and all sorts of colours are generated by the mixture. This affection is termed dazzling, and the object which produces it is called bright and flashing. There is another sort of fire which is intermediate, and which reaches and mingles with the moisture of the eye without flashing; and in this, the fire mingling with the ray of the moisture, produces a colour like blood, to which we give the name of red. A bright hue mingled with red and white gives the colour called auburn (ξανθόν). The law of proportion, however, according to which the several colours are formed, even if a man knew he would be foolish in telling, for he could not give any necessary reason, nor indeed any tolerable or probable explanation of them. Again, red, when mingled with black and white, becomes purple, but it becomes umber (ὄρφνινον) when the colours are burnt as well as mingled and the black is more thoroughly mixed with them. Flame-colour (πυρρὸν) is produced by a union of auburn and dun (φαιὸν), and dun by an admixture of black and white; pale yellow (ὠχρὸν), by an admixture of white and auburn. White and bright meeting, and falling upon a full black, become dark blue (κυανοῦν), and when dark blue mingles with white, a light blue (γλαυκὸν) colour is formed, as flame-colour with black makes leek green (πράσιον). There will be no difficulty in seeing how and by what mixtures the colours derived from these are made according to the rules of probability. He, however, who should attempt to verify all this by experiment, would forget the difference of the human and divine nature. For God only has the knowledge and also the power which are able to combine many things into one and again resolve the one into many. But no man either is or ever will be able to accomplish either the one or the other operation.

These are the elements, thus of necessity then subsisting, which the creator of the fairest and best of created things associated with himself, when he made the self-sufficing and most perfect God, using the necessary causes as his ministers in the accomplishment of his work, but himself contriving the good in all his creations. Wherefore we may distinguish two sorts of causes, the one divine and the other necessary, and may seek for the divine in all things, as far as our nature admits, with a view to the blessed life; but the necessary kind only for the sake of the divine, considering that without them and when isolated from them, these higher things for which we look cannot be apprehended or received or in any way shared by us.

Seeing, then, that we have now prepared for our use the various classes of causes which are the material out of which the remainder of our discourse must be woven, just as wood is the material of the carpenter, let us revert in a few words to the point at which we be-

The compound colours are:

a. Auburn.

b. Purple.

c. Umber.

d. Flame-colour.

e. Dun.

f. Pale yellow.

g. Dark blue.

h. Light blue.

i. Leek green.

These are the necessary causes which God used in creating the universe. They are [69] subservient to the divine, which we must seek, if we wish to attain bliss.

gan, and then endeavour to add on a suitable ending to the beginning of our tale.

As I said at first, when all things were in disorder God created in
each thing in relation to itself, and in all things in relation to each
other, all the measures and harmonies which they could possibly
receive. For in those days nothing had any proportion except by
accident; nor did any of the things which now have names deserve
to be named at all—as, for example, fire, water, and the rest of the
elements. All these the creator first set in order, and out of them
he constructed the universe, which was a single animal comprehending in itself all other animals, mortal and immortal. Now of
the divine, he himself was the creator, but the creation of the mortal
he committed to his offspring. And they, imitating him, received
from him the immortal principle of the soul; and around this they
proceeded to fashion a mortal body, and made it to be the vehicle
of the soul, and constructed within the body a soul of another nature which was mortal, subject to terrible and irresistible affections,
—first of all, pleasure, the greatest incitement to evil; then, pain,
which deters from good; also rashness and fear, two foolish counsellors, anger hard to be appeased, and hope easily led astray;—
these they mingled with irrational sense and with all-daring love[1]
according to necessary laws, and so framed man. Wherefore, fearing to pollute the divine any more than was absolutely unavoidable,
they gave to the mortal nature a separate habitation in another
part of the body, placing the neck between them to be the isthmus
and boundary, which they constructed between the head and breast,
to keep them apart. And in the breast, and in what is termed the
thorax, they encased the mortal soul; and as the one part of this
was superior and the other inferior they divided the cavity of the
thorax into two parts, as the women's and men's apartments are
divided in houses, and placed the midriff to be a wall of partition
between them. That part of the inferior soul which is endowed with
courage and passion and loves contention they settled nearer the
head, midway between the midriff and the neck, in order that it
might be under the rule of reason and might join with it in controlling and restraining the desires when they are no longer willing of
their own accord to obey the word of command issuing from the
citadel.

The heart, the knot[2] of the veins and the fountain of the blood
which races through all the limbs, was set in the place of guard,
that when the might of passion was roused by reason making proc-

---

[1] Putting a colon after εὐπαράγωγον and reading αἰσθήσει δὲ ἀλόγῳ.
[2] Reading ἅμμα.

lamation of any wrong assailing them from without or being perpetrated by the desires within, quickly the whole power of feeling in
the body, perceiving these commands and threats, might obey and
follow through every turn and alley, and thus allow the principle
of the best to have the command in all of them. But the gods, fore-
knowing that the palpitation of the heart in the expectation of
danger and the swelling and excitement of passion was caused by
fire, formed and implanted as a supporter to the heart the lung,
which was, in the first place, soft and bloodless, and also had within
hollows like the pores of a sponge, in order that by receiving the
breath and the drink, it might give coolness and the power of respiration and alleviate the heat. Wherefore they cut the air-channels
leading to the lung, and placed the lung about the heart as a soft
spring, that, when passion was rife within, the heart, beating
against a yielding body, might be cooled and suffer less, and might
thus become more ready to join with passion in the service of
reason.

The part of the soul which desires meats and drinks and the other
things of which it has need by reason of the bodily nature, they
placed between the midriff and the boundary of the navel, contriving in all this region a sort of manger for the food of the body; and
there they bound it down like a wild animal which was chained up
with man, and must be nourished if man was to exist. They appointed this lower creation his place here in order that he might be
always feeding at the manger, and have his dwelling as far as might
be from the council-chamber, making as little noise and disturbance
as possible, and permitting the best part to advise quietly for the
good of the whole. And knowing that this lower principle in man
would not comprehend reason, and even if attaining to some degree of perception would never naturally care for rational notions,
but that it would be led away by phantoms and visions night and
day,—to be a remedy for this, God combined with it the liver, and
placed it in the house of the lower nature, contriving that it should
be solid and smooth, and bright and sweet, and should also have a
bitter quality, in order that the power of thought, which proceeds
from the mind, might be reflected as in a mirror which receives
likenesses of objects and gives back images of them to the sight;
and so might strike terror into the desires, when, making use of the
bitter part of the liver, to which it is akin, it comes threatening and
invading, and diffusing this bitter element swiftly through the
whole liver produces colours like bile, and contracting every part
makes it wrinkled and rough; and twisting out of its right place and
contorting the lobe and closing and shutting up the vessels and

the neck,
and in-
tended to
assist
reason
against
desire.

The heart
acts as
herald
and exec-
utive of
reason,
carrying
its com-
mands
through-
out the
body.

It is sus-
tained
and re-
freshed
by the
softness
and cool-
ness of
the lung.

(2) De-
sire,
[71]
chained
up be-
tween
the mid-
riff and
the navel
far away
from the
council-
chamber.

Knowing
that this
part
would be
guided
by images
alone,
God con-
structed
the liver
with its

The purpose of the liver

50

Timaeus

TIMAEUS.

mirror-like surface, in which are imaged the intimations of reason.

These intimations are given to men when asleep or demented, but

[72]

can only be interpreted by the sane man who is awake.

The spleen, like a napkin, keeps the liver clean.

gates, causes pain and loathing. And the converse happens when some gentle inspiration of the understanding pictures images of an opposite character, and allays the bile and bitterness by refusing to stir or touch the nature opposed to itself, but by making use of the natural sweetness of the liver, corrects all things and makes them to be right and smooth and free, and renders the portion of the soul which resides about the liver happy and joyful, enabling it to pass the night in peace, and to practise divination in sleep, inasmuch as it has no share in mind and reason. For the authors of our being, remembering the command of their father when he bade them create the human race as good as they could, that they might correct our inferior parts and make them to attain a measure of truth, placed in the liver the seat of divination. And herein is a proof that God has given the art of divination not to the wisdom, but to the foolishness of man. No man, when in his wits, attains prophetic truth and inspiration; but when he receives the inspired word, either his intelligence is enthralled in sleep, or he is demented by some distemper or possession. And he who would understand what he remembers to have been said, whether in a dream or when he was awake, by the prophetic and inspired nature, or would determine by reason the meaning of the apparitions which he has seen, and what indications they afford to this man or that, of past, present or future good and evil, must first recover his wits. But, while he continues demented, he cannot judge of the visions which he sees or the words which he utters; the ancient saying is very true, that 'only a man who has his wits can act or judge about himself and his own affairs.' And for this reason it is customary to appoint interpreters to be judges of the true inspiration. Some persons call them prophets; they are quite unaware that they are only the expositors of dark sayings and visions, and are not to be called prophets at all, but only interpreters of prophecy.

Such is the nature of the liver, which is placed as we have described in order that it may give prophetic intimations. During the life of each individual these intimations are plainer, but after his death the liver becomes blind, and delivers oracles too obscure to be intelligible. The neighbouring organ [the spleen] is situated on the left-hand side, and is constructed with a view of keeping the liver bright and pure,—like a napkin, always ready prepared and at hand to clean the mirror. And hence, when any impurities arise in the region of the liver by reason of disorders of the body, the loose nature of the spleen, which is composed of a hollow and bloodless tissue, receives them all and clears them away, and when filled with the unclean matter, swells and festers, but, again, when the body is purged, settles down into the same place as before, and is humbled.

Concerning the soul, as to which part is mortal and which divine, and how and why they are separated, and where located, if God acknowledges that we have spoken the truth, then, and then only, can we be confident; still, we may venture to assert that what has been said by us is probable, and will be rendered more probable by investigation. Let us assume thus much.

The creation of the rest of the body follows next in order, and this we may investigate in a similar manner. And it appears to be very meet that the body should be framed on the following principles:—

The authors of our race were aware that we should be intemperate in eating and drinking, and take a good deal more than was necessary or proper, by reason of gluttony. In order then that disease might not quickly destroy us, and lest our mortal race should perish without fulfilling its end—intending to provide against this, the gods made what is called the lower belly, to be a receptacle for the superfluous meat and drink, and formed the convolution of the bowels, so that the food might be prevented from passing quickly through and compelling the body to require more food, thus producing insatiable gluttony, and making the whole race an enemy to philosophy and music, and rebellious against the divinest element within us.

The bones and flesh, and other similar parts of us, were made as follows. The first principle of all of them was the generation of the marrow. For the bonds of life which unite the soul with the body are made fast there, and they are the root and foundation of the human race. The marrow itself is created out of other materials: God took such of the primary triangles as were straight and smooth, and were adapted by their perfection to produce fire and water, and air and earth—these, I say, he separated from their kinds, and mingling them in due proportions with one another, made the marrow out of them to be a universal seed of the whole race of mankind; and in this seed he then planted and enclosed the souls, and in the original distribution gave to the marrow as many and various forms as the different kinds of souls were hereafter to receive. That which, like a field, was to receive the divine seed, he made round every way, and called that portion of the marrow, brain, intending that, when an animal was perfected, the vessel containing this substance should be the head; but that which was intended to contain the remaining and mortal part of the soul he distributed into figures at once round and elongated, and he called them all by the

Timaeus

TIMAEUS.

Our account of the soul is probable: God only knows if it is true.

The bowels intended to pre-[73] vent the food from passing away too quickly, that men might not be perpetually occupied in eating and drinking.

Bone, flesh, and similar substances are all formed from marrow. Marrow is composed of the most perfect of the elementary triangles, mingled in due proportion. To the marrow

[74]

name 'marrow;' and to these, as to anchors, fastening the bonds of the whole soul, he proceeded to fashion around them the entire framework of our body, constructing for the marrow, first of all, a complete covering of bone.

Bone was composed by him in the following manner. Having sifted pure and smooth earth he kneaded it and wetted it with marrow, and after that he put it into fire and then into water, and once more into fire and again into water—in this way by frequent transfers from one to the other he made it insoluble by either. Out of this he fashioned, as in a lathe, a globe made of bone, which he placed around the brain, and in this he left a narrow opening; and around the marrow of the neck and back he formed vertebrae which he placed under one another like pivots, beginning at the head and extending through the whole of the trunk. Thus wishing to preserve the entire seed, he enclosed it in a stone-like casing, inserting joints, and using in the formation of them the power of the other or diverse as an intermediate nature, that they might have motion and flexure. Then again, considering that the bone would be too brittle and inflexible, and when heated and again cooled would soon mortify and destroy the seed within—having this in view, he contrived the sinews and the flesh, that so binding all the members together by the sinews, which admitted of being stretched and relaxed about the vertebrae, he might thus make the body capable of flexion and extension, while the flesh would serve as a protection against the summer heat and against the winter cold, and also against falls, softly and easily yielding to external bodies, like articles made of felt; and containing in itself a warm moisture which in summer exudes and makes the surface damp, would impart a natural coolness to the whole body; and again in winter by the help of this internal warmth would form a very tolerable defence against the frost which surrounds it and attacks it from without. He who modelled us, considering these things, mixed earth with fire and water and blended them; and making a ferment of acid and salt, he mingled it with them and formed soft and succulent flesh. As for the sinews, he made them of a mixture of bone and unfermented flesh, attempered so as to be in a mean, and gave them a yellow colour; wherefore the sinews have a firmer and more glutinous nature than flesh, but a softer and moister nature than the bones. With these God covered the bones and marrow, binding them together by sinews, and then enshrouded them all in an upper covering of flesh. The more living and sensitive of the bones he enclosed in the thinnest film of flesh, and those which had the least life within them in the thickest and most solid flesh. So again on the

joints of the bones, where reason indicated that no more was required, he placed only a thin covering of flesh, that it might not interfere with the flexion of our bodies and make them unwieldy because difficult to move; and also that it might not, by being
crowded and pressed and matted together, destroy sensation by
reason of its hardness, and impair the memory and dull the edge of
intelligence. Wherefore also the thighs and the shanks and the hips,
and the bones of the arms and the forearms, and other parts which
have no joints, and the inner bones, which on account of the rarity
of the soul in the marrow are destitute of reason—all these are
abundantly provided with flesh; but such as have mind in them
are in general less fleshy, except where the creator has made some
part solely of flesh in order to give sensation,—as, for example, the
tongue. But commonly this is not the case. For the nature which
comes into being and grows up in us by a law of necessity, does not
admit of the combination of solid bone and much flesh with acute
perceptions. More than any other part the framework of the head
would have had them, if they could have co-existed, and the human
race, having a strong and fleshy and sinewy head, would have had a
life twice or many times as long as it now has, and also more healthy
and free from pain. But our creators, considering whether they
should make a longer-lived race which was worse, or a shorter-lived
race which was better, came to the conclusion that every one ought
to prefer a shorter span of life, which was better, to a longer one,
which was worse; and therefore they covered the head with thin
bone, but not with flesh and sinews, since it had no joints; and
thus the head was added, having more wisdom and sensation than
the rest of the body, but also being in every man far weaker. For
these reasons and after this manner God placed the sinews at the
extremity of the head, in a circle round the neck, and glued them
together by the principle of likeness and fastened the extremities of
the jawbones to them below the face, and the other sinews he dispersed throughout the body, fastening limb to limb. The framers
of us framed the mouth, as now arranged, having teeth and tongue
and lips, with a view to the necessary and the good, contriving the
way in for necessary purposes, the way out for the best purposes;
for that is necessary which enters in and gives food to the body;
but the river of speech, which flows out of a man and ministers to
the intelligence, is the fairest and noblest of all streams. Still the
head could neither be left a bare frame of bones, on account of the
extremes of heat and cold in the different seasons, nor yet be allowed to be wholly covered, and so become dull and senseless by
reason of an overgrowth of flesh. The fleshy nature was not there-

mingling
with
them a
[75]
ferment
of acid
and salt;
the sinews
by mixing
bone and
unfer-
mented
flesh.

The most
sensitive
of the
bones, as
well as
the joints,
are thinly
covered
with
flesh;

the least
sensitive
are thick-
ly cov-
ered.

Flesh,
however,
without
bone, is
some-
times
highly
sensitive:
e. g. the
tongue.
But this
is excep-
tional;
for the
chief pur-
pose of
the flesh
is to give
protec-
tion, not
sensation.
And be-
cause God
wished us
to live a

TIMAEUS.

rational
and not a
long life,
the head
was not
covered
with
flesh.

The
mouth
was con-
structed
with a
view to
the neces-
sary and
the good.

The skull
was not
left bare,
but en-
veloped
with skin
(= the
film
which
forms on
flesh as it
dries).

The su-
tures and
their di-
versity.

Out of
punctures
in the
skin of
the head
grew the
hair.

77
Nails are
com-
pounded
of sinew,
skin and
bone;
they were
made
with a

fore wholly dried up, but a large sort of peel was parted off and remained over, which is now called the skin. This met and grew by the help of the cerebral moisture, and became the circular envelopment of the head. And the moisture, rising up under the sutures, watered and closed in the skin upon the crown, forming a sort of knot. The diversity of the sutures was caused by the power of the courses of the soul and of the food, and the more these struggled against one another the more numerous they became, and fewer if the struggle were less violent. This skin the divine power pierced all round with fire, and out of the punctures which were thus made the moisture issued forth, and the liquid and heat which was pure came away, and a mixed part which was composed of the same material as the skin, and had a fineness equal to the punctures, was borne up by its own impulse and extended far outside the head, but being too slow to escape, was thrust back by the external air, and rolled up underneath the skin, where it took root. Thus the hair sprang up in the skin, being akin to it because it is like threads of leather, but rendered harder and closer through the pressure of the cold, by which each hair, while in process of separation from the skin, is compressed and cooled. Wherefore the creator formed the head hairy, making use of the causes which I have mentioned, and reflecting also that instead of flesh the brain needed the hair to be a light covering or guard, which would give shade in summer and shelter in winter, and at the same time would not impede our quickness of perception. From the combination of sinew, skin, and bone, in the structure of the finger, there arises a triple compound, which, when dried up, takes the form of one hard skin partaking of all three natures, and was fabricated by these second causes, but designed by mind which is the principal cause with an eye to the future. For our creators well knew that women and other animals would some day be framed out of men, and they further knew that many animals would require the use of nails for many purposes; wherefore they fashioned in men at their first creation the rudiments of nails. For this purpose and for these reasons they caused skin, hair, and nails to grow at the extremities of the limbs. And now that all the parts and members of the mortal animal had come together, since its life of necessity consisted of fire and breath, and it therefore wasted away by dissolution and depletion, the gods contrived the following remedy: They mingled a nature akin to that of man with other forms and perceptions, and thus created another kind of animal. These are the trees and plants and seeds which have been improved by cultivation and are now domesticated among us; anciently there were only the wild kinds, which are older than the cultivated. For everything that partakes of life may be truly called a living being, and the animal of which we are now speaking partakes of the third kind of soul, which is said to be seated between the midriff and the navel, having no part in opinion or reason or mind, but only in feelings of pleasure and pain and the desires which accompany them. For this nature is always in a passive state, revolving in and about itself, repelling the motion from without and using its own, and accordingly is not endowed by nature with the power of observing or reflecting on its own concerns. Wherefore it lives and does not differ from a living being, but is fixed and rooted in the same spot, having no power of self-motion.

Now after the superior powers had created all these natures to be food for us who are of the inferior nature, they cut various channels through the body as through a garden, that it might be watered as from a running stream. In the first place, they cut two hidden channels or veins down the back where the skin and the flesh join, which answered severally to the right and left side of the body. These they let down along the backbone, so as to have the marrow of generation between them, where it was most likely to flourish, and in order that the stream coming down from above might flow freely to the other parts, and equalize the irrigation. In the next place, they divided the veins about the head, and interlacing them, they sent them in opposite directions; those coming from the right side they sent to the left of the body, and those from the left they diverted towards the right, so that they and the skin might together form a bond which should fasten the head to the body, since the crown of the head was not encircled by sinews; and also in order that the sensations from both sides might be distributed over the whole body. And next, they ordered the water-courses of the body in a manner which I will describe, and which will be more easily understood if we begin by admitting that all things which have lesser parts retain the greater, but the greater cannot retain the lesser. Now of all natures fire has the smallest parts, and therefore penetrates through earth and water and air and their compounds, nor can anything hold it. And a similar principle applies to the human belly; for when meats and drinks enter it, it holds them, but it cannot hold air and fire, because the particles of which they consist are smaller than its own structure.

These elements, therefore, God employed for the sake of distributing moisture from the belly into the veins, weaving together a network of fire and air like a weel, having at the entrance two lesser weels; further he constructed one of these with two openings, and from the lesser weels he extended cords reaching all round to the ex-

Timaeus

TIMAEUS.

view to the time when women and animals should spring from man.

Seeing that mankind would need food, trees and plants were created. These are animals and have life, being endowed with the lower mortal soul.

Next the gods cut two channels down the back, [78] one on either side of the spine. After this they diverted the veins on the right of the head to the left of the body, and *vice versa*.

tremities of the network. All the interior of the net he made of fire, but the lesser weels and their cavity, of air. The network he took and spread over the newly-formed animal in the following manner: —He let the lesser weels pass into the mouth; there were two of them, and one he let down by the air-pipes into the lungs, the other by the side of the air-pipes into the belly. The former he divided into two branches, both of which he made to meet at the channels of the nose, so that when the way through the mouth did not act, the streams of the mouth as well were replenished through the nose. With the other cavity (i. e. of the greater weel) he enveloped the hollow parts of the body, and at one time he made all this to flow into the lesser weels, quite gently, for they are composed of air, and at another time he caused the lesser weels to flow back again; and the net he made to find a way in and out through the pores of the body, and the rays of fire which are bound fast within followed the passage of the air either way, never at any time ceasing so long as the mortal being holds together. This process, as we affirm, the name-giver named inspiration and expiration. And all this movement, active as well as passive, takes place in order that the body, being watered and cooled, may receive nourishment and life; for when the respiration is going in and out, and the fire, which is fast bound within, follows it, and ever and anon moving to and fro, enters through the belly and reaches the meat and drink, it dissolves them, and dividing them into small portions and guiding them through the passages where it goes, pumps them as from a fountain into the channels of the veins, and makes the stream of the veins flow through the body as through a conduit.

Let us once more consider the phenomena of respiration, and enquire into the causes which have made it what it is. They are as follows:—Seeing that there is no such thing as a vacuum into which any of those things which are moved can enter, and the breath is carried from us into the external air, the next point is, as will be clear to every one, that it does not go into a vacant space, but pushes its neighbour out of its place, and that which is thrust out in turn drives out its neighbour; and in this way everything of necessity at last comes round to that place from whence the breath came forth, and enters in there, and following the breath, fills up the vacant space; and this goes on like the rotation of a wheel, because there can be no such thing as a vacuum. Wherefore also the breast and the lungs, when they emit the breath, are replenished by the air which surrounds the body and which enters in through the pores of the flesh and is driven round in a circle; and again, the air which is sent away and passes out through the body forces the breath inwards through the passage of the mouth and the nostrils. Now the origin of this movement may be supposed to be as follows. In the interior of every animal the hottest part is that which is around the blood and veins; it is in a manner an internal fountain of fire, which we compare to the network of a creel, being woven all of fire and extended through the centre of the body, while the outer parts are composed of air. Now we must admit that heat naturally proceeds outward to its own place and to its kindred element; and as there are two exits for the heat, the one out through the body, and the other through the mouth and nostrils, when it moves towards the one, it drives round the air at the other, and that which is driven round falls into the fire and becomes warm, and that which goes forth is cooled. But when the heat changes its place, and the particles at the other exit grow warmer, the hotter air inclining in that direction and carried towards its native element, fire, pushes round the air at the other; and this being affected in the same way and communicating the same impulse, a circular motion swaying to and fro is produced by the double process, which we call inspiration and expiration.

The phenomena of medical cupping-glasses and of the swallowing of drink and of the projection of bodies, whether discharged in the air or bowled along the ground, are to be investigated on a similar principle; and swift and slow sounds, which appear to be high and low, and are sometimes discordant on account of their inequality, and then again harmonical on account of the equality of the motion which they excite in us. For when the motions of the antecedent swifter sounds begin to pause and the two are equalized, the slower sounds overtake the swifter and then propel them. When they overtake them they do not intrude a new and discordant motion, but introduce the beginnings of a slower, which answers to the swifter as it dies away, thus producing a single mixed expression out of high and low, whence arises a pleasure which even the unwise feel, and which to the wise becomes a higher sort of delight, being an imitation of divine harmony in mortal motions. Moreover, as to the flowing of water, the fall of the thunderbolt, and the marvels that are observed about the attraction of amber and the Heraclean stones,—in none of these cases is there any attraction; but he who investigates rightly, will find that such wonderful phenomena are attributable to the combination of certain conditions, —the non-existence of a vacuum, the fact that objects push one another round, and that they change places, passing severally into their proper positions as they are divided or combined.

Such as we have seen, is the nature and such are the causes of

the fire within following the air in either direction. The motion of the fire into and out of the belly dissolves the food and pumps the blood into the veins.

Expiration and inspiration take place [80] through the pores as well as through the mouth and nostrils. Expiration is due to the attraction of similars: the air on entering the body is heated, and then moves outward, seeking the place of fire. Inspiration is due to the impossibility of a vacu-

respiration,—the subject in which this discussion originated. For the fire cuts the food and following the breath surges up within, fire and breath rising together and filling the veins by drawing up out of the belly and pouring into them the cut portions of the food; and so the streams of food are kept flowing through the whole body in all animals. And fresh cuttings from kindred substances, whether the fruits of the earth or herb of the field, which God planted to be our daily food, acquire all sorts of colours by their inter-mixture; but red is the most pervading of them, being created by the cutting action of fire and by the impression which it makes on a moist substance; and hence the liquid which circulates in the body has a colour such as we have described. The liquid itself we call blood, which nourishes the flesh and the whole body, whence all parts are watered and empty places filled.

Now the process of repletion and evacuation is effected after the manner of the universal motion by which all kindred substances are drawn towards one another. For the external elements which surround us are always causing us to consume away, and distributing and sending off like to like; the particles of blood, too, which are divided and contained within the frame of the animal as in a sort of heaven, are compelled to imitate the motion of the universe. Each, therefore, of the divided parts within us, being carried to its kindred nature, replenishes the void. When more is taken away than flows in, then we decay, and when less, we grow and increase.

The frame of the entire creature when young has the triangles of each kind new, and may be compared to the keel of a vessel which is just off the stocks; they are locked firmly together and yet the whole mass is soft and delicate, being freshly formed of marrow and nurtured on milk. Now when the triangles out of which meats and drinks are composed come in from without, and are comprehended in the body, being older and weaker than the triangles already there, the frame of the body gets the bettter of them and its newer triangles cut them up, and so the animal grows great, being nourished by a multitude of similar particles. But when the roots of the triangles are loosened by having undergone many conflicts with many things in the course of time, they are no longer able to cut or assimilate the food which enters, but are themselves easily divided by the bodies which come in from without. In this way every animal is overcome and decays, and this affection is called old age. And at last, when the bonds by which the triangles of the marrow are united no longer hold, and are parted by the strain of existence, they in turn loosen the bonds of the soul, and she, obtaining a natural release, flies away with joy. For that which takes

place according to nature is pleasant, but that which is contrary to
nature is painful. And thus death, if caused by disease or produced
by wounds, is painful and violent; but that sort of death which
comes with old age and fulfils the debt of nature is the easiest of
deaths, and is accompanied with pleasure rather than with pain.

Now every one can see whence diseases arise. There are four
natures out of which the body is compacted, earth and fire and
water and air, and the unnatural excess or defect of these, or the
change of any of them from its own natural place into another, or
—since there are more kinds than one of fire and of the other elements—the assumption by any of these of a wrong kind, or any
similar irregularity, produces disorders and diseases; for when any
of them is produced or changed in a manner contrary to nature,
the parts which were previously cool grow warm, and those which
were dry become moist, and the light become heavy, and the heavy
light; all sorts of changes occur. For, as we affirm, a thing can only
remain the same with itself, whole and sound, when the same is
added to it, or subtracted from it, in the same respect and in the
same manner and in due proportion; and whatever comes or goes
away in violation of these laws causes all manner of changes and
infinite diseases and corruptions. Now there is a second class of
structures which are also natural, and this affords a second opportunity of observing diseases to him who would understand them.
For whereas marrow and bone and flesh and sinews are composed
of the four elements, and the blood, though after another manner,
is likewise formed out of them, most diseases originate in the way
which I have described; but the worst of all owe their severity to
the fact that the generation of these substances proceeds in a wrong
order; they are then destroyed. For the natural order is that the
flesh and sinews should be made of blood, the sinews out of the
fibres to which they are akin, and the flesh out of the clots which
are formed when the fibres are separated. And the glutinous and
rich matter which comes away from the sinews and the flesh, not
only glues the flesh to the bones, but nourishes and imparts growth
to the bone which surrounds the marrow; and by reason of the
solidity of the bones, that which filters through consists of the purest and smoothest and oiliest sort of triangles, dropping like dew
from the bones and watering the marrow. Now when each process
takes place in this order, health commonly results; when in the opposite order, disease. For when the flesh becomes decomposed and
sends back the wasting substance into the veins, then an over-supply
of blood of diverse kinds, mingling with air in the veins, having
variegated colours and bitter properties, as well as acid and saline

Timaeus

TIMAEUS.

attrac-
tion.

When the
body is
[82]
young,
the tri-
angles of
which it
is com-
posed are
new and
strong,
and over-
come the
triangles
of the
food; but
in old age
they are
overcome
by them.

Death
takes
place
when the
triangles
of the
marrow,
becoming
disunited,
loosen
the soul's
bonds.
A natural
death is
pleasant,
a violent,
painful.

Diseases
of the
body
arise (i)
when any
of the
four ele-
ments is
out of
place or
there is
too much
or too
little of

83
Timaeus

TIMAEUS.

them in
any part;

and (ii)
when
blood,
flesh,
and
sinews
are pro-
duced in
a wrong
order.
The pro-
per order
is that
flesh and
sinew
should be
formed
from
blood,
flesh from
the liquid
and sinew
from the
fibrous
part of it;
and that
from
these
should
exude a
glutinous
matter
which
nourishes
bone and
marrow.
When this
order is
reversed,
[84]
all sorts
of bile
and
phlegm
are gen-
erated.

qualities, contains all sorts of bile and serum and phlegm. For all things go the wrong way, and having become corrupted, first they taint the blood itself, and then ceasing to give nourishment to the body they are carried along the veins in all directions, no longer preserving the order of their natural courses, but at war with themselves, because they receive no good from one another, and are hostile to the abiding constitution of the body, which they corrupt and dissolve. The oldest part of the flesh which is corrupted, being hard to decompose, from long burning grows black, and from being everywhere corroded becomes bitter, and is injurious to every part of the body which is still uncorrupted. Sometimes, when the bitter element is refined away, the black part assumes an acidity which takes the place of the bitterness; at other times the bitterness being tinged with blood has a redder colour; and this, when mixed with black, takes the hue of grass [1]; and again, an auburn colour mingles with the bitter matter when new flesh is decomposed by the fire which surrounds the internal flame;—to all which symptoms some physician perhaps, or rather some philosopher, who had the power of seeing in many dissimilar things one nature deserving of a name, has assigned the common name of bile. But the other kinds of bile are variously distinguished by their colours. As for serum, that sort which is the watery part of blood is innocent, but that which is a secretion of black and acid bile is malignant when mingled by the power of heat with any salt substance, and is then called acid phlegm. Again, the substance which is formed by the liquefaction of new and tender flesh when air is present, if inflated and encased in liquid so as to form bubbles, which separately are invisible owing to their small size, but when collected are of a bulk which is visible, and have a white colour arising out of the generation of foam—all this decomposition of tender flesh when inter-mingled with air is termed by us white phlegm. And the whey or sediment of newly-formed phlegm is sweat and tears, and includes the various daily discharges by which the body is purified. Now all these become causes of disease when the blood is not replenished in a natural manner by food and drink but gains bulk from opposite sources in violation of the laws of nature. When the several parts of the flesh are separated by disease, if the foundation remains, the power of the disorder is only half as great, and there is still a prospect of an easy recovery; but when that which binds the flesh to the bones is diseased, and no longer being separated from the muscles and sinews [2], ceases to give nourishment

---

[1] Reading χλοῶδες.
[2] Reading αὐτό for αὖ τό and ἅμα for αἷμα.

to the bone and to unite flesh and bone, and from being oily and smooth and glutinous becomes rough and salt and dry, owing to bad regimen, then all the substance thus corrupted crumbles away under the flesh and the sinews, and separates from the bone, and the fleshy parts fall away from their foundation and leave the sinews bare and full of brine, and the flesh again gets into the circulation of the blood and makes the previously-mentioned disorders still greater. And if these bodily affections be severe, still worse are the prior disorders; as when the bone itself, by reason of the density of the flesh, does not obtain sufficient air, but becomes mouldy and hot and gangrened and receives no nutriment, and the natural process is inverted, and the bone crumbling passes into the food, and the food into the flesh, and the flesh again falling into the blood makes all maladies that may occur more virulent than those already mentioned. But the worst case of all is when the marrow is diseased, either from excess or defect; and this is the cause of the very greatest and most fatal disorders, in which the whole course of the body is reversed.

There is a third class of diseases which may be conceived of as arising in three ways; for they are produced sometimes by wind, and sometimes by phlegm, and sometimes by bile. When the lung, which is the dispenser of the air to the body, is obstructed by rheums and its passages are not free, some of them not acting, while through others too much air enters, then the parts which are unrefreshed by air corrode, while in other parts the excess of air forcing its way through the veins distorts them and decomposing the body is enclosed in the midst of it and occupies the midriff; thus numberless painful diseases are produced, accompanied by copious sweats. And oftentimes when the flesh is dissolved in the body, wind, generated within and unable to escape, is the source of quite as much pain as the air coming in from without; but the greatest pain is felt when the wind gets about the sinews and the veins of the shoulders, and swells them up, and so twists back the great tendons and the sinews which are connected with them. These disorders are called tetanus and opisthotonus, by reason of the tension which accompanies them. The cure of them is difficult; relief is in most cases given by fever supervening. The white phlegm, though dangerous when detained within by reason of the air-bubbles, yet if it can communicate with the outside air, is less severe, and only discolours the body, generating leprous eruptions and similar diseases. When it is mingled with black bile and dispersed about the courses of the head, which are the divinest part of us, the attack if coming on in sleep, is not so severe; but when assailing

Timaeus

TIMAEUS.

The various kinds of bile.

Of phlegm there is an acid and a white sort.

Stages of the disease:—
(1) When the flesh is attacked, if the foundations remain sound, there is less danger.
(2) There is more when the flesh falls away from the sinews and bones.
(3) Worse still are the prior disorders, such as crumbling away and gangrene of the bones;
[85]
and
(4) worst of all is disease of the spinal marrow.

Timaeus

TIMAEUS.

(iii) A third class of diseases is produced
a. by wind—i.e. disorders of the lungs,

tetanus and opisthotonus;

b. by phlegm— i. e. leprosy,

epilepsy,

and catarrh;

c. by bile —i. e. tumours and inflammations,

chills and shuddering,

disease of the marrow,

diarrhoea [86] and dysentery.

Excess of fire causes continuous fever, of air quotidian, of water tertian, of earth quartan.

There are two kinds

those who are awake it is hard to be got rid of, and being an affection of a sacred part, is most justly called sacred. An acid and salt phlegm, again, is the source of all those diseases which take the form of catarrh, but they have many names because the places into which they flow are manifold.

Inflammations of the body come from burnings and inflamings, and all of them originate in bile. When bile finds a means of discharge, it boils up and sends forth all sorts of tumours; but when imprisoned within, it generates many inflammatory diseases, above all when mingled with pure blood; since it then displaces the fibres which are scattered about in the blood and are designed to maintain the balance of rare and dense, in order that the blood may not be so liquefied by heat as to exude from the pores of the body, nor again become too dense and thus find a difficulty in circulating through the veins. The fibres are so constituted as to maintain this balance; and if any one brings them all together when the blood is dead and in process of cooling, then the blood which remains becomes fluid, but if they are left alone, they soon congeal by reason of the surrounding cold. The fibres having this power over the blood, bile, which is only stale blood, and which from being flesh is dissolved again into blood, at the first influx coming in little by little, hot and liquid, is congealed by the power of the fibres; and so congealing and made to cool, it produces internal cold and shuddering. When it enters with more of a flood and overcomes the fibres by its heat, and boiling up throws them into disorder, if it have power enough to maintain its supremacy, it penetrates the marrow and burns up what may be termed the cables of the soul, and sets her free; but when there is not so much of it, and the body though wasted still holds out, the bile is itself mastered, and is either utterly banished, or is thrust through the veins into the lower or upper belly, and is driven out of the body like an exile from a state in which there has been civil war; whence arise diarrhoeas and dysenteries, and all such disorders. When the constitution is disordered by excess of fire, continuous heat and fever are the result; when excess of air is the cause, then the fever is quotidian; when of water, which is a more sluggish element than either fire or air, then the fever is a tertian; when of earth, which is the most sluggish of the four, and is only purged away in a four-fold period, the result is a quartan fever, which can with difficulty be shaken off.

Such is the manner in which diseases of the body arise; the disorders of the soul, which depend upon the body, originate as follows. We must acknowledge disease of the mind to be a want of intelligence; and of this there are two kinds; to wit, madness and ignorance. In whatever state a man experiences either of them, that state may be called disease; and excessive pains and pleasures are justly to be regarded as the greatest diseases to which the soul is liable. For a man who is in great joy or in great pain, in his unseasonable eagerness to attain the one and to avoid the other, is not able to see or to hear anything rightly; but he is mad, and is at the time utterly incapable of any participation in reason. He who has the seed about the spinal marrow too plentiful and overflowing, like a tree overladen with fruit, has many throes, and also obtains many pleasures in his desires and their offspring, and is for the most part of his life deranged, because his pleasures and pains are so very great; his soul is rendered foolish and disordered by his body; yet he is regarded not as one diseased, but as one who is voluntarily bad, which is a mistake. The truth is that the intemperance of love is a disease of the soul due chiefly to the moisture and fluidity which is produced in one of the elements by the loose consistency of the bones. And in general, all that which is termed the incontinence of pleasure and is deemed a reproach under the idea that the wicked voluntarily do wrong is not justly a matter for reproach. For no man is voluntarily bad; but the bad become bad by reason of an ill disposition of the body and bad education, things which are hateful to every man and happen to him against his will. And in the case of pain too in like manner the soul suffers much evil from the body. For where the acid and briny phlegm and other bitter and bilious humours wander about in the body, and find no exit or escape, but are pent up within and mingle their own vapours with the motions of the soul, and are blended, with them, they produce all sorts of diseases, more or fewer, and in every degree of intensity; and being carried to the three places of the soul, whichever they may severally assail, they create infinite varieties of ill-temper and melancholy, of rashness and cowardice, and also of forgetfulness and stupidity. Further, when to this evil constitution of body evil forms of government are added and evil discourses are uttered in private as well as in public, and no sort of instruction is given in youth to cure these evils, then all of us who are bad become bad from two causes which are entirely beyond our control. In such cases the planters are to blame rather than the plants, the educators rather than the educated. But however that may be, we should endeavour as far as we can by education, and studies, and learning, to avoid vice and attain virtue; this, however, is part of another subject.

There is a corresponding enquiry concerning the mode of treatment by which the mind and the body are to be preserved, about

of mental disease, madness and ignorance. Vice is due to an ill-disposition of the body,

and is involuntary.

87

Bad education and bad government increase the evil.

The great means of

preventing disease is to preserve the due proportion of mind and body.

88

The soul should not be allowed to wear out the body;

nor the body to embrute the soul.

Both should be equally exercised: the mathematicion should practise gymnastic, and the gymnast should study music.

which it is meet and right that I should say a word in turn; for it is more our duty to speak of the good than of the evil. Everything that is good is fair, and the fair is not without proportion, and the animal which is to be fair must have due proportion. Now we perceive lesser symmetries or proportions and reason about them, but of the highest and greatest we take no heed; for there is no proportion or disproportion more productive of health and disease, and virtue and vice, than that between soul and body. This however we do not perceive, nor do we reflect that when a weak or small frame is the vehicle of a great and mighty soul, or conversely, when a little soul is encased in a large body, then the whole animal is not fair, for it lacks the most important of all symmetries; but the due proportion of mind and body is the fairest and loveliest of all sights to him who has the seeing eye. Just as a body which has a leg too long, or which is unsymmetrical in some other respect, is an unpleasant sight, and also, when doing its share of work, is much distressed and makes convulsive efforts, and often stumbles through awkwardness, and is the cause of infinite evil to its own self—in like manner we should conceive of the double nature which we call the living being; and when in this compound there is an impassioned soul more powerful than the body, that soul, I say, convulses and fills with disorders the whole inner nature of man; and when eager in the pursuit of some sort of learning or study, causes wasting; or again, when teaching or disputing in private or in public, and strifes and controversies arise, inflames and dissolves the composite frame of man and introduces rheums; and the nature of this phenomenon is not understood by most professors of medicine, who ascribe it to the opposite of the real cause. And once more, when a body large and too strong for the soul is united to a small and weak intelligence, then inasmuch as there are two desires natural to man,—one of food for the sake of the body, and one of wisdom for the sake of the diviner part of us—then, I say, the motions of the stronger, getting the better and increasing their own power, but making the soul dull, and stupid, and forgetful, engender ignorance, which is the greatest of diseases. There is one protection against both kinds of disproportion:—that we should not move the body without the soul or the soul without the body, and thus they will be on their guard against each other, and be healthy and well balanced. And therefore the mathematician or any one else whose thoughts are much absorbed in some intellectual pursuit, must allow his body also to have due exercise, and practise gymnastic; and he who is careful to fashion the body, should in turn impart to the soul its proper motions, and should cultivate music and all philosophy, if he would deserve to be called truly fair and truly good. And the separate parts should be treated in the same manner, in imitation of the pattern of the universe; for as the body is heated and also cooled within by the elements which enter into it, and is again dried up and moistened by external things, and experiences these and the like affections from both kinds of motions, the result is that the body if given up to motion when in a state of quiescence is overmastered and perishes; but if any one, in imitation of that which we call the foster-mother and nurse of the universe, will not allow the body ever to be inactive, but is always producing motions and agitations through its whole extent, which form the natural defence against other motions both internal and external, and by moderate exercise reduces to order according to their affinities the particles and affections which are wandering about the body, as we have already said when speaking of the universe [1], he will not allow enemy placed by the side of enemy to stir up wars and disorders in the body, but he will place friend by the side of friend, so as to create health. Now of all motions that is the best which is produced in a thing by itself, for it is most akin to the motion of thought and of the universe; but that motion which is caused by others is not so good, and worst of all is that which moves the body, when at rest, in parts only and by some external agency. Wherefore of all modes of purifying and re-uniting the body the best is gymnastic; the next best is a surging motion, as in sailing or any other mode of conveyance which is not fatiguing; the third sort of motion may be of use in a case of extreme necessity, but in any other will be adopted by no man of sense: I mean the purgative treatment of physicians; for diseases unless they are very dangerous should not be irritated by medicines, since every form of disease is in a manner akin to the living being, whose complex frame has an appointed term of life. For not the whole race only, but each individual—barring inevitable accidents—comes into the world having a fixed span, and the triangles in us are originally framed with power to last for a certain time, beyond which no man can prolong his life. And this holds also of the constitution of diseases; if any one regardless of the appointed time tries to subdue them by medicine, he only aggravates and multiplies them. Wherefore we ought always to manage them by regimen, as far as a man can spare the time, and not provoke a disagreeable enemy by medicines.

Enough of the composite animal, and of the body which is a part of him, and of the manner in which a man may train and be

[1] *Supra,* 33 A.

Timaeus

TIMAEUS.

Motion, as in the universe, so in the body, produces order and harmony.

89
The best exercise and purification is the spontaneous motion of the body, as in gymnastic; less good is an external motion, as in sailing; least good the external motion of a part only produced by medicine. The last should be employed only in extreme cases.

trained by himself so as to live most according to reason: and we must above and before all provide that the element which is to train him shall be the fairest and best adapted to that purpose. A minute discussion of this subject would be a serious task; but if, as before, I am to give only an outline, the subject may not unfitly be summed up as follows.

I have often remarked that there are three kinds of soul located within us, having each of them motions, and I must now repeat in the fewest words possible, that one part, if remaining inactive and ceasing from its natural motion, must necessarily become very weak, but that which is trained and exercised, very strong. Wherefore we should take care that the movements of the different parts of the soul should be in due proportion.

And we should consider that God gave the sovereign part of the human soul to be the divinity of each one, being that part which, as we say, dwells at the top of the body, and inasmuch as we are a plant not of an earthly but of a heavenly growth, raises us from earth to our kindred who are in heaven. And in this we say truly; for the divine power suspended the head and root of us from that place where the generation of the soul first began, and thus made the whole body upright. When a man is always occupied with the cravings of desire and ambition, and is eagerly striving to satisfy them, all his thoughts must be mortal, and, as far as it is possible altogether to become such, he must be mortal every whit, because he has cherished his mortal part. But he who has been earnest in the love of knowledge and of true wisdom, and has exercised his intellect more than any other part of him, must have thoughts immortal and divine, if he attain truth, and in so far as human nature is capable of sharing in immortality, he must altogether be immortal; and since he is ever cherishing the divine power, and has the divinity within him in perfect order, he will be perfectly happy. Now there is only one way of taking care of things, and this is to give to each the food and motion which are natural to it. And the motions which are naturally akin to the divine principle within us are the thoughts and revolutions of the universe. These each man should follow, and correct the courses of the head which were corrupted at our birth, and by learning the harmonies and revolutions of the universe, should assimilate the thinking being to the thought, renewing his original nature, and having assimilated them should attain to that perfect life which the gods have set before mankind, both for the present and the future.

Thus our original design of discoursing about the universe down to the creation of man is nearly completed. A brief mention may be made of the generation of other animals, so far as the subject admits of brevity; in this manner our argument will best attain a due proportion. On the subject of animals, then, the following remarks may be offered. Of the men who came into the world, those who were cowards or led unrighteous lives may with reason be supposed to have changed into the nature of women in the second generation. And this was the reason why at that time the gods created in us the desire of sexual intercourse, contriving in man one animated substance, and in woman another, which they formed respectively in the following manner. The outlet for drink by which liquids pass through the lung under the kidneys and into the bladder, which receives and then by the pressure of the air emits them, was so fashioned by them as to penetrate also into the body of the marrow, which passes from the head along the neck and through the back, and which in the preceding discourse we have named the seed. And the seed having life, and becoming endowed with respiration, produces in that part in which it respires a lively desire of emission, and thus creates in us the love of procreation. Wherefore also in men the organ of generation becoming rebellious and masterful, like an animal disobedient to reason, and maddened with the sting of lust, seeks to gain absolute sway; and the same is the case with the so-called womb or matrix of women; the animal within them is desirous of procreating children, and when remaining unfruitful long beyond its proper time, gets discontented and angry, and wandering in every direction through the body, closes up the passages of the breath, and, by obstructing respiration, drives them to extremity, causing all varieties of disease, until at length the desire and love of the man and the woman, bringing them together [1] and as it were plucking the fruit from the tree, sow in the womb, as in a field, animals unseen by reason of their smallness and without form; these again are separated and matured within; they are then finally brought out into the light, and thus the generation of animals is completed.

Thus were created women and the female sex in general. But the race of birds was created out of innocent light-minded men, who, although their minds were directed toward heaven, imagined, in their simplicity, that the clearest demonstration of the things above was to be obtained by sight; these were remodelled and transformed into birds, and they grew feathers instead of hair. The race of wild pedestrian animals, again, came from those who had no philosophy in any of their thoughts, and never considered at all about the nature of the heavens, because they had ceased to use

[1] Reading ξυνδυάζοντες (conj. Hermann).

the origin of man. Women and the [91] other animals were generated on this wise. Cowardly and unjust men became women in the second generation.

Simpleminded men passed into birds;

those who were the slaves of passion into beasts;

Timaeus

TIMAEUS.

92

the most
foolish
into
reptiles;

the most
ignorant
and im-
pure into
fish.

Our task
is now
com-
pleted.

the courses of the head, but followed the guidance of those parts of the soul which are in the breast. In consequence of these habits of theirs they had their front-legs and their heads resting upon the earth to which they were drawn by natural affinity; and the crowns of their heads were elongated and of all sorts of shapes, into which the courses of the soul were crushed by reason of disuse. And this was the reason why they were created quadrupeds and polypods: God gave the more senseless of them the more support that they might be more attracted to the earth. And the most foolish of them, who trail their bodies entirely upon the ground and have no longer any need of feet, he made without feet to crawl upon the earth. The fourth class were the inhabitants of the water: these were made out of the most entirely senseless and ignorant of all, whom the transformers did not think any longer worthy of pure respiration, because they possessed a soul which was made impure by all sorts of transgression; and instead of the subtle and pure medium of air, they gave them the deep and muddy sea to be their element of respiration; and hence arose the race of fishes and oysters, and other aquatic animals, which have received the most remote habitations as a punishment of their outlandish ignorance. These are the laws by which animals pass into one another, now, as ever, changing as they lose or gain wisdom and folly.

We may now say that our discourse about the nature of the universe has an end. The world has received animals, mortal and immortal, and is fulfilled with them, and has become a visible animal containing the visible—the sensible God who is the image of the intellectual [1], the greatest, best, fairest, most perfect—the one only-begotten heaven.

[1] Or reading ποιητοῦ—'of his maker.'

CRITIAS

CRITIAS

PERSONS OF THE DIALOGUE

CRITIAS	TIMAEUS
HERMOCRATES	SOCRATES

Timaeus. How thankful I am, Socrates, that I have arrived at last, and, like a weary traveller after a long journey, may be at rest! And I pray the being who always was of old, and has now been by me revealed, to grant that my words may endure in so far as they have been spoken truly and acceptably to him; but if unintentionally I have said anything wrong, I pray that he will impose upon me a just retribution, and the just retribution of him who errs is that he should be set right. Wishing, then, to speak truly in future concerning the generation of the gods, I pray him to give me knowledge, which of all medicines is the most perfect and best. And now having offered my prayer I deliver up the argument to Critias, who is to speak next according to our agreement [1].

Critias. And I, Timaeus, accept the trust, and as you at first said that you were going to speak of high matters, and begged that some forbearance might be shown to you, I too ask the same or greater forbearance for what I am about to say. And although I very well know that my request may appear to be somewhat ambitious and discourteous, I must make it nevertheless. For will any man of sense deny that you have spoken well? I can only attempt to show that I ought to have more indulgence than you, because my theme is more difficult; and I shall argue that to seem to speak well of the gods to men is far easier than to speak well of men to men: for the inexperience and utter ignorance of his hearers about any subject is a great assistance to him who has to speak of it, and we know how ignorant we are concerning the gods. But I should like to make my meaning clearer, if you will follow me. All that is said by any of us can only be imitation and representation. For if we consider the likenesses which painters make of bodies divine

[1] Tim. 27 A.

Timaeus prays to the 'ancient of days' that the truth of his words may endure, and for enlightenment where he has erred

107

Critias asks for greater indulgence than was shown to Timaeus on the ground that it is easier to speak well of the Gods,

Critias

SOCRATES,
CRITIAS,
HERMO-
CRATES.

whom we
do not
know,
than of
men,
whom we
do.

An illus-
tration.

108

Socrates
grants the
indul-
gence,
and, not
to have
the same
request
repeated,
extends it
to Her-
mocrates.

Critias
invokes

and heavenly, and the different degrees of gratification with which the eye of the spectator receives them, we shall see that we are satisfied with the artist who is able in any degree to imitate the earth and its mountains, and the rivers, and the woods, and the universe, and the things that are and move therein, and further, that knowing nothing precise about such matters, we do not examine or analyze the painting; all that is required is a sort of indistinct and deceptive mode of shadowing them forth. But when a person endeavours to paint the human form we are quick at finding out defects, and our familiar knowledge makes us severe judges of any one who does not render every point of similarity. And we may observe the same thing to happen in discourse; we are satisfied with a picture of divine and heavenly things which has very little likeness to them; but we are more precise in our criticism of mortal and human things. Wherefore if at the moment of speaking I cannot suitably express my meaning, you must excuse me, considering that to form approved likenesses of human things is the reverse of easy. This is what I want to suggest to you, and at the same time to beg, Socrates, that I may have not less, but more indulgence conceded to me in what I am about to say. Which favour, if I am right in asking, I hope that you will be ready to grant.

Socrates. Certainly, Critias, we will grant your request, and we will grant the same by anticipation to Hermocrates, as well as to you and Timaeus; for I have no doubt that when his turn comes a little while hence, he will make the same request which you have made. In order, then, that he may provide himself with a fresh beginning, and not be compelled to say the same things over again, let him understand that the indulgence is already extended by anticipation to him. And now, friend Critias, I will announce to you the judgment of the theatre. They are of opinion that the last performer was wonderfully successful, and that you will need a great deal of indulgence before you will be able to take his place.

Hermocrates. The warning, Socrates, which you have addressed to him, I must also take to myself. But remember, Critias, that faint heart never yet raised a trophy; and therefore you must go and attack the argument like a man. First invoke Apollo and the Muses, and then let us hear you sound the praises and show forth the virtues of your ancient citizens.

Crit. Friend Hermocrates, you, who are stationed last and have another in front of you, have not lost heart as yet; the gravity of the situation will soon be revealed to you; meanwhile I accept your exhortations and encouragements. But besides the gods and goddesses whom you have mentioned, I would specially invoke

Mnemosyne; for all the important part of my discourse is dependent on her favour, and if I can recollect and recite enough of what was said by the priests and brought hither by Solon, I doubt not that I shall satisfy the requirements of this theatre. And now, making no more excuses, I will proceed.

Let me begin by observing first of all, that nine thousand was the sum of years which had elapsed since the war which was said to have taken place between those who dwelt outside the pillars of Heracles and all who dwelt within them; this war I am going to describe. Of the combatants on the one side, the city of Athens was reported to have been the leader and to have fought out the war; the combatants on the other side were commanded by the kings of Atlantis, which, as I was saying, was an island greater in extent than Libya and Asia, and when afterwards sunk by an earthquake, became an impassable barrier of mud to voyagers sailing from hence to any part of the ocean. The progress of the history will unfold the various nations of barbarians and families of Hellenes which then existed, as they successively appear on the scene; but I must describe first of all Athenians of that day, and their enemies who fought with them, and then the respective powers and governments of the two kingdoms. Let us give the precedence to Athens.

In the days of old the gods had the whole earth distributed among them by allotment [1]. There was no quarrelling; for you cannot rightly suppose that the gods did not know what was proper for each of them to have, or, knowing this, that they would seek to procure for themselves by contention that which more properly belonged to others. They all of them by just apportionment obtained what they wanted, and peopled their own districts; and when they had peopled them they tended us, their nurselings and possessions, as shepherds tend their flocks, excepting only that they did not use blows or bodily force, as shepherds do, but governed us like pilots from the stern of the vessel, which is an easy way of guiding animals, holding our souls by the rudder of persuasion according to their own pleasure;—thus did they guide all mortal creatures. Now different gods had their allotments in different places which they set in order. Hephaestus and Athene, who were brother and sister, and sprang from the same father, having a common nature, and being united also in the love of philosophy and art, both obtained as their common portion this land, which was naturally adapted for wisdom and virtue; and there they implanted brave children of the soil, and put into their minds the order of government; their names are preserved, but their actions have dis-

[1] Cp. Polit. 271 ff.

Critias

CRITIAS.

the aid of Mnemosyne.

The subject is the war between Athens and Atlantis.

109

He proposes to speak first of Athens.

When the Gods divided the earth, the land of Attica was allotted to Hephaestus and Athene, who implanted there brave children of the soil. Of these the history was lost, but their names remained.

appeared by reason of the destruction of those who received the tradition, and the lapse of ages. For when there were any survivors, as I have already said, they were men who dwelt in the mountains; and they were ignorant of the art of writing, and had heard only the names of the chiefs of the land, but very little about their actions. The names they were willing enough to give to their children; but the virtues and the laws of their predecessors, they knew only by obscure traditions; and as they themselves and their children lacked for many generations the necessaries of life, they directed their attention to the supply of their wants, and of them they conversed, to the neglect of events that had happened in times long past; for mythology and the enquiry into antiquity are first introduced into cities when they begin to have leisure [1], and when they see that the necessaries of life have already been provided, but not before. And this is the reason why the names of the ancients have been preserved to us and not their actions. This I infer because Solon said that the priests in their narrative of that war mentioned most of the names which are recorded prior to the time of Theseus, such as Cecrops, and Erechtheus, and Erichthonius, and Erysichthon, and the names of the women in like manner. Moreover, since military pursuits were then common to men and women, the men of those days in accordance with the custom of the time set up a figure and image of the goddess in full armour, to be a testimony that all animals which associate together, male as well as female, may, if they please, practise in common the virtue which belongs to them without distinction of sex.

Now the country was inhabited in those days by various classes of citizens;—there were artisans, and there were husbandmen, and there was also a warrior class originally set apart by divine men. The latter dwelt by themselves, and had all things suitable for nurture and education; neither had any of them anything of their own, but they regarded all that they had as common property; nor did they claim to receive of the other citizens anything more than their necessary food. And they practised all the pursuits which we yesterday described as those of our imaginary guardians. Concerning the country the Egyptian priests said what is not only probable but manifestly true, that the boundaries were in those days fixed by the Isthmus, and that in the direction of the continent they extended as far as the heights of Cithaeron and Parnes; the boundary line came down in the direction of the sea, having the district of Oropus on the right, and with the river Asopus as the limit on the left. The land was the best in the world, and was

[1] Cp. Arist. Metaphys. I. i, § 16.

therefore able in those days to support a vast army, raised from the surrounding people. Even the remnant of Attica which now exists may compare with any region in the world for the variety and excellence of its fruits and the suitableness of its pastures to every sort of animal, which proves what I am saying; but in those days the country was fair as now and yielded far more abundant produce. How shall I establish my words? and what part of it can be truly called a remnant of the land that then was? The whole country is only a long promontory extending far into the sea away from the rest of the continent, while the surrounding basin of the sea is everywhere deep in the neighbourhood of the shore. Many great deluges have taken place during the nine thousand years, for that is the number of years which have elapsed since the time of which I am speaking; and during all this time and through so many changes, there has never been any considerable accumulation of the soil coming down from the mountains, as in other places, but the earth has fallen away all round and sunk out of sight. The consequence is, that in comparison of what then was, there are remaining only the bones of the wasted body, as they may be called, as in the case of small islands, all the richer and softer parts of the soil having fallen away, and the mere skeleton of the land being left. But in the primitive state of the country, its mountains were high hills covered with soil, and the plains, as they are termed by us, of Phelleus were full of rich earth, and there was abundance of wood in the mountains. Of this last the traces still remain, for although some of the mountains now only afford sustenance to bees, not so very long ago there were still to be seen roofs of timber cut from trees growing there, which were of a size sufficient to cover the largest houses; and there were many other high trees, cultivated by man and bearing abundance of food for cattle. Moreover, the land reaped the benefit of the annual rainfall, not as now losing the water which flows off the bare earth into the sea, but, having an abundant supply in all places, and receiving it into herself and treasuring it up in the close clay soil, it let off into the hollows the streams which it absorbed from the heights, providing everywhere abundant fountains and rivers, of which there may still be observed sacred memorials in places where fountains once existed; and this proves the truth of what I am saying.

Such was the natural state of the country, which was cultivated, as we may well believe, by true husbandmen, who made husbandry their business, and were lovers of honour, and of a noble nature, and had a soil the best in the world, and abundance of water, and in the heaven above an excellently attempered climate. Now the

Critias

CRITIAS.

III

The productiveness of the soil still equal to that of any country;

although the land is a mere skeleton from which the richer and softer parts have been washed away.

CRITIAS.

The extent of the Acropolis.

On its slopes dwelt artisans and husbandmen; on its summit the warrior class.

Their winter and summer habitations.

The fountain on the Acropolis.

The number of the population the same then as now.

city in those days was arranged on this wise. In the first place the Acropolis was not as now. For the fact is that a single night of excessive rain washed away the earth and laid bare the rock; at the same time there were earthquakes, and then occurred the extraordinary inundation, which was the third before the great destruction of Deucalion. But in primitive times the hill of the Acropolis extended to the Eridanus and Ilissus, and included the Pnyx on one side, and the Lycabettus as a boundary on the opposite side to the Pnyx, and was all well covered with soil, and level at the top, except in one or two places. Outside the Acropolis and under the sides of the hill there dwelt artisans, and such of the husbandmen as were tilling the ground near; the warrior class dwelt by themselves around the temples of Athene and Hephaestus at the summit, which moreover they had enclosed with a single fence like the garden of a single house. On the north side they had dwellings in common and had erected halls for dining in winter, and had all the buildings which they needed for their common life, besides temples, but there was no adorning of them with gold and silver, for they made no use of these for any purpose; they took a middle course between meanness and ostentation, and built modest houses in which they and their children's children grew old, and they handed them down to others who were like themselves, always the same. But in summer-time they left their gardens and gymnasia and dining halls, and then the southern side of the hill was made use of by them for the same purpose. Where the Acropolis now is there was a fountain, which was choked by the earthquake, and has left only the few small streams which still exist in the vicinity, but in those days the fountain gave an abundant supply of water for all and of suitable temperature in summer and in winter. This is how they dwelt, being the guardians of their own citizens and the leaders of the Hellenes, who were their willing followers. And they took care to preserve the same number of men and women through all time, being so many as were required for warlike purposes, then as now,—that is to say, about twenty thousand. Such were the ancient Athenians, and after this manner they righteously administered their own land and the rest of Hellas; they were renowned all over Europe and Asia for the beauty of their persons and for the many virtues of their souls, and of all men who lived in those days they were the most illustrious. And next, if I have not forgotten what I heard when I was a child, I will impart to you the character and origin of their adversaries. For friends should not keep their stories to themselves, but have them in common.

113   Yet, before proceeding further in the narrative, I ought to warn

you, that you must not be surprised if you should perhaps hear Hellenic names given to foreigners. I will tell you the reason of this: Solon, who was intending to use the tale for his poem, enquired into the meaning of the names, and found that the early Egyptians in writing them down had translated them into their own language, and he recovered the meaning of the several names and when copying them out again translated them into our language. My great-grandfather, Dropides, had the original writing, which is still in my possession, and was carefully studied by me when I was a child. Therefore if you hear names such as are used in this country, you must not be surprised, for I have told how they came to be introduced. The tale, which was of great length, began as follows:—

I have before remarked in speaking of the allotments of the gods, that they distributed the whole earth into portions differing in extent, and made for themselves temples and instituted sacrifices. And Poseidon, receiving for his lot the island of Atlantis, begat children by a mortal woman, and settled them in a part of the island, which I will describe. Looking towards the sea, but in the centre of the whole island, there was a plain which is said to have been the fairest of all plains and very fertile. Near the plain again, and also in the centre of the island at a distance of about fifty stadia, there was a mountain not very high on any side. In this mountain there dwelt one of the earth-born primeval men of that country, whose name was Evenor, and he had a wife named Leucippe, and they had an only daughter who was called Cleito. The maiden had already reached womanhood, when her father and mother died; Poseidon fell in love with her and had intercourse with her, and breaking the ground, inclosed the hill in which she dwelt all round, making alternate zones of sea and land larger and smaller, encircling one another; there were two of land and three of water, which he turned as with a lathe, each having its circumference equidistant every way from the centre, so that no man could get to the island, for ships and voyages were not as yet. He himself, being a god, found no difficulty in making special arrangements for the centre island, bringing up two springs of water from beneath the earth, one of warm water and the other of cold, and making every variety of food to spring up abundantly from the soil. He also begat and brought up five pairs of twin male children; and dividing the island of Atlantis into ten portions, he gave to the first-born of the eldest pair his mother's dwelling and the surrounding allotment, which was the largest and best, and made him king over the rest; the others he made princes, and gave them rule over many men, and a large territory. And he named them all; the eld-

Critias

CRITIAS.

Explanation of the occurrence of Greek names in the narrative.

The originals still in existence.

Atlantis the lot of Poseidon.

His love for Cleito. He surrounded the hill in which she lived with alternate zones of sea and land.

114

Critias

CRITIAS.

Their
children,
Atlas and
his
brothers,
were the
princes
of the
island.
The ex-
tent of
their do-
minion.

est, who was the first king, he named Atlas, and after him the
whole island and the ocean were called Atlantic. To his twin
brother, who was born after him, and obtained as his lot the extremity of the island towards the pillars of Heracles, facing the
country which is now called the region of Gades in that part of the
world, he gave the name which in the Hellenic language is Eumelus,
in the language of the country which is named after him, Gadeirus.
Of the second pair of twins he called one Ampheres, and the other
Evaemon. To the elder of the third pair of twins he gave the name
Mneseus, and Autochthon to the one who followed him. Of the
fourth pair of twins he called the elder Elasippus, and the younger
Mestor. And of the fifth pair he gave to the elder the name of
Azaes, and to the younger that of Diaprepes. All these and their
descendants for many generations were the inhabitants and rulers
of divers islands in the open sea; and also, as has been already
said, they held sway in our direction over the country within the
pillars as far as Egypt and Tyrrhenia. Now Atlas had a numerous
and honourable family, and they retained the kingdom, the eldest

son handing it on to his eldest for many generations; and they had
such an amount of wealth as was never before possessed by kings
and potentates, and is not likely ever to be again, and they were
furnished with everything which they needed, both in the city and
country. For because of the greatness of their empire many things
were brought to them from foreign countries, and the island itself
provided most of what was required by them for the uses of life.

In the first place, they dug out of the earth whatever was to be
found there, solid as well as fusile, and that which is now only a
name and was then something more than a name, orichalcum, was
dug out of the earth in many parts of the island, being more pre-

cious in those days than anything except gold. There was an abundance of wood for carpenter's work, and sufficient maintenance for
tame and wild animals. Moreover, there were a great number of

elephants in the island; for as there was provision for all other
sorts of animals, both for those which live in lakes and marshes and
rivers, and also for those which live in mountains and on plains, so
there was for the animal which is the largest and most voracious

of all. Also whatever fragrant things there now are in the earth,
whether roots, or herbage, or woods, or essences which distil from
fruit and flower, grew and thrived in that land; also the fruit which
admits of cultivation, both the dry sort, which is given us for
nourishment and any other which we use for food—we call them
all by the common name of pulse, and the fruits having a hard
rind, affording drinks and meats and ointments, and good store of

chestnuts and the like, which furnish pleasure and amusement, and are fruits which spoil with keeping, and the pleasant kinds of dessert, with which we console ourselves after dinner, when we are tired of eating—all these that sacred island which then beheld the light of the sun, brought forth fair and wondrous and in infinite abundance. With such blessings the earth freely furnished them; meanwhile they went on constructing their temples and palaces and harbours and docks. And they arranged the whole country in the following manner:—

First of all they bridged over the zones of sea which surrounded the ancient metropolis, making a road to and from the royal palace. And at the very beginning they built the palace in the habitation of the god and of their ancestors, which they continued to ornament in successive generations, every king surpassing the one who went before him to the utmost of his power, until they made the building a marvel to behold for size and for beauty. And beginning from the sea they bored a canal of three hundred feet in width and one hundred feet in depth and fifty stadia in length, which they carried through to the outermost zone, making a passage from the sea up to this, which became a harbour, and leaving an opening sufficient to enable the largest vessels to find ingress. Moreover, they divided at the bridges the zones of land which parted the zones of sea, leaving room for a single trireme to pass out of one zone into another, and they covered over the channels so as to leave a way underneath for the ships; for the banks were raised considerably above the water. Now the largest of the zones into which a passage was cut from the sea was three stadia in breadth, and the zone of land which came next of equal breadth; but the next two zones, the one of water, the other of land, were two stadia, and the one which surrounded the central island was a stadium only in width. The island in which the palace was situated had a diameter of five stadia. All this including the zones and the bridge, which was the sixth part of a stadium in width, they surrounded by a stone wall on every side, placing towers and gates on the bridges where the sea passed in. The stone which was used in the work they quarried from underneath the centre island, and from underneath the zones, on the outer as well as the inner side. One kind was white, another black, and a third red, and as they quarried, they at the same time hollowed out double docks, having roofs formed out of the native rock. Some of their buildings were simple, but in others they put together different stones, varying the colour to please the eye, and to be a natural source of delight. The entire circuit of the wall, which went round the outermost

The bridges over the zones.

The royal palace.

The great canal.

The harbour.

Size of the zones,

116 and of the centre island.

zone, they covered with a coating of brass, and the circuit of the next wall they coated with tin, and the third, which encompassed the citadel, flashed with the red light of orichalcum. The palaces in the interior of the citadel were constructed on this wise:—in the centre was a holy temple dedicated to Cleito and Poseidon, which remained inaccessible, and was surrounded by an enclosure of gold; this was the spot where the family of the ten princes first saw the light, and thither the people annually brought the fruits of the earth in their season from all the ten portions, to be an offering to each of the ten. Here was Poseidon's own temple which was a stadium in length, and half a stadium in width, and of a proportionate height, having a strange barbaric appearance. All the outside of the temple, with the exception of the pinnacles, they covered with silver, and the pinnacles with gold. In the interior of the temple the roof was of ivory, curiously wrought everywhere with gold and silver and orichalcum; and all the other parts, the walls and pillars and floor, they coated with orichalcum. In the temple they placed statues of gold: there was the god himself standing in a chariot—the charioteer of six winged horses—and of such a size that he touched the roof of the building with his head; around him there were a hundred Nereids riding on dolphins, for such was thought to be the number of them by the men of those days. There were also in the interior of the temple other images which had been dedicated by private persons. And around the temple on the outside were placed statues of gold of all the descendants of the ten kings and of their wives, and there were many other great offerings of kings and of private persons, coming both from the city itself and from the foreign cities over which they held sway. There was an altar too, which in size and workmanship corresponded to this magnificence, and the palaces, in like manner, answered to the greatness of the kingdom and the glory of the temple.

117

Springs.

Baths.

The grove of Poseidon.

In the next place, they had fountains, one of cold and another of hot water, in gracious plenty flowing; and they were wonderfully adapted for use by reason of the pleasantness and excellence of their waters[1]. They constructed buildings about them and planted suitable trees; also they made cisterns, some open to the heavens, others roofed over, to be used in winter as warm baths; there were the kings' baths, and the baths of private persons, which were kept apart; and there were separate baths for women, and for horses and cattle, and to each of them they gave as much adornment as was suitable. Of the water which ran off they carried some to the grove of Poseidon, where were growing all manner of trees of

[1] Reading ἑκατέρου πρὸς τὴν χρῆσιν.

wonderful height and beauty, owing to the excellence of the soil, while the remainder was conveyed by aqueducts along the bridges to the outer circles; and there were many temples built and dedicated to many gods; also gardens and places of exercise, some for men, and others for horses in both of the two islands formed by the zones; and in the centre of the larger of the two there was set apart a race-course of a stadium in width, and in length allowed to extend all round the island, for horses to race in. Also there were guard-houses at intervals for the guards, the more trusted of whom were appointed to keep watch in the lesser zone, which was nearer the Acropolis; while the most trusted of all had houses given them within the citadel, near the persons of the kings. The docks were full of triremes and naval stores, and all things were quite ready for use. Enough of the plan of the royal palace.

Leaving the palace and passing out across the three harbours, you came to a wall which began at the sea and went all round: this was everywhere distant fifty stadia from the largest zone or harbour, and enclosed the whole, the ends meeting at the mouth of the channel which led to the sea. The entire area was densely crowded with habitations; and the canal and the largest of the harbours were full of vessels and merchants coming from all parts, who, from their numbers, kept up a multitudinous sound of human voices, and din and clatter of all sorts night and day.

I have described the city and the environs of the ancient palace nearly in the words of Solon, and now I must endeavour to represent to you the nature and arrangement of the rest of the land. The whole country was said by him to be very lofty and precipitous on the side of the sea, but the country immediately about and surrounding the city was a level plain, itself surrounded by mountains which descended towards the sea; it was smooth and even, and of an oblong shape, extending in one direction three thousand stadia, but across the centre inland it was two thousand stadia. This part of the island looked towards the south, and was sheltered from the north. The surrounding mountains were celebrated for their number and size and beauty, far beyond any which still exist, having in them also many wealthy villages of country folk, and rivers, and lakes, and meadows supplying food enough for every animal, wild or tame, and much wood of various sorts, abundant for each and every kind of work.

I will now describe the plain, as it was fashioned by nature and by the labours of many generations of kings through long ages. It was for the most part rectangular and oblong, and where falling out of the straight line followed the circular ditch. The depth, and

Critias

CRITIAS.

The great foss, 100 feet in depth, 600 in width, and 10,000 stadia in length.

The cross canals.

Two harvests.

119

60,000 lots and 60,000 officers.

Military strength: 10,000 chariots, 1,200 ships, &c.

Laws affecting the kings inscribed on a column of orichalcum.

width, and length of this ditch were incredible, and gave the impression that a work of such extent, in addition to so many others, could never have been artificial. Nevertheless I must say what I was told. It was excavated to the depth of a hundred feet, and its breadth was a stadium everywhere; it was carried round the whole of the plain, and was ten thousand stadia in length. It received the streams which came down from the mountains, and winding round the plain and meeting at the city, was there let off into the sea. Further inland, likewise, straight canals of a hundred feet in width were cut from it through the plain, and again let off into the ditch leading to the sea: these canals were at intervals of a hundred stadia, and by them they brought down the wood from the mountains to the city, and conveyed the fruits of the earth in ships, cutting transverse passages from one canal into another, and to the city. Twice in the year they gathered the fruits of the earth—in winter having the benefit of the rains of heaven, and in summer the water which the land supplied by introducing streams from the canals.

As to the population, each of the lots in the plain had to find a leader for the men who were fit for military service, and the size of a lot was a square of ten stadia each way, and the total number of all the lots was sixty thousand. And of the inhabitants of the mountains and of the rest of the country there was also a vast multitude, which was distributed among the lots and had leaders assigned to them according to their districts and villages. The leader was required to furnish for the war the sixth portion of a war-chariot, so as to make up a total of ten thousand chariots; also two horses and riders for them, and a pair of chariot-horses without a seat, accompanied by a horseman who could fight on foot carrying a small shield, and having a charioteeer who stood behind the man-at-arms to guide the two horses; also, he was bound to furnish two heavy armed soldiers, two archers, two slingers, three stone-shooters and three javelin-men, who were light-armed, and four sailors to make up the complement of twelve hundred ships. Such was the military order of the royal city—the order of the other nine governments varied, and it would be wearisome to recount their several differences.

As to offices and honours, the following was the arrangement from the first. Each of the ten kings in his own division and in his own city had the absolute control of the citizens, and, in most cases, of the laws, punishing and slaying whomsoever he would. Now the order of precedence among them and their mutual relations were regulated by the commands of Poseidon which the law had handed down. These were inscribed by the first kings on a pillar of orichalcum, which was situated in the middle of the island, at the temple of Poseidon, whither the kings were gathered together every fifth and every sixth year alternately, thus giving equal honour to the odd and to the even number. And when they were gathered together they consulted about their common interests, and enquired if any one had transgressed in anything, and passed judgment, and before they passed judgment they gave their pledges to one another on this wise:—There were bulls who had the range of the temple of Poseidon; and the ten kings, being left alone in the temple, after they had offered prayers to the god that they might capture the victim which was acceptable to him, hunted the bulls, without weapons, but with staves and nooses; and the bull which they caught they led up to the pillar and cut its throat over the top of it so that the blood fell upon the sacred inscription. Now on the pillar, besides the laws, there was inscribed an oath invoking mighty curses on the disobedient. When therefore, after slaying the bull in the accustomed manner, they had burnt its limbs, they filled a bowl of wine and cast in a clot of blood for each of them; the rest of the victim they put in the fire, after having purified the column all round. Then they drew from the bowl in golden cups, and pouring a libation on the fire, they swore that they would judge according to the laws on the pillar, and would punish him who in any point had already transgressed them, and that for the future they would not, if they could help, offend against the writing on the pillar, and would neither command others, nor obey any ruler who commanded them, to act otherwise than according to the laws of their father Poseidon. This was the prayer which each of them offered up for himself and for his descendants, at the same time drinking and dedicating the cup out of which he drank in the temple of the god; and after they had supped and satisfied their needs, when darkness came on, and the fire about the sacrifice was cool, all of them put on most beautiful azure robes, and, sitting on the ground, at night, over the embers of the sacrifices by which they had sworn, and extinguishing all the fire about the temple, they received and gave judgment, if any of them had an accusation to bring against any one; and when they had given judgment, at daybreak they wrote down their sentences on a golden tablet, and dedicated it together with their robes to be a memorial.

There were many special laws affecting the several kings inscribed about the temples, but the most important was the following: They were not to take up arms against one another, and they were all to come to the rescue if any one in any of their cities

Administration of these laws by the ten kings in the temple of Poseidon, after sacrifice and prayer.

120

They put on azure robes when they gave judgment, and recorded their decisions on golden tablets.

The kings were not

Critias

CRITIAS.

to take up
arms
against
one an-
other, but
were to
unite for
mutual
defence.

The vir-
tues of
the people
of At-
lantis
were
great so
long as
[121]
the divine
element
lasted in
them; but
when this
grew
weaker,
they de-
generated.

Intima-
tion of
the over-
throw of
Atlantis.

attempted to overthrow the royal house; like their ancestors, they were to deliberate in common about war and other matters, giving the supremacy to the descendants of Atlas. And the king was not to have the power of life and death over any of his kinsmen unless he had the assent of the majority of the ten.

Such was the vast power which the god settled in the lost island of Atlantis; and this he afterwards directed against our land for the following reasons, as tradition tells: For many generations, as long as the divine nature lasted in them, they were obedient to the laws, and well-affectioned towards the god, whose seed they were; for they possessed true and in every way great spirits, uniting gentleness with wisdom in the various chances of life, and in their intercourse with one another. They despised everything but virtue, caring little for their present state of life, and thinking lightly of the possession of gold and other property, which seemed only a burden to them; neither were they intoxicated by luxury; nor did wealth deprive them of their self-control; but they were sober, and saw clearly that all these goods are increased by virtue and friendship with one another, whereas by too great regard and respect for them, they are lost and friendship with them. By such reflections and by the continuance in them of a divine nature, the qualities which we have described grew and increased among them; but when the divine portion began to fade away, and became diluted too often and too much with the mortal admixture, and the human nature got the upper hand, they then, being unable to bear their fortune, behaved unseemly, and to him who had an eye to see, grew visibly debased, for they were losing the fairest of their precious gifts; but to those who had no eye to see the true happiness, they appeared glorious and blessed at the very time when they were full of avarice and unrighteous power. Zeus, the god of gods, who rules according to law, and is able to see into such things, perceiving that an honourable race was in a woeful plight, and wanting to inflict punishment on them, that they might be chastened and improve, collected all the gods into their [1] most holy habitation, which, being placed in the centre of the world, beholds all created things. And when he had called them together, he spake as follows:—[2]

[1] Reading αὐτῶν.
[2] The fragment *Critias* thus breaks off in the middle of a sentence.

PARMENIDES

PARMENIDES

PERSONS OF THE DIALOGUE

CEPHALUS	SOCRATES
ADEIMANTUS	ZENO
GLAUCON	PARMENIDES
ANTIPHON	ARISTOTELES
PYTHODORUS	

Cephalus rehearses a dialogue which is supposed to have been narrated in his presence by Antiphon, the half-brother of Adeimantus and Glaucon, to certain Clazomenians.

WE had come from our home at Clazomenae to Athens, and met Adeimantus and Glaucon in the Agora. Welcome, Cephalus, said Adeimantus, taking me by the hand; is there anything which we can do for you in Athens?

Yes; that is why I am here; I wish to ask a favour of you.

What may that be? he said.

I want you to tell me the name of your half-brother, which I have forgotten; he was a mere child when I last came hither from Clazomenae, but that was a long time ago; his father's name, if I remember rightly, was Pyrilampes?

Yes, he said, and the name of our brother, Antiphon; but why do you ask?

Let me introduce some countrymen of mine, I said; they are lovers of philosophy, and have heard that Antiphon was intimate with a certain Pythodorus, a friend of Zeno, and remembers a conversation which took place between Socrates, Zeno, and Parmenides many years ago, Pythodorus having often recited it to him.

Quite true.

And could we hear it? I asked.

Nothing easier, he replied; when he was a youth he made a careful study of the piece; at present his thoughts run in another direction; like his grandfather Antiphon he is devoted to horses.

Steph.
126
CEPHA-
LUS,
ADEI-
MANTUS.

Preface.

The request of the Clazomenians.

*Par-
menides*

127

CEPH-
ALUS,
ADEI-
MANTUS,
ANTI-
PHON,
SOCRATES,
ZENO.

Descrip-
tive.

But, if that is what you want, let us go and look for him; he dwells at Melita, which is quite near, and he has only just left us to go home.

Accordingly we went to look for him; he was at home, and in the act of giving a bridle to a smith to be fitted. When he had done with the smith, his brothers told him the purpose of our visit; and he saluted me as an acquaintance whom he remembered from my former visit, and we asked him to repeat the dialogue. At first he was not very willing, and complained of the trouble, but at length he consented. He told us that Pythodorus had described to him the appearance of Parmenides and Zeno; they came to Athens, as he said, at the great Panathenaea; the former was, at the time of his visit, about 65 years old, very white with age, but well favoured. Zeno was nearly 40 years of age, tall and fair to look upon; in the days of h's youth he was reported to have been beloved by Parmenides. He said that they lodged with Pythodorus in the Ceramicus, outside the wall, whither Socrates, then a very young man, came to see them, and many others with him; they wanted to hear the writings of Zeno, which had been brought to Athens for the first time on the occasion of their visit. These Zeno himself read to them in the absence of Parmenides, and had very nearly finished when Pythodorous entered, and with him Parmenides and Aristoteles who was afterwards one of the Thirty, and heard the little that remained of the dialogue. Pythodorus had heard Zeno repeat them before.

The con
tention of
Zeno is,
that being
cannot be
many, be-
cause, if
it were,
it would
be like
and
unlike at
the same
time,
which is
impos-
sible.

When the recitation was completed, Socrates requested that the first thesis of the first argument might be read over again, and this having been done, he said: What is your meaning, Zeno? Do you maintain that if being is many, it must be both like and unlike, and that this is impossible, for neither can the like be unlike, nor the unlike like—is that your position?

Just so, said Zeno.

And if the unlike cannot be like, or the like unlike, then according to you, being could not be many; for this would involve an impossibility. In all that you say have you any other purpose except to disprove the being of the many? and is not each division of your treatise intended to furnish a separate proof of this, there being in all as many proofs of the not-being of the many as you have composed arguments? Is that your meaning, or have I misunderstood you?

128

No, said Zeno; you have correctly understood my general purpose.

I see, Parmenides, said Socrates, that Zeno would like to be not only one with you in friendship but your second self in his writings too; he puts what you say in another way, and would fain make believe that he is telling us something which is new. For you, in your poems, say The All is one, and of this you adduce excellent proofs; and he on the other hand says There is no many; and on behalf of this he offers overwhelming evidence. You affirm unity, he denies plurality. And so you deceive the world into believing that you are saying different things when really you are saying much the same. This is a strain of art beyond the reach of most of us.

Yes, Socrates, said Zeno. But although you are as keen as a Spartan hound in pursuing the track, you do not fully apprehend the true motive of the composition, which is not really such an artificial work as you imagine; for what you speak of was an accident; there was no pretence of a great purpose; nor any serious intention of deceiving the world. The truth is, that these writings of mine were meant to protect the arguments of Parmenides against those who make fun of him and seek to show the many ridiculous and contradictory results which they suppose to follow from the affirmation of the one. My answer is addressed to the partisans of the many, whose attack I return with interest by retorting upon them that their hypothesis of the being of many, if carried out, appears to be still more ridiculous than the hypothesis of the being of one. Zeal for my master led me to write the book in the days of my youth, but some one stole the copy; and therefore I had no choice whether it should be published or not; the motive, however, of writing, was not the ambition of an elder man, but the pugnacity of a young one. This you do not seem to see, Socrates; though in other respects, as I was saying, your notion is a very just one.

I understand, said Socrates, and quite accept your account. But tell me, Zeno, do you not further think that there is an idea of likeness in itself, and another idea of unlikeness, which is the opposite of likeness, and that in these two, you and I and all other things to which we apply the term many, participate—things which participate in likeness become in that degree and manner like; and so far as they participate in unlikeness become in that degree unlike, or both like and unlike in the degree in which they participate in both? And may not all things partake of both opposites, and be both like and unlike, by reason of this participation?—Where is the wonder? Now if a person could prove the absolute like to become unlike, or the absolute unlike to become like, that, in my opinion, would indeed be a wonder; but there is nothing extraordinary, Zeno, in showing that the things which only partake of likeness and unlikeness experience both. Nor, again, if a person

*Par-
menides*

SOCRATES,
PAR-
MEN-
IDES.

and the
things
which
partake
of them.

were to show that all is one by partaking of one, and at the same
time many by partaking of many, would that be very astonishing.
But if he were to show me that the absolute one was many, or the
absolute many one, I should be truly amazed. And so of all the rest:
I should be surprised to hear that the natures or ideas themselves
had these opposite qualities; but not if a person wanted to prove of
me that I was many and also one. When he wanted to show that I
was many he would say that I have a right and a left side, and a
front and a back, and an upper and a lower half, for I cannot deny
that I partake of multitude; when, on the other hand, he wants to
prove that I am one, he will say, that we who are here assembled are
seven, and that I am one and partake of the one. In both instances
he proves his case. So again, if a person shows that such things as
wood, stones, and the like, being many are also one, we admit that
he shows the coexistence of the one and many, but he does not show
that the many are one or the one many; he is uttering not a paradox but a truism. If however, as I just now suggested, some one
were to abstract simple notions of like, unlike, one, many, rest, motion, and similar ideas, and then to show that these admit of admixture and separation in themselves, I should be very much astonished. This part of the argument appears to be treated by you,
Zeno, in a very spirited manner; but, as I was saying, I should be
130 far more amazed if any one found in the ideas themselves which are
apprehended by reason, the same puzzle and entanglement which
you have shown to exist in visible objects.

While Socrates was speaking, Pythodorus thought that Parmenides and Zeno were not altogether pleased at the successive steps of
the argument; but still they gave the closest attention, and often
looked at one another, and smiled as if in admiration of him. When
he had finished, Parmenides expressed their feelings in the following words:—

Socrates, he said, I admire the bent of your mind towards philosophy; tell me now, was this your own distinction between ideas
in themselves and the things which partake of them? and do you
think that there is an idea of likeness apart from the likeness which
we possess, and of the one and many, and of the other things which
Zeno mentioned?

I think that there are such ideas, said Socrates.

Parmenides proceeded: And would you also make absolute ideas
of the just and the beautiful and the good, and of all that class?

Yes, he said, I should.

*Par-
menides
asks
Socrates
whether
he would*

And would you make an idea of man apart from us and from all
other human creatures, or of fire and water?

I am often undecided, Parmenides, as to whether I ought to include them or not.

And would you feel equally undecided, Socrates, about things of which the mention may provoke a smile?—I mean such things as hair, mud, dirt, or anything else which is vile and paltry; would you suppose that each of these has an idea distinct from the actual objects with which we come into contact, or not?

Certainly not, said Socrates; visible things like these are such as they appear to us, and I am afraid that there would be an absurdity in assuming any idea of them, although I sometimes get disturbed, and begin to think that there is nothing without an idea; but then again, when I have taken up this position, I run away, because I am afraid that I may fall into a bottomless pit of nonsense, and perish; and so I return to the ideas of which I was just now speaking, and occupy myself with them.

Yes, Socrates, said Parmenides; that is because you are still young; the time will come, if I am not mistaken, when philosophy will have a firmer grasp of you, and then you will not despise even the meanest things; at your age, you are too much disposed to regard the opinions of men. But I should like to know whether you mean that there are certain ideas of which all other things partake, and from which they derive their names; that similars, for example, become similar, because they partake of similarity; and great things become great, because they partake of greatness; and that just and beautiful things become just and beautiful, because they partake of justice and beauty?

Yes, certainly, said Socrates, that is my meaning.

Then each individual partakes either of the whole of the idea or else of a part of the idea? Can there be any other mode of participation?

There cannot be, he said.

Then do you think that the whole idea is one, and yet, being one, is in each one of the many?

Why not, Parmenides? said Socrates.

Because one and the same thing will exist as a whole at the same time in many separate individuals, and will therefore be in a state of separation from itself.

Nay, but the idea may be like the day which is one and the same in many places at once, and yet continuous with itself; in this way each idea may be one and the same in all at the same time.

I like your way, Socrates, of making one in many places at once. You mean to say, that if I were to spread out a sail and cover a

*Par-
menides*

SOCRATES,
PAR-
MEN-
IDES.

make
ideas of
all things.

Socrates
fears to
extend his
idealism
to mud,
dirt, etc.,

and is re-
buked by
Par-
menides
for exhib-
iting an
unphilo-
sophic
temper.
131

The
whole
idea can-
not exist
in differ-
ent ob-
jects at
the same
time;

Par-
menides

SOCRATES,
PAR-
MEN-
IDES.

number of men, there would be one whole including many—is not that your meaning?

I think so.

And would you say that the whole sail includes each man, or a part of it only, and different parts different men?

The latter.

Then, Socrates, the ideas themselves will be divisible, and things which participate in them will have a part of them only and not the whole idea existing in each of them?

That seems to follow.

Then would you like to say, Socrates, that the one idea is really divisible and yet remains one?

Certainly not, he said.

Suppose that you divide absolute greatness, and that of the many great things, each one is great in virtue of a portion of greatness less than absolute greatness—is that conceivable?

No.

Or will each equal thing, if possessing some small portion of equality less than absolute equality, be equal to some other thing by virtue of that portion only?

Impossible.

Or suppose one of us to have a portion of smallness; this is but a part of the small, and therefore the absolutely small is greater; if the absolutely small be greater, that to which the part of the small is added will be smaller and not greater than before.

How absurd!

Then in what way, Socrates, will all things participate in the ideas, if they are unable to participate in them either as parts or wholes?

Indeed, he said, you have asked a question which is not easily answered.

Well, said Parmenides, and what do you say of another question?

What question?

I imagine that the way in which you are led to assume one idea of each kind is as follows:—You see a number of great objects, and when you look at them there seems to you to be one and the same idea (or nature) in them all; hence you conceive of greatness as one.

Very true, said Socrates.

And if you go on and allow your mind in like manner to embrace in one view the idea of greatness and of great things which are not the idea, and to compare them, will not another greatness arise, which will appear to be the source of all these?

nor can objects contain only parts of ideas, for this would equally involve an absurdity. Things cannot become great or equal or small by addition of a part of greatness or equality or smallness.

132

Ideas are given by generalization.

But the general and its particulars to-

It would seem so.

Then another idea of greatness now comes into view over and above absolute greatness, and the individuals which partake of it; and then another, over and above all these, by virtue of which they will all be great, and so each idea instead of being one will be infinitely multiplied.

But may not the ideas, asked Socrates, be thoughts only, and have no proper existence except in our minds, Parmenides? For in that case each idea may still be one, and not experience this infinite multiplication.

And can there be individual thoughts which are thoughts of nothing?

Impossible, he said.

The thought must be of something?

Yes.

Of something which is or which is not?

Of something which is.

Must it not be of a single something, which the thought recognizes as attaching to all, being a single form or nature?

Yes.

And will not the something which is apprehended as one and the same in all, be an idea?

From that, again, there is no escape.

Then, said Parmenides, if you say that everything else participates in the ideas, must you not say either that everything is made up of thoughts, and that all things think; or that they are thoughts but have no thought?

The latter view, Parmenides, is no more rational than the previous one. In my opinion, the ideas are, as it were, patterns fixed in nature, and other things are like them, and resemblances of them —what is meant by the participation of other things in the ideas, is really assimilation to them.

But if, said he, the individual is like the idea, must not the idea also be like the individual, in so far as the individual is a resemblance of the idea? That which is like, cannot be conceived of as other than the like of like.

Impossible.

And when two things are alike, must they not partake of the same idea?

They must.

And will not that of which the two partake, and which makes them alike, be the idea itself?

Certainly.

Parmenides

SOCRATES,
PARMENIDES.

gether
form a
new idea;
the new
idea and
its particulars
another;
and so *ad
infinitum*.
It is suggested
that the
ideas are
thoughts
only.—
This solution is
rejected.

A fresh
attempt.
The ideas
are patterns, and
other
things
will be
like
them. But
then there
will be
likeness
of the
like to the
like, and
a common idea
including
both; and
so on *ad
infinitum*.

*Par-
menides*

133
SOCRATES,
PAR-
MEN-
IDES.

Resem-
blance
must be
given up.

Then the idea cannot be like the individual, or the individual like the idea; for if they are alike, some further idea of likeness will always be coming to light, and if that be like anything else, another; and new ideas will be always arising, if the idea resembles that which partakes of it?

Quite true.

The theory, then, that other things participate in the ideas by resemblance, has to be given up, and some other mode of participation devised?

It would seem so.

Do you see then, Socrates, how great is the difficulty of affirming the ideas to be absolute?

Yes, indeed.

And, further, let me say that as yet you only understand a small part of the difficulty which is involved if you make of each thing a single idea, parting it off from other things.

What difficulty? he said.

There are many, but the greatest of all is this:—If an opponent argues that these ideas, being such as we say they ought to be, must remain unknown, no one can prove to him that he is wrong, unless he who denies their existence be a man of great ability and knowledge, and is willing to follow a long and laborious demonstration; he will remain unconvinced, and still insist that they cannot be known.

What do you mean, Parmenides? said Socrates.

Ideas
would be
no longer
absolute,
if they
existed
within
us.
And if
without
us, then
they and
their
resem-
blances in
our
sphere
are relat-
ed among
them-
selves
only and
not to
one an-

In the first place, I think, Socrates, that you, or any one who maintains the existence of absolute essences, will admit that they cannot exist in us.

No, said Socrates; for then they would be no longer absolute.

True, he said; and therefore when ideas are what they are in relation to one another, their essence is determined by a relation among themselves, and has nothing to do with the resemblances, or whatever they are to be termed, which are in our sphere, and from which we receive this or that name when we partake of them. And the things which are within our sphere and have the same names with them, are likewise only relative to one another, and not to the ideas which have the same names with them, but belong to themselves and not to them.

What do you mean? said Socrates.

I may illustrate my meaning in this way, said Parmenides:—A master has a slave; now there is nothing absolute in the relation between them, which is simply a relation of one man to another. But there is also an idea of mastership in the abstract, which is relative to the idea of slavery in the abstract. These natures have nothing to do with us, nor we with them; they are concerned with themselves only, and we with ourselves. Do you see my meaning?

Yes, said Socrates, I quite see your meaning.

And will not knowledge—I mean absolute knowledge—answer to absolute truth?

Certainly.

And each kind of absolute knowledge will answer to each kind of absolute being?

Yes.

But the knowledge which we have, will answer to the truth which we have; and again, each kind of knowledge which we have, will be a knowledge of each kind of being which we have?

Certainly.

But the ideas themselves, as you admit, we have not, and cannot have?

No, we cannot.

And the absolute natures or kinds are known severally by the absolute idea of knowledge?

Yes.

And we have not got the idea of knowledge?

No.

Then none of the ideas are known to us, because we have no share in absolute knowledge?

I suppose not.

Then the nature of the beautiful in itself, and of the good in itself, and all other ideas which we suppose to exist absolutely, are unknown to us?

It would seem so.

I think that there is a stranger consequence still.

What is it?

Would you, or would you not say, that absolute knowledge, if there is such a thing, must be a far more exact knowledge than our knowledge; and the same of beauty and of the rest?

Yes.

And if there be such a thing as participation in absolute knowledge, no one is more likely than God to have this most exact knowledge?

Certainly.

But then, will God, having absolute knowledge, have a knowledge of human things?

Why not?

Because, Socrates, said Parmenides, we have admitted that the

134
Parmenides

PARMENIDES.

other. For example, we must distinguish the individual slave and master in the concrete from the ideas of mastership and slavery in the abstract.

The truth which we have will correspond to the knowledge which we have; and we have no knowledge of the absolute or of the ideas.

Another objection. God above has absolute knowledge. But if so, he cannot have a knowledge of human things, because

*Par-
menides*

SOCRATES,
PAR-
MEN-
IDES.

they are
in an-
other
sphere.

ideas are not valid in relation to human things; nor human things in relation to them; the relations of either are limited to their respective spheres.

Yes, that has been admitted.

And if God has this perfect authority, and perfect knowledge, his authority cannot rule us, nor his knowledge know us, or any human thing; just as our authority does not extend to the gods, nor our knowledge know anything which is divine, so by parity of reason they, being gods, are not our masters, neither do they know the things of men.

Yet, surely, said Socrates, to deprive God of knowledge is monstrous.

135

These, Socrates, said Parmenides, are a few, and only a few of the difficulties in which we are involved if ideas really are and we determine each one of them to be an absolute unity. He who hears what may be said against them will deny the very existence of them—and even if they do exist, he will say that they must of necessity be unknown to man; and he will seem to have reason on his side, and as we were remarking just now, will be very difficult to convince; a man must be gifted with very considerable ability before he can learn that everything has a class and an absolute essence; and still more remarkable will he be who discovers all these things for himself, and having thoroughly investigated them is able to teach them to others.

I agree with you, Parmenides, said Socrates; and what you say is very much to my mind.

And yet, Socrates, said Parmenides, if a man, fixing his attention on these and the like difficulties, does away with ideas of things and will not admit that every individual thing has its own determinate idea which is always one and the same, he will have nothing on which his mind can rest; and so he will utterly destroy the power of reasoning, as you seem to me to have particularly noted.

Very true, he said.

But, then, what is to become of philosophy? Whither shall we turn, if the ideas are unknown?

I certainly do not see my way at present.

Par-
menides
has ob-
served
Socrates
to be
untried in
dialectic.

Yes, said Parmenides; and I think that this arises, Socrates, out of your attempting to define the beautiful, the just, the good, and the ideas generally, without sufficient previous training. I noticed your deficiency, when I heard you talking here with your friend Aristoteles, the day before yesterday. The impulse that carries you towards philosophy is assuredly noble and divine; but there is an art which is called by the vulgar idle talking, and which is often imagined to be useless; in that you must train and exercise yourself, now that you are young, or truth will elude your grasp.

And what is the nature of this exercise, Parmenides, which you would recommend?

That which you heard Zeno practising; at the same time, I give you credit for saying to him that you did not care to examine the perplexity in reference to visible things, or to consider the question in that way; but only in reference to objects of thought, and to what may be called ideas.

Why, yes, he said, there appears to me to be no difficulty in showing by this method that visible things are like and unlike and may experience anything.

Quite true, said Parmenides; but I think that you should go a step further, and consider not only the consequences which flow from a given hypothesis, but also the consequences which flow from denying the hypothesis; and that will be still better training for you.

What do you mean? he said.

I mean, for example, that in the case of this very hypothesis of Zeno's about the many, you should inquire not only what will be the consequences to the many in relation to themselves and to the one, and to the one in relation to itself and the many, on the hypothesis of the being of the many, but also what will be the consequences to the one and the many in their relation to themselves and to each other, on the opposite hypothesis. Or, again, if likeness is or is not, what will be the consequences in either of these cases to the subjects of the hypothesis, and to other things, in relation both to themselves and to one another, and so of unlikeness; and the same holds good of motion and rest, of generation and destruction, and even of being and not-being. In a word, when you suppose anything to be or not to be, or to be in any way affected, you must look at the consequences in relation to the thing itself, and to any other things which you choose,—to each of them singly, to more than one, and to all; and so of other things, you must look at them in relation to themselves and to anything else which you suppose either to be or not to be, if you would train yourself perfectly and see the real truth.

That, Parmenides, is a tremendous business of which you speak, and I do not quite understand you; will you take some hypothesis and go through the steps?—then I shall apprehend you better.

That, Socrates, is a serious task to impose on a man of my years.

Then will you, Zeno? said Socrates.

Zeno answered with a smile:—Let us make our petition to Par-

Par- menides

SOCRATES, PAR- MEN- IDES.

He sub- gests that the con- [136] sequences of the not being, as well as of the being of anything, should be consid- ered.

Socrates asks him to give an ex- ample of this process.

*Par-
menides*

ZENO,
PAR-
MEN-
IDES,
ARISTO-
TELES.

Par-
menides
is at first
disin-
clined to
engage in
such a
[137]
laborious
pastime;
but at the
request
of the
company
he pro-
ceeds.

menides himself, who is quite right in saying that you are hardly
aware of the extent of the task which you are imposing on him;
and if there were more of us I should not ask him, for these are not
subjects which any one, especially at his age, can well speak of before a large audience; most people are not aware that this round-
about progress through all things is the only way in which the
mind can attain truth and wisdom. And therefore, Parmenides, I
join in the request of Socrates, that I may hear the process again
which I have not heard for a long time.

When Zeno had thus spoken, Pythodorus, according to Antiphon's report of him, said, that he himself and Aristoteles and the
whole company entreated Parmenides to give an example of the
process. I cannot refuse, said Parmenides; and yet I feel rather like
Ibycus, who, when in his old age, against his will, he fell in love,
compared himself to an old racehorse, who was about to run in a
chariot race, shaking with fear at the course he knew so well—this
was his simile of himself. And I also experience a trembling when I
remember through what an ocean of words I have to wade at my
time of life. But I must indulge you, as Zeno says that I ought, and
we are alone. Where shall I begin? And what shall be our first hypothesis, if I am to attempt this laborious pastime? Shall I begin
with myself, and take my own hypothesis of the one? and consider
the consequences which follow on the supposition either of the being or of the not-being of one?

By all means, said Zeno.

And who will answer me? he said. Shall I propose the youngest?
He will not make difficulties and will be the most likely to say what
he thinks; and his answers will give me time to breathe.

I am the one whom you mean, Parmenides, said Aristoteles; for
I am the youngest and at your service. Ask, and I will answer.

i. a. If the
one is, it
cannot
be many,
and
therefore
cannot
have
parts, or
be a
whole,
because a
whole is
made up
of parts;

Parmenides proceeded: i. a. If one is, he said, the one cannot be
many?

Impossible.

Then the one cannot have parts, and cannot be a whole?

Why not?

Because every part is part of a whole; is it not?

Yes.

And what is a whole? would not that of which no part is wanting
be a whole?

Certainly.

Then, in either case, the one would be made up of parts; both
as being a whole, and also as having parts?

To be sure.

And in either case, the one would be many, and not one?
True.

But, surely, it ought to be one and not many?
It ought.

Then, if the one is to remain one, it will not be a whole, and will not have parts?
No.

But if it has no parts, it will have neither beginning, middle, nor end; for these would of course be parts of it.
Right.

But then, again, a beginning and an end are the limits of everything?
Certainly.

Then the one, having neither beginning nor end, is unlimited?
Yes, unlimited.

And therefore formless; for it cannot partake either of round or straight.
But why?

Why, because the round is that of which all the extreme points are equidistant from the centre?
Yes.

And the straight is that of which the centre intercepts the view of the extremes?
True.

Then the one would have parts and would be many, if it partook either of a straight or of a circular form?
Assuredly.

But having no parts, it will be neither straight nor round?
Right.

And, being of such a nature, it cannot be in any place, for it cannot be either in another or in itself.
How so?

Because if it were in another, it would be encircled by that in which it was, and would touch it at many places and with many parts; but that which is one and indivisible, and does not partake of a circular nature, cannot be touched all round in many places.
Certainly not.

But if, on the other hand, one were in itself, it would also be contained by nothing else but itself[1]; that is to say, if it were really in itself; for nothing can be in anything which does not contain it.
Impossible.

But then, that which contains must be other than that which is

[1] Omitting ὄν.

*Par-
menides*

PAR-
MEN-
IDES,
ARISTO-
TELES.

and having no parts it cannot have a beginning, middle, and end; nor any limit or form.

It is neither circular nor straight;

138

it does not exist in any place;

*Par-
menides*

PAR-
MEN-
IDES,
ARISTO-
TELES.

it has
neither
rest nor
motion.

Two
forms of
motion—
(1)
change of
nature;
(2) loco-
motion.

contained? for the same whole cannot do and suffer both at once; and if so, one will be no longer one, but two?

True.

Then one cannot be anywhere, either in itself or in another?

No.

Further consider, whether that which is of such a nature can have either rest or motion.

Why not?

Why, because the one, if it were moved, would be either moved in place or changed in nature; for these are the only kinds of motion.

Yes.

And the one, when it changes and ceases to be itself, cannot be any longer one.

It cannot.

It cannot therefore experience the sort of motion which is change of nature?

Clearly not.

Then can the motion of the one be in place?

Perhaps.

Two
forms of
locomo-
tion—(a)
in a
place;
(b) from
one place
to an-
other.

But if the one moved in place, must it not either move round and round in the same place, or from one place to another?

It must.

And that which moves in a circle must rest upon a centre; and that which goes round upon a centre must have parts which are different from the centre; but that which has no centre and no parts cannot possibly be carried round upon a centre?

Impossible.

But perhaps the motion of the one consists in change of place?

Perhaps so, if it moves at all.

The one
does not
admit of
change of
nature,
nor of
either
form of
locomo-
tion;

And have we not already shown that it cannot be in anything?

Yes.

Then its coming into being in anything is still more impossible; is it not?

I do not see why.

Why, because anything which comes into being in anything, can neither as yet be in that other thing while still coming into being, nor be altogether out of it, if already coming into being in it.

Certainly not.

And therefore whatever comes into being in another must have parts, and then one part may be in, and another part out of that other; but that which has no parts can never be at one and the same time neither wholly within nor wholly without anything.

True.

And is there not a still greater impossibility in that which has no parts, and is not a whole, coming into being anywhere, since it cannot come into being either as a part or as a whole?

Clearly.

Then it does not change place by revolving in the same spot, nor by going somewhere and coming into being in something; nor again, by change in itself?

Very true.

Then in respect of any kind of motion the one is immoveable?

Immoveable.

But neither can the one be in anything, as we affirm?

Yes, we said so.

Then it is never in the same?

Why not?

Because if it were in the same it would be in something.

Certainly.

And we said that it could not be in itself, and could not be in other?

True.

Then one is never in the same place?

It would seem not.

But that which is never in the same place is never quiet or at rest?

Never.

One then, as would seem, is neither at rest nor in motion?

It certainly appears so.

Neither will it be the same with itself or other; nor again, other than itself or other.

How is that?

If other than itself it would be other than one, and would not be one.

True.

And if the same with other, it would be that other, and not itself; so that upon this supposition too, it would not have the nature of one, but would be other than one?

It would.

Then it will not be the same with other, or other than itself?

It will not.

Neither will it be other than other, while it remains one; for not one, but only other, can be other than other, and nothing else.

True.

Then not by virtue of being one will it be other?

*Par-
menides*

139
Par-
men-
ides,
Aristo-
teles.

Again,
the one
is never
in the
same any
more than
in the
other, and
is there-
fore in no
place and
therefore
incapable
of rest.

Neither
otherness
nor same-
ness can
be at-
tributed
to the
one, in
reference
to itself
or other;

*Par-
menides*

PAR-
MEN-
IDES,
ARISTO-
TELES.

Certainly not.

But if not by virtue of being one, not by virtue of itself; and if not by virtue of itself, not itself, and itself not being other at all, will not be other than anything?

Right.

Neither will one be the same with itself.

How not?

Surely the nature of the one is not the nature of the same.

Why not?

It is not when anything becomes the same with anything that it becomes one.

What of that?

Anything which becomes the same with the many, necessarily becomes many and not one.

True.

But, if there were no difference between the one and the same, when a thing became the same, it would always become one; and when it became one, the same?

Certainly.

And, therefore, if one be the same with itself, it is not one with itself, and will therefore be one and also not one.

Surely that is impossible.

And therefore the one can neither be other than other, nor the same with itself.

Impossible.

And thus the one can neither be the same, nor other, either in relation to itself or other?

No.

nor yet
likeness,
which is
sameness
of affec-
tions; nor
unlike-
ness,

Neither will the one be like anything or unlike itself or other.

Why not?

Because likeness is sameness of affections.

Yes.

And sameness has been shown to be of a nature distinct from oneness?

That has been shown.

140

But if the one had any other affection than that of being one, it would be affected in such a way as to be more than one; which is impossible.

True.

Then the one can never be so affected as to be the same either with another or with itself?

Clearly not.

Then it cannot be like another, or like itself?

No.

Nor can it be affected so as to be other, for then it would be affected in such a way as to be more than one.

It would.

That which is affected otherwise than itself or another, will be unlike itself or another, for sameness of affections is likeness.

True.

But the one, as appears, never being affected otherwise, is never unlike itself or other?

Never.

Then the one will never be either like or unlike itself or other?

Plainly not.

Again, being of this nature, it can neither be equal nor unequal either to itself or to other.

How is that?

Why, because the one if equal must be of the same measures as that to which it is equal.

True.

And if greater or less than things which are commensurable with it, the one will have more measures than that which is less, and fewer than that which is greater?

Yes.

And so of things which are not commensurate with it, the one will have greater measures than that which is less and smaller than that which is greater.

Certainly.

But how can that which does not partake of sameness, have either the same measures or have anything else the same?

Impossible.

And not having the same measures, the one cannot be equal either with itself or with another?

It appears so.

But again, whether it have fewer or more measures, it will have as many parts as it has measures; and thus again the one will be no longer one but will have as many parts as measures.

Right.

And if it were of one measure, it would be equal to that measure; yet it has been shown to be incapable of equality.

It has.

Then it will neither partake of one measure, nor of many, nor of few, nor of the same at all, nor be equal to itself or another; nor be greater or less than itself, or other?

Certainly.

*Par-
menides*

PAR-
MEN-
IDES,
ARISTO-
TELES.

nor
equality,
nor in-
equality
of size;

*Par-
menides*

PAR-
MEN-
IDES,
ARISTO-
TELES.

nor
equality
or in-
[141]
equality
of age;

nor time,

Well, and do we suppose that one can be older, or younger than anything, or of the same age with it?

Why not?

Why, because that which is of the same age with itself or other, must partake of equality or likeness of time; and we said that the one did not partake either of equality or of likeness?

We did say so.

And we also said, that it did not partake of inequality or unlikeness.

Very true.

How then can one, being of this nature, be either older or younger than anything, or have the same age with it?

In no way.

Then one cannot be older or younger, or of the same age, either with itself or with another?

Clearly not.

Then the one, being of this nature, cannot be in time at all; for must not that which is in time, be always growing older than itself?

Certainly.

And that which is older, must always be older than something which is younger?

True.

Then, that which becomes older than itself, also becomes at the same time younger than itself, if it is to have something to become older than.

What do you mean?

I mean this:—A thing does not need to become different from another thing which is already different; it *is* different, and if its different has become, it has become different; if its different will be, it will be different; but of that which is becoming different, there cannot have been, or be about to be, or yet be, a different—the only different possible is one which is becoming.

That is inevitable.

But, surely, the elder is a difference relative to the younger, and to nothing else.

True.

Then that which becomes older than itself must also, at the same time, become younger than itself?

Yes.

But again, it is true that it cannot become for a longer or for a shorter time than itself, but it must become, and be, and have become, and be about to be, for the same time with itself?

That again is inevitable.

*Par-
menides*

PAR-
MEN-
IDES,
ARISTO-
TELES.

Then things which are in time, and partake of time, must in every case, I suppose, be of the same age with themselves; and must also become at once older and younger than themselves?

Yes.

But the one did not partake of those affections?

Not at all.

Then it does not partake of time, and is not in any time?

So the argument shows.

Well, but do not the expressions 'was,' and 'has become,' and 'was becoming,' signify a particpation of past time?

Certainly.

And do not 'will be,' 'will become,' 'will have become,' signify a participation of future time?

Yes.

And 'is,' or 'becomes,' signifies a participation of present time?

Certainly.

And if the one is absolutely without participation in time, it never had become, or was becoming, or was at any time, or is now become or is becoming, or is, or will become, or will have become, or will be, hereafter.

Most true.

But are there any modes of partaking of being other than these?

There are none.

Then the one cannot possibly partake of being?

That is the inference.

Then the one is not at all?

Clearly not.

Then the one does not exist in such way as to be one; for if it were and partook of being, it would already be; but if the argument is to be trusted, the one neither is nor is one?

True.

But that which is not admits of no attribute or relation?

Of course not.

Then there is no name, nor expression, nor perception, nor opinion, nor knowledge of it?

Clearly not.

Then it is neither named, nor expressed, nor opined, nor known, nor does anything that is perceive it.

So we must infer.

But can all this be true about the one?

I think not.

i. b. Suppose, now, that we return once more to the original hypo-

nor
modes of
time.

But these
are the
only
modes of
partaking
of being,
and if
they are
all denied
of it, then
the one
is not,
[142]
and has
therefore
no attri-
bute or
relation,
etc.

The con-
clusion is
unsatis-
factory.

thesis; let us see whether, on a further review, any new aspect of the question appears.

I shall be very happy to do so.

We say that we have to work out together all the consequences, whatever they may be, which follow, if the one is?

Yes.

Then we will begin at the beginning:—If one is, can one be, and not partake of being?

Impossible.

Then the one will have being, but its being will not be the same with the one; for if the same, it would not be the being of the one; nor would the one have participated in being, for the proposition that one is would have been identical with the proposition that one is one; but our hypothesis is not if one is one, what will follow, but if one is:—am I not right?

Quite right.

We mean to say, that being has not the same significance as one?

Of course.

And when we put them together shortly, and say 'One is,' that is equivalent to saying, 'partakes of being'?

Quite true.

Once more then let us ask, if one is what will follow. Does not this hypothesis necessarily imply that one is of such a nature as to have parts?

How so?

In this way:—If being is predicated of the one, if the one is, and one of being, if being is one; and if being and one are not the same; and since the one, which we have assumed, is, must not the whole, if it is one, itself be, and have for its parts, one and being?

Certainly.

And is each of these parts—one and being—to be simply called a part, or must the word 'part' be relative to the word 'whole'?

The latter.

Then that which is one is both a whole and has a part?

Certainly.

Again, of the parts of the one, if it is—I mean being and one—does either fail to imply the other? is the one wanting to being, or being to the one?

Impossible.

Thus, each of the parts also has in turn both one and being, and is at the least made up of two parts; and the same principle goes on for ever, and every part whatever has always these two parts; for

*Par-
menides*

143
PAR-
MEN-
IDES,
ARISTO-
TELES.

being always involves one, and one being; so that one is always disappearing, and becoming two.

Certainly.

And so the one, if it is, must be infinite in multiplicity?

Clearly.

Let us take another direction.

What direction?

We say that the one partakes of being and therefore it is?

Yes.

And in this way, the one, if it has being, has turned out to be many?

True.

But now, let us abstract the one which, as we say, partakes of being, and try to imagine it apart from that of which, as we say, it partakes—will this abstract one be one only or many?

One, I think.

Let us see:—Must not the being of one be other than one? for the one is not being, but, considered as one, only partook of being?

Certainly.

If being and the one be two different things, it is not because the one is one that it is other than being; nor because being is being that it is other than the one; but they differ from one another in virtue of otherness and difference.

Certainly.

So that the other is not the same—either with the one or with being?

Certainly not.

And therefore whether we take being and the other, or being and the one, or the one and the other, in every such case we take two things, which may be rightly called both.

How so.

In this way—you may speak of being?

Yes.

And also of one?

Yes.

Then now we have spoken of either of them?

Yes.

Well, and when I speak of being and one, I speak of them both?

Certainly.

And if I speak of being and the other, or of the one and the other,—in any such case do I not speak of both?

Yes.

*Par-
menides*

PAR-
MEN-
IDES,
ARISTO-
TELES.

And must not that which is correctly called both, be also two?

Undoubtedly.

And of two things how can either by any possibility not be one?

It cannot.

Then, if the individuals of the pair are together two, they must be severally one?

Clearly.

*from odd
to even
numbers,*

And if each of them is one, then by the addition of any one to any pair, the whole becomes three?

Yes.

And three are odd, and two are even?

Of course.

*from ad-
dition to
multipli-
cation.*

And if there are two there must also be twice, and if there are three there must be thrice; that is, if twice one makes two, and thrice one three?

Certainly.

There are two, and twice, and therefore there must be twice two; and there are three, and there is thrice, and therefore there must be thrice three?

Of course.

If there are three and twice, there is twice three; and if there are two and thrice, there is thrice two?

Undoubtedly.

144

Here, then, we have even taken even times, and odd taken odd times, and even taken odd times, and odd taken even times.

True.

And if this is so, does any number remain which has no necessity to be?

None whatever.

Then if one is, number must also be?

It must.

*Out of
the one
that is,
has come
differ-
ence, and
from dif-
ference
number
of every
sort,*

But if there is number, there must also be many, and infinite multiplicity of being; for number is infinite in multiplicity, and partakes also of being: am I not right?

Certainly.

And if all number participates in being, every part of number will also participate?

Yes.

*and num-
ber is co-
extensive
with
being;*

Then being is distributed over the whole multitude of things, and nothing that is, however small or however great, is devoid of it? And, indeed, the very supposition of this is absurd, for how can that which is, be devoid of being?

In no way.

*Par-
menides*

PAR-
MEN-
IDES,
ARISTO-
TELES.

And it is divided into the greatest and into the smallest, and into being of all sizes, and is broken up more than all things; the divisions of it have no limit.

True.

Then it has the greatest number of parts?

Yes, the greatest number.

Is there any of these which is a part of being, and yet no part?

Impossible.

But if it is at all and so long as it is, it must be one, and cannot be none?

Certainly.

Then the one attaches to every single part of being, and does not fail in any part, whether great or small, or whatever may be the size of it?

True.

But reflect:—Can one in its entirety, be in many places at the same time?

No; I see the impossibility of that.

And if not in its entirety, then it is divided; for it cannot be present with all the parts of being, unless divided.

True.

And that which has parts will be as many as the parts are?

Certainly.

Then we were wrong in saying just now, that being was distributed into the greatest number of parts. For it is not distributed into parts more than the one, but into parts equal to the one; the one is never wanting to being, or being to the one, but being two they are co-equal and co-extensive.

Certainly that is true.

The one itself, then, having been broken up into parts by being, is many and infinite?

True.

Then not only the one which has being is many, but the one itself distributed by being, must also be many?

Certainly.

Further, inasmuch as the parts are parts of a whole, the one, as a whole, will be limited; for are not the parts contained by the whole?

Certainly.

And that which contains, is a limit?

Of course.

Then the one if it has being is one and many, whole and parts, having limits and yet unlimited in number?

for every single part of being, however small, is one.

Again, one is in as many places as being, and must therefore be divided into as many parts.

The abstract one, as well as the one [145] which is, is both one and many, finite and infinite.

It is in itself, yet in other;

*Par-
menides*

PAR-
MEN-
IDES,
ARISTO-
TELES.

Clearly.

And because having limits, also having extremes?

Certainly.

And if a whole, having beginning and middle and end. For can anything be a whole without these three? And if any one of them is wanting to anything, will that any longer be a whole?

No.

Then the one, as appears, will have beginning, middle, and end.

It will.

But, again, the middle will be equidistant from the extremes; or it would not be in the middle?

Yes.

The one, as being a whole and also finite, has a beginning, middle and end, and so partakes of figure.

Then the one will partake of figure, either rectilinear or round, or a union of the two?

True.

And if this is the case, it will be both in itself and in another too.

How?

Every part is in the whole, and none is outside the whole.

True.

And all the parts are contained by the whole?

Yes.

And the one is all its parts, and neither more nor less than all?

No.

Regarded as the sum of its parts, it is in itself;

And the one is the whole?

Of course.

But if all the parts are in the whole, and the one is all of them and the whole, and they are all contained by the whole, the one will be contained by the one; and thus the one will be in itself.

That is true.

regarded as a whole, it is in other, because it is not in the parts, neither in one, nor more than one, nor in all.

But then, again, the whole is not in the parts—neither in all the parts, nor in some one of them. For if it is in all, it must be in one; for if there were any one in which it was not, it could not be in all the parts; for the part in which it is wanting is one of all, and if the whole is not in this, how can it be in them all?

It cannot.

Nor can the whole be in some of the parts; for if the whole were in some of the parts, the greater would be in the less, which is impossible.

Yes, impossible.

But if the whole is neither in one, nor in more than one, nor in all of the parts, it must be in something else, or cease to be anywhere at all?

Certainly.

If it were nowhere, it would be nothing; but being a whole, and not being in itself, it must be in another.

Very true.

The one then, regarded as a whole, is in another, but regarded as being all its parts, is in itself; and therefore the one must be itself in itself and also in another.

Certainly.

The one then, being of this nature, is of necessity both at rest and in motion?

How?

The one is at rest since it is in itself, for being in one, and not passing out of this, it is in the same, which is itself.

True.

And that which is ever in the same, must be ever at rest?

Certainly.

Well, and must not that, on the contrary, which is ever in other, never be in the same; and if never in the same, never at rest, and if not at rest, in motion?

True.

Then the one being always itself in itself and other, must always be both at rest and in motion?

Clearly.

And must be the same with itself, and other than itself; and also the same with the others, and other than the others; this follows from its previous affections.

How so?

Every thing in relation to every other thing, is either the same or other; or if neither the same nor other, then in the relation of a part to a whole, or of a whole to a part.

Clearly.

And is the one a part of itself?

Certainly not.

Since it is not a part in relation to itself it cannot be related to itself as whole to part?

It cannot.

But is the one other than one?

No.

And therefore not other than itself?

Certainly not.

If then it be neither other, nor a whole, nor a part in relation to itself, must it not be the same with itself?

Certainly.

But then, again, a thing which is in another place from 'itself,' if

*Par-
menides*

PAR-
MEN-
IDES,
ARISTO-
TELES.

The one therefore is both at rest and in motion: at [146] rest, if in itself; in motion, if in another.

Four possible relations of two things: (1) sameness, (2) otherness, (3) part and whole, (4) whole and part.

The one stands to itself in the relation of sameness,

this 'itself' remains in the same place with itself, must be other than 'itself,' for it will be in another place?

True.

Then the one has been shown to be at once in itself and in another?

Yes.

Thus, then, as appears, the one will be other than itself?

True.

Well, then, if anything be other than anything, will it not be other than that which is other?

Certainly.

And will not all things that are not one, be other than the one, and the one other than the not-one?

Of course.

Then the one will be other than the others?

True.

But, consider:—Are not the absolute same, and the absolute other, opposites to one another?

Of course.

Then will the same ever be in the other, or the other in the same?

They will not.

If then the other is never in the same, there is nothing in which the other is during any space of time; for during that space of time, however small, the other would be in the same. Is not that true?

Yes.

And since the other is never in the same, it can never be in anything that is.

True.

Then the other will never be either in the not-one, or in the one?

Certainly not.

Then not by reason of otherness is the one other than the not-one, or the not-one other than the one.

No.

Nor by reason of themselves will they be other than one another, if not partaking of the other.

How can they be?

But if they are not other, either by reason of themselves or of the other, will they not altogether escape being other than one another?

They will.

Again, the not-one cannot partake of the one; otherwise it would not have been not-one, but would have been in some way one.

True.

Nor can the not-one be number; for having number, it would not have been not-one at all.

It would not.

Again, is the not-one part of the one; or rather, would it not in that case partake of the one?

It would.

If then, in every point of view, the one and the not-one are distinct, then neither is the one part or whole of the not-one, nor is the not-one part or whole of the one?

No.

But we said that things which are neither parts nor wholes of one another, nor other than one another, will be the same with one another:—so we said?

Yes.

Then shall we say that the one, being in this relation to the not-one, is the same with it?

Let us say so.

Then it is the same with itself and the others, and also other than itself and the others.

That appears to be the inference.

And it will also be like and unlike itself and the others?

Perhaps.

Since the one was shown to be other than the others, the others will also be other than the one.

Yes.

And the one is other than the others in the same degree that the others are other than it, and neither more nor less?

True.

And if neither more nor less, then in a like degree?

Yes.

In virtue of the affection by which the one is other than others and others in like manner other than it, the one will be affected like the others and the others like the one.

How do you mean?

I may take as an illustration the case of names: You give a name to a thing?

Yes.

And you may say the name once or oftener?

Yes.

Again, the not-one cannot partake of the one; and therefore it cannot be number; and it cannot be part or whole of the one;

and therefore, according to our former table of relations, the one is the same with the not-one, the same with and also other than itself and others.

It is like and unlike itself and other; for one and other are other than one another, yet other in the same degree.

like, yet unlike;

*Par-
menides*

PAR-
MEN-
IDES,
ARISTO-
TELES.

And
therefore
they are
affected
in the
same
manner.
For when
we apply
the same
name, we
imply the
presence
[148]
of the
same
nature.

One, in
that it is
other
than the
others, is
shown to
be like;
and
therefore,
in that it
is the
same
with the
others, to
be unlike.

And when you say it once, you mention that of which it is the name? and when more than once, is it something else which you mention? or must it always be the same thing of which you speak, whether you utter the name once or more than once?

Of course it is the same.

And is not 'other' a name given to a thing?

Certainly.

Whenever, then, you use the word 'other,' whether once or oftener, you name that of which it is the name, and to no other do you give the name?

True.

Then when we say that the others are other than the one, and the one other than the others, in repeating the word 'other' we speak of that nature to which the name is applied, and of no other?

Quite true.

Then the one which is other than others, and the other which is other than the one, in that the word 'other' is applied to both, will be in the same condition; and that which is in the same condition is like?

Yes.

Then in virtue of the affection by which the one is other than the others, every thing will be like every thing, for every thing is other than every thing.

True.

Again, the like is opposed to the unlike?

Yes.

And the other to the same?

True again.

And the one was also shown to be the same with the others?

Yes.

And to be the same with the others is the opposite of being other than the others?

Certainly.

And in that it was other it was shown to be like?

Yes.

But in that it was the same it will be unlike by virtue of the opposite affection to that which made it like; and this was the affection of otherness.

Yes.

The same then will make it unlike; otherwise it will not be the opposite of the other.

True.

Then the one will be both like and unlike the others; like in so far as it is other, and unlike in so far as it is the same.

Yes, that argument may be used.

And there is another argument.

What?

In so far as it is affected in the same way it is not affected otherwise, and not being affected otherwise is not unlike, and not being unlike, is like; but in so far as it is affected by other it is otherwise, and being otherwise affected is unlike.

True.

Then because the one is the same with the others and other than the others, on either of these two grounds, or on both of them, it will be both like and unlike the others?

Certainly.

And in the same way as being other than itself and the same with itself, on either of these two grounds and on both of them, it will be like and unlike itself?

Of course.

Again, how far can the one touch or not touch itself and others? —consider.

I am considering.

The one was shown to be in itself which was a whole?

True.

And also in other things?

Yes.

In so far as it is in other things it would touch other things, but in so far as it is in itself it would be debarred from touching them, and would touch itself only.

Clearly.

Then the inference is that it would touch both?

It would.

But what do you say to a new point of view? Must not that which is to touch another be next to that which it is to touch, and occupy the place nearest to that in which what it touches is situated?

True.

Then the one, if it is to touch itself, ought to be situated next to itself, and occupy the place next to that in which itself is?

It ought.

And that would require that the one should be two, and be in two places at once, and this, while it is one, will never happen.

No.

Par-menides

PAR-
MEN-
IDES,
ARISTO-
TELES.

From an-
other
point of
view the
opposite
conse-
quences
follow.

Again,
the one
will and
will not
touch
both it-
self and
others.
Being in
both, it
will
touch
both.

But if
contact
implies at
least two
separate
things,
one can-
[149]
not touch

*Par-
menides*

PAR-
MEN-
IDES,
ARISTO-
TELES.

itself,—
for it
cannot be
two;

or other,
—for
'other'
cannot be
'one'
thing.

Then the one cannot touch itself any more than it can be two?

It cannot.

Neither can it touch others.

Why not?

The reason is, that whatever is to touch another must be in separation from, and next to, that which it is to touch, and no third thing can be between them.

True.

Two things, then, at the least are necessary to make contact possible?

They are.

And if to the two a third be added in due order, the number of terms will be three, and the contacts two?

Yes.

And every additional term makes one additional contact, whence it follows that the contacts are one less in number than the terms; the first two terms exceeded the number of contacts by one, and the whole number of terms exceeds the whole number of contacts by one in like manner; and for every one which is afterwards added to the number of terms, one contact is added to the contacts.

True.

Whatever is the whole number of things, the contacts will be always one less.

True.

But if there be only one, and not two, there will be no contact?

How can there be?

And do we not say that the others being other than the one are not one and have no part in the one?

True.

Then they have no number, if they have no one in them?

Of course not.

Then the others are neither one nor two, nor are they called by the name of any number?

No.

One, then, alone is one, and two do not exist?

Clearly not.

And if there are not two, there is no contact?

There is not.

Then neither does the one touch the others, nor the others the one, if there is no contact?

Certainly not.

For all which reasons the one touches and does not touch itself and the others?

True.

Further—is the one equal and unequal to itself and others?

How do you mean?

If the one were greater or less than the others, or the others greater or less than the one, they would not be greater or less than each other in virtue of their being the one and the others; but, if in addition to their being what they are they had equality, they would be equal to one another, or if the one had smallness and the others greatness, or the one had greatness and the others smallness— whichever kind had greatness would be greater, and whichever had smallness would be smaller?

Certainly.

Then there are two such ideas as greatness and smallness; for if they were not they could not be opposed to each other and be present in that which is.

How could they?

If, then, smallness is present in the one it will be present either in the whole or in a part of the whole?

Certainly.

Suppose the first; it will be either co-equal and co-extensive with the whole one, or will contain the one?

Clearly.

If it be co-extensive with the one it will be co-equal with the one, or if containing the one it will be greater than the one?

Of course.

But can smallness be equal to anything or greater than anything, and have the functions of greatness and equality and not its own functions?

Impossible.

Then smallness cannot be in the whole of one, but, if at all, in a part only?

Yes.

And surely not in all of a part, for then the difficulty of the whole will recur; it will be equal to or greater than any part in which it is.

Certainly.

Then smallness will not be in anything, whether in a whole or in a part; nor will there be anything small but actual smallness.

True.

Neither will greatness be in the one, for if greatness be in anything there will be something greater other and besides greatness itself, namely, that in which greatness is; and this too when the small itself is not there, which the one, if it is great, must exceed;

*Par-
menides*

PAR-
MEN-
IDES,
ARISTO-
TELES.

The one is
equal and
unequal
to itself
and
others;

150

equal, be-
cause, not
partaking
of great-
ness and
smallness,
it must
partake
of equal-
ity to it-
self and
others:

and to other;

*Par-
menides*

PAR-
MEN-
IDES,
ARISTO-
TELES.

this, however, is impossible, seeing that smallness is wholly absent.

True.

But absolute greatness is only greater than absolute smallness, and smallness is only smaller than absolute greatness.

Very true.

Then other things are not greater or less than the one, if they have neither greatness nor smallness; nor have greatness or smallness any power of exceeding or being exceeded in relation to the one, but only in relation to one another; nor will the one be greater or less than them or others, if it has neither greatness nor smallness.

Clearly not.

Then if the one is neither greater nor less than the others, it cannot either exceed or be exceeded by them?

Certainly not.

And that which neither exceeds nor is exceeded, must be on an equality; and being on an equality, must be equal.

Of course.

And this will be true also of the relation of the one to itself; having neither greatness nor smallness in itself, it will neither exceed nor be exceeded by itself, but will be on an equality with and equal to itself.

Certainly.

Then the one will be equal to both itself and the others?

Clearly so.

And yet the one, being itself in itself, will also surround and be without itself; and, as containing itself, will be greater than itself; and, as contained in itself, will be less; and will thus be greater and less than itself.

It will.

Now there cannot possibly be anything which is not included in the one and the others?

Of course not.

But, surely, that which is must always be somewhere?

Yes.

But that which is in anything will be less, and that in which it is will be greater; in no other way can one thing be in another.

True.

And since there is nothing other or besides the one and the others, and they must be in something, must they not be in one another, the one in the others and the others in the one, if they are to be anywhere?

That is clear.

But inasmuch as the one is in the others, the others will be great-

151
Unequal
to itself,
—because
it con-
tains and
is con-
tained in
itself, and
is there-
fore
greater
and less
than it-
self

Unequal
to others,
—because
it con-
tains and
is con-
tained in
them, and

er than the one, because they contain the one, which will be less than the others, because it is contained in them; and inasmuch as the others are in the one, the one on the same principle will be greater than the others, and the others less than the one.

True.

The one, then, will be equal to and greater and less than itself and the others?

Clearly.

And if it be greater and less and equal, it will be of equal and more and less measures or divisions than itself and the others, and if of measures, also of parts?

Of course.

And if of equal and more and less measures or divisions, it will be in number more or less than itself and the others, and likewise equal in number to itself and to the others?

How is that?

It will be of more measures than those things which it exceeds, and of as many parts as measures; and so with that to which it is equal, and that than which it is less.

True.

And being greater and less than itself, and equal to itself, it will be of equal measures with itself and of more and fewer measures than itself; and if of measures then also of parts?

It will.

And being of equal parts with itself, it will be numerically equal to itself; and being of more parts, more, and being of less, less than itself?

Certainly.

And the same will hold of its relation to other things; inasmuch as it is greater than them, it will be more in number than them; and inasmuch as it is smaller, it will be less in number; and inasmuch as it is equal in size to other things, it will be equal to them in number.

Certainly.

Once more, then, as would appear, the one will be in number both equal to and more and less than both itself and all other things.

It will.

Does the one also partake of time? And is it and does it become older and younger than itself and others, and again, neither younger nor older than itself and others, by virtue of participation in time?

*Par-
menides*

PAR-
MEN-
IDES,
ARISTO-
TELES.

is there-
fore
greater
and less
than
them.

That
which is
equal and
unequal
to itself
and
others,
must be
of a num-
ber of
divisions
or parts
equal
and un-
equal to
itself and
others.

Does one
partake
of time
and be-
come
older and

Par-
menides

152

PAR-
MEN-
IDES,
ARISTO-
TELES.

younger,
and
neither
older nor
younger
than itself
and
others?

The one
is, and
therefore
partakes
of time;
and since
time is
always
moving
forward,
it be-
comes
older
than it-
self.

But older
and
younger
are rela-
tive
terms,
and
therefore
that
which
becomes
older than
itself
must be-
come also
younger
than
itself.

One be-
comes

How do you mean?

If one is, being must be predicated of it?

Yes.

But to be (εἶναι) is only participation of being in present time, and to have been is the participation of being at a past time, and to be about to be is the participation of being at a future time?

Very true.

Then the one, since it partakes of being, partakes of time?

Certainly.

And is not time always moving forward?

Yes.

Then the one is always becoming older than itself, since it moves forward in time?

Certainly.

And do you remember that the older becomes older than that which becomes younger?

I remember.

Then since the one becomes older than itself, it becomes younger at the same time?

Certainly.

Thus, then, the one becomes older as well as younger than itself?

Yes.

And it is older (is it not?) when in becoming, it gets to the point of time between 'was' and 'will be,' which is 'now': for surely in going from the past to the future, it cannot skip the present?

No.

And when it arrives at the present it stops from becoming older, and no longer becomes, but is older, for if it went on it would never be reached by the present, for it is the nature of that which goes on, to touch both the present and the future, letting go the present and seizing the future, while in process of becoming between them.

True.

But that which is becoming cannot skip the present; when it reaches the present it ceases to become, and is then whatever it may happen to be becoming.

Clearly.

And so the one, when in becoming older it reaches the present, ceases to become, and is then older.

Certainly.

And it is older than that than which it was becoming older, and it was becoming older than itself.

Yes.

And that which is older is older than that which is younger?
True.

Then the one is younger than itself, when in becoming older it reaches the present?
Certainly.

But the present is always present with the one during all its being; for whenever it is it is always now.
Certainly.

Then the one always both is and becomes older and younger than itself?
Truly.

And is it or does it become a longer time than itself or an equal time with itself?
An equal time.

But if it becomes or is for an equal time with itself, it is of the same age with itself?
Of course.

And that which is of the same age, is neither older nor younger?
No.

The one, then, becoming and being the same time with itself, neither is nor becomes older or younger than itself?
I should say not.

And what are its relations to other things? Is it or does it become older or younger than they?
I cannot tell you.

You can at least tell me that others than the one are more than the one—other would have been one, but the others have multitude, and are more than one?
They will have multitude.

And a multitude implies a number larger than one?
Of course.

And shall we say that the lesser or the greater is the first to come or to have come into existence?
The lesser.

Then the least is the first? And that is the one?
Yes.

Then the one of all things that have number is the first to come into being; but all other things have also number, being plural and not singular.
They have.

And since it came into being first it must be supposed to have come into being prior to the others, and the others later; and the

*Par-
menides*

PAR-
MEN-
IDES,
ARISTO-
TELES.

older
until it
reaches
the now
or pre-
sent;
then it
ceases to
become
and is
older;

and also
younger.

It always
is and
becomes
older and
younger
[153]
than it-
self;

and since
it is and
becomes
during
the same
time with
itself is of
the same
age, and
therefore
neither
older nor
younger
than it-
self.
Is the
one
younger
or older
than
other
things?
The less
comes
into
being

*Par-
menides*

PAR-
MEN-
IDES,
ARISTO-
TELES.

before
the
greater:
the one is
less than
the many
or others,
and
therefore
comes
into being
before
them and
is older
than they.

The one
has
parts and
comes
into being
with the
last of
them:

and
therefore
it is
younger
than the
others.
But
again,
each part
is one,

and one
comes
into be-
ing to-
gether
with
each
part, and
so the one
is neither
older nor
younger

things which came into being later, are younger than that which preceded them? And so the other things will be younger than the one, and the one older than other things?

True.

What would you say of another question? Can the one have come into being contrary to its own nature, or is that impossible?

Impossible.

And yet, surely, the one was shown to have parts; and if parts, then a beginning, middle and end?

Yes.

And a beginning, both of the one itself and of all other things, comes into being first of all; and after the beginning, the others follow, until you reach the end?

Certainly.

And all these others we shall affirm to be parts of the whole and of the one, which, as soon as the end is reached, has become whole and one?

Yes; that is what we shall say.

But the end comes last, and the one is of such a nature as to come into being with the last; and, since the one cannot come into being except in accordance with its own nature, its nature will require that it should come into being after the others, simultaneously with the end.

Clearly.

Then the one is younger than the others and the others older than the one.

That also is clear in my judgment.

Well, and must not a beginning or any other part of the one or of anything, if it be a part and not parts, being a part, be also of necessity one?

Certainly.

And will not the one come into being together with each part— together with the first part when that comes into being, and together with the second part and with all the rest, and will not be wanting to any part, which is added to any other part until it has reached the last and become one whole; it will be wanting neither to the middle, nor to the first, nor to the last, nor to any of them, while the process of becoming is going on?

True.

Then the one is of the same age with all the others, so that if the one itself does not contradict its own nature, it will be neither prior nor posterior to the others, but simultaneous; and according to this argument the one will be neither older nor younger than the others,

154

nor the others than the one, but according to the previous argument the one will be older and younger than the others and the others than the one.

Certainly.

After this manner then the one is and has become. But as to its becoming older and younger than the others, and the others than the one, and neither older nor younger, what shall we say? Shall we say as of being so also of becoming, or otherwise?

I cannot answer.

But I can venture to say, that even if one thing were older or younger than another, it could not become older or younger in a greater degree than it was at first; for equals added to unequals, whether to periods of time or to anything else, leave the difference between them the same as at first.

Of course.

Then that which is, cannot become older or younger than that which is, since the difference of age is always the same; the one is and has become older and the other younger; but they are no longer becoming so.

True.

And the one which is does not therefore become either older or younger than the others which are.

No.

But consider whether they may not become older and younger in another way.

In what way?

Just as the one was proven to be older than the others and the others than the one.

And what of that?

If the one is older than the others, it has come into being a longer time than the others.

Yes.

But consider again; if we add equal time to a greater and a less time, will the greater differ from the less time by an equal or by a smaller portion than before?

By a smaller portion.

Then the difference between the age of the one and the age of the others will not be afterwards so great as at first, but if an equal time be added to both of them they will differ less and less in age?

Yes.

And that which differs in age from some other less than formerly, from being older will become younger in relation to that other than which it was older?

Par-
menides

PAR-
MEN-
IDES,
ARISTO-
TELES.

than the
others but
coeval.

Again,
nothing
can be-
come
older or
younger
than it
was at
first in
relation
to some-
thing
else, if an
equal
amount
of time be
added to
both.
This is
true of
the one
and the
other.

But if an
equal
time be
added to
a greater
and less,
the rela-
tive dif-
ference
between
them di-
minishes;
and so the
one,

Yes, younger.

And if the one becomes younger the others aforesaid will become older than they were before, in relation to the one.

Certainly.

Then that which had become younger becomes older relatively to that which previously had become and was older; it never really is older, but is always becoming, for the one is always growing on the side of youth and the other on the side of age. And in like manner the older is always in process of becoming younger than the younger; for as they are always going in opposite directions they become in ways the opposite to one another, the younger older than the older, and the older younger than the younger. They cannot, however, have become; for if they had already become they would be and not merely become. But that is impossible; for they are always becoming both older and younger than one another: the one becomes younger than the others because it was seen to be older and prior, and the others become older than the one because they came into being later; and in the same way the others are in the same relation to the one, because they were seen to be older and prior to the one.

That is clear.

Inasmuch then, as one thing does not become older or younger than another, in that they always differ from each other by an equal number, the one cannot become older or younger than the others, nor the others than the one; but inasmuch as that which came into being earlier and that which came into being later must continually differ from each other by a different portion—in this point of view the others must become older and younger than the one, and the one than the others.

Certainly.

For all these reasons, then, the one is and becomes older and younger than itself and the others, and neither is nor becomes older or younger than itself or the others.

Certainly.

But since the one partakes of time, and partakes of becoming older and younger, must it not also partake of the past, the present, and the future?

Of course it must.

Then the one was and is and will be, and was becoming and is becoming and will become?

Certainly.

And there is and was and will be something which is in relation to it and belongs to it?

*Par-
menides*

PAR-
MEN-
IDES,
ARISTO-
TELES.

True.

And since we have at this moment opinion and knowledge and perception of the one, there is opinion and knowledge and perception of it?

Quite right.

Then there is name and expression for it, and it is named and expressed, and everything of this kind which appertains to other things appertains to the one.

Certainly, that is true.

Yet once more and for the third time, let us consider: If the one is both one and many, as we have described, and is neither one nor many, and participates in time, must it not, in as far as it is one, at times partake of being, and in as far as it is not one, at times not partake of being?

Certainly.

But can it partake of being when not partaking of being, or not partake of being when partaking of being?

Impossible.

Then the one partakes and does not partake of being at different times, for that is the only way in which it can partake and not partake of the same.

True.

And is there not also a time at which it assumes being and relinquishes being—for how can it have and not have the same thing unless it receives and also gives it up at some time?

Impossible.

And the assuming of being is what you would call becoming?

I should.

And the relinquishing of being you would call destruction?

I should.

The one then, as would appear, becomes and is destroyed by taking and giving up being.

Certainly.

And being one and many and in process of becoming and being destroyed, when it becomes one it ceases to be many, and when many, it ceases to be one?

Certainly.

And as it becomes one and many, must it not inevitably experience separation and aggregation?

Inevitably.

And whenever it becomes like and unlike it must be assimilated and dissimilated?

Opposites cannot be predicated of the same thing at the same time.

The one must therefore partake of being [156] and not-being and assume and relinquish them at different times.

How does the change take place?

Yes.

And when it becomes greater or less or equal it must grow or diminish or be equalized?

True.

And when being in motion it rests, and when being at rest it changes to motion, it can surely be in no time at all?

How can it?

But that a thing which is previously at rest should be afterwards in motion, or previously in motion and afterwards at rest, without experiencing change, is impossible.

Impossible.

And surely there cannot be a time in which a thing can be at once neither in motion nor at rest?

There cannot.

But neither can it change without changing.

True.

When then does it change; for it cannot change either when at rest, or when in motion, or when in time?

It cannot.

And does this strange thing in which it is at the time of changing really exist?

What thing?

The moment. For the moment seems to imply a something out of which change takes place into either of two states; for the change is not from the state of rest as such, nor from the state of motion as such; but there is this curious nature which we call the moment lying between rest and motion, not being in any time; and into this and out of this what is in motion changes into rest, and what is at rest into motion.

So it appears.

And the one then, since it is at rest and also in motion, will change to either, for only in this way can it be in both. And in changing it changes in a moment, and when it is changing it will be in no time, and will not then be either in motion or at rest.

It will not.

And it will be in the same case in relation to the other changes, when it passes from being into cessation of being, or from not-being into becoming—then it passes between certain states of motion and rest, and neither is nor is not, nor becomes nor is destroyed.

Very true.

And on the same principle, in the passage from one to many and from many to one, the one is neither one nor many, neither separated nor aggregated; and in the passage from like to unlike, and from unlike to like, it is neither like nor unlike, neither in a state of assimilation nor of dissimilation; and in the passage from small to great and equal and back again, it will be neither small nor great, nor equal, nor in a state of increase, or diminution, or equalization. *Par-menides*

PAR-
MEN-
IDES,
ARISTO-
TELES.

True.

All these, then, are the affections of the one, if the one has being.

Of course.

i. aa. But if one is, what will happen to the others—is not that also to be considered?

Yes.

Let us show then, if one is, what will be the affections of the others than the one.

Let us do so.

Inasmuch as there are things other than the one, the others are not the one; for if they were they could not be other than the one.

Very true.

Nor are the others altogether without the one, but in a certain way they participate in the one.

In what way?

Because the others are other than the one inasmuch as they have parts; for if they had no parts they would be simply one.

Right.

And parts, as we affirm, have relation to a whole?

So we say.

And a whole must necessarily be one made up of many; and the parts will be parts of the one, for each of the parts is not a part of many, but of a whole.

How do you mean?

If anything were a part of many, being itself one of them, it will surely be a part of itself, which is impossible, and it will be a part of each one of the other parts, if of all; for if not a part of some one, it will be a part of all the others but this one, and thus will not be a part of each one; and if not a part of each one, it will not be a part of any one of the many; and not being a part of any one, it cannot be a part or anything else of all those things of none of which it is anything.

Clearly not.

Then the part is not a part of the many, nor of all, but is of a certain single form, which we call a whole, being one perfect unity framed out of all—of this the part will be a part.

*Par-
menides*

PAR-
MEN-
IDES,
ARISTO-
TELES.

Again,
each part
[158]
is not
only a
part but
also a
perfect
whole in
itself.

The
whole
and the
part are
both one,
and
therefore
they must
partici-
pate in
the one
and be
other
than the
one, and
more
than one
and infi-
nite in
number.

Certainly.

If, then, the others have parts, they will participate in the whole and in the one.

True.

Then the others than the one must be one perfect whole, having parts.

Certainly.

And the same argument holds of each part, for the part must participate in the one; for if each of the parts is a part, this means, I suppose, that it is one separate from the rest and self-related; otherwise it is not each.

True.

But when we speak of the part participating in the one, it must clearly be other than one; for if not, it would not merely have participated, but would have been one; whereas only the one itself can be one.

Very true.

Both the whole and the part must participate in the one; for the whole will be one whole, of which the parts will be parts; and each part will be one part of the whole which is the whole of the part.

True.

And will not the things which participate in the one, be other than it?

Of course.

And the things which are other than the one will be many; for if the things which are other than the one were neither one nor more than one, they would be nothing.

True.

But, seeing that the things which participate in the one as a part, and in the one as a whole, are more than one, must not those very things which participate in the one be infinite in number?

How so?

Let us look at the matter thus:—Is it not a fact that in partaking of the one they are not one, and do not partake of the one at the very time when they are partaking of it?

Clearly.

They do so then as multitudes in which the one is not present?

Very true.

And if we were to abstract from them in idea the very smallest fraction, must not that least fraction, if it does not partake of the one, be a multitude and not one?

It must.

And if we continue to look at the other side of their nature, regarded simply, and in itself, will not they, as far as we see them, be unlimited in number?

Certainly.

And yet, when each several part becomes a part, then the parts have a limit in relation to the whole and to each other, and the whole in relation to the parts.

Just so.

The result to the others than the one is that the union of themselves and the one appears to create a new element in them which gives to them limitation in relation to one another; whereas in their own nature they have no limit.

That is clear.

Then the others than the one, both as whole and parts, are infinite, and also partake of limit.

Certainly.

Then they are both like and unlike one another and themselves.

How is that?

Inasmuch as they are unlimited in their own nature, they are all affected in the same way.

True.

And inasmuch as they all partake of limit, they are all affected in the same way.

Of course.

But inasmuch as their state is both limited and unlimited, they are affected in opposite ways.

Yes.

And opposites are the most unlike of things.

Certainly.

Considered, then, in regard to either one of their affections, they will be like themselves and one another; considered in reference to both of them together, most opposed and most unlike.

That appears to be true.

Then the others are both like and unlike themselves and one another?

True.

And they are the same and also different from one another, and in motion and at rest, and experience every sort of opposite affection, as may be proved without difficulty of them, since they have been shown to have experienced the affections aforesaid?

True.

i. bb. Suppose, now, that we leave the further discussion of these matters as evident, and consider again upon the hypothesis that

Par-
menides

PAR-
MEN-
IDES,
ARISTO-
TELES.

The others unlimited and also limited in their nature,

both as whole and parts.

Wherefore also they are like and unlike,

159

A reversal of former

the one is, whether the opposite of all this is or is not equally true of the others.

By all means.

Then let us begin again, and ask, If one is, what must be the affections of the others?

Let us ask that question.

Must not the one be distinct from the others, and the others from the one?

Why so?

Why, because there is nothing else beside them which is distinct from both of them; for the expression 'one and the others' includes all things.

Yes, all things.

Then we cannot suppose that there is anything different from them in which both the one and the others might exist?

There is nothing.

Then the one and the others are never in the same?

True.

Then they are separated from each other?

Yes.

And we surely cannot say that what is truly one has parts?

Impossible.

Then the one will not be in the others as a whole, nor as part, if it be separated from the others, and has no parts?

Impossible.

Then there is no way in which the others can partake of the one, if they do not partake either in whole or in part?

It would seem not.

Then there is no way in which the others are one, or have in themselves any unity?

There is not.

Nor are the others many; for if they were many, each part of them would be a part of the whole; but now the others, not partaking in any way of the one, are neither one nor many, nor whole, nor part.

True.

Then the others neither are nor contain two or three, if entirely deprived of the one?

True.

Then the others are neither like nor unlike the one, nor is likeness and unlikeness in them; for if they were like and unlike, or had in them likeness and unlikeness, they would have two natures in them opposite to one another.

That is clear.

But for that which partakes of nothing to partake of two things was held by us to be impossible?

Impossible.

Then the others are neither like nor unlike nor both, for if they were like or unlike they would partake of one of those two natures, which would be one thing, and if they were both they would partake of opposites which would be two things, and this has been shown to be impossible.

True.

Therefore they are neither the same, nor other, nor in motion, nor at rest, nor in a state of becoming, nor of being destroyed, nor greater, nor less, nor equal, nor have they experienced anything else of the sort; for, if they are capable of experiencing any such affection, they will participate in one and two and three, and odd and even, and in these, as has been proved, they do not participate, seeing that they are altogether and in every way devoid of the one.

Very true.

Therefore if one is, the one is all things, and also nothing, both in relation to itself and to other things.

Certainly.

ii. a. Well, and ought we not to consider next what will be the consequence if the one is not?

Yes; we ought.

What is the meaning of the hypothesis—If the one is not; is there any difference between this and the hypothesis—If the not one is not?

There is a difference, certainly.

Is there a difference only, or rather are not the two expressions— if the one is not, and if the not one is not, entirely opposed?

They are entirely opposed.

And suppose a person to say:—If greatness is not, if smallness is not, or anything of that sort, does he not mean, whenever he uses such an expression, that 'what is not' is other than other things?

To be sure.

And so when he says 'If one is not' he clearly means, that what 'is not' is other than all others; we know what he means—do we not?

Yes, we do.

When he says 'one,' he says something which is known; and secondly something which is other than all other things; it makes no difference whether he predicate of one being or not-being, for

Par-menides

160
PAR-
MEN-
IDES,
ARISTO-
TELES.

cannot partake of two things if they cannot partake of one.

The others without the one = o.

The one is all things; but also nothing (141 E., 142).

If the one is not, what then?

What is the meaning of 'the one which is not'?

It some-times

that which is said 'not to be' is known to be something all the same,
and is distinguished from other things.

Certainly.

Then I will begin again, and ask: If one is not, what are the
consequences? In the first place, as would appear, there is a knowledge of it, or the very meaning of the words, 'if one is not,' would
not be known.

True.

Secondly, the others differ from it, or it could not be described
as different from the others?

Certainly.

Difference, then, belongs to it as well as knowledge; for in
speaking of the one as different from the others, we do not speak
of a difference in the others, but in the one.

Clearly so.

Moreover, the one that is not is something and partakes of relation to 'that,' and 'this,' and 'these,' and the like, and is an attribute of 'this'; for the one, or the others than the one, could not
have been spoken of, nor could any attribute or relative of the one
that is not have been or been spoken of, nor could it have been said
to be anything, if it did not partake of 'some,' or of the other relations just now mentioned.

True.

Being, then, cannot be ascribed to the one, since it is not; but the
one that is not may or rather must participate in many things, if
it and nothing else is not; if, however, neither the one nor the one
that is not is supposed not to be, and we are speaking of something
of a different nature, we can predicate nothing of it. But supposing
that the one that is not and nothing else is not, then it must participate in the predicate 'that,' and in many others.

Certainly.

And it will have unlikeness in relation to the others, for the
others being different from the one will be of a different kind.

Certainly.

And are not things of a different kind also other in kind?

Of course.

And are not things other in kind unlike?

They are unlike.

And if they are unlike the one, that which they are unlike will
clearly be unlike them?

Clearly so.

Then the one will have unlikeness in respect of which the others
are unlike it?

That would seem to be true.

And if unlikeness to other things is attributed to it, it must have likeness to itself.

How so?

If the one have unlikeness to one, something else must be meant; nor will the hypothesis relate to one; but it will relate to something other than one?

Quite so.

But that cannot be.

No.

Then the one must have likeness to itself?

It must.

Again, it is not equal to the others; for if it were equal, then it would at once be and be like them in virtue of the equality; but if one has no being, then it can neither be nor be like?

It cannot.

But since it is not equal to the others, neither can the others be equal to it?

Certainly not.

And things that are not equal are unequal?

True.

And they are unequal to an unequal?

Of course.

Then the one partakes of inequality, and in respect of this the others are unequal to it?

Very true.

And inequality implies greatness and smallness?

Yes.

Then the one, if of such a nature, has greatness and smallness?

That appears to be true.

And greatness and smallness always stand apart?

True.

Then there is always something between them?

There is.

And can you think of anything else which is between them other than equality?

No, it is equality which lies between them.

Then that which has greatness and smallness also has equality, which lies between them?

That is clear.

Then the one, which is not, partakes, as would appear, of greatness and smallness and equality?

Clearly.

Parmenides

PAR-
MEN-
IDES,
ARISTO-
TELES.

The one which is not is unequal to the others and the others to it.

But partaking of inequality, it partakes also of greatness and smallness, and therefore of equality which lies between them;

Further, it must surely in a sort partake of being?

How so?

It must be so, for if not, then we should not speak the truth in saying that the one is not. But if we speak the truth, clearly we must say what is. Am I not right?

162
PAR-
MEN-
IDES,
ARISTO-
TELES.

Yes.

And since we affirm that we speak truly, we must also affirm that we say what is?

Certainly.

Then, as would appear, the one, when it is not, is; for if it were not to be when it is not, but [1] were to relinquish something of being, so as to become not-being, it would at once be.

it must
surely
partake
of being
in a
sense;

Quite true.

for not-
being im-
plies be-
ing and
being im-
plies not-
being.

Then the one which is not, if it is to maintain itself, must have the being of not-being as the bond of not-being, just as being must have as a bond the not-being of not-being in order to perfect its own being; for the truest assertion of the being of being and of the not-being of not-being is when being partakes of the being of being, and not of the being of not-being—that is, the perfection of being; and when not-being does not partake of the not-being of not-being but of the being of not-being—that is the perfection of not-being.

Most true.

Since then what is partakes of not-being, and what is not of being, must not the one also partake of being in order not to be?

Certainly.

Then the one, if it is not, clearly has being?

Clearly.

And has not-being also, if it is not?

Of course.

But to be
both, it
must
change
from one
to the
other, and
therefore
be in
motion.

But can anything which is in a certain state not be in that state without changing?

Impossible.

Then everything which is and is not in a certain state, implies change?

Certainly.

And change is motion—we may say that?

Yes, motion.

And the one has been proved both to be and not to be?

Yes.

And therefore is and is not in the same state?

Yes.

[1] Or, 'to remit something of existence in relation to not being.'

Thus the one that is not has been shown to have motion also, because it changes from being to not-being?

That appears to be true.

But surely if it is nowhere among what is, as is the fact, since it is not, it cannot change from one place to another?

Impossible.

Then it cannot move by changing place?

No.

Nor can it turn on the same spot, for it nowhere touches the same, for the same is, and that which is not cannot be reckoned among things that are?

It cannot.

Then the one, if it is not, cannot turn in that in which it is not?

No.

Neither can the one, whether it is or is not, be altered into other than itself, for if it altered and became different from itself, then we could not be still speaking of the one, but of something else?

True.

But if the one neither suffers alteration, nor turns round in the same place, nor changes place, can it still be capable of motion?

Impossible.

Now that which is unmoved must surely be at rest, and that which is at rest must stand still?

Certainly.

Then the one that is not, stands still, and is also in motion?

That seems to be true.

But if it be in motion it must necessarily undergo alteration, for anything which is moved, in so far as it is moved, is no longer in the same state, but in another?

Yes.

Then the one, being moved, is altered?

Yes.

And, further, if not moved in any way, it will not be altered in any way?

No.

Then, in so far as the one that is not is moved, it is altered, but in so far as it is not moved, it is not altered?

Right.

Then the one that is not is altered and is not altered?

That is clear.

And must not that which is altered become other than it previously was, and lose its former state and be destroyed; but that which is not altered can neither come into being nor be destroyed?

Parmenides

PAR-
MEN-
IDES,
ARISTO-
TELES.

How can it change? Not (*a*) by change of place, nor (*b*) by revolving in the same place, nor (*c*) by change of nature.

It is therefore unmoved;

and being unmoved, it must be at rest.

163
But motion implies alteration.

The one that is not becomes

Very true.

And the one that is not, being altered, becomes and is destroyed; and not be'ng altered, neither becomes nor is destroyed; and so the one that is not becomes and is destroyed, and neither becomes nor is destroyed?

True.

ii. b. And now, let us go back once more to the beginning, and see whether these or some other consequences will follow.

Let us do as you say.

If one is not, we ask what will happen in respect of one? That is the question.

Yes.

Do not the words 'is not' signify absence of being in that to which we apply them?

Just so.

And when we say that a thing is not, do we mean that it is not in one way but is in another? or do we mean, absolutely, that what is not has in no sort or way or kind participation of being?

Quite absolutely.

Then, that which is not cannot be, or in any way participate in being?

It cannot.

And did we not mean by becoming, and being destroyed, the assumption of being and the loss of being?

Nothing else.

And can that which has no participation in being, either assume or lose being?

Impossible.

The one then, since it in no way is, cannot have or lose or assume being in any way?

True.

Then the one that is not, since it in no way partakes of being, neither perishes nor becomes?

No.

Then it is not altered at all; for if it were it would become and be destroyed?

True.

But if it be not altered it cannot be moved?

Certainly not.

Nor can we say that it stands, if it is nowhere; for that which stands must always be in one and the same spot?

Of course.

Then we must say that the one which is not never stands still and never moves?

Neither.

Nor is there any existing thing which can be attributed to it; for if there had been, it would partake of being?

That is clear.

And therefore neither smallness, nor greatness, nor equality, can be attributed to it?

No.

Nor yet likeness nor difference, either in relation to itself or to others?

Clearly not.

Well, and if nothing should be attributed to it, can other things be attributed to it?

Certainly not.

And therefore other things can neither be like or unlike, the same, or different in relation to it?

They cannot.

Nor can what is not, be anything, or be this thing, or be related to or the attribute of this or that or other, or be past, present, or future. Nor can knowledge, or opinion, or perception, or expression, or name, or any other thing that is, have any concern with it?

No.

Then the one that is not has no condition of any kind?

Such appears to be the conclusion.

ii. aa. Yet once more; if one is not, what becomes of the others? Let us determine that.

Yes; let us determine that.

The others must surely be; for if they, like the one, were not, we could not be now speaking of them.

True.

But to speak of the others implies difference—the terms 'other' and 'different' are synonymous?

True.

Other means other than other, and different, different from the different?

Yes.

Then, if there are to be others, there is something than which they will be other?

Certainly.

And what can that be?—for if the one is not, they will not be other than the one.

*Par-
menides*

164
PAR-
MEN-
IDES,
ARISTO-
TELES.

It has no
attributes
and no
condi-
tions of
any kind.

Again, if
one is not,
what
happens
to the
others?

Other
implies
differ-
ence; it
cannot
mean
other
than the
one; and
therefore

*Par-
menides*

PAR-
MEN-
IDES,
ARISTO-
TELES.

the others
are other
than each
other,

and each
of them,
though
devoid of
the one,
appears
to be one.

They will not.

Then they will be other than each other; for the only remaining alternative is that they are other than nothing.

True.

And they are each other than one another, as being plural and not singular; for if one is not, they cannot be singular but every particle of them is infinite in number; and even if a person takes that which appears to be the smallest fraction, this, which seemed one, in a moment evanesces into many, as in a dream, and from being the smallest becomes very great, in comparison with the fractions into which it is split up?

Very true.

And in such particles the others will be other than one another, if others are, and the one is not?

Exactly.

And will there not be many particles, each appearing to be one, but not being one, if one is not?

True.

And it would seem that number can be predicated of them if each of them appears to be one, though it is really many?

It can.

And there will seem to be odd and even among them, which will also have no reality, if one is not?

Yes.

165   And there will appear to be a least among them; and even this will seem large and manifold in comparison with the many small fractions which are contained in it?

Certainly.

And each particle will be imagined to be equal to the many and little; for it could not have appeared to pass from the greater to the less without having appeared to arrive at the middle; and thus would arise the appearance of equality.

Yes.

And having neither beginning, middle, nor end, each separate particle yet appears to have a limit in relation to itself and other.

How so?

Because, when a person conceives of any one of these as such, prior to the beginning another beginning appears, and there is another end, remaining after the end, and in the middle truer middles within but smaller, because no unity can be conceived of any of them, since the one is not.

Very true.

And so all being, whatever we think of, must be broken up into fractions, for a particle will have to be conceived of without unity?

Certainly.

And such being when seen indistinctly and at a distance, appears to be one; but when seen near and with keen intellect, every single thing appears to be infinite, since it is deprived of the one, which is not?

Nothing more certain.

Then each of the others must appear to be infinite and finite, and one and many, if others than the one exist and not the one.

They must.

Then will they not appear to be like and unlike?

In what way?

Just as in a picture things appear to be all one to a person standing at a distance, and to be in the same state and alike?

True.

But when you approach them, they appear to be many and different; and because of the appearance of the difference, different in kind from, and unlike, themselves?

True.

And so must the particles appear to be like and unlike themselves and each other.

Certainly.

And must they not be the same and yet different from one another, and in contact with themselves, although they are separated, and having every sort of motion, and every sort of rest, and becoming and being destroyed, and in neither state, and the like, all which things may be easily enumerated, if the one is not and the many are?

Most true.

ii. bb. Once more, let us go back to the beginning, and ask if the one is not, and the others of the one are, what will follow.

Let us ask that question.

In the first place, the others will not be one?

Impossible.

Nor will they be many; for if they were many one would be contained in them. But if no one of them is one, all of them are nought, and therefore they will not be many.

True.

If there be no one in the others, the others are neither many nor one.

They are not.

Nor do they appear either as one or many.

PAR-
MEN-
IDES,
ARISTO-
TELES.

When
seen at a
distance
the others
appear to
be one;
when
near,
many and
infinite.

If one is
not and
the
others
are, what
then?
The
others are
not one
and
therefore
not many.

166

*Par-
menides*

PAR-
MEN-
IDES,
ARISTO-
TELES.

Again, if
the
others
appear to
be one or
many
they
must in
some
sense
partake
of not-
being;
but this
is not the
case.

Nor are
they like
or unlike,
the same
or dif-
ferent.

Why not?

Because the others have no sort or manner or way of communion with any sort of not-being, nor can anything which is not, be connected with any of the others; for that which is not has no parts.

True.

Nor is there an opinion or any appearance of not-being in connection with the others, nor is not-being ever in any way attributed to the others.

No.

Then if one is not, there is no conception of any of the others either as one or many; for you cannot conceive the many without the one.

You cannot.

Then if one is not, the others neither are, nor can be conceived to be either one or many?

It would seem not.

Nor as like or unlike?

No.

Nor as the same or different, nor in contact or separation, nor in any of those states which we enumerated as appearing to be;—the others neither are nor appear to be any of these, if one is not?

True.

Then may we not sum up the argument in a word and say truly: If one is not, then nothing is?

Certainly.

Let thus much be said; and further let us affirm what seems to be the truth, that, whether one is or is not, one and the others in relation to themselves and one another, all of them, in every way, are and are not, and appear to be and appear not to be.

Most true.

THEAETETUS

THEAETETUS

PERSONS OF THE DIALOGUE

SOCRATES   THEODORUS   THEAETETUS

Euclid and Terpsion meet in front of Euclid's house in Megara; they enter the house, and the dialogue is read to them by a servant.

Euclid. Have you only just arrived from the country, Terpsion?

Terpsion. No, I came some time ago: and I have been in the Agora looking for you, and wondering that I could not find you.

Euc. But I was not in the city.

Terp. Where then?

Euc. As I was going down to the harbour, I met Theaetetus— he was being carried up to Athens from the army at Corinth.

Terp. Was he alive or dead?

Euc. He was scarcely alive, for he has been badly wounded; but he was suffering even more from the sickness which has broken out in the army.

Terp. The dysentery, you mean?

Euc. Yes.

Terp. Alas! what a loss he will be!

Euc. Yes, Terpsion, he is a noble fellow; only to-day I heard some people highly praising his behaviour in this very battle.

Terp. No wonder; I should rather be surprised at hearing anything else of him. But why did he go on, instead of stopping at Megara?

Euc. He wanted to get home: although I entreated and advised him to remain, he would not listen to me; so I set him on his way, and turned back, and then I remembered what Socrates had said of him, and thought how remarkably this, like all his predictions, had been fulfilled. I believe that he had seen him a little before his own death, when Theaetetus was a youth, and he had a memorable conversation with him, which he repeated to me when I came to Athens; he was full of admiration of his genius, and said that he would most certainly be a great man, if he lived.

Euclid and Terpsion meet in front of Euclid's house in Megara; they converse about the dangerous condition of Theaetetus, who had ben carried away dying from the camp at Corinth.

Euclid calls to mind the great things which Socrates had early prophesied of him: and

143

Theaete-tus

143
EUCLID,
TERPSION.
SOCRATES,
THEO-
DORUS.

he has
preserved
the re-
port of a
conversa-
tion of
Theaete-
tus with
Socrates,
which
took place
just be-
fore the
latter's
death.

They
enter the
house,
and
Euclid
produces
the roll,
which his
servant
reads to
them.

Socrates,
meeting
Theo-
dorus of
Cyrene
in an
Athenian
palaestra,
asks what
youths of
promise
he has
discov-
ered at
Athens.

Theo-
dorus in
answer
expatiates
on the

Terp. The prophecy has certainly been fulfilled; but what was the conversation? can you tell me?

Euc. No, indeed, not offhand; but I took notes of it as soon as I got home; these I filled up from memory, writing them out at leisure; and whenever I went to Athens, I asked Socrates about any point which I had forgotten, and on my return I made corrections; thus I have nearly the whole conversation written down.

Terp. I remember—you told me; and I have always been intending to ask you to show me the writing, but have put off doing so; and now, why should we not read it through?—having just come from the country, I should greatly like to rest.

Euc. I too shall be very glad of a rest, for I went with Theaetetus as far as Erineum. Let us go in, then, and, while we are reposing, the servant shall read to us.

Terp. Very good.

Euc. Here is the roll, Terpsion; I may observe that I have introduced Socrates, not as narrating to me, but as actually conversing with the persons whom he mentioned—these were, Theodorus the geometrician (of Cyrene), and Theaetetus. I have omitted, for the sake of convenience, the interlocutory words 'I said,' 'I remarked,' which he used when he spoke of himself, and again, 'he agreed,' or 'disagreed,' in the answer, lest the repetition of them should be troublesome.

Terp. Quite right, Euclid.

Euc. And now, boy, you may take the roll and read.

Euclid's servant reads.

Socrates. If I cared enough about the Cyrenians, Theodorus, I would ask you whether there are any rising geometricians or philosophers in that part of the world. But I am more interested in our own Athenian youth, and I would rather know who among them are likely to do well. I observe them as far as I can myself, and I enquire of any one whom they follow, and I see that a great many of them follow you, in which they are quite right, considering your eminence in geometry and in other ways. Tell me then, if you have met with any one who is good for anything.

Theodorus. Yes, Socrates, I have become acquainted with one very remarkable Athenian youth, whom I commend to you as well worthy of your attention. If he had been a beauty I should have been afraid to praise him, lest you should suppose that I was in love with him; but he is no beauty, and you must not be offended if I say that he is very like you; for he has a snub nose and projecting eyes, although these features are less marked in him than in you.

Seeing, then, that he has no personal attractions, I may freely say, that in all my acquaintance, which is very large, I never knew any one who was his equal in natural gifts: for he has a quickness of apprehension which is almost unrivalled, and he is exceedingly gentle, and also the most courageous of men; there is a union of qualities in him such as I have never seen in any other, and should scarcely have thought possible; for those who, like him, have quick and ready and retentive wits, have generally also quick tempers; they are ships without ballast, and go darting about, and are mad rather than courageous; and the steadier sort, when they have to face study, prove stupid and cannot remember. Whereas he moves surely and smoothly and successfully in the path of knowledge and enquiry; and he is full of gentleness, flowing on silently like a river of oil; at his age, it is wonderful.

Soc. That is good news; whose son is he?

Theod. The name of his father I have forgotten, but the youth himself is the middle one of those who are approaching us; he and his companions have been anointing themselves in the outer court, and now they seem to have finished, and are coming towards us. Look and see whether you know him.

Soc. I know the youth, but I do not know his name; he is the son of Euphronius the Sunian, who was himself an eminent man, and such another as his son is, according to your account of him; I believe that he left a considerable fortune.

Theod. Theaetetus, Socrates, is his name; but I rather think that the property disappeared in the hands of trustees; notwithstanding which he is wonderfully liberal.

Soc. He must be a fine fellow; tell him to come and sit by me.

Theod. I will. Come hither, Theaetetus, and sit by Socrates.

Soc. By all means, Theaetetus, in order that I may see the reflection of myself in your face, for Theodorus says that we are alike; and yet if each of us held in his hands a lyre, and he said that they were tuned alike, should we at once take his word, or should we ask whether he who said so was or was not a musician?

Theaetetus. We should ask.

Soc. And if we found that he was, we should take his word; and if not, not?

Theaet. True.

Soc. And if this supposed likeness of our faces is a matter of any interest to us, we should enquire whether he who says that we are alike is a painter or not?

Theaet. Certainly we should.

Soc. And is Theodorus a painter?

Theaete-tus

SOCRATES,
THEAETE-
TUS.

But he is
a geome-
trician
and phil-
osopher,
not a
painter,
and
therefore
he need
not be
believed. ·

He also
praised
Theaete-
tus' intel-
lect and
disposi-
tion; and
so Theae-
tetus
must be
examined,
that
Theo-
dorus'
praises
may be
shown to
be well-
deserved
or not.

Socrates'
difficulty.
What is
knowl-
edge?

Theaet. I never heard that he was.

Soc. Is he a geometrician?

Theaet. Of course he is, Socrates.

Soc. And is he an astronomer and calculator and musician, and in general an educated man?

Theaet. I think so.

Soc. If, then, he remarks on a similarity in our persons, either by way of praise or blame, there is no particular reason why we should attend to him.

Theaet. I should say not.

Soc. But if he praises the virtue or wisdom which are the mental endowments of either of us, then he who hears the praises will naturally desire to examine him who is praised: and he again should be willing to exhibit himself.

Theaet. Very true, Socrates.

Soc. Then now is the time, my dear Theaetetus, for me to examine, and for you to exhibit; since although Theodorus has praised many a citizen and stranger in my hearing, never did I hear him praise any one as he has been praising you.

Theaet. I am glad to hear it, Socrates; but what if he was only in jest?

Soc. Nay, Theodorus is not given to jesting; and I cannot allow you to retract your consent on any such pretence as that. If you do, he will have to swear to his words; and we are perfectly sure that no one will be found to impugn him. Do not be shy then, but stand to your word.

Theaet. I suppose I must, if you wish it.

Soc. In the first place, I should like to ask what you learn of Theodorus: something of geometry, perhaps?

Theaet. Yes.

Soc. And astronomy and harmony and calculation?

Theaet. I do my best.

Soc. Yes, my boy, and so do I: and my desire is to learn of him, or of anybody who seems to understand these things. And I get on pretty well in general; but there is a little difficulty which I want you and the company to aid me in investigating. Will you answer me a question: 'Is not learning growing wiser about that which you learn?'

Theaet. Of course.

Soc. And by wisdom the wise are wise?

Theaet. Yes.

Soc. And is that different in any way from knowledge?

Theaet. What?

Soc. Wisdom; are not men wise in that which they know?

Theaet. Certainly they are.

Soc. Then wisdom and knowledge are the same?

Theaet. Yes.

Soc. Herein lies the difficulty which I can never solve to my satisfaction—What is knowledge? Can we answer that question? What say you? which of us will speak first? whoever misses shall sit down, as at a game of ball, and shall be donkey, as the boys say; he who lasts out his competitors in the game without missing, shall be our king, and shall have the right of putting to us any questions which he pleases . . . Why is there no reply? I hope, Theodorus, that I am not betrayed into rudeness by my love of conversation? I only want to make us talk and be friendly and sociable.

Theod. The reverse of rudeness, Socrates: but I would rather that you would ask one of the young fellows; for the truth is, that I am unused to your game of question and answer, and I am too old to learn; the young will be more suitable, and they will improve more than I shall, for youth is always able to improve. And so having made a beginning with Theaetetus, I would advise you to go on with him and not let him off.

Soc. Do you hear, Theaetetus, what Theodorus says? The philosopher, whom you would not like to disobey, and whose word ought to be a command to a young man, bids me interrogate you. Take courage, then, and nobly say what you think that knowledge is.

Theaet. Well, Socrates, I will answer as you and he bid me; and if I make a mistake, you will doubtless correct me.

Soc. We will, if we can.

Theaet. Then, I think that the sciences which I learn from Theodorus—geometry, and those which you just now mentioned—are knowledge; and I would include the art of the cobbler and other craftsmen; these, each and all of them, are knowledge.

Soc. Too much, Theaetetus, too much; the nobility and liberality of your nature make you give many and diverse things, when I am asking for one simple thing.

Theaet. What do you mean, Socrates?

Soc. Perhaps nothing. I will endeavour, however, to explain what I believe to be my meaning: When you speak of cobbling, you mean the art or science of making shoes?

Theaet. Just so.

Soc. And when you speak of carpentering, you mean the art of making wooden implements?

146
SOCRATES,
THEO-
DORUS,
THEAETE-
TUS.

It is wisdom.

Socrates proposes a discussion on the subject.

Who will answer? —A pause.

At the suggestion of Theodorus Theaetetus is invited to reply and consents.

In his answer, instead of giving a general definition of knowledge, he enumerates its parts.

Theaete-
tus

SOCRATES,
THEAE-
TETUS.

Such enu-
meration
is not
definition.

Theaet. I do.

Soc. In both cases you define the subject-matter of each of the two arts?

Theaet. True.

Soc. But that, Theaetetus, was not the point of my question: we wanted to know not the subjects, nor yet the number of the arts or sciences, for we were not going to count them, but we wanted to know the nature of knowledge in the abstract. Am I not right?

Theaet. Perfectly right.

147
Socrates
indicates
by an il-
lustration
the sort
of answer
required.

Soc. Let me offer an illustration: Suppose that a person were to ask about some very trivial and obvious thing—for example, What is clay? and we were to reply, that there is a clay of potters, there is a clay of oven-makers, there is a clay of brick-makers; would not the answer be ridiculous?

Theaet. Truly.

Soc. In the first place, there would be an absurdity in assuming that he who asked the question would understand from our answer the nature of 'clay,' merely because we added 'of the image-makers,' or of any other workers. How can a man understand the name of anything, when he does not know the nature of it?

Theaet. He cannot.

Soc. Then he who does not know what science or knowledge is, has no knowledge of the art or science of making shoes?

Theaet. None.

Soc. Nor of any other science?

Theaet. No.

Soc. And when a man is asked what science or knowledge is, to give in answer the name of some art or science is ridiculous; for the question is, 'What is knowledge?' and he replies, 'A knowledge of this or that.'

Theaet. True.

Soc. Moreover, he might answer shortly and simply, but he makes an enormous circuit. For example, when asked about the clay, he might have said simply, that clay is moistened earth—what sort of clay is not to the point.

Theaet. Yes, Socrates, there is no difficulty as you put the question. You mean, if I am not mistaken, something like what occurred to me and to my friend here, your namesake Socrates, in a recent discussion.

Soc. What was that, Theaetetus?

Theaet. Theodorus was writing out for us something about roots, such as the roots of three or five, showing that they are incommensurable by the unit: he selected other examples up to seventeen—there he stopped. Now as there are innumerable roots, the notion occurred to us of attempting to include them all under one name or class.

Soc. And did you find such a class?

Theaet. I think that we did; but I should like to have your opinion.

Soc. Let me hear.

Theaet. We divided all numbers into two classes: those which are made up of equal factors multiplying into one another, which we compared to square figures and called square or equilateral numbers;—that was one class.

Soc. Very good.

Theaet. The intermediate numbers, such as three and five, and every other number which is made up of unequal factors, either of a greater multiplied by a less, or of a less multiplied by a greater, and when regarded as a figure, is contained in unequal sides;—all these we compared to oblong figures, and called them oblong numbers.

Soc. Capital; and what followed?

Theaet. The lines, or sides, which have for their squares the equilateral plane numbers, were called by us lengths or magnitudes; and the lines which are the roots of (or whose squares are equal to) the oblong numbers, were called powers or roots; the reason of this latter name being, that they are commensurable with the former [i. e. with the so-called lengths or magnitudes] not in linear measurement, but in the value of the superficial content of their squares; and the same about solids.

Soc. Excellent, my boys; I think that you fully justify the praises of Theodorus, and that he will not be found guilty of false witness.

Theaet. But I am unable, Socrates, to give you a similar answer about knowledge, which is what you appear to want; and therefore Theodorus is a deceiver after all.

Soc. Well, but if some one were to praise you for running, and to say that he never met your equal among boys, and afterwards you were beaten in a race by a grown-up man, who was a great runner—would the praise be any the less true?

Theaet. Certainly not.

Soc. And is the discovery of the nature of knowledge so small a matter, as I just now said? Is it not one which would task the powers of men perfect in every way?

Theaet. By heaven, they should be the top of all perfection!

Soc. Well, then, be of good cheer; do not say that Theodorus was mistaken about you, but do your best to ascertain the true nature of knowledge, as well as of other things.

Theaet. I am eager enough, Socrates, if that would bring to light the truth.

Soc. Come, you made a good beginning just now; let your own answer about roots be your model, and as you comprehended them all in one class, try and bring the many sorts of knowledge under one definition.

Theaet. I can assure you, Socrates, that I have tried very often, when the report of questions asked by you was brought to me; but I can neither persuade myself that I have a satisfactory answer to give, nor hear of any one who answers as you would have him; and I cannot shake off a feeling of anxiety.

Soc. These are the pangs of labour, my dear Theaetetus; you have something within you which you are bringing to the birth.

Theaet. I do not know, Socrates; I only say what I feel.

Soc. And have you never heard, simpleton, that I am the son of a midwife, brave and burly, whose name was Phaenarete?

Theaet. Yes, I have.

Soc. And that I myself practise midwifery?

Theaet. No, never.

Soc. Let me tell you that I do though, my friend: but you must not reveal the secret, as the world in general have not found me out; and therefore they only say of me, that I am the strangest of mortals and drive men to their wits' end. Did you ever hear that too?

Theaet. Yes.

Soc. Shall I tell you the reason?

Theaet. By all means.

Soc. Bear in mind the whole business of the midwives, and then you will see my meaning better:—No woman, as you are probably aware, who is still able to conceive and bear, attends other women, but only those who are past bearing.

Theaet. Yes, I know.

Soc. The reason of this is said to be that Artemis—the goddess of childbirth—is not a mother, and she honours those who are like herself; but she could not allow the barren to be midwives, because human nature cannot know the mystery of an art without experience; and therefore she assigned this office to those who are too old to bear.

Theaet. I dare say.

Soc. And I dare say too, or rather I am absolutely certain, that the midwives know better than others who is pregnant and who is not?

Theaet. Very true.

Soc. And by the use of potions and incantations they are able to arouse the pangs and to soothe them at will; they can make those bear who have a difficulty in bearing, and if they think fit they can smother the embryo in the womb.

Theaet. They can.

Soc. Did you ever remark that they are also most cunning matchmakers, and have a thorough knowledge of what unions are likely to produce a brave brood?

Theaet. No, never.

Soc. Then let me tell you that this is their greatest pride, more than cutting the umbilical cord. And if you reflect, you will see that the same art which cultivates and gathers in the fruits of the earth, will be most likely to know in what soils the several plants or seeds should be deposited.

Theaet. Yes, the same art.

Soc. And do you suppose that with women the case is otherwise?

Theaet. I should think not.

Soc. Certainly not; but midwives are respectable women who have a character to lose, and they avoid this department of their profession, because they are afraid of being called procuresses, which is a name given to those who join together man and woman in an unlawful and unscientific way; and yet the true midwife is also the true and only matchmaker.

Theaet. Clearly.

Soc. Such are the midwives, whose task is a very important one, but not so important as mine; for women do not bring into the world at one time real children, and at another time counterfeits which are with difficulty distinguished from them; if they did, then the discernment of the true and false birth would be the crowning achievement of the art of midwifery—you would think so?

Theaet. Indeed I should.

Soc. Well, my art of midwifery is in most respects like theirs; but differs, in that I attend men and not women, and I look after their souls when they are in labour, and not after their bodies: and the triumph of my art is in thoroughly examining whether the thought which the mind of the young man brings forth is a false idol or a noble and true birth. And like the midwives, I am barren, and the reproach which is often made against me, that I ask questions of others and have not the wit to answer them myself,

His business is
more important
than
theirs,
yet generally
similar.
He attends
men, they
women;
he takes
care of
the mind,
they of
the body.
But, unlike the
midwives,
he dis-

tinguishes
the true
birth
from the
counter-
feit.

The be-
haviour
of his
patients.

151

Like mid-
wives, he
is a
match-
maker.

Theae-
tetus is
exhorted
to submit
himself to
the treat-
ment, and
not to
wax
wroth if
some dar-
ling idol
is taken
from him.

is very just—the reason is, that the god compels me to be a midwife, but does not allow me to bring forth. And therefore I am not myself at all wise, nor have I anything to show which is the invention or birth of my own soul, but those who converse with me profit. Some of them appear dull enough at first, but afterwards, as our acquaintance ripens, if the god is gracious to them, they all make astonishing progress; and this in the opinion of others as well as in their own. It is quite clear that they never learned anything from me; the many fine discoveries to which they cling are of their own making. But to me and the god they owe their delivery. And the proof of my words is, that many of them in their ignorance, either in their self-conceit despising me, or falling under the influence of others [1], have gone away too soon; and have not only lost the children of whom I had previously delivered them by an ill bringing up, but have stifled whatever else they had in them by evil communications, being fonder of lies and shams than of the truth; and they have at last ended by seeing themselves, as others see them, to be great fools. Aristeides, the son of Lysimachus, is one of them, and there are many others. The truants often return to me, and beg that I would consort with them again—they are ready to go to me on their knees—and then, if my familiar allows, which is not always the case, I receive them, and they begin to grow again. Dire are the pangs which my art is able to arouse and to allay in those who consort with me, just like the pangs of women in childbirth; night and day they are full of perplexity and travail which is even worse than that of the women. So much for them. And there are others, Theaetetus, who come to me apparently having nothing in them; and as I know that they have no need of my art, I coax them into marrying some one, and by the grace of God I can generally tell who is likely to do them good. Many of them I have given away to Prodicus, and many to other inspired sages. I tell you this long story, friend Theaetetus, because I suspect, as indeed you seem to think yourself, that you are in labour—great with some conception. Come then to me, who am a midwife's son and myself a midwife, and do your best to answer the questions which I will ask you. And if I abstract and expose your first-born, because I discover upon inspection that the conception which you have formed is a vain shadow, do not quarrel with me on that account, as the manner of women is when their first children are taken from them. For I have actually known some who were ready to bite me when I deprived them of a darling folly; they did not

---

[1] Reading with the Bodleian MS. ἢ αὐτοὶ ὑπ' ἄλλων πεισθέντες.

perceive that I acted from good will, not knowing that no god is the enemy of man—that was not within the range of their ideas; neither am I their enemy in all this, but it would be wrong for me to admit falsehood, or to stifle the truth. Once more, then, Theaetetus, I repeat my old question, 'What is knowledge?'—and do not say that you cannot tell; but quit yourself like a man, and by the help of God you will be able to tell.

Theaet. At any rate, Socrates, after such an exhortation I should be ashamed of not trying to do my best. Now he who knows perceives what he knows, and, as far as I can see at present, knowledge is perception.

Soc. Bravely said, boy; that is the way in which you should express your opinion. And now, let us examine together this conception of yours, and see whether it is a true birth or a mere wind-egg: —You say that knowledge is perception?

Theaet. Yes.

Soc. Well, you have delivered yourself of a very important doctrine about knowledge; it is indeed the opinion of Protagoras, who has another way of expressing it. Man, he says, is the measure of all things, of the existence of things that are, and of the non-existence of things that are not:—You have read him?

Theaet. O yes, again and again.

Soc. Does he not say that things are to you such as they appear to you, and to me such as they appear to me, and that you and I are men?

Theaet. Yes, he says so.

Soc. A wise man is not likely to talk nonsense. Let us try to understand him: the same wind is blowing, and yet one of us may be cold and the other not, or one may be slightly and the other very cold?

Theaet. Quite true.

Soc. Now is the wind, regarded not in relation to us but absolutely, cold or not; or are we to say, with Protagoras, that the wind is cold to him who is cold, and not to him who is not?

Theaet. I suppose the last.

Soc. Then it must appear so to each of them?

Theaet. Yes.

Soc. And 'appears to him' means the same as 'he perceives.'

Theaet. True.

Soc. Then appearing and perceiving coincide in the case of hot and cold, and in similar instances; for things appear, or may be supposed to be, to each one such as he perceives them?

Theaet. Yes.

Theaetetus

SOCRATES, THEAETETUS.

In answer to the invitation he boldly replies: Knowledge is perception.

This is [152] only another way of expressing Protagoras' doctrine, 'Man is the measure of all things,' i.e. things are as they appear to you or me at any moment.

This is true in some cases.

*Theaete-
ius*

SOCRATES,
THEAE-
TETUS.

But Pro-
tagoras
had also a
hidden
mean-
ing,—'All
things are
relative
and in
motion.'
In this
the an-
cients
agree
with him.

Soc. Then perception is always of existence, and being the same as knowledge is unerring?

Theaet. Clearly.

Soc. In the name of the Graces, what an almighty wise man Protagoras must have been! He spoke these things in a parable to the common herd, like you and me, but told the truth, 'his Truth[1],' in secret to his own disciples.

Theaet. What do you mean, Socrates?

Soc. I am about to speak of a high argument, in which all things are said to be relative; you cannot rightly call anything by any name, such as great or small, heavy or light, for the great will be small and the heavy light—there is no single thing or quality, but out of motion and change and admixture all things are becoming relatively to one another, which 'becoming' is by us incorrectly called being, but is really becoming, for nothing ever is, but all things are becoming. Summon all philosophers—Protagoras, Heracleitus, Empedocles, and the rest of them, one after another, and with the exception of Parmenides they will agree with you in this. Summon the great masters of either kind of poetry—Epicharmus, the prince of Comedy, and Homer of Tragedy; when the latter sings of

'Ocean whence sprang the gods, and mother Tethys,'

does he not mean that all things are the offspring of flux and motion?

Theaet. I think so.

153

Soc. And who could take up arms against such a great army having Homer for its general, and not appear ridiculous[2]?

Theaet. Who indeed, Socrates?

The
praises of
motion.

Soc. Yes, Theaetetus; and there are plenty of other proofs which will show that motion is the source of what is called being and becoming, and inactivity of not-being and destruction; for fire and warmth, which are supposed to be the parent and guardian of all other things, are born of movement and of friction, which is a kind of motion [3];—is not this the origin of fire?

Theaet. It is.

By mo-
tion all
things are
generat-
ed, and
body and
soul,
water and
air, are

Soc. And the race of animals is generated in the same way?

Theaet. Certainly.

Soc. And is not the bodily habit spoiled by rest and idleness, but preserved for a long time [4] by motion and exercise?

[1] In allusion to a book of Protagoras' which bore this title.
[2] Cp. Cratylus 401 E ff.   [3] Reading τοῦτο δὲ κίνησις.
[4] Reading ἐπὶ πολύ.

Theaet. True.

Soc. And what of the mental habit? Is not the soul informed, and improved, and preserved by study and attention, which are motions; but when at rest, which in the soul only means want of attention and study, is uninformed, and speedily forgets whatever she has learned?

Theaet. True.

Soc. Then motion is a good, and rest an evil, to the soul as well as to the body?

Theaet. Clearly.

Soc. I may add, that breathless calm, stillness and the like waste and impair, while wind and storm preserve; and the palmary argument of all, which I strongly urge, is the golden chain in Homer, by which he means the sun, thereby indicating that so long as the sun and the heavens go round in their orbits, all things human and divine are and are preserved, but if they were chained up and their motions ceased, then all things would be destroyed, and, as the saying is, turned upside down.

Theaet. I believe, Socrates, that you have truly explained his meaning.

Soc. Then now apply his doctrine to perception, my good friend, and first of all to vision; that which you call white colour is not in your eyes, and is not a distinct thing which exists out of them. And you must not assign any place to it: for if it had position it would be, and be at rest, and there would be no process of becoming.

Theaet. Then what is colour?

Soc. Let us carry out the principle which has just been affirmed, that nothing is self-existent, and then we shall see that white, black, and every other colour, arises out of the eye meeting the appropriate motion, and that what we call a colour is in each case neither the active nor the passive element, but something which passes between them, and is peculiar to each percipient; are you quite certain that the several colours appear to a dog or to any animal whatever as they appear to you?

Theaet. Far from it.

Soc. Or that anything appears the same to you as to another man? Are you so profoundly convinced of this? Rather would it not be true that it never appears exactly the same to you, because you are never exactly the same?

Theaet. The latter.

Soc. And if that with which I compare myself in size[1], or which I apprehend by touch, were great or white or hot, it could not be-

[1] Reading with the MSS. ᾧ παραμετρούμεθα.

Margin notes:

Theaetetus

SOCRATES, THEAETETUS.

alike preserved by it.

The clinching argument of the golden chain.

Again, colour is a motion passing between the eye and its object.

154

Nothing which is perceived by different men or by the same man at different times is the same.

come different by mere contact with another unless it actually
changed; nor again, if the comparing or apprehending subject were
great or white or hot, could this, when unchanged from within, become changed by any approximation or affection of any other
thing. The fact is that in our ordinary way of speaking we allow
ourselves to be driven into most ridiculous and wonderful contradictions, as Protagoras and all who take his line of argument would
remark.

Theaet. How? and of what sort do you mean?

Contra-
dictions
arising
out of
relations
of num-
bers.

Soc. A little instance will sufficiently explain my meaning: Here
are six dice, which are more by a half when compared with four,
and fewer by a half than twelve—they are more and also fewer.
How can you or any one maintain the contrary?

Theaet. Very true.

Soc. Well, then, suppose that Protagoras or some one asks
whether anything can become greater or more if not by increasing,
how would you answer him, Theaetetus?

Theaet. I should say 'No,' Socrates, if I were to speak my mind
in reference to this last question, and if I were not afraid of contradicting my former answer.

Soc. Capital! excellent! spoken like an oracle, my boy! And if
you reply 'Yes,' there will be a case for Euripides; for our tongue
will be unconvinced, but not our mind[1].

Theaet. Very true.

Soc. The thoroughbred Sophists, who know all that can be
known about the mind, and argue only out of the superfluity of
their wits, would have had a regular sparring-match over this, and
would have knocked their arguments together finely. But you and
I, who have no professional aims, only desire to see what is the
mutual relation of these principles,—whether they are consistent
with each other or not.

Theaet. Yes, that would be my desire.

Three
laws of
thought:
[155]
(1)
Nothing,
while re-
maining
equal to
itself, can
become
fewer or
more,
greater or

Soc. And mine too. But since this is our feeling, and there is
plenty of time, why should we not calmly and patiently review our
own thoughts, and thoroughly examine and see what these appearances in us really are? If I am not mistaken, they will be described
by us as follows:—first, that nothing can become greater or less,
either in number or magnitude, while remaining equal to itself—
you would agree?

Theaet. Yes.

---

[1] In allusion to the well-known line of Euripides, Hippol. 612: ἡ γλῶσσ'
ὀμώμοχ', ἡ δὲ φρὴν ἀνώμοτος.

Soc. Secondly, that without addition or subtraction there is no increase or diminution of anything, but only equality.

Theaet. Quite true.

Soc. Thirdly, that what was not before cannot be afterwards, without becoming and having become.

Theaet. Yes, truly.

Soc. These three axioms, if I am not mistaken, are fighting with one another in our minds in the case of the dice, or, again, in such a case as this—if I were to say that I, who am of a certain height and taller than you, may within a year, without gaining or losing in height, be not so tall—not that I should have lost, but that you would have increased. In such a case, I am afterwards what I once was not, and yet I have not become; for I could not have become without becoming, neither could I have become less without losing somewhat of my height; and I could give you ten thousand examples of similar contradictions, if we admit them at all. I believe that you follow me, Theaetetus; for I suspect that you have thought of these questions before now.

Theaet. Yes, Socrates, and I am amazed when I think of them; by the Gods I am! and I want to know what on earth they mean; and there are times when my head quite swims with the contemplation of them.

Soc. I see, my dear Theaetetus, that Theodorus had a true insight into your nature when he said that you were a philosopher, for wonder is the feeling of a philosopher, and philosophy begins in wonder. He was not a bad genealogist who said that Iris (the messenger of heaven) is the child of Thaumas (wonder). But do you begin to see what is the explanation of this perplexity on the hypothesis which we attribute to Protagoras?

Theaet. Not as yet.

Soc. Then you will be obliged to me if I help you to unearth the hidden 'truth' of a famous man or school.

Theaet. To be sure, I shall be very much obliged.

Soc. Take a look round, then, and see that none of the uninitiated are listening. Now by the uninitiated I mean the people who believe in nothing but what they can grasp in their hands, and who will not allow that action or generation or anything invisible can have real existence.

Theaet. Yes, indeed, Socrates, they are very hard and impenetrable mortals.

Soc. Yes, my boy, outer barbarians. Far more ingenious are the brethren whose mysteries I am about to reveal to you. Their first

Theaetetus

SOCRATES, THEAETETUS.

less. (2) Without addition or subtraction nothing can increase or diminish. (3) Nothing can be what it was not without becoming. These axioms seem to jar in certain cases.

Further development of the doctrine of Protagoras to meet the difficulty. —The uninitiated who believe only in [156] what they

*Theaete-
tus*

SOCRATES,
THEAE-
TETUS.

can hold
in their
hands are
to be kept
out of the
secret.

principle is, that all is motion, and upon this all the affections of
which we were just now speaking are supposed to depend: there is
nothing but motion, which has two forms, one active and the other
passive, both in endless number; and out of the union and friction
of them there is generated a progeny endless in number, having two
forms, sense and the object of sense, which are ever breaking forth
and coming to the birth at the same moment. The senses are variously named hearing, seeing, smelling; there is the sense of heat,
cold, pleasure, pain, desire, fear, and many more which have names,
as well as innumerable others which are without them; each has its
kindred object,—each variety of colour has a corresponding variety
of sight, and so with sound and hearing, and with the rest of the
senses and the objects akin to them. Do you see, Theaetetus, the
bearings of this tale on the preceding argument?

Theaet. Indeed I do not.

All things
are in
motion,
of a
slower
and of a
swifter
kind. The
slower
objects
move
without
changing
place,
and pro-
duce the
swifter,
which are
in loco-
motion.

Applica-
tion of
the
    [157]
theory to
vision.

Soc. Then attend, and I will try to finish the story. The purport
is that all these things are in motion, as I was saying, and that this
motion is of two kinds, a slower and a quicker; and the slower elements have their motions in the same place and with reference to
things near them, and so they beget; but what is begotten is swifter, for it is carried to and fro, and moves from place to place. Apply
this to sense:—When the eye and the appropriate object meet together and give birth to whiteness and the sensation connatural
with it, which could not have been given by either of them going
elsewhere, then, while the sight is flowing from the eye, whiteness
proceeds from the object which combines in producing the colour;
and so the eye is fulfilled with sight, and really sees, and becomes,
not sight, but a seeing eye; and the object which combined to form
the colour is fulfilled with whiteness, and becomes not whiteness
but a white thing, whether wood or stone or whatever the object
may be which happens to be coloured white[1]. And this is true of all
sensible objects, hard, warm, and the like, which are similarly to be
regarded, as I was saying before, not as having any absolute existence, but as being all of them of whatever kind generated by
motion in their intercourse with one another; for of the agent and
patient, as existing in separation, no trustworthy conception, as
they say, can be formed, for the agent has no existence until united
with the patient, and the patient has no existence until united with
the agent; and that which by uniting with something becomes an
agent, by meeting with some other thing is converted into a patient. And from all these considerations, as I said at first, there

Every-
thing be-
comes,
and

[1] Reading ὁτιοῦν or ὁτῳοῦν and omitting χρῶμα.

arises a general reflection, that there is no one self-existent thing, but everything is becoming and in relation; and being must be altogether abolished, although from habit and ignorance we are compelled even in this discussion to retain the use of the term. But great philosophers tell us that we are not to allow either the word 'something,' or 'belonging to something,' or 'to me,' or 'this' or 'that,' or any other detaining name to be used; in the language of nature all things are being created and destroyed, coming into being and passing into new forms; nor can any name fix or detain them; he who attempts to fix them is easily refuted. And this should be the way of speaking, not only of particulars but of aggregates; such aggregates as are expressed in the word 'man,' or 'stone,' or any name of an animal or of a class. O Theaetetus, are not these speculations sweet as honey? And do you not like the taste of them in the mouth?

becomes
relatively
to some-
thing
else.

This ap-
plies not
only to
indivi-
duals,
but also
to
classes.

Theaet. I do not know what to say, Socrates, for, indeed, I cannot make out whether you are giving your own opinion or only wanting to draw me out.

Soc. You forget, my friend, that I neither know, nor profess to know, anything of these matters; you are the person who is in labour, I am the barren midwife; and this is why I soothe you, and offer you one good thing after another, that you may taste them. And I hope that I may at last help to bring your own opinion into the light of day: when this has been accomplished, then we will determine whether what you have brought forth is only a wind-egg or a real and genuine birth. Therefore, keep up your spirits, and answer like a man what you think.

Socrates
is repeat-
ing these
'charming
specula-
tions'
only to
draw out
Theae-
tetus.

Theaet. Ask me.

Soc. Then once more: Is it your opinion that nothing is but what becomes?—the good and the noble, as well as all the other things which we were just now mentioning?

Theaet. When I hear you discoursing in this style, I think that there is a great deal in what you say, and I am very ready to assent.

Soc. Let us not leave the argument unfinished, then; for there still remains to be considered an objection which may be raised about dreams and diseases, in particular about madness, and the various illusions of hearing and sight, or of other senses. For you know that in all these cases the *esse-percipi* theory appears to be unmistakably refuted, since in dreams and illusions we certainly have false perceptions; and far from saying that everything is which appears, we should rather say that nothing is which appears.

Dreams
and illu-
sions are
a stum-
bling-
block to
[158]
the
theory,
as they
imply
falseness

Theaet. Very true, Socrates.

Soc. But then, my boy, how can any one contend that knowledge is perception, or that to every man what appears is?

Theaet. I am afraid to say, Socrates, that I have nothing to answer, because you rebuked me just now for making this excuse; but I certainly cannot undertake to argue that madmen or dreamers think truly, when they imagine, some of them that they are gods, and others that they can fly, and are flying in their sleep.

Soc. Do you see another question which can be raised about these phenomena, notably about dreaming and waking?

Theaet. What question?

Soc. A question which I think that you must often have heard persons ask:—How can you determine whether at this moment we are sleeping, and all our thoughts are a dream; or whether we are awake, and talking to one another in the waking state?

Theaet. Indeed, Socrates, I do not know how to prove the one any more than the other, for in both cases the facts precisely correspond; and there is no difficulty in supposing that during all this discussion we have been talking to one another in a dream; and when in a dream[1] we seem to be narrating dreams, the resemblance of the two states is quite astonishing.

Soc. You see, then, that a doubt about the reality of sense is easily raised, since there may even be a doubt whether we are awake or in a dream. And as our time is equally divided between sleeping and waking, in either sphere of existence the soul contends that the thoughts which are present to our minds at the time are true; and during one half of our lives we affirm the truth of the one, and, during the other half, of the other; and are equally confident of both.

Theaet. Most true.

Soc. And may not the same be said of madness and other disorders? the difference is only that the times are not equal.

Theaet. Certainly.

Soc. And is truth or falsehood to be determined by duration of time?

Theaet. That would be in many ways ridiculous.

Soc. But can you certainly determine by any other means which of these opinions is true?

Theaet. I do not think that I can.

Soc. Listen, then, to a statement of the other side of the argument, which is made by the champions of appearance. They would say, as I imagine—Can that which is wholly other than something, have the same quality as that from which it differs? and observe,

[1] Or perhaps, reading ὕπαρ, 'in our waking state.'

Theaetetus, that the word 'other' means not 'partially,' but 'wholly other.'

*Theaete-
tus*

159
SOCRATES,
THEAE-
TETUS.

Theaet. Certainly, putting the question as you do, that which is wholly other cannot either potentially or in any other way be the same.

Soc. And must therefore be admitted to be unlike?

Theaet. True.

Soc. If, then, anything happens to become like or unlike itself or another, when it becomes like we call it the same—when unlike, other?

Theaet. Certainly.

Soc. Were we not saying that there are agents many and infinite, and patients many and infinite?

Theaet. Yes.

Soc. And also that different combinations will produce results which are not the same, but different?

Theaet. Certainly.

Soc. Let us take you and me, or anything as an example:—There is Socrates in health, and Socrates sick—Are they like or unlike?

Theaet. You mean to compare Socrates in health as a whole, and Socrates in sickness as a whole?

Soc. Exactly; that is my meaning.

Theaet. I answer, they are unlike.

Soc. And if unlike, they are other?

Theaet. Certainly.

Soc. And would you not say the same of Socrates sleeping and waking, or in any of the states which we were mentioning?

Theaet. I should.

Soc. All agents have a different patient in Socrates, accordingly as he is well or ill.

Theaet. Of course.

Soc. And I who am the patient, and that which is the agent, will produce something different in each of the two cases?

Theaet. Certainly.

Soc. The wine which I drink when I am in health, appears sweet and pleasant to me?

Theaet. True.

Soc. For, as has been already acknowledged, the patient and agent meet together and produce sweetness and a perception of sweetness, which are in simultaneous motion, and the perception which comes from the patient makes the tongue percipient, and the quality of sweetness which arises out of and is moving about the

What is
wholly
other can
in no way
be the
same,

and dif-
ferent
agents
and pa-
tients, in
conjunc-
tion, pro-
duce
different
results.

Socrates
in health
is unlike
Socrates
in sick-
ness;

and
therefore
it is only
natural
that the
same
draught

Theaete-
tus

SOCRATES,
THEAE-
TETUS.

of wine
should
produce a
sweet
taste in
the one
case, a
bitter in
the other.

160

wine, makes the wine both to be and to appear sweet to the healthy tongue.

Theaet. Certainly; that has been already acknowledged.

Soc. But when I am sick, the wine really acts upon another and a different person?

Theaet. Yes.

Soc. The combination of the draught of wine, and the Socrates who is sick, produces quite another result; which is the sensation of bitterness in the tongue, and the motion and creation of bitterness in and about the wine, which becomes not bitterness but something bitter; as I myself become not perception but percipient?

Theaet. True.

Soc. There is no other object of which I shall ever have the same perception, for another object would give another perception, and would make the percipient other and different; nor can that object which affects me, meeting another subject, produce the same, or become similar, for that too will produce another result from another subject, and become different.

Theaet. True.

Soc. Neither can I by myself, have this sensation, nor the object by itself, this quality.

Theaet. Certainly not.

Soc. When I perceive I must become percipient of something— there can be no such thing as perceiving and perceiving nothing; the object, whether it become sweet, bitter, or of any other quality, must have relation to a percipient; nothing can become sweet which is sweet to no one.

Theaet. Certainly not.

Soc. Then the inference is, that we [the agent and patient] are or become in relation to one another; there is a law which binds us one to the other, but not to any other existence, nor each of us to himself; and therefore we can only be bound to one another; so that whether a person says that a thing is or becomes, he must say that it is or becomes to or of or in relation to something else; but he must not say or allow any one else to say that anything is or becomes absolutely:—such is our conclusion.

Theaet. Very true, Socrates.

Each object is
relative
to one
percipient
only, and
he alone
can judge
of its
truth.

Soc. Then, if that which acts upon me has relation to me and to no other, I and no other am the percipient of it?

Theaet. Of course.

Soc. Then my perception is true to me, being inseparable from my own being; and, as Protagoras says, to myself I am judge of what is and what is not to me.

Theaet. I suppose so.

Soc. How then, if I never err, and if my mind never trips in the conception of being or becoming, can I fail of knowing that which I perceive?

Theaet. You cannot.

Soc. Then you were quite right in affirming that knowledge is only perception; and the meaning turns out to be the same, whether with Homer and Heracleitus, and all that company, you say that all is motion and flux, or with the great sage Protagoras, that man is the measure of all things; or with Theaetetus, that, given these premises, perception is knowledge. Am I not right, Theaetetus, and is not this your new-born child, of which I have delivered you? What say you?

Theaet. I cannot but agree, Socrates.

Soc. Then this is the child, however he may turn out, which you and I have with difficulty brought into the world. And now that he is born, we must run round the hearth with him, and see whether he is worth rearing, or is only a wind-egg and a sham. Is he to be reared in any case, and not exposed? or will you bear to see him rejected, and not get into a passion if I take away your first-born?

Theod. Theaetetus will not be angry, for he is very good-natured. But tell me, Socrates, in heaven's name, is this, after all, not the truth?

Soc. You, Theodorus, are a lover of theories, and now you innocently fancy that I am a bag full of them, and can easily pull one out which will overthrow its predecessor. But you do not see that in reality none of these theories come from me; they all come from him who talks with me. I only know just enough to extract them from the wisdom of another, and to receive them in a spirit of fairness. And now I shall say nothing myself, but shall endeavour to elicit something from our young friend.

Theod. Do as you say, Socrates; you are quite right.

Soc. Shall I tell you, Theodorus, what amazes me in your acquaintance Protagoras?

Theod. What is it?

Soc. I am charmed with his doctrine, that what appears is to each one, but I wonder that he did not begin his book on Truth with a declaration that a pig or a dog-faced baboon, or some other yet stranger monster which has sensation, is the measure of all things; then he might have shown a magnificent contempt for our opinion of him by informing us at the outset that while we were reverencing him like a God for his wisdom he was no better than a tadpole, not to speak of his fellow-men—would not this have pro-

Theaetetus

SOCRATES, THEAE-TETUS, THEO-DORUS.

Thus knowledge is perception. Homer, Heracleitus, and their company agree in this with Protagoras.
161

Let us inspect the new-born babe.

Why did not Protagoras say, 'A pig is the measure of all things'? —for a pig has sensation.

duced an overpowering effect? For if truth is only sensation, and
no man can discern another's feelings better than he, or has any
superior right to determine whether his opinion is true or false, but
each, as we have several times repeated, is to himself the sole
judge, and everything that he judges is true and right, why, my
friend, should Protagoras be preferred to the place of wisdom and
instruction, and deserve to be well paid, and we poor ignoramuses
have to go to him, if each one is the measure of his own wisdom?
Must he not be talking 'ad captandum' in all this? I say nothing
of the ridiculous predicament in which my own midwifery and the
whole art of dialectic is placed; for the attempt to supervise or
refute the notions or opinions of others would be a tedious and
enormous piece of folly, if to each man his own are right; and this
must be the case if Protagoras' Truth is the real truth, and the
philosopher is not merely amusing himself by giving oracles out
of the shrine of his book.

Theod. He was a friend of mine, Socrates, as you were saying,
and therefore I cannot have him refuted by my lips, nor can I
oppose you when I agree with you; please, then, to take Theaetetus
again; he seemed to answer very nicely.

Soc. If you were to go into a Lacedaemonian palestra, Theodorus, would you have a right to look on at the naked wrestlers,
some of them making a poor figure, if you did not strip and give
them an opportunity of judging of your own person?

Theod. Why not, Socrates, if they would allow me, as I think
you will, in consideration of my age and stiffness; let some more
supple youth try a fall with you, and do not drag me into the
gymnasium.

Soc. Your will is my will, Theodorus, as the proverbial philosophers say, and therefore I will return to the sage Theaetetus: Tell
me, Theaetetus, in reference to what I was saying, are you not lost
in wonder, like myself, when you find that all of a sudden you are
raised to the level of the wisest of men, or indeed of the gods?—
for you would assume the measure of Protagoras to apply to the
gods as well as men?

Theaet. Certainly I should, and I confess to you that I am lost
in wonder. At first hearing, I was quite satisfied with the doctrine,
that whatever appears is to each one, but now the face of things has
changed.

Soc. Why, my dear boy, you are young, and therefore your ear
is quickly caught and your mind influenced by popular arguments.
Protagoras, or some one speaking on his behalf, will doubtless say
in reply,—Good people, young and old, you meet and harangue,

and bring in the gods, whose existence or non-existence I banish from writing and speech, or you talk about the reason of man being degraded to the level of the brutes, which is a telling argument with the multitude, but not one word of proof or demonstration do you offer. All is probability with you, and yet surely you and Theodorus had better reflect whether you are disposed to admit of probability and figures of speech in matters of such importance. He or any other mathematician who argued from probabilities and likelihoods in geometry, would not be worth an ace.

Theaet. But neither you nor we, Socrates, would be satisfied with such arguments.

Soc. Then you and Theodorus mean to say that we must look at the matter in some other way?

Theaet. Yes, in quite another way.

Soc. And the way will be to ask whether perception is or is not the same as knowledge; for this was the real point of our argument, and with a view to this we raised (did we not?) those many strange questions.

Theaet. Certainly.

Soc. Shall we say that we know every thing which we see and hear? for example, shall we say that not having learned, we do not hear the language of foreigners when they speak to us? or shall we say that we not only hear, but know what they are saying? Or again, if we see letters which we do not understand, shall we say that we do not see them? or shall we aver that, seeing them, we must know them?

Theaet. We shall say, Socrates, that we know what we actually see and hear of them—that is to say, we see and know the figure and colour of the letters, and we hear and know the elevation or depression of the sound of them; but we do not perceive by sight and hearing, or know, that which grammarians and interpreters teach about them.

Soc. Capital, Theaetetus; and about this there shall be no dispute, because I want you to grow; but there is another difficulty coming, which you will also have to repulse.

Theaet. What is it?

Soc. Some one will say, Can a man who has ever known anything, and still has and preserves a memory of that which he knows, not know that which he remembers at the time when he remembers? I have, I fear, a tedious way of putting a simple question, which is only, whether a man who has learned, and remembers, can fail to know?

Theaet. Impossible, Socrates; the supposition is monstrous.

Theaetetus

SOCRATES,
THEAE-
TETUS.

would say that he [163] had been influenced by mere claptrap.

A new start.

Is perception knowledge?

We know what we see and hear: but we see only certain forms or colours, and hear only sounds of different pitch. Yet it is possible to know more than this.

Again, according to the theory, a man cannot know what he remembers;

Soc. Am I talking nonsense, then? Think: is not seeing perceiving, and is not sight perception?

Theaet. True.

Soc. And if our recent definition holds, every man knows that which he has seen?

Theaet. Yes.

Soc. And you would admit that there is such a thing as memory?

Theaet. Yes.

Soc. And is memory of something or of nothing?

Theaet. Of something, surely.

Soc. Of things learned and perceived, that is?

Theaet. Certainly.

for, when
remem-
bering
some-
    [164]
thing
which he
has seen,
he does
not see,
and not-
seeing is
not-
knowing.

Soc. Often a man remembers that which he has seen?

Theaet. True.

Soc. And if he closed his eyes, would he forget?

Theaet. Who, Socrates, would dare to say so?

Soc. But we must say so, if the previous argument is to be maintained.

Theaet. What do you mean? I am not quite sure that I understand you, though I have a strong suspicion that you are right.

Soc. As thus: he who sees knows, as we say, that which he sees; for perception and sight and knowledge are admitted to be the same.

Theaet. Certainly.

Soc. But he who saw, and has knowledge of that which he saw, remembers, when he closes his eyes, that which he no longer sees.

Theaet. True.

Soc. And seeing is knowing, and therefore not-seeing is not-knowing?

Theaet. Very true.

And it
would be
ridiculous
to say
that what
is remem-
bered is
not
known.

Soc. Then the inference is, that a man may have attained the knowledge of something, which he may remember and yet not know, because he does not see; and this has been affirmed by us to be a monstrous supposition.

Theaet. Most true.

Soc. Thus, then, the assertion that knowledge and perception are one, involves a manifest impossibility?

Theaet. Yes.

Soc. Then they must be distinguished?

Theaet. I suppose that they must.

Soc. Once more we shall have to begin, and ask 'What is knowledge?' and yet, Theaetetus, what are we going to do?

Theaet. About what?

Soc. Like a good-for-nothing cock, without having won the victory, we walk away from the argument and crow.

Theaet. How do you mean?

Soc. After the manner of disputers [1], we were satisfied with mere verbal consistency, and were well pleased if in this way we could gain an advantage. Although professing not to be mere Eristics, but philosophers, I suspect that we have unconsciously fallen into the error of that ingenious class of persons.

Theaet. I do not as yet understand you.

Soc. Then I will try to explain myself: just now we asked the question, whether a man who had learned and remembered could fail to know, and we showed that a person who had seen might remember when he had his eyes shut and could not see, and then he would at the same time remember and not know. But this was an impossibility. And so the Protagorean fable came to nought, and yours also, who maintained that knowledge is the same as perception.

Theaet. True.

Soc. And yet, my friend, I rather suspect that the result would have been different if Protagoras, who was the father of the first of the two brats, had been alive; he would have had a great deal to say on their behalf. But he is dead, and we insult over his orphan child; and even the guardians whom he left, and of whom our friend Theodorus is one, are unwilling to give any help, and therefore I suppose that I must take up his cause myself, and see justice done?

Theod. Not I, Socrates, but rather Callias, the son of Hipponicus, is guardian of his orphans. I was too soon diverted from the abstractions of dialectic to geometry. Nevertheless, I shall be grateful to you if you assist him.

Soc. Very good, Theodorus; you shall see how I will come to the rescue. If a person does not attend to the meaning of terms as they are commonly used in argument, he may be involved even in greater paradoxes than these. Shall I explain this matter to you or to Theaetetus?

Theod. To both of us, and let the younger answer; he will incur less disgrace if he is discomfited.

Soc. Then now let me ask the awful question, which is this:— Can a man know and also not know that which he knows?

Theod. How shall we answer, Theaetetus?

Theaet. He cannot, I should say.

Soc. He can, if you maintain that seeing is knowing. When you

[1] Lys. 216 A; Phaedo 90 B, 101 E; Rep. V, 453 E ff.

Theaetetus

SOCRATES,
THEAE-
TETUS,
THEO-
DORUS.

Socrates is dissatisfied with the mode of argument.

If Protagoras had been alive he would not have allowed us to throw ridicule on his brats.

165

As Theodorus, their guardian, declines to protect them, Socrates takes up their defence.

Another difficulty: A man can know and not know the same thing at

are imprisoned in a well, as the saying is, and the self-assured adversary closes one of your eyes with his hand, and asks whether you can see his cloak with the eye which he has closed, how will you answer the inevitable man?

Theaet. I should answer, 'Not with that eye but with the other.'

Soc. Then you see and do not see the same thing at the same time.

Theaet. Yes, in a certain sense.

Soc. None of that, he will reply; I do not ask or bid you answer in what sense you know, but only whether you know that which you do not know. You have been proved to see that which you do not see; and you have already admitted that seeing is knowing, and that not-seeing is not-knowing: I leave you to draw the inference.

Theaet. Yes, the inference is the contradictory of my assertion.

Soc. Yes, my marvel, and there might have been yet worse things in store for you, if an opponent had gone on to ask whether you can have a sharp and also a dull knowledge, and whether you can know near, but not at a distance, or know the same thing with more or less intensity, and so on without end. Such questions might have been put to you by a light-armed mercenary, who argued for pay. He would have lain in wait for you, and when you took up the position, that sense is knowledge, he would have made an assault upon hearing, smelling, and the other senses;—he would have shown you no mercy; and while you were lost in envy and admiration of his wisdom, he would have got you into his net, out of which you would not have escaped until you had come to an understanding about the sum to be paid for your release. Well, you ask, and how will Protagoras reinforce his position? Shall I answer for him?

Theaet. By all means.

Soc. He will repeat all those things which we have been urging on his behalf, and then he will close with us in disdain, and say:—The worthy Socrates asked a little boy, whether the same man could remember and not know the same thing, and the boy said No, because he was frightened, and could not see what was coming, and then Socrates made fun of poor me. The truth is, O slatternly Socrates, that when you ask questions about any assertion of mine, and the person asked is found tripping, if he has answered as I should have answered, then I am refuted, but if he answers something else, then he is refuted and not I. For do you really suppose that any one would admit the memory which a man has of an impression which has passed away to be the same with that which he experienced at the time? Assuredly not. Or would he hesitate to acknowledge that the same man may know and not know the same thing? Or, if he is afraid of making this admission, would he ever grant that one who has become unlike is the same as before he became unlike? Or would he admit that a man is one at all, and not rather many and infinite as the changes which take place in him? I speak by the card in order to avoid entanglements of words. But, O my good sir, he will say, come to the argument in a more generous spirit; and either show, if you can, that our sensations are not relative and individual, or, if you admit them to be so, prove that this does not involve the consequence that the appearance becomes, or, if you will have the word, is, to the individual only. As to your talk about pigs and baboons, you are yourself behaving like a pig, and you teach your hearers to make sport of my writings in the same ignorant manner; but this is not to your credit. For I declare that the truth is as I have written, and that each of us is a measure of existence and of non-existence. Yet one man may be a thousand times better than another in proportion as different things are and appear to him. And I am far from saying that wisdom and the wise man have no existence; but I say that the wise man is he who makes the evils which appear and are to a man, into goods which are and appear to him. And I would beg you not to press my words in the letter, but to take the meaning of them as I will explain them. Remember what has been already said,—that to the sick man his food appears to be and is bitter, and to the man in health the opposite of bitter. Now I cannot conceive that one of these men can be or ought to be made wiser than the other: nor can you assert that the sick man because he has one impression is foolish, and the healthy man because he has another is wise; but the one state requires to be changed into the other, the worse into the better. As in education, a change of state has to be effected, and the sophist accomplishes by words the change which the physician works by the aid of drugs. Not that any one ever made another think truly, who previously thought falsely. For no one can think what is not, or think anything different from that which he feels; and this is always true. But as the inferior habit of mind has thoughts of kindred nature, so I conceive that a good mind causes men to have good thoughts; and these which the inexperienced call true, I maintain to be only better, and not truer than others. And, O my dear Socrates, I do not call wise men tadpoles: far from it; I say that they are the physicians of the human body, and the husbandmen of plants—for the husbandmen also take away the evil and disordered sensations of plants, and infuse into them good

Theaetetus

SOCRATES.

'What I maintain is, that sensations are relative and individual; that consequently what appears is.

'A wise man is not he who has certain impressions, but he who can make what appears evil appear good.

[167]

and healthy sensations—aye and true ones[1]; and the wise and
good rhetoricians make the good instead of the evil to seem just to
states; for whatever appears to a state to be just and fair, so long
as it is regarded as such, is just and fair to it; but the teacher of
wisdom causes the good to take the place of the evil, both in appearance and in reality. And in like manner the Sophist who is
able to train his pupils in this spirit is a wise man, and deserves to
be well paid by them. And so one man is wiser than another; and
no one thinks falsely, and you, whether you will or not, must endure to be a measure. On these foundations the argument stands
firm, which you, Socrates, may, if you please, overthrow by an
opposite argument, or if you like you may put questions to me—a
method to which no intelligent person will object, quite the reverse.
But I must beg you to put fair questions: for there is great inconsistency in saying that you have a zeal for virtue, and then always
behaving unfairly in argument. The unfairness of which I complain
is that you do not distinguish between mere disputation and dialectic: the disputer may trip up his opponent as often as he likes,
and make fun; but the dialectician will be in earnest, and only
correct his adversary when necessary, telling him the errors into
which he has fallen through his own fault, or that of the company
which he has previously kept. If you do so, your adversary will lay
the blame of his own confusion and perplexity on himself, and not
on you. He will follow and love you, and will hate himself, and
escape from himself into philosophy, in order that he may become
different from what he was. But the other mode of arguing, which
is practised by the many, will have just the opposite effect upon
him; and as he grows older, instead of turning philosopher, he
will come to hate philosophy. I would recommend you, therefore,
as I said before, not to encourage yourself in this polemical and
controversial temper, but to find out, in a friendly and congenial
spirit, what we really mean when we say that all things are in
motion, and that to every individual and state what appears, is.
In this manner you will consider whether knowledge and sensation
are the same or different, but you will not argue, as you were just
now doing, from the customary use of names and words, which the
vulgar pervert in all sorts of ways, causing infinite perplexity to
one another. Such, Theodorus, is the very slight help which I am
able to offer to your old friend[2]; had he been living, he would
have helped himself in a far more gloriose style.

[1] Reading ἀληθεῖς, but? Cp. supra 167 A: ταῦτα δὲ ἀεὶ ἀληθῆ.
[2] Reading προσήρκεσα.

Theod. You are jesting, Socrates; indeed, your defence of him has been most valorous.

Soc. Thank you, friend; and I hope that you observed Protagoras bidding us be serious, as the text, 'Man is the measure of all things,' was a solemn one; and he reproached us with making a boy the medium of discourse, and said that the boy's timidity was made to tell against his argument; he also declared that we made a joke of him.

Theod. How could I fail to observe all that, Socrates?

Soc. Well, and shall we do as he says?

Theod. By all means.

Soc. But if his wishes are to be regarded, you and I must take up the argument, and in all seriousness [1], and ask and answer one another, for you see that the rest of us are nothing but boys. In no other way can we escape the imputation, that in our fresh analysis of his thesis we are making fun with boys.

Theod. Well, but is not Theaetetus better able to follow a philosophical enquiry than a great many men who have long beards?

Soc. Yes, Theodorus, but not better than you; and therefore please not to imagine that I am to defend by every means in my power your departed friend; and that you are to defend nothing and nobody. At any rate, my good man, do not sheer off until we know whether you are a true measure of diagrams, or whether all men are equally measures and sufficient for themselves in astronomy and geometry, and the other branches of knowledge in which you are supposed to excel them.

Theod. He who is sitting by you, Socrates, will not easily avoid being drawn into an argument; and when I said just now that you would excuse me, and not, like the Lacedaemonians, compel me to strip and fight, I was talking nonsense—I should rather compare you to Scirrhon, who threw travellers from the rocks; for the Lacedaemonian rule is 'strip or depart,' but you seem to go about your work more after the fashion of Antaeus: you will not allow any one who approaches you to depart until you have stripped him, and he has been compelled to try a fall with you in argument.

Soc. There, Theodorus, you have hit off precisely the nature of my complaint; but I am even more pugnacious than the giants of old, for I have met with no end of heroes; many a Heracles, many a Theseus, mighty in words, has broken my head; nevertheless I am always at this rough exercise, which inspires me like a passion. Please, then, to try a fall with me, whereby you will do yourself good as well as me.

[1] Reading αὐτοῦ τῶν λόγων.

Socrates
insists
that out
of respect
for his old
friend,
Theo-
dorus
must
reply in-
stead of
Theae-
tetus.

Theo-
dorus
compares
Socrates
to Scir-
rhon and
Antaeus.

Socrates
replies
that he
often
gets a
broken
head for
his pains;
but that

Theod. I consent; lead me whither you will, for I know that you are like destiny; no man can escape from any argument which you may weave for him. But I am not disposed to go further than you suggest.

Soc. Once will be enough; and now take particular care that we do not again unwittingly expose ourselves to the reproach of talking childishly.

Theod. I will do my best to avoid that error.

Soc. In the first place, let us return to our old objection, and see whether we were right in blaming and taking offence at Protagoras on the ground that he assumed all to be equal and sufficient in wisdom; although he admitted that there was a better and worse, and that in respect of this, some who as he said were the wise excelled others.

Theod. Very true.

Soc. Had Protagoras been living and answered for himself, instead of our answering for him, there would have been no need of our reviewing or reinforcing the argument. But as he is not here, and some one may accuse us of speaking without authority on his behalf, had we not better come to a clearer agreement about his meaning, for a great deal may be at stake?

Theod. True.

170

Soc. Then let us obtain, not through any third person, but from his own statement and in the fewest words possible, the basis of agreement.

Theod. In what way?

Soc. In this way:—His words are, 'What seems to a man, is to him.'

Theod. Yes, so he says.

Soc. And are not we, Protagoras, uttering the opinion of man, or rather of all mankind, when we say that every one thinks himself wiser than other men in some things, and their inferior in others? In the hour of danger, when they are in perils of war, or of the sea, or of sickness, do they not look up to their commanders as if they were gods, and expect salvation from them, only because they excel them in knowledge? Is not the world full of men in their several employments, who are looking for teachers and rulers of themselves and of the animals? and there are plenty who think that they are able to teach and able to rule. Now, in all this is implied that ignorance and wisdom exist among them, at least in their own opinion.

Theod. Certainly.

Soc. And wisdom is assumed by them to be true thought, and ignorance to be false opinion.

Theod. Exactly.

Soc. How then, Protagoras, would you have us treat the argument? Shall we say that the opinions of men are always true, or sometimes true and sometimes false? In either case, the result is the same, and their opinions are not always true, but sometimes true and sometimes false. For tell me, Theodorus, do you suppose that you yourself, or any other follower of Protagoras, would contend that no one deems another ignorant or mistaken in his opinion?

Theod. The thing is incredible, Socrates.

Soc. And yet that absurdity is necessarily involved in the thesis which declares man to be the measure of all things.

Theod. How so?

Soc. Why, suppose that you determine in your own mind something to be true, and declare your opinion to me; let us assume, as he argues, that this is true to you. Now, if so, you must either say that the rest of us are not the judges of this opinion or judgment of yours, or that we judge you always to have a true opinion? But are there not thousands upon thousands who, whenever you form a judgment, take up arms against you and are of an opposite judgment and opinion, deeming that you judge falsely?

Theod. Yes, indeed, Socrates, thousands and tens of thousands, as Homer says, who give me a world of trouble.

Soc. Well, but are we to assert that what you think is true to you and false to the ten thousand others?

Theod. No other inference seems to be possible.

Soc. And how about Protagoras himself? If neither he nor the multitude thought, as indeed they do not think, that man is the measure of all things, must it not follow that the truth of which Protagoras wrote would be true to no one? But if you suppose that he himself thought this, and that the multitude does not agree with him, you must begin by allowing that in whatever proportion the many are more than one, in that proportion his truth is more untrue than true.

Theod. That would follow if the truth is supposed to vary with individual opinion.

Soc. And the best of the joke is, that he acknowledges the truth of their opinion who believe his own opinion to be false; for he admits that the opinions of all men are true.

Theod. Certainly.

*Theaete-
tus*

Socrates,
Theo-
dorus.

and this is
enough to
show that
opinions
clash,—
a fact
denied by
Prota-
goras,

though
very
obvious.

When
opinions
conflict,
[177]
numbers
ought to
decide:
this goes
all
against
Prota-
goras.

In any
case he
acknowl-
edges that
their
opinion is

true who
declare
his to be
false,
and so de-
nies the
truth of
his own
doctrine.

Soc. And does he not allow that his own opinion is false, if he admits that the opinion of those who think him false is true?

Theod. Of course.

Soc. Whereas the other side do not admit that they speak falsely?

Theod. They do not.

Soc. And he, as may be inferred from his writings, agrees that this opinion is also true.

Theod. Clearly.

Soc. Then all mankind, beginning with Protagoras, will contend, or rather, I should say that he will allow, when he concedes that his adversary has a true opinion—Protagoras, I say, will himself allow that neither a dog nor any ordinary man is the measure of anything which he has not learned—am I not right?

Theod. Yes.

Soc. And the truth of Protagoras being doubted by all, will be true neither to himself nor to any one else?

Theod. I think, Socrates, that we are running my old friend too hard.

But are
we doing
him jus-
tice?

Soc. But I do not know that we are going beyond the truth. Doubtless, as he is older, he may be expected to be wiser than we are. And if he could only just get his head out of the world below, he would have overthrown both of us again and again, me for talking nonsense and you for assenting to me, and have been off and underground in a trice. But as he is not within call, we must make the best use of our own faculties, such as they are, and speak out what appears to us to be true. And one thing which no one will deny is, that there are great differences in the understandings of men.

Theod. In that opinion I quite agree.

A conces-
sion.

His posi-
tion is
only true,
if at all,
in refer-
ence to
sensible
things;

Soc. And is there not most likely to be firm ground in the distinction which we were indicating on behalf of Protagoras, viz. that most things, and all immediate sensations, such as hot, dry, sweet, are only such as they appear; if however difference of opinion is to be allowed at all, surely we must allow it in respect of health or disease? for every woman, child, or living creature has not such a knowledge of what conduces to health as to enable them to cure themselves.

Theod. I quite agree.

172

and he
himself
admits
that in
politics
one man

Soc. Or again, in politics, while affirming that just and unjust, honourable and disgraceful, holy and unholy, are in reality to each state such as the state thinks and makes lawful, and that in determining these matters no individual or state is wiser than another, still the followers of Protagoras will not deny that in determining what is or is not expedient for the community one state is wiser and one counsellor better than another—they will scarcely venture to maintain, that what a city enacts in the belief that it is expedient will always be really expedient. But in the other case, I mean when they speak of justice and injustice, piety and impiety, they are confident that in nature these have no existence or essence of their own —the truth is that which is agreed on at the time of the agreement, and as long as the agreement lasts; and this is the philosophy of many who do not altogether go along with Protagoras. Here arises a new question, Theodorus, which threatens to be more serious than the last.

Theod. Well, Socrates, we have plenty of leisure.

Soc. That is true, and your remark recalls to my mind an observation which I have often made, that those who have passed their days in the pursuit of philosophy are ridiculously at fault when they have to appear and speak in court. How natural is this!

Theod. What do you mean?

Soc. I mean to say, that those who have been trained in philosophy and liberal pursuits are as unlike those who from their youth upwards have been knocking about in the courts and such places, as a freeman is in breeding unlike a slave.

Theod. In what is the difference seen?

Soc. In the leisure spoken of by you, which a freeman can always command: he has his talk out in peace, and, like ourselves, he wanders at will from one subject to another, and from a second to a third,—if the fancy takes him, he begins again, as we are doing now, caring not whether his words are many or few; his only aim is to attain the truth. But the lawyer is always in a hurry; there is the water of the clepsydra driving him on, and not allowing him to expatiate at will: and there is his adversary standing over him, enforcing his rights; the indictment, which in their phraseology is termed the affidavit, is recited at the time: and from this he must not deviate. He is a servant, and is continually disputing about a fellow-servant before his master, who is seated, and has the cause in his hands; the trial is never about some indifferent matter, but always concerns himself; and often the race is for his life. The consequence has been, that he has become keen and shrewd; he has learned how to flatter his master in word and indulge him in deed; but his soul is small and unrighteous. His condition, which has been that of a slave from his youth upwards, has deprived him of growth and uprightness and independence; dangers and fears, which were too much for his truth and honesty, came upon him in early years, when the tenderness of youth was unequal to them, and he has been driven into crooked ways; from the first he has

is wiser than another.

A larger question appears.

An apparent digression, in which is set forth, not the opposition of sense and knowledge, but a parallel contrast between the ways of the lawyer and philosopher.

173

The lawyer is the slave of this world, the philosopher is the freeman.

practised deception and retaliation, and has become stunted and warped. And so he has passed out of youth into manhood, having no soundness in him; and is now, as he thinks, a master in wisdom. Such is the lawyer, Theodorus. Will you have the companion picture of the philosopher, who is of our brotherhood; or shall we return to the argument? Do not let us abuse the freedom of digression which we claim.

Theod. Nay, Socrates, not until we have finished what we are about; for you truly said that we belong to a brotherhood which is free, and are not the servants of the argument; but the argument is our servant, and must wait our leisure. Who is our judge? Or where is the spectator having any right to censure or control us, as he might the poets?

Soc. Then, as this is your wish, I will describe the leaders; for there is no use in talking about the inferior sort. In the first place, the lords of philosophy have never, from their youth upwards, known their way to the Agora, or the dicastery, or the council, or any other political assembly; they neither see nor hear the laws or decrees, as they are called, of the state written or recited; the eagerness of political societies in the attainment of offices—clubs, and banquets, and revels, and singing-maidens,—do not enter even into their dreams. Whether any event has turned out well or ill in the city, what disgrace may have descended to any one from his ancestors, male or female, are matters of which the philosopher no more knows than he can tell, as they say, how many pints are contained in the ocean. Neither is he conscious of his ignorance. For he does not hold aloof in order that he may gain a reputation; but the truth is, that the outer form of him only is in the city: his mind, disdaining the littlenesses and nothingnesses of human things, is 'flying all abroad' as Pindar says, measuring earth and heaven and the things which are under and on the earth and above the heaven, interrogating the whole nature of each and all in their entirety, but not condescending to anything which is within reach.

Theod. What do you mean, Socrates?

Soc. I will illustrate my meaning, Theodorus, by the jest which the clever witty Thracian handmaid is said to have made about Thales, when he fell into a well as he was looking up at the stars. She said, that he was so eager to know what was going on in heaven, that he could not see what was before his feet. This is a jest which is equally applicable to all philosophers. For the philosopher is wholly unacquainted with his next-door neighbour; he is ignorant, not only of what he is doing, but he hardly knows whether he is a man or an animal; he is searching into the essence of man, and busy in enquiring what belongs to such a nature to do or suffer different from any other;—I think that you understand me, Theodorus?

Theod. I do, and what you say is true.

Soc. And thus, my friend, on every occasion, private as well as public, as I said at first, when he appears in a law-court, or in any place in which he has to speak of things which are at his feet and before his eyes, he is the jest, not only of Thracian handmaids but of the general herd, tumbling into wells and every sort of disaster through his inexperience. His awkwardness is fearful, and gives the impression of imbecility. When he is reviled, he has nothing personal to say in answer to the civilities of his adversaries, for he knows no scandals of any one, and they do not interest him; and therefore he is laughed at for his sheepishness; and when others are being praised and glorified, in the simplicity of his heart he cannot help going into fits of laughter, so that he seems to be a downright idiot. When he hears a tyrant or king eulogized, he fancies that he is listening to the praises of some keeper of cattle—a swineherd, or shepherd, or perhaps a cowherd, who is congratulated on the quantity of milk which he squeezes from them; and he remarks that the creature whom they tend, and out of whom they squeeze the wealth, is of a less tractable and more insidious nature. Then, again, he observes that the great man is of necessity as ill-mannered and uneducated as any shepherd—for he has no leisure, and he is surrounded by a wall, which is his mountain-pen. Hearing of enormous landed proprietors of ten thousand acres and more, our philosopher deems this to be a trifle, because he has been accustomed to think of the whole earth; and when they sing the praises of family, and say that someone is a gentleman because he can show seven generations of wealthy ancestors, he thinks that their sentiments only betray a dull and narrow vision in those who utter them, and who are not educated enough to look at the whole, nor to consider that every man has had thousands and ten thousands of progenitors, and among them have been rich and poor, kings and slaves, Hellenes and barbarians, innumerable. And when people pride themselves on having a pedigree of twenty-five ancestors, which goes back to Heracles, the son of Amphitryon, he cannot understand their poverty of ideas. Why are they unable to calculate that Amphitryon had a twenty-fifth ancestor, who might have been anybody, and was such as fortune made him, and he had a fiftieth, and so on? He amuses himself with the notion that they cannot count, and thinks that a little arithmetic would have got rid of their senseless vanity. Now, in all these cases our philos-

Theaetetus

Socrates, Theodorus.

He is the laughing-stock of mankind whenever he appears in public.

His irony: his ideas of kings and tyrants,

of landed property, and of long pedigrees.

175

To the world he is a fool.

He has his
revenge
upon the
lawyer.

opher is derided by the vulgar, partly because he is thought to despise them, and also because he is ignorant of what is before him, and always at a loss.

Theod. That is very true, Socrates.

Soc. But, O my friend, when he draws the other into upper air, and gets him out of his pleas and rejoinders into the contemplation of justice and injustice in their own nature and in their difference from one another and from all other things; or from the commonplaces about the happiness of a king or of a rich man to the consideration of government, and of human happiness and misery in general—what they are, and how a man is to attain the one and avoid the other—when that narrow, keen, little legal mind is called to account about all this, he gives the philosopher his revenge; for dizzied by the height at which he is hanging, whence he looks down into space, which is a strange experience to him, he being dismayed, and lost, and stammering broken words, is laughed at, not by Thracian handmaidens or any other uneducated persons, for they have no eye for the situation, but by every man who has not been brought up a slave. Such are the two characters, Theodorus: the one of the freeman, who has been trained in liberty and leisure, whom you call the philosopher,—him we cannot blame because he appears simple and of no account when he has to perform some menial task, such as packing up bed-clothes, or flavouring a sauce or fawning speech; the other character is that of the man who is able to do all this kind of service smartly and neatly, but knows not how to wear his cloak like a gentleman; still less with the music of discourse can he hymn the true life aright which is lived by immortals or men blessed of heaven.

Theod. If you could only persuade everybody, Socrates, as you do me, of the truth of your words, there would be more peace and fewer evils among men.

Soc. Evils, Theodorus, can never pass away; for there must always remain something which is antagonistic to good. Having no place among the gods in heaven, of necessity they hover around the mortal nature, and this earthly sphere. Wherefore we ought to fly away from earth to heaven as quickly as we can; and to fly away is to become like God, as far as this is possible; and to become like him, is to become holy, just, and wise. But, O my friend, you cannot easily convince mankind that they should pursue virtue or avoid vice, not merely in order that a man may seem to be good, which is the reason given by the world, and in my judgment is only a repetition of an old wives' fable. Whereas, the truth is that God is never in any way unrighteous—he is perfect righteousness; and he

176

Evil a
necessary
part of
human
nature,
from
which
men can
only fly
away
when
they be-
come like
God.

of us who is the most righteous is most like him. Herein is seen the true cleverness of a man, and also his nothingness and want of manhood. For to know this is true wisdom and virtue, and ignorance of this is manifest folly and vice. All other kinds of wisdom or cleverness, which seem only, such as the wisdom of politicians, or the wisdom of the arts, are coarse and vulgar. The unrighteous man, or the sayer and doer of unholy things, had far better not be encouraged in the illusion that his roguery is clever; for men glory in their shame—they fancy that they hear others saying of them, 'These are not mere good-for-nothing persons, mere burdens of the earth, but such as men should be who mean to dwell safely in a state.' Let us tell them that they are all the more truly what they do not think they are because they do not know it; for they do not know the penalty of injustice, which above all things they ought to know—not stripes and death, as they suppose, which evil-doers often escape, but a penalty which cannot be escaped.

Theod. What is that?

Soc. There are two patterns eternally set before them; the one blessed and divine, the other godless and wretched: but they do not see them, or perceive that in their utter folly and infatuation they are growing like the one and unlike the other, by reason of their evil deeds; and the penalty is, that they lead a life answering to the pattern which they are growing like. And if we tell them, that unless they depart from their cunning, the place of innocence will not receive them after death; and that here on earth, they will live ever in the likeness of their own evil selves, and with evil friends—when they hear this they in their superior cunning will seem to be listening to the talk of idiots.

Theod. Very true, Socrates.

Soc. Too true, my friend, as I well know; there is, however, one peculiarity in their case: when they begin to reason in private about their dislike of philosophy, if they have the courage to hear the argument out, and do not run away, they grow at last strangely discontented with themselves; their rhetoric fades away, and they become helpless as children. These however are digressions from which we must now desist, or they will overflow, and drown the original argument; to which, if you please, we will now return.

Theod. For my part, Socrates, I would rather have the digressions, for at my age I find them easier to follow; but if you wish, let us go back to the argument.

Soc. Had we not reached the point at which the partisans of the perpetual flux, who say that things are as they seem to each one, were confidently maintaining that the ordinances which the state

177

The wicked will only laugh at the truth.

A strange thing: when they consent to reason about philosophy, they are as helpless as children.

End of digression.

The partisans of

commanded and thought just, were just to the state which imposed them, while they were in force; this was especially asserted of justice; but as to the good, no one had any longer the hardihood to contend of any ordinances which the state thought and enacted to be good that these, while they were in force, were really good;— he who said so would be playing with the name 'good,' and would not touch the real question—it would be a mockery, would it not?

Theod. Certainly it would.

Soc. He ought not to speak of the name, but of the thing which is contemplated under the name.

Theod. Right.

Soc. Whatever be the term used, the good or expedient is the aim of legislation, and as far as she has an opinion, the state imposes all laws with a view to the greatest expediency; can legislation have any other aim?

Theod. Certainly not.

Soc. But is the aim attained always? do not mistakes often happen?

Theod. Yes, I think that there are mistakes.

Soc. The possibility of error will be more distinctly recognised, if we put the question in reference to the whole class under which the good or expedient falls. That whole class has to do with the future, and laws are passed under the idea that they will be useful in after-time; which, in other words, is the future.

Theod. Very true.

Soc. Suppose now, that we ask Protagoras, or one of his disciples, a question:—O, Protagoras, we will say to him, Man is, as you declare, the measure of all things—white, heavy, light: of all such things he is the judge; for he has the criterion of them in himself, and when he thinks that things are such as he experiences them to be, he thinks what is and is true to himself. Is it not so?

Theod. Yes.

Soc. And do you extend your doctrine, Protagoras (as we shall further say), to the future as well as to the present; and has he the criterion not only of what in his opinion is but of what will be, and do things always happen to him as he expected? For example, take the case of heat:—When an ordinary man thinks that he is going to have a fever, and that this kind of heat is coming on, and another person, who is a physician, thinks the contrary, whose opinion is likely to prove right? Or are they both right?—he will have a heat and fever in his own judgment, and not have a fever in the physician's judgment?

Theod. How ludicrous!

Soc. And the vinegrower, if I am not mistaken, is a better judge of the sweetness or dryness of the vintage which is not yet gathered than the harp-player?

Theod. Certainly.

Soc. And in musical composition the musician will know better than the training master what the training master himself will hereafter think harmonious or the reverse?

Theod. Of course.

Soc. And the cook will be a better judge than the guest, who is not a cook, of the pleasure to be derived from the dinner which is in preparation; for of present or past pleasure we are not as yet arguing; but can we say that every one will be to himself the best judge of the pleasure which will seem to be and will be to him in the future?—nay, would not you, Protagoras, better guess which arguments in a court would convince any one of us than the ordinary man?

Theod. Certainly, Socrates, he used to profess in the strongest manner that he was the superior of all men in this respect.

Soc. To be sure, friend: who would have paid a large sum for the privilege of talking to him, if he had really[1] persuaded his visitors that neither a prophet nor any other man was better able to judge what will be and seem to be in the future than every one could for himself?

Theod. Who indeed?

Soc. And legislation and expediency are all concerned with the future; and every one will admit that states, in passing laws, must often fail of their highest interests?

Theod. Quite true.

Soc. Then we may fairly argue against your master, that he must admit one man to be wiser than another, and that the wiser is a measure: but I, who know nothing, am not at all obliged to accept the honour which the advocate of Protagoras was just now forcing upon me, whether I would or not, of being a measure of anything.

Theod. That is the best refutation of him, Socrates; although he is also caught when he ascribes truth to the opinions of others, who give the lie direct to his own opinion.

Soc. There are many ways, Theodorus, in which the doctrine that every opinion of every man is true may be refuted; but there is more difficulty in proving that states of feeling, which are present to a man, and out of which arise sensations and opinions in accordance with them, are also untrue. And very likely I have been talking nonsense about them; for they may be unassailable, and those

---

[1] Reading δή.

Theaetetus

SOCRATES, THEODORUS.

nor of vinegrowing;

nor of cookery;

nor of rhetoric, legislation, &c.
179

Protagoras himself was wiser than the ordinary man about the future, and was well paid for it.

The refutation is complete.

who say that there is clear evidence of them, and that they are matters of knowledge, may probably be right; in which case our friend
Theaetetus was not so far from the mark when he identified perception and knowledge. And therefore let us draw nearer, as the advocate of Protagoras desires, and give the truth of the universal flux
a ring: is the theory sound or not? at any rate, no small war is raging about it, and there are combatants not a few.

Theod. No small war, indeed, for in Ionia the sect makes rapid
strides; the disciples of Heracleitus are most energetic upholders of
the doctrine.

Soc. Then we are the more bound, my dear Theodorus, to examine the question from the foundation as it is set forth by themselves.

Theod. Certainly we are. About these speculations of Heracleitus, which, as you say, are as old as Homer, or even older still, the
Ephesians themselves, who profess to know them, are downright
mad, and you cannot talk with them on the subject. For, in accordance with their text-books, they are always in motion; but as for
dwelling upon an argument or a question, and quietly asking and
answering in turn, they can no more do so than they can fly; or
rather, the determination of these fellows not to have a particle of
rest in them is more than the utmost powers of negation can express. If you ask any of them a question, he will produce, as from
a quiver, sayings brief and dark, and shoot them at you; and if
you inquire the reason of what he has said, you will be hit by some
other new-fangled word, and will make no way with any of them,
nor they with one another; their great care is, not to allow of any
settled principle either in their arguments or in their minds, conceiving, as I imagine, that any such principle would be stationary;
for they are at war with the stationary, and do what they can to
drive it out everywhere.

Soc. I suppose, Theodorus, that you have only seen them when
they were fighting, and have never stayed with them in time of
peace, for they are no friends of yours; and their peace doctrines
are only communicated by them at leisure, as I imagine, to those
disciples of theirs whom they want to make like themselves.

Theod. Disciples! my good sir, they have none; men of their sort
are not one another's disciples, but they grow up at their own sweet
will, and get their inspiration anywhere, each of them saying of his
neighbour that he knows nothing. From these men, then, as I was
going to remark, you will never get a reason, whether with their
will or without their will; we must take the question out of their
hands, and make the analysis ourselves, as if we were doing a geometrical problem.

The
friends of
Hera-
cleitus
wage a
violent
contro-
versy
about the
universal
flux. But
we must
take the
argument
[180]
out of the
hands of
these
lunatics
and fana-
tics, if we
would
test it.

Soc. Quite right too; but as touching the aforesaid problem, have we not heard from the ancients, who concealed their wisdom from the many in poetical figures, that Oceanus and Tethys, the origin of all things, are streams, and that nothing is at rest? And now the moderns, in their superior wisdom, have declared the same openly, that the cobbler too may hear and learn of them, and no longer foolishly imagine that some things are at rest and others in motion —having learned that all is motion, he will duly honour his teachers. I had almost forgotten the opposite doctrine, Theodorus,

'Alone Being remains unmoved, which is the name for the all.'

This is the language of Parmenides, Melissus, and their followers, who stoutly maintain that all being is one and self-contained, and has no place in which to move. What shall we do, friend, with all these people; for, advancing step by step, we have imperceptibly got between the combatants, and, unless we can protect our retreat, we shall pay the penalty of our rashness—like the players in the palaestra who are caught upon the line, and are dragged different ways by the two parties. Therefore I think that we had better begin by considering those whom we first accosted, 'the river-gods,' and, if we find any truth in them, we will help them to pull us over, and try to get away from the others. But if the partisans of 'the whole' appear to speak more truly, we will fly off from the party which would move the immovable, to them. And if we find that neither of them have anything reasonable to say, we shall be in a ridiculous position, having so great a conceit of our own poor opinion and rejecting that of ancient and famous men. O Theodorus, do you think that there is any use in proceeding when the danger is so great?

Theod. Nay, Socrates, not to examine thoroughly what the two parties have to say would be quite intolerable.

Soc. Then examine we must, since you, who were so reluctant to begin, are so eager to proceed. The nature of motion appears to be the question with which we begin. What do they mean when they say that all things are in motion? Is there only one kind of motion, or, as I rather incline to think, two? I should like to have your opinion upon this point in addition to my own, that I may err, if I must err, in your company; tell me, then, when a thing changes from one place to another, or goes round in the same place, is not that what is called motion?

Theod. Yes.

Soc. Here then we have one kind of motion. But when a thing, remaining on the same spot, grows old, or becomes black from being

The ancients held similar views, which they veiled in poetical figures. Then came the opposite doctrine [181] of Parmenides and Melissus.

Which side shall we take— motion or rest?

The advocates o motion

*Theaete-
tus*

SOCRATES,
THEO-
DORUS.

must of
necessity
maintain
that all
things
partake
of all
kinds of
motion.

white, or hard from being soft, or undergoes any other change, may not this be properly called motion of another kind?

Theod. I think so.

Soc. Say rather that it must be so. Of motion then there are these two kinds, 'change,' and 'motion in place[1].'

Theod. You are right.

Soc. And now, having made this distinction, let us address ourselves to those who say that all is motion, and ask them whether all things according to them have the two kinds of motion, and are changed as well as move in place, or is one thing moved in both ways, and another in one only?

Theod. Indeed, I do not know what to answer; but I think they would say that all things are moved in both ways.

Soc. Yes, comrade; for, if not, they would have to say that the same things are in motion and at rest, and there would be no more truth in saying that all things are in motion, than that all things are at rest.

Theod. To be sure.

Soc. And if they are to be in motion, and nothing is to be devoid of motion, all things must always have every sort of motion?

Theod. Most true.

Recapitu-
lation of
the Hera-
clitean
theory of
sensation
and
qualities.

Soc. Consider a further point: did we not understand them to explain the generation of heat, whiteness, or anything else, in some such manner as the following:—were they not saying that each of them is moving between the agent and the patient, together with a perception, and that the patient ceases to be a perceiving power and becomes a percipient, and the agent a quale instead of a quality? I suspect that quality may appear a strange and uncouth term to you, and that you do not understand the abstract expression. Then I will take concrete instances: I mean to say that the producing power or agent becomes neither heat nor whiteness, but hot and white, and the like of other things. For I must repeat what I said before, that neither the agent nor patient have any absolute existence, but when they come together and generate sensations and their objects, the one becomes a thing of a certain quality, and the other a percipient. You remember?

Theod. Of course.

Soc. We may leave the details of their theory unexamined, but we must not forget to ask them the only question with which we are concerned: Are all things in motion and flux?

Theod. Yes, they will reply.

Soc. And they are moved in both those ways which we distin-

---

[1] Reading φοράν: Lib. περιφοράν.

guished; that is to say, they move in place and are also changed?

Theod. Of course, if the motion is to be perfect.

Soc. If they only moved in place and were not changed, we should be able to say what is the nature of the things which are in motion and flux

Theod. Exactly.

Soc. But now, since not even white continues to flow white, and whiteness itself is a flux or change which is passing into another colour, and is never to be caught standing still, can the name of any colour be rightly used at all?

Theod. How is that possible, Socrates, either in the case of this or of any other quality—if while we are using the word the object is escaping in the flux?

Soc. And what would you say of perceptions, such as sight and hearing, or any other kind of perception? Is there any stopping in the act of seeing and hearing?

Theod. Certainly not, if all things are in motion.

Soc. Then we must not speak of seeing any more than of not-seeing, nor of any other perception more than of any non-perception, if all things partake of every kind of motion?

Theod. Certainly not.

Soc. Yet perception is knowledge: so at least Theaetetus and I were saying.

Theod. Very true.

Soc. Then when we were asked what is knowledge, we no more answered what is knowledge than what is not knowledge?

Theod. I suppose not.

Soc. Here, then, is a fine result: we corrected our first answer in our eagerness to prove that nothing is at rest. But if nothing is at rest, every answer upon whatever subject is equally right: you may say that a thing is or is not thus; or, if you prefer, 'becomes' thus; and if we say 'becomes,' we shall not then hamper them with words expressive of rest.

Theod. Quite true.

Soc. Yes, Theodorus, except in saying 'thus' and 'not thus.' But you ought not to use the word 'thus,' for there is no motion in 'thus' or in 'not thus.' The maintainers of the doctrine have as yet no words in which to express themselves, and must get a new language. I know of no word that will suit them, except perhaps 'no how,' which is perfectly indefinite.

Theod. Yes, that is a manner of speaking in which they will be quite at home.

Soc. And so, Theodorus, we have got rid of your friend without

*Theaete-
tus*

SOCRATES,
THEO-
DORUS.

Since each
quality
not only
moves in
place, but
changes
at the
same
time, one
name
cannot be
more ap-
propriate
to it than
another.

So too
with sen-
sations:
seeing
might
just as
well be
called
not-
seeing;
and to
come to
our defi-
nition,
[183]
knowl-
edge is no
more per-
ception
than non-
percep-
tion.

*Theaete-
tus*

SOCRATES,
THEO-
DORUS,
THEAE-
TETUS.

The
theory is
refuted so
far as it is
based on
a per-
petual
flux.

Theaete-
tus wishes
to hear a
discussion
of the
opposite
doctrine
of rest.

Socrates
is afraid
of enter-
ing on the
question.
He has so
great an
awe of
Parmeni-
[184]
des, and
he has
not yet
'delivered'
Theae-
tetus of
his con-
ception of
knowl-
edge.

assenting to his doctrine, that every man is the measure of all things —a wise man only is a measure; neither can we allow that knowledge is perception, certainly not on the hypothesis of a perpetual flux, unless perchance our friend Theaetetus is able to convince us that it is.

Theod. Very good, Socrates; and now that the argument about the doctrine of Protagoras has been completed, I am absolved from answering; for this was the agreement.

Theaet. Not, Theodorus, until you and Socrates have discussed the doctrine of those who say that all things are at rest, as you were proposing.

Theod. You, Theaetetus, who are a young rogue, must not instigate your elders to a breach of faith, but should prepare to answer Socrates in the remainder of the argument.

Theaet. Yes, if he wishes; but I would rather have heard about the doctrine of rest.

Theod. Invite Socrates to an argument—invite horsemen to the open plain; do but ask him, and he will answer.

Soc. Nevertheless, Theodorus, I am afraid that I shall not be able to comply with the request of Theaetetus.

Theod. Not comply! for what reason?

Soc. My reason is that I have a kind of reverence; not so much for Melissus and the others, who say that 'All is one and at rest,' as for the great leader himself, Parmenides, venerable and awful, as in Homeric language he may be called;—him I should be ashamed to approach in a spirit unworthy of him. I met him when he was an old man, and I was a mere youth, and he appeared to me to have a glorious depth of mind. And I am afraid that we may not understand his words, and may be still further from understanding his meaning; above all I fear that the nature of knowledge, which is the main subject of our discussion, may be thrust out of sight by the unbidden guests who will come pouring in upon our feast of discourse, if we let them in—besides, the question which is now stirring is of immense extent, and will be treated unfairly if only considered by the way; or if treated adequately and at length, will put into the shade the other question of knowledge. Neither the one nor the other can be allowed; but I must try by my art of midwifery to deliver Theaetetus of his conceptions about knowledge.

Theaet. Very well; do so if you will.

Soc. Then now, Theaetetus, take another view of the subject: you answered that knowledge is perception?

Theaet. I did.

Soc. And if any one were to ask you: With what does a man see black and white colours? and with what does he hear high and low sounds?—you would say, if I am not mistaken, 'With the eyes and with the ears.'

Theaet. I should.

Soc. The free use of words and phrases, rather than minute precision, is generally characteristic of a liberal education, and the opposite is pedantic; but sometimes precision is necessary, and I believe that the answer which you have just given is open to the charge of incorrectness; for which is more correct, to say that we see or hear with the eyes and with the ears, or through the eyes and through the ears.

Theaet. I should say 'through,' Socrates, rather than 'with.'

Soc. Yes, my boy, for no one can suppose that in each of us, as in a sort of Trojan horse, there are perched a number of unconnected senses, which do not all meet in some one nature, the mind, or whatever we please to call it, of which they are the instruments, and with which through them we perceive objects of sense.

Theaet. I agree with you in that opinion.

Soc. The reason why I am thus precise is, because I want to know whether, when we perceive black and white through the eyes, and again, other qualities through other organs, we do not perceive them with one and the same part of ourselves, and, if you were asked, you might refer all such perceptions to the body. Perhaps, however, I had better allow you to answer for yourself and not interfere. Tell me, then, are not the organs through which you perceive warm and hard and light and sweet, organs of the body?

Theaet. Of the body, certainly.

Soc. And you would admit that what you perceive through one faculty you cannot perceive through another; the objects of hearing, for example, cannot be perceived through sight, or the objects of sight through hearing?

Theaet. Of course not.

Soc. If you have any thought about both of them, this common perception cannot come to you, either through the one or the other organ?

Theaet. It cannot.

Soc. How about sounds and colours: in the first place you would admit that they both exist?

Theaet. Yes.

Soc. And that either of them is different from the other, and the same with itself?

Theaet. Certainly.

Soc. And that both are two and each of them one?

Theaete-tus

SOCRATES,
THEAE-
TETUS.

Another
point of
view.

We per-
ceive
sensible
things not
through,
but with
the mind,
and not
with, but
through
the
senses.

185
The
senses dif-
fer from
each
other,
and have
no ob-
jects in
common.

Theaet. Yes.

Soc. You can further observe whether they are like or unlike one another?

Theaet. I dare say.

Soc. But through what do you perceive all this about them? for neither through hearing nor yet through seeing can you apprehend that which they have in common. Let me give you an illustration of the point at issue:—If there were any meaning in asking whether sounds and colours are saline or not, you would be able to tell me what faculty would consider the question. It would not be sight or hearing, but some other.

Theaet. Certainly; the faculty of taste.

Soc. Very good; and now tell me what is the power which discerns, not only in sensible objects, but in all things, universal notions, such as those which are called being and not-being, and those others about which we were just asking—what organs will you assign for the perception of these notions?

General
ideas are
perceived
by the
mind
alone
without
the help
of the
senses.

Theaet. You are thinking of being and not-being, likeness and unlikeness, sameness and difference, and also of unity and other numbers which are applied to objects of sense; and you mean to ask, through what bodily organ the soul perceives odd and even numbers and other arithmetical conceptions.

Soc. You follow me excellently, Theaetetus; that is precisely what I am asking.

Theaet. Indeed, Socrates, I cannot answer; my only notion is, that these, unlike objects of sense, have no separate organ, but that the mind, by a power of her own, contemplates the universals in all things.

Soc. You are a beauty, Theaetetus, and not ugly, as Theodorus was saying; for he who utters the beautiful is himself beautiful and good. And besides being beautiful, you have done me a kindness in releasing me from a very long discussion, if you are clear that the soul views some things by herself and others through the bodily organs. For that was my own opinion, and I wanted you to agree with me.

Theaet. I am quite clear.

186

Soc. And to which class would you refer being or essence; for this, of all our notions, is the most universal?

Theaet. I should say, to that class which the soul aspires to know of herself.

Soc. And would you say this also of like and unlike, same and other?

Theaet. Yes.

Soc. And would you say the same of the noble and base, and of good and evil?

Theaet. These I conceive to be notions which are essentially relative, and which the soul also perceives by comparing in herself things past and present with the future.

Soc. And does she not perceive the hardness of that which is hard by the touch, and the softness of that which is soft equally by the touch?

Theaet. Yes.

Soc. But their essence and what they are, and their opposition to one another, and the essential nature of this opposition, the soul herself endeavors to decide for us by the review and comparison of them?

Theaet. Certainly.

Soc. The simple sensations which reach the soul through the body are given at birth to men and animals by nature, but their reflections on the being and use of them are slowly and hardly gained, if they are ever gained, by education and long experience.

Theaet. Assuredly.

Soc. And can a man attain truth who fails of attaining being?

Theaet. Impossible.

Soc. And can he who misses the truth of anything, have a knowledge of that thing?

Theaet. He cannot.

Soc. Then knowledge does not consist in impressions of sense, but in reasoning about them; in that only, and not in the mere impression, truth and being can be attained?

Theaet. Clearly.

Soc. And would you call the two processes by the same name, when there is so great a difference between them?

Theaet. That would certainly not be right.

Soc. And what name would you give to seeing, hearing, smelling, being cold and being hot?

Theaet. I should call all of them perceiving—what other name could be given to them?

Soc. Perception would be the collective name of them?

Theaet. Certainly.

Soc. Which, as we say, has no part in the attainment of truth any more than of being?

Theaet. Certainly not.

Soc. And therefore not in science or knowledge?

Theaetetus

SOCRATES, THEAETETUS.

The senses perceive objects of sense, but the mind alone can compare them.

Sensations are given at birth, but truth and being, which are essential to knowledge, are acquired by reflection later on.

Theaete-
tus

SOCRATES,
THEAE-
TETUS.

187

We have
found out
then what
knowl-
edge is
not. But
what is
it?

Theaete-
tus boldly
answers,
'True
opinion.'

But false
opinion is
impos-
sible, (1)
in the
sphere of
knowl-
edge:

Theaet. No.

Soc. Then perception, Theaetetus, can never be the same as knowledge or science?

Theaet. Clearly not, Socrates; and knowledge has now been most distinctly proved to be different from perception.

Soc. But the original aim of our discussion was to find out rather what knowledge is than what it is not; at the same time we have made some progress, for we no longer seek for knowledge in perception at all, but in that other process, however called, in which the mind is alone and engaged with being.

Theaet. You mean, Socrates, if I am not mistaken, what is called thinking or opining.

Soc. You conceive truly. And now, my friend, please to begin again at this point; and having wiped out of your memory all that has preceded, see if you have arrived at any clearer view, and once more say what is knowledge.

Theaet. I cannot say, Socrates, that all opinion is knowledge, because there may be a false opinion; but I will venture to assert, that knowledge is true opinion: let this then be my reply; and if this is hereafter disproved, I must try to find another.

Soc. That is the way in which you ought to answer, Theaetetus, and not in your former hesitating strain, for if we are bold we shall gain one of two advantages; either we shall find what we seek, or we shall be less likely to think that we know what we do not know —in either case we shall be richly rewarded. And now, what are you saying?—Are there two sorts of opinion, one true and the other false; and do you define knowledge to be the true?

Theaet. Yes, according to my present view.

Soc. Is it still worth our while to resume the discussion touching opinion?

Theaet. To what are you alluding?

Soc. There is a point which often troubles me, and is a great perplexity to me, both in regard to myself and others. I cannot make out the nature or origin of the mental experience to which I refer.

Theaet. Pray what is it?

Soc. How there can be false opinion—that difficulty still troubles the eye of my mind; and I am uncertain whether I shall leave the question, or begin over again in a new way.

Theaet. Begin again, Socrates,—at least if you think that there is the slightest necessity for doing so. Were not you and Theodorus just now remarking very truly, that in discussions of this kind we may take our own time?

Soc. You are quite right, and perhaps there will be no harm in retracing our steps and beginning again. Better a little which is well done, than a great deal imperfectly.

Theaet. Certainly.

Soc. Well, and what is the difficulty? Do we not speak of false opinion, and say that one man holds a false and another a true opinion, as though there were some natural distinction between them?

Theaet. We certainly say so.

Soc. All things and everything are either known or not known. I leave out of view the intermediate conceptions of learning and forgetting, because they have nothing to do with our present question.

Theaet. There can be no doubt, Socrates, if you exclude these, that there is no other alternative but knowing or not knowing a thing.

Soc. That point being now determined, must we not say that he who has an opinion, must have an opinion about something which he knows or does not know?

Theaet. He must.

Soc. He who knows, cannot but know; and he who does not know, cannot know?

Theaet. Of course.

Soc. What shall we say then? When a man has a false opinion does he think that which he knows to be some other thing which he knows, and knowing both, is he at the same time ignorant of both?

Theaet. That, Socrates, is impossible.

Soc. But perhaps he thinks of something which he does not know as some other thing which he does not know; for example, he knows neither Theaetetus nor Socrates, and yet he fancies that Theaetetus is Socrates, or Socrates Theaetetus?

Theaet. How can he?

Soc. But surely he cannot suppose what he knows to be what he does not know, or what he does not know to be what he knows?

Theaet. That would be monstrous.

Soc. Where, then, is false opinion? For if all things are either known or unknown, there can be no opinion which is not comprehended under this alternative, and so false opinion is excluded.

Theaet. Most true.

Soc. Suppose that we remove the question out of the sphere of knowing or not knowing, into that of being and not-being.

Theaet. What do you mean?

Soc. May we not suspect the simple truth to be that he who thinks about anything, that which is not, will necessarily think

Theaete-
tus

SOCRATES,
THEAE-
TETUS.

188
for all
things are
either
known or
not
known;

and a
man can-
not think
one thing,
which he
knows or
does not
know, to
be an-
other
thing
which he
knows or
does not
know;
nor what
he does
not know
to be
what he
knows, or
vice
versa:

and (2)
in the
sphere of
being:

what is false, whatever in other respects may be the state of his mind?

Theaet. That, again, is not unlikely, Socrates.

Soc. Then suppose some one to say to us, Theaetetus:—Is it possible for any man to think that which is not, either as a self-existent substance or as a predicate of something else? And suppose that we answer, 'Yes, he can, when he thinks what is not true.' —That will be our answer?

Theaet. Yes.

Soc. But is there any parallel to this?

Theaet. What do you mean?

for it is impossible when seeing or hearing not to see or hear some existing thing.

189

Soc. Can a man see something and yet see nothing?

Theaet. Impossible.

Soc. But if he sees any one thing, he sees something that exists. Do you suppose that what is one is ever to be found among non-existing things?

Theaet. I do not.

Soc. He then who sees some one thing, sees something which is?

Theaet. Clearly.

Soc. And he who hears anything, hears some one thing, and hears that which is?

Theaet. Yes.

Soc. And he who touches anything, touches something which is one and therefore is?

Theaet. That again is true.

Soc. And does not he who thinks, think some one thing?

Theaet. Certainly.

Soc. And does not he who thinks some one thing, think something which is?

Theaet. I agree.

Soc. Then he who thinks of that which is not, thinks of nothing?

Theaet. Clearly.

Soc. And he who thinks of nothing, does not think at all?

Theaet. Obviously.

Soc. Then no one can think that which is not, either as a self-existent substance or as a predicate of something else?

Theaet. Clearly not.

Soc. Then to think falsely is different from thinking that which is not?

Theaet. It would seem so.

Soc. Then false opinion has no existence in us, either in the sphere of being or of knowledge?

Theaet. Certainly not.

Soc. But may not the following be the description of what we express by this name?

Theaet. What?

Soc. May we not suppose that false opinion or thought is a sort of heterodoxy; a person may make an exchange in his mind, and say that one real object is another real object. For thus he always thinks that which is, but he puts one thing in place of another, and missing the aim of his thoughts, he may be truly said to have false opinion.

Theaet. Now you appear to me to have spoken the exact truth: when a man puts the base in the place of the noble, or the noble in the place of the base, then he has truly false opinion.

Soc. I see, Theaetetus, that your fear has disappeared, and that you are beginning to despise me.

Theaet. What makes you say so?

Soc. You think, if I am not mistaken, that your 'truly false' is safe from censure, and that I shall never ask whether there can be a swift which is slow, or a heavy which is light, or any other self-contradictory thing, which works, not according to its own nature, but according to that of its opposite. But I will not insist upon this, for I do not wish needlessly to discourage you. And so you are satisfied that false opinion is heterodoxy, or the thought of something else?

Theaet. I am.

Soc. It is possible then upon your view for the mind to conceive of one thing as another?

Theaet. True.

Soc. But must not the mind, or thinking power, which misplaces them, have a conception either of both objects or of one of them?

Theaet. Certainly.

Soc. Either together or in succession?

Theaet. Very good.

Soc. And do you mean by conceiving, the same which I mean?

Theaet. What is that?

Soc. I mean the conversation which the soul holds with herself in considering of anything. I speak of what I scarcely understand; but the soul when thinking appears to me to be just talking—asking questions of herself and answering them, affirming and denying. And when she has arrived at a decision, either gradually or by a sudden impulse, and has at last agreed, and does not doubt, this is called her opinion. I say, then, that to form an opinion is to speak, and opinion is a word spoken,—I mean, to oneself and in silence, not aloud or to another: What think you?

Theaete-
tus

SOCRATES,
THEAE-
TETUS.

But how
can one
thing be
thought
to be
another?

e. g. no
one ever
says to
himself
that the
noble is
the base,
or that
odd is
even.

It is ad-
mitted on
all hands
that no
one can
confuse
two
things,
either
when he
has both
in his
mind, or
when he
has only
one.

Theaet. I agree.

Soc. Then when any one thinks of one thing as another, he is saying to himself that one thing is another?

Theaet. Yes.

Soc. But do you ever remember saying to yourself that the noble is certainly base, or the unjust just; or, best of all—have you ever attempted to convince yourself that one thing is another? Nay, not even in sleep, did you ever venture to say to yourself that odd is even, or anything of the kind?

Theaet. Never.

Soc. And do you suppose that any other man, either in his senses or out of them, ever seriously tried to persuade himself that an ox is a horse, or that two are one?

Theaet. Certainly not.

Soc. But if thinking is talking to oneself, no one speaking and thinking of two objects, and apprehending them both in his soul, will say and think that the one is the other of them, and I must add, that even you, lover of dispute as you are, had better let the word 'other' alone [i. e. not insist that 'one' and 'other' are the same [1]]. I mean to say, that no one thinks the noble to be base, or anything of the kind.

Theaet. I will give up the word 'other,' Socrates; and I agree to what you say.

Soc. If a man has both of them in his thoughts, he cannot think that the one of them is the other?

Theaet. True.

Soc. Neither, if he has one of them only in his mind and not the other, can he think that one is the other?

Theaet. True; for we should have to suppose that he apprehends that which is not in his thoughts at all.

Soc. Then no one who has either both or only one of the two objects in his mind can think that the one is the other. And therefore, he who maintains that false opinion is heterodoxy is talking nonsense; for neither in this, any more than in the previous way, can false opinion exist in us.

Theaet. No.

Soc. But if, Theaetetus, this is not admitted, we shall be driven into many absurdities.

Theaet. What are they?

Soc. I will not tell you until I have endeavoured to consider the matter from every point of view. For I should be ashamed of us if we were driven in our perplexity to admit the absurd consequences

191

[1] Both words in Greek are called ἕτερον: cp. Parmen. 147 C; Euthyd. 301 A.

of which I speak. But if we find the solution, and get away from them, we may regard them only as the difficulties of others, and the ridicule will not attach to us. On the other hand, if we utterly fail, I suppose that we must be humble, and allow the argument to trample us under foot, as the sea-sick passenger is trampled upon by the sailor, and to do anything to us. Listen, then, while I tell you how I hope to find a way out of our difficulty.

Theaet. Let me hear.

Soc. I think that we were wrong in denying that a man could think what he knew to be what he did not know; and that there is a way in which such a deception is possible.

Theaet. You mean to say, as I suspected at the time, that I may know Socrates, and at a distance see some one who is unknown to me, and whom I mistake for him—then the deception will occur?

Soc. But has not that position been relinquished by us, because involving the absurdity that we should know and not know the things which we know?

Theaet. True.

Soc. Let us make the assertion in another form, which may or may not have a favourable issue; but as we are in a great strait, every argument should be turned over and tested. Tell me, then, whether I am right in saying that you may learn a thing which at one time you did not know?

Theaet. Certainly you may.

Soc. And another and another?

Theaet. Yes.

Soc. I would have you imagine, then, that there exists in the mind of man a block of wax, which is of different sizes in different men; harder, moister, and having more or less of purity in one than another, and in some of an intermediate quality.

Theaet. I see.

Soc. Let us say that this tablet is a gift of Memory, the mother of the Muses; and that when we wish to remember anything which we have seen, or heard, or thought in our own minds, we hold the wax to the perceptions and thoughts, and in that material receive the impression of them as from the seal of a ring; and that we remember and know what is imprinted as long as the image lasts; but when the image is effaced, or cannot be taken, then we forget and do not know.

Theaet. Very good.

Soc. Now, when a person has this knowledge, and is considering something which he sees or hears, may not false opinion arise in the following manner?

Theaetetus

SOCRATES, THEAE-
TETUS.

We are in great straits.

A way out of the difficulty: Theaetetus may know Socrates, and yet mistake another whom he sees, but does not know, for him.

The image of the waxen tablet having different qualities of wax.

Theaete-
tus

SOCRATES,
THEAE-
TETUS.

192
Confu-
sion is
impos-
sible, (1)
between
two
things not
perceived
by sense,
when we
know one
or both or
neither of
them ;
(2) be-
tween
two
things
when we
have a
sensible
impres-
sion of
one or
both or
neither of
them ;
(3) still
more im-
possible
between
two
things,
both of
which are
known
and per-
ceived,
and of
which the
impres-
sion coin-
cides with
sense ;
(4) be-
tween
two
things of
which
both or

Theaet. In what manner?

Soc. When he thinks what he knows, sometimes to be what he knows, and sometimes to be what he does not know. We were wrong before in denying the possibility of this.

Theaet. And how would you amend the former statement?

Soc. I should begin by making a list of the impossible cases which must be excluded. (1) No one can think one thing to be another when he does not perceive either of them, but has the memorial or seal of both of them in his mind; nor can any mistaking of one thing for another occur, when he only knows one, and does not know, and has no impression of the other; nor can he think that one thing which he does not know is another thing which he does not know, or that what he does not know is what he knows; nor (2) that one thing which he perceives is another thing which he perceives, or that something which he perceives is something which he does not perceive; or that something which he does not perceive is something else which he does not perceive; or that something which he does not perceive is something which he perceives; nor again (3) can he think that something which he knows and perceives, and of which he has the impression coinciding with sense, is something else which he knows and perceives, and of which he has the impression coinciding with sense;—this last case, if possible, is still more inconceivable than the others; nor (4) can he think that something which he knows and perceives, and of which he has the memorial coinciding with sense, is something else which he knows; nor so long as these agree, can he think that a thing which he knows and perceives is another thing which he perceives; or that a thing which he does not know and does not perceive, is the same as another thing which he does not know and does not perceive;—nor again, can he suppose that a thing which he does not know and does not perceive is the same as another thing which he does not know; or that a thing which he does not know and does not perceive is another thing which he does not perceive:—All these utterly and absolutely exclude the possibility of false opinion. The only cases, if any, which remain, are the following.

Theaet. What are they? If you tell me, I may perhaps understand you better; but at present I am unable to follow you.

Soc. A person may think that some things which he knows, or which he perceives and does not know, are some other things which he knows and perceives; or that some things which he knows and perceives, are other things which he knows and perceives.

Theaet. I understand you less than ever now.

Soc. Hear me once more, then:—I, knowing Theodorus, and remembering in my own mind what sort of person he is, and also what sort of person Theaetetus is, at one time see them, and at another time do not see them, and sometimes I touch them, and at another time not, or at one time I may hear them or perceive them in some other way, and at another time not perceive them, but still I remember them, and know them in my own mind.

Theaet. Very true.

Soc. Then, first of all, I want you to understand that a man may or may not perceive sensibly that which he knows.

Theaet. True.

Soc. And that which he does not know will sometimes not be perceived by him and sometimes will be perceived and only perceived?

Theaet. That is also true.

Soc. See whether you can follow me better now: Socrates can recognize Theodorus and Theaetetus, but he sees neither of them, nor does he perceive them in any other way; he cannot then by any possibility imagine in his own mind that Theaetetus is Theodorus. Am I not right?

Theaet. You are quite right.

Soc. Then that was the first case of which I spoke.

Theaet. Yes.

Soc. The second case was, that I, knowing one of you and not knowing the other, and perceiving neither, can never think him whom I know to be him whom I do not know.

Theaet. True.

Soc. In the third case, not knowing and not perceiving either of you, I cannot think that one of you whom I do not know is the other whom I do not know. I need not again go over the catalogue of excluded cases, in which I cannot form a false opinion about you and Theodorus, either when I know both or when I am in ignorance of both, or when I know one and not the other. And the same of perceiving: do you understand me?

Theaet. I do.

Soc. The only possibility of erroneous opinion is, when knowing you and Theodorus, and having on the waxen block the impression of both of you given as by a seal, but seeing you imperfectly and at a distance, I try to assign the right impression of memory to the right visual impression, and to fit this into its own print: if I succeed, recognition will take place; but if I fail and transpose them, putting the foot into the wrong shoe—that is to say, putting the vision of either of you on to the wrong impression, or if my mind, like the sight in a mirror, which is transferred from right

Theaetetus

SOCRATES, THEAE-TETUS.

one only or neither are known and perceived and have an impression corresponding to sense.

193 Confusion arises when for things already known and perceived we mistake other things, either known, or perceived and not known, or both known and perceived.

Recapitulation.

False opinion **is** the erroneous combination of sensation and thought.

to left, err by reason of some similar affection, then 'heterodoxy' and false opinion ensues.

Theaet. Yes, Socrates, you have described the nature of opinion with wonderful exactness.

Soc. Or again, when I know both of you, and perceive as well as know one of you, but not the other, and my knowledge of him does not accord with perception—that was the case put by me just now which you did not understand.

Theaet. No, I did not.

Soc. I meant to say, that when a person knows and perceives one of you, and his knowledge coincides with his perception, he will never think him to be some other person, whom he knows and perceives, and the knowledge of whom coincides with his perception—for that also was a case supposed.

Theaet. True.

Soc. But there was an omission of the further case, in which, as we now say, false opinion may arise, when knowing both, and seeing, or having some other sensible perception of both, I fail in holding the seal over against the corresponding sensation; like a bad archer, I miss and fall wide of the mark—and this is called falsehood.

Theaet. Yes; it is rightly so called.

Soc. When, therefore, perception is present to one of the seals or impressions but not to the other, and the mind fits the seal of the absent perception on the one which is present, in any case of this sort the mind is deceived; in a word, if our view is sound, there can be no error or deception about things which a man does not know and has never perceived, but only in things which are known and perceived; in these alone opinion turns and twists about, and becomes alternately true and false;—true when the seals and impressions of sense meet straight and opposite—false when they go awry and crooked.

Theaet. And is not that, Socrates, nobly said?

Soc. Nobly! yes; but wait a little and hear the explanation, and then you will say so with more reason; for to think truly is noble and to be deceived is base.

Theaet. Undoubtedly.

Soc. And the origin of truth and error is as follows:—When the wax in the soul of any one is deep and abundant, and smooth and perfectly tempered, then the impressions which pass through the senses and sink into the heart of the soul, as Homer says in a parable, meaning to indicate the likeness of the soul to wax (κῆρ κηρὸς); these, I say, being pure and clear, and having a

The differences in the kinds and degrees of knowledge depend on

sufficient depth of wax, are also lasting, and minds, such as these,
easily learn and easily retain, and are not liable to confusion, but
have true thoughts, for they have plenty of room, and having
clear impressions of things, as we term them, quickly distribute
them into their proper places on the block. And such men are
called wise. Do you agree?

Theaet. Entirely.

Soc. But when the heart of any one is shaggy—a quality which
the all-wise poet commends, or muddy and of impure wax, or
very soft, or very hard, then there is a corresponding defect in
the mind—the soft are good at learning, but apt to forget; and the
hard are the reverse; the shaggy and rugged and gritty, or those
who have an admixture of earth or dung in their composition,
have the impressions indistinct, as also the hard, for there is no
depth in them; and the soft too are indistinct, for their impressions are easily confused and effaced. Yet greater is the indistinct-
ness when they are all jostled together in a little soul, which has
no room. These are the natures which have false opinion; for
when they see or hear or think of anything, they are slow in assigning the right objects to the right impressions—in their stupidity they confuse them, and are apt to see and hear and think
amiss—and such men are said to be deceived in their knowledge
of objects, and ignorant.

Theaet. No man, Socrates, can say anything truer than that.

Soc. Then now we may admit the existence of false opinion in
us?

Theaet. Certainly.

Soc. And of true opinion also?

Theaet. Yes.

Soc. We have at length satisfactorily proven that beyond a
doubt there are these two sorts of opinion?

Theaet. Undoubtedly.

Soc. Alas, Theaetetus, what a tiresome creature is a man who
is fond of talking!

Theaet. What makes you say so?

Soc. Because I am disheartened at my own stupidity and tiresome garrulity; for what other term will describe the habit of a
man who is always arguing on all sides of a question; whose dul-
ness cannot be convinced, and who will never leave off?

Theaet. But what puts you out of heart?

Soc. I am not only out of heart, but in positive despair; for I
do not know what to answer if any one were to ask me:—O Socrates, have you indeed discovered that false opinion arises neither

the extent
and the
qualities
of the
wax.

195

Our simile
does not
explain
all the

Theaete-tus

SOCRATES,
THEAE-
TETUS.

facts; for
error may
arise
not only
in the
combina-
tion of
thought
and
sense, but
in pure
thought.

196

For ex-
ample, a
man may
think that
5+7=11,
instead of
12, and so
confuse
two im-
pressions
on the
wax.

We must
therefore
admit
either
that false

in the comparison of perceptions with one another nor yet in thought, but in the union of thought and perception? Yes, I shall say, with the complacence of one who thinks that he has made a noble discovery.

Theaet. I see no reason why we should be ashamed of our demonstration, Socrates.

Soc. He will say: You mean to argue that the man whom we only think of and do not see, cannot be confused with the horse which we do not see or touch, but only think of and do not perceive? That I believe to be my meaning, I shall reply.

Theaet. Quite right.

Soc. Well, then, he will say, according to that argument, the number eleven, which is only thought, can never be mistaken for twelve, which is only thought: How would you answer him?

Theaet. I should say that a mistake may very likely arise between the eleven or twelve which are seen or handled, but that no similar mistake can arise between the eleven and twelve which are in the mind.

Soc. Well, but do you think that no one ever put before his own mind five and seven,—I do not mean five or seven men or horses, but five or seven in the abstract, which, as we say, are recorded on the waxen block, and in which false opinion is held to be impossible;—did no man ever ask himself how many these numbers make when added together, and answer that they are eleven, while another thinks that they are twelve, or would all agree in thinking and saying that they are twelve?

Theaet. Certainly not; many would think that they are eleven, and in the higher numbers the chance of error is greater still; for I assume you to be speaking of numbers in general.

Soc. Exactly; and I want you to consider whether this does not imply that the twelve in the waxen block are supposed to be eleven?

Theaet. Yes, that seems to be the case.

Soc. Then do we not come back to the old difficulty? For he who makes such a mistake does think one thing which he knows to be another thing which he knows; but this, as we said, was impossible, and afforded an irresistible proof of the non-existence of false opinion, because otherwise the same person would inevitably know and not know the same thing at the same time.

Theaet. Most true.

Soc. Then false opinion cannot be explained as a confusion of thought and sense, for in that case we could not have been mistaken about pure conceptions of thought; and thus we are obliged to say, either that false opinion does not exist, or that a man may not know that which he knows;—which alternative do you prefer?

Theaet. It is hard to determine, Socrates.

Soc. And yet the argument will scarcely admit of both. But, as we are at our wits' end, suppose that we do a shameless thing?

Theaet. What is it?

Soc. Let us attempt to explain the verb 'to know.'

Theaet. And why should that be shameless?

Soc. You seem not to be aware that the whole of our discussion from the very beginning has been a search after knowledge, of which we are assumed not to know the nature.

Theaet. Nay, but I am well aware.

Soc. And is it not shameless when we do not know what knowledge is, to be explaining the verb 'to know'? The truth is, Theaetetus, that we have long been infected with logical impurity. Thousands of times have we repeated the words 'we know,' and 'do not know,' and 'we have or have not science or knowledge,' as if we could understand what we are saying to one another, so long as we remain ignorant about knowledge; and at this moment we are using the words 'we understand,' 'we are ignorant,' as though we could still employ them when deprived of knowledge or science.

Theaet. But if you avoid these expressions, Socrates, how will you ever argue at all?

Soc. I could not, being the man I am. The case would be different if I were a true hero of dialectic: and O that such an one were present! for he would have told us to avoid the use of these terms; at the same time he would not have spared in you and me the faults which I have noted. But, seeing that we are no great wits, shall I venture to say what knowing is? for I think that the attempt may be worth making.

Theaet. Then by all means venture, and no one shall find fault with you for using the forbidden terms.

Soc. You have heard the common explanation of the verb 'to know'?

Theaet. I think so, but I do not remember it at the moment.

Soc. They explain the word 'to know' as meaning 'to have knowledge.'

Theaet. True.

Soc. I should like to make a slight change, and say 'to possess' knowledge.

Theaet. How do the two expressions differ?

Soc. Perhaps there may be no difference; but still I should like you to hear my view, that you may help me to test it.

Theaet. I will, if I can.

Theaetetus

SOCRATES, THEAE-TETUS.

opinion does not exist, or that a man may not know what he knows.

As a last resource let us ask, What is the meaning of 'knowing'?

But how can we answer the question while we are [197] still ignorant of what knowledge is?

Still we had better try.

'To know' is not 'to have,' but 'to possess knowledge.'

To illus-
trate this
distinc-
tion let us
compare
the mind
to an
aviary
which is
gradually
filled with
different
kinds of
birds,
corre-
sponding
to the
varieties
of knowl-
edge.

Soc. I should distinguish 'having' from 'possessing': for example, a man may buy and keep under his control a garment which he does not wear; and then we should say, not that he has, but that he possesses the garment.

Theaet. It would be the correct expression.

Soc. Well, may not a man 'possess' and yet not 'have' knowledge in the sense of which I am speaking? As you may suppose a man to have caught wild birds—doves or any other birds—and to be keeping them in an aviary which he has constructed at home; we might say of him in one sense, that he always has them because he possesses them, might we not?

Theaet. Yes.

Soc. And yet, in another sense, he has none of them; but they are in his power, and he has got them under his hand in an enclosure of his own, and can take and have them whenever he likes; —he can catch any which he likes, and let the bird go again, and he may do so as often as he pleases.

Theaet. True.

Soc. Once more, then, as in what preceded we made a sort of waxen figment in the mind, so let us now suppose that in the mind of each man there is an aviary of all sorts of birds—some flocking together apart from the rest, others in small groups, others solitary, flying anywhere and everywhere.

Theaet. Let us imagine such an aviary—and what is to follow?

Soc. We may suppose that the birds are kinds of knowledge, and that when we were children, this receptacle was empty; whenever a man has gotten and detained in the enclosure a kind of knowledge, he may be said to have learned or discovered the thing which is the subject of the knowledge: and this is to know.

Theaet. Granted.

Three
stages of
posses-
sion:—
(1) the
original
capture;
(2) the
[198]
detention
in the
cage;
(3) the
second
capture
for use.

Soc. And further, when any one wishes to catch any of these knowledges or sciences, and having taken, to hold it, and again to let them go, how will he express himself?—will he describe the 'catching' of them and the original 'possession' in the same words? I will make my meaning clearer by an example:—You admit that there is an art of arithmetic?

Theaet. To be sure.

Soc. Conceive this under the form of a hunt after the science of odd and even in general.

Theaet. I follow.

Soc. Having the use of the art, the arithmetician, if I am not mistaken, has the conceptions of number under his hand, and can transmit them to another.

Theaet. Yes.

Soc. And when transmitting them he may be said to teach them, and when receiving to learn them, and when having them in possession in the aforesaid aviary he may be said to know them.

Theaet. Exactly.

Soc. Attend to what follows: must not the perfect arithmetician know all numbers, for he has the science of all numbers in his mind?

Theaet. True.

Soc. And he can reckon abstract numbers in his head, or things about him which are numerable?

Theaet. Of course he can.

Soc. And to reckon is simply to consider how much such and such a number amounts to?

Theaet. Very true.

Soc. And so he appears to be searching into something which he knows, as if he did not know it, for we have already admitted that he knows all numbers;—you have heard these perplexing questions raised?

Theaet. I have.

Soc. May we not pursue the image of the doves, and say that the chase after knowledge is of two kinds? one kind is prior to possession and for the sake of possession, and the other for the sake of taking and holding in the hands that which is possessed already. And thus, when a man has learned and known something long ago, he may resume and get hold of the knowledge which he has long possessed, but has not at hand in his mind.

Theaet. True.

Soc. That was my reason for asking how we ought to speak when an arithmetician sets about numbering, or a grammarian about reading? Shall we say, that although he knows, he comes back to himself to learn what he already knows?

Theaet. It would be too absurd, Socrates.

Soc. Shall we say then that he is going to read or number what he does not know, although we have admitted that he knows all letters and all numbers?

Theaet. That, again, would be an absurdity.

Soc. Then shall we say that about names we care nothing?—any one may twist and turn the words 'knowing' and 'learning' in any way which he likes, but since we have determined that the possession of knowledge is not the having or using it, we do assert that a man cannot not possess that which he possesses; and, therefore, in no case can a man not know that which he knows, but he

The three stages of knowl-edge:—
(1) acquisition;
(2) latent possession;
(3) conscious possession and use.

199

False opinion arises if the arithmetician, when searching for a certain number, catches the wrong one.

For a moment the explanation appears satisfactory.

But again the old difficulty returns; for when a man has knowledge in his hand, how can he mistake it for ignorance?

Theaetetus suggests that there are forms of ignorance, as well as of knowledge, flying about [200] in the aviary. But the man who makes a

may get a false opinion about it; for he may have the knowledge, not of this particular thing, but of some other;—when the various numbers and forms of knowledge are flying about in the aviary, and wishing to capture a certain sort of knowledge out of the general store, he takes the wrong one by mistake, that is to say, when he thought eleven to be twelve, he got hold of the ring-dove which he had in his mind, when he wanted the pigeon.

Theaet. A very rational explanation.

Soc. But when he catches the one which he wants, then he is not deceived, and has an opinion of what is, and thus false and true opinion may exist, and the difficulties which were previously raised disappear. I dare say that you agree with me, do you not?

Theaet. Yes.

Soc. And so we are rid of the difficulty of a man's not knowing what he knows, for we are not driven to the inference that he does not possess what he possesses, whether he be or be not deceived. And yet I fear that a greater difficulty is looking in at the window.

Theaet. What is it?

Soc. How can the exchange of one knowledge for another ever become false opinion?

Theaet. What do you mean?

Soc. In the first place, how can a man who has the knowledge of anything be ignorant of that which he knows, not by reason of ignorance, but by reason of his own knowledge? And, again, is it not an extreme absurdity that he should suppose another thing to be this, and this to be another thing;—that, having knowledge present with him in his mind, he should still know nothing and be ignorant of all things?—you might as well argue that ignorance may make a man know, and blindness make him see, as that knowledge can make him ignorant.

Theaet. Perhaps, Socrates, we may have been wrong in making only forms of knowledge our birds: whereas there ought to have been forms of ignorance as well, flying about together in the mind, and then he who sought to take one of them might sometimes catch a form of knowledge, and sometimes a form of ignorance; and thus he would have a false opinion from ignorance, but a true one from knowledge, about the same thing.

Soc. I cannot help praising you, Theaetetus, and yet I must beg you to reconsider your words. Let us grant what you say—then, according to you, he who takes ignorance will have a false opinion —am I right?

Theaet. Yes.

Soc. He will certainly not think that he has a false opinion?

Theaet. Of course not.

Soc. He will think that his opinion is true, and he will fancy that he knows the things about which he has been deceived?

Theaet. Certainly.

Soc. Then he will think that he has captured knowledge and not ignorance?

Theaet. Clearly.

Soc. And thus, after going a long way round, we are once more face to face with our original difficulty. The hero of dialectic will retort upon us:—'O my excellent friends, he will say, laughing, if a man knows the form of ignorance and the form of knowledge, can he think that one of them which he knows is the other which he knows? or, if he knows neither of them, can he think that the one which he knows not is another which he knows not? or, if he knows one and not the other, can he think the one which he knows to be the one which he does not know? or the one which he does not know to be the one which he knows? or will you tell me that there are other forms of knowledge which distinguish the right and wrong birds, and which the owner keeps in some other aviaries or graven on waxen blocks according to your foolish images, and which he may be said to know while he possesses them, even though he have them not at hand in his mind? And thus, in a perpetual circle, you will be compelled to go round and round, and you will make no progress.' What are we to say in reply, Theaetetus?

Theaet. Indeed, Socrates, I do not know what we are to say.

Soc. Are not his reproaches just, and does not the argument truly show that we are wrong in seeking for false opinion until we know what knowledge is; that must be first ascertained; then, the nature of false opinion?

Theaet. I cannot but agree with you, Socrates, so far as we have yet gone.

Soc. Then, once more, what shall we say that knowledge is?—for we are not going to lose heart as yet.

Theaet. Certainly, I shall not lose heart, if you do not.

Soc. What definition will be most consistent with our former views?

Theaet. I cannot think of any but our old one, Socrates.

Soc. What was it?

Theaet. Knowledge was said by us to be true opinion; and true opinion is surely unerring, and the results which follow from it are all noble and good.

Soc. He who led the way into the river, Theaetetus, said 'The experiment will show;' and perhaps if we go forward in the search,

mistake will take a form of ignorance for a form of knowledge; and so we are brought back to the original difficulty.

It will be ridiculous to attempt to get rid of this by the help of another aviary, containing other birds, i.e. forms of knowledge.

Our discomfiture is due to the fact that we seek false opinion before knowledge.

What then is knowledge?

An old friend reappears: 'Knowl-

[201]

we may stumble upon the thing which we are looking for; but if we
stay where we are, nothing will come to light.

Theaet. Very true; let us go forward and try.

Soc. The trail soon comes to an end, for a whole profession is
against us.

Theaet. How is that, and what profession do you mean?

Soc. The profession of the great wise ones who are called orators
and lawyers; for these persuade men by their art and make them
think whatever they like, but they do not teach them. Do you
imagine that there are any teachers in the world so clever as to
be able to convince others of the truth about acts of robbery or
violence, of which they were not eye-witnesses, while a little water
is flowing in the clepsydra?

Theaet. Certainly not, they can only persuade them.

Soc. And would you not say that persuading them is making
them have an opinion?

Theaet. To be sure.

Soc. When, therefore, judges are justly persuaded about matters
which you can know only by seeing them, and not in any other way,
and when thus judging of them from report they attain a true
opinion about them, they judge without knowledge and yet are
rightly persuaded, if they have judged well.

Theaet. Certainly.

Soc. And yet, O my friend, if true opinion in law courts [1] and
knowledge are the same, the perfect judge could not have judged
rightly without knowledge; and therefore I must infer that they
are not the same.

Theaet. That is a distinction, Socrates, which I have heard
made by some one else, but I had forgotten it. He said that true
opinion, combined with reason, was knowledge, but that the opinion which had no reason was out of the sphere of knowledge; and
that things of which there is no rational account are not knowable—such was the singular expression which he used—and that
things which have a reason or explanation are knowable.

Soc. Excellent; but then, how did he distinguish between things
which are and are not 'knowable'? I wish that you would repeat to
me what he said, and then I shall know whether you and I have
heard the same tale.

Theaet. I do not know whether I can recall it; but if another
person would tell me, I think that I could follow him.

Soc. Let me give you, then, a dream in return for a dream:—

---

[1] Reading κατὰ δικαστήρια: an emendation suggested by Professor Campbell.

Methought that I too had a dream, and I heard in my dream that the primeval letters or elements out of which you and I and all other things are compounded, have no reason or explanation; you can only name them, but no predicate can be either affirmed or denied of them, for in the one case existence, in the other non-existence is already implied, neither of which must be added, if you mean to speak of this or that thing by itself alone. It should not be called itself, or that, or each, or alone, or this, or the like; for these go about everywhere and are applied to all things, but are distinct from them; whereas, if the first elements could be described, and had a definition of their own, they would be spoken of apart from all else. But none of these primeval elements can be defined; they can only be named, for they have nothing but a name, and the things which are compounded of them, as they are complex, are expressed by a combination of names, for the combination of names is the essence of a definition. Thus, then, the elements or letters are only objects of perception, and cannot be defined or known; but the syllables or combinations of them are known and expressed, and are apprehended by true opinion. When, therefore, any one forms the true opinion of anything without rational explanation, you may say that his mind is truly exercised, but has no knowledge; for he who cannot give and receive a reason for a thing, has no knowledge of that thing; but when he adds rational explanation, then, he is perfected in knowledge and may be all that I have been denying of him. Was that the form in which the dream appeared to you?

Theaet. Precisely.

Soc. And you allow and maintain that true opinion, combined with definition or rational explanation, is knowledge?

Theaet. Exactly.

Soc. Then may we assume, Theaetetus, that to-day, and in this casual manner, we have found a truth which in former times many wise men have grown old and have not found?

Theaet. At any rate, Socrates, I am satisfied with the present statement.

Soc. Which is probably correct—for how can there be knowledge apart from definition and true opinion? And yet there is one point in what has been said which does not quite satisfy me.

Theaet. What was it?

Soc. What might seem to be the most ingenious notion of all:— That the elements or letters are unknown, but the combination or syllables known.

Theaetetus

202
SOCRATES,
THEAE-
TETUS.

The same notion expressed by Socrates in a different manner.

The simple and primeval elements can only be named; it is the combination of them in the proposition which gives knowledge.

The theory states that the ele-

*Theaete-
tus*

Socrates,
Theae-
tetus.

ments are
unknown,
but that
[203]
the com-
bination
of them is
known.
Can this
be true?

We are, at
any rate,
right in
saying
that the
elements
have no
definition.

Theaet. And was that wrong?

Soc. We shall soon know; for we have as hostages the instances which the author of the argument himself used.

Theaet. What hostages?

Soc. The letters, which are the elements; and the syllables, which are the combinations;—he reasoned, did he not, from the letters of the alphabet?

Theaet. Yes; he did.

Soc. Let us take them and put them to the test, or rather, test ourselves:—What was the way in which we learned letters? and, first of all, are we right in saying that syllables have a definition, but that letters have no definition?

Theaet. I think so.

Soc. I think so too; for, suppose that some one asks you to spell the first syllable of my name:—Theaetetus, he says, what is SO?

Theaet. I should reply S and O.

Soc. That is the definition which you would give of the syllable?

Theaet. I should.

Soc. I wish that you would give me a similar definition of the S.

Theaet. But how can any one, Socrates, tell the elements of an element? I can only reply, that S is a consonant, a mere noise, as of the tongue hissing; B, and most other letters, again, are neither vowel-sounds nor noises. Thus letters may be most truly said to be undefined; for even the most distinct of them, which are the seven vowels, have a sound only, but no definition at all.

Soc. Then, I suppose, my friend, that we have been so far right in our idea about knowledge?

Theaet. Yes; I think that we have.

But are
they
therefore
un-
known?

Soc. Well, but have we been right in maintaining that the syllables can be known, but not the letters?

Theaet. I think so.

Soc. And do we mean by a syllable two letters, or if there are more, all of them, or a single idea which arises out of the combination of them?

If by syl-
lable we
mean the
letters
which
compose
it,

Theaet. I should say that we mean all the letters.

Soc. Take the case of the two letters S and O, which form the first syllable of my own name; must not he who knows the syllable, know both of them?

Theaet. Certainly.

Soc. He knows, that is, the S and O?

Theaet. Yes.

a man
cannot

Soc. But can he be ignorant of either singly and yet know both together?

Theaet. Such a supposition, Socrates, is monstrous and unmeaning.

Soc. But if he cannot know both without knowing each, then if he is ever to know the syllable, he must know the letters first; and thus the fine theory has again taken wings and departed.

Theaet. Yes, with wonderful celerity.

Soc. Yes, we did not keep watch properly. Perhaps we ought to have maintained that a syllable is not the letters, but rather one single idea framed out of them, having a separate form distinct from them.

Theaet. Very true; and a more likely notion than the other.

Soc. Take care; let us not be cowards and betray a great and imposing theory.

Theaet. No, indeed.

Soc. Let us assume then, as we now say, that the syllable is a simple form arising out of the several combinations of harmonious elements—of letters or of any other elements.

Theaet. Very good.

Soc. And it must have no parts.

Theaet. Why?

Soc. Because that which has parts must be a whole of all the parts. Or would you say that a whole, although formed out of the parts, is a single notion different from all the parts?

Theaet. I should.

Soc. And would you say that all and the whole are the same, or different?

Theaet. I am not certain; but, as you like me to answer at once, I shall hazard the reply, that they are different.

Soc. I approve of your readiness, Theaetetus, but I must take time to think whether I equally approve of your answer.

Theaet. Yes; the answer is the point.

Soc. According to this new view, the whole is supposed to differ from all?

Theaet. Yes.

Soc. Well, but is there any difference between all [in the plural] and the all [in the singular]? Take the case of number:—When we say one, two, three, four, five, six; or when we say twice three, or three times two, or four and two, or three and two and one, are we speaking of the same or of different numbers?

Theaet. Of the same.

Soc. That is of six?

Theaet. Yes.

Soc. And in each form of expression we spoke of all the six?

Theaet. True.

Soc. Again, in speaking of all [in the plural], is there not one thing which we express [1]?

Theaet. Of course there is.

Soc. And that is six?

Theaet. Yes.

Soc. Then in predicating the word 'all' of things measured by number, we predicate at the same time a singular and a plural?

Theaet. Clearly we do.

Soc. Again, the number of the acre and the acre are the same; are they not?

Theaet. Yes.

Soc. And the number of the stadium in like manner is the stadium?

Theaet. Yes.

Soc. And the army is the number of the army; and in all similar cases, the entire number of anything is the entire thing?

Theaet. True.

Soc. And the number of each is the parts of each?

Theaet. Exactly.

Soc. Then as many things as have parts are made up of parts?

Theaet. Clearly.

and therefore it implies parts.

Soc. But all the parts are admitted to be the all, if the entire number is the all?

Theaet. True.

Soc. Then the whole is not made up of parts, for it would be the all, if consisting of all the parts?

Theaet. That is the inference.

But the whole being different from the all, cannot have parts;

[205]

Soc. But is a part a part of anything but the whole?

Theaet. Yes, of the all.

Soc. You make a valiant defence, Theaetetus. And yet is not the all that of which nothing is wanting?

Theaet. Certainly.

which is absurd.

Soc. And is not a whole likewise that from which nothing is absent? but that from which anything is absent is neither a whole nor all;—if wanting in anything, both equally lose their entirety of nature.

Theaet. I now think that there is no difference between a whole and all.

Accordingly there can be no difference between the whole

Soc. But were we not saying that when a thing has parts, all the parts will be a whole and all?

Theaet. Certainly.

[1] Reading οὐδ' ἕν.

Soc. Then, as I was saying before, must not the alternative be that either the syllable is not the letters, and then the letters are not parts of the syllable, or that the syllable will be the same with the letters, and will therefore be equally known with them?

Theaet. You are right.

Soc. And, in order to avoid this, we suppose it to be different from them?

Theaet. Yes.

Soc. But if letters are not parts of syllables, can you tell me of any other parts of syllables, which are not letters?

Theaet. No, indeed, Socrates; for if I admit the existence of parts in a syllable, it would be ridiculous in me to give up letters and seek for other parts.

Soc. Quite true, Theaetetus, and therefore, according to our present view, a syllable must surely be some indivisible form?

Theaet. True.

Soc. But do you remember, my friend, that only a little while ago we admitted and approved the statement, that of the first elements out of which all other things are compounded there could be no definition, because each of them when taken by itself is uncompounded; nor can one rightly attribute to them the words 'being' or 'this,' because they are alien and inappropriate words, and for this reason the letters or elements were indefinable and unknown?

Theaet. I remember.

Soc. And is not this also the reason why they are simple and indivisible? I can see no other.

Theaet. No other reason can be given.

Soc. Then is not the syllable in the same case as the elements or letters, if it has no parts and is one form?

Theaet. To be sure.

Soc. If, then, a syllable is a whole, and has many parts or letters, the letters as well as the syllable must be intelligible and expressible, since all the parts are acknowledged to be the same as the whole?

Theaet. True.

Soc. But if it be one and indivisible, then the syllables and the letters are alike undefined and unknown, and for the same reason?

Theaet. I cannot deny that.

Soc. We cannot, therefore, agree in the opinion of him who says that the syllable can be known and expressed, but not the letters.

Theaet. Certainly not; if we may trust the argument.

Soc. Well, but will you not be equally inclined to disagree with him, when you remember your own experience in learning to read?

Theaetetus

SOCRATES, THEAETETUS.

and the all. But the whole, if distinct from the elements, cannot have these for its parts; and, since it can have no other parts, it must be without parts altogether. The syllable is therefore an uncompounded element, and consequently unknown.

If the syllable is the sum of its letters, letters and syllable must be equally intelligible. If [206] it is indivisible, letters and syl-

lable must
be equally
unknown.
It is un-
true to
say that
the syl-
lables are
known,
but the
letters un-
known.

And in
learning
to read
and play
on the
lyre we
are taught
the ele-
ments,
which are
the letters
or notes,
first of all.

We said
that
knowl-
edge is
right
opinion
with
rational
explana-
tion.

But what
is expla-
nation?

(1) The
reflection
of
thought
in
speech.—
But this is
not pecu-
liar to

Theaet. What experience?

Soc. Why, that in learning you were kept trying to distinguish
the separate letters both by the eye and by the ear, in order that,
when you heard them spoken or saw them written, you might not
be confused by their position.

Theaet. Very true.

Soc. And is the education of the harp-player complete unless
he can tell what string answers to a particular note; the notes, as
every one would allow, are the elements or letters of music?

Theaet. Exactly.

Soc. Then, if we argue from the letters and syllables which we
know to other simples and compounds, we shall say that the letters
or simple elements as a class are much more certainly known than
the syllables, and much more indispensable to a perfect knowledge
of any subject; and if some one says that the syllable is known and
the letter unknown, we shall consider that either intentionally or
unintentionally he is talking nonsense?

Theaet. Exactly.

Soc. And there might be given other proofs of this belief, if I am
not mistaken. But do not let us in looking for them lose sight of the
question before us, which is the meaning of the statement, that
right opinion with rational definition or explanation is the most
perfect form of knowledge.

Theaet. We must not.

Soc. Well, and what is the meaning of the term 'explanation'? I
think that we have a choice of three meanings.

Theat. What are they?

Soc. In the first place, the meaning may be, manifesting one's
thought by the voice with verbs and nouns, imaging an opinion in
the stream which flows from the lips, as in a mirror or water. Does
not explanation appear to be of this nature?

Theaet. Certainly; he who so manifests his thought, is said to
explain himself.

Soc. And every one who is not born deaf or dumb is able sooner
or later to manifest what he thinks of anything; and if so, all those
who have a right opinion about anything will also have right explanation; nor will right opinion be anywhere found to exist apart
from knowledge.

Theaet. True.

Soc. Let us not, therefore, hastily charge him who gave this
account of knowledge with uttering an unmeaning word; for perhaps he only intended to say, that when a person was asked what

was the nature of anything, he should be able to answer his questioner by giving the elements of the thing.

Theaet. As for example, Socrates . . .?

Soc. As, for example, when Hesiod says that a waggon is made up of a hundred planks. Now, neither you nor I could describe all of them individually; but if any one asked what is a waggon, we should be content to answer, that a waggon consists of wheels, axle, body, rims, yoke.

Theaet. Certainly.

Soc. And our opponent will probably laugh at us, just as he would if we professed to be grammarians and to give a grammatical account of the name of Theaetetus, and yet could only tell the syllables and not the letters of your name—that would be true opinion, and not knowledge; for knowledge, as has been already remarked, is not attained until, combined with true opinion, there is an enumeration of the elements out of which anything is composed.

Theaet. Yes.

Soc. In the same general way, we might also have true opinion about a waggon; but he who can describe its essence by an enumeration of the hundred planks, adds rational explanation to true opinion, and instead of opinion has art and knowledge of the nature of a waggon, in that he attains to the whole through the elements.

Theaet. And do you not agree in that view, Socrates?

Soc. If you do, my friend; but I want to know first, whether you admit the resolution of all things into their elements to be a rational explanation of them, and the consideration of them in syllables or larger combinations of them to be irrational—is this your view?

Theaet. Precisely.

Soc. Well, and do you conceive that a man has knowledge of any element who at one time affirms and at another time denies that element of something, or thinks that the same thing is composed of different elements at different times?

Theaet. Assuredly not.

Soc. And do you not remember that in your case and in that of others this often occurred in the process of learning to read?

Theaet. You mean that I mistook the letters and misspelt the syllables?

Soc. Yes.

Theaet. To be sure; I perfectly remember, and I am very far from supposing that they who are in this condition have knowledge.

Soc. When a person at the time of learning writes the name of

207
Theaetetus

SOCRATES,
THEAE-
TETUS.

those who
know.

(2) The
enumeration of
the parts
of a
thing.

But there
may be
enumeration of
parts
without
knowledge.

208
*Theaete-
tus*

SOCRATES,
THEAE-
TETUS.

Theaetetus, and thinks that he ought to write and does write *Th* and *e*; but, again, meaning to write the name of Theodorus, thinks that he ought to write and does write *T* and *e*—can we suppose that he knows the first syllables of your two names?

Theaet. We have already admitted that such a one has not yet attained knowledge.

Soc. And in like manner he may enumerate without knowing them the second and third and fourth syllables of your name?

Theaet. He may.

Soc. And in that case, when he knows the order of the letters and can write them out correctly, he has right opinion?

Theaet. Clearly.

Soc. But although we admit that he has right opinion, he will still be without knowledge?

Theaet. Yes.

Soc. And yet he will have explanations, as well as right opinion, for he knew the order of the letters when he wrote; and this we admit to be explanation.

Theaet. True.

Soc. Then, my friend, there is such a thing as right opinion united with definition or explanation, which does not as yet attain to the exactness of knowledge.

Theaet. It would seem so.

Soc. And what we fancied to be a perfect definition of knowledge is a dream only. But perhaps we had better not say so as yet, for were there not three explanations of knowledge, one of which must, as we said, be adopted by him who maintains knowledge to be true opinion combined with rational explanation? And very likely there may be found some one who will not prefer this but the third.

Theaet. You are quite right; there is still one remaining. The first was the image or expression of the mind in speech; the second, which has just been mentioned, is a way of reaching the whole by an enumeration of the elements. But what is the third definition?

(3 True
opinion
about a
thing
with the
addition
of a mark
or sign of
difference.

Soc. There is, further, the popular notion of telling the mark or sign of difference which distinguishes the thing in question from all others.

Theaet. Can you give me any example of such a definition?

Soc. As, for example, in the case of the sun, I think that you would be contented with the statement that the sun is the brightest of the heavenly bodies which revolve about the earth.

Theaet. Certainly.

Soc. Understand why:—the reason is, as I was just now saying, that if you get at the difference and distinguishing characteristic of each thing, then, as many persons affirm, you will get at the definition or explanation of it; but while you lay hold only of the common and not of the characteristic notion, you will only have the definition of those things to which this common quality belongs.

Theaet. I understand you, and your account of definition is in my judgment correct.

Soc. But he, who having right opinion about anything, can find out the difference which distinguishes it from other things will know that of which before he had only an opinion.

Theaet. Yes; that is what we are maintaining.

Soc. Nevertheless, Theaetetus, on a nearer view, I find myself quite disappointed; the picture, which at a distance was not so bad, has now become altogether unintelligible.

Theaet. What do you mean?

Soc. I will endeavour to explain: I will suppose myself to have true opinion of you, and if to this I add your definition, then I have knowledge, but if not, opinion only.

209

Theaet. Yes.

Soc. The definition was assumed to be the interpretation of your difference.

Theaet. True.

Soc. But when I had only opinion, I had no conception of your distinguishing characteristics.

Theaet. I suppose not.

Soc. Then I must have conceived of some general or common nature which no more belonged to you than to another.

Theaet. True.

But right
opinion
already
implies a
knowl-
edge of
difference.

Soc. Tell me, now—How in that case could I have formed a judgment of you any more than of any one else? Suppose that I imagine Theaetetus to be a man who has nose, eyes, and mouth, and every other member complete; how would that enable me to distinguish Theaetetus from Theodorus, or from some outer barbarian?

Theaet. How could it?

Soc. Or if I had further conceived of you, not only as having nose and eyes, but as having a snub nose and prominent eyes, should I have any more notion of you than of myself and others who resemble me?

Theaet. Certainly not.

Soc. Surely I can have no conception of Theaetetus until your snub-nosedness has left an impression on my mind different from the snub-nosedness of all others whom I have ever seen, and until your other peculiarities have a like distinctness; and so when I meet you to-morrow the right opinion will be re-called?

Theaet. Most true.

Soc. Then right opinion implies the perception of differences?

Theaet. Clearly.

Soc. What, then, shall we say of adding reason or explanation to right opinion? If the meaning is, that we should form an opinion of the way in which something differs from another thing, the proposal is ridiculous.

Theaet. How so?

Soc. We are supposed to acquire a right opinion of the differences which distinguish one thing from another when we have already a right opinion of them, and so we go round and round:— the revolution of the scytal, or pestle, or any other rotatory machine, in the same circles, is as nothing compared with such a requirement; and we may be truly described as the blind directing the blind; for to add those things which we already have, in order that we may learn what we already think, is like a soul utterly benighted.

Theaet. Tell me; what were you going to say just now, when you asked the question?

Soc. If, my boy, the argument, in speaking of adding the definition, had used the word to 'know,' and not merely 'have an opinion' of the difference, this which is the most promising of all the definitions of knowledge would have come to a pretty end, for to know is surely to acquire knowledge.

Theaet. True.

Soc. And so, when the question is asked, What is knowledge? this fair argument will answer 'Right opinion with knowledge,'— knowledge, that is, of difference, for this, as the said argument maintains, is adding the definition.

Theaet. That seems to be true.

Soc. But how utterly foolish, when we are asking what is knowledge, that the reply should only be, right opinion with knowledge of difference or of anything! And so, Theaetetus, knowledge is neither sensation nor true opinion, nor yet definition and explanation accompanying and added to true opinion?

Theaet. I suppose not.

Soc. And are you still in labour and travail, my dear friend, or have you brought all that you have to say about knowledge to the birth?

How ab-
surd it
would be
to repeat
the word
we are de-
fining in
our defi-
nition,
[210]
and say
that
knowl-
edge is
knowl-
edge of
differ-
ence!

Theaet. I am sure, Socrates, that you have elicited from me a good deal more than ever was in me.

Soc. And does not my art show that you have brought forth wind, and that the offspring of your brain are not worth bringing up?

Theaet. Very true.

Soc. But if, Theaetetus, you should ever conceive afresh, you will be all the better for the present investigation, and if not, you will be soberer and humbler and gentler to other men, and will be too modest to fancy that you know what you do not know. These are the limits of my art; I can no further go, nor do I know aught of the things which great and famous men know or have known in this or former ages. The office of a midwife I, like my mother, have received from God; she delivered women, and I deliver men; but they must be young and noble and fair.

And now I have to go to the porch of the King Archon, where I am to meet Meletus and his indictment. To-morrow morning, Theodorus, I shall hope to see you again at this place.

Theaete-tus

SOCRATES, THEAE-TETUS.

Theae-tetus has brought forth wind. But to know that they know nothing makes men better and humbler.

Socrates is expecting his trial (cp. Euthyph. *sub fin.*; Meno *sub fin.*).

SOPHIST

SOPHIST

PERSONS OF THE DIALOGUE

THEODORUS   THEAETETUS   SOCRATES

AN ELEATIC STRANGER, *whom Theodorus and Theaetetus bring with them. The younger* SOCRATES, *who is a silent auditor.*

Theodorus. HERE we are, Socrates, true to our agreement of yesterday; and we bring with us a stranger from Elea, who is a disciple of Parmenides and Zeno, and a true philosopher.

Socrates. Is he not rather a god, Theodorus, who comes to us in the disguise of a stranger? For Homer says that all the gods, and especially the god of strangers, are companions of the meek and just, and visit the good and evil among men. And may not your companion be one of those higher powers, a cross-examining deity, who has come to spy out our weakness in argument, and to cross-examine us?

Theod. Nay, Socrates, he is not one of the disputatious sort—he is too good for that. And, in my opinion, he is not a god at all; but divine he certainly is, for this is a title which I should give to all philosophers.

Soc. Capital, my friend! and I may add that they are almost as hard to be discerned as the gods. For the true philosophers, and such as are not merely made up for the occasion, appear in various forms unrecognized by the ignorance of men, and they 'hover about cities,' as Homer declares, looking from above upon human life; and some think nothing of them, and others can never think enough; and sometimes they appear as statesmen, and sometimes as sophists; and then, again, to many they seem to be no better than madmen. I should like to ask our Eleatic friend, if he would tell us, what is thought about them in Italy, and to whom the terms are applied.

Theod. What terms?

Soc. Sophist, statesman, philosopher.

Theod. What is your difficulty about them, and what made you ask?

The Eleatic stranger, who is introduced by Theodorus, is taken by Socrates for some cross-examining deity; and Theodorus acknowledges that, though not a god, he is at any rate a divine man.

217

A question is put to him: Are the sophist,

Sophist

SOCRATES,
THEO-
DORUS,
STRANGER,
THEAE-
TETUS.

statesman, and philosopher different, or the same?

The stranger may either speak at length or adopt the method of question and answer.

On the present occasion he prefers the latter, and accepts the proposal [218] of Socrates that Theaetetus should be his respondent.

Soc. I want to know whether by his countrymen they are regarded as one or two; or do they, as the names are three, distinguish also three kinds, and assign one to each name?

Theod. I dare say that the Stranger will not object to discuss the question. What do you say, Stranger?

Stranger. I am far from objecting, Theodorus, nor have I any difficulty in replying that by us they are regarded as three. But to define precisely the nature of each of them is by no means a slight or easy task.

Theod. You have happened to light, Socrates, almost on the very question which we were asking our friend before we came hither, and he excused himself to us, as he does now to you; although he admitted that the matter had been fully discussed, and that he remembered the answer.

Soc. Then do not, Stranger, deny us the first favour which we ask of you: I am sure that you will not, and therefore I shall only beg of you to say whether you like and are accustomed to make a long oration on a subject which you want to explain to another, or to proceed by the method of question and answer. I remember hearing a very noble discussion in which Parmenides employed the latter of the two methods, when I was a young man, and he was far advanced in years. [1]

Str. I prefer to talk with another when he responds pleasantly, and is light in hand; if not, I would rather have my own say.

Soc. Any one of the present company will respond kindly to you, and you can choose whom you like of them; I should recommend you to take a young person—Theaetetus, for example—unless you have a preference for some one else.

Str. I feel ashamed, Socrates, being a new-comer into your society, instead of talking a little and hearing others talk, to be spinning out a long soliloquy or address, as if I wanted to show off. For the true answer will certainly be a very long one, a great deal longer than might be expected from such a short and simple question. At the same time, I fear that I may seem rude and ungracious if I refuse your courteous request, especially after what you have said. For I certainly cannot object to your proposal, that Theaetetus should respond, having already conversed with him myself, and being recommended by you to take him.

Theaetetus. But are you sure, Stranger, that this will be quite so acceptable to the rest of the company as Socrates imagines?

Str. You hear them applauding, Theaetetus; after that, there is

[1] Cp. Parm., 137 ff.

nothing more to be said. Well then, I am to argue with you, and if you tire of the argument, you may complain of your friends and not of me.

Theaet. I do not think that I shall tire, and if I do, I shall get my friend here, young Socrates, the namesake of the elder Socrates, to help; he is about my own age, and my partner at the gymnasium, and is constantly accustomed to work with me.

Str. Very good; you can decide about that for youself as we proceed. Meanwhile you and I will begin together and enquire into the nature of the Sophist, first of the three: I should like you to make out what he is and bring him to light in a discussion; for at present we are only agreed about the name, but of the thing to which we both apply the name possibly you have one notion and I another; whereas we ought always to come to an understanding about the the thing itself in terms of a definition, and not merely about the name minus the definition. Now the tribe of Sophists which we are investigating is not easily caught or defined; and the world has long ago agreed, that if great subjects are to be adequately treated, they must be studied in the lesser and easier instances of them before we proceed to the greatest of all. And as I know that the tribe of Sophists is troublesome and hard to be caught, I should recommend that we practise beforehand the method which is to be applied to him on some simple and smaller thing, unless you can suggest a better way.

First of all, What is the Sophist?

As he is not easy to catch, we had better begin with something simpler;

Theaet. Indeed I cannot.

Str. Then suppose that we work out some lesser example which will be a pattern of the greater?

Theaet. Good.

Str. What is there which is well known and not great, and is yet as susceptible of definition as any larger thing? Shall I say an angler? He is familiar to all of us, and not a very interesting or important person.

e.g. with the angler.

Theaet. He is not.

Str. Yet I suspect that he will furnish us with the sort of definition and line of enquiry which we want.

219

Theaet. Very good.

Str. Let us begin by asking whether he is a man having art or not having art, but some other power.

He is an artist, and all art is either creative or acquisitive.

Theaet. He is clearly a man of art.

Str. And of arts there are two kinds?

Theaet. What are they?

Str. There is agriculture, and the tending of mortal creatures, and the art of constructing or moulding vessels, and there is the art of imitation—all these may be appropriately called by a single name.

Theaet. What do you mean? And what is the name?

Str. He who brings into existence something that did not exist before is said to be a producer, and that which is brought into existence is said to be produced.

Theaet. True.

Str. And all the arts which were just now mentioned are characterized by this power of producing?

Theaet. They are.

Str. Then let us sum them up under the name of productive or creative art.

Theaet. Very good.

Str. Next follows the whole class of learning and cognition; then comes trade, fighting, hunting. And since none of these produces anything, but is only engaged in conquering by word or deed, or in preventing others from conquering, things which exist and have been already produced—in each and all of these branches there appears to be an art which may be called acquisitive.

Theaet. Yes, that is the proper name.

Str. Seeing, then, that all arts are either acquisitive or creative, in which class shall we place the art of the angler?

Theaet. Clearly in the acquisitive class.

Str. And the acquisitive may be subdivided into two parts: there is exchange, which is voluntary and is effected by gifts, hire, purchase; and the other part of acquisitive, which takes by force of word or deed, may be termed conquest?

Theaet. That is implied in what has been said.

Str. And may not conquest be again subdivided?

Theaet. How?

Str. Open force may be called fighting, and secret force may have the general name of hunting?

Theaet. Yes.

Str. And there is no reason why the art of hunting should not be further divided.

Theaet. How would you make the division?

Str. Into the hunting of living and of lifeless prey.

Theaet. Yes, if both kinds exist.

Str. Of course they exist; but the hunting after lifeless things having no special name, except some sorts of diving, and other small matters, may be omitted; the hunting after living things may be called animal hunting.

The angler is to be placed in the acquisitive class.

Acquisition is voluntary (=exchange) or forcible (=conquest).

Conquest is open (=fighting) or secret (=hunting).

220

There is hunting of animals, and

Theaet. Yes.

Str. And animal hunting may be truly said to have two divisions, land-animal hunting, which has many kinds and names, and water-animal hunting, or the hunting after animals who swim?

Theaet. True.

Str. And of swimming animals, one class lives on the wing and the other in the water?

Theaet. Certainly.

Str. Fowling is the general term under which the hunting of all birds is included.

Theaet. True.

Str. The hunting of animals who live in the water has the general name of fishing.

Theaet. Yes.

Str. And this sort of hunting may be further divided also into two principal kinds?

Theaet. What are they?

Str. There is one kind which takes them in nets, another which takes them by a blow.

Theaet. What do you mean, and how do you distinguish them?

Str. As to the first kind—all that surrounds and encloses anything to prevent egress, may be rightly called an enclosure.

Theaet. Very true.

Str. For which reason twig baskets, casting-nets, nooses, creels, and the like may all be termed 'enclosures'?

Theaet. True.

Str. And therefore this first kind of capture may be called by us capture with enclosures, or something of that sort?

Theaet. Yes.

Str. The other kind, which is practised by a blow with hooks and three-pronged spears, when summed up under one name, may be called striking, unless you, Theaetetus, can find some better name?

Theaet. Never mind the name—what you suggest will do very well.

Str. There is one mode of striking, which is done at night, and by the light of a fire, and is by the hunters themselves called firing, or spearing by firelight.

Theaet. True.

Str. And the fishing by day is called by the general name of barbing, because the spears, too, are barbed at the point.

Theaet. Yes, that is the term.

Str. Of this barb-fishing, that which strikes the fish who is be-

of lifeless
prey;

the former includes the hunting of land animals and of water animals.
Water animals live on the wing or in the water:
the fowler hunts the former, the fisherman the latter.

There are two kinds of fishing—
fishing with enclosures and by striking.

There is striking by day, and striking by night: the former is called barbing.

The angler hooked

Sophist

STRANGER,
THEAE-
TETUS.

Barbing is
of two
kinds,—
spearing
[221]
and AN-
GLING.

Recapitu-
lation.

The defi-
nition of
the So-
phist:

Like the
angler, he
is a skilled
person.

and a
hunter,—
not how-

low from above is called spearing, because this is the way in which the three-pronged spears are mostly used.

Theaet. Yes, it is often called so.

Str. Then now there is only one kind remaining.

Theaet. What is that?

Str. When a hook is used, and the fish is not struck in any chance part of his body, as he is with the spear, but only about the head and mouth, and is then drawn out from below upwards with reeds and rods:—What is the right name of that mode of fishing, Theaetetus?

Theaet. I suspect that we have now discovered the object of our search.

Str. Then now you and I have come to an understanding not only about the name of the angler's art, but about the definition of the thing itself. One half of all art was acquisitive—half of the acquisitive art was conquest or taking by force, half of this was hunting, and half of hunting was hunting animals, half of this was hunting water animals—of this again, the under half was fishing, half of fishing was striking; a part of striking was fishing with a barb, and one half of this again, being the kind which strikes with a hook and draws the fish from below upwards, is the art which we have been seeking, and which from the nature of the operation is denoted angling or drawing up (ἀσπαλιευτική, ἀνασπᾶσθαι).

Theaet. The result has been quite satisfactorily brought out.

Str. And now, following this pattern, let us endeavour to find out what a Sophist is.

Theaet. By all means.

Str. The first question about the angler was, whether he was a skilled artist or unskilled?

Theaet. True.

Str. And shall we call our new friend unskilled, or a thorough master of his craft?

Theaet. Certainly not unskilled, for his name, as, indeed, you imply, must surely express his nature.

Str. Then he must be supposed to have some art.

Theaet. What art?

Str. By heaven, they are cousins! it never occurred to us.

Theaet. Who are cousins?

Str. The angler and the Sophist.

Theaet. In what way are they related?

Str. They both appear to me to be hunters.

Theaet. How the Sophist? Of the other we have spoken.

Str. You remember our division of hunting, into hunting after swimming animals and land animals?

Theaet. Yes.

Str. And you remember that we subdivided the swimming and left the land animals, saying that there were many kinds of them?

Theaet. Certainly.

Str. Thus far, then, the Sophist and the angler, starting from the art of acquiring, take the same road?

Theaet. So it would appear.

Str. Their paths diverge when they reach the art of animal hunting; the one going to the sea-shore, and to the rivers and to the lakes, and angling for the animals which are in them.

Theaet. Very true.

Str. While the other goes to land and water of another sort— rivers of wealth and broad meadow-lands of generous youth; and he also is intending to take the animals which are in them.

Theaet. What do you mean?

Str. Of hunting on land there are two principal divisions.

Theaet. What are they?

Str. One is the hunting of tame, and the other of wild animals.

Theaet. But are tame animals ever hunted?

Str. Yes, if you include man under tame animals. But if you like you may say that there are no tame animals, or that, if there are, man is not among them; or you may say that man is a tame animal but is not hunted—you shall decide which of these alternatives you prefer.

Theaet. I should say, Stranger, that man is a tame animal, and I admit that he is hunted.

Str. Then let us divide the hunting of tame animals into two parts.

Theaet. How shall we make the division?

Str. Let us define piracy, man-stealing, tyranny, the whole military art, by one name, as hunting with violence.

Theaet. Very good.

Str. But the art of the lawyer, of the popular orator, and the art of conversation may be called in one word the art of persuasion.

Theaet. True.

Str. And of persuasion, there may be said to be two kinds?

Theaet. What are they?

Str. One is private, and the other public.

Theaet. Yes; each of them forms a class.

Sophist

STRANGER,
THEAE-
TETUS.

222

ever of a swimming, but of a land animal— man.

The angler goes to the rivers and to the sea; the Sophist to the broad meadowlands of youth.

Hunting on land is of tame and of wild animals.

Under tame animals man is included.

Tame animals are hunted with violence, or by persuasion.

Persuasion is public or private.

The
hunter in
private
brings
gifts, like
the
lover, or
receives
hire.

The hire-
ling may
seek to
give
[223]
pleasure,
or to
teach
virtue.

The latter
is the So-
PHIST.

Recapitu-
lation.

A new
defini-
tion:

Acquisi-
tion is
partly
hunting,
partly ex-
change;
and the
latter

Str. And of private hunting, one sort receives hire, and the other brings gifts.

Theaet. I do not understand you.

Str. You seem never to have observed the manner in which lovers hunt.

Theaet. To what do you refer?

Str. I mean that they lavish gifts on those whom they hunt in addition to other inducements.

Theaet. Most true.

Str. Let us admit this, then, to be the amatory art.

Theaet. Certainly.

Str. But that sort of hireling whose conversation is pleasing and who baits his hook only with pleasure and exacts nothing but his maintenance in return, we should all, if I am not mistaken, describe as possessing flattery or an art of making things pleasant.

Theaet. Certainly.

Str. And that sort, which professes to form acquaintances only for the sake of virtue, and demands a reward in the shape of money, may be fairly called by another name?

Theaet. To be sure.

Str. And what is the name? Will you tell me?

Theaet. It is obvious enough; for I believe that we have discovered the Sophist: which is, as I conceive, the proper name for the class described.

Str. Then now, Theaetetus, his art may be traced as a branch of the appropriative [1], acquisitive family—which hunts animals, —living—land—tame animals; which hunts man,—privately— for hire,—taking money in exchange—having the semblance of education; and this is termed Sophistry, and is a hunt after young men of wealth and rank—such is the conclusion.

Theaet. Just so.

Str. Let us take another branch of his genealogy; for he is a professor of a great and many-sided art; and if we look back at what has preceded we see that he presents another aspect, besides that of which we are speaking.

Theaet. In what respect?

Str. There were two sorts of acquisitive art; the one concerned with hunting, the other with exchange.

Theaet. There were.

Str. And of the art of exchange there are two divisions, the one of giving, and the other of selling.

Theaet. Let us assume that.

[1] Omitting χειρωτικῆς and πεζοθηρίας.

Str. Next, we will suppose the art of selling to be divided into two parts.

Theaet. How?

Str. There is one part which is distinguished as the sale of a man's own productions; another, which is the exchange of the works of others.

Theaet. Certainly.

Str. And is not that part of exchange which takes place in the city, being about half of the whole, termed retailing?

Theaet. Yes.

Str. And that which exchanges the goods of one city for those of another by selling and buying is the exchange of the merchant?

Theaet. To be sure.

Str. And you are aware that this exchange of the merchant is of two kinds: it is partly concerned with food for the use of the body, and partly with the food of the soul which is bartered and received in exchange for money.

Theaet. What do you mean?

Str. You want to know what is the meaning of food for the soul; the other kind you surely understand.

Theaet. Yes.

Str. Take music in general and painting and marionette playing and many other things, which are purchased in one city, and carried away and sold in another—wares of the soul which are hawked about either for the sake of instruction or amusement;— may not he who takes them about and sells them be quite as truly called a merchant as he who sells meats and drinks?

Theaet. To be sure he may.

Str. And would you not call by the same name him who buys up knowledge and goes about from city to city exchanging his wares for money?

Theaet. Certainly I should.

Str. Of this merchandise of the soul, may not one part be fairly termed the art of display? And there is another part which is certainly not less ridiculous, but being a trade in learning must be called by some name germane to the matter?

Theaet. Certainly.

Str. The latter should have two names,—one descriptive of the sale of the knowledge of virtue, and the other of the sale of other kinds of knowledge.

Theaet. Of course.

Str. The name of art-seller corresponds well enough to the latter; but you must try and tell me the name of the other.

Sophist

STRANGER, THEAE- TETUS.

partly giving, partly selling.

The seller may sell his own productions, or exchange those of others: the exchanger may be a retailer or a merchant.

The merchant may sell food for the body [224] or food for the soul.

The latter may be supplied by the art of display or by a trade in learning.

The trader in

Theaet. He must be the Sophist, whom we are seeking; no other name can possibly be right.

Str. No other; and so this trader in virtue again turns out to be our friend the Sophist, whose art may now be traced from the art of acquisition through exchange, trade, merchandise, to a merchandise of the soul which is concerned with speech and the knowledge of virtue.

Theaet. Quite true.

Str. And there may be a third reappearance of him;—for he may have settled down in a city, and may fabricate as well as buy these same wares, intending to live by selling them, and he would still be called a Sophist?

Theaet. Certainly.

Str. Then that part of acquisitive art which exchanges, and of exchange which either sells a man's own productions or retails those of others, as the case may be, and in either way sells the knowledge of virtue, you would again term Sophistry?

Theaet. I must, if I am to keep pace with the argument.

Str. Let us consider once more whether there may not be yet another aspect of sophistry.

Theaet. What is it?

Str. In the acquisitive there was a subdivision of the combative or fighting art.

Theaet. There was.

Str. Perhaps we had better divide it.

Theaet. What shall be the divisions?

Str. There shall be one division of the competitive, and another of the pugnacious.

Theaet. Very good.

Str. That part of the pugnacious which is a contest of bodily strength may be properly called by some such name as violent.

Theaet. True.

Str. And when the war is one of words, it may be termed controversy?

Theaet. Yes.

Str. And controversy may be of two kinds.

Theaet. What are they?

Str. When long speeches are answered by long speeches, and there is public discussion about the just and unjust, that is forensic controversy.

Theaet. Yes.

Str. And there is a private sort of controversy, which is cut up into questions and answers, and this is commonly called disputation?

Theaet. Yes, that is the name.

Str. And of disputation, that sort which is only a discussion about contracts, and is carried on at random, and without rules of art, is recognized by the reasoning faculty to be a distinct class, but has hitherto had no distinctive name, and does not deserve to receive one from us.

Theaet. No; for the different sorts of it are too minute and heterogeneous.

Str. But that which proceeds by rules of art to dispute about justice and injustice in their own nature, and about things in general, we have been accustomed to call argumentation (Eristic)?

Theaet. Certainly.

Str. And of argumentation, one sort wastes money, and the other makes money.

Theaet. Very true.

Str. Suppose we try and give to each of these two classes a name.

Theaet. Let us do so.

Str. I should say that the habit which leads a man to neglect his own affairs for the pleasure of conversation, of which the style is far from being agreeable to the majority of his hearers, may be fairly termed loquacity: such is my opinion.

Theaet. That is the common name for it.

Str. But now who the other is, who makes money out of private disputation, it is your turn to say.

Theaet. There is only one true answer: he is the wonderful Sophist, of whom we are in pursuit, and who reappears again for the fourth time.

Str. Yes, and with a fresh pedigree, for he is the money-making species of the Eristic, disputatious, controversial, pugnacious, combative, acquisitive family, as the argument has already proven.

Theaet. Certainly.

Str. How true was the observation that he was a many-sided animal, and not to be caught with one hand, as they say!

Theaet. Then you must catch him with two.

Str. Yes, we must, if we can. And therefore let us try another track in our pursuit of him: You are aware that there are certain menial occupations which have names among servants?

Theaet. Yes, there are many such; which of them do you mean?

Str. I mean such as sifting, straining, winnowing, threshing [1].

---

[1] Reading δίνειν, a conjecture of Professor Campbell's.

Sophist

STRANGER
THEAE-
TETUS.

kinds, public (forensic) and private (disputation).

Disputation, when proceeding by rules of art, is called argumentation; and this either wastes or makes money.

That which makes money is [226] the art of the So-PHIST.

Another track: There are arts of dividing used by servants.

Theaet. Certainly.

Str. And besides these there are a great many more, such as carding, spinning, adjusting the warp and the woof; and thousands of similar expressions are used in the arts.

Theaet. Of what are they to be patterns, and what are we going to do with them all?

Str. I think that in all of these there is implied a notion of division.

Theaet. Yes.

These afford examples of the great art of discerning,

Str. Then if, as I was saying, there is one art which includes all of them, ought not that art to have one name?

Theaet. And what is the name of the art?

Str. The art of discerning or discriminating.

Theaet. Very good.

Str. Think whether you cannot divide this.

Theaet. I should have to think a long while.

which either separates like from like, or the better from the worse.

Str. In all the previously named processes either like has been separated from like or the better from the worse.

Theaet. I see now what you mean.

Str. There is no name for the first kind of separation; of the second, which throws away the worse and preserves the better, I do know a name.

Theaet. What is it?

In the latter case it is called purification.

Str. Every discernment or discrimination of that kind, as I have observed, is called a purification.

Theaet. Yes, that is the usual expression.

Str. And any one may see that purification is of two kinds.

Theaet. Perhaps so, if he were allowed time to think; but I do not see at this moment.

Str. There are many purifications of bodies which may with propriety be comprehended under a single name.

Theaet. What are they, and what is their name?

227

Purification is of bodies animate (which may be internal or external), and of bodies inanimate: the latter

Str. There is the purification of living bodies in their inward and in their outward parts, of which the former is duly effected by medicine and gymnastic, the latter by the not very dignified art of the bath-man; and there is the purification of inanimate substances—to this the arts of fulling and of furbishing in general attend in a number of minute particulars, having a variety of names which are thought ridiculous.

Theaet. Very true.

Str. There can be no doubt that they are thought ridiculous, Theaetetus; but then the dialectical art never considers whether the benefit to be derived from the purge is greater or less than that to be derived from the sponge, and has not more interest in the one than in the other; her endeavour is to know what is and is not kindred in all arts, with a view to the acquisition of intelligence; and having this in view, she honours them all alike, and when she makes comparisons, she counts one of them not a whit more ridiculous than another; nor does she esteem him who adduces as his example of hunting, the general's art, at all more decorous than another who cites that of the vermin-destroyer, but only as the greater pretender of the two. And as to your question concerning the name which was to comprehend all these arts of purification, whether of animate or inanimate bodies, the art of dialectic is in no wise particular about fine words, if she may be only allowed to have a general name for all other purifications, binding them up together and separating them off from the purification of the soul or intellect. For this is the purification at which she wants to arrive, and this we should understand to be her aim.

sort has
ridiculous
names ap-
plied to it.

But scien-
tific
method
ignores
distinc-
tions of
high and
low.

There is
also a
purifica-
tion of
the soul.

Theaet. Yes, I understand; and I agree that there are two sorts of purification, and that one of them is concerned with the soul, and that there is another which is concerned with the body.

Str. Excellent; and now listen to what I am going to say, and try to divide further the first of the two.

Theaet. Whatever line of division you suggest, I will endeavour to assist you.

Str. Do we admit that virtue is distinct from vice in the soul?

Theaet. Certainly.

Str. And purification was to leave the good and to cast out whatever is bad?

Theaet. True.

Str. Then any taking away of evil from the soul may be properly called purification?

Theaet. Yes.

Str. And in the soul there are two kinds of evil.

Theaet. What are they?

Str. The one may be compared to disease in the body, the other to deformity.

Theaet. I do not understand.

Str. Perhaps you have never reflected that disease and discord are the same.

Theaet. To this, again, I know not what I should reply.

Str. Do you not conceive discord to be a dissolution of kindred elements, originating in some disagreement?

Theaet. Just that.

228
There are
two evils
of the
body,—
disease or
discord,
and de-
formity
or want
of
measure;

Str. And is deformity anything but the want of measure, which is always unsightly?

Theaet. Exactly.

Str. And do we not see that opinion is opposed to desire, pleasure to anger, reason to pain, and that all these elements are opposed to one another in the souls of bad men?

Theaet. Certainly.

and two
corre-
sponding
evils of
the
soul,—
vice and
ignorance.

Str. And yet they must all be akin?

Theaet. Of course.

Str. Then we shall be right in calling vice a discord and disease of the soul?

Theaet. Most true.

Str. And when things having motion, and aiming at an appointed mark, continually miss their aim and glance aside, shall we say that this is the effect of symmetry among them, or of the want of symmetry?

Theaet. Clearly of the want of symmetry.

Str. But surely we know that no soul is voluntarily ignorant of anything?

Theaet. Certainly not.

Str. And what is ignorance but the aberration of a mind which is bent on truth, and in which the process of understanding is perverted?

Theaet. True.

Str. Then we are to regard an unintelligent soul as deformed and devoid of symmetry?

Theaet. Very true.

Str. Then there are these two kinds of evil in the soul—the one which is generally called vice, and is obviously a disease of the soul . . .

Theaet. Yes.

Str. And there is the other, which they call ignorance, and which, because existing only in the soul [1], they will not allow to be vice.

Theaet. I certainly admit what I at first disputed—that there are two kinds of vice in the soul, and that we ought to consider cowardice, intemperance, and injustice to be all alike forms of disease in the soul, and ignorance, of which there are all sorts of varieties, to be deformity.

Str. And in the case of the body are there not two arts which have to do with the two bodily states?

Theaet. What are they?

---

[1] Or, 'although there is no other vice in the soul but this.'

Sophist

229
STRANGER,
THEAE-
TETUS.

Str. There is gymnastic, which has to do with deformity, and medicine, which has to do with disease.

Theaet. True.

Str. And where there is insolence and injustice and cowardice, is not chastisement the art which is most required [1]?

Theaet. That certainly appears to be the opinion of mankind.

Str. Again, of the various kinds of ignorance, may not instruction be rightly said to be the remedy?

Theaet. True.

Str. And of the art of instruction, shall we say that there is one or many kinds? At any rate there are two principal ones. Think.

Theaet. I will.

Str. I believe that I can see how we shall soonest arrive at the answer to this question.

Theaet. How?

Str. If we can discover a line which divides ignorance into two halves. For a division of ignorance into two parts will certainly imply that the art of instruction is also two-fold, answering to the two divisions of ignorance.

Theaet. Well, and do you see what you are looking for?

Str. I do seem to myself to see one very large and bad sort of ignorance which is quite separate, and may be weighed in the scale against all other sorts of ignorance put together.

Theaet. What is it?

Str. When a person supposes that he knows, and does not know; this appears to be the great source of all the errors of the intellect.

Theaet. True.

Str. And this, if I am not mistaken, is the kind of ignorance which specially earns the title of stupidity.

Theaet. True.

Str. What name, then, shall be given to the sort of instruction which gets rid of this?

Theaet. The instruction which you mean, Stranger, is, I should imagine, not the teaching of handicraft arts, but what, thanks to us, has been termed education in this part of the world.

Str. Yes, Theaetetus, and by nearly all Hellenes. But we have still to consider whether education admits of any further division.

Theaet. We have.

Str. I think that there is a point at which such a division is possible.

Theaet. Where?

of the body are medicine and gymnastic.

The arts which take away the evils of the soul are correction and instruction.

A division of instruction can only be obtained by dividing ignorance.

One sort of ignorance is unconscious.

The instruction corresponding to this is called education.

[1] Omitting δίκη, or reading δίκῃ.

Sophist

STRANGER,
THEAE-
TETUS.

230
Of edu-
cation
there are
two
kinds: the
old ad-
monitory
system,
based on
the doc-
trine that
ignorance
is volun-
tary, and
another,
based on
the oppo-
site doc-
trine,
which
proceeds
by driv-
ing men
into
contra-
dictions
and so
teaching
them to
think;
and by
refuting
them and
purging
away
their
preju-
dices and
vanity.

Refuta-
tion is the
greatest
of purifi-
cations.

Str. Of education, one method appears to be rougher, and another smoother.

Theaet. How are we to distinguish the two?

Str. There is the time-honoured mode which our fathers commonly practised towards their sons, and which is still adopted by many—either of roughly reproving their errors, or of gently advising them; which varieties may be correctly included under the general term of admonition.

Theaet. True.

Str. But whereas some appear to have arrived at the conclusion that all ignorance is involuntary, and that no one who thinks himself wise is willing to learn any of those things in which he is conscious of his own cleverness, and that the admonitory sort of instruction gives much trouble and does little good——

Theaet. There they are quite right.

Str. Accordingly, they set to work to eradicate the spirit of conceit in another way.

Theaet. In what way?

Str. They cross-examine a man's words, when he thinks that he is saying something and is really saying nothing, and easily convict him of inconsistencies in his opinions; these they then collect by the dialectical process, and placing them side by side, show that they contradict one another about the same things, in relation to the same things, and in the same respect. He, seeing this, is angry with himself, and grows gentle towards others, and thus is entirely delivered from great prejudices and harsh notions, in a way which is most amusing to the hearer, and produces the most lasting good effect on the person who is the subject of the operation. For as the physician considers that the body will receive no benefit from taking food until the internal obstacles have been removed, so the purifier of the soul is conscious that his patient will receive no benefit from the application of knowledge until he is refuted, and from refutation learns modesty; he must be purged of his prejudices first and made to think that he knows only what he knows, and no more.

Theaet. That is certainly the best and wisest state of mind.

Str. For all these reasons, Theaetetus, we must admit that refutation is the greatest and chiefest of purifications, and he who has not been refuted, though he be the Great King himself, is in an awful state of impurity; he is uninstructed and deformed in those things in which he who would be truly blessed ought to be fairest and purest.

Theaet. Very true.

Str. And who are the ministers of this art? I am afraid to say the Sophists.

Theaet. Why?

Str. Lest we should assign to them too high a prerogative.

Theaet. Yet the Sophist has a certain likeness to our minister of purification.

Str. Yes, the same sort of likeness which a wolf, who is the fiercest of animals, has to a dog, who is the gentlest. But he who would not be found tripping, ought to be very careful in this matter of comparisons, for they are most slippery things. Nevertheless, let us assume that the Sophists are the men. I say this provisionally, for I think that the line which divides them will be marked enough if proper care is taken.

Theaet. Likely enough.

Str. Let us grant, then, that from the discerning art comes purification, and from purification let there be separated off a part which is concerned with the soul; of this mental purification instruction is a portion, and of instruction education, and of education, that refutation of vain conceit which has been discovered in the present argument; and let this be called by you and me the nobly-descended art of Sophistry.

Theaet. Very well; and yet, considering the number of forms in which he has presented himself, I begin to doubt how I can with any truth or confidence describe the real nature of the Sophist.

Str. You naturally feel perplexed; and yet I think that he must be still more perplexed in his attempt to escape us, for as the proverb says, when every way is blocked, there is no escape; now, then, is the time of all others to set upon him.

Theaet. True.

Str. First let us wait a moment and recover breath, and while we are resting, we may reckon up in how many forms he has appeared. In the first place, he was discovered to be a paid hunter after wealth and youth.

Theaet. Yes.

Str. In the second place, he was a merchant in the goods of the soul.

Theaet. Certainly.

Str. In the third place, he has turned out to be a retailer of the same sort of wares.

Theaet. Yes; and in the fourth place, he himself manufactured the learned wares which he sold.

Let us assume that the Sophist practises this art.

Recapitulation.

Thus far the Sophist has been (1) a paid hunter of wealth and youth;

(2) a merchant in the goods of the soul;

Sophist

STRANGER,
THEAE-
  TETUS.

(3) a re-
tailer,

and (4) a
manufac-
turer of
    [232]
learned
wares;

(5) a hero
of de-
bate;

(6) a
purger of
souls.

But what
is the
common
principle
which
unites his
many
callings?

His chief
charac-
teristic is
disputa-
tion and
the teach-
ing of dis-
putation.

Str. Quite right; I will try and remember the fifth myself. He belonged to the fighting class, and was further distinguished as a hero of debate, who professed the eristic art.

Theaet. True.

Str. The sixth point was doubtful, and yet we at last agreed that he was a purger of souls, who cleared away notions obstructive to knowledge.

Theaet. Very true.

Str. Do you not see that when the professor of any art has one name and many kinds of knowledge, there must be something wrong? The multiplicity of names which is applied to him shows that the common principle to which all these branches of knowledge are tending, is not understood.

Theaet. I should imagine this to be the case.

Str. At any rate we will understand him, and no indolence shall prevent us. Let us begin again, then, and re-examine some of our statements concerning the Sophist; there was one thing which appeared to me especially characteristic of him.

Theaet. To what are you referring?

Str. We were saying of him, if I am not mistaken, that he was a disputer?

Theaet. We were.

Str. And does he not also teach others the art of disputation?

Theaet. Certainly he does.

Str. And about what does he profess that he teaches men to dispute? To begin at the beginning—Does he make them able to dispute about divine things, which are invisible to men in general?

Theaet. At any rate, he is said to do so.

Str. And what do you say of the visible things in heaven and earth, and the like?

Theaet. Certainly he disputes, and teaches to dispute about them.

Str. Then, again, in private conversation, when any universal assertion is made about generation and essence, we know that such persons are tremendous argufiers, and are able to impart their own skill to others.

Theaet. Undoubtedly.

Str. And do they not profess to make men able to dispute about law and about politics in general?

Theaet. Why, no one would have anything to say to them, if they did not make these professions.

Str. In all and every art, what the craftsman ought to say in

answer to any question is written down in a popular form, and he
who likes may learn.

Theaet. I suppose that you are referring to the precepts of Protagoras about wrestling and the other arts?

Str. Yes, my friend, and about a good many other things. In a
word, is not the art of disputation a power of disputing about all
things?

Theaet. Certainly; there does not seem to be much which is left
out.

Str. But oh! my dear youth, do you suppose this possible? for
perhaps your young eyes may see things which to our duller sight
do not appear.

Theaet. To what are you alluding? I do not think that I understand your present question.

Str. I ask whether anybody can understand all things.

Theaet. Happy would mankind be if such a thing were possible!

Str. But how can any one who is ignorant dispute in a rational
manner against him who knows?

Theaet. He cannot.

Str. Then why has the sophistical art such a mysterious power?

Theaet. To what do you refer?

Str. How do the Sophists make young men believe in their supreme and universal wisdom? For if they neither disputed nor were
thought to dispute rightly, or being thought to do so were deemed
no wiser for their controversial skill, then, to quote your own observation, no one would give them money or be willing to learn
their art.

Theaet. They certainly would not.

Str. But they are willing.

Theaet. Yes, they are.

Str. Yes, and the reason, as I should imagine, is that they are
supposed to have knowledge of those things about which they
dispute?

Theaet. Certainly.

Str. And they dispute about all things?

Theaet. True.

Str. And therefore, to their disciples, they appear to be all-wise?

Theaet. Certainly.

Str. But they are not; for that was shown to be impossible.

Theaet. Impossible, of course.

Str. Then the Sophist has been shown to have a sort of conjec-
tural or apparent knowledge only of all things, which is not the
truth?

Let us, as
an illus-
tration,
imagine a
creator of
all things,
which he
makes by
a single
art and
with the
greatest
ease.—
What
would he
be?

234

Theaet. Exactly; no better description of him could be given.

Str. Let us now take an illustration, which will still more clearly explain his nature.

Theaet. What is it?

Str. I will tell you, and you shall answer me, giving your very closest attention. Suppose that a person were to profess, not that he could speak or dispute, but that he knew how to make and do all things, by a single art.

Theaet. All things?

Str. I see that you do not understand the first word that I utter, for you do not understand the meaning of 'all.'

Theaet. No, I do not.

Str. Under all things, I include you and me, and also animals and trees.

Theaet. What do you mean?

Str. Suppose a person to say that he will make you and me, and all creatures.

Theaet. What would he mean by 'making'? He cannot be a husbandman;—for you said that he is a maker of animals.

Str. Yes; and I say that he is also the maker of the sea, and the earth, and the heavens, and the gods, and of all other things; and, further, that he can make them in no time, and sell them for a few pence.

Theaet. That must be a jest.

Str. And when a man says that he knows all things, and can teach them to another at a small cost, and in a short time, is not that a jest?

Theaet. Certainly.

Str. And is there any more artistic or graceful form of jest than imitation?

Theaet. Certainly not; and imitation is a very comprehensive term, which includes under one class the most diverse sorts of things.

Not really
a maker,
but a
painter or
imitator.

Str. We know, of course, that he who professes by one art to make all things is really a painter, and by the painter's art makes resemblances of real things which have the same name with them; and he can deceive the less intelligent sort of young children, to whom he shows his pictures at a distance, into the belief that he has the absolute power of making whatever he likes.

Theaet. Certainly.

So there is
an imi-
tative art
of reason-

Str. And may there not be supposed to be an imitative art of reasoning? Is it not possible to enchant the hearts of young men by words poured through their ears, when they are still at a distance from the truth of facts, by exhibiting to them fictitious arguments, and making them think that they are true, and that the speaker is the wisest of men in all things?

Theaet. Yes; why should there not be another such art?

Str. But as time goes on, and their hearers advance in years, and come into closer contact with realities, and have learnt by sad experience to see and feel the truth of things, are not the greater part of them compelled to change many opinions which they formerly entertained, so that the great appears small to them, and the easy difficult, and all their dreamy speculations are overturned by the facts of life?

Theaet. That is my view, as far as I can judge, although, at my age, I may be one of those who see things at a distance only.

Str. And the wish of all of us, who are your friends, is and always will be to bring you as near to the truth as we can without the sad reality. And now I should like you to tell me, whether the Sophist is not visibly a magician and imitator of true being; or are we still disposed to think that he may have a true knowledge of the various matters about which he disputes?

Theaet. But how can he, Stranger? Is there any doubt, after what has been said, that he is to be located in one of the divisions of children's play?

Str. Then we must place him in the class of magicians and mimics.

Theaet. Certainly we must.

Str. And now our business is not to let the animal out, for we have got him in a sort of dialectical net, and there is one thing which he decidedly will not escape.

Theaet. What is that?

Str. The inference that he is a juggler.

Theat. Precisely my own opinion of him.

Str. Then, clearly, we ought as soon as possible to divide the image-making art, and go down into the net, and, if the Sophist does not run away from us, to seize him according to orders and deliver him over to reason, who is the lord of the hunt, and proclaim the capture of him; and if he creeps into the recesses of the imitative art, and secretes himself in one of them, to divide again and follow him up until in some sub-section of imitation he is caught. For our method of tackling each and all is one which neither he nor any other creature will ever escape in triumph.

Theaet. Well said; and let us do as you propose.

Str. Well, then, pursuing the same analytic method as before, I think that I can discern two divisions of the imitative art, but I

ing which imposes upon youth, who see truth only at a distance.

235
The Sophist is a magician and imitator.

Accordingly we must subdivide imitation.

Two kinds of

Sophist

STRANGER,
THEAE-
TETUS.

imitation:
—There is
(1) like-
ness-mak-
ing which
repro-
duces
exactly
    [236]
the pro-
portions
of the
original.

But in
colossal
works of
painting
and sculp-
ture a cer-
tain
amount
of decep-
tion is
neces-
sary;

and there-
fore
(2) there
is another
kind of
imitation,
phantas-
tic, which
makes ap-
pearances.

am not as yet able to see in which of them the desired form is to
be found.

Theaet. Will you tell me first what are the two divisions of
which you are speaking?

Str. One is the art of likeness-making;—generally a likeness of
anything is made by producing a copy which is executed according
to the proportions of the original, similar in length and breadth and
depth, each thing receiving also its appropriate colour.

Theaet. Is not this always the aim of imitation?

Str. Not always; in works either of sculpture or of painting,
which are of any magnitude, there is a certain degree of deception;
for if artists were to give the true proportions of their fair works,
the upper part, which is farther off, would appear to be out of proportion in comparison with the lower, which is nearer; and so
they give up the truth in their images and make only the proportions which appear to be beautiful, disregarding the real ones.

Theaet. Quite true.

Str. And that which being other is also like, may we not fairly
call a likeness or image?

Theaet. Yes.

Str. And may we not, as I did just now, call that part of the imitative art which is concerned with making such images the art of
likeness-making?

Theaet. Let that be the name.

Str. And what shall we call those resemblances of the beautiful,
which appear such owing to the unfavourable position of the spectator, whereas if a person had the power of getting a correct view
of works of such magnitude, they would appear not even like that
to which they profess to be like? May we not call these 'appearances,' since they appear only and are not really like?

Theaet. Certainly.

Str. There is a great deal of this kind of thing in painting, and
in all imitation.

Theaet. Of course.

Str. And may we not fairly call the sort of art, which produces
an appearance and not an image, phantastic art?

Theaet. Most fairly.

Str. These then are the two kinds of image-making—the art of
making likenesses, and phantastic or the art of making appearances?

Theaet. True.

Str. I was doubtful before in which of them I should place the
Sophist, nor am I even now able to see clearly; verily he is a

wonderful and inscrutable creature. And now in the cleverest manner he has got into an impossible place.

Theaet. Yes, he has.

Str. Do you speak advisedly, or are you carried away at the moment by the habit of assenting into giving a hasty answer?

Theaet. May I ask to what you are referring?

Str. My dear friend, we are engaged in a very difficult speculation—there can be no doubt of that; for how a thing can appear and seem, and not be, or how a man can say a thing which is not true, has always been and still remains a very perplexing question. Can any one say or think that falsehood really exists, and avoid being caught in a contradiction? Indeed, Theaetetus, the task is a difficult one.

Theaet. Why?

Str. He who says that falsehood exists has the audacity to assert the being of not-being; for this is implied in the possibility of falsehood. But, my boy, in the days when I was a boy, the great Parmenides protested against this doctrine, and to the end of his life he continued to inculcate the same lesson—always repeating both in verse and out of verse:

'Keep your mind from this way of enquiry, for never will you show [1] that not-being is.'

Such is his testimony, which is confirmed by the very expression when sifted a little. Would you object to begin with the consideration of the words themselves?

Theaet. Never mind about me; I am only desirous that you should carry on the argument in the best way, and that you should take me with you.

Str. Very good; and now say, do we venture to utter the forbidden word 'not-being'?

Theaet. Certainly we do.

Str. Let us be serious then, and consider the question neither in strife nor play: suppose that one of the hearers of Parmenides was asked, 'To what is the term "not-being" to be applied?'—do you know what sort of object he would single out in reply, and what answer he would make to the enquirer?

Theaet. That is a difficult question, and one not to be answered at all by a person like myself.

Str. There is at any rate no difficulty in seeing that the predicate 'not-being' is not applicable to any being.

Theaet. None, certainly.

[1] Reading τοῦτο φανῇ.

Sophist

STRANGER,
THEAE-
TETUS.

In which
shall we
place the
Sophist?

A grave
difficulty:
[237]
If false-
hood can
exist,
then what
is not
must be.

But Par-
menides
always
denied the
existence
of not-
being.

Let us
ask: Of
what is
not-being
predi-
cable?

Certainly
not of
any being,

and there-
fore not
of some-
thing, or
of two or
more
things.

Str. And if not to being, then not to something.

Theaet. Of course not.

Str. It is also plain, that in speaking of something we speak of being, for to speak of an abstract something naked and isolated from all being is impossible.

Theaet. Impossible.

Str. You mean by assenting to imply that he who says something must say some one thing?

Theaet. Yes.

Str. Some in the singular (τὶ) you would say is the sign of one, some in the dual (τινὲ) of two, some in the plural (τινὲς) of many?

Theaet. Exactly.

Str. Then he who says 'not something' must say absolutely nothing.

Theaet. Most assuredly.

It is
nothing;

Str. And as we cannot admit that a man speaks and says nothing, he who says 'not-being' does not speak at all.

Theaet. The difficulty of the argument can no further go.

238

Str. Not yet, my friend, is the time for such a word; for there still remains of all perplexities the first and greatest, touching the very foundation of the matter.

Theaet. What do you mean? Do not be afraid to speak.

Str. To that which is, may be attributed some other thing which is?

Theaet. Certainly.

and
nothing
that is
can be
predi-
cated of
it; and
therefore
not num-
ber
either
singular
or plural.

Str. But can anything which is, be attributed to that which is not?

Theaet. Impossible.

Str. And all number is to be reckoned among things which are?

Theaet. Yes, surely number, if anything, has a real existence.

Str. Then we must not attempt to attribute to not-being number either in the singular or plural?

Theaet. The argument implies that we should be wrong in doing so.

Str. But how can a man either express in words or even conceive in thought things which are not or a thing which is not without number?

Theaet. How indeed?

And yet
we do
speak of
not-being,

Str. When we speak of things which are not, are we not attributing plurality to not-being?

Theaet. Certainly.

Str. But, on the other hand, when we say 'what is not,' do we not attribute unity?

Theaet. Manifestly.

Str. Nevertheless, we maintain that you may not and ought not to attribute being to not-being?

Theaet. Most true.

Str. Do you see, then, that not-being in itself can neither be spoken, uttered, or thought, but that it is unthinkable, unutterable, unspeakable, indescribable?

Theaet. Quite true.

Str. But, if so, I was wrong in telling you just now that the difficulty which was coming is the greatest of all.

Theaet. What! is there a greater still behind?

Str. Well, I am surprised, after what has been said already, that you do not see the difficulty in which he who would refute the notion of not-being is involved. For he is compelled to contradict himself as soon as he makes the attempt.

Theaet. What do you mean? Speak more clearly.

Str. Do not expect clearness from me. For I, who maintain that not-being has no part either in the one or many, just now spoke and am still speaking of not-being as one; for I say 'not-being.' Do you understand?

Theaet. Yes.

Str. And a little while ago I said that not-being is unutterable, unspeakable, indescribable: do you follow?

Theaet. I do after a fashion.

Str. When I introduced the word 'is,' did I not contradict what I said before?

Theaet. Clearly.

Str. And in using the singular verb, did I not speak of not-being as one?

Theaet. Yes.

Str. And when I spoke of not-being as indescribable and unspeakable and unutterable, in using each of these words in the singular, did I not refer to not-being as one?

Theaet. Certainly.

Str. And yet we say that, strictly speaking, it should not be defined as one or many, and should not even be called 'it,' for the use of the word 'it' would imply a form of unity.

Theaet. Quite true.

Str. How, then, can any one put any faith in me? For now, as always, I am unequal to the refutation of not-being. And there-

Sophist

STRANGER, THEAE-TETUS.

both in the singular and plural.

The greatest difficulty: The mere use of the word is a contradiction.

239

Sophist

STRANGER,
THEAE-
TETUS.

Let the
youthful
might of
Theae-
tetus try
to find
some bet-
ter ex-
pression.

fore, as I was saying, do not look to me for the right way of speaking about not-being; but come, let us try the experiment with you.

Theaet. What do you mean?

Str. Make a noble effort, as becomes youth, and endeavour with all your might to speak of not-being in a right manner, without introducing into it either existence or unity or plurality.

Theaet. It would be a strange boldness in me which would attempt the task when I see you thus discomfited.

Str. Say no more of ourselves; but until we find some one or other who can speak of not-being without number, we must acknowledge that the Sophist is a clever rogue who will not be got out of his hole.

Theaet. Most true.

Str. And if we say to him that he professes an art of making appearances, he will grapple with us and retort our argument upon ourselves; and when we call him an image-maker he will say, 'Pray what do you mean at all by an image?'—and I should like to know, Theaetetus, how we can possibly answer the younker's question?

Theaet. We shall doubtless tell him of the images which are reflected in water or in mirrors; also of sculptures, pictures, and other duplicates.

Str. I see, Theaetetus, that you have never made the acquaintance of the Sophist.

Theaet. Why do you think so?

Str. He will make believe to have his eyes shut, or to have none.

Theaet. What do you mean?

Str. When you tell him of something existing in a mirror, or in sculpture, and address him as though he had eyes, he will laugh you to scorn, and will pretend that he knows nothing of mirrors and streams, or of sight at all; he will say that he is asking about an idea.

Theaet. What can he mean?

Str. The common notion pervading all these objects, which you speak of as many, and yet call by the single name of image, as though it were the unity under which they were all included. How will you maintain your ground against him?

Theaet. How, Stranger, can I describe an image except as something fashioned in the likeness of the true?

Str. And do you mean this something to be some other true thing, or what do you mean?

Theaet. Certainly not another true thing, but only a resemblance.

If we call
the So-
phist an
image-
maker, he
will ask
us, out of
his hole,
'What is
an
image?'—
and will
be satis-
fied with
nothing
short of a
definition
of the
idea of it.

240

It is a re-
semblance
of the
true or
real, and
is not it-
self real.

Str. And you mean by true that which really is?

Theaet. Yes.

Str. And the not true is that which is the opposite of the true?

Theaet. Exactly.

Str. A resemblance, then, is not really real, if, as you say, not true?

Theaet. Nay, but it is in a certain sense.

Str. You mean to say, not in a true sense?

Theaet. Yes; it is in reality only an image.

Str. Then what we call an image is in reality really unreal.

Theaet. In what a strange complication of being and not-being we are involved!

Str. Strange! I should think so. See how, by his reciprocation of opposites, the many-headed Sophist has compelled us, quite against our will, to admit the existence of not-being.

Theaet. Yes, indeed, I see.

Str. The difficulty is how to define his art without falling into a contradiction.

Theaet. How do you mean? And where does the danger lie?

Str. When we say that he deceives us with an illusion, and that his art is illusory, do we mean that our soul is led by his art to think falsely, or what do we mean?

Theaet. There is nothing else to be said.

Str. Again, false opinion is that form of opinion which thinks the opposite of the truth:—You would assent?

Theaet. Certainly.

Str. You mean to say that false opinion thinks what is not?

Theaet. Of course.

Str. Does false opinion think that things which are not are not, or that in a certain sense they are?

Theaet. Things that are not must be imagined to exist in a certain sense, if any degree of falsehood is to be possible.

Str. And does not false opinion also think that things which most certainly exist do not exist at all?

Theaet. Yes.

Str. And here, again, is falsehood?

Theaet. Falsehood—yes.

Str. And in like manner, a false proposition will be deemed to be one which asserts the non-existence of things which are, and the existence of things which are not.

Theaet. There is no other way in which a false proposition can arise.

Str. There is not; but the Sophist will deny these statements.

Yet it has a sort of reality.

It is really unreal.

And thus we are forced to admit the existence of not-being.

Our definition of the Sophist's art, which creates false opinion, or again of a false proposition will contain the same paradox.

Sophist

STRANGER,
THEAE-
TETUS.

The So-
phist will
show us
no mercy.

And indeed how can any rational man assent to them, when the very expressions which we have just used were before acknowledged by us to be unutterable, unspeakable, indescribable, unthinkable? Do you see his point, Theaetetus?

Theaet. Of course he will say that we are contradicting ourselves when we hazard the assertion, that falsehood exists in opinion and in words; for in maintaining this, we are compelled over and over again to assert being of not-being, which we admitted just now to be an utter impossibility.

Str. How well you remember! And now it is high time to hold a consultation as to what we ought to do about the Sophist; for if we persist in looking for him in the class of false workers and magicians, you see that the handles for objection and the difficulties which will arise are very numerous and obvious.

Theaet. They are indeed.

Str. We have gone through but a very small portion of them, and they are really infinite.

Theaet. If that is the case, we cannot possibly catch the Sophist.

Str. Shall we then be so faint-hearted as to give him up?

Theaet. Certainly not, I should say, if we can get the slightest hold upon him.

Str. Will you then forgive me, and, as your words imply, not be altogether displeased if I flinch a little from the grasp of such a sturdy argument?

Theaet. To be sure I will.

Str. I have a yet more urgent request to make.

Theaet. Which is—?

Str. That you will promise not to regard me as a parricide.

Theaet. And why?

There is
one way
of escape:
we must
put the
revered
words of
Parmen-
ides to the
test, and
prove
that there
is a sense
in which
[242]
not-being
is and
being is
not.

Str. Because, in self-defence, I must test the philosophy of my father Parmenides, and try to prove by main force that in a certain sense not-being is, and that being, on the other hand, is not.

Theaet. Some attempt of the kind is clearly needed.

Str. Yes, a blind man, as they say, might see that, and, unless these questions are decided in one way or another, no one when he speaks of false words, or false opinion, or idols, or images, or imitations, or appearances, or about the arts which are concerned with them, can avoid falling into ridiculous contradictions.

Theaet. Most true.

Str. And therefore I must venture to lay hands on my father's argument; for if I am to be over-scrupulous, I shall have to give the matter up.

Theaet. Nothing in the world should ever induce us to do so.

Str. I have a third little request which I wish to make.

Theaet. What is it?

Str. You heard me say what I have always felt and still feel—that I have no heart for this argument?

Theaet. I did.

Str. I tremble at the thought of what I have said, and expect that you will deem me mad, when you hear of my sudden changes and shiftings; let me therefore observe, that I am examining the question entirely out of regard for you.

Theaet. There is no reason for you to fear that I shall impute any impropriety to you, if you attempt this refutation and proof; take heart, therefore, and proceed.

Str. And where shall I begin the perilous enterprise? I think that the road which I must take is—

Theaet. Which?—Let me hear.

Str. I think that we had better, first of all, consider the points which at present are regarded as self-evident, lest we may have fallen into some confusion, and be too ready to assent to one another, fancying that we are quite clear about them.

Theaet. Say more distinctly what you mean.

Str. I think that Parmenides, and all who ever yet undertook to determine the number and nature of existences, talked to us in rather a light and easy strain.

Theaet. How?

Str. As if we had been children, to whom they repeated each his own mythus or story;—one said that there were three principles, and that at one time there was war between certain of them; and then again there was peace, and they were married and begat children, and brought them up; and another spoke of two principles,—a moist and a dry, or a hot and a cold, and made them marry and cohabit. The Eleatics, however, in our part of the world, say that all things are many in name, but in nature one; this is their mythus, which goes back to Xenophanes, and is even older. Then there are Ionian, and in more recent times Sicilian muses, who have arrived at the conclusion that to unite the two principles is safer, and to say that being is one and many, and that these are held together by enmity and friendship, ever parting, ever meeting, as the severer Muses assert, while the gentler ones do not insist on the perpetual strife and peace, but admit a relaxation and alternation of them; peace and unity sometimes prevailing under the sway of Aphrodite, and then again plurality and war, by reason of a principle of strife. Whether any of them spoke the truth in all this is hard to determine; besides, antiquity and famous men

We must examine some ideas which are thought to be clear, but may prove to be confused.

The early Greek philosophers and their doctrines.

Sophist

STRANGER,
THEAE-
TETUS.

These
great men
did not
care to
explain
them-
selves to
the com-
mon herd.

In the
days of
our youth
we
seemed to
under-
stand
what not-
being
meant:
now we
are in
difficulties
about
being.

Let us
examine
the notion
in the
light of
existing
philoso-
phies.
First, let
us ask the
dualists
whether
being is a
third
principle
over and
above the
other two,
or one of
them or
both. In
any case
the two
principles

should have reverence, and not be liable to accusations so serious. Yet one thing may be said of them without offence—

Theaet. What thing?

Str. That they went on their several ways disdaining to notice people like ourselves; they did not care whether they took us with them, or left us behind them.

Theaet. How do you mean?

Str. I mean to say, that when they talk of one, two, or more elements, which are or have become or are becoming, or again of heat mingling with cold, assuming in some other part of their works separations and mixtures,—tell me, Theaetetus, do you understand what they mean by these expressions? When I was a younger man, I used to fancy that I understood quite well what was meant by the term 'not-being,' which is our present subject of dispute; and now you see in what a fix we are about it.

Theaet. I see.

Str. And very likely we have been getting into the same perplexity about 'being,' and yet may fancy that when anybody utters the word, we understand him quite easily, although we do not know about not-being. But we may be equally ignorant of both.

Theaet. I dare say.

Str. And the same may be said of all the terms just mentioned.

Theaet. True.

Str. The consideration of most of them may be deferred; but we had better now discuss the chief captain and leader of them.

Theaet. Of what are you speaking? You clearly think that we must first investigate what people mean by the word 'being.'

Str. You follow close at my heels, Theaetetus. For the right method, I conceive, will be to call into our presence the dualistic philosophers and to interrogate them. 'Come,' we will say, 'Ye, who affirm that hot and cold or any other two principles are the universe, what is this term which you apply to both of them, and what do you mean when you say that both and each of them "are"? How are we to understand the word "are"? Upon your view, are we to suppose that there is a third principle over and above the other two,—three in all, and not two? For clearly you cannot say that one of the two principles is being, and yet attribute being equally to both of them; for, if you did, whichever of the two is identified with being, will comprehend the other; and so they will be one and not two.'

Theaet. Very true.

Str. But perhaps you mean to give the name of 'being' to both of them together?

Theaet. Quite likely.

Str. 'Then, friends,' we shall reply to them, 'the answer is plainly that the two will still be resolved into one.'

Theaet. Most true.

Str. 'Since then, we are in a difficulty, please to tell us what you mean, when you speak of being; for there can be no doubt that you always from the first understood your own meaning, whereas we once thought that we understood you, but now we are in a great strait. Please to begin by explaining this matter to us, and let us no longer fancy that we understand you, when we entirely misunderstand you.' There will be no impropriety in our demanding an answer to this question, either of the dualists or of the pluralists?

Theaet. Certainly not.

Str. And what about the assertors of the oneness of the all— must we not endeavour to ascertain from them what they mean by 'being'?

Theaet. By all means.

Str. Then let them answer this question: One, you say, alone is? 'Yes,' they will reply.

Theaet. True.

Str. And there is something which you call 'being'?

Theaet. 'Yes.'

Str. And is being the same as one, and do you apply two names to the same thing?

Theaet. What will be their answer, Stranger?

Str. It is clear, Theaetetus, that he who asserts the unity of being will find a difficulty in answering this or any other question.

Theaet. Why so?

Str. To admit of two names, and to affirm that there is nothing but unity, is surely ridiculous?

Theaet. Certainly.

Str. And equally irrational to admit that a name is anything?

Theaet. How so?

Str. To distinguish the name from the thing, implies duality.

Theaet. Yes.

Str. And yet he who identifies the name with the thing will be compelled to say that it is the name of nothing, or if he says that it is the name of something, even then the name will only be the name of a name, and of nothing else.

Theaet. True.

will be
resolved
into one.

What
again do
those who
assert the
oneness
of the
all mean
by being?
Are being
and unity
two
names for
the same
thing?—
But to
admit
this, or to
admit
that the
name is
different
from the
thing, is
to admit
plurality.

And if the
name be
identified
with the
thing, it is
either the
name of

Sophist

STRANGER,
THEAE-
TETUS.

nothing
or of a
name.
This is
true of
the one.

They
identify
the whole
with the
one which
is: but a
whole, as
[245]
having
parts,
cannot
be abso-
lute
unity,
which is
indi-
visible.

Str. And the one will turn out to be only one of one, [1] and being absolute unity, will represent a mere name [1].

Theaet. Certainly.

Str. And would they say that the whole is other than the one that is, or the same with it?

Theaet. To be sure they would, and they actually say so.

Str. If being is a whole, as Parmenides sings,—

> 'Every way like unto the fullness of a well-rounded sphere,
> Evenly balanced from the centre on every side,
> And must needs be neither greater nor less in any way,
> Neither on this side nor on that—'

then being has a centre and extremes, and, having these, must also have parts.

Theaet. True.

Str. Yet that which has parts may have the attribute of unity in all the parts, and in this way being all and a whole, may be one?

Theaet. Certainly.

Str. But that of which this is the condition cannot be absolute unity?

Theaet. Why not?

Str. Because, according to right reason, that which is truly one must be affirmed to be absolutely indivisible.

Theaet. Certainly.

Str. But this indivisible, if made up of many parts, will contradict reason.

Theaet. I understand.

Is being,
then, one
by par-
ticipation
in unity,
or is it not
a whole?

In either
case we
have to
admit
plurality.

Str. Shall we say that being [2] is one and a whole, because it has the attribute of unity? Or shall we say that being is not a whole at all?

Theaet. That is a hard alternative to offer.

Str. Most true; for being, having in a certain sense the attribute of one, is yet proved not to be the same as one, and the all is therefore more than one.

Theaet. Yes.

Str. And yet if being be not a whole, through having the attribute of unity, and there be such a thing as an absolute whole, being lacks something of its own nature?

Theaet. Certainly.

Str. Upon this view, again, being, having a defect of being, will become not-being?

Theaet. True.

[1] Reading with the MSS. καὶ τοῦ ὀνόματος αὐτὸ ἓν ὄν.
[2] Reading τὸ ὄν.

Str. And, again, the all becomes more than one, for being and the whole will each have their separate nature.

Theaet. Yes.

Str. But if the whole does not exist at all, all the previous difficulties remain the same, and there will be the further difficulty, that besides having no being, being can never have come into being.

Theaet. Why so?

Str. Because that which comes into being always comes into being as a whole, so that he who does not give whole a place among beings, cannot speak either of essence or generation as existing.

Theaet. Yes, that certainly appears to be true.

Str. Again; how can that which is not a whole have any quantity? For that which is of a certain quantity must necessarily be the whole of that quantity.

Theaet. Exactly.

Str. And there will be innumerable other points, each of them causing infinite trouble to him who says that being is either one or two.

Theaet. The difficulties which are dawning upon us prove this; for one objection connects with another, and they are always involving what has preceded in a greater and worse perplexity.

Str. We are far from having exhausted the more exact thinkers who treat of being and not-being. But let us be content to leave them, and proceed to view those who speak less precisely; and we shall find as the result of all, that the nature of being is quite as difficult to comprehend as that of not-being.

Theaet. Then now we will go to the others.

Str. There appears to be a sort of war of Giants and Gods going on amongst them; they are fighting with one another about the nature of essence.

Theaet. How is that?

Str. Some of them are dragging down all things from heaven and from the unseen to earth, and they literally grasp in their hands rocks and oaks; of these they lay hold, and obstinately maintain, that the things only which can be touched or handled have being or essence, because they define being and body as one, and if any one else says that what is not a body exists they altogether despise him, and will hear of nothing but body.

Theaet. I have often met with such men, and terrible fellows they are.

Str. And that is the reason why their opponents cautiously de-

And if the whole does not exist at all, being cannot have come into being; for everything which comes into being, comes into being as a whole.

Nor can it partake of quantity.

246

Let us now ask the Materialists and Idealists to give an account of essence.

fend themselves from above, out of an unseen world, mightily contending that true essence consists of certain intelligible and incorporeal ideas; the bodies of the materialists, which by them are maintained to be the very truth, they break up into little bits by their arguments, and affirm them to be, not essence, but generation and motion. Between the two armies, Theaetetus, there is always an endless conflict raging concerning these matters.

Theaet. True.

Str. Let us ask each party in turn, to give an account of that which they call essence.

Theaet. How shall we get it out of them?

Str. With those who make being to consist in ideas, there will be less difficulty, for they are civil people enough; but there will be very great difficulty, or rather an absolute impossibility, in getting an opinion out of those who drag everything down to matter. Shall I tell you what we must do?

Theaet. What?

Str. Let us, if we can, really improve them; but if this is not possible, let us imagine them to be better than they are, and more willing to answer in accordance with the rules of argument, and then their opinion will be more worth having; for that which better men acknowledge has more weight than that which is acknowledged by inferior men. Moreover we are no respecters of persons, but seekers after truth.

Theaet. Very good.

Str. Then now, on the supposition that they are improved, let us ask them to state their views, and do you interpret them.

Theaet. Agreed.

Str. Let them say whether they would admit that there is such a thing as a mortal animal.

Theaet. Of course they would.

Str. And do they not acknowledge this to be a body having a soul?

Theaet. Certainly they do.

Str. Meaning to say the soul is something which exists?

Theaet. True.

Str. And do they not say that one soul is just, and another unjust, and that one soul is wise, and another foolish?

Theaet. Certainly.

Str. And that the just and wise soul becomes just and wise by the possession of justice and wisdom[1], and the opposite under opposite circumstances?

[1] Reading with Professor Campbell δικαιοσύνης ἕξει καὶ φρονήσεως.

The Idealists are civil enough, but the Materialists must be improved before they can be reasoned with.

The latter would admit that in the mortal animal there is a soul, and that the soul may [247] be just and wise; and whatever they may say of soul, they would never venture to

Theaet. Yes, they do.

Str. But surely that which may be present or may be absent will be admitted by them to exist?

Theaet. Certainly.

Str. And, allowing that justice, wisdom, the other virtues, and their opposites exist, as well as a soul in which they inhere, do they affirm any of them to be visible and tangible, or are they all invisible?

Theaet. They would say that hardly any of them are visible.

Str. And would they say that they are corporeal?

Theaet. They would distinguish: the soul would be said by them to have a body; but as to the other qualities of justice, wisdom, and the like, about which you asked, they would not venture either to deny their existence, or to maintain that they were all corporeal.

Str. Verily, Theaetetus, I perceive a great improvement in them; the real aborigines, children of the dragon's teeth, would have been deterred by no shame at all, but would have obstinately asserted that nothing is which they are not able to squeeze in their hands.

Theaet. That is pretty much their notion.

Str. Let us push the question; for if they will admit that any, even the smallest particle of being, is incorporeal, it is enough; they must then say what that nature is which is common to both the corporeal and incorporeal, and which they have in their mind's eye when they say of both of them that they 'are.' Perhaps they may be in a difficulty; and if this is the case, there is a possibility that they may accept a notion of ours respecting the nature of being, having nothing of their own to offer.

Theaet. What is the notion? Tell me, and we shall soon see.

Str. My notion would be, that anything which possesses any sort of power to affect another, or to be affected by another, if only for a single moment, however trifling the cause and however slight the effect, has real existence; and I hold that the definition of being is simply power.

Theaet. They accept your suggestion, having nothing better of their own to offer.

Str. Very good; perhaps we, as well as they, may one day change our minds; but, for the present, this may be regarded as the understanding which is established with them.

Theaet. Agreed.

Str. Let us now go to the friends of ideas; of their opinions, too, you shall be the interpreter.

Theaet. I will.

assert that the moral qualities are corporeal.

What is the nature, common to the corporeal and incorporeal, which we indicate when we say that both 'are'?

It is a power of affecting and being affected by another.

248

Now we turn to the friends of

ideas.—
They
acknowl-
edge a
distinc-
tion
between
genera-
tion and
essence,
and that
we parti-
cipate in
the
former
with the
body and
in the lat-
ter with
the soul.

And what
is this
participa-
tion?
Is it to be
defined,
like being,
to be a
power of
doing and
suffering?

But they
deny the
appro-
priateness
of this
definition
of being.

They ad-
mit how-
ever that
the soul
knows
and that
being is
known.
But
knowing
and being
known
are active

Str. To them we say—You would distinguish essence from generation?

Theaet. 'Yes,' they reply.

Str. And you would allow that we participate in generation with the body, and through perception, but we participate with the soul through thought in true essence; and essence you would affirm to be always the same and immutable, whereas generation or becoming varies?

Theaet. Yes; that is what we should affirm.

Str. Well, fair sirs, we say to them, what is this participation, which you assert of both? Do you agree with our recent definition?

Theaet. What definition?

Str. We said that being was an active or passive energy, arising out of a certain power which proceeds from elements meeting with one another. Perhaps your ears, Theaetetus, may fail to catch their answer, which I recognize because I have been accustomed to hear it.

Theaet. And what is their answer?

Str. They deny the truth of what we were just now saying to the aborigines about existence.

Theaet. What was that?

Str. Any power of doing or suffering in a degree however slight was held by us to be a sufficient definition of being?

Theaet. True.

Str. They deny this, and say that the power of doing or suffering is confined to becoming, and that neither power is applicable to being.

Theaet. And is there not some truth in what they say?

Str. Yes; but our reply will be that we want to ascertain from them more distinctly, whether they further admit that the soul knows, and that being or essence is known.

Theaet. There can be no doubt that they say so.

Str. And is knowing and being known doing or suffering, or both, or is the one doing and the other suffering, or has neither any share in either?

Theaet. Clearly, neither has any share in either; for if they say anything else, they will contradict themselves.

Str. I understand; but they will allow that if to know is active, then, of course, to be known is passive. And on this view being, in so far as it is known, is acted upon by knowledge, and is therefore in motion; for that which is in a state of rest cannot be acted upon, as we affirm.

Theaet. True.

Str. And, O heavens, can we ever be made to believe that motion and life and soul and mind are not present with perfect being? Can we imagine that being is devoid of life and mind, and exists in awful unmeaningness an everlasting fixture?

Theaet. That would be a dreadful thing to admit, Stranger.

Str. But shall we say that being has mind and not life?

Theaet. How is that possible?

Str. Or shall we say that both inhere in perfect being, but that it has no soul which contains them?

Theaet. And in what other way can it contain them?

Str. Or that being has mind and life and soul, but although endowed with soul remains absolutely unmoved?

Theaet. All three suppositions appear to me to be irrational.

Str. Under being, then, we must include motion, and that which is moved.

Theaet. Certainly.

Str. Then, Theaetetus, our inference is, that if there is no motion, neither is there any mind anywhere, or about anything or belonging to any one.

Theaet. Quite true.

Str. And yet this equally follows, if we grant that all things are in motion—upon this view too mind has no existence.

Theaet. How so?

Str. Do you think that sameness of condition and mode and subject could ever exist without a principle of rest?

Theaet. Certainly not.

Str. Can you see how without them mind could exist, or come into existence anywhere?

Theaet. No.

Str. And surely contend we must in every possible way against him who would annihilate knowledge and reason and mind, and yet ventures to speak confidently about anything.

Theaet. Yes, with all our might.

Str. Then the philosopher, who has the truest reverence for these qualities, cannot possibly accept the notion of those who say that the whole is at rest, either as unity or in many forms: and he will be utterly deaf to those who assert universal motion. As children say entreatingly 'Give us both,' so he will include both the moveable and immoveable in his definition of being and all.

Theaet. Most true.

Str. And now, do we seem to have gained a fair notion of being?

Theaet. Yes truly.

Str. Alas, Theaetetus, methinks that we are now only beginning

249
Sophist

STRANGER,
THEAE-
TETUS.

and passive.

If being is acted upon, it must be in motion, —an attribute which, with life and soul, certainly belongs to perfect being.

But rest, as well as motion, is necessary to the existence of mind;

and the philosopher will demand both.

to see the real difficulty of the enquiry into the nature of it.

Theaet. What do you mean?

Str. O my friend, do you not see that nothing can exceed our ignorance, and yet we fancy that we are saying something good?

Theaet. I certainly thought that we were; and I do not at all understand how we never found out our desperate case.

250
We must
question
ourselves
as we
ques-
tioned
the Dual-
ists.—
Rest and
motion,
we say,
both
exist:
but what
is
existence?

Str. Reflect: after having made these admissions, may we not be justly asked the same questions which we ourselves were asking of those who said that all was hot and cold?

Theaet. What were they? Will you recall them to my mind?

Str. To be sure I will, and I will remind you of them, by putting the same questions to you which I did to them, and then we shall get on.

Theaet. True.

Str. Would you not say that rest and motion are in the most entire opposition to one another?

Theaet. Of course.

Str. And yet you would say that both and either of them equally are?

Theaet. I should.

Str. And when you admit that both or either of them are, do you mean to say that both or either of them are in motion?

Theaet. Certainly not.

Str. Or do you wish to imply that they are both at rest, when you say that they are?

Theaet. Of course not.

It is some
third
thing in-
cluding
rest and
motion,
yet nei-
ther of
them.

Str. Then you conceive of being as some third and distinct nature, under which rest and motion are alike included; and, observing that they both participate in being, you declare that they are.

Theaet. Truly we seem to have an intimation that being is some third thing, when we say that rest and motion are.

Str. Then being is not the combination of rest and motion, but something different from them.

Theaet. So it would appear.

Str. Being, then, according to its own nature, is neither in motion nor at rest.

Theaet. That is very much the truth.

Str. Where, then, is a man to look for help who would have any clear or fixed notion of being in his mind?

Theaet. Where, indeed?

Str. I scarcely think that he can look anywhere; for that which is not in motion must be at rest, and again, that which is not at rest must be in motion; but being is placed outside of both these classes. Is this possible?

Theaet. Utterly impossible.

Str. Here, then, is another thing which we ought to bear in mind.

Theaet. What?

Str. When we were asked to what we were to assign the appellation of not-being, we were in the greatest difficulty:—do you remember?

Theaet. To be sure.

Str. And are we not now in as great a difficulty about being?

Theaet. I should say, Stranger, that we are in one which is, if possible, even greater.

Str. Then let us acknowledge the difficulty; and as being and not-being are involved in the same perplexity, there is hope that when the one appears more or less distinctly, the other will equally appear; and if we are able to see neither, there may still be a chance of steering our way in between them, without any great discredit.

Theaet. Very good.

Str. Let us enquire, then, how we come to predicate many names of the same thing.

Theaet. Give an example.

Str. I mean that we speak of man, for example, under many names—that we attribute to him colours and forms and magnitudes and virtues and vices, in all of which instances and in ten thousand others we not only speak of him as a man, but also as good, and having numberless other attributes, and in the same way anything else which we originally supposed to be one is described by us as many, and under many names.

Theaet. That is true.

Str. And thus we provide a rich feast for tyros, whether young or old; for there is nothing easier than to argue that the one cannot be many, or the many one; and great is their delight in denying that a man is good; for man, they insist, is man and good is good. I dare say that you have met with persons who take an interest in such matters—they are often elderly men, whose meagre sense is thrown into amazement by these discoveries of theirs, which they believe to be the height of wisdom.

Theaet. Certainly, I have.

Str. Then, not to exclude any one who has ever speculated at all upon the nature of being, let us put our questions to them as well as to our former friends.

Theaet. What questions?

thing be neither at rest nor in motion?

We are as perplexed about existence or being as we were about not-being.

251

A way of escape: How is predication possible?

Let us interrogate those who deny it.

There are
three
alterna-
tives:—
(1) no
partici-
pation;
(2) indis-
    [252]
criminate
partici-
pation;
(3) par-
ticipation
of some
with
some.

The first
cannot be
accepted:
it is dis-
astrous to
all philo-
sophies,

Str. Shall we refuse to attribute being to motion and rest, or any-thing to anything, and assume that they do not mingle, and are incapable of participating in one another? Or shall we gather all into one class of things communicable with one another? Or are some things communicable and others not?—Which of these alter-natives, Theaetetus, will they prefer?

Theaet. I have nothing to answer on their behalf. Suppose that you take all these hypotheses in turn, and see what are the conse-quences which follow from each of them.

Str. Very good, and first let us assume them to say that nothing is capable of participating in anything else in any respect; in that case rest and motion cannot participate in being at all.

Theaet. They cannot.

Str. But would either of them be if not participating in being?

Theaet. No.

Str. Then by this admission everything is instantly overturned, as well the doctrine of universal motion as of universal rest, and also the doctrine of those who distribute being into immutable and everlasting kinds; for all these add on a notion of being, some affirming that things 'are' truly in motion, and others that they 'are' truly at rest.

Theaet. Just so.

Str. Again, those who would at one time compound, and at an-other resolve all things, whether making them into one and out of one creating infinity, or dividing them into finite elements, and forming compounds out of these; whether they suppose the pro-cesses of creation to be successive or continuous, would be talking nonsense in all this if there were no admixture.

Theaet. True.

and those
who as-
sert it,
contradict
them-
selves.

Str. Most ridiculous of all will the men themselves be who want to carry out the argument and yet forbid us to call anything, be-cause participating in some affection from another, by the name of that other.

Theaet. Why so?

Str. Why, because they are compelled to use the words 'to be,' 'apart,' 'from others,' 'in itself,' and ten thousand more, which they cannot give up, but must make the connecting links of discourse; and therefore they do not require to be refuted by others, but their enemy, as the saying is, inhabits the same house with them; they are always carrying about with them an adversary, like the won-derful ventriloquist, Eurycles, who out of their own bellies audibly contradicts them.

Theaet. Precisely so; a very true and exact illustration.

Str. And now, if we suppose that all things have the power of communion with one another—what will follow?

Theaet. Even I can solve that riddle.

Str. How?

Theaet. Why, because motion itself would be at rest, and rest again in motion, if they could be attributed to one another.

Str. But this is utterly impossible.

Theaet. Of course.

Str. Then only the third hypothesis remains.

Theaet. True.

Str. For, surely, either all things have communion with all; or nothing with any other thing; or some things communicate with some things and others not.

Theaet. Certainly.

Str. And two out of these three suppositions have been found to be impossible.

Theaet. Yes.

Str. Every one then, who desires to answer truly, will adopt the third and remaining hypothesis of the communion of some with some.

Theaet. Quite true.

Str. This communion of some with some may be illustrated by the case of letters; for some letters do not fit each other, while others do.

Theaet. Of course.

Str. And the vowels, especially, are a sort of bond which pervades all the other letters, so that without a vowel one consonant cannot be joined to another.

Theaet. True.

Str. But does every one know what letters will unite with what? Or is art required in order to do so [1]?

Theaet. Art is required.

Str. What art?

Theaet. The art of grammar.

Str. And is not this also true of sounds high and low?—Is not he who has the art to know what sounds mingle, a musician, and he who is ignorant, not a musician?

Theaet. Yes.

Str. And we shall find this to be generally true of art or the absence of art.

Theaet. Of course.

Str. And as classes are admitted by us in like manner to be

The second alternative is impossible; for if it were true, rest would move and motion would rest.

The third alternative of communion of some with some.

253
The analogy of letters, vowels and consonants,

and of musical notes.

---

[1] Reading δρᾶν ἱκανῶς αὐτά (? αὐτό).

As the
gram-
marian
and mu-
sician
know
what let-
ters and
notes
rightly
combine
with one
another,
so the
dialec-
tician
knows
what
classes
have
com-
munion
with each
other and
what not.

He is the
classifier
and only
true
philoso-
pher.

some of them capable and others incapable of intermixture, must
not he who would rightly show what kinds will unite and what will
not, proceed by the help of science in the path of argument? And
will he not ask if the connecting links are universal, and so capable of intermixture with all things; and again, in divisions,
whether there are not other universal classes, which make them
possible?

Theaet. To be sure he will require science, and, if I am not mistaken, the very greatest of all sciences.

Str. How are we to call it? By Zeus, have we not lighted unwittingly upon our free and noble science, and in looking for the
Sophist have we not entertained the philosopher unawares?

Theaet. What do you mean?

Str. Should we not say that the division according to classes,
which neither makes the same other, nor makes other the same, is
the business of the dialectical science?

Theaet. That is what we should say.

Str. Then, surely, he who can divide rightly is able to see clearly
one form pervading a scattered multitude, and many different
forms contained under one higher form; and again, one form knit
together into a single whole and pervading many such wholes, and
many forms, existing only in separation and isolation. This is the
knowledge of classes which determines where they can have communion with one another and where not.

Theaet. Quite true.

Str. And the art of dialectic would be attributed by you only to
the philosopher pure and true?

Theaet. Who but he can be worthy?

254   *Str.* In this region we shall always discover the philosopher, if
we look for him; like the Sophist, he is not easily discovered, but
for a different reason.

Theaet. For what reason?

Str. Because the Sophist runs away into the darkness of not-
being, in which he has learned by habit to feel about, and cannot
be discovered because of the darkness of the place. Is not that
true?

Theaet. It seems to be so.

The
philoso-
pher is
hidden
from ex-
cess of
light; the

Str. And the philosopher, always holding converse through
reason with the idea of being, is also dark from excess of light; for
the souls of the many have no eye which can endure the vision of
the divine.

Theaet. Yes; that seems to be quite as true as the other.

Str. Well, the philosopher may hereafter be more fully considered by us, if we are disposed; but the Sophist must clearly not be allowed to escape until we have had a good look at him.

Theaet. Very good.

Str. Since, then, we are agreed that some classes have a communion with one another, and others not, and some have communion with a few and others with many, and that there is no reason why some should not have universal communion with all, let us now pursue the enquiry, as the argument suggests, not in relation to all ideas, lest the multitude of them should confuse us, but let us select a few of those which are reckoned to be the principal ones, and consider their several natures and their capacity of communion with one another, in order that if we are not able to apprehend with perfect clearness the notions of being and not-being, we may at least not fall short in the consideration of them, so far as they come within the scope of the present enquiry, if peradventure we may be allowed to assert the reality of not-being, and yet escape unscathed.

Theaet. We must do so.

Str. The most important of all the genera are those which we were just now mentioning—being and rest and motion.

Theaet. Yes, by far.

Str. And two of these are, as we affirm, incapable of communion with one another.

Theaet. Quite incapable.

Str. Whereas being surely has communion with both of them, for both of them are?

Theaet. Of course.

Str. That makes up three of them.

Theaet. To be sure.

Str. And each of them is other than the remaining two, but the same with itself.

Theaet. True.

Str. But then, what is the meaning of these two words, 'same' and 'other'? Are they two new kinds other than the three, and yet always of necessity intermingling with them, and are we to have five kinds instead of three; or when we speak of the same and other, are we unconsciously speaking of one of the three first kinds?

Theaet. Very likely we are.

Str. But, surely, motion and rest are neither the other nor the same.

Sophist from the darkness of the place in which he lives.

Let us examine some of the principal kinds, with reference to their power of intercommunion.

Most important of all are being, rest, and motion, of which the two latter hold communion with being, but not with one another.

They are other than one another, but the same with themselves.

[255]

'Same' and 'other'

again are
two new
kinds.
For they
are not
identical
with mo-
tion and
rest;

nor is
being
identical
with 'the
same';

nor yet
with 'the
other,'
which is
relative
only, and
never
absolute.

Theaet. How is that?

Str. Whatever we attribute to motion and rest in common, cannot be either of them.

Theaet. Why not?

Str. Because motion would be at rest and rest in motion, for either of them, being predicated of both, will compel the other to change into the opposite of its own nature, because partaking of its opposite.

Theaet. Quite true.

Str. Yet they surely both partake of the same and of the other?

Theaet. Yes.

Str. Then we must not assert that motion, any more than rest, is either the same or the other.

Theaet. No; we must not.

Str. But are we to conceive that being and the same are identical?

Theaet. Possibly.

Str. But if they are identical, then again in saying that motion and rest have being, we should also be saying that they are the same.

Theaet. Which surely cannot be.

Str. Then being and the same cannot be one.

Theaet. Scarcely.

Str. Then we may suppose the same to be a fourth class, which is now to be added to the three others.

Theaet. Quite true.

Str. And shall we call the other a fifth class? Or should we consider being and other to be two names of the same class?

Theaet. Very likely.

Str. But you would agree, if I am not mistaken, that existences are relative as well as absolute?

Theaet. Certainly.

Str. And the other is always relative to other?

Theaet. True.

Str. But this would not be the case unless being and the other entirely differed; for, if the other, like being, were absolute as well as relative, then there would have been a kind of other which was not other than other. And now we find that what is other must of necessity be what it is in relation to some other.

Theaet. That is the true state of the case.

Str. Then we must admit the other as the fifth of our selected classes.

Theaet. Yes.

Str. And the fifth class pervades all classes, for they all differ from one another, not by reason of their own nature, but because they partake of the idea of the other.

Theaet. Quite true.

Str. Then let us now put the case with reference to each of the five.

Theaet. How?

Str. First there is motion, which we affirm to be absolutely 'other' than rest: what else can we say?

Theaet. It is so.

Str. And therefore is not rest.

Theaet. Certainly not.

Str. And yet is, because partaking of being.

Theaet. True.

Str. Again, motion is other than the same?

Theaet. Just so.

Str. And is therefore not the same.

Theaet. It is not.

Str. Yet, surely, motion is the same, because all things partake of the same.

Theaet. Very true.

Str. Then we must admit, and not object to say, that motion is the same and is not the same, for we do not apply the terms 'same' and 'not the same,' in the same sense; but we call it the 'same,' in relation to itself, because partaking of the same; and not the same, because having communion with the other, it is thereby severed from the same, and has become not that but other, and is therefore rightly spoken of as 'not the same.'

Theaet. To be sure.

Str. And if absolute motion in any point of view partook of rest, there would be no absurdity in calling motion stationary.

Theaet. Quite right,—that is, on the supposition that some classes mingle with one another, and others not.

Str. That such a communion of kinds is according to nature, we had already proved [1] before we arrived at this part of our discussion.

Theaet. Certainly.

Str. Let us proceed, then. May we not say that motion is other than the other, having been also proved by us to be other than the same and other than rest?

Theaet. That is certain.

This fifth class of 'the other' pervades all classes, and helps to distinguish them.

Thus motion is other [256] than rest,—i.e. is not rest; yet it *is,* since it partakes of being.

It is other than the same and not the same, but in different senses.

Again, motion is other than the other;

---

[1] Cp. *supra,* 252.

Str. Then, according to this view, motion is other and also not other?

Theaet. True.

Str. What is the next step? Shall we say that motion is other than the three and not other than the fourth,—for we agreed that there are five classes about and in the sphere of which we proposed to make enquiry?

Theaet. Surely we cannot admit that the number is less than it appeared to be just now.

Str. Then we may without fear contend that motion is other than being?

Theaet. Without the least fear.

Str. The plain result is that motion, since it partakes of being, really is and also is not?

Theaet. Nothing can be plainer.

Str. Then not-being necessarily exists in the case of motion and of every class; for the nature of the other entering into them all, makes each of them other than being, and so non-existent; and therefore of all of them, in like manner, we may truly say that they are not; and again, inasmuch as they partake of being, that they are and are existent.

Theaet. So we may assume.

Str. Every class, then, has plurality of being and infinity of not-being.

Theaet. So we must infer.

Str. And being itself may be said to be other than the other kinds.

Theaet. Certainly.

Str. Then we may infer that being is not, in respect of as many other things as there are; for not being these it is itself one, and is not the other things, which are infinite in number.

Theaet. That is not far from the truth.

Str. And we must not quarrel with this result, since it is of the nature of classes to have communion with one another; and if any one denies our present statement [viz. that being is not, etc.], let him first argue with our former conclusion [i.e. respecting the communion of ideas], and then he may proceed to argue with what follows.

Theaet. Nothing can be fairer.

Str. Let me ask you to consider a further question.

Theaet. What question?

Str. When we speak of not-being, we speak, I suppose, not of something opposed to being, but only different.

Theaet. What do you mean?

Str. When we speak of something as not great, does the expression seem to you to imply what is little any more than what is equal?

Theaet. Certainly not.

Str. The negative particles, οὐ and μή, when prefixed to words, do not imply opposition, but only difference from the words, or more correctly from the things represented by the words, which follow them.

Theaet. Quite true.

Str. There is another point to be considered, if you do not object.

Theaet. What is it?

Str. The nature of the other appears to me to be divided into fractions like knowledge.

Theaet. How so?

Str. Knowledge, like the other, is one; and yet the various parts of knowledge have each of them their own particular name, and hence there are many arts and kinds of knowledge.

Theaet. Quite true.

Str. And is not the case the same with the parts of the other, which is also one?

Theaet. Very likely; but will you tell me how?

Str. There is some part of the other which is opposed to the beautiful?

Theaet. There is.

Str. Shall we say that this has or has not a name?

Theaet. It has; for whatever we call not-beautiful is other than the beautiful, not than something else.

Str. And now tell me another thing.

Theaet. What?

Str. Is the not-beautiful anything but this—an existence parted off from a certain kind of existence, and again from another point of view opposed to an existing something?

Theaet. True.

Str. Then the not-beautiful turns out to be the opposition of being to being?

Theaet. Very true.

Str. But upon this view, is the beautiful a more real and the not-beautiful a less real existence?

Theaet. Not at all.

Str. And the not-great may be said to exist, equally with the great?

Theaet. Yes.

A negative particle does not imply opposition, but only difference.

The parts of otherness or difference and of knowledge correspond: the former are expressed by prefixing 'not' to the names of the corresponding parts of knowledge.

Thus the not-beautiful is the other of the beautiful, and is equally real with it.

258

And so of
other
things.

The op-
position
between
the parts
of being
and other
is also
being.

Not-being
is a kind
of being,

which in-
cludes all
things
other
than some
given
thing.

Str. And, in the same way, the just must be placed in the same category with the not-just—the one cannot be said to have any more existence than the other.

Theaet. True.

Str. The same may be said of other things; seeing that the nature of the other has a real existence, the parts of this nature must equally be supposed to exist.

Theaet. Of course.

Str. Then, as would appear, the opposition of a part of the other, and of a part of being, to one another, is, if I may venture to say so, as truly essence as being itself, and implies not the opposite of being, but only what is other than being.

Theaet. Beyond question.

Str. What then shall we call it?

Theaet. Clearly, not being; and this is the very nature for which the Sophist compelled us to search.

Str. And has not this, as you were saying, as real an existence as any other class? May I not say with confidence that not-being has an assured existence, and a nature of its own? Just as the great was found to be great and the beautiful beautiful, and the not-great not-great, and the not-beautiful not-beautiful, in the same manner not-being has been found to be and is not-being, and is to be reckoned one among the many classes of being. Do you, Theaetetus, still feel any doubt of this?

Theaet. None whatever.

Str. Do you observe that our scepticism has carried us beyond the range of Parmenides' prohibition?

Theaet. In what?

Str. We have advanced to a further point, and shown him more than he forbad us to investigate.

Theaet. How is that?

Str. Why, because he says—

'Not-being never is [1], and do thou keep thy thoughts from this way of enquiry.'

Theaet. Yes, he says so.

Str. Whereas, we have not only proved that things which are not are, but we have shown what form of being not-being is; for we have shown that the nature of the other is, and is distributed over all things in their relations to one another, and whatever part of the other is contrasted with being, this is precisely what we have ventured to call not-being.

[1] Reading τοῦτο φανῇ.

Theaet. And surely, Stranger, we were quite right.

Str. Let not any one say, then, that while affirming the opposition of not-being to being, we still assert the being of not-being; for as to whether there is an opposite of being, to that enquiry we have long said good-bye—it may or may not be, and may or may not be capable of definition. But as touching our present account of not-being, let a man either convince us of error, or, so long as he cannot, he too must say, as we are saying, that there is a communion of classes, and that being, and difference or other, traverse all things and mutually interpenetrate, so that the other partakes of being, and by reason of this participation is, and yet is not that of which it partakes, but other, and being other than being, it is clearly a necessity that not-being should be. And again, being, through partaking of the other, becomes a class other than the remaining classes, and being other than all of them, is not each one of them, and is not all the rest, so that undoubtedly there are thousands upon thousands of cases in which being is not, and all other things, whether regarded individually or collectively, in many respects are, and in many respects are not.

Theaet. True.

Str. And he who is sceptical of this contradiction, must think how he can find something better to say; or if he sees a puzzle, and his pleasure is to drag words this way and that, the argument will prove to him, that he is not making a worthy use of his faculties; for there is no charm in such puzzles, and there is no difficulty in detecting them; but we can tell him of something else the pursuit of which is noble and also difficult.

Theaet. What is it?

Str. A thing of which I have already spoken;—letting alone these puzzles as involving no difficulty, he should be able to follow and criticize in detail every argument, and when a man says that the same is in a manner other, or that other is the same, to understand and refute him from his own point of view, and in the same respect in which he asserts either of these affections. But to show that somehow and in some sense the same is other, or the other same, or the great small, or the like unlike; and to delight in always bringing forward such contradictions, is no real refutation, but is clearly the new-born babe of some one who is only beginning to approach the problem of being.

Theaet. To be sure.

Str. For certainly, my friend, the attempt to separate all existences from one another is a barbarism and utterly unworthy of an educated or philosophical mind.

Sophist

STRANGER,
THEAE-
TETUS.

259
Our
theory
rests upon
the com-
munion
of kinds.

We
should
let alone
verbal
puzzles.

The utter
separa-
tion of all
existences
would de-
prive us
of dis-
course,
and with-
out dis-
course we
could
have no
philoso-
phy.

Theaet. Why so?

Str. The attempt at universal separation is the final annihila-
tion of all reasoning; for only by the union of conceptions with one
another do we attain to discourse of reason.

Theaet. True.

Str. And, observe that we were only just in time in making a
resistance to such separatists, and compelling them to admit that
one thing mingles with another.

Theaet. Why so?

Str. Why, that we might be able to assert discourse to be a kind
of being; for if we could not, the worst of all consequences would
follow; we should have no philosophy. Moreover, the necessity for
determining the nature of discourse presses upon us at this moment; if utterly deprived of it, we could no more hold discourse;
and deprived of it we should be if we admitted that there was no
admixture of natures at all.

Theaet. Very true. But I do not understand why at this moment
we must determine the nature of discourse.

Str. Perhaps you will see more clearly by the help of the following explanation.

Theaet. What explanation?

Str. Not-being has been acknowledged by us to be one among
many classes diffused over all being.

Theaet. True.

Str. And thence arises the question, whether not-being mingles
with opinion and language.

Theaet. How so?

Str. If not-being has no part in the proposition, then all things
must be true; but if not-being has a part, then false opinion and
false speech are possible, for to think or to say what is not—is
falsehood, which thus arises in the region of thought and in speech.

Theaet. That is quite true.

Str. And where there is falsehood surely there must be deceit.

Theaet. Yes.

Str. And if there is deceit, then all things must be full of idols
and images and fancies.

Theaet. To be sure.

We left
the So-
phist, in
the region
of images,
denying
the possi-
bility of
false-
hood.
But now
that not-

Str. Into that region the Sophist, as we said, made his escape,
and, when he had got there, denied the very possibility of falsehood; no one, he argued, either conceived or uttered falsehood, inasmuch as not-being did not in any way partake of being.

Theaet. True.

Str. And now, not-being has been shown to partake of being,

and therefore he will not continue fighting in this direction, but he will probably say that some ideas partake of not-being, and some not, and that language and opinion are of the non-partaking class; and he will still fight to the death against the existence of the image-making and phantastic art, in which we have placed him, because, as he will say, opinion and language do not partake of not-being, and unless this participation exists, there can be no such thing as falsehood. And, with the view of meeting this evasion, we must begin by enquiring into the nature of language, opinion, and imagination, in order that when we find them we may find also that they have communion with not-being, and, having made out the connection of them, may thus prove that falsehood exists; and therein we will imprison the Sophist, if he deserves it, or, if not, we will let him go again and look for him in another class.

Theaet. Certainly, Stranger, there appears to be truth in what was said about the Sophist at first, that he was of a class not easily caught, for he seems to have abundance of defences, which he throws up, and which must every one of them be stormed before we can reach the man himself. And even now, we have with difficulty got through his first defence, which is the not-being of not-being, and lo! here is another; for we have still to show that falsehood exists in the sphere of language and opinion, and there will be another and another line of defence without end.

Str. Any one, Theaetetus, who is able to advance even a little ought to be of good cheer, for what would he who is dispirited at a little progress do, if he were making none at all, or even undergoing a repulse? Such a faint heart, as the proverb says, will never take a city: but now that we have succeeded thus far, the citadel is ours, and what remains is easier.

Theaet. Very true.

Str. Then, as I was saying, let us first of all obtain a conception of language and opinion, in order that we may have clearer grounds for determining, whether not-being has any concern with them, or whether they are both always true, and neither of them ever false.

Theaet. True.

Str. Then, now, let us speak of names, as before we were speaking of ideas and letters; for that is the direction in which the answer may be expected.

Theaet. And what is the question at issue about names?

Str. The question at issue is whether all names may be connected with one another, or none, or only some of them.

Theaet. Clearly the last is true.

being has been shown to partake of being, this line of defence can no [261] longer be maintained. Yet he will still evade us by denying that opinion and language partake of not-being.

We want to obtain a clear conception of language and opinion.

As with letters, so with names: only some

Str. I understand you to say that words which have a meaning when in sequence may be connected, but that words which have no meaning when in sequence cannot be connected?

Theaet. What are you saying?

Str. What I thought that you intended when you gave your assent; for there are two sorts of intimation of being which are given by the voice.

Theaet. What are they?

Str. One of them is called nouns, and the other verbs.

Theaet. Describe them.

Str. That which denotes action we call a verb.

Theaet. True.

Str. And the other, which is an articulate mark set on those who do the actions, we call a noun.

Theaet. Quite true.

Str. A succession of nouns only is not a sentence, any more than of verbs without nouns.

Theaet. I do not understand you.

Str. I see that when you gave your assent you had something else in your mind. But what I intended to say was, that a mere succession of nouns or of verbs is not discourse.

Theaet. What do you mean?

Str. I mean that words like 'walks,' 'runs,' 'sleeps,' or any other words which denote action, however many of them you string together, do not make discourse.

Theaet. How can they?

Str. Or, again, when you say 'lion,' 'stag,' 'horse,' or any other words which denote agents—neither in this way of stringing words together do you attain to discourse; for there is no expression of action or inaction, or of the existence of existence or non-existence indicated by the sounds, until verbs are mingled with nouns; then the words fit, and the smallest combination of them forms language, and is the simplest and least form of discourse.

Theaet. Again I ask, What do you mean?

Str. When any one says 'A man learns,' should you not call this the simplest and least of sentences?

Theaet. Yes.

Str. Yes, for he now arrives at the point of giving an intimation about something which is, or is becoming, or has become, or will be. And he not only names, but he does something, by connecting verbs with nouns; and therefore we say that he discourses, and to this connection of words we give the name of discourse.

Theaet. True.

Str. And as there are some things which fit one another, and other things which do not fit, so there are some vocal signs which do, and others which do not, combine and form discourse.

Theaet. Quite true.

Str. There is another small matter.

Theaet. What is it?

Str. A sentence must and cannot help having a subject.

Theaet. True.

Str. And must be of a certain quality.

Theaet. Certainly.

Str. And now let us mind what we are about.

Theaet. We must do so.

Str. I will repeat a sentence to you in which a thing and an action are combined, by the help of a noun and a verb; and you shall tell me of whom the sentence speaks.

Theaet. I will, to the best of my power.

Str. 'Theaetetus sits'—not a very long sentence.

Theaet. Not very.

Str. Of whom does the sentence speak, and who is the subject? that is what you have to tell.

Theaet. Of me; I am the subject.

Str. Or this sentence, again—

Theaet. What sentence?

Str. 'Theaetetus, with whom I am now speaking, is flying.'

Theaet. That also is a sentence which will be admitted by every one to speak of me, and to apply to me.

Str. We agreed that every sentence must necessarily have a certain quality.

Theaet. Yes.

Str. And what is the quality of each of these two sentences?

Theaet. The one, as I imagine, is false, and the other true.

Str. The true says what is true about you?

Theaet. Yes.

Str. And the false says what is other than true?

Theaet. Yes.

Str. And therefore speaks of things which are not as if they were?

Theaet. True.

Str. And says that things are real of you which are not; for, as we were saying, in regard to each thing or person, there is much that is and much that is not.

Theaet. Quite true.

Str. The second of the two sentences which related to you was

---

Sophist

STRANGER, THEAE-TETUS.

A sentence must have a subject, and be of a certain quality,— i. e. true or false.

Examples.

263

A true sentence says what is true of its subject, a false sentence what is false.

first of all an example of the shortest form consistent with our definition.

Theaet. Yes, this was implied in our recent admission.

Str. And, in the second place, it related to a subject?

Theaet. Yes.

Str. Who must be you, and can be nobody else?

Theaet. Unquestionably.

Str. And it would be no sentence at all if there were no subject, for, as we proved, a sentence which has no subject is impossible.

Theaet. Quite true.

Thus false discourse is possible, and therefore false thought, opinion, imagination, which are akin to it, are also possible.

Str. When other, then, is asserted of you as the same, and not-being as being, such a combination of nouns and verbs is really and truly false discourse.

Theaet. Most true.

Str. And therefore thought, opinion, and imagination are now proved to exist in our minds both as true and false.

Theaet. How so?

Str. You will know better if you first gain a knowledge of what they are, and in what they severally differ from one another.

Theaet. Give me the knowledge which you would wish me to gain.

Thought is the un-uttered conversation of the soul, which, when uttered, becomes speech.

Str. Are not thought and speech the same, with this exception, that what is called thought is the unuttered conversation of the soul with herself?

Theaet. Quite true.

Str. But the stream of thought which flows through the lips and is audible is called speech?

Theaet. True.

Str. And we know that there exists in speech . . .

Theaet. What exists?

Opinion is silent [264] affirmation or denial.

Str. Affirmation.

Theaet. Yes, we know it.

Str. When the affirmation or denial takes place in silence and in the mind only, have you any other name by which to call it but opinion?

Theaet. There can be no other name.

Imagination is opinion expressed in a form of sense.

Str. And when opinion is presented, not simply, but in some form of sense, would you not call it imagination?

Theaet. Certainly.

Str. And seeing that language is true and false, and that thought is the conversation of the soul with herself, and opinion is the end of thinking, and imagination or phantasy is the union of sense and opinion, the inference is that some of them, since they are akin to language, should have an element of falsehood as well as of truth?

Theaet. Certainly.

Str. Do you perceive, then, that false opinion and speech have been discovered sooner than we expected?—For just now we seemed to be undertaking a task which would never be accomplished.

Theaet. I perceive.

Str. Then let us not be discouraged about the future; but now having made this discovery, let us go back to our previous classification.

Theaet. What classification?

Str. We divided image-making into two sorts; the one likeness-making, the other imaginative or phantastic.

Theaet. True.

Str. And we said that we were uncertain in which we should place the Sophist.

Theaet. We did say so.

Str. And our heads began to go round more and more when it was asserted that there is no such thing as an image or idol or appearance, because in no manner or time or place can there ever be such a thing as falsehood.

Theaet. True.

Str. And now, since there has been shown to be false speech and false opinion, there may be imitations of real existences, and out of this condition of the mind an art of deception may arise.

Theaet. Quite possible.

Str. And we have already admitted, in what preceded, that the Sophist was lurking in one of the divisions of the likeness-making art?

Theaet. Yes.

Str. Let us, then, renew the attempt, and in dividing any class, always take the part to the right, holding fast to that which holds the Sophist, until we have stripped him of all his common properties, and reached his difference or peculiar. Then we may exhibit him in his true nature, first to ourselves and then to kindred dialectical spirits.

Theaet. Very good.

Str. You may remember that all art was originally divided by us into creative and acquisitive.

Theaet. Yes.

Str. And the Sophist was flitting before us in the acquisitive class, in the subdivisions of hunting, contests, merchandize, and the like.

Recapitulation from 235 ff. (*supra*). —We divided image-making into likeness-making and phantastic, and then the difficulty which we have just solved arose.

265

We have traced the Sophist's descent

through
the sub-
divisions
of acqui-
sitive: let
us now
look for
him in the
branches
of creat-
ive, of
which
imitation
is one.
Creative
art is (1)
human,
(2) di-
vine.

Nature is
to be at-
tributed
to an in-
telligent
cause, not
to an un-
intelli-
gent.

Theaet. Very true.

Str. But now that the imitative art has enclosed him, it is clear that we must begin by dividing the art of creation; for imitation is a kind of creation—of images, however, as we affirm, and not of real things.

Theaet. Quite true.

Str. In the first place, there are two kinds of creation.

Theaet. What are they?

Str. One of them is human and the other divine.

Theaet. I do not follow.

Str. Every power, as you may remember our saying originally, which causes things to exist, not previously existing, was defined by us as creative.

Theaet. I remember.

Str. Looking, now, at the world and all the animals and plants, at things which grow upon the earth from seeds and roots, as well as at inanimate substances which are formed within the earth, fusile or non-fusile, shall we say that they come into existence— not having existed previously—by the creation of God, or shall we agree with vulgar opinion about them?

Theaet. What is it?

Str. The opinion that nature brings them into being from some spontaneous and unintelligent cause. Or shall we say that they are created by a divine reason and a knowledge which comes from God?

Theaet. I dare say that, owing to my youth, I may often waver in my view, but now when I look at you and see that you incline to refer them to God, I defer to your authority.

Str. Nobly said, Theaetetus, and if I thought that you were one of those who would hereafter change your mind, I would have gently argued with you, and forced you to assent; but as I perceive that you will come of yourself and without any argument of mine, to that belief which, as you say, attracts you, I will not forestall the work of time. Let me suppose, then, that things which are said to be made by nature are the work of divine art, and that things which are made by man out of these are work of human art. And so there are two kinds of making and production, the one human and the other divine.

Theaet. True.

Str. Then, now, subdivide each of the two sections which we have already.

Theaet. How do you mean?

Str. I mean to say that you should make a vertical division of production or invention, as you have already made a lateral one.

Theaet. I have done so.

Str. Then, now, there are in all four parts or segments—two of them have reference to us and are human, and two of them have reference to the gods and are divine.

Theaet. True.

Str. And, again, in the division which was supposed to be made in the other way, one part in each subdivision is the making of the things themselves, but the two remaining parts may be called the making of likenesses; and so the productive art is again divided into two parts.

Theaet. Tell me the divisions once more.

Str. I suppose that we, and the other animals, and the elements out of which things are made—fire, water, and the like—are known by us to be each and all the creation and work of God.

Theaet. True.

Str. And there are images of them, which are not them, but which correspond to them; and these are also the creation of a wonderful skill.

Theaet. What are they?

Str. The appearances which spring up of themselves in sleep or by day, such as a shadow when darkness arises in a fire, or the reflection which is produced when the light in bright and smooth objects meets on their surface with an external light, and creates a perception the opposite of our ordinary sight.

Theaet. Yes; and the images as well as the creation are equally the work of a divine hand.

Str. And what shall we say of human art? Do we not make one house by the art of building, and another by the art of drawing, which is a sort of dream created by man for those who are awake?

Theaet. Quite true.

Str. And other products of human creation are also twofold and go in pairs; there is the thing, with which the art of making the thing is concerned, and the image, with which imitation is concerned.

Theaet. Now I begin to understand, and am ready to acknowledge that there are two kinds of production, and each of them twofold; in the lateral division there is both a divine and a human production; in the vertical there are realities and a creation of a kind of similitudes.

Str. And let us not forget that of the imitative class the one part

266
Sophist

STRANGER,
THEAE-
TETUS.

Both in divine and in human creation there is a division for realities and a division for images and likenesses.

Divinely made images are such as dreams, shadows, transposed likenesses.

A human image is (e. g.) the drawing of a house.

Such un-
realities
are pro-
duced by
[267]
phantas-
tic.

Phantas-
tic is
further
divided
into
mimicry
or imita-
tion and a
nameless
section.

was to have been likeness-making, and the other phantastic, if it could be shown that falsehood is a reality and belongs to the class of real being.

Theaet. Yes.

Str. And this appeared to be the case; and therefore now, without hesitation, we shall number the different kinds as two.

Theaet. True.

Str. Then, now, let us again divide the phantastic art.

Theaet. Where shall we make the division?

Str. There is one kind which is produced by an instrument, and another in which the creator of the appearance is himself the instrument.

Theaet. What do you mean?

Str. When any one makes himself appear like another in his figure or his voice, imitation is the name for this part of the phantastic art.

Theaet. Yes.

Str. Let this, then, be named the art of mimicry, and this the province assigned to it; as for the other division, we are weary and will give that up, leaving to some one else the duty of making the class and giving it a suitable name.

Theaet. Let us do as you say—assign a sphere to the one and leave the other.

A further
distinc-
tion is to
be drawn
between
the mimic
who
knows,
and the
mimic
who is
ignorant.

Str. There is a further distinction, Theaetetus, which is worthy of our consideration, and for a reason which I will tell you.

Theaet. Let me hear.

Str. There are some who imitate, knowing what they imitate, and some who do not know. And what line of distinction can there possibly be greater than that which divides ignorance from knowledge?

Theaet. There can be no greater.

Str. Was not the sort of imitation of which we spoke just now the imitation of those who know? For he who would imitate you would surely know you and your figure?

Theaet. Naturally.

Str. And what would you say of the figure or form of justice or of virtue in general? Are we not well aware that many, having no knowledge of either, but only a sort of opinion, do their best to show that this opinion is really entertained by them, by expressing it, as far as they can, in word and deed?

Theaet. Yes, that is very common.

Str. And do they always fail in their attempt to be thought just, when they are not? Or is not the very opposite true?

Theaet. The very opposite.

Str. Such a one, then, should be described as an imitator—to be distinguished from the other, as he who is ignorant is distinguished from him who knows?

Theaet. True.

Str. Can we find a suitable name for each of them? This is clearly not an easy task; for among the ancients there was some confusion of ideas, which prevented them from attempting to divide genera into species; wherefore there is no great abundance of names. Yet, for the sake of distinctness, I will make bold to call the imitation which coexists with opinion, the imitation of appearance—that which coexists with science, a scientific or learned imitation.

Theaet. Granted.

Str. The former is our present concern, for the Sophist was classed with imitators indeed, but not among those who have knowledge.

Theaet. Very true.

Str. Let us, then, examine our imitator of appearance, and see whether he is sound, like a piece of iron, or whether there is still some crack in him.

Theaet. Let us examine him.

Str. Indeed there is a very considerable crack; for if you look, you find that one of the two classes of imitators is a simple creature, who thinks that he knows that which he only fancies; the other sort has knocked about among arguments, until he suspects and fears that he is ignorant of that which to the many he pretends to know.

Theaet. There are certainly the two kinds which you describe.

Str. Shall we regard one as the simple imitator—the other as the dissembling or ironical imitator?

Theaet. Very good.

Str. And shall we further speak of this latter class as having one or two divisions?

Theaet. Answer yourself.

Str. Upon consideration, then, there appear to me to be two; there is the dissembler, who harangues a multitude in public in a long speech, and the dissembler, who in private and in short speeches compels the person who is conversing with him to contradict himself.

Theaet. What you say is most true.

Str. And who is the maker of the longer speeches? Is he the statesman or the popular orator?

STRANGER,
THEAE-
TETUS.

The latter
is the
mimic of
appear-
ance; the
former,
the
learned
mimic.

The
mimic of
appear-
ance may
be un-
conscious
of his ig-
norance
[268]
or a dis-
sembler.

There is a
dis-
sembler
in public
and a dis-
sembler in
private.
The latter
is the
SOPHIST.

Theaet. The latter.

Str. And what shall we call the other? Is he the philosopher or the Sophist?

Theaet. The philosopher he cannot be, for upon our view he is ignorant; but since he is an imitator of the wise he will have a name which is formed by an adaptation of the word σοφός. What shall we name him? I am pretty sure that I cannot be mistaken in terming him the true and very Sophist.

Str. Shall we bind up his name as we did before, making a chain from one end of his genealogy to the other?

Theaet. By all means.

His full
gene-
alogy.

Str. He, then [1], who traces the pedigree of his art as follows— who, belonging to the conscious or dissembling section of the art of causing self-contradiction, is an imitator of appearance, and is separated from the class of phantastic which is a branch of image-making into that further division of creation, the juggling of words, a creation human, and not divine—any one who affirms the real Sophist to be of this blood and lineage will say the very truth.

Theaet. Undoubtedly.

[1] Reading τὸν δή.

STATESMAN

STATESMAN

PERSONS OF THE DIALOGUE

THEODORUS   THE ELEATIC STRANGER

SOCRATES   THE YOUNGER SOCRATES

Socrates. I OWE you many thanks, indeed, Theodorus, for the acquaintance both of Theaetetus and of the Stranger.

Theodorus. And in a little while, Socrates, you will owe me three times as many, when they have completed for you the delineation of the Statesman and of the Philosopher, as well as of the Sophist.

Soc. Sophist, statesman, philosopher! O my dear Theodorus, do my ears truly witness that this is the estimate formed of them by the great calculator and geometrician?

Theod. What do you mean, Socrates?

Soc. I mean that you rate them all at the same value, whereas they are really separated by an interval, which no geometrical ratio can express.

Theod. By Ammon, the god of Cyrene, Socrates, that is a very fair hit; and shows that you have not forgotten your geometry. I will retaliate on you at some other time, but I must now ask the Stranger, who will not, I hope, tire of his goodness to us, to proceed either with the Statesman or with the Philosopher, whichever he prefers.

Stranger. That is my duty, Theodorus; having begun I must go on, and not leave the work unfinished. But what shall be done with Theaetetus?

Theod. In what respect?

Str. Shall we relieve him, and take his companion, the Young Socrates, instead of him? What do you advise?

Theod. Yes, give the other a turn, as you propose. The young always do better when they have intervals of rest.

Soc. I think, Stranger, that both of them may be said to be in some way related to me; for the one, as you affirm, has the cut of

Steph.

257

SOCRATES,
THEO-
dorus,
STRANGER.

Only a third of our task is done, or rather much less than a third; such a geometrician as Theodorus must know that the Statesman rises above the Sophist, and the Philosopher above the Statesman, in more than a geometrical ratio.

[258]

my ugly face [1], the other is called by my name. And we should always be on the look-out to recognize a kinsman by the style of his conversation. I myself was discoursing with Theaetetus yesterday, and I have just been listening to his answers; my namesake I have not yet examined, but I must. Another time will do for me; to-day let him answer you.

Str. Very good. Young Socrates, do you hear what the elder Socrates is proposing?

Young Socrates. I do.

Str. And do you agree to his proposal?

Y. Soc. Certainly.

Str. As you do not object, still less can I. After the Sophist, then, I think that the Statesman naturally follows next in the order of enquiry. And please to say, whether he, too, should be ranked among those who have science.

Y. Soc. Yes.

Str. Then the sciences must be divided as before?

Y. Soc. I dare say.

Str. But yet the division will not be the same?

Y. Soc. How then?

Str. They will be divided at some other point.

Y. Soc. Yes.

Str. Where shall we discover the path of the Statesman? We must find and separate off, and set our seal upon this, and we will set the mark of another class upon all diverging paths. Thus the soul will conceive of all kinds of knowledge under two classes.

Y. Soc. To find the path is your business, Stranger, and not mine.

Str. Yes, Socrates, but the discovery, when once made, must be yours as well as mine.

Y. Soc. Very good.

Str. Well, and are not arithmetic and certain other kindred arts, merely abstract knowledge, wholly separated from action?

Y. Soc. True.

Str. But in the art of carpentering and all other handicrafts, the knowledge of the workman is merged in his work; he not only knows, but he also makes things which previously did not exist.

Y. Soc. Certainly.

Str. Then let us divide sciences in general into those which are practical and those which are purely intellectual.

Y. Soc. Let us assume these two divisions of science, which is one whole.

_____
[1] Cp. Theaet. 143 E.

Str. And are 'statesman,' 'king,' 'master,' or 'householder,' one and the same; or is there a science or art answering to each of these names? Or rather, allow me to put the matter in another way.

Y. Soc. Let me hear.

Str. If any one who is in a private station has the skill to advise one of the public physicians, must not he also be called a physician?

Y. Soc. Yes.

Str. And if any one who is in a private station is able to advise the ruler of a country, may not he be said to have the knowledge which the ruler himself ought to have?

Y. Soc. True.

Str. But surely the science of a true king is royal science?

Y. Soc. Yes.

Str. And will not he who possesses this knowledge, whether he happens to be a ruler or a private man, when regarded only in reference to his art, be truly called 'royal'?

Y. Soc. He certainly ought to be.

Str. And the householder and master are the same?

Y. Soc. Of course.

Str. Again, a large household may be compared to a small state:—will they differ at all, as far as government is concerned?

Y. Soc. They will not.

Str. Then, returning to the point which we were just now discussing, do we not clearly see that there is one science of all of them; and this science may be called either royal or political or economical; we will not quarrel with any one about the name.

Y. Soc. Certainly not.

Str. This, too, is evident, that the king cannot do much with his hands, or with his whole body, towards the maintenance of his empire, compared with what he does by the intelligence and strength of his mind.

Y. Soc. Clearly not.

Str. Then, shall we say that the king has a greater affinity to knowledge than to manual arts and to practical life in general?

Y. Soc. Certainly he has.

Str. Then we may put all together as one and the same—statesmanship and the statesman—the kingly science and the king.

Y. Soc. Clearly.

Str. And now we shall only be proceeding in due order if we go on to divide the sphere of knowledge?

Y. Soc. Very good.

States-man

259
STRANGER,
YOUNG
SOCRATES.

We note that royal science may be possessed by a private man as well as by a king, and that a large household is like a small state; whence we draw the inference that king, statesman, master, householder are the same.

The royal science has a greater affinity to knowledge than to the manual arts or to practical life.

States-
man

STRANGER,
YOUNG
SOCRATES.

Arith-
metic is
the type
of one
kind of
abstract
science,—
which
judges;
the art of
building
of an-
other,—
which
com-
mands.

260

The
king's
knowl-
edge is of

Str. Think whether you can find any joint or parting in knowl-edge.

Y. Soc. Tell me of what sort.

Str. Such as this: You may remember that we made an art of calculation?

Y. Soc. Yes.

Str. Which was, unmistakeably, one of the arts of knowledge?

Y. Soc. Certainly.

Str. And to this art of calculation which discerns the differences of numbers shall we assign any other function except to pass judgment on their differences?

Y. Soc. How could we?

Str. You know that the master-builder does not work himself, but is the ruler of workmen?

Y. Soc. Yes.

Str. He contributes knowledge, not manual labour?

Y. Soc. True.

Str. And may therefore be justly said to share in theoretical science?

Y. Soc. Quite true.

Str. But he ought not, like the calculator, to regard his func-tions as at an end when he has formed a judgment;—he must assign to the individual workmen their appropriate task until they have completed the work.

Y. Soc. True.

Str. Are not all such sciences, no less than arithmetic and the like, subjects of pure knowledge; and is not the difference be-tween the two classes, that the one sort has the power of judging only, and the other of ruling as well?

Y. Soc. That is evident.

Str. May we not very properly say, that of all knowledge, there are two divisions—one which rules, and the other which judges?

Y. Soc. I should think so.

Str. And when men have anything to do in common, that they should be of one mind is surely a desirable thing?

Y. Soc. Very true.

Str. Then while we are at unity among ourselves, we need not mind about the fancies of others?

Y. Soc. Certainly not.

Str. And now, in which of these divisions shall we place the king?—Is he a judge and a kind of spectator? Or shall we assign to him the art of command—for he is a ruler?

Y. Soc. The latter, clearly.

Str. Then we must see whether there is any mark of division in the art of command too. I am inclined to think that there is a distinction similar to that of manufacturer and retail dealer, which parts off the king from the herald.

Y. Soc. How is this?

Str. Why, does not the retailer receive and sell over again the productions of others, which have been sold before?

Y. Soc. Certainly he does.

Str. And is not the herald under command, and does he not receive orders, and in his turn give them to others?

Y. Soc. Very true.

Str. Then shall we mingle the kingly art in the same class with the art of the herald, the interpreter, the boatswain, the prophet, and the numerous kindred arts which exercise command; or, as in the preceding comparison we spoke of manufacturers, or sellers for themselves, and of retailers,—seeing, too, that the class of supreme rulers, or rulers for themselves, is almost nameless— shall we make a word following the same analogy, and refer kings to a supreme or ruling-for-self science, leaving the rest to receive a name from some one else? For we are seeking the ruler; and our enquiry is not concerned with him who is not a ruler.

Y. Soc. Very good.

Str. Thus a very fair distinction has been attained between the man who gives his own commands, and him who gives another's. And now let us see if the supreme power allows of any further division.

Y. Soc. By all means.

Str. I think that it does; and please to assist me in making the division.

Y. Soc. At what point?

Str. May not all rulers be supposed to command for the sake of producing something?

Y. Soc. Certainly.

Str. Nor is there any difficulty in dividing the things produced into two classes.

Y. Soc. How would you divide them?

Str. Of the whole class, some have life and some are without life.

Y. Soc. True.

Str. And by the help of this distinction we may make, if we please, a subdivision of the section of knowledge which commands.

Y. Soc. At what point?

the com-
manding
sort, and
falls in
that divi-
sion of it
which is
supreme,
not
subordi-
nate.

261

Com-
mand is
for the
sake of
produc-
tion,

States-
man

STRANGER,
YOUNG
SOCRATES.

which is
either (1)
of life-
less, or
(2) of
living
objects.—
The latter
is the
function
of the
king;

and he
is the
manager,
not mere-
ly of indi-
viduals,
but of
creatures
united in
flocks.

It matters
not
whether
we call
his art
managing
a herd or
collective
[262]
manage-
ment. If
a man is
not too
particular
about
words, he
will be all
the richer
in wisdom
when he
grows old.

Manage-
ment of
herds is of
two
kinds,—of
men, and

Str. One part may be set over the production of lifeless, the other of living objects; and in this way the whole will be divided.

Y. Soc. Certainly.

Str. That division, then, is complete; and now we may leave one half, and take up the other; which may also be divided into two.

Y. Soc. Which of the two halves do you mean?

Str. Of course that which exercises command about animals. For, surely, the royal science is not like that of a master-work-man, a science presiding over lifeless objects;—the king has a nobler function, which is the management and control of living beings.

Y. Soc. True.

Str. And the breeding and tending of living beings may be observed to be sometimes a tending of the individual; in other cases, a common care of creatures in flocks?

Y. Soc. True.

Str. But the statesman is not a tender of individuals—not like the driver or groom of a single ox or horse; he is rather to be compared with the keeper of a drove of horses or oxen.

Y. Soc. Yes, I see, thanks to you.

Str. Shall we call this art of tending many animals together, the art of managing a herd, or the art of collective management?

Y. Soc. No matter;—whichever suggests itself to us in the course of conversation.

Str. Very good, Socrates; and, if you continue to be not too particular about names, you will be all the richer in wisdom when you are an old man. And now, as you say, leaving the discussion of the name,—can you see a way in which a person, by showing the art of herding to be of two kinds, may cause that which is now sought amongst twice the number of things, to be then sought amongst half that number?

Y. Soc. I will try;—there appears to me to be one manage-ment of men and another of beasts.

Str. You have certainly divided them in a most straightfor-ward and manly style; but you have fallen into an error which hereafter I think that we had better avoid.

Y. Soc. What is the error?

Str. I think that we had better not cut off a single small por-tion which is not a species, from many larger portions; the part should be a species. To separate off at once the subject of investi-gation, is a most excellent plan, if only the separation be rightly made; and you were under the impression that you were right, because you saw that you would come to man; and this led you to hasten the steps. But you should not chip off too small a piece, my friend; the safer way is to cut through the middle; which is also the more likely way of finding classes. Attention to this principle makes all the difference in a process of enquiry.

Y. Soc. What do you mean, Stranger?

Str. I will endeavour to speak more plainly out of love to your good parts, Socrates; and, although I cannot at present entirely explain myself, I will try, as we proceed, to make my meaning a little clearer.

Y. Soc. What was the error of which, as you say, we were guilty in our recent division?

Str. The error was just as if some one who wanted to divide the human race, were to divide them after the fashion which prevails in this part of the world; here they cut off the Hellenes as one species, and all the other species of mankind, which are innumerable, and have no ties or common language, they include under the single name of 'barbarians,' and because they have one name they are supposed to be of one species also. Or suppose that in dividing numbers you were to cut off ten thousand from all the rest, and make of it one species, comprehending the rest under another separate name, you might say that here too was a single class, because you had given it a single name. Whereas you would make a much better and more equal and logical classification of numbers, if you divided them into odd and even; or of the human species, if you divided them into male and female; and only separated off Lydians or Phrygians, or any other tribe, and arrayed them against the rest of the world, when you could no longer make a division into parts which were also classes.

Y. Soc. Very true; but I wish that this distinction between a part and a class could still be made somewhat plainer.

Str. O Socrates, best of men, you are imposing upon me a very difficult task. We have already digressed further from our original intention than we ought, and you would have us wander still further away. But we must now return to our subject; and hereafter, when there is a leisure hour, we will follow up the other track; at the same time, I wish you to guard against imagining that you ever heard me declare—

Y. Soc. What?

Str. That a class and a part are distinct.

Y. Soc. What did I hear, then?

Str. That a class is necessarily a part, but there is no similar

of beasts.
—But not
so fast.

We have
omitted
inter-
mediate
steps,
having
only cut
off one
class from
all the
rest.

Hellenes
and bar-
barians is
a similar
example
of false
division.

263
Part and
class.

necessity that a part should be a class; that is the view which I should always wish you to attribute to me, Socrates.

Y. Soc. So be it.

Str. There is another thing which I should like to know.

Y. Soc. What is it?

Str. The point at which we digressed; for, if I am not mistaken, the exact place was at the question, Where you would divide the management of herds. To this you appeared rather too ready to answer that there were two species of animals; man being one, and all brutes making up the other.

Y. Soc. True.

Str. I thought that in taking away a part, you imagined that the remainder formed a class, because you were able to call them by the common name of brutes.

Y. Soc. That again is true.

The crane would divide living creatures into 'cranes and all other animals.'

Str. Suppose now, O most courageous of dialecticians, that some wise and understanding creature, such as a crane is reputed to be, were, in imitation of you, to make a similar division, and set up cranes against all other animals to their own special glorification, at the same time jumbling together all the others, including man, under the appellation of brutes,—here would be the sort of error which we must try to avoid.

Y. Soc. How can we be safe?

Str. If we do not divide the whole class of animals, we shall be less likely to fall into that error.

Y. Soc. We had better not take the whole?

Str. Yes, there lay the source of error in our former division.

Y. Soc. How?

Str. You remember how that part of the art of knowledge which was concerned with command, had to do with the rearing of living creatures,—I mean, with animals in herds?

Y. Soc. Yes.

264

In our haste we omitted the division of animals into tame and wild.

Str. In that case, there was already implied a division of all animals into tame and wild; those whose nature can be tamed are called tame, and those which cannot be tamed are called wild.

Y. Soc. True.

Str. And the political science of which we are in search, is and ever was concerned with tame animals, and is also confined to gregarious animals.

Y. Soc. Yes.

Str. But then we ought not to divide, as we did, taking the whole class at once. Neither let us be in too great haste to arrive quickly at the political science; for this mistake has already brought upon us the misfortune of which the proverb speaks.

Y. Soc. What misfortune?

Str. The misfortune of too much haste, which is too little speed.

Y. Soc. And all the better, Stranger; we got what we deserved.

Str. Very well: Let us then begin again, and endeavour to divide the collective rearing of animals; for probably the completion of the argument will best show what you are so anxious to know. Tell me, then—

Y. Soc. What?

Str. Have you ever heard, as you very likely may—for I do not suppose that you ever actually visited them—of the preserves of fishes in the Nile, and in the ponds of the Great King; or you may have seen similar preserves in wells at home?

Y. Soc. Yes, to be sure, I have seen them, and I have often heard the others described.

Str. And you may have heard also, and may have been assured by report, although you have not travelled in those regions, of nurseries of geese and cranes in the plains of Thessaly?

Y. Soc. Certainly.

Str. I asked you, because here is a new division of the management of herds, into the managment of land and of water herds.

Y. Soc. There is.

Str. And do you agree that we ought to divide the collective rearing of herds into two corresponding parts, the one the rearing of water, and the other the rearing of land herds?

Y. Soc. Yes.

Str. There is surely no need to ask which of these two contains the royal art, for it is evident to everybody.

Y. Soc. Certainly.

Str. Any one can divide the herds which feed on dry land?

Y. Soc. How would you divide them?

Str. I should distinguish between those which fly and those which walk.

Y. Soc. Most true.

Str. And where shall we look for the political animal? Might not an idiot, so to speak, know that he is a pedestrian?

Y. Soc. Certainly.

Str. The art of managing the walking animal has to be further divided, just as you might halve an even number

Y. Soc. Clearly.

Str. Let me note that here appear in view two ways to that part or class which the argument aims at reaching,—the one a speedier way, which cuts off a small portion and leaves a large; the other

The collective rearing of animals includes the rearing of both land and water herds.

Land herds are of flying or walking animals.

265
At this point we

States-
man

STRANGER,
YOUNG
SOCRATES.

may take
either a
shorter or
a longer
way.

Let us
begin
with the
longer
one.

The tame
walking
and herd-
ing
animals
fall into
two
classes, as
they are
with or
without
horns;

agrees better with the principle which we were laying down, that as far as we can we should divide in the middle; but it is longer. We can take either of them, whichever we please.

Y. Soc. Cannot we have both ways?

Str. Together? What a thing to ask! but, if you take them in turn, you clearly may.

Y. Soc. Then I should like to have them in turn.

Str. There will be no difficulty, as we are near the end; if we had been at the beginning, or in the middle, I should have demurred to your request; but now, in accordance with your desire, let us begin with the longer way; while we are fresh, we shall get on better. And now attend to the division.

Y. Soc. Let me hear.

Str. The tame walking herding animals are distributed by nature into two classes.

Y. Soc. Upon what principle?

Str. The one grows horns; and the other is without horns.

Y. Soc. Clearly.

Str. Suppose that you divide the science which manages pedestrian animals into two corresponding parts, and define them; for if you try to invent names for them, you will find the intricacy too great.

Y. Soc. How must I speak of them, then?

Str. In this way: let the science of managing pedestrian animals be divided into two parts, and one part assigned to the horned herd, and the other to the herd that has no horns.

Y. Soc. All that you say has been abundantly proved, and may therefore be assumed.

Str. The king is clearly the shepherd of a polled herd, who have no horns.

Y. Soc. That is evident.

Str. Shall we break up this hornless herd into sections, and endeavour to assign to him what is his?

Y. Soc. By all means.

and the
latter into
those who
do and do
not mix
the breed.

Str. Shall we distinguish them by their having or not having cloven feet, or by their mixing or not mixing the breed? You know what I mean.

Y. Soc. What?

Str. I mean that horses and asses naturally breed from one another.

Y. Soc. Yes.

Str. But the remainder of the hornless herd of tame animals will not mix the breed.

Y. Soc. Very true.

Str. And of which has the Statesman charge,—of the mixed or of the unmixed race?

Y. Soc. Clearly of the unmixed.

Str. I suppose that we must divide this again as before.

Y. Soc. We must.

Str. Every tame and herding animal has now been split up, with the exception of two species; for I hardly think that dogs should be reckoned among gregarious animals.

Y. Soc. Certainly not; but how shall we divide the two remaining species?

Str. There is a measure of difference which may be appropriately employed by you and Theaetetus, who are students of geometry.

Y. Soc. What is that?

Str. The diameter; and, again, the diameter of a diameter [1].

Y. Soc. What do you mean?

Str. How does man walk, but as a diameter whose power is two feet?

Y. Soc. Just so.

Str. And the power of the remaining kind, being the power of twice two feet, may be said to be the diameter of our diameter.

Y. Soc. Certainly; and now I think that I pretty nearly understand you.

Str. In these divisions, Socrates, I descry what would make another famous jest.

Y. Soc. What is it?

Str. Human beings have come out in the same class with the freest and airiest of creation, and have been running a race with them.

Y. Soc. I remark that very singular coincidence.

Str. And would you not expect the slowest to arrive last?

Y. Soc. Indeed I should.

Str. And there is a still more ridiculous consequence, that the king is found running about with the herd, and in close competition with the bird-catcher, who of all mankind is most of an adept at the airy life [2].

Y. Soc. Certainly.

States-man

STRANGER,
YOUNG
SOCRATES.

The States-
[266]
man has
to do
with the
unmixed.

Dogs are
not herd-
ing ani-
mals, and
may
therefore
be ex-
cluded.

Next
follows
the divi-
sion into
bipeds
and quad-
rupeds,
who may
be de-
scribed
mathe-
matically
as having
a power
of two
and four
feet.

What
fun ! Men
and birds
alone re-
main, and
the bird-
catcher is
running a
race with
the king.

---

[1] Cp. Meno 82 ff.

[2] Plato is here introducing a new subdivision, i. e. that of bipeds into men and birds. Others however refer the passage to the division into quadrupeds and bipeds, making pigs compete with human beings and the pig-driver with the king. According to this explanation we must translate the words above, 'freest and airiest of creation,' 'worthiest and laziest of creation.'

Truly
dialectic
is no re-
garder of
persons.

The
shorter
road.—
Land-
animals
are bipeds
or quad-
rupeds,
and bi-
peds
feathered
or with-
out
feathers:
    [267]
the latter
=man.

Recapitu-
lation.

Str. Then here, Socrates, is still clearer evidence of the truth of what was said in the enquiry about the Sophist [1].

Y. Soc. What?

Str. That the dialectical method is no respecter of persons, and does not set the great above the small, but always arrives in her own way at the truest result.

Y. Soc. Clearly.

Str. And now, I will not wait for you to ask me, but will of my own accord take you by the shorter road to the definition of a king.

Y. Soc. By all means.

Str. I say that we should have begun at first by dividing land animals into biped and quadruped; and since the winged herd, and that alone, comes out in the same class with man, we should divide bipeds into those which have feathers and those which have not, and when they have been divided, and the art of the management of mankind is brought to light, the time will have come to produce our Statesman and ruler, and set him like a charioteer in his place, and hand over to him the reins of state, for that too is a vocation which belongs to him.

Y. Soc. Very good; you have paid me the debt,—I mean, that you have completed the argument, and I suppose that you added the digression by way of interest [2].

Str. Then now, let us go back to the beginning, and join the links, which together make the definition of the name of the Statesman's art.

Y. Soc. By all means.

Str. The science of pure knowledge had, as we said originally, a part which was the science of rule or command, and from this was derived another part, which was called command-for-self, on the analogy of selling-for-self; an important section of this was the management of living animals, and this again was further limited to the management of them in herds, and again in herds of pedestrian animals. The chief division of the latter was the art of managing pedestrian animals which are without horns; this again has a part which can only be comprehended under one term by joining together three names,—shepherding pure-bred animals. The only further subdivision is the art of man-herding,—this has to do with bipeds, and is what we were seeking after, and have now found, being at once the royal and political.

Y. Soc. To be sure.

[1] Cp. Soph. 227 B.
[2] Cp. Rep. VI. 507 A.

Str. And do you think, Socrates, that we really have done as you say?

Y. Soc. What?

Str. Do you think, I mean, that we have really fulfilled our intention?—There has been a sort of discussion, and yet the investigation seems to me not to be perfectly worked out: this is where the enquiry fails.

Y. Soc. I do not understand.

Str. I will try to make the thought, which is at this moment present in my mind, clearer to us both.

Y. Soc. Let me hear.

Str. There were many arts of shepherding, and one of them was the political, which had the charge of one particular herd?

Y. Soc. Yes.

Str. And this the argument defined to be the art of rearing, not horses or other brutes, but the art of rearing man collectively?

Y. Soc. True.

Str. Note, however, a difference which distinguishes the king from all other shepherds.

Y. Soc. To what do you refer?

Str. I want to ask, whether any one of the other herdsmen has a rival who professes and claims to share with him in the management of the herd [1]?

Y. Soc. What do you mean?

Str. I mean to say that merchants, husbandmen, providers of food, and also training-masters and physicians, will all contend with the herdsmen of humanity, whom we call Statesmen, declaring that they themselves have the care of rearing or managing mankind, and that they rear not only the common herd, but also the rulers themselves.

Y. Soc. Are they not right in saying so?

Str. Very likely they may be, and we will consider their claim. But we are certain of this,—that no one will raise a similar claim as against the herdsman, who is allowed on all hands to be the sole and only feeder and physician of his herd; he is also their match-maker and accoucheur; no one else knows that department of science. And he is their merry-maker and musician, as far as their nature is susceptible of such influences, and no one can console and soothe his own herd better than he can, either with the natural tones of his voice or with instruments. And the same may be said of tenders of animals in general.

STRANGER,
YOUNG
SOCRATES.

But the
argument
is not
really at
an end.

The king,
unlike
other
herdsmen,
[268]
has many
rivals,
who dispute his
claims to
the management
of the
herd.

[1] Reading εἴ τις τῶν ἄλλων τῳ.

*States-
man*

STRANGER,
YOUNG
SOCRATES.

How then
can we
maintain
his posi-
tion?

Y. Soc. Very true.

Str. But if this is as you say, can our argument about the king be true and unimpeachable? Were we right in selecting him out of ten thousand other claimants to be the shepherd and rearer of the human flock?

Y. Soc. Surely not.

Str. Had we not reason just now [1] to apprehend, that although we may have described a sort of royal form, we have not as yet accurately worked out the true image of the Statesman? and that we cannot reveal him as he truly is in his own nature, until we have disengaged and separated him from those who hang about him and claim to share in his prerogatives?

Y. Soc. Very true.

Str. And that, Socrates, is what we must do, if we do not mean to bring disgrace upon the argument at its close.

Y. Soc. We must certainly avoid that.

Str. Then let us make a new beginning, and travel by a different road.

Y. Soc. What road?

We reply
by telling
a famous
tale,
which is
amusing
as well as
instruc-
tive.

Str. I think that we may have a little amusement; there is a famous tale, of which a good portion may with advantage be interwoven, and then we may resume our series of divisions, and proceed in the old path until we arrive at the desired summit. Shall we do as I say?

Y. Soc. By all means.

Str. Listen, then, to a tale which a child would love to hear; and you are not too old for childish amusement.

Y. Soc. Let me hear.

Str. There did really happen, and will again happen, like many other events of which ancient tradition has preserved the record, the portent which is traditionally said to have occurred in the quarrel of Atreus and Thyestes. You have heard, no doubt, and remember what they say happened at that time?

Y. Soc. I suppose you to mean the token of the birth of the golden lamb.

269
We have
all heard
fragments
of it, such
as the
reversal
of the

Str. No, not that; but another part of the story, which tells how the sun and the stars once rose in the west, and set in the east, and that the god reversed their motion, and gave them that which they now have as a testimony to the right of Atreus.

Y. Soc. Yes; there is that legend also.

Str. Again, we have been often told of the reign of Cronos.

[1] Cp. supra, 267 C, D.

Y. Soc. Yes, very often.

Str. Did you ever hear that the men of former times were earth-born, and not begotten of one another?

Y. Soc. Yes, that is another old tradition.

Str. All these stories, and ten thousand others which are still more wonderful, have a common origin; many of them have been lost in the lapse of ages, or are repeated only in a disconnected form; but the origin of them is what no one has told, and may as well be told now; for the tale is suited to throw light on the nature of the king.

Y. Soc. Very good; and I hope that you will give the whole story, and leave out nothing.

Str. Listen, then. There is a time when God himself guides and helps to roll the world in its course; and there is a time, on the completion of a certain cycle, when he lets go, and the world being a living creature, and having originally received intelligence from its author and creator, turns about and by an inherent necessity revolves in the opposite direction.

Y. Soc. Why is that?

Str. Why, because only the most divine things of all remain ever unchanged and the same, and body is not included in this class. Heaven and the universe, as we have termed them, although they have been endowed by the Creator with many glories, partake of a bodily nature, and therefore cannot be entirely free from perturbation. But their motion is, as far as possible, single and in the same place, and of the same kind; and is therefore only subject to a reversal, which is the least alteration possible. For the lord of all moving things is alone able to move of himself; and to think that he moves them at one time in one direction and at another time in another is blasphemy. Hence we must not say that the world is either self-moved always, or all made to go round by God in two opposite courses; or that two Gods, having opposite purposes, make it move round. But as I have already said (and this is the only remaining alternative) the world is guided at one time by an external power which is divine and receives fresh life and immortality from the renewing hand of the Creator, and again, when let go, moves spontaneously, being set free at such a time as to have, during infinite cycles of years, a reverse movement: this is due to its perfect balance, to its vast size, and to the fact that it turns on the smallest pivot.

Y. Soc. Your account of the world seems to be very reasonable indeed.

Str. Let us now reflect and try to gather from what has been said

motion of sun and stars, the reign of Cronos, and the story of the earth-born men.

The whole of the story.— There is a time when God moves and guides the world, and there is a time when he lets go, and the world moves itself but in an opposite direction. This change of motion, which is [270] the slightest possible, is due to the material element in the world.

the nature of the phenomenon which we affirmed to be the cause
of all these wonders. It is this.

Y. Soc. What?

Str. The reversal which takes place from time to time of the motion of the universe.

Y. Soc. How is that the cause?

Str. Of all changes of the heavenly motions, we may consider
this to be the greatest and most complete.

Y. Soc. I should imagine so.

Str. And it may be supposed to result in the greatest changes to
the human beings who are the inhabitants of the world at the time.

Y. Soc. Such changes would naturally occur.

Str. And animals, as we know, survive with difficulty great and
serious changes of many different kinds when they come upon them
at once.

Y. Soc. Very true.

Str. Hence there necessarily occurs a great destruction of them,
which extends also to the life of man; few survivors of the race
are left, and those who remain become the subjects of several
novel and remarkable phenomena, and of one in particular, which
takes place at the time when the transition is made to the cycle
opposite to that in which we are now living.

Y. Soc. What is it?

At the
time of
transition
from our
cycle to
the oppo-
site, a
retro-
gression
takes
place in
the life of
men and
animals.

Str. The life of all animals first came to a standstill, and the
mortal nature ceased to be or look older, and was then reversed
and grew young and delicate; the white locks of the aged darkened
again, and the cheeks of the bearded man became smooth, and
recovered their former bloom; the bodies of youths in their prime
grew softer and smaller, continually by day and night returning
and becoming assimilated to the nature of a newly-born child in
mind as well as body; in the succeeding stage they wasted away
and wholly disappeared. And the bodies of those who died by
violence at that time quickly passed through the like changes, and
in a few days were no more seen.

Y. Soc. Then how, Stranger, were the animals created in those
days; and in what way were they begotten of one another?

Men, in
the age of
Cronos,
sprang,
not from
one an-
other, but
from the
earth.

Str. It is evident, Socrates, that there was no such thing in the
then order of nature as the procreation of animals from one another; the earth-born race, of which we hear in story, was the one
which existed in those days—they rose again from the ground;
and of this tradition, which is now-a-days often unduly discredited,
our ancestors, who were nearest in point of time to the end of the
last period and came into being at the beginning of this, are to us

the heralds. And mark how consistent the sequel of the tale is; after the return of age to youth, follows the return of the dead, who are lying in the earth, to life; simultaneously with the reversal of the world the wheel of their generation has been turned back, and they are put together and rise and live in the opposite order, unless God has carried any of them away to some other lot. According to this tradition they of necessity sprang from the earth and have the name of earth-born, and so the above legend clings to them.

Y. Soc. Certainly that is quite consistent with what has preceded; but tell me, was the life which you said existed in the reign of Cronos in that cycle of the world, or in this? For the change in the course of the stars and the sun must have occurred in both.

Str. I see that you enter into my meaning;—no, that blessed and spontaneous life does not belong to the present cycle of the world, but to the previous one, in which God superintended the whole revolution of the universe; and the several parts of the universe were distributed under the rule of certain inferior deities, as is the way in some places still. There were demigods, who were the shepherds of the various species and herds of animals, and each one was in all respects sufficient for those of whom he was the shepherd; neither was there any violence, or devouring of one another, or war or quarrel among them; and I might tell of ten thousand other blessings, which belonged to that dispensation. The reason why the life of man was, as tradition says, spontaneous, is as follows: In those days God himself was their shepherd, and ruled over them, just as man, who is by comparison a divine being, still rules over the lower animals. Under him there were no forms of government or separate possession of women and children; for all men rose again from the earth, having no memory of the past. And although they had nothing of this sort, the earth gave them fruits in abundance, which grew on trees and shrubs unbidden, and were not planted by the hand of man. And they dwelt naked, and mostly in the open air, for the temperature of their seasons was mild; and they had no beds, but lay on soft couches of grass, which grew plentifully out of the earth. Such was the life of man in the days of Cronos, Socrates; the character of our present life, which is said to be under Zeus, you know from your own experience. Can you, and will you, determine which of them you deem the happier?

Y. Soc. Impossible.

Str. Then shall I determine for you as well as I can?

Y. Soc. By all means.

Str. Suppose that the nurslings of Cronos, having this bound-

States-man

STRANGER, YOUNG SOCRATES.

The tale is so consistent that it must be true.

Description of the life of innocence which prevailed in the days when God governed the world.

272

Which would you call happier, that life or our own?

*States-
man*

STRANGER,
YOUNG
SOCRATES.

We can-
not say;
for the
life of
innocence
might be
a life of
philoso-
phy,
or of mere
eating
and
drinking.

273

When
God let
the world
go, at first
there was
a great
earth-
quake,
but
things
soon
settled
down.

The
creature
at first re-
membered
his
Creator,
but after-
wards
forgot
him. And
so there
arose
great dis-
order,

less leisure, and the power of holding intercourse, not only with men, but with the brute creation, had used all these advantages with a view to philosophy, conversing with the brutes as well as with one another, and learning of every nature which was gifted with any special power, and was able to contribute some special experience to the store of wisdom, there would be no difficulty in deciding that they would be a thousand times happier than the men of our own day. Or, again, if they had merely eaten and drunk until they were full, and told stories to one another and to the animals—such stories as are now attributed to them—in this case also, as I should imagine, the answer would be easy. But until some satisfactory witness can be found of the love of that age for knowledge and discussion, we had better let the matter drop, and give the reason why we have unearthed this tale, and then we shall be able to get on. In the fulness of time, when the change was to take place, and the earth-born race had all perished, and every soul had completed its proper cycle of births and been sown in the earth her appointed number of times, the pilot of the universe let the helm go, and retired to his place of view; and then Fate and innate desire reversed the motion of the world. Then also all the inferior deities who share the rule of the supreme power, being informed of what was happening, let go the parts of the world which were under their control. And the world turning round with a sudden shock, being impelled in an opposite direction from beginning to end, was shaken by a mighty earthquake, which wrought a new destruction of all manner of animals. Afterwards, when sufficient time had elapsed, the tumult and confusion and earthquake ceased, and the universal creature, once more at peace, attained to a calm, and settled down into his own orderly and accustomed course, having the charge and rule of himself and of all the creatures which are contained in him, and executing, as far as he remembered them, the instructions of his Father and Creator, more precisely at first, but afterwards with less exactness. The reason of the falling off was the admixture of matter in him; this was inherent in the primal nature, which was full of disorder, until attaining to the present order. From God, the constructor, the world received all that is good in him, but from a previous state came elements of evil and unrighteousness, which, thence derived, first of all passed into the world, and were then transmitted to the animals. While the world was aided by the pilot in nurturing the animals, the evil was small, and great the good which he produced, but after the separation, when the world was let go, at first all proceeded well enough; but, as time went on, there was more and more forgetting, and the old discord again held sway and burst forth in full glory; and at last small was the good, and great was the admixture of evil, and there was a danger of universal ruin to the world, and to the things contained in him. Wherefore God, the orderer of all, in his tender care, seeing that the world was in great straits, and fearing that all might be dissolved in the storm and disappear in infinite chaos, again seated himself at the helm; and bringing back the elements which had fallen into dissolution and disorder to the motion which had prevailed under his dispensation, he set them in order and restored them, and made the world imperishable and immortal. And this is the whole tale, of which the first part will suffice to illustrate the nature of the king. For when the world turned towards the present cycle of generation, the age of man again stood still, and a change opposite to the previous one was the result. The small creatures which had almost disappeared grew in stature, and the newly-born children of the earth became grey and died and sank into the earth again. All things changed, imitating and following the condition of the universe, and of necessity agreeing with that in their mode of conception and generation and nurture; for no animal was any longer allowed to come into being in the earth through the agency of other creative beings, but as the world was ordained to be the lord of his own progress, in like manner the parts were ordained to grow and generate and give nourishment, as far as they could, of themselves, impelled by a similar movement. And so we have arrived at the real end of this discourse; for although there might be much to tell of the lower animals, and of the condition out of which they changed and of the causes of the change, about men there is not much, and that little is more to the purpose. Deprived of the care of God, who had possessed and tended them, they were left helpless and defenceless, and were torn in pieces by the beasts, who were naturally fierce and had now grown wild. And in the first ages they were still without skill or resource; the food which once grew spontaneously had failed, and as yet they knew not how to procure it, because they had never felt the pressure of necessity. For all these reasons they were in a great strait; wherefore also the gifts spoken of in the old tradition were imparted to man by the gods, together with so much teaching and education as was indispensable; fire was given to them by Prometheus, the arts by Hephaestus and his fellow-worker, Athene, seeds and plants by others. From these is derived all that has helped to frame human life; since the care of the Gods, as I was saying, had now failed men, and they had to order their course of life for themselves, and were their own masters, just like the uni-

which continued until God once more took the helm and the old order was reinstated.

At the begining of our cycle there was [274] another change in the life of man, opposite to the former.

Man, being found unequal to the struggle for existence, is helped by Prometheus, Hephaestus, and Athene.

Two mis-
takes
made by
us:—(1)
[275]
we did
not speak
of a king
or states-
man of
the
present
cycle; or
(2) define
the nature
of his
rule.

versal creature whom they imitate and follow, ever changing, as he changes, and ever living and growing, at one time in one manner, and at another time in another. Enough of the story, which may be of use in showing us how greatly we erred in the delineation of the king and the statesman in our previous discourse.

Y. Soc. What was this great error of which you speak?

Str. There were two; the first a lesser one, the other was an error on a much larger and grander scale.

Y. Soc. What do you mean?

Str. I mean to say that when we were asked about a king and statesman of the present cycle and generation, we told of a shepherd of a human flock who belonged to the other cycle, and of one who was a god when he ought to have been a man; and this was a great error. Again, we declared him to be the ruler of the entire State, without explaining how: this was not the whole truth, nor very intelligible; but still it was true, and therefore the second error was not so great as the first.

Y. Soc. Very good.

Str. Before we can expect to have a perfect description of the statesman we must define the nature of his office.

Y. Soc. Certainly.

Str. And the myth was introduced in order to show, not only that all others are rivals of the true shepherd who is the object of our search, but in order that we might have a clearer view of him who is alone worthy to receive this appellation, because he alone of shepherds and herdsmen, according to the image which we have employed, has the care of human beings.

Y. Soc. Very true.

The true
shepherd
is greater
even than
a king;
for now-
a-days
kings and
their sub-
jects are
much
upon a
level.

Str. And I cannot help thinking, Socrates, that the form of the divine shepherd is even higher than that of a king; whereas the statesmen who are now on earth seem to be much more like their subjects in character, and much more nearly to partake of their breeding and education.

Y. Soc. Certainly.

Str. Still they must be investigated all the same, to see whether, like the divine shepherd, they are above their subjects or on a level with them.

Y. Soc. Of course.

Com-
mand-
for-self
over
herds
should be

Str. To resume:—Do you remember that we spoke of a command-for-self exercised over animals, not singly but collectively, which we called the art of rearing a herd?

Y. Soc. Yes, I remember.

Str. There, somewhere, lay our error; for we never included or mentioned the Statesman; and we did not observe that he had no place in our nomenclature.

Y. Soc. How was that?

Str. All other herdsmen 'rear' their herds, but this is not a suitable term to apply to the Statesman; we should use a name which is common to them all.

Y. Soc. True, if there be such a name.

Str. Why, is not 'care' of herds applicable to all? For this implies no feeding, or any special duty; if we say either 'tending' the herds, or 'managing' the herds, or 'having the care' of them, the same word will include all, and then we may wrap up the Statesman with the rest, as the argument seems to require.

Y. Soc. Quite right; but how shall we take the next step in the division?

Str. As before we divided the art of 'rearing' herds accordingly as they were land or water herds, winged and wingless, mixing or not mixing the breed, horned and hornless, so we may divide by these same differences the 'tending' of herds, comprehending in our definition the kingship of to-day and the rule of Cronos.

Y. Soc. That is clear; but I still ask, what is to follow.

Str. If the word had been 'managing' herds, instead of feeding or rearing them, no one would have argued that there was no care of men in the case of the politician, although it was justly contended, that there was no human art of feeding them which was worthy of the name, or at least, if there were, many a man had a prior and greater right to share in such an art than any king.

Y. Soc. True.

Str. But no other art or science will have a prior or better right than the royal science to care for human society and to rule over men in general.

Y. Soc. Quite true.

Str. In the next place, Socrates, we must surely notice that a great error was committed at the end of our analysis.

Y. Soc. What was it?

Str. Why, supposing we were ever so sure that there is such an art as the art of rearing or feeding bipeds, there was no reason why we should call this the royal or political art, as though there were no more to be said.

Y. Soc. Certainly not.

Str. Our first duty, as we were saying, was to remodel the name, so as to have the notion of care rather than of feeding, and then to divide, for there may be still considerable divisions.

Y. Soc. How can they be made?

Statesman

STRANGER,
YOUNG
SOCRATES.

called not 'rearing of herds,' but by some more general term, such as 'tending' or [276] 'management' of herds, which will include the king.

We may then subdivide the 'tending' of herds as we subdivided the 'rearing' of herds.

But we should not, as before, hastily call the art of managing bipeds the royal art.

Str. First, by separating the divine shepherd from the human guardian or manager.

Y. Soc. True.

Str. And the art of management which is assigned to man would again have to be subdivided.

Y. Soc. On what principle?

Str. On the principle of voluntary and compulsory.

Y. Soc. Why?

Str. Because, if I am not mistaken, there has been an error here; for our simplicity led us to rank king and tyrant together, whereas they are utterly distinct, like their modes of government.

Y. Soc. True.

Str. Then, now, as I said, let us make the correction and divide human care into two parts, on the principle of voluntary and compulsory.

Y. Soc. Certainly.

Str. And if we call the management of violent rulers tyranny, and the voluntary management of herds of voluntary bipeds politics, may we not further assert that he who has this latter art of management is the true king and statesman?

Y. Soc. I think, Stranger, that we have now completed the account of the Statesman.

Str. Would that we had, Socrates, but I have to satisfy myself as well as you; and in my judgment the figure of the king is not yet perfected; like statuaries who, in their too great haste, having overdone the several parts of their work, lose time in cutting them down, so too we, partly out of haste, partly out of a magnanimous desire to expose our former error, and also because we imagined that a king required grand illustrations, have taken up a marvellous lump of fable, and have been obliged to use more than was necessary. This made us discourse at large, and, nevertheless, the story never came to an end. And our discussion might be compared to a picture of some living being which had been fairly drawn in outline, but had not yet attained the life and clearness which is given by the blending of colours. Now to intelligent persons a living being had better be delineated by language and discourse than by any painting or work of art: to the duller sort by works of art.

Y. Soc. Very true; but what is the imperfection which still remains? I wish that you would tell me.

Str. The higher ideas, my dear friend, can hardly be set forth except through the medium of examples; every man seems to know all things in a dreamy sort of way, and then again to wake up and to know nothing.

Statesman

STRANGER, YOUNG SOCRATES.

It must first be subdivided into divine and human management; and the latter into voluntary and compulsory, that the king may be distinguished from the tyrant.

277

Alas! the picture of the king is both overdone and defective.

We seem only to know the higher ideas

Y. Soc. What do you mean?

Str. I fear that I have been unfortunate in raising a question about our experience of knowledge.

Y. Soc. Why so?

Str. Why, because my 'example' requires the assistance of another example.

Y. Soc. Proceed; you need not fear that I shall tire.

Str. I will proceed, finding, as I do, such a ready listener in you: when children are beginning to know their letters—

Y. Soc. What are you going to say?

Str. That they distinguish the several letters well enough in very short and easy syllables, and are able to tell them correctly.

Y. Soc. Certainly.

Str. Whereas in other syllables they do not recognize them, and think and speak falsely of them.

Y. Soc. Very true.

Str. Will not the best and easiest way of bringing them to a knowledge of what they do not as yet know be—

Y. Soc. Be what?

Str. To refer them first of all to cases in which they judge correctly about the letters in question, and then to compare these with the cases in which they do not as yet know, and to show them that the letters are the same, and have the same character in both combination, until all cases in which they are right have been placed side by side with all cases in which they are wrong. In this way they have examples, and are made to learn that each letter in every combination is always the same and not another, and is always called by the same name.

Y. Soc. Certainly.

Str. Are not examples formed in this manner? We take a thing and compare it with another distinct instance of the same thing, of which we have a right conception, and out of the comparison there arises one true notion, which includes both of them.

Y. Soc. Exactly.

Str. Can we wonder, then, that the soul has the same uncertainty about the alphabet of things, and sometimes and in some cases is firmly fixed by the truth in each particular, and then, again, in other cases is altogether at sea; having somehow or other a correct notion of combinations; but when the elements are transferred into the long and difficult language (syllables) of facts, is again ignorant of them?

Y. Soc. There is nothing wonderful in that.

Str. Could any one, my friend, who began with false opinion

through
examples
dimly.

The use
of examples
illustrated
by the
[278]
way
in which
children
learn to
know letters in
different
combinations.

The
method
by which
we learn
'the long
and difficult language
of facts' is
similar.

*States-
man*

STRANGER,
YOUNG
SOCRATES.

ever expect to arrive even at a small portion of truth and to attain
wisdom?

Y. Soc. Hardly.

Str. Then you and I will not be far wrong in trying to see the
nature of example in general in a small and particular instance;
afterwards from lesser things we intend to pass to the royal class,
which is the highest form of the same nature, and endeavour to
discover by rules of art what the management of cities is; and then
the dream will become a reality to us.

Y. Soc. Very true.

279

Str. Then, once more, let us resume the previous argument, and
as there were innumerable rivals of the royal race who claim to
have the care of states, let us part them all off, and leave him
alone; and, as I was saying, a model or example of this process
has first to be framed.

Y. Soc. Exactly.

Weaving
may be
made a
model of
the
States-
man's art.

Str. What model is there which is small, and yet has any analogy
with the political occupation? Suppose, Socrates, that if we have
no other example at hand, we choose weaving, or, more precisely,
weaving of wool—this will be quite enough, without taking the
whole of weaving, to illustrate our meaning?

Y. Soc. Certainly.

Str. Why should we not apply to weaving the same processes of
division and subdivision which we have already applied to other
classes; going once more as rapidly as we can through all the
steps until we come to that which is needed for our purpose?

Y. Soc. How do you mean?

Str. I shall reply by actually performing the process.

Y. Soc. Very good.

Partings-
off of
larger
classes
from
which
weaving
is de-
scended.

Str. All things which we make or acquire are either creative or
preventive; of the preventive class are antidotes, divine and human, and also defences; and defences are either military weapons
or protections; and protections are veils, and also shields against
heat and cold, and shields against heat and cold are shelters
and coverings; and coverings are blankets and garments; and garments are some of them in one piece, and others of them are made
in several parts; and of these latter some are stitched, others are
fastened and not stitched; and of the not stitched, some are made
of the sinews of plants, and some of hair; and of these, again, some
are cemented with water and earth, and others are fastened together by themselves. And these last defences and coverings which are
fastened together by themselves are called clothes, and the art
which superintends them we may call, from the nature of the oper-

ation, the art of clothing, just as before the art of the Statesman was derived from the State; and may we not say that the art of weaving, at least that largest portion of it which was concerned with the making of clothes (cp. 279 B), differs only in name from this art of clothing, in the same way that, in the previous case, the royal science differed from the political?

Y. Soc. Most true.

Str. In the next place, let us make the reflection, that the art of weaving clothes, which an incompetent person might fancy to have been sufficiently described, has been separated off from several others which are of the same family, but not from the co-operative arts.

Y. Soc. And which are the kindred arts?

Str. I see that I have not taken you with me. So I think that we had better go backwards, starting from the end. We just now parted off from the weaving of clothes, the making of blankets, which differ from each other in that one is put under and the other is put around! and these are what I termed kindred arts.

Y. Soc. I understand.

Str. And we have subtracted the manufacture of all articles made of flax and cords, and all that we just now metaphorically termed the sinews of plants, and we have also separated off the process of felting and the putting together of materials by stitching and sewing, of which the most important part is the cobbler's art.

Y. Soc. Precisely.

Str. Then we separated off the currier's art, which prepared coverings in entire pieces, and the art of sheltering, and subtracted the various arts of making water-tight which are employed in building, and in general in carpentering, and in other crafts, and all such arts as furnish impediments to thieving and acts of violence, and are concerned with making the lids of boxes and the fixing of doors, being divisions of the art of joining; and we also cut off the manufacture of arms, which is a section of the great and manifold art of making defences; and we originally began by parting off the whole of the magic art which is concerned with antidotes, and have left, as would appear, the very art of which we were in search, the art of protection against winter cold, which fabricates woollen defences, and has the name of weaving.

Y. Soc. Very true.

Str. Yes, my boy, but that is not all; for the first process to which the material is subjected is the opposite of weaving.

Y. Soc. How so?

Str. Weaving is a sort of uniting?

Y. Soc. Yes.

280
Statesman

STRANGER,
YOUNG
SOCRATES.

The art of weaving and the art of making clothes differ only in name, like the royal and the political sciences.

Recapitulation of the arts which have been parted off from weaving.

Weaving is an art of protection against cold, which fabricates woollen defences.
[281]
But it must be further distinguished.

Str. But the first process is a separation of the clotted and matted fibres?

Y. Soc. What do you mean?

Str. I mean the work of the carder's art; for we cannot say that carding is weaving, or that the carder is a weaver.

Y. Soc. Certainly not.

Str. Again, if a person were to say that the art of making the warp and the woof was the art of weaving, he would say what was paradoxical and false.

Y. Soc. To be sure.

Str. Shall we say that the whole art of the fuller or of the mender has nothing to do with the care and treatment of clothes, or are we to regard all these as arts of weaving?

Y. Soc. Certainly not.

Str. And yet surely all these arts will maintain that they are concerned with the treatment and production of clothes; they will dispute the exclusive prerogative of weaving, and though assigning a larger sphere to that, will still reserve a considerable field for themselves.

Y. Soc. Very true.

Str. Besides these, there are the arts which make tools and instruments of weaving, and which will claim at least to be co-operative causes in every work of the weaver.

Y. Soc. Most true.

Str. Well, then, suppose that we define weaving, or rather that part of it which has been selected by us, to be the greatest and noblest of arts which are concerned with woollen garments—shall we be right? Is not the definition, although true, wanting in clearness and completeness; for do not all those other arts require to be first cleared away?

Y. Soc. True.

Str. Then the next thing will be to separate them, in order that the argument may proceed in a regular manner?

Y. Soc. By all means.

Str. Let us consider, in the first place, that there are two kinds of arts entering into everything which we do.

Y. Soc. What are they?

Str. The one kind is the conditional or co-operative, the other the principal cause.

Y. Soc. What do you mean?

Str. The arts which do not manufacture the actual thing, but which furnish the necessary tools for the manufacture, without which the several arts could not fulfil their appointed work, are co-operative; but those which make the things themselves are causal.

Y. Soc. A very reasonable distinction.

Str. Thus the arts which make spindles, combs, and other instruments of the production of clothes, may be called co-operative, and those which treat and fabricate the things themselves, causal.

Y. Soc. Very true.

Str. The arts of washing and mending, and the other preparatory arts which belong to the causal class, and form a division of the great art of adornment, may be all comprehended under what we call the fuller's art.

Y. Soc. Very good.

Str. Carding and spinning threads and all the parts of the process which are concerned with the actual manufacture of a woollen garment form a single art, which is one of those universally acknowledged,—the art of working in wool.

Y. Soc. To be sure.

Str. Of working in wool, again, there are two divisions, and both these are parts of two arts at once.

Y. Soc. How is that?

Str. Carding and one half of the use of the comb, and the other processes of wool-working which separate the composite, may be classed together as belonging both to the art of wool-working, and also to one of the two great arts which are of universal application —the art of composition and the art of division.

Y. Soc. Yes.

Str. To the latter belong carding and the other processes of which I was just now speaking; the art of discernment or division in wool and yarn, which is effected in one manner with the comb and in another with the hands, is variously described under all the names which I just now mentioned.

Y. Soc. Very true.

Str. Again, let us take some process of wool-working which is also a portion of the art of composition, and, dismissing the elements of division which we found there[1], make two halves, one on the principle of composition, and the other on the principle of division.

Y. Soc. Let that be done.

Str. And once more, Socrates, we must divide the part which belongs at once both to wool-working and composition, if we are ever to discover satisfactorily the aforesaid art of weaving.

Y. Soc. We must.

[1] Reading ὅσα δὲ τῆς διακριτικῆς ἦν αὐτόθι, μεθιῶμεν ξύμπαντα,

make tools, the [282] causal use them in production.

In the case of working in wool, washing, mending, carding, spinning, etc. belong to the causal class.

Of wool-working there are two great sections, which fall respectively under the art of composition and the art of division.

We are concerned with the former, of which there are two parts, one which twists, and another which combines.

States-
man

STRANGER,
YOUNG
SOCRATES.

Both
warp and
woof are
made by
twisting;
but the
thread of
the warp
is firm,
whereas
the thread
of the
woof is
loose and
soft.

283

Weaving
is that
portion of
the art of
compo-
sition
which
forms a
web by
the inter-
texture of
warp and
woof.

But could
we not
have de-
fined it
more
speedily?
—This
question
cannot be
answered
until we
have con-

Str. Yes, certainly, and let us call one part of the art the art of twisting threads, the other the art of combining them.

Y. Soc. Do I understand you, in speaking of twisting, to be referring to manufacture of the warp?

Str. Yes, and of the woof too; how, if not by twisting, is the woof made?

Y. Soc. There is no other way.

Str. Then suppose that you define the warp and the woof, for I think that the definition will be of use to you.

Y. Soc. How shall I define them?

Str. As thus: A piece of carded wool which is drawn out lengthwise and breadthwise is said to be pulled out.

Y. Soc. Yes.

Str. And the wool thus prepared, when twisted by the spindle, and made into a firm thread, is called the warp, and the art which regulates these operations the art of spinning the warp.

Y. Soc. True.

Str. And the threads which are more loosely spun, having a softness proportioned to the intertexture of the warp and to the degree of force used in dressing the cloth,—the threads which are thus spun are called the woof, and the art which is set over them may be called the art of spinning the woof.

Y. Soc. Very true.

Str. And, now, there can be no mistake about the nature of the part of weaving which we have undertaken to define. For when that part of the art of composition which is employed in the working of wool forms a web by the regular intertexture of warp and woof, the entire woven substance is called by us a woollen garment, and the art which presides over this is the art of weaving.

Y. Soc. Very true.

Str. But why did we not say at once that weaving is the art of entwining warp and woof, instead of making a long and useless circuit?

Y. Soc. I thought, Stranger, that there was nothing useless in what was said.

Str. Very likely, but you may not always think so, my sweet friend; and in case any feeling of dissatisfaction should hereafter arise in your mind, as it very well may, let me lay down a principle which will apply to arguments in general.

Y. Soc. Proceed.

Str. Let us begin by considering the whole nature of excess and defect, and then we shall have a rational ground on which we may praise or blame too much length or too much shortness in discussions of this kind.

Y. Soc. Let us do so.

Str. The points on which I think that we ought to dwell are the following:—

Y. Soc. What?

Str. Length and shortness, excess and defect; with all of these the art of measurement is conversant.

Y. Soc. Yes.

Str. And the art of measurement has to be divided into two parts, with a view to our present purpose.

Y. Soc. Where would you make the division?

Str. As thus: I would make two parts, one having regard to the relativity of greatness and smallness to each other; and there is another, without which the existence of production would be impossible.

Y. Soc. What do you mean?

Str. Do you not think that it is only natural for the greater to be called greater with reference to the less alone, and the less less with reference to the greater alone?

Y. Soc. Yes.

Str. Well, but is there not also something exceeding and exceeded by the principle of the mean, both in speech and action, and is not this a reality, and the chief mark of difference between good and bad men?

Y. Soc. Plainly.

Str. Then we must suppose that the great and small exist and are discerned in both these ways, and not, as we were saying before, only relatively to one another, but there must also be another comparison of them with the mean or ideal standard; would you like to hear the reason why?

Y. Soc. Certainly.

Str. If we assume the greater to exist only in relation to the less, there will never be any comparison of either with the mean.

Y. Soc. True.

Str. And would not this doctrine be the ruin of all the arts and their creations; would not the art of the Statesman and the aforesaid art of weaving disappear? For all these arts are on the watch against excess and defect, not as unrealities, but as real evils, which occasion a difficulty in action; and the excellence of beauty of every work of art is due to this observance of measure.

Y. Soc. Certainly.

States-man

STRANGER,
YOUNG
SOCRATES.

sidered the whole nature of excess and defect.

There are two divisions of the art of measurement: the first compares excess and defect with each other;

the second, with the principle of the mean.

284

The excellence of the arts depends on their observance of the mean; the ne-

States-
man

STRANGER,
YOUNG
SOCRATES.

glect of it
is their
ruin.

It is no
easy
matter to
show the
truth of
the state-
ment that
excess
and defect
are rela-
tive to a
mean, as
well as to
each
other.

At present
we will
not at-
tempt the
task; it is
enough
that the
existence
of the
arts de-
pends on
the possi-
bility of a
mean
standard.

285
The art of
measure-
ment is
said by
many to
be uni-
versal,
and with
a certain

Str. But if the science of the Statesman disappears, the search for the royal science will be impossible.

Y. Soc. Very true.

Str. Well, then, as in the case of the Sophist we extorted the in-ference that not-being had an existence, because here was the point at which the argument eluded our grasp, so in this we must en-deavour to show that the greater and less are not only to be meas-ured with one another, but also have to do with the production of the mean; for if this is not admitted, neither a statesman nor any other man of action can be an undisputed master of his science.

Y. Soc. Yes, we must certainly do again what we did then.

Str. But this, Socrates, is a greater work than the other, of which we only too well remember the length. I think, however, that we may fairly assume something of this sort:—

Y. Soc. What?

Str. That we shall some day require this notion of a mean with a view to the demonstration of absolute truth; meanwhile, the argu-ment that the very existence of the arts must be held to depend on the possibility of measuring more or less, not only with one another, but also with a view to the attainment of the mean, seems to afford a grand support and satisfactory proof of the doctrine which we are maintaining; for if there are arts, there is a standard of meas-ure, and if there is a standard of measure, there are arts; but if either is wanting, there is neither.

Y. Soc. True; and what is the next step?

Str. The next step clearly is to divide the art of measurement into two parts, as we have said already, and to place in the one part all the arts which measure number, length, depth, breadth, swiftness[1] with their opposites; and to have another part in which they are measured with the mean, and the fit, and the opportune, and the due, and with all those words, in short, which denote a mean or standard removed from the extremes.

Y. Soc. Here are two vast divisions, embracing two very differ-ent spheres.

Str. There are many accomplished men, Socrates, who say, be-lieving themselves to speak wisely, that the art of measurement is universal, and has to do with all things. And this means what we are now saying; for all things which come within the province of art do certainly in some sense partake of measure. But these per-sons, because they are not accustomed to distinguish classes accord-ing to real forms, jumble together two widely different things, relation to one another, and to a standard, under the idea that they

---

[1] Reading ταχύτητας.

are the same, and also fall into the converse error of dividing other
things not according to their real parts. Whereas the right way is,
if a man has first seen the unity of things, to go on with the enquiry
and not desist until he has found all the differences contained in it
which form distinct classes; nor again should he be able to rest contented with the manifold diversities which are seen in a multitude
of things until he has comprehended all of them that have any affinity within the bounds of one similarity and embraced them within the reality of a single kind. But we have said enough on this
head, and also of excess and defect; we have only to bear in mind
that two divisions of the art of measurement have been discovered
which are concerned with them, and not forget what they are.

Y. Soc. We will not forget.

Str. And now that this discussion is completed, let us go on to
consider another question, which concerns not this argument only
but the conduct of such arguments in general.

Y. Soc. What is this new question?

Str. Take the case of a child who is engaged in learning his letters: when he is asked what letters make up a word, should we say
that the question is intended to improve his grammatical knowledge
of that particular word, or of all words?

Y. Soc. Clearly, in order that he may have a better knowledge
of all words.

Str. And is our enquiry about the Statesman intended only to
improve our knowledge of politics, or our power of reasoning
generally?

Y. Soc. Clearly, as in the former example, the purpose is general.

Str. Still less would any rational man seek to analyse the notion
of weaving for its own sake. But people seem to forget that some
things have sensible images, which are readily known, and can be
easily pointed out when any one desires to answer an enquirer without any trouble or argument; whereas the greatest and highest
truths have no outward image of themselves visible to man, which
he who wishes to satisfy the soul of the enquirer can adapt to the
eye of sense[1], and therefore we ought to train ourselves to give and
accept a rational account of them; for immaterial things, which
are the noblest and greatest, are shown only in thought and idea,
and in no other way, and all that we are now saying is said for the
sake of them. Moreover, there is always less difficulty in fixing the
mind on small matters than on great.

Y. Soc. Very good.

Str. Let us call to mind the bearing of all this.

[1] Cp. Phaedr. 250 D, E.

amount
of truth;
but they
confuse
the two
divisions
of
the art
and also
make
false dis-
tinctions.

Our en-
quiry
about the
States-
man is
intended
to make
us better
dialecti-
cians; and
the illus-
[286]
trations
and an-
alogies
which we
employ in
order to
throw
light upon
it have
the same
purpose.

States-man

STRANGER,
YOUNG
SOCRATES.

Y. Soc. What is it?

Str. I wanted to get rid of any impression of tediousness which we may have experienced in the discussion about weaving, and the reversal of the universe, and in the discussion concerning the Sophist and the being of not-being. I know that they were felt to be too long, and I reproached myself with this, fearing that they might be not only tedious but irrelevant; and all that I have now said is only designed to prevent the recurrence of any such disagreeables for the future.

Y. Soc. Very good. Will you proceed?

Str. Then I would like to observe that you and I, remembering what has been said, should praise or blame the length or shortness of discussions, not by comparing them with one another, but with what is fitting, having regard to the part of measurement, which, as we said, was to be borne in mind.

Y. Soc. Very true.

Str. And yet, not everything is to be judged even with a view to what is fitting; for we should only want such a length as is suited to give pleasure, if at all, as a secondary matter; and reason tells us, that we should be contented to make the ease or rapidity of an enquiry, not our first, but our second object; the first and highest of all being to assert the great method of division according to species—whether the discourse be shorter or longer is not to the point. No offence should be taken at length, but the longer and shorter are to be employed indifferently, according as either of them is better calculated to sharpen the wits of the auditors. Reason would also say to him who censures the length of discourses on such occasions and cannot away with their circumlocution, that he should not be in such a hurry to have done with them, when he can only complain that they are tedious, but he should prove that if they had been shorter they would have made those who took part in them better dialecticians, and more capable of expressing the truth of things; about any other praise and blame, he need not trouble himself—he should pretend not to hear them. But we have had enough of this, as you will probably agree with me in thinking. Let us return to our Statesman, and apply to his case the aforesaid example of weaving.

Y. Soc. Very good;—let us do as you say.

Str. The art of the king has been separated from the similar arts of shepherds, and, indeed, from all those which have to do with herds at all. There still remain, however, of the causal and co-operative arts those which are immediately concerned with States, and which must first be distinguished from one another.

The standard by which excess and defect should be determined is what is fitting, but not what is fitting to give pleasure; for the chief aim of an enquiry should be, not to give pleasure, but to assert the method of division
[287]
according to species.

Would our discourse, if shorter, have made the listeners better dialecticians?

Let us now apply our example

Y. Soc. Very good.

Str. You know that these arts cannot easily be divided into two halves; the reason will be very evident as we proceed.

Y. Soc. Then we had better do so.

Str. We must carve them like a victim into members or limbs, since we cannot bisect them[1]. For we certainly should divide everything into as few parts as possible.

Y. Soc. What is to be done in this case?

Str. What we did in the example of weaving—all those arts which furnish the tools were regarded by us as co-operative.

Y. Soc. Yes.

Str. So now, and with still more reason, all arts which make any implement in a State, whether great or small, may be regarded by us as co-operative, for without them neither State nor Statesmanship would be possible; and yet we are not inclined to say that any of them is a product of the kingly art.

Y. Soc. No, indeed.

Str. The task of separating this class from others is not an easy one; for there is plausibility in saying that anything in the world is the instrument of doing something. But there is another class of possessions in a city, of which I have a word to say.

Y. Soc. What class do you mean?

Str. A class which may be described as not having this power[2]; that is to say, not like an instrument, framed for production, but designed for the preservation of that which is produced.

Y. Soc. To what do you refer?

Str. To the class of vessels, as they are comprehensively termed, which are constructed for the preservation of things moist and dry, of things prepared in the fire or out of the fire; this is a very large class, and has, if I am not mistaken, literally nothing to do with the royal art of which we are in search.

Y. Soc. Certainly not.

Str. There is also a third class of possessions to be noted, different from these and very extensive, moving or resting on land or water, honourable and also dishonourable. The whole of this class has one name, because it is intended to be sat upon, being always a seat for something.

Y. Soc. What is it?

Str. A vehicle, which is certainly not the work of the Statesman, but of the carpenter, potter, and coppersmith.

---

[1] Cp. Phaedr. 265 E.
[2] Or, taking the words in a different context, 'As not having political power —I say another class, because not like an instrument,' &c.

Statesman

STRANGER, YOUNG SOCRATES.

of weaving to the Statesman.

From kingship the other arts of tending herds have been separated: certain causal and co-operative arts remain. These cannot be bisected, and must therefore be neatly carved.

Thus we set aside the arts which provide [288] (1) instruments,— under this head we might place anything;

(2) vessels;

(3) seats or vehicles;

Y. Soc. I understand.

Str. And is there not a fourth class which is again different, and in which most of the things formerly mentioned are contained,—every kind of dress, most sorts of arms, walls and enclosures, whether of earth or stone, and ten thousand other things? all of which being made for the sake of defence, may be truly called defences, and are for the most part to be regarded as the work of the builder or of the weaver, rather than of the Statesman.

Y. Soc. Certainly.

Str. Shall we add a fifth class, of ornamentation and drawing, and of the imitations produced by drawing and music, which are designed for amusement only, and may be fairly comprehended under one name?

Y. Soc. What is it?

Str. Plaything is the name.

Y. Soc. Certainly.

Str. That one name may be fitly predicated of all of them, for none of these things have a serious purpose—amusement is their sole aim.

Y. Soc. That again I understand.

Str. Then there is a class which provides materials for all these, out of which and in which the arts already mentioned fabricate their works;—this manifold class, I say, which is the creation and offspring of many other arts, may I not rank sixth?

Y. Soc. What do you mean?

Str. I am referring to gold, silver, and other metals, and all that wood-cutting and shearing of every sort provides for the art of carpentry and plaiting; and there is the process of barking and stripping the cuticle of plants, and the currier's art, which strips off the skins of animals, and other similar arts which manufacture corks and papyri and cords, and provide for the manufacture of composite species out of simple kinds—the whole class may be termed the primitive and simple possession of man, and with this the kingly science has no concern at all.

Y. Soc. True.

Str. The provision of food and of all other things which mingle their particles with the particles of the human body, and minister to the body, will form a seventh class, which may be called by the general term of nourishment, unless you have any better name to offer. This, however, appertains rather to the husbandman, huntsman, trainer, doctor, cook, and is not to be assigned to the Statesman's art.

Y. Soc. Certainly not.

Str. These seven classes include nearly every description of property, with the exception of tame animals. Consider;—there was the original material, which ought to have been placed first; next come instruments, vessels, vehicles, defences, playthings, nourishment; small things, which may be included under one of these—as for example, coins, seals and stamps, are omitted, for they have not in them the character of any larger kind which includes them; but some of them may, with a little forcing, be placed among ornaments, and others may be made to harmonize with the class of implements. The art of herding, which has been already divided into parts, will include all property in tame animals, except slaves.

Y. Soc. Very true.

Str. The class of slaves and ministers only remains, and I suspect that in this the real aspirants for the throne, who are the rivals of the king in the formation of the political web, will be discovered; just as spinners, carders, and the rest of them, were the rivals of the weaver. All the others, who were termed co-operators, have been got rid of among the occupations already mentioned, and separated from the royal and political science.

Y. Soc. I agree.

Str. Let us go a little nearer, in order that we may be more certain of the complexion of this remaining class.

Y. Soc. Let us do so.

Str. We shall find from our present point of view that the greatest servants are in a case and condition which is the reverse of what we anticipated.

Y. Soc. Who are they?

Str. Those who have been purchased, and have so become possessions; these are unmistakably slaves, and certainly do not claim royal science.

Y. Soc. Certainly not.

Str. Again, freemen who of their own accord become the servants of the other classes in a State, and who exchange and equalise the products of husbandry and the other arts, some sitting in the market-place, others going from city to city by land or sea, and giving money in exchange for money or for other productions— the money-changer, the merchant, the ship-owner, the retailer, will not put in any claim to statecraft or politics?

Y. Soc. No; unless, indeed, to the politics of commerce.

Str. But surely men whom we see acting as hirelings and serfs, and too happy to turn their hand to anything, will not profess to share in royal science?

Y. Soc. Certainly not.

Statesman

STRANGER, YOUNG SOCRATES.

These seven classes include almost all possessions, except tame animals; and all tame animals, except slaves, have been included under herding.

Thus slaves and ministers alone remain; and among them we must look for the rivals of the king.

But slaves certainly do not claim royal science;

nor traders;

290

nor hirelings;

States-
man

STRANGER,
YOUNG
SOCRATES.

nor state
officials;

Str. But what would you say of some other serviceable officials?

Y. Soc. Who are they, and what services do they perform?

Str. There are heralds, and scribes perfected by practice, and divers others who have great skill in various sorts of business connected with the government of states—what shall we call them?

Y. Soc. They are the officials, and servants of the rulers, as you just now called them, but not themselves rulers.

Str. There may be something strange in any servant pretending to be a ruler, and yet I do not think that I could have been dreaming when I imagined that the principal claimants to political science would be found somewhere in this neighbourhood.

Y. Soc. Very true.

nor
diviners;

Str. Well, let us draw nearer, and try the claims of some who have not yet been tested; in the first place, there are diviners, who have a portion of servile or ministerial science, and are thought to be the interpreters of the gods to men.

Y. Soc. True.

nor
priests.

Str. There is also the priestly class, who, as the law declares, know how to give the gods gifts from men in the form of sacrifices which are acceptable to them, and to ask on our behalf blessings in return from them. Now both these are branches of the servile or ministerial art.

Y. Soc. Yes, clearly.

But here
we are
getting on
the right
track; for
both
priest and
diviner
are am-
bitious.

Str. And here I think that we seem to be getting on the right track; for the priest and the diviner are swollen with pride and prerogative, and they create an awful impression of themselves by the magnitude of their enterprises; in Egypt, the king himself is not allowed to reign, unless he have priestly powers, and if he should be of another class and has thrust himself in, he must get enrolled in the priesthood. In many parts of Hellas, the duty of offering the most solemn propitiatory sacrifices is assigned to the highest magistracies, and here, at Athens, the most solemn and national of the ancient sacrifices are supposed to be celebrated by him who has been chosen by lot to be the King Archon.

Y. Soc. Precisely.

291

At last
the false
politician,
the great-
est of
Sophists
and
wizards,
appears in

Str. But who are these other kings and priests elected by lot who now come into view followed by their retainers and a vast throng, as the former class disappears and the scene changes?

Y. Soc. Whom can you mean?

Str. They are a strange crew.

Y. Soc. Why strange?

Str. A minute ago I thought that they were animals of every tribe; for many of them are like lions and centaurs, and many more like satyrs and such weak and shifty creatures;—Protean shapes quickly changing into one another's forms and natures; and now, Socrates, I begin to see who they are.

Y. Soc. Who are they? You seem to be gazing on some strange vision.

Str. Yes; every one looks strange when you do not know him; and just now I myself fell into this mistake—at first sight, coming suddenly upon him, I did not recognize the politician and his troop.

Y. Soc. Who is he?

Str. The chief of Sophists and most accomplished of wizards, who must at any cost be separated from the true king or Statesman, if we are ever to see daylight in the present enquiry.

Y. Soc. That is a hope not lightly to be renounced.

Str. Never, if I can help it; and, first, let me ask you a question.

Y. Soc. What?

Str. Is not monarchy a recognized form of government?

Y. Soc. Yes.

Str. And, after monarchy, next in order comes the government of the few?

Y. Soc. Of course.

Str. Is not the third form of government the rule of the multitude, which is called by the name of democracy?

Y. Soc. Certainly.

Str. And do not these three expand in a manner into five, producing out of themselves two other names?

Y. Soc. What are they?

Str. There is a criterion of voluntary and involuntary, poverty and riches, law and the absence of law, which men now-a-days apply to them; the two first they subdivide accordingly, and ascribe to monarchy two forms and two corresponding names, royalty and tyranny.

Y. Soc. Very true.

Str. And the government of the few they distinguish by the names of aristocracy and oligarchy.

Y. Soc. Certainly.

Str. Democracy alone, whether rigidly observing the laws or not, and whether the multitude rule over the men of property with their consent or against their consent, always in ordinary language has the same name.

Y. Soc. True.

Str. But do you suppose that any form of government which is defined by these characteristics of the one, the few, or the many,

---

States-man

STRANGER, YOUNG SOCRATES.

view, surrounded by his troop who take Protean shapes.

He must be separated from the king at any cost.

There are three chief forms of government; monarchy, the rule of the few, and democracy; these expand into five by the division of monarchy into royalty and tyranny, and of the government of the few into aristocracy [292] and oligarchy.

But these forms of govern-

320 The true criterion of government

*States-
man*

STRANGER,
YOUNG
SOCRATES.

ment are
based on
false
principles.

of poverty or wealth, of voluntary or compulsory submission, of written law or the absence of law, can be a right one?

Y. Soc. Why not?

Str. Reflect; and follow me.

Y. Soc. In what direction?

Str. Shall we abide by what we said at first, or shall we retract our words?

Y. Soc. To what do you refer?

Str. If I am not mistaken, we said that royal power was a science?

Y. Soc. Yes.

Str. And a science of a peculiar kind, which was selected out of the rest as having a character which is at once judicial and authoritative?

Y. Soc. Yes.

Str. And there was one kind of authority over lifeless things and another over living animals; and so we proceeded in the division step by step up to this point, not losing the idea of science, but unable as yet to determine the nature of the particular science?

Y. Soc. True.

The char-
acteristic
of a true
govern-
ment is
not that
it is of
few or
many,
voluntary
or invol-
untary,
but that it
is scien-
tific.

Str. Hence we are led to observe that the distinguishing principle of the State cannot be the few or many, the voluntary or involuntary, poverty or riches; but some notion of science must enter into it, if we are to be consistent with what has preceded.

Y. Soc. And we must be consistent.

Str. Well, then, in which of these various forms of States may the science of government, which is among the greatest of all sciences and most difficult to acquire, be supposed to reside? That we must discover, and then we shall see who are the false politicians who pretend to be politicians but are not, although they persuade many, and shall separate them from the wise king.

Y. Soc. That, as the argument has already intimated, will be our duty.

Str. Do you think that the multitude in a State can attain political science?

Y. Soc. Impossible.

Str. But, perhaps, in a city of a thousand men, there would be a hundred, or say fifty, who could?

Y. Soc. In that case political science would certainly be the easiest of all sciences; there could not be found in a city of that number as many really first-rate draught-players, if judged by the standard of the rest of Hellas, and there would certainly not be as many kings. For kings we may truly call those who possess royal science, whether they rule or not, as was shown in the previous argument[1].

Str. Thank you for reminding me; and the consequence is that any true form of government can only be supposed to be the government of one, two, or, at any rate, of a few.

Y. Soc. Certainly.

Str. And these, whether they rule with the will, or against the will, of their subjects, with written laws or without written laws, and whether they are poor or rich, and whatever be the nature of their rule, must be supposed, according to our present view, to rule on some scientific principle; just as the physician, whether he cures us against our will or with our will, and whatever be his mode of treatment,—incision, burning, or the infliction of some other pain, —whether he practises out of a book or not out of a book, and whether he be rich or poor, whether he purges or reduces in some other way, or even fattens his patients, is a physician all the same, so long as he exercises authority over them according to rules of art, if he only does them good and heals and saves them. And this we lay down to be the only proper test of the art of medicine, or of any other art of command.

Y. Soc. Quite true.

Str. Then that can be the only true form of government in which the governors are really found to possess science, and are not mere pretenders, whether they rule according to law or without law, over willing or unwilling subjects, and are rich or poor themselves— none of these things can with any propriety be included in the notion of the ruler.

Y. Soc. True.

Str. And whether with a view to the public good they purge the State by killing some, or exiling some; whether they reduce the size of the body corporate by sending out from the hive swarms of citizens, or, by introducing persons from without, increase it; while they act according to the rules of wisdom and justice, and use their power with a view to the general security and improvement, the city over which they rule, and which has these characteristics, may be described as the only true State. All other governments are not genuine or real, but only imitations of this, and some of them are better and some of them are worse; the better are said to be well governed, but they are mere imitations like the others.

Y. Soc. I agree, Stranger, in the greater part of what you say; but as to their ruling without laws—the expression has a harsh sound.

[1] Cp. *supra*, 259 A.

*States-
man*

293
STRANGER,
YOUNG
SOCRATES.

The
science of
govern-
ment can
only be
attained
by a very
few.

So long as
the gov-
ernors
rule scien-
tifically, it
matters
not
whether
they rule
with or
without
law, over
willing or
unwilling
subjects.

Young
Socrates
objects to
govern-

294
*States-
man*

STRANGER,
YOUNG
SOCRATES.

ment
without
laws.

He is an-
swered
that the
rule of a
wise man
is better
than the
rule of
law; for
the com-
plexity of
human
affairs
cannot be
met by
legisla-
tion.

Law is
like an
obstinate
and ig-
norant
tyrant.

Why then
are laws
made?

As the
training-
master
makes
rules, not
for each
particular
case—
that
would be
impos-
sible—but
for the
gener-
ality,

Str. You have been too quick for me, Socrates; I was just going to ask you whether you objected to any of my statements. And now I see that we shall have to consider this notion of there being good government without laws.

Y. Soc. Certainly.

Str. There can be no doubt that legislation is in a manner the business of a king, and yet the best thing of all is not that the law should rule, but that a man should rule, supposing him to have wisdom and royal power. Do you see why this is?

Y. Soc. Why?

Str. Because the law does not perfectly comprehend what is noblest and most just for all and therefore cannot enforce what is best. The differences of men and actions, and the endless irregular movements of human things, do not admit of any universal and simple rule. And no art whatsoever can lay down a rule which will last for all time.

Y. Soc. Of course not.

Str. But the law is always striving to make one;—like an obstinate and ignorant tyrant, who will not allow anything to be done contrary to his appointment, or any question to be asked—not even in sudden changes of circumstances, when something happens to be better than what he commanded for some one.

Y. Soc. Certainly; the law treats us all precisely in the manner which you describe.

Str. A perfectly simple principle can never be applied to a state of things which is the reverse of simple.

Y. Soc. True.

Str. Then if the law is not the perfection of right, why are we compelled to make laws at all? The reason of this has next to be investigated.

Y. Soc. Certainly.

Str. Let me ask, whether you have not meetings for gymnastic contests in your city, such as there are in other cities, at which men compete in running, wrestling, and the like?

Y. Soc. Yes; they are very common among us.

Str. And what are the rules which are enforced on their pupils by professional trainers or by others having similar authority? Can you remember?

Y. Soc. To what do you refer?

Str. The training-masters do not issue minute rules for individuals, or give every individual what is exactly suited to his constitution; they think that they ought to go more roughly to work, and to prescribe generally the regimen which will benefit the majority.

Y. Soc. Very true.

Str. And therefore they assign equal amounts of exercise to them all; they send them forth together, and let them rest together from their running, wrestling, or whatever the form of bodily exercise may be.

Y. Soc. True.

Str. And now observe that the legislator who has to preside over the herd, and to enforce justice in their dealings with one another, will not be able, in enacting for the general good, to provide exactly what is suitable for each particular case.

Y. Soc. He cannot be expected to do so.

Str. He will lay down laws in a general form for the majority, roughly meeting the cases of individuals; and some of them he will deliver in writing, and others will be unwritten; and these last will be traditional customs of the country.

Y. Soc. He will be right.

Str. Yes, quite right; for how can he sit at every man's side all through his life, prescribing for him the exact particulars of his duty? Who, Socrates, would be equal to such a task? No one who really had the royal science, if he had been able to do this, would have imposed upon himself the restriction of a written law.

Y. Soc. So I should infer from what has now been said.

Str. Or rather, my good friend, from what is going to be said.

Y. Soc. And what is that?

Str. Let us put to ourselves the case of a physician, or trainer, who is about to go into a far country, and is expecting to be a long time away from his patients—thinking that his instructions will not be remembered unless they are written down, he will leave notes of them for the use of his pupils or patients.

Y. Soc. True.

Str. But what would you say, if he came back sooner than he had intended, and, owing to an unexpected change of the winds or other celestial influences, something else happened to be better for them, —would he not venture to suggest this new remedy, although not contemplated in his former prescription? Would he persist in observing the original law, neither himself giving any new commandments, nor the patient daring to do otherwise than was prescribed, under the idea that this course only was healthy and medicinal, all others noxious and heterodox? Viewed in the light of science and true art, would not all such enactments be utterly ridiculous?

States-
man

STRANGER,
YOUNG
SOCRATES.

296

he will
disregard
his former
prescrip-
tion.

The legis-
lator, in
like man-
ner,
would not
hesitate to
change his
own laws,
if he came
to life
again.

A reform-
er should
carry
mankind
with him;
but even
if he use
a little
violence,
what
harm?

A phy-
sician is
not
blamed
for curing
a patient
against
his will;

and we
should
not con-
demn any
one who
compels
men to
act more
justly.

Y. Soc. Utterly.

Str. And if he who gave laws, written or unwritten, determining what was good or bad, honourable or dishonourable, just or unjust, to the tribes of men who flock together in their several cities, and are governed in accordance with them; if, I say, the wise legislator were suddenly to come again, or another like to him, is he to be prohibited from changing them?—would not this prohibition be in reality quite as ridiculous as the other?

Y. Soc. Certainly.

Str. Do you know a plausible saying of the common people which is in point?

Y. Soc. I do not recall what you mean at the moment.

Str. They say that if any one knows how the ancient laws may be improved, he must first persuade his own State of the improve-ment, and then he may legislate, but not otherwise.

Y. Soc. And are they not right?

Str. I dare say. But supposing that he does use some gentle vio-lence for their good, what is this violence to be called? Or rather, before you answer, let me ask the same question in reference to our previous instances.

Y. Soc. What do you mean?

Str. Suppose that a skilful physician has a patient, of whatever sex or age, whom he compels against his will to do something for his good which is contrary to the written rules; what is this com-pulsion to be called? Would you ever dream of calling it a viola-tion of the art, or a breach of the laws of health? Nothing could be more unjust than for the patient to whom such violence is applied, to charge the physician who practises the violence with wanting skill or aggravating his disease.

Y. Soc. Most true.

Str. In the political art error is not called disease, but evil, or disgrace, or injustice.

Y. Soc. Quite true.

Str. And when the citizen, contrary to law and custom, is com-pelled to do what is juster and better and nobler than he did before, the last and most absurd thing which he could say about such violence is that he has incurred disgrace or evil or injustice at the hands of those who compelled him.

Y. Soc. Very true.

Str. And shall we say that the violence, if exercised by a rich man, is just, and if by a poor man, unjust? May not any man, rich or poor, with or without laws, with the will of the citizens or against the will of the citizens, do what is for their interest? Is not this the true principle of government, according to which the wise and good man will order the affairs of his subjects? As the pilot, by watching continually over the interests of the ship and of the crew,—not by laying down rules, but by making his art a law,—preserves the lives of his fellow-sailors, even so, and in the self-same way, may there not be a true form of polity created by those who are able to govern in a similar spirit, and who show a strength of art which is superior to the law? Nor can wise rulers ever err while they, observing the one great rule of distributing justice to the citizens with intelligence and skill, are able to preserve them, and, as far as may be, to make them better from being worse.

Y. Soc. No one can deny what has been now said.

Str. Neither, if you consider, can any one deny the other statement.

Y. Soc. What was it?

Str. We said that no great number of persons, whoever they may be, can attain political knowledge, or order a State wisely, but that the true government is to be found in a small body, or in an individual, and that other States are but imitations of this, as we said a little while ago, some for the better and some for the worse.

Y. Soc. What do you mean? I cannot have understood your previous remark about imitations.

Str. And yet the mere suggestion which I hastily threw out is highly important, even if we leave the question where it is, and do not seek by the discussion of it to expose the error which prevails in this matter.

Y. Soc. What do you mean?

Str. The idea which has to be grasped by us is not easy or familiar; but we may attempt to express it thus:—Supposing the government of which I have been speaking to be the only true model, then the others must use the written laws of this—in no other way can they be saved; they will have to do what is now generally approved, although not the best thing in the world.

Y. Soc. What is this?

Str. No citizen should do anything contrary to the laws, and any infringement of them should be punished with death and the most extreme penalties; and this is very right and good when regarded as the second best thing, if you set aside the first, of which I was just now speaking. Shall I explain the nature of what I call the second best?

Y. Soc. By all means.

Str. I must again have recourse to my favourite images; through them, and them alone, can I describe kings and rulers.

297

Statesman

STRANGER,
YOUNG
SOCRATES.

In government, as in seamanship, art is superior to law.

The true form of government, as we said, is of few or of an individual: other forms are imitations of this.

They copy its laws and punish very severely the infringement of them — Yet this is not the best thing, but only the second best.

The real nature of

States-
man

STRANGER,
YOUNG
SOCRATES.

298

Y. Soc. What images?

Str. The noble pilot and the wise physician, who 'is worth many another man'—in the similitude of these let us endeavour to discover some image of the king.

Y. Soc. What sort of an image?

Str. Well, such as this:—Every man will reflect that he suffers strange things at the hands of both of them; the physician saves any whom he wishes to save, and any whom he wishes to maltreat he maltreats—cutting or burning them, and at the same time requiring them to bring him payments, which are a sort of tribute, of which little or nothing is spent upon the sick man, and the greater part is consumed by him and his domestics; and the finale is that he receives money from the relations of the sick man or from some enemy of his, and puts him out of the way. And the pilots of ships are guilty of numberless evil deeds of the same kind; they intentionally play false and leave you ashore when the hour of sailing arrives; or they cause mishaps at sea and cast away their freight; and are guilty of other rogueries. Now suppose that we, bearing all this in mind, were to determine, after consideration, that neither of these arts shall any longer be allowed to exercise absolute control either over freemen or over slaves, but that we will summon an assembly either of all the people, or of the rich only, that anybody who likes, whatever may be his calling, or even if he have no calling, may offer an opinion either about seamanship or about diseases—whether as to the manner in which physic or surgical instruments are to be applied to the patient, or again about the vessels and the nautical implements which are required in navigation, and how to meet the dangers of winds and waves which are incidental to the voyage, how to behave when encountering pirates, and what is to be done with the old-fashioned galleys, if they have to fight with others of a similar build—and that, whatever shall be decreed by the multitude on these points, upon the advice of persons skilled or unskilled, shall be written down on triangular tablets and columns, or enacted although unwritten to be national customs; and that in all future time vessels shall be navigated and remedies administered to the patient after this fashion.

Y. Soc. What a strange notion!

Str. Suppose further, that the pilots and physicians are appointed annually, either out of the rich, or out of the whole people, and that they are elected by lot; and that after their election they navigate vessels and heal the sick according to the written rules.

Y. Soc. Worse and worse.

Str. But hear what follows:—When the year of office has expired,

this second best may be shown with the help of our favourite images.

Suppose the crimes of physicians and pilots to be such that it is necessary to put some check upon them: an assembly of non-professional persons is called to make minute regulations which must be observed in the practice of medicine or seamanship.

Pilots and physicians are elected annually and called to account at

the pilot or physician has to come before a court of review, in which the judges are either selected from the wealthy classes or chosen by lot out of the whole people; and anybody who pleases may be their accuser, and may lay to their charge, that during the past year they have not navigated their vessels or healed their patients according to the letter of the law and the ancient customs of their ancestors; and if either of them is condemned, some of the judges must fix what he is to suffer or pay.

Y. Soc. He who is willing to take a command under such conditions, deserves to suffer any penalty.

Str. Yet once more, we shall have to enact that if any one is detected enquiring into piloting and navigation, or into health and the true nature of medicine, or about the winds, or other conditions of the atmosphere, contrary to the written rules, and has any ingenious notions about such matters, he is not to be called a pilot or physician, but a cloudy prating sophist;—further, on the ground that he is a corrupter of the young, who would persuade them to follow the art of medicine or piloting in an unlawful manner, and to exercise an arbitrary rule over their patients or ships, any one who is qualified by law may inform against him, and indict him in some court, and then if he is found to be persuading any, whether young or old, to act contrary to the written law, he is to be punished with the utmost rigour; for no one should presume to be wiser than the laws; and as touching healing and health and piloting and navigation, the nature of them is known to all, for anybody may learn the written laws and the national customs. If such were the mode of procedure, Socrates, about these sciences and about generalship, and any branch of hunting, or about painting or imitation in general, or carpentry, or any sort of handicraft, or husbandry, or planting, or if we were to see an art of rearing horses, or tending herds, or divination, or any ministerial service, or draught-playing, or any science conversant with number, whether simple or square or cube, or comprising motion,—I say, if all these things were done in this way according to written regulations, and not according to art, what would be the result?

Y. Soc. All the arts would utterly perish, and could never be recovered, because enquiry would be unlawful. And human life, which is bad enough already, would then become utterly unendurable.

Str. But what, if while compelling all these operations to be regulated by written law, we were to appoint as the guardian of the laws some one elected by a show of hands, or by lot, and he caring nothing about the laws, were to act contrary to them from motives

299
Statesman

STRANGER, YOUNG SOCRATES.

the end of their year of office, and punished if they have violated any of the written rules.

Speculation about medicine or seamanship is to be forbidden on pain of death.

What would be the consequence of such procedure to these or to other arts?

They would utterly perish.

300
But the consequence if the

of interest or favour, and without knowledge,—would not this be a still worse evil than the former?

Y. Soc. Very true.

Str. To go against the laws, which are based upon long experience, and the wisdom of counsellors who have graciously recommended them and persuaded the multitude to pass them, would be a far greater and more ruinous error than any adherence to written law?

Y. Soc. Certainly.

Str. Therefore, as there is a danger of this, the next best thing in legislating is not to allow either the individual or the multitude to break the law in any respect whatever.

Y. Soc. True.

Str. The laws would be copies of the true particulars of action as far as they admit of being written down from the lips of those who have knowledge?

Y. Soc. Certainly they would.

Str. And, as we were saying, he who has knowledge and is a true Statesman, will do many things within his own sphere of action by his art without regard to the laws, when he is of opinion that something other than that which he has written down and enjoined to be observed during his absence would be better.

Y. Soc. Yes, we said so.

Str. And any individual or any number of men, having fixed laws, in acting contrary to them with a view to something better, would only be acting, as far as they are able, like the true Statesman?

Y. Soc. Certainly.

Str. If they had no knowledge of what they were doing, they would imitate the truth, and they would always imitate ill; but if they had knowledge, the imitation would be the perfect truth, and an imitation no longer.

Y. Soc. Quite true.

Str. And the principle that no great number of men are able to acquire a knowledge of any art has been already admitted by us.

Y. Soc. Yes, it has.

Str. Then the royal or political art, if there be such an art, will never be attained either by the wealthy or by the other mob.

Y. Soc. Impossible.

Str. Then the nearest approach which these lower forms of government can ever make to the true government of the one scientific ruler, is to do nothing contrary to their own written laws and national customs.

Y. Soc. Very good.

Str. When the rich imitate the true form, such a government is called aristocracy; and when they are regardless of the laws, oligarchy.

Y. Soc. True.

Str. Or again, when an individual rules according to law in imitation of him who knows, we call him a king; and if he rules according to law, we give him the same name, whether he rules with opinion or with knowledge.

Y. Soc. To be sure.

Str. And when an individual truly possessing knowledge rules, his name will surely be the same—he will be called a king; and thus the five names of governments, as they are now reckoned, become one.

Y. Soc. That is true.

Str. And when an individual ruler governs neither by law nor by custom, but following in the steps of the true man of science pretends that he can only act for the best by violating the laws, while in reality appetite and ignorance are the motives of the imitation, may not such an one be called a tyrant?

Y. Soc. Certainly.

Str. And this we believe to be the origin of the tyrant and the king, of oligarchies, and aristocracies, and democracies,—because men are offended at the one monarch, and can never be made to believe that any one can be worthy of such authority, or is able and willing in the spirit of virtue and knowledge to act justly and holily to all; they fancy that he will be a despot who will wrong and harm and slay whom he pleases of us; for if there could be such a despot as we describe, they would acknowledge that we ought to be too glad to have him, and that he alone would be the happy ruler of a true and perfect State.

Y. Soc. To be sure.

Str. But then, as the State is not like a beehive, and has no natural head who is at once recognized to be the superior both in body and in mind, mankind are obliged to meet and make laws, and endeavour to approach as nearly as they can to the true form of government.

Y. Soc. True.

Str. And when the foundation of politics is in the letter only and in custom, and knowledge is divorced from action, can we wonder, Socrates, at the miseries which there are, and always will be, in States? Any other art, built on such a foundation and thus conducted, would ruin all that it touched. Ought we not rather to won-

States-
man

STRANGER,
YOUNG
SOCRATES.

custom
rules?
Yet, in
spite of it,
states
survive.

Which of
the un-
true
forms of
govern-
ment is
best,
which
worst?

One of
the three
chief
forms is
best and
worst.

If we
divide
these
three
forms and
add the
perfect
state,
there will
be, alto-
gether,
seven
forms.

der at the natural strength of the political bond? For States have endured all this, time out of mind, and yet some of them still remain and are not overthrown, though many of them, like ships at sea, founder from time to time, and perish and have perished and will hereafter perish, through the badness of their pilots and crews, who have the worst sort of ignorance of the highest truths—I mean to say, that they are wholly unacquainted with politics, of which, above all other sciences, they believe themselves to have acquired the most perfect knowledge.

Y. Soc. Very true.

Str. Then the question arises:—which of these untrue forms of government is the least oppressive to their subjects, though they are all oppressive; and which is the worst of them? Here is a consideration which is beside our present purpose, and yet having regard to the whole it seems to influence all our actions: we must examine it.

Y. Soc. Yes, we must.

Str. You may say that of the three forms, the same is at once the hardest and the easiest.

Y. Soc. What do you mean?

Str. I am speaking of the three forms of government, which I mentioned at the beginning of this discussion—monarchy, the rule of the few, and the rule of the many.

Y. Soc. True.

Str. If we divide each of these we shall have six, from which the true one may be distinguished as a seventh.

Y. Soc. How would you make the division?

Str. Monarchy divides into royalty and tyranny; the rule of the few into aristocracy, which has an auspicious name, and oligarchy; and democracy or the rule of the many, which before was one, must now be divided.

Y. Soc. On what principle of division?

Str. On the same principle as before, although the name is now discovered to have a twofold meaning. For the distinction of ruling with law or without law, applies to this as well as to the rest.

Y. Soc. Yes.

Str. The division made no difference when we were looking for the perfect State, as we showed before. But now that this has been separated off, and, as we said, the others alone are left for us, the principle of law and the absence of law will bisect them all.

Y. Soc. That would seem to follow, from what has been said.

Str. Then monarchy, when bound by good prescriptions or laws, is the best of all the six, and when lawless is the most bitter and oppressive to the subject.

Y. Soc. True.

Str. The government of the few, which is intermediate between that of the one and many, is also intermediate in good and evil; but the government of the many is in every respect weak and unable to do either any great good or any great evil, when compared with the others, because the offices are too minutely subdivided and too many hold them. And this therefore is the worst of all lawful governments, and the best of all lawless ones. If they are all without the restraints of law, democracy is the form in which to live is best; if they are well ordered, then this is the last which you should choose, as royalty, the first form, is the best, with the exception of the seventh, for that excels them all, and is among States what God is among men.

Y. Soc. You are quite right, and we should choose that above all.

Str. The members of all these States, with the exception of the one which has knowledge, may be set aside as being not Statesmen but partisans,—upholders of the most monstrous idols, and themselves idols; and, being the greatest imitators and magicians, they are also the greatest of Sophists.

Y. Soc. The name of Sophist after many windings in the argument appears to have been most justly fixed upon the politicians, as they are termed.

Str. And so our satyric drama has been played out; and the troop of Centaurs and Satyrs, however unwilling to leave the stage, have at last been separated from the political science.

Y. Soc. So I perceive.

Str. There remain, however, natures still more troublesome, because they are more nearly akin to the king, and more difficult to discern; the examination of them may be compared to the process of refining gold.

Y. Soc. What is your meaning?

Str. The workmen begin by sifting away the earth and stones and the like; there remain in a confused mass the valuable elements akin to gold, which can only be separated by fire,—copper, silver, and other precious metals; these are at last refined away by the use of tests, until the gold is left quite pure.

Y. Soc. Yes, that is the way in which these things are said to be done.

Str. In like manner, all alien and uncongenial matter has been separated from political science, and what is precious and of a

States-
man

303
STRANGER,
YOUNG
SOCRATES.

Monarchy, in the form of royalty, is the best; and in the form of tyranny the worst.

The government of the few is intermediate in good and evil. Democracy is the best of lawless and the worst of lawful governments. The seventh form is among states what God is among men.

The upholders of the untrue forms of government are mere partisans and the greatest of Sophists.

*States-
man*

304
STRANGER,
YOUNG
SOCRATES.

The im-
postors
depart.

Like re-
finers of
gold, we
have now
got rid of
the earth
and
dross:
there re-
main the
arts of the
general,
judge,
orator,
which are
nearly
akin to
States-
manship,
and for
that rea-
son diffi-
cult to
separate
from it.

The case
of music
may help
us.

There is
an art
above it,
which
decides
whether
it shall be
learnt or
not.

This art is
the art of

kindred nature has been left; there remain the nobler arts of the
general and the judge, and the higher sort of oratory which is an
ally of the royal art, and persuades men to do justice, and assists in
guiding the helm of States:—How can we best clear away all these,
leaving him whom we seek alone and unalloyed?

Y. Soc. That is obviously what has in some way to be attempted.

Str. If the attempt is all that is wanting, he shall certainly be
brought to light; and I think that the illustration of music may
assist in exhibiting him. Please to answer me a question.

Y. Soc. What question?

Str. There is such a thing as learning music or handicraft arts
in general?

Y. Soc. There is.

Str. And is there any higher art or science, having power to decide which of these arts are and are not to be learned;—what do
you say?

Y. Soc. I should answer that there is.

Str. And do we acknowledge this science to be different from
the others?

Y. Soc. Yes.

Str. And ought the other sciences to be superior to this, or no
single science to any other? Or ought this science to be the overseer
and governor of all the others?

Y. Soc. The latter.

Str. You mean to say that the science which judges whether we
ought to learn or not, must be superior to the science which is
learned or which teaches?

Y. Soc. Far superior.

Str. And the science which determines whether we ought to persuade or not, must be superior to the science which is able to
persuade?

Y. Soc. Of course.

Str. Very good; and to what science do we assign the power of
persuading a multitude by a pleasing tale and not by teaching?

Y. Soc. That power, I think, must clearly be assigned to rhetoric.

Str. And to what science do we give the power of determining
whether we are to employ persuasion or force towards any one, or
to refrain altogether?

Y. Soc. To that science which governs the arts of speech and
persuasion.

Str. Which, if I am not mistaken, will be politics?

Y. Soc. Very good.

Str. Rhetoric seems to be quickly distinguished from politics, being a different species, yet ministering to it.

Y. Soc. Yes.

Str. But what would you think of another sort of power or science?

Y. Soc. What science?

Str. The science which has to do with military operations against our enemies—is that to be regarded as a science or not?

Y. Soc. How can generalship and military tactics be regarded as other than a science?

Str. And is the art which is able and knows how to advise when we are to go to war, or to make peace, the same as this or different?

Y. Soc. If we are to be consistent, we must say different.

Str. And we must also suppose that this rules the other, if we are not to give up our former notion?

Y. Soc. True.

Str. And, considering how great and terrible the whole art of war is, can we imagine any which is superior to it but the truly royal?

Y. Soc. No other.

Str. The art of the general is only ministerial, and therefore not political?

Y. Soc. Exactly.

Str. Once more let us consider the nature of the righteous judge.

Y. Soc. Very good.

Str. Does he do anything but decide the dealings of men with one another to be just or unjust in accordance with the standard which he receives from the king and legislator,—showing his own peculiar virtue only in this, that he is not perverted by gifts, or fears, or pity, or by any sort of favour or enmity, into deciding the suits of men with one another contrary to the appointment of the legislator?

Y. Soc. No; his office is such as you describe.

Str. Then the inference is that the power of the judge is not royal, but only the power of a guardian of the law which ministers to the royal power?

Y. Soc. True.

Str. The review of all these sciences shows that none of them is political or royal. For the truly royal ought not itself to act, but to rule over those who are able to act; the king ought to know what is ·and what is not a fitting opportunity for taking the initiative in matters of the greatest importance, whilst others should execute his orders.

States-
man

STRANGER,
YOUNG
 SOCRATES.

politics,
which is
also
superior
to
rhetoric,

and to
general-
ship,

305

and to the
adminis-
tration of
justice.

The po-
litical or
royal art
com-
mands all
the
others;

Y. Soc. True.

Str. And, therefore, the arts which we have described, as they have no authority over themselves or one another, but are each of them concerned with some special action of their own, have, as they ought to have, special names corresponding to their several actions.

Y. Soc. I agree.

Str. And the science which is over them all, and has charge of the laws, and of all matters affecting the State, and truly weaves them all into one, if we would describe under a name characteristic of their common nature, most truly we may call politics.

Y. Soc. Exactly so.

Str. Then, now that we have discovered the various classes in a State[1], shall I analyse politics after the pattern which weaving supplied?

Y. Soc. I greatly wish that you would.

Str. Then I must describe the nature of the royal web, and show how the various threads are woven into one piece.

Y. Soc. Clearly.

Str. A task has to be accomplished, which, although difficult, appears to be necessary.

Y. Soc. Certainly the attempt must be made.

Str. To assume that one part of virtue differs in kind from another, is a position easily assailable by contentious disputants, who appeal to popular opinion.

Y. Soc. I do not understand.

Str. Let me put the matter in another way: I suppose that you would consider courage to be a part of virtue?

Y. Soc. Certainly I should.

Str. And you would think temperance to be different from courage; and likewise to be a part of virtue?

Y. Soc. True.

Str. I shall venture to put forward a strange theory about them.

Y. Soc. What is it?

Str. That they are two principles which thoroughly hate one another and are antagonistic throughout a great part of nature.

Y. Soc. How singular!

Str. Yes very—for all the parts of virtue are commonly said to be friendly to one another.

Y. Soc. Yes.

Str. Then let us carefully investigate whether this is universally true, or whether there are not parts of virtue which are at war with their kindred in some respect.

---

[1] Cp. supra, 287-90, 303-5.

and
weaves
them to-
gether in
the po-
litical
web.

306

The na-
ture of
this web
must now
be con-
sidered.

Certain
parts of
virtue,
such as
courage
and tem-
perance,
are an-
tagonistic.

Common
opinion
however
does not
allow
this.

Let us
investi-
gate the
matter.

Y. Soc. Tell me how we shall consider that question.

Str. We must extend our enquiry to all those things which we consider beautiful and at the same time place in two opposite classes.

Y. Soc. Explain; what are they?

Str. Acuteness and quickness, whether in body or soul or in the movement of sound, and the imitations of them which painting and music supply, you must have praised yourself before now, or been present when others praised them.

Y. Soc. Certainly.

Str. And do you remember the terms in which they are praised?

Y. Soc. I do not.

Str. I wonder whether I can explain to you in words the thought which is passing in my mind.

Y. Soc. Why not?

Str. You fancy that this is all so easy: Well, let us consider these notions with reference to the opposite classes of action under which they fall. When we praise quickness and energy and acuteness, whether of mind or body or sound, we express our praise of the quality which we admire by one word, and that one word is manliness or courage.

Y. Soc. How?

Str. We speak of an action as energetic and brave, quick and manly, and vigorous too; and when we apply the name of which I speak as the common attribute of all these natures, we certainly praise them.

Y. Soc. True.

Str. And do we not often praise the quiet strain of action also?

Y. Soc. To be sure.

Str. And do we not then say the opposite of what we said of the other?

Y. Soc. How do you mean?

Str. We exclaim How calm! How temperate! in admiration of the slow and quiet working of the intellect, and of steadiness and gentleness in action, of smoothness and depth of voice, and of all rhythmical movement and of music in general, when these have a proper solemnity. Of all such actions we predicate not courage, but a name indicative of order.

Y. Soc. Very true.

Str. But when, on the other hand, either of these is out of place, the names of either are changed into terms of censure.

Y. Soc. How so?

Str. Too great sharpness or quickness or hardness is termed vio-

We express our admiration for quick and energetic action by applying the epithet 'brave' to it,

307
and for gentle and quiet action by calling it 'calm' or 'temperate.'

But when
these
qualities
are in
excess, we
call them
violence
or mad-
ness, cow-
ardice or
sluggish-
ness.—
These ex-
tremes do
not meet
in the
same
persons.

The
gentle are
willing to
pay any
price for
peace;

308

the
coura-
geous are
always
anxious
for war.

These
two
classes are
always
antago-
nistic.
And so
we have

lence or madness; too great slowness or gentleness is called cowardice or sluggishness; and we may observe, that for the most part
these qualities, and the temperance and manliness of the opposite
characters, are arrayed as enemies on opposite sides, and do not
mingle with one another in their respective actions; and if we pursue the enquiry, we shall find that men who have these different
qualities of mind differ from one another.

Y. Soc. In what respect?

Str. In respect of all the qualities which I mentioned, and very
likely of many others. According to their respective affinities to either class of actions they distribute praise and blame,—praise to
the actions which are akin to their own, blame to those of the opposite party—and out of this many quarrels and occasions of quarrel arise among them.

Y. Soc. True.

Str. The difference between the two classes is often a trivial concern; but in a state, and when affecting really important matters,
becomes of all disorders the most hateful.

Y. Soc. To what do you refer?

Str. To nothing short of the whole regulation of human life. For
the orderly class are always ready to lead a peaceful life, quietly
doing their own business; this is their manner of behaving with all
men at home, and they are equally ready to find some way of keeping the peace with foreign States. And on account of this fondness
of theirs for peace, which is often out of season where their influence prevails, they become by degrees unwarlike, and bring up
their young men to be like themselves; they are at the mercy of
their enemies; whence in a few years they and their children and
the whole city often pass imperceptibly from the condition of freemen into that of slaves.

Y. Soc. What a cruel fate!

Str. And now think of what happens with the more courageous
natures. Are they not always inciting their country to go to war,
owing to their excessive love of the military life? they raise up enemies against themselves many and mighty, and either utterly ruin
their native-land or enslave and subject it to its foes?

Y. Soc. That, again, is true.

Str. Must we not admit, then, that where these two classes exist,
they always feel the greatest antipathy and antagonism towards
one another?

Y. Soc. We cannot deny it.

Str. And returning to the enquiry with which we began, have we
not found that considerable portions of virtue are at variance with

one another, and give rise to a similar opposition in the characters who are endowed with them?

Y. Soc. True.

Str. Let us consider a further point.

Y. Soc. What is it?

Str. I want to know, whether any constructive art will make any, even the most trivial thing, out of bad and good materials indifferently, if this can be helped? does not all art rather reject the bad as far as possible, and accept the good and fit materials, and from these elements, whether like or unlike, gathering them all into one, work out some nature or idea?

Y. Soc. To be sure.

Str. Then the true and natural art of statesmanship will never allow any State to be formed by a combination of good and bad men, if this can be avoided; but will begin by testing human natures in play, and after testing them, will entrust them to proper teachers who are the ministers of her purposes—she will herself give orders, and maintain authority; just as the art of weaving continually gives orders and maintains authority over the carders and all the others who prepare the material for the work, commanding the subsidiary arts to execute the works which she deems necessary for making the web.

Y. Soc. Quite true.

Str. In like manner, the royal science appears to me to be the mistress of all lawful educators and instructors, and having this queenly power, will not permit them to train men in what will produce characters unsuited to the political constitution which she desires to create, but only in what will produce such as are suitable. Those which have no share of manliness and temperance, or any other virtuous inclination, and, from the necessity of an evil nature, are violently carried away to godlessness and insolence and injustice, she gets rid of by death and exile, and punishes them with the greatest of disgraces.

Y. Soc. That is commonly said.

Str. But those who are wallowing in ignorance and baseness she bows under the yoke of slavery.

Y. Soc. Quite right.

Str. The rest of the citizens, out of whom, if they have education, something noble may be made, and who are capable of being united by the Statesman, the kingly art blends and weaves together; taking on the one hand those whose natures tend rather to courage, which is the stronger element and may be regarded as the warp, and on the other hand those which incline to order and gentleness,

found
what we
sought.

A further
point.
No con-
structive
art will
use bad
material,
if this
can be
avoided.

And
states-
manship
will not
weave
bad men
into the
political
web. She
will select
and train
suitable
natures,

but will
extermi-
nate the
evil,

309
and en-
slave the
ignorant.

The rest
of the
citizens
she will
weave in-
to one,
combin-

*States-
man*

STRANGER,
YOUNG
SOCRATES.

ing
courage,
which is
thc warp,
with
gentle-
ness and
order,
which
form the
woof.

She binds
the divine
element
with a
divine,
the
human
with a
human
cord.
True
opinion
about the
just and
good,
when
confirmed
by reason,
is a divine
principle,
and the
states-
man alone
can im-
plant it in
the citi-
zen.

310
The
coura-
geous soul
is civil-
ized by it,

the peace-
ful is
rendered

and which are represented in the figure as spun thick and soft, after the manner of the woof—these, which are naturally opposed, she seeks to bind and weave together in the following manner:

Y. Soc. In what manner?

Str. First of all, she takes the eternal element of the soul and binds it with a divine cord, to which it is akin, and then the animal nature, and binds that with human cords.

Y. Soc. I do not understand what you mean.

Str. The meaning is, that the opinion about the honourable and the just and good and their opposites, which is true and confirmed by reason, is a divine principle, and when implanted in the soul, is implanted, as I maintain, in a nature of heavenly birth.

Y. Soc. Yes; what else should it be?

Str. Only the Statesman and the good legislator, having the inspiration of the royal muse, can implant this opinion, and he, only in the rightly educated, whom we were just now describing.

Y. Soc. Likely enough.

Str. But him who cannot, we will not designate by any of the names which are the subject of the present enquiry.

Y. Soc. Very right.

Str. The courageous soul when attaining this truth becomes civilized, and rendered more capable of partaking of justice; but when not partaking, is inclined to brutality. Is not that true?

Y. Soc. Certainly.

Str. And again, the peaceful and orderly nature, if sharing in these opinions, becomes temperate and wise, as far as this may be in a State, but if not, deservedly obtains the ignominious name of silliness.

Y. Soc. Quite true.

Str. Can we say that such a connection as this will lastingly unite the evil with one another or with the good, or that any science would seriously think of using a bond of this kind to join such materials?

Y. Soc. İmpossible.

Str. But in those who were originally of a noble nature, and who have been nurtured in noble ways, and in those only, may we not say that union is implanted by law, and that this is the medicine which art prescribes for them, and of all the bonds which unite the dissimilar and contrary parts of virtue is not this, as I was saying, the divinest?

Y. Soc. Very true.

Str. Where this divine bond exists there is no difficulty in imagining, or when you have imagined, in creating the other bonds, which are human only.

Y. Soc. How is that, and what bonds do you mean?

Str. Rights of intermarriage, and ties which are formed between States by giving and taking children in marriage, or between individuals by private betrothals and espousals. For most persons form marriage connections without due regard to what is best for the procreation of children.

Y. Soc. In what way?

Str. They seek after wealth and power, which in matrimony are objects not worthy even of a serious censure.

Y. Soc. There is no need to consider them at all.

Str. More reason is there to consider the practice of those who make family their chief aim, and to indicate their error.

Y. Soc. Quite true.

Str. They act on no true principle at all; they seek their ease and receive with open arms those who are like themselves, and hate those who are unlike them, being too much influenced by feelings of dislike.

Y. Soc. How so?

Str. The quiet orderly class seek for natures like their own, and as far as they can they marry and give in marriage exclusively in this class, and the courageous do the same; they seek natures like their own, whereas they should both do precisely the opposite.

Y. Soc. How and why is that?

Str. Because courage, when untempered by the gentler nature during many generations, may at first bloom and strengthen, but at last bursts forth into downright madness.

Y. Soc. Like enough.

Str. And then, again, the soul which is over-full of modesty and has no element of courage in many successive generations, is apt to grow too indolent, and at last to become utterly paralyzed and useless.

Y. Soc. That, again, is quite likely.

Str. It was of these bonds I said that there would be no difficulty in creating them, if only both classes originally held the same opinion about the honourable and good;—indeed, in this single work, the whole process of royal weaving is comprised—never to allow temperate natures to be separated from the brave, but to weave them together, like the warp and the woof, by common sentiments and honours and reputation, and by the giving of pledges to one another; and out of them forming one smooth and even web, to entrust to them the offices of State.

States-man

STRANGER,
YOUNG
SOCRATES.

temperate and wise.

Where the divine bond exists it is easy to create the human bonds, i.e. ties of intermarriage.—The true object of marriage is the procreation of children, not wealth or power or rank.

Like should not consort with like, or courage will degenerate into madness and modesty into helplessness.

Royal science prevents this by weaving together the temperate [311] and courageous.

Y. Soc. How do you mean?

Str. Where one officer only is needed, you must choose a ruler who has both these qualities—-when many, you must mingle some of each, for the temperate ruler is very careful and just and safe, but is wanting in thoroughness and go.

Y. Soc. Certainly, that is very true.

Str. The character of the courageous, on the other hand, falls short of the former in justice and caution, but has the power of action in a remarkable degree, and where either of these two qualities is wanting, there cities cannot altogether prosper either in their public or private life.

Y. Soc. Certainly they cannot.

Str. This then we declare to be the completion of the web of political action, which is created by a direct intertexture of the brave and temperate natures, whenever the royal science has drawn the two minds into communion with one another by unanimity and friendship, and having perfected the noblest and best of all the webs which political life admits, and enfolding therein all other inhabitants of cities, whether slaves or freemen, binds them in one fabric and governs and presides over them, and, in so far as to be happy is vouchsafed to a city, in no particular fails to secure their happiness.

Y. Soc. Your picture, Stranger, of the king and statesman, no less than of the Sophist, is quite perfect.

PHILEBUS

PHILEBUS

PERSONS OF THE DIALOGUE

SOCRATES   PROTARCHUS   PHILEBUS

Socrates. OBSERVE, Protarchus, the nature of the position which you are now going to take from Philebus, and what the other position is which I maintain, and which, if you do not approve of it, is to be controverted by you. Shall you and I sum up the two sides?

Protarchus. By all means.

Soc. Philebus was saying that enjoyment and pleasure and delight, and the class of feelings akin to them, are a good to every living being, whereas I contend, that not these, but wisdom and intelligence and memory, and their kindred, right opinion and true reasoning, are better and more desirable than pleasure for all who are able to partake of them, and that to all such who are or ever will be they are the most advantageous of all things. Have I not given, Philebus, a fair statement of the two sides of the argument?

Philebus. Nothing could be fairer, Socrates.

Soc. And do you, Protarchus, accept the position which is assigned to you?

Pro. I cannot do otherwise, since our excellent Philebus has left the field.

Soc. Surely the truth about these matters ought, by all means, to be ascertained.

Pro. Certainly.

Soc. Shall we further agree—

Pro. To what?

Soc. That you and I must now try to indicate some state and disposition of the soul which has the property of making all men happy.

Pro. Yes, by all means.

Soc. And you say that pleasure, and I say that wisdom, is such a state?

Pro. True.

Soc. And what if there be a third state, which is better than ei-

Steph.
11
SOCRATES,
PROTAR-
CHUS,
PHILE-
BUS.

Philebus, who is now to be succeeded by Protarchus, maintains that pleasure is the good; Socrates prefers wisdom.

Which of these two positions is the truer?

12

SOCRATES,
PROTAR-
CHUS,
PHILE-
BUS.

In the
course of
our en-
quiry
some-
thing
superior
both to
pleasure
and to
wisdom
may ap-
pear. In
that case,
if plea-
sure be
more
akin to
this
superior
nature,
pleasure
must be
adjudged
conquer-
or: but if
wisdom,
wisdom.

We will
begin
with
pleasure,
which is
one, but
also has
many
varieties,
some of
them
being
mutually
opposed.

Pleasures
are op-
posed
when

ther? Then both of us are vanquished—are we not? But if this life, which really has the power of making men happy, turn out to be more akin to pleasure than to wisdom, the life of pleasure may still have the advantage over the life of wisdom.

Pro. True.

Soc. Or suppose that the better life is more nearly allied to wisdom, then wisdom conquers, and pleasure is defeated;—do you agree?

Pro. Certainly.

Soc. And what do you say, Philebus?

Phi. I say, and shall always say, that pleasure is easily the conqueror; but you must decide for yourself, Protarchus.

Pro. You, Philebus, have handed over the argument to me, and have no longer a voice in the matter?

Phi. True enough. Nevertheless I would clear myself and deliver my soul of you; and I call the goddess herself to witness that I now do so.

Pro. You may appeal to us; we too will be the witnesses of your words. And now, Socrates, whether Philebus is pleased or displeased, we will proceed with the argument.

Soc. Then let us begin with the goddess herself, of whom Philebus says that she is called Aphrodite, but that her real name is Pleasure.

Pro. Very good.

Soc. The awe which I always feel, Protarchus, about the names of the gods is more than human—it exceeds all other fears. And now I would not sin against Aphrodite by naming her amiss; let her be called what she pleases. But Pleasure I know to be manifold, and with her, as I was just now saying, we must begin, and consider what her nature is. She has one name, and therefore you would imagine that she is one; and yet surely she takes the most varied and even unlike forms. For do we not say that the intemperate has pleasure, and that the temperate has pleasure in his very temperance,—that the fool is pleased when he is full of foolish fancies and hopes, and that the wise man has pleasure in his wisdom? and how foolish would any one be who affirmed that all these opposite pleasures are severally alike!

Pro. Why, Socrates, they are opposed in so far as they spring from opposite sources, but they are not in themselves opposite. For must not pleasure be of all things most absolutely like pleasure,—that is, like itself?

Soc. Yes, my good friend, just as colour is like colour;—in so far as colours are colours, there is no difference between them; and yet

we all know that black is not only unlike, but even absolutely opposed to white: or again, as figure is like figure, for all figures are
comprehended under one class; and yet particular figures may be
absolutely opposed to one another, and there is an infinite diversity
of them. And we might find similar examples in many other things;
therefore do not rely upon this argument, which would go to prove
the unity of the most extreme opposites. And I suspect that we
shall find a similar opposition among pleasures.

Pro. Very likely; but how will this invalidate the argument?

Soc. Why, I shall reply, that dissimilar as they are, you apply to
them a new predicate, for you say that all pleasant things are good;
now although no one can argue that pleasure is not pleasure, he
may argue, as we are doing, that pleasures are oftener bad than
good; but you call them all good, and at the same time are compelled, if you are pressed, to acknowledge that they are unlike. And
so you must tell us what is the identical quality existing alike in
good and bad pleasures, which makes you designate all of them as
good.

Pro. What do you mean, Socrates? Do you think that any one
who asserts pleasure to be the good, will tolerate the notion that
some pleasures are good and others bad?

Soc. And yet you will acknowledge that they are different from
one another, and sometimes opposed?

Pro. Not in so far as they are pleasures.

Soc. That is a return to the old position, Protarchus, and so we
are to say (are we?) that there is no difference in pleasures, but
that they are all alike; and the examples which have just been cited
do not pierce our dull minds, but we go on arguing all the same,
like the weakest and most inexperienced reasoners?[1]

Pro. What do you mean?

Soc. Why, I mean to say, that in self-defence I may, if I like, follow your example, and assert boldly that the two things most unlike are most absolutely alike; and the result will be that you and I
will prove ourselves to be very tyros in the art of disputing; and
the argument will be blown away and lost. Suppose that we put
back, and return to the old position; then perhaps we may come to
an understanding with one another.

Pro. How do you mean?

Soc. Shall I, Protarchus, have my own question asked of me by
you?

Pro. What question?

Soc. Ask me whether wisdom and science and mind, and those

springing
from
opposite
sources:
in them-
selves
they are
all alike.

But this
proves
only that
all
pleasures
are plea-
sures, and
not that
all
pleasures
are good.

We shall
not be
able to
proceed,
if obvious
facts are
ignored.

---

[1] Probably corrupt.

Philebus

SOCRATES,
PROTAR-
CHUS.

To say
that there
are no
[14]
differ-
ences
between
pleasures,
is as ab-
surd as to
say that
there are
no differ-
ences
between
sciences.

other qualities which I, when asked by you at first what is the nature of the good, affirmed to be good, are not in the same case with
the pleasures of which you spoke.

Pro. What do you mean?

Soc. The sciences are a numerous class, and will be found to present great differences. But even admitting that, like the pleasures,
they are opposite as well as different, should I be worthy of the
name of dialectician if, in order to avoid this difficulty, I were to
say (as you are saying of pleasure) that there is no difference between one science and another;—would not the argument founder
and disappear like an idle tale, although we might ourselves escape
drowning by clinging to a fallacy?

Pro. May none of this befall us, except the deliverance! Yet I
like the even-handed justice which is applied to both our arguments. Let us assume, then, that there are many and diverse pleasures, and many and different sciences.

Soc. And let us have no concealment, Protarchus, of the differences between my good and yours; but let us bring them to the
light in the hope that, in the process of testing them, they may
show whether pleasure is to be called the good, or wisdom, or some
third quality; for surely we are not now simply contending in order that my view or that yours may prevail, but I presume that we
ought both of us to be fighting for the truth.

Pro. Certainly we ought.

Soc. Then let us have a more definite understanding and establish the principle on which the argument rests.

Pro. What principle?

Soc. A principle about which all men are always in a difficulty,
and some men sometimes against their will.

Pro. Speak plainer.

Soc. The principle which has just turned up, which is a marvel of
nature; for that one should be many or many one, are wonderful
propositions; and he who affirms either is very open to attack.

Pro. Do you mean, when a person says that I, Protarchus, am
by nature one and also many, dividing the single 'me' into many
'me's,' and even opposing them as great and small, light and heavy,
and in ten thousand other ways?

Soc. Those, Protarchus, are the common and acknowledged paradoxes about the one and many, which I may say that everybody
has by this time agreed to dismiss as childish and obvious and
detrimental to the true course of thought; and no more favour is
shown to that other puzzle, in which a person proves the members
and parts of anything to be divided, and then confessing that they

We have
lighted
upon the
old prob-
lem of the
One and
Many.

The co-
existence
of the
One and
Many in
concrete
objects
presents
no diffi-
culty.

are all one, says laughingly in disproof of his own words: Why, here is a miracle, the one is many and infinite, and the many are only one.

Pro. But what, Socrates, are those other marvels connected with this subject which, as you imply, have not yet become common and acknowledged?

Soc. When, my boy, the one does not belong to the class of things that are born and perish, as in the instances which we were giving, for in those cases, and when unity is of this concrete nature, there is, as I was saying, a universal consent that no refutation is needed; but when the assertion is made that man is one, or ox is one, or beauty one, or the good one, then the interest which attaches to these and similar unities and the attempt which is made to divide them gives birth to a controversy.

Pro. Of what nature?

Soc. In the first place, as to whether these unities have a real existence; and then how each individual unity, being always the same, and incapable either of generation or of destruction, but retaining a permanent individuality, can be conceived either as dispersed and multiplied in the infinity of the world of generation, or as still entire and yet divided from itself, which latter would seem to be the greatest impossibility of all, for how can one and the same thing be at the same time in one and in many things? These, Protarchus, are the real difficulties, and this is the one and many to which they relate; they are the source of great perplexity if ill decided, and the right determination of them is very helpful.

Pro. Then, Socrates, let us begin by clearing up these questions.

Soc. That is what I should wish.

Pro. And I am sure that all my other friends will be glad to hear them discussed; Philebus, fortunately for us, is not disposed to move, and we had better not stir him up with questions.

Soc. Good; and where shall we begin this great and multifarious battle, in which such various points are at issue? Shall we begin thus?

Pro. How?

Soc. We say that the one and many become identified by thought, and that now, as in time past, they run about together, in and out of every word which is uttered, and that this union of them will never cease, and is not now beginning, but is, as I believe, an everlasting quality of thought itself, which never grows old. Any young man, when he first tastes these subtleties, is delighted, and fancies that he has found a treasure of wisdom; in the first enthusiasm of his joy he leaves no stone, or rather no thought unturned,

Philebus

SOCRATES,
PROTAR-
CHUS.

15

Our troubles begin with abstract unities.

What is the relation of ideas and phenomena?

The co-existence of one and many is a consequence of thought.
—The enthusiasm of young

now rolling up the many into the one, and kneading them together, now unfolding and dividing them; he puzzles himself first and above all, and then he proceeds to puzzle his neighbours, whether they are older or younger, or of his own age—that makes no difference; neither father nor mother does he spare; no human being who has ears is safe from him, hardly even his dog, and a barbarian would have no chance of escaping him, if an interpreter could only be found.

Pro. Considering, Socrates, how many we are, and that all of us are young men, is there not a danger that we and Philebus may all set upon you, if you abuse us? We understand what you mean; but is there no charm by which we may dispel all this confusion, no more excellent way of arriving at the truth? If there is, we hope that you will guide us into that way, and we will do our best to follow, for the enquiry in which we are engaged, Socrates, is not unimportant.

Soc. The reverse of unimportant, my boys, as Philebus calls you, and there neither is nor ever will be a better than my own favourite way, which has nevertheless already often deserted me and left me helpless in the hour of need.

Pro. Tell us what that is.

Soc. One which may be easily pointed out, but is by no means easy of application; it is the parent of all the discoveries in the arts.

Pro. Tell us what it is.

Soc. A gift of heaven, which, as I conceive, the gods tossed among men by the hands of a new Prometheus, and therewith a blaze of light; and the ancients, who were our betters and nearer the gods than we are, handed down the tradition, that whatever things are said to be are composed of one and many, and have the finite and infinite implanted in them: seeing, then, that such is the order of the world, we too ought in every enquiry to begin by laying down one idea of that which is the subject of enquiry; this unity we shall find in everything. Having found it, we may next proceed to look for two, if there be two, or, if not, then for three or some other number, subdividing each of these units, until at last the unity with which we began is seen not only to be one and many and infinite, but also a definite number; the infinite must not be suffered to approach the many until the entire number of the species intermediate between unity and infinity has been discovered,—then, and not till then, we may rest from division, and without further troubling ourselves about the endless individuals may allow them to drop into infinity. This, as I was saying, is the way of considering and learning and teaching one another, which the gods have handed down to us. But the wise men of our time are either too quick or too slow in conceiving plurality in unity. Having no method, they make their one and many anyhow, and from unity pass at once to infinity; the intermediate steps never occur to them. And this, I repeat, is what makes the difference between the mere art of disputation and true dialectic.

Pro. I think that I partly understand you, Socrates, but I should like to have a clearer notion of what you are saying.

Soc. I may illustrate my meaning by the letters of the alphabet, Protarchus, which you were made to learn as a child.

Pro. How do they afford an illustration?

Soc. The sound which passes through the lips whether of an individual or of all men is one and yet infinite.

Pro. Very true.

Soc. And yet not by knowing either that sound is one or that sound is infinite are we perfect in the art of speech, but the knowledge of the number and nature of sounds is what makes a man a grammarian.

Pro. Very true.

Soc. And the knowledge which makes a man a musician is of the same kind.

Pro. How so?

Soc. Sound is one in music as well as in grammar?

Pro. Certainly.

Soc. And there is a higher note and a lower note, and a note of equal pitch:—may we affirm so much?

Pro. Yes.

Soc. But you would not be a real musician if this was all that you knew; though if you did not know this you would know almost nothing of music.

Pro. Nothing.

Soc. But when you have learned what sounds are high and what low, and the number and nature of the intervals and their limits or proportions, and the systems compounded out of them, which our fathers discovered, and have handed down to us who are their descendants under the name of harmonies; and the affections corresponding to them in the movements of the human body, which when measured by numbers ought, as they say, to be called rhythms and measures; and they tell us that the same principle should be applied to every one and many;—when, I say, you have learned all this, then, my dear friend, you are perfect; and you may be said to understand any other subject, when you have a similar grasp of it. But the infinity of kinds and the infinity of individuals

The true
method
applied to
grammar,

and to
music.

which there is in each of them, when not classified, creates in every one of us a state of infinite ignorance; and he who never looks for number in anything, will not himself be looked for in the number of famous men.

18
Socrates,
Protar-
chus,
Phile-
bus.

If a man
has to
start with
infinity,
he should
not jump
at once to
unity, but
should
proceed
first to
some
definite
quantity.
—An il-
lustration
of this
process
taken
from
grammar.

Pro. I think that what Socrates is now saying is excellent, Philebus.

Phi. I think so too, but how do his words bear upon us and upon the argument?

Soc. Philebus is right in asking that question of us, Protarchus.

Pro. Indeed he is, and you must answer him.

Soc. I will; but you must let me make one little remark first about these matters; I was saying, that he who begins with any individual unity, should proceed from that, not to infinity, but to a definite number, and now I say conversely, that he who has to begin with infinity should not jump to unity, but he should look about for some number representing a certain quantity, and thus out of all end in one. And now let us return for an illustration of our principle to the case of letters.

Pro. What do you mean?

Soc. Some god or divine man, who in the Egyptian legend is said to have been Theuth, observing that the human voice was infinite, first distinguished in this infinity a certain number of vowels, and then other letters which had sound, but were not pure vowels (i. e. the semivowels); these too exist in a definite number; and lastly, he distinguished a third class of letters which we now call mutes, without voice and without sound, and divided these, and likewise the two other classes of vowels and semivowels, into the individual sounds, and told the number of them, and gave to each and all of them the name of letters; and observing that none of us could learn any one of them and not learn them all, and in consideration of this common bond which in a manner united them, he assigned to them all a single art, and this he called the art of grammar or letters.

Phi. The illustration, Protarchus, has assisted me in understanding the original statement, but I still feel the defect of which I just now complained.

Soc. Are you going to ask, Philebus, what this has to do with the argument?

Phi. Yes, that is a question which Protarchus and I have been long asking.

Soc. Assuredly you have already arrived at the answer to the question which, as you say, you have been so long asking?

Phi. How so?

Soc. Did we not begin by enquiring into the comparative eligibility of pleasure and wisdom?

Phi. Certainly.

Soc. And we maintain that they are each of them one?

Phi. True.

Soc. And the precise question to which the previous discussion desires an answer is, how they are one and also many [i. e. how they have one genus and many species], and are not at once infinite, and what number of species is to be assigned to either of them before they pass into infinity[1].

Pro. That is a very serious question, Philebus, to which Socrates has ingeniously brought us round, and please to consider which of us shall answer him; there may be something ridiculous in my being unable to answer, and therefore imposing the task upon you, when I have undertaken the whole charge of the argument, but if neither of us were able to answer, the result methinks would be still more ridiculous. Let us consider, then, what we are to do:— Socrates, if I understood him rightly, is asking whether there are not kinds of pleasure, and what is the number and nature of them, and the same of wisdom.

Soc. Most true, O son of Callias; and the previous argument showed that if we are not able to tell the kinds of everything that has unity, likeness, sameness, or their opposites, none of us will be of the smallest use in any enquiry.

Pro. That seems to be very near the truth, Socrates. Happy would the wise man be if he knew all things, and the next best thing for him is that he should know himself. Why do I say so at this moment? I will tell you. You, Socrates, have granted us this opportunity of conversing with you, and are ready to assist us in determining what is the best of human goods. For when Philebus said that pleasure and delight and enjoyment and the like were the chief good, you answered—No, not those, but another class of goods; and we are constantly reminding ourselves of what you said, and very properly, in order that we may not forget to examine and compare the two. And these goods, which in your opinion are to be designated as superior to pleasure, and are the true objects of pursuit, are mind and knowledge and understanding and art, and the like. There was a dispute about which were the best, and we playfully threatened that you should not be allowed to go home until the question was settled; and you agreed, and placed yourself at our disposal. And now, as children say, what has been

Philebus

SOCRATES, PROTAR-CHUS, PHILE-BUS.

We wish to compare pleasure and wisdom. [19] If then we would follow the true method of investigation, we must seek to discover the number and nature of their kinds.

---

[1] i. e. into the infinite number of individuals.

SOCRATES,
PROTAR-
CHUS,
PHILE-
BUS.

Philebus
and Pro-
tarchus
confess
them-
selves in-
capable of
doing
this. They
therefore
ask help
of
Socrates.

Socrates
has heard
some one
say that
neither
pleasure
nor wis-
dom is
the good,
but some
third
thing. If
this be
brought
to light,
there will
be no
need to
distin-
guish the
kinds of
pleasure
and
wisdom.

Let us
first ad-
mit that
the good
is perfect,
and suffi-
cient, and

fairly given cannot be taken back; cease then to fight against us in this way.

Soc. In what way?

Phi. Do not perplex us, and keep asking questions of us to which we have not as yet any sufficient answer to give; let us not imagine that a general puzzling of us all is to be the end of our discussion, but if we are unable to answer, do you answer, as you have promised. Consider, then, whether you will divide pleasure and knowledge according to their kinds; or you may let the matter drop, if you are able and willing to find some other mode of clearing up our controversy.

Soc. If you say that, I have nothing to apprehend, for the words 'if you are willing' dispel all my fear; and, moreover, a god seems to have recalled something to my mind.

Phi. What is that?

Soc. I remember to have heard long ago certain discussions about pleasure and wisdom, whether awake or in a dream I cannot tell; they were to the effect that neither the one nor the other of them was the good, but some third thing, which was different from them, and better than either. If this be clearly established, then pleasure will lose the victory, for the good will cease to be identified with her:—Am I not right?

Pro. Yes.

Soc. And there will cease to be any need of distinguishing the kinds of pleasures, as I am inclined to think, but this will appear more clearly as we proceed.

Pro. Capital, Socrates; pray go on as you propose.

Soc. But, let us first agree on some little points.

Pro. What are they?

Soc. Is the good perfect or imperfect?

Pro. The most perfect, Socrates, of all things.

Soc. And is the good sufficient?

Pro. Yes, certainly, and in a degree surpassing all other things.

Soc. And no one can deny that all percipient beings desire and hunt after good, and are eager to catch and have the good about them, and care not for the attainment of anything which is not accompanied by good.

Pro. That is undeniable.

Soc. Now let us part off the life of pleasure from the life of wisdom, and pass them in review.

Pro. How do you mean?

Soc. Let there be no wisdom in the life of pleasure, nor any pleasure in the life of wisdom, for if either of them is the chief good, it cannot be supposed to want anything, but if either is shown to want anything, then it cannot really be the chief good.

Pro. Impossible.

Soc. And will you help us to test these two lives?

Pro. Certainly.

Soc. Then answer.

Pro. Ask.

Soc. Would you choose, Protarchus, to live all your life long in the enjoyment of the greatest pleasures?

Pro. Certainly I should.

Soc. Would you consider that there was still anything wanting to you if you had perfect pleasure?

Pro. Certainly not.

Soc. Reflect; would you not want wisdom and intelligence and forethought, and similar qualities? would you not at any rate want sight?

Pro. Why should I? Having pleasure I should have all things.

Soc. Living thus, you would always throughout your life enjoy the greatest pleasures?

Pro. I should.

Soc. But if you had neither mind, nor memory, nor knowledge, nor true opinion, you would in the first place be utterly ignorant of whether you were pleased or not, because you would be entirely devoid of intelligence.

Pro. Certainly.

Soc. And similarly, if you had no memory you would not recollect that you had ever been pleased, nor would the slightest recollection of the pleasure which you feel at any moment remain with you; and if you had no true opinion you would not think that you were pleased when you were; and if you had no power of calculation you would not be able to calculate on future pleasure, and your life would be the life, not of a man, but of an oyster or 'pulmo marinus.' Could this be otherwise?

Pro. No.

Soc. But is such a life eligible?

Pro. I cannot answer you, Socrates; the argument has taken away from me the power of speech.

Soc. We must keep up our spirits;—let us now take the life of mind and examine it in turn.

Pro. And what is this life of mind?

Soc. I want to know whether any one of us would consent to

above all things to be desired.

Next let us separate the life of pleasure from the life of wisdom, and examine each apart.

Pleasure without knowledge is pleasure of which we are unconscious,— the life of an oyster.

Philebus

SOCRATES,
PROTAR-
CHUS,
PHILE-
BUS.

22

And knowl-
edge,
without
pleasure,
is equally
undesir-
able.

The
mixed
life of
pleasure
and wis-
dom is to
be pre-
ferred.

'And so
pleasure,'
says
Socrates,
'is not the
same with
the good.'
—'Nor
your
mind',
rejoins
Philebus.
—'Not
my mind,
certainly,
but the
divine,
yes. And
I might
add that
the excel-
lence of
the mixed
life is due

live, having wisdom and mind and knowledge and memory of all things, but having no sense of pleasure or pain, and wholly unaffected by these and the like feelings?

Pro. Neither life, Socrates, appears eligible to me, or is likely, as I should imagine, to be chosen by any one else.

Soc. What would you say, Protarchus, to both of these in one, or to one that was made out of the union of the two?

Pro. Out of the union, that is, of pleasure with mind and wisdom?

Soc. Yes, that is the life which I mean.

Pro. There can be no difference of opinion; not some but all would surely choose this third rather than either of the other two, and in addition to them.

Soc. But do you see the consequence?

Pro. To be sure I do. The consequence is, that two out of the three lives which have been proposed are neither sufficient nor eligible for man or for animal.

Soc. Then now there can be no doubt that neither of them has the good, for the one which had would certainly have been sufficient and perfect and eligible for every living creature or thing that was able to live such a life; and if any of us had chosen any other, he would have chosen contrary to the nature of the truly eligible, and not of his own free will, but either through ignorance or from some unhappy necessity.

Pro. Certainly that seems to be true.

Soc. And now have I not sufficiently shown that Philebus' goddess is not to be regarded as identical with the good?

Phi. Neither is your 'mind' the good, Socrates, for that will be open to the same objections.

Soc. Perhaps, Philebus, you may be right in saying so of my 'mind'; but of the true, which is also the divine mind, far otherwise. However, I will not at present claim the first place for mind as against the mixed life; but we must come to some understanding about the second place. For you might affirm pleasure and I mind to be the cause of the mixed life; and in that case although neither of them would be the good, one of them might be imagined to be the cause of the good. And I might proceed further to argue in opposition to Philebus, that the element which makes this mixed life eligible and good, is more akin and more similar to mind than to pleasure. And if this is true, pleasure cannot be truly said to share either in the first or second place, and does not, if I may trust my own mind, attain even to the third.

Pro. Truly, Socrates, pleasure appears to me to have had a fall;

in fighting for the palm, she has been smitten by the argument, and is laid low. I must say that mind would have fallen too, and may therefore be thought to show discretion in not putting forward a similar claim. And if pleasure were deprived not only of the first but of the second place, she would be terribly damaged in the eyes of her admirers, for not even to them would she still appear as fair as before.

Soc. Well, but had we not better leave her now, and not pain her by applying the crucial test, and finally detecting her?

Pro. Nonsense, Socrates.

Soc. Why? because I said that we had better not pain pleasure, which is an impossibility?

Pro. Yes, and more than that, because you do not seem to be aware that none of us will let you go home until you have finished the argument.

Soc. Heavens! Protarchus, that will be a tedious business, and just at present not at all an easy one. For in going to war in the cause of mind, who is aspiring to the second prize, I ought to have weapons of another make from those which I used before; some, however, of the old ones may do again. And must I then finish the argument?

Pro. Of course you must.

Soc. Let us be very careful in laying the foundation.

Pro. What do you mean?

Soc. Let us divide all existing things into two, or rather, if you do not object, into three classes.

Pro. Upon what principle would you make the division?

Soc. Let us take some of our newly-found notions.

Pro. Which of them?

Soc. Were we not saying that God revealed a finite element of existence, and also an infinite?

Pro. Certainly.

Soc. Let us assume these two principles, and also a third, which is compounded out of them; but I fear that I am ridiculously clumsy at these processes of division and enumeration.

Pro. What do you mean, my good friend?

Soc. I say that a fourth class is still wanted.

Pro. What will that be?

Soc. Find the cause of the third or compound, and add this as a fourth class to the three others.

Pro. And would you like to have a fifth class or cause of resolution as well as a cause of composition?

23
Philebus

SOCRATES,
PROTAR-
CHUS.

rather to wisdom than to pleasure.'

In supporting the claims of mind to the second place, some new weapons will be required.

All things may be divided into three or four classes: (1) the finite, (2) the infinite, (3) the union of the two, and (4) the cause of the union.

Soc. Not, I think, at present; but if I want a fifth at some future time you shall allow me to have it.

Pro. Certainly.

Soc. Let us begin with the first three; and as we find two out of the three greatly divided and dispersed, let us endeavour to reunite them, and see how in each of them there is a one and many.

Pro. If you would explain to me a little more about them, perhaps I might be able to follow you.

Soc. Well, the two classes are the same which I mentioned before, one the finite, and the other the infinite; I will first show that the infinite is in a certain sense many, and the finite may be hereafter discussed.

Pro. I agree.

Soc. And now consider well; for the question to which I invite your attention is difficult and controverted. When you speak of hotter and colder, can you conceive any limit in those qualities? Does not the more and less, which dwells in their very nature, prevent their having any end? for if they had an end, the more and less would themselves have an end.

Pro. That is most true.

Soc. Ever, as we say, into the hotter and the colder there enters a more and a less.

Pro. Yes.

Soc. Then, says the argument, there is never any end of them, and being endless they must also be infinite.

Pro. Yes, Socrates, that is exceedingly true.

Soc. Yes, my dear Protarchus, and your answer reminds me that such an expression as 'exceedingly,' which you have just uttered, and also the term 'gently,' have the same significance as more or less; for whenever they occur they do not allow of the existence of quantity—they are always introducing degrees into actions, instituting a comparison of a more or a less excessive or a more or a less gentle, and at each creation of more or less, quantity disappears. For, as I was just now saying, if quantity and measure did not disappear, but were allowed to intrude in the sphere of more and less and the other comparatives, these last would be driven out of their own domain. When definite quantity is once admitted, there can be no longer a 'hotter' or a 'colder' (for these are always progressing, and are never in one stay); but definite quantity is at rest, and has ceased to progress. Which proves that comparatives, such as the hotter and the colder, are to be ranked in the class of the infinite.

Pro. Your remark certainly has the look of truth, Socrates; but these subjects, as you were saying, are difficult to follow at first. I think, however, that if I could hear the argument repeated by you once or twice, there would be a substantial agreement between us.

Soc. Yes, and I will try to meet your wish; but, as I would rather not waste time in the enumeration of endless particulars, let me know whether I may not assume as a note of the infinite—

Pro. What?

Soc. I want to know whether such things as appear to us to admit of more or less, or are denoted by the words 'exceedingly,' 'gently,' 'extremely,' and the like, may not be referred to the class of the infinite, which is their unity, for, as was asserted in the previous argument, all things that were divided and dispersed should be brought together, and have the mark or seal of some one nature, if possible, set upon them—do you remember?

Pro. Yes.

Soc. And all things which do not admit of more or less, but admit their opposites, that is to say, first of all, equality, and the equal, or again, the double, or any other ratio of number and measure—all these may, I think, be rightly reckoned by us in the class of the limited or finite; what do you say?

Pro. Excellent, Socrates.

Soc. And now what nature shall we ascribe to the third or compound kind?

Pro. You, I think, will have to tell me that.

Soc. Rather God will tell you, if there be any God who will listen to my prayers.

Pro. Offer up a prayer, then, and think.

Soc. I am thinking, Protarchus, and I believe that some God has befriended us.

Pro. What do you mean, and what proof have you to offer of what you are saying?

Soc. I will tell you, and do you listen to my words.

Pro. Proceed.

Soc. Were we not speaking just now of hotter and colder?

Pro. True.

Soc. Add to them drier, wetter, more, less, swifter, slower, greater, smaller, and all that in the preceding argument we placed under the unity of more and less.

Pro. In the class of the infinite, you mean?

Soc. Yes; and now mingle this with the other.

Pro. What is the other?

Soc. The class of the finite which we ought to have brought to-

The union
of finite
and infi-
nite gives
rise to the
third
class,

gether as we did the infinite; but, perhaps, it will come to the same
thing if we do so now;—when the two are combined, a third will
appear.

Pro. What do you mean by the class of the finite?

Soc. The class of the equal and the double, and any class which
puts an end to difference and opposition, and by introducing number creates harmony and proportion among the different elements.

Pro. I understand; you seem to me to mean that the various opposites, when you mingle with them the class of the finite, takes
certain forms.

Soc. Yes, that is my meaning.

Pro. Proceed.

under
which are
included
health
[26]
and har-
mony and
beauty
and the
seasons
and every
sort of
good.

Soc. Does not the right participation in the finite give health—
in disease, for instance?

Pro. Certainly.

Soc. And whereas the high and low, the swift and the slow are
infinite or unlimited, does not the addition of the principles aforesaid introduce a limit, and perfect the whole frame of music?

Pro. Yes, certainly.

Soc. Or, again, when cold and heat prevail, does not the introduction of them take away excess and indefiniteness, and infuse
moderation and harmony?

Pro. Certainly.

Soc. And from a like admixture of the finite and infinite come
the seasons, and all the delights of life?

Pro. Most true.

Soc. I omit ten thousand other things, such as beauty and health
and strength, and the many beauties and high perfections of the
soul: O my beautiful Philebus, the goddess, methinks, seeing the
universal wantonness and wickedness of all things, and that there
was in them no limit to pleasures and self-indulgence, devised the
limit of law and order, whereby, as you say, Philebus, she torments,
or as I maintain, delivers the soul.—What think you, Protarchus?

Pro. Her ways are much to my mind, Socrates.

Soc. You will observe that I have spoken of three classes?

Pro. Yes, I think that I understand you: you mean to say that
the infinite is one class, and that the finite is a second class of existences; but what you would make the third I am not so certain.

The third
class
takes an
amazing
variety
of forms,

Soc. That is because the amazing variety of the third class is too
much for you, my dear friend; but there was not this difficulty
with the infinite, which also comprehended many classes, for all
of them were sealed with the note of more and less, and therefore
appeared one.

Pro. True.

Soc. And the finite or limit had not many divisions, and we readily acknowledged it to be by nature one?

Pro. Yes.

Soc. Yes, indeed; and when I speak of the third class, understand me to mean any offspring of these, being a birth into true being, effected by the measure which the limit introduces.

Pro. I understand.

Soc. Still there was, as we said, a fourth class to be investigated, and you must assist in the investigation; for does not everything which comes into being, of necessity come into being through a cause?

Pro. Yes, certainly; for how can there be anything which has no cause?

Soc. And is not the agent the same as the cause in all except name; the agent and the cause may be rightly called one?

Pro. Very true.

Soc. And the same may be said of the patient, or effect; we shall find that they too differ, as I was saying, only in name—shall we not?

Pro. We shall.

Soc. The agent or cause always naturally leads, and the patient or effect naturally follows it?

Pro. Certainly.

Soc. Then the cause and what is subordinate to it in generation are not the same, but different?

Pro. True.

Soc. Did not the things which were generated, and the things out of which they were generated, furnish all the three classes?

Pro. Yes.

Soc. And the creator or cause of them has been satisfactorily proven to be distinct from them—and may therefore be called a fourth principle?

Pro. So let us call it.

Soc. Quite right; but now, having distinguished the four, I think that we had better refresh our memories by recapitulating each of them in order.

Pro. By all means.

Soc. Then the first I will call the infinite or unlimited, and the second the finite or limited; then follows the third, an essence compound and generated; and I do not think that I shall be far wrong in speaking of the cause of mixture and generation as the fourth.

Pro. Certainly not.

Philebus

SOCRATES,
PROTAR-
CHUS.

and is therefore more difficult to conceive than the two first classes.

The fourth class is the cause of the union of finite and infinite.

27

Order of the classes: (1) the infinite; (2) the finite;

Philebus

SOCRATES,
PROTAR-
CHUS.
PHILE-
BUS.

(3) the
union of
these;
(4) the
cause of
the union.

To the
third be-
longs the
mixed
life of
pleasure
and
wisdom.

Pleasure
and also
pain be-
long to
the first
class.

28

To which
does mind
belong?

Soc. And now what is the next question, and how came we hither? Were we not enquiring whether the second place belonged to pleasure or wisdom?

Pro. We were.

Soc. And now, having determined these points, shall we not be better able to decide about the first and second place, which was the original subject of dispute?

Pro. I dare say.

Soc. We said, if you remember, that the mixed life of pleasure and wisdom was the conqueror—did we not?

Pro. True.

Soc. And we see what is the place and nature of this life and to what class it is to be assigned?

Pro. Beyond a doubt.

Soc. This is evidently comprehended in the third or mixed class; which is not composed of any two particular ingredients, but of all the elements of infinity, bound down by the finite, and may therefore be truly said to comprehend the conqueror life.

Pro. Most true.

Soc. And what shall we say, Philebus, of your life which is all sweetness; and in which of the aforesaid classes is that to be placed? Perhaps you will allow me to ask you a question before you answer?

Phi. Let me hear.

Soc. Have pleasure and pain a limit, or do they belong to the class which admits of more and less?

Phi. They belong to the class which admits of more, Socrates; for pleasure would not be perfectly good if she were not infinite in quantity and degree.

Soc. Nor would pain, Philebus, be perfectly evil. And therefore the infinite cannot be that element which imparts to pleasure some degree of good. But now—admitting, if you like, that pleasure is of the nature of the infinite—in which of the aforesaid classes, O Protarchus and Philebus, can we without irreverence place wisdom and knowledge and mind? And let us be careful, for I think that the danger will be very serious if we err on this point.

Phi. You magnify, Socrates, the importance of your favourite god.

Soc. And you, my friend, are also magnifying your favourite goddess; but still I must beg you to answer the question.

Pro. Socrates is quite right, Philebus, and we must submit to him.

Phi. And did not you, Protarchus, propose to answer in my place?

Philebus

SOCRATES,
PROTAR-
CHUS.
PHILE-
BUS.

Pro. Certainly I did; but I am now in a great strait, and I must entreat you, Socrates, to be our spokesman, and then we shall not say anything wrong or disrespectful of your favourite.

Soc. I must obey you, Protarchus; nor is the task which you impose a difficult one; but did I really, as Philebus implies, disconcert you with my playful solemnity, when I asked the question to what class mind and knowledge belong?

Pro. You did, indeed, Socrates.

Soc. Yet the answer is easy, since all philosophers assert with one voice that mind is the king of heaven and earth—in reality they are magnifying themselves. And perhaps they are right. But still I should like to consider the class of mind, if you do not object, a little more fully.

To the highest, as philosophers declare. But they are interested witnesses, and therefore further proof is needed.

Phi. Take your own course, Socrates, and never mind length; we shall not tire of you.

Soc. Very good; let us begin then, Protarchus, by asking a question.

Pro. What question?

Soc. Whether all this which they call the universe is left to the guidance of unreason and chance medley, or, on the contrary, as our fathers have declared, ordered and governed by a marvellous intelligence and wisdom.

First, we agree that the world is governed by mind, and not by chance.

Pro. Wide asunder are the two assertions, illustrious Socrates, for that which you were just now saying to me appears to be blasphemy; but the other assertion, that mind orders all things, is worthy of the aspect of the world, and of the sun, and of the moon, and of the stars and of the whole circle of the heavens; and never will I say or think otherwise.

Soc. Shall we then[1] agree with them of old time in maintaining[1] this doctrine,—not merely reasserting the notions of others, without risk to ourselves,—but shall we share in the danger, and take our part of the reproach which will await us, when an ingenious individual declares that all is disorder?

29

Pro. That would certainly be my wish.

Soc. Then now please to consider the next stage of the argument.

Pro. Let me hear.

Soc. We see that the elements which enter into the nature of the bodies of all animals, fire, water, air, and, as the storm-tossed sailor cries, 'land' [i. e. earth], reappear in the constitution of the world.

Next, our bodies are dependent on the body of the

Pro. The proverb may be applied to us; for truly the storm gathers over us, and we are at our wit's end.

[1] Or, 'maintain in accordance with our previous statements:' but cf. supra 28 D, and infra 30 D.

Philebus

SOCRATES,
PROTAR-
CHUS.

universe,
whence
the ele-
ments,
which
compose
them,
are de-
rived.

Soc. There is something to be remarked about each of these elements.

Pro. What is it?

Soc. Only a small fraction of any one of them exists in us, and that of a mean sort, and not in any way pure, or having any power worthy of its nature. One instance will prove this of all of them; there is fire within us, and in the universe.

Pro. True.

Soc. And is not our fire small and weak and mean? But the fire in the universe is wonderful in quantity and beauty, and in every power that fire has.

Pro. Most true.

Soc. And is the fire in the universe nourished and generated and ruled by the fire in us, or is the fire in you and me, and in other animals, dependent on the universal fire?

Pro. That is a question which does not deserve an answer.

Soc. Right; and you would say the same, if I am not mistaken, of the earth which is in animals and the earth which is in the universe, and you would give a similar reply about all the other elements?

Pro. Why, how could any man who gave any other be deemed in his senses?

Soc. I do not think that he could—but now go on to the next step. When we saw those elements of which we have been speaking gathered up in one, did we not call them a body?

Pro. We did.

Soc. And the same may be said of the cosmos, which for the same reason may be considered to be a body, because made up of the same elements.

Pro. Very true.

Soc. But is our body nourished wholly by this body, or is this body nourished by our body, thence deriving and having the qualities of which we were just now speaking?

Pro. That again, Socrates, is a question which does not deserve to be asked.

30

Soc. Well, tell me, is this question worth asking?

Pro. What question?

Soc. May our body be said to have a soul?

Pro. Clearly.

And,
following
out the
analogy,
we must
conclude
that our
souls and

Soc. And whence comes that soul, my dear Protarchus, unless the body of the universe, which contains elements like those in our bodies but in every way fairer, had also a soul? Can there be another source?

Pro. Clearly, Socrates, that is the only source.

Soc. Why, yes, Protarchus; for surely we cannot imagine that of the four classes, the finite, the infinite, the composition of the two, and the cause, the fourth, which enters into all things, giving to our bodies souls, and the art of self-management, and of healing disease, and operating in other ways to heal and organize, having too all the attributes of wisdom;—we cannot, I say, imagine that whereas the self-same elements exist, both in the entire heaven and in great provinces of the heaven, only fairer and purer, this last should not also in that higher sphere have designed the noblest and fairest things?

Pro. Such a supposition is quite unreasonable.

Soc. Then if this be denied, should we not be wise in adopting the other view and maintaining that there is in the universe a mighty infinite and an adequate limit, of which we have often spoken, as well as a presiding cause of no mean power, which orders and arranges years and seasons and months, and may be justly called wisdom and mind?

Pro. Most justly.

Soc. And wisdom and mind cannot exist without soul?

Pro. Certainly not.

Soc. And in the divine nature of Zeus would you not say that there is the soul and mind of a king, because there is in him the power of the cause? And other gods have other attributes, by which they are pleased to be called.

Pro. Very true.

Soc. Do not then suppose that these words are rashly spoken by us, O Protarchus, for they are in harmony with the testimony of those who said of old time that mind rules the universe.

Pro. True.

Soc. And they furnish an answer to my enquiry (cp. 28 A); for they imply that mind is the parent of that class of the four which we called the cause of all; and I think that you now have my answer.

Pro. I have indeed, and yet I did not observe that you had answered.

Soc. A jest is sometimes refreshing, Protarchus, when it interrupts earnest.

Pro. Very true.

Soc. I think, friend, that we have now pretty clearly set forth the class to which mind belongs and what is the power of mind.

Pro. True.

Soc. And the class to which pleasure belongs has also been long ago discovered?

Pro. Yes.

Soc. And let us remember, too, of both of them, (1) that mind was akin to the cause and of this family; and (2) that pleasure is infinite and belongs to the class which neither has, nor ever will have in itself, a beginning, middle, or end of its own.

Pro. I shall be sure to remember.

Soc. We must next examine what is their place and under what conditions they are generated. And we will begin with pleasure, since her class was first examined; and yet pleasure cannot be rightly tested apart from pain.

Pro. If this is the road, let us take it.

Soc. I wonder whether you would agree with me about the origin of pleasure and pain.

Pro. What do you mean?

Soc. I mean to say that their natural seat is in the mixed class.

Pro. And would you tell me again, sweet Socrates, which of the aforesaid classes is the mixed one?

Soc. I will, my fine fellow, to the best of my ability.

Pro. Very good.

Soc. Let us then understand the mixed class to be that which we placed third in the list of four.

Pro. That which followed the infinite and the finite; and in which you ranked health, and, if I am not mistaken, harmony.

Soc. Capital; and now will you please to give me your best attention?

Pro. Proceed; I am attending.

Soc. I say that when the harmony in animals is dissolved, there is also a dissolution of nature and a generation of pain.

Pro. That is very probable.

Soc. And the restoration of harmony and return to nature is the source of pleasure, if I may be allowed to speak in the fewest and shortest words about matters of the greatest moment.

Pro. I believe that you are right, Socrates; but will you try to be a little plainer?

Soc. Do not obvious and every-day phenomena furnish the simplest illustration?

Pro. What phenomena do you mean?

Soc. Hunger, for example, is a dissolution and a pain.

Pro. True.

Soc. Whereas eating is a replenishment and a pleasure?

Pro. Yes.

Soc. Thirst again is a destruction and a pain, but the effect of moisture replenishing the dry place is a pleasure: once more, the unnatural separation and dissolution caused by heat is painful, and the natural restoration and refrigeration is pleasant.

Pro. Very true.

Soc. And the unnatural freezing of the moisture in an animal is pain, and the natural process of resolution and return of the elements to their original state is pleasure. And would not the general proposition seem to you to hold, that the destroying of the natural union of the finite and infinite, which, as I was observing before, make up the class of living beings, is pain, and that the process of return of all things to their own nature is pleasure?

Pro. Granted; what you say has a general truth.

Soc. Here then is one kind of pleasures and pains originating severally in the two processes which we have described?

Pro. Good.

Soc. Let us next assume that in the soul herself there is an antecedent hope of pleasure which is sweet and refreshing, and an expectation of pain, fearful and anxious.

Pro. Yes; this is another class of pleasures and pains, which is of the soul only, apart from the body, and is produced by expectation.

Soc. Right; for in the analysis of these, pure, as I suppose them to be, the pleasures being unalloyed with pain and the pains with pleasure, methinks that we shall see clearly whether the whole class of pleasure is to be desired, or whether this quality of entire desirableness is not rather to be attributed to another of the classes which have been mentioned; and whether pleasure and pain, like heat and cold, and other things of the same kind, are not sometimes to be desired and sometimes not to be desired, as being not in themselves good, but only sometimes and in some instances admitting of the nature of good.

Pro. You say most truly that this is the track which the investigation should pursue.

Soc. Well, then, assuming that pain ensues on the dissolution, and pleasure on the restoration of the harmony, let us now ask what will be the condition of animated beings who are neither in process of restoration nor of dissolution. And mind what you say: I ask whether any animal who is in that condition can possibly have any feeling of pleasure or pain, great or small?

Pro. Certainly not.

Soc. Then here we have a third state, over and above that of pleasure and of pain?

Pro. Very true.

In the soul there are pleasures and pains of expectation corresponding to these.

But besides dissolution and restoration, there is a neutral state of the body,

33

Philebus

SOCRATES,
PROTAR-
CHUS.

in which,
if he
pleases,
the man
who
chooses
the life
of wis-
dom may
live, like
the gods,
having
neither
joy nor
sorrow.

Soc. And do not forget that there is such a state; it will make a great difference in our judgment of pleasure, whether we remember this or not. And I should like to say a few words about it.

Pro. What have you to say?

Soc. Why, you know that if a man chooses the life of wisdom, there is no reason why he should not live in this neutral state.

Pro. You mean that he may live neither rejoicing nor sorrowing?

Soc. Yes; and if I remember rightly, when the lives were compared, no degree of pleasure, whether great or small, was thought to be necessary to him who chose the life of thought and wisdom.

Pro. Yes, certainly, we said so.

Soc. Then he will live without pleasure; and who knows whether this may not be the most divine of all lives?

Pro. If so, the gods, at any rate, cannot be supposed to have either joy or sorrow.

Soc. Certainly not—there would be a great impropriety in the assumption of either alternative. But whether the gods are or are not indifferent to pleasure is a point which may be considered hereafter if in any way relevant to the argument, and whatever is the conclusion we will place it to the account of mind in her contest for the second place, should she have to resign the first.

Pro. Just so.

Soc. The other class of pleasures, which as we were saying is purely mental, is entirely derived from memory.

Pro. What do you mean?

Soc. I must first of all analyze memory, or rather perception which is prior to memory, if the subject of our discussion is ever to be properly cleared up.

Pro. How will you proceed?

Some
affections
of the
body do
not reach
the soul;
those
which do
are con-
scious
affections.

Soc. Let us imagine affections of the body which are extinguished before they reach the soul, and leave her unaffected; and again, other affections which vibrate through both soul and body, and impart a shock to both and to each of them.

Pro. Granted.

Soc. And the soul may be truly said to be oblivious of the first but not of the second?

Pro. Quite true.

Soc. When I say oblivious, do not suppose that I mean forgetfulness in a literal sense; for forgetfulness is the exit of memory, which in this case has not yet entered; and to speak of the loss of that which is not yet in existence, and never has been, is a contradiction; do you see?

Pro. Yes.

Soc. Then just be so good as to change the terms.

Pro. How shall I change them?

Soc. Instead of the oblivion of the soul, when you are describing the state in which she is unaffected by the shocks of the body, say unconsciousness.

Pro. I see.

Soc. And the union or communion of soul and body in one feeling and motion would be properly called consciousness?

Pro. Most true.

Soc. Then now we know the meaning of the word?

Pro. Yes.

Soc. And memory may, I think, be rightly described as the preservation of consciousness?

Pro. Right.

Soc. But do we not distinguish memory from recollection?

Pro. I think so.

Soc. And do we not mean by recollection the power which the soul has of recovering, when by herself, some feeling which she experienced when in company with the body?

Pro. Certainly.

Soc. And when she recovers of herself the lost recollection of some consciousness or knowledge, the recovery is termed recollection and reminiscence?

Pro. Very true.

Soc. There is a reason why I say all this.

Pro. What is it?

Soc. I want to attain the plainest possible notion of pleasure and desire, as they exist in the mind only, apart from the body; and the previous analysis helps to show the nature of both.

Pro. Then now, Socrates, let us proceed to the next point.

Soc. There are certainly many things to be considered in discussing the generation and whole complexion of pleasure. At the outset we must determine the nature and seat of desire.

Pro. Ay; let us enquire into that, for we shall lose nothing.

Soc. Nay, Protarchus, we shall surely lose the puzzle if we find the answer.

Pro. A fair retort; but let us proceed.

Soc. Did we not place hunger, thirst, and the like, in the class of desires?

Pro. Certainly.

Soc. And yet they are very different; what common nature have we in view when we call them by a single name?

Philebus

34
SOCRATES,
PROTAR-
CHUS.

Memory
is the
preserva-
tion of
conscious
affec-
tions; re-
collection
is the re-
covery
of them.

These
prelimi-
nary
remarks
will help
us to
under-
stand the
nature of
pleasure
and
desire.

What is
desire?—
The wish
for re-
plenish-
ment.

Desire is a mental act

Pro. By heavens, Socrates, that is a question which is not easily answered; but it must be answered.

Soc. Then let us go back to our examples.

Pro. Where shall we begin?

Soc. Do we mean anything when we say 'a man thirsts'?

Pro. Yes.

Soc. We mean to say that he 'is empty'?

Pro. Of course.

Soc. And is not thirst desire?

Pro. Yes, of drink.

35

Soc. Would you say of drink, or of replenishment with drink?

Pro. I should say, of replenishment with drink.

Soc. Then he who is empty desires, as would appear, the opposite of what he experiences; for he is empty and desires to be full?

Pro. Clearly so.

But how
can a
man,
when first
empty,
desire
replenish-
ment of
which he
has no ex-
perience?

Soc. But how can a man who is empty for the first time, attain either by perception or memory to any apprehension of replenishment, of which he has no present or past experience?

Pro. Impossible.

Soc. And yet he who desires, surely desires something?

Pro. Of course.

Soc. He does not desire that which he experiences, for he experiences thirst, and thirst is emptiness; but he desires replenishment?

Pro. True.

Soc. Then there must be something in the thirsty man which in some way apprehends replenishment?

Pro. There must.

Yet he
does de-
sire it,
not how-
ever with
his body,
but with
his mind
by the
help of
memory.

Soc. And that cannot be the body, for the body is supposed to be emptied?

Pro. Yes.

Soc. The only remaining alternative is that the soul apprehends the replenishment by the help of memory; as is obvious, for what other way can there be?

Pro. I cannot imagine any other.

Soc. But do you see the consequence?

Pro. What is it?

Soc. That there is no such thing as desire of the body.

Pro. Why so?

Soc. Why, because the argument shows that the endeavour of every animal is to the reverse of his bodily state.

Pro. Yes.

Soc. And the impulse which leads him to the opposite of what he is experiencing proves that he has a memory of the opposite state.

Pro. True.

Soc. And the argument, having proved that memory attracts us towards the objects of desire, proves also that the impulses and the desires and the moving principle in every living being have their origin in the soul.

Pro. Most true.

Soc. The argument will not allow that our body either hungers or thirsts or has any similar experience.

Pro. Quite right.

Soc. Let me make a further observation; the argument appears to me to imply that there is a kind of life which consists in these affections.

Pro. Of what affections, and of what kind of life, are you speaking?

Soc. I am speaking of being emptied and replenished, and of all that relates to the preservation and destruction of living beings, as well as of the pain which is felt in one of these states and of the pleasure which succeeds to it.

Pro. True.

Soc. And what would you say of the intermediate state?

Pro. What do you mean by 'intermediate'?

Soc. I mean when a person is in actual suffering and yet remembers past pleasures which, if they would only return, would relieve him; but as yet he has them not. May we not say of him, that he is in an intermediate state?

Pro. Certainly.

Soc. Would you say that he was wholly pained or wholly pleased?

Pro. Nay, I should say that he has two pains; in his body there is the actual experience of pain, and in his soul longing and expectation.

Soc. What do you mean, Protarchus, by the two pains? May not a man who is empty have at one time a sure hope of being filled, and at other times be quite in despair?

Pro. Very true.

Soc. And has he not the pleasure of memory when he is hoping to be filled, and yet in that he is empty is he not at the same time in pain?

Pro. Certainly.

Soc. Then man and the other animals have at the same time both pleasure and pain?

The mind, then, is the seat of desire.

There is an intermediate life, which combines a bodily [36] pain with the mental pleasure of hope.

Philebus

SOCRATES,
PROTAR-
CHUS.

But when
the hope
is turned
into
despair,
there is a
double
pain.

A ques-
tion.—
Can there
be false
pleasures,
as there
are false
opinions?
'No,' re-
joins Pro-
tarchus;
'opinions
may be
false, but
not plea-
sures.'

Pro. I suppose so.

Soc. But when a man is empty and has no hope of being filled, there will be the double experience of pain. You observed this and inferred that the double experience was the single case possible.

Pro. Quite true, Socrates.

Soc. Shall the enquiry into these states of feeling be made the occasion of raising a question?

Pro. What question?

Soc. Whether we ought to say that the pleasures and pains of which we are speaking are true or false? or some true and some false?

Pro. But how, Socrates, can there be false pleasures and pains?

Soc. And how, Protarchus, can there be true and false fears, or true and false expectations, or true and false opinions?

Pro. I grant that opinions may be true or false, but not pleasures.

Soc. What do you mean? I am afraid that we are raising a very serious enquiry.

Pro. There I agree.

Soc. And yet, my boy, for you are one of Philebus' boys (cp. 16 A), the point to be considered, is, whether the enquiry is relevant to the argument.

Pro. Surely.

Soc. No tedious and irrelevant discussion can be allowed; what is said should be pertinent.

Pro. Right.

Soc. I am always wondering at the question which has now been raised.

Pro. How so?

Soc. Do you deny that some pleasures are false, and others true?

Pro. To be sure I do.

Soc. Would you say that no one ever seemed to rejoice and yet did not rejoice, or seemed to feel pain and yet did not feel pain, sleeping or waking, mad or lunatic?

Pro. So we have always held, Socrates.

Soc. But were you right? Shall we enquire into the truth of your opinion?

Pro. I think that we should.

Soc. Let us then put into more precise terms the question which has arisen about pleasure and opinion. Is there such a thing as opinion?

Pro. Yes.

Soc. And such a thing as pleasure?

Pro. Yes.

Soc. And an opinion must be of something?

Pro. True.

Soc. And a man must be pleased by something?

Pro. Quite correct.

Soc. And whether the opinion be right or wrong, makes no difference; it will still be an opinion?

Pro. Certainly.

Soc. And he who is pleased, whether he is rightly pleased or not will always have a real feeling of pleasure?

Pro. Yes; that is also quite true.

Soc. Then, how can opinion be both true and false, and pleasure true only, although pleasure and opinion are both equally real?

Pro. Yes; that is the question.

Soc. You mean that opinion admits of truth and falsehood, and hence becomes not merely opinion, but opinion of a certain quality; and this is what you think should be examined?

Pro. Yes.

Soc. And further, even if we admit the existence of qualities in other objects, may not pleasure and pain be simple and devoid of quality?

Pro. Clearly.

Soc. But there is no difficulty in seeing that pleasure and pain as well as opinion have qualities, for they are great or small, and have various degrees of intensity; as was indeed said long ago by us.

Pro. Quite true.

Soc. And if badness attaches to any of them, Protarchus, then we should speak of a bad opinion or of a bad pleasure?

Pro. Quite true, Socrates.

Soc. And if rightness attaches to any of them, should we not speak of a right opinion or right pleasure; and in like manner of the reverse of rightness?

Pro. Certainly.

Soc. And if the thing opined be erroneous, might we not say that opinion, being erroneous, is not right or rightly opined?

Pro. Certainly.

Soc. And if we see a pleasure or pain which errs in respect of its object, shall we call that right or good, or by any honourable name?

Pro. Not if the pleasure is mistaken; how could we?

Soc. And surely pleasure often appears to accompany an opinion which is not true, but false?

Pro. Certainly it does; and in that case, Socrates, as we were saying, the opinion is false, but no one could call the actual pleasure false.

All pleasures and opinions, whether right or wrong, are real.

But do pleasures, like opinions, admit of quality? Certainly they do.

False pleasures are pleasures based on false opinion.
38

Philebus

SOCRATES,
PROTAR-
CHUS.

How do
these
differ
from
pleasures
based on
true
opinion?

Soc. How eagerly, Protarchus, do you rush to the defence of pleasure!

Pro. Nay, Socrates, I only repeat what I hear.

Soc. And is there no difference, my friend, between that pleasure which is associated with right opinion and knowledge, and that which is often found in all of us associated with falsehood and ignorance?

Pro. There must be a very great difference between them.

Soc. Then, now let us proceed to contemplate this difference.

Pro. Lead, and I will follow.

Soc. Well, then, my view is—

Pro. What is it?

Soc. We agree—do we not?—that there is such a thing as false, and also such a thing as true opinion?

Pro. Yes.

Soc. And pleasure and pain, as I was just now saying, are often consequent upon these—upon true and false opinion, I mean.

Pro. Very true.

Opinions
spring
from
memory
and per-
ception,

Soc. And do not opinion and the endeavour to form an opinion always spring from memory and perception?

Pro. Certainly.

Soc. Might we imagine the process to be something of this nature?

Pro. Of what nature?

Soc. An object may be often seen at a distance not very clearly, and the seer may want to determine what it is which he sees.

Pro. Very likely.

Soc. Soon he begins to interrogate himself.

Pro. In what manner?

Soc. He asks himself—'What is that which appears to be standing by the rock under the tree?' This is the question which he may be supposed to put to himself when he sees such an appearance.

Pro. True.

Soc. To which he may guess the right answer, saying as if in a whisper to himself—'It is a man.'

Pro. Very good.

Soc. Or again, he may be misled, and then he will say—'No, it is a figure made by the shepherds.'

Pro. Yes.

Soc. And if he has a companion, he repeats his thought to him in articulate sounds, and what was before an opinion, has now become a proposition.

Pro. Certainly.

Soc. But if he be walking alone when these thoughts occur to him, he may not unfrequently keep them in his mind for a considerable time.

Pro. Very true.

Soc. Well, now, I wonder whether you would agree in my explanation of this phenomenon.

Pro. What is your explanation?

Soc. I think that the soul at such times is like a book.

Pro. How so?

Soc. Memory and perception meet, and they and their attendant feelings seem to me almost to write down words in the soul, and when the inscribing feeling writes truly, then true opinion and true propositions which are the expressions of opinion, come into our souls—but when the scribe within us writes falsely, the result is false.

Pro. I quite assent and agree to your statement.

Soc. I must bespeak your favour also for another artist, who is busy at the same time in the chambers of the soul.

Pro. Who is he?

Soc. The painter, who, after the scribe has done his work, draws images in the soul of the things which he has described.

Pro. But when and how does he do this?

Soc. When a man, besides receiving from sight or some other sense certain opinions or statements, sees in his mind the images of the subjects of them;—is not this a very common mental phenomenon?

Pro. Certainly.

Soc. And the images answering to true opinions and words are true, and to false opinions and words false; are they not?

Pro. They are.

Soc. If we are right so far, there arises a further question.

Pro. What is it?

Soc. Whether we experience the feeling of which I am speaking only in relation to the present and the past, or in relation to the future also?

Pro. I should say in relation to all times alike.

Soc. Have not purely mental pleasures and pains been described already as in some cases anticipations of the bodily ones; from which we may infer that anticipatory pleasures and pains have to do with the future?

Pro. Most true.

which write down in the soul propositions relating to objects perceived. Imagination at the same time draws pictures of them. These propositions and pictures may be true or false.

Do the propositions and pictures refer to the future, as well as to the past and present?

Certainly
they do;
and then
they are
hopes.

40

Soc. And do all those writings and paintings which, as we were saying a little while ago, are produced in us, relate to the past and present only, and not to the future?

Pro. To the future, very much.

Soc. When you say, 'Very much,' you mean to imply that all these representations are hopes about the future, and that mankind are filled with hopes in every stage of existence?

Pro. Exactly.

Soc. Answer me another question.

Pro. What question?

Soc. A just and pious and good man is the friend of the gods; is he not?

Pro. Certainly he is.

Soc. And the unjust and utterly bad man is the reverse?

Pro. True.

Soc. And all men, as we were saying just now, are always filled with hopes?

Pro. Certainly.

Soc. And these hopes, as they are termed, are propositions which exist in the minds of each of us?

Pro. Yes.

Soc. And the fancies of hope are also pictured in us; a man may often have a vision of a heap of gold, and pleasures ensuing, and in the picture there may be a likeness of himself mightily rejoicing over his good fortune.

Pro. True.

And the
good have
true
hopes
presented
to their
minds by
the gods,
the bad
have false
pleasures
painted in
their
fancies.

Soc. And may we not say that the good, being friends of the gods, have generally true pictures presented to them, and the bad false pictures?

Pro. Certainly.

Soc. The bad, too, have pleasures painted in their fancy as well as the good; but I presume that they are false pleasures.

Pro. They are.

Soc. The bad then commonly delight in false pleasures, and the good in true pleasures?

Pro. Doubtless.

Soc. Then upon this view there are false pleasures in the souls of men which are a ludicrous imitation of the true, and there are pains of a similar character?

Pro. There are.

Soc. And did we not allow that a man who had an opinion at all had a real opinion, but often about things which had no existence either in the past, present, or future?

Pro. Quite true.

Soc. And this was the source of false opinion and opining; am I not right?

Pro. Yes.

Soc. And must we not attribute to pleasure and pain a similar real but illusory character?

Pro. How do you mean?

Soc. I mean to say that a man must be admitted to have real pleasure who is pleased with anything or anyhow; and he may be pleased about things which neither have nor have ever had any real existence, and, more often than not, are never likely to exist.

Pro. Yes, Socrates, that again is undeniable.

Soc. And may not the same be said about fear and anger and the like; are they not often false?

Pro. Quite so.

Soc. And can opinions be good or bad except in as far as they are true or false?

Pro. In no other way.

Soc. Nor can pleasures be conceived to be bad except in so far as they are false.

Pro. Nay, Socrates, that is the very opposite of truth; for no one would call pleasures and pains bad because they are false, but by reason of some other great corruption to which they are liable.

Soc. Well, of pleasures which are corrupt and caused by corruption we will hereafter speak, if we care to continue the enquiry; for the present I would rather show by another argument that there are many false pleasures existing or coming into existence in us, because this may assist our final decision.

Pro. Very true; that is to say, if there are such pleasures.

Soc. I think that there are, Protarchus; but this is an opinion which should be well assured, and not rest upon a mere assertion.

Pro. Very good.

Soc. Then now, like wrestlers, let us approach and grasp this new argument.

Pro. Proceed.

Soc. We were maintaining a little while since, that when desires, as they are termed, exist in us, then the body has separate feelings apart from the soul—do you remember?

Pro. Yes, I remember that you said so.

Soc. And the soul was supposed to desire the opposite of the bodily state, while the body was the source of any pleasure or pain which was experienced.

Pro. True.

But these false pleasures have a real existence.

Opinions are only bad if they are [41] false: Is this the case with plea-sures?—Protar-chus reclaims against the notion.

Recapitu-lation.

Soc. Then now you may infer what happens in such cases.

Pro. What am I to infer?

Soc. That in such cases pleasure and pains come simultaneously; and there is a juxtaposition of the opposite sensations which correspond to them, as has been already shown.

Pro. Clearly.

Soc. And there is another point to which we have agreed.

Pro. What is it?

Soc. That pleasure and pain both admit of more and less, and that they are of the class of infinites.

Pro. Certainly, we said so.

Soc. But how can we rightly judge of them?

Pro. How can we?

Soc. It is our intention to judge of their comparative importance and intensity, measuring pleasure against pain, and pain against pain, and pleasure against pleasure?

Pro. Yes, such is our intention, and we shall judge of them accordingly.

42   *Soc.* Well, take the case of sight. Does not the nearness or distance of magnitudes obscure their true proportions, and make us opine falsely; and do we not find the same illusion happening in the case of pleasures and pains?

Pro. Yes, Socrates, and in a degree far greater.

Soc. Then what we are now saying is the opposite of what we were saying before.

Pro. What was that?

Soc. Then the opinions were true and false, and infected the pleasures and pains with their own falsity.

Pro. Very true.

*Pleasures
and pains
are often
false, be-
cause
they are
seen at
various
distances
and in
various
relations.*

Soc. But now it is the pleasures which are said to be true and false because they are seen at various distances, and subjected to comparison; the pleasures appear to be greater and more vehement when placed side by side with the pains, and the pains when placed side by side with the pleasures.

Pro. Certainly, and for the reason which you mention.

Soc. And suppose you part off from pleasures and pains the element which makes them appear to be greater or less than they really are: you will acknowledge that this element is illusory, and you will never say that the corresponding excess or defect of pleasure or pain is real or true.

Pro. Certainly not.

Soc. Next let us see whether in another direction we may not find pleasures and pains existing and appearing in living beings, which are still more false than these.

Pro. What are they, and how shall we find them?

Soc. If I am not mistaken, I have often repeated that pains and aches and suffering and uneasiness of all sorts arise out of a corruption of nature caused by concretions, and dissolutions, and repletions, and evacuations, and also by growth and decay?

Pro. Yes, that has been often said.

Soc. And we have also agreed that the restoration of the natural state is pleasure?

Pro. Right.

Soc. But now let us suppose an interval of time at which the body experiences none of these changes.

Pro. When can that be, Socrates?

Soc. Your question, Protarchus, does not help the argument.

Pro. Why not, Socrates?

Soc. Because it does not prevent me from repeating mine.

Pro. And what was that?

Soc. Why, Protarchus, admitting that there is no such interval, I may ask what would be the necessary consequence if there were?

Pro. You mean, what would happen if the body were not changed either for good or bad?

Soc. Yes.

Pro. Why then, Socrates, I should suppose that there would be neither pleasure nor pain.

Soc. Very good; but still, if I am not mistaken, you do assert that we must always be experiencing one of them; that is what the wise tell us; for, say they, all things are ever flowing up and down.

Pro. Yes, and their words are of no mean authority.

Soc. Of course, for they are no mean authorities themselves; and I should like to avoid the brunt of their argument. Shall I tell you how I mean to escape from them? And you shall be the partner of my flight.

Pro. How?

Soc. To them we will say: 'Good; but are we, or living things in general, always conscious of what happens to us—for example, of our growth, or the like? Are we not, on the contrary, almost wholly unconscious of this and similar phenomena?' You must answer for them.

Pro. The latter alternative is the true one.

Soc. Then we were not right in saying, just now, that motions going up and down cause pleasures and pains?

Philebus

SOCRATES,
PROTAR-
CHUS.

These are
not the
only in-
stances of
false
pleasures
and pains.
Pleasure
and pain
may arise
from
certain
changes in
the bodily
constitu-
tion.

43
Such
changes
are al-
ways
going on,
though
they are
not al-
ways per-
ceptible;
only the
greatest
are ac-
com-
panied by
pleasure
and pain.

Pro. True.

Soc. A better and more unexceptionable way of speaking will be—

Pro. What?

Soc. If we say that the great changes produce pleasures and pains, but that the moderate and lesser ones do neither.

Pro. That, Socrates, is the more correct mode of speaking.

Soc. But if this be true, the life to which I was just now referring again appears.

Thus the
neutral
life re-
appears.

Pro. What life?

Soc. The life which we affirmed to be devoid either of pain or of joy.

Pro. Very true.

Soc. We may assume then that there are three lives, one pleasant, one painful, and the third which is neither; what say you?

Pro. I should say as you do that there are three of them.

This
neutral
life,
though
painless,
is not
pleasant.

Soc. But if so, the negation of pain will not be the same with pleasure.

Pro. Certainly not.

Soc. Then when you hear a person saying, that always to live without pain is the pleasantest of all things, what would you understand him to mean by that statement?

Pro. I think that by pleasure he must mean the negative of pain.

Soc. Let us take any three things; or suppose that we embellish a little and call the first gold, the second silver, and there shall be a third which is neither.

Pro. Very good.

Soc. Now, can that which is neither be either gold or silver?

Pro. Impossible.

Soc. No more can that neutral or middle life be rightly or reasonably spoken or thought of as pleasant or painful.

Pro. Certainly not.

44

Yet some
people
think that
it is.

Soc. And yet, my friend, there are, as we know, persons who say and think so.

Pro. Certainly.

Soc. And do they think that they have pleasure when they are free from pain?

Pro. They say so.

Soc. And they must think or they would not say that they have pleasure.

Pro. I suppose not.

Soc. And yet if pleasure and the negation of pain are of distinct natures, they are wrong.

Pro. But they are undoubtedly of distinct natures.

Soc. Then shall we take the view that they are three, as we were just now saying, or that they are two only—the one being a state of pain, which is an evil, and the other a cessation of pain, which is of itself a good, and is called pleasant?

Pro. But why, Socrates, do we ask the question at all? I do not see the reason.

Soc. You, Protarchus, have clearly never heard of certain enemies of our friend Philebus.

Pro. And who may they be?

Soc. Certain persons who are reputed to be masters in natural philosophy, who deny the very existence of pleasure.

Pro. Indeed!

Soc. They say that what the school of Philebus calls pleasures are all of them only avoidances of pain.

Pro. And would you, Socrates, have us agree with them?

Soc. Why, no, I would rather use them as a sort of diviners, who divine the truth, not by rules of art, but by an instinctive repugnance and extreme detestation which a noble nature has of the power of pleasure, in which they think that there is nothing sound, and her seductive influence is declared by them to be witchcraft, and not pleasure. This is the use which you may make of them. And when you have considered the various grounds of their dislike, you shall hear from me what I deem to be true pleasures. Having thus examined the nature of pleasure from both points of view, we will bring her up for judgment.

Pro. Well said.

Soc. Then let us enter into an alliance with these philosophers and follow in the track of their dislike. I imagine that they would say something of this sort; they would begin at the beginning, and ask whether, if we wanted to know the nature of any quality, such as hardness, we should be more likely to discover it by looking at the hardest things, rather than at the least hard? You, Protarchus, shall answer these severe gentlemen as you answer me.

Pro. By all means, and I reply to them, that you should look at the greatest instances.

Soc. Then if we want to see the true nature of pleasures as a class, we should not look at the most diluted pleasures, but at the most extreme and most vehement?

Pro. In that every one will agree.

Soc. And the obvious instances of the greatest pleasures, as we have often said, are the pleasures of the body?

Pro. Certainly.

Philebus

SOCRATES, PROTAR-CHUS.

They are certain physical philosophers who affirm pleasure to be only the absence of pain.

The grounds of their dislike to pleasure may throw light on our present enquiry.

The nature of things is best seen in their greatest instances.

45

The greatest pleasures are of the

body,
not in a
healthy,

Soc. And are they felt by us to be or become greater, when we are sick or when we are in health? And here we must be careful in our answer, or we shall come to grief.

Pro. How will that be?

Soc. Why, because we might be tempted to answer, 'When we are in health.'

Pro. Yes, that is the natural answer.

Soc. Well, but are not those pleasures the greatest of which mankind have the greatest desires?

Pro. True.

but in a
morbid
state.

Soc. And do not people who are in a fever, or any similar illness, feel cold or thirst or other bodily affections more intensely? Am I not right in saying that they have a deeper want and greater pleasure in the satisfaction of their want?

Pro. That is obvious as soon as it is said.

Soc. Well, then, shall we not be right in saying, that if a person would wish to see the greatest pleasures he ought to go and look, not at health, but at disease? And here you must distinguish:—do not imagine that I mean to ask whether those who are very ill have more pleasures than those who are well, but understand that I am speaking of the magnitude of pleasure; I want to know where pleasures are found to be most intense. For, as I say, we have to discover what is pleasure, and what they mean by pleasure who deny her very existence.

Pro. I think I follow you.

The
pleasures
of wan-
tonness
are more
intense
than
those of
temper-
ance.

Soc. You will soon have a better opportunity of showing whether you do or not, Protarchus. Answer now, and tell me whether you see, I will not say more, but more intense and excessive pleasures in wantonness than in temperance? Reflect before you speak.

Pro. I understand you, and see that there is a great difference between them; the temperate are restrained by the wise man's aphorism of 'Never too much,' which is their rule, but excess of pleasure possessing the minds of fools and wantons becomes madness and makes them shout with delight.

Soc. Very good, and if this be true, then the greatest pleasures and pains will clearly be found in some vicious state of soul and body, and not in a virtuous state.

46

Pro. Certainly.

Soc. And ought we not to select some of these for examination, and see what makes them the greatest?

Pro. To be sure we ought.

Soc. Take the case of the pleasures which arise out of certain disorders.

Pro. What disorders?

Soc. The pleasures of unseemly disorders, which our severe friends utterly detest.

Pro. What pleasures?

Soc. Such, for example, as the relief of itching and other ailments by scratching, which is the only remedy required. For what in Heaven's name is the feeling to be called which is thus produced in us?—Pleasure or pain?

Pro. A villainous mixture of some kind, Socrates, I should say.

Soc. I did not introduce the argument, O Protarchus, with any personal reference to Philebus, but because, without the consideration of these and similar pleasures, we shall not be able to determine the point at issue.

Pro. Then we had better proceed to analyze this family of pleasures.

Soc. You mean the pleasures which are mingled with pain?

Pro. Exactly.

Soc. There are some mixtures which are of the body, and only in the body, and others which are of the soul, and only in the soul; while there are other mixtures of pleasures with pains, common both to soul and body, which in their composite state are called sometimes pleasures and sometimes pains.

Pro. How is that?

Soc. Whenever, in the restoration or in the derangement of nature, a man experiences two opposite feelings; for example, when he is cold and is growing warm, or again, when he is hot and is becoming cool, and he wants to have the one and be rid of the other;—the sweet has a bitter, as the common saying is, and both together fasten upon him and create irritation and in time drive him to distraction.

Pro. That description is very true to nature.

Soc. And in these sorts of mixtures the pleasures and pains are sometimes equal, and sometimes one or other of them predominates?

Pro. True.

Soc. Of cases in which the pain exceeds the pleasure, an example is afforded by itching, of which we were just now speaking, and by the tingling which we feel when the boiling and fiery element is within, and the rubbing and motion[1] only relieves the surface, and does not reach the parts affected; then if you put them to the fire, and as a last resort apply cold to them, you may often produce the most intense pleasure or pain in the inner parts, which contrasts

---

[1] Reading with the MSS. κινήσει.

Philebus

SOCRATES,
PROTAR-
CHUS.

Morbid pleasures are such as those of scratching, which are of a mixed character.

Mixed pleasures may be of the body, of the soul, or common to both.

Either element may predominate in the mixture.

Instances of mixed pleasures: (1) of the body only —the relief of itching

Philebus

47

SOCRATES,
PROTAR-
CHUS.

by
scratch-
ing;

and mingles with the pain or pleasure, as the case may be, of the outer parts; and this is due to the forcible separation of what is united, or to the union of what is separated, and to the juxtaposition of pleasure and pain.

Pro. Quite so.

Soc. Sometimes the element of pleasure prevails in a man, and the slight undercurrent of pain makes him tingle, and causes a gentle irritation; or again, the excessive infusion of pleasure creates an excitement in him,—he even leaps for joy, he assumes all sorts of attitudes, he changes all manner of colours, he gasps for breath, and is quite amazed, and utters the most irrational exclamations.

Pro. Yes, indeed.

Soc. He will say of himself, and others will say of him, that he is dying with these delights; and the more dissipated and good-for-nothing he is, the more vehemently he pursues them in every way; of all pleasures he declares them to be the greatest; and he reckons him who lives in the most constant enjoyment of them to be the happiest of mankind.

Pro. That, Socrates, is a very true description of the opinions of the majority about pleasures.

(2) com-
mon to
body and
mind—
vacuity
accom-
panied by
hope;

Soc. Yes, Protarchus, quite true of the mixed pleasures, which arise out of the communion of external and internal sensations in the body; there are also cases in which the mind contributes an opposite element to the body[1], whether of pleasure or pain, and the two unite and form one mixture. Concerning these I have already remarked, that when a man is empty he desires to be full, and has pleasure in hope and pain in vacuity. But now I must further add what I omitted before, that in all these and similar emotions in which body and mind are opposed (and they are innumerable), pleasure and pain coalesce in one.

Pro. I believe that to be quite true.

Soc. There still remains one other sort of admixture of pleasures and pains.

Pro. What is that?

Soc. The union which, as we were saying, the mind often experiences of purely mental feelings.

Pro. What do you mean?

Soc. Why, do we not speak of anger, fear, desire, sorrow, love, emulation, envy, and the like, as pains which belong to the soul only?

Pro. Yes.

[1] Reading περὶ δὲ τῶν ἐν αἷς ψυχὴ σώματι τἀναντία ξυμβάλλεται.

Philebus

SOCRATES,
PROTAR-
CHUS.

Soc. And shall we not find them also full of the most wonderful pleasures? need I remind you of the anger

> 'Which stirs even a wise man to violence,
> And is sweeter than honey and the honeycomb?'

a. anger;
48
b. sor-
row;

And you remember how pleasures mingle with pains in lamentation and bereavement?

Pro. Yes, there is a natural connection between them.

Soc. And you remember also how at the sight of tragedies the spectators smile through their tears?

Pro. Certainly I do.

Soc. And are you aware that even at a comedy the soul experiences a mixed feeling of pain and pleasure?

Pro. I do not quite understand you.

Soc. I admit, Protarchus, that there is some difficulty in recognizing this mixture of feelings at a comedy.

Pro. There is, I think.

Soc. And the greater the obscurity of the case the more desirable is the examination of it, because the difficulty in detecting other cases of mixed pleasures and pains will be less.

Pro. Proceed.

c. the
mixed
feelings
with
which
spectators
regard
tragedy
and
comedy;

Soc. I have just mentioned envy; would you not call that a pain of the soul?

Pro. Yes.

Soc. And yet the envious man finds something in the misfortunes of his neighbours at which he is pleased?

Pro. Certainly.

d. envy.

Soc. And ignorance, and what is termed clownishness, are surely an evil?

Pro. To be sure.

Soc. From these considerations learn to know the nature of the ridiculous.

Pro. Explain.

Soc. The ridiculous is in short the specific name which is used to describe the vicious form of a certain habit; and of vice in general it is that kind which is most at variance with the inscription at Delphi.

Pro. You mean, Socrates, 'Know thyself.'

Soc. I do; and the opposite would be, 'Know not thyself.'

Pro. Certainly.

Soc. And now, O Protarchus, try to divide this into three.

Pro. Indeed I am afraid that I cannot.

Soc. Do you mean to say that I must make the division for you?

From
envy we
proceed
to the
considera-
tion of
the ridi-
culous.

The sense
of the
ridiculous
is excited
by self-
deception;

Pro. Yes, and what is more, I beg that you will.

Soc. Are there not three ways in which ignorance of self may be shown?

Pro. What are they?

Soc. In the first place, about money; the ignorant may fancy himself richer than he is.

Pro. Yes, that is a very common error.

Soc. And still more often he will fancy that he is taller or fairer than he is, or that he has some other advantage of person which he really has not.

Pro. Of course.

Soc. And yet surely by far the greatest number err about the goods of the mind; they imagine themselves to be much better men than they are.

Pro. Yes, that is by far the commonest delusion.

Soc. And of all the virtues, is not wisdom the one which the mass of mankind are always claiming, and which most arouses in them a spirit of contention and lying conceit of wisdom?

Pro. Certainly.

Soc. And may not all this be truly called an evil condition?

Pro. Very evil.

Soc. But we must pursue the division a step further, Protarchus, if we would see in envy of the childish sort a singular mixture of pleasure and pain.

Pro. How can we make the further division which you suggest?

Soc. All who are silly enough to entertain this lying conceit of themselves may of course be divided, like the rest of mankind, into two classes—one having power and might; and the other the reverse.

Pro. Certainly.

Soc. Let this, then, be the principle of division; those of them who are weak and unable to revenge themselves, when they are laughed at, may be truly called ridiculous, but those who can defend themselves may be more truly described as strong and formidable; for ignorance in the powerful is hateful and horrible, because hurtful to others both in reality and in fiction, but powerless ignorance may be reckoned, and in truth is, ridiculous.

Pro. That is very true, but I do not as yet see where is the admixture of pleasures and pains.

Soc. Well, then, let us examine the nature of envy.

Pro. Proceed.

Soc. Is not envy an unrighteous pleasure, and also an unrighteous pain?

Pro. Most true.

Soc. There is nothing envious or wrong in rejoicing at the misfortunes of enemies?

Pro. Certainly not.

Soc. But to feel joy instead of sorrow at the sight of our friends' misfortunes—is not that wrong?

We laugh at a friend's misfortunes through envy. Laughter is pleasant, envy is painful.

Pro. Undoubtedly.

Soc. Did we not say that ignorance was always an evil?

Pro. True.

Soc. And the three kinds of vain conceit in our friends which we enumerated—the vain conceit of beauty, of wisdom, and of wealth, are ridiculous if they are weak, and detestable when they are powerful: May we not say, as I was saying before, that our friends who are in this state of mind, when harmless to others, are simply ridiculous?

Pro. They are ridiculous.

Soc. And do we not acknowledge this ignorance of theirs to be a misfortune?

Pro. Certainly.

Soc. And do we feel pain or pleasure in laughing at it?

Pro. Clearly we feel pleasure.

Soc. And was not envy the source of this pleasure which we feel at the misfortunes of friends?

50

Pro. Certainly.

Soc. Then the argument shows that when we laugh at the folly of our friends, pleasure, in mingling with envy, mingles with pain, for envy has been acknowledged by us to be mental pain, and laughter is pleasant; and so we envy and laugh at the same instant.

Pro. True.

Soc. And the argument implies that there are combinations of pleasure and pain in lamentations, and in tragedy and comedy, not only on the stage, but on the greater stage of human life; and so in endless other cases.

Combinations of pleasure and pain take place, not only on the stage, but in human life, and arise out of many other causes besides sorrow, envy, and anger.

Pro. I do not see how any one can deny what you say, Socrates, however eager he may be to assert the opposite opinion.

Soc. I mentioned anger, desire, sorrow, fear, love, emulation, envy, and similar emotions, as examples in which we should find a mixture of the two elements so often named; did I not?

Pro. Yes.

Soc. We may observe that our conclusions hitherto have had reference only to sorrow and envy and anger.

Pro. I see.

Soc. Then many other cases still remain?

But these
instances
will
suffice.

After the
mixed
pleasures
[51]
we must
consider
the un-
mixed
or true.

True
pleasures
are given
(1) by
beauty of
form,

Pro. Certainly.

Soc. And why do you suppose me to have pointed out to you the admixture which takes place in comedy? Why but to convince you that there was no difficulty in showing the mixed nature of fear and love and similar affections; and I thought that when I had given you the illustration, you would have let me off, and have acknowledged as a general truth that the body without the soul, and the soul without the body, as well as the two united, are susceptible of all sorts of admixtures of pleasures and pains; and so further discussion would have been unnecessary. And now I want to know whether I may depart; or will you keep me here until midnight? I fancy that I may obtain my release without many words; —if I promise that to-morrow I will give you an account of all these cases. But at present I would rather sail in another direction, and go to other matters which remain to be settled, before the judgment can be given which Philebus demands.

Pro. Very good, Socrates; in what remains take your own course.

Soc. Then after the mixed pleasures the unmixed should have their turn; this is the natural and necessary order.

Pro. Excellent.

Soc. These, in turn, then, I will now endeavour to indicate; for with the maintainers of the opinion that all pleasures are a cessation of pain, I do not agree, but, as I was saying, I use them as witnesses, that there are pleasures which seem only and are not, and there are others again which have great power and appear in many forms, yet are intermingled with pains, and are partly alleviations of agony and distress, both of body and mind.

Pro. Then what pleasures, Socrates, should we be right in conceiving to be true?

Soc. True pleasures are those which are given by beauty of colour and form, and most of those which arise from smells; those of sound, again, and in general those of which the want is painless and unconscious, and of which the fruition is palpable to sense and pleasant and unalloyed with pain.

Pro. Once more, Socrates, I must ask what you mean.

Soc. My meaning is certainly not obvious, and I will endeavour to be plainer. I do not mean by beauty of form such beauty as that of animals or pictures, which the many would suppose to be my meaning; but, says the argument, understand me to mean straight lines and circles, and the plane or solid figures which are formed out of them by turning-lathes and rulers and measurers of angles; for these I affirm to be not only relatively beautiful, like other things, but they are eternally and absolutely beautiful, and they have peculiar pleasures, quite unlike the pleasures of scratching. And there are colours which are of the same character, and have similar pleasures; now do you understand my meaning?

Pro. I am trying to understand, Socrates, and I hope that you will try to make your meaning clearer.

Soc. When sounds are smooth and clear, and have a single pure tone, then I mean to say that they are not relatively but absolutely beautiful, and have natural pleasures associated with them.

Pro. Yes, there are such pleasures.

Soc. The pleasures of smell are of a less ethereal sort, but they have no necessary admixture of pain; and all pleasures, however and wherever experienced, which are unattended by pains, I assign to an analogous class. Here then are two kinds of pleasures.

Pro. I understand.

Soc. To these may be added the pleasures of knowledge, if no hunger of knowledge and no pain caused by such hunger precede them.

Pro. And this is the case.

Soc. Well, but if a man who is full of knowledge loses his knowledge, are there not pains of forgetting?

Pro. Not necessarily, but there may be times of reflection, when he feels grief at the loss of his knowledge.

Soc. Yes, my friend, but at present we are enumerating only the natural perceptions, and have nothing to do with reflection.

Pro. In that case you are right in saying that the loss of knowledge is not attended with pain.

Soc. These pleasures of knowledge, then, are unmixed with pain; and they are not the pleasures of the many but of a very few.

Pro. Quite true.

Soc. And now, having fairly separated the pure pleasures and those which may be rightly termed impure, let us further add to our description of them, that the pleasures which are in excess have no measure, but that those which are not in excess have measure; the great, the excessive, whether more or less frequent, we shall be right in referring to the class of the infinite, and of the more and less, which pours through body and soul alike; and the others we shall refer to the class which has measure.

Pro. Quite right, Socrates.

Soc. Still there is something more to be considered about pleasures.

Pro. What is it?

(2) co-
lour,

(3)
sound;

(4) by
sweet
smells,

52
and (5)
by
knowl-
edge.

Excessive
pleasures
are in-
finite;
moderate
pleasures
have
measure
or limit.

We must
select the
pure and
not the
impure
kinds of
pleasure
and
knowl-
edge for
com-
parison.

53

Purity is
given,
not by
quantity,
but by
quality.

Wise men
say that
pleasure
is a gen-
eration.
What
does this
mean?

Soc. When you speak of purity and clearness, or of excess, abundance, greatness and sufficiency, in what relation do these terms stand to truth?

Pro. Why do you ask, Socrates?

Soc. Because, Protarchus, I should wish to test pleasure and knowledge in every possible way, in order that if there be a pure and impure element in either of them, I may present the pure element for judgment, and then they will be more easily judged of by you and by me and by all of us.

Pro. Most true.

Soc. Let us investigate all the pure kinds; first selecting for consideration a single instance.

Pro. What instance shall we select?

Soc. Suppose that we first of all take whiteness.

Pro. Very good.

Soc. How can there be purity in whiteness, and what purity? Is that purest which is greatest or most in quantity, or that which is most unadulterated and freest from any admixture of other colours?

Pro. Clearly that which is most unadulterated.

Soc. True, Protarchus; and so the purest white, and not the greatest or largest in quantity, is to be deemed truest and most beautiful?

Pro. Right.

Soc. And we shall be quite right in saying that a little pure white is whiter and fairer and truer than a great deal that is mixed.

Pro. Perfectly right.

Soc. There is no need of adducing many similar examples in illustration of the argument about pleasure; one such is sufficient to prove to us that a small pleasure or a small amount of pleasure, if pure or unalloyed with pain, is always pleasanter and truer and fairer than a great pleasure or a great amount of pleasure of another kind.

Pro. Assuredly; and the instance you have given is quite sufficient.

Soc. But what do you say of another question:—have we not heard that pleasure is always a generation, and has no true being? Do not certain ingenious philosophers teach this doctrine, and ought not we to be grateful to them?

Pro. What do they mean?

Soc. I will explain to you, my dear Protarchus, what they mean, by putting a question.

Pro. Ask, and I will answer.

Soc. I assume that there are two natures, one self-existent, and the other ever in want of something.

Pro. What manner of natures are they?

Soc. The one majestic ever, the other inferior.

Pro. You speak riddles.

Soc. You have seen loves good and fair, and also brave lovers of them.

Pro. I should think so.

Soc. Search the universe for two terms which are like these two and are present everywhere.

Pro. Yet a third time I must say[1], Be a little plainer, Socrates.

Soc. There is no difficulty, Protarchus; the argument is only in play, and insinuates that some things are for the sake of something else (relatives), and that other things are the ends to which the former class subserve (absolutes).

Pro. Your many repetitions make me slow to understand.

Soc. As the argument proceeds, my boy, I dare say that the meaning will become clearer.

Pro. Very likely.

Soc. Here are two new principles.

Pro. What are they?

Soc. One is the generation of all things, and the other is essence.

Pro. I readily accept from you both generation and essence.

Soc. Very right; and would you say that generation is for the sake of essence, or essence for the sake of generation?

Pro. You want to know whether that which is called essence is, properly speaking, for the sake of generation?

Soc. Yes.

Pro. By the gods, I wish that you would repeat your question.

Soc. I mean, O my Protarchus, to ask whether you would tell me that ship-building is for the sake of ships, or ships for the sake of ship-building? and in all similar cases I should ask the same question.

Pro. Why do you not answer yourself, Socrates?

Soc. I have no objection, but you must take your part.

Pro. Certainly.

Soc. My answer is, that all things instrumental, remedial, material, are given to us with a view to generation, and that each generation is relative to, or for the sake of, some being or essence, and that the whole of generation is relative to the whole of essence.

Pro. Assuredly.

There are two natures, the absolute and the relative: the latter is for the sake of the former.

54

Generation is relative to essence, which is an absolute.

---

[1] Reading τὸ τρίτον ἔτ' ἐρῶ (conj. Badham).

Absolutes
are to be
placed in
the class
of good,
relatives
in some
other
class.
Thus
pleasure,
which is a
genera-
tion and
relative,
is not a
good.
(Many
thanks to
him who
first
pointed
this out.)

It is ab-
surd to
[55]
make
pleasure
consist in
genera-
tion and
destruc-
tion;

and ab-
surd to
say (1)
that in
the body
there is
nothing
good;
(2) that
the only
good of

Soc. Then pleasure, being a generation, must surely be for the sake of some essence?

Pro. True.

Soc. And that for the sake of which something else is done must be placed in the class of good, and that which is done for the sake of something else, in some other class, my good friend.

Pro. Most certainly.

Soc. Then pleasure, being a generation, will be rightly placed in some other class than that of good?

Pro. Quite right.

Soc. Then, as I said at first, we ought to be very grateful to him who first pointed out that pleasure was a generation only, and had no true being at all; for he is clearly one who laughs at the notion of pleasure being a good.

Pro. Assuredly.

Soc. And he would surely laugh also at those who make generation their highest end.

Pro. Of whom are you speaking, and what do they mean?

Soc. I am speaking of those who when they are cured of hunger or thirst or any other defect by some process of generation are delighted at the process as if it were pleasure; and they say that they would not wish to live without these and other feelings of a like kind which might be mentioned.

Pro. That is certainly what they appear to think.

Soc. And is not destruction universally admitted to be the opposite of generation?

Pro. Certainly.

Soc. Then he who chooses thus, would choose generation and destruction rather than that third sort of life, in which, as we were saying, was neither pleasure nor pain, but only the purest possible thought.

Pro. He who would make us believe pleasure to be a good is involved in great absurdities, Socrates.

Soc. Great, indeed; and there is yet another of them.

Pro. What is it?

Soc. Is there not an absurdity in arguing that there is nothing good or noble in the body, or in anything else, but that good is in the soul only, and that the only good of the soul is pleasure; and that courage or temperance or understanding, or any other good of the soul, is not really a good?—and is there not yet a further absurdity in our being compelled to say that he who has a feeling of pain and not of pleasure is bad at the time when he is suffering pain, even though he be the best of men; and again, that he who has a feeling of pleasure, in so far as he is pleased at the time when he is pleased, in that degree excels in virtue?

Pro. Nothing, Socrates, can be more irrational than all this.

Soc. And now, having subjected pleasure to every sort of test, let us not appear to be too sparing of mind and knowledge: let us ring their metal bravely, and see if there be unsoundness in any part, until we have found out what in them is of the purest nature; and then the truest elements both of pleasure and knowledge may be brought up for judgment.

Pro. Right.

Soc. Knowledge has two parts,—the one productive, and the other educational?

Pro. True.

Soc. And in the productive or handicraft arts, is not one part more akin to knowledge, and the other less; and may not the one part be regarded as the pure, and the other as the impure?

Pro. Certainly.

Soc. Let us separate the superior or dominant elements in each of them.

Pro. What are they, and how do you separate them?

Soc. I mean to say, that if arithmetic, mensuration, and weighing be taken away from any art, that which remains will not be much.

Pro. Not much, certainly.

Soc. The rest will be only conjecture, and the better use of the senses which is given by experience and practice, in addition to a certain power of guessing, which is commonly called art, and is perfected by attention and pains.

Pro. Nothing more, assuredly.

Soc. Music, for instance, is full of this empiricism; for sounds are harmonized, not by measure, but by skilful conjecture; the music of the flute is always trying to guess the pitch of each vibrating note, and is therefore mixed up with much that is doubtful and has little which is certain.

Pro. Most true.

Soc. And the same will be found to hold good of medicine and husbandry and piloting and generalship.

Pro. Very true.

Soc. The art of the builder, on the other hand, which uses a number of measures and instruments, attains by their help to a greater degree of accuracy than the other arts.

Pro. How is that?

Soc. In ship-building and house-building, and in other branches

---

Philebus

SOCRATES,
PROTAR-
CHUS.

the soul is pleasure; (3) that a man is vicious when in pain and virtuous when he is pleased.

And now for knowledge: Are some kinds purer than others?

Knowledge is (1) productive and (2) educational; of the former there is a [56] pure and impure sort.

The pure elements in the productive arts are arithmetic, mensuration, and weighing; the rest is guesswork and experience.

Music,
medicine,
etc. are
less accu-
rate than
the art of
building.

Arts may
be
divided
into more
and less
exact.

Of arith-
metic and
mensu-
ration,
which
belong to
the
former
class,
there are
two
kinds,—
one pure,
the other
impure.

57

Thus we
see that as
of plea-
sure, so
of knowl-
edge,
there are
two sorts,
and one is
purer
than the
other.

of the art of carpentering, the builder has his rule, lathe, compass, line, and a most ingenious machine for straightening wood.

Pro. Very true, Socrates.

Soc. Then now let us divide the arts of which we were speaking into two kinds,—the arts which, like music, are less exact in their results, and those which, like carpentering, are more exact.

Pro. Let us make that division.

Soc. Of the latter class, the most exact of all are those which we just now spoke of as primary.

Pro. I see that you mean arithmetic, and the kindred arts of weighing and measuring.

Soc. Certainly, Protarchus; but are not these also distinguishable into two kinds?

Pro. What are the two kinds?

Soc. In the first place, arithmetic is of two kinds, one of which is popular, and the other philosophical.

Pro. How would you distinguish them?

Soc. There is a wide difference between them, Protarchus; some arithmeticians reckon unequal units; as for example, two armies, two oxen, two very large things or two very small things. The party who are opposed to them insist that every unit in ten thousand must be the same as every other unit.

Pro. Undoubtedly there is, as you say, a great difference among the votaries of the science; and there may be reasonably supposed to be two sorts of arithmetic.

Soc. And when we compare the art of mensuration which is used in building with philosophical geometry, or the art of computation which is used in trading with exact calculation, shall we say of either of the pairs that it is one or two?

Pro. On the analogy of what has preceded, I should be of opinion that they were severally two.

Soc. Right; but do you understand why I have discussed the subject?

Pro. I think so, but I should like to be told by you.

Soc. The argument has all along been seeking a parallel to pleasure, and true to that original design, has gone on to ask whether one sort of knowledge is purer than another, as one pleasure is purer than another.

Pro. Clearly; that was the intention.

Soc. And has not the argument in what has preceded, already shown that the arts have different provinces, and vary in their degrees of certainty?

Pro. Very true.

Soc. And just now did not the argument first designate a particular art by a common term, thus making us believe in the unity of that art; and then again, as if speaking of two different things, proceed to enquire whether the art as pursued by philosophers, or as pursued by non-philosophers, has more of certainty and purity?

Pro. That is the very question which the argument is asking.

Soc. And how, Protarchus, shall we answer the enquiry?

Pro. O Socrates, we have reached a point at which the difference of clearness in different kinds of knowledge is enormous.

Soc. Then the answer will be the easier.

Pro. Certainly; and let us say in reply, that those arts into which arithmetic and mensuration enter, far surpass all others; and that of these the arts or sciences which are animated by the pure philosophic impulse are infinitely superior in accuracy and truth.

The purer sort consists of those arts into which mathematics enter; and of mathematics themselves there is a purer and an impurer kind.

Soc. Then this is your judgment; and this is the answer which, upon your authority, we will give to all masters of the art of misinterpretation?

Pro. What answer?

Soc. That there are two arts of arithmetic, and two of mensuration; and also several other arts which in like manner have this double nature, and yet only one name.

Pro. Let us boldly return this answer to the masters of whom you speak, Socrates, and hope for good luck.

Soc. We have explained what we term the most exact arts or sciences.

Pro. Very good.

Soc. And yet, Protarchus, dialectic will refuse to acknowledge us, if we do not award to her the first place.

Where shall we place dialectic, the truest of sciences?

Pro. And pray, what is dialectic?

Soc. Clearly the science which has to do with all that knowledge of which we are now speaking; for I am sure that all men who have a grain of intelligence will admit that the knowledge which has to do with being and reality, and sameness and unchangeableness, is by far the truest of all. But how would you decide this question, Protarchus?

Pro. I have often heard Gorgias maintain, Socrates, that the art of persuasion far surpassed every other; this, as he says, is by far the best of them all, for to it all things submit, not by compulsion, but of their own free will. Now, I should not like to quarrel either with you or with him.

Protarchus is afraid that he will offend Gorgias, if he assigns

Soc. You mean to say that you would like to desert, if you were not ashamed?

the first
place to
dialectic,
and So-
crates, if
to
rhetoric.

Socrates
assures
him that
if he does
not deny
that
rhetoric
is the
most
useful of
arts and
sciences,
Gorgias
will not
quarrel
with him
[59]
for saying
that dia-
lectic is
the truest.

Dialectic
differs
from the
generality
of arts
which
have to
do with
the
change-
able and
therefore
never
attain
certainty.

Pro. As you please.

Soc. May I not have led you into a misapprehension?

Pro. How?

Soc. Dear Protarchus, I never asked which was the greatest or best or usefullest of arts or sciences, but which had clearness and accuracy, and the greatest amount of truth, however humble and little useful an art. And as for Gorgias, if you do not deny that his art has the advantage in usefulness to mankind, he will not quarrel with you for saying that the study of which I am speaking is superior in this particular of essential truth; as in the comparison of white colours, a little whiteness, if that little be only pure, was said to be superior in truth to a great mass which is impure. And now let us give our best attention and consider well, not the comparative use or reputation of the sciences, but the power or faculty, if there be such, which the soul has of loving the truth, and of doing all things for the sake of it; let us search into the pure element of mind and intelligence, and then we shall be able to say whether the science of which I have been speaking is most likely to possess the faculty, or whether there be some other which has higher claims.

Pro. Well, I have been considering, and I can hardly think that any other science or art has a firmer grasp of the truth than this.

Soc. Do you say so because you observe that the arts in general and those engaged[1] in them make use of opinion, and are resolutely engaged in the investigation of matters of opinion? Even he who supposes himself to be occupied with nature is really occupied with the things of this world, how created, how acting or acted upon. Is not this the sort of enquiry in which his life is spent?

Pro. True.

Soc. He is labouring, not after eternal being, but about things which are becoming, or which will or have become.

Pro. Very true.

Soc. And can we say that any of these things which neither are nor have been nor will be unchangeable, when judged by the strict rule of truth, ever become certain?

Pro. Impossible.

Soc. How can anything fixed be concerned with that which has no fixedness?

Pro. How indeed?

Soc. Then mind and science when employed about such changing things do not attain the highest truth?

Pro. I should imagine not.

Soc. And now let us bid farewell, a long farewell, to you or me or

[1] Reading ὅσοι.

Philebus or Gorgias, and urge on behalf of the argument a single point.

Pro. What point?

Soc. Let us say that the stable and pure and true and unalloyed has to do with the things which are eternal and unchangeable and unmixed, or if not, at any rate what is most akin to them has; and that all other things are to be placed in a second or inferior class.

Pro. Very true.

Soc. And of the names expressing cognition, ought not the fairest to be given to the fairest things?

Pro. That is natural.

Soc. And are not mind and wisdom the names which are to be honoured most?

Pro. Yes.

Soc. And these names may be said to have their truest and most exact application when the mind is engaged in the contemplation of true being?

Pro. Certainly.

Soc. And these were the names which I adduced of the rivals of pleasure?

Pro. Very true, Socrates.

Soc. In the next place, as to the mixture, here are the ingredients, pleasure and wisdom, and we may be compared to artists who have their materials ready to their hands.

Pro. Yes.

Soc. And now we must begin to mix them?

Pro. By all means.

Soc. But had we not better have a preliminary word and refresh our memories?

Pro. Of what?

Soc. Of that which I have already mentioned. Well says the proverb, that we ought to repeat twice and even thrice that which is good.

Pro. Certainly.

Soc. Well then, by Zeus, let us proceed, and I will make what I believe to be a fair summary of the argument.

Pro. Let me hear.

Soc. Philebus says that pleasure is the true end of all living beings, at which all ought to aim, and moreover that it is the chief good of all, and that the two names 'good' and 'pleasant' are correctly given to one thing and one nature; Socrates, on the other hand, begins by denying this, and further says, that in nature as in name they are two, and that wisdom partakes more than pleasure

Being con-
cerned
with the
eternal
and un-
change-
able, it
ranks
first.

The fair-
est
names
should be
given to
the fair-
est
things—
therefore
mind and
wisdom
are to be
assigned
to the
contem-
plation of
true
being.

Before
mixing
let us
sum up.

60

By Phile-
bus
pleasure
was af-
firmed to
be the
good:
Socrates

Philebus

SOCRATES,
PROTAR-
CHUS.

preferred
wisdom.

We
agreed
that the
good
must be
character-
ised by
self-suf-
fiency;

but we
found
that both
pleasure
and wis-
dom by
them-
selves are
devoid of
this
quality.

of the good. Is not and was not this what we were saying, Protarchus?

Pro. Certainly.

Soc. And is there not and was there not a further point which was conceded between us?

Pro. What was it?

Soc. That the good differs from all other things.

Pro. In what respect?

Soc. In that the being who possesses good always everywhere and in all things has the most perfect sufficiency, and is never in need of anything else.

Pro. Exactly.

Soc. And did we not endeavour to make an imaginary separation of wisdom and pleasure, assigning to each a distinct life, so that pleasure was wholly excluded from wisdom, and wisdom in like manner had no part whatever in pleasure?

Pro. We did.

Soc. And did we think that either of them alone would be sufficient?

Pro. Certainly not.

Soc. And if we erred in any point, then let any one who will, take up the enquiry again and set us right; and assuming memory and wisdom and knowledge and true opinion to belong to the same class, let him consider whether he would desire to possess or acquire,—I will not say pleasure, however abundant or intense, if he has no real perception that he is pleased, nor any consciousness of what he feels, nor any recollection, however momentary, of the feeling,—but would he desire to have anything at all, if these faculties were wanting to him? And about wisdom I ask the same question; can you conceive that any one would choose to have all wisdom absolutely devoid of pleasure, rather than with a certain degree of pleasure, or all pleasure devoid of wisdom, rather than with a certain degree of wisdom?

Pro. Certainly not, Socrates; but why repeat such questions any more?

61

Neither
therefore
ranks
first.
And be-
fore the
second
place can
be as-

Soc. Then the perfect and universally eligible and entirely good cannot possibly be either of them?

Pro. Impossible.

Soc. Then now we must ascertain the nature of the good more or less accurately, in order, as we were saying, that the second place may be duly assigned?

Pro. Right.

Soc. Have we not found a road which leads towards the good?

Pro. What road?

Soc. Supposing that a man had to be found, and you could discover in what house he lived, would not that be a great step towards the discovery of the man himself?

Pro. Certainly.

Soc. And now reason intimates to us, as at our first beginning, that we should seek the good, not in the unmixed life but in the mixed.

Pro. True.

Soc. There is greater hope of finding that which we are seeking in the life which is well mixed than in that which is not?

Pro. Far greater.

Soc. Then now let us mingle, Protarchus, at the same time offering up a prayer to Dionysus or Hephaestus, or whoever is the god who presides over the ceremony of mingling.

Pro. By all means.

Soc. Are not we the cup-bearers? and here are two fountains which are flowing at our side: one, which is pleasure, may be likened to a fountain of honey; the other, wisdom, a sober draught in which no wine mingles, is of water unpleasant but healthful; out of these we must seek to make the fairest of all possible mixtures.

Pro. Certainly.

Soc. Tell me first;—should we be most likely to succeed if we mingled every sort of pleasure with every sort of wisdom?

Pro. Perhaps we might.

Soc. But I should be afraid of the risk, and I think that I can show a safer plan.

Pro. What is it?

Soc. One pleasure was supposed by us to be truer than another, and one art to be more exact than another.

Pro. Certainly.

Soc. There was also supposed to be a difference in sciences; some of them regarding only the transient and perishing, and others the permanent and imperishable and everlasting and immutable; and when judged by the standard of truth, the latter, as we thought, were truer than the former.

Pro. Very good and right.

Soc. If, then, we were to begin by mingling the sections of each class which have the most of truth, will not the union suffice to give us the loveliest of lives, or shall we still want some elements of another kind?

Pro. I think that we ought to do what you suggest.

signed,
we must
discover
the na-
ture of
the good.

Reason
tells us
that we
should
look for
it in the
mixed
class.

Let us
then
mingle
pleasure
and wis-
dom.

Shall we
mingle
all kinds
of them,
or the
pure
only?

We can-
not ex-
clude the
impure
kinds of
knowl-
edge, for
they are
required
by the
needs of
every-
day life.

Soc. Let us suppose a man who understands justice, and has reason as well as understanding about the true nature of this and of all other things.

Pro. We will suppose such a man.

Soc. Will he have enough of knowledge if he is acquainted only with the divine circle and sphere, and knows nothing of our human spheres and circles, but uses only divine circles and measures in the building of a house?

Pro. The knowledge which is only superhuman, Socrates, is ridiculous in man.

Soc. What do you mean? Do you mean that you are to throw into the cup and mingle the impure and uncertain art which uses the false measure and the false circle?

Pro. Yes, we must, if any of us is ever to find his way home.

Soc. And am I to include music, which, as I was saying just now, is full of guesswork and imitation, and is wanting in purity?

Pro. Yes, I think that you must, if human life is to be a life at all.

Soc. Well, then, suppose that I give way, and, like a doorkeeper who is pushed and overborne by the mob, I open the door wide, and let knowledge of every sort stream in, and the pure mingle with the impure?

All the
sciences
may be
admitted,
but the
pleasures
require
more
consider-
ation.

Pro. I do not know, Socrates, that any great harm would come of having them all, if only you have the first sort.

Soc. Well, then, shall I let them all flow into what Homer poetically terms 'a meeting of the waters'?

Pro. By all means.

Soc. There—I have let him in, and now I must return to the fountain of pleasure. For we were not permitted to begin by mingling in a single stream the true portions of both according to our original intention; but the love of all knowledge constrained us to let all the sciences flow in together before the pleasures.

Pro. Quite true.

Soc. And now the time has come for us to consider about the pleasures also, whether we shall in like manner let them go all at once, or at first only the true ones.

First, let
us have
the true
ones;
secondly,
we must
have the
necessary.

Pro. It will be by far the safer course to let flow the true ones first.

Soc. Let them flow, then; and now, if there are any necessary pleasures, as there were arts and sciences necessary, must we not mingle them?

Pro. Yes; the necessary pleasures should certainly be allowed to mingle.

Soc. The knowledge of the arts has been admitted to be innocent and useful always; and if we say of pleasures in like manner that all of them are good and innocent for all of us at all times, we must let them all mingle?

Pro. What shall we say about them, and what course shall we take?

Soc. Do not ask me, Protarchus; but ask the daughters of pleasure and wisdom to answer for themselves.

Pro. How?

Soc. Tell us, O beloved—shall we call you pleasures or by some other name?—would you rather live with or without wisdom? I am of opinion that they would certainly answer as follows:

Pro. How?

Soc. They would answer, as we said before, that for any single class to be left by itself pure and isolated is not good, nor altogether possible; and that if we are to make comparisons of one class with another and choose, there is no better companion than knowledge of things in general, and likewise the perfect knowledge, if that may be, of ourselves in every respect[1].

Pro. And our answer will be:—In that ye have spoken well.

Soc. Very true. And now let us go back and interrogate wisdom and mind: Would you like to have any pleasures in the mixture? And they will reply:—'What pleasures do you mean?'

Pro. Likely enough.

Soc. And we shall take up our parable and say: Do you wish to have the greatest and most vehement pleasures for your companions in addition to the true ones? 'Why, Socrates,' they will say, 'how can we? seeing that they are the source of ten thousand hindrances to us; they trouble the souls of men, which are our habitation, with their madness; they prevent us from coming to the birth, and are commonly the ruin of the children which are born to us, causing them to be forgotten and unheeded; but the true and pure pleasures, of which you spoke, know to be of our family, and also those pleasures which accompany health and temperance, and which every Virtue, like a goddess has in her train to follow her about wherever she goes,—mingle these and not the others; there would be great want of sense in any one who desires to see a fair and perfect mixture, and to find in it what is the highest good in man and in the universe, and to divine what is the true form of good—there would be great want of sense in his allowing the pleasures, which are always in the company of folly and vice, to mingle with mind in the cup.'—Is not this a very rational and

Philebus

SOCRATES, PROTAR-CHUS.

Let us consult the pleasures and wisdom.

The pleasures say that they cannot live alone or without knowledge;

and wisdom, that she desires only true and virtuous pleasures, not all of them.

64

---

[1] Reading αὐτῶν ἡμῶν.

Truth is
an indis-
pensable
element
in the
mixture.

suitable reply, which mind has made, both on her own behalf, as well as on the behalf of memory and true opinion?

Pro. Most certainly.

Soc. And still there must be something more added, which is a necessary ingredient in every mixture.

Pro. What is that?

Soc. Unless truth enter into the composition, nothing can truly be created or subsist.

Pro. Impossible.

Soc. Quite impossible; and now you and Philebus must tell me whether anything is still wanting in the mixture, for to my way of thinking the argument is now completed, and may be compared to an incorporeal law, which is going to hold fair rule over a living body.

Pro. I agree with you, Socrates.

We are
now at
the vesti-
bule of
the good.

Soc. And may we not say with reason that we are now at the vestibule of the habitation of the good?

Pro. I think that we are.

What is
the most
precious
element
in the
mixture?

Soc. What, then, is there in the mixture which is most precious, and which is the principal cause why such a state is universally beloved by all? When we have discovered it, we will proceed to ask whether this omnipresent nature is more akin to pleasure or to mind.

Pro. Quite right; in that way we shall be better able to judge.

Soc. And there is no difficulty in seeing the cause which renders any mixture either of the highest value or of none at all.

Pro. What do you mean?

Soc. Every man knows it.

Pro. What?

Measure,
which is
the es-
sence of
beauty
and
virtue.

Soc. He knows that any want of measure and symmetry in any mixture whatever must always of necessity be fatal, both to the elements and to the mixture, which is then not a mixture, but only a confused medley which brings confusion on the possessor of it.

Pro. Most true.

Soc. And now the power of the good has retired into the region of the beautiful; for measure and symmetry are beauty and virtue all the world over.

Pro. True.

Soc. Also we said that truth was to form an element in the mixture.

Pro. Certainly.

65

Sym-
metry,

Soc. Then, if we are not able to hunt the good with one idea only, with three we may catch our prey; Beauty, Symmetry, Truth are the three, and these taken together we may regard as the single cause of the mixture, and the mixture as being good by reason of the infusion of them.

Pro. Quite right.

Soc. And now, Protarchus, any man could decide well enough whether pleasure or wisdom is more akin to the highest good, and more honourable among gods and men.

Pro. Clearly, and yet perhaps the argument had better be pursued to the end.

Soc. We must take each of them separately in their relation to pleasure and mind, and pronounce upon them; for we ought to see to which of the two they are severally most akin.

Pro. You are speaking of beauty, truth, and measure?

Soc. Yes, Protarchus, take truth first, and, after passing in review mind, truth, pleasure, pause awhile and make answer to yourself, —as to whether pleasure or mind is more akin to truth.

Pro. There is no need to pause, for the difference between them is palpable; pleasure is the veriest impostor in the world; and it is said that in the pleasures of love, which appear to be the greatest, perjury is excused by the gods; for pleasures, like children, have not the least particle of reason in them; whereas mind is either the same as truth, or the most like truth, and the truest.

Soc. Shall we next consider measure, in like manner, and ask whether pleasure has more of this than wisdom, or wisdom than pleasure?

Pro. Here is another question which may be easily answered; for I imagine that nothing can ever be more immoderate than the transports of pleasure, or more in conformity with measure than mind and knowledge.

Soc. Very good; but there still remains the third test: Has mind a greater share of beauty than pleasure, and is mind or pleasure the fairer of the two?

Pro. No one, Socrates, either awake or dreaming, ever saw or imagined mind or wisdom to be in aught unseemly, at any time, past, present, or future.

Soc. Right.

Pro. But when we see some one indulging in pleasures, perhaps in the greatest of pleasures, the ridiculous or disgraceful nature of the action makes us ashamed; and so we put them out of sight, and consign them to darkness, under the idea that they ought not to meet the eye of day.

Soc. Then, Protarchus, you will proclaim everywhere, by word of mouth to this company, and by messengers bearing the tidings

beauty, and truth are the cause of the mixture and of the good in it.

Of each of these three elements wisdom has a larger share than pleasure.

66

The order of

Philebus

SOCRATES,
PROTAR-
CHUS.

goods:—
(1) meas-
ure, the
eternal
nature;

(2) the
sym-
metrical
and per-
fect;

(3) mind
and
wisdom;

(4) sci-
ences,
arts, and
true
opinions;

(5) pure
pleasures.

far and wide, that pleasure is not the first of possessions, nor yet the second, but that in measure, and the mean, and the suitable, and the like, the eternal nature has been found.

Pro. Yes, that seems to be the result of what has been now said.

Soc. In the second class is contained the symmetrical and beautiful and perfect or sufficient, and all which are of that family.

Pro. True.

Soc. And if you reckon in the third class mind and wisdom, you will not be far wrong, if I divine aright.

Pro. I dare say.

Soc. And would you not put in the fourth class the goods which we were affirming to appertain specially to the soul—sciences and arts and true opinions as we called them? These come after the third class, and form the fourth, as they are certainly more akin to good than pleasure is.

Pro. Surely.

Soc. The fifth class are the pleasures which were defined by us as painless, being the pure pleasures of the soul herself, as we termed them, which accompany, some the sciences, and some the senses[1].

Pro. Perhaps.

Soc. And now, as Orpheus says,

'With the sixth generation cease the glory of my song.'

Here, at the sixth award, let us make an end; all that remains is to set the crown on our discourse.

Pro. True.

Soc. Then let us sum up and reassert what has been said, thus offering the third libation to the saviour Zeus.

Pro. How?

Soc. Philebus affirmed that pleasure was always and absolutely the good.

Pro. I understand; this third libation, Socrates, of which you spoke, meant a recapitulation.

Soc. Yes, but listen to the sequel; convinced of what I have just been saying, and feeling indignant at the doctrine, which is maintained, not by Philebus only, but by thousands of others, I affirmed that mind was far better and far more excellent, as an element of human life, than pleasure.

Pro. True.

Soc. But, suspecting that there were other things which were also better, I went on to say that if there was anything better than

---

[1] Reading ἐπιστήμαις, τὰς δὲ κ.τ.λ.

either, then I would claim the second place for mind over pleasure, and pleasure would lose the second place as well as the first.

Pro. You did.

Soc. Nothing could be more satisfactorily shown than the unsatisfactory nature of both of them.

Pro. Very true.

Soc. The claims both of pleasure and mind to be the absolute good have been entirely disproven in this argument, because they are both wanting in self-sufficiency and also in adequacy and perfection.

Pro. Most true.

Soc. But, though they must both resign in favour of another, mind is ten thousand times nearer and more akin to the nature of the conqueror than pleasure.

Pro. Certainly.

Soc. And, according to the judgment which has now been given, pleasure will rank fifth.

Pro. True.

Soc. But not first; no, not even if all the oxen and horses and animals in the world by their pursuit of enjoyment proclaim her to be so;—although the many trusting in them, as diviners trust in birds, determine that pleasures make up the good of life, and deem the lusts of animals to be better witnesses than the inspirations of divine philosophy.

Pro. And now, Socrates, we tell you that the truth of what you have been saying is approved by the judgment of all of us.

Soc. And will you let me go?

Pro. There is a little which yet remains, and I will remind you of it, for I am sure that you will not be the first to go away from an argument.

Philebus

67
SOCRATES,
PROTAR-
CHUS.

Pleasure is the last and lowest of goods, and not first, even if asserted to be so by all the animals in the world.

perfection.

divine philosophy.

argument.

LAWS

LAWS

BOOK I

PERSONS OF THE DIALOGUE

An ATHENIAN STRANGER   CLEINIAS, *a Cretan*

MEGILLUS, *a Lacedaemonian*

Athenian Stranger. TELL me, Strangers, is a God or some man supposed to be the author of your laws?

Cleinias. A God, Stranger; in very truth a God: among us Cretans he is said to have been Zeus, but in Lacedaemon, whence our friend here comes, I believe they would say that Apollo is their lawgiver: would they not, Megillus?

Megillus. Certainly.

Ath. And do you, Cleinias, believe, as Homer tells, that every ninth year Minos went to converse with his Olympian sire, and was inspired by him to make laws for your cities?

Cle. Yes, that is our tradition; and there was Rhadamanthus, a brother of his, with whose name you are familiar; he is reputed to have been the justest of men, and we Cretans are of opinion that he earned this reputation from his righteous administration of justice when he was alive.

Ath. Yes, and a noble reputation it was, worthy of a son of Zeus. As you and Megillus have been trained in these institutions, I dare say that you will not be unwilling to give an account of your government and laws; on our way we can pass the time pleasantly in talking about them, for I am told that the distance from Cnosus to the cave and temple of Zeus is considerable; and doubtless there are shady places under the lofty trees, which will protect us from this scorching sun. Being no longer young, we may often stop to rest beneath them, and get over the whole journey without difficulty, beguiling the time by conversation.

Cle. Yes, Stranger, and if we proceed onward we shall come to groves of cypresses, which are of rare height and beauty, and there are green meadows, in which we may repose and converse.

Steph.
624
ATHEN-
IAN,
CLEINIAS,
MEGIL-
LUS.

Crete and Lacedae-mon both received their laws from a God, [625] Crete from Zeus, Lacedae-mon from Apollo.

Laws I

ATHEN-
IAN,
CLEINIAS,
MEGIL-
LUS.

The
Cretan
institu-
tions are
designed
with a
view to
war,
which the
lawgiver
thought
to be the
natural
state of
man.

626

Ath. Very good.

Cle. Very good, indeed; and still better when we see them; let us move on cheerily.

Ath. I am willing.—And first, I want to know why the law has ordained that you shall have common meals and gymnastic exercises, and wear arms.

Cle. I think, Stranger, that the aim of our institutions is easily intelligible to any one. Look at the character of our country: Crete is not like Thessaly, a large plain; and for this reason they have horsemen in Thessaly, and we have runners—the inequality of the ground in our country is more adapted to locomotion on foot; but then, if you have runners you must have light arms,—no one can carry a heavy weight when running, and bows and arrows are convenient because they are light. Now all these regulations have been made with a view to war, and the legislator appears to me to have looked to this in all his arrangements:—the common meals, if I am not mistaken, were instituted by him for a similar reason, because he saw that while they are in the field the citizens are by the nature of the case compelled to take their meals together for the sake of mutual protection. He seems to me to have thought the world foolish in not understanding that all men are always at war with one another; and if in war there ought to be common meals and certain persons regularly appointed under others to protect an army, they should be continued in peace. For what men in general term peace would be said by him to be only a name; in reality every city is in a natural state of war with every other, not indeed proclaimed by heralds, but everlasting. And if you look closely, you will find that this was the intention of the Cretan legislator; all institutions, private as well as public, were arranged by him with a view to war; in giving them he was under the impression that no possessions or institutions are of any value to him who is defeated in battle; for all the good things of the conquered pass into the hands of the conquerors.

Ath. You appear to me, Stranger, to have been thoroughly trained in the Cretan institutions, and to be well informed about them; will you tell me a little more explicitly what is the principle of government which you would lay down? You seem to imagine that a well-governed state ought to be so ordered as to conquer all other states in war: am I right in supposing this to be your meaning?

There is
war, not
only be-
tween
cities,

Cle. Certainly; and our Lacedaemonian friend, if I am not mistaken, will agree with me.

Meg. Why, my good friend, how could any Lacedaemonian say anything else?

Ath. And is what you say applicable only to states, or also to villages?

Cle. To both alike.

Ath. The case is the same?

Cle. Yes.

Ath. And in the village will there be the same war of family against family, and of individual against individual?

Cle. The same.

Ath. And should each man conceive himself to be his own enemy:—what shall we say?

Cle. O Athenian Stranger,—inhabitant of Attica I will not call you, for you seem to deserve rather to be named after the goddess herself, because you go back to first principles,—you have thrown a light upon the argument, and will now be better able to understand what I was just saying,—that all men are publicly one another's enemies, and each man privately his own.

(*Ath.* My good sir, what do you mean?)—

Cle. . . . . Moreover, there is a victory and defeat,—the first and best of victories, the lowest and worst of defeats,—which each man gains or sustains at the hands, not of another, but of himself; this shows that there is a war, against ourselves going on within every one of us.

Ath. Let us now reverse the order of the argument: Seeing that every individual is either his own superior or his own inferior, may we say that there is the same principle in the house, the village, and the state?

Cle. You mean that in each of them there is a principle of superiority or inferiority to self?

Ath. Yes.

Cle. You are quite right in asking the question, for there certainly is such a principle, and above all in states; and the state in which the better citizens win a victory over the mob and over the inferior classes may be truly said to be better than itself, and may be justly praised, where such a victory is gained, or censured in the opposite case.

Ath. Whether the better is ever really conquered by the worse, is a question which requires more discussion, and may be therefore left for the present. But I now quite understand your meaning when you say that citizens who are of the same race and live in the same cities may unjustly conspire, and having the superiority in numbers may overcome and enslave the few just; and when they prevail, the state may be truly called its own inferior and therefore

Laws I

ATHENIAN,
CLEINIAS.

but between villages,

between families, between individuals and individuals.

The best victory and the worst defeat.

627

The state superior to itself when the better citizens win a victory over the mob; inferior when the mob wins a victory over them.

Laws I

ATHEN-
IAN,
CLEINIAS,
MEGIL-
LUS.

The
parallel
of the
family

bad; and when they are defeated, its own superior and therefore good.

Cle. Your remark, Stranger, is a paradox, and yet we cannot possibly deny it.

Ath. Here is another case for consideration;—in a family there may be several brothers, who are the offspring of a single pair; very possibly the majority of them may be unjust, and the just may be in a minority.

Cle. Very possibly.

Ath. And you and I ought not to raise a question of words as to whether this family and household are rightly said to be superior when they conquer, and inferior when they are conquered; for we are not now considering what may or may not be the proper or customary way of speaking, but we are considering the natural principles of right and wrong in laws.

Cle. What you say, Stranger, is most true.

Meg. Quite excellent, in my opinion, as far as we have gone.

Ath. Again; might there not be a judge over these brethren, of whom we were speaking?

Cle. Certainly.

628

Ath. Now, which would be the better judge,—one who destroyed the bad and appointed the good to govern themselves; or one who, while allowing the good to govern, let the bad live, and made them voluntarily submit? Or third, I suppose, in the scale of excellence might be placed a judge, who, finding the family distracted, not only did not destroy any one, but reconciled them to one another for ever after, and gave them laws which they mutually observed, and was able to keep them friends.

Cle. The last would be by far the best sort of judge and legislator.

Ath. And yet the aim of all the laws which he gave would be the reverse of war.

Cle. Very true.

trans-
ferred to
the state.

Ath. And will he who constitutes the state and orders the life of man have in view external war, or that kind of intestine war called civil, which no one, if he could prevent, would like to have occurring in his own state; and when occurring, every one would wish to be quit of as soon as possible?

Cle. He would have the latter chiefly in view.

Is it bet-
ter in
civil war
for one
party to
conquer

Ath. And would he prefer that this civil war should be terminated by the destruction of one of the parties, and by the victory of the other, or that peace and friendship should be re-established, and that, being reconciled, they should give their attention to foreign enemies?

Cle. Every one would desire the latter in the case of his own state.

Ath. And would not that also be the desire of the legislator?

Cle. Certainly.

Ath. And would not every one always make laws for the sake of the best?

Cle. To be sure.

Ath. But war, whether external or civil, is not the best, and the need of either is to be deprecated; but peace with one another, and good will, are best. Nor is the victory of the state over itself to be regarded as a really good thing, but as a necessity; a man might as well say that the body was in the best state when sick and purged by medicine, forgetting that there is also a state of the body which needs no purge. And in like manner no one can be a true statesman, whether he aims at the happiness of the individual or state, who looks only, or first of all, to external warfare; nor will he ever be a sound legislator who orders peace for the sake of war, and not war for the sake of peace.

Cle. I suppose that there is truth, Stranger, in that remark of yours; and yet I am greatly mistaken if war is not the entire aim and object of our own institutions, and also of the Lacedaemonian.

Ath. I dare say; but there is no reason why we should rudely quarrel with one another about your legislators, instead of gently questioning them, seeing that both we and they are equally in earnest. Please follow me and the argument closely:—And first I will put forward Tyrtaeus, an Athenian by birth, but also a Spartan citizen, who of all men was most eager about war: Well, he says,

'I sing not, I care not, about any man,

even if he were the richest of men, and possessed every good (and then he gives a whole list of them), if he be not at all times a brave warrior.' I imagine that you, too, must have heard his poems; our Lacedaemonian friend has probably heard more than enough of them.

Meg. Very true.

Cle. And they have found their way from Lacedaemon to Crete.

Ath. Come now and let us all join in asking this question of Tyrtaeus: O most divine poet, we will say to him, the excellent praise which you have bestowed on those who excel in war sufficiently proves that you are wise and good, and I and Megillus and Cleinias of Cnosus do, as I believe, entirely agree with you. But we should like to be quite sure that we are speaking of the same men; tell us, then, do you agree with us in thinking that there are two kinds of war; or what would you say? A far inferior man to Tyrtaeus

Laws I

ATHEN-
IAN,
CLEINIAS,
MEGIL-
LUS.

the other, or for both to unite and conquer their enemies?

Peace better than victory in war, just as health is better than the cure of disease.

629

The praise of Tyrtaeus is bestowed on those who excel in war,

would have no difficulty in replying quite truly, that war is of two kinds,—one which is universally called civil war, and is, as we were just now saying, of all wars the worst; the other, as we should all admit, in which we fall out with other nations who are of a different race, is a far milder form of warfare.

Cle. Certainly, far milder.

and by war he means foreign war.

Ath. Well, now, when you praise and blame war in this high-flown strain, whom are you praising or blaming, and to which kind of war are you referring? I suppose that you must mean foreign war, if I am to judge from expressions of yours in which you say that you abominate those

'Who refuse to look upon fields of blood, and will not draw near and strike at their enemies.'

And we shall naturally go on to say to him,—You, Tyrtaeus, as it seems, praise those who distinguish themselves in external and foreign war; and he must admit this.

Cle. Evidently.

Ath. They are good; but we say that there are still better men whose virtue is displayed in the greatest of all battles. And we too have a poet whom we summon as a witness, Theognis, citizen of Megara in Sicily:—

630

But the civil strife of which Theognis speaks is a far higher test of a man's character, because it demands the other virtues as well as courage.

'Cyrnus,' he says, 'he who is faithful in a civil broil is worth his weight in gold and silver.'

And such an one is far better, as we affirm, than the other in a more difficult kind of war, much in the same degree as justice and temperance and wisdom, when united with courage, are better than courage only; for a man cannot be faithful and good in civil strife without having all virtue. But in the war of which Tyrtaeus speaks, many a mercenary soldier will take his stand and be ready to die at his post, and yet they are generally and almost without exception insolent, unjust, violent men, and the most senseless of human beings. You will ask what the conclusion is, and what I am seeking to prove: I maintain that the divine legislator of Crete, like any other who is worthy of consideration, will always and above all things in making laws have regard to the greatest virtue; which, according to Theognis, is loyalty in the hour of danger, and may be truly called perfect justice. Whereas, that virtue which Tyrtaeus highly praises is well enough, and was praised by the poet at the right time, yet in place and dignity may be said to be only fourth-rate[1].

And the legislator must aim, not at one virtue only, but at virtue whole and complete.

Cle. Stranger, we are degrading our inspired lawgiver to a rank which is far beneath him.

[1] i. e., it ranks after justice, temperance, and wisdom.

Ath. Nay, I think that we degrade not him but ourselves, if we imagine that Lycurgus and Minos laid down laws both in Lacedaemon and Crete mainly with a view to war.

Cle. What ought we to say then?

Ath. What truth and what justice require of us, if I am not mistaken, when speaking in behalf of[1] divine excellence[1];—that the legislator when making his laws had in view not a part only, and this the lowest part of virtue, but all virtue, and that he devised classes of laws answering to the kinds of virtue; not in the way in which modern inventors of laws make the classes, for they only investigate and offer laws whenever a want is felt, and one man has a class of laws about allotments and heiresses, another about assaults; others about ten thousand other such matters. But we maintain that the right way of examining into laws is to proceed as we have now done, and I admired the spirit of your exposition; for you were quite right in beginning with virtue, and saying that this was the aim of the giver of the law, but I thought that you went wrong when you added that all his legislation had a view only to a part, and the least part of virtue, and this called forth my subsequent remarks. Will you allow me then to explain how I should have liked to have heard you expound the matter?

Cle. By all means.

Ath. You ought to have said, Stranger,—The Cretan laws are with reason famous among the Hellenes; for they fulfil the object of laws, which is to make those who use them happy; and they confer every sort of good. Now goods are of two kinds: there are human and there are divine goods, and the human hang upon the divine; and the state which attains the greater, at the same time acquires the less, or, not having the greater, has neither. Of the lesser goods the first is health, the second beauty, the third strength, including swiftness in running and bodily agility generally, and the fourth is wealth, not the blind god [Pluto], but one who is keen of sight, if only he has wisdom for his companion. For wisdom is chief and leader of the divine class of goods, and next follows temperance; and from the union of these two with courage springs justice, and fourth in the scale of virtue is courage. All these naturally take precedence of the other goods, and this is the order in which the legislator must place them, and after them he will enjoin the rest of his ordinances on the citizens with a view to these, the human looking to the divine, and the divine looking to their leader mind. Some of his ordinances will relate to contracts of marriage which they make one with another, and then to the procreation and education of children,

631

Virtue the foundation of law.

Two kinds of goods, (1) the lesser or human: (2) the greater or divine goods.

The legislator will base the first on the second.

[1] Some word, such as ἀρετῆς or πολιτείας, seems to have fallen out.

Laws I

ATHEN-
IAN,
CLEINIAS,
MEGIL-
LUS.

He will
[632]
regulate
all the
relations
and cir-
cum-
stances
of life;

both male and female; the duty of the lawgiver will be to take charge of his citizens, in youth and age, and at every time of life, and to give them punishments and rewards; and in reference to all their intercourse with one another, he ought to consider their pains and pleasures and desires, and the vehemence of all their passions; he should keep a watch over them, and blame and praise them rightly by the mouth of the laws themselves. Also with regard to anger and terror, and the other perturbations of the soul, which arise out of misfortune, and the deliverances from them which prosperity brings, and the experiences which come to men in diseases, or in war, or poverty, or the opposite of these; in all these states he should determine and teach what is the good and evil of the condition of each. In the next place, the legislator has to be careful how the citizens make their money and in what way they spend it, and to have an eye to their mutual contracts and dissolutions of contracts, whether voluntary or involuntary: he should see how they order all this, and consider where justice as well as injustice is found or is wanting in their several dealings with one another; and honour those who obey the law, and impose fixed penalties on those who disobey, until the round of civil life is ended, and the time has come for the consideration of the proper funeral rites and honours

and will
appoint
guardians
to take
care that
his regu-
lations
are ob-
served.

of the dead. And the lawgiver reviewing his work, will appoint guardians to preside over these things,—some who walk by intelligence, others by true opinion only, and then mind will bind together all his ordinances and show them to be in harmony with temperance and justice, and not with wealth or ambition. This is the spirit, Stranger, in which I was and am desirous that you should pursue the subject. And I want to know the nature of all these things, and how they are arranged in the laws of Zeus, as they are termed, and in those of the Pythian Apollo, which Minos and Lycurgus gave; and how the order of them is discovered to his eyes, who has experience in laws gained either by study or habit, although they are far from being self-evident to the rest of mankind like ourselves.

Cle. How shall we proceed, Stranger?

Ath. I think that we must begin again as before, and first consider the habit of courage; and then we will go on and discuss another and then another form of virtue, if you please. In this way we shall have a model of the whole; and with these and similar discourses we will beguile the way. And when we have gone through all the virtues, we will show, by the grace of God, that the institutions of which I was speaking look to virtue.

633

Meg. Very good; and suppose that you first criticize this praiser of Zeus and the laws of Crete.

Ath. I will try to criticize you and myself, as well as him, for the argument is a common concern. Tell me,—were not first the syssitia, and secondly the gymnasia, invented by your legislator with a view to war?

Meg. Yes.

Ath. And what comes third, and what fourth? For that, I think, is the sort of enumeration which ought to be made of the remaining parts of virtue, no matter whether you call them parts or what their name is, provided the meaning is clear.

Meg. Then I, or any other Lacedaemonian, would reply that hunting is third in order.

Ath. Let us see if we can discover what comes fourth and fifth.

Meg. I think that I can get as far as the fourth head, which is the frequent endurance of pain, exhibited among us Spartans in certain hand-to-hand fights; also in stealing with the prospect of getting a good beating; there is, too, the so-called Crypteia, or secret service, in which wonderful endurance is shown,—our people wander over the whole country by day and by night, and even in winter have not a shoe to their foot, and are without beds to lie upon, and have to attend upon themselves. Marvellous, too, is the endurance which our citizens show in their naked exercises, contending against the violent summer heat; and there are many similar practices, to speak of which in detail would be endless.

Ath. Excellent, O Lacedaemonian stranger. But how ought we to define courage? Is it to be regarded only as a combat against fears and pains, or also against desires and pleasures, and against flatteries; which exercise such a tremendous power, that they make the hearts even of respectable citizens to melt like wax?

Meg. I should say the latter.

Ath. In what preceded, as you will remember, our Cnosian friend was speaking of a man or a city being inferior to themselves:—Were you not, Cleinias?

Cle. I was.

Ath. Now, which is in the truest sense inferior, the man who is overcome by pleasure or by pain?

Cle. I should say the man who is overcome by pleasure; for all men deem him to be inferior in a more disgraceful sense, than the other who is overcome by pain.

Ath. But surely the lawgivers of Crete and Lacedaemon have not legislated for a courage which is lame of one leg, able only to meet attacks which come from the left, but impotent against the insidious flatteries which come from the right?

Cle. Able to meet both, I should say.

Laws I

ATHEN-
IAN,
CLEINIAS,
MEGIL-
LUS.

At Sparta the (1) common meals, (2) gymnastic, (3) hunting, (4) Crypteia and other trials of endurance, are all designed with a view to war, and to inure men against pain.

But courage is not merely endurance of pain;

it is also shown in resistance to pleasure.
634

Ath. Then let me once more ask, what institutions have you in either of your states which give a taste of pleasures, and do not avoid them any more than they avoid pains; but which set a person in the midst of them, and compel or induce him by the prospect of reward to get the better of them? Where is an ordinance about pleasure similar to that about pain to be found in your laws? Tell me what there is of this nature among you:—What is there which makes your citizen equally brave against pleasure and pain, conquering what they ought to conquer, and superior to the enemies who are most dangerous and nearest home?

Meg. I was able to tell you, Stranger, many laws which were directed against pain; but I do not know that I can point out any great or obvious examples of similar institutions which are concerned with pleasure; there are some lesser provisions, however, which I might mention.

Cle. Neither can I show anything of that sort which is at all equally prominent in the Cretan laws.

Ath. No wonder, my dear friends; and if, as is very likely, in our search after the true and good, one of us may have to censure the laws of the others, we must not be offended, but take kindly what another says.

Cle. You are quite right, Athenian Stranger, and we will do as you say.

Ath. At our time of life, Cleinias, there should be no feeling of irritation.

Cle. Certainly not.

Ath. I will not at present determine whether he who censures the Cretan or Lacedaemonian polities is right or wrong. But I believe that I can tell better than either of you what the many say about them. For assuming that you have reasonably good laws, one of the best of them will be the law forbidding any young men to enquire which of them are right or wrong; but with one mouth and one voice they must all agree that the laws are all good, for they came from God; and any one who says the contrary is not to be listened to. But an old man who remarks any defect in your laws may communicate his observation to a ruler or to an equal in years when no young man is present.

Cle. Exactly so, Stranger; and like a diviner, although not there at the time, you seem to me quite to have hit the meaning of the legislator, and to say what is most true.

Ath. As there are no young men present, and the legislator has given old men free licence, there will be no impropriety in our discussing these very matters now that we are alone.

Cle. True. And therefore you may be as free as you like in your censure of our laws, for there is no discredit in knowing what is wrong; he who receives what is said in a generous and friendly spirit will be all the better for it.

Ath. Very good; however, I am not going to say anything against your laws until to the best of my ability I have examined them, but I am going to raise doubts about them. For you are the only people known to us, whether Greek or barbarian, whom the legislator commanded to eschew all great pleasures and amusements and never to touch them; whereas in the matter of pains or fears which we have just been discussing, he thought that they who from infancy had always avoided pains and fears and sorrows, when they were compelled to face them would run away from those who were hardened in them, and would become their subjects. Now the legislator ought to have considered that this was equally true of pleasure; he should have said to himself, that if our citizens are from their youth upward unacquainted with the greatest pleasures, and unused to endure amid the temptations of pleasure, and are not disciplined to refrain from all things evil, the sweet feeling of pleasure will overcome them just as fear would overcome the former class; and in another, and even a worse manner, they will be the slaves of those who are able to endure amid pleasures, and have had the opportunity of enjoying them, they being often the worst of mankind. One half of their souls will be a slave, the other half free; and they will not be worthy to be called in the true sense men and freemen. Tell me whether you assent to my words?

Cle. On first hearing, what you say appears to be the truth; but to be hasty in coming to a conclusion about such important matters would be very childish and simple.

Ath. Suppose, Cleinias and Megillus, that we consider the virtue which follows next of those which we intended to discuss (for after courage comes temperance), what institutions shall we find relating to temperance, either in Crete or Lacedaemon, which, like your military institutions, differ from those of any ordinary state.

Meg. That is not an easy question to answer; still I should say that the common meals and gymnastic exercises have been excellently devised for the promotion both of temperance and courage.

Ath. There seems to be a difficulty, Stranger, with regard to states, in making words and facts coincide so that there can be no dispute about them. As in the human body, the regimen which does good in one way does harm in another; and we can hardly say that any one course of treatment is adapted to a particular constitution. Now the gymnasia and common meals do a great deal of good, and

Laws I

ATHEN-
IAN,
CLEINIAS
MEGIL-
LUS.

The legislators of Sparta and Crete never reflected that he who cannot resist pleasure will be the slave of any bad man who has this power of endurance.

Enough of courage.

Next let us consider [636] temperance.

The syssitia and gymnasia were intended to promote this vir-

Laws I

ATHEN-
IAN,
MEGIL-
LUS.

tue, but
they have
the effect
of en-
couraging
unnatu-
ral love.

The story
of Zeus
and
Gany-
mede in-
vented in
Crete.

Yet
surely
the
Spartan
lawgiver
[637]
was
right. For
Sparta is
a most
orderly
city:
there is
no drunk-
enness
such as is
found at
Athens or
at Taren-
tum.

Those are
matters
of cus-
tom.

yet they are a source of evil in civil troubles; as is shown in the case of the Milesian, and Boeotian, and Thurian youth, among whom these institutions seem always to have had a tendency to degrade the ancient and natural custom of love below the level, not only of man, but of the beasts. The charge may be fairly brought against your cities above all others, and is true also of most other states which especially cultivate gymnastics. Whether such matters are to be regarded jestingly or seriously, I think that the pleasure is to be deemed natural which arises out of the intercourse between men and women; but that the intercourse of men with men, or of women with women, is contrary to nature, and that the bold attempt was originally due to unbridled lust. The Cretans are always accused of having invented the story of Ganymede and Zeus because they wanted to justify themselves in the enjoyment of unnatural pleasures by the practice of the god whom they believe to have been their lawgiver. Leaving the story, we may observe that any speculation about laws turns almost entirely on pleasure and pain, both in states and in individuals: these are two fountains which nature lets flow, and he who draws from them where and when, and as much as he ought, is happy; and this holds of men and animals—of individuals as well as states; and he who indulges in them ignorantly and at the wrong time, is the reverse of happy.

Meg. I admit, Stranger, that your words are well spoken, and I hardly know what to say in answer to you; but still I think that the Spartan lawgiver was quite right in forbidding pleasure. Of the Cretan laws, I shall leave the defence to my Cnosian friend. But the laws of Sparta, in as far as they relate to pleasure, appear to me to be the best in the world; for that which leads mankind in general into the wildest pleasure and licence, and every other folly, the law has clean driven out; and neither in the country nor in towns which are under the control of Sparta, will you find revelries and the many incitements of every kind of pleasure which accompany them; and any one who meets a drunken and disorderly person, will immediately have him most severely punished, and will not let him off on any pretence, not even at the time of a Dionysiac festival; although I have remarked that this may happen at your performances 'on the cart,' as they are called; and among our Tarentine colonists I have seen the whole city drunk at a Dionysiac festival; but nothing of the sort happens among us.

Ath. O Lacedaemonian Stranger, these festivities are praiseworthy where there is a spirit of endurance, but are very senseless when they are under no regulations. In order to retaliate, an Athenian has only to point out the licence which exists among your women. To all such accusations, whether they are brought against the Tarentines, or us, or you, there is one answer which exonerates the practice in question from impropriety. When a stranger expresses wonder at the singularity of what he sees, any inhabitant will naturally answer him:—Wonder not, O stranger; this is our custom, and you may very likely have some other custom about the same things. Now we are speaking, my friends, not about men in general, but about the merits and defects of the lawgivers themselves. Let us then discourse a little more at length about intoxication, which is a very important subject, and will seriously task the discrimination of the legislator. I am not speaking of drinking, or not drinking, wine at all, but of intoxication. Are we to follow the custom of the Scythians, and Persians, and Carthaginians, and Celts, and Iberians, and Thracians, who are all warlike nations, or that of your countrymen, for they, as you say, altogether abstain? But the Scythians and Thracians, both men and women, drink unmixed wine, which they pour on their garments, and this they think a happy and glorious institution. The Persians, again, are much given to other practices of luxury which you reject, but they have more moderation in them than the Thracians and Scythians.

Meg. O best of men, we have only to take arms into our hands, and we send all these nations flying before us.

Ath. Nay, my good friend, do not say that; there have been, as there always will be, flights and pursuits of which no account can be given, and therefore we cannot say that victory or defeat in battle affords more than a doubtful proof of the goodness or badness of institutions. For when the greater states conquer and enslave the lesser, as the Syracusans have done the Locrians, who appear to be the best-governed people in their part of the world, or as the Athenians have done the Ceans (and there are ten thousand other instances of the same sort of thing), all this is not to the point; let us endeavour rather to form a conclusion about each institution in itself and say nothing, at present, of victories and defeats. Let us only say that such and such a custom is honourable, and another not. And first permit me to tell you how good and bad are to be estimated in reference to these very matters.

Meg. How do you mean?

Ath. All those who are ready at a moment's notice to praise or censure any practice which is matter of discussion, seem to me to proceed in a wrong way. Let me give you an illustration of what I mean:—You may suppose a person to be praising wheat as a good kind of food, whereupon another person instantly blames wheat, without ever enquiring into its effect or use, or in what way, or to

Laws I

ATHEN-
IAN,
MEGIL-
LUS.

But customs vary: for instance, intoxication is encouraged among many war-like nations, and disallowed at Sparta.

The question is, which custom is the bet-
[638]
ter?

'Give us arms, and we can conquer all other men.'
Victory may be a matter of chance.

No ques-
tion can
be de-
termined
by num-
bers.

639

Fallacy of
*a dicto se-
cundum
quem ad
dictum
simplic-
iter.*

A feast
should
have a
president
to main-
tain
order.

whom, or with what, or in what state and how, wheat is to be given. And that is just what we are doing in this discussion. At the very mention of the word intoxication, one side is ready with their praises and the other with their censures; which is absurd. For either side adduce their witnesses and approvers, and some of us think that we speak with authority because we have many witnesses; and others because they see those who abstain conquering in battle, and this again is disputed by us. Now I cannot say that I shall be satisfied, if we go on discussing each of the remaining laws in the same way. And about this very point of intoxication I should like to speak in another way, which I hold to be the right one; for if number is to be the criterion, are there not myriads upon myriads of nations ready to dispute the point with you, who are only two cities?

Meg. I shall gladly welcome any method of enquiry which is right.

Ath. Let me put the matter thus:—Suppose a person to praise the keeping of goats, and the creatures themselves as capital things to have, and then some one who had seen goats feeding without a goatherd in cultivated spots, and doing mischief, were to censure a goat or any other animal who has no keeper, or a bad keeper, would there be any sense or justice in such censure?

Meg. Certainly not.

Ath. Does a captain require only to have nautical knowledge in order to be a good captain, whether he is sea-sick or not? What do you say?

Meg. I say that he is not a good captain if, although he have nautical skill, he is liable to sea-sickness.

Ath. And what would you say of the commander of an army? Will he be able to command merely because he has military skill if he be a coward, who, when danger comes, is sick and drunk with fear?

Meg. Impossible.

Ath. And what if besides being a coward he has no skill?

Meg. He is a miserable fellow, not fit to be a commander of men, but only of old women.

Ath. And what would you say of some one who blames or praises any sort of meeting which is intended by nature to have a ruler, and is well enough when under his presidency? The critic, however, has never seen the society meeting together at an orderly feast under the control of a president, but always without a ruler or with a bad one:—when observers of this class praise or blame such meetings, are we to suppose that what they say is of any value?

Meg. Certainly not, if they have never seen or been present at such a meeting when rightly ordered.

Ath. Reflect; may not banqueters and banquets be said to constitute a kind of meeting?

Meg. Of course.

Ath. And did any one ever see this sort of convivial meeting rightly ordered? Of course you two will answer that you have never seen them at all, because they are not customary or lawful in your country; but I have come across many of them in many different places, and moreover I have made enquiries about them wherever I went, as I may say, and never did I see or hear of anything of the kind which was carried on altogether rightly; in some few particulars they might be right, but in general they were utterly wrong.

Cle. What do you mean, Stranger, by this remark? Explain. For we, as you say, from our inexperience in such matters, might very likely not know, even if they came in our way, what was right or wrong in such societies.

Ath. Likely enough; then let me try to be your instructor: You would acknowledge, would you not, that in all gatherings of mankind, of whatever sort, there ought to be a leader?

Cle. Certainly I should.

Ath. And we were saying just now, that when men are at war the leader ought to be a brave man?

Cle. We were.

Ath. The brave man is less likely than the coward to be disturbed by fears?

Cle. That again is true.

Ath. And if there were a possibility of having a general of an army who was absolutely fearless and imperturbable, should we not by all means appoint him?

Cle. Assuredly.

Ath. Now, however, we are speaking not of a general who is to command an army, when foe meets foe in time of war, but of one who is to regulate meetings of another sort, when friend meets friend in time of peace.

Cle. True.

Ath. And that sort of meeting, if attended with drunkenness, is apt to be unquiet.

Cle. Certainly; the reverse of quiet.

Ath. In the first place, then, the revellers as well as the soldiers will require a ruler?

Cle. To be sure; no men more so.

Ath. And we ought, if possible, to provide them with a quiet ruler?

Cle. Of course.

Laws I

ATHENIAN, CLEINIAS, MEGILLUS.

Feasts are almost always disorderly.

640

As the leader of an army should be brave,

so the ruler of a feast should be sober,

genial,

sociable,

sensible.

He who
has only
seen
feasts
which
have a
bad ruler
should
not con-
demn
[641]
those
which
have a
good one.

The good
of a well-
ordered
feast is
great;
for social
meetings
are an im-
portant
part of
education.

Ath. And he should be a man who understands society; for his duty is to preserve the friendly feelings which exist among the company at the time, and to increase them for the future by his use of the occasion.

Cle. Very true.

Ath. Must we not appoint a sober man and a wise to be our master of the revels? For if the ruler of drinkers be himself young and drunken, and not over-wise, only by some special good fortune will he be saved from doing some great evil.

Cle. It will be by a singular good fortune that he is saved.

Ath. Now suppose such associations to be framed in the best way possible in states, and that some one blames the very fact of their existence—he may very likely be right. But if he blames a practice which he only sees very much mismanaged, he shows in the first place that he is not aware of the mismanagement, and also not aware that everything done in this way will turn out to be wrong, because done without the superintendence of a sober ruler. Do you not see that a drunken pilot or a drunken ruler of any sort will ruin ship, chariot, army—anything, in short, of which he has the direction?

Cle. The last remark is very true, Stranger; and I see quite clearly the advantage of an army having a good leader—he will give victory in war to his followers, which is a very great advantage; and so of other things. But I do not see any similar advantage which either individuals or states gain from the good management of a feast; and I want you to tell me what great good will be effected, supposing that this drinking ordinance is duly established.

Ath. If you mean to ask what great good accrues to the state from the right training of a single youth, or of a single chorus,—when the question is put in that form, we cannot deny that the good is not very great in any particular instance. But if you ask what is the good of education in general, the answer is easy—that education makes good men, and that good men act nobly, and conquer their enemies in battle, because they are good. Education certainly gives victory, although victory sometimes produces forgetfulness of education; for many have grown insolent from victory in war, and this insolence has engendered in them innumerable evils; and many a victory has been and will be suicidal to the victors; but education is never suicidal.

Cle. You seem to imply, my friend, that convivial meetings, when rightly ordered, are an important element of education.

Ath. Certainly I do.

Cle. And can you show that what you have been saying is true?

Ath. To be absolutely sure of the truth of matters concerning which there are many opinions, is an attribute of the Gods not given to man, Stranger; but I shall be very happy to tell you what I think, especially as we are now proposing to enter on a discussion concerning laws and constitutions.

Cle. Your opinion, Stranger, about the questions which are now being raised, is precisely what we want to hear.

Ath. Very good; I will try to find a way of explaining my meaning, and you shall try to have the gift of understanding me. But first let me make an apology. The Athenian citizen is reputed among all the Hellenes to be a great talker, whereas Sparta is renowned for brevity, and the Cretans have more wit than words. Now I am afraid of appearing to elicit a very long discourse out of very small materials. For drinking indeed may appear to be a slight matter, and yet is one which cannot be rightly ordered according to nature, without correct principles of music; these are necessary to any clear or satisfactory treatment of the subject, and music again runs up into education generally, and there is much to be said about all this. What would you say then to leaving these matters for the present, and passing on to some other question of law?

Meg. O Athenian Stranger, let me tell you what perhaps you do not know, that our family is the proxenus of your state. I imagine that from their earliest youth all boys, when they are told that they are the proxeni of a particular state, feel kindly towards their second country; and this has certainly been my own feeling. I can well remember from the days of my boyhood, how, when any Lacedaemonians praised or blamed the Athenians, they used to say to me,— 'See, Megillus, how ill or how well,' as the case might be, 'has your state treated us;' and having always had to fight your battles against detractors when I heard you assailed, I became warmly attached to you. And I always like to hear the Athenian tongue spoken; the common saying is quite true, that a good Athenian is more than ordinarily good, for he is the only man who is freely and genuinely good by the divine inspiration of his own nature, and is not manufactured. Therefore be assured that I shall like to hear you say whatever you have to say.

Cle. Yes, Stranger; and when you have heard me speak, say boldly what is in your thoughts. Let me remind you of a tie which unites you to Crete. You must have heard here the story of the prophet Epimenides, who was of my family, and came to Athens ten years before the Persian war, in accordance with the response of the Oracle, and offered certain sacrifices which the God commanded. The Athenians were at that time in dread of the Persian invasion;

Laws I

ATHE-
NIAN,
CLEINIAS,
MEGIL-
LUS.

I am afraid of bestowing upon you my [642] Athenian tediousness; but the subject runs up into music and education generally.

The Lacedaemonian is the proxenus of Athens.

The Cretan, too, is connected with Athens through Epimenides.

and he said that for ten years they would not come, and that when they came, they would go away again without accomplishing any of their objects, and would suffer more evil than they inflicted. At that time my forefathers formed ties of hospitality with you; thus ancient is the friendship which I and my parents have had for you.

643

Ath. You seem to be quite ready to listen; and I am also ready to perform as much as I can of an almost impossible task, which I will nevertheless attempt. At the outset of the discussion, let me define the nature and power of education; for this is the way by which our argument must travel onwards to the God Dionysus.

Cle. Let us proceed, if you please.

Ath. Well, then, if I tell you what are my notions of education, will you consider whether they satisfy you?

Cle. Let us hear.

What is education?

Ath. According to my view, any one who would be good at anything must practise that thing from his youth upwards, both in sport and earnest, in its several branches: for example, he who is to be a good builder, should play at building children's houses; he who is to be a good husbandman, at tilling the ground; and those who have the care of their education should provide them when young with mimic tools. They should learn beforehand the knowledge which they will afterwards require for their art. For example, the future carpenter should learn to measure or apply the line in play; and the future warrior should learn riding, or some other exercise, for amusement, and the teacher should endeavour to direct the children's inclinations and pleasures, by the help of amusements, to their final aim in life. The most important part of education is right training in the nursery. The soul of the child in his play should be guided to the love of that sort of excellence in which when he grows up to manhood he will have to be perfected. Do you agree with me thus far?

Education is training for the work of after-life.

It should begin with the right direction of children's sports.

Cle. Certainly.

The true education fits men, not for mere success in life, but to be perfect citizens.

Ath. Then let us not leave the meaning of education ambiguous or ill-defined. At present, when we speak in terms of praise or blame about the bringing-up of each person, we call one man educated and another uneducated, although the uneducated man may be sometimes very well educated for the calling of a retail trader, or of a captain of a ship, and the like. For we are not speaking of education in this narrower sense, but of that other education in virtue from youth upwards, which makes a man eagerly pursue the ideal perfection of citizenship, and teaches him how rightly to rule and how to obey. This is the only education which, upon our view, deserves the name; that other sort of training, which aims at the acquisition of

644

wealth or bodily strength, or mere cleverness apart from intelligence and justice, is mean and illiberal, and is not worthy to be called education at all. But let us not quarrel with one another about a word, provided that the proposition which has just been granted hold good: to wit, that those who are rightly educated generally become good men. Neither must we cast a slight upon education, which is the first and fairest thing that the best of men can ever have, and which, though liable to take a wrong direction, is capable of reformation. And this work of reformation is the great business of every man while he lives.

Cle. Very true; and we entirely agree with you.

Ath. And we agreed before that they are good men who are able to rule themselves, and bad men who are not.

Cle. You are quite right.

Ath. Let me now proceed, if I can, to clear up the subject a little further by an illustration which I will offer you.

Cle. Proceed.

Ath. Do we not consider each of ourselves to be one?

Cle. We do.

Ath. And each one of us has in his bosom two counsellors, both foolish and also antagonistic; of which we call the one pleasure, and the other pain.

Cle. Exactly.

Ath. Also there are opinions about the future, which have the general name of expectations; and the specific name of fear, when the expectation is of pain; and of hope, when of pleasure; and further, there is reflection about the good or evil of them, and this, when embodied in a decree by the State, is called Law.

Cle. I am hardly able to follow you; proceed, however, as if I were.

Meg. I am in the like case.

Ath. Let us look at the matter thus: May we not conceive each of us living beings to be a puppet of the Gods, either their plaything only, or created with a purpose—which of the two we cannot certainly know? But we do know, that these affections in us are like cords and strings, which pull us different and opposite ways, and to opposite actions; and herein lies the difference between virtue and vice. According to the argument there is one among these cords which every man ought to grasp and never let go, but to pull with it against all the rest; and this is the sacred and golden cord of reason, called by us the common law of the State; there are others which are hard and of iron, but this one is soft because golden; and there are several other kinds. Now we ought always to co-operate with the lead of the best, which is law. For inasmuch as reason is

Laws I

ATHE-
NIAN,
CLEINIAS,
MEGIL-
LUS.

It is the first and fairest thing which the best of men can have.

Man the puppet of the Gods.

He is pulled opposite [645] ways by the strings of his affections, but

must
himself
pull
against
them
with the
golden
cord of
reason.

beautiful and gentle, and not violent, her rule must needs have ministers in order to help the golden principle in vanquishing the other principles. And thus the moral of the tale about our being puppets will not have been lost, and the meaning of the expression 'superior or inferior to a man's self' will become clearer; and the individual, attaining to right reason in this matter of pulling the strings of the puppet, should live according to its rule; while the city, receiving the same from some god or from one who has knowledge of these things, should embody it in a law, to be her guide in her dealings with herself and with other states. In this way virtue and vice will be more clearly distinguished by us. And when they have become clearer, education and other institutions will in like manner become clearer; and in particular that question of convivial entertainment, which may seem, perhaps, to have been a very trifling matter, and to have taken a great many more words than were necessary.

Cle. Perhaps, however, the theme may turn out not to be unworthy of the length of discourse.

Ath. Very good; let us proceed with any enquiry which really bears on our present object.

Cle. Proceed.

Ath. Suppose that we give this puppet of ours drink,—what will be the effect on him?

Cle. Having what in view do you ask that question?

When the
puppet
drinks,
his desires
increase
in
strength
and his
rational
faculties
diminish.

Ath. Nothing as yet; but I ask generally, when the puppet is brought to the drink, what sort of result is likely to follow. I will endeavour to explain my meaning more clearly: what I am now asking is this—Does the drinking of wine heighten and increase pleasures and pains, and passions and loves?

Cle. Very greatly.

Ath. And are perception and memory, and opinion and prudence, heightened and increased? Do not these qualities entirely desert a man if he becomes saturated with drink?

Cle. Yes, they entirely desert him.

Ath. Does he not return to the state of soul in which he was when a young child?

Cle. He does.

Ath. Then at that time he will have the least control over himself?

Cle. The least.

646

Ath. And will he not be in a most wretched plight?

Cle. Most wretched.

He be-
comes a
child
again.

Ath. Then not only an old man but also a drunkard becomes a second time a child?

Cle. Well said, Stranger.

Ath. Is there any argument which will prove to us that we ought to encourage the taste for drinking instead of doing all we can to avoid it?

Cle. I suppose that there is; you, at any rate, were just now saying that you were ready to maintain such a doctrine.

Ath. True, I was; and I am ready still, seeing that you have both declared that you are anxious to hear me.

Cle. To be sure we are, if only for the strangeness of the paradox, which asserts that a man ought of his own accord to plunge into utter degradation.

Ath. Are you speaking of the soul?

Cle. Yes.

Ath. And what would you say about the body, my friend? Are you not surprised at any one of his own accord bringing upon himself deformity, leanness, ugliness, decrepitude?

Cle. Certainly.

Ath. Yet when a man goes of his own accord to a doctor's shop, and takes medicine, is he not quite aware that soon, and for many days afterwards, he will be in a state of body which he would die rather than accept as the permanent condition of his life? Are not those who train in gymnasia, at first beginning reduced to a state of weakness?

Cle. Yes, all that is well known.

Ath. Also that they go of their own accord for the sake of the subsequent benefit?

Cle. Very good.

Ath. And we may conceive this to be true in the same way of other practices?

Cle. Certainly.

Ath. And the same view may be taken of the pastime of drinking wine, if we are right in supposing that the same good effect follows?

Cle. To be sure.

Ath. If such convivialities should turn out to have any advantage equal in importance to that of gymnastic, they are in their very nature to be preferred to mere bodily exercise, inasmuch as they have no accompaniment of pain.

Cle. True; but I hardly think that we shall be able to discover any such benefits to be derived from them.

Ath. That is just what we must endeavour to show. And let me ask you a question:—Do we not distinguish two kinds of fear, which are very different?

Cle. What are they?

Ath. There is the fear of expected evil.

Laws I

ATHE-
NIAN,
CLEINIAS.

But, although drinking degrades both soul and body, it may be of use in some other way.

Two kinds of fear: one, the expectation of pain

and evil;
the other,
the dread
of dis-
grace.

The latter
is termed
reverence.

Cle. Yes.

Ath. And there is the fear of an evil reputation; we are afraid of being thought evil, because we do or say some dishonourable thing, which fear we and all men term shame.

Cle. Certainly.

Ath. These are the two fears, as I called them; one of which is the opposite of pain and other fears, and the opposite also of the greatest and most numerous sort of pleasures.

Cle. Very true.

Ath. And does not the legislator and every one who is good for anything, hold this fear in the greatest honour? This is what he terms reverence, and the confidence which is the reverse of this he terms insolence; and the latter he always deems to be a very great evil both to individuals and to states.

Cle. True.

Ath. Does not this kind of fear preserve us in many important ways? What is there which so surely gives victory and safety in war? For there are two things which give victory—confidence before enemies, and fear of disgrace before friends.

Cle. There are.

Ath. Then each of us should be fearless and also fearful; and why we should be either has now been determined.

Cle. Certainly.

Ath. And when we want to make any one fearless, we and the law bring him face to face with many fears.

Cle. Clearly.

Reverence
is trained
amid con-
flicts with
shame-
lessness,
as cour-
age is
amid con-
flicts with
danger.

Ath. And when we want to make him rightly fearful, must we not introduce him to shameless pleasures, and train him to take up arms against them, and to overcome them? Or does this principle apply to courage only, and must he who would be perfect in valour fight against and overcome his own natural character,—since if he be unpractised and inexperienced in such conflicts, he will not be half the man which he might have been,—and are we to suppose, that with temperance it is otherwise, and that he who has never fought with the shameless and unrighteous temptations of his pleasures and lusts, and conquered them, in earnest and in play, by word, deed, and act, will still be perfectly temperate?

Cle. A most unlikely supposition.

Suppose
there
were a
potion
which
tested
courage:

Ath. Suppose that some God had given a fear-potion to men, and that the more a man drank of this the more he regarded himself at every draught as a child of misfortune, and that he feared everything happening or about to happen to him; and that at last the most courageous of men utterly lost his presence of mind for a time,

and only came to himself again when he had slept off the influence
of the draught.

Cle. But has such a draught, Stranger, ever really been known
among men?

Ath. No; but, if there had been, might not such a draught have
been of use to the legislator as a test of courage? Might we not go
and say to him, 'O legislator, whether you are legislating for the
Cretan, or for any other state, would you not like to have a touchstone of the courage and cowardice of your citizens?'

Cle. 'I should,' will be the answer of every one.

Ath. 'And you would rather have a touchstone in which there is
no risk and no great danger than the reverse?'

Cle. In that proposition every one may safely agree.

Ath. 'And in order to make use of the draught, you would lead
them amid these imaginary terrors, and prove them, when the affection of fear was working upon them, and compel them to be fearless, exhorting and admonishing them; and also honouring them,
but dishonouring any one who will not be persuaded by you to be
in all respects such as you command him; and if he underwent the
trial well and manfully, you would let him go unscathed; but if ill,
you would inflict a punishment upon him? Or would you abstain
from using the potion altogether, although you have no reason for
abstaining?'

Cle. He would be certain, Stranger, to use the potion.

Ath. This would be a mode of testing and training which would
be wonderfully easy in comparison with those now in use, and might
be applied to a single person, or to a few, or indeed to any number;
and he would do well who provided himself with the potion only,
rather than with any number of other things, whether he preferred
to be by himself in solitude, and there contend with his fears, because he was ashamed to be seen by the eye of man until he was
perfect; or trusting to the force of his own nature and habits, and
believing that he had been already disciplined sufficiently, he did
not hesitate to train himself in company with any number of others,
and display his power in conquering the irresistible change effected
by the draught—his virtue being such, that he never in any instance
fell into any great unseemliness, but was always himself, and left off
before he arrived at the last cup, fearing that he, like all other men,
might be overcome by the potion.

Cle. Yes, Stranger, in that last case, too, he might equally show
his self-control.

Ath. Let us return to the lawgiver, and say to him:—'Well, lawgiver, there is certainly no such fear-potion which man has either

648
Laws I
ATHE-
NIAN,
CLEINIAS.

should we
not em-
ploy it?

The
drinker of
the fear-
potion
might test
his own
quality,
either
alone or
among
other
men.

649

Laws I

ATHE-
NIAN,
CLEINIAS,
MEGIL-
LUS.

There is
no such
potion,
but there
is a
potion
which
will test
a man's
self-
control.

received from the Gods or himself discovered; for witchcraft has no place at our board. But is there any potion which might serve as a test of overboldness and excessive and indiscreet boasting?'

Cle. I suppose that he will say, Yes,—meaning that wine is such a potion.

Ath. Is not the effect of this quite the opposite of the effect of the other? When a man drinks wine he begins to be better pleased with himself, and the more he drinks the more he is filled full of brave hopes, and conceit of his power, and at last the string of his tongue is loosened, and fancying himself wise, he is brimming over with lawlessness, and has no more fear or respect, and is ready to do or say anything.

Cle. I think that every one will admit the truth of your description.

Meg. Certainly.

Ath. Now, let us remember, as we were saying, that there are two things which should be cultivated in the soul: first, the greatest courage; secondly, the greatest fear—

Cle. Which you said to be characteristic of reverence, if I am not mistaken.

Ath. Thank you for reminding me. But now, as the habit of courage and fearlessness is to be trained amid fears, let us consider whether the opposite quality is not also to be trained among opposites.

Cle. That is probably the case.

Ath. There are times and seasons at which we are by nature more than commonly valiant and bold; now we ought to train ourselves on these occasions to be as free from impudence and shamelessness as possible, and to be afraid to say or suffer or do anything that is base.

Cle. True.

A man's
nature
should be
proved,
not in the
business
of
life, but
in festive
inter-
course.

Ath. Are not the moments in which we are apt to be bold and shameless such as these?—when we are under the influence of anger, love, pride, ignorance, avarice, cowardice? or when wealth, beauty, strength, and all the intoxicating workings of pleasure madden us? What is better adapted than the festive use of wine, in the first place to test, and in the second place to train the character of a man, if care be taken in the use of it? What is there cheaper, or more innocent? For do but consider which is the greater risk:—Would you rather test a man of a morose and savage nature, which is the source of ten thousand acts of injustice, by making bargains with him at a risk to yourself, or by having him as a companion at the festival of Dionysus? Or would you, if you wanted to apply a touchstone to a man who is prone to love, entrust your wife, or your sons, or daughters to him, perilling your dearest interests in order to have a view of the condition of his soul? I might mention numberless cases, in which the advantage would be manifest of getting to know a character in sport, and without paying dearly for experience. And I do not believe that either a Cretan, or any other man, will doubt that such a test is a fair test, and safer, cheaper, and speedier than any other.

Cle. That is certainly true.

Ath. And this knowledge of the natures and habits of men's souls will be of the greatest use in that art which has the management of them; and that art, if I am not mistaken, is politics.

Cle. Exactly so.

BOOK II

Athenian Stranger. AND now we have to consider whether the insight into human nature is the only benefit derived from well-ordered potations, or whether there are not other advantages great and much to be desired. The argument seems to imply that there are. But how and in what way these are to be attained, will have to be considered attentively, or we may be entangled in error.

Cleinias. Proceed.

Ath. Let me once more recall our doctrine of right education; which, if I am not mistaken, depends on the due regulation of convivial intercourse.

Cle. You talk rather grandly.

Ath. Pleasure and pain I maintain to be the first perceptions of children, and I say that they are the forms under which virtue and vice are originally present to them. As to wisdom and true and fixed opinions, happy is the man who acquires them, even when declining in years; and we may say that he who possesses them, and the blessings which are contained in them, is a perfect man. Now I mean by education that training which is given by suitable habits to the first instincts of virtue in children;—when pleasure, and friendship, and pain, and hatred, are rightly implanted in souls not yet capable of understanding the nature of them, and who find them, after they have attained reason, to be in harmony with her. This harmony of the soul, taken as a whole, is virtue; but the particular training in respect of pleasure and pain, which leads you always to hate what

652
Laws II

ATHE-
NIAN,
CLEINIAS.

653

Our first impressions are of pleasure and pain: wisdom comes later.

Education is the right training of these impressions.

you ought to hate, and love what you ought to love from the beginning of life to the end, may be separated off; and, in my view, will be rightly called education.

Cle. I think, Stranger, that you are quite right in all that you have said and are saying about education.

Ath. I am glad to hear that you agree with me; for, indeed, the discipline of pleasure and pain which, when rightly ordered, is a principle of education, has been often relaxed and corrupted in human life. And the Gods, pitying the toils which our race is born to undergo, have appointed holy festivals, wherein men alternate rest with labour; and have given them the Muses and Apollo, the leader of the Muses, and Dionysus, to be companions in their revels, that they may improve their education by taking part in the festivals of the Gods, and with their help. I should like to know whether a common saying is in our opinion true to nature or not. For men say that the young of all creatures cannot be quiet in their bodies or in their voices; they are always wanting to move and cry out; some leaping and skipping, and overflowing with sportiveness and delight at something, others uttering all sorts of cries. But, whereas the animals have no perception of order or disorder in their movements, that is, of rhythm or harmony, as they are called, to us, the Gods, who, as we say, have been appointed to be our companions in the dance, have given the pleasurable sense of harmony and rhythm; and so they stir us into life, and we follow them, joining hands together in dances and songs; and these they call choruses, which is a term naturally expressive of cheerfulness[1]. Shall we begin, then, with the acknowledgment that education is first given through Apollo and the Muses? What do you say?

Cle. I assent.

Ath. And the uneducated is he who has not been trained in the chorus, and the educated is he who has been well trained?

Cle. Certainly.

Ath. And the chorus is made up of two parts, dance and song?

Cle. True.

Ath. Then he who is well educated will be able to sing and dance well?

Cle. I suppose that he will.

Ath. Let us see; what are we saying?

Cle. What?

Ath. He sings well and dances well; now must we add that he sings what is good and dances what is good?

Cle. Let us make the addition.

The Gods have appointed festivals for our improvement. They are our partners in the dance, and have given us the sense of harmony and rhythm.

654

---

[1] χορός, erroneously connected with χαίρειν.

Ath. We will suppose that he knows the good to be good, and the bad to be bad, and makes use of them accordingly: which now is the better trained in dancing and music—he who is able to move his body and to use his voice in what is understood to be the right manner, but has no delight in good or hatred of evil; or he who is incorrect in gesture and voice, but is right in his sense of pleasure and pain, and welcomes what is good, and is offended at what is evil?

Cle. There is a great difference, Stranger, in the two kinds of education.

Ath. If we three know what is good in song and dance, then we truly know also who is educated and who is uneducated; but if not, then we certainly shall not know wherein lies the safeguard of education, and whether there is any or not.

Cle. True.

Ath. Let us follow the scent like hounds, and go in pursuit of beauty of figure, and melody, and song, and dance; if these escape us, there will be no use in talking about true education, whether Hellenic or barbarian.

Cle. Yes.

What makes the beauty of figure, melody, song, dance?

Ath. And what is beauty of figure, or beautiful melody? When a manly soul is in trouble, and when a cowardly soul is in similar case, are they likely to use the same figures and gestures, or to give utterance to the same sounds?

655

Cle. How can they, when the very colours of their faces differ?

Ath. Good, my friend; I may observe, however, in passing, that in music there certainly are figures and there are melodies: and music is concerned with harmony and rhythm, so that you may speak of a melody or figure having good rhythm or good harmony—the term is correct enough; but to speak metaphorically of a melody or figure having a 'good colour,' as the masters of choruses do, is not allowable, although you can speak of the melodies or figures of the brave and the coward, praising the one and censuring the other. And not to be tedious, let us say that the figures and melodies which are expressive of virtue of soul or body, or of images of virtue, are without exception good, and those which are expressive of vice are the reverse of good.

(Note that you cannot speak of the 'colour' of a melody.)

Melodies which express virtue are good; those which express vice are the reverse.

Cle. Your suggestion is excellent; and let us answer that these things are so.

Ath. Once more, are all of us equally delighted with every sort of dance?

Cle. Far otherwise.

Ath. What, then, leads us astray? Are beautiful things not the same to us all, or are they the same in themselves, but not in our

But some
blasphe-
mously
say that
the ex-
cellence
of music
is to give
pleasure;
and so it
becomes
a matter
of likes
and dis-
likes.

656

opinion of them? For no one will admit that forms of vice in the dance are more beautiful than forms of virtue, or that he himself delights in the forms of vice, and others in a muse of another character. And yet most persons say, that the excellence of music is to give pleasure to our souls. But this is intolerable and blasphemous; there is, however, a much more plausible account of the delusion.

Cle. What?

Ath. The adaptation of art to the characters of men. Choric movements are imitations of manners occurring in various actions, fortunes, dispositions,—each particular is imitated, and those to whom the words, or songs, or dances are suited, either by nature or habit or both, cannot help feeling pleasure in them and applauding them, and calling them beautiful. But those whose natures, or ways, or habits are unsuited to them, cannot delight in them or applaud them, and they call them base. There are others, again, whose natures are right and their habits wrong, or whose habits are right and their natures wrong, and they praise one thing, but are pleased at another. For they say that all these imitations are pleasant, but not good. And in the presence of those whom they think wise, they are ashamed of dancing and singing in the baser manner, or of deliberately lending any countenance to such proceedings; and yet, they have a secret pleasure in them.

Cle. Very true.

Ath. And is any harm done to the lover of vicious dances or songs, or any good done to the approver of the opposite sort of pleasure?

Cle. I think that there is.

The effect
of good
and bad
music like
that of
good and
bad com-
pany.

Ath. 'I think' is not the word, but I would say, rather, 'I am certain.' For must they not have the same effect as when a man associates with bad characters, whom he likes and approves rather than dislikes, and only censures playfully because he has a suspicion of his own badness? In that case, he who takes pleasure in them will surely become like those in whom he takes pleasure, even though he be ashamed to praise them. And what greater good or evil can any destiny ever make us undergo?

Cle. I know of none.

Ath. Then in a city which has good laws, or in future ages is to have them, bearing in mind the instruction and amusement which are given by music, can we suppose that the poets are to be allowed to teach in the dance anything which they themselves like, in the way of rhythm, or melody, or words, to the young children of any well-conditioned parents? Is the poet to train his choruses as he pleases, without reference to virtue or vice?

Cle. That is surely quite unreasonable, and is not to be thought of.

Ath. And yet he may do this in almost any state with the exception of Egypt.

Cle. And what are the laws about music and dancing in Egypt?

Ath. You will wonder when I tell you: Long ago they appear to have recognized the very principle of which we are now speaking—that their young citizens must be habituated to forms and strains of virtue. These they fixed, and exhibited the patterns of them in their temples; and no painter or artist is allowed to innovate upon them, or to leave the traditional forms and invent new ones. To this day, no alteration is allowed either in these arts, or in music at all. And you will find that their works of art are painted or moulded in the same forms which they had ten thousand years ago;—this is literally true and no exaggeration,—their ancient paintings and sculptures are not a whit better or worse than the work of to-day, but are made with just the same skill.

Cle. How extraordinary!

Ath. I should rather say, How statesmanlike, how worthy of a legislator! I know that other things in Egypt are not so well. But what I am telling you about music is true and deserving of consideration, because showing that a lawgiver may institute melodies which have a natural truth and correctness without any fear of failure. To do this, however, must be the work of God, or of a divine person; in Egypt they have a tradition that their ancient chants which have been preserved for so many ages are the composition of the Goddess Isis. And therefore, as I was saying, if a person can only find in any way the natural melodies, he may confidently embody them in a fixed and legal form. For the love of novelty which arises out of pleasure in the new and weariness of the old, has not strength enough to corrupt the consecrated song and dance, under the plea that they have become antiquated. At any rate, they are far from being corrupted in Egypt.

Cle. Your arguments seem to prove your point.

Ath. May we not confidently say that the true use of music and of choral festivities is as follows: We rejoice when we think that we prosper, and again we think that we prosper when we rejoice?

Cle. Exactly.

Ath. And when rejoicing in our good fortune, we are unable to be still?

Cle. True.

Ath. Our young men break forth into dancing and singing, and we who are their elders deem that we are fulfilling our part in life when we look on at them. Having lost our agility, we delight in their sports and merry-making, because we love to think of our former

Laws II

ATHE-
NIAN,
CLEINIAS.

Egypt has
fixed
forms of
art which
have ex-
isted for
ten thou-
sand
years.

657

The
Egyptian
chants
were
originally
composed
by the
Goddess
Isis, and
their
sacred
character
preserves
them.

Music
begins in
rejoicing;
our
young
men sing
and
dance,
and the

selves; and gladly institute contests for those who are able to awaken in us the memory of our youth.

Cle. Very true.

Ath. Is it altogether unmeaning to say, as the common people do about festivals, that he should be adjudged the wisest of men, and the winner of the palm, who gives us the greatest amount of pleasure and mirth? For on such occasions, and when mirth is the order of the day, ought not he to be honoured most, and, as I was saying, bear the palm, who gives most mirth to the greatest number? Now is this a true way of speaking or of acting?

Cle. Possibly.

Ath. But, my dear friend, let us distinguish between different cases, and not be hasty in forming a judgment: One way of considering the question will be to imagine a festival at which there are entertainments of all sorts, including gymnastic, musical, and equestrian contests: the citizens are assembled; prizes are offered, and proclamation is made that any one who likes may enter the lists, and that he is to bear the palm who gives the most pleasure to the spectators—there is to be no regulation about the manner how; but he who is most successful in giving pleasure is to be crowned victor, and deemed to be the pleasantest of the candidates: What is likely to be the result of such a proclamation?

Cle. In what respect?

Ath. There would be various exhibitions: one man, like Homer, will exhibit a rhapsody, another a performance on the lute; one will have a tragedy, and another a comedy. Nor would there be anything astonishing in some one imagining that he could gain the prize by exhibiting a puppet-show. Suppose these competitors to meet, and not these only, but innumerable others as well—can you tell me who ought to be the victor?

Cle. I do not see how any one can answer you, or pretend to know, unless he has heard with his own ears the several competitors; the question is absurd.

Ath. Well, then, if neither of you can answer, shall I answer this question which you deem so absurd?

Cle. By all means.

Ath. If very small children are to determine the question, they will decide for the puppet-show.

Cle. Of course.

Ath. The older children will be advocates of comedy; educated women, and young men, and people in general, will favour tragedy.

Cle. Very likely.

Ath. And I believe that we old men would have the greatest pleasure in hearing a rhapsodist recite well the Iliad and Odyssey, or one of the Hesiodic poems, and would award the victory to him. But, who would really be the victor?—that is the question.

Cle. Yes.

Ath. Clearly you and I will have to declare that those whom we old men adjudge victors ought to win; for our ways are far and away better than any which at present exist anywhere in the world.

Cle. Certainly.

Ath. Thus far I too should agree with the many, that the excellence of music is to be measured by pleasure. But the pleasure must not be that of chance persons; the fairest music is that which delights the best and best educated, and especially that which delights the one man who is pre-eminent in virtue and education. And therefore the judges must be men of character, for they will require both wisdom and courage; the true judge must not draw his inspiration from the theatre, nor ought he to be unnerved by the clamour of the many and his own incapacity; nor again, knowing the truth, ought he through cowardice and unmanliness carelessly to deliver a lying judgment, with the very same lips which have just appealed to the Gods before he judged. He is sitting not as the disciple of the theatre, but, in his proper place, as their instructor, and he ought to be the enemy of all pandering to the pleasure of the spectators. The ancient and common custom of Hellas, which still prevails in Italy and Sicily, did certainly leave the judgment to the body of spectators, who determined the victor by show of hands. But this custom has been the destruction of the poets; for they are now in the habit of composing with a view to please the bad taste of their judges, and the result is that the spectators instruct themselves;— and also it has been the ruin of the theatre; they ought to be having characters put before them better than their own, and so receiving a higher pleasure, but now by their own act the opposite result follows. What inference is to be drawn from all this? Shall I tell you?

Cle. What?

Ath. The inference at which we arrive for the third or fourth time is, that education is the constraining and directing of youth towards that right reason, which the law affirms, and which the experience of the eldest and best has agreed to be truly right. In order, then, that the soul of the child may not be habituated to feel joy and sorrow in a manner at variance with the law, and those who obey the law, but may rather follow the law and rejoice and sorrow at the same things as the aged—in order, I say, to produce this effect, chants appear to have been invented, which really enchant, and are designed to implant that harmony of which we speak. And, because

Laws II

ATHE-
NIAN,
CLEINIAS.

educated women and young men and people in general for tragedy: [659] older men will say, 'Give us Homer and Hesiod.'

The criterion of excellence should be pleasure, but not the pleasure of chance persons.

The judge should be the instructor, not the disciple, of the theatre.

The souls of the young should be charmed by song into harmony with the law.

the mind of the child is incapable of enduring serious training, they are called plays and songs, and are performed in play; just as when men are sick and ailing in their bodies, their attendants give them wholesome diet in pleasant meats and drinks, but unwholesome diet in disagreeable things, in order that they may learn, as they ought, to like the one, and to dislike the other. And similarly the true legislator will persuade, and, if he cannot persuade, will compel the poet to express, as he ought, by fair and noble words, in his rhythms, the figures, and in his melodies, the music of temperate and brave and in every way good men.

Cle. But do you really imagine, Stranger, that this is the way in which poets generally compose in States at the present day? As far as I can observe, except among us and among the Lacedaemonians, there are no regulations like those of which you speak; in other places novelties are always being introduced in dancing and in music, generally not under the authority of any law, but at the instigation of lawless pleasures; and these pleasures are so far from being the same, as you describe the Egyptian to be, or having the same principles, that they are never the same.

But all
this is an
ideal. No
fixed
principles
of music
except
among
Cretans
and Lace-
daemo-
nians.

Ath. Most true, Cleinias; and I daresay that I may have expressed myself obscurely, and so led you to imagine that I was speaking of some really existing state of things, whereas I was only saying what regulations I would like to have about music; and hence there occurred a misapprehension on your part. For when evils are far gone and irremediable, the task of censuring them is never pleasant, although at times necessary. But as we do not really differ, will you let me ask you whether you consider such institutions to be more prevalent among the Cretans and Lacedaemonians than among the other Hellenes?

Cle. Certainly they are.

Ath. And if they were extended to the other Hellenes, would it be an improvement on the present state of things?

Cle. A very great improvement, if the customs which prevail among them were such as prevail among us and the Lacedaemonians, and such as you were just now saying ought to prevail.

Ath. Let us see whether we understand one another:—Are not the principles of education and music which prevail among you as follows: you compel your poets to say that the good man, if he be temperate and just, is fortunate and happy; and this whether he be great and strong or small and weak, and whether he be rich or poor; and, on the other hand, if he have a wealth passing that of Cinyras or Midas, and be unjust, he is wretched and lives in misery? As the poet says, and with truth: I sing not, I care not about him who accomplishes all noble things, not having justice; let him who 'draws near and stretches out his hand against his enemies be a just man.' But if he be unjust, I would not have him 'look calmly upon bloody death,' nor 'surpass in swiftness the Thracian Boreas;' and let no other thing that is called good ever be his. For the goods of which the many speak are not really good: first in the catalogue is placed health, beauty next, wealth third; and then innumerable others, as for example to have a keen eye or a quick ear, and in general to have all the senses perfect; or, again, to be a tyrant and do as you like; and the final consummation of happiness is to have acquired all these things, and when you have acquired them to become at once immortal. But you and I say, that while to the just and holy all these things are the best of possessions, to the unjust they are all, including even health, the greatest of evils. For in truth, to have sight, and hearing, and the use of the senses, or to live at all without justice and virtue, even though a man be rich in all the so-called goods of fortune, is the greatest of evils, if life be immortal; but not so great, if the bad man lives only a very short time. These are the truths which, if I am not mistaken, you will persuade or compel your poets to utter with suitable accompaniments of harmony and rhythm, and in these they must train up your youth. Am I not right? For I plainly declare that evils as they are termed are goods to the unjust, and only evils to the just, and that goods are truly good to the good, but evil to the evil. Let me ask again, Are you and I agreed about this?

Cle. I think that we partly agree and partly do not.

Ath. When a man has health and wealth and a tyranny which lasts, and when he is pre-eminent in strength and courage, and has the gift of immortality, and none of the so-called evils which counter-balance these goods, but only the injustice and insolence of his own nature—of such an one you are, I suspect, unwilling to believe that he is miserable rather than happy.

Cle. That is quite true.

Ath. Once more: Suppose that he be valiant and strong, and handsome and rich, and does throughout his whole life whatever he likes, still, if he be unrighteous and insolent, would not both of you agree that he will of necessity live basely? You will surely grant so much?

Cle. Certainly.

Ath. And an evil life too?

Cle. I am not equally disposed to grant that.

Ath. Will he not live painfully and to his own disadvantage?

Cle. How can I possibly say so?

Laws II

661
ATHE-
NIAN,
CLEINIAS.

have a man a brave warrior unless he be a just man.

He who has external goods only is miserable.

Injustice naturally base, and [662] also evil and painful.

Men are
not
always
agreed in
their
opinions;
but the
Gods and
the legis-
lator will
never
cease to
affirm
that the
just is
also the
pleasant.

Ath. How! Then may Heaven make us to be of one mind, for now we are of two. To me, dear Cleinias, the truth of what I am saying is as plain as the fact that Crete is an island. And, if I were a law-giver, I would try to make the poets and all the citizens speak in this strain; and I would inflict the heaviest penalties on any one in all the land who should dare to say that there are bad men who lead pleasant lives, or that the profitable and gainful is one thing, and the just another; and there are many other matters about which I should make my citizens speak in a manner different from the Cretans and Lacedaemonians of this age, and I may say, indeed, from the world in general. For tell me, my good friends, by Zeus and Apollo tell me, if I were to ask these same Gods who were your legislators,—Is not the most just life also the pleasantest? or are there two lives, one of which is the justest and the other the pleasantest? —and they were to reply that there are two; and thereupon I proceeded to ask, (that would be the right way of pursuing the enquiry), Which are the happier—those who lead the justest, or those who lead the pleasantest life? and they replied, Those who lead the pleasantest—that would be a very strange answer, which I should not like to put into the mouth of the Gods. The words will come with more propriety from the lips of fathers and legislators, and therefore I will repeat my former questions to one of them, and suppose him to say again that he who leads the pleasantest life is the happiest. And to that I rejoin:—O my father, did you not wish me to live as happily as possible? And yet you also never ceased telling me that I should live as justly as possible. Now, here the giver of the rule, whether he be legislator or father, will be in a dilemma, and will in vain endeavour to be consistent with himself. But if he were to declare that the justest life is also the happiest, every one hearing him would enquire, if I am not mistaken, what is that good and noble principle in life which the law approves, and which is superior to pleasure. For what good can the just man have which is separated from pleasure? Shall we say that glory and fame, coming from Gods and men, though good and noble, are nevertheless unpleasant, and infamy pleasant? Certainly not, sweet legislator. Or shall we say that the not-doing of wrong and there being no wrong done is good and honourable, although there is no pleasure in it, and that the doing wrong is pleasant, but evil and base?

Cle. Impossible.

Ath. The view which identifies the pleasant and the just and the good and the noble has an excellent moral and religious tendency. And the opposite view is most at variance with the designs of the legislator, and is, in his opinion, infamous; for no one, if he can help,

The different

will be persuaded to do that which gives him more pain than pleasure. But as distant prospects are apt to make us dizzy, especially in childhood, the legislator will try to purge away the darkness and exhibit the truth; he will persuade the citizens, in some way or other, by customs and praises and words, that just and unjust are shadows only, and that injustice, which seems opposed to justice, when contemplated by the unjust and evil man appears pleasant and the just most unpleasant; but that from the just man's point of view, the very opposite is the appearance of both of them.

Cle. True.

Ath. And which may be supposed to be the truer judgment—that of the inferior or of the better soul?

Cle. Surely, that of the better soul.

Ath. Then the unjust life must not only be more base and depraved, but also more unpleasant than the just and holy life?

Cle. That seems to be implied in the present argument.

Ath. And even supposing this were otherwise, and not as the argument has proven, still the lawgiver, who is worth anything, if he ever ventures to tell a lie to the young for their good, could not invent a more useful lie than this, or one which will have a better effect in making them do what is right, not on compulsion but voluntarily.

Cle. Truth, Stranger, is a noble thing and a lasting, but a thing of which men are hard to be persuaded.

Ath. And yet the story of the Sidonian Cadmus, which is so improbable, has been readily believed, and also innumerable other tales.

Cle. What is that story?

Ath. The story of armed men springing up after the sowing of teeth, which the legislator may take as a proof that he can persuade the minds of the young of anything; so that he has only to reflect and find out what belief will be of the greatest public advantage, and then use all his efforts to make the whole community utter one and the same word in their songs and tales and discourses all their life long. But if you do not agree with me, there is no reason why you should not argue on the other side.

Cle. I do not see that any argument can fairly be raised by either of us against what you are now saying.

Ath. The next suggestion which I have to offer is, that all our three choruses shall sing to the young and tender souls of children, reciting in their strains all the noble thoughts of which we have already spoken, or are about to speak; and the sum of them shall be, that the life which is by the Gods deemed to be the happiest is also

Laws II

ATHE-
NIAN,
CLEINIAS.

points of
view
taken by
the lower
and the
higher
soul.

Even if
the higher
soul did
not speak
the truth
about the
unplea-
santness
of in-
justice, it
would be
a useful
lie, and
much
more
credible
than the
tale of
Cadmus.
664

That the
holiest life
is the
happiest,
—this is
the strain

to be sung
by all the
three
choruses
of
children,
young
men, old
men.

the best;—we shall affirm this to be a most certain truth; and the minds of our young disciples will be more likely to receive these words of ours than any others which we might address to them.

Cle. I assent to what you say.

Ath. First will enter in their natural order the sacred choir composed of children, which is to sing lustily the heaven-taught lay to the whole city. Next will follow the choir of young men under the age of thirty, who will call upon the God Paean to testify to the truth of their words, and will pray him to be gracious to the youth and to turn their hearts. Thirdly, the choir of elder men, who are from thirty to sixty years of age, will also sing. There remain those who are too old to sing, and they will tell stories, illustrating the same virtues, as with the voice of an oracle.

Cle. Who are those who compose the third choir, Stranger? for I do not clearly understand what you mean to say about them.

Ath. And yet almost all that I have been saying has been said with a view to them.

Cle. Will you try to be a little plainer?

Ath. I was speaking at the commencement of our discourse, as you will remember, of the fiery nature of young creatures: I said that they were unable to keep quiet either in limb or voice, and that they called out and jumped about in a disorderly manner; and that no other animal attained to any perception of order, but man only. Now the order of motion is called rhythm, and the order of the voice, in which high and low are duly mingled, is called harmony; and both together are termed choric song. And I said that the Gods had pity on us, and gave us Apollo and the Muses to be our playfellows and leaders in the dance; and Dionysus, as I dare say that you will remember, was the third.

Cle. I quite remember.

Ath. Thus far I have spoken of the chorus of Apollo and the Muses, and I have still to speak of the remaining chorus, which is that of Dionysus.

Cle. How is that arranged? There is something strange, at any rate on first hearing, in a Dionysiac chorus of old men, if you really mean that those who are above thirty, and may be fifty, or from fifty to sixty years of age, are to dance in his honour.

Ath. Very true; and therefore it must be shown that there is good reason for the proposal.

Cle. Certainly.

Ath. Are we agreed thus far?

Cle. About what?

Ath. That every man and boy, slave and free, both sexes, and the

Recapitu-
lation.
Apollo
and the
Muses
[665]
our play-
fellows;
also
Dionysus.
The cries
and
move-
ments of
children
are con-
verted
into
harmony
and
rhythm.

The
Dion-
ysiac
chorus of
old men.

whole city, should never cease charming themselves with the strains
of which we have spoken; and that there should be every sort of
change and variation of them in order to take away the effect of
sameness, so that the singers may always receive pleasure from their
hymns, and may never weary of them?

Cle. Every one will agree.

Ath. Where, then, will that best part of our city which, by reason
of age and intelligence, has the greatest influence, sing these fairest
of strains, which are to do so much good? Shall we be so foolish as
to let them off who would give us the most beautiful and also the
most useful of songs?

Cle. But, says the argument, we cannot let them off.

Ath. Then how can we carry out our purpose with decorum? Will
this be the way?

Cle. What?

Ath. When a man is advancing in years, he is afraid and reluctant
to sing;—he has no pleasure in his own performances; and if compulsion is used, he will be more and more ashamed, the older and
more discreet he grows;—is not this true?

Cle. Certainly.

Ath. Well, and will he not be yet more ashamed if he has to stand
up and sing in the theatre to a mixed audience?—and if moreover
when he is required to do so, like the other choirs who contend for
prizes, and have been trained under a singing master, he is pinched
and hungry, he will certainly have a feeling of shame and discom-
fort which will make him very unwilling to exhibit.

Cle. No doubt.

Ath. How, then, shall we reassure him, and get him to sing? Shall
we begin by enacting that boys shall not taste wine at all until they
are eighteen years of age; we will tell them that fire must not be
poured upon fire, whether in the body or in the soul, until they begin
to go to work—this is a precaution which has to be taken against
the excitableness of youth;—afterwards they may taste wine in
moderation up to the age of thirty, but while a man is young he
should abstain altogether from intoxication and from excess of wine;
when, at length, he has reached forty years, after dinner at a public
mess, he may invite not only the other Gods, but Dionysus above
all, to the mystery and festivity of the elder men, making use of the
wine which he has given men to lighten the sourness of old age; that
in age we may renew our youth, and forget our sorrows; and also in
order that the nature of the soul, like iron melted in the fire, may
become softer and so more impressible. In the first place, will not
any one who is thus mellowed be more ready and less ashamed to

Laws II

ATHE-
NIAN,
CLEINIAS.

The
whole
city will
break out
into sing-
ing, and
the songs
will be
varied to
avoid
sameness.

Least of
all can the
chorus of
old men
be ex-
cused; for
they will
give us
the best
and
fairest
strains.

666

But they
must be
encour-
aged by
the use
of wine.

sing,—I do not say before a large audience, but before a moderate company; nor yet among strangers, but among his familiars, and, as we have often said, to chant, and to enchant?

Cle. He will be far more ready.

Ath. There will be no impropriety in our using such a method of persuading them to join with us in song.

Cle. None at all.

Ath. And what strain will they sing, and what muse will they hymn? The strain should clearly be one suitable to them.

Cle. Certainly.

Ath. And what strain is suitable for heroes? Shall they sing a choric strain?

At Sparta
and Crete
only
martial
strains
are
heard.

Cle. Truly, Stranger, we of Crete and Lacedaemon know no strain other than that which we have learnt and been accustomed to sing in our chorus.

Ath. I dare say; for you have never acquired the knowledge of the most beautiful kind of song, in your military way of life, which is modelled after the camp, and is not like that of dwellers in cities; and you have your young men herding and feeding together like young colts. No one takes his own individual colt and drags him away from his fellows against his will, raging and foaming, and gives him a groom to attend to him alone, and trains and rubs him down privately, and gives him the qualities in education which will make him not only a good soldier, but also a governor of a state and of cities. Such an one, as we said at first, would be a greater warrior

than he of whom Tyrtaeus sings; and he would honour courage everywhere, but always as the fourth, and not as the first part of virtue, either in individuals or states.

Cle. Once more, Stranger, I must complain that you depreciate our lawgivers.

The
common
forms of
song are
not the
highest.

Ath. Not intentionally, if at all, my good friend; but whither the argument leads, thither let us follow; for if there be indeed some strain of song more beautiful than that of the choruses or the public theatres, I should like to impart it to those who, as we say, are ashamed of these, and want to have the best.

Cle. Certainly.

Ath. When things have an accompanying charm, either the best thing in them is this very charm, or there is some rightness or utility possessed by them;—for example, I should say that eating and drinking, and the use of food in general, have an accompanying charm which we call pleasure; but that this rightness and utility is just the healthfulness of the things served up to us, which is their true rightness.

Cle. Just so.

Ath. Thus, too, I should say that learning has a certain accompanying charm which is the pleasure; but that the right and the profitable, the good and the noble, are qualities which the truth gives to it.

Cle. Exactly.

Ath. And so in the imitative arts,—if they succeed in making likenesses, and are accompanied by pleasure, may not their works be said to have a charm?

Cle. Yes.

Ath. But equal proportions, whether of quality or quantity, and not pleasure, speaking generally, would give them truth or rightness.

Cle. Yes.

Ath. Then that only can be rightly judged by the standard of pleasure, which makes or furnishes no utility or truth or likeness, nor on the other hand is productive of any hurtful quality, but exists solely for the sake of the accompanying charm; and the term 'pleasure' is most appropriately applied to it when these other qualities are absent.

Cle. You are speaking of harmless pleasure, are you not?

Ath. Yes; and this I term amusement, when doing neither harm nor good in any degree worth speaking of.

Cle. Very true.

Ath. Then, if such be our principles, we must assert that imitation is not to be judged of by pleasure and false opinion; and this is true of all equality, for the equal is not equal or the symmetrical symmetrical, because somebody thinks or likes something, but they are to be judged of by the standard of truth, and by no other whatever.

Cle. Quite true.

Ath. Do we not regard all music as representative and imitative?

Cle. Certainly.

Ath. Then, when any one says that music is to be judged of by pleasure, his doctrine cannot be admitted; and if there be any music of which pleasure is the criterion, such music is not to be sought out or deemed to have any real excellence, but only that other kind of music which is an imitation of the good.

Cle. Very true.

Ath. And those who seek for the best kind of song and music ought not to seek for that which is pleasant, but for that which is true; and the truth of imitation consists, as we were saying, in rendering the thing imitated according to quantity and quality.

Cle. Certainly.

Many things have an accompanying charm, but this is no criterion of their excellence, if there be any higher one.

The goodness of an imitation is to be determined by its truth, 668 not by the pleasure which it gives.

Ath. And every one will admit that musical compositions are all imitative and representative. Will not poets and spectators and actors all agree in this?

Cle. They will.

Ath. Surely then he who would judge correctly must know what each composition is; for if he does not know what is the character and meaning of the piece, and what it represents, he will never discern whether the intention is true or false.

Cle. Certainly not.

Ath. And will he who does not know what is true be able to distinguish what is good and bad? My statement is not very clear; but perhaps you will understand me better if I put the matter in another way.

Cle. How?

Ath. There are ten thousand likenesses of objects of sight?

Cle. Yes.

But to know whether an imitation is faithful, we must know, (1) of what it is the imitation; (2) whether it is true;

[669]

(3) whether it is beautiful or well executed.

Ath. And can he who does not know what the exact object is which is imitated, ever know whether the resemblance is truthfully executed? I mean, for example, whether a statue has the proportions of a body, and the true situation of the parts; what those proportions are, and how the parts fit into one another in due order; also their colours and conformations, or whether this is all confused in the execution: do you think that any one can know about this, who does not know what the animal is which has been imitated?

Cle. Impossible.

Ath. But even if we know that the thing pictured or sculptured is a man, who has received at the hand of the artist all his proper parts and colours and shapes, must we not also know whether the work is beautiful or in any respect deficient in beauty?

Cle. If this were not required, Stranger, we should all of us be judges of beauty.

Ath. Very true; and may we not say that in everything imitated, whether in drawing, music, or any other art, he who is to be a competent judge must possess three things;—he must know, in the first place, of what the imitation is; secondly, he must know that it is true; and thirdly, that it has been well executed in words and melodies and rhythms?

Cle. Certainly.

Injurious influence of some kinds of music.

Ath. Then let us not faint in discussing the peculiar difficulty of music. Music is more celebrated than any other kind of imitation, and therefore requires the greatest care of them all. For if a man makes a mistake here, he may do himself the greatest injury by welcoming evil dispositions, and the mistake may be very difficult to discern, because the poets are artists very inferior in character to the Muses themselves, who would never fall into the monstrous error of assigning to the words of men the gestures and songs of women; nor after combining the melodies with the gestures of free-men would they add on the rhythms of slaves and men of the baser sort; nor, beginning with the rhythms and gestures of freemen, would they assign to them a melody or words which are of an opposite character; nor would they mix up the voices and sounds of animals and of men and instruments, and every other sort of noise, as if they were all one. But human poets are fond of introducing this sort of inconsistent mixture, and so make themselves ridiculous in the eyes of those who, as Orpheus says, 'are ripe for true pleasure.' The experienced see all this confusion, and yet the poets go on and make still further havoc by separating the rhythm and the figure of the dance from the melody, setting bare words to metre, and also separating the melody and the rhythm from the words, using the lyre or the flute alone. For when there are no words, it is very difficult to recognize the meaning of the harmony and rhythm, or to see that any worthy object is imitated by them. And we must acknowledge that all this sort of thing, which aims only at swiftness and smoothness and a brutish noise, and uses the flute and the lyre not as the mere accompaniments of the dance and song, is exceedingly coarse and tasteless. The use of either instrument, when unaccompanied, leads to every sort of irregularity and trickery. This is all rational enough. But we are considering not how our choristers, who are from thirty to fifty years of age, and may be over fifty, are not to use the Muses, but how they are to use them. And the considerations which we have urged seem to show in what way these fifty-year-old choristers who are to sing, may be expected to be better trained. For they need to have a quick perception and knowledge of harmonies and rhythms; otherwise, how can they ever know whether a melody would be rightly sung to the Dorian mode, or to the rhythm which the poet has assigned to it?

Cle. Clearly they cannot.

Ath. The many are ridiculous in imagining that they know what is in proper harmony and rhythm, and what is not, when they can only be made to sing and step in rhythm by force; it never occurs to them that they are ignorant of what they are doing. Now every melody is right when it has suitable harmony and rhythm, and wrong when unsuitable.

Cle. That is most certain.

Ath. But can a man who does not know a thing, as we were saying, know that the thing is right?

Laws II

ATHE-
NIAN,
CLEINIAS.

Incongru-
ous
unions of
gestures,
styles,
melodies,
rhythms,
sounds.

Absurd-
ity of
song
without
rhythm
and fig-
ure, and
of in-
strument-
al music
and
rhythm
without
words.
670

Only
learned
and ex-
perienced
judges,
like our
fifty-
year-old
choristers,
can see
their way
through
all this.

They will
have a
far more
complete
knowl-
edge of
the art of
music
than the
people
and even
than the
poets
[671]
them-
selves.

Cle. Impossible.

Ath. Then now, as would appear, we are making the discovery that our newly-appointed choristers, whom we hereby invite and, although they are their own masters, compel to sing, must be educated to such an extent as to be able to follow the steps of the rhythm and the notes of the song, that they may know the harmonies and rhythms, and be able to select what are suitable for men of their age and character to sing; and may sing them, and have innocent pleasure from their own performance, and also lead younger men to welcome with dutiful delight good dispositions. Having such training, they will attain a more accurate knowledge than falls to the lot of the common people, or even of the poets themselves. For the poet need not know the third point, viz. whether the imitation is good or not, though he can hardly help knowing the laws of melody and rhythm. But the aged chorus must know all the three, that they may choose the best, and that which is nearest to the best; for otherwise they will never be able to charm the souls of young men in the way of virtue. And now the original design of the argument which was intended to bring eloquent aid to the Chorus of Dionysus, has been accomplished to the best of our ability, and let us see whether we were right:—I should imagine that a drinking assembly is likely to become more and more tumultuous as the drinking goes on: this, as we were saying at first, will certainly be the case.

The
drinking
assembly
is apt to
be tu-
multuous.
Every
man
grows
light-
headed.

At such
times the
soul may
be easily
fashioned
by the
legislator
who
should
prescribe
rules of
behav-
iour.

Cle. Certainly.

Ath. Every man has a more than natural elevation; his heart is glad within him, and he will say anything and will be restrained by nobody at such a time; he fancies that he is able to rule over himself and all mankind.

Cle. Quite true.

Ath. Were we not saying that on such occasions the souls of the drinkers become like iron heated in the fire, and grow softer and younger, and are easily moulded by him who knows how to educate and fashion them, just as when they were young, and that this fashioner of them is the same who prescribed for them in the days of their youth, viz. the good legislator; and that he ought to enact laws of the banquet, which, when a man is confident, bold, and impudent, and unwilling to wait his turn and have his share of silence and speech, and drinking and music, will change his character into the opposite—such laws as will infuse into him a just and noble fear, which will take up arms at the approach of insolence, being that divine fear which we have called reverence and shame?

Cle. True.

Ath. And the guardians of these laws and fellow-workers with them are the calm and sober generals of the drinkers; and without their help there is greater difficulty in fighting against drink than in fighting against enemies when the commander of an army is not himself calm; and he who is unwilling to obey them and the commanders of Dionysiac feasts who are more than sixty years of age, shall suffer a disgrace as great as he who disobeys military leaders, or even greater.

Cle. Right.

Ath. If, then, drinking and amusement were regulated in this way, would not the companions of our revels be improved? they would part better friends than they were, and not, as now, enemies. Their whole intercourse would be regulated by law and observant of it, and the sober would be the leaders of the drunken.

Cle. I think so too, if drinking were regulated as you propose.

Ath. Let us not then simply censure the gift of Dionysus as bad and unfit to be received into the State. For wine has many excellences, and one pre-eminent one, about which there is a difficulty in speaking to the many, from a fear of their misconceiving and misunderstanding what is said.

Cle. To what do you refer?

Ath. There is a tradition or story, which has somehow crept about the world, that Dionysus was robbed of his wits by his stepmother Here, and that out of revenge he inspires Bacchic furies and dancing madnesses in others; for which reason he gave men wine. Such traditions concerning the Gods I leave to those who think that they may be safely uttered[1]; I only know that no animal at birth is mature or perfect in intelligence; and in the intermediate period, in which he has not yet acquired his own proper sense, he rages and roars without rhyme or reason; and when he has once got on his legs he jumps about without rhyme or reason; and this, as you will remember, has been already said by us to be the origin of music and gymnastic[2].

Cle. To be sure, I remember.

Ath. And did we not say that the sense of harmony and rhythm sprang from this beginning among men, and that Apollo and the Muses and Dionysus were the Gods whom we had to thank for them?

Cle. Certainly.

Ath. The other story implied that wine was given man out of revenge, and in order to make him mad; but our present doctrine, on the contrary, is, that wine was given him as a balm, and in order to

Laws II

ATHE-
NIAN,
CLEINIAS.

But there must be sober generals of the feast under whose [672] command men will fight against drink.

There is a good as well as a bad tradition about Dionysus. He is not only said to have given men wine to make them mad, but also as a balm.

---

[1] Cp. Euthyph. 6, ff.; Rep. ii. 378; iii. 388, 408 C.   [2] *Supra*, 653 D, E.

implant modesty in the soul, and health and strength in the body.

Cle. That, Stranger, is precisely what was said.

Ath. Then half the subject may now be considered to have been discussed; shall we proceed to the consideration of the other half?

Cle. What is the other half, and how do you divide the subject?

Ath. The whole choral art is also in our view the whole of education; and of this art, rhythms and harmonies form the part which has to do with the voice.

Cle. Yes.

Ath. The movement of the body has rhythm in common with the movement of the voice, but gesture is peculiar to it, whereas song is simply the movement of the voice.

Cle. Most true.

Ath. And the sound of the voice which reaches and educates the soul, we have ventured to term music.

Cle. We were right.

Ath. And the movement of the body, when regarded as an amusement, we termed dancing; but when extended and pursued with a view to the excellence of the body, this scientific training may be called gymnastic.

Cle. Exactly.

Ath. Music, which was one half of the choral art, may be said to have been completely discussed. Shall we proceed to the other half or not? What would you like?

Cle. My good friend, when you are talking with a Cretan and Lacedaemonian, and we have discussed music and not gymnastic, what answer are either of us likely to make to such an enquiry?

Ath. An answer is contained in your question; and I understand and accept what you say not only as an answer, but also as a command to proceed with gymnastic.

Cle. You quite understand me; do as you say.

Ath. I will; and there will not be any difficulty in speaking intelligibly to you about a subject with which both of you are far more familiar than with music.

Cle. There will not.

Ath. Is not the origin of gymnastics, too, to be sought in the tendency to rapid motion which exists in all animals; man, as we were saying, having attained the sense of rhythm, created and invented dancing; and melody arousing and awakening rhythm, both united formed the choral art?

Cle. Very true.

Ath. And one part of this subject has been already discussed by us, and there still remains another to be discussed[1]?

Cle. Exactly.

Ath. I have first a final word to add to my discourse about drink, if you will allow me to do so.

Cle. What more have you to say?

Ath. I should say that if a city seriously means to adopt the practice of drinking under due regulation and with a view to the enforcement of temperance, and in like manner, and on the same principle, will allow of other pleasures, designing to gain the victory over them —in this way all of them may be used. But if the State makes drinking an amusement only, and whoever likes may drink whenever he likes, and with whom he likes, and add to this any other indulgences, I shall never agree or allow that this city or this man should practise drinking. I would go farther than the Cretans and Lacedaemonians, and am disposed rather to the law of the Carthaginians, that no one while he is on a campaign should be allowed to taste wine at all, but that he should drink water during all that time, and that in the city no slave, male or female, should ever drink wine; and that no magistrates should drink during their year of office, nor should pilots of vessels or judges while on duty taste wine at all, nor any one who is going to hold a consultation about any matter of importance; nor in the day-time at all, unless in consequence of exercise or as medicine; nor again at night, when any one, either man or woman, is minded to get children. There are numberless other cases also in which those who have good sense and good laws ought not to drink wine, so that if what I say is true, no city will need many vineyards. Their husbandry and their way of life in general will follow an appointed order, and their cultivation of the vine will be the most limited and the least common of their employments. And this, Stranger, shall be the crown of my discourse about wine, if you agree.

Cle. Excellent: we agree.

BOOK III

Athenian Stranger. ENOUGH of this. And what, then, is to be regarded as the origin of government? Will not a man be able to judge of it best from a point of view in which he may behold the progress of states and their transitions to good or evil?

[1] Cp. *infra*, vii. 813, 814.

Laws II

ATHENIAN, CLEINIAS.

The final word. Drinking should only be allowed with a view to [674] the promotion of temperance.

The law of the Carthaginians about drinking.

676
Laws III
ATHENIAN.

Laws III

ATHE-
NIAN,
CLEINIAS.

The
point of
view of
time.

Innumer-
able
forms of
govern-
ment
have
arisen in
the
course of
ages:

677

and many
destruc-
tions of
mankind
have
taken
place
through
deluges
and
plagues.

A few
survivors.

Cleinias. What do you mean?

Ath. I mean that he might watch them from the point of view of time, and observe the changes which take place in them during infinite ages.

Cle. How so?

Ath. Why, do you think that you can reckon the time which has elapsed since cities first existed and men were citizens of them?

Cle. Hardly.

Ath. But you are sure that it must be vast and incalculable?

Cle. Certainly.

Ath. And have not thousands and thousands of cities come into being during this period and as many perished? And has not each of them had every form of government many times over, now growing larger, now smaller, and again improving or declining?

Cle. To be sure.

Ath. Let us endeavour to ascertain the cause of these changes; for that will probably explain the first origin and development of forms of government.

Cle. Very good. You shall endeavour to impart your thoughts to us, and we will make an effort to understand you.

Ath. Do you believe that there is any truth in ancient traditions?

Cle. What traditions?

Ath. The traditions about the many destructions of mankind which have been occasioned by deluges and pestilences, and in many other ways, and of the survival of a remnant?

Cle. Every one is disposed to believe them.

Ath. Let us consider one of them, that which was caused by the famous deluge.

Cle. What are we to observe about it?

Ath. I mean to say that those who then escaped would only be hill shepherds,—small sparks of the human race preserved on the tops of mountains.

Cle. Clearly.

Ath. Such survivors would necessarily be unacquainted with the arts and the various devices which are suggested to the dwellers in cities by interest or ambition, and with all the wrongs which they contrive against one another.

Cle. Very true.

Ath. Let us suppose, then, that the cities in the plain and on the sea-coast were utterly destroyed at that time.

Cle. Very good.

Ath. Would not all implements have then perished and every other excellent invention of political or any other sort of wisdom have utterly disappeared?

Cle. Why, yes, my friend; and if things had always continued as they are at present ordered, how could any discovery have ever been made even in the least particular? For it is evident that the arts were unknown during ten thousand times ten thousand years. And no more than a thousand or two thousand years have elapsed since the discoveries of Daedalus, Orpheus and Palamedes,—since Marsyas and Olympus invented music, and Amphion the lyre,—not to speak of numberless other inventions which are but of yesterday.

Ath. Have you forgotten, Cleinias, the name of a friend who is really of yesterday?

Cle. I suppose that you mean Epimenides[1].

Ath. The same, my friend; he does indeed far overleap the heads of all mankind by his invention; for he carried out in practice, as you declare, what of old Hesiod[2] only preached.

Cle. Yes, according to our tradition.

Ath. After the great destruction, may we not suppose that the state of man was something of this sort:—In the beginning of things there was a fearful illimitable desert and a vast expanse of land; a herd or two of oxen would be the only survivors of the animal world; and there might be a few goats, these too hardly enough to maintain the shepherds who tended them?

Cle. True.

Ath. And of cities or governments or legislation, about which we are now talking, do you suppose that they could have any recollection at all?

Cle. None whatever.

Ath. And out of this state of things has there not sprung all that we now are and have: cities and governments, and arts and laws, and a great deal of vice and a great deal of virtue?

Cle. What do you mean?

Ath. Why, my good friend, how can we possibly suppose that those who knew nothing of all the good and evil of cities could have attained their full development, whether of virtue or of vice?

Cle. I understand your meaning, and you are quite right.

Ath. But, as time advanced and the race multiplied, the world came to be what the world is.

Cle. Very true.

Ath. Doubtless the change was not made all in a moment, but little by little, during a very long period of time.

[1] Cp. i. 642 D.   [2] Works and Days, ll. 40, 41.

Laws III

ATHE-
NIAN,
CLEINIAS.

The arts
perished.

The last
recovery
of civil-
ization
quite
recent.
Famous
dis-
coveries;
Daedalus,
&c.

Hesiod
and
Epimen-
ides.

Growth
of society.
A few
poor
[678]
shepherds
left with
their
scanty
flocks

have de-
veloped
into gov-
ernments
and cities.

Cle. A highly probable supposition.

Ath. At first, they would have a natural fear ringing in their ears which would prevent their descending from the heights into the plain.

Cle. Of course.

Ath. The fewness of the survivors at that time would have made them all the more desirous of seeing one another; but then the means of travelling either by land or sea had been almost entirely lost, as I may say, with the loss of the arts, and there was great difficulty in getting at one another; for iron and brass and all metals were jumbled together and had disappeared in the chaos; nor was there any possibility of extracting ore from them; and they had scarcely any means of felling timber. Even if you suppose that some implements might have been preserved in the mountains, they must quickly have worn out and vanished, and there would be no more of them until the art of metallurgy had again revived.

After the deluge no arts or metals or implements or means of transit.

Cle. There could not have been.

Ath. In how many generations would this be attained?

Cle. Clearly, not for many generations.

Ath. During this period, and for some time afterwards, all the arts which require iron and brass and the like would disappear.

Cle. Certainly.

Ath. Faction and war would also have died out in those days, and for many reasons.

Cle. How would that be?

Isolation; friendliness:

Ath. In the first place, the desolation of these primitive men would create in them a feeling of affection and good-will towards one another; and, secondly, they would have no occasion to quarrel about their subsistence, for they would have pasture in abundance, except just at first, and in some particular cases; and from their pasture-land they would obtain the greater part of their food in a primitive age, having plenty of milk and flesh; moreover they would procure other food by the chase, not to be despised either in quantity or quality. They would also have abundance of clothing, and bedding, and dwellings, and utensils either capable of standing on the fire or not; for the plastic and weaving arts do not require any use of iron: and God has given these two arts to man in order to provide him with all such things, that, when reduced to the last extremity, the human race may still grow and increase. Hence in those days mankind were not very poor; nor was poverty a cause of difference among them; and rich they could not have been, having neither gold nor silver:—such at that time was their condition. And the community which has neither poverty nor riches will always

679

no wants; no wars:

plastic and weaving arts:

have the noblest principles; in it there is no insolence or injustice, nor, again, are there any contentions or envyings. And therefore they were good, and also because they were what is called simpleminded; and when they were told about good and evil, they in their simplicity believed what they heard to be very truth and practised it. No one had the wit to suspect another of a falsehood, as men do now; but what they heard about Gods and men they believed to be true, and lived accordingly; and therefore they were in all respects such as we have described them.

Cle. That quite accords with my views, and with those of my friend here.

Ath. Would not many generations living on in a simple manner, although ruder, perhaps, and more ignorant of the arts generally, and in particular of those of land or naval warfare, and likewise of other arts, termed in cities legal practices and party conflicts, and including all conceivable ways of hurting one another in word and deed;—although inferior to those who lived before the deluge, or to the men of our day in these respects, would they not, I say, be simpler and more manly, and also more temperate and altogether more just? The reason has been already explained.

Cle. Very true.

Ath. I should wish you to understand that what has preceded and what is about to follow, has been, and will be said, with the intention of explaining what need the men of that time had of laws, and who was their lawgiver.

Cle. And thus far what you have said has been very well said.

Ath. They could hardly have wanted lawgivers as yet; nothing of that sort was likely to have existed in their days, for they had no letters at this early period; they lived by habit and the customs of their ancestors, as they are called.

Cle. Probably.

Ath. But there was already existing a form of government which, if I am not mistaken, is generally termed a lordship, and this still remains in many places, both among Hellenes and barbarians[1], and is the government which is declared by Homer to have prevailed among the Cyclopes:—

'They have neither councils nor judgments, but they dwell in hollow caves on the tops of high mountains, and every one gives law to his wife and children, and they do not busy themselves about one another[2].'

Cle. That seems to be a charming poet of yours; I have read some other verses of his, which are very clever; but I do not know much

[1] Cp. Arist. Pol. i. 2, §§ 6, 7.   [2] Odyss. ix. 112, ff.

Laws III

ATHE-
NIAN,
CLEINIAS.

simplicity
of life
and character.

Men were
ruder, but
also better, than
a later
generation.

No laws.

680

No
letters.

The oldest form
of government
a lordship:
men lived
by custom, like
the Cyclopes.
(Homer
unknown

Laws III

ATHE-
NIAN,
CLEINIAS,
MEGIL-
LUS.

in Crete,
but well
known at
Sparta.)

The Ho-
meric
way of
life
Ionian
rather
than
Spartan.

The
origin of
society
patri-
archal.

681

The
second
stage:—
larger
settle-
ments at
the foot
of the
moun-
tain; be-
ginning
of agri-
culture.

The
lesser
settle-
ments
bring
with
them into
the
larger
society
family
customs
peculiar
to them-
selves.

of him, for foreign poets are very little read among the Cretans.

Meg. But they are in Lacedaemon, and he appears to be the prince of them all; the manner of life, however, which he describes is not Spartan, but rather Ionian, and he seems quite to confirm what you are saying, when he traces up the ancient state of mankind by the help of tradition to barbarism.

Ath. Yes, he does confirm it; and we may accept his witness to the fact that such forms of government sometimes arise.

Cle. We may.

Ath. And were not such states composed of men who had been dispersed in single habitations and families by the poverty which attended the devastations; and did not the eldest then rule among them, because with them government originated in the authority of a father and a mother, whom, like a flock of birds, they followed, forming one troop under the patriarchal rule and sovereignty of their parents, which of all sovereignties is the most just?

Cle. Very true.

Ath. After this they came together in greater numbers, and increased the size of their cities, and betook themselves to husbandry, first of all at the foot of the mountains, and made enclosures of loose walls and works of defence, in order to keep off wild beasts; thus creating a single large and common habitation.

Cle. Yes; at least we may suppose so.

Ath. There is another thing which would probably happen.

Cle. What?

Ath. When these larger habitations grew up out of the lesser original ones, each of the lesser ones would survive in the larger; every family would be under the rule of the eldest, and, owing to their separation from one another, would have peculiar customs in things divine and human, which they would have received from their several parents who had educated them; and these customs would incline them to order, when the parents had the element of order in their nature, and to courage, when they had the element of courage. And they would naturally stamp upon their children, and upon their children's children, their own likings[1]; and, as we are saying, they would find their way into the larger society, having already their own peculiar laws.

Cle. Certainly.

Ath. And every man surely likes his own laws best, and the laws of others not so well.

Cle. True.

---

[1] Reading αἱρέσεις: but ?

Ath. Then now we seem to have stumbled upon the beginnings of legislation.

Cle. Exactly.

Ath. The next step will be that these persons who have met together, will select some arbiters, who will review the laws of all of them, and will publicly present such as they approve to the chiefs who lead the tribes, and who are in a manner their kings, allowing them to choose those which they think best. These persons will themselves be called legislators, and will appoint the magistrates, framing some sort of aristocracy, or perhaps monarchy, out of the dynasties or lordships, and in this altered state of the government they will live.

Cle. Yes, that would be the natural order of things.

Ath. Then, now let us speak of a third form of government, in which all other forms and conditions of polities and cities concur.

Cle. What is that?

Ath. The form which in fact Homer indicates as following the second. This third form arose when, as he says, Dardanus founded Dardania:—

The third
stage: the
city
finally
settled in
the plain.

'For not as yet had the holy Ilium been built on the plain to be a city of speaking men; but they were still dwelling at the foot of many-fountained Ida[1].'

For indeed, in these verses, and in what he said of the Cyclopes, he speaks the words of God and nature; for poets are a divine race[2] and often in their strains, by the aid of the Muses and the Graces, they attain truth.

Cle. Yes.

Ath. Then now let us proceed with the rest of our tale, which will probably be found to illustrate in some degree our proposed design:—Shall we do so?

Cle. By all means.

Ath. Ilium was built, when they had descended from the mountain, in a large and fair plain, on a sort of low hill, watered by many rivers descending from Ida.

Cle. Such is the tradition.

Ath. And we must suppose this event to have taken place many ages after the deluge?

Ath. A marvellous forgetfulness of the former destruction would appear to have come over them, when they placed their town right under numerous streams flowing from the heights, trusting for their security to not very high hills, either.

[1] Il. xx. 216, ff.   [2] Omitting ἐνθεαστικόν.

Laws III

ATHE-
NIAN,
CLEINIAS.
MEGIL-
LUS.

Cle. There must have been a long interval, clearly.

Ath. And, as population increased, many other cities would begin to be inhabited.

Cle. Doubtless.

Ath. Those cities made war against Troy—by sea as well as land—for at that time men were ceasing to be afraid of the sea.

Cle. Clearly.

Ath. The Achaeans remained ten years, and overthrew Troy.

Cle. True.

Ath. And during the ten years in which the Achaeans were besieging Illium, the homes of the besiegers were falling into an evil plight. Their youth revolted; and when the soldiers returned to their own cities and families, they did not receive them properly, and as they ought to have done, and numerous deaths, murders, exiles, were the consequence. The exiles came again, under a new name, no longer Achaeans, but Dorians,—a name which they derived from Dorieus; for it was he who gathered them together. The rest of the story is told by you Lacedaemonians as part of the history of Sparta.

The return of the Achaeans under the new name of Dorians.

Meg. To be sure.

Ath. Thus, after digressing from the original subject of laws into music and drinking-bouts, the argument has, providentially, come back to the same point, and presents to us another handle. For we have reached the settlement of Lacedaemon; which, as you truly say, is in laws and in institutions the sister of Crete. And we are all the better for the digression, because we have gone through various governments and settlements, and have been present at the foundation of a first, second, and third state, succeeding one another in infinite time. And now there appears on the horizon a fourth state or nation which was once in process of settlement and has continued settled to this day. If, out of all this, we are able to discern what is well or ill settled, and what laws are the salvation and what are the destruction of cities, and what changes would make a state happy, O Megillus and Cleinias, we may now begin again, unless we have some fault to find with the previous discussion.

683

Settlement of Lacedaemon, the sister settlement of Crete.

The fourth stage: a nation or federation.

Meg. If some God, Stranger, would promise us that our new enquiry about legislation would be as good and full as the present, I would go a great way to hear such another, and would think that a day as long as this—and we are now approaching the longest day of the year—was too short for the discussion.

Ath. Then I suppose that we must consider this subject?

Meg. Certainly.

Ath. Let us place ourselves in thought at the moment when La-

cedaemon and Argos and Messene and the rest of the Peloponnesus
were all in complete subjection, Megillus, to your ancestors; for
afterwards, as the legend informs us, they divided their army into
three portions, and settled three cities, Argos, Messene, Lacedaemon.

Meg. True.

Ath. Temenus was the king of Argos, Cresphontes of Messene,
Procles and Eurysthenes of Lacedaemon.

Meg. Certainly.

Ath. To these kings all the men of that day made oath that they
would assist them, if any one subverted their kingdom.

Meg. True.

Ath. But can a kingship be destroyed, or was any other form of
government ever destroyed, by any but the rulers themselves? No
indeed, by Zeus. Have we already forgotten what was said a little
while ago[1]?

Meg. No.

Ath. And may we not now further confirm what was then mentioned? For we have come upon facts which have brought us back
again to the same principle; so that, in resuming the discussion, we
shall not be enquiring about an empty theory, but about events
which actually happened. The case was as follows:—Three royal
heroes made oath to three cities which were under a kingly government, and the cities to the kings, that both rulers and subjects
should govern and be governed according to the laws which were
common to all of them: the rulers promised that as time and the
race went forward they would not make their rule more arbitrary;
and the subjects said that, if the rulers observed these conditions,
they would never subvert or permit others to subvert those kingdoms; the kings were to assist kings and peoples when injured, and
the peoples were to assist peoples and kings in like manner. Is not
this the fact?

Meg. Yes.

Ath. And the three states to whom these laws were given, whether
their kings or any others were the authors of them, had therefore
the greatest security for the maintenance of their constitutions?

Meg. What security?

Ath. That the other two states were always to come to the rescue
against a rebellious third.

Meg. True.

Ath. Many persons say that legislators ought to impose such laws
as the mass of the people will be ready to receive; but this is just as

[1] Cp. *supra*, 682 D, E.

Laws III

ATHE-
NIAN,
MEGIL-
LUS.

The time
of the
conquest.

684

The three
Dorian
kingdoms
were to
be gov-
erned by
common
laws, and
to help
one an-
other in
case of
need.

Laws III

ATHE-
NIAN,
MEGIL-
LUS.

And be-
sides this
close al-
liance
there was
another
advant-
age. The
early
legislators
had a
clear
stage.

No debts
or vested
interests.

Yet the
Dorian
settlement
[685]
turned
out bad-
ly, and
the laws
originally
given to
the three
kingdoms
were only
retained
by
Sparta.

The
Dorian
con-
federacy
was de-

if one were to command gymnastic masters or physicians to treat or cure their pupils or patients in an agreeable manner.

Meg. Exactly.

Ath. Whereas the physician may often be too happy if he can re-store health, and make the body whole, with out any very great in-fliction of pain.

Meg. Certainly.

Ath. There was also another advantage possessed by the men of that day, which greatly lightened the task of passing laws[1].

Meg. What advantage?

Ath. The legislators of that day, when they equalized property, escaped the great accusation which generally arises in legislation, if a person attempts to disturb the possession of land, or to abolish debts, because he sees that without this reform there can never be any real equality. Now, in general, when the legislator attempts to make a new settlement of such matters, every one meets him with the cry, that 'he is not to disturb vested interests,'—declaring with imprecations that he is introducing agrarian laws and cancelling of debts, until a man is at his wits' end; whereas no one could quarrel with the Dorians for distributing the land,—there was nothing to hinder them; and as for debts, they had none which were consider-able or of old standing.

Meg. Very true.

Ath. But then, my good friends, why did the settlement and legis-lation of their country turn out so badly?

Meg. How do you mean; and why do you blame them?

Ath. There were three kingdoms, and of these, two quickly cor-rupted their original constitution and laws, and the only one which remained was the Spartan.

Meg. The question which you ask is not easily answered.

Ath. And yet must be answered when we are enquiring about laws, this being our old man's sober game of play, whereby we be-guile the way, as I was saying when we first set out on our journey[2].

Meg. Certainly; and we must find out why this was.

Ath. What laws are more worthy of our attention than those which have regulated such cities? or what settlements of states are greater or more famous?

Meg. I know of none.

Ath. Can we doubt that your ancestors intended these institu-tions not only for the protection of Peloponnesus, but of all the Hellenes, in case they were attacked by the barbarian? For the in-habitants of the region about Ilium, when they provoked by their

[1] Cp. *infra*, v. 736 C.   [2] Cp. *supra*, i. 625.

insolence the Trojan war, relied upon the power of the Assyrians and the Empire of Ninus, which still existed and had a great prestige; the people of those days fearing the united Assyrian Empire just as we now fear the Great King. And the second capture of Troy was a serious offence against them, because Troy was a portion of the Assyrian Empire. To meet the danger the single army was distributed between three cities by the royal brothers, sons of Heracles,—a fair device, as it seemed, and a far better arrangement than the expedition against Troy. For, firstly, the people of that day had, as they thought, in the Heraclidae better leaders than the Pelopidae; in the next place, they considered that their army was superior in valour to that which went against Troy; for, although the latter conquered the Trojans, they were themselves conquered by the Heraclidae—Achaeans by Dorians. May we not suppose that this was the intention with which the men of those days framed the constitutions of their states?

Meg. Quite true.

Ath. And would not men who had shared with one another many dangers, and were governed by a single race of royal brothers, and had taken the advice of oracles, and in particular of the Delphian Apollo, be likely to think that such states would be firmly and lastingly established?

Meg. Of course they would.

Ath. Yet these institutions, of which such great expectations were entertained, seem to have all rapidly vanished away; with the exception, as I was saying, of that small part of them which existed in your land. And this third part has never to this day ceased warring against the two others; whereas, if the original idea had been carried out, and they had agreed to be one, their power would have been invincible in war.

Meg. No doubt.

Ath. But what was the ruin of this glorious confederacy? Here is a subject well worthy of consideration.

Meg. Certainly, no one will ever find more striking instances of laws or governments being the salvation or destruction of great and noble interests, than are here presented to his view.

Ath. Then now we seem to have happily arrived at a real and important question.

Meg. Very true.

Ath. Did you never remark, sage friend, that all men, and we ourselves at this moment, often fancy that they see some beautiful thing which might have effected wonders if any one had only known how to make a right use of it in some way; and yet this mode of

signed to protect the Hellenes against the Assyrian Empire.

686
Why, with its great prestige and many advantages, did it fall to pieces?

The con-
federates
did not
under-
stand
how to
keep to-
gether.
Had they
only been
united,
[687]
they
might
have done
anything.

looking at things may turn out after all to be a mistake, and not according to nature, either in our own case or in any other?

Meg. To what are you referring, and what do you mean?

Ath. I was thinking of my own admiration of the aforesaid Heracleid expedition, which was so noble, and might have had such wonderful results for the Hellenes, if only rightly used; and I was just laughing at myself.

Meg. But were you not right and wise in speaking as you did, and we in assenting to you?

Ath. Perhaps; and yet I cannot help observing that any one who sees anything great or powerful, immediately has the feeling that— 'If the owner only knew how to use his great and noble possession, how happy would he be, and what great results would he achieve!'

Meg. And would he not be justified?

Ath. Reflect; in what point of view does this sort of praise appear just: First, in reference to the question in hand:—If the then commanders had known how to arrange their army properly, how would they have attained success? Would not this have been the way? They would have bound them all firmly together and preserved them for ever, giving them freedom and dominion at pleasure, combined with the power of doing in the whole world, Hellenic and barbarian, whatever they and their descendants desired. What other aim would they have had?

Meg. Very good.

Ath. Suppose any one were in the same way to express his admiration at the sight of great wealth or family honour, or the like, he would praise them under the idea that through them he would attain either all or the greater and chief part of what he desires.

Meg. He would.

Ath. Well, now, and does not the argument show that there is one common desire of all mankind?

Meg. What is it?

Ath. The desire which a man has, that all things, if possible,—at any rate, things human,—may come to pass in accordance with his soul's desire.

Meg. Certainly.

Men
desire
things
which are
not for
their
good.

Ath. And having this desire always, and at every time of life, in youth, in manhood, in age, he cannot help always praying for the fulfilment of it.

Meg. No doubt.

Ath. And we join in the prayers of our friends, and ask for them what they ask for themselves.

Meg. We do.

Ath. Dear is the son to the father—the younger to the elder.

Meg. Of course.

Ath. And yet the son often prays to obtain things which the father prays that he may not obtain.

Meg. When the son is young and foolish, you mean?

Ath. Yes; or when the father, in the dotage of age or the heat of youth, having no sense of right and justice, prays with fervour, under the influence of feelings akin to those of Theseus when he cursed the unfortunate Hippolytus, do you imagine that the son, having a sense of right and justice, will join in his father's prayers?

Meg. I understand you to mean that a man should not desire or be in a hurry to have all things according to his wish, for his wish may be at variance with his reason. But every state and every individual ought to pray and strive for wisdom.

Ath. Yes; and I remember, and you will remember, what I said at first, that a statesman and legislator ought to ordain laws with a view to wisdom; while you were arguing that the good lawgiver ought to order all with a view to war. And to this I replied that there were four virtues, but that upon your view one of them only was the aim of legislation; whereas you ought to regard all virtue, and especially that which comes first, and is the leader of all the rest—I mean wisdom and mind and opinion, having affection and desire in their train. And now the argument returns to the same point, and I say once more, in jest if you like, or in earnest if you like, that the prayer of a fool is full of danger, being likely to end in the opposite of what he desires. And if you would rather receive my words in earnest, I am willing that you should; and you will find, I suspect, as I have said already, that not cowardice was the cause of the ruin of the Dorian kings and of their whole design, nor ignorance of military matters, either on the part of the rulers or of their subjects; but their misfortunes were due to their general degeneracy, and especially to their ignorance of the most important human affairs. That was then, and is still, and always will be the case, as I will endeavour, if you will allow me, to make out and demonstrate as well as I am able to you who are my friends, in the course of the argument.

Cle. Pray go on, Stranger;—compliments are troublesome, but we will show, not in word but in deed, how greatly we prize your words, for we will give them our best attention; and that is the way in which a freeman best shows his approval or disapproval.

Meg. Excellent, Cleinias; let us do as you say.

Cle. By all means, if Heaven wills. Go on.

Ath. Well, then, proceeding in the same train of thought, I say

Laws III

ATHE-
NIAN,
CLEINIAS,
MEGIL-
LUS.

688

The statesman in making laws should have in view all the four virtues, and not one only

Ignorance of the highest things the ruin of the Dorian power.

that the greatest ignorance was the ruin of the Dorian power, and
that now, as then, ignorance is ruin. And if this be true, the legislator must endeavour to implant wisdom in states, and banish ignorance to the utmost of his power.

Cle. That is evident.

689 *Ath.* Then now consider what is really the greatest ignorance. I
should like to know whether you and Megillus would agree with me
in what I am about to say; for my opinion is——

Cle. What?

The
greatest
ignorance
is to
know
and not
to do the
good and
noble.

Ath. That the greatest ignorance is when a man hates that which
he nevertheless thinks to be good and noble, and loves and embraces
that which he knows to be unrighteous and evil. This disagreement
between the sense of pleasure and the judgment of reason in the
soul is, in my opinion, the worst ignorance; and also the greatest,
because affecting the great mass of the human soul; for the principle which feels pleasure and pain in the individual is like the mass
or populace in a state. And when the soul is opposed to knowledge,
or opinion, or reason, which are her natural lords, that I call folly,
just as in the state, when the multitude refuses to obey their rulers
and the laws; or, again, in the individual, when fair reasonings have
their habitation in the soul and yet do no good, but rather the reverse of good. All these cases I term the worst ignorance, whether in
individuals or in states. You will understand, Stranger, that I am
speaking of something which is very different from the ignorance of
handicraftsmen.

Cle. Yes, my friend, we understand and agree.

Ath. Let us, then, in the first place declare and affirm that the
citizen who does not know these things ought never to have any
kind of authority entrusted to him: he must be stigmatized as ignorant, even though he be versed in calculation and skilled in all sorts
of accomplishments, and feats of mental dexterity; and the opposite
are to be called wise, even although, in the words of the proverb,
they know neither how to read nor how to swim; and to them, as to

No
wisdom
where
there is
no har-
mony.

men of sense, authority is to be committed. For, O my friends, how
can there be the least shadow of wisdom when there is no harmony?
There is none; but the noblest and greatest of harmonies may be
truly said to be the greatest wisdom; and of this he is a partaker
who lives according to reason; whereas he who is devoid of reason is
the destroyer of his house and the very opposite of a saviour of the
state: he is utterly ignorant of political wisdom. Let this, then, as I
was saying, be laid down by us.

Cle. Let it be so laid down.

Ath. I suppose that there must be rulers and subjects in states?

Cle. Certainly.

Ath. And what are the principles on which men rule and obey in cities, whether great or small; and similarly in families? What are they, and how many in number? Is there not one claim of authority which is always just,—that of fathers and mothers and in general of progenitors to rule over their offspring?

Cle. There is.

Ath. Next follows the principle that the noble should rule over the ignoble; and, thirdly, that the elder should rule and the younger obey?

Cle. To be sure.

Ath. And, fourthly, that slaves should be ruled, and their masters rule?

Cle. Of course.

Ath. Fifthly, if I am not mistaken, comes the principle that the stronger shall rule, and the weaker be ruled?

Cle. That is a rule not to be disobeyed.

Ath. Yes, and a rule which prevails very widely among all creatures, and is according to nature, as the Theban poet Pindar once said; and the sixth principle, and the greatest of all, is, that the wise should lead and command, and the ignorant follow and obey; and yet, O thou most wise Pindar, as I should reply to him, this surely is not contrary to nature, but according to nature, being the rule of law over willing subjects, and not a rule of compulsion.

Cle. Most true.

Ath. There is a seventh kind of rule which is awarded by lot, and is dear to the Gods and a token of good fortune: he on whom the lot falls is a ruler, and he who fails in obtaining the lot goes away and is the subject; and this we affirm to be quite just.

Cle. Certainly.

Ath. 'Then now,' as we say playfully to any of those who lightly undertake the making of laws, 'you see, legislator, the principles of government, how many they are, and that they are naturally opposed to each other. There we have discovered a fountain-head of seditions, to which you must attend. And, first, we will ask you to consider with us, how and in what respect the kings of Argos and Messene violated these our maxims, and ruined themselves and the great and famous Hellenic power of the olden time. Was it because they did not know how wisely Hesiod spoke when he said that the half is often more than the whole? His meaning was, that when to take the whole would be dangerous, and to take the half would be the safe and moderate course, then the moderate or better was more than the immoderate or worse.'

690
Laws III

ATHE-
NIAN,
CLEINIAS

The
various
kinds of
author-
ity:—
(1) of
parents
over
children;
(2) of
noble
over
ignoble;
(3) of
elder over
younger;
(4) of
master
over
slave;
(5) of
stronger
over
weaker;
(6) of
wise over
ignorant;
(7) of the
winner of
the lot
over the
loser.

The
kings of
Argos and
Messene
did
not know
that 'the
half is
often
more
than the
whole.'

Cle. Very true.

Ath. And may we suppose this immoderate spirit to be more fatal when found among kings than when among peoples?

691

ATHE-
NIAN,
CLEINIAS,
MEGIL-
LUS.

Cle. The probability is that ignorance will be a disorder especially prevalent among kings, because they lead a proud and luxurious life.

Ath. Is it not palpable that the chief aim of the kings of that time was to get the better of the established laws, and that they were not in harmony with the principles which they had agreed to observe by word and oath? This want of harmony may have had the appearance of wisdom, but was really, as we assert, the greatest ignorance, and utterly overthrew the whole empire by dissonance and harsh discord.

Cle. Very likely.

Ath. Good; and what measures ought the legislator to have then taken in order to avert this calamity? Truly there is no great wisdom in knowing, and no great difficulty in telling, after the evil has happened; but to have foreseen the remedy at the time would have taken a much wiser head than ours.

Meg. What do you mean?

Ath. Any one who looks at what has occurred with you Lacedaemonians, Megillus, may easily know and may easily say what ought to have been done at that time.

Meg. Speak a little more clearly.

Ath. Nothing can be clearer than the observation which I am about to make.

Meg. What is it?

Too much of anything is fatal to any man, especially too much power to a despot.

Ath. That if any one gives too great a power to anything, too large a sail to a vessel, too much food to the body, too much authority to the mind, and does not observe the mean, everything is overthrown, and, in the wantonness of excess runs in the one case to disorders, and in the other to injustice, which is the child of excess. I mean to say, my dear friends, that there is no soul of man, young and irresponsible, who will be able to sustain the temptation of arbitrary power—no one who will not, under such circumstances, become filled with folly, that worst of diseases, and be hated by his nearest and dearest friends: when this happens his kingdom is undermined, and all his power vanishes from him. And great legislators who know the mean should take heed of the danger. As far as we can guess at this distance of time, what happened was as follows:—

Meg. What?

Sparta was

Ath. A God, who watched over Sparta, seeing into the future, gave you two families of kings instead of one; and thus brought you

Laws III

ATHE-
NIAN,
CLEINIAS.

692

saved by
the dual
monarchy
and the
institu-
tion of
Elders
and
Ephors.

more within the limits of moderation. In the next place, some human wisdom mingled with divine power, observing that the constitution of your government was still feverish and excited, tempered your inborn strength and pride of birth with the moderation which comes of age, making the power of your twenty-eight elders equal with that of the kings in the most important matters. But your third saviour, perceiving that your government was still swelling and foaming, and desirous to impose a curb upon it, instituted the Ephors, whose power he made to resemble that of magistrates elected by lot; and by this arrangement the kingly office, being compounded of the right elements and duly moderated, was preserved, and was the means of preserving all the rest. Since, if there had been only the original legislators, Temenus, Cresphontes, and their contemporaries, as far as they were concerned not even the portion of Aristodemus would have been preserved; for they had no proper experience in legislation, or they would surely not have imagined that oaths would moderate a youthful spirit invested with a power which might be converted into a tyranny. Now that God has instructed us what sort of government would have been or will be lasting, there is no wisdom, as I have already said, in judging after the event; there is no difficulty in learning from an example which has already occurred. But if any one could have foreseen all this at the time, and had been able to moderate the government of the three kingdoms and unite them into one, he might have saved all the excellent institutions which were then conceived; and no Persian or any other armament would have dared to attack us, or would have regarded Hellas as a power to be despised.

Cle. True.

Ath. There was small credit to us, Cleinias, in defeating them; and the discredit was, not that the conquerors did not win glorious victories both by land and sea, but what, in my opinion, brought discredit was, first of all, the circumstance that of the three cities one only fought on behalf of Hellas, and the two others were so utterly good for nothing that the one was waging a mighty war against Lacedaemon, and was thus preventing her from rendering assistance, while the city of Argos, which had the precedence at the time of the distribution, when asked to aid in repelling the barbarian, would not answer to the call, or give aid. Many things might be told about Hellas in connection with that war which are far from honourable; nor, indeed, can we rightly say that Hellas repelled the invader; for the truth is, that unless the Athenians and Lacedaemonians, acting in concert, had warded off the impending yoke, all the tribes of Hellas would have been fused in a chaos of Hellenes ming-

The
Athenians
were as-
sisted
against
the Per-
sians by
the
Spartans
alone.
Disgrace-
ful con-
duct of
Messene
and
Argos.

693

ling with one another, of barbarians mingling with Hellenes, and Hellenes with barbarians; just as nations who are now subject to the Persian power, owing to unnatural separations and combinations of them, are dispersed and scattered, and live miserably. These, Cleinias and Megillus, are the reproaches which we have to make against statesmen and legislators, as they are called, past and present, if we would analyze the causes of their failure, and find out what else might have been done. We said, for instance, just now, that there ought to be no great and unmixed powers; and this was under the idea that a state ought to be free and wise and harmonious, and that a legislator ought to legislate with a view to this end. Nor is there any reason to be surprised at our continually proposing aims for the legislator which appear not to be always the same; but we should consider when we say that temperance is to be the aim, or wisdom is to be the aim, or friendship is to be the aim, that all these aims are really the same; and if so a variety in the modes of expression ought not to disturb us.

Cle. Let us resume the argument in that spirit. And now, speaking of friendship and wisdom and freedom, I wish that you would tell me at what, in your opinion, the legislator should aim.

Ath. Hear me, then: there are two mother forms of states from which the rest may be truly said to be derived; and one of them may be called monarchy and the other democracy: the Persians have the highest form of the one, and we of the other; almost all the rest, as I was saying, are variations of these. Now, if you are to have liberty and the combination of friendship with wisdom, you must have both these forms of government in a measure; the argument emphatically declares that no city can be well governed which is not made up of both[1].

Cle. Impossible.

Ath. Neither the one, if it be exclusively and excessively attached to monarchy, nor the other, if it be similarly attached to freedom, observes moderation; but your states, the Laconian and Cretan, have more of it; and the same was the case with the Athenians and Persians of old time, but now they have less. Shall I tell you why?

Cle. By all means, if it will tend to elucidate our subject.

Ath. Hear, then:—There was a time when the Persians had more of the state which is a mean between slavery and freedom. In the reign of Cyrus they were freemen and also lords of many others: the rulers gave a share of freedom to the subjects, and being treated as equals, the soldiers were on better terms with their generals, and showed themselves more ready in the hour of danger. And if there

[1] Cp. *infra*, vi. 756 E; Arist. Pol. ii. 6, § 18.

was any wise man among them, who was able to give good counsel, he imparted his wisdom to the public; for the king was not jealous, but allowed him full liberty of speech, and gave honour to those who could advise him in any matter. And the nation waxed in all respects, because there was freedom and friendship and communion of mind among them.

Cle. That certainly appears to have been the case.

Ath. How, then, was this advantage lost under Cambyses, and again recovered under Darius? Shall I try to divine?

Cle. The enquiry, no doubt, has a bearing upon our subject.

Ath. I imagine that Cyrus, though a great and patriotic general, had never given his mind to education, and never attended to the order of his household.

Cle. What makes you say so?

Ath. I think that from his youth upwards he was a soldier, and entrusted the education of his children to the women; and they brought them up from their childhood as the favourites of fortune, who were blessed already, and needed no more blessings. They thought that they were happy enough, and that no one should be allowed to oppose them in any way, and they compelled every one to praise all that they said or did. This was how they brought them up.

Cle. A splendid education truly!

Ath. Such an one as women were likely to give them, and especially princesses who had recently grown rich, and in the absence of the men, too, who were occupied in wars and dangers, and had no time to look after them.

Cle. What would you expect?

Ath. Their father had possessions of cattle and sheep, and many herds of men and other animals; but he did not consider that those to whom he was about to make them over were not trained in his own calling, which was Persian; for the Persians are shepherds— sons of a rugged land, which is a stern mother, and well fitted to produce a sturdy race able to live in the open air and go without sleep, and also to fight, if fighting is required[1]. He did not observe that his sons were trained differently; through the so-called blessing of being royal they were educated in the Median fashion by women and eunuchs, which led to their becoming such as people do become when they are brought up unreproved. And so, after the death of Cyrus, his sons, in the fulness of luxury and licence, took the kingdom, and first one slew the other because he could not endure a rival; and, afterwards, the slayer himself, mad with wine and bru-

Laws III

ATHE-
NIAN,
CLEINIAS.

they lost
under
Camby-
ses.

Cyrus
himself
had been
brought
up well,
but he
neglected
the edu-
cation of
his chil-
dren.

695

[1] Cp. Arist. Pol. vii, 2, § 10.

Laws III

ATHE-
NIAN,
CLEINIAS,
MEGIL-
LUS.

Darius,
too, was
an ex-
cellent
prince:

but, like
Cyrus, he
took no
care
about his
children's
educa-
tion.

696

tality, lost his kingdom through the Medes and the Eunuch, as they called him, who despised the folly of Cambyses.

Cle. So runs the tale, and such probably were the facts.

Ath. Yes; and the tradition says, that the empire came back to the Persians, through Darius and the seven chiefs.

Cle. True.

Ath. Let us note the rest of the story. Observe, that Darius was not the son of a king, and had not received a luxurious education. When he came to the throne, being one of the seven, he divided the country into seven portions, and of this arrangement there are some shadowy traces still remaining; he made laws upon the principle of introducing universal equality in the order of the state, and he embodied in his laws the settlement of the tribute which Cyrus promised,—thus creating a feeling of friendship and community among all the Persians, and attaching the people to him with money and gifts. Hence his armies cheerfully acquired for him countries as large as those which Cyrus had left behind him. Darius was succeeded by his son Xerxes; and he again was brought up in the royal and luxurious fashion. Might we not most justly say: 'O Darius, how came you to bring up Xerxes in the same way in which Cyrus brought up Cambyses, and not to see his fatal mistake?' For Xerxes, being the creation of the same education, met with much the same fortune as Cambyses; and from that time until now there has never been a really great king among the Persians, although they are all called Great. And their degeneracy is not to be attributed to chance, as I maintain; the reason is rather the evil life which is generally led by the sons of very rich and royal persons; for never will boy or man, young or old, excel in virtue, who has been thus educated. And this, I say, is what the legislator has to consider, and what at the present moment has to be considered by us. Justly may you, O Lacedaemonians, be praised, in that you do not give special honour or a special education to wealth rather than to poverty, or to a royal rather than to a private station, where the divine and inspired lawgiver has not originally commanded them to be given. For no man ought to have pre-eminent honour in a state because he surpasses others in wealth, any more than because he is swift of foot or fair or strong, unless he have some virtue in him; nor even if he have virtue, unless he have this particular virtue of temperance.

Meg. What do you mean, Stranger?

Ath. I suppose that courage is a part of virtue?

Meg. To be sure.

Ath. Then, now hear and judge for yourself:—Would you like to have for a fellow-lodger or neighbour a very courageous man, who had no control over himself?

Meg. Heaven forbid!

Ath. Or an artist, who was clever in his profession, but a rogue?

Meg. Certainly not.

Ath. And surely justice does not grow apart from temperance?

Meg. Impossible.

Ath. Any more than our pattern wise man, whom we exhibited as having his pleasures and pains in accordance with and corresponding to true reason, can be intemperate[1]?

Meg. No.

Ath. There is a further consideration relating to the due and undue award of honours in states.

Meg. What is it?

Ath. I should like to know whether temperance without the other virtues, existing alone in the soul of man, is rightly to be praised or blamed?

Meg. I cannot tell.

Ath. And that is the best answer; for whichever alternative you had chosen, I think that you would have gone wrong.

Meg. I am fortunate.

Ath. Very good; a quality, which is a mere appendage of things which can be praised or blamed, does not deserve an expression of opinion, but is best passed over in silence.

Meg. You are speaking of temperance?

Ath. Yes; but of the other virtues, that which having this appendage is also most beneficial, will be most deserving of honour, and next that which is beneficial in the next degree; and so each of them will be rightly honoured according to a regular order.

Meg. True.

Ath. And ought not the legislator to determine these classes?

Meg. Certainly he should.

Ath. Suppose that we leave to him the arrangement of details. But the general division of laws according to their importance into a first and second and third class, we who are lovers of law may make ourselves.

Meg. Very good.

Ath. We maintain, then, that a State which would be safe and happy, as far as the nature of man allows, must and ought to distribute honour and dishonour in the right way. And the right way is to place the goods of the soul first and highest in the scale, always

[1] Cp *supra*, 689 D.

Temperance not a virtue, but rather an appendage or condition of the virtues. Not much to be said about it.

697

The order in which the law should arrange

Laws III

ATHE-
NIAN,
MEGIL-
LUS.

goods:—
(1) goods
of the
soul;
(2) goods
of the
body; (3)
money
and pro-
perty.

The
growth
of des-
potism
among
the Per-
sians was
the ruin
of their
nation-
ality.

698

assuming temperance to be the condition of them; and to assign the second place to the goods of the body; and the third place to money and property. And if any legislator or state departs from this rule by giving money the place of honour, or in any way preferring that which is really last; may we not say, that he or the state is doing an unholy and unpatriotic thing?

Meg. Yes; let that be plainly declared.

Ath. The consideration of the Persian governments led us thus far to enlarge. We remarked that the Persians grew worse and worse. And we affirm the reason of this to have been, that they too much diminished the freedom of the people, and introduced too much of despotism, and so destroyed friendship and community of feeling. And when there is an end of these, no longer do the governors govern on behalf of their subjects or of the people, but on behalf of themselves; and if they think that they can gain ever so small an advantage for themselves, they devastate cities, and send fire and desolation among friendly races. And as they hate ruthlessly and horribly, so are they hated; and when they want the people to fight for them, they find no community of feeling or willingness to risk their lives on their behalf; their untold myriads are useless to them on the field of battle, and they think that their salvation depends on the employment of mercenaries and strangers whom they hire, as if they were in want of more men. And they cannot help being stupid, since they proclaim by their actions that the ordinary distinctions of right and wrong which are made in a state are a trifle, when compared with gold and silver.

Meg. Quite true.

Ath. And now enough of the Persians, and their present maladministration of their government, which is owing to the excess of slavery and despotism among them.

Meg. Good.

The
Athenian
constitu-
tion was
excellent
at the
time of
the
Persian
invasion.

Ath. Next, we must pass in review the government of Attica in like manner, and from this show that entire freedom and the absence of all superior authority is not by any means so good as government by others when properly limited, which was our ancient Athenian constitution at the time when the Persians made their attack on Hellas, or, speakingly more correctly, on the whole continent of Europe. There were four classes, arranged according to a property census, and reverence was our queen and mistress, and made us willing to live in obedience to the laws which then prevailed. Also the vastness of the Persian armament, both by sea and on land, caused a helpless terror, which made us more and more the servants of our rulers and of the laws; and for all these reasons an exceeding harmony prevailed among us. About ten years before the naval engagement at Salamis, Datis came, leading a Persian host by command of Darius, which was expressly directed against the Athenians and Eretrians, having orders to carry them away captive; and these orders he was to execute under pain of death. Now Datis and his myriads soon became complete masters of Eretria, and he sent a fearful report to Athens that no Eretrian had escaped him; for the soldiers of Datis had joined hands and netted the whole of Eretria. And this report, whether well or ill founded, was terrible to all the Hellenes, and above all to the Athenians, and they dispatched embassies in all directions, but no one was willing to come to their relief, with the exception of the Lacedaemonians; and they, either because they were detained by the Messenian war, which was then going on, or for some other reason of which we are not told, came a day too late for the battle of Marathon. After a while, the news arrived of mighty preparations being made, and innumerable threats came from the king. Then, as time went on, a rumour reached us that Darius had died, and that his son, who was young and hotheaded, had come to the throne and was persisting in his design. The Athenians were under the impression that the whole expedition was directed against them, in consequence of the battle of Marathon; and hearing of the bridge over the Hellespont, and the canal of Athos, and the host of ships, considering that there was no salvation for them either by land or by sea, for there was no one to help them, and remembering that in the first expedition, when the Persians destroyed Eretria, no one came to their help, or would risk the danger of an alliance with them, they thought that this would happen again, at least on land; nor, when they looked to the sea, could they descry any hope of salvation; for they were attacked by a thousand vessels and more. One chance of safety remained, slight indeed and desperate, but their only one. They saw that on the former occasion they had gained a seemingly impossible victory, and borne up by this hope, they found that their only refuge was in themselves and in the Gods. All these things created in them the spirit of friendship; there was the fear of the moment, and there was that higher fear, which they had acquired by obedience to their ancient laws, and which I have several times in the preceding discourse called reverence, of which the good man ought to be a willing servant, and of which the coward is independent and fearless. If this fear had not possessed them, they would never have met the enemy, or defended their temples and sepulchres and their country, and everything that was near and dear to them, as they did; but little by little they would have been all scattered and dispersed.

Laws III

ATHE-
NIAN.

699
Renewal
of the
attack by
Xerxes.

The
Athe-
nians,
though
unsup-
ported,
con-
quered,
because
they were
a united
people,
and
trusted to
them-
selves
and God.

Their
habit of
obedi-

Laws III

ATHE-
NIAN,
MEGIL-
LUS.

ence to
law in-
spired in
them the
fear of
disgrace.

Too much
rule the
ruin of
[700]
the Per-
sians, too
much
liberty of
the
Athe-
nians.

Ancient
simplicity
and good
order of
music.

The reign
of mis-
rule
intro-
duced by
the poets.

Meg. Your words, Athenian, are quite true, and worthy of your-self and of your country.

Ath. They are true, Megillus; and to you, who have inherited the virtues of your ancestors, I may properly speak of the actions of that day. And I would wish you and Cleinias to consider whether my words have not also a bearing on legislation; for I am not discoursing only for the pleasure of talking, but for the argument's sake. Please to remark that the experience both of ourselves and the Persians was, in a certain sense, the same; for as they led their people into utter servitude, so we too led ours into all freedom. And now, how shall we proceed? for I would like you to observe that our previous arguments have a good deal to say for themselves.

Meg. True; but I wish that you would give us a fuller explanation.

Ath. I will. Under the ancient laws, my friends, the people was not as now the master, but rather the willing servant of the laws.

Meg. What laws do you mean?

Ath. In the first place, let us speak of the laws about music,—that is to say, such music as then existed,—in order that we may trace the growth of the excess of freedom from the beginning. Now music was early divided among us into certain kinds and manners. One sort consisted of prayers to the Gods, which were called hymns; and there was another and opposite sort called lamentations, and another termed paeans, and another, celebrating the birth of Dionysus, called, I believe, 'dithyrambs.' And they used the actual word 'laws,' or νόμοι, for another kind of song; and to this they added the term 'citharoedic.' All these and others were duly distinguished, nor were the performers allowed to confuse one style of music with another. And the authority which determined and gave judgment, and punished the disobedient, was not expressed in a hiss, nor in the most unmusical shouts of the multitude, as in our days, nor in applause and clapping of hands. But the directors of public instruction insisted that the spectators should listen in silence to the end; and boys and their tutors, and the multitude in general, were kept quiet by a hint from a stick. Such was the good order which the multitude were willing to observe; they would never have dared to give judgment by noisy cries. And then, as time went on, the poets themselves introduced the reign of vulgar and lawless innovation. They were men of genius, but they had no perception of what is just and lawful in music; raging like Bacchanals and possessed with inordinate delights—mingling lamentations with hymns, and paeans with dithyrambs; imitating the sounds of the flute on the lyre, and making one general confusion; ignorantly affirming that music has no truth, and, whether good or bad, can only be judged of rightly by the pleasure of the hearer[1]. And by composing such licentious works, and adding to them words as licentious, they have inspired the multitude with lawlessness and boldness, and made them fancy that they can judge for themselves about melody and song. And in this way the theatres from being mute have become vocal, as though they had understanding of good and bad in music and poetry; and instead of an aristocracy, an evil sort of theatrocracy has grown up[2]. For if the democracy which judged had only consisted of educated persons, no fatal harm would have been done; but in music there first arose the universal conceit of omniscience and general lawlessness;—freedom came following afterwards, and men, fancying that they knew what they did not know, had no longer any fear, and the absence of fear begets shamelessness. For what is this shamelessness, which is so evil a thing, but the insolent refusal to regard the opinion of the better by reason of an over-daring sort of liberty?

Meg. Very true.

Ath. Consequent upon this freedom comes the other freedom, of disobedience to rulers[3]; and then the attempt to escape the control and exhortation of father, mother, elders, and when near the end, the control of the laws also; and at the very end there is the contempt of oaths and pledges, and no regard at all for the Gods,—herein they exhibit and imitate the old so-called Titanic nature, and come to the same point as the Titans when they rebelled against God, leading a life of endless evils. But why have I said all this? I ask, because the argument ought to be pulled up from time to time, and not be allowed to run away, but held with bit and bridle, and then we shall not, as the proverb says, fall off our ass. Let us then once more ask the question, To what end has all this been said?

Meg. Very good.

Ath. This, then, has been said for the sake——

Meg. Of what?

Ath. We were maintaining that the lawgiver ought to have three things in view: first, that the city for which he legislates should be free; and secondly, be at unity with herself; and thirdly, should have understanding;—these were our principles, were they not?

Meg. Certainly.

Ath. With a view to this we selected two kinds of government, the one the most despotic, and the other the most free; and now we are considering which of them is the right form: we took a mean in both cases, of despotism in the one, and of liberty in the other, and we saw that in a mean they attained their perfection; but that when

---

Laws III

701
ATHE-
NIAN,
MEGIL-
LUS.

The conceit of omniscience led to lawlessness.

Three chief objects of legislation:—freedom, harmony, good sense.

[1] Cp. Rep. iii. 397 foll.   [2] Cp. Ar. Pol. viii. 6.   [3] Cp. Rep. iv. 424 E.

Laws III

702
ATHE-
NIAN,
CLEINIAS,
MEGIL-
LUS.

they were carried to the extreme of either, slavery or licence, neither party were the gainers.

Meg. Very true.

Ath. And that was our reason for considering the settlement of the Dorian army, and of the city built by Dardanus at the foot of the mountains, and the removal of cities to the seashore, and of our mention of the first men, who were the survivors of the deluge. And all that was previously said about music and drinking, and what preceded, was said with the view of seeing how a state might be best administered, and how an individual might best order his own life. And now, Megillus and Cleinias, how can we put to the proof the value of our words?

Cle. Stranger, I think that I see how a proof of their value may be obtained. This discussion of ours appears to me to have been singularly fortunate, and just what I at this moment want; most auspiciously have you and my friend Megillus come in my way. For I will tell you what has happened to me; and I regard the coincidence as a sort of omen. The greater part of Crete is going to send out a colony, and they have entrusted the management of the affair to the Cnosians; and the Cnosian government to me and nine others. And they desire us to give them any laws which we please, whether taken from the Cretan model or from any other; and they do not mind about their being foreign if they are better. Grant me then this favour, which will also be a gain to yourselves:—Let us make a selection from what has been said, and then let us imagine a State of which we will suppose ourselves to be the original founders. Thus we shall proceed with our enquiry, and, at the same time, I may have the use of the framework which you are constructing, for the city which is in contemplation.

Ath. Good news, Cleinias; if Megillus has no objection, you may be sure that I will do all in my power to please you.

Cle. Thank you.

Meg. And so will I.

Cle. Excellent; and now let us begin to frame the State.

A lucky
omen.

Cleinias
and nine
other
Cnosians
have been
empow-
ered by
the
Cretan
states to
superin-
tend the
arrange-
ments of
a colony.

The three
proceed
to make
laws for
it.

BOOK IV

Athenian Stranger. And now, what will this city be? I do not mean to ask what is or will hereafter be the name of the place; that may be determined by the accident of locality or of the original settlement,—a river or fountain, or some local deity may give the sanction of a name to the newly-founded city; but I do want to know what the situation is, whether maritime or inland.

Cleinias. I should imagine, Stranger, that the city of which we are speaking is about eighty stadia distant from the sea.

Ath. And are there harbours on the seaboard?

Cle. Excellent harbours, Stranger; there could not be better.

Ath. Alas! what a prospect! And is the surrounding country productive, or in need of importations?

Cle. Hardly in need of anything.

Ath. And is there any neighbouring State?

Cle. None whatever, and that is the reason for selecting the place; in days of old, there was a migration of the inhabitants, and the region has been deserted from time immemorial.

Ath. And has the place a fair proportion of hill, and plain, and wood?

Cle. Like the rest of Crete in that.

Ath. You mean to say that there is more rock than plain?

Cle. Exactly.

Ath. Then there is some hope that your citizens may be virtuous: had you been on the sea, and well provided with harbours, and an importing rather than a producing country, some mighty saviour would have been needed, and lawgivers more than mortal, if you were ever to have a chance of preserving your state from degeneracy and discordance of manners[1]. But there is comfort in the eighty stadia; although the sea is too near, especially if, as you say, the harbours are so good. Still we may be content. The sea is pleasant enough as a daily companion, but has indeed also a bitter and brackish quality; filling the streets with merchants and shopkeepers, and begetting in the souls of men uncertain and unfaithful ways —making the state unfriendly and unfaithful both to her own citizens, and also to other nations. There is a consolation, therefore, in the country producing all things at home; and yet, owing to the ruggedness of the soil, not providing anything in great abundance. Had there been abundance, there might have been a great export trade, and a great return of gold and silver; which, as we may safely affirm, has the most fatal results on a State whose aim is the attainment of just and noble sentiments: this was said by us, if you remember, in the previous discussion[2].

Cle. I remember, and am of opinion that we both were and are in the right.

Ath. Well, but let me ask, how is the country supplied with timber for ship-building?

[1] Cp. Ar. Pol. vii. 6, §§ 1-4.   [2] *sup.* iii. 679 B.

Laws IV

ATHE-
NIAN,
CLEINIAS.

The situation of the new colony:

near the sea, and therefore favourable to virtue:

705

self-supporting:

deficient
in
timber;

and
therefore
not
adapted
for
maritime
warfare,
which is
an ad-
vantage.

706

For mari-
time war-
fare often
teaches
men to be
cowards.

Illustra-
tion of
this from
Homer.

Cle. There is no fir of any consequence, nor pine, and not much cypress; and you will find very little stone-pine or plane-wood, which shipwrights always require for the interior of ships.

Ath. These are also natural advantages.

Cle. Why so?

Ath. Because no city ought to be easily able to imitate its enemies in what is mischievous.

Cle. How does that bear upon any of the matters of which we have been speaking?

Ath. Remember, my good friend, what I said at first[1] about the Cretan laws, that they look to one thing only, and this, as you both agreed, was war; and I replied that such laws, in so far as they tended to promote virtue, were good; but in that they regarded a part only, and not the whole of virtue, I disapproved of them. And now I hope that you in your turn will follow and watch me if I legislate with a view to anything but virtue, or with a view to a part of virtue only. For I consider that the true lawgiver, like an archer, aims only at that on which some eternal beauty is always attending, and dismisses everything else, whether wealth or any other benefit, when separated from virtue. I was saying that the imitation of enemies was a bad thing; and I was thinking of a case in which a maritime people are harassed by enemies, as the Athenians were by Minos (I do not speak from any desire to recall past grievances); but he, as we know, was a great naval potentate, who compelled the inhabitants of Attica to pay him a cruel tribute; and in those days they had no ships of war as they now have, nor was the country filled with ship-timber, and therefore they could not readily build them. Hence they could not learn how to imitate their enemy at sea, and in this way, becoming sailors themselves, directly repel their enemies. Better for them to have lost many times over the seven youths, than that heavy-armed and stationary troops should have been turned into sailors, and accustomed to be often leaping on shore, and again to come running back to their ships; or should have fancied that there was no disgrace in not awaiting the attack of an enemy and dying boldly; and that there were good reasons, and plenty of them, for a man throwing away his arms, and betaking himself to flight,—which is not dishonourable, as people say, at certain times. This is the language of naval warfare, and is anything but worthy of extraordinary praise. For we should not teach bad habits, least of all to the best part of the citizens. You may learn the evil of such a practice from Homer, by whom Odysseus is introduced, rebuking Agamemnon, because he desires to draw down the

[1] Cp. i. 625 D.

ships to the sea at a time when the Achaeans are hard pressed by the Trojans,—he gets angry with him, and says:—

'Who, at a time when the battle is in full cry, biddest to drag the well-benched ships into the sea, that the prayers of the Trojans may be accomplished yet more, and high ruin fall upon us. For the Achaeans will not maintain the battle, when the ships are drawn into the sea, but they will look behind and will cease from strife; in that the counsel which you give will prove injurious.'

You see that he quite knew triremes on the sea, in the neighbourhood of fighting men, to be an evil;—lions might be trained in that way to fly from a herd of deer. Moreover, naval powers which owe their safety to ships, do not give honour to that sort of warlike excellence which is most deserving of it. For he who owes his safety to the pilot and the captain, and the oarsman, and all sorts of rather inferior persons, cannot rightly give honour to whom honour is due. But how can a state be in a right condition which cannot justly award honour?

Cle. It is hardly possible, I admit; and yet, Stranger, we Cretans are in the habit of saying that the battle of Salamis was the salvation of Hellas.

Ath. Why, yes; and that is an opinion which is widely spread both among Hellenes and barbarians. But Megillus and I say rather, that the battle of Marathon was the beginning, and the battle of Plataea the completion, of the great deliverance, and that these battles by land made the Hellenes better; whereas the sea-fights of Salamis and Artemisium—for I may as well put them both together—made them no better, if I may say so without offence about the battles which helped to save us. And in estimating the goodness of a state, we regard both the situation of the country and the order of the laws, considering that the mere preservation and continuance of life is not the most honourable thing for men, as the vulgar think, but the continuance of the best life, while we live; and that again, if I am not mistaken, is a remark which has been made already[1].

Cle. Yes.

Ath. Then we have only to ask, whether we are taking the course which we acknowledge to be the best for the settlement and legislation of states.

Cle. The best by far.

Ath. And now let me proceed to another question: Who are to be the colonists? May any one come out of all Crete; and is the idea that the population in the several states is too numerous for the means of subsistence? For I suppose that you are not going to send

[1] Cp. ii. 661.

The victories of Marathon and Plataea, not those of Salamis and Artemisium, the salvation of Hellas.

Not the mere preservation of life, but the continuance of the best life, the true end of the state.

Who are to be the colonists?

Laws IV

708

ATHE-
NIAN,
CLEINIAS.

They are
to be
drawn
from all
Crete. Of
other
Hellenes
Pelopon-
nesians
will be
specially
accept-
able.

Should
colonists
be of one
or of
many
races?

709

It some-
times ap-
pears as
if man
never
legislated,

out a general invitation to any Hellene who likes to come. And yet I observe that to your country settlers have come from Argos and Aegina and other parts of Hellas. Tell me, then, whence do you draw your recruits in the present enterprise?

Cle. They will come from all Crete; and of other Hellenes, Peloponnesians will be most acceptable. For, as you truly observe, there are Cretans of Argive descent; and the race of Cretans which has the highest character at the present day is the Gortynian, and this has come from Gortys in the Peloponnesus.

Ath. Cities find colonization in some respects easier if the colonists are one race, which like a swarm of bees is sent out from a single country, either when friends leave friends, owing to some pressure of population or other similar necessity, or when a portion of a state is driven by factions to emigrate. And there have been whole cities which have taken flight when utterly conquered by a superior power in war. This, however, which is in one way an advantage to the colonist or legislator, in another point of view creates a difficulty. There is an element of friendship in the community of race, and language, and laws, and in common temples and rites of worship; but colonies which are of this homogeneous sort are apt to kick against any laws or any form of constitution differing from that which they had at home; and although the badness of their own laws may have been the cause of the factions which prevailed among them, yet from the force of habit they would fain preserve the very customs which were their ruin, and the leader of the colony, who is their legislator, finds them troublesome and rebellious. On the other hand, the conflux of several populations might be more disposed to listen to new laws; but then, to make them combine and pull together, as they say of horses, is a most difficult task, and the work of years. And yet there is nothing which tends more to the improvement of mankind than legislation and colonization.

Cle. No doubt; but I should like to know why you say so.

Ath. My good friend, I am afraid that the course of my speculations is leading me to say something depreciatory of legislators; but if the word be to the purpose, there can be no harm. And yet, why am I disquieted, for I believe that the same principle applies equally to all human things?

Cle. To what are you referring?

Ath. I was going to say that man never legislates, but accidents of all sorts, which legislate for us in all sorts of ways. The violence of war and the hard necessity of poverty are constantly overturning governments and changing laws. And the power of disease has often caused innovations in the state, when there have been pestilences,

ATHENIAN, CLEINIAS.

or when there has been a succession of bad seasons continuing during many years. Any one who sees all this, naturally rushes to the conclusion of which I was speaking, that no mortal legislates in anything, but that in human affairs chance is almost everything. And this may be said of the arts of the sailor, and the pilot, and the physician, and the general, and may seem to be well said; and yet there is another thing which may be said with equal truth of all of them.

but that every-thing were left to chance.

Cle. What is it?

Ath. That God governs all things, and that chance and opportunity co-operate with Him in the government of human affairs. There is, however, a third and less extreme view, that art should be there also; for I should say that in a storm there must surely be a great advantage in having the aid of the pilot's art. You would agree?

The truth is that God directs all, chance working with Him. Art too is a cause.

Cle. Yes.

Ath. And does not a like principle apply to legislation as well as to other things: even supposing all the conditions to be favourable which are needed for the happiness of the state, yet the true legislator must from time to time appear on the scene?

Cle. Most true.

Ath. In each case the artist would be able to pray rightly for certain conditions, and if these were granted by fortune, he would then only require to exercise his art?

Cle. Certainly.

Ath. And all the other artists just now mentioned, if they were bidden to offer up each their special prayer, would do so?

All artists must desire favourable conditions; and so the legislator.

Cle. Of course.

Ath. And the legislator would do likewise?

Cle. I believe that he would.

Ath. 'Come, legislator,' we will say to him; 'what are the conditions which you require in a state before you can organize it?' How ought he to answer this question? Shall I give his answer?

Cle. Yes.

Ath. He will say—'Give me a state which is governed by a tyrant, and let the tyrant be young and have a good memory; let him be quick at learning, and of a courageous and noble nature; let him have that quality which, as I said before, is the inseparable companion of all the other parts of virtue, if there is to be any good in them.'

He would say:—'Let there be a tyrant who [710] has every virtue,

Cle. I suppose, Megillus, that this companion virtue of which the Stranger speaks, must be temperance?

Ath. Yes, Cleinias, temperance in the vulgar sense; not that which in the forced and exaggerated language of some philosophers is

and temperance

Laws IV

ATHE-
NIAN,
CLEINIAS.

as the
condition
of all the
rest.'

called prudence, but that which is the natural gift of children and animals, of whom some live continently and others incontinently, but when isolated, was, as we said, hardly worth reckoning in the catalogue of goods[1]. I think that you must understand my meaning.

Cle. Certainly.

Ath. Then our tyrant must have this as well as the other qualities, if the state is to acquire in the best manner and in the shortest time the form of government which is most conducive to happiness; for there neither is nor ever will be a better or speedier way of establishing a polity than by a tyranny.

Cle. By what possible arguments, Stranger, can any man persuade himself of such a monstrous doctrine?

Ath. There is surely no difficulty in seeing, Cleinias, what is in accordance with the order of nature?

Cle. You would assume, as you say, a tyrant who was young, temperate, quick at learning, having a good memory, courageous, of a noble nature?

The ty-
rant must
be the
contem-
porary of
a great
legis-
lator.

Ath. Yes; and you must add fortunate; and his good fortune must be that he is the contemporary of a great legislator, and that some happy chance brings them together. When this has been accomplished, God has done all that He ever does for a state which He desires to be eminently prosperous; He has done second best for a state in which there are two such rulers, and third best for a state in which there are three. The difficulty increases with the increase, and diminishes with the diminution of the number.

Cle. You mean to say, I suppose, that the best government is produced from a tyranny, and originates in a good lawgiver and an orderly tyrant, and that the change from such a tyranny into a perfect form of government takes place most easily; less easily when from an oligarchy; and, in the third degree, from a democracy: is not that your meaning?

The per-
fect state
may be
formed,
(1) most
easily
from a
tyranny:
(2) less
so from
a mon-

711

Ath. Not so; I mean rather to say that the change is best made out of a tyranny; and secondly, out of a monarchy; and thirdly, out of some sort of democracy: fourth, in the capacity for improvement, comes oligarchy, which has the greatest difficulty in admitting of such a change, because the government is in the hands of a number of potentates. I am supposing that the legislator is by nature of the true sort, and that his strength is united with that of the chief men of the state; and when the ruling element is numerically small, and at the same time very strong, as in a tyranny, there the change is likely to be easiest and most rapid.

[1] Cp. *supra*, iii. 696 D.

Cle. How? I do not understand.

Ath. And yet I have repeated what I am saying a good many times; but I suppose that you have never seen a city which is under a tyranny?

Cle. No, and I cannot say that I have any great desire to see one.

Ath. And yet, where there is a tyranny, you might certainly see that of which I am now speaking.

Cle. What do you mean?

Ath. I mean that you might see how, without trouble and in no very long period of time, the tyrant, if he wishes, can change the manners of a state: he has only to go in the direction of virtue or of vice, whichever he prefers, he himself indicating by his example the lines of conduct, praising and rewarding some actions and reproving others, and degrading those who disobey.

Cle. But how can we imagine that the citizens in general will at once follow the example set to them; and how can he have this power both of persuading and of compelling them?

Ath. Let no one, my friends, persuade us that there is any quicker and easier way in which states change their laws than when the rulers lead: such changes never have, nor ever will, come to pass in any other way. The real impossibility or difficulty is of another sort, and is rarely surmounted in the course of ages; but when once it is surmounted, ten thousand or rather all blessings follow.

Cle. Of what are you speaking?

Ath. The difficulty is to find the divine love of temperate and just institutions existing in any powerful forms of government, whether in a monarchy or oligarchy of wealth or of birth. You might as well hope to reproduce the character of Nestor, who is said to have excelled all men in the power of speech, and yet more in his temperance. This, however, according to the tradition, was in the times of Troy; in our own days there is nothing of the sort; but if such an one either has or ever shall come into being, or is now among us, blessed is he and blessed are they who hear the wise words that flow from his lips. And this may be said of power in general: When the supreme power in man coincides with the greatest wisdom and temperance, then the best laws and the best constitution come into being; but in no other way. And let what I have been saying be regarded as a kind of sacred legend or oracle, and let this be our proof that, in one point of view, there may be a difficulty for a city to have good laws, but that there is another point of view in which nothing can be easier or sooner effected, granting our supposition.

Cle. How do you mean?

archy:
(3) still less from a democracy:
(4) least easily from an oligarchy.

The change is speedily effected by the example and by the power of a tyrant.

Rare is the combination of power and wisdom.

712

Laws IV

ATHE-
NIAN,
CLEINIAS,
MEGIL-
LUS.

What is
to be the
govern-
ment of
the
colony?

What are
your
own
govern-
ments?

Sparta
seems to
be a mix-
ture of
tyranny,
mon-
archy,
aristoc-
racy, de-
mocracy.

So too
Cnosus.

Most
states
named
[713]
after the
ruling
power.

The per-
fect state
should be
called the
City of
God.

Ath. Let us try to amuse ourselves, old boys as we are, by moulding in words the laws which are suitable to your state[1].

Cle. Let us proceed without delay.

Ath. Then let us invoke God at the settlement of our state; may
He hear and be propitious to us, and come and set in order the State
and the laws!

Cle. May He come!

Ath. But what form of polity are we going to give the city?

Cle. Tell us what you mean a little more clearly. Do you mean
some form of democracy, or oligarchy, or aristocracy, or monarchy?
For we cannot suppose that you would include tyranny.

Ath. Which of you will first tell me to which of these classes his
own government is to be referred?

Meg. Ought I to answer first, since I am the elder?

Cle. Perhaps you should.

Meg. And yet, Stranger, I perceive that I cannot say, without
more thought, what I should call the government of Lacedaemon,
for it seems to me to be like a tyranny,—the power of our Ephors is
marvellously tyrannical; and sometimes it appears to me to be of all
cities the most democratical; and who can reasonably deny that it is
an aristocracy[2]? We have also a monarchy which is held for life, and
is said by all mankind, and not by ourselves only, to be the most
ancient of all monarchies; and, therefore, when asked on a sudden, I
cannot precisely say which form of government the Spartan is.

Cle. I am in the same difficulty, Megillus; for I do not feel confident that the polity of Cnosus is any of these.

Ath. The reason is, my excellent friends, that you really have
polities, but the states of which we were just now speaking are
merely aggregations of men dwelling in cities who are the subjects
and servants of a part of their own state, and each of them is named
after the dominant power; they are not polities at all. But if states
are to be named after their rulers, the true state ought to be called
by the name of the God who rules over wise men.

Cle. And who is this God?

Ath. May I still make use of fable to some extent, in the hope that
I may be better able to answer your question: shall I?

Cle. By all means.

Ath. In the primeval world, and a long while before the cities
came into being whose settlements we have described, there is said
to have been in the time of Cronos a blessed rule and life, of which
the best-ordered of existing states is a copy[3].

Cle. It will be very necessary to hear about that.

[1] Cp. v. 746 A.　　[2] Cp. Ar. Pol. ii. 6, § 17.　　[3] Cp. Statesman 271.

Ath. I quite agree with you; and therefore I have introduced the subject.

Cle. Most appropriately; and since the tale is to the point, you will do well in giving us the whole story.

Ath. I will do as you suggest. There is a tradition of the happy life of mankind in days when all things were spontaneous and abundant. And of this the reason is said to have been as follows:—Cronos knew what we ourselves were declaring[1], that no human nature invested with supreme power is able to order human affairs and not overflow with insolence and wrong. Which reflection led him to appoint not men but demigods, who are of a higher and more divine race, to be the kings and rulers of our cities; he did as we do with flocks of sheep and other tame animals. For we do not appoint oxen to be the lords of oxen, or goats of goats; but we ourselves are a superior race, and rule over them. In like manner God, in His love of mankind, placed over us the demons, who are a superior race, and they with great ease and pleasure to themselves, and no less to us, taking care of us and giving us peace and reverence and order and justice never failing, made the tribes of men happy and united. And this tradition, which is true, declares that cities of which some mortal man and not God is the ruler, have no escape from evils and toils. Still we must do all that we can to imitate the life which is said to have existed in the days of Cronos, and, as far as the principle of immortality dwells in us, to that we must hearken, both in private and public life, and regulate our cities and houses according to law, meaning by the very term 'law,' the distribution of mind[2]. But if either a single person or an oligarchy or a democracy has a soul eager after pleasures and desires—wanting to be filled with them, yet retaining none of them, and perpetually afflicted with an endless and insatiable disorder; and this evil spirit, having first trampled the laws under foot, becomes the master either of a state or of an individual,—then, as I was saying, salvation is hopeless. And now, Cleinias, we have to consider whether you will or will not accept this tale of mine.

Cle. Certainly we will.

Ath. You are aware,—are you not?—that there are often said to be as many forms of laws as there are of governments, and of the latter we have already mentioned[3] all those which are commonly recognized. Now you must regard this as a matter of first-rate importance. For what is to be the standard of just and unjust, is once more the point at issue. Men say that the law ought not to regard either military virtue, or virtue in general, but only the interests and power and preservation of the established form of government;

In the days of Cronos men were governed by demigods, who were to mankind what shepherds are to animals.

To the divine rule we must return, as [714] far as we can.

Men commonly define justice to be

---

[1] *supra*, iii. 691.   [2] νόμος=νοῦ διανομή.   [3] *supra*, 712 C.

Laws IV

Athe-
nian,
Cleinias.

the in-
terest of
the
stronger,

meaning
by this
the se-
curity
and con-
tinuance
of the
ruling
class.

this is thought by them to be the best way of expressing the natural definition of justice.

Cle. How?

Ath. Justice is said by them to be the interest of the stronger[1].

Cle. Speak plainer.

Ath. I will:—'Surely,' they say, 'the governing power makes whatever laws have authority in any state'?

Cle. True.

Ath. 'Well,' they would add, 'and do you suppose that tyranny or democracy, or any other conquering power, does not make the continuance of the power which is possessed by them the first or principal object of their laws'?

Cle. How can they have any other?

Ath. 'And whoever transgresses these laws is punished as an evildoer by the legislator, who calls the laws just'?

Cle. Naturally.

Ath. 'This, then, is always the mode and fashion in which justice exists.'

Cle. Certainly, if they are correct in their view.

Ath. Why, yes, this is one of those false principles of government to which we were referring[2].

Cle. Which do you mean?

Ath. Those which we were examining when we spoke of who ought to govern whom. Did we not arrive at the conclusion that parents ought to govern their children, and the elder the younger, and the noble the ignoble? And there were many other principles, if you remember, and they were not always consistent. One principle was this very principle of might, and we said that Pindar considered violence natural and justified it.

715

But the
forms of
govern-
ment
which are
based on
this prin-
ciple are
not gov-
ernments
at all.

Cle. Yes; I remember.

Ath. Consider, then, to whom our state is to be entrusted. For there is a thing which has occurred times without number in states——

Cle. What thing?

Ath. That when there has been a contest for power, those who gain the upper hand so entirely monopolize the government, as to refuse all share to the defeated party and their descendants—they live watching one another, the ruling class being in perpetual fear that some one who has a recollection of former wrongs will come into power and rise up against them. Now, according to our view, such governments are not polities at all, nor are laws right which are passed for the good of particular classes and not for the good of

[1] Rep. i. 338, ii. 367.　　[2] *Supra*, iii. 690 B.

the whole state. States which have such laws are not polities but parties, and their notions of justice are simply unmeaning. I say this, because I am going to assert that we must not entrust the government in your state to any one because he is rich, or because he possesses any other advantage, such as strength, or stature, or again birth: but he who is most obedient to the laws of the state, he shall win the palm; and to him who is victorious in the first degree shall be given the highest office and chief ministry of the gods; and the second to him who bears the second palm; and on a similar principle shall all the other offices be assigned to those who come next in order. And when I call the rulers servants or ministers of the law, I give them this name not for the sake of novelty, but because I certainly believe that upon such service or ministry depends the well- or ill-being of the state. For that state in which the law is subject and has no authority, I perceive to be on the highway to ruin; but I see that the state in which the law is above the rulers, and the rulers are the inferiors of the law, has salvation, and every blessing which the Gods can confer.

Cle. Truly, Stranger, you see with the keen vision of age[1].

Ath. Why, yes; every man when he is young has that sort of vision dullest, and when he is old keenest.

Cle. Very true.

Ath. And now, what is to be the next step? May we not suppose the colonists to have arrived, and proceed to make our speech to them?

Cle. Certainly.

Ath. 'Friends,' we say to them,—'God, as the old tradition declares, holding in His hand the beginning, middle, and end of all that is, travels according to His nature in a straight line towards the accomplishment of His end. Justice always accompanies Him, and is the punisher of those who fall short of the divine law. To justice, he who would be happy holds fast, and follows in her company with all humility and order; but he who is lifted up with pride, or elated by wealth or rank, or beauty, who is young and foolish, and has a soul hot with insolence, and thinks that he has no need of any guide or ruler, but is able himself to be the guide of others, he, I say, is left deserted of God; and being thus deserted, he takes to him others who are like himself, and dances about, throwing all things into confusion, and many think that he is a great man, but in a short time he pays a penalty which justice cannot but approve, and is utterly destroyed, and his family and city with him. Wherefore, see-

---

[1] Or:—'for a man of your age you have a keen sight.'

Marginalia:

Laws IV
ATHE-
NIAN,
CLEINIAS.

Rule should be given, not to the richest or the strongest, but to him who is most obedient to the law.

The keen sight of the aged.

Address to the colonists.

God moves in a [716] straight path according to a divine law, and those who would be happy should hold fast to that law.

Seeing
these
things,
what
should
we do
or be?

God is
the meas-
ure of
all
things;
and they
who are
like Him
conform
to His
measure.
They are
His
friends
and He
accepts
[717]
their
offerings.

The first
honour is
to be
given to
the Gods
of Olym-
pus and
of the
state; the
second to
the Gods
below;
the third
honour
to
demons,
heroes,
ancestral
Gods;
next
comes the

ing that human things are thus ordered, what should a wise man do or think, or not do or think'?

Cle. Every man ought to make up his mind that he will be one of the followers of God; there can be no doubt of that.

Ath. Then what life is agreeable to God, and becoming in His followers? One only, expressed once for all in the old saying that 'like agrees with like, with measure measure,' but things which have no measure agree neither with themselves nor with the things which have. Now God ought to be to us the measure of all things, and not man[1], as men commonly say (Protagoras): the words are far more true of Him. And he who would be dear to God must, as far as is possible, be like Him and such as He is. Wherefore the temperate man is the friend of God, for he is like Him; and the intemperate man is unlike Him, and different from Him, and unjust. And the same applies to other things; and this is the conclusion, which is also the noblest and truest of all sayings,—that for the good man to offer sacrifice to the Gods, and hold converse with them by means of prayers and offerings and every kind of service, is the noblest and best of all things, and also the most conducive to a happy life, and very fit and meet. But with the bad man, the opposite of this is true: for the bad man has an impure soul, whereas the good is pure; and from one who is polluted, neither a good man nor God can without impropriety receive gifts. Wherefore the unholy do only waste their much service upon the Gods, but when offered by any holy man, such service is most acceptable to them. This is the mark at which we ought to aim. But what weapons shall we use, and how shall we direct them? In the first place, we affirm that next after the Olympian Gods and the Gods of the State, honour should be given to the Gods below; they should receive everything in even numbers, and of the second choice, and ill omen, while the odd numbers, and the first choice, and the things of lucky omen, are given to the Gods above, by him who would rightly hit the mark of piety. Next to these Gods, a wise man will do service to the demons or spirits, and then to the heroes, and after them will follow the private and ancestral Gods, who are worshipped as the law prescribes in the places which are sacred to them. Next comes the honour of living parents, to whom, as is meet, we have to pay the first and greatest and oldest of all debts, considering that all which a man has belongs to those who gave him birth and brought him up, and that he must do all that he can to minister to them, first, in his property, secondly, in his person, and thirdly, in his soul, in return for the endless care and travail which they bestowed upon him of old, in the days of his

[1] Cp. Crat. 386 A foll.; Theaet. 152 A.

infancy, and which he is now to pay back to them when they are old and in the extremity of their need. And all his life long he ought never to utter, or to have uttered, an unbecoming word to them; for of light and fleeting words the penalty is most severe; Nemesis, the messenger of justice, is appointed to watch over all such matters. When they are angry and want to satisfy their feelings in word or deed, he should give way to them; for a father who thinks that he has been wronged by his son may be reasonably expected to be very angry. At their death, the most moderate funeral is best, neither exceeding the customary expense, nor yet falling short of the honour which has been usually shown by the former generation to their parents. And let a man not forget to pay the yearly tribute of respect to the dead, honouring them chiefly by omitting nothing that conduces to a perpetual remembrance of them, and giving a reasonable portion of his fortune to the dead. Doing this, and living after this manner, we shall receive our reward from the Gods and those who are above us [i.e. the demons]; and we shall spend our days for the most part in good hope. And how a man ought to order what relates to his descendants and his kindred and friends and fellow-citizens, and the rites of hospitality taught by Heaven, and the intercourse which arises out of all these duties, with a view to the embellishment and orderly regulation of his own life—these things, I say, the laws, as we proceed with them, will accomplish, partly persuading, and partly when natures do not yield to the persuasion of custom, chastising them by might and right, and will thus render our state, if the Gods co-operate with us, prosperous and happy. But of what has to be said, and must be said by the legislator who is of my way of thinking, and yet, if said in the form of law, would be out of place— of this I think that he may give a sample for the instruction of himself and of those for whom he is legislating; and then when, as far as he is able, he has gone through all the preliminaries, he may proceed to the work of legislation. Now, what will be the form of such prefaces? There may be a difficulty in including or describing them all under a single form, but I think that we may get some notion of them if we can guarantee one thing.

Cle. What is that?

Ath. I should wish the citizens to be as readily persuaded to virtue as possible; this will surely be the aim of the legislator in all his laws.

Cle. Certainly.

Ath. The proposal appears to me to be of some value; and I think that a person will listen with more gentleness and good-will to the precepts addressed to him by the legislator, when his soul is not altogether unprepared to receive them. Even a little done in the way

Laws IV

ATHE-
NIAN,
CLEINIAS.

honour
of par-
ents, liv-
ing or
dead.

718

Hospi-
tality and
the other
duties of
social life
will also
be regu-
lated by
law.

And the
laws will
have pre-
faces,
which
may be
summed
up in a
general
preface,
or prep-
aration
for
virtue;

for the
way is
[719]
difficult,
as Hesiod
says.

of conciliation gains his ear, and is always worth having. For there is no great inclination or readiness on the part of mankind to be made as good, or as quickly good, as possible. The case of the many proves the wisdom of Hesiod, who says that the road to wickedness is smooth and can be travelled without perspiring, because it is so very short:—

'But before virtue the immortal Gods have placed the sweat of labour, and long and steep is the way thither, and rugged at first; but when you have reached the top, although difficult before, it is then easy [1].'

Cle. Yes; and he certainly speaks well.

Ath. Very true: and now let me tell you the effect which the preceding discourse has had upon me.

Cle. Proceed.

Ath. Suppose that we have a little conversation with the legislator, and say to him—'O, legislator, speak; if you know what we ought to say and do, you can surely tell.'

Cle. Of course he can.

Ath. 'Did we not hear you just now saying [2], that the legislator ought not to allow the poets to do what they liked? For that they would not know in which of their words they went against the laws, to the hurt of the state.'

Cle. That is true.

Ath. May we not fairly make answer to him on behalf of the poets?

Cle. What answer shall we make to him?

The poet
may con-
tradict
himself as
often as
he pleases,
but the
legislator
must be
definite
and con-
sistent.

Ath. That the poet, according to the tradition which has ever prevailed among us, and is accepted of all men, when he sits down on the tripod of the muse, is not in his right mind; like a fountain, he allows to flow out freely whatever comes in, and his art being imitative, he is often compelled to represent men of opposite dispositions, and thus to contradict himself; neither can he tell whether there is more truth in one thing that he has said than in another. But this is not the case in a law; the legislator must give not two rules about the same thing, but one only. Take an example from what you have just been saying [3]. Of three kinds of funerals, there is one which is too extravagant, another is too niggardly, the third in a mean; and you choose and approve and order the last without qualification. But if I had an extremely rich wife, and she bade me bury her and describe her burial in a poem, I should praise the extravagant sort; and a poor miserly man, who had not much money to spend, would approve of the niggardly; and the man of moderate means, who was himself moderate, would praise a moderate funeral.

[1] Works and Days, 287 sqq.   [2] ii. 656 foll.   [3] Cp. *supra*, 717 E.

Now you in the capacity of legislator must not barely say 'a moderate funeral,' but you must define what moderation is, and how much; unless you are definite, you must not suppose that you are speaking a language that can become law.

Cle. Certainly not.

Ath. And is our legislator to have no preface to his laws, but to say at once Do this, avoid that—and then holding the penalty in terrorem, to go on to another law; offering never a word of advice or exhortation to those for whom he is legislating, after the manner of some doctors? For of doctors, as I may remind you, some have a gentler, others a ruder method of cure; and as children ask the doctor to be gentle with them, so we will ask the legislator to cure our disorders with the gentlest remedies. What I mean to say is, that besides doctors there are doctors' servants, who are also styled doctors.

Cle. Very true.

Ath. And whether they are slaves or freemen makes no difference; they acquire their knowledge of medicine by obeying and observing their masters; empirically and not according to the natural way of learning, as the manner of freemen is, who have learned scientifically themselves the art which they impart scientifically to their pupils. You are aware that there are these two classes of doctors?

Cle. To be sure.

Ath. And did you ever observe that there are two classes of patients in states, slaves and freemen; and the slave doctors run about and cure the slaves, or wait for them in the dispensaries—practitioners of this sort never talk to their patients individually, or let them talk about their own individual complaints? The slave-doctor prescribes what mere experience suggests, as if he had exact knowledge; and when he has given his orders, like a tyrant, he rushes off with equal assurance to some other servant who is ill; and so he relieves the master of the house of the care of his invalid slaves. But the other doctor, who is a freeman, attends and practises upon freemen; and he carries his enquiries far back, and goes into the nature of the disorder; he enters into discourse with the patient and with his friends, and is at once getting information from the sick man, and also instructing him as far as he is able, and he will not prescribe for him until he has first convinced him; at last, when he has brought the patient more and more under his persuasive influences and set him on the road to health, he attempts to effect a cure. Now which is the better way of proceeding in a physician and in a trainer? Is he the better who accomplishes his ends in a double way, or he who works in one way, and that the ruder and inferior?

Laws IV

ATHE-
NIAN,
CLEINIAS.

Ambiguous terms, such as 'moderate,'
[720] should be defined.

Illustration taken from doctors and their assistants.

The slave-doctor a very peremptory and tyrannical person; the doctor who attends freemen is courteous and persuasive.

Cle. I should say, Stranger, that the double way is far better.

Ath. Should you like to see an example of the double and single method in legislation?

Cle. Certainly I should.

721

ATHE-
NIAN,
CLEINIAS,
MEGIL-
LUS.

Ath. What will be our first law? Will not the legislator, observing the order of nature, begin by making regulations for states about births?

Cle. He will.

Ath. In all states the birth of children goes back to the connection of marriage?

Cle. Very true.

The
double
method,
which in-
cludes
both per-
suasion
and com-
mand, is
the better
both in
medicine
and in
legisla-
tion.

Ath. And, according to the true order, the laws relating to marriage should be those which are first determined in every state?

Cle. Quite so.

Ath. Then let me first give the law of marriage in a simple form; it may run as follows:—A man shall marry between the ages of thirty and thirty-five, or, if he does not, he shall pay such and such a fine, or shall suffer the loss of such and such privileges. This would be the simple law about marriage. The double law would run thus:—A man shall marry between the ages of thirty and thirty-five, consid-

Simple
and
double
law of
marriage.

ering that in a manner the human race naturally partakes of immortality, which every man is by nature inclined to desire to the utmost; for the desire of every man that he may become famous, and not lie in the grave without a name, is only the love of continuance. Now mankind are coeval with all time, and are ever following, and will ever follow, the course of time; and so they are immortal, because they leave children's children behind them, and partake of immortality in the unity of generation. And for a man voluntarily to deprive himself of this gift, as he deliberately does who will not have a wife or children, is impiety. He who obeys the law shall be free, and shall pay no fine; but he who is disobedient, and does not marry, when he has arrived at the age of thirty-five, shall pay a yearly fine of a certain amount, in order that he may not imagine his celibacy to bring ease and profit to him; and he shall not share in the honours which the young men in the state give to the aged. Comparing now the two forms of the law, you will be able to arrive at a judgment about any other laws—whether they should be double in length even when shortest, because they have to persuade as well as threaten, or whether they shall only threaten and be of half the length.

The
shorter
form
would be

Meg. The shorter form, Stranger, would be more in accordance with Lacedaemonian custom; although, for my own part, if any one were to ask me which I myself prefer in the state, I should certainly determine in favour of the longer; and I would have every law made after the same pattern, if I had to choose. But I think that Cleinias is the person to be consulted, for his is the state which is going to use these laws.

Cle. Thank you, Megillus.

Ath. Whether, in the abstract, words are to be many or few, is a very foolish question; the best form, and not the shortest, is to be approved; nor is length at all to be regarded. Of the two forms of law which have been recited, the one is not only twice as good in practical usefulness as the other, but the case is like that of the two kinds of doctors, which I was just now mentioning. And yet legislators never appear to have considered that they have two instruments which they might use in legislation—persuasion and force; for in dealing with the rude and uneducated multitude, they use the one only as far as they can; they do not mingle persuasion with coercion, but employ force pure and simple. Moreover, there is a third point, sweet friends, which ought to be, and never is, regarded in our existing laws.

Cle. What is it?

Ath. A point arising out of our previous discussion, which comes into my mind in some mysterious way. All this time, from early dawn until noon, have we been talking about laws in this charming retreat: now we are going to promulgate our laws, and what has preceded was only the prelude of them. Why do I mention this? For this reason:—Because all discourses and vocal exercises have preludes and overtures, which are a sort of artistic beginnings intended to help the strain which is to be performed; lyric measures and music of every other kind have preludes framed with wonderful care. But of the truer and higher strain of law and politics, no one has ever yet uttered any prelude, or composed or published any, as though there was no such thing in nature. Whereas our present discussion seems to me to imply that there is;—these double laws, of which we were speaking, are not exactly double, but they are in two parts, the law and the prelude of the law. The arbitrary command, which was compared to the commands of doctors, whom we described as of the meaner sort, was the law pure and simple; and that which preceded, and was described by our friend here as being hortatory only, was, although in fact, an exhortation, likewise analogous to the preamble of a discourse[1]. For I imagine that all this language of conciliation, which the legislator has been uttering in the preface of the law, was intended to create good-will in the person whom he addressed, in order that, by reason of this good-will, he

[1] Cp. *supra*, 718.

preferred by the Lacedaemonians.

Legislators should use persuasion as well as force:

and the law should contain a [723] preamble or exhortation as well as a command.

The preamble is intended to create

good-will
towards
the law,
and to
make it
more ac-
ceptable.

Pre-
ambles
are nat-
ural, but
not al-
ways
necessary.

The prin-
ciples al-
ready laid
down
about the
honour of
[724]
the Gods
and the
respect of
parents
are a part
of our
pre-
amble.

might more intelligently receive his command, that is to say, the law. And therefore, in my way of speaking, this is more rightly described as the preamble than as the matter of the law. And I must further proceed to observe, that to all his laws, and to each separately, the legislator should prefix a preamble; he should remember how great will be the difference between them, according as they have, or have not, such preambles, as in the case already given.

Cle. The lawgiver, if he asks my opinion, will certainly legislate in the form which you advise.

Ath. I think that you are quite right, Cleinias, in affirming that all laws have preambles, and that throughout the whole of this work of legislation every single law should have a suitable preamble at the beginning; for that which is to follow is most important, and it makes all the difference whether we clearly remember the preambles or not. Yet we should be wrong in requiring that all laws, small and great alike, should have preambles of the same kind, any more than all songs or speeches; although they may be natural to all, they are not always necessary, and whether they are to be employed or not has in each case to be left to the judgment of the speaker or the musician, or, in the present instance, of the lawgiver.

Cle. That I think is most true. And now, Stranger, without delay let us return to the argument, and, as people say in play, make a second and better beginning, if you please, with the principles which we have been laying down, which we never thought of regarding as a preamble before, but of which we may now make a preamble, and not merely consider them to be chance topics of discourse. Let us acknowledge, then, that we have a preamble. About the honour of the Gods and the respect of parents, enough has been already said; and we may proceed to the topics which follow next in order, until the preamble is deemed by you to be complete; and after that you shall go through the laws themselves.

Ath. I understand you to mean that we have made a sufficient preamble about Gods and demigods, and about parents living or dead; and now you would have us bring the rest of the subject into the light of day?

Cle. Exactly.

Ath. After this, as is meet and for the interest of us all, I the speaker, and you the listeners, will try to estimate all that relates to the souls and bodies and properties of the citizens, as regards both their occupations and amusements, and thus arrive, as far as in us lies, at the nature of education. These then are the topics which follow next in order.

Cle. Very good.

BOOK V

Athenian Stranger. LISTEN, all ye who have just now heard the laws about Gods, and about our dear forefathers:—Of all the things which a man has, next to the Gods, his soul is the most divine and most truly his own. Now in every man there are two parts: the better and superior, which rules, and the worse and inferior, which serves; and the ruling part of him is always to be preferred to the subject. Wherefore I am right in bidding every one next to the Gods, who are our masters, and those who in order follow them [i.e. the demons], to honour his own soul, which every one seems to honour, but no one honours as he ought; for honour is a divine good, and no evil thing is honourable; and he who thinks that he can honour the soul by word or gift, or any sort of compliance, without making her in any way better, seems to honour her, but honours her not at all. For example, every man, from his very boyhood, fancies that he is able to know everything, and thinks that he honours his soul by praising her, and he is very ready to let her do whatever she may like. But I mean to say that in acting thus he injures his soul, and is far from honouring her; whereas, in our opinion, he ought to honour her as second only to the Gods. Again, when a man thinks that others are to be blamed, and not himself, for the errors which he has committed from time to time, and the many and great evils which befell him in consequence, and is always fancying himself to be exempt and innocent, he is under the idea that he is honouring his soul; whereas the very reverse is the fact, for he is really injuring her. And when, disregarding the word and approval of the legislator, he indulges in pleasure, then again he is far from honouring her; he only dishonours her, and fills her full of evil and remorse; or when he does not endure to the end the labours and fears and sorrows and pains which the legislator approves, but gives way before them, then, by yielding, he does not honour the soul, but by all such conduct he makes her to be dishonourable; nor when he thinks that life at any price is a good, does he honour her, but yet once more he dishonours her; for the soul having a notion that the world below is all evil, he yields to her, and does not resist and teach or convince her that, for aught she knows, the world of the Gods below, instead of being evil, may be the greatest of all goods. Again, when any one prefers beauty to virtue, what is this but the real and utter dishonour of the soul? For such a preference implies that the body is more honourable than the soul; and this is false, for there is nothing

726
Laws V
ATHE-
NIAN.

727
Next to
the Gods,
a man
should
honour
his own
soul.

False
ways of
honour-
ing the
soul:—

(1) by
praise;

(2) by
excuse;

(3) by
self-in-
dulgence;

(4) by
want of
endur-
ance;

(5) by
excessive
love of
life;

(6) by
preferring
beauty to
virtue;

(7) by
making
dishonest
gains.

of earthly birth which is more honourable than the heavenly, and he
who thinks otherwise of the soul has no idea how greatly he under-
values this wonderful possession; nor, again, when a person is willing, or not unwilling, to acquire dishonest gains, does he then honour his soul with gifts—far otherwise; he sells her glory and honour
for a small piece of gold; but all the gold which is under or upon the
earth is not enough to give in exchange for virtue. In a word, I may
say that he who does not estimate the base and evil, the good and
noble, according to the standard of the legislator, and abstain in
every possible way from the one and practise the other to the utmost of his power, does not know that in all these respects he is
most foully and disgracefully abusing his soul, which is the divinest

The pen-
alty of
yielding
to evil is
to grow
into its
likeness.

part of man; for no one, as I may say, ever considers that which is
declared to be the greatest penalty of evil-doing—namely, to grow
into the likeness of bad men, and growing like them to fly from the
conversation of the good, and be cut off from them, and cleave to
and follow after the company of the bad. And he who is joined to
them must do and suffer what such men by nature do and say to
one another,—a suffering which is not justice but retribution; for
justice and the just are noble, whereas retribution is the suffering
which waits upon injustice; and whether a man escape or endure
this, he is miserable,—in the former case, because he is not cured;
while in the latter, he perishes in order that the rest of mankind may
be saved.

Speaking generally, our glory is to follow the better and improve
the inferior, which is susceptible of improvement, as far as this is
possible. And of all human possessions, the soul is by nature most
inclined to avoid the evil, and track out and find the chief good;
which when a man has found, he should take up his abode with it
during the remainder of his life. Wherefore the soul also is second
[or next to God] in honour; and third, as every one will perceive,

The hon-
our of the
body
comes
next after
the
honour of
the soul;
the mean,
not the
excess, of
bodily ex-
cellence is
best.

comes the honour of the body in natural order. Having determined
this, we have next to consider that there is a natural honour of the
body, and that of honours some are true and some are counterfeit.
To decide which are which is the business of the legislator; and he,
I suspect, would intimate that they are as follows:—Honour is not
to be given to the fair body, or to the strong or the swift or the tall,
or to the healthy body (although many may think otherwise), any
more than to their opposites; but the mean states of all these habits
are by far the safest and most moderate; for the one extreme makes
the soul braggart and insolent, and the other, illiberal and base; and
money, and property, and distinction all go to the same tune. The

729

excess of any of these things is apt to be a source of hatreds and divisions among states and individuals; and the defect of them is commonly a cause of slavery. And, therefore, I would not have any one fond of heaping up riches for the sake of his children, in order that he may leave them as rich as possible. For the possession of great wealth is of no use, either to them or to the state. The condition of youth which is free from flattery, and at the same time not in need of the necessaries of life, is the best and most harmonious of all, being in accord and agreement with our nature, and making life to be most entirely free from sorrow. Let parents, then, bequeath to their children not a heap of riches, but the spirit of reverence. We, indeed, fancy that they will inherit reverence from us, if we rebuke them when they show a want of reverence. But this quality is not really imparted to them by the present style of admonition, which only tells them that the young ought always to be reverential. A sensible legislator will rather exhort the elders to reverence the younger, and above all to take heed that no young man sees or hears one of themselves doing or saying anything disgraceful; for where old men have no shame, there young men will most certainly be devoid of reverence. The best way of training the young is to train yourself at the same time; not to admonish them, but to be always carrying out your own admonitions in practice. He who honours his kindred, and reveres those who share in the same Gods and are of the same blood and family, may fairly expect that the Gods who preside over generation will be propitious to him, and will quicken his seed. And he who deems the services which his friends and acquaintances do for him, greater and more important than they themselves deem them, and his own favours to them less than theirs to him, will have their good-will in the intercourse of life. And surely in his relations to the state and his fellow-citizens, he is by far the best, who rather than the Olympic or any other victory of peace or war, desires to win the palm of obedience to the laws of his country, and who, of all mankind, is the person reputed to have obeyed them best through life. In his relations to strangers, a man should consider that a contract is a most holy thing, and that all concerns and wrongs of strangers are more directly dependent on the protection of God, than wrongs done to citizens; for the stranger, having no kindred and friends, is more to be pitied by Gods and men. Wherefore, also, he who is most able to avenge him is most zealous in his cause; and he who is most able is the genius and the god of the stranger, who follow in the train of Zeus, the god of strangers. And for this reason, he who has a spark of caution in him, will do his best to pass through life without sinning against the stranger. And of offences committed, whether against strangers or

Parents should bequeath to their children not money, but the spirit of reverence.

The younger should reverence the elder; the elder the younger.

The best way of training the young is to train yourself.

Honour kindred, that you may have offspring.

Esteem others more than yourself.

Obey the laws.

730
Respect strangers and suppliants.

fellow-countrymen, that against suppliants is the greatest. For the God who witnessed to the agreement made with the suppliant, becomes in a special manner the guardian of the sufferer; and he will certainly not suffer unavenged.

Thus we have fairly described the manner in which a man is to act about his parents, and himself, and his own affairs; and in relation to the state, and his friends, and kindred, both in what concerns his own countrymen, and in what concerns the stranger. We will now consider what manner of man he must be who would best pass through life in respect of those other things which are not matters of law, but of praise and blame only; in which praise and blame educate a man, and make him more tractable and amenable to the laws which are about to be imposed.

Truth the beginning of every good.

Truth is the beginning of every good thing, both to Gods and men; and he who would be blessed and happy, should be from the first a partaker of the truth, that he may live a true man as long as possible, for then he can be trusted; but he is not to be trusted who loves voluntary falsehood, and he who loves involuntary falsehood is a fool. Neither condition is enviable, for the untrustworthy and ignorant has no friend, and as time advances he becomes known, and lays up in store for himself isolation in crabbed age when life is on the wane: so that, whether his children or friends are alive or not, he is equally solitary.—Worthy of honour is he who does no injustice, and of more than twofold honour, if he not only does no injustice himself, but hinders others from doing any; the first may count as one man, the second is worth many men, because he informs the rulers of the injustice of others. And yet more highly to be esteemed is he who co-operates with the rulers in correcting the citizens as far as he can—he shall be proclaimed the great and perfect citizen, and bear away the palm of virtue. The same praise may be given about temperance and wisdom, and all other goods which may be imparted to others, as well as acquired by a man for himself; he who imparts them shall be honoured as the man of men, and he who is willing, yet is not able, may be allowed the second place; but he who is jealous and will not, if he can help, allow others to partake in a friendly way of any good, is deserving of blame: the good, however, which he has, is not to be undervalued by us because it is possessed by him, but must be acquired by us also to the utmost of our power. Let every man, then, freely strive for the prize of virtue, and let there be no envy. For the unenvious nature increases the greatness of states—he himself contends in the race, blasting the fair fame of no man; but the envious, who thinks that he ought to get the better by defaming others, is less energetic himself in the

The misery of being ignorant and untrustworthy.

Justice is to be honoured and vindicated.

To impart the good
[731]
more than only to possess it.

The contrast of the envious and unenvious natures.

pursuit of true virtue, and reduces his rivals to despair by his unjust slanders of them. And so he makes the whole city to enter the arena untrained in the practice of virtue, and diminishes her glory as far as in him lies. Now every man should be valiant, but he should also be gentle. From the cruel, or hardly curable, or altogether incurable acts of injustice done to him by others, a man can only escape by fighting and defending himself and conquering, and by never ceasing to punish them; and no man who is not of a noble spirit is able to accomplish this. As to the actions of those who do evil, but whose evil is curable, in the first place, let us remember that the unjust man is not unjust of his own free will. For no man of his own free will would choose to possess the greatest of evils, and least of all in the most honourable part of himself. And the soul, as we said, is of a truth deemed by all men the most honourable. In the soul, then, which is the most honourable part of him, no one, if he could help, would admit, or allow to continue the greatest of evils[1]. The unrighteous and vicious are always to be pitied in any case; and one can afford to forgive as well as pity him who is curable, and refrain and calm one's anger, not getting into a passion, like a woman, and nursing ill-feeling. But upon him who is incapable of reformation and wholly evil, the vials of our wrath should be poured out; wherefore I say that good men ought, when occasion demands, to be both gentle and passionate.

Of all evils the greatest is one which in the souls of most men is innate, and which a man is always excusing in himself and never correcting; I mean, what is expressed in the saying that 'Every man by nature is and ought to be his own friend.' Whereas the excessive love of self is in reality the source to each man of all offences; for the lover is blinded about the beloved, so that he judges wrongly of the just, the good, and the honourable, and thinks that he ought always to prefer himself to the truth. But he who would be a great man ought to regard, not himself or his interests, but what is just, whether the just act be his own or that of another. Through a similar error men are induced to fancy that their own ignorance is wisdom, and thus we who may be truly said to know nothing, think that we know all things; and because we will not let others act for us in what we do not know, we are compelled to act amiss ourselves. Wherefore let every man avoid excess of self-love, and condescend to follow a better man than himself, not allowing any false shame to stand in the way. There are also minor precepts which are often repeated, and are quite as useful; a man should recollect them and remind himself of them. For when a stream is flowing out, there

[1] Cp. Rep. ii. 382.

Side notes:

Laws V

ATHE-NIAN.

The incurable must be punished.

But the unjust are always to be pitied, and when curable may be forgiven.

Selfishness the greatest of evils.

732
A great man should be above his own interests.

Every man should be willing to follow another who is

Laws V

ATHE-
NIAN.

wiser or
better
than him-
self.

The
necessity
of self-
control.

The con-
solation
of hope.

should be water flowing in too; and recollection flows in while wisdom is departing. Therefore I say that a man should refrain from excess either of laughter or tears, and should exhort his neighbour to do the same; he should veil his immoderate sorrow or joy, and seek to behave with propriety, whether the genius of his good fortune remains with him, or whether at the crisis of his fate, when he seems to be mounting high and steep places, the Gods oppose him in some of his enterprises. Still he may ever hope, in the case of good men, that whatever afflictions are to befall them in the future God will lessen, and that present evils He will change for the better; and as to the goods which are the opposite of these evils, he will not doubt that they will be added to them, and that they will be fortunate. Such should be men's hopes, and such should be the exhortations with which they admonish one another, never losing an opportunity, but on every occasion distinctly reminding themselves and others of all these things, both in jest and earnest.

Enough has now been said of divine matters, both as touching the practices which men ought to follow, and as to the sort of persons who they ought severally to be. But of human things we have not as yet spoken, and we must; for to men we are discoursing and not to Gods. Pleasures and pains and desires are a part of human nature, and on them every mortal being must of necessity hang and depend with the most eager interest. And therefore we must praise the noblest life, not only as the fairest in appearance, but as being one which, if a man will only taste, and not, while still in his youth, desert for another, he will find to surpass also in the very thing which we all of us desire,—I mean in having a greater amount of pleasure and less of pain during the whole of life. And this will be plain, if a man has a true taste of them, as will be quickly and clearly seen. But what is a true taste? That we have to learn from the argument,—the point being what is according to nature, and what is not according to nature. One life must be compared with another, the more pleasurable with the more painful, after this manner:—We desire to have pleasure, but we neither desire nor choose pain; and the neutral state we are ready to take in exchange, not for pleasure but for pain; and we also wish for less pain and greater pleasure, but less pleasure and greater pain we do not wish for; and an equal balance of either we cannot venture to assert that we should desire. And all these differ or do not differ severally in number and magnitude and intensity and equality, and in the opposites of these when regarded as objects of choice, in relation to desire. And such being the necessary order of things, we wish for that life in which there are many great and intense elements of pleasure and

There
must be a
true
sense or
taste of
pleasure
and pain.

[733]

Men
choose

pain, and in which the pleasures are in excess, and do not wish for that in which the opposites exceed; nor, again, do we wish for that in which the elements of either are small and few and feeble, and the pains exceed. And when, as I said before, there is a balance of pleasure and pain in life, this is to be regarded by us as the balanced life; while other lives are preferred by us because they exceed in what we like, or are rejected by us because they exceed in what we dislike. All the lives of men may be regarded by us as bound up in these, and we must also consider what sort of lives we by nature desire. And if we wish for any others, I say that we desire them only through some ignorance and inexperience of the lives which actually exist.

Now, what lives are they, and how many in which, having searched out and beheld the objects of will and desire and their opposites, and making of them a law, choosing, I say, the dear and the pleasant and the best and noblest, a man may live in the happiest way possible? Let us say that the temperate life is one kind of life, and the rational another, and the courageous another, and the healthful another; and to these four let us oppose four other lives,— the foolish, the cowardly, the intemperate, the diseased. He who knows the temperate life will describe it as in all things gentle, having gentle pains and gentle pleasures, and placid desires and loves not insane; whereas the intemperate life is impetuous in all things, and has violent pains and pleasures, and vehement and stinging desires, and loves utterly insane; and in the temperate life the pleasures exceed the pains, but in the intemperate life the pains exceed the pleasures in greatness and number and frequency. Hence one of the two lives is naturally and necessarily more pleasant and the other more painful, and he who would live pleasantly cannot possibly choose to live intemperately. And if this is true, the inference clearly is that no man is voluntarily intemperate; but that the whole multitude of men lack temperance in their lives, either from ignorance, or from want of self-control, or both. And the same holds of the diseased and healthy life; they both have pleasures and pains, but in health the pleasure exceeds the pain, and in sickness the pain exceeds the pleasure. Now our intention in choosing the lives is not that the painful should exceed, but the life in which pain is exceeded by pleasure we have determined to be the more pleasant life. And we should say that the temperate life has the elements both of pleasure and pain fewer and smaller and less frequent than the intemperate, and the wise life than the foolish life, and the life of courage than the life of cowardice; one of each pair exceeding in pleasure and the other in pain, the courageous surpassing the cow-

the life which has great pleasures and pains, and in which the pleasure exceeds the pain.

The most pleasant and the noblest lives are (1) the temperate; (2) the rational; (3) the courageous; [734] (4) the healthful.

The pleasures of the temperate, wise, courageous and healthy life are greater than those of the intemperate, foolish, cowardly and diseased life. How then can a man volun-

tarily
choose
the
latter?

ardly, and the wise exceeding the foolish. And so the one class of
lives exceeds the other class in pleasure; the temperate and courageous and wise and healthy exceed the cowardly and foolish and intemperate and diseased lives; and generally speaking, that which
has any virtue, whether of body or soul, is pleasanter than the
vicious life, and far superior in beauty and rectitude and excellence
and reputation, and causes him who lives accordingly to be infinitely happier than the opposite.

Enough of the preamble; and now the laws should follow; or, to
speak more correctly, an outline of them. As, then, in the case of a
web or any other tissue, the warp and the woof cannot be made of
the same materials[1], but the warp is necessarily superior as being
stronger, and having a certain character of firmness, whereas the
woof is softer and has a proper degree of elasticity;—in a similar
manner those who are to hold great offices in states, should be distinguished truly in each case from those who have been but slen
derly proven by education. Let us suppose that there are two parts
in the constitution of a state—one the creation of offices, the other
the laws which are assigned to them to administer.

But, before all this, comes the following consideration:—The
shepherd or herdsman, or breeder of horses or the like, when he has
received his animals will not begin to train them until he has first
purified them in a manner which befits a community of animals; he
will divide the healthy and unhealthy, and the good breed and the
bad breed, and will send away the unhealthy and badly bred to
other herds, and tend the rest, reflecting that his labours will be
vain and have no effect, either on the souls or bodies of those whom
nature and ill nurture have corrupted, and that they will involve in
destruction the pure and healthy nature and being of every other
animal, if he should neglect to purify them. Now the case of other
animals is not so important—they are only worth introducing for
the sake of illustration; but what relates to man is of the highest
importance; and the legislator should make enquiries, and indicate
what is proper for each one in the way of purification and of any
other procedure. Take, for example, the purification of a city—there
are many kinds of purification, some easier and others more difficult; and some of them, and the best and most difficult of them, the
legislator, if he be also a despot, may be able to effect; but the legislator, who, not being a despot, sets up a new government and laws,
even if he attempt the mildest of purgations, may think himself
happy if he can complete his work. The best kind of purification is
painful, like similar cures in medicine, involving righteous punish-

735

As in a
web the
warp is
firmer
than the
woof, so
in the
state the
magis-
trates
should be
stronger
than the
people.

There are
incurable

[1] Cp. Statesman 309 A, B.

ment and inflicting death or exile in the last resort. For in this way we commonly dispose of great sinners who are incurable, and are the greatest injury of the whole state. But the milder form of purification is as follows:—when men who have nothing, and are in want of food, show a disposition to follow their leaders in an attack on the property of the rich—these, who are the natural plague of the state, are sent away by the legislator in a friendly spirit as far as he is able; and this dismissal of them is euphemistically termed a colony. And every legislator should contrive to do this at once. Our present case, however, is peculiar. For there is no need to devise any colony or purifying separation under the circumstances in which we are placed. But as, when many streams flow together from many sources, whether springs or mountain torrents, into a single lake, we ought to attend and take care that the confluent waters should be perfectly clear, and in order to effect this, should pump and draw off and divert impurities, so in every political arrangement there may be trouble and danger. But, seeing that we are now only discoursing and not acting, let our selection be supposed to be completed, and the desired purity attained. Touching evil men, who want to join and be citizens of our state, after we have tested them by every sort of persuasion and for a sufficient time, we will prevent them from coming; but the good we will to the utmost of our ability receive as friends with open arms.

Another piece of good fortune must not be forgotten, which, as we were saying[1], the Heraclid colony had, and which is also ours,—that we have escaped division of land and the abolition of debts; for these are always a source of dangerous contention, and a city which is driven by necessity to legislate upon such matters can neither allow the old ways to continue, nor yet venture to alter them. We must have recourse to prayers, so to speak, and hope that a slight change may be cautiously effected in a length of time. And such a change can be accomplished[2] by those who have abundance of land, and having also many debtors, are willing, in a kindly spirit, to share with those who are in want, sometimes remitting and sometimes giving, holding fast in a path of moderation, and deeming poverty to be the increase of a man's desires and not the diminution of his property. For this is the great beginning of salvation to a state, and upon this lasting basis may be erected afterwards whatever political order is suitable under the circumstances; but if the change be based upon an unsound principle, the future administration of the country will be full of difficulties. That is a danger which, as I am saying, is escaped by us, and yet we had better say how, if

[1] Cp. *supra*, iii. 684 D, E.   [2] Reading ὑπάρχει.

Laws V

ATHE-
NIAN.

and cur-
able dis-
[736]
eases in a
state.

The first
are
purged
away by
exile or
death;
the
second by
coloniza-
tion.

But in
our state,
no purga-
tion will
be need-
ed; for
we shall
only ad-
mit good
citizens;
nor shall
we re-
quire a
division
of lands
or the
abolition
of debts.

737

That is a
danger
which our
colony
has
escaped;
and
which in
another
can only
be
escaped
by inspir-
ing con-
tentment
among
the
citizens.

The citi-
zens must
be suffi-
ciently
numerous
to protect
them-
selves,
and to
assist
their
neigh-
bours in
the hour
of need.

738

5040 is a
very good
number
because it
has so
many di-
visions.

we had not escaped, we might have escaped; and we may venture
now to assert that no other way of escape, whether narrow or broad,
can be devised but freedom from avarice and a sense of justice—
upon this rock our city shall be built; for there ought to be no disputes among citizens about property. If there are quarrels of long
standing among them, no legislator of any degree of sense will proceed a step in the arrangement of the state until they are settled.
But that they to whom God has given, as He has to us, to be the
founders of a new state as yet free from enmity—that they should
create themselves enmities by their mode of distributing lands and
houses, would be superhuman folly and wickedness.

How then can we rightly order the distribution of the land? In
the first place, the number of the citizens has to be determined, and
also the number and size of the divisions into which they will have
to be formed; and the land and the houses will then have to be ap-
portioned by us as fairly as we can. The number of citizens can only
be estimated satisfactorily in relation to the territory and the neighbouring states. The territory must be sufficient to maintain a certain number of inhabitants in a moderate way of life—more than
this is not required; and the number of citizens should be sufficient
to defend themselves against the injustice of their neighbours, and
also to give them the power of rendering efficient aid to their neighbours when they are wronged. After having taken a survey of theirs
and their neighbours' territory, we will determine the limits of them
in fact as well as in theory. And now, let us proceed to legislate with
a view to perfecting the form and outline of our state. The number
of our citizens shall be 5040—this will be a convenient number; and
these shall be owners of the land and protectors of the allotment.
The houses and the land will be divided in the same way, so that
every man may correspond to a lot. Let the whole number be first
divided into two parts, and then into three; and the number is
further capable of being divided into four or five parts, or any number of parts up to ten. Every legislator ought to know so much
arithmetic as to be able to tell what number is most likely to be
useful to all cities; and we are going to take that number which contains the greatest and most regular and unbroken series of divisions.
The whole of number has every possible division, and the number
5040 can be divided by exactly fifty-nine divisors, and ten of these
proceed without interval from one to ten: this will furnish numbers
for war and peace, and for all contracts and dealings, including
taxes and divisions of the land. These properties of number should
be ascertained at leisure by those who are bound by law to know

them; for they are true, and should be proclaimed at the foundation of the city, with a view to use. Whether the legislator is establishing a new state or restoring an old and decayed one, in respect of Gods and temples,—the temples which are to be built in each city, and the Gods or demi-gods after whom they are to be called,—if he be a man of sense, he will make no change in anything which the oracle of Delphi, or Dodona, or the God Ammon, or any ancient tradition has sanctioned in whatever manner, whether by apparitions or reputed inspiration of Heaven, in obedience to which mankind have established sacrifices in connection with mystic rites, either originating on the spot, or derived from Tyrrhenia or Cyprus or some other place, and on the strength of which traditions they have consecrated oracles and images, and altars and temples, and portioned out a sacred domain for each of them. The least part of all these ought not to be disturbed by the legislator; but he should assign to the several districts some God, or demi-god, or hero, and, in the distribution of the soil, should give to these first their chosen domain and all things fitting, that the inhabitants of the several districts may meet at fixed times, and that they may readily supply their various wants, and entertain one another with sacrifices, and become friends and acquaintances; for there is no greater good in a state than that the citizens should be known to one another. When not light but darkness and ignorance of each other's characters prevails among them, no one will receive the honour of which he is deserving, or the power or the justice to which he is fairly entitled: wherefore, in every state, above all things, every man should take heed that he have no deceit in him, but that he be always true and simple; and that no deceitful person take any advantage of him.

The next move in our pastime of legislation, like the withdrawal of the stone from the holy line in the game of draughts, being an unusual one, will probably excite wonder when mentioned for the first time. And yet, if a man will only reflect and weigh the matter with care, he will see that our city is ordered in a manner which, if not the best, is the second best. Perhaps also some one may not approve this form, because he thinks that such a constitution is ill adapted to a legislator who has not despotic power. The truth is, that there are three forms of government, the best, the second and the third best, which we may just mention, and then leave the selection to the ruler of the settlement. Following this method in the present instance, let us speak of the states which are respectively first, second, and third in excellence, and then we will leave the choice to Cleinias now, or to any one else who may hereafter have to make a similar

Laws V

ATHE-
NIAN.

Ancient religious traditions and customs should be retained.

The country to be divided into districts, and to each of these is to be assigned a God or hero.

The citizens should know and trust one another.

739

The form of constitution not the best, but the second best.

The best
is that in
which
there is
absolute
com-
munity.

This is
our pat-
tern.

The es-
tablish-
[740]
ment of
the
second-
best state.
Distribu-
tion of
land and
houses.

The heir
of the lot.

choice among constitutions, and may desire to give to his state some feature which is congenial to him and which he approves in his own country.

The first and highest form of the state and of the government and of the law is that in which there prevails most widely the ancient saying, that 'Friends have all things in common.' Whether there is anywhere now, or will ever be, this communion of women and children and of property, in which the private and individual is altogether banished from life, and things which are by nature private, such as eyes and ears and hands, have become common, and in some way see and hear and act in common, and all men express praise and blame and feel joy and sorrow on the same occasions, and whatever laws there are unite the city to the utmost[1],—whether all this is possible or not, I say that no man, acting upon any other principle, will ever constitute a state which will be truer or better or more exalted in virtue. Whether such a state is governed by Gods or sons of Gods, one, or more than one, happy are the men who, living after this manner, dwell there; and therefore to this we are to look for the pattern of the state, and to cling to this, and to seek with all our might for one which is like this. The state which we have now in hand, when created, will be nearest to immortality and the only one which takes the second place; and after that, by the grace of God, we will complete the third one. And we will begin by speaking of the nature and origin of the second.

Let the citizens at once distribute their land and houses, and not till the land in common, since a community of goods goes beyond their proposed origin, and nurture, and education. But in making the distribution, let the several possessors feel that their particular lots also belong to the whole city; and seeing that the earth is their parent, let them tend her more carefully than children do their mother. For she is a goddess and their queen, and they are her mortal subjects. Such also are the feelings which they ought to entertain to the Gods and demi-gods of the country. And in order that the distribution may always remain, they ought to consider further that the present number of families should be always retained, and neither increased nor diminished. This may be secured for the whole city in the following manner:—Let the possessor of a lot leave the one of his children who is his best beloved, and one only, to be the heir of his dwelling, and his successor in the duty of ministering to the Gods, the state and the family, as well the living members of it as those who are departed when he comes into the inheritance; but of his other children, if he have more than one, he shall

[1] Cp. Rep. v. 462 foll.

give the females in marriage according to the law to be hereafter enacted[1], and the males he shall distribute as sons to those citizens who have no children, and are disposed to receive them; or if there should be none such, and particular individuals have too many children, male or female, or too few, as in the case of barrenness—in all these cases let the highest and most honourable magistracy created by us judge and determine what is to be done with the redundant or deficient, and devise a means that the number of 5040 houses shall always remain the same. There are many ways of regulating numbers; for they in whom generation is affluent may be made to refrain[2], and, on the other hand, special care may be taken to increase the number of births by rewards and stigmas, or we may meet the evil by the elder men giving advice and administering rebuke to the younger—in this way the object may be attained. And if after all there be very great difficulty about the equal preservation of the 5040 houses, and there be an excess of citizens, owing to the too great love of those who live together, and we are at our wits' end, there is still the old device often mentioned by us of sending out a colony, which will part friends with us, and be composed of suitable persons. If, on the other hand, there come a wave bearing a deluge of disease, or a plague of war, and the inhabitants become much fewer than the appointed number by reason of bereavement, we ought not to introduce citizens of spurious birth and education, if this can be avoided; but even God is said not to be able to fight against necessity.

Wherefore let us suppose this 'high argument' of ours to address us in the following terms:—Best of men, cease not to honour according to nature similarity and equality and sameness and agreement, as regards number and every good and noble quality. And, above all, observe the aforesaid number 5040 throughout life; in the second place, do not disparage the small and modest proportions of the inheritances which you received in the distribution, by buying and selling them to one another. For then neither will the God who gave you the lot be your friend, nor will the legislator; and indeed the law declares to the disobedient that these are the terms upon which he may or may not take the lot. In the first place, the earth as he is informed is sacred to the Gods; and in the next place, priests and priestesses will offer up prayers over a first, and second, and even a third sacrifice, that he who buys or sells the houses or lands which he has received, may suffer the punishment which he deserves; and these their prayers they shall write down in the temples, on tablets of cypress-wood, for the instruction of posterity. Moreover they will

[1] Cp. *infra*, xi. 923-926.   [2] Cp. Arist. Pol. vii. 16, § 15.

Laws V

ATHE-
NIAN.

What is
to be
done with
the other
children?

Regula-
tion of re-
dundant
or defi-
cient
popula-
tion.

741

Honour
equality
and ob-
serve the
number
5040.

Laws V

ATHE-
NIAN.

set a watch over all these things, that they may be observed;—the magistracy which has the sharpest eyes shall keep watch that any infringement of these commands may be discovered and punished as offences both against the law and the God. How great is the benefit of such an ordinance to all those cities, which obey and are administered accordingly, no bad man can ever know, as the old proverb says; but only a man of experience and good habits. For in such an order of things there will not be much opportunity for making money; no man either ought, or indeed will be allowed, to exercise any ignoble occupation, of which the vulgarity is a matter of reproach to a freeman, and should never want to acquire riches by any such means.

742

No man should possess gold and silver except in money. Foreign and domestic currency.

Further, the law enjoins that no private man shall be allowed to possess gold and silver, but only coin for daily use, which is almost necessary in dealing with artisans, and for payment of hirelings, whether slaves or immigrants, by all those persons who require the use of them. Wherefore our citizens, as we say, should have a coin passing current among themselves, but not accepted among the rest of mankind; with a view, however, to expeditions and journeys to other lands,—for embassies, or for any other occasion which may arise of sending out a herald, the state must also possess a common Hellenic currency. If a private person is ever obliged to go abroad, let him have the consent of the magistrates and go; and if when he returns he has any foreign money remaining, let him give the surplus back to the treasury, and receive a corresponding sum in the local currency. And if he is discovered to appropriate it, let it be confiscated, and let him who knows and does not inform be subject to curse and dishonour equally with him who brought the money, and also to a fine not less in amount than the foreign money which has been brought back. In marrying and giving in marriage, no one

No dow-
:ies,

or lending money upon interest.

shall give or receive any dowry at all; and no one shall deposit money with another whom he does not trust as a friend, nor shall he lend money upon interest; and the borrower should be under no obligation to repay either capital or interest. That these principles are best, any one may see who compares them with the first principle and intention of a state. The intention, as we affirm, of a reasonable statesman, is not what the many declare to be the object of

The state to be good rather than rich; since neither

a good legislator, namely, that the state for the true interests of which he is advising should be as great and as rich as possible, and should possess gold and silver, and have the greatest empire by sea and land;—this they imagine to be the real object of legislation, at the same time adding, inconsistently, that the true legislator desires to have the city the best and happiest possible. But they do not see that some of these things are possible, and some of them are impossible; and he who orders the state will desire what is possible, and will not indulge in vain wishes or attempts to accomplish that which is impossible. The citizen must indeed be happy and good, and the legislator will seek to make him so; but very rich and very good at the same time he cannot be, not, at least, in the sense in which the many speak of riches. For they mean by 'the rich' the few who have the most valuable possessions, although the owner of them may quite well be a rogue. And if this is true, I can never assent to the doctrine that the rich man will be happy—he must be good as well as rich. And good in a high degree, and rich in a high degree at the same time, he cannot be. Some one will ask, why not? And we shall answer,—Because acquisitions which come from sources which are just and unjust indifferently, are more than double those which come from just sources only; and the sums which are expended neither honourably nor disgracefully, are only half as great as those which are expended honourably and on honourable purposes. Thus, if the one acquires double and spends half, the other who is in the opposite case and is a good man cannot possibly be wealthier than he. The first—I am speaking of the saver and not of the spender—is not always bad; he may indeed in some cases be utterly bad, but, as I was saying, a good man he never is. For he who receives money unjustly as well as justly, and spends neither justly nor unjustly, will be a rich man if he be also thrifty. On the other hand, the utterly bad is in general profligate, and therefore very poor; while he who spends on noble objects, and acquires wealth by just means only, can hardly be remarkable for riches, any more than he can be very poor. Our statement, then, is true, that the very rich are not good, and, if they are not good, they are not happy. But the intention of our laws was, that the citizens should be as happy as may be, and as friendly as possible to one another. And men who are always at law with one another, and amongst whom there are many wrongs done, can never be friends to one another, but only those among whom crimes and lawsuits are few and slight. Therefore we say that gold and silver ought not to be allowed in the city, nor much of the vulgar sort of trade which is carried on by lending money, or rearing the meaner kinds of live stock; but only the produce of agriculture, and only so much of this as will not compel us in pursuing it to neglect that for the sake of which riches exist,—I mean, soul and body, which without gymnastics, and without education, will never be worth anything; and therefore, as we have said not once but many times, the care of riches should have the last place in our thoughts. For there are in all three things about which every man has an in-

Laws V

ATHE-
NIAN.

state nor individual can be both.
743

The good man gains half as much as the bad and spends twice as much; so that he cannot easily be rich.

The making of money not to be allowed to interfere with education.

terest; and the interest about money, when rightly regarded, is the
third and lowest of them: midway comes the interest of the body;
and, first of all, that of the soul; and the state which we are describing will have been rightly constituted if it ordains honours according
to this scale. But if, in any of the laws which have been ordained,
health has been preferred to temperance, or wealth to health and
temperate habits, that law must clearly be wrong. Wherefore, also,
the legislator ought often to impress upon himself the question—
'What do I want?' and 'Do I attain my aim, or do I miss the mark?'
In this way, and in this way only, he may acquit himself and free
others from the work of legislation.

Let the allottee then hold his lot upon the conditions which we
have mentioned[1].

It would be well that every man should come to the colony having
all things equal; but seeing that this is not possible, and one man
will have greater possessions than another, for many reasons and in
particular in order to preserve equality in special crises of the state,
qualifications of property must be unequal, in order that offices and
contributions and distributions may be proportioned to the value of
each person's wealth, and not solely to the virtue of his ancestors or
himself, nor yet to the strength and beauty of his person, but also to
the measure of his wealth or poverty; and so by a law of inequality,
which will be in proportion to his wealth, he will receive honours
and offices as equally as possible, and there will be no quarrels and
disputes. To which end there should be four different standards appointed according to the amount of property: there should be a first
and a second and a third and a fourth class, in which the citizens will
be placed, and they will be called by these or similar names: they
may continue in the same rank, or pass into another in any individual case, on becoming richer from being poorer, or poorer from
being richer. The form of law which I should propose as the natural
sequel would be as follows:—In a state which is desirous of being
saved from the greatest of all plagues—not faction, but rather distraction—there should exist among the citizens neither extreme
poverty, nor, again, excess of wealth, for both are productive of
both these evils. Now the legislator should determine what is to be
the limit of poverty or wealth. Let the limit of poverty be the value
of the lot; this ought to be preserved, and no ruler, nor any one else
who aspires after a reputation for virtue, will allow the lot to be impaired in any case. This the legislator gives as a measure, and he will
permit a man to acquire double or triple, or as much as four times
the amount of this[1]. But if a person have yet greater riches, whether

The citi-
zens to be
arranged
in classes
according
to their
census.

There are
to be four
such
classes,
the lowest
not fall-
ing below
the lot,
and the
highest
not ex-
ceeding
five times
the lot.

[1] *Supra,* 740, 741.   [2] Cp. Arist. Pol. ii. 6, § 15.

he has found them, or they have been given to him, or he has made them in business, or has acquired by any stroke of fortune that which is in excess of the measure, if he give back the surplus to the state, and to the Gods who are the patrons of the state, he shall suffer no penalty or loss of reputation; but if he disobeys this our law, any one who likes may inform against him and receive half the value of the excess, and the delinquent shall pay a sum equal to the excess out of his own property, and the other half of the excess shall belong to the Gods. And let every possession of every man, with the exception of the lot, be publicly registered before the magistrates whom the law appoints, so that all suits about money may be easy and quite simple.

The next thing to be noted is, that the city should be placed as nearly as possible in the centre of the country; we should choose a place which possesses what is suitable for a city, and this may easily be imagined and described. Then we will divide the city into twelve portions, first founding temples to Hestia, to Zeus and to Athene, in a spot which we will call the Acropolis, and surround with a circular wall, making the division of the entire city and country radiate from this point. The twelve portions shall be equalized by the provision that those which are of good land shall be smaller, while those of inferior quality shall be larger. The number of the lots shall be 5040, and each of them shall be divided into two, and every allotment shall be composed of two such sections; one of land near the city, the other of land which is at a distance[1]. This arrangement shall be carried out in the following manner: The section which is near the city shall be added to that which is on the borders, and form one lot, and the portion which is next nearest shall be added to the portion which is next farthest; and so of the rest. Moreover, in the two sections of the lots the same principle of equalization of the soil ought to be maintained; the badness and goodness shall be compensated by more and less. And the legislator shall divide the citizens into twelve parts, and arrange the rest of their property, as far as possible, so as to form twelve equal parts; and there shall be a registration of all. After this they shall assign twelve lots to twelve Gods, and call them by their names, and dedicate to each God their several portions, and call the tribes after them. And they shall distribute the twelve divisions of the city in the same way in which they divided the country; and every man shall have two habitations[2], one in the centre of the country, and the other at the extremity. Enough of the manner of settlement.

Now we ought by all means to consider that there can never be

[1] Cp. Arist. Pol. vii. 10, § 11.   [2] Cp. ibid. ii. 6, § 15.

Twelve-
fold divi-
sion of
city and
country.

The land
to be dis-
tributed
into 5040
lots.
Each lot
to be
divided,
—half to
be near
the city,
half more
distant.

Less of
good land
to be
given,
more of
inferior.

Twelve
tribes,
named

Laws V
746
ATHE-
NIAN.

after
twelve
Gods.

Every
citizen to
have a
town and
a country
house.

But this
is only
a dream.

The legis-
lator
should
first be al-
lowed to
perfect
his design,
and then
we may
consider
how far it
can be
executed.

such a happy concurrence of circumstances as we have described; neither can all things coincide as they are wanted. Men who will not take offence at such a mode of living together, and will endure all their life long to have their property fixed at a moderate limit, and to beget children in accordance with our ordinances, and will allow themselves to be deprived of gold and other things which the legislator, as is evident from these enactments, will certainly forbid them; and will endure, further, the situation of the land with the city in the middle and dwellings round about;—all this is as if the legislator were telling his dreams, or making a city and citizens of wax. There is truth in these objections, and therefore every one should take to heart what I am going to say. Once more, then, the legislator shall appear and address us:—'O my friends,' he will say to us, 'do not suppose me ignorant that there is a certain degree of truth in your words; but I am of opinion that, in matters which are not present but future, he who exhibits a pattern of that at which he aims, should in nothing fall short of the fairest and truest; and that if he finds any part of this work impossible of execution he should avoid and not execute it, but he should contrive to carry out that which is nearest and most akin to it; you must allow the legislator to perfect his design, and when it is perfected, you should join with him in considering what part of his legislation is expedient and what will arouse opposition; for surely the artist who is to be deemed worthy of any regard at all, ought always to make his work self-consistent.'

Having determined that there is to be a distribution into twelve parts, let us now see in what way this may be accomplished. There is no difficulty in perceiving that the twelve parts admit of the greatest number of divisions of that which they include, or in seeing the other numbers which are consequent upon them, and are produced out of them up to 5040; wherefore the law ought to order phratries and demes and villages, and also military ranks and movements, as well as coins and measures, dry and liquid, and weights, so as to be commensurable and agreeable to one another. Nor should we fear the appearance of minuteness, if the law commands that all the vessels which a man possesses should have a common measure, when we consider generally that the divisions and variations of numbers have a use in respect of all the variations of which they are susceptible, both in themselves and as measures of height and depth, and in all sounds, and in motions, as well those which proceed in a straight direction, upwards or downwards, as in those which go round and round. The legislator is to consider all these things and to bid the citizens, as far as possible, not to lose sight of numerical order; for no single instrument of youthful education has such mighty power, both as regards domestic economy and politics, and in the arts, as the study of arithmetic. Above all, arithmetic stirs up him who is by nature sleepy and dull, and makes him quick to learn, retentive, shrewd, and aided by art divine he makes progress quite beyond his natural powers[1]. All such things, if only the legislator, by other laws and institutions, can banish meanness and covetousness from the souls of men, so that they can use them properly and to their own good, will be excellent and suitable instruments of education. But if he cannot, he will unintentionally create in them, instead of wisdom, the habit of craft, which evil tendency may be observed in the Egyptians and Phoenicians, and many other races, through the general vulgarity of their pursuits and acquisitions, whether some unworthy legislator of theirs has been the cause, or some impediment of chance or nature. For we must not fail to observe, O Megillus and Cleinias, that there is a difference in places, and that some beget better men and others worse; and we must legislate accordingly. Some places are subject to strange and fatal influences by reason of diverse winds and violent heats, some by reason of waters; or, again, from the character of the food given by the earth, which not only affects the bodies of men for good or evil, but produces similar results in their souls. And in all such qualities those spots excel in which there is a divine inspiration, and in which the demigods have their appointed lots, and are propitious, not adverse, to the settlers in them. To all these matters the legislator, if he have any sense in him, will attend as far as man can, and frame his laws accordingly. And this is what you, Cleinias, must do, and to matters of this kind you must turn you mind since you are going to colonize a new country.

Cleinias. Your words, Athenian Stranger, are excellent, and I will do as you say.

The study of arithmetic the most powerful instrument of education. But it may also encourage meanness, as among the Egyptians and Phoenicians.

Effects of soil and climate on national character.

BOOK VI

Athenian Stranger. AND now having made an end of the preliminaries we will proceed to the appointment of magistracies.

Cleinias. Very good.

Ath. In the ordering of a state there are two parts: first, the number of the magistracies, and the mode of establishing them; and,

[1] Cp. Rep. vii. 526 B.

The appointment of officials a matter too important to be left to chance uneducated persons who are brought together for the first time.

secondly, when they have been established, laws again will have to be provided for each of them, suitable in nature and number. But before electing the magistrates let us stop a little and say a word in season about the election of them.

Cle. What have you got to say?

Ath. This is what I have to say;—every one can see, that although the work of legislation is a most important matter, yet if a well-ordered city superadd to good laws unsuitable offices, not only will there be no use in having the good laws,—not only will they be ridiculous and useless, but the greatest political injury and evil will accrue from them.

Cle. Of course.

Ath. Then now, my friend, let us observe what will happen in the constitution of our intended state. In the first place, you will acknowledge that those who are duly appointed to magisterial power, and their families, should severally have given satisfactory proof of what they are, from youth upward until the time of election; in the next place, those who are to elect should have been trained in habits of law, and be well educated, that they may have a right judgment, and may be able to select or reject men whom they approve or disapprove, as they are worthy of either. But how can we imagine that those who are brought together for the first time, and are strangers to one another, and also uneducated, will avoid making mistakes in the choice of magistrates?

Cle. Impossible.

Ath. The matter is serious, and excuses will not serve the turn. I will tell you, then, what you and I will have to do, since you, as you tell me, with nine others, have offered to settle the new state on behalf of the people of Crete, and I am to help you by the invention of the present romance. I certainly should not like to leave the tale wandering all over the world without a head;—a headless monster is such a hideous thing.

Cle. Excellent, Stranger.

Ath. Yes; and I will be as good as my word.

Cle. Let us by all means do as you propose.

Ath. That we will, by the grace of God, if old age will only permit us.

Cle. But God will be gracious.

Ath. Yes; and under His guidance let us consider a further point.

Cle. What is it?

Ath. Let us remember what a courageously mad and daring creation this our city is.

Cle. What had you in your mind when you said that?

752

Ath. I had in my mind the free and easy manner in which we are ordaining that the inexperienced colonists shall receive our laws. Now a man need not be very wise, Cleinias, in order to see that no one can easily receive laws at their first imposition. But if we could anyhow wait until those who have been imbued with them from childhood, and have been nurtured in them, and become habituated to them, take their part in the public elections of the state; I say, if this could be accomplished, and rightly accomplished by any way or contrivance,—then, I think that there would be very little danger, at the end of the time, of a state thus trained not being permanent.

Cle. A reasonable supposition.

Ath. Then let us consider if we can find any way out of the difficulty; for I maintain, Cleinias, that the Cnosians, above all the other Cretans, should not be satisfied with barely discharging their duty to the colony, but they ought to take the utmost pains to establish the offices which are first created by them in the best and surest manner. Above all, this applies to the selection of the guardians of the law, who must be chosen first of all, and with the greatest care; the others are of less importance.

Cle. What method can we devise of electing them?

Ath. This will be the method:—Sons of the Cretans, I shall say to them, inasmuch as the Cnosians have precedence over the other states, they should, in common with those who join this settlement, choose a body of thirty-seven in all, nineteen of them being taken from the settlers, and the remainder from the citizens of Cnosus. Of those latter the Cnosians shall make a present to your colony, and you yourself shall be one of the eighteen, and shall become a citizen of the new state; and if you and they cannot be persuaded to go, the Cnosians may fairly use a little violence in order to make you.

Cle. But why, Stranger, do not you and Megillus take a part in our new city?

Ath. O, Cleinias, Athens is proud, and Sparta too; and they are both a long way off. But you and likewise the other colonists are conveniently situated as you describe. I have been speaking of the way in which the new citizens may be best managed under present circumstances; but in after-ages, if the city continues to exist, let the election be on this wise. All who are horse or foot soldiers, or have seen military service at the proper ages when they were severally fitted for it[1], shall share in the election of magistrates; and the election shall be held in whatever temple the state deems most venerable, and every one shall carry his vote to the altar of the God,

[1] Cp. Arist. Pol. ii. 6, § 16.

Laws VI

ATHE-
NIAN,
CLEINIAS.

The first magistrates must be elected by some already existing authority.

The Cnosians, acting in concert with the [753] new colonists, should appoint a body of 37 guardians of the law.

In after ages they shall be elected by the military class.

Manner
of elec-
tion.

writing down on a tablet the name of the person for whom he votes, and his father's name, and his tribe, and ward; and at the side he shall write his own name in like manner. Any one who pleases may take away any tablet which he does not think properly filled up, and exhibit it in the Agora for a period of not less than thirty days. The tablets which are judged to be first, to the number of 300, shall be shown by the magistrates to the whole city, and the citizens shall in like manner select from these the candidates whom they prefer; and this second selection, to the number of 100, shall be again exhibited to the citizens; in the third, let any one who pleases select whom he pleases out of the 100, walking through the parts of victims, and let them choose for magistrates and proclaim the seven-and-thirty who have the greatest number of votes. But who, Cleinias and Megillus. will order for us in the colony all this matter of the magistrates, and the scrutinies of them? If we reflect, we shall see that cities which are in process of construction like ours must have some such persons, who cannot possibly be elected before there are any magistrates[1]; and yet they must be elected in some way, and they are not to be inferior men, but the best possible. For as the proverb says, 'a good beginning is half the business;' and 'to have begun well' is praised by all, and in my opinion is a great deal more than half the business, and has never been praised by any one enough.

754

Cle. That is very true.

Ath. Then let us recognize the difficulty, and make clear to our own minds how the beginning is to be accomplished. There is only one proposal which I have to offer, and that is one which, under our circumstances, is both necessary and expedient.

Cle. What is it?

Cnosus,
the parent
state,
should
take an
interest
in her
offspring.

Ath. I maintain that this colony of ours has a father and mother, who are no other than the colonizing state. Well I know that many colonies have been, and will be, at enmity with their parents. But in early days the child, as in a family, loves and is beloved; even if there come a time later when the tie is broken, still, while he is in want of education, he naturally loves his parents and is beloved by them, and flies to his relatives for protection, and finds in them his only natural allies in time of need; and this parental feeling already exists in the Cnosians, as is shown by their care of the new city; and there is a similar feeling on the part of the young city towards Cnosus. And I repeat what I was saying—for there is no harm in repeating a good thing—that the Cnosians should take a common interest in all these matters, and choose, as far as they can, the eldest and best of the colonists, to the number of not less than a hundred;

[1] Reading πρὸ πασῶν.

and let there be another hundred of the Cnosians themselves. These, I say, on their arrival, should have a joint care that the magistrates should be appointed according to law, and that when they are appointed they should undergo a scrutiny. When this has been effected, the Cnosians shall return home, and the new city do the best she can for her own preservation and happiness. I would have the seven-and-thirty now, and in all future time, chosen to fulfil the following duties:—Let them, in the first place, be the guardians of the law; and, secondly, of the registers in which each one registers before the magistrate the amount of his property, excepting four minae which are allowed to citizens of the first class, three allowed to the second, two to the third, and a single mina to the fourth. And if any one, despising the laws for the sake of gain, be found to possess anything more which has not been registered, let all that he has in excess be confiscated, and let him be liable to a suit which shall be the reverse of honourable or fortunate. And let any one who will, indict him on the charge of loving base gains, and proceed against him before the guardians of the law. And if he be cast, let him lose his share of the public possessions, and when there is any public distribution, let him have nothing but his original lot; and let him be written down a condemned man as long as he lives, in some place in which any one who pleases can read about his offences. The guardian of the law shall not hold office longer than twenty years, and shall not be less than fifty years of age when he is elected; or if he is elected when he is sixty years of age, he shall hold office for ten years only; and upon the same principle, he must not imagine that he will be permitted to hold such an important office as that of guardian of the laws after he is seventy years of age, if he live so long.

These are the three first ordinances about the guardians of the law; as the work of legislation progresses, each law in turn will assign to them their further duties. And now we may proceed in order to speak of the election of other officers; for generals have to be elected, and these again must have their ministers, commanders, and colonels of horse, and commanders of brigades of foot, who would be more rightly called by their popular name of brigadiers. The guardians of the law shall propose as generals men who are natives of the city, and a selection from the candidates proposed shall be made by those who are or have been of the age for military service. And if one who is not proposed is thought by somebody to be better than one who is, let him name whom he prefers in the place of whom, and make oath that he is better, and propose him; and whichever of them is approved by vote shall be admitted to the final selection; and the three who have the greatest number of votes

who are
or have
been
soldiers.
The
generals
shall ap-
point 12
briga-
diers.

756

The elec-
tion of
cavalry
officers.

The coun-
cil to con-
sist of 360
persons.
The
penalty
for not
voting at
elections
to the
council
shall vary
with the
class.
Details of
the mode
of elec-
tion.

shall be appointed generals, and superintendents of military affairs, after previously undergoing a scrutiny, like the guardians of the law. And let the generals thus elected propose twelve brigadiers, one for each tribe; and there shall be a right of counter-proposal as in the case of the generals, and the voting and decision shall take place in the same way. Until the prytanes and council are elected, the guardians of the law shall convene the assembly in some holy spot which is suitable to the purpose, placing the hoplites by themselves, and the cavalry by themselves, and in a third division all the rest of the army. All are to vote for the generals [and for the colonels of horse], but the brigadiers are to be voted for only by those who carry shields [i. e. the hoplites]. Let the body of cavalry choose phylarchs for the generals; but captains of light troops, or archers, or any other division of the army, shall be appointed by the generals for themselves. There only remains the appointment of officers of cavalry: these shall be proposed by the same persons who proposed the generals, and the election and the counter-proposal of other candidates shall be arranged in the same way as in the case of the generals, and let the cavalry vote and the infantry look on at the election; the two who have the greatest number of votes shall be the leaders of all the horse. Disputes about the voting may be raised once or twice; but if the dispute be raised a third time, the officers who preside at the several elections shall decide.

The council shall consist of 30 × 12 members,—360 will be a convenient number for sub-division. If we divide the whole number into four parts of ninety each, we get ninety counsellors for each class. First, all the citizens shall select candidates from the first class; they shall be compelled to vote, and, if they do not, shall be duly fined. When the candidates have been selected, some one shall mark them down; this shall be the business of the first day. And on the following day, candidates shall be selected from the second class in the same manner and under the same conditions as on the previous day; and on the third day a selection shall be made from the third class, at which every one may if he likes vote, and the three first classes shall be compelled to vote; but the fourth and lowest class shall be under no compulsion, and any member of this class who does not vote shall not be punished. On the fourth day candidates shall be selected from the fourth and smallest class; they shall be selected by all, but he who is of the fourth class shall suffer no penalty, nor he who is of the third, if he be not willing to vote; but he who is of the first or second class, if he does not vote shall be punished;—he who is of the second class shall pay a fine of triple the amount which was exacted at first, and he who is of the first class quadruple. On the fifth day the rulers shall bring out the names noted down, for all the citizens to see, and every man shall choose out of them, under pain, if he do not, of suffering the first penalty; and when they have chosen 180 out of each of the classes, they shall choose one-half of them by lot, who shall undergo a scrutiny:— These are to form the council for the year.

The mode of election which has been described is in a mean between monarchy and democracy, and such a mean the state ought always to observe; for servants and masters never can be friends, nor good and bad, merely because they are declared to have equal privileges. For to unequals equals become unequal, if they are not harmonised by measure; and both by reason of equality, and by reason of inequality, cities are filled with seditions. The old saying, that 'equality makes friendship,' is happy and also true; but there is obscurity and confusion as to what sort of equality is meant. For there are two equalities which are called by the same name, but are in reality in many ways almost the opposite of one another; one of them may be introduced without difficulty, by any state or any legislator in the distribution of honours: this is the rule of measure, weight, and number, which regulates and apportions them. But there is another equality, of a better and higher kind, which is not so easily recognized. This is the judgment of Zeus; among men it avails but little; that little, however, is the source of the greatest good to individuals and states. For it gives to the greater more, and to the inferior less and in proportion to the nature of each; and, above all, greater honour always to the greater virtue, and to the less less; and to either in proportion to their respective measure of virtue and education. And this is justice, and is ever the true principle of states, at which we ought to aim, and according to this rule order the new city which is now being founded, and any other city which may be hereafter founded. To this the legislator should look, —not to the interests of tyrants one or more, or to the power of the people, but to justice always; which, as I was saying, is the distribution of natural equality among unequals in each case. But there are times at which every state is compelled to use the words, 'just,' 'equal,' in a secondary sense, in the hope of escaping in some degree from factions. For equity and indulgence are infractions of the perfect and strict rule of justice. And this is the reason why we are obliged to use the equality of the lot, in order to avoid the discontent of the people; and so we invoke God and fortune in our prayers, and beg that they themselves will direct the lot with a view to su-

Laws VI

ATHE-
NIAN.

757
The state
to be in a
mean
between
monarchy
and de-
mocracy.

Two
kinds of
equality,
simple,
and pro-
portion-
ate—

that is,
the dis-
tribution
of more
to the
superior,
and of
less to the
inferior.

Equality,
like
justice, is
often used
in a lax
sense, as
when ap-
plied to
the lot:
the less

Laws VI

758

ATHE-
NIAN,
CLEINIAS.

there is
of chance
the better.

The coun-
cil to be
divided
into
twelve
parts,
each of
which
will serve
for a
month.

Their
duties.

preme justice. And therefore, although we are compelled to use both equalities, we should use that into which the element of chance enters as seldom as possible.

Thus, O my friends, and for the reasons given, should a state act which would endure and be saved. But as a ship sailing on the sea has to be watched night and day, in like manner a city also is sailing on a sea of politics, and is liable to all sorts of insidious assaults; and therefore from morning to night, and from night to morning, rulers must join hands with rulers, and watchers with watchers, receiving and giving up their trust in a perpetual succession. Now a multitude can never fulfil a duty of this sort with anything like energy. Moreover, the greater number of the senators will have to be left during the greater part of the year to order their concerns at their own homes. They will therefore have to be arranged in twelve portions, answering to the twelve months, and furnish guardians of the state, each portion for a single month. Their business is to be at hand and receive any foreigner or citizen who comes to them, whether to give information, or to put one of those questions, to which, when asked by other cities, a city should give an answer, and to which, if she ask them herself, she should receive an answer; or again, when there is a likelihood of internal commotions, which are always liable to happen in some form or other, they will, if they can, prevent their occurring; or if they have already occurred, will lose no time in making them known to the city, and healing the evil. Wherefore, also, this which is the presiding body of the state ought always to have the control of their assemblies, and of the dissolutions of them, ordinary as well as extraordinary. All this is to be ordered by the twelfth part of the council, which is always to keep watch together with the other officers of the state during one portion of the year, and to rest during the remaining eleven portions.

Thus will the city be fairly ordered. And now, who is to have the superintendence of the country, and what shall be the arrangement? Seeing that the whole city and the entire country have been both of them divided into twelve portions, ought there not to be appointed superintendents of the streets of the city, and of the houses, and buildings, and harbours, and the agora, and fountains, and sacred domains, and temples, and the like?

Cle. To be sure there ought.

Ath. Let us assume, then, that there ought to be servants of the temples, and priests and priestesses. There must also be superintendents of roads and buildings, who will have a care of men, that they may do no harm, and also of beasts, both within the enclosure and in the suburbs. Three kinds of officers will thus have to be ap-

759
Three
kinds of
officers
necessary
for the

pointed, in order that the city may be suitably provided according to her needs. Those who have the care of the city shall be called wardens of the city; and those who have the care of the agora shall be called wardens of the agora; and those who have the care of the temples shall be called priests. Those who hold hereditary offices as priests or priestesses, shall not be disturbed; but if there be few or none such, as is probable at the foundation of a new city, priests and priestesses shall be appointed to be servants of the Gods who have no servants. Some of our officers shall be elected, and others appointed by lot, those who are of the people and those who are not of the people mingling in a friendly manner in every place and city, that the state may be as far as possible of one mind. The officers of the temples shall be appointed by lot; in this way their election will be committed to God, that He may do what is agreeable to Him. And he who obtains a lot shall undergo a scrutiny, first, as to whether he is sound of body and of legitimate birth; and in the second place, in order to show that he is of a perfectly pure family, not stained with homicide or any similar impiety in his own person, and also that his father and mother have led a similar unstained life. Now the laws about all divine things should be brought from Delphi, and interpreters appointed, under whose direction they should be used. The tenure of the priesthood should always be for a year and no longer; and he who will duly execute the sacred office, according to the laws of religion, must be not less than sixty years of age,—the laws shall be the same about priestesses. As for the interpreters, they shall be appointed thus:—let the twelve tribes be distributed into groups of four, and let each group select four, one out of each tribe within the group, three times; and let the three who have the greatest number of votes [out of the twelve appointed by each group], after undergoing a scrutiny, nine in all, be sent to Delphi, in order that the God may return one out of each triad; their age shall be the same as that of the priests, and the scrutiny of them shall be conducted in the same manner; let them be interpreters for life, and when any one dies let the four tribes select another from the tribe of the deceased. Moreover, besides priests and interpreters, there must be treasurers, who will take charge of the property of the several temples, and of the sacred domains, and shall have authority over the produce and the letting of them; and three of them shall be chosen from the highest classes for the greater temples, and two for the lesser, and one for the least of all; the manner of their election and the scrutiny of them shall be the same as that of the generals[1]. This shall be the order of the temples.

[1] Cp. *supra*, 755 C.

Laws VI

ATHE-
NIAN.

city:—
(1)
Priests,
Inter-
preters,
and
Temple-
Treasur-
ers: (2)
Wardens
of the
city: (3)
Wardens
of the
Agora.

Mixture
of classes
in election
to offices.

Election
of priests
and
priest-
esses,

of inter-
preters,

and of
temple-
treasur-
ers.

760

Laws VI

ATHE-
NIAN.

The war-
dens of
the
country.

Five to
keep
watch in
each divi-
sion with
twelve
young
men ap-
pointed
by them.

A differ-
ent divi-
sion to
be taken
every
month,
and the
circuit of
the land
twice
made in
their two
years'
service.

Their
duties:—
Protec-
tion of
the
country;

761

road-
making;

Let everything have a guard as far as possible. Let the defence of the city be committed to the generals, and taxiarchs, and hipparchs, and phylarchs, and prytanes, and the wardens of the city, and of the agora, when the election of them has been completed. The defence of the country shall be provided for as follows:—The entire land has been already distributed into twelve as nearly as possible equal parts, and let the tribe allotted to a division provide annually for it five wardens of the country and commanders of the watch; and let each body of five have the power of selecting twelve others out of the youth of their own tribe,—these shall be not less than twenty-five years of age, and not more than thirty. And let there be allotted to them severally every month the various districts, in order that they may all acquire knowledge and experience of the whole country. The term of service for commanders and for watchers shall continue during two years. After having had their stations allotted to them, they will go from place to place in regular order, making their round from left to right as their commanders direct them; (when I speak of going to the right, I mean that they are to go to the east). And at the commencement of the second year, in order that as many as possible of the guards may not only get a knowledge of the country at any one season of the year, but may also have experience of the manner in which different places are affected at different seasons of the year, their then commanders shall lead them again towards the left, from place to place in succession, until they have completed the second year. In the third year other wardens of the country shall be chosen and commanders of the watch, five for each division, who are to be the superintendents of the bands of twelve. While on service at each station, their attention shall be directed to the following points:—In the first place, they shall see that the country is well protected against enemies; they shall trench and dig wherever this is required, and, as far as they can, they shall by fortifications keep off the evil-disposed, in order to prevent them from doing any harm to the country or the property; they shall use the beasts of burden and the labourers whom they find on the spot: these will be their instruments whom they will superintend, taking them, as far as possible, at the times when they are not engaged in their regular business. They shall make every part of the country inaccessible to enemies, and as accessible as possible to friends[1]; there shall be ways for man and beasts of burden and for cattle, and they shall take care to have them always as smooth as they can; and shall provide against the rains doing harm instead of good to the land, when they come down from the mountains into the hollow

[1] Cp. Arist. Pol. vii. 5, § 3.

dells; and shall keep in the overflow by the help of works and
ditches, in order that the valleys, receiving and drinking up the rain
from heaven, and providing fountains and streams in the fields and
regions which lie underneath, may furnish even to the dry places
plenty of good water. The fountains of water, whether of rivers or of
springs, shall be ornamented with plantations and buildings for
beauty; and let them bring together the streams in subterraneous
channels, and make all things plenteous; and if there be a sacred
grove or dedicated precinct in the neighbourhood, they shall conduct the water to the actual temples of the Gods, and so beautify
them at all seasons of the year. Everywhere in such places the youth
shall make gymnasia for themselves, and warm baths for the aged,
placing by them abundance of dry wood, for the benefit of those
labouring under disease—there the weary frame of the rustic, worn
with toil, will receive a kindly welcome[1], far better than he would at
the hands of a not over-wise doctor.

The building of these and the like works will be useful and orna-
mental; they will provide a pleasing amusement, but they will be a
serious employment too; for the sixty wardens will have to guard
their several divisions, not only with a view to enemies, but also
with an eye to professing friends. When a quarrel arises among
neighbours or citizens, and any one whether slave or freeman wrongs
another, let the five wardens decide small matters on their own authority; but where the charge against another relates to greater
matters, the seventeen composed of the fives and twelves, shall determine any charges which one man brings against another, not involving more than three minae[2]. Every judge and magistrate shall
be liable to give an account of his conduct in office, except those
who, like kings, have the final decision. Moreover, as regards the
aforesaid wardens of the country, if they do any wrong to those of
whom they have the care, whether by imposing upon them unequal
tasks, or by taking the produce of the soil or implements of husbandry without their consent; also if they receive anything in the
way of a bribe, or decide suits unjustly, or if they yield to the influences of flattery, let them be publicly dishonoured; and in regard to
any other wrong which they do to the inhabitants of the country, if
the question be of a mina, let them submit to the decision of the
villagers in the neighbourhood; but in suits of greater amount, or in
the case of lesser if they refuse to submit, trusting that their
monthly removal into another part of the country will enable them
to escape—in such cases the injured party may bring his suit in the

the care
of foun-
tains and
streams;

and of
irrigation.

Gymnasia
for youth.

Warm
baths for
the aged
rustic,
better
than a
doctor.

The war-
dens of
the
country
shall
decide
minor
cases.

They
should be
careful
of op-
[762]
pressing
the in-
habitants.

---

[1] Reading δέξιν.   [2] Cp. *infra*, viii. 843 D.

Common
meals.

No sleep-
ing out.

common court, and if he obtain a verdict he may exact from the defendant, who refused to submit, a double penalty.

The wardens and the overseers of the country, while on their two years' service, shall have common meals at their several stations, and shall all live together; and he who is absent from the common meal, or sleeps out, if only for one day or night, unless by order of his commanders, or by reason of absolute necessity, if the five denounce him and inscribe his name in the agora as not having kept his guard, let him be deemed to have betrayed the city, as far as lay in his power, and let him be disgraced and beaten with impunity by any one who meets him and is willing to punish him. If any of the commanders is guilty of such an irregularity, the whole company of sixty shall see to it, and he who is cognisant of the offence, and does not bring the offender to trial, shall be amenable to the same laws as the younger offender himself, and shall pay a heavier fine, and be incapable of ever commanding the young. The guardians of the law are to be careful inspectors of these matters, and shall either prevent or punish offenders. Every man should remember the universal rule, that he who is not a good servant will not be a good master; a man should pride himself more upon serving well than upon commanding

The ser-
vice of
the laws
is the
service of
the Gods.

well: first upon serving the laws, which is also the service of the Gods; in the second place, upon having served ancient and honourable men in the days of his youth. Furthermore, during the two years in which any one is a warden of the country, his daily food ought to be of a simple and humble kind. When the twelve have

763
The war-
dens of
the
country
are to
wait on
them-
selves.

been chosen, let them and the five meet together, and determine that they will be their own servants, and, like servants, will not have other slaves and servants for their own use, neither will they use those of the villagers and husbandmen for their private advantage, but for the public service only; and in general they should make up their minds to live independently by themselves, servants of each other and of themselves. Further, at all seasons of the year, summer and winter alike, let them be under arms and survey minutely the whole country; thus they will at once keep guard, and at

A man
should
acquire
an exact
knowl-
edge of
his own
country.

the same time acquire a perfect knowledge of every locality. There can be no more important kind of information than the exact knowledge of a man's own country; and for this as well as for more general reasons of pleasure and advantage, hunting with dogs and other kinds of sports should be pursued by the young. The service to whom this is committed may be called the secret police[1] or wardens of the country; the name does not much signify, but every one

---

[1] Cp. *supra*, i. 633 C.

who has the safety of the state at heart will use his utmost diligence in this service.

After the wardens of the country, we have to speak of the election of wardens of the agora and of the city. The wardens of the country were sixty in number, and the wardens of the city will be three, and will divide the twelve parts of the city into three; like the former, they shall have care of the ways, and of the different high roads which lead out of the country into the city, and of the buildings, that they may be all made according to law;—also of the waters, which the guardians of the supply preserve and convey to them, care being taken that they may reach the fountains pure and abundant, and be both an ornament and a benefit to the city. These also should be men of influence, and at leisure to take care of the public interest. Let every man propose as warden of the city any one whom he likes out of the highest class, and when the vote has been given on them, and the number is reduced to the six who have the greatest number of votes, let the electing officers choose by lot three out of the six, and when they have undergone a scrutiny let them hold office according to the laws laid down for them. Next, let the wardens of the agora be elected in like manner, out of the first and second class, five in number: ten are to be first elected, and out of the ten five are to be chosen by lot, as in the election of the wardens of the city:—these when they have undergone a scrutiny are to be declared magistrates. Every one shall vote for every one, and he who will not vote, if he be informed against before the magistrates, shall be fined fifty drachmae, and shall also be deemed a bad citizen. Let any one who likes go to the assembly and to the general council; it shall be compulsory to go on citizens of the first and second class, and they shall pay a fine of ten drachmae if they be found not answering to their names at the assembly. But the third and fourth class shall be under no compulsion, and shall be let off without a fine, unless the magistrates have commanded all to be present, in consequence of some urgent necessity. The wardens of the agora shall observe the order appointed by law for the agora, and shall have the charge of the temples and fountains which are in the agora; and they shall see that no one injures anything, and punish him who does, with stripes and bonds, if he be a slave or stranger; but if he be a citizen who misbehaves in this way, they shall have the power themselves of inflicting a fine upon him to the amount of a hundred drachmae, or with the consent of the wardens of the city up to double that amount. And let the wardens of the city have a similar power of imposing punishments and fines in their own department; and let them impose fines by their own authority, up to a mina, or

Laws VI

ATHE-
NIAN.

The wardens of the city are to be three, the wardens of the agora to be five in number.

The manner of electing them.

764
Attendance at the assembly and general council.

Powers of the wardens of the city and agora.

Two
kinds of
directors
of music
and of
gymnas-
tic:—
(1) in-
structors;
(2) judges.

The three
judges of
gymnas-
tic shall
judge
of horses
[765]
also. In
music
there
shall be
one judge
of the
solo
singers,
and one
of the
choruses.

The
manner
of elect-
ing the
judges.

up to two minae with the consent of the wardens of the agora.

In the next place, it will be proper to appoint directors of music
and gymnastic, two kinds of each—of the one kind the business will
be education, of the other, the superintendence of contests. In
speaking of education, the law means to speak of those who have
the care of order and instruction in gymnasia and schools, and of the
going to school, and of school buildings for boys and girls; and in
speaking of contests, the law refers to the judges of gymnastics and
of music; these again are divided into two classes, the one having to
do with music, the other with gymnastics; and the same who judge
of the gymnastic contests of men, shall judge of horses; but in music
there shall be one set of judges of solo singing, and of imitation—I
mean of rhapsodists, players on the harp, the flute and the like, and
another who shall judge of choral song. First of all, we must choose
directors for the choruses of boys, and men, and maidens, whom
they shall follow in the amusement of the dance, and for our other
musical arrangements;—one director will be enough for the choruses, and he should be not less than forty years of age. One director
will also be enough to introduce the solo singers, and to give judgment on the competitors, and he ought not to be less than thirty
years of age. The director and manager of the choruses shall be
elected after the following manner:—Let any persons who commonly take an interest in such matters go to the meeting, and be
fined if they do not go (the guardians of the law shall judge of their
fault), but those who have no interest shall not be compelled. The
elector shall propose as director some one who understands music,
and he in the scrutiny may be challenged on the one part by those
who say he has no skill, and defended on the other hand by those
who say that he has. Ten are to be elected by vote, and he of the ten
who is chosen by lot shall undergo a scrutiny, and lead the choruses
for a year according to law. And in like manner the competitor who
wins the lot shall be leader of the solo and concert music for that
year; and he who is thus elected shall deliver the award to the
judges. In the next place, we have to choose judges in the contests
of horses and of men; these shall be selected from the third and also
from the second class of citizens, and the three first classes shall be
compelled to go to the election, but the lowest may stay away with
impunity; and let there be three elected by lot out of the twenty
who have been chosen previously, and they must also have the vote
and approval of the examiners. But if any one is rejected in the
scrutiny at any ballot or decision, others shall be chosen in the same
manner, and undergo a similar scrutiny.

There remains the minister of the education of youth, male and female; he too will rule according to law; one such minister will be sufficient, and he must be fifty years old, and have children lawfully begotten, both boys and girls by preference, at any rate, one or the other. He who is elected, and he who is the elector, should consider that of all the great offices of state this is the greatest; for the first shoot of any plant, if it makes a good start towards the attainment of its natural excellence, has the greatest effect on its maturity; and this is not only true of plants, but of animals wild and tame, and also of men. Man, as we say, is a tame or civilized animal; nevertheless, he requires proper instruction and a fortunate nature, and then of all animals he becomes the most divine and most civilized[1]; but if he be insufficiently or ill educated he is the most savage of earthly creatures. Wherefore the legislator ought not to allow the education of children to become a secondary or accidental matter. In the first place, he who would be rightly provident about them, should begin by taking care that he is elected, who of all the citizens is in every way best; him the legislator shall do his utmost to appoint guardian and superintendent. To this end all the magistrates, with the exception of the council and prytanes, shall go to the temple of Apollo, and elect by ballot him of the guardians of the law whom they severally think will be the best superintendent of education. And he who has the greatest number of votes, after he has undergone a scrutiny at the hands of all the magistrates who have been his electors, with the exception of the guardians of the law,—shall hold office for five years; and in the sixth year let another be chosen in like manner to fill his office.

If any one dies while he is holding a public office, and more than thirty days before his term of office expires, let those whose business it is elect another to the office in the same manner as before. And if any one who is entrusted with orphans dies, let the relations both on the father's and mother's side, who are residing at home, including cousins, appoint another guardian within ten days, or be fined a drachma a day for neglect to do so.

A city which has no regular courts of law ceases to be a city; and again, if a judge is silent and says no more in preliminary proceedings than the litigants, as is the case in arbitrations, he will never be able to decide justly; wherefore a multitude of judges will not easily judge well, nor a few if they are bad. The point in dispute between the parties should be made clear; and time, and deliberation, and repeated examination, greatly tend to clear up doubts. For this reason, he who goes to law with another, should go first of all to his neighbours and friends who know best the questions at issue. And

[1] Arist. Pol. i. 2, §§ 15, 16.

Laws VI

ATHE-
NIAN.

The minister of the education of youth [766] the greatest of the officers of state.

He is to be elected by the magistrates, and to hold office for five years.

Disputes to be referred (1) to a

767
Laws VI

ATHE-
NIAN.

council of
friends
and
neigh-
bours:
(2) to an
ordinary
court:
(3) to a
court of
appeal.

Litigants
may ap-
point
their own
tribunal.

There will
be courts
(1) for
private,
and (2)
for public
causes.

The court
of appeal:
the judges
to be
selected
from each
magis-
tracy.

if he be unable to obtain from them a satisfactory decision, let him have recourse to another court; and if the two courts cannot settle the matter, let a third put an end to the suit.

Now the establishment of courts of justice may be regarded as a choice of magistrates, for every magistrate must also be a judge of some things; and the judge, though he be not a magistrate, yet in certain respects is a very important magistrate on the day on which he is determining a suit. Regarding then the judges also as magistrates, let us say who are fit to be judges, and of what they are to be judges, and how many of them are to judge in each suit. Let that be the supreme tribunal which the litigants appoint in common for themselves, choosing certain persons by agreement. And let there be two other tribunals: one for private causes, when a citizen accuses another of wronging him and wishes to get a decision; the other for public causes, in which some citizen is of opinion that the public has been wronged by an individual, and is willing to vindicate the common interests. And we must not forget to mention how the judges are to be qualified, and who they are to be. In the first place, let there be a tribunal open to all private persons who are trying causes one against another for the third time, and let this be composed as follows:—All the officers of state, as well annual as those holding office for a longer period, when the new year is about to commence, in the month following after the summer solstice, on the last day but one of the year, shall meet in some temple, and calling God to witness, shall dedicate one judge from every magistracy to be their first-fruits, choosing in each office him who seems to them to be the best, and whom they deem likely to decide the causes of his fellow-citizens during the ensuing year in the best and holiest manner. And when the election is completed, a scrutiny shall be held in the presence of the electors themselves, and if any one be rejected another shall be chosen in the same manner. Those who have undergone the scrutiny shall judge the causes of those who have declined the inferior courts, and shall give their vote openly. The councillors and other magistrates who have elected them shall be required to be hearers and spectators of the causes; and any one else may be present who pleases. If one man charges another with having intentionally decided wrong, let him go to the guardians of the law and lay his accusation before them, and he who is found guilty in such a case shall pay damages to the injured party equal to half the injury; but if he shall appear to deserve a greater penalty, the judges shall determine what additional punishment he shall suffer, and how much more he ought to pay to the public treasury, and to the party who brought the suit.

In the judgment of offences against the state, the people ought to participate, for when any one wrongs the state all are wronged, and may reasonably complain if they are not allowed to share in the decision. Such causes ought to originate with the people, and they ought also to have the final decision of them, but the trial of them shall take place before three of the highest magistrates, upon whom the plaintiff and the defendant shall agree; and if they are not able to come to an agreement themselves, the council shall choose one of the two proposed. And in private suits, too, as far as is possible, all should have a share; for he who has no share in the administration of justice, is apt to imagine that he has no share in the state at all. And for this reason there shall be a court of law in every tribe, and the judges shall be chosen by lot;—they shall give their decisions at once, and shall be inaccessible to entreaties. The final judgment shall rest with that court which, as we maintain, has been established in the most incorruptible form of which human things admit: this shall be the court established for those who are unable to get rid of their suits either in the courts of neighbours or of the tribes.

Thus much of the courts of law, which, as I was saying, cannot be precisely defined either as being or not being offices; a superficial sketch has been given of them, in which some things have been told and others omitted. For the right place of an exact statement of the laws respecting suits, under their several heads, will be at the end of the body of legislation;—let us then expect them at the end[1]. Hitherto our legislation has been chiefly occupied with the appointment of offices. Perfect unity and exactness, extending to the whole and every particular of political administration, cannot be attained to the full, until the discussion shall have a beginning, middle, and end, and is complete in every part. At present we have reached the election of magistrates, and this may be regarded as a sufficient termination of what has preceded. And now there need no longer be any delay or hesitation in beginning the work of legislation.

Cle. I like what you have said, Stranger; and I particularly like your manner of tacking on the beginning of your new discourse to the end of the former one.

Ath. Thus far, then, the old men's rational pastime has gone off well.

Cle. You mean, I suppose, their serious and noble pursuit?

Ath. Perhaps; but I should like to know whether you and I are agreed about a certain thing.

Cle. About what thing?

Ath. You know the endless labour which painters expend upon

[1] Cp. *infra*, ix. 853 foll.; xii. 956 foll.

Public suits should originate with the people, and should be decided by them. In private suits, too, all should share.

The courts of the tribes.

From magistrates we proceed to laws.

769

Laws, like
pictures,
require
renewal in
the course
of ages.

their pictures—they are always putting in or taking out colours, or whatever be the term which artists employ; they seem as if they would never cease touching up their works, which are always being made brighter and more beautiful.

Cle. I know something of these matters from report, although I have never had any great acquaintance with the art.

Ath. No matter; we may make use of the illustration notwithstanding:—Suppose that some one had a mind to paint a figure in the most beautiful manner, in the hope that his work instead of losing would always improve as time went on—do you not see that being a mortal, unless he leaves some one to succeed him who will correct the flaws which time may introduce, and be able to add what is left imperfect through the defect of the artist, and who will further brighten up and improve the picture, all his great labour will last but a short time?

Cle. True.

Ath. And is not the aim of the legislator similar? First, he desires that his laws should be written down with all possible exactness; in the second place, as time goes on and he has made an actual trial of his decrees, will he not find omissions? Do you imagine that there ever was a legislator so foolish as not to know that many things are necessarily omitted, which some one coming after him must correct, if the constitution and the order of government is not to deteriorate, but to improve in the state which he has established?

Cle. Assuredly, that is the sort of thing which every one would desire.

The
guardians
of the law
should be
also legis-
lators.

Ath. And if any one possesses any means of accomplishing this by word or deed, or has any way great or small by which he can teach a person to understand how he can maintain and amend the laws, he should finish what he has to say, and not leave the work incomplete.

Cle. By all means.

770

Ath. And is not this what you and I have to do at the present moment?

Cle. What have we to do?

Ath. As we are about to legislate and have chosen our guardians of the law, and are ourselves in the evening of life, and they as compared with us are young men, we ought not only to legislate for them, but to endeavour to make them not only guardians of the law but legislators themselves, as far as this is possible.

Cle. Certainly; if we can.

Ath. At any rate, we must do our best.

Cle. Of course.

Ath. We will say to them,—O friends and saviours of our laws, in

laying down any law, there are many particulars which we shall
omit, and this cannot be helped; at the same time, we will do our
utmost to describe what is important, and will give an outline which
you shall fill up. And I will explain on what principle you are to act.
Megillus and Cleinias and I have often spoken to one another
touching these matters, and we are of opinion that we have spoken
well. And we hope that you will be of the same mind with us, and
become our disciples, and keep in view the things which in our
united opinion the legislator and guardian of the law ought to keep
in view. There was one main point about which we were agreed—
that a man's whole energies throughout life should be devoted to
the acquisition of the virtue proper to a man, whether this was to be
gained by study, or habit, or some mode of acquisition, or desire, or
opinion, or knowledge—and this applies equally to men and women,
old and young—the aim of all should always be such as I have described; anything which may be an impediment, the good man
ought to show that he utterly disregards. And if at last necessity
plainly compels him to be an outlaw from his native land, rather
than bow his neck to the yoke of slavery and be ruled by inferiors,
and he has to fly, an exile he must be and endure all such trials,
rather than accept another form of government, which is likely to
make men worse. These are our original principles; and do you now,
fixing your eyes upon the standard of what a man and a citizen
ought or ought not to be, praise and blame the laws—blame those
which have not this power of making the citizen better, but embrace
those which have; and with gladness receive and live in them;
bidding a long farewell to other institutions which aim at goods, as
they are termed, of a different kind.

Let us proceed to another class of laws, beginning with their
foundation in religion. And we must first return to the number
5040—the entire number had, and has, a great many convenient
divisions, and the number of the tribes which was a twelfth part of
the whole, being correctly formed by 21 × 20 [5040 ÷ (21 × 20),
i.e. 5040 ÷ 420 = 12], also has them. And not only is the whole
number divisible by twelve, but also the number of each tribe is
divisible by twelve. Now every portion should be regarded by us as
a sacred gift of Heaven, corresponding to the months and to the
revolution of the universe[1]. Every city has a guiding and sacred
principle given by nature, but in some the division or distribution
has been more right than in others, and has been more sacred and
fortunate. In our opinion, nothing can be more right than the selection of the number 5040, which may be divided by all numbers

[1] Cp. Tim. 39, 47 A.

Laws VI

ATHE-
NIAN.

A man's
whole
energies
to be de-
voted to
virtue.

If the
govern-
ment of
his
country
grows
corrupt,
he must
go into
exile.

771

The
number
5040 and
its nu-
merous
divisors.

from one to twelve with the single exception of eleven, and that admits of a very easy correction; for if, turning to the dividend (5040), we deduct two families, the defect in the division is cured. And the truth of this may be easily proved when we have leisure. But for the present, trusting to the mere assertion of this principle, let us divide the state; and assigning to each portion some God or son of a God, let us give them altars and sacred rites, and at the altars let us hold assemblies for sacrifice twice in the month—twelve assemblies for the tribes, and twelve for the city, according to their divisions; the first in honour of the Gods and divine things, and the second to promote friendship and 'better acquaintance,' as the phrase is, and every sort of good fellowship with one another. For

people must be acquainted with those into whose families and whom they marry and with those to whom they give in marriage; in such matters, as far as possible, a man should deem it all important to avoid a mistake, and with this serious purpose let games be instituted[1] in which youths and maidens shall dance together, seeing one another and being seen naked, at a proper age, and on a suitable occasion, not transgressing the rules of modesty.

The directors of choruses will be the superintendents and regulators of these games, and they, together with the guardians of the law, will legislate in any matters which we have omitted; for, as we said[2], where there are numerous and minute details, the legislator must leave out something. And the annual officers who have experience, and know what is wanted, must make arrangements and improvements year by year, until such enactments and provisions are sufficiently determined. A ten years' experience of sacrifices and dances, if extending to all particulars, will be quite sufficient; and if the legislator be alive they shall communicate with him, but if he be dead then the several officers shall refer the omissions which come under their notice to the guardians of the law, and correct

them, until all is perfect; and from that time there shall be no more change, and they shall establish and use the new laws with the others which the legislator originally gave them, and of which they are never, if they can help, to change aught; or, if some necessity overtakes them, the magistrates must be called into counsel, and the whole people, and they must go to all the oracles of the Gods; and if they are all agreed, in that case they may make the change, but if they are not agreed, by no manner of means, and any one who dissents shall prevail, as the law ordains.

Whenever any one over twenty-five years of age, having seen and

[1] Cp. Rep. v. 459 E.   [2] Cp. *supra*, 770 B.

been seen by others, believes himself to have found a marriage connection which is to his mind, and suitable for the procreation of children, let him marry if he be still under the age of five-and-thirty years; but let him first hear how he ought to seek after what is suitable and appropriate[1]. For, as Cleinias says[2], every law should have a suitable prelude.

Cle. You recollect at the right moment, Stranger, and do not miss the opportunity which the argument affords of saying a word in season.

Ath. I thank you. We will say to him who is born of good parents, —O my son, you ought to make such a marriage as wise men would approve. Now they would advise you neither to avoid a poor marriage, nor specially to desire a rich one; but if other things are equal, always to honour inferiors, and with them to form connections;—this will be for the benefit of the city and of the families which are united; for the equable and symmetrical tends infinitely more to virtue than the unmixed. And he who is conscious of being too headstrong, and carried away more than is fitting in all his actions, ought to desire to become the relation of orderly parents; and he who is of the opposite temper ought to seek the opposite alliance. Let there be one word concerning all marriages:—Every man shall follow, not after the marriage which is most pleasing to himself, but after that which is most beneficial to the state. For somehow every one is by nature prone to that which is likest to himself, and in this way the whole city becomes unequal in property and in disposition; and hence there arise in most states the very results which we least desire to happen. Now, to add to the law an express provision, not only that the rich man shall not marry into the rich family, nor the powerful into the family of the powerful, but that the slower natures shall be compelled to enter into marriage with the quicker, and the quicker with the slower, may awaken anger as well as laughter in the minds of many; for there is a difficulty in perceiving that the city ought to be well mingled like a cup, in which the maddening wine is hot and fiery, but when chastened by a soberer God, receives a fair associate and becomes an excellent and temperate drink[3]. Yet in marriage no one is able to see that the same result occurs. Wherefore also the law must let alone such matters, but we should try to charm the spirits of men into believing the equability of their children's disposition to be of more importance than equality in excessive fortune when they marry; and him who is too desirous of making a rich marriage we should endeavour

Laws VI

ATHE-
NIAN,
CLEINIAS.

773

In marriage there should be a union of opposite qualities.

In marriage every man should seek, not what is pleasantest to himself, but what is best for the state: the rich should marry the poor, the quicker natures the slower.

These principles can only be suggested; they can-

---

[1] Cp. *supra*, iv. 721, and Arist. Pol. vii. 16, § 9.   [2] *Supra*, iv. 723 C.
[3] Cp. Statesman, 306 foll.

774

not be en-
forced by
law.

The un-
married
shall be
fined
and dis-
honoured.

No one
need
marry for
money.

Marriage
garments
to be in-
expensive.

Be-
trothals.

to turn aside by reproaches, not, however, by any compulsion of written law.

Let this then be our exhortation concerning marriage, and let us remember what was said before[1]—that a man should cling to immortality, and leave behind him children's children to be the servants of God in his place for ever. All this and much more may be truly said by way of prelude about the duty of marriage. But if a man will not listen, and remains unsocial and alien among his fellow-citizens, and is still unmarried at thirty-five years of age, let him pay a yearly fine;—he who is of the highest class shall pay a fine of a hundred drachmae, and he who is of the second class a fine of seventy drachmae; the third class shall pay sixty drachmae, and the fourth thirty drachmae, and let the money be sacred to Herè; he who does not pay the fine annually shall owe ten times the sum, which the treasurer of the goddess shall exact; and if he fails in doing so, let him be answerable and give an account of the money at his audit. He who refuses to marry shall be thus punished in money, and also be deprived of all honour which the younger show to the elder; let no young man voluntarily obey him, and, if he attempt to punish any one, let every one come to the rescue and defend the injured person, and he who is present and does not come to the rescue, shall be pronounced by the law to be a coward and a bad citizen. Of the marriage portion I have already spoken[2]; and again I say for the instruction[3] of poor men that he who neither gives nor receives a dowry on account of poverty, has a compensation; for the citizens of our state are provided with the necessaries of life, and wives will be less likely to be insolent, and husbands to be mean and subservient to them on account of property. And he who obeys this law will do a noble action; but he who will not obey, and gives or receives more than fifty drachmae as the price of the marriage garments if he be of the lowest, or more than a mina, or a mina-and-a-half, if he be of the third or second classes, or two minae if he be of the highest class, shall owe to the public treasury a similar sum, and that which is given or received shall be sacred to Herè and Zeus; and let the treasurers of these Gods exact the money, as was said before about the unmarried—that the treasurers of Herè were to exact the money, or pay the fine themselves.

The betrothal by a father shall be valid in the first degree, that by a grandfather in the second degree, and in the third degree, betrothal by brothers who have the same father; but if there are none

---

[1] *Supra*, iv. 721.   [2] Cp. *supra*, v. 742 C.
[3] Reading with Stallbaum, διδάσκειν.

of these alive, the betrothal by a mother shall be valid in like manner; in cases of unexampled fatality, the next of kin and the guardians shall have authority. What are to be the rites before marriages, or any other sacred acts, relating either to future, present, or past marriages, shall be referred to the interpreters; and he who follows their advice may be satisfied. Touching the marriage festival, they shall assemble not more than five male and five female friends of both families, and a like number of members of the family of either sex, and no man shall spend more than his means will allow; he who is of the richest class may spend a mina,—he who is of the second, half a mina, and in the same proportion as the census of each decreases: all men shall praise him who is obedient to the law; but he who is disobedient shall be punished by the guardians of the law as a man wanting in true taste, and uninstructed in the laws of bridal song. Drunkenness is always improper, except at the festivals of the God who gave wine; and peculiarly dangerous, when a man is engaged in the business of marriage; at such a crisis of their lives a bride and bridegroom ought to have all their wits about them— they ought to take care that their offspring may be born of reasonable beings; for on what day or night Heaven will give them increase, who can say? Moreover, they ought not to be begetting children when their bodies are dissipated by intoxication, but their offspring should be compact and solid, quiet and compounded properly; whereas the drunkard is all abroad in all his actions, and beside himself both in body and soul. Wherefore, also, the drunken man is bad and unsteady in sowing the seed of increase, and is likely to beget offspring who will be unstable and untrustworthy, and cannot be expected to walk straight either in body or mind. Hence during the whole year and all his life long, and expecially while he is begetting children, he ought to take care and not intentionally do what is injurious to health, or what involves insolence and wrong; for he cannot help leaving the impression of himself on the souls and bodies of his offspring, and he begets children in every way inferior. And especially on the day and night of marriage should a man abstain from such things. For the beginning, which is also a God dwelling in man, preserves all things, if it meet with proper respect from each individual. He who marries is further to consider, that one of the two houses in the lot is the nest and nursery of his young, and there he is to marry and make a home for himself and bring up his children, going away from his father and mother. For in friendships there must be some degree of desire, in order to cement and bind together diversities of character; but excessive intercourse not having the desire which is created by time,

Laws VI

ATHE-
NIAN.

775
Marriage
festivals
to be
moderate.

A man
should be
sober
when he
is engaged
in the
business
of marriage; for
children
receive
the impress of
their
parents,
both in
body and
soul.

776
'A man
shall leave
his father
and
mother,
and
cleave
unto his
wife.'

Laws VI

ATHE-
NIAN,
CLEINIAS,
MEGIL-
LUS.

'Handing
on the
torch of
life.'

Slaves the
most
trouble-
some kind
of pro-
perty.

Two
kinds of
slaves.
There are
good
slaves,
'better
than
brethren
or sons.'

Another
class are
like brute
animals,
[777]
or are
made so
by the
treatment
of their
masters.

insensibly dissolves friendships from a feeling of satiety; wherefore a man and his wife shall leave to his and her father and mother their own dwelling-places, and themselves go as to a colony and dwell there, and visit and be visited by their parents; and they shall beget and bring up children, handing on the torch of life from one generation to another, and worshipping the Gods according to law for ever.

In the next place, we have to consider what sort of property will be most convenient. There is no difficulty either in understanding or acquiring most kinds of property, but there is great difficulty in what relates to slaves. And the reason is, that we speak about them in a way which is right and which is not right; for what we say about our slaves is consistent and also inconsistent with our practice about them.

Meg. I do not understand, Stranger, what you mean.

Ath. I am not surprised, Megillus, for the state of the Helots among the Lacedaemonians is of all Hellenic forms of slavery the most controverted and disputed about, some approving and some condemning it; there is less dispute about the slavery which exists among the Heracleots, who have subjugated the Mariandynians, and about the Thessalian Penestae. Looking at these and the like examples, what ought we to do concerning property in slaves? I made a remark, in passing, which naturally elicited a question about my meaning from you. It was this:—We know that all would agree that we should have the best and most attached slaves whom we can get. For many a man has found his slaves better in every way than brethren or sons, and many times they have saved the lives and property of their masters and their whole house—such tales are well known.

Meg. To be sure.

Ath. But may we not also say that the soul of the slave is utterly corrupt, and that no man of sense ought to trust them? And the wisest of our poets, speaking of Zeus, says:

'Far-seeing Zeus takes away half the understanding of men whom the day of slavery subdues.'

Different persons have got these two different notions of slaves in their minds—some of them utterly distrust their servants, and, as if they were wild beasts, chastise them with goads and whips, and make their souls three times, or rather many times, as slavish as they were before;—and others do just the opposite.

Meg. True.

Cle. Then what are we to do in our own country, Stranger, seeing that there are such differences in the treatment of slaves by their owners?

Ath. Well, Cleinias, there can be no doubt that man is a troublesome animal, and therefore he is not very manageable, nor likely to become so, when you attempt to introduce the necessary division of slave, and freeman, and master.

Cle. That is obvious.

Ath. He is a troublesome piece of goods, as has been often shown by the frequent revolts of the Messenians, and the great mischiefs which happen in states having many slaves who speak the same language, and the numerous robberies and lawless life of the Italian banditti, as they are called. A man who considers all this is fairly at a loss. Two remedies alone remain to us,—not to have the slaves of the same country, nor if possible, speaking the same language[1]; in this way they will more easily be held in subjection: secondly, we should tend them carefully, not only out of regard to them, but yet more out of respect to ourselves. And the right treatment of slaves is to behave properly to them, and to do to them, if possible, even more justice than to those who are our equals; for he who naturally and genuinely reverences justice, and hates injustice, is discovered in his dealings with any class of men to whom he can easily be unjust. And he who in regard to the natures and actions of his slaves is undefiled by impiety and injustice, will best sow the seeds of virtue in them; and this may be truly said of every master, and tyrant, and of every other having authority in relation to his inferiors. Slaves ought to be punished as they deserve, and not admonished as if they were freemen, which will only make them conceited. The language used to a servant ought always to be that of a command[2], and we ought not to jest with them, whether they are males or females—this is a foolish way which many people have of setting up their slaves, and making the life of servitude more disagreeable both for them and for their masters.

Cle. True.

Ath. Now that each of the citizens is provided, as far as possible, with a sufficient number of suitable slaves who can help him in what he has to do, we may next proceed to describe their dwellings.

Cle. Very good.

Ath. The city being new and hitherto uninhabited, care ought to be taken of all the buildings, and the manner of building each of them, and also of the temples and walls. These, Cleinias, were matters which properly came before the marriages; but, as we are only talking, there is no objection to changing the order. If, how-

[1] Cp. Arist. Pol. vii. 10, § 13.   [2] Cp. Arist. Pol. i. 13, § 14.

Laws VI

ATHE-
NIAN,
CLEINIAS.

Slaves
should
not be of
the same
country;
they
should be
tended
carefully
and
treated
justly.

778

The
houses
should
have
come be-
fore mar-

riages;
but no
matter.

The city
to be
placed
on the
heights,
and the
temples,
near
which are
the law-
courts, to
be built
round the
Agora.

The walls
should
slumber
in the
earth.

779

If cities
are to
have
walls, the
private
houses
should
form
them.

ever, our plan of legislation is ever to take effect, then the house shall precede the marriage if God so will, and afterwards we will come to the regulations about marriage; but at present we are only describing these matters in a general outline.

Cle. Quite true.

Ath. The temples are to be placed all round the agora, and the whole city built on the heights in a circle[1], for the sake of defence and for the sake of purity. Near the temples are to be placed buildings for the magistrates and the courts of law; in these plaintiff and defendant will receive their due, and the places will be regarded as most holy, partly because they have to do with holy things, and partly because they are the dwelling-places of holy Gods: and in them will be held the courts in which cases of homicide and other trials of capital offenses may fitly take place. As to the walls, Megillus, I agree with Sparta in thinking that they should be allowed to sleep in the earth, and that we should not attempt to disinter them[2]; there is a poetical saying, which is finely expressed, that 'walls ought to be of steel and iron, and not of earth;' besides, how ridiculous of us to be sending out our young men annually into the country to dig and to trench, and to keep off the enemy by fortifications, under the idea that they are not to be allowed to set foot in our territory, and then, that we should surround ourselves with a wall, which, in the first place, is by no means conducive to the health of cities, and is also apt to produce a certain effeminacy in the minds of the inhabitants, inviting men to run thither instead of repelling their enemies, and leading them to imagine that their safety is due not to their keeping guard day and night, but that when they are protected by walls and gates, then they may sleep in safety; as if they were not meant to labour, and did not know that true repose comes from labour, and that disgraceful indolence and a careless temper of mind is only the renewal of trouble. But if men must have walls, the private houses ought to be so arranged from the first that the whole city may be one wall, having all the houses capable of defence by reason of their uniformity and equality towards the streets[3]. The form of the city being that of a single dwelling will have an agreeable aspect, and being easily guarded will be infinitely better for security. Until the original building is completed, these should be the principal objects of the inhabitants; and the wardens of the city should superintend the work, and should impose a fine on him who is negligent; and in all that relates to the city they should have a care of cleanliness, and not

[1] Cp. Arist. Pol. vii. 12, § 3.   [2] Cp. Arist. Pol. vii. 11, § 8.
[3] Cp. Arist. Pol. vii. 11, § 6.

allow a private person to encroach upon any public property either by buildings or excavations. Further, they ought to take care that the rains from heaven flow off easily, and of any other matters which may have to be administered either within or without the city. The guardians of the law shall pass any further enactments which their experience may show to be necessary, and supply any other points in which the law may be deficient. And now that these matters, and the buildings about the agora, and the gymnasia, and places of instruction, and theatres, are all ready and waiting for scholars and spectators, let us proceed to the subjects which follow marriage in the order of legislation.

Cle. By all means.

Ath. Assuming that marriages exist already, Cleinias, the mode of life during the year after marriage, before children are born, will follow next in order. In what way bride and bridegroom ought to live in a city which is to be superior to other cities, is a matter not at all easy for us to determine. There have been many difficulties already, but this will be the greatest of them, and the most disagreeable to the many. Still I cannot but say what appears to me to be right and true, Cleinias.

Cle. Certainly.

Ath. He who imagines that he can give laws for the public conduct of states, while he leaves the private life of citizens wholly to take care of itself; who thinks that individuals may pass the day as they please, and that there is no necessity of order in all things; he, I say, who gives up the control of their private lives, and supposes that they will conform to law in their common and public life, is making a great mistake. Why have I made this remark? Why, because I am going to enact that the bridegrooms should live at the common tables, just as they did before marriage. This was a singularity when first enacted by the legislator in your parts of the world, Megillus and Cleinias, as I should suppose, on the occasion of some war or other similar danger[1], which caused the passing of the law, and which would be likely to occur in thinly-peopled places, and in times of pressure. But when men had once tried and been accustomed to a common table, experience showed that the institution greatly conduced to security; and in some such manner the custom of having common tables arose among you.

Cle. Likely enough.

Ath. I said that there may have been singularity and danger in imposing such a custom at first, but that now there is not the same difficulty. There is, however, another institution which is the

[1] Cp. *supra,* i. 625, 633.

Laws VI

ATHE-
NIAN,
CLEINIAS.

The rain
should be
made to
flow off
easily.

Life after
marriage.

780

As at
Sparta
and
Crete, the
bride-
groom
should
continue
to live
at the
common
tables

natural sequel to this, and would be excellent, if it existed any-where, but at present it does not. The institution of which I am about to speak is not easily described or executed; and would be like the legislator 'combing wool into the fire,' as people say, or performing any other impossible and useless feat.

Cle. What is the cause, Stranger, of this extreme hesitation?

Ath. You shall hear without any fruitless loss of time. That which has law and order in a state is the cause of every good, but that which is disordered or ill-ordered is often the ruin of that which is well-ordered; and at this point the argument is now waiting. For with you, Cleinias and Megillus, the common tables of men are, as I said, a heaven-born and admirable institution, but you are mistaken in leaving the women unregulated by law. They have no similar institution of public tables in the light of day, and just that part of the human race which is by nature prone to secrecy and stealth on account of their weakness—I mean the female sex—has been left without regulation by the legislator, which is a great mis-take. And, in consequence of this neglect, many things have grown lax among you, which might have been far better, if they had been only regulated by law; for the neglect of regulations about women may not only be regarded as a neglect of half the entire matter[1], but in proportion as woman's nature is inferior to that of men in capacity for virtue, in that degree the consequence of such neglect is more than twice as important. The careful consideration of this matter, and the arranging and ordering on a common principle of all our institutions relating both to men and women, greatly con-duces to the happiness of the state. But at present, such is the un-fortunate condition of mankind, that no man of sense will even ven-ture to speak of common tables in places and cities in which they have never been established at all; and how can any one avoid being utterly ridiculous, who attempts to compel women to show in public how much they eat and drink? There is nothing at which the sex is more likely to take offence. For women are accustomed to creep into dark places, and when dragged out into the light they will exert their utmost powers of resistance, and be far too much for the legislator. And therefore, as I said before, in most places they will not endure to have the truth spoken without raising a tremen-dous outcry, but in this state perhaps they may. And if we may assume that our whole discussion about the state has not been mere idle talk, I should like to prove to you, if you will consent to listen, that this institution is good and proper; but if you had rather not, I will refrain.

[1] Arist. Pol. i. 13, §§ 15, 16.

781

Women should be drawn into the light of day, and not be left to them-selves.

No one ventures to intro-duce common tables where they do not exist already; and women certainly will not submit to them.

Cle. There is nothing which we should both of us like better, Stranger, than to hear what you have to say.

Ath. Very good; and you must not be surprised if I go back a little, for we have plenty of leisure, and there is nothing to prevent us from considering in every point of view the subject of law.

Cle. True.

Ath. Then let us return once more to what we were saying at first. Every man should understand that the human race either had no beginning at all, and will never have an end, but always will be and has been; or that it began an immense while ago[1].

Cle. Certainly.

Ath. Well, and have there not been constitutions and destructions of states, and all sorts of pursuits both orderly and disorderly, and diverse desires of meats and drinks always, and in all the world, and all sorts of changes of the seasons in which animals may be expected to have undergone innumerable transformations of themselves?

Cle. No doubt.

Ath. And may we not suppose that vines appeared, which had previously no existence, and also olives, and the gifts of Demeter and her daughter, of which one Triptolemus was the minister, and that, before these existed, animals took to devouring each other as they do still?

Cle. True.

Ath. Again, the practice of men sacrificing one another still exists among many nations; while, on the other hand, we hear of other human beings who did not even venture to taste[2] the flesh of a cow and had no animal sacrifices, but only cakes and fruits dipped in honey, and similar pure offerings, but no flesh of animals; from these they abstained under the idea that they ought not to eat them, and might not stain the altars of the Gods with blood. For in those days men are said to have lived a sort of Orphic life, having the use of all lifeless things, but abstaining from all living things.

Cle. Such has been the constant tradition, and is very likely true.

Ath. Some one might say to us, What is the drift of all this?

Cle. A very pertinent question, Stranger.

Ath. And therefore I will endeavour, Cleinias, if I can, to draw the natural inference.

Cle. Proceed.

Ath. I see that among men all things depend upon three wants and desires, of which the end is virtue, if they are rightly led by them, or the opposite if wrongly. Now these are eating and drinking, which begin at birth—every animal has a natural desire for

---

[1] Cp. iii. *supra*, 676. [2] Reading ὅτι and ἐτόλμων.

Laws VI
ATHE-
NIAN,
CLEINIAS.

Antiquity
of man-
kind.

782

All sorts
of
changes
have oc-
curred in
the course
of ages.

The
growth of
vines,
olives,
corn.

Some na-
tions still
sacrifice
human
beings;
others are
said to
have ab-
stained
from ani-
mal food.

Three
great de-
sires:—
(1) of
eating;

Laws VI

783

ATHE-
NIAN,
CLEINIAS.

(2) of
drinking;
(3) of
sexual
inter-
course.

Three
counter-
acting
princi-
ples:—
fear, law,
and right
reason.

them, and is violently excited, and rebels against him who says that he must not satisfy all his pleasures and appetites, and get rid of all the corresponding pains—and the third and greatest and sharpest want and desire breaks out last, and is the fire of sexual lust, which kindles in men every species of wantonness and madness. And these three disorders we must endeavour to master by the three great principles of fear and law and right reason; turning them away from that which is called pleasantest to the best, using the Muses and the Gods who preside over contests to extinguish their increase and influx.

But to return:—After marriage let us speak of the birth of children, and after their birth of their nurture and education. In the course of discussion the several laws will be perfected, and we shall at last arrive at the common tables. Whether such associations are to be confined to men, or extended to women also, we shall see better when we approach and take a nearer view of them; and we may then determine what previous institutions are required and will have to precede them. As I said before, we shall see them more in detail, and shall be better able to lay down the laws which are proper or suited to them.

Cle. Very true.

Ath. Let us keep in mind the words which have now been spoken; for hereafter there may be need of them.

Cle. What do you bid us keep in mind?

Ath. That which we comprehended under the three words—first, eating, secondly, drinking, thirdly, the excitement of love.

Cle. We shall be sure to remember, Stranger.

Ath. Very good. Then let us now proceed to marriage, and teach persons in what way they shall beget children, threatening them, if they disobey, with the terrors of the law.

Cle. What do you mean?

The bride
and
bride-
groom
should at-
tend to
their
business.

Ath. The bride and bridegroom should consider that they are to produce for the state the best and fairest specimens of children which they can. Now all men who are associated in any action always succeed when they attend and give their mind to what they are doing, but when they do not give their mind or have no mind, they fail; wherefore let the bridegroom give his mind to the bride and to the begetting of children, and the bride in like manner give her mind to the bridegroom, and particularly at the time when their children are not yet born. And let the women whom we have chosen be the overseers of such matters, and let them in whatever number, large or small, and at whatever time the magistrates may command, assemble every day in the temple of Eileithyia during a

third part of the day, and being there assembled, let them inform
one another of any one whom they see, whether man or woman, of
those who are begetting children, disregarding the ordinances given
at the time when the nuptial sacrifices and ceremonies were performed. Let the begetting of children and the supervision of those
who are begetting them continue ten years and no longer, during the
time when marriage is fruitful. But if any continue without
children up to this time, let them take counsel with their kindred
and with the women holding the office of overseer and be divorced
for their mutual benefit. If, however, any dispute arises about what
is proper and for the interest of either party, they shall choose ten
of the guardians of the law and abide by their permission and appointment. The women who preside over these matters shall enter
into the houses of the young, and partly by admonitions and partly
by threats make them give over their folly and error: if they persist, let the women go and tell the guardians of the law, and the
guardians shall prevent them. But if they too cannot prevent them,
they shall bring the matter before the people; and let them write up
their names and make oath that they cannot reform such and such
an one; and let him who is thus written up, if he cannot in a court of
law convict those who have inscribed his name, be deprived of the
privileges of a citizen in the following respects:—let him not go to
weddings nor to the thanksgivings after the birth of children;
and if he go, let any one who pleases strike him with impunity; and
let the same regulations hold about women: let not a woman be
allowed to appear abroad, or receive honour, or go to nuptial and
birthday festivals, if she in like manner be written up as acting disorderly and cannot obtain a verdict. And if, when they themselves
have done begetting children according to the law, a man or
woman have connection with another man or woman who are
still begetting children, let the same penalties be inflicted upon
them as upon those who are still having a family; and when the
time for procreation has passed let the man or woman who refrains
in such matters be held in esteem, and let those who do not refrain
be held in the contrary of esteem—that is to say, disesteem. Now,
if the greater part of mankind behave modestly, the enactments of
law may be left to slumber; but, if they are disorderly, the enactments having been passed, let them be carried into execution. To
every man the first year is the beginning of life, and the time of
birth ought to be written down in the temples of their fathers as the
beginning of existence to every child, whether boy or girl. Let every
phratria have inscribed on a whited wall the names of the successive
archons by whom the years are reckoned. And near to them let the

Laws VI

ATHE-
NIAN.

seers of
marriage
shall see
that the
provisions
of the
law are
observed.

785

Every
phratry
to have
inscribed
upon a
wall the
names of
its living
members.

Laws VI

ATHE-
NIAN.

The ages
for mar-
riage, for
office, and
for war.

living members of the phratria be inscribed, and when they depart
life let them be erased. The limit of marriageable ages for a woman
shall be from sixteen to twenty years at the longest,—for a man,
from thirty to thirty-five years; and let a woman hold office at
forty, and a man at thirty years. Let a man go out to war from
twenty to sixty years, and for a woman, if there appear any need to
make use of her in military service, let the time of service be after
she shall have brought forth children up to fifty years of age; and
let regard be had to what is possible and suitable to each.

BOOK VII

788
Laws VII

ATHE-
NIAN,
CLEINIAS.

Educa-
tion
comes
next.

There are
many
small
matters
which
cannot be
legislated
about,
but need
some
other
kind of
regula-
tion.

AND now, assuming children of both sexes to have been born,
it will be proper for us to consider, in the next place, their nurture
and education; this cannot be left altogether unnoticed, and yet may
be thought a subject fitted rather for precept and admonition than
for law. In private life there are many little things, not always apparent, arising out of the pleasures and pains and desires of individuals, which run counter to the intention of the legislator, and make
the characters of the citizens various and dissimilar:—this is an
evil in states; for by reason of their smallness and frequent occurrence, there would be an unseemliness and want of propriety in
making them penal by law; and if made penal, they are the destruction of the written law because mankind get the habit of frequently
transgressing the law in small matters. The result is that you cannot
legislate about them, and still less can you be silent. I speak somewhat darkly, but I shall endeavour also to bring my wares into the
light of day, for I acknowledge that at present there is a want of
clearness in what I am saying.

Cle. Very true.

Ath. Am I not right in maintaining that a good education is that
which tends most to the improvement of mind and body?

Cle. Undoubtedly.

Ath. And nothing can be plainer than that the fairest bodies are
those which grow up from infancy in the best and straightest manner?

Cle. Certainly.

Ath. And do we not further observe that the first shoot of every
living thing is by far the greatest and fullest? Many will even con-

tend that a man at twenty-five does not reach twice the height which he attained at five.

Cle. True.

Ath. Well, and is not rapid growth without proper and abundant exercise the source of endless evils in the body?

Cle. Yes.

Ath. And the body should have the most exercise when it receives most nourishment?

Cle. But, Stranger, are we to impose this great amount of exercise upon newly-born infants?

Ath. Nay, rather on the bodies of infants still unborn.

Cle. What do you mean, my good sir? In the process of gestation?

Ath. Exactly. I am not at all surprised that you have never heard of this very peculiar sort of gymnastic applied to such little creatures, which, although strange, I will endeavour to explain to you.

Cle. By all means.

Ath. The practice is more easy for us to understand than for you, by reason of certain amusements which are carried to excess by us at Athens. Not only boys, but often older persons, are in the habit of keeping quails and cocks[1], which they train to fight one another. And they are far from thinking that the contests in which they stir them up to fight with one another are sufficient exercise; for, in addition to this, they carry them about tucked beneath their armpits, holding the smaller birds in their hands, the larger under their arms, and go for a walk of a great many miles for the sake of health, that is to say, not their own health, but the health of the birds; whereby they prove to any intelligent person, that all bodies are benefited by shakings and movements, when they are moved without weariness, whether the motion proceeds from themselves, or is caused by a swing, or at sea, or on horseback, or by other bodies in whatever way moving, and that thus gaining the mastery over food and drink, they are able to impart beauty and health and strength. But admitting all this, what follows? Shall we make a ridiculous law that the pregnant woman shall walk about and fashion the embryo within as we fashion wax before it hardens, and after birth swathe the infant for two years? Suppose that we compel nurses, under penalty of a legal fine, to be always carrying the children somewhere or other, either to the temples, or into the country, or to their relations' houses, until they are well able to stand, and to take care that their limbs are not distorted by leaning on them when they are too young[2],—they should continue to carry

----

Laws VII

ATHE-
NIAN,
CLEINIAS.

During the first years of [789] life the body grows most rapidly, and therefore needs most exercise.

The Athenians and their quails and cocks.

The benefit of motion to health and digestion.

Pregnant women should walk about, and infants should be carried in the arms of strong nurses,

----

[1] Cp. Rep. v. 459.   [2] Cp. Arist. Pol. vii. 17, § 2.

them until the infant has completed its third year; the nurses should be strong, and there should be more than one of them. Shall these be our rules, and shall we impose a penalty for the neglect of

790

them? No, no; the penalty of which we were speaking will fall upon

ATHE-
NIAN,
CLEINIAS.

our own heads more than enough.

Cle. What penalty?

until they
are three
years old.

Ath. Ridicule, and the difficulty of getting the feminine and servant-like dispositions of the nurses to comply.

Cle. Then why was there any need to speak of the matter at all?

Public
law is
based
upon the
customs
of priv-
ate life.

Ath. The reason is, that masters and freemen in states, when they hear of it, are very likely to arrive at a true conviction that without due regulation of private life in cities, stability in the laying down of laws is hardly to be expected[1]; and he who makes this reflection may himself adopt the laws just now mentioned, and, adopting them, may order his house and state well and be happy.

Cle. Likely enough.

Ath. And therefore let us proceed with our legislation until we have determined the exercises which are suited to the souls of young children, in the same manner in which we have begun to go through the rules relating to their bodies.

Cle. By all means.

Motion is
good for
the soul
as well as
for the
body.

Ath. Let us assume, then, as a first principle in relation both to the body and soul of very young creatures, that nursing and moving about by day and night is good for them all, and that the younger they are, the more they will need it[2]; infants should live, if that were possible, as if they were always rocking at sea. This is the lesson which we may gather from the experience of nurses, and likewise from the use of the remedy of motion in the rites of the Corybantes; for when mothers want their restless children to go to sleep they do not employ rest, but, on the contrary, motion—rocking them in their arms; nor do they give them silence, but they sing to them and lap them in sweet strains; and the Bacchic women are cured of their frenzy in the same manner by the use of the dance and of music.

Cle. Well, Stranger, and what is the reason of this?

Ath. The reason is obvious.

Cle. What?

It quiets
fear.

Ath. The affection both of the Bacchantes and of the children is an emotion of fear, which springs out of an evil habit of the soul.

791

And when some one applies external agitation to affections of this sort, the motion coming from without gets the better of the terrible and violent internal one, and produces a peace and calm in the soul,

[1] Cp. Rep. v. 449 E.   [2] Cp. Arist. Pol. vii 17, § 2.

and quiets the restless palpitation of the heart, which is a thing much to be desired, sending the children to sleep, and making the Bacchantes, although they remain awake, to dance to the pipe with the help of the Gods to whom they offer acceptable sacrifices, and producing in them a sound mind, which takes the place of their frenzy. And, to express what I mean in a word, there is a good deal to be said in favour of this treatment.

Cle. Certainly.

Ath. But if fear has such a power we ought to infer from these facts, that every soul which from youth upward has been familiar with fears, will be made more liable to fear[1], and every one will allow that this is the way to form a habit of cowardice and not of courage.

Cle. No doubt.

Ath. And, on the other hand, the habit of overcoming, from our youth upwards, the fears and terrors which beset us, may be said to be an exercise of courage.

Cle. True.

Ath. And we may say that the use of exercise and motion in the earliest years of life greatly contributes to create a part of virtue in the soul.

Cle. Quite true.

Ath. Further, a cheerful temper, or the reverse, may be regarded as having much to do with high spirit on the one hand, or with cowardice on the other.

Cle. To be sure.

Ath. Then now we must endeavour to show how and to what extent we may, if we please, without difficulty implant either character in the young.

Cle. Certainly.

Ath. There is a common opinion, that luxury makes the disposition of youth discontented and irascible and vehemently excited by trifles; that on the other hand excessive and savage servitude makes men mean and abject, and haters of their kind, and therefore makes them undesirable associates.

Cle. But how must the state educate those who do not as yet understand the language of the country, and are therefore incapable of appreciating any sort of instruction?

Ath. I will tell you how:—Every animal that is born is wont to utter some cry, and this is especially the case with man, and he is also affected with the inclination to weep more than any other animal.

[1] Cp. Rep. iii. 386 A.

Laws VII

ATHE-
NIAN,
CLEINIAS.

Familiar-
ity with
fear in
childhood
breeds
coward-
ice;

the habit
of over-
coming it,
courage.

Luxury
creates
discon-
tent in
the
young;
constrain‍
makes
them
sullen.

The
infant
manifests
his dis-
likes by
tears and
cries; his
likes by
silence.

Very
young
children
should
be made
happy.

Seek not
for plea-
sures, nor
avoid
pains;
but em-
brace the
middle
state,
which is
divine.

Applica-
tion of
this pre-
cept to
infants
and to
pregnant
women.

793

Cle. Quite true.

Ath. Do not nurses, when they want to know what an infant desires, judge by these signs?—when anything is brought to the infant
and he is silent, then he is supposed to be pleased, but, when he
weeps and cries out, then he is not pleased. For tears and cries are
the inauspicious signs by which children show what they love and
hate. Now the time which is thus spent is no less than three years,
and is a very considerable portion of life to be passed ill or well.

Cle. True.

Ath. Does not the discontented and ungracious nature appear to
you to be full of lamentations and sorrows more than a good man
ought to be?

Cle. Certainly.

Ath. Well, but if during these three years every possible care were
taken that our nursling should have as little of sorrow and fear, and
in general of pain as was possible, might we not expect in early
childhood to make his soul more gentle and cheerful[1]?

Cle. To be sure, Stranger,—more especially if we could procure
him a variety of pleasures.

Ath. There I can no longer agree, Cleinias: you amaze me. To
bring him up in such a way would be his utter ruin; for the beginning is always the most critical part of education. Let us see whether
I am right.

Cle. Proceed.

Ath. The point about which you and I differ is of great importance, and I hope that you, Megillus, will help to decide between
us. For I maintain that the true life should neither seek for pleasures, nor, on the other hand, entirely avoid pains, but should embrace the middle state[2], which I just spoke of as gentle and benign,
and is a state which we by some divine presage and inspiration
rightly ascribe to God. Now, I say, he among men, too, who would
be divine ought to pursue after this mean habit—he should not rush
headlong into pleasures, for he will not be free from pains; nor
should we allow any one, young or old, male or female, to be thus
given any more than ourselves, and least of all the newly-born infant, for in infancy more than at any other time the character is en-
grained by habit. Nay, more, if I were not afraid of appearing to be
ridiculous, I would say that a woman during her year of pregnancy
should of all women be most carefully tended, and kept from violent or excessive pleasures and pains, and should at that time cultivate gentleness and benevolence and kindness.

Cle. You need not ask Megillus, Stranger, which of us has most

[1] Cp. Arist. Pol. vii. 17, § 6.　　　　　[2] Cp. Rep. x. 619 A.

truly spoken; for I myself agree that all men ought to avoid the life of unmingled pain or pleasure, and pursue always a middle course. And having spoken well, may I add that you have been well answered?

Ath. Very good, Cleinias; and now let us all three consider a further point.

Cle. What is it?

Ath. That all the matters which we are now describing are commonly called by the general name of unwritten customs, and what are termed the laws of our ancestors are all of similar nature. And the reflection which lately arose in our minds[1], that we can neither call these things laws, nor yet leave them unmentioned, is justified; for they are the bonds of the whole state, and come in between the written laws which are or are hereafter to be laid down; they are just ancestral customs of great antiquity, which, if they are rightly ordered and made habitual, shield and preserve the previously existing written law; but if they depart from right and fall into disorder, then they are like the props of builders which slip away out of their place and cause a universal ruin—one part drags another down, and the fair superstructure falls because the old foundations are undermined. Reflecting upon this, Cleinias, you ought to bind together the new state in every possible way, omitting nothing, whether great or small, of what are called laws or manners or pursuits, for by these means a city is bound together, and all these things are only lasting when they depend upon one another; and, therefore, we must not wonder if we find that many apparently trifling customs or usages come pouring in and lengthening out our laws.

Cle. Very true: we are disposed to agree with you.

Ath. Up to the age of three years, whether of boy or girl, if a person strictly carries out our previous regulations and makes them a principal aim, he will do much for the advantage of the young creatures. But at three, four, five, and even six years the childish nature will require sports; now is the time to get rid of self-will in him, punishing him, but not so as to disgrace him. We were saying about slaves[2], that we ought neither to add insult to punishment so as to anger them, nor yet to leave them unpunished lest they become self-willed; and a like rule is to be observed in the case of the free-born. Children at that age have certain natural modes of amusement which they find out for themselves when they meet. And all the children who are between the ages of three and six ought to meet at the temples of the villages, the several families of a

Custom
fills up
the in-
terstices
of laws,

and is the
supple-
ment and
prop of
them.

The age
for
amuse-
ment
between
3 and 6.

794

Between
these

[1] Cp. *supra*, 788 A.   [2] vi. 777 D, E.

ages,
children
should
meet
daily at
the
village
temples
under the
superin-
tendence
of
matrons
and
nurses.

At six,
boys and
girls
should be
sep-
arated;
and the
boys, and
the girls
too,
should
learn the
use of
weapons.

They
should be
taught to
use the
left hand
[795]
as well as
the right.

This is
very im-
portant
for the
warrior.

village uniting on one spot. The nurses are to see that the children behave properly and orderly,—they themselves and all their companies are to be under the control of twelve matrons, one for each company, who are annually selected to inspect them from the women previously mentioned[1], [i.e. the women who have authority over marriage], whom the guardians of the law appoint. These matrons shall be chosen by the women who have authority over marriage, one out of each tribe; all are to be of the same age; and let each of them, as soon as she is appointed, hold office and go to the temples every day, punishing all offenders, male or female, who are slaves or strangers, by the help of some of the public slaves; but if any citizen disputes the punishment, let her bring him before the wardens of the city; or, if there be no dispute, let her punish him herself. After the age of six years the time has arrived for the separation of the sexes,—let boys live with boys, and girls in like manner with girls. Now they must begin to learn—the boys going to teachers of horsemanship and the use of the bow, the javelin, and sling, and the girls too, if they do not object, at any rate until they know how to manage these weapons, and especially how to handle heavy arms; for I may note, that the practice which now prevails is almost universally misunderstood.

Cle. In what respect?

Ath. In that the right and left hand are supposed to be by nature differently suited for our various uses of them; whereas no difference is found in the use of the feet and the lower limbs; but in the use of the hands we are, as it were, maimed by the folly of nurses and mothers; for although our several limbs are by nature balanced, we create a difference in them by bad habit. In some cases this is of no consequence, as, for example, when we hold the lyre in the left hand, and the plectrum in the right, but it is downright folly to make the same distinction in other cases. The custom of the Scythians proves our error; for they not only hold the bow from them with the left hand and draw the arrow to them with their right, but use either hand for both purposes. And there are many similar examples in charioteering and other things, from which we may learn that those who make the left side weaker than the right act contrary to nature. In the case of the plectrum, which is of horn only, and similar instruments, as I was saying, it is of no consequence, but makes a great difference, and may be of very great importance to the warrior who has to use iron weapons, bows and javelins, and the like; above all, when in heavy armour, he has to fight against heavy armour. And there is a very great difference between

[1] vi. 784 A.

one who has learnt and one who has not, and between one who has been trained in gymnastic exercises and one who has not been. For as he who is perfectly skilled in the Pancratium or boxing or wrestling, is not unable to fight from his left side, and does not limp and draggle in confusion when his opponent makes him change his position, so in heavy-armed fighting, and in all other things, if I am not mistaken, the like holds—he who has these double powers of attack and defence ought not in any case to leave them either unused or untrained, if he can help; and if a person had the nature of Geryon or Briareus he ought to be able with his hundred hands to throw a hundred darts. Now, the magistrates, male and female, should see to all these things, the women superintending the nursing and amusements of the children, and the men superintending their education, that all of them, boys and girls alike, may be sound hand and foot, and may not, if they can help, spoil the gifts of nature by bad habits.

Education has two branches,—one of gymnastic, which is concerned with the body, and the other of music, which is designed for the improvement of the soul[1]. And gymnastic has also two branches—dancing and wrestling; and one sort of dancing imitates musical recitation, and aims at preserving dignity and freedom, the other aims at producing health, agility, and beauty in the limbs and parts of the body, giving the proper flexion and extension to each of them, a harmonious motion being diffused everywhere, and forming a suitable accompaniment to the dance. As regards wrestling, the tricks which Antaeus and Cercyon devised in their systems out of a vain spirit of competition, or the tricks of boxing which Epeius or Amycus invented, are useless and unsuitable for war, and do not deserve to have much said about them; but the art of wrestling erect and keeping free the neck and hands and sides, working with energy and constancy, with a composed strength, and for the sake of health —these are always useful, and are not to be neglected, but to be enjoined alike on masters and scholars, when we reach that part of legislation; and we will desire the one to give their instructions freely, and the others to receive them thankfully[2]. Nor, again, must we omit suitable imitations of war in our choruses; here in Crete you have the armed dances of the Curetes, and the Lacedaemonians have those of the Dioscuri. And our virgin lady, delighting in the amusement of the dance, thought it not fit to amuse herself with empty hands; she must be clothed in a complete suit of armour, and in this attire go through the dance[3]; and youths and maidens should in every respect imitate her, esteeming highly the favour of the

Two branches of education, gymnastic and music; and two parts of gymnastic, [796] dancing and wrestling.

Only those forms of wrestling which are useful in war to be practised.

Imitations of war to be given also by dances in armour, &c.

[1].-Cp. Rep. ii. 376 E; iii. 403, 410.   [2] Cp. *infra*, 814 D.   [3] Cp. Crit. 110 B.

Laws VII

Athe-
nian,
Cleinias.

Goddess, both with a view to the necessities of war, and to festive occasions: it will be right also for the boys, until such time as they go out to war, to make processions and supplications to all the Gods in goodly array, armed and on horseback, in dances, and marches, fast or slow, offering up prayers to the Gods and to the sons of Gods; and also engaging in contests and preludes of contests, if at all, with these objects. For these sorts of exercises, and no others, arc useful both in peace and war, and are beneficial alike to states and to private houses. But other labours and sports and exercises of the body are unworthy of freemen, O Megillus and Cleinias.

I have now completely described the kind of gymnastic which I said at first ought to be described; if you know of any better, will you communicate your thoughts?

Cle. It is not easy, Stranger, to put aside these principles of gymnastic and wrestling and to enunciate better ones.

Music
again.

Ath. Now we must say what has yet to be said about the gifts of the Muses and of Apollo: before, we fancied that we had said all, and that gymnastic alone remained[1]; but now we see clearly what points have been omitted, and should be first proclaimed; of these, then, let us proceed to speak.

797

Cle. By all means.

Ath. Let me tell you once more—although you have heard me say the same before—that caution must be always exercised, both by the speaker and by the hearer, about anything that is very singular and unusual. For my tale is one which many a man would be afraid to tell, and yet I have a confidence which makes me go on.

Cle. What have you to say, Stranger?

The plays
of
children
should be
fixed that
their cha-
racters
may
become
fixed.

Ath. I say that in states generally no one has observed that the plays of childhood have a great deal to do with the permanence or want of permanence in legislation. For when plays are ordered with a view to children having the same plays, and amusing themselves after the same manner, and finding delight in the same playthings, the more solemn institutions of the state are allowed to remain undisturbed. Whereas if sports are disturbed, and innovations are made in them, and they constantly change, and the young never speak of their having the same likings, or the same established notions of good and bad taste, either in the bearing of their bodies or in their dress, but he who devises something new and out of the way in figures and colours and the like is held in special honour, we may truly say that no greater evil can happen in a state[2]; for he who changes the sports is secretly changing the manners of the young,

[1] Cp. *supra*, ii. 673.   [2] Cp. Rep. iv. 424 C.

and making the old to be dishonoured among them and the new to be honoured. And I affirm that there is nothing which is a greater injury to all states than saying or thinking thus. Will you hear me tell how great I deem the evil to be?

Cle. You mean the evil of blaming antiquity in states?

Ath. Exactly.

Cle. If you are speaking of that, you will find in us hearers who are disposed to receive what you say not unfavourably but most favourably.

Ath. I should expect so.

Cle. Proceed.

Ath. Well, then, let us give all the greater heed to one another's words. The argument affirms that any change whatever except from evil is the most dangerous of all things; this is true in the case of the seasons and of the winds, in the management of our bodies and the habits of our minds—true of all things except, as I said before, of the bad. He who looks at the constitution of individuals accustomed to eat any sort of meat, or drink any drink, or to do any work which they can get, may see that they are at first disordered by them, but afterwards, as time goes on, their bodies grow adapted to them, and they learn to know and like variety, and have good health and enjoyment of life; and if ever afterwards they are confined again to a superior diet, at first they are troubled with disorders, and with difficulty become habituated to their new food. A similar principle we may imagine to hold good about the minds of men and the natures of their souls. For when they have been brought up in certain laws, which by some Divine Providence have remained unchanged during long ages, so that no one has any memory or tradition of their ever having been otherwise than they are, then every one is afraid and ashamed to change that which is established. The legislator must somehow find a way of implanting this reverence for antiquity, and I would propose the following way:—People are apt to fancy, as I was saying before, that when the plays of children are altered they are merely plays, not seeing that the most serious and detrimental consequences arise out of the change; and they readily comply with the child's wishes instead of deterring him, not considering that these children who make innovations in their games, when they grow up to be men, will be different from the last generation of children, and, being different, will desire a different sort of life, and under the influence of this desire will want other institutions and laws; and no one of them reflects that there will follow what I just now called the greatest of evils to states. Changes in bodily fashions are no such serious evils, but frequent changes in the

Changes
are
generally
danger-
ous,

798

for the
mind as
well as
for the
body.

Children
who
make in-
novation
in their
games
will de-
velop
into revo-
lutionists.

praise and censure of manners are the greatest of evils, and require the utmost prevision.

Cle. To be sure.

Ath. And now do we still hold to our former assertion, that rhythms and music in general are imitations of good and evil characters in men[1]? What say you?

Cle. That is the only doctrine which we can admit.

Ath. Must we not, then, try in every possible way to prevent our youth from even desiring to imitate new modes either in dance or song[2]? nor must any one be allowed to offer them varieties of pleasures.

Cle. Most true.

799

Ath. Can any of us imagine a better mode of effecting this object than that of the Egyptians?

Cle. What is their method?

We, like the Egyptians, should consecrate the forms of song and dance.

Ath. To consecrate every sort of dance or melody. First we should ordain festivals,—calculating for the year what they ought to be, and at what time, and in honour of what Gods, sons of Gods, and heroes they ought to be celebrated; and, in the next place, what hymns ought to be sung at the several sacrifices, and with what dances the particular festival is to be honoured. This has to be arranged at first by certain persons, and, when arranged, the whole assembly of the citizens are to offer sacrifices and libations to the Fates and all the other Gods, and to consecrate the several odes to Gods and heroes: and if any one offers any other hymns or dances to any one of the Gods, the priests and priestesses, acting in concert with the guardians of the law, shall, with the sanction of religion and the law, exclude him, and he who is excluded, if he do not submit, shall be liable all his life long to have a suit of impiety brought against him by any one who likes.

Cle. Very good.

Ath. In the consideration of this subject, let us remember what is due to ourselves.

Cle. To what are you referring?

Before stating our paradoxical law about music, we should ponder and reflect.

Ath. I mean that any young man, and much more any old one, when he sees or hears anything strange or unaccustomed, does not at once run to embrace the paradox, but he stands considering, like a person who is at a place where three paths meet, and does not very well know his way—he may be alone or he may be walking with others, and he will say to himself and them,'Which is the way?' and will not move forward until he is satisfied that he is going right. And this is what we must do in the present instance:—A strange discus-

---

[1] Cp. *supra*, ii. 655 D foll. [2] Cp. Rep. iv. 424.

sion on the subject of law has arisen, which requires the utmost consideration, and we should not at our age be too ready to speak about such great matters, or be confident that we can say anything certain all in a moment.

Cle. Most true.

Ath. Then we will allow time for reflection, and decide when we have given the subject sufficient consideration. But that we may not be hindered from completing the natural arrangement of our laws, let us proceed to the conclusion of them in due order; for very possibly, if God will, the exposition of them, when completed, may throw light on our present perplexity.

Cle. Excellent, Stranger; let us do as you propose.

Ath. Let us then affirm the paradox that strains of music are our laws (νόμοι), and this latter being the name which the ancients gave to lyric songs[1], they probably would not have very much objected to our proposed application of the word. Some one, either asleep or awake, must have had a dreamy suspicion of their nature. And let our decree be as follows:—No one in singing or dancing shall offend against public and consecrated models, and the general fashion among the youth, any more than he would offend against any other law. And he who observes this law shall be blameless; but he who is disobedient, as I was saying, shall be punished by the guardians of the laws, and by the priests and priestesses. Suppose that we imagine this to be our law.

Cle. Very good.

Ath. Can any one who makes such laws escape ridicule? Let us see. I think that our only safety will be in first framing certain models for composers. One of these models shall be as follows:—If when a sacrifice is going on, and the victims are being burnt according to law,—if, I say, any one who may be a son or brother, standing by another at the altar and over the victims, horribly blasphemes, will not his words inspire despondency and evil omens and forebodings in the mind of his father and of his other kinsmen?

Cle. Of course.

Ath. And this is just what takes place in almost all our cities. A magistrate offers a public sacrifice, and there come in not one but many choruses, who take up a position a little way from the altar, and from time to time pour forth all sorts of horrible blasphemies on the sacred rites, exciting the souls of the audience with words and rhythms and melodies most sorrowful to hear; and he who at the moment when the city is offering sacrifice makes the citizens weep most, carries away the palm of victory. Now, ought we not to forbid

[1] Cp. *supra,* iii. 700 B.

such strains as these? And if ever our citizens must hear such lamentations, then on some unblest and inauspicious day let there be choruses of foreign and hired minstrels, like those hirelings who accompany the departed at funerals with barbarous Carian chants. That is the sort of thing which will be appropriate if we have such strains at all; and let the apparel of the singers be, not circlets and ornaments of gold, but the reverse. Enough of all this. I will simply ask once more whether we shall lay down as one of our principles of song——

Cle. What?

801

Ath. That we should avoid every word of evil omen; let that kind of song which is of good omen be heard everywhere and always in our state. I need hardly ask again, but shall assume that you agree with me.

Cle. By all means; that law is approved by the suffrages of us all.

Ath. But what shall be our next musical law or type? Ought not prayers to be offered up to the Gods when we sacrifice?

Cle. Certainly.

Ath. And our third law, if I am not mistaken, will be to the effect that our poets, understanding prayers to be requests which we make to the Gods, will take especial heed that they do not by mistake ask for evil instead of good. To make such a prayer would surely be too ridiculous.

Cle. Very true.

Ath. Were we not a little while ago quite convinced that no silver or golden Plutus should dwell in our state[1]?

Cle. To be sure.

Ath. And what has it been the object of our argument to show? Did we not imply that the poets are not always quite capable of knowing what is good or evil? And if one of them utters a mistaken prayer in song or words, he will make our citizens pray for the opposite of what is good in matters of the highest import; than which, as I was saying, there can be few greater mistakes. Shall we then propose as one of our laws and models relating to the Muses——

Cle. What?—will you explain the law more precisely?

Ath. Shall we make a law that the poet shall compose nothing contrary to the ideas of the lawful, or just, or beautiful, or good, which are allowed in the state? nor shall he be permitted to communicate his compositions to any private individuals, until he shall have shown them to the appointed judges and the guardians of the law, and they are satisfied with them. As to the persons whom we

[1] Cp. *supra,* v. 741 E.

appoint to be our legislators about music[1] and as to the director of education[2], these have been already indicated. Once more then, as I have asked more than once, shall this be our third law, and type, and model—What do you say?

Cle. Let it be so, by all means.

Ath. Then it will be proper to have hymns and praises of the Gods[3], intermingled with prayers; and after the Gods prayers and praises should be offered in like manner to demigods and heroes, suitable to their several characters.

Cle. Certainly.

Ath. In the next place there will be no objection to a law, that citizens who are departed and have done good and energetic deeds, either with their souls or with their bodies, and have been obedient to the laws, should receive eulogies; this will be very fitting.

Cle. Quite true.

Ath. But to honour with hymns and panegyrics those who are still alive is not safe; a man should run his course, and make a fair ending, and then we will praise him; and let praise be given equally to women as well as men who have been distinguished in virtue. The order of songs and dances shall be as follows:—There are many ancient musical compositions and dances which are excellent, and from these the newly-founded city may freely select what is proper and suitable; and they shall choose judges of not less than fifty years of age, who shall make the selection, and any of the old poems which they deem sufficient they shall include; any that are deficient or altogether unsuitable, they shall either utterly throw aside, or examine and amend, taking into their counsel poets and musicians, and making use of their poetical genius; but explaining to them the wishes of the legislator in order that they may regulate dancing, music, and all choral strains, according to the mind of the judges; and not allowing them to indulge, except in some few matters, their individual pleasures and fancies. Now the irregular strain of music is always made ten thousand times better by attaining to law and order, and rejecting the honeyed Muse—not however that we mean wholly to exclude pleasure, which is the characteristic of all music. And if a man be brought up from childhood to the age of discretion and maturity in the use of the orderly and severe music, when he hears the opposite he detests it, and calls it illiberal; but if trained in the sweet and vulgar music, he deems the severer kind cold and displeasing[4]. So that, as I was saying before, while he who hears them gains no more pleasure from the one than from the other, the

Laws VII

ATHE-
NIAN,
CLEINIAS.

which the state approves.

(4) There shall be suitable hymns for Gods, demigods, and heroes.

(5) The good to [802] be honoured after death.

The law respecting the order of songs and dances.

---

[1] Cp. *supra*, vi. 764 C.   [2] Cp. *supra*, vi. 765 D.
[3] Cp. Rep. x. 607 A.   [4] Cp. Arist. Pol. viii. 6, § 8; 7, § 7.

one has the advantage of making those who are trained in it better men, whereas the other makes them worse.

Cle. Very true.

Ath. Again, we must distinguish and determine on some general principle what songs are suitable to women, and what to men, and must assign to them their proper melodies and rhythms. It is shocking for a whole harmony to be inharmonical, or for a rhythm to be unrhythmical, and this will happen when the melody is inappropriate to them. And therefore the legislator must assign to these also their forms. Now both sexes have melodies and rhythms which of necessity belong to them; and those of women are clearly enough indicated by their natural difference. The grand, and that which tends to courage, may be fairly called manly; but that which inclines to moderation and temperance, may be declared both in law and in ordinary speech to be the more womanly quality. This, then, will be the general order of them.

Let us now speak of the manner of teaching and imparting them, and the persons to whom, and the time when, they are severally to be imparted. As the shipwright first lays down the lines of the keel, and thus, as it were, draws the ship in outline, so do I seek to distinguish the patterns of life, and lay down their keels according to the nature of different men's souls; seeking truly to consider by what means, and in what ways, we may go through the voyage of life best. Now human affairs are hardly worth considering in earnest, and yet we must be in earnest about them,—a sad necessity constrains us. And having got thus far, there will be a fitness in our completing the matter, if we can only find some suitable method of doing so. But what do I mean? Some one may ask this very question, and quite rightly, too.

Cle. Certainly.

Ath. I say that about serious matters a man should be serious, and about a matter which is not serious he should not be serious; and that God is the natural and worthy object of our most serious and blessed endeavours, for man, as I said before[1], is made to be the plaything of God, and this, truly considered, is the best of him; wherefore also every man and woman should walk seriously, and pass life in the noblest of pastimes, and be of another mind from what they are at present.

Cle. In what respect?

Ath. At present they think that their serious pursuits should be for the sake of their sports, for they deem war a serious pursuit, which must be managed well for the sake of peace; but the truth is,

[1] Cp. *supra*, i. 644 D, E.

that there neither is, nor has been, nor ever will be, either amusement or instruction in any degree worth speaking of in war, which is nevertheless deemed by us to be the most serious of our pursuits. And therefore, as we say, every one of us should live the life of peace as long and as well as he can[1]. And what is the right way of living? Are we to live in sports always? If so, in what kind of sports? We ought to live sacrificing, and singing, and dancing, and then a man will be able to propitiate the Gods, and to defend himself against his enemies and conquer them in battle. The type of song or dance by which he will propitiate them has been described, and the paths along which he is to proceed have been cut for him. He will go forward in the spirit of the poet[2]:—

'Telemachus, some things thou wilt thyself find in thy heart, but other things God will suggest; for I deem that thou wast not born or brought up without the will of the Gods.'

And this ought to be the view of our alumni; they ought to think that what has been said is enough for them, and that any other things their Genius and God will suggest to them—he will tell them to whom, and when, and to what Gods severally they are to sacrifice and perform dances, and how they may propitiate the deities, and live according to the appointment of nature; being for the most part puppets, but having some little share of reality.

Meg. You have a low opinion of mankind, Stranger.

Ath. Nay, Megillus, be not amazed, but forgive me:—I was comparing them with the Gods; and under that feeling I spoke. Let us grant, if you wish, that the human race is not to be despised, but is worthy of some consideration.

Next follow the buildings for gymnasia and schools open to all; these are to be in three places in the midst of the city; and outside the city and in the surrounding country, also in three places, there shall be schools for horse exercise, and large grounds arranged with a view to archery and the throwing of missiles, at which young men may learn and practise. Of these mention has already been made[3]; and if the mention be not sufficiently explicit, let us speak further of them and embody them in laws. In these several schools let there be dwellings for teachers, who shall be brought from foreign parts by pay, and let them teach those who attend the schools the art of war and the art of music, and the children shall come not only if their parents please, but if they do not please; there shall be compulsory education, as the saying is, of all and sundry, as far as this is possible; and the pupils shall be regarded as belonging to the

---

[1] Cp. *supra*, i. 628.   [2] Homer, Odyss. iii. 26 foll.   [3] Cp. *supra*, vi. 764, 779.

The life of peace better than the life of war.

But what is [804] the life of peace?— The life of dance and song.

A new subject: —Gymnasia; schools; places for horse exercise; open spaces for archery.

The teachers to be foreigners and paid.

Laws VII

ATHE-
NIAN,
CLEINIAS.

Educa-
tion to be
compuls-
ory on
both
sexes.

[805]

The state
is re-
duced to
a half, if
the train-
ing of
women
be neg-
lected.

It is a
well-
known
fact that
women
are able
to share
men's
pursuits.
If they
do not
they must
have an
inferior
life.

Lives of
women in
different
countries.

806

state rather than to their parents[1]. My law would apply to females as well as males; they shall both go through the same exercises. I assert without fear of contradiction that gymnastic and horsemanship are as suitable to women as to men[2]. Of the truth of this I am persuaded from ancient tradition, and at the present day there are said to be countless myriads of women in the neighbourhood of the Black Sea, called Sauromatides, who not only ride on horseback like men, but have enjoined upon them the use of bows and other weapons equally with the men. And I further affirm, that if these things are possible, nothing can be more absurd than the practice which prevails in our own country, of men and women not following the same pursuits with·all their strength and with one mind, for thus the state, instead of being a whole, is reduced to a half[3], but has the same imposts to pay and the same toils to undergo; and what can be a greater mistake for any legislator to make than this?

Cle. Very true; yet much of what has been asserted by us, Stranger, is contrary to the custom of states; still, in saying that the discourse should be allowed to proceed, and that when the discussion is completed, we should choose what seems best, you spoke very properly[4], and I now feel compunction for what I have said. Tell me, then, what you would next wish to say.

Ath. I should wish to say, Cleinias, as I said before, that if the possibility of these things were not sufficiently proven in fact, then there might be an objection to the argument, but the fact being as I have said, he who rejects the law must find some other ground of objection; and, failing this, our exhortation will still hold good, nor will any one deny that women ought to share as far as possible in education and in other ways with men. For consider;—if women do not share in their whole life with men, then they must have some other order of life.

Cle. Certainly.

Ath. And what arrangement of life to be found anywhere is preferable to this community which we are now assigning to them? Shall we prefer that which is adopted by the Thracians and many other races who use their women to till the ground and to be shepherds of their herds and flocks, and to minister to them like slaves? —Or shall we do as we and people in our part of the world do—getting together, as the phrase is, all our goods and chattels into one dwelling, we entrust them to our women, who are the stewards of them, and who also preside over the shuttles and the whole art of spinning? Or shall we take a middle course, as in Lacedaemon, Me-

---

[1] Cp. Arist. Pol. viii. 1, §§ 3, 4. [2] Cp. Rep. v. 451 foll.
[3] Cp. *supra.* vi. 781 B; Arist. Pol. i. 13, §§ 15, 16. [4] *Supra,* 799 C.

gillus—letting the girls share in gymnastic and music, while the
grown-up women, no longer employed in spinning wool, are hard at
work weaving the web of life, which will be no cheap or mean employment, and in the duty of serving and taking care of the household and bringing up children, in which they will observe a sort of
mean, not participating in the toils of war; and if there were any
necessity that they should fight for their city and families, unlike
the Amazons, they would be unable to take part in archery or any
other skilled use of missiles, nor could they, after the example of the
Goddess, carry shield or spear, or stand up nobly for their country
when it was being destroyed, and strike terror into their enemies, if
only because they were seen in regular order? Living as they do, they
would never dare at all to imitate the Sauromatides, who, when
compared with ordinary women, would appear to be like men. Let
him who will, praise your legislators, but I must say what I think.
The legislator ought to be whole and perfect, and not half a man
only; he ought not to let the female sex live softly and waste money
and have no order of life, while he takes the utmost care of the male
sex, and leaves half of life only blest with happiness, when he might
have made the whole state happy.

Meg. What shall we do, Cleinias? Shall we allow a stranger to run
down Sparta in this fashion?

Cle. Yes; for as we have given him liberty of speech we must let
him go on until we have perfected the work of legislation.

Meg. Very true.

Ath. Then now I may proceed?

Cle. By all means.

Ath. What will be the manner of life among men who may be
supposed to have their food and clothing provided for them in moderation, and who have entrusted the practice of the arts to others,
and whose husbandry, committed to slaves paying a part of the produce, brings them a return sufficient for men living temperately;
who, moreover, have common tables in which the men are placed
apart, and near them are the common tables of their families, of
their daughters and mothers, which day by day, the officers, male
and female, are to inspect—they shall see to the behaviour of the
company, and so dismiss them; after which the presiding magistrate and his attendants shall honour with libations those Gods
to whom that day and night are dedicated, and then go home? To
men whose lives are thus ordered, is there no work remaining to be
done which is necessary and fitting, but shall each one of them
live fattening like a beast? Such a life is neither just nor honourable, nor can he who lives it fail of meeting his due; and the due

---

Laws VII

ATHE-
NIAN,
CLEINIAS,
MEGIL-
LUS.

The
Spartan
type falls
short
of the
Sauro-
matid.

Our
citizens
are not to
live like
cattle;
they have
a work
to do.

807

Laws VII

ATHE-
NIAN.

The per-
fect life
can only
be led by
men who
have all
things in
common.
Yet even
when
there is
private
property,
the due
ordering
of home
life is a
more ar-
duous
task than
the pur-
suit of
Olympian
victories.

The duty
of wake-
fulness.

808

The
citizens
and their
wives
should
rise early.

reward of the idle fatted beast is that he should be torn in pieces
by some other valiant beast whose fatness is worn down by brave
deeds and toil. These regulations, if we duly consider them, will
never be exactly carried into execution under present circumstances, nor as long as women and children and houses and all other
things are the private property of individuals; but if we can attain
the second-best form of polity, we shall be very well off. And to men
living under this second polity there remains a work to be accomplished which is far from being small or insignificant, but is the
greatest of all works, and ordained by the appointment of righteous
law. For the life which may be truly said to be concerned with the
virtue of body and soul is twice, or more than twice, as full of toil and
trouble as the pursuit after Pythian and Olympic victories[1], which
debars a man from every employment of life. For there ought to be
no bye-work interfering with the greater work of providing the necessary exercise and nourishment for the body, and instruction and
education for the soul. Night and day are not long enough for the
accomplishment of their perfection and consummation; and therefore to this end all freemen ought to arrange the way in which they
will spend their time during the whole course of the day, from morning till evening and from evening till the morning of the next sun-
rise. There may seem to be some impropriety in the legislator determining minutely the numberless details of the management of the
house, including such particulars as the duty of wakefulness in those
who are to be perpetual watchmen of the whole city; for that any
citizen should continue during the whole of any night in sleep, instead of being seen by all his servants, always the first to awake and
get up—this, whether the regulation is to be called a law or only a
practice, should be deemed base and unworthy of a freeman; also
that the mistress of the house should be awakened by her handmaidens instead of herself first awakening them, is what the slaves,
male and female, and the serving-boys, and, if that were possible,
everybody and everything in the house should regard as base. If
they rise early, they may all of them do much of their public and of
their household business, as magistrates in the city, and masters and
mistresses in their private houses, before the sun is up. Much sleep
is not required by nature, either for our souls or bodies, or for the
actions which they perform. For no one who is asleep is good for
anything, any more than if he were dead; but he of us who has the
most regard for life and reason keeps awake as long as he can, re-
serving only so much time for sleep as is expedient for health; and
much sleep is not required, if the habit of moderation be once right-

[1] Cp. Rep. v. 465 D, 466 A.

ly formed. Magistrates in states who keep awake at night are terrible to the bad, whether enemies or citizens, and are honoured and reverenced by the just and temperate, and are useful to themselves and to the whole state.

A night which is passed in such a manner, in addition to all the above-mentioned advantages, infuses a sort of courage into the minds of the citizens. When the day breaks, the time has arrived for youth to go to their schoolmasters. Now neither sheep nor any other animals can live without a shepherd, nor can children be left without tutors, or slaves without masters. And of all animals the boy is the most unmanageable, inasmuch as he has the fountain of reason in him not yet regulated[1]; he is the most insidious, sharp-witted, and insubordinate of animals. Wherefore he must be bound with many bridles; in the first place, when he gets away from mothers and nurses, he must be under the management of tutors on account of his childishness and foolishness; then, again, being a freeman, he must be controlled by teachers, no matter what they teach, and by studies; but he is also a slave, and in that regard any freeman who comes in his way may punish him and his tutor and his instructor, if any of them does anything wrong; and he who comes across him and does not inflict upon him the punishment which he deserves, shall incur the greatest disgrace; and let the guardian of the law, who is the director of education, see to him who coming in the way of the offences which we have mentioned, does not chastise them when he ought, or chastises them in a way which he ought not; let him keep a sharp look-out, and take especial care of the training of our children, directing their natures, and always turning them to good according to the law.

But how can our law sufficiently train the director of education himself; for as yet all has been imperfect, and nothing has been said either clear or satisfactory? Now, as far as possible, the law ought to leave nothing to him, but to explain everything, that he may be an interpreter and tutor to others. About dances and music and choral strains, I have already spoken both as to the character of the selection of them, and the manner in which they are to be amended and consecrated. But we have not as yet spoken, O illustrious guardian of education, of the manner in which your pupils are to use those strains which are written in prose, although you have been informed what martial strains they are to learn and practise; what relates in the first place to the learning of letters, and secondly, to the lyre, and also to calculation, which, as we were saying[2], is needful for them all to learn, and any other things which are required

[1] Cp. *supra,* vi. 766 A.   [2] Cp. *supra,* v. 747.

Laws VII

ATHE-
NIAN.

At daybreak the boy is to be taken to school.

The nature of that animal.

809

The Director of Education is to proceed according to fixed rules.

Laws VII

ATHE-
NIAN,
CLEINIAS.

with a view to war and the management of house and city, and,
looking to the same object, what is useful in the revolutions of the
heavenly bodies—the stars and sun and moon, and the various regulations about these matters which are necessary for the whole
state—I am speaking of the arrangements of days in periods of
months, and of months in years, which are to be observed, in order
that seasons and sacrifices and festivals may have their regular and
natural order, and keep the city alive and awake, the Gods receiving
the honours due to them, and men having a better understanding
about them[1]: all these things, O my friend, have not yet been sufficiently declared to you by the legislator. Attend, then, to what I am
now going to say:— We were telling you, in the first place, that you
were not sufficiently informed about letters, and the objection was
to this effect,—that you were never told whether he who was meant
to be a respectable citizen should apply himself in detail to that sort
of learning, or not apply himself at all; and the sane remark holds
good of the study of the lyre. But now we say that he ought to at-

810

tend to them. A fair time for a boy of ten years old to spend in
letters is three years; the age of thirteen is the proper time for him to
begin to handle the lyre, and he may continue at this for another
three years, neither more nor less, and whether his father or himself like or dislike the study, he is not to be allowed to spend more or
less time in learning music than the law allows. And let him who
disobeys the law be deprived of those youthful honours of which we
shall hereafter speak[2]. Hear, however, first of all, what the young
ought to learn in the early years of life, and what their instructors
ought to teach them. They ought to be occupied with their letters
until they are able to read and write; but the acquisition of perfect
beauty or quickness in writing, if nature has not stimulated them to
acquire these accomplishments in the given number of years, they
should let alone. And as to the learning of compositions committed
to writing which are not set to the lyre, whether metrical or without
rhythmical divisions, compositions in prose, as they are termed,
having no rhythm or harmony—seeing how dangerous are the writings handed down to us by many writers of this class—what will you
do with them, O most excellent guardians of the law? or how can the
lawgiver rightly direct you about them? I believe that he will be in
great difficulty.

Cle. What troubles you, Stranger? and why are you so perplexed
in your mind?

Ath. You naturally ask, Cleinias, and to you and Megillus, who

Three
years
(10-13)
to be
spent in
learning
to read
and
write:
another
three
years in
learning
music.

Danger-
ous tend-
ency of
many
prose
writings.

[1] Cp. *infra*, viii. 828.   [2] Cp. *infra*, viii. 829 C.

are my partners in the work of legislation, I must state the more difficult as well as the easier parts of the task.

Cle. To what do you refer in this instance?

Ath. I will tell you. There is a difficulty in opposing many myriads of mouths.

Cle. Well, and have we not already opposed the popular voice in many important enactments?

Ath. That is quite true; and you mean to imply that the road which we are taking may be disagreeable to some but is agreeable to as many others, or if not to as many, at any rate to persons not inferior to the others, and in company with them you bid me, at whatever risk, to proceed along the path of legislation which has opened out of our present discourse, and to be of good cheer, and not to faint.

Cle. Certainly.

Ath. And I do not faint; I say, indeed, that we have a great many poets writing in hexameter, trimeter, and all sorts of measures— some who are serious, others who aim only at raising a laugh—and all mankind declare that the youth who are rightly educated should be brought up in them and saturated with them; some insist that they should be constantly hearing them read aloud, and always learning them, so as to get by heart entire poets; while others select choice passages and long speeches, and make compendiums of them, saying that these ought to be committed to memory, if a man is to be made good and wise by experience and learning of many things. And you want me now to tell them plainly in what they are right and in what they are wrong.

Cle. Yes, I do.

Ath. But how can I in one word rightly comprehend all of them? I am of opinion, and, if I am not mistaken, there is a general agreement, that every one of these poets has said many things well and many things the reverse of well; and if this be true, then I do affirm that much learning is dangerous to youth.

Cle. How would you advise the guardian of the law to act?

Ath. In what respect?

Cle. I mean to what pattern should he look as his guide in permitting the young to learn some things and forbidding them to learn others. Do not shrink from answering.

Ath. My good Cleinias, I rather think that I am fortunate.

Cle. How so?

Ath. I think that I am not wholly in want of a pattern, for when I consider the words which we have spoken from early dawn until now, and which, as I believe, have been inspired by Heaven, they

The Di-
rector of
Educa-
tion shall
author-
ize the
teachers
to in-
struct
their pu-
pils in
[812]
our laws
and in
works of
a similar
character.

appear to me to be quite like a poem. When I reflected upon all these words of ours, I naturally felt pleasure, for of all the discourses which I have ever learnt or heard, either in poetry or prose, this seemed to me to be the justest, and most suitable for young men to hear; I cannot imagine any better pattern than this which the guardian of the law who is also the director of education can have. He cannot do better than advise the teachers to teach the young these words and any which are of a like nature, if he should happen to find them, either in poetry or prose, or if he come across un-written discourses akin to ours, he should certainly preserve them, and commit them to writing. And, first of all, he shall constrain the teachers themselves to learn and approve them, and any of them who will not, shall not be employed by him, but those whom he finds agreeing in his judgment, he shall make use of and shall commit to them the instruction and education of youth. And here and on this wise let my fanciful tale about letters and teachers of letters come to an end.

Cle. I do not think, Stranger, that we have wandered out of the proposed limits of the argument; but whether we are right or not in our whole conception, I cannot be very certain.

Ath. The truth, Cleinias, may be expected to become clearer when, as we have often said, we arrive at the end of the whole discussion about laws.

Cle. Yes.

The
teaching
of the
lyre.

Ath. And now that we have done with the teacher of letters, the teacher of the lyre has to receive orders from us.

Cle. Certainly.

Ath. I think that we have only to recollect our previous discus-sions, and we shall be able to give suitable regulations touching all this part of instruction and education to the teachers of the lyre.

Cle. To what do you refer?

Ath. We were saying, if I remember rightly, that the sixty-year-old choristers of Dionysus were to be specially quick in their per-ceptions of rhythm and musical composition, that they might be able to distinguish good and bad imitation, that is to say, the imi-tation of the good or bad soul when under the influence of passion, rejecting the one and displaying the other in hymns and songs, charming the souls of youth, and inviting them to follow and attain virtue by the way of imitation[1].

Cle. Very true.

Ath. And with this view the teacher and the learner ought to use the sounds of the lyre, because its notes are pure, the player who

[1] Cp. *supra*, ii. 664 foll.

teaches and his pupil rendering note for note in unison; but complexity, and variation of notes, when the strings give one sound and the poet or composer of the melody gives another,—also when they make concords and harmonies in which lesser and greater intervals, slow and quick, or high and low notes, are combined,—or, again, when they make complex variations of rhythms, which they adapt to the notes of the lyre[1],—all that sort of thing is not suited to those who have to acquire a speedy and useful knowledge of music in three years; for opposite principles are confusing, and create a difficulty in learning, and our young men should learn quickly, and their mere necessary acquirements are not few or trifling, as will be shown in due course. Let the director of education attend to the principles concerning music which we are laying down. As to the songs and words themselves which the masters of choruses are to teach and the character of them, they have been already described by us, and are the same which, when consecrated and adapted to the different festivals, we said were to benefit cities by affording them an innocent amusement[2].

Variety and complexity of notes and rhythms to be avoided.

813

Cle. That, again, is true.

Ath. Then let him who has been elected a director of music[3] receive these rules from us as containing the very truth; and may he prosper in his office! Let us now proceed to lay down other rules in addition to the preceding about dancing and gymnastic exercise in general. Having said what remained to be said about the teaching of music, let us speak in like manner about gymnastic. For boys and girls ought to learn to dance and practise gymnastic exercises— ought they not?

The teaching of gymnastic.

Cle. Yes.

Ath. Then the boys ought to have dancing masters, and the girls dancing mistresses to exercise them.

Cle. Very good.

Ath. Then once more let us summon him who has the chief concern in the business, the superintendent of youth [i. e. the director of education]; he will have plenty to do, if he is to have the charge of music and gymnastic.

Cle. But how will an old man be able to attend to such great charges?

Ath. O my friend, there will be no difficulty, for the law has already given and will give him permission to select as his assistants in this charge any citizens, male or female, whom he desires; and he will know whom he ought to choose, and will be anxious not to make a mistake, from a due sense of responsibility, and from a con-

---

[1] Cp. Rep. iii. 397. [2] Cp. *supra,* 799. [3] Cp. *supra,* vi. 764 C.

Laws VII

ATHE-
NIAN,
CLEINIAS.

Gymnas-
tics
(under
which,
besides
dancing,
all mili-
tary ex-
ercises are
included)
are to be
learned
[814]
by wom-
en as well
as by
men.

Women,
like birds,
should be
willing to
fight for
their
young.

Wrestling
most akin
to the
military
art.

sciousness of the importance of his office, and also because he will consider that if young men have been and are well brought up, then all things go swimmingly, but if not, it is not meet to say, nor do we say, what will follow, lest the regarders of omens should take alarm about our infant state. Many things have been said by us about dancing and about gymnastic movements in general; for we include under gymnastics all military exercises, such as archery, and all hurling of weapons, and the use of the light shield, and all fighting with heavy arms, and military evolutions, and movements of armies, and encampings, and all that relates to horsemanship. Of all these things there ought to be public teachers, receiving pay from the state, and their pupils should be the men and boys in the state, and also the girls and women, who are to know all these things. While they are yet girls they should have practised dancing in arms and the whole art of fighting—when grown-up women, they should apply themselves to evolutions and tactics, and the mode of grounding and taking up arms; if for no other reason, yet in case the whole military force should have to leave the city and carry on operations of war outside, that those who will have to guard the young and the rest of the city may be equal to the task; and, on the other hand, when enemies, whether barbarian or Hellenic, come from without with mighty force and make a violent assault upon them, and thus compel them to fight for the possession of the city, which is far from being an impossibility, great would be the disgrace to the state, if the women had been so miserably trained that they could not fight for their young, as birds will, against any creature however strong, and die or undergo any danger, but must instantly rush to the temples and crowd at the altars and shrines, and bring upon human nature the reproach, that of all animals man is the most cowardly!

Cle. Such a want of education, Stranger, is certainly an unseemly thing to happen in a state, as well as a great misfortune.

Ath. Suppose that we carry our law to the extent of saying that women ought not to neglect military matters, but that all citizens, male and female alike, shall attend to them?

Cle. I quite agree.

Ath. Of wrestling we have spoken in part, but of what I should call the most important part we have not spoken, and cannot easily speak without showing at the same time by gesture as well as in word what we mean; when word and action combine, and not till then, we shall explain clearly what has been said, pointing out that of all movements wrestling is most akin to the military art, and is to be pursued for the sake of this, and not this for the sake of wrestling.

Cle. Excellent.

Ath. Enough of wrestling; we will now proceed to speak of other movements of the body. Such motion may be in general called dancing, and is of two kinds: one of nobler figures, imitating the honourable, the other of the more ignoble figures, imitating the mean; and of both these there are two further subdivisions. Of the serious, one kind is of those engaged in war and vehement action, and is the exercise of a noble person and a manly heart; the other exhibits a temperate soul in the enjoyment of prosperity and modest pleasures, and may be truly called and is the dance of peace. The warrior dance is different from the peaceful one, and may be rightly termed Pyrrhic; this imitates the modes of avoiding blows and missiles by dropping or giving way, or springing aside, or rising up or falling down; also the opposite postures which are those of action, as, for example, the imitation of archery and the hurling of javelins, and of all sorts of blows. And when the imitation is of brave bodies and souls, and the action is direct and muscular, giving for the most part a straight movement to the limbs of the body—that, I say, is the true sort; but the opposite is not right. In the dance of peace what we have to consider is whether a man bears himself naturally and gracefully, and after the manner of men who duly conform to the law. But before proceeding I must distinguish the dancing about which there is any doubt, from that about which there is no doubt. Which is the doubtful kind, and how are the two to be distinguished? There are dances of the Bacchic sort, both those in which, as they say, they imitate drunken men, and which are named after the Nymphs, and Pan, and Silenuses, and Satyrs; and also those in which purifications are made or mysteries celebrated,—all this sort of dancing cannot be rightly defined as having either a peaceful or a warlike character, or indeed as having any meaning whatever, and may, I think, be most truly described as distinct from the warlike dance, and distinct from the peaceful, and not suited for a city at all. There let it lie; and so leaving it to lie, we will proceed to the dances of war and peace, for with these we are undoubtedly concerned. Now the unwarlike muse, which honours in dance the Gods and the sons of the Gods, is entirely associated with the consciousness of prosperity; this class may be subdivided into two lesser classes, of which one is expressive of an escape from some labour or danger into good, and has greater pleasures, the other expressive of preservation and increase of former good, in which the pleasure is less exciting;—in all these cases, every man when the pleasure is greater, moves his body more, and less when the pleasure is less; and, again, if he be more orderly and has learned courage from

Two forms of the dance, a noble and an ignoble. Of the [815] former there are again two kinds:—

(1) the Pyrrhic dance, imitating the postures of attack and defence;

(2) the dance of peace, Emmeleia, easy and graceful.

The Bacchic dance condemned.

The peaceful dance may express increase of good or escape from evil:

and has more or

816

Laws VII

ATHE-
NIAN.

less of
motion,
as the
pleasure
is greater
or less.

discipline he moves less, but if he be a coward, and has no training or self-control, he makes greater and more violent movements, and in general when he is speaking or singing he is not altogether able to keep his body still; and so out of the imitation of words in gestures the whole art of dancing has arisen. And in these various kinds of imitation one man moves in an orderly, another in a disorderly manner; and as the ancients may be observed to have given many names which are according to nature and deserving of praise, so there is an excellent one which they have given to the dances of men who in their times of prosperity are moderate in their pleasures— the giver of names, whoever he was, assigned to them a very true, and poetical, and rational name, when he called them Emmeleiai, or dances of order, thus establishing two kinds of dances of the nobler sort, the dance of war which he called the Pyrrhic, and the dance of peace which he called Emmeleia, or the dance of order; giving to each their appropriate and becoming name[1]. These things the legislator should indicate in general outline, and the guardian of the law should enquire into them and search them out, combining dancing with music, and assigning to the several sacrificial feasts that which is suitable to them; and when he has consecrated all of them in due order, he shall for the future change nothing, whether of dance or song. Thenceforward the city and the citizens shall continue to have the same pleasures, themselves being as far as possible alike, and shall live well and happily.

Laugh-
able
things to
be under-
stood by
our citi-
zens as
well as
serious,
but not
to be
imitated
by them.

Comedies
to be per-
formed
only by
slaves and
hirelings.

I have described the dances which are appropriate to noble bodies and generous souls. But it is necessary also to consider and know uncomely persons and thoughts, and those which are intended to produce laughter in comedy, and have a comic character in respect of style, song, and dance, and of the imitations which these afford. For serious things cannot be understood without laughable things, nor opposites at all without opposites, if a man is really to have intelligence of either; but he cannot carry out both in action, if he is to have any degree of virtue. And for this very reason he should learn them both, in order that he may not in ignorance do or say anything which is ridiculous and out of place—he should command slaves and hired strangers to imitate such things, but he should never take any serious interest in them himself, nor should any freeman or freewoman be discovered taking pains to learn them; and there should always be some element of novelty in the imitation. Let these then be laid down, both in law and in our discourse, as the regulations of laughable amusements which are generally called comedy. And, if any of the serious poets, as they are termed, who

817

[1] Cp. Crat. 388 E foll.

write tragedy, come to us and say—'O strangers, may we go to your city and country or may we not, and shall we bring with us our poetry—what is your will about these matters?'—how shall we answer the divine men? I think that our answer should be as follows[1]: —Best of strangers, we will say to them, we also according to our ability are tragic poets, and our tragedy is the best and noblest; for our whole state is an imitation of the best and noblest life, which we affirm to be indeed the very truth of tragedy. You are poets and we are poets, both makers of the same strains, rivals and antagonists in the noblest of dramas, which true law can alone perfect, as our hope is. Do not then suppose that we shall all in a moment allow you to erect your stage in the agora, or introduce the fair voices of your actors, speaking above our own, and permit you to harangue our women and children, and the common people, about our institutions, in language other than our own, and very often the opposite of our own. For a state would be mad which gave you this licence, until the magistrates had determined whether your poetry might be recited, and was fit for publication or not. Wherefore, O ye sons and scions of the softer Muses, first of all show your songs to the magistrates, and let them compare them with our own, and if they are the same or better we will give you a chorus; but if not, then, my friends, we cannot. Let these, then, be the customs ordained by law about all dances and the teaching of them, and let matters relating to slaves be separated from those relating to masters, if you do not object.

Cle. We can have no hesitation in assenting when you put the matter thus.

Ath. There still remain three studies suitable for freemen. Arithmetic is one of them; the measurement of length, surface, and depth is the second; and the third has to do with the revolutions of the stars in relation to one another. Not every one has need to toil through all these things in a strictly scientific manner, but only a few, and who they are to be we will hereafter indicate at the end, which will be the proper place[2]; not to know what is necessary for mankind in general, and what is the truth, is disgraceful to every one: and yet to enter into these matters minutely is neither easy, nor at all possible for every one; but there is something in them which is necessary and cannot be set aside, and probably he who made the proverb about God originally had this in view when he said, that 'not even God himself can fight against necessity;'—he meant, if I am not mistaken, divine necessity; for as to the human necessities of which the many speak, when they talk in this manner,

[1] Cp. Rep. iii. 398 A; x. 607 A.   [2] Cp. *infra,* xii. 967.

The serious poet too is required to conform to our models.

Three subjects of education remain: (1) Arithmetic; (2) Geometry; (3) Astronomy. Of all three there is a scientific knowledge for the few; a popular

Laws VII

ATHE-
NIAN,
CLEINIAS.

knowl-
edge for
the many.

(1) In
arith-
metic
there is a
divine
necessity;

and it is a
necessary
prelimin-
ary to the
higher
kinds of
knowl-
edge.

nothing can be more ridiculous than such an application of the words.

Cle. And what necessities of knowledge are there, Stranger, which are divine and not human?

Ath. I conceive them to be those of which he who has no use nor any knowledge at all cannot be a God, or demi-god, or hero to mankind, or able to take any serious thought or charge of them. And very unlike a divine man would he be, who is unable to count one, two, three, or to distinguish odd and even numbers[1], or is unable to count at all, or reckon night and day, and who is totally unacquainted with the revolution of the sun and moon, and the other stars. There would be great folly in supposing that all these are not necessary parts of knowledge to him who intends to know anything about the highest kinds of knowledge[2]; but which these are, and how many there are of them, and when they are to be learned, and what is to be learned together and what apart, and the whole correlation of them, must be rightly apprehended first; and these leading the way we may proceed to the other parts of knowledge. For so necessity grounded in nature constrains us, against which we say that no God contends, or ever will contend.

Cle. I think, Stranger, that what you have now said is very true and agreeable to nature.

Ath. Yes, Cleinias, that is so. But it is difficult for the legislator to begin with these studies; at a more convenient time we will make regulations for them.

819

Cle. You seem, Stranger, to be afraid of our habitual ignorance of the subject: there is no reason why that should prevent you from speaking out.

Clever-
ness ill-
directed
often
more
fatal than
ignor-
ance.

Ath. I certainly am afraid of the difficulties to which you allude, but I am still more afraid of those who apply themselves to this sort of knowledge, and apply themselves badly. For entire ignorance is not so terrible or extreme an evil, and is far from being the greatest of all; too much cleverness and too much learning, accompanied with an ill bringing up, are far more fatal[3].

Cle. True.

Arith-
metical
games
practised
by the
Egyp-
tians and
their
uses.

Ath. All freemen, I conceive, should learn as much of these branches of knowledge as every child in Egypt is taught when he learns the alphabet. In that country arithmetical games have been invented for the use of mere children, which they learn as a pleasure and amusement. They have to distribute apples and garlands, using the same number sometimes for a larger and sometimes for a lesser number of persons; and they arrange pugilists and wrestlers as they

[1] Cp. *Rep.* vii. 522.   [2] Cp. *ibid.* 523, 524, 525, &c.   [3] Cp. *Rep.* vii. 519.

pair together by lot or remain over, and show how their turns come in natural order. Another mode of amusing them is to distribute vessels, sometimes of gold, brass, silver, and the like, intermixed with one another, sometimes of one metal only; as I was saying they adapt to their amusement the numbers in common use, and in this way make more intelligible to their pupils the arrangements and movements of armies and expeditions, and in the management of a household they make people more useful to themselves, and more wide awake; and again in measurements of things which have length, and breadth, and depth, they free us from that natural ignorance of all these things which is so ludicrous and disgraceful[1].

(2) Geo-
metry.

Cle. What kind of ignorance do you mean?

Ath. O my dear Cleinias, I, like yourself, have late in life heard with amazement of our ignorance in these matters; to me we appear to be more like pigs than men, and I am quite ashamed, not only of myself, but of all Hellenes.

Cle. About what? Say, Stranger, what you mean.

Ath. I will; or rather I will show you my meaning by a question, and do you please to answer me: You know, I suppose, what length is?

Illustra-
tions of
the ignor-
ance of
the Hel-
lenes:
(a) Their
mistaken
notion
that
various
dimen-
sions are
commen-
surable.

Cle. Certainly.

Ath. And what breadth is?

Cle. To be sure.

Ath. And you know that these are two distinct things, and that there is a third thing called depth?

Cle. Of course.

Ath. And do not all these seem to you to be commensurable with themselves?

Cle. Yes.

Ath. That is to say, length is naturally commensurable with length, and breadth with breadth, and depth in like manner with depth?

820

Cle. Undoubtedly.

Ath. But if some things are commensurable and others wholly incommensurable, and you think that all things are commensurable, what is your position in regard to them?

Cle. Clearly, far from good.

Ath. Concerning length and breadth when compared with depth, or breadth and length when compared with one another, are not all the Hellenes agreed that these are commensurable with one another in some way?

Cle. Quite true.

[1] Cp. *ibid.* 528.

Ath. But if they are absolutely incommensurable, and yet all of us regard them as commensurable, have we not reason to be ashamed of our compatriots; and might we not say to them:—O ye best of Hellenes, is not this one of the things of which we were saying that not to know them is disgraceful, and of which to have a bare knowledge only is no great distinction?

Cle. Certainly.

Ath. And there are other things akin to these, in which there spring up other errors of the same family.

Cle. What are they?

(b) Their
inability
to dis-
tinguish
between
the
commen-
surable
and the
incom-
mensur-
able.

Ath. The natures of commensurable and incommensurable quantities in their relation to one another. A man who is good for anything ought to be able, when he thinks, to distinguish them; and different persons should compete with one another in asking questions, which will be a far better and more graceful way of passing their time than the old man's game of draughts.

Cle. I dare say; and these pastimes are not so very unlike a game of draughts.

Ath. And these, as I maintain, Cleinias, are the studies which our youth ought to learn, for they are innocent and not difficult; the learning of them will be an amusement, and they will benefit the state. If any one is of another mind, let him say what he has to say.

Cle. Certainly.

Ath. Then if these studies are such as we maintain, we will include them; if not, they shall be excluded.

Cle. Assuredly: but may we not now, Stranger, prescribe these studies as necessary, and so fill up the lacunae of our laws?

Ath. They shall be regarded as pledges which may be hereafter redeemed and removed from our state, if they do not please either us who give them, or you who accept them.

Cle. A fair condition.

Ath. Next let us see whether we are or are not willing that the study of astronomy shall be proposed for our youth[1].

Cle. Proceed.

Ath. Here occurs a strange phenomenon, which certainly cannot in any point of view be tolerated.

Cle. To what are you referring?

Enquiries
respect-
ing the
nature of
God and
the

Ath. Men say that we ought not to enquire into the supreme God and the nature of the universe, nor busy ourselves in searching out the causes of things, and that such enquiries are impious; whereas the very opposite is the truth.

Cle. What do you mean?

[1] Cp. Rep. vii. 527 foll.

Ath. Perhaps what I am saying may seem paradoxical, and at variance with the usual language of age. But when any one has any good and true notion which is for the advantage of the state and in every way acceptable to God, he cannot abstain from expressing it.

Cle. Your words are reasonable enough; but shall we find any good or true notion about the stars?

Ath. My good friends, at this hour all of us Hellenes tell lies, if I may use such an expression, about those great Gods, the Sun and the Moon.

Cle. Lies of what nature?

Ath. We say that they and divers other stars do not keep the same path, and we call them planets or wanderers.

Cle. Very true, Stranger; and in the course of my life I have often myself seen the morning star and the evening star and divers others not moving in their accustomed course, but wandering out of their path in all manner of ways, and I have seen the sun and moon doing what we all know that they do.

Ath. Just so, Megillus and Cleinias; and I maintain that our citizens and our youth ought to learn about the nature of the Gods in heaven, so far as to be able to offer sacrifices and pray to them in pious language, and not to blaspheme about them.

Cle. There you are right, if such a knowledge be only attainable; and if we are wrong in our mode of speaking now, and can be better instructed and learn to use better language, then I quite agree with you that such a degree of knowledge as will enable us to speak rightly should be acquired by us. And now do you try to explain to us your whole meaning, and we, on our part, will endeavour to understand you.

Ath. There is some difficulty in understanding my meaning, but not a very great one, nor will any great length of time be required. And of this I am myself a proof; for I did not know these things long ago, nor in the days of my youth, and yet I can explain them to you in a brief space of time; whereas if they had been difficult I could certainly never have explained them all, old as I am, to old men like yourselves.

Cle. True; but what is this study which you describe as wonderful and fitting for youth to learn, but of which we are ignorant? Try and explain the nature of it to us as clearly as you can.

Ath. I will. For, O my good friends, that other doctrine about the wandering of the sun and the moon and the other stars is not the truth, but the very reverse of the truth. Each of them moves in the same path—not in many paths, but in one only, which is circular, and the varieties are only apparent. Nor are we right in supposing

universe, the reverse of impious.

At present the sun, moon, and other stars are blasphemously said to be wanderers.

822

All the stars move in a circle; their wander-

ings are
only ap-
parent.

that the swiftest of them is the slowest, nor conversely, that the slowest is the quickest. And if what I say is true, only just imagine that we had a similar notion about horses running at Olympia, or about men who ran in the long course, and that we addressed the swiftest as the slowest and the slowest as the swiftest, and sang the praises of the vanquished as though he were the victor,—in that case our praises would not be true, nor very agreeable to the runners, though they be but men; and now, to commit the same error about the Gods which would have been ludicrous and erroneous in the case of men,—is not that ludicrous and erroneous?

Cle. Worse than ludicrous, I should say.

Ath. At all events, the Gods cannot like us to be spreading a false report of them.

Cle. Most true, if such is the fact.

Ath. And if we can show that such is really the fact, then all these matters ought to be learned so far as is necessary for the avoidance of impiety; but if we cannot, they may be let alone, and let this be our decision.

Cle. Very good.

Hunting.

Ath. Enough of laws relating to education and learning. But hunting and similar pursuits in like manner claim our attention. For the legislator appears to have a duty imposed upon him which goes beyond mere legislation. There is something over and above law which lies in a region between admonition and law, and has several times occurred to us in the course of discussion; for example, in the education of very young children there were things, as we maintain, which are not to be defined, and to regard them as matters of positive law is a great absurdity. Now, our laws and the whole constitution of our state having been thus delineated, the praise of the virtuous citizen is not complete when he is described as the person who serves the laws best and obeys them most, but the higher form of praise is that which describes him as the good citizen who passes through life undefiled and is obedient to the words of the legislator, both when he is giving laws and when he assigns praise and blame. This is the truest word that can be spoken in praise of a citizen; and the true legislator ought not only to write his laws, but also to interweave with them all such things as seem to him honourable and dishonourable. And the perfect citizen ought to seek to strengthen these no less than the principles of law which are sanctioned by punishments. I will adduce an example which will clear up my meaning, and will be a sort of witness to my words. Hunting is of wide extent, and has a name under which many things are included, for there is a hunting of creatures in the water, and of

The
highest
honour to
be given
to him
who not
[823]
only
obeys the
laws, but
earns the
praise of
the legis-
lator.

creatures in the air, and there is a great deal of hunting of land animals of all kinds, and not of wild beasts only. The hunting after man
is also worthy of consideration; there is the hunting after him in
war, and there is often a hunting after him in the way of friendship,
which is praised and also blamed; and there is thieving, and the
hunting which is practised by robbers, and that of armies against
armies. Now the legislator, in laying down laws about hunting, can
neither abstain from noting these things, nor can he make threatening ordinances which will assign rules and penalties about all of
them. What is he to do? He will have to praise and blame hunting
with a view to the exercise and pursuits of youth. And, on the other
hand, the young man must listen obediently; neither pleasure nor
pain should hinder him, and he should regard as his standard of action the praises and injunctions of the legislator rather than the
punishments which he imposes by law. This being premised, there
will follow next in order moderate praise and censure of hunting;
the praise being assigned to that kind which will make the souls of
young men better, and the censure to that which has the opposite
effect. And now let us address young men in the form of a prayer
for their welfare: O friends, we will say to them, may no desire or
love of hunting in the sea, or of angling or of catching the creatures
in the waters, ever take possession of you, either when you are
awake or when you are asleep, by hook or with weels, which latter
is a very lazy contrivance; and let not any desire of catching men
and of piracy by sea enter into your souls and make you cruel and
lawless hunters. And as to the desire of thieving in town or country,
may it never enter into your most passing thoughts; nor let the insidious fancy of catching birds, which is hardly worthy of freemen,
come into the head of any youth. There remains therefore for our
athletes only the hunting and catching of land animals, of which the
one sort is called hunting by night, in which the hunters sleep in
turn and are lazy; this is not to be commended any more than that
which has intervals of rest, in which the wild strength of beasts is
subdued by nets and snares, and not by the victory of a laborious
spirit. Thus, only the best kind of hunting is allowed at all—that of
quadrupeds, which is carried on with horses and dogs and men's
own persons, and they get the victory over the animals by running
them down and striking them and hurling at them, those who have
a care of godlike manhood taking them with their own hands. The
praise and blame which is assigned to all these things has now been
declared; and let the law be as follows:—Let no one hinder these
who verily are sacred hunters from following the chase wherever
and whithersoever they will; but the hunter by night, who trusts to

Forms of
hunting
which are
approved,
disap-
proved,
and for-
bidden.

824

his nets and gins, shall not be allowed to hunt anywhere. The fowler in the mountains and waste places shall be permitted, but on culti-vated ground and on consecrated wilds he shall not be permitted; and any one who meets him may stop him. As to the hunter in waters, he may hunt anywhere except in harbours or sacred streams or marshes or pools, provided only that he do not pollute the water with poisonous juices. And now we may say that all our enactments about education are complete.

Cle. Very good.

BOOK VIII

828
Laws VIII

ATHE-
NIAN,
CLEINIAS.

Festivals
and sacri-
fices.

There
shall be
daily sac-
rifices:

also a
monthly
feast to
each of
the
twelve
Gods of
the
tribes;
and festi-
vals set
apart for
women.

The rites
of the
Gods

Athenian Stranger. NEXT, with the help of the Delphian oracle, we have to institute festivals and make laws about them, and to determine what sacrifices will be for the good of the city, and to what Gods they shall be offered; but when they shall be offered, and how often, may be partly regulated by us.

Cleinias. The number—yes.

Ath. Then we will first determine the number; and let the whole number be 365—one for every day,—so that one magistrate at least will sacrifice daily to some God or demi-god on behalf of the city, and the citizens, and their possessions. And the interpreters, and priests, and priestesses, and prophets shall meet, and, in company with the guardians of the law, ordain those things which the legis-lator of necessity omits; and I may remark that they are the very persons who ought to take note of what is omitted[1]. The law will say that there are twelve feasts dedicated to the twelve Gods, after whom the several tribes are named; and that to each of them they shall sacrifice every month, and appoint choruses, and musical and gymnastic contests, assigning them so as to suit the Gods and sea-sons of the year. And they shall have festivals for women, distin-guishing those which ought to be separated from the men's festivals, and those which ought not. Further, they shall not confuse the in-fernal deities and their rites with the Gods who are termed heavenly and their rites, but shall separate them, giving to Pluto his own in the twelfth month, which is sacred to him, according to the law. To such a deity warlike men should entertain no aversion, but they should honour him as being always the best friend of man[2]. For the

---

[1] Cp. *supra,* vi. 770, and Rep. v. 458 C.　　[2] Cp. Crat. 403; Rep. iii. 386.

connection of soul and body is no way better than the dissolution of them, as I am ready to maintain quite seriously. Moreover, those who would regulate these matters rightly should consider, that our city among existing cities has no fellow, either in respect of leisure or command of the necessaries of life, and that like an individual she ought to live happily. And those who would live happily should in the first place do no wrong to one another, and ought not themselves to be wronged by others; to attain the first is not difficult, but there is great difficulty in acquiring the power of not being wronged. No man can be perfectly secure against wrong, unless he has become perfectly good; and cities are like individuals in this, for a city if good has a life of peace, but if evil, a life of war within and without. Wherefore the citizens ought to practise war—not in time of war, but rather while they are at peace. And every city which has any sense, should take the field at least for one day in every month, and for more if the magistrates think fit, having no regard to winter cold or summer heat; and they should go out *en masse*, including their wives and their children, when the magistrates determine to lead forth the whole people, or in separate portions when summoned by them; and they should always provide that there should be games and sacrificial feasts, and they should have tournaments, imitating in as lively a manner as they can real battles. And they should distribute prizes of victory and valour to the competitors, passing censures and encomiums on one another according to the characters which they bear in the contests and in their whole life, honouring him who seems to be the best, and blaming him who is the opposite. And let poets celebrate the victors,—not however every poet, but only one who in the first place is not less than fifty years of age; nor should he be one who, although he may have musical and poetical gifts, has never in his life done any noble or illustrious action; but those who are themselves good and also honourable in the state, creators of noble actions—let their poems be sung, even though they be not very musical. And let the judgment of them rest with the instructor of youth[1] and the other guardians of the laws, who shall give them this privilege, and they alone shall be free to sing; but the rest of the world shall not have this liberty. Nor shall any one dare to sing a song which has not been approved by the judgment of the guardians of the laws, not even if his strain be sweeter than the songs of Thamyras and Orpheus; but only such poems as have been judged sacred and dedicated to the Gods, and such as are the works of good men, in which praise or blame has

above and of [829] the Gods below should be kept distinct.

The God of Death the best friend of man.

Neither individual nor city can live happily if not perfectly good.

With a view to war there should be military festivals.

The victors in these are to be celebrated by poets who have themselves done noble actions.

All songs to be approved by the guardians of the law.

---

[1] i. e. the director of education.

The reflections of the legislator

LawsVIII

ATHE-
NIAN,
CLEINIAS.

830

Our
citizens
are com-
petitors
in the
greatest
of con-
tests, and
must en-
ter it
well-pre-
pared.

Gymnas-
tics and
military
drill to be
practised
continu-
ally.

831

been awarded and which have been deemed to fulfil their design
fairly.

The regulations about war, and about liberty of speech in poetry,
ought to apply equally to men and women. The legislator may be
supposed to argue the question in his own mind:—Who are my
citizens for whom I have set in order the city? Are they not competitors in the greatest of all contests[1], and have they not innumerable rivals? To be sure, will be the natural reply. Well, but if we
were training boxers, or pancratiasts, or any other sort of athletes,
would they never meet until the hour of contest arrived; and should
we do nothing to prepare ourselves previously by daily practice?
Surely, if we were boxers, we should have been learning to fight for
many days before, and exercising ourselves in imitating all those
blows and wards which we were intending to use in the hour of conflict; and in order that we might come as near to reality as possible,
instead of cestuses we should put on boxing-gloves, that the blows
and the wards might be practised by us to the utmost of our power.
And if there were a lack of competitors, the ridicule of fools would
not deter us from hanging up a lifeless image and practising at that.
Or if we had no adversary at all, animate or inanimate, should we
not venture in the dearth of antagonists to spar by ourselves? In
what other manner could we ever study the art of self-defence?

Cle. The way which you mention, Stranger, would be the only
way.

Ath. And shall the warriors of our city, who are destined when
occasion calls to enter the greatest of all contests, and to fight for
their lives, and their children, and their property, and the whole
city, be worse prepared than boxers? And will the legislator, because he is afraid that their practising with one another may appear
to some ridiculous, abstain from commanding them to go out and
fight; will he not ordain that soldiers shall perform lesser exercises
without arms every day, making dancing and all gymnastic tend to
this end; and also will he not require that they shall practise some
gymnastic exercises, greater as well as lesser, as often as every
month; and that they shall have contests one with another in every
part of the country, seizing upon posts and lying in ambush, and
imitating in every respect the reality of war; fighting with boxing-
gloves and hurling javelins, and using weapons somewhat dangerous, and as nearly as possible like the true ones, in order that the
sport may not be altogether without fear, but may have terrors and
to a certain degree show the man who has and who has not courage;
and that the honour and dishonour which are assigned to them re-

[1] Cp. Rep. iii. 403 E.

spectively, may prepare the whole city for the true conflict of life? If any one dies in these mimic contests, the homicide is involuntary, and we will make the slayer, when he has been purified according to law, to be pure of blood, considering that if a few men should die, others as good as they will be born; but that if fear is dead, then the citizens will never find a test of superior and inferior natures, which is a far greater evil to the state than the loss of a few.

Cle. We are quite agreed, Stranger, that we should legislate about such things, and that the whole state should practise them.

Ath. And what is the reason that dances and contests of this sort hardly ever exist in states, at least not to any extent worth speaking of? Is this due to the ignorance of mankind and their legislators?

Cle. Perhaps.

Ath. Certainly not, sweet Cleinias; there are two causes, which are quite enough to account for the deficiency.

Cle. What are they?

Ath. One cause is the love of wealth, which wholly absorbs men, and never for a moment allows them to think of anything but their own private possessions; on this the soul of every citizen hangs suspended, and can attend to nothing but his daily gain; mankind are ready to learn any branch of knowledge, and to follow any pursuit which tends to this end, and they laugh at every other:—that is one reason why a city will not be in earnest about such contests or any other good and honourable pursuit. But from an insatiable love of gold and silver, every man will stoop to any art or contrivance, seemly or unseemly, in the hope of becoming rich; and will make no objection to performing any action, holy, or unholy and utterly base, if only like a beast he have the power of eating and drinking all kinds of things, and procuring for himself in every sort of way the gratification of his lusts.

Cle. True.

Ath. Let this, then, be deemed one of the causes which prevent states from pursuing in an efficient manner the art of war, or any other noble aim, but makes the orderly and temperate part of mankind into merchants, and captains of ships, and servants, and converts the valiant sort into thieves and burglars, and robbers of temples, and violent, tyrannical persons; many of whom are not without ability, but they are unfortunate[1].

Cle. What do you mean?

Ath. Must not they be truly unfortunate whose souls are compelled to pass through life always hungering?

Cle. Then that is one cause, Stranger; but you spoke of another.

[1] Cp. Rep. vi. 491 E, 495 B.

One of the reasons (1) why martial dances and contests are neglected is the love of money.

The orderly become traders, the valiant robbers.

832

The latter have often considerable natural gifts.

Laws VIII

ATHE-
NIAN,
CLEINIAS.

Ath. Thank you for reminding me.

Cle. The insatiable lifelong love of wealth, as you were saying, is one cause which absorbs mankind, and prevents them from rightly practising the arts of war:—Granted; and now tell me, what is the other?

Ath. Do you imagine that I delay because I am in a perplexity?

Cle. No; but we think that you are too severe upon the money-loving temper, of which you seem in the present discussion to have a peculiar dislike.

Ath. That is a very fair rebuke, Cleinias; and I will now proceed to the second cause.

Cle. Proceed.

(2) Bad govern-ments are a second cause.

Ath. I say that governments are a cause—democracy, oligarchy, tyranny, concerning which I have often spoken in the previous discourse[1]; or rather governments they are not, for none of them exercises a voluntary rule over voluntary subjects; but they may be truly called states of discord, in which while the government is voluntary, the subjects always obey against their will, and have to be coerced; and the ruler fears the subject, and will not, if he can help, allow him to become either noble, or rich, or strong, or valiant, or warlike at all[2]. These two are the chief causes of almost all evils, and of the evils of which I have been speaking they are notably the causes. But our state has escaped both of them; for her citizens have the greatest leisure, and they are not subject to one another, and will, I think, be made by these laws the reverse of lovers of money. Such a constitution may be reasonably supposed to be the only one existing which will accept the education which we have described, and the martial pastimes which have been perfected according to our idea.

Our state is free from both these evils.

Cle. True.

Military gymnas-tics to be alone en-couraged.

Ath. Then next we must remember, about all gymnastic contests, that only the warlike sort of them are to be practised and to have prizes of victory; and those which are not military are to be given up. The military sort had better be completely described and established by law; and first, let us speak of running and swiftness.

Cle. Very good.

833

Ath. Certainly the most military of all qualities is general activity of body, whether of foot or hand. For escaping or for capturing an enemy, quickness of foot is required; but hand-to-hand conflict and combat need vigour and strength.

Cle. Very true.

[1] Cp. *supra,* iv. 712 E, 715 B.
[2] Cp. Arist. Pol. v. 11, §§ 5, 13.

Ath. Neither of them can attain their greatest efficiency without arms.

Cle. How can they?

Ath. Then our herald, in accordance with the prevailing practice, will first summon the runner;—he will appear armed, for to an unarmed competitor we will not give a prize. And he shall enter first who is to run the single course bearing arms; next, he who is to run the double course; third, he who is to run the horse-course; and fourthly, he who is to run the long course; the fifth whom we start, shall be the first sent forth in heavy armour, and shall run a course of sixty stadia to some temple of Ares—and we will send forth another, whom we will style the more heavily armed, to run over smoother ground. There remains the archer; and he shall run in the full equipments of an archer a distance of 100 stadia over mountains, and across every sort of country, to a temple of Apollo and Artemis; this shall be the order of the contest, and we will wait for them until they return, and will give a prize to the conqueror in each.

Cle. Very good.

Ath. Let us suppose that there are three kinds of contests,—one of boys, another of beardless youths, and a third of men. For the youths we will fix the length of the contest at two-thirds, and for the boys at half of the entire course, whether they contend as archers or as heavy-armed. Touching the women, let the girls who are not grown up compete naked in the stadium and the double course, and the horse-course and the long course, and let them run on the race-ground itself; those who are thirteen years of age and upwards until their marriage shall continue to share in contests if they are not more than twenty, and shall be compelled to run up to eighteen; and they shall descend into the arena in suitable dresses. Let these be the regulations about contests in running both for men and women.

Respecting contests of strength, instead of wrestling and similar contests of the heavier sort, we will institute conflicts in armour of one against one, and two against two, and so on up to ten against ten. As to what a man ought not to suffer or do, and to what extent, in order to gain the victory—as in wrestling, the masters of the art have laid down what is fair and what is not fair, so in fighting in armour—we ought to call in skilful persons, who shall judge for us and be our assessors in the work of legislation; they shall say who deserves to be victor in combats of this sort, and what he is not to do or have done to him, and in like manner what rule determines who is defeated; and let these ordinances apply to women until they

Laws VIII

ATHE-
NIAN,
CLEINIAS.

Contests
of swift-
ness.

The
seven
courses
of run-
ning in
light or
heavy
armour.

Different
courses
for boys,
for
youths,
and for
men.

Women
and girls
to share
in the
contests.

Contests
of
strength.
Men and
women to
contend
in
armour.

The mili-
tary pan-
cration.

are married as well as to men. The pancration shall have a counterpart in a combat of the light-armed; they shall contend with bows
and with light shields and with javelins and in the throwing of
stones by slings and by hand: and laws shall be made about it, and
rewards and prizes given to him who best fulfils the ordinances of
the law.

No
prizes for
chariot-
races, but
only for
single
horses,

Next in order we shall have to legislate about the horse contests.
Now we do not need many horses, for they cannot be of much use
in a country like Crete[1], and hence we naturally do not take great
pains about the rearing of them or about horse races. There is no
one who keeps a chariot among us, and any rivalry in such matters
would be altogether out of place; there would be no sense nor any
shadow of sense in instituting contests which are not after the manner of our country. And therefore we give our prizes for single
horses,—for colts who have not yet cast their teeth, and for those
who are intermediate, and for the full-grown horses themselves; and
thus our equestrian games will accord with the nature of the country. Let them have conflict and rivalry in these matters in accordance with the law, and let the colonels and generals of horse decide
together about all courses and about the armed competitors in
them. But we have nothing to say to the unarmed either in gym-

and for
mounted
archers
and
spearmen.

nastic exercises or in these contests. On the other hand, the Cretan
bowman or javelin-man who fights in armour on horseback is useful,
and therefore we may as well place a competition of this sort among
our amusements. Women are not to be forced to compete by laws
and ordinances; but if from previous training they have acquired
the habit and are strong enough and like to take part, let them do
so, girls as well as boys, and no blame to them.

The ar-
range-
ments for
recita-
tions and
choruses.

835

Thus the competition in gymnastic and the mode of learning it
have been described; and we have spoken also of the toils of the
contest, and of daily exercises under the superintendence of masters[2]. Likewise, what relates to music has been, for the most part,
completed. But as to rhapsodes and the like, and the contests of
choruses which are to perform at feasts, all this shall be arranged
when the months and days and years have been appointed for Gods
and demi-gods, whether every third year, or again every fifth year,
or in whatever way or manner the Gods may put into men's minds
the distribution and order of them. At the same time, we may expect that the musical contests will be celebrated in their turn by the
command of the judges and the director of education and the guardians of the law meeting together for this purpose, and themselves
becoming legislators of the times and nature and conditions of the

[1] Cp. *supra*, i. 625 D.   [2] Omitting ἐν, a conjecture of Winkelmann.

choral contests and of dancing in general. What they ought severally to be in language and song, and in the admixture of harmony
with rhythm and the dance, has been often declared by the original
legislator; and his successors ought to follow him, making the games
and sacrifices duly to correspond at fitting times, and appointing
public festivals. It is not difficult to determine how these and the
like matters may have a regular order; nor, again, will the alteration
of them do any great good or harm to the state. There is, however,
another matter of great importance and difficulty, concerning which
God should legislate, if there were any possibility of obtaining from
Him an ordinance about it. But seeing that divine aid is not to be
had, there appears to be a need of some bold man who specially
honours plainness of speech, and will say outright what he thinks
best for the city and citizens,—ordaining what is good and convenient for the whole state amid the corruptions of human souls,
opposing the mightiest lusts, and having no man his helper but himself standing alone and following reason only.

Cle. What is this, Stranger, that you are saying? For we do not as
yet understand your meaning.

Ath. Very likely; I will endeavour to explain myself more clearly.
When I came to the subject of education, I beheld young men and
maidens holding friendly intercourse with one another. And there
naturally arose in my mind a sort of apprehension—I could not help
thinking how one is to deal with a city in which youths and maidens
are well nurtured, and have nothing to do, and are not undergoing
the excessive and servile toils which extinguish wantonness, and
whose only cares during their whole life are sacrifices and festivals
and dances. How, in such a state as this, will they abstain from desires which thrust many a man and woman into perdition; and from
which reason, assuming the functions of law, commands them to
abstain? The ordinances already made may possibly get the better
of most of these desires; the prohibition of excessive wealth is a very
considerable gain in the direction of temperance, and the whole education of our youth imposes a law of moderation on them; moreover, the eye of the rulers is required always to watch over the
young, and never to lose sight of them; and these provisions do, as
far as human means can effect anything, exercise a regulating influence upon the desires in general. But how can we take precautions
against the unnatural loves of either sex, from which innumerable
evils have come upon individuals and cities? How shall we devise a
remedy and way of escape out of so great a danger? Truly, Cleinias,
here is a difficulty. In many ways Crete and Lacedaemon furnish a
great help to those who make peculiar laws; but in the matter of

How can
men and
women
living at
ease be
saved
from their
lusts?

836

The evil
of un-
natural
loves.

Bad ex-
ample set
by Crete

Laws VIII

ATHE-
NIAN,
CLEINIAS.

and Lace-
daemon.

love, as we are alone, I must confess that they are quite against us. For if any one following nature should lay down the law which existed before the days of Laius, and denounce these lusts as contrary to nature, adducing the animals as a proof that such unions were monstrous, he might prove his point, but he would be wholly at variance with the custom of your states. Further, they are repugnant to a principle which we say that a legislator should always observe; for we are always enquiring which of our enactments tends to virtue and which not[1]. And suppose we grant that these loves are accounted by law to be honourable, or at least not disgraceful, in what degree will they contribute to virtue? Will such passions implant in the soul of him who is seduced the habit of courage, or in the soul of the seducer the principle of temperance? Who will ever believe this?—or rather, who will not blame the effeminacy of him who yields to pleasures and is unable to hold out against them? Will not all men censure as womanly him who imitates the woman? And who would ever think of establishing such a practice by law? Certainly no one who had in his mind the image of true law. How can we prove that what I am saying is true? He who would rightly consider these matters must see the nature of friendship and desire, and of these so-called loves, for they are of two kinds, and out of the two arises a third kind, having the same name; and this similarity of name causes all the difficulty and obscurity.

837

Cle. How is that?

Ath. Dear is the like in virtue to the like, and the equal to the equal; dear also, though unlike, is he who has abundance to him who is in want. And when either of these friendships becomes excessive, we term the excess love.

Cle. Very true.

Ath. The friendship which arises from contraries is horrible and coarse, and has often no tie of communion; but that which arises from likeness is gentle, and has a tie of communion which lasts through life. As to the mixed sort which is made up of them both, there is, first of all, a difficulty in determining what he who is possessed by this third love desires; moreover, he is drawn different ways, and is in doubt between the two principles; the one exhorting him to enjoy the beauty of youth, and the other forbidding him. For the one is a lover of the body, and hungers after beauty, like ripe fruit, and would fain satisfy himself without any regard to the character of the beloved; the other holds the desire of the body to be a secondary matter, and looking rather than loving and with his soul desiring the soul of the other in a becoming manner, regards the

[1] Cp. iii. 693 B; iv. 705 E; vi. 770; xii. 963 A.

satisfaction of the bodily love as wantonness[1]; he reverences and respects temperance and courage and magnanimity and wisdom, and wishes to live chastely with the chaste object of his affection. Now the sort of love which is made up of the other two is that which we have described as the third. Seeing then that there are these three sorts of love, ought the law to prohibit and forbid them all to exist among us? Is it not rather clear that we should wish to have in the state the love which is of virtue and which desires the beloved youth to be the best possible; and the other two, if possible, we should hinder? What do you say, friend Megillus?

Meg. I think, Stranger, that you are perfectly right in what you have been now saying.

Ath. I knew well, my friend, that I should obtain your assent, which I accept, and therefore have no need to analyze your custom any further. Cleinias shall be prevailed upon to give me his assent at some other time. Enough of this; and now let us proceed to the laws.

Meg. Very good.

Ath. Upon reflection I see a way of imposing the law, which, in one respect, is easy, but, in another, is of the utmost difficulty.

Meg. What do you mean?

Ath. We are all aware that most men, in spite of their lawless natures, are very strictly and precisely restrained from intercourse with the fair, and this is not at all against their will, but entirely with their will.

Meg. When do you mean?

Ath. When any one has a brother or sister who is fair; and about a son or daughter the same unwritten law holds, and is a most perfect safeguard, so that no open or secret connection ever takes place between them. Nor does the thought of such a thing ever enter at all into the minds of most of them.

Meg. Very true.

Ath. Does not a little word extinguish all pleasures of that sort?

Meg. What word?

Ath. The declaration that they are unholy, hated of God, and most infamous; and is not the reason of this that no one has ever said the opposite, but every one from his earliest childhood has heard men speaking in the same manner about them always and everywhere, whether in comedy or in the graver language of tragedy? When the poet introduces on the stage a Thyestes or an Oedipus, or a Macareus having secret intercourse with his sister, he

Laws VIII

ATHE-
NIAN,
MEGIL-
LUS.

We approve only of the second.

838

An encouraging circumstance that the purity of the family is perfectly preserved.

The reason of this is that incestuous connections have ever been deemed infamous.

---

[1] Cp. Phaedr. 251.

represents him, when found out, ready to kill himself as the penalty of his sin.

Meg. You are very right in saying that tradition, if no breath of opposition ever assails it, has a marvellous power.

Ath. Am I not also right in saying that the legislator who wants to master any of the passions which master man may easily know how to subdue them? He will consecrate the tradition of their evil character among all, slaves and freemen, women and children, throughout the city:—that will be the surest foundation of the law which he can make.

Meg. Yes; but will he ever succeed in making all mankind use the same language about them?

Ath. A good objection; but was I not just now saying that I had a way to make men use natural love and abstain from unnatural, not intentionally destroying the seeds of human increase, or sowing them in stony places, in which they will take no root; and that I would command them to abstain too from any female field of increase in which that which is sown is not likely to grow? Now if a law to this effect could only be made perpetual, and gain an authority such as already prevents intercourse of parents and children—such a law, extending to other sensual desires, and conquering them, would be the source of ten thousand blessings. For, in the first place, moderation is the appointment of nature, and deters men from all frenzy and madness of love, and from all adulteries and immoderate use of meats and drinks, and makes them good friends to their own wives. And innumerable other benefits would result if such a law could only be enforced. I can imagine some lusty youth who is standing by, and who, on hearing this enactment, declares in scurrilous terms that we are making foolish and impossible laws, and fills the world with his outcry. And therefore I said that I knew a way of enacting and perpetuating such a law, which was very easy in one respect, but in another most difficult. There is no difficulty in seeing that such a law is possible, and in what way; for, as I was saying, the ordinance once consecrated would master the soul of every man, and terrify him into obedience. But matters have now come to such a pass that even then the desired result seems as if it could not be attained, just as the continuance of an entire state in the practice of common meals is also deemed impossible. And although this latter is partly disproven by the fact of their existence among you, still even in your cities the common meals of women would be regarded as unnatural and impossible. I was thinking of the rebelliousness of the human heart when I said that the permanent establishment of these things is very difficult.

Meg. Very true.

Ath. Shall I try and find some sort of persuasive argument which will prove to you that such enactments are possible, and not beyond human nature?

Cle. By all means.

Ath. Is a man more likely to abstain from the pleasures of love and to do what he is bidden about them, when his body is in a good condition, or when he is in an ill condition, and out of training?

Cle. He will be far more temperate when he is in training.

Ath. And have we not heard of Iccus of Tarentum, who, with a view to the Olympic and other contests, in his zeal for his art, and also because he was of a manly and temperate disposition, never had any connection with a woman or a youth during the whole time of his training? And the same is said of Crison and Astylus and Diopompus and many others; and yet, Cleinias, they were far worse educated in their minds than your and my citizens, and in their bodies far more lusty.

Cle. No doubt this fact has been often affirmed positively by the ancients of these athletes.

Ath. And had they the courage to abstain from what is ordinarily deemed a pleasure for the sake of a victory in wrestling, running, and the like; and shall our young men be incapable of a similar endurance for the sake of a much nobler victory, which is the noblest of all, as from their youth upwards we will tell them, charming them, as we hope, into the belief of this by tales and sayings and songs?

Cle. Of what victory are you speaking?

Ath. Of the victory over pleasure, which if they win, they will live happily; or if they are conquered, the reverse of happily. And, further, may we not suppose that the fear of impiety will enable them to master that which other inferior people have mastered?

Cle. I dare say.

Ath. And since we have reached this point in our legislation, and have fallen into a difficulty by reason of the vices of mankind, I affirm that our ordinance should simply run in the following terms: Our citizens ought not to fall below the nature of birds and beasts in general, who are born in great multitudes, and yet remain until the age for procreation virgin and unmarried, but when they have reached the proper time of life are coupled, male and female, and lovingly pair together, and live the rest of their lives in holiness and innocence, abiding firmly in their original compact:—surely, we will say to them, you should be better than the animals. But if they are corrupted by the other Hellenes and the common practice of bar-

Laws VIII

ATHE-
NIAN,
MEGIL-
LUS,
CLEINIAS.

840
Iccus of
Tarentum
and other
athletes
have
practised
entire
contin-
ence to
gain a
prize at
Olympia.

And shall
not our
citizens
endure
that they
may win
the prize
of a far
nobler
victory?

The first
law:—

Our
citizens
should
not be
less inno-
cent than
the ani-
mals.

Laws VIII

ATHE-
NIAN,
MEGIL-
LUS,
CLEINIAS.

841

The
second
law:—

Labour
should di-
vert the
aliment
of pas-
sion into
other
parts of
the body.

Conceal-
ment bet-
ter than
open vice.

Three
correc-
tive prin-
ciples.

barians, and they see with their eyes and hear with their ears of the so-called free love everywhere prevailing among them, and they themselves are not able to get the better of the temptation, the guardians of the law, exercising the functions of lawgivers, shall devise a second law against them.

Cle. And what law would you advise them to pass if this one failed?

Ath. Clearly, Cleinias, the one which would naturally follow.

Cle. What is that?

Ath. Our citizens should not allow pleasures to strengthen with indulgence, but should by toil divert the aliment and exuberance of them into other parts of the body; and this will happen if no immodesty be allowed in the practice of love. Then they will be ashamed of frequent intercourse, and they will find pleasure, if seldom enjoyed, to be a less imperious mistress. They should not be found out doing anything of the sort. Concealment shall be honourable, and sanctioned by custom and made law by unwritten prescription; on the other hand, to be detected shall be esteemed dishonourable, but not, to abstain wholly. In this way there will be a second legal standard of honourable and dishonourable, involving a second notion of right. Three principles will comprehend all those corrupt natures whom we call inferior to themselves, and who form but one class, and will compel them not to transgress.

Cle. What are they?

Ath. The principle of piety, the love of honour, and the desire of beauty, not in the body but in the soul. These are, perhaps, romantic aspirations; but they are the noblest of aspirations, if they could only be realized in all states, and, God willing, in the matter of love we may be able to enforce one of two things—either that no one shall venture to touch any person of the freeborn or noble class except his wedded wife, or sow the unconsecrated and bastard seed among harlots, or in barren and unnatural lusts; or at least we may abolish altogether the connection of men with men; and as to women, if any man has to do with any but those who come into his house duly married by sacred rites, whether they be bought or acquired in any other way, and he offends publicly in the face of all mankind, we shall be right in enacting that he be deprived of civic honours and privileges, and be deemed to be, as he truly is, a stranger. Let this law, then, whether it is one, or ought rather to be called two, be laid down respecting love in general, and the intercourse of the sexes which arises out of the desires, whether rightly or wrongly indulged.

No man
shall
touch a
woman
except his
wedded
wife.
Prohibi-
tion of
loves be-
tween
man and
man.

842

Meg. I, for my part, Stranger, would gladly receive this law. Cleinias shall speak for himself, and tell you what is his opinion.

Cle. I will, Megillus, when an opportunity offers; at present, I think that we had better allow the Stranger to proceed with his laws.

Meg. Very good.

Ath. We had got about as far as the establishment of the common tables, which in most places would be difficult, but in Crete no one would think of introducing any other custom. There might arise a question about the manner of them—whether they shall be such as they are here in Crete, or such as they are in Lacedaemon,—or is there a third kind which may be better than either of them[1]? The answer to this question might be easily discovered, but the discovery would do no great good, for at present they are very well ordered.

Leaving the common tables, we may therefore proceed to the means of providing food. Now, in cities the means of life are gained in many ways and from divers sources, and in general from two sources, whereas our city has only one. For most of the Hellenes obtain their food from sea and land, but our citizens from land only. And this makes the task of the legislator less difficult—half as many laws will be enough, and much less than half; and they will be of a kind better suited to free men. For he has nothing to do with laws about shipowners and merchants and retailers and innkeepers and tax collectors and mines and moneylending and compound interest and innumerable other things—bidding good-bye to these, he gives laws to husbandmen and shepherds and bee-keepers, and to the guardians and superintendents of their implements; and he has already legislated for greater matters, as for example, respecting marriage and the procreation and nurture of children, and for education, and the establishment of offices—and now he must direct his laws to those who provide food and labour in preparing it.

The way of providing food being more simple than in other states, the laws relating to this subject will also be more simple.

Let us first of all, then, have a class of laws which shall be called the laws of husbandmen. And let the first of them be the law of Zeus, the god of boundaries. Let no one shift the boundary line either of a fellow-citizen who is a neighbour, or, if he dwells at the extremity of the land, of any stranger who is conterminous with him, considering that this is truly 'to move the immovable,' and every one should be more willing to move the largest rock which is not a landmark, than the least stone which is the sworn mark of friendship and hatred between neighbours; for Zeus, the god of kindred, is the witness of the citizen, and Zeus, the god of strangers, of the stranger, and when aroused, terrible are the wars which they stir up. He who obeys the law will never know the fatal conse-

Laws concerning husbandmen:—

843

Let boundaries not be disturbed.

[1] Cp. Arist. Pol. vii. 10, § 10.

Laws VIII

ATHE-
NIAN.

Let no
man en-
croach in
any way.

844

The an-
cient laws
about
water
quite suf-
ficient.

quences of disobedience, but he who despises the law shall be liable to a double penalty, the first coming from the Gods, and the second from the law. For let no one wilfully remove the boundaries of his neighbour's land, and if any one does, let him who will inform the landowners, and let them bring him into court, and if he be convicted of re-dividing the land by stealth or by force, let the court determine what he ought to suffer or pay. In the next place, many small injuries done by neighbours to one another, through their multiplication, may cause a weight of enmity, and make neighbourhood a very disagreeable and bitter thing. Wherefore a man ought to be very careful of committing any offence against his neighbour, and especially of encroaching on his neighbour's land; for any man may easily do harm, but not every man can do good to another. He who encroaches on his neighbour's land, and transgresses his boundaries, shall make good the damage, and, to cure him of his impudence and also of his meanness, he shall pay a double penalty to the injured party. Of these and the like matters the wardens of the country shall take cognizance, and be the judges of them and assessors of the damage; in the more important cases, as has been already said[1], the whole number of them belonging to any one of the twelve divisions shall decide, and in the lesser cases the commanders: or, again, if any one pastures his cattle on his neighbour's land, they shall see the injury, and adjudge the penalty. And if any one, by decoying the bees, gets possession of another's swarms, and draws them to himself by making noises, he shall pay the damage; or if any one sets fire to his own wood and takes no care of his neighbour's property, he shall be fined at the discretion of the magistrates. And if in planting he does not leave a fair distance between his own and his neighbour's land, he shall be punished, in accordance with the enactments of many lawgivers, which we may use, not deeming it necessary that the great legislator of our state should determine all the trifles which might be decided by any body; for example, husbandmen have had of old excellent laws about waters, and there is no reason why we should propose to divert their course: He who likes may draw water from the fountain-head of the common stream on to his own land, if he do not cut off the spring which clearly belongs to some other owner; and he may take the water in any direction which he pleases, except through a house or temple or sepulchre, but he must be careful to do no harm beyond the channel. And if there be in any place a natural dryness of the earth, which keeps in the rain from heaven, and causes a deficiency in the supply of water, let him dig down on his own land as far as the clay, and

[1] Cp. *supra*, vi. 761 D, E.

if at this depth he finds no water, let him obtain water from his neighbours, as much as is required for his servants' drinking, and if his neighbours, too, are limited in their supply, let him have a fixed measure, which shall be determined by the wardens of the country. This he shall receive each day, and on these terms have a share of his neighbours' water. If there be heavy rain, and one of those on the lower ground injures some tiller of the upper ground, or some one who has a common wall, by refusing to give them an outlet for water; or, again, if some one living on the higher ground recklessly lets off the water on his lower neighbour, and they cannot come to terms with one another, let him who will call in a warden of the city, if he be in the city, or if he be in the country, a warden of the country, and let him obtain a decision determining what each of them is to do. And he who will not abide by the decision shall suffer for his malignant and morose temper, and pay a fine to the injured party, equivalent to double the value of the injury, because he was unwilling to submit to the magistrates.

Now the participation of fruits shall be ordered on this wise. The goddess of Autumn has two gracious gifts: one, the joy[1] of Dionysus which is not treasured up; the other, which nature intends to be stored. Let this be the law, then, concerning the fruits of autumn: He who tastes the common or storing fruits of autumn, whether grapes or figs, before the season of vintage which coincides with Arcturus, either on his own land or on that of others,—let him pay fifty drachmae, which shall be sacred to Dionysus, if he pluck them from his own land; and if from his neighbour's land, a mina, and if from any others', two-thirds of a mina. And he who would gather the 'choice' grapes or the 'choice' figs, as they are now termed, if he take them off his own land, let him pluck them how and when he likes; but if he take them from the ground of others without their leave, let him in that case be always punished in accordance with the law which ordains that he should not move what he has not laid down[2]. And if a slave touches any fruit of this sort, without the consent of the owner of the land, he shall be beaten with as many blows as there are grapes on the bunch, or figs on the fig-tree. Let a metic purchase the 'choice' autumnal fruit, and then, if he pleases, he may gather it; but if a stranger is passing along the road, and desires to eat, let him take of the 'choice' grape for himself and a single follower without payment, as a tribute of hospitality. The law however forbids strangers from sharing in the sort which is not used for eating; and if any one, whether he be master or slave, takes of them in ignorance, let the slave be beaten, and the freeman dismissed

The citizen may not pluck the storing fruit anywhere, but he may pluck the choice grapes or figs on his own land.

845

A stranger may take of the choice grape, but not of the storing.

---

[1] Reading παιδιάν.   [2] Cp. *infra*, xi. 913.

Pears and
apples
may be
taken
secretly;
but any
one under
thirty
who is
caught
may be
beaten
off.

with admonitions, and instructed to take of the other autumnal fruits which are unfit for making raisins and wine, or for laying by as dried figs. As to pears, and apples, and pomegranates, and similar fruits, there shall be no disgrace in taking them secretly; but he who is caught, if he be of less than thirty years of age, shall be struck and beaten off, but not wounded; and no freeman shall have any right of satisfaction for such blows. Of these fruits the stranger may partake, just as he may of the fruits of autumn. And if an elder, who is more than thirty years of age, eat of them on the spot, let him, like the stranger, be allowed to partake of all such fruits, but he must carry away nothing. If, however, he will not obey the law, let him run the risk of failing in the competition of virtue, in case any one takes notice of his actions before the judges at the time.

The
penalty
for pol-
luting
water.

Water is the greatest element of nutrition in gardens, but is easily polluted. You cannot poison the soil, or the sun, or the air, which are the other elements of nutrition in plants, or divert them, or steal them; but all these things may very likely happen in regard to water, which must therefore be protected by law. And let this be the law:—If any one intentionally pollutes the water of another, whether the water of a spring, or collected in reservoirs, either by poisonous substances, or by digging, or by theft, let the injured party bring the cause before the wardens of the city, and claim in writing the value of the loss; if the accused be found guilty of injuring the water by deleterious substances, let him not only pay damages, but purify the stream or the cistern which contains the water, in such manner as the laws of the interpreters[1] order the purification to be made by the offender in each case.

Regula-
tions
    [846]
about
harvest-
ing.

With respect to the gathering in of the fruits of the soil, let a man, if he pleases, carry his own fruits through any place in which he either does no harm to any one, or himself gains three times as much as his neighbour loses. Now of these things the magistrates should be cognisant, as of all other things in which a man intentionally does injury to another or to the property of another, by fraud or force, in the use which he makes of his own property. All these matters a man should lay before the magistrates, and receive damages, supposing the injury to be not more than three minae; or if he have a charge against another which involves a larger amount, let him bring his suit into the public courts and have the evil-doer punished. But if any of the magistrates appear to adjudge the penalties which he imposes in an unjust spirit, let him be liable to pay double to the injured party. Any one may bring the offences of magistrates, in any particular case, before the public courts. There

[1] Cp. *supra*, vi. 759 C.

are innumerable little matters relating to the modes of punishment, and applications for suits, and summonses and the witnesses to summonses—for example, whether two witnesses should be required for a summons, or how many—and all such details, which cannot be omitted in legislation, but are beneath the wisdom of an aged legislator. These lesser matters, as they indeed are in comparison with the greater ones, let a younger generation regulate by law, after the patterns which have preceded, and according to their own experience of the usefulness and necessity of such laws; and when they are duly regulated let there be no alteration, but let the citizens live in the observance of them.

Now of artisans, let the regulations be as follows:—In the first place, let no citizen or servant of a citizen be occupied in handicraft arts; for he who is to secure and preserve the public order of the state, has an art which requires much study and many kinds of knowledge, and does not admit of being made a secondary occupation; and hardly any human being is capable of pursuing two professions or two arts rightly, or of practising one art himself, and superintending some one else who is practising another. Let this, then, be our first principle in the state:—No one who is a smith shall also be a carpenter, and if he be a carpenter, he shall not superintend the smith's art rather than his own, under the pretext that in superintending many servants who are working for him, he is likely to superintend them better, because more revenue will accrue to him from them than from his own art; but let every man in the state have one art, and get his living by that. Let the wardens of the city labour to maintain this law, and if any citizen incline to any other art than the study of virtue, let them punish him with disgrace and infamy, until they bring him back into his own right course; and if any stranger profess two arts, let them chastise him with bonds and money penalties, and expulsion from the state, until they compel him to be one only and not many[1].

But as touching payments for hire, and contracts of work, or in case any one does wrong to any of the citizens, or they do wrong to any other, up to fifty drachmae, let the wardens of the city decide the case; but if a greater amount be involved, then let the public courts decide according to law. Let no one pay any duty either on the importation or exportation of goods; and as to frankincense and similar perfumes, used in the service of the Gods, which come from abroad, and purple and other dyes which are not produced in the country, or the materials of any art which have to be imported, and which are not necessary—no one should import them; nor, again,

[1] Cp. Rep. iii. 397 E.

Laws VIII

ATHE-
NIAN.

No citizen to be an artisan.

No man should have more than one craft.

847

Free trade.

should any one export anything which is wanted in the country. Of all these things let there be inspectors and superintendents, taken from the guardians of the law; and they shall be the twelve next in order to the five seniors. Concerning arms, and all implements which are required for military purposes, if there be need of introducing any art, or plant, or metal, or chains of any kind, or animals for use in war, let the commanders of the horse and the generals have authority over their importation and exportation; the city shall send them out and also receive them, and the guardians of the law shall make fit and proper laws about them. But let there be no retail trade[1] for the sake of moneymaking, either in these or any other articles, in the city or country at all.

The produce of the land shall be divided into twelve [848] portions, and each portion into three parts,— one for freemen; another for slaves; another for strangers.

With respect to food and the distribution of the produce of the country, the right and proper way seems to be nearly that which is the custom of Crete[2]; for all should be required to distribute the fruits of the soil into twelve parts, and in this way consume them. Let the twelfth portion of each (as for instance of wheat and barley, to which the rest of the fruits of the earth shall be added, as well as the animals which are for sale in each of the twelve divisions) be divided in due proportion into three parts; one part for freemen, another for their servants, and a third for craftsmen and in general for strangers, whether sojourners who may be dwelling in the city, and like other men must live, or those who come on some business which they have with the state, or with some individual. Let only this third part of all necessaries be required to be sold; out of the other two-thirds no one shall be compelled to sell. And how will they be best distributed? In the first place, we see clearly that the distribution will be of equals in one point of view, and in another point of view of unequals.

Cle. What do you mean?

Ath. I mean that the earth of necessity produces and nourishes the various articles of food, sometimes better and sometimes worse.

Cle. Of course.

Ath. Such being the case, let no one of the three portions be greater than either of the other two;—neither that which is assigned to masters or to slaves, nor again that of the stranger; but let the distribution to all be equal and alike, and let every citizen take his two portions and distribute them among slaves and freemen, he having power to determine the quantity and quality. And what remains he shall distribute by measure and number among the animals who have to be sustained from the earth, taking the whole number of them.

[1] Cp. Arist. Pol. vii. 9, § 7.   [2] Cp. *ibid*. ii. 10, § 8.

In the second place, our citizens should have separate houses duly ordered; and this will be the order proper for men like them. There shall be twelve hamlets, one in the middle of each twelfth portion, and in each hamlet they shall first set apart a market-place, and the temples of the Gods, and of their attendant demi-gods; and if there be any local deities of the Magnetes, or holy seats of other ancient deities, whose memory has been preserved, to these let them pay their ancient honours[1]. But Hestia, and Zeus, and Athene will have temples everywhere together with the God who presides in each of the twelve districts[2]. And the first erection of houses shall be around these temples, where the ground is highest, in order to provide the safest and most defensible place of retreat for the guards. All the rest of the country they shall settle in the following manner:—They shall make thirteen divisions of the craftsmen; one of them they shall establish in the city, and this, again, they shall subdivide into twelve lesser divisions, among the twelve districts of the city, and the remainder shall be distributed in the country round about; and in each village they shall settle various classes of craftsmen, with a view to the convenience of the husbandmen. And the chief officers of the wardens of the country shall superintend all these matters, and see how many of them, and which class of them, each place requires; and fix them where they are likely to be least troublesome, and most useful to the husbandman. And the wardens of the city shall see to similar matters in the city.

Now the wardens of the agora ought to see to the details of the agora. Their first care, after the temples which are in the agora have been seen to, should be to prevent any one from doing any wrong in dealings between man and man; in the second place, as being inspectors of temperance and violence, they should chastise him who requires chastisement. Touching articles of sale, they should first see whether the articles which the citizens are under regulations to sell to strangers are sold to them, as the law ordains. And let the law be as follows:—On the first day of the month, the persons in charge, whoever they are, whether strangers or slaves, who have the charge on behalf of the citizens, shall produce to the strangers the portion which falls to them, in the first place, a twelfth portion of the corn;—the stranger shall purchase corn for the whole month, and other cereals, on the first market day; and on the tenth day of the month the one party shall sell, and the other buy, liquids sufficient to last during the whole month; and on the twenty-third day there shall be a sale of animals by those who are willing to sell to the people who want to buy, and of implements and other things

[1] Cp. *supra*, v. 738 C.   [2] Cp. *ibid.* 745.

Laws VIII

ATHE-
NIAN.

Twelve
hamlets,
one in the
middle of
each of
the
twelve di-
visions,
and
temples
in each.

Of the
thirteen
divisions
of the
crafts-
men, one
to be set-
tled in the
city, the
rest in the
country.

849

Duties of
the war-
dens of
the
agora.

The
market
days.

Laws VIII

ATHE-
NIAN.

Prohibi-
tion of
retail
trade
except
among
strangers.

850

Credit
not to be
recog-
nized by
law.

Metics
may
dwell in
the land
for
twenty
years;
(or
longer,
with
special
permis-
sion;)
and their
children
for the
same
term,
reckon-
ing from
the age of
fifteen.

which husbandmen sell, (such as skins and all kinds of clothing, either woven or made of felt and other goods of the same sort,) and which strangers are compelled to buy and purchase of others. As to the retail trade in these things, whether of barley or wheat set apart for meal and flour, or any other kind of food, no one shall sell them to citizens or their slaves, nor shall any one buy of a citizen; but let the stranger sell them in the market of strangers, to artisans and their slaves, making an exchange of wine and food, which is commonly called retail trade. And butchers shall offer for sale parts of dismembered animals to the strangers, and artisans, and their servants. Let any stranger who likes buy fuel from day to day wholesale, from those who have the care of it in the country, and let him sell to the strangers as much as he pleases and when he pleases. As to other goods and implements which are likely to be wanted, they shall sell them in the common market, at any place which the guardians of the law and the wardens of the market and city, choosing according to their judgment, shall determine; at such places they shall exchange money for goods, and goods for money, neither party giving credit to the other[1]; and he who gives credit must be satisfied, whether he obtain his money or not, for in such exchanges he will not be protected by law. But whenever property has been bought or sold, greater in quantity or value than is allowed by the law, which has determined within what limits a man may increase and diminish his possessions, let the excess be registered in the books of the guardians of the law; or in case of diminution, let there be an erasure made. And let the same rule be observed about the registration of the property of the metics. Any one who likes may come and be a metic on certain conditions; a foreigner, if he likes, and is able to settle, may dwell in the land, but he must practise an art, and not abide more than twenty years from the time at which he has registered himself; and he shall pay no sojourner's tax, however small, except good conduct, nor any other tax for buying and selling. But when the twenty years have expired, he shall take his property with him and depart. And if in the course of these years he should chance to distinguish himself by any considerable benefit which he confers on the state, and he thinks that he can persuade the council and assembly, either to grant him delay in leaving the country, or to allow him to remain for the whole of his life, let him go and persuade the city, and whatever they assent to at his instance shall take effect. For the children of the metics, being artisans, and of fifteen years of age, let the time of their sojourn commence after their fifteenth year; and let them remain for twenty

[1] Cp. *infra*, xi. 915 D.

years, and then go where they like; but any of them who wishes to remain, may do so, if he can persuade the council and assembly. And if he depart, let him erase all the entries which have been made by him in the register kept by the magistrates.

BOOK IX

NEXT to all the matters which have preceded in the natural order of legislation will come suits of law. Of suits those which relate to agriculture have been already described, but the more important have not been described. Having mentioned them severally under their usual names, we will proceed to say what punishments are to be inflicted for each offence, and who are to be the judges of them.

Cle. Very good.

Ath. There is a sense of disgrace in legislating, as we are about to do, for all the details of crime in a state which, as we say, is to be well regulated and will be perfectly adapted to the practice of virtue. To assume that in such a state there will arise some one who will be guilty of crimes as heinous as any which are ever perpetrated in other states, and that we must legislate for him by anticipation, and threaten and make laws against him if he should arise, in order to deter him, and punish his acts, under the idea that he will arise— this, as I was saying, is in a manner disgraceful. Yet seeing that we are not like the ancient legislators, who gave laws to heroes and sons of gods, being, according to the popular belief, themselves the offspring of the gods, and legislating for others, who were also the children of divine parents, but that we are only men who are legislating for the sons of men, there is no uncharitableness in apprehending that some one of our citizens may be like a seed which has touched the ox's horn, having a heart so hard that it cannot be softened any more than those seeds can be softened by fire. Among our citizens there may be those who cannot be subdued by all the strength of the laws; and for their sake, though an ungracious task, I will proclaim my first law about the robbing of temples, in case any one should dare to commit such a crime. I do not expect or imagine that any well-brought-up citizen will ever take the infection, but their servants, and strangers, and strangers' servants may be guilty of many impieties. And with a view to them especially, and yet not without a provident eye to the weakness of human nature generally, I will proclaim the law about robbers of temples

'It must be that offences come,' since we are legislating for men and not for heroes or demigods.

854

The pre-
lude to
the law
about
sacri-
lege:—

Sacri-
lege is
an in-
herited
malady,
begotten
of crime,
which
men
should do
their ut-
most to
cure.

and similar incurable, or almost incurable, criminals. Having already agreed that such enactments ought always to have a short prelude, we may speak to the criminal, whom some tormenting desire by night and by day tempts to go and rob a temple, the fewest possible words of admonition and exhortation:—O sir, we will say to him, the impulse which moves you to rob temples is not an ordinary human malady, nor yet a visitation of heaven, but a madness which is begotten in a man from ancient and unexpiated crimes of his race, an ever-recurring curse;—against this you must guard with all your might, and how you are to guard we will explain to you. When any such thought comes into your mind, go and perform expiations, go as a suppliant to the temples of the Gods who avert evils, go to the society of those who are called good men among you; hear them tell and yourself try to repeat after them, that every man should honour the noble and the just. Fly from the company of the wicked—fly and turn not back; and if your disorder is lightened by these remedies, well and good, but if not, then acknowledge death to be nobler than life, and depart hence.

The
law:—
The slave
or
stranger
who robs
a temple
shall be
branded,
beaten,
and cast
out of the
land;—

the citi-
zen shall
be put to
death;
[855]
for he is
incurable.

'The fa-
ther and
the chil-
dren.'

Such are the preludes which we sing to all who have thoughts of unholy and treasonable actions, and to him who hearkens to them the law has nothing to say. But to him who is disobedient when the prelude is over, cry with a loud voice—He who is taken in the act of robbing temples, if he be a slave or stranger, shall have his evil deed engraven on his face and hands, and shall be beaten with as many stripes as may seem good to the judges, and be cast naked beyond the borders of the land. And if he suffers this punishment he will probably return to his right mind and be improved; for no penalty which the law inflicts is designed for evil, but always makes him who suffers either better or not so much worse as he would have been[1]. But if any citizen be found guilty of any great or unmentionable wrong, either in relation to the gods, or his parents, or the state, let the judge deem him to be incurable, remembering that after receiving such an excellent education and training from youth upward, he has not abstained from the greatest of crimes[2]. His punishment shall be death, which to him will be the least of evils; and his example will benefit others, if he perish ingloriously, and be cast beyond the borders of the land. But let his children and family, if they avoid the ways of their father, have glory, and let honourable mention be made of them, as having nobly and manfully escaped out of evil into good. None of them should have their goods confiscated to the state, for the lots of the citizens ought always to continue the same and equal.

[1] Cp. Protag. 323 D foll.; Gorg. 525.   [2] Cp. Statesman 308 E.

Touching the exaction of penalties, when a man appears to have done anything which deserves a fine, he shall pay the fine, if he have anything in excess of the lot which is assigned to him; but more than that he shall not pay. And to secure exactness, let the guardians of the law refer to the registers, and inform the judges of the precise truth, in order that none of the lots may go uncultivated for want of money. But if any one seems to deserve a greater penalty, let him undergo a long and public imprisonment and be dishonoured, unless some of his friends are willing to be surety for him, and liberate him by assisting him to pay the fine. No criminal shall go unpunished, not even for a single offence, nor if he have fled the country; but let the penalty be according to his deserts,—death, or bonds, or blows, or degrading places of sitting or standing, or removal to some temple on the borders of the land; or let him pay fines, as we said before. In cases of death, let the judges be the guardians of the law, and a court selected by merit from the last year's magistrates. But how the causes are to be brought into court, how the summonses are to be served, and the like, these things may be left to the younger generation of legislators to determine; the manner of voting we must determine ourselves.

No criminal to escape.

Let the vote be given openly; but before they come to the vote let the judges sit in order of seniority over against plaintiff and defendant, and let all the citizens who can spare time hear and take a serious interest in listening to such causes. First of all the plaintiff shall make one speech, and then the defendant shall make another; and after the speeches have been made the eldest judge shall begin to examine the parties, and proceed to make an adequate enquiry into what has been said; and after the oldest has spoken, the rest shall proceed in order to examine either party as to what he finds defective in the evidence, whether of statement or omission; and he who has nothing to ask shall hand over the examination to another. And on so much of what has been said as is to the purpose all the judges shall set their seals, and place the writings on the altar of Hestia. On the next day they shall meet again, and in like manner put their questions and go through the cause, and again set their seals upon the evidence; and when they have three times done this, and have had witnesses and evidence enough, they shall each of them give a holy vote, after promising by Hestia that they will decide justly and truly to the utmost of their power; and so they shall put an end to the suit.

Manner of procedure.

856

Next, after what relates to the Gods, follows what relates to the dissolution of the state:—Whoever by promoting a man to power enslaves the laws, and subjects the city to factions, using violence

The factious person is the great-

est enemy
of the
state;
and the
magis-
trate who
does not
suppress
him is
nearly as
bad.

He shall
be pun-
ished
with
death.

The law
about
traitors.

857

One law
for thefts
of all
kinds;
restitu-
tion of
double
the
amount
stolen.

and stirring up sedition contrary to law, him we will deem the greatest enemy of the whole state. But he who takes no part in such proceedings, and, being one of the chief magistrates of the state, has no knowledge of the treason, or, having knowledge of it, by reason of cowardice does not interfere on behalf of his country, such an one we must consider nearly as bad. Every man who is worth anything will inform the magistrates, and bring the conspirator to trial for making a violent and illegal attempt to change the government. The judges of such cases shall be the same as of the robbers of temples; and let the whole proceeding be carried on in the same way, and the vote of the majority condemn to death. But let there be a general rule, that the disgrace and punishment of the father is not to be visited on the children, except in the case of some one whose father, grandfather, and great-grandfather have successively undergone the penalty of death. Such persons the city shall send away with all their possessions to the city and country of their ancestors, retaining only and wholly their appointed lot. And out of the citizens who have more than one son of not less than ten years of age, they shall select ten whom their father or grandfather by the mother's or father's side shall appoint, and let them send to Delphi the names of those who are selected, and him whom the God chooses they shall establish as heir of the house which has failed; and may he have better fortune than his predecessors!

Cle. Very good.

Ath. Once more let there be a third general law respecting the judges who are to give judgment, and the manner of conducting suits against those who are tried on an accusation of treason; and as concerning the remaining or departure of their descendants,—there shall be one law for all three, for the traitor, and the robber of temples, and the subverter by violence of the laws of the state. For a thief, whether he steal much or little, let there be one law, and one punishment for all alike: in the first place, let him pay double the amount of the theft if he be convicted, and if he have so much over and above the allotment;—if he have not, he shall be bound until he pay the penalty, or persuade him who has obtained the sentence against him to forgive him. But if a person be convicted of a theft against the state, then if he can persuade the city, or if he will pay back twice the amount of the theft, he shall be set free from his bonds[1].

Cle. What makes you say, Stranger, that a theft is all one, whether the thief may have taken much or little, and either from sacred or secular places—and these are not the only differences in

[1] Cp. *infra*, xi. 933 E; xii. 941.

thefts:—seeing, then, that they are of many kinds, ought not the legislator to adapt himself to them, and impose upon them entirely different penalties?

Ath. Excellent. I was running on too fast, Cleinias, and you impinged upon me, and brought me to my senses, reminding me of what, indeed, had occurred to my mind already, that legislation was never yet rightly worked out, as I may say in passing.—Do you remember the image in which I likened the men for whom laws are now made to slaves who are doctored by slaves[1]? For of this you may be very sure, that if one of those empirical physicians, who practise medicine without science, were to come upon the gentleman physician talking to his gentleman patient, and using the language almost of philosophy, beginning at the beginning of the disease and discoursing about the whole nature of the body, he would burst into a hearty laugh—he would say what most of those who are called doctors always have at their tongue's end:—Foolish fellow, he would say, you are not healing the sick man, but you are educating him; and he does not want to be made a doctor, but to get well.

Cle. And would he not be right?

Ath. Perhaps he would; and he might remark upon us, that he who discourses about laws, as we are now doing, is giving the citizens education and not laws; that would be rather a telling observation.

Cle. Very true.

Ath. But we are fortunate.

Cle. In what way?

Ath. Inasmuch as we are not compelled to give laws, but we may take into consideration every form of government, and ascertain what is best and what is most needful, and how they may both be carried into execution; and we may also, if we please, at this very moment choose what is best, or, if we prefer, what is most necessary —which shall we do?

Cle. There is something ridiculous, Stranger, in our proposing such an alternative, as if we were legislators, simply bound under some great necessity which cannot be deferred to the morrow. But we, as I may by the grace of Heaven affirm, like gatherers of stones or beginners of some composite work, may gather a heap of materials, and out of this, at our leisure, select what is suitable for our projected construction. Let us then suppose ourselves to be at leisure, not of necessity building, but rather like men who are partly providing materials, and partly putting them together. And we may

The Athenian compares his own case to that of the scientific doctor, who talks to his patient so much that he seems to be educating rather than curing him.

858

The truth is that we are collecting materials.

[1] Cp. *supra*, iv. 720.

truly say that some of our laws, like stones, are already fixed in their places, and others lie at hand.

Ath. Certainly, in that case, Cleinias, our view of law will be more in accordance with nature. For there is another matter affecting legislators, which I must earnestly entreat you to consider.

Cle. What is it?

Ath. There are many writings to be found in cities, and among them there are discourses composed by legislators as well as by other persons.

Cle. To be sure.

Poets and
others
have laid
down
rules of
life, but
the pre-
cepts of
legisla-
tors
should be
far su-
perior.

Ath. Shall we give heed rather to the writings of those others,— poets and the like, who either in metre or out of metre have recorded their advice about the conduct of life, and not to the writings of legislators? or shall we give heed to them above all?

Cle. Yes; to them far above all others.

Ath. And ought the legislator alone among writers to withhold his opinion about the beautiful, the good, and the just, and not to teach what they are, and how they are to be pursued by those who intend to be happy?

Cle. Certainly not.

Ath. And is it disgraceful for Homer and Tyrtaeus and other poets to lay down evil precepts in their writings respecting life and the pursuits of men, but not so disgraceful for Lycurgus and Solon and others who were legislators as well as writers? Is it not true that of all the writings to be found in cities, those which relate to laws, when you unfold and read them, ought to be by far the noblest and the best? and should not other writings either agree with them, or if they disagree, be deemed ridiculous? We should consider whether the laws of states ought not to have the character of loving and wise parents, rather than of tyrants and masters, who command and threaten, and, after writing their decrees on walls, go their ways; and whether, in discoursing of laws, we should not take the gentler view of them which may or may not be attainable,—at any rate, we will show our readiness to entertain such a view, and be prepared to undergo whatever may be the result. And may the result be good, and if God be gracious, it will be good!

Cle. Excellent; let us do as you say.

Ath. Then we will now consider accurately, as we proposed, what relates to robbers of temples, and all kinds of thefts, and offences in general; and we must not be annoyed if, in the course of legislation, we have enacted some things, and have not made up our minds about some others; for as yet we are not legislators, but we may soon be. Let us, if you please, consider these matters.

Cle. By all means.

Ath. Concerning all things honourable and just, let us then endeavour to ascertain how far we are consistent with ourselves, and how far we are inconsistent, and how far the many, from whom at any rate we should profess a desire to differ, agree and disagree among themselves.

Cle. What are the inconsistencies which you observe in us?

Ath. I will endeavour to explain. If I am not mistaken, we are all agreed that justice, and just men and things and actions, are all fair, and, if a person were to maintain that just men, even when they are deformed in body, are still perfectly beautiful in respect of the excellent justice of their minds, no one would say that there was any inconsistency in this.

Cle. They would be quite right.

Ath. Perhaps; but let us consider further, that if all things which are just are fair and honourable, in the term 'all' we must include just sufferings which are the correlatives of just actions.

Cle. And what is the inference?

Ath. The inference is, that a just action in partaking of the just partakes also in the same degree of the fair and honourable.

Cle. Certainly.

Ath. And must not a suffering which partakes of the just principle be admitted to be in the same degree fair and honourable, if the argument is consistently carried out?

Cle. True.

Ath. But then if we admit suffering to be just and yet dishonourable, and the term 'dishonourable' is applied to justice, will not the just and the honourable disagree?

Cle. What do you mean?

Ath. A thing not difficult to understand; the laws which have been already enacted would seem to announce principles directly opposed to what we are saying.

Cle. To what?

Ath. We had enacted, if I am not mistaken, that the robber of temples, and he who was the enemy of law and order, might justly be put to death, and we were proceeding to make divers other enactments of a similar nature. But we stopped short, because we saw that these sufferings are infinite in number and degree, and that they are, at once, the most just and also the most dishonourable of all sufferings. And if this be true, are not the just and the honourable at one time all the same, and at another time in the most diametrical opposition?

Cle. Such appears to be the case.

We say —'the just is the honourable': this is true of just actions, but not of just sufferings or punishments.

[860]

Ath. In this discordant and inconsistent fashion does the language of the many rend asunder the honourable and just.

Cle. Very true, Stranger.

Ath. Then now, Cleinias, let us see how far we ourselves are consistent about these matters.

Cle. Consistent in what?

Ath. I think that I have clearly stated in the former part of the discussion, but if I did not, let me now state——

Cle. What?

Ath. That all bad men are always involuntarily bad; and from this I must proceed to draw a further inference.

Cle. What is it?

All un-
just acts
are not
volun-
tary, but
involun-
tary: but
how then
can we
punish
them?

Ath. That the unjust man may be bad, but that he is bad against his will. Now that an action which is voluntary should be done involuntarily is a contradiction; wherefore he who maintains that injustice is involuntary will deem that the unjust does injustice involuntarily. I too admit that all men do injustice involuntarily, and if any contentious or disputatious person says that men are unjust against their will, and yet that many do injustice willingly, I do not agree with him. But, then, how can I avoid being inconsistent with myself, if you, Cleinias, and you, Megillus, say to me,—Well, Stranger, if all this be as you say, how about legislating for the city of the Magnetes—shall we legislate or not—what do you advise? Certainly we will, I should reply. Then will you determine for them what are voluntary and what are involuntary crimes, and shall we make the punishments greater of voluntary errors and crimes and less for the involuntary? or shall we make the punishment of all to

861

be alike, under the idea that there is no such thing as voluntary crime?

Cle. Very good, Stranger; and what shall we say in answer to these objections?

Ath. That is a very fair question. In the first place, let us——

Cle. Do what?

Ath. Let us remember what has been well said by us already, that our ideas of justice are in the highest degree confused and contradictory. Bearing this in mind, let us proceed to ask ourselves once more whether we have discovered a way out of the difficulty. Have we ever determined in what respect these two classes of actions differ from one another? For in all states and by all legislators whatsoever, two kinds of actions have been distinguished—the one, voluntary, the other, involuntary; and they have legislated about them accordingly. But shall this new word of ours, like an oracle of God, be only spoken, and get away without giving any explanation

All legis-
lators
have
distin-
guished
the vol-

or verification of itself? How can a word not understood be the basis of legislation? Impossible. Before proceeding to legislate, then, we must prove that they are two, and what is the difference between them, that when we impose the penalty upon either, every one may understand our proposal, and be able in some way to judge whether the penalty is fitly or unfitly inflicted.

Cle. I agree with you, Stranger; for one of two things is certain: either we must not say that all unjust acts are involuntary, or we must show the meaning and truth of this statement.

Ath. Of these two alternatives, the one is quite intolerable—not to speak what I believe to be the truth would be to me unlawful and unholy. But if acts of injustice cannot be divided into voluntary and involuntary, I must endeavour to find some other distinction between them.

Cle. Very true, Stranger; there cannot be two opinions among us upon that point.

Ath. Reflect, then; there are hurts of various kinds done by the citizens to one another in the intercourse of life, affording plentiful examples both of the voluntary and involuntary.

Cle. Certainly.

Ath. I would not have any one suppose that all these hurts are injuries, and that these injuries are of two kinds,—one, voluntary, and the other, involuntary; for the involuntary hurts of all men are quite as many and as great as the voluntary[1]. And please to consider whether I am right or quite wrong in what I am going to say; for I deny, Cleinias and Megillus, that he who harms another involuntarily does him an injury involuntarily, nor should I legislate about such an act under the idea that I am legislating for an involuntary injury. But I should rather say that such a hurt, whether great or small, is not an injury at all; and, on the other hand, if I am right, when a benefit is wrongly conferred, the author of the benefit may often be said to injure. For I maintain, O my friends, that the mere giving or taking away of anything is not to be described either as just or unjust; but the legislator has to consider whether mankind do good or harm to one another out of a just principle and intention. On the distinction between injustice and hurt he must fix his eye; and when there is hurt, he must, as far as he can, make the hurt good by law, and save that which is ruined, and raise up that which is fallen, and make that which is dead or wounded whole. And when compensation has been given for injustice, the law must always seek to win over the doers and sufferers of the several hurts from feelings of enmity to those of friendship.

[1] Cp. Arist. N. E. iii. cc. 1-5; v. c. 8.

Laws IX

ATHE-
NIAN,
CLEINIAS.

untary
from the
involun-
tary.

If we dis-
card this
distinc-
tion, we
must find
another.

For vol-
untary
and in-
voluntary
[862]
injus-
tice we
must sub-
stitute in-
justice
and
hurt.

In judg-
ing of
acts we
should
look to
the in-
tention.

The true
aim of
punish-
ment is
the re-
formation
of the
offender.

Death
only for
the in-
curable.

863

Three
causes of
crime:—
(1) Pas-
sion
working
by vio-
lence;

(2) pleas-
ure, by
persua-
sion and
deceit;

(3) ig-
norance,
of which
there are
two
kinds,
simple
ignorance
and con-

Cle. Very good.

Ath. Then as to unjust hurts (and gains also, supposing the injustice to bring gain), of these we may heal as many as are capable of being healed, regarding them as diseases of the soul; and the cure of injustice will take the following direction.

Cle. What direction?

Ath. When any one commits any injustice, small or great, the law will admonish and compel him either never at all to do the like again, or never voluntarily, or at any rate in a far less degree; and he must in addition pay for the hurt. Whether the end is to be attained by word or action, with pleasure or pain, by giving or taking away privileges, by means of fines or gifts, or in whatsoever way the law shall proceed to make a man hate injustice, and love or not hate the nature of the just,—this is quite the noblest work of law. But if the legislator sees any one who is incurable, for him he will appoint a law and a penalty. He knows quite well that to such men themselves there is no profit in the continuance of their lives, and that they would do a double good to the rest of mankind if they would take their departure, inasmuch as they would be an example to other men not to offend, and they would relieve the city of bad citizens. In such cases, and in such cases only, the legislator ought to inflict death as the punishment of offences.

Cle. What you have said appears to me to be very reasonable, but will you favour me by stating a little more clearly the difference between hurt and injustice, and the various complications of the voluntary and involuntary which enter into them?

Ath. I will endeavour to do as you wish:—Concerning the soul, thus much would be generally said and allowed, that one element in her nature is passion, which may be described either as a state or a part of her, and is hard to be striven against and contended with, and by irrational force overturns many things.

Cle. Very true.

Ath. And pleasure is not the same with passion, but has an opposite power, working her will by persuasion and by the force of deceit in all things.

Cle. Quite true.

Ath. A man may truly say that ignorance is a third cause of crimes. Ignorance, however, may be conveniently divided by the legislator into two sorts: there is simple ignorance, which is the source of lighter offences, and double ignorance, which is accompanied by a conceit of wisdom; and he who is under the influence of the latter fancies that he knows all about matters of which he knows nothing. This second kind of ignorance, when possessed of power and strength, will be held by the legislator to be the source of great and monstrous crimes, but when attended with weakness, will only result in the errors of children and old men; and these he will treat as errors, and will make laws accordingly for those who commit them, which will be the mildest and most merciful of all laws.

Cle. You are perfectly right.

Ath. We all of us remark of one man that he is superior to pleasure and passion, and of another that he is inferior to them; and this is true[1].

Cle. Certainly.

Ath. But no one was ever yet heard to say that one of us is superior and another inferior to ignorance.

Cle. Very true.

Ath. We are speaking of motives which incite men to the fulfilment of their will; although an individual may be often drawn by them in opposite directions at the same time.

Cle. Yes, often.

Ath. And now I can define to you clearly, and without ambiguity, what I mean by the just and unjust, according to my notion of them:—When anger and fear, and pleasure and pain, and jealousies and desires, tyrannize over the soul, whether they do any harm or not,—I call all this injustice. But when the opinion of the best, in whatever part of human nature states or individuals may suppose that to dwell, has dominion in the soul and orders the life of every man, even if it be sometimes mistaken, yet what is done in accordance therewith, and the principle in individuals which obeys this rule, and is best for the whole life of man, is to be called just; although the hurt done by mistake is thought by many to be involuntary injustice. Leaving the question of names, about which we are not going to quarrel, and having already delineated three sources of error, we may begin by recalling them somewhat more vividly to our memory:—One of them was of the painful sort, which we denominate anger and fear.

Cle. Quite right.

Ath. There was a second consisting of pleasures and desires, and a third of hopes, which aimed at true opinion about the best. The latter being subdivided into three, we now get five sources of actions, and for these five we will make laws of two kinds.

Cle. What are the two kinds?

Ath. There is one kind of actions done by violence and in the light of day, and another kind of actions which are done in dark-

[1] Cp. Rep. iv. 430 E; *supra*, i. 626 E, foll.

ceit of wisdom; and the latter may be either powerful or weak.

Passions and pleasures may be controlled, but not ignorance.

864
The unjust soul is mastered by passion and desire; the just soul follows the opinion of the best.

Recapitulation.

Two kinds of

actions,
and two
kinds of
laws.

ness and with secret deceit, or sometimes both with violence and deceit; the laws concerning these last ought to have a character of severity.

Cle. Naturally.

Ath. And now let us return from this digression and complete the work of legislation. Laws have been already enacted by us concerning the robbers of the Gods, and concerning traitors, and also concerning those who corrupt the laws for the purpose of subverting the government. A man may very likely commit some of these crimes, either in a state of madness or when affected by disease, or under the influence of extreme old age, or in a fit of childish wantonness, himself no better than a child. And if this be made evident to the judges elected to try the cause, on the appeal of the criminal or his advocate, and he be judged to have been in this state when he committed the offence, he shall simply pay for the hurt which he may have done to another; but he shall be exempt from other penalties, unless he have slain some one, and have on his hands the stain of blood. And in that case he shall go to another land and country, and there dwell for a year; and if he return before the expiration of the time which the law appoints, or even set his foot at all on his native land, he shall be bound by the guardians of the law in the public prison for two years, and then go free.

865

Cases of
involun-
tary
homi-
cide:—
(1) He
who kills
another
at the
games
must be
purified,
but is
guiltless;

so also is
(2) the
doctor
whose pa-
tient
dies.

(3) If a
man kill
another's
slave, he
must

Having begun to speak of homicide, let us endeavour to lay down laws concerning every different kind of homicide; and, first of all, concerning violent and involuntary homicides. If any one in an athletic contest, and at the public games, involuntarily kills a friend, and he dies either at the time or afterwards of the blows which he has received; or if the like misfortune happens to any one in war, or military exercises, or mimic contests of which the magistrates enjoin the practice, whether with or without arms, when he has been purified according to the law brought from Delphi relating to these matters, he shall be innocent. And so in the case of physicians: if their patient dies against their will, they shall be held guiltless by the law. And if one slay another with his own hand, but unintentionally, whether he be unarmed or have some instrument or dart in his hand; or if he kill him by administering food or drink, or by the application of fire or cold, or by suffocating him, whether he do the deed by his own hand, or by the agency of others, he shall be deemed the agent, and shall suffer one of the following penalties:—
If he kill the slave of another in the belief that he is his own, he shall bear the master of the dead man harmless from loss, or shall pay a penalty of twice the value of the dead man, which the judges shall assess; but purifications must be used greater and more numer-

ous than for those who committed homicide at the games;—what they are to be, the interpreters whom the God appoints[1] shall be authorized to declare. And if a man kills his own slave, when he has been purified according to law, he shall be quit of the homicide. And if a man kills a freeman unintentionally, he shall undergo the same purification as he did who killed the slave. But let him not forget also a tale of olden time, which is to this effect:—He who has suffered a violent end, when newly dead, if he has had the soul of a freeman in life, is angry with the author of his death; and being himself full of fear and panic by reason of his violent end, when he sees his murderer walking about in his own accustomed haunts, he is stricken with terror and becomes disordered, and this disorder of his, aided by the guilty recollection of the other, is communicated by him with overwhelming force to the murderer and his deeds. Wherefore also the murderer must go out of the way of his victim for the entire period of a year, and not himself be found in any spot which was familiar to him throughout the country. And if the dead man be a stranger, the homicide shall be kept from the country of the stranger during a like period. If any one voluntarily obeys this law, the next of kin to the deceased, seeing all that has happened, shall take pity on him, and make peace with him, and show him all gentleness. But if any one is disobedient, and either ventures to go to any of the temples and sacrifice unpurified, or will not continue in exile during the appointed time, the next of kin to the deceased shall proceed against him for murder; and if he be convicted, every part of his punishment shall be doubled. And if the next of kin do not proceed against the perpetrator of the crime, then the pollution shall be deemed to fall upon his own head;—the murdered man will fix the guilt upon his kinsman, and he who has a mind to proceed against him may compel him to be absent from his country during five years, according to law. If a stranger unintentionally kill a stranger who is dwelling in the city, he who likes shall prosecute the cause according to the same rules. If he be a metic, let him be absent for a year, or if he be an entire stranger, in addition to the purification, whether he have slain a stranger, or a metic, or a citizen, he shall be banished for life from the country which is in possession of our laws. And if he return contrary to law, let the guardians of the law punish him with death; and let them hand over his property, if he have any, to him who is next of kin to the sufferer. And if he be wrecked, and driven on the coast against his will, he shall take up his abode on the seashore, wetting his feet in the sea, and watching for an opportunity of sailing; but if he be brought by land, and is

[1] Cp. *supra*, vi. 759.

make restitution to the owner; and undergo purification, like him (4) who kills his own slave.

(5) The slayer of a freeman, [866] whether citizen or stranger, must be purified and avoid the ghost of the sufferer for a year.

If he obeys the law he shall be forgiven by the next of kin, or if he disobey the law the next of kin shall prosecute him for murder or be himself prosecuted for neglect.

Laws IX

ATHE-
NIAN,
CLEINIAS.

(6) A
metic
who kills
a
stranger
must be
purified
and go
into exile
for a
year; but
[867]
(7) a
stranger
who kills
any one
shall be
banished
for life.

Homicide
arising
from pas-
sion, if
premedi-
tated, is
the shad-
ow of the
volun-
tary; if
unpre-
medi-
tated, of
the in-
volun-
tary.

The
former
kind de-
serves a
heavier
punish-
ment.

Cases of
homicide
done in
passion:
—(1) If
a man
kills a
freeman
without

not his own master, let the magistrate whom he first comes across in the city, release him and send him unharmed over the border.

If any one slays a freeman with his own hand, and the deed be done in passion, in the case of such actions we must begin by making a distinction. For a deed is done from passion either when men suddenly, and without intention to kill, cause the death of another by blows and the like on a momentary impulse, and are sorry for the deed immediately afterwards; or again, when after having been insulted in deed or word, men pursue revenge, and kill a person intentionally, and are not sorry for the act. And, therefore, we must assume that these homicides are of two kinds, both of them arising from passion, which may be justly said to be in a mean between the voluntary and involuntary; at the same time, they are neither of them anything more than a likeness or shadow of either. He who treasures up his anger, and avenges himself, not immediately and at the moment, but with insidious design, and after an interval, is like the voluntary; but he who does not treasure up his anger, and takes vengeance on the instant, and without malice prepense, approaches to the involuntary; and yet even he is not altogether involuntary, but is only the image or shadow of the involuntary; wherefore about homicides committed in hot blood, there is a difficulty in determining whether in legislating we shall reckon them as voluntary or as partly involuntary. The best and truest view is to regard them respectively as likenesses only of the voluntary and involuntary, and to distinguish them accordingly as they are done with or without premeditation. And we should make the penalties heavier for those who commit homicide with angry premeditation, and lighter for those who do not premeditate, but smite upon the instant; for that which is like a greater evil should be punished more severely, and that which is like a less evil should be punished less severely: this shall be the rule of our laws.

Cle. Certainly.

Ath. Let us proceed:—If any one slays a freeman with his own hand, and the deed be done in a moment of anger, and without premeditation, let the offender suffer in other respects as the involuntary homicide would have suffered, and also undergo an exile of two years, that he may learn to school his passions. But he who slays another from passion, yet with premeditation, shall in other respects suffer as the former; and to this shall be added an exile of three instead of two years,—his punishment is to be longer because his passion is greater. The manner of their return shall be on this wise: (and here the law has difficulty in determining exactly; for in some cases the murderer who is judged by the law to be the worse may really be the less cruel, and he who is judged the less cruel may be really the worse, and may have executed the murder in a more savage manner, whereas the other may have been gentler. But in general the degrees of guilt will be such as we have described them. Of all these things the guardians of the law must take cognizance): —When a homicide of either kind has completed his term of exile, the guardians shall send twelve judges to the borders of the land; these during the interval shall have informed themselves of the actions of the criminals, and they shall judge respecting their pardon and reception; and the homicides shall abide by their judgment. But if after they have returned home, any one of them in a moment of anger repeats the deed, let him be an exile, and return no more; or if he returns, let him suffer as the stranger was to suffer in a similar case. He who kills his own slave shall undergo a purification, but if he kills the slave of another in anger, he shall pay twice the amount of the loss to his owner. And if any homicide is disobedient to the law, and without purification pollutes the agora, or the games, or the temples, he who pleases may bring to trial the next of kin to the dead man for permitting him, and the murderer with him, and may compel the one to exact and the other to suffer a double amount of fines and purifications; and the accuser shall himself receive the fine in accordance with the law. If a slave in a fit of passion kills his master, the kindred of the deceased man may do with the murderer (provided only they do not spare his life) whatever they please, and they will be pure; or if he kills a freeman, who is not his master, the owner shall give up the slave to the relatives of the deceased, and they shall be under an obligation to put him to death, but this may be done in any manner which they please. And if (which is a rare occurrence, but does sometimes happen) a father or a mother in a moment of passion slays a son or daughter by blows, or some other violence, the slayer shall undergo the same purification as in other cases, and be exiled during three years; but when the exile returns the wife shall separate from the husband, and the husband from the wife, and they shall never afterwards beget children together, or live under the same roof, or partake of the same sacred rites with those whom they have deprived of a child or of a brother. And he who is impious and disobedient in such a case shall be brought to trial for impiety by any one who pleases. If in a fit of anger a husband kills his wedded wife, or the wife her husband, the slayer shall undergo the same purification, and the term of exile shall be three years. And when he who has committed any such crime returns, let him have no communication in sacred rites with his children, neither let him sit at the same table with

Laws IX

ATHE-
NIAN.

premedi-
tation,
he shall
be exiled
for two
years;
(2) if
with pre-
[868]
medita-
tion, for
three
years.

The re-
turn of
the exiles.

The
second
offence.

(3) If a
man kills
his own
slave, he
shall be
purified;
(4) if an-
other's,
pay to the
owner
double his
value.

(5) The
slave who
kills a
freeman
to be
punished
with
death.

(6) The
parent
who kills
a child
shall be
exiled for
three
years and
debarred
from

Laws IX

ATHE-
NIAN.

sharing in
the family
rites:

869

so too
(7) the
husband
who kills
his wife
or the
wife who
kills her
husband;

and (8)
the bro-
ther or
sister who
kills a
brother
or sister.

(9) The
child who
kills a
parent to
be pun-
ished
with
death, if
not for-
given.

Homicide
in civil
war or in
self-de-
fence (ex-
cept when
a slave
kills a
freeman)
is free
from
guilt.

A homi-
cide, if
forgiven
by his
victim, to
be ban-
ished for
a year.

them, and the father or son who disobeys shall be liable to be brought to trial for impiety by any one who pleases. If a brother or a sister in a fit of passion kills a brother or a sister, they shall undergo purification and exile, as was the case with parents who killed their offspring: they shall not come under the same roof, or share in the sacred rites of those whom they have deprived of their brethren, or of their children. And he who is disobedient shall be justly liable to the law concerning impiety, which relates to these matters. If any one is so violent in his passion against his parents, that in the madness of his anger he dares to kill one of them, if the murdered person before dying freely forgives the murderer, let him undergo the purification which is assigned to those who have been guilty of involuntary homicide, and do as they do, and he shall be pure. But if he be not acquitted, the perpetrator of such a deed shall be amenable to many laws;—he shall be amenable to the extreme punishments for assault, and impiety, and robbing of temples, for he has robbed his parent of life; and if a man could be slain more than once, most justly would he who in a fit of passion has slain father or mother, undergo many deaths. How can he, whom, alone of all men, even in defence of his life, and when about to suffer death at the hands of his parents, no law will allow to kill his father or his mother who are the authors of his being, and whom the legislator will command to endure any extremity rather than do this—how can he, I say, lawfully receive any other punishment? Let death then be the appointed punishment of him who in a fit of passion slays his father or his mother. But if brother kills brother in a civil broil, or under other like circumstances, if the other has begun, and he only defends himself, let him be free from guilt, as he would be if he had slain an enemy; and the same rule will apply if a citizen kill a citizen, or a stranger a stranger. Or if a stranger kill a citizen or a citizen a stranger in self-defence, let him be free from guilt in like manner; and so in the case of a slave who has killed a slave; but if a slave have killed a freeman in self-defence, let him be subject to the same law as he who has killed a father; and let the law about the remission of penalties in the case of parricide apply equally to every other remission. Whenever any sufferer of his own accord remits the guilt of homicide to another, under the idea that his act was involuntary, let the perpetrator of the deed undergo a purification and remain in exile for a year, according to law.

Enough has been said of murders violent and involuntary and committed in passion: we have now to speak of voluntary crimes done with injustice of every kind and with premeditation, through the influence of pleasures, and desires, and jealousies.

Cle. Very good.

Ath. Let us first speak, as far as we are able, of their various kinds. The greatest cause of them is lust, which gets the mastery of the soul maddened by desire; and this is most commonly found to exist where the passion reigns which is strongest and most prevalent among the mass of mankind: I mean where the power of wealth breeds endless desires of never-to-be-satisfied acquisition, originating in natural disposition, and a miserable want of education. Of this want of education, the false praise of wealth which is bruited about both among Hellenes and barbarians is the cause; they deem that to be the first of goods which in reality is only the third. And in this way they wrong both posterity and themselves, for nothing can be nobler and better than that the truth about wealth should be spoken in all states—namely, that riches are for the sake of the body, as the body is for the sake of the soul. They are good, and wealth is intended by nature to be for the sake of them, and is therefore inferior to them both, and third in order of excellence. This argument teaches us that he who would be happy ought not to seek to be rich, or rather he should seek to be rich justly and temperately, and then there would be no murders in states requiring to be purged away by other murders. But now, as I said at first, avarice is the chiefest cause and source of the worst trials for voluntary homicide. A second cause is ambition: this creates jealousies, which are troublesome companions, above all to the jealous man himself, and in a less degree to the chiefs of the state. And a third cause is cowardly and unjust fear, which has been the occasion of many murders. When a man is doing or has done something which he desires that no one should know him to be doing or to have done, he will take the life of those who are likely to inform of such things, if he have no other means of getting rid of them. Let this be said as a prelude concerning crimes of violence in general; and I must not omit to mention a tradition which is firmly believed by many, and has been received by them from those who are learned in the mysteries: they say that such deeds will be punished in the world below, and also that when the perpetrators return to this world they will pay the natural penalty which is due to the sufferer, and end their lives in like manner by the hand of another. If he who is about to commit murder believes this, and is made by the mere prelude to dread such a penalty, there is no need to proceed with the proclamation of the law. But if he will not listen, let the following law be declared and registered against him:—Whoever shall wrongfully and of design slay with his own hand any of his kinsmen, shall in the first place be deprived of legal privileges; and he shall not pol-

Laws IX

ATHE-
NIAN.
870
Crimes
com-
mitted
volun-
tarily and
with pre-
medita-
tion are
due to
three
causes:—

(1) ava-
rice:

(2) am-
bition:

(3) cow-
ardly
fear.

The pun-
ishments
of the
world be-
low and
when
men re-
turn to
earth.
871
The law:
—Excom-

munica-
tion of
slayers of
kindred.

Duties of
the near-
est kins-
men, and
the pun-
ishment
of him
who neg-
lects
them.

lute the temples, or the agora, or the harbours, or any other place of meeting, whether he is forbidden of men or not; for the law, which represents the whole state, forbids him, and always is and will be in the attitude of forbidding him. And if a cousin or nearer relative of the deceased, whether on the male or female side, does not prosecute the homicide when he ought, and have him proclaimed an outlaw, he shall in the first place be involved in the pollution, and incur the hatred of the Gods, even as the curse of the law stirs up the voices of men against him; and in the second place he shall be liable to be prosecuted by any one who is willing to inflict retribution on behalf of the dead. And he who would avenge a murder shall observe all the precautionary ceremonies of lavation, and any others which the God commands in cases of this kind. Let him have proclamation made, and then go forth and compel the perpetrator to suffer the execution of justice according to the law. Now the legislator may easily show that these things must be accomplished by prayers and sacrifices to certain Gods, who are concerned with the prevention of murders in states. But who these Gods are, and what should be the true manner of instituting such trials with due regard to religion, the guardians of the law, aided by the interpreters, and the prophets, and the God, shall determine, and when they have determined let them carry on the prosecution at law. The cause shall have the same judges[1] who are appointed to decide in the case of those who plunder temples. Let him who is convicted be punished with death, and let him not be buried in the country of the murdered man, for this would be shameless as well as impious. But if he fly and will not stand his trial, let him fly for ever; or, if he set foot anywhere on any part of the murdered man's country, let any relation of the deceased, or any other citizen who may first happen to meet with him, kill him with impunity, or bind and deliver him to those among the judges of the case who are magistrates, that they may put him to death. And let the prosecutor demand surety of him whom he prosecutes; three sureties sufficient in the opinion of the magistrates who try the cause shall be provided by him, and they shall undertake to produce him at the trial. But if he be unwilling or unable to provide sureties, then the magistrates shall take him and keep him in bonds, and produce him at the day of trial.

The mur-
derer to
be pun-
ished
with
death if
convicted.
He may
fly, but
must not
return.

872

The insti-
gator of a
murder is
as guilty

If a man do not commit a murder with his own hand, but contrives the death of another, and is the author of the deed in intention and design, and he continues to dwell in the city, having his soul not pure of the guilt of murder, let him be tried in the same

[1] Cp. *supra*, 855 C.

way, except in what relates to the sureties; and also, if he be found guilty, his body after execution may have burial in his native land, but in all other respects his case shall be as the former; and whether a stranger shall kill a citizen, or a citizen a stranger, or a slave a slave, there shall be no difference as touching murder by one's own hand or by contrivance, except in the matter of sureties; and these, as has been said, shall be required of the actual murderer only, and he who brings the accusation shall bind them over at the time. If a slave be convicted of slaying a freeman voluntarily, either by his own hand or by contrivance, let the public executioner take him in the direction of the sepulchre, to a place whence he can see the tomb of the dead man, and inflict upon him as many stripes as the person who caught him orders, and if he survive, let him put him to death. And if any one kills a slave who has done no wrong, because he is afraid that he may inform of some base and evil deeds of his own, or for any similar reason, in such a case let him pay the penalty of murder, as he would have done if he had slain a citizen. There are things about which it is terrible and unpleasant to legislate, but impossible not to legislate. If, for example, there should be murders of kinsmen, either perpetrated by the hands of kinsmen, or by their contrivance, voluntary and purely malicious, which most often happen in ill-regulated and ill-educated states, and may perhaps occur even in a country where a man would not expect to find them, we must repeat once more the tale which we narrated a little while ago, in the hope that he who hears us will be the more disposed to abstain voluntarily on these grounds from murders which are utterly abominable. For the myth, or saying, or whatever we ought to call it[1], has been plainly set forth by priests of old; they have pronounced that the justice which guards and avenges the blood of kindred, follows the law of retaliation, and ordains that he who has done any murderous act should of necessity suffer that which he has done. He who has slain a father shall himself be slain at some time or other by his children,—if a mother, he shall of necessity take a woman's nature, and lose his life at the hands of his offspring in after ages; for where the blood of a family has been polluted there is no other purification, nor can the pollution be washed out until the homicidal soul which did the deed has given life for life, and has propitiated and laid to sleep the wrath of the whole family. These are the retributions of Heaven, and by such punishments men should be deterred. But if they are not deterred, and any one should be incited by some fatality to deprive his father or mother, or brethren, or children, of life voluntarily and of pur-

[1] Cp. *supra*, 870 D.

Laws IX

ATHE-
NIAN.

as the doer, and like him, shall suffer death.

Various cases of murder and their punishments.

The retribution of heaven on the slayers of kinsmen.

873

The earthly law.

The pun-
ishment
and the
manner of
executing
it.

The sui-
cide to be
buried
alone in
no-man's-
land.

Animals
which
take away
life to be
slain and
cast forth.

Lifeless
things
also to be
cast forth.

874

When a
murderer
is un-
known,
he shall
still be

pose, for him the earthly lawgiver legislates as follows:—There shall be the same proclamations about outlawry, and there shall be the same sureties which have been enacted in the former cases. But in his case, if he be convicted, the servants of the judges and the magistrates shall slay him at an appointed place without the city where three ways meet, and there expose his body naked, and each of the magistrates on behalf of the whole city shall take a stone and cast it upon the head of the dead man, and so deliver the city from pollution; after that, they shall bear him to the borders of the land, and cast him forth unburied, according to law. And what shall he suffer who slays him who of all men, as they say, is his own best friend? I mean the suicide, who deprives himself by violence of his appointed share of life, not because the law of the state requires him, nor yet under the compulsion of some painful and inevitable misfortune which has come upon him, nor because he has had to suffer from irremediable and intolerable shame, but who from sloth or want of manliness imposes upon himself an unjust penalty. For him, what ceremonies there are to be of purification and burial God knows, and about these the next of kin should enquire of the interpreters and of the laws thereto relating, and do according to their injunctions. They who meet their death in this way shall be buried alone, and none shall be laid by their side; they shall be buried ingloriously in the borders of the twelve portions of the land, in such places as are uncultivated and nameless, and no column or inscription shall mark the place of their interment. And if a beast of burden or other animal cause the death of any one, except in the case of anything of that kind happening to a competitor in the public contests, the kinsmen of the deceased shall prosecute the slayer for murder, and the wardens of the country, such, and so many as the kinsmen appoint, shall try the cause, and let the beast when condemned be slain by them, and let them cast it beyond the borders. And if any lifeless thing deprive a man of life, except in the case of a thunderbolt or other fatal dart sent from the Gods,—whether a man is killed by lifeless objects falling upon him, or by his falling upon them, the nearest of kin shall appoint the nearest neighbour to be a judge, and thereby acquit himself and the whole family of guilt. And he shall cast forth the guilty thing beyond the border, as has been said about the animals.

If a man is found dead, and his murderer be unknown, and after a diligent search cannot be detected, there shall be the same proclamation as in the previous cases, and the same interdict on the murderer; and having proceeded against him, they shall proclaim in the agora by a herald, that he who has slain such and such a person, and has been convicted of murder, shall not set his foot in the temples, nor at all in the country of the murdered man, and if he appears and is discovered, he shall die, and be cast forth unburied beyond the border. Let this one law then be laid down by us about murder; and let cases of this sort be so regarded.

And now let us say in what cases and under what circumstances the murderer is rightly free from guilt:—If a man catch a thief coming into his house by night to steal, and he take and kill him, or if he slay a footpad in self-defence, he shall be guiltless. And any one who does violence to a free woman or a youth, shall be slain with impunity by the injured person, or by his or her father or brothers or sons. If a man find his wife suffering violence, he may kill the violator, and be guiltless in the eye of the law; or if a person kill another in warding off death from his father or mother or children or brethren or wife who are doing no wrong, he shall assuredly be guiltless.

Thus much as to the nurture and education of the living soul of man, having which, he can, and without which, if he unfortunately be without them, he cannot live; and also concerning the punishments which are to be inflicted for violent deaths, let thus much be enacted. Of the nurture and education of the body we have spoken before, and next in order we have to speak of deeds of violence, voluntary and involuntary, which men do to one another; these we will now distinguish, as far as we are able, according to their nature and number, and determine what will be the suitable penalties of each, and so assign to them their proper place in the series of our enactments. The poorest legislator will have no difficulty in determining that wounds and mutilations arising out of wounds should follow next in order after deaths. Let wounds be divided as homicides were divided—into those which are involuntary, and which are given in passion or from fear, and those inflicted voluntarily and with premeditation. Concerning all this, we must make some such proclamation as the following:—Mankind must have laws, and conform to them, or their life would be as bad as that of the most savage beast[1]. And the reason of this is that no man's nature is able to know what is best for human society; or knowing, always able and willing to do what is best. In the first place, there is a difficulty in apprehending that the true art of politics is concerned, not with private but with public good (for public good binds together states, but private only distracts them); and that both the public and private good as well of individuals as of states is greater when the state and not the individual is first considered. In the second

[1] Cp. Arist. Pol. i. 2, § 15.

Laws IX

ATHE-
NIAN.

tried, and
if after-
wards
dis-
covered,
he shall
die.

Cases of
justifiable
homicide.

875
Prelude
to the law
about
wound-
ing:—

Laws are
necessary
because of
the self-
ishness of
human
nature.

place, although a person knows in the abstract that this is true, yet if he be possessed of absolute and irresponsible power, he will never remain firm in his principles or persist in regarding the public good as primary in the state, and the private good as secondary. Human nature will be always drawing him into avarice and selfishness, avoiding pain and pursuing pleasure without any reason, and will bring these to the front, obscuring the juster and better; and so working darkness in his soul will at last fill with evils both him and the whole city[1]. For if a man were born so divinely gifted that he could naturally apprehend the truth, he would have no need of laws to rule over him[2]; for there is no law or order which is above knowledge, nor can mind, without impiety, be deemed the subject or slave of any man, but rather the lord of all. I speak of mind, true and free, and in harmony with nature. But then there is no such mind anywhere, or at least not much; and therefore we must choose law and order, which are second best. These look at things as they exist for the most part only, and are unable to survey the whole of them. And therefore I have spoken as I have.

And now we will determine what penalty he ought to pay or suffer who has hurt or wounded another. Any one may easily imagine the questions which have to be asked in all such cases:—What did he wound, or whom, or how, or when? for there are innumerable particulars of this sort which greatly vary from one another. And to allow courts of law to determine all these things, or not to determine any of them, is alike impossible. There is one particular which they must determine in all cases—the question of fact. And then, again, that the legislator should not permit them to determine what punishment is to be inflicted in any of these cases, but should himself decide about all of them, small or great, is next to impossible.

876

Cle. Then what is to be the inference?

Ath. The inference is, that some things should be left to courts of law; others the legislator must decide for himself.

Cle. And what ought the legislator to decide, and what ought he to leave to the courts of law?

Ath. I may reply, that in a state in which the courts are bad and mute, because the judges conceal their opinions and decide causes clandestinely; or what is worse, when they are disorderly and noisy, as in a theatre, clapping or hooting in turn this or that orator—I say that then there is a very serious evil, which affects the whole state. Unfortunate is the necessity of having to legislate for such courts, but where the necessity exists, the legislator should only allow them to ordain the penalties for the smallest offences; if the

If the
courts of
law are
bad they

[1] Cp. *supra,* iii. 691; iv. 711 E, 713 C, 716 A.   [2] Cp. Statesman, 297 A.

state for which he is legislating be of this character, he must take most matters into his own hands and speak distinctly. But when a state has good courts, and the judges are well trained and scrupulously tested, the determination of the penalties or punishments which shall be inflicted on the guilty may fairly and with advantage be left to them. And we are not to be blamed for not legislating concerning all that large class of matters which judges far worse educated than ours would be able to determine, assigning to each offence what is due both to the perpetrator and to the sufferer. We believe those for whom we are legislating to be best able to judge, and therefore to them the greater part may be left. At the same time, as I have often said[1], we should exhibit to the judges, as we have done, the outline and form of the punishments to be inflicted, and then they will not transgress the just rule. That was an excellent practice, which we observed before, and which now that we are resuming the work of legislation, may with advantage be repeated by us.

Let the enactment about wounding be in the following terms:— If any one has a purpose and intention to slay another who is not his enemy, and whom the law does not permit him to slay, and he wounds him, but is unable to kill him, he who had the intent and has wounded him is not to be pitied—he deserves no consideration, but should be regarded as a murderer and be tried for murder. Still having respect to the fortune which has in a manner favoured him, and to the providence which in pity to him and to the wounded man saved the one from a fatal blow, and the other from an accursed fate and calamity—as a thank-offering to this deity, and in order not to oppose his will—in such a case the law will remit the punishment of death, and only compel the offender to emigrate to a neighbouring city for the rest of his life, where he shall remain in the enjoyment of all his possessions. But if he have injured the wounded man, he shall make such compensation for the injury as the court deciding the cause shall assess, and the same judges shall decide who would have decided if the man had died of his wounds. And if a child intentionally wound his parents, or a servant his master, death shall be the penalty. And if a brother or a sister intentionally wound a brother or a sister, and is found guilty, death shall be the penalty. And if a husband wound a wife, or a wife a husband, with intent to kill, let him or her undergo perpetual exile; if they have sons or daughters who are still young, the guardians shall take care of their property, and have charge of the children as orphans. If their sons are grown up, they shall be under no obliga-

[1] Cp. *supra*, v. 734 E; vi. 770.

Laws IX

ATHE-
NIAN.

should have little or no power of determining penalties: to good courts much may be left.

Wounding with intent to kill to be [877] deemed murder, but only when children wound their parents or one another, or a slave wounds a master, to be punished with death.

Husband wounding wife or wife husband shall be

Laws IX

ATHE-
NIAN.

exiled for
life.

When the
lot be-
comes
vacant
through
crime, the
kinsmen
and the
guardians
of the law
shall se-
lect some
one of a
virtuous
family to
succeed.

878

Punish-
ments for
wounds
inflicted
in pas-
sion.

tion to support the exiled parent, but they shall possess the property themselves. And if he who meets with such a misfortune has no children, the kindred of the exiled man to the degree of sons of cousins, both on the male and female side, shall meet together, and after taking counsel with the guardians of the law and the priests, shall appoint a 5040th citizen to be the heir of the house, considering and reasoning that no house of all the 5040 belongs to the inhabitant or to the whole family, but is the public and private property of the state. Now the state should seek to have its houses as holy and happy as possible. And if any one of the houses be unfortunate, and stained with impiety, and the owner leave no posterity, but dies unmarried, or married and childless, having suffered death as the penalty of murder or some other crime committed against the Gods or against his fellow-citizens, of which death is the penalty distinctly laid down in the law; or if any of the citizens be in perpetual exile, and also childless, that house shall first of all be purified and undergo expiation according to law; and then let the kinsmen of the house, as we were just now saying, and the guardians of the law, meet and consider what family there is in the state which is of the highest repute for virtue and also for good fortune, in which there are a number of sons; from that family let them take one and introduce him to the father and forefathers of the dead man as their son, and, for the sake of the omen, let him be called so, that he may be the continuer of their family, the keeper of their hearth, and the minister of their sacred rites with better fortune than his father had; and when they have made this supplication, they shall make him heir according to law, and the offending person they shall leave nameless and childless and portionless when calamities such as these overtake him.

Now the boundaries of some things do not touch one another, but there is a borderland which comes in between, preventing them from touching. And we were saying that actions done from passion are of this nature, and come in between the voluntary and involuntary. If a person be convicted of having inflicted wounds in a passion, in the first place he shall pay twice the amount of the injury, if the wound be curable, or, if incurable, four times the amount of the injury; or if the wound be curable, and at the same time cause great and notable disgrace to the wounded person, he shall pay fourfold. And whenever any one in wounding another injures not only the sufferer, but also the city, and makes him incapable of defending his country against the enemy, he, besides the other penalties, shall pay a penalty for the loss which the state has incurred. And the penalty shall be, that in addition to his own times of service, he shall serve on behalf of the disabled person, and shall take his place in war; or, if he refuse, he shall be liable to be convicted by law of refusal to serve. The compensation for the injury, whether to be twofold or threefold or fourfold, shall be fixed by the judges who convict him. And if, in like manner, a brother wounds a brother, the parents and kindred of either sex, including the children of cousins, whether on the male or female side, shall meet, and when they have judged the cause, they shall entrust the assessment of damages to the parents, as is natural; and if the estimate be disputed, then the kinsmen on the male side shall make the estimate, or if they cannot, they shall commit the matter to the guardians of the law. And when similar charges of wounding are brought by children against their parents, those who are more than sixty years of age, having children of their own, not adopted, shall be required to decide; and if any one is convicted, they shall determine whether he or she ought to die, or suffer some other punishment either greater than death, or, at any rate, not much less. A kinsman of the offender shall not be allowed to judge the cause, not even if he be of the age which is prescribed by the law. If a slave in a fit of anger wound a freeman, the owner of the slave shall give him up to the wounded man, who may do as he pleases with him, and if he do not give him up he shall himself make good the injury. And if any one says that the slave and the wounded man are conspiring together, let him argue the point, and if he is cast, he shall pay for the wrong three times over, but if he gains his case, the freeman who conspired with the slave shall be liable to an action for kidnapping. And if any one unintentionally wounds another he shall simply pay for the harm, for no legislator is able to control chance. In such a case the judges shall be the same as those who are appointed in the case of children suing their parents; and they shall estimate the amount of the injury.

All the preceding injuries and every kind of assault are deeds of violence; and every man, woman, or child ought to consider that the elder has the precedence of the younger in honour[1], both among the Gods and also among men who would live in security and happiness. Wherefore it is a foul thing and hateful to the Gods to see an elder man assaulted by a younger in the city; and it is reasonable that a young man when struck by an elder should lightly endure his anger, laying up in store for himself a like honour when he is old. Let this be the law:—Every one shall reverence his elder in word and deed; he shall respect any one who is twenty years older than himself, whether male or female, regarding him or her as his father

[1] Cp. Rep. v. 465 A.

Laws IX

ATHE-
NIAN.

The case of a brother who wounds a brother;

of parents who wound their children;

879

of a slave who wounds a freeman.

Unintentional hurts not to be punished, but only compensated.

The law respecting assaults committed by elders and strangers.

The elder, if he commits an assault, not to be

Laws IX
ATHE-
NIAN.

struck in
return;

the stran-
ger to be
taken be-
fore the
wardens
of the
city.

880
Cases of
assault
(1) on
equals in
age;

(2) on
elders,—
by citi-
zens;

and by
strangers
or metics.

or mother; and he shall abstain from laying hands on any one who is of an age to have been his father or his mother, out of reverence to the Gods who preside over birth; similarly he shall keep his hands from a stranger, whether he be an old inhabitant or newly arrived; he shall not venture to correct such an one by blows, either as the aggressor or in self-defence. If he thinks that some stranger has struck him out of wantonness or insolence, and ought to be punished, he shall take him to the wardens of the city, but let him not strike him, that the stranger may be kept far away from the possibility of lifting up his hand against a citizen, and let the wardens of the city take the offender and examine him, not forgetting their duty to the God of Strangers, and in case the stranger appears to have struck the citizen unjustly, let them inflict upon him as many blows with the scourge as he has himself inflicted, and quell his presumption. But if he be innocent, they shall threaten and rebuke the man who arrested him, and let them both go. If a person strikes another of the same age or somewhat older than himself, who has no children, whether he be an old man who strikes an old man or a young man who strikes a young man, let the person struck defend himself in the natural way without a weapon and with his hands only. He who, being more than forty years of age, dares to fight with another, whether he be the aggressor or in self-defence, shall be regarded as rude and ill-mannered and slavish;—this will be a disgraceful punishment, and therefore suitable to him. The obedient nature will readily yield to such exhortations, but the disobedient, who heeds not the prelude, shall have the law ready for him:—If any man smite another who is older than himself, either by twenty or by more years, in the first place, he who is at hand, not being younger than the combatants, nor their equal in age, shall separate them, or be disgraced according to law; but if he be the equal in age of the person who is struck or younger, he shall defend the person injured as he would a brother or father or still older relative. Further, let him who dares to smite an elder be tried for assault, as I have said, and if he be found guilty, let him be imprisoned for a period of not less than a year, or if the judges approve of a longer period, their decision shall be final. But if a stranger or metic smite one who is older by twenty years or more, the same law shall hold about the bystanders assisting, and he who is found guilty in such a suit, if he be a stranger but not resident, shall be imprisoned during a period of two years; and a metic who disobeys the laws shall be imprisoned for three years, unless the court assign him a longer term. And let him who was present in any of these cases and did not assist according to law be punished, if he be of the highest class, by paying a fine of a mina; or if he be of the second class, of fifty drachmas; or if of the third class, by a fine of thirty drachmas; or if he be of the fourth class, by a fine of twenty drachmas; and the generals and taxiarchs and phylarchs and hipparchs shall form the court in such cases.

Laws are partly framed for the sake of good men, in order to instruct them how they may live on friendly terms with one another, and partly for the sake of those who refuse to be instructed, whose spirit cannot be subdued, or softened, or hindered from plunging into evil. These are the persons who cause the word to be spoken which I am about to utter; for them the legislator legislates of necessity, and in the hope that there may be no need of his laws. He who shall dare to lay violent hands upon his father or mother, or any still older relative, having no fear either of the wrath of the Gods above, or of the punishments that are spoken of in the world below, but transgresses in contempt of ancient and universal traditions as though he were too wise to believe in them, requires some extreme measure of prevention. Now death is not the worst that can happen to men; far worse are the punishments which are said to pursue them in the world below. But although they are most true tales, they work on such souls no prevention; for if they had any effect there would be no slayers of mothers, or impious hands lifted up against parents; and therefore the punishments of this world which are inflicted during life ought not in such cases to fall short, if possible, of the terrors of the world below. Let our enactment then be as follows:—If a man dare to strike his father or his mother, or their fathers or mothers, he being at the time of sound mind, then let any one who is at hand come to the rescue as has been already said, and the metic or stranger who comes to the rescue shall be called to the first place in the games; but if he do not come he shall suffer the punishment of perpetual exile. He who is not a metic, if he comes to the rescue, shall have praise, and if he do not come, blame. And if a slave come to the rescue, let him be made free, but if he do not come to the rescue, let him receive 100 strokes of the whip, by order of the wardens of the agora, if the occurrence take place in the agora; or if somewhere in the city beyond the limits of the agora, any warden of the city who is in residence shall punish him; or if in the country, then the commanders of the wardens of the country[1]. If those who are near at the time be inhabitants of the same place, whether they be youths, or men, or women, let them come to the rescue and denounce him as the impious one; and he who does not come to the rescue shall fall under the curse of Zeus,

Laws
partly for
instruc-
tion,
partly for
those who
will not
listen to
instruc-
tion.

881
Hard-
ened
criminals
are not
affected
by the
tales of
the world
below:
and must
therefore
be pun-
ished on
earth.

Law
about
striking a
parent.

[1] Cp. *supra*, vi. 760 B.

Laws IX

ATHE-
NIAN.

The pun-
ishment
for the
offence is
perpetual
exile from
the city.

the God of kindred and of ancestors, according to law. And if any one is found guilty of assaulting a parent, let him in the first place be for ever banished from the city into the country, and let him abstain from the temples; and if he do not abstain, the wardens of the country shall punish him with blows, or in any way which they please, and if he return he shall be put to death. And if any freeman eat or drink, or have any other sort of intercourse with him, or only meeting him have voluntarily touched him, he shall not enter into any temple, nor into the agora, nor into the city, until he is purified; for he should consider that he has become tainted by a curse. And if he disobeys the law, and pollutes the city and the temples contrary to law, and one of the magistrates sees him and does not indict him, when he gives in his account this omission shall be a most serious charge.

882

The pun-
ishment
of the
slave who
strikes a
freeman.

If a slave strike a freeman, whether a stranger or a citizen, let any one who is present come to the rescue, or pay the penalty already mentioned; and let the bystanders bind him, and deliver him up to the injured person, and he receiving him shall put him in chains, and inflict on him as many stripes as he pleases; but having punished him he must surrender him to his master according to law, and not deprive him of his property. Let the law be as follows: —The slave who strikes a freeman, not at the command of the magistrates, his owner shall receive bound from the man whom he has stricken, and not release him until the slave has persuaded the man whom he has stricken that he ought to be released. And let there be the same laws about women in relation to women, and about men and women in relation to one another.

BOOK X

884

Laws X

ATHE-
NIAN.

A gen-
eral law
about
deeds of
violence.

885

AND now having spoken of assaults, let us sum up all acts of violence under a single law, which shall be as follows:—No one shall take or carry away any of his neighbour's goods, neither shall he use anything which is his neighbour's without the consent of the owner; for these are the offences which are and have been, and will ever be, the source of all the aforesaid evils. The greatest of them are excesses and insolences of youth, and are offences against the greatest when they are done against religion; and especially great when in violation of public and holy rites, or of the partly-common rites in which tribes and phratries share; and in the second degree great when they are committed against private rites and sepulchres, and in the third degree (not to repeat the acts formerly mentioned), when insults are offered to parents; the fourth kind of violence is when any one, regardless of the authority of the rulers, takes or carries away or makes use of anything which belongs to them, not having their consent; and the fifth kind is when the violation of the civil rights of an individual demands reparation. There should be a common law embracing all these cases. For we have already said in general terms what shall be the punishment of sacrilege, whether fraudulent or violent, and now we have to determine what is to be the punishment of those who speak or act insolently toward the Gods. But first we must give them an admonition which may be in the following terms:—No one who in obedience to the laws believed that there were Gods, ever intentionally did any unholy act, or uttered any unlawful word; but he who did must have supposed one of three things,—either that they did not exist,—which is the first possibility, or secondly, that, if they did, they took no care of man, or thirdly, that they were easily appeased and turned aside from their purpose by sacrifices and prayers.

Cle. What shall we say or do to these persons?

Ath. My good friend, let us first hear the jests which I suspect that they in their superiority will utter against us.

Cle. What jests?

Ath. They will make some irreverent speech of this sort:—'O inhabitants of Athens, and Sparta, and Cnosus,' they will reply, 'in that you speak truly; for some of us deny the very existence of the Gods, while others, as you say, are of opinion that they do not care about us; and others that they are turned from their course by gifts. Now we have a right to claim, as you yourself allowed, in the matter of laws, that before you are hard upon us and threaten us, you should argue with us and convince us[1]—you should first attempt to teach and persuade us that there are Gods by reasonable evidences, and also that they are too good to be unrighteous, or to be propitiated, or turned from their course by gifts. For when we hear such things said of them by those who are esteemed to be the best of poets, and orators, and prophets, and priests, and by innumerable others, the thoughts of most of us are not set upon abstaining from unrighteous acts, but upon doing them and atoning for them[2]. When lawgivers profess that they are gentle and not stern, we think that they should first of all use persuasion to us, and show us the existence of Gods, if not in a better manner than other men, at any rate in a truer; and who knows but that we shall hearken to you?

Insolence
towards
the Gods
arises
from ir-
religion,
of which
there are
three
forms.

The un-
believers
demand
that they
should be
reasoned
with be-
fore they
are con-
demned.

---

[1] Cp. *supra,* iv. 718 foll.   [2] Cp. Rep. ii. 364.

The ex-
istence of
the Gods
is proved
by the
order of
the uni-
verse.

Impiety
arises out
of con-
ceit of
wisdom.

Supersti-
tion of
the
ancients;
irreligion
of the
moderns.

The lat-
ter say
that the
sun, moon
and stars
are earth
and stone
only.

If then our request is a fair one, please to accept our challenge.'

Cle. But is there any difficulty in proving the existence of the Gods?

Ath. How would you prove it?

Cle. How? In the first place, the earth and the sun, and the stars and the universe, and the fair order of the seasons, and the division of them into years and months, furnish proofs of their existence; and also there is the fact that all Hellenes and barbarians believe in them.

Ath. I fear, my sweet friend, though I will not say that I much regard, the contempt with which the profane will be likely to assail us. For you do not understand the nature of their complaint, and you fancy that they rush into impiety only from a love of sensual pleasure.

Cle. Why, Stranger, what other reason is there?

Ath. One which you who live in a different atmosphere would never guess.

Cle. What is it?

Ath. A very grievous sort of ignorance which is imagined to be the greatest wisdom.

Cle. What do you mean?

Ath. At Athens there are tales preserved in writing which the virtue of your state, as I am informed, refuses to admit. They speak of the Gods in prose as well as verse, and the oldest of them tell of the origin of the heavens and of the world, and not far from the beginning of their story they proceed to narrate the birth of the Gods, and how after they were born they behaved to one another. Whether these stories have in other ways a good or a bad influence, I should not like to be severe upon them, because they are ancient; but, looking at them with reference to the duties of children to their parents, I cannot praise them, or think that they are useful, or at all true[1]. Of the words of the ancients I have nothing more to say; and I should wish to say of them only what is pleasing to the Gods. But as to our younger generation and their wisdom, I cannot let them off when they do mischief. For do but mark the effect of their words: when you and I argue for the existence of the Gods, and produce the sun, moon, stars, and earth, claiming for them a divine being, if we would listen to the aforesaid philosophers we should say[2] that they are earth and stones only[3], which can have no care at all of human affairs, and that all religion is a cooking up of words and a make-believe.

[1] Cp. *Rep.* ii. 378 foll.   [2] Reading λέγοιμεν.   [3] Cp. *Apology*, 26 foll.

Cle. One such teacher, O Stranger, would be bad enough, and you imply that there are many of them, which is worse.

Ath. Well, then; what shall we say or do?—Shall we assume that some one is accusing us among unholy men, who are trying to escape from the effect of our legislation; and that they say of us— How dreadful that you should legislate on the supposition that there are Gods! Shall we make a defence of ourselves? or shall we leave them and return to our laws, lest the prelude should become longer than the law? For the discourse will certainly extend to great length, if we are to treat the impiously disposed as they desire, partly demonstrating to them at some length the things of which they demand an explanation, partly making them afraid or dissatisfied, and then proceed to the requisite enactments.

Cle. Yes, Stranger; but then how often have we repeated already that on the present occasion there is no reason why brevity should be preferred to length[1]; for who is 'at our heels?'—as the saying goes, and it would be paltry and ridiculous to prefer the shorter to the better. It is a matter of no small consequence, in some way or other to prove that there are Gods, and that they are good, and regard justice more than men do. The demonstration of this would be the best and noblest prelude of all our laws. And therefore, without impatience, and without hurry, let us unreservedly consider the whole matter, summoning up all the power of persuasion which we possess.

Ath. Seeing you thus in earnest, I would fain offer up a prayer that I may succeed:—but I must proceed at once. Who can be calm when he is called upon to prove the existence of the Gods? Who can avoid hating and abhorring the men who are and have been the cause of this argument; I speak of those who will not believe the tales which they have heard as babes and sucklings from their mothers and nurses, repeated by them both in jest and earnest, like charms, who have also heard them in the sacrificial prayers, and seen sights accompanying them,—sights and sounds delightful to children,—and their parents during the sacrifices showing an intense earnestness on behalf of their children and of themselves, and with eager interest talking to the Gods, and beseeching them, as though they were firmly convinced of their existence; who likewise see and hear the prostrations and invocations which are made by Hellenes and barbarians at the rising and setting of the sun and moon, in all the vicissitudes of life, not as if they thought that there were no Gods, but as if there could be no doubt of their existence, and no suspicion of their non-existence; when men, knowing all

[1] Cp. *supra,* iv. 719 E foll.; ix. 857-8.

The prelude will extend to a great length.

It should be the best and noblest prelude of all.

Can we suppose that all the practices of religion with which we have been familiar from childhood, and which are common to Greeks and barbarians, have no meaning?

We say
to the
young:—
Do not
meddle
with
things
above
you; but
know
that no
one ever
continues
through
life an
unbe-
liever.

these things, despise them on no real grounds, as would be admitted by all who have any particle of intelligence, and when they force us to say what we are now saying, how can any one in gentle terms remonstrate with the like of them, when he has to begin by proving to them the very existence of the Gods? Yet the attempt must be made; for it would be unseemly that one half of mankind should go mad in their lust of pleasure, and the other half in their indignation at such persons. Our address to these lost and perverted natures should not be spoken in passion; let us suppose ourselves to select some one of them, and gently reason with him, smothering our anger:—O my son, we will say to him, you are young, and the advance of time will make you reverse many of the opinions which you now hold. Wait awhile, and do not attempt to judge at present of the highest things; and that is the highest of which you now think nothing—to know the Gods rightly and to live accordingly. And in the first place let me indicate to you one point which is of great importance, and about which I cannot be deceived:—You and your friends are not the first who have held this opinion about the Gods. There have always been persons more or less numerous who have had the same disorder. I have known many of them, and can tell you, that no one who had taken up in youth this opinion, that the Gods do not exist, ever continued in the same until he was old; the two other notions certainly do continue in some cases, but not in many; the notion, I mean, that the Gods exist, but take no heed of human things, and the other notion that they do take heed of them, but are easily propitiated with sacrifices and prayers. As to the opinion about the Gods which may some day become clear to you, I advise you go wait and consider if it be true or not; ask of others, and above all of the legislator. In the meantime take care that you do not offend against the Gods. For the duty of the legislator is and always will be to teach you the truth of these matters.

Cle. Our address, Stranger, thus far, is excellent.

Ath. Quite true, Megillus and Cleinias, but I am afraid that we have unconsciously lighted on a strange doctrine.

Cle. What doctrine do you mean?

Ath. The wisest of all doctrines, in the opinion of many.

Cle. I wish that you would speak plainer.

Ath. The doctrine that all things do become, have become, and will become, some by nature, some by art, and some by chance.

Cle. Is not that true?

Ath. Well, philosophers are probably right; at any rate we may as well follow in their track, and examine what is the meaning of them and their disciples.

Cle. By all means.

Ath. They say that the greatest and fairest things are the work of nature and of chance, the lesser of art, which, receiving from nature the greater and primeval creations, moulds and fashions all those lesser works which are generally termed artificial.

Cle. How is that?

Ath. I will explain my meaning still more clearly. They say that fire and water, and earth and air, all exist by nature and chance, and none of them by art, and that as to the bodies which come next in order,—earth, and sun, and moon, and stars,—they have been created by means of these absolutely inanimate existences. The elements are severally moved by chance and some inherent force according to certain affinities among them—of hot with cold, or of dry with moist, or of soft with hard, and according to all the other accidental admixtures of opposites which have been formed by necessity. After this fashion and in this manner the whole heaven has been created, and all that is in the heaven, as well as animals and all plants, and all the seasons come from these elements, not by the action of mind, as they say, or of any God, or from art, but as I was saying, by nature and chance only. Art sprang up afterwards and out of these, mortal and of mortal birth, and produced in play certain images and very partial imitations of the truth, having an affinity to one another, such as music and painting create and their companion arts. And there are other arts which have a serious purpose, and these co-operate with nature, such, for example, as medicine, and husbandry, and gymnastic. And they say that politics co-operate with nature, but in a less degree, and have more of art; also that legislation is entirely a work of art, and is based on assumptions which are not true.

Cle. How do you mean?

Ath. In the first place, my dear friend, these people would say that the Gods exist not by nature, but by art, and by the laws of states, which are different in different places, according to the agreement of those who make them; and that the honourable is one thing by nature and another thing by law, and that the principles of justice have no existence at all in nature, but that mankind are always disputing about them and altering them; and that the alterations which are made by art and by law have no basis in nature, but are of authority for the moment and at the time at which they are made.—These, my friends, are the sayings of wise men, poets and prose writers, which find a way into the minds of youth. They are told by them that the highest right is might, and in this way the young fall into impieties, under the idea that the Gods are not such

Laws X

ATHE-
NIAN,
CLEINIAS.

The doctrine of certain philosophers explained.

They say that the elements exist, and the heavenly bodies are created out of them, by nature and chance. Art comes later, sometimes working alone, sometimes co-operating with nature.

They maintain further that religion and morality are a mere convention; and [890] that 'The highest right is might.'

as the law bids them imagine; and hence arise factions, these philosophers inviting them to lead a true life according to nature, that is, to live in real dominion over others, and not in legal subjection to them[1].

Cle. What a dreadful picture, Stranger, have you given, and how great is the injury which is thus inflicted on young men to the ruin both of states and families!

The laws
should
persuade
rather
than
threaten.

Ath. True, Cleinias; but then what should the lawgiver do when this evil is of long standing? should he only rise up in the state and threaten all mankind, proclaiming that if they will not say and think that the Gods are such as the law ordains (and this may be extended generally to the honourable, the just, and to all the highest things, and to all that relates to virtue and vice), and if they will not make their actions conform to the copy which the law gives them, then he who refuses to obey the law shall die, or suffer stripes and bonds, or privation of citizenship, or in some cases be punished by loss of property and exile? Should he not rather, when he is making laws for men, at the same time infuse the spirit of persuasion into his words, and mitigate the severity of them as far as he can?

Cle. Why, Stranger, if such persuasion be at all possible, then a legislator who has anything in him ought never to weary of persuading men; he ought to leave nothing unsaid in support of the ancient opinion that there are Gods, and of all those other truths which you were just now mentioning; he ought to support the law and also art, and acknowledge that both alike exist by nature, and no less than nature, if they are the creations of mind in accordance with right reason, as you appear to me to maintain, and I am disposed to agree with you in thinking.

Ath. Yes, my enthusiastic Cleinias; but are not these things when spoken to a multitude hard to be understood, not to mention that they take up a dismal length of time?

The laws
if once
[891]
written
down
may in
time be
under-
stood.

Cle. Why, Stranger, shall we, whose patience failed not when drinking or music were the themes of discourse, weary now of discoursing about the Gods, and about divine things? And the greatest help to rational legislation is that the laws when once written down are always at rest; they can be put to the test at any future time, and therefore, if on first hearing they seem difficult, there is no reason for apprehension about them, because any man however dull can go over them and consider them again and again; nor if they are tedious but useful, is there any reason or religion, as it seems

---

[1] Cp. Gorg. 483.

to me, in any man refusing to maintain the principles of them to the utmost of his power.

Laws X

ATHE-
NIAN,
CLEINIAS,
MEGIL-
LUS.

Meg. Stranger, I like what Cleinias is saying.

Ath. Yes, Megillus, and we should do as he proposes; for if impious discourses were not scattered, as I may say, throughout the world, there would have been no need for any vindication of the existence of the Gods—but seeing that they are spread far and wide, such arguments are needed; and who should come to the rescue of the greatest laws, when they are being undermined by bad men, but the legislator himself?

Meg. There is no more proper champion of them.

Ath. Well, then, tell me, Cleinias,—for I must ask you to be my partner,—does not he who talks in this way conceive fire and water and earth and air to be the first elements of all things[1]? these he calls nature, and out of these he supposes the soul to be formed afterwards; and this is not a mere conjecture of ours about his meaning, but is what he really means.

The error of the physical philosophers is that they speak of the four elements as the first elements.

Cle. Very true.

Ath. Then, by Heaven, we have discovered the source of this vain opinion of all those physical investigators; and I would have you examine their arguments with the utmost care, for their impiety is a very serious matter; they not only make a bad and mistaken use of argument, but they lead away the minds of others: that is my opinion of them.

Cle. You are right; but I should like to know how this happens.

Ath. I fear that the argument may seem singular.

Cle. Do not hesitate, Stranger; I see that you are afraid of such a discussion carrying you beyond the limits of legislation. But if there be no other way of showing our agreement in the belief that there are Gods, of whom the law is said now to approve, let us take this way, my good sir.

Ath. Then I suppose that I must repeat the singular argument of those who manufacture the soul according to their own impious notions; they affirm that which is the first cause of the generation and destruction of all things, to be not first, but last, and that which is last to be first, and hence they have fallen into error about the true nature of the Gods.

They put what is first last; they do not know that the soul is prior to the body.
892

Cle. Still I do not understand you.

Ath. Nearly all of them, my friends, seem to be ignorant of the nature and power of the soul, especially in what relates to her origin: they do not know that she is among the first of things, and before all

[1] Cp. Tim. 46 D.

Mind and
art and
law come
first, and
then the
works
of nature,
which
are, how-
ever, so
termed in
error.

The Athe-
nian is
willing to
under-
take the
entire
risk of the
argu-
ment in
his own
person.

893

bodies, and is the chief author of their changes and transpositions. And if this is true, and if the soul is older than the body, must not the things which are of the soul's kindred be of necessity prior to those which appertain to the body?

Cle. Certainly.

Ath. Then thought and attention and mind and art and law will be prior to that which is hard and soft and heavy and light; and the great and primitive works and actions will be works of art; they will be the first, and after them will come nature and works of nature, which however is a wrong term for men to apply to them; these will follow, and will be under the government of art and mind.

Cle. But why is the word 'nature' wrong?

Ath. Because those who use the term mean to say that nature is the first creative power; but if the soul turn out to be the primeval element, and not fire or air, then in the truest sense and beyond other things the soul may be said to exist by nature; and this would be true if you proved that the soul is older than the body, but not otherwise.

Cle. You are quite right.

Ath. Shall we, then, take this as the next point to which our attention should be directed?

Cle. By all means.

Ath. Let us be on our guard lest this most deceptive argument with its youthful looks, beguiling us old men, give us the slip and make a laughing-stock of us. Who knows but we may be aiming at the greater, and fail of attaining the lesser? Suppose that we three have to pass a rapid river, and I, being the youngest of the three and experienced in rivers, take upon me the duty of making the attempt first by myself; leaving you in safety on the bank, I am to examine whether the river is passable by older men like yourselves, and if such appears to be the case then I shall invite you to follow, and my experience will help to convey you across; but if the river is impassable by you, then there will have been no danger to anybody but myself,—would not that seem to be a very fair proposal? I mean to say that the argument in prospect is likely to be too much for you, out of your depth and beyond your strength, and I should be afraid that the stream of my questions might create in you who are not in the habit of answering, giddiness and confusion of mind, and hence a feeling of unpleasantness and unsuitableness might arise. I think therefore that I had better first ask the questions and then answer them myself while you listen in safety; in that way I can carry on the argument until I have completed the proof that the soul is prior to the body.

Cle. Excellent, Stranger, and I hope that you will do as you propose.

Ath. Come, then, and if ever we are to call upon the Gods, let us call upon them now in all seriousness to come to the demonstration of their own existence. And so holding fast to the rope we will venture upon the depths of the argument. When questions of this sort are asked of me, my safest answer would appear to be as follows:— Some one says to me, 'O Stranger, are all things at rest and nothing in motion, or is the exact opposite of this true, or are some things in motion and others at rest?'—To this I shall reply that some things are in motion and others at rest. 'And do not things which move move in a place, and are not the things which are at rest at rest in a place?' Certainly. 'And some move or rest in one place and some in more places than one?' You mean to say, we shall rejoin, that those things which rest at the centre move in one place, just as the circumference goes round of globes which are said to be at rest? 'Yes.' And we observe that, in the revolution, the motion which carries round the larger and the lesser circle at the same time is proportionally distributed to greater and smaller, and is greater and smaller in a certain proportion. Here is a wonder which might be thought an impossibility, that the same motion should impart swiftness and slowness in due proportion to larger and lesser circles. 'Very true.' And when you speak of bodies moving in many places, you seem to me to mean those which move from one place to another, and sometimes have one centre of motion and sometimes more than one because they turn upon their axis; and whenever they meet anything, if it be stationary, they are divided by it; but if they get in the midst between bodies which are approaching and moving towards the same spot from opposite directions, they unite with them. 'I admit the truth of what you are saying.' Also when they unite they grow, and when they are divided they waste away, —that is, supposing the constitution of each to remain, or if that fails, then there is a second reason of their dissolution. 'And when are all things created and how?' Clearly, they are created when the first principle receives increase and attains to the second dimension, and from this arrives at the one which is neighbour to this, and after reaching the third becomes perceptible to sense. Everything which is thus changing and moving is in process of generation; only when at rest has it real existence, but when passing into another state it is destroyed utterly. Have we not mentioned all motions that there are, and comprehended them under their kinds and numbered them with the exception, my friends, of two?

Cle. Which are they?

Some things are in motion; others at rest.

Of motion there are ten kinds:—

(1) Motion on an axis;

(2) locomotion;

(3) a combination of these;

(4) separation;

(5) composition;

(6) growth;
894
(7) decay;

(8) destruction;

Laws X

ATHE-
NIAN,
CLEINIAS.

Ath. Just the two, with which our present enquiry is concerned

Cle. Speak plainer.

Ath. I suppose that our enquiry has reference to the soul?

Cle. Very true.

Ath. Let us assume that there is a motion able to move other things, but not to move itself;—that is one kind; and there is another kind which can move itself as well as other things, working in composition and decomposition, by increase and diminution and generation and destruction,—that is also one of the many kinds of motion.

Cle. Granted.

(9) external, and

(10) spontaneous, motion.

The last is superior to the other kinds,

Ath. And we will assume that which moves other, and is changed by other, to be the ninth, and that which changes itself and others, and is co-incident with every action and every passion, and is the true principle of change and motion in all that is,—that we shall be inclined to call the tenth.

Cle. Certainly.

Ath. And which of these ten motions ought we to prefer as being the mightiest and most efficient?

Cle. I must say that the motion which is able to move itself is ten thousand times superior to all the others[1].

Ath. Very good; but may I make one or two corrections in what I have been saying?

Cle. What are they?

and should rank first, being the ultimate source of all motion.

The ninth should rank second.

Ath. When I spoke of the tenth sort of motion, that was not quite correct.

Cle. What was the error?

Ath. According to the true order, the tenth was really the first in generation and power; then follows the second, which was strangely enough termed the ninth by us.

Cle. What do you mean?

A demonstra-
[895]
tion of the priority of spontaneous to external motion.

Ath. I mean this: when one thing changes another, and that another, of such will there be any primary changing element? How can a thing which is moved by another ever be the beginning of change? Impossible. But when the self-moved changes other, and that again other, and thus thousands upon tens of thousands of bodies are set in motion, must not the beginning of all this motion be the change of the self-moving principle[2]?

Cle. Very true, and I quite agree.

Ath. Or, to put the question in another way, making answer to ourselves:—If, as most of these philosophers have the audacity to affirm, all things were at rest in one mass, which of the above-

[1] Cp. Tim. 89 A.   [2] Cp. Phaedr. 245 D.

mentioned principles of motion would first spring up among them?

Cle. Clearly the self-moving; for there could be no change in them arising out of any external cause; the change must first take place in themselves.

Ath. Then we must say that self-motion being the origin of all motions, and the first which arises among things at rest as well as among things in motion, is the eldest and mightiest principle of change, and that which is changed by another and yet moves other is second.

Cle. Quite true.

Ath. At this stage of the argument let us put a question.

Cle. What question?

Ath. If we were to see this power existing in any earthy, watery, or fiery substance, simple or compound—how should we describe it?

Cle. You mean to ask whether we should call such a self-moving power life?

The self-moving principle is life and soul.

Ath. I do.

Cle. Certainly we should.

Ath. And when we see soul in anything, must we not do the same —must we not admit that this is life?

Cle. We must.

Ath. And now, I beseech you, reflect;—you would admit that we have a threefold knowledge of things?

Cle. What do you mean?

The knowl-edge of things is three-fold:— of the essence, the defi-nition, and the name.

Ath. I mean that we know the essence, and that we know the definition of the essence, and the name,—these are the three; and there are two questions which may be raised about anything.

Cle. How two?

Ath. Sometimes a person may give the name and ask the defini-tion; or he may give the definition and ask the name. I may illus-trate what I mean in this way.

Cle. How?

Ath. Number like some other things is capable of being divided into equal parts; when thus divided, number is named 'even,' and the definition of the name 'even' is 'number divisible into two equal parts'?

Cle. True.

Ath. I mean, that when we are asked about the definition and give the name, or when we are asked about the name and give the definition—in either case, whether we give name or definition, we speak of the same thing, calling 'even' the number which is divided into two equal parts.

Cle. Quite true.

The soul
may be
defined
as the
self-
moved,
and is the
source of
motion in
all things.

External
motion is
posterior
to spon-
taneous,
and
therefore
the body
to the
soul.

And
mental
qualities
are prior
to the
qualities
of body.

The soul
(or two
souls) of
the world
is the
source of
good and
evil,

Ath. And what is the definition of that which is named 'soul'? Can we conceive of any other than that which has been already given—the motion which can move itself?

Cle. You mean to say that the essence which is defined as the self-moved is the same with that which has the name soul?

Ath. Yes; and if this is true, do we still maintain that there is anything wanting in the proof that the soul is the first origin and moving power of all that is, or has become, or will be, and their contraries, when she has been clearly shown to be the source of change and motion in all things?

Cle. Certainly not; the soul as being the source of motion, has been most satisfactorily shown to be the oldest of all things.

Ath. And is not that motion which is produced in another, by reason of another, but never has any self-moving power at all, being in truth the change of an inanimate body, to be reckoned second, or by any lower number which you may prefer?

Cle. Exactly.

Ath. Then we are right, and speak the most perfect and absolute truth, when we say that the soul is prior to the body, and that the body is second and comes afterwards, and is born to obey the soul, which is the ruler?

Cle. Nothing can be more true.

Ath. Do you remember our old admission, that if the soul was prior to the body the things of the soul were also prior to those of the body?

Cle. Certainly.

Ath. Then characters and manners, and wishes and reasonings, and true opinions, and reflections, and recollections are prior to length and breadth and depth and strength of bodies, if the soul is prior to the body.

Cle. To be sure.

Ath. In the next place, must we not of necessity admit that the soul is the cause of good and evil, base and honourable, just and unjust, and of all other opposites, if we suppose her to be the cause of all things?

Cle. We must.

Ath. And as the soul orders and inhabits all things that move, however moving, must we not say that she orders also the heavens?

Cle. Of course.

Ath. One soul or more? More than one—I will answer for you; at any rate, we must not suppose that there are less than two—one the author of good, and the other of evil.

Cle. Very true.

Ath. Yes, very true; the soul then directs all things in heaven, and earth, and sea by her movements, and these are described by the terms—will, consideration, attention, deliberation, opinion true and false, joy and sorrow, confidence, fear, hatred, love, and other primary motions akin to these; which again receive the secondary motions of corporeal substances, and guide all things to growth and decay, to composition and decomposition, and to the qualities which accompany them, such as heat and cold, heaviness and lightness, hardness and softness, blackness and whiteness, bitterness and sweetness, and all those other qualities which the soul uses, herself a goddess, when truly receiving the divine mind she disciplines all things rightly to their happiness; but when she is the companion of folly, she does the very contrary of all this. Shall we assume so much, or do we still entertain doubts?

Cle. There is no room at all for doubt.

Ath. Shall we say then that it is the soul which controls heaven and earth, and the whole world?—that it is a principle of wisdom and virtue, or a principle which has neither wisdom nor virtue? Suppose that we make answer as follows:—

Cle. How would you answer?

Ath. If, my friend, we say that the whole path and movement of heaven, and of all that is therein, is by nature akin to the movement and revolution and calculation of mind, and proceeds by kindred laws, then, as is plain, we must say that the best soul takes care of the world and guides it along the good path.

Cle. True.

Ath. But if the world moves wildly and irregularly, then the evil soul guides it.

Cle. True again.

Ath. Of what nature is the movement of mind?—To this question it is not easy to give an intelligent answer; and therefore I ought to assist you in framing one.

Cle. Very good.

Ath. Then let us not answer as if we would look straight at the sun, making ourselves darkness at midday[1],—I mean as if we were under the impression that we could see with mortal eyes, or know adequately the nature of mind;—it will be safer to look at the image only.

Cle. What do you mean?

Ath. Let us select of the ten motions the one which mind chiefly resembles; this I will bring to your recollection, and will then make the answer on behalf of us all.

[1] Cp. Rep. vii. 515.

Laws X

897
ATHE-
NIAN,
CLEINIAS.

and or-
ders all
things in
heaven
and earth.

Is the
world
governed
by the
better of
the two
souls?

Yes:—
for its
motion is
akin to
that of
mind,
which is
circular.

Cle. That will be excellent.

Ath. You will surely remember our saying that all things were either at rest or in motion?

Cle. I do.

Ath. And that of things in motion some were moving in one place, and others in more than one?

898

Cle. Yes.

Ath. Of these two kinds of motion, that which moves in one place must move about a centre like globes made in a lathe, and is most entirely akin and similar to the circular movement of mind.

Cle. What do you mean?

Ath. In saying that both mind and the motion which is in one place move in the same and like manner, in and about the same, and in relation to the same, and according to one proportion and order, and are like the motion of a globe, we invented a fair image, which does no discredit to our ingenuity.

Cle. It does us great credit.

The ir-
regular
motion is
the mo-
tion of
senseless-
ness and
folly.

Ath. And the motion of the other sort which is not after the same manner, nor in the same, nor about the same, nor in relation to the same, nor in one place, nor in order, nor according to any rule or proportion, may be said to be akin to senselessness and folly?

Cle. That is most true.

Ath. Then, after what has been said, there is no difficulty in distinctly stating, that since soul carries all things round, either the best soul or the contrary must of necessity carry round and order and arrange the revolution of the heaven.

Cle. And judging from what has been said, Stranger, there would be impiety in asserting that any but the most perfect soul or souls carries round the heavens.

Ath. You have understood my meaning right well, Cleinias, and now let me ask you another question.

Cle. What are you going to ask?

The soul
or mind
carries
round the
whole;—
does it
carry
round
each of
the
heavenly
bodies?
e.g., the
sun?

Ath. If the soul carries round the sun and moon, and the other stars, does she not carry round each individual of them?

Cle. Certainly.

Ath. Then of one of them let us speak, and the same argument will apply to all.

Cle. Which will you take?

Ath. Every one sees the body of the sun, but no one sees his soul, nor the soul of any other body living or dead; and yet there is great reason to believe that this nature, unperceived by any of our senses, is circumfused around them all, but is perceived by mind; and therefore by mind and reflection only let us apprehend the following point.

Cle. What is that?

Ath. If the soul carries round the sun, we shall not be far wrong in supposing one of three alternatives.

Cle. What are they?

Ath. Either the soul which moves the sun this way and that, resides within the circular and visible body, like the soul which carries us about every way; or the soul provides herself with an external body of fire or air, as some affirm, and violently propels body by body; or thirdly, she is without such a body, but guides the sun by some extraordinary and wonderful power.

Cle. Yes, certainly; the soul can only order all things in one of these three ways.

Ath. And this soul of the sun, which is therefore better than the sun, whether taking the sun about in a chariot to give light to men, or acting from without, or in whatever way, ought by every man to be deemed a God[1].

Cle. Yes, by every man who has the least particle of sense.

Ath. And of the stars too, and of the moon, and of the years and months and seasons, must we not say in like manner, that since a soul or souls having every sort of excellence are the causes of all of them, those souls are Gods, whether they are living beings and reside in bodies, and in this way order the whole heaven, or whatever be the place and mode of their existence;—and will any one who admits all this venture to deny that all things are full of Gods?

Cle. No one, Stranger, would be such a madman.

Ath. And now, Megillus and Cleinias, let us offer terms to him who has hitherto denied the existence of the Gods, and leave him.

Cle. What terms?

Ath. Either he shall teach us that we were wrong in saying that the soul is the original of all things, and arguing accordingly; or, if he be not able to say anything better, then he must yield to us and live for the remainder of his life in the belief that there are Gods.— Let us see, then, whether we have said enough or not enough to those who deny that there are Gods.

Cle. Certainly,—quite enough, Stranger.

Ath. Then to them we will say no more. And now we are to address him who, believing that there are Gods, believes also that they take no heed of human affairs: To him we say,—O thou best of men, in believing that there are Gods you are led by some affinity

[1] Cp. *infra*, xii. 966, 967.

Laws X

ATHE-
NIAN,
CLEINIAS.

900
take no
heed of
man, we
say:—
You feel
that you
are the
kindred
of the
Gods, and
you
cannot
believe
that the
injustice
of this
world is
to be
ascribed
to them.

We will
justify
the ways
of God
to you.

The Gods
are
perfectly
good:

to them, which attracts you towards your kindred and makes you honour and believe in them. But the fortunes of evil and unrighteous men in private as well as public life, which, though not really happy, are wrongly counted happy in the judgment of men, and are celebrated both by poets and prose writers[1]—these draw you aside from your natural piety. Perhaps you have seen impious men growing old and leaving their children's children in high offices, and their prosperity shakes your faith—you have known or heard or been yourself an eyewitness of many monstrous impieties, and have beheld men by such criminal means from small beginnings attaining to sovereignty and the pinnacle of greatness; and considering all these things you do not like to accuse the Gods of them, because they are your relatives; and so from some want of reasoning power, and also from an unwillingness to find fault with them, you have come to believe that they exist indeed, but have no thought or care of human things. Now, that your present evil opinion may not grow to still greater impiety, and that we may if possible use arguments which may conjure away the evil before it arrives, we will add another argument to that originally addressed to him who utterly denied the existence of the Gods. And do you, Megillus and Cleinias, answer for the young man as you did before; and if any impediment comes in our way, I will take the word out of your mouths, and carry you over the river as I did just now.

Cle. Very good; do as you say, and we will help you as well as we can.

Ath. There will probably be no difficulty in proving to him that the Gods care about the small as well as about the great. For he was present and heard what was said, that they are perfectly good, and that the care of all things is most entirely natural to them[2].

Cle. No doubt he heard that.

Ath. Let us consider together in the next place what we mean by this virtue which we ascribe to them. Surely we should say that to be temperate and to possess mind belongs to virtue, and the contrary to vice?

Cle. Certainly.

Ath. Yes; and courage is a part of virtue, and cowardice of vice?

Cle. True.

Ath. And the one is honourable, and the other dishonourable?

Cle. To be sure.

Ath. And the one, like other meaner things, is a human quality, but the Gods have no part in anything of the sort?

Cle. That again is what everybody will admit.

[1] Cp. Rep. ii. 364 A.   [2] Cp. *supra*, 899 B.

Ath. But do we imagine carelessness and idleness and luxury to be virtues? What do you think?

Cle. Decidedly not.

Ath. They rank under the opposite class?

Cle. Yes.

Ath. And their opposites, therefore, would fall under the opposite class?

Cle. Yes.

Ath. But are we to suppose that one who possesses all these good qualities will be luxurious and heedless and idle, like those whom the poet compares to stingless drones[1]?

Cle. And the comparison is a most just one.

Ath. Surely God must not be supposed to have a nature which He Himself hates?—he who dares to say this sort of thing must not be tolerated for a moment.

Cle. Of course not. How could He have?

Ath. Should we not on any principle be entirely mistaken in praising any one who has some special business entrusted to him, if he have a mind which takes care of great matters and no care of small ones? Reflect; he who acts in this way, whether he be God or man, must act from one of two principles.

Cle. What are they?

Ath. Either he must think that the neglect of the small matters is of no consequence to the whole, or if he knows that they are of consequence, and he neglects them, his neglect must be attributed to carelessness and indolence. Is there any other way in which his neglect can be explained? For surely, when it is impossible for him to take care of all, he is not negligent if he fails to attend to these things great or small, which a God or some inferior being might be wanting in strength or capacity to manage?

Cle. Certainly not.

Ath. Now, then, let us examine the offenders, who both alike confess that there are Gods, but with a difference,—the one saying that they may be appeased, and the other that they have no care of small matters: there are three of us and two of them, and we will say to them,—In the first place, you both acknowledge that the Gods hear and see and know all things, and that nothing can escape them which is matter of sense and knowledge:—do you admit this?

Cle. Yes.

Ath. And do you admit also that they have all power which mortals and immortals can have?

Cle. They will, of course, admit this also.

[1] Hesiod, Works and Days, 307.

Laws X

ATHE-
NIAN,
CLEINIAS.

901

and therefore cannot be charged with idleness and carelessness.

We and our adversaries alike admit that the Gods see and know all things; that they have all power;

and that
they are
good and
perfect.

Ath. And surely we three and they two—five in all—have acknowledged that they are good and perfect?

Cle. Assuredly.

Ath. But, if they are such as we conceive them to be, can we possibly suppose that they ever act in the spirit of carelessness and indolence? For in us inactivity is the child of cowardice, and carelessness of inactivity and indolence.

Cle. Most true.

They
cannot
therefore
neglect
small
[902]
matters
from idle-
ness;

Ath. Then not from inactivity and carelessness is any God ever negligent; for there is no cowardice in them.

Cle. That is very true.

Ath. Then the alternative which remains is, that if the Gods neglect the lighter and lesser concerns of the universe, they neglect them because they know that they ought not to care about such matters—what other alternative is there but the opposite of their knowing?

Cle. There is none.

but ei-
ther they
think
them un-
worthy of
regard, or
are ig-
norant:—
they can-
not be
ignorant,
and they
will not
knowing-
ly neg-
lect man
who is
their pos-
session.

Ath. And, O most excellent and best of men, do I understand you to mean that they are careless because they are ignorant, and do not know that they ought to take care, or that they know, and yet like the meanest sort of men, knowing the better, choose the worse because they are overcome by pleasures and pains?

Cle. Impossible.

Ath. Do not all human things partake of the nature of soul? And is not man the most religious of all animals[1]?

Cle. That is not to be denied.

Ath. And we acknowledge that all mortal creatures are the property of the Gods, to whom also the whole of heaven belongs[2]?

Cle. Certainly.

Ath. And, therefore, whether a person says that these things are to the Gods great or small—in either case it would not be natural for the Gods who own us, and who are the most careful and the best of owners, to neglect us.—There is also a further consideration.

Cle. What is it?

Ath. Sensation and power are in an inverse ratio to each other in respect to their ease and difficulty.

Cle. What do you mean?

Small
things
harder to
be seen,
but more
easily

Ath. I mean that there is greater difficulty in seeing and hearing the small than the great, but more facility in moving and controlling and taking care of small and unimportant things than of their opposites.

Cle. Far more.

[1] Cp. Tim. 42 A.   [2] Cp. Phaedo 62.

Ath. Suppose the case of a physician who is willing and able to cure some living thing as a whole,—how will the whole fare at his hands if he takes care only of the greater and neglects the parts which are lesser?

Cle. Decidedly not well.

Ath. No better would be the result with pilots or generals, or householders or statesmen, or any other such class, if they neglected the small and regarded only the great;—as the builders say, the larger stones do not lie well without the lesser.

Cle. Of course not.

Ath. Let us not, then, deem God inferior to human workmen, who, in proportion to their skill, finish and perfect their works, small as well as great, by one and the same art; or that God, the wisest of beings, who is both willing and able to take care, is like a lazy good-for-nothing, or a coward, who turns his back upon labour and gives no thought to smaller and easier matters, but to the greater only.

Cle. Never, Stranger, let us admit a supposition about the Gods which is both impious and false.

Ath. I think that we have now argued enough with him who delights to accuse the Gods of neglect.

Cle. Yes.

Ath. He has been forced to acknowledge that he is in error, but he still seems to me to need some words of consolation.

Cle. What consolation will you offer him?

Ath. Let us say to the youth:—The ruler of the universe has ordered all things with a view to the excellence and preservation of the whole, and each part, as far as may be, has an action and passion appropriate to it. Over these, down to the least fraction of them, ministers have been appointed to preside, who have wrought out their perfection with infinitesimal exactness. And one of these portions of the universe is thine own, unhappy man, which, however little, contributes to the whole; and you do not seem to be aware that this and every other creation is for the sake of the whole, and in order that the life of the whole may be blessed; and that you are created for the sake of the whole, and not the whole for the sake of you. For every physician and every skilled artist does all things for the sake of the whole, directing his effort towards the common good, executing the part for the sake of the whole, and not the whole for the sake of the part. And you are annoyed because you are ignorant how what is best for you happens to you and to the universe, as far as the laws of the common creation admit. Now, as the soul combining first with one body and then with another undergoes all sorts

managed than great.

The physician, the pilot, the general, &c., take care of [903] small things as well as great: will the all-wise God neglect them?

Words of consolation:—

Let the youth remember that God created him for the whole, not the whole for the sake of him.

of changes, either of herself, or through the influence of another soul, all that remains to the player of the game is that he should shift the pieces; sending the better nature to the better place, and the worse to the worse, and so assigning to them their proper portion.

Cle. In what way do you mean?

Ath. In a way which may be supposed to make the care of all things easy to thc Gods. If any one were to form or fashion all things without any regard to the whole[1],—if, for example, he formed a living element of water out of fire, instead of forming many things out of one or one out of many in regular order attaining to a first or second or third birth[2], the transmutation would have been infinite; but now the ruler of the world has a wonderfully easy task.

Cle. How so?

Ath. I will explain:—When the king saw that our actions had life, and that there was much virtue in them and much vice, and that the soul and body, although not, like the Gods of popular opinion, eternal, yet having once come into existence, were inde-structible (for if either of them had been destroyed, there would have been no generation of living beings); and when he observed that the good of the soul was ever by nature designed to profit men, and the evil to harm them—he, seeing all this, contrived so to place each of the parts that their position might in the easiest and best manner procure the victory of good and the defeat of evil in the whole. And he contrived a general plan by which a thing of a certain nature found a certain seat and room. But the formation of qual-ities[3] he left to the wills of individuals. For every one of us is made pretty much what he is by the bent of his desires and the nature of his soul.

Cle. Yes, that is probably true.

Ath. Then all things which have a soul change, and possess in themselves a principle of change, and in changing move according to law and to the order of destiny: natures which have undergone a lesser change move less and on the earth's surface, but those which have suffered more change and have become more criminal sink into the abyss, that is to say, into Hades and other places in the world below, of which the very names terrify men, and which they picture to themselves as in a dream, both while alive and when released from the body. And whenever the soul receives more of good or evil from her own energy and the strong influence of others—when she has communion with divine virtue and becomes divine, she is car-ried into another and better place, which is perfect in holiness; but

God as-
signs to
human
souls
their
places in
such a
manner
as to en-
sure the
defeat of
evil.

The
fashion-
ing of
men's
char-
acters he
leaves to
them-
selves.

If a soul
grows
better, it
goes to a

---

[1] Reading μὴ πρὸς τὸ ὅλον.   [2] Cp. Timaeus 42 B, C.   [3] Reading τοῦ ποίου.

when she has communion with evil, then she also changes the place of her life.

'This is the justice of the Gods who inhabit Olympus [1].'

O youth or young man, who fancy that you are neglected by the Gods, know that if you become worse you shall go to the worse souls, or if better to the better, and in every succession of life and death you will do and suffer what like may fitly suffer at the hands of like. This is the justice of heaven, which neither you nor any other unfortunate will ever glory in escaping, and which the ordaining powers have specially ordained; take good heed thereof, for it will be sure to take heed of you. If you say:—I am small and will creep into the depths of the earth, or I am high and will fly up to heaven, you are not so small or so high but that you shall pay the fitting penalty, either here or in the world below or in some still more savage place whither you shall be conveyed. This is also the explanation of the fate of those whom you saw, who had done unholy and evil deeds, and from small beginnings had grown great, and you fancied that from being miserable they had become happy; and in their actions, as in a mirror, you seemed to see the universal neglect of the Gods, not knowing how they make all things work together and contribute to the great whole. And thinkest thou, bold man, that thou needest not to know this?—he who knows it not can never form any true idea of the happiness or unhappiness of life or hold any rational discourse respecting either. If Cleinias and this our reverend company succeed in proving to you that you know not what you say of the Gods, then will God help you; but should you desire to hear more, listen to what we say to the third opponent, if you have any understanding whatsoever. For I think that we have sufficiently proved the existence of the Gods, and that they care for men:—The other notion that they are appeased by the wicked, and take gifts, is what we must not concede to any one, and what every man should disprove to the utmost of his power.

Cle. Very good; let us do as you say.

Ath. Well, then, by the Gods themselves I conjure you to tell me,—if they are to be propitiated, how are they to be propitiated? Who are they, and what is their nature? Must they not be at least rulers who have to order unceasingly the whole heaven?

Cle. True.

Ath. And to what earthly rulers can they be compared, or who to them? How in the less can we find an image of the greater? Are they charioteers of contending pairs of steeds, or pilots of vessels?

better place; if worse, to a worse.
905

You complain of the prosperity of the wicked, not seeing how all things work together for the good of the whole.

We turn to him who believes that the Gods may be appeased.

The Gods are our allies in the great

[1] Hom. Odyss. xix. 43.

conflict
which is
going on
between
good and
evil.

But some
men
fawn
upon
them in
the be-
lief that
they can
be flat-
tered and
bribed
into the
betrayal
of
justice.

Perhaps they might be compared to the generals of armies, or they might be likened to physicians providing against the diseases which make war upon the body, or to husbandmen observing anxiously the effects of the seasons on the growth of plants; or perhaps to shepherds of flocks. For as we acknowledge the world to be full of many goods and also of evils, and of more evils than goods, there is, as we affirm, an immortal conflict going on among us, which requires marvellous watchfulness; and in that conflict the Gods and demigods are our allies, and we are their property. Injustice and insolence and folly are the destruction of us, and justice and temperance and wisdom are our salvation; and the place of these latter is in the life of the Gods, although some vestige of them may occasionally be discerned among mankind. But upon this earth we know that there dwell souls possessing an unjust spirit[1], who may be compared to brute animals, which fawn upon their keepers, whether dogs or shepherds, or the best and most perfect masters; for they in like manner, as the voices of the wicked declare, prevail by flattery and prayers and incantations, and are allowed to make their gains with impunity. And this sin, which is termed dishonesty, is an evil of the same kind as what is termed disease in living bodies or pestilence in years or seasons of the year, and in cities and governments has another name, which is injustice.

Cle. Quite true.

Ath. What else can he say who declares that the Gods are always lenient to the doers of unjust acts, if they divide the spoil with them? As if wolves were to toss a portion of their prey to the dogs, and they, mollified by the gift, suffered them to tear the flocks[2]. Must not he who maintains that the Gods can be propitiated argue thus?

Cle. Precisely so.

Ath. And to which of the above-mentioned classes of guardians would any man compare the Gods without absurdity? Will he say that they are like pilots, who are themselves turned away from their duty by 'libations of wine and the savour of fat,' and at last overturn both ship and sailors?

Cle. Assuredly not.

Ath. And surely they are not like charioteers who are bribed to give up the victory to other chariots?

Cle. That would be a fearful image of the Gods.

Ath. Nor are they like generals, or physicians, or husbandmen, or shepherds; and no one would compare them to dogs who have been silenced by wolves.

[1] Reading λῆμα. [2] Cp. Rep. ii. 365 E.

Cle. A thing not to be spoken of.

Ath. And are not all the Gods the chiefest of all guardians, and do they not guard our highest interests?

Cle. Yes; the chiefest.

Ath. And shall we say that those who guard our noblest interests, and are the best of guardians, are inferior in virtue to dogs, and to men even of moderate excellence, who would never betray justice for the sake of gifts which unjust men impiously offer them?

Cle. Certainly not; nor is such a notion to be endured, and he who holds this opinion may be fairly singled out and characterized as of all impious men the wickedest and most impious.

Ath. Then are the three assertions—that the Gods exist, and that they take care of men, and that they can never be persuaded to do injustice, now sufficiently demonstrated? May we say that they are?

Cle. You have our entire assent to your words.

Ath. I have spoken with vehemence because I am zealous against evil men; and I will tell you, dear Cleinias, why I am so. I would not have the wicked think that, having the superiority in argument, they may do as they please and act according to their various imaginations about the Gods; and this zeal has led me to speak too vehemently; but if we have at all succeeded in persuading the men to hate themselves and love their opposites, the prelude of our laws about impiety will not have been spoken in vain.

Cle. So let us hope; and even if we have failed, the style of our argument will not discredit the lawgiver.

Ath. After the prelude shall follow a discourse, which will be the interpreter of the law; this shall proclaim to all impious persons that they must depart from their ways and go over to the pious. And to those who disobey, let the law about impiety be as follows:—If a man is guilty of any impiety in word or deed, any one who happens to be present shall give information to the magistrates, in aid of the law; and let the magistrates who first receive the information bring him before the appointed court according to the law; and if a magistrate, after receiving information, refuses to act, he shall be tried for impiety at the instance of any one who is willing to vindicate the laws; and if any one be cast, the court shall estimate the punishment of each act of impiety; and let all such criminals be imprisoned. There shall be three prisons in the state: the first of them is to be the common prison in the neighbourhood of the agora for the safe-keeping of the generality of offenders; another is to be in the neighbourhood of the nocturnal council[1], and is to be called the

[1] Cp. *infra,* xii. 951, 961.

We cannot, however, suppose the Gods to be worse than even moderately good men.

A righteous zeal must excuse our warmth.

The law about impiety.

Method of procedure.

908

The three
sorts of
impious
persons
are
either
(1) hon-
est, or
(2) dis-
honest.

'House of Reformation'; another, to be situated in some wild and desolate region in the centre of the country, shall be called by some name expressive of retribution. Now, men fall into impiety from three causes, which have been already mentioned, and from each of these causes arise two sorts of impiety, in all six, which are worth distinguishing, and should not all have the same punishment. For he who does not believe in the Gods, and yet has a righteous nature, hates the wicked and dislikes and refuses to do injustice, and avoids unrighteous men, and lóves the righteous. But they who besides believing that the world is devoid of Gods are intemperate, and have at the same time good memories and quick wits, are worse; although both of them are unbelievers, much less injury is done by the one than by the other. The one may talk loosely about the Gods and about sacrifices and oaths, and perhaps by laughing at other men he may make them like himself, if he be not punished. But the other who holds the same opinions and is called a clever man, is full of stratagem and deceit—men of this class deal in prophecy and jugglery of all kinds, and out of their ranks sometimes come tyrants and demagogues and generals and hierophants of private mysteries and the Sophists, as they are termed, with their ingenious devices. There are many kinds of unbelievers, but two only for whom legis-lation is required; one the hypocritical sort, whose crime is deserv-ing of death many times over, while the other needs only bonds and admonition. In like manner also the notion that the Gods take no thought of men produces two other sorts of crimes, and the notion that they may be propitiated produces two more. Assuming these divisions, let those who have been made what they are only from want of understanding, and not from malice or an evil nature, be placed by the judge in the House of Reformation, and ordered to suffer imprisonment during a period of not less than five years. And in the meantime let them have no intercourse with the other citi-zens, except with members of the nocturnal council, and with them let them converse with a view to the improvement of their soul's health. And when the time of their imprisonment has expired, if any of them be of sound mind let him be restored to sane company, but if not, and if he be condemned a second time, let him be punished with death. As to that class of monstrous natures who not only be-lieve that there are no Gods, or that they are negligent, or to be propitiated, but in contempt of mankind conjure the souls of the living[1] and say that they can conjure the dead and promise to charm the Gods with sacrifices and prayers, and will utterly over-throw individuals and whole houses and states for the sake of

The first
class are
to be
placed in
solitary
confine-
[909]
ment for
five
years;
and, if
they re-
pent, at
the end
of that
time they
shall be
restored
to so-
ciety.

If they
again of-
fend, they
shall die.

[1] Cp. Rep. ii. 364.

money—let him who is guilty of any of these things be condemned by the court to be bound according to law in the prison which is in the centre of the land, and let no freeman ever approach him, but let him receive the rations of food appointed by the guardians of the law from the hands of the public slaves; and when he is dead let him be cast beyond the borders unburied, and if any freeman assist in burying him, let him pay the penalty of impiety to any one who is willing to bring a suit against him. But if he leaves behind him children who are fit to be citizens, let the guardians of orphans take care of them, just as they would of any other orphans, from the day on which their father is convicted.

In all these cases there should be one law, which will make men in general less liable to transgress in word or deed, and less foolish, because they will not be allowed to practise religious rites contrary to law. And let this be the simple form of the law:—No man shall have sacred rites in a private house. When he would sacrifice, let him go to the temples and hand over his offerings to the priests and priestesses, who see to the sanctity of such things, and let him pray himself, and let any one who pleases join with him in prayer. The reason of this is as follows:—Gods and temples are not easily instituted, and to establish them rightly is the work of a mighty intellect. And women especially, and men too, when they are sick or in danger, or in any sort of difficulty, or again on their receiving any good fortune, have a way of consecrating the occasion, vowing sacrifices, and promising shrines to Gods, demigods, and sons of Gods; and when they are awakened by terrible apparitions and dreams or remember visions, they find in altars and temples the remedies of them, and will fill every house and village with them, placing them in the open air, or wherever they may have had such visions; and with a view to all these cases we should obey the law. The law has also regard to the impious, and would not have them fancy that by the secret performance of these actions—by raising temples and by building altars in private houses, they can propitiate the God secretly with sacrifices and prayers, while they are really multiplying their crimes infinitely, bringing guilt from heaven upon themselves, and also upon those who permit them, and who are better men than they are; and the consequence is that the whole state reaps the fruit of their impiety, which, in a certain sense, is deserved. Assuredly God will not blame the legislator, who will enact the following law: —No one shall possess shrines of the Gods in private houses, and he who is found to possess them, and perform any sacred rites not publicly authorized,—supposing the offender to be some man or woman who is not guilty of any other great and impious crime,—

Laws X

ATHE-
NIAN.

The
second
class are
to be im-
prisoned
for life,
and when
dead to
be cast
beyond
the
border.

Their
children
to be
cared for,
like
other
orphans.

Men must
not make
a re-
ligion for
them-
selves.
910
Only a
great in-
telligence
can
establish
Gods and
temples.

Private
rites
to be
trans-
ferred to
temples
under a
penalty.

shall be informed against by him who is acquainted with the fact, which shall be announced by him to the guardians of the law; and let them issue orders that he or she shall carry away their private rites to the public temples, and if they do not persuade them, let them inflict a penalty on them until they comply. And if a person be proven guilty of impiety, not merely from childish levity, but such as grown-up men may be guilty of, whether he have sacrificed publicly or privately to any Gods, let him be punished with death, for his sacrifice is impure. Whether the deed has been done in earnest, or only from childish levity, let the guardians of the law determine, before they bring the matter into court and prosecute the offender for impiety.

BOOK XI

913
Laws XI

ATHE-
NIAN.

Dealings
between
man and
man: the
princi-
ples
which
should
regulate
them.

Treasure-
trove.

IN the next place, dealings between man and man require to be suitably regulated. The principle of them is very simple:—Thou shalt not, if thou canst help, touch that which is mine, or remove the least thing which belongs to me without my consent; and may I be of a sound mind, and do to others as I would that they should do to me. First, let us speak of treasure trove:—May I never pray the Gods to find the hidden treasure, which another has laid up for himself and his family, he not being one of my ancestors, nor lift, if I should find, such a treasure. And may I never have any dealings with those who are called diviners, and who in any way or manner counsel me to take up the deposit entrusted to the earth, for I should not gain so much in the increase of my possessions, if I take up the prize, as I should grow in justice and virtue of soul, if I abstain; and this will be a better possession to me than the other in a better part of myself; for the possession of justice in the soul is preferable to the possession of wealth. And of many things it is well said,—'Move not the immovables,' and this may be regarded as one of them. And we shall do well to believe the common tradition which says, that such deeds prevent a man from having a family. Now as to him who is careless about having children and regardless of the legislator, taking up that which neither he deposited, nor any ancestor of his, without the consent of the depositor, violating the simplest and noblest of laws which was the enactment of no mean man:—'Take not up that which was not laid down by thee,'—of him, I say, who despises these two legislators, and takes up, not small matter which he has not deposited, but perhaps a great heap of treasure, what he ought to suffer at the hands of the Gods, God only knows; but I would have the first person who sees him go and tell the wardens of the city, if the occurrence has taken place in the city, or if the occurrence has taken place in the agora he shall tell the wardens of the agora, or if in the country he shall tell the wardens of the country and their commanders[1]. When information has been received the city shall send to Delphi, and, whatever the God answers about the money and the remover of the money, that the city shall do in obedience to the oracle; the informer, if he be a freeman, shall have the honour of doing rightly, and he who informs not, the dishonour of doing wrongly; and if he be a slave who gives information, let him be freed, as he ought to be, by the state, which shall give his master the price of him; but if he do not inform he shall be punished with death. Next in order shall follow a similar law, which shall apply equally to matters great and small:—If a man happens to leave behind him some part of his property, whether intentionally or unintentionally, let him who may come upon the left property suffer it to remain, reflecting that such things are under the protection of the Goddess of ways, and are dedicated to her by the law. But if any one defies the law, and takes the property home with him, let him, if the thing is of little worth, and the man who takes it a slave, be beaten with many stripes by him, being a person of not less than thirty years of age. Or if he be a freeman, in addition to being thought a mean person and a despiser of the laws, let him pay ten times the value of the treasure which he has moved to the leaver. And if some one accuses another of having anything which belongs to him, whether little or much, and the other admits that he has this thing, but denies that the property in dispute belongs to the other, if the property be registered with the magistrates according to law, the claimant shall summon the possessor, who shall bring it before the magistrates; and when it is brought into court, if it be registered in the public registers, to which of the litigants it belonged, let him take it and go his way. Or if the property be registered as belonging to some one who is not present, whoever will offer sufficient surety on behalf of the absent person that he will give it up to him, shall take it away as the representative of the other. But if the property which is deposited be not registered with the magistrates, let it remain until the time of trial with three of the eldest of the magistrates; and if it be an animal which is deposited, then he who loses the suit shall pay the magis-

914
The punishment of a man who removes treasure to be fixed by the God of Delphi.

The penalties of the law for those who take away what others leave behind.

How cases of disputed ownership are to be determined.

---

[1] Cp. *supra*, vi. 760.

Laws XI

ATHE-
NIAN.

A man
may car-
ry off his
own
slave, the
runaway
slave of a
friend, or
a dis-
loyal
freedman.

915

The du-
ties and
condi-
tions of
freed-
manship.

Disputed
posses-
sions.

Goods to
be sold at

trates for its keep, and they shall determine the cause within three days.

Any one who is of sound mind may arrest his own slave, and do with him whatever he will of such things as are lawful; and he may arrest the runaway slave of any of his friends or kindred with a view to his safe-keeping. And if any one takes away him who is being carried off as a slave, intending to liberate him, he who is carrying him off shall let him go; but he who takes him away shall give three sufficient sureties; and if he give them, and not without giving them, he may take him away, but if he take him away after any other manner he shall be deemed guilty of violence, and being convicted shall pay as a penalty double the amount of the damages claimed to him who has been deprived of the slave. Any man may also carry off a freedman, if he do not pay respect or sufficient respect to him who freed him. Now the respect shall be, that the freedman go three times in the month to the hearth of the person who freed him, and offer to do whatever he ought, so far as he can; and he shall agree to make such a marriage as his former master approves. He shall not be permitted to have more property than he who gave him liberty, and what more he has shall belong to his master. The freedman shall not remain in the state more than twenty years, but like other foreigners[1] shall go away, taking his entire property with him, unless he has the consent of the magistrates and of his former master to remain. If a freedman or any other stranger has a property greater than the census of the third class, at the expiration of thirty days from the day on which this comes to pass, he shall take that which is his and go his way, and in this case he shall not be allowed to remain any longer by the magistrates. And if any one disobeys this regulation, and is brought into court and convicted, he shall be punished with death, and his property shall be confiscated. Suits about these matters shall take place before the tribes, unless the plaintiff and defendant have got rid of the accusation either before their neighbours or before judges chosen by them. If a man lay claim to any animal or anything else which he declares to be his, let the possessor refer to the seller or to some honest and trustworthy person, who has given, or in some legitimate way made over the property to him; if he be a citizen or a metic, sojourning in the city, within thirty days, or, if the property have been delivered to him by a stranger, within five months, of which the middle month shall include the summer solstice[2]. When goods are exchanged by selling and buying, a man shall deliver them, and receive the price of them, at a fixed place in

[1] Cp. *supra*, viii. 850.   [2] Cp. *infra*. xii. 952 E.

the agora, and have done with the matter; but he shall not buy or sell anywhere else, nor give credit. And if in any other manner or in any other place there be an exchange of one thing for another, and the seller give credit to the man who buys from him, he must do this on the understanding that the law gives no protection in cases of things sold not in accordance with these regulations[1]. Again, as to contributions, any man who likes may go about collecting contributions as a friend among friends, but if any difference arises about the collection, he is to act on the understanding that the law gives no protection in such cases. He who sells anything above the value of fifty drachmas shall be required to remain in the city for ten days, and the purchaser shall be informed of the house of the seller, with a view to the sort of charges which are apt to arise in such cases, and the restitutions which the law allows. And let legal restitution be on this wise:—If a man sells a slave who is in a consumption, or who has the disease of the stone, or of strangury, or epilepsy, or some other tedious and incurable disorder of body or mind, which is not discernible to the ordinary man, if the purchaser be a physician or trainer, he shall have no right of restitution; nor shall there be any right of restitution if the seller has told the truth beforehand to the buyer. But if a skilled person sells to another who is not skilled, let the buyer appeal for restitution within six months, except in the case of epilepsy, and then the appeal may be made within a year. The cause shall be determined by such physicians as the parties may agree to choose; and the defendant, if he lose the suit, shall pay double the price at which he sold. If a private person sell to another private person, he shall have the right of restitution, and the decision shall be given as before, but the defendant, if he be cast, shall only pay back the price of the slave. If a person sells a homicide to another, and they both know of the fact, let there be no restitution in such a case, but if he do not know of the fact, there shall be a right of restitution, whenever the buyer makes the discovery; and the decision shall rest with the five youngest guardians of the law, and if the decision be that the seller was cognisant of the fact, he shall purify the house of the purchaser, according to the law of the interpreters, and shall pay back three times the purchase-money.

If a man exchanges either money for money, or anything whatever for anything else, either with or without life, let him give and receive them genuine and unadulterated, in accordance with the law. And let us have a prelude about all this sort of roguery, like the preludes of our other laws. Every man should regard adulteration

[1] Cp. *supra,* viii. 849 E.

Laws XI

ATHE-
NIAN.

a fixed place: no credit to be given.

There will be no laws [916] about contributions.

Precaution against fraudulent sale.

When restitution is or is not to be made.

Prelude to the law about adulteration:— Adul-

Laws XI

ATHE-
NIAN.

teration
is a kind
of false-
hood and
perjury.

917

The
law:—
One
price to
be asked;
no puf-
fing, or
taking of
oaths.

Penalties
for adul-
teration.

as of one and the same class with falsehood and deceit, concerning which the many are too fond of saying that at proper times and places the practice may often be right. But they leave the occasion, and the when, and the where, undefined and unsettled, and from this want of definiteness in their language they do a great deal of harm to themselves and to others. Now a legislator ought not to leave the matter undetermined; he ought to prescribe some limit, either greater or less. Let this be the rule prescribed:—No one shall call the Gods to witness, when he says or does anything false or deceitful or dishonest, unless he would be the most hateful of mankind to them. And he is most hateful to them who takes a false oath, and pays no heed to the Gods; and in the next degree, he who tells a falsehood in the presence of his superiors. Now better men are the superiors of worse men, and in general elders are the superiors of the young; wherefore also parents are the superiors of their offspring, and men of women and children, and rulers of their subjects; for all men ought to reverence any one who is in any position of authority, and especially those who are in state offices. And this is the reason why I have spoken of these matters. For every one who is guilty of adulteration in the ágora tells a falsehood, and deceives, and when he invokes the Gods, according to the customs and cautions of the wardens of the agora, he does but swear without any respect for God or man. Certainly, it is an excellent rule not lightly to defile the names of the Gods, after the fashion of men in general, who care little about piety and purity in their religious actions. But if a man will not conform to this rule, let the law be as follows:—He who sells anything in the agora shall not ask two prices for that which he sells, but he shall ask one price, and if he do not obtain this, he shall take away his goods; and on that day he shall not value them either at more or less; and there shall be no praising of any goods, or oath taken about them. If a person disobeys this command, any citizen who is present, not being less than thirty years of age, may with impunity chastise and beat the swearer, but if instead of obeying the laws he takes no heed, he shall be liable to the charge of having betrayed them. If a man sells any adulterated goods and will not obey these regulations, he who knows and can prove the fact, and does prove it in the presence of the magistrates, if he be a slave or a metic, shall have the adulterated goods; but if he be a citizen, and do not pursue the charge, he shall be called a rogue, and deemed to have robbed the Gods of the agora; or if he proves the charge, he shall dedicate the goods to the Gods of the agora. He who is proved to have sold any adulterated goods, in addition to losing the goods themselves, shall be beaten with stripes,—a stripe for a drachma, according to the price of the goods; and the herald shall proclaim in the agora the offence for which he is going to be beaten. The wardens of the agora and the guardians of the law shall obtain information from experienced persons about the rogueries and adulterations of the sellers, and shall write up what the seller ought and ought not to do in each case; and let them inscribe their laws on a column in front of the court of the wardens of the agora, that they may be clear instructors of those who have business in the agora. Enough has been said in what has preceded about the wardens of the city, and if anything seems to be wanting, let them communicate with the guardians of the law, and write down the omission, and place on a column in the court of the wardens of the city the primary and secondary regulations which are laid down for them about their office.

After the practices of adulteration naturally follow the practices of retail trade. Concerning these, we will first of all give a word of counsel and reason, and the law shall come afterwards. Retail trade in a city is not by nature intended to do any harm, but quite the contrary; for is not he a benefactor who reduces the inequalities and incommensurabilities of goods to equality and common measure? And this is what the power of money accomplishes, and the merchant may be said to be appointed for this purpose. The hireling and the tavern-keeper, and many other occupations, some of them more and others less seemly—alike have this object;—they seek to satisfy our needs and equalize our possessions[1]. Let us then endeavour to see what has brought retail trade into ill-odour, and wherein lies the dishonour and unseemliness of it, in order that if not entirely, we may yet partially, cure the evil by legislation. To effect this is no easy matter, and requires a great deal of virtue.

Cle. What do you mean?

Ath. Dear Cleinias, the class of men is small—they must have been rarely gifted by nature, and trained by education,—who, when assailed by wants and desires, are able to hold out and observe moderation, and when they might make a great deal of money are sober in their wishes, and prefer a moderate to a large gain. But the mass of mankind are the very opposite: their desires are unbounded, and when they might gain in moderation they prefer gains without limit; wherefore all that relates to retail trade, and merchandise, and the keeping of taverns, is denounced and numbered among dishonourable things. For if what I trust may never be and will not be, we were to compel, if I may venture to say a ridiculous thing, the best men everywhere to keep taverns for a time, or carry on re-

[1] Cp. Arist. Pol. i. 9, §§ 1-11.

Laws XI

ATHE-
NIAN,
CLEINIAS.

918

Retail
trade.

Its ob-
jects are
laudable:

why,
then, is it
so des-
pised?

Because
it en-
courages
the love
of gain.

If good
men and
women
only kept

Laws XI

ATHE-
NIAN.

shops and
taverns,
retail
[919]
trade
would be
thought a
bene-
ficent oc-
cupation.

The ex-
tortionate
practices
now-a-
days have
brought
it into ill-
repute.

The rem-
edy:—
Retailers
to be few,
of the
meaner
sort, and
well
looked
after.

The
law:—
Retail
traders to
be, not
citizens,
but
metics or
strangers.

tail trade, or do anything of that sort; or if, in consequence of some fate or necessity, the best women were compelled to follow similar callings, then we should know how agreeable and pleasant all these things are; and if all such occupations were managed on incorrupt principles, they would be honoured as we honour a mother or a nurse. But now that a man goes to desert places and builds houses which can only be reached by long journeys, for the sake of retail trade, and receives strangers who are in need at the welcome resting-place, and gives them peace and calm when they are tossed by the storm, or cool shade in the heat; and then instead of behaving to them as friends, and showing the duties of hospitality to his guests, treats them as enemies and captives who are at his mercy, and will not release them until they have paid the most unjust, abominable, and extortionate ransom,—these are the sort of practices, and foul evils they are, which cast a reproach upon the succour of adversity. And the legislator ought always to be devising a remedy for evils of this nature. There is an ancient saying, which is also a true one—'To fight against two opponents is a difficult thing,' as is seen in diseases and in many other cases. And in this case also the war is against two enemies—wealth and poverty; one of whom corrupts the soul of man with luxury, while the other drives him by pain into utter shamelessness. What remedy can a city of sense find against this disease? In the first place, they must have as few retail traders as possible; and in the second place, they must assign the occupation to that class of men whose corruption will be the least injury to the state; and in the third place, they must devise some way whereby the followers of these occupations themselves will not readily fall into habits of unbridled shamelessness and meanness.

After this preface let our law run as follows, and may fortune favour us:—No landowner among the Magnetes, whose city the God is restoring and resettling—no one, that is, of the 5040 families, shall become a retail trader either voluntarily or involuntarily; neither shall he be a merchant, or do any service for private persons unless they equally serve him, except for his father or his mother, and their fathers and mothers; and in general for his elders who are freemen[1], and whom he serves as a freeman. Now it is difficult to determine accurately the things which are worthy or unworthy of a freeman, but let those who have obtained the prize of virtue give judgment about them in accordance with their feelings of right and wrong. He who in any way shares in the illiberality of retail trades may be indicted for dishonouring his race by any one who likes, be-

---

[1] Placing a comma after ἐλεύθεροι.

fore those who have been judged to be the first in virtue; and if he appear to throw dirt upon his father's house by an unworthy occupation, let him be imprisoned for a year and abstain from that sort of thing; and if he repeat the offence, for two years; and every time that he is convicted let the length of his imprisonment be doubled. This shall be the second law:—He who engages in retail trade must be either a metic or a stranger. And a third law shall be:—In order that the retail trader who dwells in our city may be as good or as little bad as possible, the guardians of the law shall remember that they are not only guardians of those who may be easily watched and prevented from becoming lawless or bad, because they are well-born and bred; but still more should they have a watch over those who are of another sort, and follow pursuits which have a very strong tendency to make men bad. And, therefore, in respect of the multifarious occupations of retail trade, that is to say, in respect of such of them as are allowed to remain, because they seem to be quite necessary in a state,—about these the guardians of the law should meet and take counsel with those who have experience of the several kinds of retail trade, as we before commanded concerning adulteration (which is a matter akin to this), and when they meet they shall consider what amount of receipts, after deducting expenses, will produce a moderate gain to the retail trades, and they shall fix in writing and strictly maintain what they find to be the right percentage of profit; this shall be seen to by the wardens of the agora, and by the wardens of the city, and by the wardens of the country. And so retail trade will benefit every one, and do the least possible injury to those in the state who practise it.

When a man makes an agreement which he does not fulfil, unless the agreement be of a nature which the law or a vote of the assembly does not allow, or which he has made under the influence of some unjust compulsion, or which he is prevented from fulfilling against his will by some unexpected chance, the other party may go to law with him in the courts of the tribes, for not having completed his agreement, if the parties are not able previously to come to terms before arbiters or before their neighbours. The class of craftsmen who have furnished human life with the arts is dedicated to Hephaestus and Athene; and there is a class of craftsmen who preserve the works of all craftsmen by arts of defence, the votaries of Ares and Athene, to which divinities they too are rightly dedicated. All these continue through life serving the country and the people; some of them are leaders in battle; others make for hire implements and works, and they ought not to deceive in such matters, out of respect to the Gods who are their ancestors. If any craftsman

The punishment for citizens who disobey.

The guardians of the law shall determine the rate of profit.

Breaches of contract to be actionable.

Laws XI

ATHE-
NIAN.

Punish-
ment for
not ful-
filling a
contract
within
the ap-
pointed
time.

No over-
charge.

through indolence omit to execute his work in a given time, not
reverencing the God who gives him the means of life, but considering, foolish fellow, that he is his own God and will let him off easily,
in the first place, he shall suffer at the hands of the God, and in the
second place, the law shall follow in a similar spirit. He shall owe to
him who contracted with him the price of the works which he has
failed in performing, and he shall begin again and execute them
gratis in the given time. When a man undertakes a work, the law
gives him the same advice which was given to the seller, that he
should not attempt to raise the price, but simply ask the value; this
the law enjoins also on the contractor; for the craftsman assuredly
knows the value of his work. Wherefore, in free states the man of
art ought not to attempt to impose upon private individuals by the
help of his art, which is by nature a true thing; and he who is
wronged in a matter of this sort, shall have a right of action against
the party who has wronged him. And if any one lets out work to a
craftsman, and does not pay him duly according to the lawful a-
greement, disregarding Zeus the guardian of the city and Athene,
who are the partners of the state, and overthrows the foundations
of society for the sake of a little gain, in his case let the law and the

The price,
if not
paid at
the time
agreed,
shall be
doubled.

Soldiers
and gen-
erals, also,
like other
crafts-
men,
should
have their
reward,
though
not the
highest;
—this is
  [922]
reserved
for men
who hon-
our the
law.

Gods maintain the common bonds of the state. And let him who,
having already received the work in exchange, does not pay the
price in the time agreed, pay double the price; and if a year has e-
lapsed, although interest is not to be taken on loans, yet for every
drachma which he owes to the contractor let him pay a monthly
interest of an obol. Suits about these matters are to be decided by
the courts of the tribes; and by the way, since we have mentioned
craftsmen at all, we must not forget the other craft of war, in which
generals and tacticians are the craftsmen, who undertake voluntarily the work of our safety, as other craftsmen undertake other
public works;—if they execute their work well the law will never
tire of praising him who gives them[1] those honours which are the
just rewards of the soldier; but if any one, having already received
the benefit of any noble service in war, does not make the due return of honour, the law will blame him. Let this then be the law,
having an ingredient of praise, not compelling but advising the
great body of the citizens to honour the brave men who are the saviours of the whole state, whether by their courage or by their military skill;—they should honour them, I say, in the second place; for
the first and highest tribute of respect is to be given to those who
are able above other men to honour the words of good legislators.

  The greater part of the dealings between man and man have been

---

[1] Reading, according to Schneider, ὃς τούτοις αὖ.

now regulated by us with the exception of those that relate to orphans and the supervision of orphans by their guardians. These
follow next in order, and must be regulated in some way. But to
arrive at them we must begin with the testamentary wishes of the
dying and the case of those who may have happened to die intestate. When I said, Cleinias, that we must regulate them, I had in my
mind the difficulty and perplexity in which all such matters are involved. You cannot leave them unregulated, for individuals would
make regulations at variance with one another, and repugnant to
the laws and habits of the living and to their own previous habits,
if a person were simply allowed to make any will which he pleased,
and this were to take effect in whatever state he may have been at
the end of his life; for most of us lose our senses in a manner, and
feel crushed when we think that we are about to die.

The
wishes
of the
dying to
be made
subject to
the in-
terests of
the living.

Cle. What do you mean, Stranger?

Ath. O Cleinias, a man when he is about to die is an intractable
creature, and is apt to use language which causes a great deal of
anxiety and trouble to the legislator.

Cle. In what way?

Ath. He wants to have the entire control of all his property, and
will use angry words.

Cle. Such as what?

Ath. O ye Gods, he will say, how monstrous that I am not allowed
to give, or not to give, my own to whom I will—less to him who has
been bad to me, and more to him who has been good to me, and
whose badness and goodness have been tested by me in time of
sickness or in old age and in every other sort of fortune!

The fret-
ful com-
paints of
the dying
man;

Cle. Well, Stranger, and may he not very fairly say so?

Ath. In my opinion, Cleinias, the ancient legislators were too
good-natured, and made laws without sufficient observation or consideration of human things.

Cle. What do you mean?

Ath. I mean, my friend, that they were afraid of the testator's
reproaches, and so they passed a law to the effect that a man should
be allowed to dispose of his property in all respects as he liked; but
you and I, if I am not mistaken, will have something better to say
to our departing citizens.

923

Cle. What?

Ath. O my friends, we will say to them, hard is it for you, who are
creatures of a day, to know what is yours,—hard too, as the Delphic
oracle says, to know yourselves at this hour. Now I, as the legislator, regard you and your possessions, not as belonging to yourselves, but as belonging to your whole family, both past and future,

and the
legisla-
tor's an-
swer to
them.

and yet more do I regard both family and possessions as belonging to the state; wherefore, if some one steals upon you with flattery, when you are tossed on the sea of disease or old age, and persuades you to dispose of your property in a way that is not for the best, I will not, if I can help, allow this; but I will legislate with a view to the whole, considering what is best both for the state and for the family, esteeming as I ought the feelings of an individual at a lower rate; and I hope that you will depart in peace and kindness towards us, as you are going the way of all mankind; and we will impartially take care of all your concerns, not neglecting any of them, if we can possibly help. Let this be our prelude and consolation to the living and dying, Cleinias, and let the law be as follows:
—He who makes a disposition in a testament, if he be the father of a family, shall first of all inscribe as his heir any one of his sons whom he may think fit; and if he gives any of his children to be adopted by another citizen, let the adoption be inscribed. And if he has a son remaining over and above who has not been adopted upon any lot, and who may be expected to be sent out to a colony according to law, to him his father may give as much as he pleases of the rest of his property, with the exception of the paternal lot and the fixtures on the lot. And if there are other sons, let him distribute among them what there is more than the lot in such portions as he pleases. And if one of the sons has already a house of his own, he shall not give him of the money, nor shall he give money to a daughter who has been betrothed, but if she is not betrothed he may give her money. And if any of the sons or daughters shall be found to have another lot of land in the country, which has accrued after the testament has been made, they shall leave the lot which they have inherited to the heir of the man who has made the will. If the testator has no sons, but only daughters, let him choose the husband of any one of his daughters whom he pleases, and leave and inscribe him as his son and heir. And if a man have lost his son, when he was a child, and before he could be reckoned among grown-up men, whether his own or an adopted son, let the testator make mention of the circumstance and inscribe whom he will to be his second son in hope of better fortune. If the testator has no children at all, he may select and give to any one whom he pleases the tenth part of the property which he has acquired; but let him not be blamed if he gives all the rest to his adopted son, and makes a friend of him according to the law. If the sons of a man require guardians, and the father when he dies leaves a will appointing guardians, those who have been named by him, whoever they are and whatever their number be, if they are able and willing to take charge of the

children, shall be recognized according to the provisions of the will. But if he dies and has made no will, or a will in which he has appointed no guardians, then the next of kin, two on the father's and two on the mother's side, and one of the friends of the deceased, shall have the authority of guardians, whom the guardians of the law shall appoint when the orphans require guardians. And the fifteen eldest guardians of the law shall have the whole care and charge of the orphans, divided into threes according to seniority,— a body of three for one year, and then another body of three for the next year, until the cycle of the five periods is complete; and this, as far as possible, is to continue always. If a man dies, having made no will at all, and leaves sons who require the care of guardians, they shall share in the protection which is afforded by these laws. And if a man dying by some unexpected fate leaves daughters behind him, let him pardon the legislator if when he gives them in marriage, he have a regard only to two out of three conditions,—nearness of kin and the preservation of the lot, and omits the third condition, which a father would naturally consider, for he would choose out of all the citizens a son for himself, and a husband for his daughter, with a view to his character and disposition—the father, I say, shall forgive the legislator if he disregards this, which to him is an impossible consideration. Let the law about these matters where practicable be as follows:—If a man dies without making a will, and leaves behind him daughters, let his brother, being the son of the same father or of the same mother, having no lot, marry the daughter and have the lot of the dead man. And if he have no brother, but only a brother's son, in like manner let them marry, if they be of a suitable age; and if there be not even a brother's son, but only the son of a sister, let them do likewise, and so in the fourth degree, if there be only the testator's father's brother, or in the fifth degree, his father's brother's son, or in a sixth degree, the child of his father's sister. Let kindred be always reckoned in this way: if a person leaves daughters the relationship shall proceed upwards through brothers and sisters, and brothers' and sisters' children, and first the males shall come, and after them the females in the same family. The judge shall consider and determine the suitableness or unsuitableness of age in marriage; he shall make an inspection of the males naked, and of the women naked down to the navel. And if there be a lack of kinsmen in a family extending to grandchildren of a brother, or to the grandchildren of a grandfather's children, the maiden may choose with the consent of her guardians any one of the citizens who is willing and whom she wills, and he shall be the heir of the dead man, and the husband of his daughter. Circumstances vary, and there may sometimes be a still greater lack of relations within the limits of the state; and if any maiden has no kindred living in the city, and there is some one who has been sent out to a colony, and she is disposed to make him the heir of her father's possessions, if he be indeed of her kindred, let him proceed to take the lot according to the regulation of the law; but if he be not of her kindred, she having no kinsmen within the city, and he be chosen by the daughter of the dead man, and empowered to marry by the guardians, let him return home and take the lot of him who died intestate. And if a man has no children, either male or female, and dies without making a will, let the previous law in general hold; and let a man and a woman go forth from the family and share the deserted house, and let the lot belong absolutely to them; and let the heiress in the first degree be a sister, and in a second degree a daughter of a brother, and in the third, a daughter of a sister, in the fourth degree the sister of a father, and in the fifth degree the daughter of a father's brother, and in a sixth degree of a father's sister; and these shall dwell with their male kinsmen, according to the degree of relationship and right, as we enacted before. Now we must not conceal from ourselves that such laws are apt to be oppressive and that there may sometimes be a hardship in the lawgiver commanding the kinsman of the dead man to marry his relation; he may be thought not to have considered the innumerable hindrances which may arise among men in the execution of such ordinances; for there may be cases in which the parties refuse to obey, and are ready to do anything rather than marry, when there is some bodily or mental malady or defect among those who are bidden to marry or be married. Persons may fancy that the legislator never thought of this, but they are mistaken; wherefore let us make a common prelude on behalf of the lawgiver and of his subjects, the law begging the latter to forgive the legislator, in that he, having to take care of the common weal, cannot order at the same time the various circumstances of individuals, and begging him to pardon them if naturally they are sometimes unable to fulfil the act which he in his ignorance imposes upon them.

The legislator is well aware that his law may
[926]
be oppressive, but he must sometimes sacrifice individuals for the state.

Cle. And how, Stranger, can we act most fairly under the circumstances?

Ath. There must be arbiters chosen to deal with such laws and the subjects of them.

Cle. What do you mean?

Ath. I mean to say, that a case may occur in which the nephew, having a rich father, will be unwilling to marry the daughter of his uncle; he will have a feeling of pride, and he will wish to look higher. And there are cases in which the legislator will be imposing upon him the greatest calamity, and he will be compelled to disobey the law, if he is required, for example, to take a wife who is mad, or has some other terrible malady of soul or body, such as makes life intolerable to the sufferer. Then let what we are saying concerning these cases be embodied in a law:—If any one finds fault with the established laws respecting testaments, both as to other matters and especially in what relates to marriage, and asserts that the legislator, if he were alive and present, would not compel him to obey,—that is to say, would not compel those who are by our law required to marry or be given in marriage, to do either,—and some kinsman or guardian dispute this, the reply is that the legislator left fifteen of the guardians of the law to be arbiters and fathers of orphans, male or female, and to them let the disputants have recourse, and by their aid determine any matters of the kind, admitting their decision to be final. But if any one thinks that too great power is thus given to the guardians of the law, let him bring his adversaries into the court of the select judges, and there have the points in dispute determined. And he who loses the cause shall have censure and blame from the legislator, which, by a man of sense, is felt to be a penalty far heavier than a great loss of money.

Thus will orphan children have a second birth. After their first birth we spoke of their nurture and education, and after their second birth, when they have lost their parents, we ought to take measures that the misfortune of orphanhood may be as little sad to them as possible. In the first place, we say that the guardians of the law are lawgivers and fathers to them, not inferior to their natural fathers. Moreover, they shall take charge of them year by year[1] as of their own kindred; and we have given both to them and to the children's own guardians a suitable admonition concerning the nurture of orphans. And we seem to have spoken opportunely in our former discourse[2], when we said that the souls of the dead have the power after death of taking an interest in human affairs, about which there are many tales and traditions, long indeed, but true; and seeing that they are so many and so ancient, we must believe them, and we must also believe the lawgivers, who tell us that these things are true, if they are not to be regarded as utter fools. But if these things are really so, in the first place men should have a fear of the Gods above, who regard the loneliness of the orphans; and in the second place of the souls of the departed, who by nature incline to take an especial care of their own children, and are

[1] Cp. *supra,* 924 C.   [2] Cp. *supra,* ix. 865 E.

look upon
them, and
aged and
venerable
persons
have a
care of
them.

friendly to those who honour, and unfriendly to those who dishon-our them. Men should also fear the souls of the living who are aged and high in honour; wherever a city is well ordered and prosperous, their descendants cherish them, and so live happily; old persons are quick to see and hear all that relates to them, and are propitious to those who are just in the fulfilment of such duties, and they punish those who wrong the orphan and the desolate, considering that they are the greatest and most sacred of trusts. To all which matters the guardian and magistrate ought to apply his mind, if he has any, and take heed of the nurture and education of the orphans, seeking in every possible way to do them good, for he is making a contri-bution[1] to his own good and that of his children. He who obeys the tale which precedes the law, and does no wrong to an orphan, will never experience the wrath of the legislator. But he who is disobe-dient, and wrongs any one who is bereft of father or mother, shall

The
guard-
ian shall
educate
the
orphan
and man-
age his
property
as if he
were his
own child.

pay twice the penalty which he would have paid if he had wronged one whose parents had been alive. As touching other legislation concerning guardians in their relation to orphans, or concerning magistrates and their superintendence of the guardians, if they did not possess[2] examples of the manner in which children of freemen should be brought up in the bringing up of their own children, and of the care of their property in the care of their own, or if they had not just laws fairly stated about these very things,—there would have been reason in making laws for them, under the idea that they were a peculiar class, and we might distinguish and make separate rules for the life of those who are orphans and of those who are not orphans. But as the case stands, the condition of orphans with us is not different from the case of those who have a father, though in regard to honour and dishonour, and the attention given to them, the two are not usually placed upon a level. Wherefore, touching

928

the legislation about orphans, the law speaks in serious accents, both of persuasion and threatening, and such a threat as the follow-ing will be by no means out of place:—He who is the guardian of an orphan of either sex, and he among the guardians of the law to whom the superintendence of this guardian has been assigned, shall love the unfortunate orphan as though he were his own child, and he shall be as careful and diligent in the management of his possessions as he would be if they were his own, or even more care-ful and diligent. Let every one who has the care of an orphan ob-serve this law. But any one who acts contrary to the law on these

Punish-
ment of
the fraud-
ulent or

matters, if he be a guardian of the child, may be fined by a magis-trate, or, if he be himself a magistrate, the guardian may bring him

---

[1] Or, 'as if he were making a contribution.'   [2] Reading εἰ μὲν μή.

before the court of select judges, and punish him, if convicted, by exacting a fine of double the amount of that inflicted by the court. And if a guardian appears to the relations of the orphan, or to any other citizen, to act negligently or dishonestly, let them bring him before the same court, and whatever damages are given against him, let him pay fourfold, and let half belong to the orphan and half to him who procured the conviction. If any orphan arrives at years of discretion, and thinks that he has been ill-used by his guardians, let him within five years of the expiration of the guardianship be allowed to bring them to trial; and if any of them be convicted, the court shall determine what he shall pay or suffer. And if a magistrate shall appear to have wronged the orphan by neglect, and he be convicted, let the court determine what he shall suffer or pay to the orphan, and if there be dishonesty in addition to neglect, besides paying the fine, let him be deposed from his office of guardian of the law, and let the state appoint another guardian of the law for the city and for the country in his room.

Greater differences than there ought to be sometimes arise between fathers and sons, on the part either of fathers who will be of opinion that the legislator should enact that they may, if they wish, lawfully renounce their son by the proclamation of a herald in the face of the world, or of sons who think that they should be allowed to indict their fathers on the charge of imbecility when they are disabled by disease or old age. These things only happen, as a matter of fact, where the natures of men are utterly bad; for where only half is bad, as, for example, if the father be not bad, but the son be bad, or conversely, no great calamity is the result of such an amount of hatred as this. In another state, a son disowned by his father would not of necessity cease to be a citizen, but in our state, of which these are to be the laws, the disinherited must necessarily emigrate into another country, for no addition can be made even of a single family to the 5040 households; and, therefore, he who deserves to suffer these things must be renounced not only by his father, who is a single person, but by the whole family, and what is done in these cases must be regulated by some such law as the following:—He who in the sad disorder of his soul has a mind, justly or unjustly, to expel from his family a son whom he has begotten and brought up, shall not lightly or at once execute his purpose; but first of all he shall collect together his own kinsmen, extending to cousins, and in like manner his son's kinsmen by the mother's side, and in their presence he shall accuse his son, setting forth that he deserves at the hands of them all to be dismissed from the family; and the son shall be allowed to address them in a similar manner,

Laws XI

ATHE-
NIAN.

negligent
trustee or
magis-
trate.

Quarrels
between
fathers
and sons.

A son can
only
be re-
[929]
nounced
by a fa-
ther with
the con-
sent of
the fam-
ily. When
re-
nounced,
he may
be
adopted
by an-
other
citizen:
but if he
be not

Laws XI

ATHE-
NIAN.

adopted
within
ten years,
he must
emigrate.

The char-
acters of
young
men are
subject to
many
changes.

An im-
becile
father
may be
deprived
of the
control
of his
affairs.

If hus-
band and
wife do
not agree,
[930]
let them
separate
and find
other
partners.

Regula-
tions re-
specting

and show that he does not deserve to suffer any of these things. And if the father persuades them, and obtains the suffrages of more than half of his kindred, exclusive of the father and mother and the offender himself—I say, if he obtains more than half the suffrages of all the other grown-up members of the family, of both sexes, the father shall be permitted to put away his son, but not otherwise. And if any other citizen is willing to adopt the son who is put away, no law shall hinder him; for the characters of young men are subject to many changes in the course of their lives. And if he has been put away, and in a period of ten years no one is willing to adopt him, let those who have the care of the superabundant population which is sent out into colonies, see to him, in order that he may be suitably provided for in the colony. And if disease or age or harshness of temper, or all these together, makes a man to be more out of his mind than the rest of the world are,—but this is not observable, except to those who live with him,—and he, being master of his property, is the ruin of the house, and his son doubts and hesitates about indicting his father for insanity, let the law in that case ordain that he shall first of all go to the eldest guardians of the law and tell them of his father's misfortune, and they shall duly look into the matter, and take counsel as to whether he shall indict him or not. And if they advise him to proceed, they shall be both his witnesses and his advocates; and if the father is cast, he shall henceforth be incapable of ordering the least particular of his life; let him be as a child dwelling in the house for the remainder of his days. And if a man and his wife have an unfortunate incompatibility of temper, ten of the guardians of the law, who are impartial[1], and ten of the women who regulate marriages[2], shall look to the matter, and if they are able to reconcile them they shall be formally reconciled; but if their souls are too much tossed with passion, they shall endeavour to find other partners. Now they are not likely to have very gentle tempers; and, therefore, we must endeavour to associate with them deeper and softer natures. Those who have no children, or only a few, at the time of their separation, should choose their new partners with a view to the procreation of children; but those who have a sufficient number of children should separate and marry again in order that they may have some one to grow old with and that the pair may take care of one another in age. If a woman dies, leaving children, male or female, the law will advise rather than compel the husband to bring up the children without introducing into the house

---

[1] *Or,* 'who are intermediate in age':—i. e. who are neither the youngest nor the oldest guardians of the law.
[2] Cp. *supra,* vi. 784 A foll.; vii. 794.

a stepmother. But if he have no children, then he shall be compelled to marry until he has begotten a sufficient number of sons to his family and to the state. And if a man dies leaving a sufficient number of children, the mother of his children shall remain with them and bring them up. But if she appears to be too young to live virtuously without a husband, let her relations communicate with the women who superintend marriage, and let both together do what they think best in these matters; if there is a lack of children, let the choice be made with a view to having them; two children, one of either sex, shall be deemed sufficient in the eye of the law. When a child is admitted to be the offspring of certain parents and is acknowledged by them, but there is need of a decision as to which parent the child is to follow,—in case a female slave have intercourse with a male slave, or with a freeman or freedman, the offspring shall always belong to the master of the female slave. Again, if a free woman have intercourse with a male slave, the offspring shall belong to the master of the slave; but if a child be born either of a slave by her master, or of his mistress by a slave—and this be proven—the offspring of the woman and its father shall be sent away by the women who superintend marriage into another country, and the guardians of the law shall send away the offspring of the man and its mother.

Neither God, nor a man who has understanding, will ever advise any one to neglect his parents. To a discourse concerning the honour and dishonour of parents, a prelude such as the following, about the service of the Gods, will be a suitable introduction:—There are ancient customs about the Gods which are universal, and they are of two kinds: some of the Gods we see with our eyes and we honour them, of others we honour the images, raising statues of them which we adore; and though they are lifeless, yet we imagine that the living Gods have a good will and gratitude to us on this account. Now, if a man has a father or mother, or their fathers or mothers treasured up in his house stricken in years, let him consider that no statue can be more potent to grant his requests than they are, who are sitting at his hearth, if only he knows how to show true service to them.

Cle. And what do you call the true mode of service?

Ath. I will tell you, O my friend, for such things are worth listening to.

Cle. Proceed.

Ath. Oedipus, as tradition says, when dishonoured by his sons, invoked on them curses which every one declares to have been heard and ratified by the Gods, and Amyntor in his wrath invoked

Laws XI

ATHE-
NIAN,
CLEINIAS.

widowers
and
widows.

The custody of
children
of whom
one or
both parents are
slaves.

931

A father
or mother
stricken
in years
is as potent to
grant a
request
as any
lifeless
image.

The
curses of
parents
upon

their
children
are heard
by the
Gods, and
so are the
prayers
which
they of-
fer for
their
welfare.

The wor-
ship of a
living an-
cestor
higher
than of a
lifeless
image.

932

The pen-
alty for
the neg-
lect of
parents
in the
case of
the young
will be
bonds and
stripes;

curses on his son Phoenix, and Theseus upon Hippolytus, and innumerable others have also called down wrath upon their children,
whence it is clear that the Gods listen to the imprecations of
parents; for the curses of parents are, as they ought to be, mighty
against their children as no others are. And shall we suppose that
the prayers of a father or mother who is specially dishonoured by
his or her children, are heard by the Gods in accordance with nature; and that if a parent is honoured by them, and in the gladness
of his heart earnestly entreats the Gods in his prayers to do them
good, he is not equally heard, and that they do not minister to his
request? If not, they would be very unjust ministers of good, and
that we affirm to be contrary to their nature.

Cle. Certainly.

Ath. May we not think, as I was saying just now, that we can
possess no image which is more honoured by the Gods, than that of
a father or grandfather, or of a mother stricken in years? whom
when a man honours, the heart of the God rejoices, and he is ready
to answer their prayers. And, truly, the figure of an ancestor is a
wonderful thing, far higher than that of a lifeless image. For the
living, when they are honoured by us, join in our prayers, and when
they are dishonoured, they utter imprecations against us; but lifeless objects do neither. And therefore, if a man makes a right use of
his father and grandfather and other aged relations, he will have
images which above all others will win him the favour of the Gods.

Cle. Excellent.

Ath. Every man of any understanding fears and respects the
prayers of parents, knowing well that many times and to many persons they have been accomplished. Now these things being thus ordered by nature, good men think it a blessing from heaven if their
parents live to old age and reach the utmost limit of human life, or if
taken away before their time they are deeply regretted by them; but
to bad men parents are always a cause of terror. Wherefore let every
man honour with every sort of lawful honour his own parents,
agreeably to what has now been said. But if this prelude be an unmeaning sound in the ears of any one, let the law follow, which may
be rightly imposed in these terms:—If any one in this city be not
sufficiently careful of his parents, and do not regard and gratify in
every respect their wishes more than those of his sons and of his
other offspring or of himself,—let him who experiences this sort of
treatment either come himself, or send some one to inform the three
eldest guardians of the law, and three of the women who have the
care of marriages; and let them look to the matter and punish
youthful evil-doers with stripes and bonds if they are under thirty

years of age, that is to say, if they be men, or if they be women, let them undergo the same punishment up to forty years of age. But if, when they are still more advanced in years, they continue the same neglect of their parents, and do any hurt to any of them, let them be brought before a court in which every single one of the eldest citizens shall be the judges, and if the offender be convicted, let the court determine what he ought to pay or suffer, and any penalty may be imposed on him which a man can pay or suffer. If the person who has been wronged be unable to inform the magistrates, let any freeman who hears of his case inform, and if he do not, he shall be deemed base, and shall be liable to have a suit for damage brought against him by any one who likes. And if a slave inform, he shall receive freedom; and if he be the slave of the injurer or injured party, he shall be set free by the magistrates, or if he belong to any other citizen, the public shall pay a price on his behalf to the owner; and let the magistrates take heed that no one wrongs him out of revenge, because he has given information.

Cases in which one man injures another by poisons, and which prove fatal, have been already discussed[1]; but about other cases in which a person intentionally and of malice harms another with meats, or drinks, or ointments, nothing has as yet been determined. For there are two kinds of poisons used among men, which cannot clearly be distinguished. There is the kind just now explicitly mentioned, which injures bodies by the use of other bodies according to a natural law; there is also another kind which persuades the more daring class that they can do injury by sorceries, and incantations, and magic knots, as they are termed, and makes others believe that they above all persons are injured by the powers of the magician. Now it is not easy to know the nature of all these things; nor if a man do know can he readily persuade others to believe him. And when men are disturbed in their minds at the sight of waxen images fixed either at their doors, or in a place where three ways meet, or on the sepulchres of parents, there is no use in trying to persuade them that they should despise all such things because they have no certain knowledge about them. But we must have a law in two parts, concerning poisoning, in whichever of the two ways the attempt is made, and we must entreat, and exhort, and advise men not to have recourse to such practices, by which they scare the multitude out of their wits, as if they were children, compelling the legislator and the judge to heal the fears which the sorcerer arouses, and to tell them in the first place, that he who attempts to poison or enchant others knows not what he is doing, either as regards the body (un-

Laws XI

ATHE-
NIAN.

if they persist they shall be brought before a court of elders and punished more severely.

Two kinds of poison-[933]-ing: (1) by meats and drinks; (2) by magic.

Men cannot be taught to despise sorcery, and therefore the practice of it must be punished.

[1] i. e. they are cases of murder: cp. *supra*, ix. 870 foll.

Laws XI

ATHE-
NIAN.

The phy-
sician
who em-
ploys
poison,
and the
profes-
sional
sorcerer,
shall be
put to
death.

less he has a knowledge of medicine), or as regards his enchantments (unless he happens to be a prophet or diviner). Let the law, then, run as follows about poisoning or witchcraft:—He who employs poison to do any injury, not fatal, to a man himself, or to his servants, or any injury, whether fatal or not, to his cattle or his bees, if he be a physician, and be convicted of poisoning, shall be punished with death; or if he be a private person, the court shall determine what he is to pay or suffer. But he who seems to be the sort of man who injures others by magic knots, or enchantments, or incantations, or any of the like practices, if he be a prophet or diviner, let him die; and if, not being a prophet, he be convicted of witchcraft, as in the previous case, let the court fix what he ought to pay or suffer.

He who
does an
injury
shall not
only
make
[934]
compen-
sation,
but suf-
fer pun-
ishment.

Punish-
ment not
vindic-
tive, but
preven-
tive.

When a man does another any injury by theft or violence, for the greater injury let him pay greater damages to the injured man, and less for the smaller injury; but in all cases, whatever the injury may have been, as much as will compensate the loss. And besides the compensation of the wrong, let a man pay a further penalty for the chastisement of his offence: he who has done the wrong instigated by the folly of another[1], through the lightheartedness of youth or the like, shall pay a lighter penalty; but he who has injured another through his own folly, when overcome by pleasure or pain, in cowardly fear, or lust, or envy, or implacable anger, shall endure a heavier punishment. Not that he is punished because he did wrong, for that which is done can never be undone, but in order that in future times, he, and those who see him corrected, may utterly hate injustice, or at any rate abate much of their evil-doing. Having an eye to all these things, the law, like a good archer, should aim at the right measure of punishment, and in all cases at the deserved punishment. In the attainment of this the judge shall be a fellow-worker with the legislator, whenever the law leaves to him to determine what the offender shall suffer or pay; and the legislator, like a painter, shall give a rough sketch of the cases in which the law is to be applied. This is what we must do, Megillus and Cleinias, in the best and fairest manner that we can, saying what the punishments are to be of all actions of theft and violence, and giving laws of such a kind as the Gods and sons of Gods would have us give.

A mad-
man must
be kept
at home
by his
relations.

If a man is mad he shall not be at large in the city, but his relations shall keep him at home in any way which they can; or if not, let them pay a penalty,—he who is of the highest class shall pay a penalty of one hundred drachmas, whether he be a slave or a freeman whom he neglects; and he of the second class shall pay four-

[1] Putting the comma after ἀλλοτρίᾳ.

fifths of a mina; and he of the third class three-fifths; and he of the fourth class two-fifths. Now there are many sorts of madness, some arising out of disease, which we have already mentioned; and there are other kinds, which originate in an evil and passionate temperament, and are increased by bad education; out of a slight quarrel this class of madmen will often raise a storm of abuse against one another, and nothing of that sort ought to be allowed to occur in a well-ordered state. Let this, then, be the law about abuse, which shall relate to all cases:—No one shall speak evil of another; and when a man disputes with another he shall teach and learn of the disputant and the company, but he shall abstain from evil-speaking; for out of the imprecations which men utter against one another, and the feminine habit of casting aspersions on one another, and using foul names, out of words light as air, in very deed the greatest enmities and hatreds spring up. For the speaker gratifies his anger, which is an ungracious element of his nature; and nursing up his wrath by the entertainment of evil thoughts, and exacerbating that part of his soul which was formerly civilized by education, he lives in a state of savageness and moroseness, and pays a bitter penalty for his anger. And in such cases almost all men take to saying something ridiculous about their opponent, and there is no man who is in the habit of laughing at another who does not miss virtue and earnestness altogether, or lose the better half of greatness. Wherefore let no one utter any taunting word at a temple, or at the public sacrifices, or at the games, or in the agora, or in a court of justice, or in any public assembly. And let the magistrate who presides on these occasions chastise an offender, and he shall be blameless; but if he fails in doing so, he shall not claim the prize of virtue; for he is one who heeds not the laws, and does not do what the legislator commands. And if in any other place any one indulges in these sort of revilings, whether he has begun the quarrel or is only retaliating, let any elder who is present support the law, and control with blows those who indulge in passion, which is another great evil; and if he do not, let him be liable to pay the appointed penalty. And we say now, that he who deals in reproaches against others cannot reproach them without attempting to ridicule them; and this, when done in a moment of anger, is what we make matter of reproach against him. But then, do we admit into our state the comic writers[1] who are so fond of making mankind ridiculous, if they attempt in a good-natured manner to turn the laugh against our citizens? or do we draw the distinction of jest and earnest, and allow a man to make use of ridicule in jest and without

---

[1] Cp. Rep. iii. 394; x. 606; Arist. Pol. vii. 17, § 11.

Laws XI

ATHE-
NIAN.

The madness (1) of disease, (2) of passion.

The law respecting abuse.

935

He who ridicules another misses virtue and loses the better half of greatness.

The punishment of the offender.

Jesting in verse without anger may be allowed,

anger about any thing or person; though as we were saying, not if he be angry and have a set purpose? We forbid earnest—that is unalterably fixed; but we have still to say who are to be sanctioned or not to be sanctioned by the law in the employment of innocent humour. A comic poet, or maker of iambic or satirical lyric verse, shall not be permitted to ridicule any of the citizens, either by word or likeness, either in anger or without anger. And if any one is disobedient, the judges shall either at once expel him from the country, or he shall pay a fine of three minae, which shall be dedicated to the God who presides over the contests. Those only who have received permission shall be allowed to write verses at one another, but they shall be without anger and in jest; in anger and in serious earnest they shall not be allowed. The decision of this matter shall be left to the superintendent of the general education of the young, and whatever he may license, the writer shall be allowed to produce, and whatever he rejects let not the poet himself exhibit, or ever teach anybody else, slave or freeman, under the penalty of being dishonoured, and held disobedient to the laws.

Now he is not to be pitied who is hungry, or who suffers any bodily pain, but he who is temperate, or has some other virtue, or part of a virtue, and at the same time suffers from misfortune; it would be an extraordinary thing if such an one, whether slave or freeman, were utterly forsaken and fell into the extremes of poverty in any tolerably well-ordered city or government. Wherefore the legislator
may safely make a law applicable to such cases in the following terms:—Let there be no beggars in our state; and if anybody begs, seeking to pick up a livelihood by unavailing prayers, let the wardens of the agora turn him out of the agora, and the wardens of the city out of the city, and the wardens of the country send him out of any other parts of the land across the border, in order that the land may be cleared of this sort of animal.

If a slave of either sex injure anything, which is not his or her own, through inexperience, or some improper practice, and the person who suffers damage be not himself in part to blame, the master of the slave who has done the harm shall either make full satisfaction, or give up the slave who has done the injury. But if the master argue that the charge has arisen by collusion between the injured party and the injurer, with the view of obtaining the slave, let him sue the person, who says that he has been injured, for malpractices. And if he gain a conviction, let him receive double the value which the court fixes as the price of the slave; and if he lose his suit, let him make amends for the injury, and give up the slave. And if a beast of burden, or horse, or dog, or any other animal, injure the property of a neighbour, the owner shall in like manner pay for the injury.

If any man refuses to be a witness, he who wants him shall summon him, and he who is summoned shall come to the trial; and if he knows and is willing to bear witness, let him bear witness, but if he says he does not know let him swear by the three divinities Zeus, and Apollo, and Themis, that he does not, and have no more to do with the cause. And he who is summoned to give witness and does not answer to his summoner, shall be liable for the harm which ensues according to law. And if a person calls up as a witness any one who is acting as a judge, let him give his witness, but he shall not afterwards vote in the cause. A free woman may give her witness and plead, if she be more than forty years of age, and may bring an action if she have no husband; but if her husband be alive she shall only be allowed to bear witness. A slave of either sex and a child shall be allowed to give evidence and to plead, but only in cases of murder; and they must produce sufficient sureties that they will certainly remain until the trial, in case they should be charged with false witness. And either of the parties in a cause may bring an accusation of perjury against witnesses, touching their evidence in whole or in part, if he asserts that such evidence has been given; but the accusation must be brought previous to the final decision of the cause. The magistrates shall preserve the accusations of false witness, and have them kept under the seal of both parties, and produce them on the day when the trial for false witness takes place. If a man be twice convicted of false witness, he shall not be required, and if thrice, he shall not be allowed to bear witness; and if he dare to witness after he has been convicted three times, let any one who pleases inform against him to the magistrates, and let the magistrates hand him over to the court, and if he be convicted he shall be punished with death. And in any case in which the evidence is rightly found to be false, and yet to have given the victory to him who wins the suit, and more than half the witnesses are condemned, the decision which was gained by these means shall be rescinded, and there shall be a discussion and a decision as to whether the suit was determined by that false evidence or not; and in whichever way the decision may be given, the previous suit shall be determined accordingly.

There are many noble things in human life, but to most of them attach evils which are fated to corrupt and spoil them. Is not justice noble, which has been the civilizer of humanity? How then can the advocate of justice be other than noble? And yet upon this profession which is presented to us under the fair name of art has come

Laws XI
ATHE-
NIAN.

Regulations respecting witnesses.

937

False witness.

Penalties for false witness.

Good and evil lie near together in human life. The

Laws XI

938
ATHE-
NIAN.

ends of
the law
apt to be
defeated
by the in-
genuity
of law-
yers.

The pun-
ishment
of un-
scrupu-
lous ad-
vocacy,
which in
certain
cases is to
be death.

an evil reputation[1]. In the first place, we are told that by ingenious pleas and the help of an advocate the law enables a man to win a particular cause, whether just or unjust; and that both the art, and the power of speech which is thereby imparted, are at the service of him who is willing to pay for them. Now in our state this so-called art, whether really an art[2] or only an experience and practice destitute of any art, ought if possible never to come into existence, or if existing among us should listen to the request of the legislator and go away into another land, and not speak contrary to justice. If the offenders obey we say no more; but for those who disobey, the voice of the law is as follows:—If any one thinks that he will pervert the power of justice in the minds of the judges, and unseasonably litigate or advocate, let any one who likes indict him for malpractices of law and dishonest advocacy, and let him be judged in the court of select judges; and if he be convicted, let the court determine whether he may be supposed to act from a love of money or from contentiousness. And if he is supposed to act from contentiousness, the court shall fix a time during which he shall not be allowed to institute or plead a cause; and if he is supposed to act as he does from love of money, in case he be a stranger, he shall leave the country, and never return under penalty of death; but if he be a citizen, he shall die, because he is a lover of money, in whatever manner gained; and equally, if he be judged to have acted more than once from contentiousness, he shall die.

BOOK XII

941
Laws XII

ATHE-
NIAN.

Miscon-
duct of
heralds or
ambas-
sadors.

No God
or son of
a God

IF a herald or an ambassador carry a false message from our city to any other, or bring back a false message from the city to which he is sent, or be proved to have brought back, whether from friends or enemies, in his capacity of herald or ambassador, what they have never said, let him be indicted for having violated, contrary to the law, the commands and duties imposed upon him by Hermes and Zeus, and let there be a penalty fixed, which he shall suffer or pay if he be convicted.

Theft is a mean, and robbery a shameless thing; and none of the sons of Zeus delight in fraud and violence, or ever practised either. Wherefore let no one be deluded by poets or mythologers into a mis-

---

[1] The text is probably corrupt.   [2] Cp. Gorg. 463 A.

taken belief of such things, nor let him suppose, when he thieves or is guilty of violence, that he is doing nothing base, but only what the Gods themselves do. For such tales are untrue and improbable; and he who steals or robs contrary to the law, is never either a God or the son of a God; of this the legislator ought to be better informed than all the poets put together[1]. Happy is he and may he be for ever happy, who is persuaded and listens to our words; but he who disobeys shall have to contend against the following law:—If a man steal anything belonging to the public, whether that which he steals be much or little, he shall have the same punishment. For he who steals a little steals with the same wish as he who steals much, but with less power, and he who takes up a greater amount, not having deposited it, is wholly unjust. Wherefore the law is not disposed to inflict a less penalty on the one than on the other because his theft is less, but on the ground that the thief may possibly be in one case still curable, and may in another case be incurable. If any one convict in a court of law a stranger or a slave of a theft of public property, let the court determine what punishment he shall suffer, or what penalty he shall pay, bearing in mind that he is probably not incurable. But the citizen who has been brought up as our citizens will have been, if he be found guilty of robbing his country by fraud or violence, whether he be caught in the act or not, shall be punished with death; for he is incurable[2].

Now for expeditions of war much consideration and many laws are required; the great principle of all is that no one of either sex should be without a commander[3]; nor should the mind of any one be accustomed to do anything, either in jest or earnest, of his own motion, but in war and in peace he should look to and follow his leader, even in the least things being under his guidance; for example, he should stand or move, or exercise, or wash, or take his meals, or get up in the night to keep guard and deliver messages when he is bidden; and in the hour of danger he should not pursue and not retreat except by order of his superior; and in a word, not teach the soul or accustom her to know or understand how to do anything apart from others. Of all soldiers the life should be always and in all things as far as possible in common and together; there neither is nor ever will be a higher, or better, or more scientific principle than this for the attainment of salvation and victory in war. And we ought in time of peace from youth upwards to practise this

Punish-
ment for
theft of
public
property.

The
stranger
or slave,
as cur-
able, to
be dealt
with leni-
ently; the
citizen, as
incurable,
[942]
to suffer
death.

Obedi-
ence the
great
military
virtue.

Soldiers
to have a
common
life.

[1] Cp. Rep. iii. 388 C, 391 D.
[2] This passage is not consistent with ix. 857 A, where theft of public property is punished by imprisonment.
[3] Cp. Thucyd. v. 66.

Agility
and en-
durance
to be cul-
tivated.

Care of
the ex-
tremities.

943

The man-
ner of
trial and
punish-
ment of
those who
fail to
serve.

The
award of
prizes of
valour.

Desertion
to re-
ceive the
same
punish-
ment as
refusal to
serve.

habit of commanding others, and of being commanded by others; anarchy should have no place in the life of man or of the beasts who are subject to man. I may add that all dances ought to be performed with a view to military excellence[1]; and agility and ease should be cultivated for the same object, and also endurance of the want of meats and drinks, and of winter cold and summer heat, and of hard couches; and, above all, care should be taken not to destroy the peculiar qualities of the head and the feet by surrounding them with extraneous coverings, and so hindering their natural growth of hair and soles. For these are the extremities, and of all the parts of the body, whether they are preserved or not is of the greatest consequence; the one is the servant of the whole body, and the other the master, in whom all the ruling senses are by nature set. Let the young man imagine that he hears in what has preceded the praises of the military life; the law shall be as follows:—He shall serve in war who is on the roll or appointed to some special service, and if any one is absent from cowardice, and without the leave of the generals, he shall be indicted before the military commanders for failure of service when the army comes home; and the soldiers shall be his judges; the heavy-armed, and the cavalry, and the other arms of the service shall form separate courts; and they shall bring the heavy-armed before the heavy-armed, and the horsemen before the horsemen, and the others in like manner before their peers; and he who is found guilty shall never be allowed to compete for any prize of valour, or indict another for not serving on an expedition, or be an accuser at all in any military matters. Moreover, the court shall further determine what punishment he shall suffer, or what penalty he shall pay. When the suits for failure of service are completed, the leaders of the several kinds of troops shall again hold an assembly, and they shall adjudge the prizes of valour; and he who likes shall give judgment in his own branch of the service, saying nothing about any former expedition, nor producing any proof or witnesses to confirm his statement, but speaking only of the present occasion. The crown of victory shall be an olive wreath which the victor shall offer up at the temple of any war-god whom he likes, adding an inscription for a testimony to last during life, that such an one has received the first, the second, or the third prize. If any one goes on an expedition, and returns home before the appointed time, when the generals have not withdrawn the army, he shall be indicted for desertion before the same persons who took cognizance of failure of service, and if he be found guilty, the same punishment shall be inflicted on him. Now every man who is engaged in any suit ought to

[1] Cp. *supra*, vii. 796 B.

be very careful of bringing false witness against any one, either intentionally or unintentionally, if he can help; for justice is truly said to be an honourable maiden[1], and falsehood is naturally repugnant to honour and justice. A witness ought to be very careful not to sin against justice, as for example in what relates to the throwing away of arms—he must distinguish the throwing them away when necessary, and not make that a reproach, or bring an action against some innocent person on that account. To make the distinction may be difficult; but still the law must attempt to define the different kinds in some way. Let me endeavour to explain my meaning by an ancient tale:—If Patroclus had been brought to the tent still alive but without his arms (and this has happened to innumerable persons), the original arms, which the poet says were presented to Peleus by the Gods as a nuptial gift when he married Thetis, remaining in the hands of Hector, then the base spirits of that day might have reproached the son of Menoetius with having cast away his arms. Again, there is the case of those who have been thrown down precipices and lost their arms; and of those who at sea, and in stormy places, have been suddenly overwhelmed by floods of water; and there are numberless things of this kind which one might adduce by way of extenuation, and with the view of justifying a misfortune which is easily misrepresented. We must, therefore, endeavour to divide to the best of our power the greater and more serious evil from the lesser. And a distinction may be drawn in the use of terms of reproach. A man does not always deserve to be called the thrower away of his shield; he may be only the loser of his arms. For there is a great or rather absolute difference between him who is deprived of his arms by a sufficient force, and him who voluntarily lets his shield go. Let the law then be as follows:—If a person having arms is overtaken by the enemy and does not turn round and defend himself, but lets them go voluntarily or throws them away, choosing a base life and a swift escape rather than a courageous and noble and blessed death—in such a case of the throwing away of arms let justice be done, but the judge need take no note of the case just now mentioned; for the bad man ought always to be punished, in the hope that he may be improved, but not the unfortunate, for there is no advantage in that. And what shall be the punishment suited to him who has thrown away his weapons of defence? Tradition says that Caeneus, the Thessalian, was changed by a God from a woman into a man; but the converse miracle cannot now be wrought, or no punishment would be more proper than that the man who throws away his shield should be changed into a

[1] Reading αἰδοίη.

Laws XII

ATHE-
NIAN.

Witnesses
to be
careful
not to
confound
[944]
the losing
and the
throwing
away of
arms.

The law
respect-
ing cow-
ardice.

Would
that the
coward
could be
changed

Laws XII
ATHE-
NIAN.

into a
woman!

Since
such a
[945]
punish-
ment is
impossi-
ble, let
him not
be al-
lowed to
serve, and
let him
incur a
fine.

Examin-
ers to be
better
men than
the other
magis-
trates.

Import-
ance of
the of-
fice.

Three
men pre-
eminent
in virtue
to be

woman[1]. This however is impossible, and therefore let us make a law as nearly like this as we can—that he who loves his life too well shall be in no danger for the remainder of his days, but shall live for ever under the stigma of cowardice. And let the law be in the following terms:—When a man is found guilty of disgracefully throwing away his arms in war, no general or military officer shall allow him to serve as a soldier, or give him any place at all in the ranks of soldiers; and the officer who gives the coward any place, shall suffer a penalty which the public examiner shall exact of him; and if he be of the highest class, he shall pay a thousand drachmae; or if he be of the second class, five minae; or if he be of the third, three minae; or if he be of the fourth class, one mina. And he who is found guilty of cowardice, shall not only be dismissed from manly dangers, which is a disgrace appropriate to his nature, but he shall pay a thousand drachmae, if he be of the highest class, and five minae if he be of the second class, and three if he be of the third class, and a mina, like the preceding, if he be of the fourth class.

What regulations will be proper about examiners, seeing that some of our magistrates are elected by lot, and for a year, and some for a longer time and from selected persons? Of such magistrates, who will be a sufficient censor or examiner, if any of them, weighed down by the pressure of office or his own inability to support the dignity of his office, be guilty of any crooked practice? It is by no means easy to find a magistrate who excels other magistrates in virtue, but still we must endeavour to discover some censor or examiner who is more than man. For the truth is, that there are many elements of dissolution in a state, as there are also in a ship, or in an animal; they all have their cords, and girders, and sinews,—one nature diffused in many places, and called by many names; and the office of examiner is a most important element in the preservation and dissolution of states. For if the examiners are better than the magistrates, and their duty is fulfilled justly and without blame, then the whole state and country flourishes and is happy; but if the examination of the magistrates is carried on in a wrong way, then, by the relaxation of that justice which is the uniting principle of all constitutions, every power in the state is rent asunder from every other; they no longer incline in the same direction, but fill the city with faction, and make many cities out of one[2], and soon bring all to destruction. Wherefore the examiners ought to be admirable in every sort of virtue. Let us invent a mode of creating them, which shall be as follows:—Every year, after the summer solstice, the whole city shall meet in the common precincts of Helios and Apollo,

[1] Cp. Tim. 90 E.   [2] Cp. Rep. iv. 422 E.

and shall present to the God three men out of their own number in
the manner following:—Each citizen shall select, not himself, but
some other citizen whom he deems in every way the best, and who
is not less than fifty years of age. And out of the selected persons
who have the greatest number of votes, they shall make a further
selection until they reduce them to one-half, if they are an even
number; but if they are not an even number, they shall subtract the
one who has the smallest number of votes, and make them an even
number, and then leave the half which have the greater number of
votes. And if two persons have an equal number of votes, and thus
increase the number beyond one-half, they shall withdraw the
younger of the two and do away the excess; and then including all
the rest they shall again vote, until there are left three having an
unequal number of votes. But if all the three, or two out of the
three, have equal votes, let them commit the election to good fate
and fortune, and separate off by lot the first, and the second, and
the third; these they shall crown with an olive wreath and give them
the prize of excellence, at the same time proclaiming to all the world
that the city of the Magnetes, by the providence of the Gods, is
again preserved, and presents to the Sun and to Apollo her three
best men as first-fruits, to be a common offering to them, according
to the ancient law, as long as their lives answer to the judgment
formed of them. And these shall appoint in their first year twelve
examiners, to continue until each has completed seventy-five years,
to whom three shall afterwards be added yearly; and let these divide
all the magistracies into twelve parts, and prove the holders of them
by every sort of test to which a freeman may be subjected; and let
them live while they hold office in the precinct of Helios and Apollo,
in which they were chosen, and let each one form a judgment of
some things individually, and of others in company with his colleagues; and let him place a writing in the agora about each magistracy, and what the magistrate ought to suffer or pay, according to
the decision of the examiners. And if a magistrate does not admit
that he has been justly judged, let him bring the examiners before
the select judges, and if he be acquitted by their decision, let him, if
he will, accuse the examiners themselves; if, however, he be convicted, and have been condemned to death by the examiners, let
him die (and of course he can only die once):—but any other penalties which admit of being doubled let him suffer twice over.

And now let us pass under review the examiners themselves;
what will their examination be, and how conducted? During the life
of these men, whom the whole state counts worthy of the rewards of
virtue, they shall have the first seat at all public assemblies, and at

Laws XII

946
ATHE-
NIAN.

elected
annually
from
among
the citi-
zens.

Honours
to be paid
to them.

Examin-
ers to be
appointed
by them,
who shall
have
power to
punish
the
magis-
trates.

The
magis-
trates
may
appeal
against
them to
the court
of select
judges.

947
The
honours

during
life and
after
death of
the ex-
aminers,
if they
pass the
scrutiny.

all Hellenic sacrifices and sacred missions, and other public and holy ceremonies in which they share. The chiefs of each sacred mission shall be selected from them, and they only of all the citizens shall be adorned with a crown of laurel; they shall all be priests of Apollo and Helios; and one of them, who is judged first of the priests created in that year, shall be high priest; and they shall write up his name in each year to be a measure of time as long as the city lasts; and after their death they shall be laid out and carried to the grave and entombed in a manner different from the other citizens. They shall be decked in a robe all of white, and there shall be no crying or lamentation over them; but a chorus of fifteen maidens, and another of boys, shall stand around the bier on either side, hymning the praises of the departed priests in alternate responses, declaring their blessedness in song all day long; and at dawn a hundred of the youths who practise gymnastic exercises, and whom the relations of the departed shall choose, shall carry the bier to the sepulchre, the young men marching first, dressed in the garb of warriors,—the cavalry with their horses, the heavy-armed with their arms, and the others in like manner. And boys near the bier and in front of it shall sing their national hymn, and maidens shall follow behind, and with them the women who have passed the age of child-bearing; next, although they are interdicted from other burials, let priests and priestesses follow, unless the Pythian oracle forbid them; for this burial is free from pollution. The place of burial shall be an oblong vaulted chamber underground, constructed of tufa, which will last for ever, having stone couches placed side by side. And here they will lay the blessed person, and cover the sepulchre with a circular mound of earth and plant a grove of trees around on every side but one; and on that side the sepulchre shall be allowed to extend for ever, and a new mound will not be required. Every year they shall have contests in music and gymnastics, and in horsemanship, in honour of the dead. These are the honours which shall be given to

But if
after the
scrutiny
they do
[948]
wrong,
they shall
be de-
prived
of their
honours.

those who at the examination are found blameless; but if any of them, trusting to the scrutiny being over, should, after the judgment has been given, manifest the wickedness of human nature, let the law ordain that he who pleases shall indict him, and let the cause be tried in the following manner. In the first place, the court shall be composed of the guardians of the law, and to them the surviving examiners shall be added, as well as the court of select judges; and let the pursuer lay his indictment in this form—he shall say that so-and-so is unworthy of the prize of virtue and of his office; and if the defendant be convicted let him be deprived of his office, and of the burial, and of the other honours given him. But if the

prosecutor do not obtain the fifth part of the votes, let him, if he be
of the first class, pay twelve minae, and eight if he be of the second
class, and six if he be of the third class, and two minae if he be of
the fourth class.

The so-called decision of Rhadamanthus is worthy of all admiration. He knew that the men of his own time believed and had no
doubt that there were Gods, which was a reasonable belief in those
days, because most men were the sons of Gods[1], and according to
tradition he was one himself. He appears to have thought that he
ought to commit judgment to no man, but to the Gods only, and in
this way suits were simply and speedily decided by him. For he
made the two parties take an oath respecting the points in dispute,
and so got rid of the matter speedily and safely. But now that a
certain portion of mankind do not believe at all in the existence of
the Gods, and others imagine that they have no care of us, and the
opinion of most men, and of the worst men, is that in return for a
small sacrifice and a few flattering words they will be their accom-
plices in purloining large sums and save them from many terrible
punishments, the way of Rhadamanthus is no longer suited to the
needs of justice; for as the opinions of men about the Gods are
changed, the laws should also be changed;—in the granting of suits
a rational legislation ought to do away with the oaths of the parties
on either side—he who obtains leave to bring an action should write
down the charges, but should not add an oath; and the defendant
in like manner should give his denial to the magistrates in writing,
and not swear; for it is a dreadful thing to know, when many lawsuits are going on in a state, that almost half the people who meet
one another quite unconcernedly at the public meals and in other
companies and relations of private life are perjured. Let the law,
then, be as follows:—A judge who is about to give judgment shall
take an oath, and he who is choosing magistrates for the state shall
either vote on oath or with a voting tablet which he brings from a
temple; so too the judge of dances and of all music, and the superintendents and umpires of gymnastic and equestrian contests, and
any matters in which, as far as men can judge, there is nothing to
be gained by a false oath; but all cases in which a denial confirmed
by an oath clearly results in a great advantage to the taker of the
oath, shall be decided without the oath of the parties to the suit,
and the presiding judges shall not permit either of them to use an
oath for the sake of persuading, nor to call down curses on himself
and his race, nor to use unseemly supplications or womanish la-
ments. But they shall ever be teaching and learning what is just in

[1] Cp. Tim. 40 D.

Laws XII

ATHE-
NIAN.

The
oath of
Rhada-
manthus
suited to
a God-
fearing
age, but
not to
our own.

Oaths are
not to be
taken by
the
parties to
a suit.

Judges,
however,
and citi-
zens when
[949]
electing
magis-
trates,
and the
umpires
of con-
tests, shall
take an
oath.

Laws XII

ATHE-
NIAN.

Note;—
the pro-
hibition
of oaths
does not
extend to
strangers.

Penalty
for neg-
lect of
certain
public
duties.

Admis-
sion of
foreign-
ers, and
foreign
travel,

950

are evils
in a well-
ordered
state, but
of no con-
sequence
in an
ordinary
state.

Inhospi-
tality
con-
demned
by the
many;
the good

auspicious words; and he who does otherwise shall be supposed to speak beside the point, and the judges shall again bring him back to the question at issue. On the other hand, strangers in their dealings with strangers shall as at present have power to give and receive oaths, for they will not often grow old in the city or leave a fry of young ones like themselves to be the sons and heirs of the land.

As to the initiation of private suits, let the manner of deciding causes between all citizens be the same as in cases in which any freeman is disobedient to the state in minor matters, of which the penalty is not stripes, imprisonment, or death. But as regards attendance at choruses or processions or other shows, and as regards public services, whether the celebration of sacrifice in peace, or the payment of contributions in war—in all these cases, first comes the necessity of providing a remedy for the loss; and by those who will not obey, there shall be security given to the officers whom the city and the law empower to exact the sum due; and if they forfeit their security, let the goods which they have pledged be sold and the money given to the city; but if they ought to pay a larger sum, the several magistrates shall impose upon the disobedient a suitable penalty, and bring them before the court, until they are willing to do what they are ordered.

Now a state which makes money from the cultivation of the soil only, and has no foreign trade, must consider what it will do about the emigration of its own people to other countries, and the reception of strangers from elsewhere. About these matters the legislator has to consider, and he will begin by trying to persuade men as far as he can. The intercourse of cities with one another is apt to create a confusion of manners; strangers are always suggesting novelties to strangers[1]. When states are well governed by good laws the mixture causes the greatest possible injury; but seeing that most cities are the reverse of well-ordered, the confusion which arises in them from the reception of strangers, and from the citizens themselves rushing off into other cities, when any one either young or old desires to travel anywhere abroad at whatever time, is of no consequence. On the other hand, the refusal of states to receive others, and for their own citizens never to go to other places, is an utter impossibility, and to the rest of the world is likely to appear ruthless and uncivilized; it is a practice adopted by people who use harsh words, such as xenelasia or banishment of strangers, and who have harsh and morose ways, as men think. And to be thought or not to be thought well of by the rest of the world is no light matter; for the many are not so far wrong in their judgment of who are bad and

[1] Cp. *supra,* iv. 704 E.

who are good, as they are removed from the nature of virtue in themselves. Even bad men have a divine instinct which guesses rightly, and very many who are utterly depraved form correct notions and judgments of the differences between the good and bad. And the generality of cities are quite right in exhorting us to value a good reputation in the world, for there is no truth greater and more important than this—that he who is really good (I am speaking of the man who would be perfect) seeks for reputation with, but not without, the reality of goodness. And our Cretan colony ought also to acquire the fairest and noblest reputation for virtue from other men; and there is every reason to expect that, if the reality answers to the idea, she will be one of the few well-ordered cities which the sun and the other Gods behold. Wherefore, in the matter of journeys to other countries and the reception of strangers, we enact as follows:—In the first place, let no one be allowed to go anywhere at all into a foreign country who is less than forty years of age; and no one shall go in a private capacity, but only in some public one, as a herald, or on an embassy, or on a sacred mission. Going abroad on an expedition or in war is not to be included among travels of the class authorized by the state. To Apollo at Delphi and to Zeus at Olympia and to Nemea and to the Isthmus, citizens should be sent to take part in the sacrifices and games there dedicated to the Gods; and they should send as many as possible, and the best and fairest that can be found, and they will make the city renowned at holy meetings in time of peace, procuring a glory which shall be the converse of that which is gained in war; and when they come home they shall teach the young that the institutions of other states are inferior to their own. And they shall send spectators of another sort, if they have the consent of the guardians, being such citizens as desire to look a little more at leisure at the doings of other men; and these no law shall hinder. For a city which has no experience of good and bad men or intercourse with them, can never be thoroughly and perfectly civilized, nor, again, can the citizens of a city properly observe the laws by habit only, and without an intelligent understanding of them[1]. And there always are in the world a few inspired men whose acquaintance is beyond price, and who spring up quite as much in ill-ordered as in well-ordered cities. These are they whom the citizens of a well-ordered city should be ever seeking out, going forth over sea and over land to find him who is incorruptible—that he may establish more firmly institutions in his own state which are good already, and amend what is deficient; for without this examination and enquiry a city

[1] Cp. *Rep.* x. 619.

Laws XII

ATHE-
NIAN.

opinion
of man-
kind to be
desired,

both by
cities, and
individu-
als, but it
should be
also de-
served.

The
law:—

No one to
travel in
a foreign
country
under
forty
years of
age, or in
a private
capacity.

951

The state
to send
out men
to be
specta-
tors of
the
world.

Saints
and
sages are
to be
found
even in
ill-gov-
erned
cities.

The spec-
tator to
be a
model
citizen of
his own
city.

He shall
report to
the
assembly
which re-
vises the
laws.

The
assembly
to con-
sist of
elders and
of young-
[952]
er men
co-opted
by them.

The city
to have
an eye for
young
men
distin-
guished
in the as-
sembly.

The re-
wards
and pun-
ishments
of spec-
tators ac-
cordingly
as they

will never continue perfect any more than if the examination is ill-conducted.

Cle. How can we have an examination and also a good one?

Ath. In this way:—In the first place, our spectator shall be of not less than fifty years of age; he must be a man of reputation, especially in war, if he is to exhibit to other cities a model of the guardians of the law, but when he is more than sixty years of age he shall no longer continue in his office of spectator. And when he has carried on his inspection during as many out of the ten years of his office as he pleases, on his return home let him go to the assembly of those who review the laws. This shall be a mixed body of young and old men, who shall be required to meet daily between the hour of dawn and the rising of the sun. They shall consist, in the first place, of the priests who have obtained the rewards of virtue[1]; and, in the second place, of guardians of the law, the ten eldest being chosen; the general superintendent of education shall also be a member, as well the last appointed as those who have been released from the office; and each of them shall take with him as his companion a young man, whomsoever he chooses, between the ages of thirty and forty. These shall be always holding conversation and discourse about the laws of their own city or about any specially good ones which they may hear to be existing elsewhere; also about kinds of knowledge which may appear to be of use and will throw light upon the examination, or of which the want will make the subject of laws dark and uncertain to them. Any knowledge of this sort which the elders approve, the younger men shall learn with all diligence; and if any one of those who have been invited appear to be unworthy, the whole assembly shall blame him who invited him. The rest of the city shall watch over those among the young men who distinguish themselves, having an eye upon them, and especially honouring them if they succeed, but dishonouring them above the rest if they turn out to be inferior. This is the assembly to which he who has visited the institutions of other men, on his return home shall straightway go, and if he have discovered any one who has anything to say about the enactment of laws or education or nurture, or if he have himself made any observations, let him communicate his discoveries to the whole assembly. And if he be seen to have come home neither better nor worse, let him be praised at any rate for his enthusiasm; and if he be much better, let him be praised so much the more; and not only while he lives but after his death let the assembly honour him with fitting honours. But if on his return home he appear to have been corrupted, pretending to be wise when he is

[1] Cp. *supra*, 947.

not, let him hold no communication with any one, whether young or old; and if he will hearken to the rulers, then he shall be permitted to live as a private individual; but if he will not, let him die, if he be convicted in a court of law of interfering about education and the laws. And if he deserve to be indicted, and none of the magistrates indict him, let that be counted as a disgrace to them when the rewards of virtue are decided.

Let such be the character of the person who goes abroad, and let him go abroad under these conditions. In the next place, the stranger who comes from abroad should be received in a friendly spirit. Now there are four kinds of strangers, of whom we must make some mention—the first is he who comes and stays throughout the summer[1]; this class are like birds of passage, taking wing in pursuit of commerce, and flying over the sea to other cities, while the season lasts; he shall be received in market-places and harbours and public buildings, near the city but outside[2], by those magistrates who are appointed to superintend these matters; and they shall take care that a stranger, whoever he be, duly receives justice; but he shall not be allowed to make any innovation. They shall hold the intercourse with him which is necessary, and this shall be as little as possible. The second kind is just a spectator who comes to see with his eyes and hear with his ears the festivals of the Muses; such ought to have entertainment provided them at the temples by hospitable persons, and the priests and ministers of the temples should see and attend to them. But they should not remain more than a reasonable time; let them see and hear that for the sake of which they came, and then go away, neither having suffered nor done any harm. The priests shall be their judges, if any of them receive or do any wrong up to the sum of fifty drachmae, but if any greater charge be brought, in such cases the suit shall come before the wardens of the agora. The third kind of stranger is he who comes on some public business from another land, and is to be received with public honours. He is to be received only by the generals and commanders of horse and foot, and the host by whom he is entertained, in conjunction with the Prytanes, shall have the sole charge of what concerns him. There is a fourth class of persons answering to our spectators, who come from another land to look at ours. In the first place, such visits will be rare, and the visitor should be at least fifty years of age; he may possibly be wanting to see something that is rich and rare in other states, or himself to show something in like manner to another city. Let such an one, then, go unbidden to the doors of the wise and rich, being one of them himself: let him go,

Laws XII

ATHE-
NIAN.

return
home
better or
worse.

Regula-
tions
about
strangers.

Four
kinds:—

(1) the
bird of
passage,
who
comes in
the sum-
mer to
trade;

953

(2) the
visitor of
festivals;

(3) the
repre-
senta-
tive of a
foreign
country;

(4) the
official
specta-
tor.

---

[1] Cp. *supra*, xi. 915 D. 　　　　[2] Cp. Arist. Pol. vii. 6, § 5.

for example, to the house of the superintendent of education, confident that he is a fitting guest of such a host, or let him go to the house of some of those who have gained the prize of virtue and hold discourse with them, both learning from them, and also teaching them; and when he has seen and heard all, he shall depart, as a friend taking leave of friends, and be honoured by them with gifts and suitable tributes of respect. These are the customs, according to which our city should receive all strangers of either sex who come from other countries, and should send forth her own citizens, showing respect to Zeus, the God of hospitality, not forbidding strangers at meals and sacrifices, as is the manner which prevails among the children of the Nile, nor driving them away by savage proclamations[1].

When a man becomes surety, let him give the security in a distinct form, acknowledging the whole transaction in a written document, and in the presence of not less than three witnesses if the sum be under a thousand drachmae, and of not less than five witnesses

if the sum be above a thousand drachmae. The agent of a dishonest or untrustworthy seller shall himself be responsible; both the agent and the principal shall be equally liable. If a person wishes to find

anything in the house of another, he shall enter naked, or wearing only a short tunic and without a girdle, having first taken an oath by the customary Gods that he expects to find it there; he shall then make his search, and the other shall throw open his house and allow him to search things both sealed and unsealed. And if a person

will not allow the searcher to make his search, he who is prevented shall go to law with him, estimating the value of the goods after which he is searching, and if the other be convicted he shall pay twice the value of the article. If the master be absent from home, the dwellers in the house shall let him search the unsealed property, and on the sealed property the searcher shall set another seal, and shall appoint any one whom he likes to guard them during five days; and if the master of the house be absent during a longer time, he shall take with him the wardens of the city, and so make his search, opening the sealed property as well as the unsealed, and then, together with the members of the family and the wardens of the city, he shall seal them up again as they were before. There shall

be a limit of time in the case of disputed things, and he who has had possession of them during a certain time shall no longer be liable to be disturbed. As to houses and lands there can be no dispute in this state of ours; but if a man has any other possessions which he has used and openly shown in the city and in the agora and in the

[1] Cp. *supra.* 950 A, B.

temples, and no one has put in a claim to them, and some one says
that he was looking for them during this time, and the possessor is
proved to have made no concealment, if they have continued for a
year, the one having the goods and the other looking for them, the
claim of the seeker shall not be allowed after the expiration of the
year; or if he does not use or show the lost property in the market
or in the city, but only in the country, and no one offers himself as
the owner during five years, at the expiration of the five years the
claim shall be barred for ever after; or if he uses them in the city but
within the house, then the appointed time of claiming the goods
shall be three years, or ten years if he has them in the country in
private. And if he has them in another land, there shall be no limit
of time or prescription, but whenever the owner finds them he may
claim them.

If any one prevents another by force from being present at a trial,
whether a principal party or his witnesses; if the person prevented
be a slave, whether his own or belonging to another, the suit shall
be incomplete and invalid; but if he who is prevented be a freeman,
besides the suit being incomplete, the other who has prevented him
shall be imprisoned for a year, and shall be prosecuted for kidnapping by any one who pleases. And if any one hinders by force a rival
competitor in gymnastic or music, or any other sort of contest, from
being present at the contest, let him who has a mind inform the presiding judges, and they shall liberate him who is desirous of competing; and if they are not able, and he who hinders the other from
competing wins the prize, then they shall give the prize of victory
to him who is prevented, and inscribe him as the conqueror in any
temples which he pleases; and he who hinders the other shall not be
permitted to make any offering or inscription having reference to
that contest, and in any case he shall be liable for damages, whether
he be defeated or whether he conquer.

If any one knowingly receives anything which has been stolen, he
shall undergo the same punishment as the thief, and if a man receives an exile he shall be punished with death. Every man should
regard the friend and enemy of the state as his own friend and
enemy; and if any one makes peace or war with another on his own
account, and without the authority of the state, he, like the receiver
of the exile, shall undergo the penalty of death. And if any fraction
of the city declare war or peace against any, the generals shall indict
the authors of this proceeding, and if they are convicted death shall
be the penalty. Those who serve their country ought to serve without receiving gifts, and there ought to be no excusing or approving
the saying, 'Men should receive gifts as the reward of good, but not

Laws XII

ATHE-
NIAN.

than land
or
houses.

Penalty
for pre-
venting
the ap-
pearance
[955]
of a per-
son in the
courts or
at con-
tests.

The
receiver
as bad as
the thief.

Death to
be the
punish-
ment of
those who
(1) re-
ceive
exiles, or

Laws XII

ATHE-
NIAN.

who (2)
make war
or peace
on their
own ac-
count, or
who (3)
take
bribes.

Registra-
tion of
property
with a
view to
income-
tax.

956
Offerings
to the
Gods to
be simple
and inex-
pensive.

Private
suits to
be tried,

(1) be-
fore arbi-
ters:

(2) there
may be
an appeal
from
their de-
cision to
the tribal
courts:

and (3)
from the
tribal
courts to
the court
of select

of evil deeds'; for to know which we are doing, and to stand fast by our knowledge, is no easy matter. The safest course is to obey the law which says, 'Do no service for a bribe,' and let him who disobeys, if he be convicted, simply die. With a view to taxation, for various reasons, every man ought to have had his property valued: and the tribesmen should likewise bring a register of the yearly produce to the wardens of the country, that in this way there may be two valuations; and the public officers may use annually whichever on consideration they deem the best, whether they prefer to take a certain portion of the whole value, or of the annual revenue, after subtracting what is paid to the common tables.

Touching offerings to the Gods, a moderate man should observe moderation in what he offers. Now the land and the hearth of the house of all men is sacred to all Gods; wherefore let no man dedicate them a second time to the Gods. Gold and silver, whether possessed by private persons or in temples, are in other cities provocative of envy, and ivory, the product of a dead body, is not a proper offering; brass and iron, again, are instruments of war; but of wood let a man bring what offering he likes, provided it be a single block, and in like manner of stone, to the public temples; of woven work let him not offer more than one woman can execute in a month. White is a colour suitable to the Gods, especially in woven works, but dyes should only be used for the adornments of war. The most divine of gifts are birds and images, and they should be such as one painter can execute in a single day. And let all other offerings follow a similar rule.

Now that the whole city has been divided into parts of which the nature and number have been described, and laws have been given about all the most important contracts as far as this was possible, the next thing will be to have justice done. The first of the courts shall consist of elected judges, who shall be chosen by the plaintiff and the defendant in common: these shall be called arbiters rather than judges. And in the second court there shall be judges of the villages and tribes corresponding to the twelvefold division of the land, and before these the litigants shall go to contend for greater damages, if the suit be not decided before the first judges; the defendant, if he be defeated the second time, shall pay a fifth more than the damages mentioned in the indictment; and if he find fault with his judges and would try a third time, let him carry the suit before the select judges, and if he be again defeated, let him pay the whole of the damages and half as much again. And the plaintiff, if when defeated before the first judges he persist in going on to the second, shall if he wins receive in addition to the damages a fifth part more, and if defeated he shall pay a like sum; but if he is not satisfied with the previous decision, and will insist on proceeding to a third court, then if he win he shall receive from the defendant the amount of the damages and, as I said before, half as much again, and the plaintiff, if he lose, shall pay half of the damages claimed. Now the assignment by lot of judges to courts and the completion of the number of them, and the appointment of servants to the different magistrates, and the times at which the several causes should be heard, and the votings and delays, and all the things that necessarily concern suits, and the order of causes, and the time in which answers have to be put in and parties are to appear—of these and other things akin to these we have indeed already spoken[1], but there is no harm in repeating what is right twice or thrice:—All lesser and easier matters which the elder legislator has omitted may be supplied by the younger one. Private courts will be sufficiently regulated in this way, and the public and state courts, and those which the magistrates must use in the administration of their several offices, exist in many other states. Many very respectable institutions of this sort have been framed by good men, and from them the guardians of the law may by reflection derive what is necessary for the order of our new state, considering and correcting them, and bringing them to the test of experience, until every detail appears to be satisfactorily determined; and then putting the final seal upon them, and making them irreversible, they shall use them for ever afterwards. As to what relates to the silence of judges and the abstinence from words of evil omen and the reverse, and the different notions of the just and good and honourable which exist in our own as compared with other states, they have been partly mentioned already, and another part of them will be mentioned hereafter as we draw near the end. To all these matters he who would be an equal judge shall justly look, and he shall possess writings about them that he may learn them. For of all kinds of knowledge the knowledge of good laws has the greatest power of improving the learner; otherwise there would be no meaning in the divine and admirable law possessing a name akin to mind (νοῦς, νόμος). And of all other words, such as the praises and censures of individuals which occur in poetry and also in prose, whether written down or uttered in daily conversation, whether men dispute about them in the spirit of contention or weakly assent to them, as is often the case—of all these the one sure test is the writings of the legislator[2], which the righteous judge ought to have in his mind as the antidote of all other words, and thus make himself and the city stand up-

Laws XII

ATHE-
NIAN.

judges; in the two last cases with an increase of the penalty.

The younger legislator [957] will arrange minor matters.

The judge should study the writings of the legislator and test all other writings by their standard, and then he will give righteous judgment.

---

[1] Cp. *supra*, vi. 766; ix. 853 foll.   [2] Cp. *supra*, vii. 811 D.

958

The
goods of
the losing
party in a
suit to be
handed
over to
the gain-
er if the
damages
are not
paid
within a
month.

Con-
tempt of
court to
be pun-
ished
with
death.

The dead
are to be
buried in
some
barren
region,
where
they will
do least

right, procuring for the good the continuance and increase of justice, and for the bad, on the other hand, a conversion from ignorance and intemperance, and in general from all unrighteousness,
as far as their evil minds can be healed, but to those whose web of
life is in reality finished, giving death, which is the only remedy for
souls in their condition, as I may say truly again and again. And
such judges and chiefs of judges will be worthy of receiving praise
from the whole city.

When the suits of the year are completed the following laws shall
regulate their execution:—In the first place, the judge shall assign
to the party who wins the suit the whole property of him who loses,
with the exception of mere necessaries[1], and the assignment shall
be made through the herald immediately after each decision in the
hearing of the judges; and when the month arrives following the
month in which the courts are sitting (unless the gainer of the suit
has been previously satisfied), the court shall follow up the case,
and hand over to the winner the goods of the loser; but if they find
that he has not the means of paying, and the sum deficient is not
less than a drachma, the insolvent person shall not have any right
of going to law with any other man until he have satisfied the debt
of the winning party; but other persons shall still have the right of
bringing suits against him. And if any one after he is condemned
refuses to acknowledge the authority which condemned him, let the
magistrates who are thus deprived of their authority bring him before the court of the guardians of the law, and if he be cast, let him
be punished with death, as a subverter of the whole state and of
the laws.

Thus a man is born and brought up, and after this manner he
begets and brings up his own children, and has his share of dealings
with other men, and suffers if he has done wrong to any one, and
receives satisfaction if he has been wronged, and so at length in due
time he grows old under the protection of the laws, and his end
comes in the order of nature. Concerning the dead of either sex, the
religious ceremonies which may fittingly be performed, whether ap-
pertaining to the Gods of the under-world or of this, shall be decided
by the interpreters with absolute authority. Their sepulchres are
not to be in places which are fit for cultivation, and there shall be
no monuments in such spots, either large or small, but they shall
occupy that part of the country which is naturally adapted for receiving and concealing the bodies of the dead with as little hurt as
possible to the living. No man, living or dead, shall deprive the living of the sustenance which the earth, their foster-parent, is natur-

[1] Cp. *supra*, ix. 855 B.

ally inclined to provide for them. And let not the mound be piled higher than would be the work of five men completed in five days; nor shall the stone which is placed over the spot be larger than would be sufficient to receive the praises of the dead included in four heroic lines. Nor shall the laying out of the dead in the house continue for a longer time than is sufficient to distinguish between him who is in a trance only and him who is really dead, and speaking generally, the third day after death will be a fair time for carrying out the body to the sepulchre. Now we must believe the legislator when he tells us that the soul is in all respects superior to the body, and that even in life what makes each one of us to be what we are is only the soul; and that the body follows us about in the likeness of each of us, and therefore, when we are dead, the bodies of the dead are quite rightly said to be our shades or images; for the true and immortal being of each one of us which is called the soul goes on her way to other Gods[1], before them to give an account— which is an inspiring hope to the good, but very terrible to the bad, as the laws of our fathers tell us; and they also say that not much can be done in the way of helping a man after he is dead. But the living—he should be helped by all his kindred, that while in life he may be the holiest and justest of men, and after death may have no great sins to be punished in the world below. If this be true, a man ought not to waste his substance under the idea that all this lifeless mass of flesh which is in process of burial is connected with him; he should consider that the son, or brother, or the beloved one, whoever he may be, whom he thinks he is laying in the earth, has gone away to complete and fulfil his own destiny, and that his duty is rightly to order the present, and to spend moderately on the lifeless altar of the Gods below. But the legislator does not intend moderation to be taken in the sense of meanness[2]. Let the law, then, be as follows:—The expenditure on the entire funeral of him who is of the highest class, shall not exceed five minae; and for him who is of the second class, three minae, and for him who is of the third class, two minae, and for him who is of the fourth class, one mina, will be a fair limit of expense. The guardians of the law ought to take especial care of the different ages of life, whether childhood, or manhood, or any other age. And at the end of all, let there be some one guardian of the law presiding, who shall be chosen by the friends of the deceased to superintend, and let it be glory to him to manage with fairness and moderation what relates to the dead, and a discredit to him if they are not well managed. Let the laying out and other ceremonies be in accordance with custom, but to the states-

959
harm to
the liv-
ing.

The body
is our
shadow:
the soul
or true
being
goes to
judgment
after
death.

Burials
should be
simple.
The living
need the
help of
kindred
more than
the dead.

The
law:—
The cost
of fune-
rals.

The
funeral
cere-
monies to
be super-
intended
by some
guardian
of the
law.

---

[1] Cp. Phaedo 63 B.   [2] Cp. *supra*, iv. 717 E, 719.

Ostenta-
tious
grief to be
repres-
sed, but
some al-
lowance
to be
made for
human
weakness.

We have
still to
provide
for the
continu-
ance of
our laws.

We want
some
power,
like
Atropos
among
the fates,
to make
them ir-
reversible.

man who adopts custom as his law we must give way in certain particulars. It would be monstrous for example that he should command any man to weep or abstain from weeping over the dead; but
he may forbid cries of lamentation, and not allow the voice of the
mourner to be heard outside the house; also, he may forbid the
bringing of the dead body into the open streets, or the processions
of mourners in the streets, and may require that before daybreak
they should be outside the city. Let these, then, be our laws relating
to such matters, and let him who obeys be free from penalty; but
he who disobeys even a single guardian of the law shall be punished
by them all with a fitting penalty. Other modes of burial, or again
the denial of burial, which is to be refused in the case of robbers of
temples and parricides and the like, have been devised and are embodied in the preceding laws, so that now our work of legislation is
pretty nearly at an end; but in all cases the end does not consist in
doing something or acquiring something or establishing something,
—the end will be attained and finally accomplished, when we have
provided for the perfect and lasting continuance of our institutions
until then our creation is incomplete.

Cle. That is very good, Stranger; but I wish you would tell me
more clearly what you mean.

Ath. O Cleinias, many things of old time were well said and sung;
and the saying about the Fates was one of them.

Cle. What is it?

Ath. The saying that Lachesis or the giver of the lots is the first
of them, and that Clotho or the spinster is the second of them, and
that Atropos or the unchanging one is the third of them[1]; and that
she is the preserver of the things which we have spoken, and which
have been compared in a figure to things woven by fire, they both
(i. e. Atropos and the fire) producing[2] the quality of unchangeableness. I am speaking of the things which in a state and government
give not only health and salvation to the body, but law, or rather
preservation of the law, in the soul; and, if I am not mistaken, this
seems to be still wanting in our laws: we have still to see how we
can implant in them this irreversible nature.

Cle. It will be no small matter if we can only discover how such
a nature can be implanted in anything.

Ath. But it certainly can be; so much I clearly see.

Cle. Then let us not think of desisting until we have imparted

[1] Cp. Rep. x. 620 E.

[2] Reading ἀπεργαζομένων with the MSS. and as in the text, not as in the
notes of Stallbaum. The construction is harsh; but ἀπεικασμένα may be taken
as if in apposition with the previous sentence. With τῇ may be supplied
δυνάμει, and ἀπεργαζομένων may be regarded as a 'genitive absolute.'

Laws XII
ATHE-
NIAN,
CLEINIAS,
MEGIL-
LUS.

this quality to our laws; for it is ridiculous, after a great deal of labour has been spent, to place a thing at last on an insecure foundation.

Meg. I approve of your suggestion, and am quite of the same mind with you.

Cle. Very good: And now what, according to you, is to be the salvation of our government and of our laws, and how is it to be effected?

Ath. Were we not saying that there must be in our city a council which was to be of this sort:—The ten oldest guardians of the law, and all those who have obtained prizes of virtue, were to meet in the same assembly, and the council was also to include those who had visited foreign countries in the hope of hearing something that might be of use in the preservation of the laws, and who, having come safely home, and having been tested in these same matters, had proved themselves to be worthy to take part in the assembly;— each of the members was to select some young man of not less than thirty years of age, he himself judging in the first instance whether the young man was worthy by nature and education, and then suggesting him to the others, and if he seemed to them also to be worthy they were to adopt him; but if not, the decision at which they arrived was to be kept a secret from the citizens at large, and, more especially, from the rejected candidate. The meeting of the council was to be held early in the morning, when everybody was most at leisure from all other business, whether public or private— was not something of this sort said by us before?

961
The noc-
turnal
council
will be
such a
preserv-
ing power
in our
state.

Cle. True.

Ath. Then, returning to the council, I would say further, that if we let it down to be the anchor of the state, our city, having everything which is suitable to her, will preserve all that we wish to preserve.

Cle. What do you mean?

Ath. Now is the time for me to speak the truth in all earnestness.

Cle. Well said, and I hope that you will fulfil your intention.

Ath. Know, Cleinias, that everything, in all that it does, has a natural saviour, as of an animal the soul and the head are the chief saviours.

Cle. Once more, what do you mean?

Ath. The well-being of those two is obviously the preservation of every living thing.

Cle. How is that?

Ath. The soul, besides other things, contains mind, and the head, besides other things, contains sight and hearing; and the mind,

Laws XII

ATHE-
NIAN,
CLEINIAS,

are the
salvation
of all
things.

mingling with the noblest of the senses, and becoming one with them, may be truly called the salvation of all.

Cle. Yes, quite so.

Ath. Yes, indeed; but with what is that intellect concerned which, mingling with the senses, is the salvation of ships in storms as well as in fair weather? In a ship, when the pilot and the sailors unite their perceptions with the piloting mind, do they not save both themselves and their craft?

Cle. Very true.

Ath. We do not want many illustrations about such matters:— What aim would the general of an army, or what aim would a physician propose to himself, if he were seeking to attain salvation?

Cle. Very good.

Ath. Does not the general aim at victory and superiority in war, and do not the physician and his assistants aim at producing health in the body?

Cle. Certainly.

Ath. And a physician who is ignorant about the body, that is to say, who knows not that which we just now called health, or a general who knows not victory, or any others who are ignorant of the particulars of the arts which we mentioned, cannot be said to have understanding about any of these matters.

Cle. They cannot.

Ath. And what would you say of the state? If a person proves to be ignorant of the aim to which the statesman should look, ought he, in the first place, to be called a ruler at all; and further, will he ever be able to preserve that of which he does not even know the aim?

Cle. Impossible.

Ath. And therefore, if our settlement of the country is to be perfect, we ought to have some institution, which, as I was saying, will tell what is the aim of the state, and will inform us how we are to attain this, and what law or what man will advise us to that end. Any state which has no such institution is likely to be devoid of mind and sense, and in all her actions will proceed by mere chance.

Cle. Very true.

Ath. In which, then, of the parts or institutions of the state is any such guardian power to be found? Can we say?

Cle. I am not quite certain, Stranger; but I have a suspicion that you are referring to the assembly which you just now said was to meet at night.

Ath. You understand me perfectly, Cleinias; and we must assume, as the argument implies, that this council possesses all virtue;

As the
general
and the
physician
[962]
must
know the
aim of
their arts:

so too the
nocturnal
council
must
know the
aim of
the state.

and the beginning of virtue is not to make mistakes by guessing many things, but to look steadily at one thing, and on this to fix all our aims.

Cle. Quite true.

Ath. Then now we shall see why there is nothing wonderful in states going astray—the reason is that their legislators have such different aims; nor is there anything wonderful in some laying down as their rule of justice, that certain individuals should bear rule in the state, whether they be good or bad, and others that the citizens should be rich, not caring whether they are the slaves of other men or not. The tendency of others, again, is towards freedom; and some legislate with a view to two things at once,—they want to be at the same time free and the lords of other states; but the wisest men, as they deem themselves to be, look to all these and similar aims, and there is no one of them which they exclusively honour, and to which they would have all things look.

Cle. Then, Stranger, our former assertion will hold, for we were saying that laws generally should look to one thing only; and this, as we admitted, was rightly said to be virtue.

Ath. Yes.

Cle. And we said that virtue was of four kinds?

Ath. Quite true.

Cle. And that mind was the leader of the four, and that to her the three other virtues and all other things ought to have regard?

Ath. You follow me capitally, Cleinias, and I would ask you to follow me to the end, for we have already said that the mind of the pilot, the mind of the physician and of the general look to that one thing to which they ought to look; and now we may turn to mind political, of which, as of a human creature, we will ask a question:— O wonderful being, and to what are you looking? The physician is able to tell his single aim in life, but you, the superior, as you declare yourself to be, of all intelligent beings, when you are asked are not able to tell. Can you, Megillus, and you, Cleinias, say distinctly what is the aim of mind political, in return for the many explanations of things which I have given you?

Cle. We cannot, Stranger.

Ath. Well, but ought we not to desire to see it, and to see where it is to be found?

Cle. For example, where?

Ath. For example, we were saying that there are four kinds of virtue, and as there are four of them, each of them must be one.

Cle. Certainly.

Ath. And further, all four of them we call one; for we say that

Laws XII

ATHE-
NIAN,
CLEINIAS.

which is
not privi-
lege,
wealth, or
freedom,

963
but
virtue.

We have
seen the
end of
the mind
of the
general
and the
physi-
cian;—
but what
is the end
of mind
political?

The four
virtues
are dis-
tinct, yet
one.

It is easy
to see
how they
differ;

courage is virtue, and that prudence is virtue, and the same of the two others, as if they were in reality not many but one, that is, virtue.

Cle. Quite so.

Ath. There is no difficulty in seeing in what way the two differ from one another, and have received two names, and so of the rest. But there is more difficulty in explaining why we call these two and the rest of them by the single name of virtue.

Cle. How do you mean?

Ath. I have no difficulty in explaining what I mean. Let us distribute the subject into questions and answers.

Cle. Once more, what do you mean?

e.g. how
courage
differs
from wis-
dom;

Ath. Ask me what is that one thing which I call virtue, and then again speak of as two, one part being courage and the other wisdom. I will tell you how that occurs:—One of them has to do with fear; in this the beasts also participate[1], and quite young children,—I mean courage; for a courageous temper is a gift of nature and not of reason. But without reason there never has been, or is, or will be a wise and understanding soul; it is of a different nature.

Cle. That is true.

964

but how
are they
all one?

Ath. I have now told you in what way the two are different, and do you in return tell me in what way they are one and the same. Suppose that I ask you in what way the four are one, and when you have answered me, you will have a right to ask of me in return in what way they are four; and then let us proceed to enquire whether in the case of things which have a name and also a definition to them, true knowledge consists in knowing the name only and not the definition. Can he who is good for anything be ignorant of all this without discredit where great and glorious truths are concerned?

Cle. I suppose not.

Ath. And is there anything greater to the legislator and the guardian of the law, and to him who thinks that he excels all other men in virtue, and has won the palm of excellence, than these very qualities of which we are now speaking,—courage, temperance, wisdom, justice?

Cle. How can there be anything greater?

The na-
ture of
virtue
must be
taught by
lawgivers
and
guardians,

Ath. And ought not the interpreters, the teachers, the lawgivers, the guardians of the other citizens, to excel the rest of mankind, and perfectly to show him who desires to learn and know or whose evil actions require to be punished and reproved, what is the nature of virtue and vice? Or shall some poet who has found his way into the city, or some chance person who pretends to be an instructor of

[1] Cp. Laches 196 D.

youth, show himself to be better than him who has won the prize
for every virtue? And can we wonder that when the guardians are
not adequate in speech or action, and have no adequate knowledge
of virtue, the city being unguarded should experience the common
fate of cities in our day?

Cle. Wonder! no.

Ath. Well, then, must we do as we said? Or can we give our
guardians a more precise knowledge of virtue in speech and action
than the many have? or is there any way in which our city can be
made to resemble the head and senses of rational beings because
possessing such a guardian power?

Cle. What, Stranger, is the drift of your comparison?

Ath. Do we not see that the city is the trunk, and are not the
younger guardians, who are chosen for their natural gifts, placed in
the head of the state, having their souls all full of eyes, with which
they look about the whole city? They keep watch and hand over
their perceptions to the memory, and inform the elders of all that
happens in the city; and those whom we compared to the mind,
because they have many wise thoughts—that is to say, the old
men—take counsel, and making use of the younger men as their
ministers, and advising with them,—in this way both together truly
preserve the whole state:—Shall this or some other be the order of
our state? Are all our citizens to be equal in acquirements, or shall
there be special persons among them who have received a more
careful training and education?

Cle. That they should be equal, my good sir, is impossible.

Ath. Then we ought to proceed to some more exact training than
any which has preceded.

Cle. Certainly.

Ath. And must not that of which we are in need be the one to
which we were just now alluding?

Cle. Very true.

Ath. Did we not say that the workman or guardian, if he be perfect in every respect, ought not only to be able to see the many
aims, but he should press onward to the one[1]? this he should know,
and knowing, order all things with a view to it.

Cle. True.

Ath. And can any one have a more exact way of considering or
contemplating anything, than the being able to look at one idea
gathered from many different things?

Cle. Perhaps not.

Ath. Not 'Perhaps not,' but 'Certainly not,' my good sir, is the

[1] Cp. Rep. vii. 537 B.

Laws XII

ATHE-
NIAN,
CLEINIAS.

not by the
poets.

The
younger
guardians
are the
eyes of
the city,
and they
[965]
tell what
they have
seen to
the elders,
who are
the mind
of the
city.

The
guardians
should
have a
special
training.

which
will en-
able them
to see the
unity as
well as
plurality
of virtue,

right answer. There never has been a truer method than this discovered by any man.

Cle. I bow to your authority, Stranger; let us proceed in the way
which you propose.

Ath. Then, as would appear, we must compel the guardians of
our divine state to perceive, in the first place, what that principle is
which is the same in all the four—the same, as we affirm, in courage
and in temperance, and in justice and in prudence, and which, being
one, we call as we ought, by the single name of virtue. To this, my
friends, we will, if you please, hold fast, and not let go until we
have sufficiently explained what that is to which we are to look,
whether to be regarded as one, or as a whole, or as both, or in
whatever way. Are we likely ever to be in a virtuous condition, if
we cannot tell whether virtue is many, or four, or one? Certainly,
if we take counsel among ourselves, we shall in some way contrive
that this principle has a place amongst us; but if you have made up
your mind that we should let the matter alone, we will.

Cle. We must not, Stranger, by the God of strangers I swear that
we must not, for in our opinion you speak most truly; but we should
like to know how you will accomplish your purpose.

966

Ath. Wait a little before you ask; and let us, first of all, be quite
agreed with one another that the purpose has to be accomplished.

Cle. Certainly, it ought to be, if it can be.

and of the
good and
honour-
able.

Ath. Well, and about the good and the honourable, are we to take
the same view? Are our guardians only to know that each of them
is many, or also how and in what way they are one?

Cle. They must consider also in what sense they are one.

Ath. And are they to consider only, and to be unable to set forth
what they think?

Cle. Certainly not; that would be the state of a slave.

Ath. And may not the same be said of all good things—that the
true guardians of the laws ought to know the truth about them, and
to be able to interpret them in words, and carry them out in action,
judging of what is and of what is not well, according to nature?

Cle. Certainly.

They
must also
know
about the
Gods.

Ath. Is not the knowledge of the Gods which we have set forth
with so much zeal one of the noblest sorts of knowledge;—to know
that they are, and know how great is their power, as far as in man
lies? We do indeed excuse the mass of the citizens, who only follow
the voice of the laws, but we refuse to admit as guardians any who
do not labour to obtain every possible evidence that there is respecting the Gods; our city is forbidden and not allowed to choose
as a guardian of the law, or to place in the select order of virtue,

him who is not an inspired man, and has not laboured at these things.

Cle. It is certainly just, as you say, that he who is indolent about such matters or incapable should be rejected, and that things honourable should be put away from him.

Ath. Are we assured that there are two things which lead men to believe in the Gods, as we have already stated?

Cle. What are they?

Ath. One is the argument about the soul, which has been already mentioned—that it is the eldest and most divine of all things, to which motion attaining generation gives perpetual existence[1]; the other was an argument from the order of the motion of the stars, and of all things under the dominion of the mind which ordered the universe[2]. If a man look upon the world not lightly or ignorantly, there was never any one so godless who did not experience an effect opposite to that which the many imagine. For they think that those who handle these matters by the help of astronomy, and the accompanying arts of demonstration, may become godless, because they see, as far as they can see, things happening by necessity, and not by an intelligent will accomplishing good.

Cle. But what is the fact?

Ath. Just the opposite, as I said, of the opinion which once prevailed among men, that the sun and stars are without soul. Even in those days men wondered about them, and that which is now ascertained was then conjectured by some who had a more exact knowledge of them—that if they had been things without soul, and had no mind, they could never have moved with numerical exactness so wonderful; and even at that time some ventured to hazard the conjecture that mind was the orderer of the universe. But these same persons again mistaking the nature of the soul, which they conceived to be younger and not older than the body, once more overturned the world, or rather, I should say, themselves; for the bodies which they saw moving in heaven all appeared to be full of stones, and earth, and many other lifeless substances, and to these they assigned the causes of all things. Such studies gave rise to much atheism and perplexity, and the poets took occasion to be abusive, —comparing the philosophers to she-dogs uttering vain howlings, and talking other nonsense of the same sort. But now, as I said, the case is reversed[3].

Cle. How so?

Ath. No man can be a true worshipper of the Gods who does not know these two principles—that the soul is the eldest of all things

Two arguments for the existence of Gods: —(1) the priority of the soul; (2) [967] the order of the universe.

Astronomy need not tend to Atheism, as the many think.

Long ago it was suspected that mind was the orderer of the heavens. But mankind went wrong by putting body before mind.

The true ruler must

[1] Cp. *supra*, x. 893 A.   [2] Cp. *ib.* 896 C.   [3] *Cp.* Rep. x. 607.

have
grasped
true prin-
[968]
ciples,
and have
gone
through
the pre-
vious
training
and seen
the con-
nection of
the sci-
ences.

The noc-
turnal
council
the guard
of the
state.

We can
proceed
no further
in deter-
mining
either the
powers of
the coun-
cil,

or the
qualifica-
tions and
education
of the
guardians.

which are born, and is immortal and rules over all bodies; moreover, as I have now said several times, he who has not contemplated the mind of nature which is said to exist in the stars, and gone through the previous training, and seen the connection of music with these things, and harmonized them all with laws and institutions, is not able to give a reason of such things as have a reason[1]. And he who is unable to acquire this in addition to the ordinary virtues of a citizen, can hardly be a good ruler of a whole state; but he should be the subordinate of other rulers. Wherefore, Cleinias and Megillus, let us consider whether we may not add to all the other laws which we have discussed this further one,—that the nocturnal assembly of the magistrates, which has also shared in the whole scheme of education proposed by us, shall be a guard set according to law for the salvation of the state. Shall we propose this?

Cle. Certainly, my good friend, we will if the thing is in any degree possible.

Ath. Let us make a common effort to gain such an object; for I too will gladly share in the attempt. Of these matters I have had much experience, and have often considered them, and I dare say that I shall be able to find others who will also help.

Cle. I agree, Stranger, that we should proceed along the road in which God is guiding us; and how we can proceed rightly has now to be investigated and explained.

Ath. O Megillus and Cleinias, about these matters we cannot legislate further until the council is constituted; when that is done, then we will determine what authority they shall have of their own; but the explanation of how this is all to be ordered would only be given rightly in a long discourse.

Cle. What do you mean, and what new thing is this?

Ath. In the first place, a list would have to be made out of those who by their ages and studies and dispositions and habits are well fitted for the duty of a guardian. In the next place, it will not be easy for them to discover themselves what they ought to learn, or become the disciple of one who has already made the discovery. Furthermore, to write down the times at which, and during which, they ought to receive the several kinds of instruction, would be a vain thing; for the learners themselves do not know what is learned to advantage until the knowledge which is the result of learning has found a place in the soul of each. And so these details, although they could not be truly said to be secret, might be said to be incapable of being stated beforehand, because when stated they would have no meaning.

[1] Cp. Rep. vii. 531 foll.

Cle. What then are we to do, Stranger, under these circumstances?

Ath. As the proverb says, the answer is no secret, but open to all of us:—We must risk the whole on the chance of throwing, as they say, thrice six or thrice ace, and I am willing to share with you the danger by stating and explaining to you my views about education and nurture, which is the question coming to the surface again. The danger is not a slight or ordinary one, and I would advise you, Cleinias, in particular, to see to the matter; for if you order rightly the city of the Magnetes, or whatever name God may give it, you will obtain the greatest glory; or at any rate you will be thought the most courageous of men in the estimation of posterity. Dear companions, if this our divine assembly can only be established, to them we will hand over the city; none of the present company of legislators, as I may call them, would hesitate about that. And the state will be perfected and become a waking reality, which a little while ago we attempted to create as a dream[1] and in idea only, mingling together reason and mind in one image, in the hope that our citizens might be duly mingled and rightly educated; and being educated, and dwelling in the citadel of the land, might become perfect guardians, such as we have never seen in all our previous life, by reason of the saving virtue which is in them.

Meg. Dear Cleinias, after all that has been said, either we must detain the Stranger, and by supplications and in all manner of ways make him share in the foundation of the city, or we must give up the undertaking.

Cle. Very true, Megillus; and you must join with me in detaining him.

Meg. I will.

[1] Cp. Rep. ix. 592.

Laws XII

969
ATHE-
NIAN,
CLEINIAS.
MEGIL-
LUS.

We must stake everything on the successful establishment of the council. To its care we will then hand over the new city, and so our dream will become a reality.

The Athenian must give his help.

960

APPENDIX I

APPENDIX I.

INTRODUCTION

IT seems impossible to separate by any exact line the genuine writings of Plato from the spurious. The only external evidence to them which is of much value is that of Aristotle; for the Alexandrian catalogues of a century later include manifest forgeries. Even the value of the Aristotelian authority is a good deal impaired by the uncertainty concerning the date and authorship of the writings which are ascribed to him. And several of the citations of Aristotle omit the name of Plato, and some of them omit the name of the dialogue from which they are taken. Prior, however, to the enquiry about the writings of a particular author, general considerations which equally affect all evidence to the genuineness of ancient writings are the following: Shorter works are more likely to have been forged, or to have received an erroneous designation, than longer ones; and some kinds of composition, such as epistles or panegyrical orations, are more liable to suspicion than others; those, again, which have a taste of sophistry in them, or the ring of a later age, or the slighter character of a rhetorical exercise, or in which a motive or some affinity to spurious writings can be detected, or which seem to have originated in a name or statement really occurring in some classical author, are also of doubtful credit; while there is no instance of any ancient writing proved to be a forgery, which combines excellence with length. A really great and original writer would have no object in fathering his works on Plato; and to the forger or imitator, the 'literary hack' of Alexandria and Athens, the Gods did not grant originality or genius. Further, in attempting to balance the evidence for and against a Platonic dialogue, we must not forget that the form of the Platonic writing was common to several of his contemporaries. Aeschines, Euclid, Phaedo, Antisthenes, and in the next generation Aristotle, are all said to have composed dialogues; and mistakes of names are very likely to have occurred. Greek literature in the third century before Christ was almost as voluminous as our own, and without the safeguards of regular publication, or printing, or binding, or even of distinct titles. An unknown writing was naturally attributed to a known writer whose works bore the same character; and the name once appended easily obtained authority. A tendency may also be observed to blend the works and opinions of the master with those of his scholars. To a later Platonist, the difference between Plato and his imitators was not so perceptible as to ourselves. The Memorabilia of Xenophon and the Dialogues of Plato are but a part of a considerable Socratic literature which has passed away. And we must consider how we should regard the question of the genuineness of a particular writing, if this lost literature had been preserved to us.

These considerations lead us to adopt the following criteria of genuineness: (1) That is most certainly Plato's which Aristotle attributes to him by name, which (2) is of considerable length, of (3) great excellence, and also (4) in harmony with the general spirit of the Platonic writings. But the testimony of Aristotle cannot always be distinguished from that of a later age (see above); and has various degrees of importance. Those writings which he cites without mentioning Plato, under their own names, e.g. the Hippias, the Funeral Oration, the Phaedo, etc., have an inferior degree of evidence in their favour. They may have been supposed by him to be the writings of another, although in the case of really great works, e.g. the Phaedo, this is not credible; those again which are quoted but not named, are still more defective in their external credentials. There may be also a possibility that Aristotle was mistaken, or may have confused the master and his scholars in the case of a short writing; but this is inconceivable about a more important work, e.g. the Laws, especially when we remember that he was living at Athens, and a frequenter of the groves of the Academy, during the last twenty years of Plato's life. Nor must we forget that in all his numerous citations from the Platonic writings he never attributes any passage found in the extant dialogues to any one but Plato. And lastly, we may remark that one or two great writings, such as the Parmenides and the Politicus, which are wholly devoid of Aristotelian (1) credentials may be fairly attributed to Plato, on the ground of (2) length, (3) excellence, and (4) accordance with the general spirit of his writings. Indeed the greater part of the evidence for the genuineness of ancient Greek authors may be summed up under two heads only: (1) excellence; and (2) uniformity of tradition—a kind of evidence, which though in many cases sufficient, is of inferior value.

Proceeding upon these principles we appear to arrive at the conclusion that nineteen-twentieths of all the writings which have ever been ascribed to Plato, are undoubtedly genuine. There is another portion of them, including the Epistles, the Epinomis, the dialogues rejected by the ancients themselves, namely, the Axiochus, De justo, De virtute, Demodocus, Sisyphus, Eryxias, which on grounds, both of internal and external evidence, we are able with equal certainty to reject. But there still remains a small portion of which we are unable to affirm either that they are genuine or spurious. They may have been written in youth, or possibly like the works of some painters, may be partly or wholly the compositions of pupils; or they may have been the writings of some contemporary transferred by accident to the more celebrated name of Plato, or of some Platonist in the next generation who aspired to imitate his master. Not that on grounds either of language or philosophy we should lightly reject them. Some difference of style, or inferiority of execution, or inconsistency of thought, can hardly be considered decisive of their spurious character. For who always does justice to himself, or who writes with equal care at all times? Certainly not Plato, who exhibits the greatest differences in dramatic power, in the formation of sentences, and in the use of words, if his earlier writings are compared with his later ones, say the Protagoras or Phaedrus with the Laws. Or who can be expected to think in the same manner during a period of authorship extending over above fifty years, in an age of great intellectual activity, as well as of political and literary transition? Certainly not Plato, whose earlier writings are separated from his later ones by as wide an interval of philosophical speculation as that which separates his later writings from Aristotle.

The dialogues which have been translated in the first Appendix, and which appear to have the next claim to genuineness among the Platonic writings, are the Lesser Hippias, the Menexenus or Funeral Oration, the First Alcibiades. Of these, the Lesser Hippias and the Funeral Oration are cited by Aristotle; the first in the Metaphysics, iv. 29, 5, the latter in the Rhetoric, iii. 14, 11. Neither of them are expressly attributed to Plato, but in his citation of both of them he seems to be referring to passages in the extant dialogues. From the mention of 'Hippias' in the singular by Aristotle, we may perhaps infer that he was unacquainted with a second dialogue bearing the same name. Moreover, the mere existence of a Greater and Lesser Hippias, and of a First and Second Alcibiades, does to a certain extent throw a doubt upon both of them. Though a very clever and ingenious work, the Lesser Hippias does not appear to contain anything beyond the power of an imitator, who was also a careful student of the earlier Platonic writings, to invent. The motive or leading thought of the dialogue may be detected in Xen. Mem. iv. 2, 21, and there is no similar instance of a 'motive' which is taken from Xenophon in an undoubted dialogue of Plato. On the other hand, the upholders of the genuineness of the dialogue will find in the Hippias a true Socratic spirit; they will compare the Ion as being akin both in subject and treatment; they will urge the authority of Aristotle; and they will detect in the treatment of the Sophist, in the satirical reasoning upon Homer, in the *reductio ad absurdum* of the doctrine that vice is ignorance, traces of a Platonic authorship. In reference to the last point we are doubtful, as in some of the other dialogues, whether the author is asserting or overthrowing the paradox of Socrates, or merely following the argument 'whither the wind blows.' That no conclusion is arrived at is also in accordance with the character of the earlier dialogues. The resemblances or imitations of the Gorgias, Protagoras, and Euthydemus, which have been observed in the Hippias, cannot with certainty be adduced on either side of the argument. On the whole, more may be said in favour of the genuineness of the Hippias than against it.

The Menexenus or Funeral Oration is cited by Aristotle, and is interesting as supplying an example of the manner in which the orators praised 'the Athenians among the Athenians,' falsifying persons and dates, and casting a veil over the gloomier events of Athenian history. It exhibits an acquaintance with the funeral oration of Thucydides, and was, perhaps, intended to rival that great work. If genuine, the proper place of the Menexenus would be at the end of the Phaedrus. The satirical opening and the concluding words bear a great resemblance to the earlier dialogues; the oration itself is professedly a mimetic work, like the speeches in the Phaedrus, and cannot therefore be tested by a comparison of the other writings of Plato. The funeral oration of Pericles is expressly mentioned in the Phaedrus, and this may have suggested the subject, in the same manner that the Cleitophon appears to be suggested by the slight mention of Cleitophon and his attachment to Thrasymachus in the Republic, cp. 465 A; and the Theages by the mention of Theages in the Apology and Republic; or as the Second Alcibiades seems to be founded upon the text of Xenophon, Mem. i. 3, 1. A similar taste for parody appears not only in the Phaedrus, but in the Protagoras, in the Symposium, and to a certain extent in the Parmenides.

To these two doubtful writings of Plato I have added the First Alcibiades, which, of all the disputed dialogues of Plato, has the greatest merit, and is somewhat longer than any other of them, though not verified by the testimony of Aristotle, and in many respects at variance with the Symposium in the description of the relations of Socrates and Alcibiades. Like the Lesser Hippias and the Menexenus, it is to be compared to the earlier writings of Plato. The motive of the piece may, perhaps, be found in that passage of the Symposium in which Alcibiades describes himself as self-convicted by the words of Socrates (216 B, C). For the disparaging manner in which Schleiermacher has spoken of this dialogue there seems to be no sufficient foundation. At the same time, the lesson imparted is simple, and the irony more transparent than in the undoubted dialogues of Plato. We know, too, that Alcibiades was a favourite thesis, and that at least five or six dialogues bearing this name passed current in antiquity, and are attributed to contemporaries of Socrates and Plato. (1) In the entire absence of real external evidence (for the catalogues of the Alexandrian librarians cannot be regarded as trustworthy); and (2) in the absence of the highest marks either of poetical or philosophical excellence; and (3) considering that we have express testimony to the existence of contemporary writings bearing the name of Alcibiades, we are compelled to suspend our judgment on the genuineness of the extant dialogue.

Neither at this point, nor at any other, do we propose to draw an absolute line of demarcation between genuine and spurious writings of Plato. They fade off imperceptibly from one class to another. There may have been degrees of genuineness in the dialogues themselves, as there are certainly degrees of evidence by which they are supported. The traditions of the oral discourses both of Socrates and Plato may have formed the basis of semi-Platonic writings; some of them may be of the same mixed character which is apparent in Aristotle and Hippocrates, although the form of them is different. But the writings of Plato, unlike the writings of Aristotle, seem never to have been confused with the writings of his disciples: this was probably due to their definite form, and to their inimitable excellence. The three dialogues which we have offered in the Appendix to the criticism of the reader may be partly spurious and partly genuine; they may be altogether spurious;—that is an alternative which must be frankly admitted. Nor can we maintain of some other dialogues, such as the Parmenides, and the Sophist, and Politicus, that no considerable objection can be urged against them, though greatly overbalanced by the weight (chiefly) of internal evidence in their favour. Nor, on the other hand, can we exclude a bare possibility that some dialogues which are usually rejected, such as the Greater Hippias and the Cleitophon, may be genuine. The nature and object of these semi-Platonic writings require more careful study and more comparison of them with one another, and with forged writings in general, than they have yet received, before we can finally decide on their character. We do not consider them all as genuine until they can be proved to be spurious, as is often maintained and still more often implied in this and similar discussions; but should say of some of them, that their genuineness is neither proven nor disproven until further evidence about them can be adduced. And we are as confident that the Epistles are spurious, as that the Republic, the Timaeus, and the Laws are genuine.

On the whole, not a twentieth part of the writings which pass under the name of Plato, if we exclude the works rejected by the ancients themselves and two or three other plausible inventions, can be fairly doubted by those who are willing to allow that a considerable change and growth may have taken place in his philosophy (see above). That twentieth debatable portion scarcely in any degree affects our judgment of Plato, either as a thinker or a writer, and though suggesting some interesting questions to the scholar and critic, is of little importance to the general reader.

LESSER HIPPIAS

LESSER HIPPIAS

PERSONS OF THE DIALOGUE

EUDICUS, SOCRATES, HIPPIAS

Steph.

363

SOCRATES,
EUDICUS,
HIPPIAS.

Eudicus. WHY are you silent, Socrates, after the magnificent display which Hippias has been making? Why do you not either refute his words, if he seems to you to have been wrong in any point, or join with us in commending him? There is the more reason why you should speak, because we are now alone, and the audience is confined to those who may fairly claim to take part in a philosophical discussion.

Socrates. I should greatly like, Eudicus, to ask Hippias the meaning of what he was saying just now about Homer. I have heard your father, Apemantus, declare that the Iliad of Homer is a finer poem than the Odyssey in the same degree that Achilles was a better man than Odysseus; Odysseus, he would say, is the central figure of the one poem and Achilles of the other. Now, I should like to know, if Hippias has no objection to tell me, what he thinks about these two heroes, and which of them he maintains to be the better; he has already told us in the course of his exhibition many things of various kinds about Homer and divers other poets.

Eud. I am sure that Hippias will be delighted to answer anything which you would like to ask; tell me, Hippias, if Socrates asks you a question, will you answer him?

Hippias. Indeed, Eudicus, I should be strangely inconsistent if I refused to answer Socrates, when at each Olympic festival, as I went up from my house at Elis to the temple of Olympia, where all the Hellenes were assembled, I continually professed my willingness to perform any of the exhibitions which I had prepared, and to answer any questions which any one had to ask.

Soc. Truly, Hippias, you are to be congratulated, if at every Olympic festival you have such an encouraging opinion of your own wisdom when you go up to the temple. I doubt whether any muscular hero would be so fearless and confident in offering his body to the combat at Olympia, as you are in offering your mind.

The Iliad
of Homer
a finer
work
than the
Odyssey,
because
Achilles,
the hero
of the
poem, is
greater
than
Odysseus.

364

715

Hip. And with good reason, Socrates; for since the day when I first entered the lists at Olympia I have never found any man who was my superior in anything[1].

Soc. What an ornament, Hippias, will the reputation of your wisdom be to the city of Elis and to your parents! But to return: what say you of Odysseus and Achilles? Which is the better of the two? and in what particular does either surpass the other? For when you were exhibiting and there was company in the room, though I could not follow you, I did not like to ask what you meant, because a crowd of people were present, and I was afraid that the question might interrupt your exhibition. But now that there are not so many of us, and my friend Eudicus bids me ask, I wish you would tell me what you were saying about these two heroes, so that I may clearly understand; how did you distinguish them?

Achilles the bravest, Nestor the wisest, and Odysseus the wiliest of the Greeks at Troy.

Hip. I shall have much pleasure, Socrates, in explaining to you more clearly than I could in public my views about these and also about other heroes. I say that Homer intended Achilles to be the bravest of the men who went to Troy, Nestor the wisest, and Odysseus the wiliest.

Soc. O rare Hippias, will you be so good as not to laugh, if I find a difficulty in following you, and repeat my questions several times over? Please to answer me kindly and gently.

Hip. I should be greatly ashamed of myself, Socrates, if I, who teach others and take money of them, could not, when I was asked by you, answer in a civil and agreeable manner.

Soc. Thank you: the fact is, that I seemed to understand what you meant when you said that the poet intended Achilles to be the bravest of men, and also that he intended Nestor to be the wisest; but when you said that he meant Odysseus to be the wiliest, I must confess that I could not understand what you were saying. Will you tell me, and then I shall perhaps understand you better; has not Homer made Achilles wily?

Hip. Certainly not, Socrates; he is the most straightforward of mankind, and when Homer introduces them talking with one another in the passage called the Prayers, Achilles is supposed by the poet to say to Odysseus:—

365

'Son of Laertes, sprung from heaven, crafty Odysseus, I will speak out plainly the word which I intend to carry out in act, and which will, I believe, be accomplished. For I hate him like the gates of death who thinks one thing and says another. But I will speak that which shall be accomplished.'

Now, in these verses he clearly indicates the character of the two

[1] Cp. Gorgias 448 A.

men; he shows Achilles to be true and simple, and Odysseus to be wily and false; for he supposes Achilles to be addressing Odysseus in these lines.

Soc. Now, Hippias, I think that I understand your meaning; when you say that Odysseus is wily, you clearly mean that he is false?

Hip. Exactly so, Socrates; it is the character of Odysseus, as he is represented by Homer in many passages both of the Iliad and Odyssey.

Soc. And Homer must be presumed to have meant that the true man is not the same as the false?

Hip. Of course, Socrates.

Soc. And is that your own opinion, Hippias?

Hip. Certainly; how can I have any other?

Soc. Well, then, as there is no possibility of asking Homer what he meant in these verses of his, let us leave him; but as you show a willingness to take up his cause, and your opinion agrees with what you declare to be his, will you answer on behalf of yourself and him?

Hip. I will; ask shortly anything which you like.

Soc. Do you say that the false, like the sick, have no power to do things, or that they have the power to do things?

Hip. I should say that they have power to do many things, and in particular to deceive mankind.

Soc. Then, according to you, they are both powerful and wily, are they not?

Hip. Yes.

Soc. And are they wily, and do they deceive by reason of their simplicity and folly, or by reason of their cunning and a certain sort of prudence?

Hip. By reason of their cunning and prudence, most certainly.

Soc. Then they are prudent, I suppose?

Hip. So they are—very.

Soc. And if they are prudent, do they know or do they not know what they do?

Hip. Of course, they know very well; and that is why they do mischief to others.

Soc. And having this knowledge, are they ignorant, or are they wise?

Hip. Wise, certainly; at least, in so far as they can deceive.

And the
false have
the power
of deceiv-
ing man-
kind:
they
are pru
dent and
knowing
and wise,
and have
the ability
to speak
falsely.

Soc. Stop, and let us recall to mind what you are saying; are you not saying that the false are powerful and prudent and knowing and wise in those things about which they are false?

Hip. To be sure.

366

Soc. And the true differ from the false—the true and the false are the very opposite of each other?

Hip. That is my view.

Soc. Then, according to your view, it would seem that the false are to be ranked in the class of the powerful and wise?

Hip. Assuredly.

Soc. And when you say that the false are powerful and wise in so far as they are false, do you mean that they have or have not the power of uttering their falsehoods if they like?

Hip. I mean to say that they have the power.

Soc. In a word, then, the false are they who are wise and have the power to speak falsely?

Hip. Yes.

Soc. Then a man who has not the power of speaking falsely and is ignorant cannot be false?

Hip. You are right.

Soc. And every man has power who does that which he wishes at the time when he wishes. I am not speaking of any special case in which he is prevented by disease or something of that sort, but I am speaking generally, as I might say of you, that you are able to write my name when you like. Would you not call a man able who could do that?

Hip. Yes.

Soc. And tell me, Hippias, are you not a skilful calculator and arithmetician?

Hip. Yes, Socrates, assuredly I am.

Soc. And if some one were to ask you what is the sum of 3 multiplied by 700, you would tell him the true answer in a moment, if you pleased?

Hip. Certainly I should.

Soc. Is not that because you are the wisest and ablest of men in these matters?

Hip. Yes.

Soc. And being as you are the wisest and ablest of men in these matters of calculation, are you not also the best?

Hip. To be sure, Socrates, I am the best.

Soc. And therefore you would be the most able to tell the truth about these matters, would you not?

Hip. Yes, I should.

**They
must
truly
know
that**

Soc. And could you speak falsehoods about them equally well? I must beg, Hippias, that you will answer me with the same frankness and magnanimity which has hitherto characterized you. If a person were to ask you what is the sum of 3 multiplied by 700, would not you be the best and most consistent teller of a falsehood, having always the power of speaking falsely as you have of speaking truly, about these same matters, if you wanted to tell a falsehood, and not to answer truly? Would the ignorant man be better able to tell a falsehood in matters of calculation than you would be, if you chose? Might he not sometimes stumble upon the truth, when he wanted to tell a lie, because he did not know, whereas you who are the wise man, if you wanted to tell a lie would always and consistently lie?

Hip. Yes; there you are quite right.

Soc. Does the false man tell lies about other things, but not about number, or when he is making a calculation?

Hip. To be sure; he would tell as many lies about number as about other things.

Soc. Then may we further assume, Hippias, that there are men who are false about calculation and number?

Hip. Yes.

Soc. Who can they be? For you have already admitted that he who is false must have the ability to be false: you said, as you will remember, that he who is unable to be false will not be false?

Hip. Yes, I remember; it was so said.

Soc. And were you not yourself just now shown to be best able to speak falsely about calculation?

Hip. Yes; that was another thing which was said.

Soc. And are you not likewise said to speak truly about calculation?

Hip. Certainly.

Soc. Then the same person is able to speak both falsely and truly about calculation? And that person is he who is good at calculation—the arithmetician?

Hip. Yes.

Soc. Who, then, Hippias, is discovered to be false at calculation? Is he not the good man? For the good man is the able man, and he is the true man.

Hip. That is evident.

Soc. Do you not see, then, that the same man is false and also true about the same matters? And the true man is not a whit better than the false; for indeed he is the same with him and not the very opposite, as you were just now imagining.

Hip. Not in that instance, clearly.

Soc. Shall we examine other instances?

Hip. Certainly, if you are disposed.

Soc. Are you not also skilled in geometry?

Lesser Hippias

367
SOCRATES,
HIPPIAS.

about which they falsely speak or they will fall into the error of speaking the truth by mistake.

Therefore the same man must be true if he is to be truly false, in astronomy, in geometry,

*Lesser
Hippias*

SOCRATES,
HIPPIAS.

and in all
the sci-
ences.

Hip. I am.

Soc. Well, and does not the same hold in that science also? Is not the same person best able to speak falsely or to speak truly about diagrams; and he is—the geometrician?

Hip. Yes.

Soc. He and no one else is good at it?

Hip. Yes, he and no one else.

Soc. Then the good and wise geometer has this double power in the highest degree; and if there be a man who is false about diagrams the good man will be he, for he is able to be false; whereas the bad is unable, and for this reason is not false, as has been admitted.

Hip. True.

Soc. Once more—let us examine a third case; that of the astronomer, in whose art, again, you, Hippias, profess to be a still greater proficient than in the preceding—do you not?

368

Hip. Yes, I am.

Soc. And does not the same hold of astronomy?

Hip. True, Socrates.

Soc. And in astronomy, too, if any man be able to speak falsely he will be the good astronomer, but he who is not able will not speak falsely, for he has no knowledge.

Hip. Clearly not.

Soc. Then in astronomy also, the same man will be true and false?

Hip. It would seem so.

Socrates
compli-
ments
Hippias
on his
skill in
engraving
gems, in
making
clothes
and shoes
and the
finest fab-
rics, in
writing
poetry
and prose
of the
most
varied
kind, and
on the art

Soc. And now, Hippias, consider the question at large about all the sciences, and see whether the same principle does not always hold. I know that in most arts you are the wisest of men, as I have heard you boasting in the agora at the tables of the money-changers, when you were setting forth the great and enviable stores of your wisdom; and you said that upon one occasion, when you went to the Olympic games, all that you had on your person was made by yourself. You began with your ring, which was of your own workmanship, and you said that you could engrave rings; and you had another seal which was also of your own workmanship, and a strigil and an oil flask, which you had made yourself; you said also that you had made the shoes which you had on your feet, and the cloak and the short tunic; but what appeared to us all most extraordinary and a proof of singular art, was the girdle of your tunic, which, you said, was as fine as the most costly Persian fabric, and of your own weaving; moreover, you told us that you had brought with you poems, epic, tragic, and dithyrambic, as well as prose writings of the most various kinds; and you said that your skill was also pre-eminent in the arts which I was just now mentioning, and in the true principles of rhythm and harmony and of orthography; and if I remember rightly, there were a great many other accomplishments in which you excelled. I have forgotten to mention your art of memory, which you regard as your special glory, and I dare say that I have forgotten many other things; but, as I was saying, only look to your own arts—and there are plenty of them—and to those of others; and tell me, having regard to the admissions which you and I have made, whether you discover any department of art or any description of wisdom or cunning, whichever name you use, in which the true and false are different and not the same: tell me, if you can, of any. But you cannot.

Hip. Not without consideration, Socrates.

Soc. Nor will consideration help you, Hippias, as I believe; but then if I am right, remember what the consequence will be.

Hip. I do not know what you mean, Socrates.

Soc. I suppose that you are not using your art of memory, doubtless because you think that such an accomplishment is not needed on the present occasion. I will therefore remind you of what you were saying: were you not saying that Achilles was a true man, and Odysseus false and wily?

Hip. I was.

Soc. And now do you perceive that the same person has turned out to be false as well as true? If Odysseus is false he is also true, and if Achilles is true he is also false, and so the two men are not opposed to one another, but they are alike.

Hip. O Socrates, you are always weaving the meshes of an argument, selecting the most difficult point, and fastening upon details instead of grappling with the matter in hand as a whole. Come now, and I will demonstrate to you, if you will allow me, by many satisfactory proofs, that Homer has made Achilles a better man than Odysseus, and a truthful man too; and that he has made the other crafty, and a teller of many untruths, and inferior to Achilles. And then, if you please, you shall make a speech on the other side, in order to prove that Odysseus is the better man; and this may be compared to mine, and then the company will know which of us is the better speaker.

Soc. O Hippias, I do not doubt that you are wiser than I am. But I have a way, when anybody else says anything, of giving close attention to him, especially if the speaker appears to me to be a wise man. Having a desire to understand, I question him, and I examine and analyse and put together what he says, in order that I

Yet he who knows and remembers all things can call to mind no instance in which the false is not also true, although he was saying just now that Achilles is true and Odysseus false.

Socrates pays Hippias the compliment which he

Lesser Hippias

SOCRATES, HIPPIAS.

always pays to a wise man, of attending to him. He proves [370] by example that Achilles, the true man, is always uttering falsehoods, Odysseus, the false man, never.

may understand; but if the speaker appears to me to be a poor hand, I do not interrogate him, or trouble myself about him, and you may know by this who they are whom I deem to be wise men, for you will see that when I am talking with a wise man, I am very attentive to what he says; and I ask questions of him, in order that I may learn, and be improved by him. And I could not help remarking while you were speaking, that when you recited the verses in which Achilles, as you argued, attacks Odysseus as a deceiver, that you must be strangely mistaken, because Odysseus, the man of wiles, is never found to tell a lie; but Achilles is found to be wily on your own showing. At any rate he speaks falsely; for first he utters these words, which you just now repeated,—

'He is hateful to me even as the gates of death who thinks one thing and says another:'—

And then he says, a little while afterwards, he will not be persuaded by Odysseus and Agamemnon, neither will he remain at Troy; but, says he,—

'To-morrow, when I have offered sacrifices to Zeus and all the Gods, having loaded my ships well, I will drag them down into the deep; and then you shall see, if you have a mind, and if such things are a care to you, early in the morning my ships sailing over the fishy Hellespont, and my men eagerly plying the oar; and, if the illustrious shaker of the earth gives me a good voyage, on the third day I shall reach the fertile Phthia.'

And before that, when he was reviling Agamemnon, he said,—

'And now to Phthia I will go, since to return home in the beaked ships is far better, nor am I inclined to stay here in dishonour and amass wealth and riches for you.'

But although on that occasion, in the presence of the whole army, he spoke after this fashion, and on the other occasion to his companions, he appears never to have made any preparation or attempt to draw down the ships, as if he had the least intention of sailing home; so nobly regardless was he of the truth. Now I, Hippias, originally asked you the question, because I was in doubt as to which of the two heroes was intended by the poet to be the best, and because I thought that both of them were the best, and that it would be difficult to decide which was the better of them, not only in respect of truth and falsehood, but of virtue generally, for even in this matter of speaking the truth they are much upon a par.

Hip. There you are wrong, Socrates; for in so far as Achilles speaks falsely, the falsehood is obviously unintentional. He is compelled against his will to remain and rescue the army in their misfortune. But when Odysseus speaks falsely he is voluntarily and intentionally false.

Soc. You, sweet Hippias, like Odysseus, are a deceiver yourself.

Hip. Certainly not, Socrates; what makes you say so?

Soc. Because you say that Achilles does not speak falsely from design, when he is not only a deceiver, but besides being a braggart, in Homer's description of him is so cunning, and so far superior to Odysseus in lying and pretending, that he dares to contradict himself, and Odysseus does not find him out; at any rate he does not appear to say anything to him which would imply that he perceived his falsehood.

Hip. What do you mean, Socrates?

Soc. Did you not observe that afterwards, when he is speaking to Odysseus, he says that he will sail away with the early dawn; but to Ajax he tells quite a different story?

Hip. Where is that?

Soc. Where he says,—

'I will not think about bloody war until the son of warlike Priam, illustrious Hector, comes to the tents and ships of the Myrmidons, slaughtering the Argives, and burning the ships with fire; and about my tent and dark ship, I suspect that Hector, although eager for the battle, will nevertheless stay his hand.'

Now, do you really think, Hippias, that the son of Thetis, who had been the pupil of the sage Cheiron, had such a bad memory, or would have carried the art of lying to such an extent (when he had been assailing liars in the most violent terms only the instant before) as to say to Odysseus that he would sail away, and to Ajax that he would remain, and that he was not rather practising upon the simplicity of Odysseus, whom he regarded as an ancient, and thinking that he would get the better of him by his own cunning and falsehood?

Hip. No, I do not agree with you, Socrates; but I believe that Achilles is induced to say one thing to Ajax, and another to Odysseus in the innocence of his heart, whereas Odysseus, whether he speaks falsely or truly, speaks always with a purpose.

Soc. Then Odysseus would appear after all to be better than Achilles?

Hip. Certainly not, Socrates.

Soc. Why, were not the voluntary liars only just now shown to be better than the involuntary?

Hip. And how, Socrates, can those who intentionally err, and voluntarily and designedly commit iniquities, be better than those who err and do wrong involuntarily? Surely there is a great excuse to be made for a man telling a falsehood, or doing an injury or any sort of harm to another in ignorance. And the laws are obviously

Lesser Hippias

SOCRATES, EUDICUS.

Socrates is convinced of his own ignorance because he never agrees with wise men. But he is willing to learn,

far more severe on those who lie or do evil, voluntarily, than on those who do evil involuntarily.

Soc. You see, Hippias, as I have already told you, how pertinacious I am in asking questions of wise men. And I think that this is the only good point about me, for I am full of defects, and always getting wrong in some way or other. My deficiency is proved to me by the fact that when I meet one of you who are famous for wisdom, and to whose wisdom all the Hellenes are witnesses, I am found out to know nothing. For speaking generally, I hardly ever have the same opinion about anything which you have, and what proof of ignorance can be greater than to differ from wise men? But I have one singular good quality, which is my salvation; I am not ashamed to learn, and I ask and enquire, and am very grateful to those who answer me, and never fail to give them my grateful thanks; and when I learn a thing I never deny my teacher, or pretend that the lesson is a discovery of my own; but I praise his wisdom, and proclaim what I have learned from him. And now I cannot agree in what you are saying, but I strongly disagree. Well, I know that this is my own fault, and is a defect in my character, but I will not pretend to be more than I am; and my opinion, Hippias, is the very contrary of what you are saying. For I maintain that those who hurt or injure mankind, and speak falsely and deceive, and err voluntarily, are better far than those who do wrong involuntarily. Sometimes, however, I am of the opposite opinion; for I am all abroad in my ideas about this matter, a condition obviously occasioned by ignorance. And just now I happen to be in a crisis of my disorder at which those who err voluntarily appear to me better than those who err involuntarily. My present state of mind is due to our previous argument, which inclines me to believe that in general those who do wrong involuntarily are worse than those who do wrong voluntarily, and therefore I hope that you will be good to me, and not refuse to heal me; for you will do me a much greater benefit if you cure my soul of ignorance, than you would if you were to cure my body of disease. I must, however, tell you beforehand, that if you make a long oration to me you will not cure me, for I shall not be able to follow you; but if you will answer me, as you did just now, you will do me a great deal of good, and I do not think that you will be any the worse yourself. And I have some claim upon you also, O son of Apemantus, for you incited me to converse with Hippias; and now, if Hippias will not answer me, you must entreat him on my behalf.

Eud. But I do not think, Socrates, that Hippias will require any

373

and he desires to be cured by Hippias of his ignorance in as few words as possible.

entreaty of mine; for he has already said that he will refuse to answer no man.—Did you not say so, Hippias?

Hip. Yes, I did; but then, Eudicus, Socrates is always troublesome in an argument, and appears to be dishonest[1].

Soc. Excellent Hippias, I do not do so intentionally (if I did, it would show me to be a wise man and a master of wiles, as you would argue), but unintentionally, and therefore you must pardon me; for, as you say, he who is unintentionally dishonest should be pardoned.

Eud. Yes, Hippias, do as he says; and for our sake, and also that you may not belie your profession, answer whatever Socrates asks you.

Hip. I will answer, as you request me; and do you ask whatever you like.

Soc. I am very desirous, Hippias, of examining this question, as to which are the better—those who err voluntarily or involuntarily? And if you will answer me, I think that I can put you in the way of approaching the subject: You would admit, would you not, that there are good runners?

Hip. Yes.

Soc. And there are bad runners?

Hip. Yes.

Soc. And he who runs well is a good runner, and he who runs ill is a bad runner?

Hip. Very true.

Soc. And he who runs slowly runs ill, and he who runs quickly runs well?

Hip. Yes.

Soc. Then in a race, and in running, swiftness is a good, and slowness is an evil quality?

Hip. To be sure.

Soc. Which of the two then is a better runner? He who runs slowly voluntarily, or he who runs slowly involuntarily?

Hip. He who runs slowly voluntarily.

Soc. And is not running a species of doing?

Hip. Certainly.

Soc. And if a species of doing, a species of action?

Hip. Yes.

Soc. Then he who runs badly does a bad and dishonourable action in a race?

Hip. Yes; a bad action, certainly.

Soc. And he who runs slowly runs badly?

[1] Cp. Gorgias 499, 505; Rep. vi. 487.

Hip. Yes.

Soc. Then the good runner does this bad and disgraceful action voluntarily, and the bad involuntarily?

Hip. That is to be inferred.

Soc. Then he who involuntarily does evil actions, is worse in a race than he who does them voluntarily?

Hip. Yes, in a race.

Soc. Well; but at a wrestling match—which is the better wrestler, he who falls voluntarily or involuntarily?

Hip. He who falls voluntarily, doubtless.

Soc. And is it worse or more dishonourable at a wrestling match, to fall, or to throw another?

Hip. To fall.

Soc. Then, at a wrestling match, he who voluntarily does base and dishonourable actions is a better wrestler than he who does them involuntarily?

Hip. That appears to be the truth.

Soc. And what would you say of any other bodily exercise—is not he who is better made able to do both that which is strong and that which is weak—that which is fair and that which is foul?—so that when he does bad actions with the body, he who is better made does them voluntarily, and he who is worse made does them involuntarily.

Hip. Yes, that appears to be true about strength.

Soc. And what do you say about grace, Hippias? Is not he who is better made able to assume evil and disgraceful figures and postures voluntarily, as he who is worse made assumes them involuntarily?

Hip. True.

Soc. Then voluntary ungracefulness comes from excellence of the bodily frame, and involuntary from the defect of the bodily frame?

Hip. True.

Soc. And what would you say of an unmusical voice; would you prefer the voice which is voluntarily or involuntarily out of tune?

Hip. That which is voluntarily out of tune.

Soc. The involuntary is the worse of the two?

Hip. Yes.

Soc. And would you choose to possess goods or evils?

Hip. Goods.

Soc. And would you rather have feet which are voluntarily or involuntarily lame?

Hip. Feet which are voluntarily lame.

Soc. But is not lameness a defect or deformity?

Hip. Yes.

Soc. And is not blinking a defect in the eyes?

Hip. Yes.

Soc. And would you rather always have eyes with which you might voluntarily blink and not see, or with which you might involuntarily blink?

Hip. I would rather have eyes which voluntarily blink.

Soc. Then in your own case you deem that which voluntarily acts ill, better than that which involuntarily acts ill?

Hip. Yes, certainly, in cases such as you mention.

Soc. And does not the same hold of ears, nostrils, mouth, and of all the senses—those which involuntarily act ill are not to be desired, as being defective; and those which voluntarily act ill are to be desired as being good?

Hip. I agree.

Soc. And what would you say of instruments;—which are the better sort of instruments to have to do with?—those with which a man acts ill voluntarily or involuntarily? For example, had a man better have a rudder with which he will steer ill, voluntarily or involuntarily?

Hip. He had better have a rudder with which he will steer ill voluntarily.

Soc. And does not the same hold of the bow and the lyre, the flute and all other things?

Hip. Very true.

Soc. And would you rather have a horse of such a temper that you may ride him ill voluntarily or involuntarily?

Hip. I would rather have a horse which I could ride ill voluntarily.

Soc. That would be the better horse?

Hip. Yes.

Soc. Then with a horse of better temper, vicious actions would be produced voluntarily; and with a horse of bad temper involuntarily?

Hip. Certainly.

Soc. And that would be true of a dog, or of any other animal?

Hip. Yes.

Soc. And is it better to possess the mind of an archer who voluntarily or involuntarily misses the mark?

Hip. Of him who voluntarily misses.

Soc. This would be the better mind for the purposes of archery?

Hip. Yes.

Soc. Then the mind which involuntarily errs is worse than the mind which errs voluntarily?

Hip. Yes, certainly, in the use of the bow.

Soc. And what would you say of the art of medicine;—has not the mind which voluntarily works harm to the body, more of the healing art?

Hip. Yes.

Soc. Then in the art of medicine the voluntary is better than the involuntary?

Hip. Yes.

Soc. Well, and in lute-playing and in flute-playing, and in all arts and sciences, is not that mind the better which voluntarily does what is evil and dishonourable, and goes wrong, and is not the worse that which does so involuntarily?

Hip. That is evident.

Soc. And what would you say of the characters of slaves? Should we not prefer to have those who voluntarily do wrong and make mistakes, and are they not better in their mistakes than those who commit them involuntarily?

Hip. Yes.

Soc. And should we not desire to have our own minds in the best state possible?

Hip. Yes.

Soc. And will our minds be better if they do wrong and make mistakes voluntarily or involuntarily?

Hip. O, Socrates, it would be a monstrous thing to say that those who do wrong voluntarily are better than those who do wrong involuntarily!

Soc. And yet that appears to be the only inference.

Hip. I do not think so.

Soc. But I imagined, Hippias, that you did. Please to answer once more: Is not justice a power, or knowledge, or both? Must not justice, at all events, be one of these?

Hip. Yes.

Soc. But if justice is a power of the soul, then the soul which has the greater power is also the more just; for that which has the greater power, my good friend, has been proved by us to be the better.

Hip. Yes, that has been proved.

Soc. And if justice is knowledge, then the wiser will be the juster soul, and the more ignorant the more unjust?

Hip. Yes.

Soc. But if justice be power as well as knowledge—then will not the soul which has both knowledge and power be the more just, and that which is the more ignorant be the more unjust? Must it not be so?

Hip. Clearly.

Soc. And is not the soul which has the greater power and wisdom also better, and better able to do both good and evil in every action?

Hip. Certainly.

Soc. The soul, then, which acts ill, acts voluntarily by power and art—and these either one or both of them are elements of justice?

376

Hip. That seems to be true.

Soc. And to do injustice is to do ill, and not to do injustice is to do well?

Hip. Yes.

Soc. And will not the better and abler soul when it does wrong, do wrong voluntarily, and the bad soul involuntarily?

Hip. Clearly.

Soc. And the good man is he who has the good soul, and the bad man is he who has the bad?

Hip. Yes.

Soc. Then the good man will voluntarily do wrong, and the bad man involuntarily, if the good man is he who has the good soul?

Hip. Which he certainly has.

Soc. Then, Hippias, he who voluntarily does wrong and disgraceful things, if there be such a man, will be the good man?

Hip. There I cannot agree with you.

Soc. Nor can I agree with myself, Hippias; and yet that seems to be the conclusion which, as far as we can see at present, must follow from our argument. As I was saying before, I am all abroad, and being in perplexity am always changing my opinion. Now, that I or any ordinary man should wander in perplexity is not surprising; but if you wise men also wander, and we cannot come to you and rest from our wandering, the matter begins to be serious both to us and to you.

Hippias, who has admitted the previous deductions, rebels at the final one. Socrates is himself dissatisfied. What remains if Socrates and a wiser than Socrates are alike in doubt?

ALCIBIADES I

ALCIBIADES I

PERSONS OF THE DIALOGUE

ALCIBIADES, SOCRATES

Socrates. I DARE SAY that you may be surprised to find, O son of
Cleinias, that I, who am your first lover, not having spoken to you
for many years, when the rest of the world were wearying you with
their attentions, am the last of your lovers who still speaks to you.
The cause of my silence has been that I was hindered by a power
more than human, of which I will some day explain to you the
nature; this impediment has now been removed; I therefore here
present myself before you, and I greatly hope that no similar hin-
drance will again occur. Meanwhile, I have observed that your pride
has been too much for the pride of your admirers; they were numerous and high-spirited, but they have all run away, overpowered by
your superior force of character; not one of them remains. And I
want you to understand the reason why you have been too much for
them. You think that you have no need of them or of any other
man, for you have great possessions and lack nothing, beginning
with the body, and ending with the soul. In the first place, you say
to yourself that you are the fairest and tallest of the citizens, and
this every one who has eyes may see to be true; in the second place,
that you are among the noblest of them, highly connected both on
the father's and the mother's side, and sprung from one of the most
distinguished families in your own state, which is the greatest in
Hellas, and having many friends and kinsmen of the best sort, who
can assist you when in need; and there is one potent relative, who is
more to you than all the rest, Pericles the son of Xanthippus, whom
your father left guardian of you, and of your brother, and who can
do as he pleases not only in this city, but in all Hellas, and among
many and mighty barbarous nations. Moreover, you are rich; but I
must say that you value yourself least of all upon your possessions.
And all these things have lifted you up; you have overcome your
lovers, and they have acknowledged that you were too much for
them. Have you not remarked their absence? And now I know that

The pride
of Alcibi-
ades has
been too
[104]
much for
his lovers.

733

you wonder why I, unlike the rest of them, have not gone away, and what can be my motive in remaining.

Alcibiades. Perhaps, Socrates, you are not aware that I was just going to ask you the very same question—What do you want? And what is your motive in annoying me, and always, wherever I am, making a point of coming[1]? I do really wonder what you mean, and should greatly like to know.

Soc. Then if, as you say, you desire to know, I suppose that you will be willing to hear, and I may consider myself to be speaking to an auditor who will remain, and will not run away?

Al. Certainly, let me hear.

Soc. You had better be careful, for I may very likely be as unwilling to end as I have hitherto been to begin.

Al. Proceed, my good man, and I will listen.

Soc. I will proceed; and, although no lover likes to speak with one who has no feeling of love in him[2], I will make an effort, and tell you what I meant: My love, Alcibiades, which I hardly like to confess, would long ago have passed away, as I flatter myself, if I saw you loving your good things, or thinking that you ought to pass life in the enjoyment of them. But I shall reveal other thoughts of yours, which you keep to yourself; whereby you will know that I have always had my eye on you. Suppose that at this moment some God came to you and said: Alcibiades, will you live as you are, or die in an instant if you are forbidden to make any further acquisition?—I verily believe that you would choose death. And I will tell you the hope in which you are at present living: Before many days have elapsed, you think that you will come before the Athenian assembly, and will prove to them that you are more worthy of honour than Pericles, or any other man that ever lived, and having proved this, you will have the greatest power in the state. When you have gained the greatest power among us, you will go on to other Hellenic states, and not only to Hellenes, but to all the barbarians who inhabit the same continent with us. And if the God were then to say to you again: Here in Europe is to be your seat of empire, and you must not cross over into Asia or meddle with Asiatic affairs, I do not believe that you would choose to live upon these terms; but the world, as I may say, must be filled with your power and name—no man less than Cyrus and Xerxes is of any account with you. Such I know to be your hopes—I am not guessing only—and very likely you, who know that I am speaking the truth, will reply, Well, Socrates, but what have my hopes to do with the explanation which you promised of your unwillingness to leave me? And that is what I

105

Alcibiades
a lover,
not of
pleasure,
but of
ambition;
and he re-
quires the
help of
Socrates
for the
accom-
plishment
of his de-
signs.

---

[1] Cp. Symp. 213 C.   [2] Cp. Symp. 217 E ff.

am now going to tell you, sweet son of Cleinias and Dinomachè. The explanation is, that all these designs of yours cannot be accomplished by you without my help; so great is the power which I believe myself to have over you and your concerns; and this I conceive to be the reason why the God has hitherto forbidden me to converse with you, and I have been long expecting his permission. For, as you hope to prove your own great value to the state, and having proved it, to attain at once to absolute power, so do I indulge a hope that I shall have the supreme power over you, if I am able to prove my own great value to you, and to show you that neither guardian, nor kinsman, nor any one is able to deliver into your hands the power which you desire, but I only, God being my helper. When you were young[1] and your hopes were not yet matured, I should have wasted my time, and therefore, as I conceive, the God forbade me to converse with you; but now, having his permission, I will speak, for now you will listen to me.

Al. Your silence, Socrates, was always a surprise to me. I never could understand why you followed me about, and now that you have begun to speak again, I am still more amazed. Whether I think all this or not, is a matter about which you seem to have already made up your mind, and therefore my denial will have no effect upon you. But granting, if I must, that you have perfectly divined my purposes, why is your assistance necessary to the attainment of them? Can you tell me why?

Soc. You want to know whether I can make a long speech, such as you are in the habit of hearing; but that is not my way. I think, however, that I can prove to you the truth of what I am saying, if you will grant me one little favour.

Al. Yes, if the favour which you mean be not a troublesome one.

Soc. Will you be troubled at having questions to answer?

Al. Not at all.

Soc. Then please to answer.

Al. Ask me.

Soc. Have you not the intention which I attribute to you?

Al. I will grant anything you like, in the hope of hearing what more you have to say.

Soc. You do, then, mean, as I was saying, to come forward in a little while in the character of an adviser of the Athenians? And suppose that when you are ascending the bema, I pull you by the sleeve and say, Alcibiades, you are getting up to advise the Athenians—do you know the matter about which they are going to deliberate, better than they?—How would you answer?

[1] Cp. Symp. 181 E.

And this is the reason why Socrates has clung to him; he is hoping when Alcibiades has become the [106] ruler of Athens to rule over him.

Alcibiades does not deny the impeachment.

Alcibiades is willing to answer questions.

Alcibiades I

SOCRATES, ALCIBIA- DES.

He is go- ing to ad- vise the Athenians about matters which he knows better than they.

Al. I should reply, that I was going to advise them about a matter which I do know better than they.

Soc. Then you are a good adviser about the things which you know?

Al. Certainly.

Soc. And do you know anything but what you have learned of others, or found out yourself?

Al. That is all.

Soc. And would you have ever learned or discovered anything, if you had not been willing either to learn of others or to examine yourself?

Al. I should not.

Soc. And would you have been willing to learn or to examine what you supposed that you knew?

Al. Certainly not.

Soc. Then there was a time when you thought that you did not know what you are now supposed to know?

Al. Certainly.

Soc. I think that I know tolerably well the extent of your acquirements; and you must tell me if I forget any of them: according to my recollection, you learned the arts of writing, of playing on the lyre, and of wrestling; the flute you never would learn; this is the sum of your accomplishments, unless there were some which you acquired in secret; and I think that secrecy was hardly possible, as you could not have come out of your door, either by day or night, without my seeing you.

Al. Yes, that was the whole of my schooling.

Soc. And are you going to get up in the Athenian assembly, and give them advice about writing?

Al. No, indeed.

Soc. Or about the touch of the lyre?

Al. Certainly not.

Soc. And they are not in the habit of deliberating about wrestling, in the assembly?

Al. Hardly.

Soc. Then what are the deliberations in which you propose to advise them? Surely not about building?

Al. No.

Soc. For the builder will advise better than you will about that?

Al. He will.

Soc. Nor about divination?

Al. No.

Soc. About that again the diviner will advise better than you will?

Al. True.

Soc. Whether he be little or great, good or ill-looking, noble or ignoble—makes no difference.

Al. Certainly not.

Soc. A man is a good adviser about anything, not because he has riches, but because he has knowledge?

Al. Assuredly.

Soc. Whether their counsellor is rich or poor, is not a matter which will make any difference to the Athenians when they are deliberating about the health of the citizens; they only require that he should be a physician.

Al. Of course.

Soc. Then what will be the subject of deliberation about which you will be justified in getting up and advising them?

Al. About their own concerns, Socrates.

Soc. You mean about shipbuilding, for example, when the question is what sort of ships they ought to build?

Al. No, I should not advise them about that.

Soc. I suppose, because you do not understand shipbuilding:—is that the reason?

Al. It is.

Soc. Then about what concerns of theirs will you advise them?

Al. About war, Socrates, or about peace, or about any other concerns of the state.

Soc. You mean, when they deliberate with whom they ought to make peace, and with whom they ought to go to war, and in what manner?

Al. Yes.

Soc. And they ought to go to war with those against whom it is better to go to war?

Al. Yes.

Soc. And when it is better?

Al. Certainly.

Soc. And for as long a time as is better?

Al. Yes.

Soc. But suppose the Athenians to deliberate with whom they ought to close in wrestling, and whom they should grasp by the hand, would you, or the master of gymnastics, be a better adviser of them?

Al. Clearly, the master of gymnastics.

Soc. And can you tell me on what grounds the master of gymnastics would decide, with whom they ought or ought not to close, and when and how? To take an instance: Would he not say that

Alcibiades I

SOCRATES, ALCIBIADES.

He will advise them about war and peace, and with whom they had better go to war, and when and how long.

they should wrestle with those against whom it is best to wrestle?

Al. Yes.

Soc. And as much as is best?

Al. Certainly.

Soc. And at such times as are best?

Al. Yes.

Soc. Again; you sometimes accompany the lyre with the song and dance?

Al. Yes.

Soc. When it is well to do so?

Al. Yes.

Soc. And as much as is well?

Al. Just so.

Soc. And as you speak of an excellence or art of the best in wrestling, and of an excellence in playing the lyre, I wish you would tell me what this latter is;—the excellence of wrestling I call gymnastic, and I want to know what you call the other.

Al. I do not understand you.

Soc. Then try to do as I do; for the answer which I gave is universally right, and when I say right, I mean according to rule.

Al. Yes.

Soc. And was not the art of which I spoke gymnastic?

Al. Certainly.

Soc. And I called the excellence in wrestling gymnastic?

Al. You did.

Soc. And I was right?

Al. I think that you were.

Soc. Well, now,—for you should learn to argue prettily—let me ask you in return to tell me, first, what is that art of which playing and singing, and stepping properly in the dance, are parts,—what is the name of the whole? I think that by this time you must be able to tell.

Al. Indeed I cannot.

Soc. Then let me put the matter in another way: what do you call the Goddesses who are the patronesses of art?

Al. The Muses do you mean, Socrates?

Soc. Yes, I do; and what is the name of the art which is called after them?

Al. I suppose that you mean music.

Soc. Yes, that is my meaning; and what is the excellence of the art of music, as I told you truly that the excellence of wrestling was gymnastic—what is the excellence of music—to be what?

Al. To be musical, I suppose.

Soc. Very good; and now please to tell me what is the excellence of war and peace; as the more musical was the more excellent, or the more gymnastical was the more excellent, tell me, what name do you give to the more excellent in war and peace?

Al. But I really cannot tell you.

Soc. But if you were offering advice to another and said to him— This food is better than that, at this time and in this quantity, and he said to you—What do you mean, Alcibiades, by the word 'better'? you would have no difficulty in replying that you meant 'more wholesome,' although you do not profess to be a physician: and when the subject is one of which you profess to have knowledge, and about which you are ready to get up and advise as if you knew, are you not ashamed, when you are asked, not to be able to answer the question? Is it not disgraceful?

Al. Very.

Soc. Well, then, consider and try to explain what is the meaning of 'better,' in the matter of making peace and going to war with those against whom you ought to go to war? To what does the word refer?

Al. I am thinking, and I cannot tell.

Soc. But you surely know what are the charges which we bring against one another, when we arrive at the point of making war, and what name we give them?

Al. Yes, certainly; we say that deceit or violence has been employed, or that we have been defrauded.

Soc. And how does this happen? Will you tell me how? For there may be a difference in the manner.

Al. Do you mean by 'how,' Socrates, whether we suffered these things justly or unjustly?

Soc. Exactly.

Al. There can be no greater difference than between just and unjust.

Soc. And would you advise the Athenians to go to war with the just or with the unjust?

Al. That is an awkward question; for certainly, even if a person did intend to go to war with the just, he would not admit that they were just.

Soc. He would not go to war, because it would be unlawful?

Al. Neither lawful nor honourable.

Soc. Then you, too, would address them on principles of justice?

Al. Certainly.

Alcibiades I

SOCRATES, ALCIBIA- DES.

'the more excellent.'

The term better, when applied to food, means more wholesome.

109

In going
to war or
not going
to war,
the better
is the
more just.

But
where did
Alcibiades
acquire
this no-
tion of
just and
unjust?

Soc. What, then, is justice but that better, of which I spoke, in going to war or not going to war with those against whom we ought or ought not, and when we ought or ought not to go to war?

Al. Clearly.

Soc. But how is this, friend Alcibiades? Have you forgotten that you do not know this, or have you been to the schoolmaster without my knowledge, and has he taught you to discern the just from the unjust? Who is he? I wish you would tell me, that I may go and learn of him—you shall introduce me.

Al. You are mocking, Socrates.

Soc. No, indeed; I most solemnly declare to you by Zeus, who is the God of our common friendship, and whom I never will forswear, that I am not; tell me, then, who this instructor is, if he exists.

Al. But, perhaps, he does not exist; may I not have acquired the knowledge of just and unjust in some other way?

Soc. Yes; if you have discovered them.

Al. But do you not think that I could discover them?

Soc. I am sure that you might, if you enquired about them.

Al. And do you not think that I would enquire?

Soc. Yes; if you thought that you did not know them.

Al. And was there not a time when I did so think?

Soc. Very good; and can you tell me how long it is since you thought that you did not know the nature of the just and the unjust? What do you say to a year ago? Were you then in a state of conscious ignorance and enquiry? or did you think that you knew? And please to answer truly, that our discussion may not be in vain.

Al. Well, I thought that I knew.

Soc. And two years ago, and three years ago, and four years ago, you knew all the same?

Al. I did.

Soc. And more than four years ago you were a child—were you not?

Al. Yes.

Soc. And then I am quite sure that you thought you knew.

Al. Why are you so sure?

He al-
ways had
them.

Soc. Because I often heard you when a child, in your teacher's house, or elsewhere, playing at dice or some other game with the boys, not hesitating at all about the nature of the just and unjust; but very confident—crying and shouting that one of the boys was a rogue and a cheat, and had been cheating. Is it not true?

Al. But what was I to do, Socrates, when anybody cheated me?

Soc. And how can you say, 'What was I to do'? if at the time you did not know whether you were wronged or not?

110

Al. To be sure I knew; I was quite aware that I was being cheated.

Soc. Then you suppose yourself even when a child to have known the nature of just and unjust?

Al. Certainly; and I did know then.

Soc. And when did you discover them—not, surely, at the time when you thought that you knew them?

Al. Certainly not.

Soc. And when did you think that you were ignorant—if you consider, you will find that there never was such a time?

Al. Really, Socrates, I cannot say.

Soc. Then you did not learn them by discovering them?

Al. Clearly not.

Soc. But just before you said that you did not know them by learning; now, if you have neither discovered nor learned them, how and whence do you come to know them?

Al. I suppose that I was mistaken in saying that I knew them through my own discovery of them; whereas, in truth, I learned them in the same way that other people learn.

Soc. So you said before, and I must again ask, of whom? Do tell me.

Al. Of the many.

Soc. Do you take refuge in them? I cannot say much for your teachers.

Al. Why, are they not able to teach?

Soc. They could not teach you how to play at draughts, which you would acknowledge (would you not) to be a much smaller matter than justice?

Al. Yes.

Soc. And can they teach the better who are unable to teach the worse?

Al. I think that they can; at any rate, they can teach many far better things than to play at draughts.

Soc. What things?

Al. Why, for example, I learned to speak Greek of them, and I cannot say who was my teacher, or to whom I am to attribute my knowledge of Greek, if not to those good-for-nothing teachers, as you call them.

Soc. Why, yes, my friend; and the many are good enough teachers of Greek, and some of their instructions in that line may be justly praised.

Al. Why is that?

Soc. Why, because they have the qualities which good teachers ought to have.

He
learned
them of
the many,

111

as he
learned
Greek;—
of those
who knew
it.

Al. What qualities?

Soc. Why, you know that knowledge is the first qualification of any teacher?

Al. Certainly.

Soc. And if they know, they must agree together and not differ?

Al. Yes.

Soc. And would you say that they knew the things about which they differ?

Al. No.

Soc. Then how can they teach them?

Al. They cannot.

Yes: the many can teach things about which they are agreed.

Soc. Well, but do you imagine that the many would differ about the nature of wood and stone? are they not agreed if you ask them what they are? and do they not run to fetch the same thing, when they want a piece of wood or a stone? And so in similar cases, which I suspect to be pretty nearly all that you mean by speaking Greek.

Al. True.

Soc. These, as we were saying, are matters about which they are agreed with one another and with themselves; both individuals and states use the same words about them; they do not use some one word and some another.

Al. They do not.

Soc. Then they may be expected to be good teachers of these things?

Al. Yes.

Soc. And if we want to instruct any one in them, we shall be right in sending him to be taught by our friends the many?

Al. Very true.

Soc. But if we wanted further to know not only which are men and which are horses, but which men or horses have powers of running, would the many still be able to inform us?

Al. Certainly not.

Soc. And you have a sufficient proof that they do not know these things and are not the best teachers of them, inasmuch as they are never agreed about them?

Al. Yes.

But could the many teach things about which they are dis-agreed?

Soc. And suppose that we wanted to know not only what men are like, but what healthy or diseased men are like—would the many be able to teach us?

Al. They would not.

Soc. And you would have a proof that they were bad teachers of these matters, if you saw them at variance?

Al. I should.

Soc. Well, but are the many agreed with themselves, or with one another, about the justice or injustice of men and things?

Al. Assuredly not, Socrates.

Soc. There is no subject about which they are more at variance?

Al. None.

Soc. I do not suppose that you ever saw or heard of men quarrelling over the principles of health and disease to such an extent as to go to war and kill one another for the sake of them?

Al. No, indeed.

Soc. But of the quarrels about justice and injustice, even if you have never seen them, you have certainly heard from many people, including Homer; for you have heard of the Iliad and Odyssey?

Al. To be sure, Socrates.

Soc. A difference of just and unjust is the argument of those poems?

Al. True.

Soc. Which difference caused all the wars and deaths of Trojans and Achaeans, and the deaths of the suitors of Penelope in their quarrel with Odysseus.

Al. Very true.

Soc. And when the Athenians and Lacedaemonians and Boeotians fell at Tanagra, and afterwards in the battle of Coronea, at which your father Cleinias met his end, the question was one of justice—this was the sole cause of the battles, and of their deaths.

Al. Very true.

Soc. But can they be said to understand that about which they are quarrelling to the death?

Al. Clearly not.

Soc. And yet those whom you thus allow to be ignorant are the teachers to whom you are appealing.

Al. Very true.

Soc. But how are you ever likely to know the nature of justice and injustice, about which you are so perplexed, if you have neither learned them of others nor discovered them yourself?

Al. From what you say, I suppose not.

Soc. See, again, how inaccurately you speak, Alcibiades!

Al. In what respect?

Soc. In saying that I say so.

Al. Why, did you not say that I know nothing of the just and unjust?

Soc. No; I did not.

Al. Did I, then?

Soc. Yes.

112
*Alcibiades
I*

SOCRATES,
ALICIBIA-
DES.

And one of these things is justice.

Did not a question of justice cause the war between the Trojans and Achaeans, and between the Athenians and Lacedaemonians?

And yet they did not know what they were fighting about?

Al. How was that?

Soc. Let me explain. Suppose I were to ask you which is the greater number, two or one; you would reply 'two'?

Al. I should.

Soc. And by how much greater?

Al. By one.

Soc. Which of us now says that two is more than one?

Al. I do.

Soc. Did not I ask, and you answer the question?

Al. Yes.

113

Soc. Then who is speaking? I who put the question, or you who answer me?

Al. I am.

The
answerer,
not the
question-
er, has
been
drawing
these in-
ferences.

Soc. Or suppose that I ask and you tell me the letters which make up the name Socrates, which of us is the speaker?

Al. I am.

Soc. Now let us put the case generally: whenever there is a question and answer, who is the speaker,—the questioner or the answerer?

Al. I should say, Socrates, that the answerer was the speaker.

Soc. And have I not been the questioner all through?

Al. Yes.

Soc. And you the answerer?

Al. Just so.

Soc. Which of us, then, was the speaker?

Al. The inference is, Socrates, that I was the speaker.

Soc. Did not some one say that Alcibiades, the fair son of Cleinias, not understanding about just and unjust, but thinking that he did understand, was going to the assembly to advise the Athenians about what he did not know? Was not that said?

Al. Very true.

How can
you teach
what you
do not
know?

Soc. Then, Alcibiades, the result may be expressed in the language of Euripides. I think that you have heard all this 'from yourself, and not from me'; nor did I say this, which you erroneously attribute to me, but you yourself, and what you said was very true. For indeed, my dear fellow, the design which you meditate of teaching what you do not know, and have not taken any pains to learn, is downright insanity.

But the
expedient,
not the
just, is
the sub-
ject about

Al. But, Socrates, I think that the Athenians and the rest of the Hellenes do not often advise as to the more just or unjust; for they see no difficulty in them, and therefore they leave them, and consider which course of action will be most expedient; for there is a difference between justice and expediency. Many persons have done great wrong and profited by their injustice; others have done rightly and come to no good.

Soc. Well, but granting that the just and the expedient are ever so much opposed, you surely do not imagine that you know what is expedient for mankind, or why a thing is expedient?

Al. Why not, Socrates?—But I am not going to be asked again from whom I learned, or when I made the discovery.

Soc. What a way you have! When you make a mistake which might be refuted by a previous argument, you insist on having a new and different refutation; the old argument is a worn-out garment which you will no longer put on, but some one must produce another which is clean and new. Now I shall disregard this move of yours, and shall ask over again,—Where did you learn and how do you know the nature of the expedient, and who is your teacher? All this I comprehend in a single question, and now you will manifestly be in the old difficulty, and will not be able to show that you know the expedient, either because you learned or because you discovered it yourself. But, as I perceive that you are dainty, and dislike the taste of a stale argument, I will enquire no further into your knowledge of what is expedient or what is not expedient for the Athenian people, and simply request you to say why you do not explain whether justice and expediency are the same or different? And if you like you may examine me as I have examined you, or, if you would rather, you may carry on the discussion by yourself.

Al. But I am not certain, Socrates, whether I shall be able to discuss the matter with you.

Soc. Then imagine, my dear fellow, that I am the demus and the ecclesia; for in the ecclesia, too, you will have to persuade men individually.

Al. Yes.

Soc. And is not the same person able to persuade one individual singly and many individuals of the things which he knows? The grammarian, for example, can persuade one and he can persuade many about letters.

Al. True.

Soc. And about number, will not the same person persuade one and persuade many?

Al. Yes.

Soc. And this will be he who knows number, or the arithmetician?

Al. Quite true.

Soc. And cannot you persuade one man about that of which you can persuade many?

Al. I suppose so.

Alcibiades I

SOCRATES, ALCIBIA-DES.

which men commonly debate.

Alcibiades insists that he will not [114] have the old argument over again.

He who can persuade many can

*Alcibiades
I*

SOCRATES,
ALCIBIA-
DES.

persuade
one.
Alcibiades
should
therefore
be able to
persuade
Socrates.

Soc. And that of which you can persuade either is clearly what you know?

Al. Yes.

Soc. And the only difference between one who argues as we are doing, and the orator who is addressing an assembly, is that the one seeks to persuade a number, and the other an individual, of the same things.

Al. I suppose so.

Soc. Well, then, since the same person who can persuade a multitude can persuade individuals, try conclusions upon me, and prove to me that the just is not always expedient.

Al. You take liberties, Socrates.

Soc. I shall take the liberty of proving to you the opposite of that which you will not prove to me.

Al. Proceed.

Soc. Answer my questions—that is all.

Al. Nay, I should like you to be the speaker.

Soc. What, do you not wish to be persuaded?

Al. Certainly I do.

Soc. And can you be persuaded better than out of your own mouth?

Al. I think not.

Soc. Then you shall answer; and if you do not hear the words, that the just is the expedient, coming from your own lips, never believe another man again.

Al. I won't; but answer I will, for I do not see how I can come to any harm.

A man
may do
what is
expedient
and not
just, but
he cannot
do what
is hon-
ourable
and not
just and
good.

Soc. A true prophecy! Let me begin then by enquiring of you whether you allow that the just is sometimes expedient and sometimes not?

Al. Yes.

Soc. And sometimes honourable and sometimes not?

Al. What do you mean?

Soc. I am asking if you ever knew any one who did what was dishonourable and yet just?

Al. Never.

Soc. All just things are honourable?

Al. Yes.

Soc. And are honourable things sometimes good and sometimes not good, or are they always good?

Al. I rather think, Socrates, that some honourable things are evil.

Soc. And are some dishonourable things good?

Al. Yes.

Soc. You mean in such a case as the following:—In time of war, men have been wounded or have died in rescuing a companion or kinsman, when others who have neglected the duty of rescuing them have escaped in safety?

Al. True.

Soc. And to rescue another under such circumstances is honourable, in respect of the attempt to save those whom we ought to save; and this is courage?

Al. True.

Soc. But evil in respect of death and wounds?

Al. Yes.

Soc. And the courage which is shown in the rescue is one thing, and the death another?

Al. Certainly.

Soc. Then the rescue of one's friends is honourable in one point of view, but evil in another?

Al. True.

Soc. And if honourable, then also good: Will you consider now whether I may not be right, for you were acknowledging that the courage which is shown in the rescue is honourable? Now is this courage good or evil? Look at the matter thus: which would you rather choose, good or evil?

Al. Good.

Soc. And the greatest goods you would be most ready to choose, and would least like to be deprived of them?

Al. Certainly.

Soc. What would you say of courage? At what price would you be willing to be deprived of courage?

Al. I would rather die than be a coward.

Soc. Then you think that cowardice is the worst of evils?

Al. I do.

Soc. As bad as death, I suppose?

Al. Yes.

Soc. And life and courage are the extreme opposites of death and cowardice?

Al. Yes.

Soc. And they are what you would most desire to have, and their opposites you would least desire?

Al. Yes.

Soc. Is this because you think life and courage the best, and death and cowardice the worst?

But good
may con-
tain an
element
[116]
of evil.
Good and
evil are to
be judged
of by
their con-
sequences.

The hon-
ourable is
identified
with the
good, and
the good
is the ex-
pedient,

Al. Yes.

Soc. And you would term the rescue of a friend in battle honourable, in as much as courage does a good work?

Al. I should.

Soc. But evil because of the death which ensues?

Al. Yes.

Soc. Might we not describe their different effects as follows:— You may call either of them evil in respect of the evil which is the result, and good in respect of the good which is the result of either of them?

Al. Yes.

Soc. And they are honourable in so far as they are good, and dishonourable in so far as they are evil?

Al. True.

Soc. Then when you say that the rescue of a friend in battle is honourable and yet evil, that is equivalent to saying that the rescue is good and yet evil?

Al. I believe that you are right, Socrates.

Soc. Nothing honourable, regarded as honourable, is evil; nor anything base, regarded as base, good.

Al. Clearly not.

Soc. Look at the matter yet once more in a further light: he who acts honourably acts well?

Al. Yes.

Soc. And he who acts well is happy?

Al. Of course.

Soc. And the happy are those who obtain good?

Al. True.

Soc. And they obtain good by acting well and honourably?

Al. Yes.

Soc. Then acting well is a good?

Al. Certainly.

Soc. And happiness is a good?

Al. Yes.

Soc. Then the good and the honourable are again identified.

Al. Manifestly.

Soc. Then, if the argument holds, what we find to be honourable we shall also find to be good?

Al. Certainly.

Soc. And is the good expedient or not?

Al. Expedient.

Soc. Do you remember our admissions about the just?

Al. Yes; if I am not mistaken, we said that those who acted justly must also act honourably.

Soc. And the honourable is the good?

Al. Yes.

Soc. And the good is expedient?

Al. Yes.

Soc. Then, Alcibiades, the just is expedient?

Al. I should infer so.

Soc. And all this I prove out of your own mouth, for I ask and you answer?

Al. I must acknowledge it to be true.

Soc. And having acknowledged that the just is the same as the expedient, are you not (let me ask) prepared to ridicule any one who, pretending to understand the principles of justice and injustice, gets up to advise the noble Athenians or the ignoble Peparethians, that the just may be the evil?

Al. I solemnly declare, Socrates, that I do not know what I am saying. Verily, I am in a strange state, for when you put questions to me I am of different minds in successive instants.

Soc. And are you not aware of the nature of this perplexity, my friend?

Al. Indeed I am not.

Soc. Do you suppose that if some one were to ask you whether you have two eyes or three, or two hands or four, or anything of that sort, you would then be of different minds in successive instants?

Al. I begin to distrust myself, but still I do not suppose that I should.

Soc. You would feel no doubt; and for this reason—because you would know?

Al. I suppose so.

Soc. And the reason why you involuntarily contradict yourself is clearly that you are ignorant?

Al. Very likely.

Soc. And if you are perplexed in answering about just and unjust, honourable and dishonourable, good and evil, expedient and inexpedient, the reason is that you are ignorant of them, and therefore in perplexity. Is not that clear?

Al. I agree.

Soc. But is this always the case, and is a man necessarily perplexed about that of which he has no knowledge?

Al. Certainly he is.

and therefore the just which is the honourable is also the expedient. All this has been proved by Alcibiades himself.

Yet he still finds himself in a perplexity,

117

and this is because he thinks that he knows, but if he knew that he were ignorant he would be in no perplexity.

Soc. And do you know how to ascend into heaven?

Al. Certainly not.

Soc. And in this case, too, is your judgment perplexed?

Al. No.

Soc. Do you see the reason why, or shall I tell you?

Al. Tell me.

Soc. The reason is, that you not only do not know, my friend, but you do not think that you know.

Al. There again; what do you mean?

Soc. Ask yourself; are you in any perplexity about things of which you are ignorant? You know, for example, that you know nothing about the preparation of food.

Al. Very true.

Soc. And do you think and perplex yourself about the preparation of food: or do you leave that to some one who understands the art?

Al. The latter.

Soc. Or if you were on a voyage, would you bewilder yourself by considering whether the rudder is to be drawn inwards or outwards, or do you leave that to the pilot, and do nothing?

Al. It would be the concern of the pilot.

Soc. Then you are not perplexed about what you do not know, if you know that you do not know it?

Al. I imagine not.

The
people
who
make
mistakes
are
neither
those who
know, nor
those who
do not
know, but
those who
think that
they
know and
do not
know.

Soc. Do you not see, then, that mistakes in life and practice are likewise to be attributed to the ignorance which has conceit of knowledge?

Al. Once more, what do you mean?

Soc. I suppose that we begin to act when we think that we know what we are doing?

Al. Yes.

Soc. But when people think that they do not know, they entrust their business to others?

Al. Yes.

Soc. And so there is a class of ignorant persons who do not make mistakes in life, because they trust others about things of which they are ignorant?

Al. True.

Soc. Who, then, are the persons who make mistakes? They cannot, of course, be those who know?

Al. Certainly not.

Soc. But if neither those who know, nor those who know that they do not know, make mistakes, there remain those only who do not know and think that they know.

Al. Yes, only those.

Soc. Then this is ignorance of the disgraceful sort which is mischievous?

Al. Yes.

Soc. And most mischievous and most disgraceful when having to do with the greatest matters?

Al. By far.

Soc. And can there be any matters greater than the just, the honourable, the good, and the expedient?

Al. There cannot be.

Soc. And these, as you were saying, are what perplex you?

Al. Yes.

Soc. But if you are perplexed, then, as the previous argument has shown, you are not only ignorant of the greatest matters, but being ignorant you fancy that you know them?

Al. I fear that you are right.

Soc. And now see what has happened to you, Alcibiades! I hardly like to speak of your evil case, but as we are alone I will: My good friend, you are wedded to ignorance of the most disgraceful kind, and of this you are convicted, not by me, but out of your own mouth and by your own argument; wherefore also you rush into politics before you are educated. Neither is your case to be deemed singular. For I might say the same of almost all our statesmen, with the exception, perhaps, of your guardian, Pericles.

And you, like other statesmen, rush into politics without being trained. Pericles, alone of them all, associated with the philosophers.

Al. Yes, Socrates; and Pericles is said not to have got his wisdom by the light of nature, but to have associated with several of the philosophers; with Pythocleides, for example, and with Anaxagoras, and now in advanced life with Damon, in the hope of gaining wisdom.

Soc. Very good; but did you ever know a man wise in anything who was unable to impart his particular wisdom? For example, he who taught you letters was not only wise, but he made you and any others whom he liked wise.

Al. Yes.

Soc. And you, whom he taught, can do the same?

Al. True.

Soc. And in like manner the harper and gymnastic-master?

Al. Certainly.

Soc. When a person is enabled to impart knowledge to another, he thereby gives an excellent proof of his own understanding of any matter.

And even
he could
not teach
his own
sons, or
your
brother
Cleinias,
nor did
any one
ever grow
[119]
wiser in
his so-
ciety.

But if
other
statesmen
are un-
educated,
what need
has Alci-
biades of
educa-
tion?

The lover
is pained
at hearing
from the
lips of
Alcibiades
so un-
worthy a
senti-
ment. He
should
have a
higher
ambition
than this.

Al. I agree.

Soc. Well, and did Pericles make any one wise; did he begin by making his sons wise?

Al. But, Socrates, if the two sons of Pericles were simpletons, what has that to do with the matter?

Soc. Well, but did he make your brother, Cleinias, wise?

Al. Cleinias is a madman; there is no use in talking of him.

Soc. But if Cleinias is a madman and the two sons of Pericles were simpletons, what reason can be given why he neglects you, and lets you be as you are?

Al. I believe that I am to blame for not listening to him.

Soc. But did you ever hear of any other Athenian or foreigner, bond or free, who was deemed to have grown wiser in the society of Pericles,—as I might cite Pythodorus, the son of Isolochus, and Callias, the son of Calliades, who have grown wiser in the society of Zeno, for which privilege they have each of them paid him the sum of a hundred minae[1] to the increase of their wisdom and fame.

Al. I certainly never did hear of any one.

Soc. Well, and in reference to your own case, do you mean to remain as you are, or will you take some pains about yourself?

Al. With your aid, Socrates, I will. And indeed, when I hear you speak, the truth of what you are saying strikes home to me, and I agree with you, for our statesmen, all but a few, do appear to be quite uneducated.

Soc. What is the inference?

Al. Why, that if they were educated they would be trained athletes, and he who means to rival them ought to have knowledge and experience when he attacks them; but now, as they have become politicians without any special training, why should I have the trouble of learning and practising? For I know well that by the light of nature I shall get the better of them.

Soc. My dear friend, what a sentiment! And how unworthy of your noble form and your high estate!

Al. What do you mean, Socrates; why do you say so?

Soc. I am grieved when I think of our mutual love.

Al. At what?

Soc. At your fancying that the contest on which you are entering is with people here.

Al. Why, what others are there?

Soc. Is that a question which a magnanimous soul should ask?

Al. Do you mean to say that the contest is not with these?

[1] About £406.

Soc. And suppose that you were going to steer a ship into action, would you only aim at being the best pilot on board? Would you not, while acknowledging that you must possess this degree of excellence, rather look to your antagonists, and not, as you are now doing, to your fellow combatants? You ought to be so far above these latter, that they will not even dare to be your rivals; and, being regarded by you as inferiors, will do battle for you against the enemy; this is the kind of superiority which you must establish over them, if you mean to accomplish any noble action really worthy of yourself and of the state.

Al. That would certainly be my aim.

Soc. Verily, then, you have good reason to be satisfied, if you are better than the soldiers; and you need not, when you are their superior and have your thoughts and actions fixed upon them, look away to the generals of the enemy.

Al. Of whom are you speaking, Socrates?

Soc. Why, you surely know that our city goes to war now and then with the Lacedaemonians and with the great king?

Al. True enough.

Soc. And if you meant to be the ruler of this city, would you not be right in considering that the Lacedaemonian and Persian king were your true rivals?

Al. I believe that you are right.

Soc. Oh no, my friend, I am quite wrong, and I think that you ought rather to turn your attention to Midias the quail-breeder and others like him, who manage our politics; in whom, as the women would remark, you may still see the slaves' cut of hair, cropping out in their minds as well as on their pates; and they come with their barbarous lingo to flatter us and not to rule us. To these, I say, you should look, and then you need not trouble yourself about your own fitness to contend in such a noble arena: there is no reason why you should either learn what has to be learned, or practise what has to be practised, and only when thoroughly prepared enter on a political career.

Al. There, I think, Socrates, that you are right; I do not suppose, however, that the Spartan generals or the great king are really different from anybody else.

Soc. But, my dear friend, do consider what you are saying.

Al. What am I to consider?

Soc. In the first place, will you be more likely to take care of yourself, if you are in a wholesome fear and dread of them, or if you are not?

Al. Clearly, if I have such a fear of them.

120
His rivals
should be
the Spar-
tan and
Persian
kings, not
any
chance
persons.

Alcibiades I

SOCRATES,
ALCIBIA-
DES.

Soc. And do you think that you will sustain any injury if you take care of yourself?

Al. No, I shall be greatly benefited.

Soc. And this is one very important respect in which that notion of yours is bad.

Al. True.

Soc. In the next place, consider that what you say is probably false.

Al. How so?

Soc. Let me ask you whether better natures are likely to be found in noble races or not in noble races?

Al. Clearly in noble races.

Soc. Are not those who are well born and well bred most likely to be perfect in virtue?

Al. Certainly.

We too
have our
pride of
birth, but
how in-
ferior are
we to
[121]
those who
are de-
scended
from Zeus
through a
line of
kings!

Soc. Then let us compare our antecedents with those of the Lacedaemonian and Persian kings; are they inferior to us in descent? Have we not heard that the former are sprung from Heracles, and the latter from Achaemenes, and that the race of Heracles and the race of Achaemenes go back to Perseus, son of Zeus?

Al. Why, so does mine go back to Eurysaces, and he to Zeus!

Soc. And mine, noble Alcibiades, to Daedalus, and he to Hephaestus, son of Zeus. But, for all that, we are far inferior to them. For they are descended 'from Zeus,' through a line of kings—either kings of Argos and Lacedaemon, or kings of Persia, a country which the descendants of Achaemenes have always possessed, besides being at various times sovereigns of Asia, as they now are; whereas, we and our fathers were but private persons. How ridiculous would you be thought if you were to make a display of your ancestors and of Salamis the island of Eurysaces, or of Aegina, the habitation of the still more ancient Aeacus, before Artaxerxes, son of Xerxes. You should consider how inferior we are to them both in the derivation of our birth and in other particulars. Did you never observe how great is the property of the Spartan kings? And their wives are under the guardianship of the Ephori, who are public officers and watch over them, in order to preserve as far as possible the purity of the Heracleid blood. Still greater is the difference among the Persians; for no one entertains a suspicion that the father of a prince of Persia can be any one but the king. Such is the awe which invests the person of the queen, that any other guard is needless. And when the heir of the kingdom is born, all the subjects of the king feast; and the day of his birth is for ever afterwards kept as a holiday and time of sacrifice by all Asia; whereas, when you and I were born,

The
wealth
and dig-
nity of
the Spar-
tan kings
is great,
but it is
as no-
thing
compared
with that
of the
Persians.

Alcibiades, as the comic poet says, the neighbours hardly knew of the important event. After the birth of the royal child, he is tended, not by a good-for-nothing woman-nurse, but by the best of the royal eunuchs, who are charged with the care of him, and especially with the fashioning and right formation of his limbs, in order that he may be as shapely as possible; which being their calling, they are held in great honour. And when the young prince is seven years old he is put upon a horse and taken to the riding-masters, and begins to go out hunting. And at fourteen years of age he is handed over to the royal schoolmasters, as they are termed: these are four chosen men, reputed to be the best among the Persians of a certain age; and one of them is the wisest, another the justest, a third the most temperate, and a fourth the most valiant. The first instructs him in the magianism of Zoroaster, the son of Oromasus, which is the worship of the Gods, and teaches him also the duties of his royal office; the second, who is the justest, teaches him always to speak the truth; the third, or most temperate, forbids him to allow any pleasure to be lord over him, that he may be accustomed to be a freeman and king indeed,—lord of himself first, and not a slave; the most valiant trains him to be bold and fearless, telling him that if he fears he is to deem himself a slave; whereas Pericles gave you, Alcibiades, for a tutor Zopyrus the Thracian, a slave of his who was past all other work. I might enlarge on the nurture and education of your rivals, but that would be tedious; and what I have said is a sufficient sample of what remains to be said. I have only to remark, by way of contrast, that no one cares about your birth or nurture or education, or, I may say, about that of any other Athenian, unless he has a lover who looks after him. And if you cast an eye on the wealth, the luxury, the garments with their flowing trains, the anointings with myrrh, the multitudes of attendants, and all the other bravery of the Persians, you will be ashamed when you discern your own inferiority; or if you look at the temperance and orderliness and ease and grace and magnanimity and courage and endurance and love of toil and desire of glory and ambition of the Lacedaemonians—in all these respects you will see that you are but a child in comparison of them. Even in the matter of wealth, if you value yourself upon that, I must reveal to you how you stand; for if you form an estimate of the wealth of the Lacedaemonians, you will see that our possessions fall far short of theirs. For no one here can compete with them either in the extent and fertility of their own and the Messenian territory, or in the number of their slaves, and especially of the Helots, or of their horses, or of the animals which feed on the Messenian pastures. But I have said enough of this:

Alcibiades I

SOCRATES.

The birth of the Persian princes is a world-famous event, and the utmost pains is taken with their education, [122] which is entrusted to great and noble persons.

When Alcibiades was born nobody knew or cared, and his education was handed over to a worn-out slave of his guardian's.

Alcibiades
I

SOCRATES.

123

The
country
called the
'queen's
girdle,'
the
'queen's
veil,' and
the like.

The
queen of
Persia or
of Sparta,
if they
heard
that a
youth of
twenty,
without
resources
and with-
out edu-
cation,
was going
to attack
their son
or hus-
band,
would
deem him
mad.

124

and as to gold and silver, there is more of them in Lacedaemon than in all the rest of Hellas, for during many generations gold has been always flowing in to them from the whole Hellenic world, and often from the barbarian also, and never going out, as in the fable of Aesop the fox said to the lion, 'The prints of the feet of those going in are distinct enough;' but who ever saw the trace of money going out of Lacedaemon? and therefore you may safely infer that the inhabitants are the richest of the Hellenes in gold and silver, and that their kings are the richest of them, for they have a larger share of these things, and they have also a tribute paid to them which is very considerable. Yet the Spartan wealth, though great in comparison of the wealth of the other Hellenes, is as nothing in comparison of that of the Persians and their kings. Why, I have been informed by a credible person who went up to the king [at Susa], that he passed through a large tract of excellent land, extending for nearly a day's journey, which the people of the country called the queen's girdle, and another, which they called her veil; and several other fair and fertile districts, which were reserved for the adornment of the queen, and are named after her several habiliments. Now, I cannot help thinking to myself, What if some one were to go to Amestris, the wife of Xerxes and mother of Artaxerxes, and say to her, There is a certain Dinomachè, whose whole wardrobe is not worthy fifty minae—and that will be more than the value—and she has a son who is possessed of a three-hundred-acre patch at Erchiae, and he has a mind to go to war with your son—would she not wonder to what this Alcibiades trusts for success in the conflict? 'He must rely,' she would say to herself, 'upon his training and wisdom —these are the things which Hellenes value.' And if she heard that this Alcibiades who is making the attempt is not as yet twenty years old, and is wholly uneducated, and when his lover tells him that he ought to get education and training first, and then go and fight the king, he refuses, and says that he is well enough as he is, would she not be amazed, and ask, 'On what, then, does the youth rely?' And if we replied: He relies on his beauty, and stature, and birth, and mental endowments, she would think that we were mad, Alcibiades, when she compared the advantages which you possess with those of her own people. And I believe that even Lampido, the daughter of Leotychides, the wife of Archidamus and mother of Agis, all of whom were kings, would have the same feeling; if, in your present uneducated state, you were to turn your thoughts against her son, she too would be equally astonished. But how disgraceful, that we should not have as high a notion of what is required in us as our enemies' wives and mothers have of the qualities which are required in their assailants! O my friend, be persuaded by me, and hear the Delphian inscription, 'Know thyself'—not the men whom you think, but these kings are our rivals, and we can only overcome them by pains and skill. And if you fail in the required qualities, you will fail also in becoming renowned among Hellenes and Barbarians, which you seem to desire more than any other man ever desired anything.

Al. I entirely believe you; but what are the sort of pains which are required, Socrates,—can you tell me?

Soc. Yes, I can; but we must take counsel together concerning the manner in which both of us may be most improved. For what I am telling you of the necessity of education applies to myself as well as to you; and there is only one point in which I have an advantage over you.

Al. What is that?

Soc. I have a guardian who is better and wiser than your guardian, Pericles.

Al. Who is he, Socrates?

Soc. God, Alcibiades, who up to this day has not allowed me to converse with you; and he inspires in me the faith that I am especially designed to bring you to honour.

Al. You are jesting, Socrates.

Soc. Perhaps; at any rate, I am right in saying that all men greatly need pains and care, and you and I above all men.

Al. You are not far wrong about me.

Soc. And certainly not about myself.

Al. But what can we do?

Soc. There must be no hesitation or cowardice, my friend.

Al. That would not become us, Socrates.

Soc. No, indeed, and we ought to take counsel together: for do we not wish to be as good as possible?

Al. We do.

Soc. In what sort of virtue?

Al. Plainly, in the virtue of good men.

Soc. Who are good in what?

Al. Those, clearly, who are good in the management of affairs.

Soc. What sort of affairs? Equestrian affairs?

Al. Certainly not.

Soc. You mean that about them we should have recourse to horsemen?

Al. Yes.

Soc. Well; naval affairs?

I too need educa- tion; and God, who is my guardian, inspires me with the belief that I shall bring you to honour.

We must take counsel together, (not about eques- trian or naval af- fairs), but

125

about the
things
which oc-
cupy the
minds of
wise men.

Al. No.

Soc. You mean that we should have recourse to sailors about them?

Al. Yes.

Soc. Then what affairs? And who do them?

Al. The affairs which occupy Athenian gentlemen.

Soc. And when you speak of gentlemen, do you mean the wise or the unwise?

Al. The wise.

Soc. And a man is good in respect of that in which he is wise?

Al. Yes.

Soc. And evil in respect of that in which he is unwise?

Al. Certainly.

Soc. The shoemaker, for example, is wise in respect of the making of shoes?

Al. Yes.

Soc. Then he is good in that?

Al. He is.

Soc. But in respect of the making of garments he is unwise?

Al. Yes.

Soc. Then in that he is bad?

Al. Yes.

Soc. Then upon this view of the matter the same man is good and also bad?

Al. True.

Soc. But would you say that the good are the same as the bad?

Al. Certainly not.

Soc. Then whom do you call the good?

And the
wise are
those who
take
counsel
for the
better
order and
improve-
ment of
the city.

Al. I mean by the good those who are able to rule in the city.

Soc. Not, surely, over horses?

Al. Certainly not.

Soc. But over men?

Al. Yes.

Soc. When they are sick?

Al. No.

Soc. Or on a voyage?

Al. No.

Soc. Or reaping the harvest?

Al. No.

Soc. When they are doing something or nothing?

Al. When they are doing something, I should say.

Soc. I wish that you would explain to me what this something is.

*Alcibiades
I*

SOCRATES,
ALCIBIA-
DES.

Illustra-
tions.

Al. When they are having dealings with one another, and using one another's services, as we citizens do in our daily life.

Soc. Those of whom you speak are ruling over men who are using the services of other men?

Al. Yes.

Soc. Are they ruling over the signal-men who give the time to the rowers?

Al. No; they are not.

Soc. That would be the office of the pilot?

Al. Yes.

Soc. But, perhaps you mean that they rule over flute-players, who lead the singers and use the services of the dancers?

Al. Certainly not.

Soc. That would be the business of the teacher of the chorus?

Al. Yes.

Soc. Then what is the meaning of being able to rule over men who use other men?

Al. I mean that they rule over men who have common rights of citizenship, and dealings with one another.

Soc. And what sort of an art is this? Suppose that I ask you again, as I did just now, What art makes men know how to rule over their fellow-sailors,—how would you answer?

Al. The art of the pilot.

Soc. And, if I may recur to another old instance, what art enables them to rule over their fellow-singers?

Al. The art of the teacher of the chorus, which you were just now mentioning.

Soc. And what do you call the art of fellow-citizens?

Al. I should say, good counsel, Socrates.

Soc. And is the art of the pilot evil counsel?

Al. No.

Soc. But good counsel?

Al. Yes, that is what I should say,—good counsel, of which the aim is the preservation of the voyagers.

Soc. True. And what is the aim of that other good counsel of which you speak?

Al. The aim is the better order and preservation of the city.

Soc. And what is that of which the absence or presence improves and preserves the order of the city? Suppose you were to ask me, what is that of which the presence or absence improves or preserves the order of the body? I should reply, the presence of health and the absence of disease. You would say the same?

Al. Yes.

Soc. And if you were to ask me the same question about the eyes, I should reply in the same way, 'the presence of sight and the absence of blindness;' or about the ears, I should reply, that they were improved and were in better case, when deafness was absent, and hearing was present in them.

Al. True.

And this
improve-
ment is
given by
friend-
ship and
agree-
ment,

Soc. And what would you say of a state? What is that by the presence or absence of which the state is improved and better managed and ordered?

Al. I should say, Socrates:—the presence of friendship and the absence of hatred and division.

Soc. And do you mean by friendship agreement or disagreement?

Al. Agreement.

Soc. What art makes cities agree about numbers?

Al. Arithmetic.

Soc. And private individuals?

Al. The same.

Soc. And what art makes each individual agree with himself?

Al. The same.

Soc. And what art makes each of us agree with himself about the comparative length of the span and of the cubit? Does not the art of measure?

Al. Yes.

Soc. Individuals are agreed with one another about this; and states, equally?

Al. Yes.

Soc. And the same holds of the balance?

Al. True.

Soc. But what is the other agreement of which you speak, and about what? what art can give that agreement? And does that which gives it to the state give it also to the individual, so as to make him consistent with himself and with another?

Al. I should suppose so.

Soc. But what is the nature of the agreement?—answer, and faint not.

such as
exists
between
the mem-
bers of a
family,
however
they may

Al. I mean to say that there should be such friendship and agreement as exists between an affectionate father and mother and their son, or between brothers, or between husband and wife.

Soc. But can a man, Alcibiades, agree with a woman about the spinning of wool, which she understands and he does not?

Al. No, truly.

Soc. Nor has he any need, for spinning is a female accomplishment.

Al. Yes.

Soc. And would a woman agree with a man about the science of arms, which she has never learned?

Al. Certainly not.

Soc. I suppose that the use of arms would be regarded by you as a male accomplishment?

Al. It would.

Soc. Then, upon your view, women and men have two sorts of knowledge?

Al. Certainly.

Soc. Then in their knowledge there is no agreement of women and men?

Al. There is not.

Soc. Nor can there be friendship, if friendship is agreement?

Al. Plainly not.

Soc. Then women are not loved by men when they do their own work?

Al. I suppose not.

Soc. Nor men by women when they do their own work?

Al. No.

Soc. Nor are states well administered, when individuals do their own work?

Al. I should rather think, Socrates, that the reverse is the truth[1].

Soc. What! do you mean to say that states are well administered when friendship is absent, the presence of which, as we were saying, alone secures their good order?

Al. But I should say that there is friendship among them, for this very reason, that the two parties respectively do their own work.

Soc. That was not what you were saying before; and what do you mean now by affirming that friendship exists when there is no agreement? How can there be agreement about matters which the one party knows, and of which the other is in ignorance?

Al. Impossible.

Soc. And when individuals are doing their own work, are they doing what is just or unjust?

Al. What is just, certainly.

Soc. And when individuals do what is just in the state, is there no friendship among them?

Al. I suppose that there must be, Socrates.

[1] Cp. *Rep.* i. 332 foll.

Marginal notes:

127
SOCRATES,
ALCIBIADES.

differ in their qualities and accomplishments.

If everybody is doing his own business, how can this promote friendship? And yet when individuals are doing each his own work, they are doing what is just.

Soc. Then what do you mean by this friendship or agreement about which we must be wise and discreet in order that we may be good men? I cannot make out where it exists or among whom; according to you, the same persons may sometimes have it, and sometimes not.

Al. But, indeed, Socrates, I do not know what I am saying; and I have long been, unconsciously to myself, in a most disgraceful state.

Soc. Nevertheless, cheer up; at fifty, if you had discovered your deficiency, you would have been too old, and the time for taking care of yourself would have passed away, but yours is just the age at which the discovery should be made.

Al. And what should he do, Socrates, who would make the discovery?

The way
to clear
up diffi-
culties is
to answer

questions.
Alcibiades
is willing
to have
recourse
to this
method
of im-
prove-
ment.

Soc. Answer questions, Alcibiades; and that is a process which, by the grace of God, if I may put any faith in my oracle, will be very improving to both of us.

Al. If I can be improved by answering, I will answer.

[128]

Soc. And first of all, that we may not peradventure be deceived by appearances, fancying, perhaps, that we are taking care of ourselves when we are not, what is the meaning of a man taking care of himself? and when does he take care? Does he take care of himself when he takes care of what belongs to him?

Al. I should think so.

Soc. When does a man take care of his feet? Does he not take care of them when he takes care of that which belongs to his feet?

Al. I do not understand.

Soc. Let me take the hand as an illustration; does not a ring belong to the finger, and to the finger only?

Al. Yes.

Soc. And the shoe in like manner to the foot?

Al. Yes.

Soc. And when we take care of our shoes, do we not take care of our feet?

Al. I do not comprehend, Socrates.

Soc. But you would admit, Alcibiades, that to take proper care of a thing is a correct expression?

Al. Yes.

Soc. And taking proper care means improving?

Al. Yes.

Soc. And what is the art which improves our shoes?

Al. Shoemaking.

Soc. Then by shoemaking we take care of our shoes?

Al. Yes.

Soc. And do we by shoemaking take care of our feet, or by some other art which improves the feet?

Al. By some other art.

Soc. And the same art improves the feet which improves the rest of the body?

Al. Very true.

Soc. Which is gymnastic?

Al. Certainly.

Soc. Then by gymnastic we take care of our feet, and by shoemaking of that which belongs to our feet?

Al. Very true.

Soc. And by gymnastic we take care of our hands, and by the art of graving rings of that which belongs to our hands?

Al. Yes.

Soc. And by gymnastic we take care of the body, and by the art of weaving and the other arts we take care of the things of the body?

Al. Clearly.

Soc. Then the art which takes care of each thing is different from that which takes care of the belongings of each thing?

Al. True.

Soc. Then in taking care of what belongs to you, you do not take care of yourself?

Al. Certainly not.

Soc. For the art which takes care of our belongings appears not to be the same as that which takes care of ourselves?

Al. Clearly not.

Soc. And now let me ask you what is the art with which we take care of ourselves?

Al. I cannot say.

Soc. At any rate, thus much has been admitted, that the art is not one which makes any of our possessions, but which makes ourselves better?

Al. True.

Soc. But should we ever have known what art makes a shoe better, if we did not know a shoe?

Al. Impossible.

Soc. Nor should we know what art makes a ring better, if we did not know a ring?

Al. That is true.

Soc. And can we ever know what art makes a man better, if we do not know what we are ourselves?

Al. Impossible.

Soc. And is self-knowledge such an easy thing, and was he to be

It has
been
shown by
examples
that a
man does
not take
care of
himself,
when he
only takes
care of
what be-
longs to
him.

129
A man
must
know
himself

Alcibiades
1

SOCRATES,
ALCIBIA-
DES.

before he
can im-
prove
himself or
know
what be-
longs to
him.

lightly esteemed who inscribed the text on the temple at Delphi? Or is self-knowledge a difficult thing, which few are able to attain?

Al. At times I fancy, Socrates, that anybody can know himself; at other times the task appears to be very difficult.

Soc. But whether easy or difficult, Alcibiades, still there is no other way; knowing what we are, we shall know how to take care of ourselves, and if we are ignorant we shall not know.

Al. That is true.

Soc. Well, then, let us see in what way the self-existent can be discovered by us; that will give us a chance of discovering our own existence, which otherwise we can never know.

Al. You say truly.

Soc. Come, now, I beseech you, tell me with whom you are conversing?—with whom but with me?

Al. Yes.

Soc. As I am, with you?

Al. Yes.

Soc. That is to say, I, Socrates, am talking?

Al. Yes.

Soc. And Alcibiades is my hearer?

Al. Yes.

Soc. And I in talking use words?

Al. Certainly.

Soc. And talking and using words have, I suppose, the same meaning?

Al. To be sure.

Soc. And the user is not the same as the thing which he uses?

Al. What do you mean?

Soc. I will explain; the shoemaker, for example, uses a square tool, and a circular tool, and other tools for cutting?

Al. Yes.

Soc. But the tool is not the same as the cutter and user of the tool?

Al. Of course not.

Soc. And in the same way the instrument of the harper is to be distinguished from the harper himself?

Al. It is.

Soc. Now the question which I asked was whether you conceive the user to be always different from that which he uses?

Al. I do.

Soc. Then what shall we say of the shoemaker? Does he cut with his tools only or with his hands?

Al. With his hands as well.

Soc. He uses his hands too?

Al. Yes.

Soc. And does he use his eyes in cutting leather?

Al. He does.

Soc. And we admit that the user is not the same with the things which he uses?

Al. Yes.

Soc. Then the shoemaker and the harper are to be distinguished from the hands and feet which they use?

Al. Clearly.

Soc. And does not a man use the whole body?

Al. Certainly.

Soc. And that which uses is different from that which is used?

Al. True.

Soc. Then a man is not the same as his own body?

Al. That is the inference.

Soc. What is he, then?

Al. I cannot say.

Soc. Nay, you can say that he is the user of the body.

Al. Yes.

Soc. And the user of the body is the soul?

Al. Yes, the soul.

Soc. And the soul rules?

Al. Yes.

Soc. Let me make an assertion which will, I think, be universally admitted.

Al. What is it?

Soc. That man is one of three things.

Al. What are they?

Soc. Soul, body, or both together forming a whole.

Al. Certainly.

Soc. But did we not say that the actual ruling principle of the body is man?

Al. Yes, we did.

Soc. And does the body rule over itself?

Al. Certainly not.

Soc. It is subject, as we were saying?

Al. Yes.

Soc. Then that is not the principle which we are seeking?

Al. It would seem not.

Soc. But may we say that the union of the two rules over the body, and consequently that this is man?

Al. Very likely.

Alcibiades I

SOCRATES, ALCIBIA-DES.

He is distinct from what he uses; and therefore distinct from his own body.

130

But he must be one of three things:— Soul, body, or the union of the two. What is the ruling principle in him? Clearly the soul.

Soc. The most unlikely of all things; for if one of the members is subject, the two united cannot possibly rule.

Al. True.

Soc. But since neither the body, nor the union of the two, is man, either man has no real existence, or the soul is man?

Al. Just so.

Soc. Is anything more required to prove that the soul is man?

Al. Certainly not; the proof is, I think, quite sufficient.

Soc. And if the proof, although not perfect, be sufficient, we shall be satisfied;—more precise proof will be supplied when we have discovered that which we were led to omit, from a fear that the enquiry would be too much protracted.

Al. What was that?

Soc. What I meant, when I said that absolute existence must be first considered; but now, instead of absolute existence, we have been considering the nature of individual existence, and this may, perhaps, be sufficient; for surely there is nothing which may be called more properly ourselves than the soul?

Al. There is nothing.

Soc. Then we may truly conceive that you and I are conversing with one another, soul to soul?

Al. Very true.

Soc. And that is just what I was saying before—that I, Socrates, am not arguing or talking with the face of Alcibiades, but with the real Alcibiades; or in other words, with his soul.

Al. True.

Soc. Then he who bids a man know himself, would have him know his soul?

Al. That appears to be true.

Soc. He whose knowledge only extends to the body, knows the things of a man, and not the man himself?

Al. That is true.

Soc. Then neither the physician regarded as a physician, nor the trainer regarded as a trainer, knows himself?

Al. He does not.

Soc. The husbandmen and the other craftsmen are very far from knowing themselves, for they would seem not even to know their own belongings? When regarded in relation to the arts which they practise they are even further removed from self-knowledge, for they only know the belongings of the body. which minister to the body.

Al. That is true.

There remains a question of absolute existence, which has not been considered by us, or rather is being considered by us when we speak of the soul.

You and I are talking soul to soul.

131

But if the soul is the man, he who knows only the arts which concern man does not know himself.

Soc. Then if temperance is the knowledge of self, in respect of his art none of them is temperate?

Al. I agree.

Soc. And this is the reason why their arts are accounted vulgar, and are not such as a good man would practise?

Al. Quite true.

Soc. Again, he who cherishes his body cherishes not himself, but what belongs to him?

Al. That is true.

Soc. But he who cherishes his money, cherishes neither himself nor his belongings, but is in a stage yet further removed from himself?

Al. I agree.

Soc. Then the money-maker has really ceased to be occupied with his own concerns?

Al. True.

Soc. And if any one has fallen in love with the person of Alcibiades, he loves not Alcibiades, but the belongings of Alcibiades?

Al. True.

Soc. But he who loves your soul is the true lover?

Al. That is the necessary inference.

Soc. The lover of the body goes away when the flower of youth fades?

Al. True.

The lover of the soul is the true lover.

Soc. But he who loves the soul goes not away, as long as the soul follows after virtue?

Al. Yes.

Soc. And I am the lover who goes not away, but remains with you, when you are no longer young and the rest are gone?

Al. Yes, Socrates; and therein you do well, and I hope that you will remain.

Soc. Then you must try to look your best.

Al. I will.

He only remains and goes not away, so long as the soul of his be- loved fol- lows after virtue.

Soc. The fact is, that there is only one lover of Alcibiades the son of Cleinias; there neither is nor ever has been seemingly any other; and he is his darling,—Socrates, the son of Sophroniscus and Phaenarete.

Al. True.

Soc. And did you not say, that if I had not spoken first, you were on the point of coming to me, and enquiring why I only remained?

Al. That is true.

Soc. The reason was that I loved you for your own sake, whereas other men love what belongs to you; and your beauty, which is not you, is fading away, just as your true self is beginning to bloom. And I will never desert you, if you are not spoiled and deformed by the Athenian people; for the danger which I most fear is that you will become a lover of the people and will be spoiled by them. Many a noble Athenian has been ruined in this way. For the demus of the great-hearted Erechtheus is of a fair countenance, but you should see him naked; wherefore observe the caution which I give you.

Al. What caution?

Soc. Practise yourself, sweet friend, in learning what you ought to know, before you enter on politics; and then you will have an antidote which will keep you out of harm's way.

Al. Good advice, Socrates, but I wish that you would explain to me in what way I am to take care of myself.

Soc. Have we not made an advance? for we are at any rate tolerably well agreed as to what we are, and there is no longer any danger, as we once feared, that we might be taking care not of ourselves, but of something which is not ourselves.

Al. That is true.

Soc. And the next step will be to take care of the soul, and look to that?

Al. Certainly.

Soc. Leaving the care of our bodies and of our properties to others?

Al. Very good.

Soc. But how can we have a perfect knowledge of the things of the soul?—For if we know them, then I suppose we shall know ourselves. Can we really be ignorant of the excellent meaning of the Delphian inscription, of which we were just now speaking?

Al. What have you in your thoughts, Socrates?

Soc. I will tell you what I suspect to be the meaning and lesson of that inscription. Let me take an illustration from sight, which I imagine to be the only one suitable to my purpose.

Al. What do you mean?

Soc. Consider; if some one were to say to the eye, 'See thyself,' as you might say to a man, 'Know thyself,' what is the nature and meaning of this precept? Would not his meaning be:—That the eye should look at that in which it would see itself?

Al. Clearly.

Soc. And what are the objects in looking at which we see ourselves?

Al. Clearly, Socrates, in looking at mirrors and the like.

And So-
crates will
never de-
sert Alci-
biades so
long as he
is not
spoiled by
the Athe-
nian
people.

He who
would
take care
of him-
self must
first of all
know
himself.

The eye
which
would see
itself
must look
into the
pupil of

Soc. Very true; and is there not something of the nature of a mirror in our own eyes?

Al. Certainly.

Soc. Did you ever observe that the face of the person looking into the eye of another is reflected as in a mirror; and in the visual organ which is over against him, and which is called the pupil, there is a sort of image of the person looking?

Al. That is quite true.

Soc. Then the eye, looking at another eye, and at that in the eye which is most perfect, and which is the instrument of vision, will there see itself?

Al. That is evident.

Soc. But looking at anything else either in man or in the world, and not to what resembles this, it will not see itself?

Al. Very true.

Soc. Then if the eye is to see itself, it must look at the eye, and at that part of the eye where sight which is the virtue of the eye resides?

Al. True.

Soc. And if the soul, my dear Alcibiades, is ever to know herself, must she not look at the soul; and especially at that part of the soul in which her virtue resides, and to any other which is like this?

Al. I agree, Socrates.

Soc. And do we know of any part of our souls more divine than that which has to do with wisdom and knowledge?

Al. There is none.

Soc. Then this is that part of the soul which resembles the divine; and he who looks at this and at the whole class of things divine, will be most likely to know himself?

Al. Clearly.

Soc. And self-knowledge we agree to be wisdom?

Al. True.

Soc. But if we have no self-knowledge and no wisdom, can we ever know our own good and evil?

Al. How can we, Socrates?

Soc. You mean, that if you did not know Alcibiades, there would be no possibility of your knowing that what belonged to Alcibiades was really his?

Al. It would be quite impossible.

Soc. Nor should we know that we were the persons to whom anything belonged, if we did not know ourselves?

Al. How could we?

---

another, which is the divinest part of the eye, and will then behold itself.

And the soul which would know herself must look especially at that part of herself in which she resembles the divine.

He who knows not himself and

Alcibiades
I

SOCRATES,
ALCIBIA-
DES.

his be-
longings,
will not
know
others
and their
belong-
ings,

Soc. And if we did not know our own belongings, neither should we know the belongings of our belongings?

Al. Clearly not.

Soc. Then we were not altogether right in acknowledging just now that a man may know what belongs to him and yet not know himself; nay, rather he cannot even know the belongings of his belongings; for the discernment of the things of self, and of the things which belong to the things of self, appear all to be the business of the same man, and of the same art.

Al. So much may be supposed.

Soc. And he who knows not the things which belong to himself, will in like manner be ignorant of the things which belong to others?

Al. Very true.

and
therefore
he will
not know
the affairs
of states.

Soc. And if he knows not the affairs of others, he will not know the affairs of states?

Al. Very true.

Soc. Then if the events lessen itself, it must attain that part of—besides?

Al. True.

Soc. And if the soul, my dear Alcibiades, is over-

Soc. Then such a man can never be a statesman?

Al. He cannot.

Soc. Nor an economist?

Al. He cannot.

Soc. He will not know what he is doing?

Al. He will not.

Soc. And will not he who is ignorant fall into error?

Al. Assuredly.

And, if he
knows
not what
he is do-
ing, he
will be
miserable
and will
make
others
miserable.

Soc. And if he falls into error will he not fail both in his public and private capacity?

Al. Yes, indeed.

Soc. And failing, will he not be miserable?

Al. Very.

Soc. And what will become of those for whom he is acting?

Al. They will be miserable also.

Soc. Then he who is not wise and good cannot be happy?

Al. He cannot.

Soc. The bad, then, are miserable?

Al. Yes, very.

Soc. And if so, not he who has riches, but he who has wisdom, is delivered from his misery?

Al. Clearly.

Soc. Cities, then, if they are to be happy, do not want walls, or triremes, or docks, or numbers, or size, Alcibiades, without virtue[1]

Al. Indeed they do not.

Soc. And you must give the citizens virtue, if you mean to administer their affairs rightly or nobly?

[1] Cp. Arist. Pol. vii. 1. § 5.

Al. Certainly.

Soc. But can a man give that which he has not?

Al. Impossible.

Soc. Then you or any one who means to govern and superintend, not only himself and the things of himself, but the state and the things of the state, must in the first place acquire virtue.

Al. That is true.

Soc. You have not therefore to obtain power or authority, in order to enable you to do what you wish for yourself and the state, but justice and wisdom.

Al. Clearly.

Soc. You and the state, if you act wisely and justly, will act according to the will of God?

Al. Certainly.

Soc. As I was saying before, you will look only at what is bright and divine, and act with a view to them?

Al. Yes.

Soc. In that mirror you will see and know yourselves and your own good?

Al. Yes.

Soc. And so you will act rightly and well?

Al. Yes.

Soc. In which case, I will be security for your happiness.

Al. I accept the security.

Soc. But if you act unrighteously, your eye will turn to the dark and godless, and being in darkness and ignorance of yourselves, you will probably do deeds of darkness.

Al. Very possibly.

Soc. For if a man, my dear Alcibiades, has the power to do what he likes, but has no understanding, what is likely to be the result, either to him as an individual or to the state—for example, if he be sick and is able to do what he likes, not having the mind of a physician—having moreover tyrannical power, and no one daring to reprove him, what will happen to him? Will he not be likely to have his constitution ruined?

Al. That is true.

Soc. Or again, in a ship, if a man having the power to do what he likes, has no intelligence or skill in navigation, do you see what will happen to him and to his fellow-sailors?

Al. Yes; I see that they will all perish.

Soc. And in like manner, in a state, and where there is any power and authority which is wanting in virtue, will not misfortune, in like manner, ensue?

Al. Certainly.

He must give the citizens wisdom and justice, and he cannot give what he has not got.

If he acts wisely and justly he will act according to the will of God.

In the mirror of the divine he will see his own good and will act rightly and be happy.

135

*Alcibiades
I*

SOCRATES,
ALCIBIA-
DES.

Not
power,
but vir-
tue,
should be
the aim
both of
individ-
uals and
of states:
and he
only is a
freeman
who has
virtue.

Soc. Not tyrannical power, then, my good Alcibiades, should be the aim either of individuals or states, if they would be happy, but virtue.

Al. That is true.

Soc. And before they have virtue, to be commanded by a superior is better for men as well as for children[1]?

Al. That is evident.

Soc. And that which is better is also nobler?

Al. True.

Soc. And what is nobler is more becoming?

Al. Certainly.

Soc. Then to the bad man slavery is more becoming, because better?

Al. True.

Soc. Then vice is only suited to a slave?

Al. Yes.

Soc. And virtue to a freeman?

Al. Yes.

Soc. And, O my friend, is not the condition of a slave to be avoided?

Al. Certainly, Socrates.

Soc. And are you now conscious of your own state? And do you know whether you are a freeman or not?

Al. I think that I am very conscious indeed of my own state.

Soc. And do you know how to escape out of a state which I do not even like to name to my beauty?

Al. Yes, I do.

Soc. How?

Al. By your help, Socrates.

Soc. That is not well said, Alcibiades.

Al. What ought I to have said?

Soc. By the help of God.

Al. I agree; and I further say, that our relations are likely to be reversed. From this day forward, I must and will follow you as you have followed me; I will be the disciple, and you shall be my master.

Soc. O that is rare! My love breeds another love: and so like the stork I shall be cherished by the bird whom I have hatched.

Al. Strange, but true; and henceforward I shall begin to think about justice.

Soc. And I hope that you will persist; although I have fears, not because I doubt you; but I see the power of the state, which may be too much for both of us.

[1] Cp. Arist. Pol. i. 5. § 7.

MENEXENUS

MENEXENUS

PERSONS OF THE DIALOGUE

SOCRATES AND MENEXENUS

Socrates. Whence come you, Menexenus? Are you from the Agora?

Menexenus. Yes, Socrates; I have been at the Council.

Soc. And what might you be doing at the Council? And yet I need hardly ask, for I see that you, believing yourself to have arrived at the end of education and of philosophy, and to have had enough of them, are mounting upwards to things higher still, and, though rather young for the post, are intending to govern us elder men, like the rest of your family, which has always provided some one who kindly took care of us.

Men. Yes, Socrates, I shall be ready to hold office, if you allow and advise that I should, but not if you think otherwise. I went to the council chamber because I heard that the Council was about to choose some one who was to speak over the dead. For you know that there is to be a public funeral?

Soc. Yes, I know. And whom did they choose?

Men. No one; they delayed the election until to-morrow, but I believe that either Archinus or Dion will be chosen.

Soc. O Menexenus! death in battle is certainly in many respects a noble thing. The dead man gets a fine and costly funeral, although he may have been poor, and an elaborate speech is made over him by a wise man who has long ago prepared what he has to say, although he who is praised may not have been good for much. The speakers praise him for what he has done and for what he has not done—that is the beauty of them—and they steal away our souls with their embellished words; in every conceivable form they praise the city; and they praise those who died in war, and all our ancestors who went before us; and they praise ourselves also who are still alive, until I feel quite elevated by their laudations, and I stand listening to their words, Menexenus, and become enchanted by them, and all in a moment I imagine myself to have become a

The gain of dying in battle.

235
The effect upon Socrates of panegyrical oratory.

775

greater and nobler and finer man than I was before. And if, as often happens, there are any foreigners who accompany me to the speech, I become suddenly conscious of having a sort of triumph over them, and they seem to experience a corresponding feeling of admiration at me, and at the greatness of the city, which appears to them, when they are under the influence of the speaker, more wonderful than ever. This consciousness of dignity lasts me more than three days, and not until the fourth or fifth day do I come to my senses and know where I am; in the meantime I have been living in the Islands of the Blest. Such is the art of our rhetoricians, and in such manner does the sound of their words keep ringing in my ears.

Men. You are always making fun of the rhetoricians, Socrates; this time, however, I am inclined to think that the speaker who is chosen will not have much to say, for he has been called upon to speak at a moment's notice, and he will be compelled almost to improvise.

Soc. But why, my friend, should he not have plenty to say? Every rhetorician has speeches ready made; nor is there any difficulty in improvising that sort of stuff. Had the orator to praise Athenians among Peloponnesians, or Peloponnesians among Athenians, he must be a good rhetorician who could succeed and gain credit. But there is no difficulty in a man's winning applause when he is contending for fame among the persons whom he is praising.

Men. Do you think not, Socrates?

Soc. Certainly 'not.'

Men. Do you think that you could speak yourself if there should be a necessity, and if the Council were to choose you?

Soc. That I should be able to speak is no great wonder, Menexenus, considering that I have an excellent mistress in the art of rhetoric,—she who has made so many good speakers, and one who was the best among all the Hellenes—Pericles, the son of Xanthippus.

Men. And who is she? I suppose that you mean Aspasia.

Soc. Yes, I do; and besides her I had Connus, the son of Metrobius, as a master, and he was my master in music, as she was in rhetoric. No wonder that a man who has received such an education should be a finished speaker; even the pupil of very inferior masters, say, for example, one who had learned music of Lamprus, and rhetoric of Antiphon the Rhamnusian, might make a figure if he were to praise the Athenians among the Athenians.

Men. And what would you be able to say if you had to speak?

Soc. Of my own wit, most likely nothing; but yesterday I heard Aspasia composing a funeral oration about these very dead. For she had been told, as you were saying, that the Athenians were going to choose a speaker, and she repeated to me the sort of speech which he should deliver, partly improvising and partly from previous thought, putting together fragments of the funeral oration which Pericles spoke, but which, as I believe, she composed.

Men. And can you remember what Aspasia said?

Soc. I ought to be able, for she taught me, and she was ready to strike me because I was always forgetting.

Men. Then why will you not rehearse what she said?

Soc. Because I am afraid that my mistress may be angry with me if I publish her speech.

Men. Nay, Socrates, let us have the speech, whether Aspasia's or any one else's, no matter. I hope that you will oblige me.

Soc. But I am afraid that you will laugh at me if I continue the games of youth in old age.

Men. Far otherwise, Socrates; let us by all means have the speech.

Soc. Truly I have such a disposition to oblige you, that if you bid me dance naked I should not like to refuse, since we are alone. Listen then: If I remember rightly, she began as follows, with the mention of the dead[1]:—

There is a tribute of deeds and of words. The departed have already had the first, when going forth on their destined journey they were attended on their way by the state and by their friends; the tribute of words remains to be given to them, as is meet and by law ordained. For noble words are a memorial and a crown of noble actions, which are given to the doers of them by the hearers. A word is needed which will duly praise the dead and gently admonish the living, exhorting the brethren and descendants of the departed to imitate their virtue, and consoling their fathers and mothers and the survivors, if any, who may chance to be alive of the previous generation. What sort of a word will this be, and how shall we rightly begin the praises of these brave men? In their life they rejoiced their own friends with their valour, and their death they gave in exchange for the salvation of the living. And I think that we should praise them in the order in which nature made them good, for they were good because they were sprung from good fathers. Wherefore let us first of all praise the goodness of their birth; secondly, their nurture and education; and then let us set forth how noble their actions were, and how worthy of the education which they had received.

And first as to their birth. Their ancestors were not strangers,

237

[1] Thucyd. ii. 35-46.

*Menexe-
nus*

SOCRATES.

The de-
parted
were the
children
of the
soil;

and their
country is
dear to
the Gods,
who con-
tended
for the
possession
of her.

She first
brought
forth
man, and
proved
her true
mother-
hood by
providing
[238]
food for
her own
offspring.

The Gods
were the
rulers of
primitive
men, and
gave them
arts.

nor are these their descendants sojourners only, whose fathers have come from another country; but they are the children of the soil, dwelling and living in their own land. And the country which brought them up is not like other countries, a stepmother to her children, but their own true mother; she bore them and nourished them and received them, and in her bosom they now repose. It is meet and right, therefore, that we should begin by praising the land which is their mother, and that will be a way of praising their noble birth.

The country is worthy to be praised, not only by us, but by all mankind; first, and above all, as being dear to the Gods. This is proved by the strife and contention of the Gods respecting her. And ought not the country which the Gods praise to be praised by all mankind? The second praise which may be fairly claimed by her, is that at the time when the whole earth was sending forth and creating diverse animals, tame and wild, she our mother was free and pure from savage monsters, and out of all animals selected and brought forth man, who is superior to the rest in understanding, and alone has justice and religion. And a great proof that she brought forth the common ancestors of us and of the departed, is that she provided the means of support for her offspring. For as a woman proves her motherhood by giving milk to her young ones (and she who has no fountain of milk is not a mother), so did this our land prove that she was the mother of men, for in those days she alone and first of all brought forth wheat and barley for human food, which is the best and noblest sustenance for man, whom she regarded as her true offspring. And these are truer proofs of mother-hood in a country than in a woman, for the woman in her conception and generation is but the imitation of the earth, and not the earth of the woman. And of the fruit of the earth she gave a plente-ous supply, not only to her own, but to others also; and afterwards she made the olive to spring up to be a boon to her children, and to help them in their toils. And when she had herself nursed them and brought them up to manhood, she gave them Gods to be their rulers and teachers, whose names are well known, and need not now be repeated. They are the Gods who first ordered our lives, and in-structed us in the arts for the supply of our daily needs, and taught us the acquisition and use of arms for the defence of the country.

Thus born into the world and thus educated, the ancestors of the departed lived and made themselves a government, which I ought briefly to commemorate. For government is the nurture of man, and the government of good men is good, and of bad men bad. And I must show that our ancestors were trained under a good government, and for this reason they were good, and our contemporaries are also good, among whom our departed friends are to be reckoned. Then as now, and indeed always, from that time to this, speaking generally, our government was an aristocracy—a form of government which receives various names, according to the fancies of men, and is sometimes called democracy, but is really an aristocracy or government of the best which has the approval of the many. For kings we have always had, first hereditary and then elected, and authority is mostly in the hands of the people, who dispense offices and power to those who appear to be most deserving of them. Neither is a man rejected from weakness or poverty or obscurity of origin, nor honoured by reason of the opposite, as in other states, but there is one principle—he who appears to be wise and good is a governor and ruler. The basis of this our government is equality of birth; for other states are made up of all sorts and unequal conditions of men, and therefore their governments are unequal; there are tyrannies and there are oligarchies, in which the one party are slaves and the others masters. But we and our citizens are brethren, the children all of one mother, and we do not think it right to be one another's masters or servants; but the natural equality of birth compels us to seek for legal equality, and to recognize no superiority except in the reputation of virtue and wisdom.

And so their and our fathers, and these, too, our brethren, being nobly born and having been brought up in all freedom, did both in their public and private capacity many noble deeds famous over the whole world. They were the deeds of men who thought that they ought to fight both against Hellenes for the sake of Hellenes on behalf of freedom, and against barbarians in the common interest of Hellas. Time would fail me to tell of their defence of their country against the invasion of Eumolpus and the Amazons, or of their defence of the Argives against the Cadmeians, or of the Heracleids against the Argives; besides, the poets have already declared in song to all mankind their glory, and therefore any commemoration of their deeds in prose which we might attempt would hold a second place. They already have their reward, and I say no more of them; but there are other worthy deeds of which no poet has worthily sung, and which are still wooing the poet's muse. Of these I am bound to make honourable mention, and shall invoke others to sing of them also in lyric and other strains, in a manner becoming the actors. And first I will tell how the Persians, lords of Asia, were enslaving Europe, and how the children of this land, who were our fathers, held them back. Of these I will speak first, and praise their valour, as is meet and fitting. He who would rightly estimate them

Menexenus

SOCRATES.

We have a good government, which is sometimes called a democracy, but is really an aristocracy, for the best rule with the consent of the many.

239
The principle of our government is equality; the only superiority is that of virtue and wisdom.

The greatness of Persia.

should place himself in thought at that time, when the whole of Asia was subject to the third king of Persia. The first king, Cyrus, by his valour freed the Persians, who were his countrymen, and subjected the Medes, who were their lords, and he ruled over the rest of Asia, as far as Egypt; and after him came his son, who ruled all the accessible part of Egypt and Libya; the third king was Darius, who extended the land boundaries of the empire to Scythia, and with his fleet held the sea and the islands. None presumed to be his equal; the minds of all men were enthralled by him—so many and mighty and warlike nations had the power of Persia subdued. Now Darius had a quarrel against us and the Eretrians, because, as he said, we had conspired against Sardis, and he sent 500,000 men in transports and vessels of war, and 300 ships, and Datis as commander, telling him to bring the Eretrians and Athenians to the king, if he wished to keep his head on his shoulders. He sailed against the Eretrians, who were reputed to be amongst the noblest and most warlike of the Hellenes of that day, and they were numerous, but he conquered them all in three days; and when he had conquered them, in order that no one might escape, he searched the whole country after this manner: his soldiers, coming to the borders of Eretria and spreading from sea to sea, joined hands and passed through the whole country, in order that they might be able to tell the king that no one had escaped them. And from Eretria they went to Marathon with a like intention, expecting to bind the Athenians in the same yoke of necessity in which they had bound the Eretrians. Having effected one-half of their purpose, they were in the act of attempting the other, and none of the Hellenes dared to assist either the Eretrians or the Athenians, except the Lacedaemonians, and they arrived a day too late for the battle; but the rest were panic-stricken and kept quiet, too happy in having escaped for a time. He who has present to his mind that conflict will know what manner of men they were who received the onset of the barbarians at Marathon, and chastened the pride of the whole of Asia, and by the victory which they gained over the barbarians first taught other men that the power of the Persians was not invincible, but that hosts of men and the multitude of riches alike yield to valour. And I assert that those men are the fathers not only of ourselves, but of our liberties and of the liberties of all who are on the continent, for that was the action to which the Hellenes looked back when they ventured to fight for their own safety in the battles which ensued: they became disciples of the men of Marathon. To them, therefore, I assign in my speech the first place, and the second to those who fought and conquered in the sea fights at Salamis and Artemisium;

240

Yet at Marathon the army of Darius was overcome by the Athenians almost singlehanded.

241

for of them, too, one might have many things to say—of the assaults which they endured by sea and land, and how they repelled
them. I will mention only that act of theirs which appears to me to
be the noblest, and which followed that of Marathon and came
nearest to it; for the men of Marathon only showed the Hellenes
that it was possible to ward off the barbarians by land, the many
by the few; but there was no proof that they could be defeated by
ships, and at sea the Persians retained the reputation of being invincible in numbers and wealth and skill and strength. This is the
glory of the men who fought at sea, that they dispelled the second
terror which had hitherto possessed the Hellenes, and so made the
fear of numbers, whether of ships or men, to cease among them.
And so the soldiers of Marathon and the sailors of Salamis became
the schoolmasters of Hellas; the one teaching and habituating the
Hellenes not to fear the barbarians at sea, and the others not to fear
them by land. Third in order, for the number and valour of the
combatants, and third in the salvation of Hellas, I place the battle
of Plataea. And now the Lacedaemonians as well as the Athenians
took part in the struggle; they were all united in this greatest and
most terrible conflict of all; wherefore their virtues will be celebrated in times to come, as they are now celebrated by us. But at a
later period many Hellenic tribes were still on the side of the barbarians, and there was a report that the great king was going to
make a new attempt upon the Hellenes, and therefore justice requires that we should also make mention of those who crowned the
previous work of our salvation, and drove and purged away all barbarians from the sea. These were the men who fought by sea at the
river Eurymedon, and who went on the expedition to Cyprus, and
who sailed to Egypt and divers other places; and they should be
gratefully remembered by us, because they compelled the king in
fear for himself to look to his own safety instead of plotting the
destruction of Hellas.

And so the war against the barbarians was fought out to the end
by the whole city on their own behalf, and on behalf of their countrymen. There was peace, and our city was held in honour; and
then, as prosperity makes men jealous, there succeeded a jealousy
of her, and jealousy begat envy, and so she became engaged against
her will in a war with the Hellenes. On the breaking out of war, our
citizens met the Lacedaemonians at Tanagra, and fought for the
freedom of the Boeotians; the issue was doubtful, and was decided
by the engagement which followed. For when the Lacedaemonians
had gone on their way, leaving the Boeotians, whom they were aid-
ing, on the third day after the battle of Tanagra, our countrymen

*Menexe-
nus*

SOCRATES.

The men
of
Marathon
should
have the
first
place:
those who
followed
in the war
were their
disciples,
except the
men who
defeated
the Per-
sians at
Salamis
and first
made
proof of
them at
sea: these
have the
second
place.

And the
third
place is to
be as-
signed to
those who
fought at
Plataea.

Euryme-
don;
Cyprus;
Egypt.
242

Tanagra;
Oeno-
phyta.

*Menexe-
nus*

SOCRATES.

conquered at Oenophyta, and righteously restored those who had
been unrighteously exiled. And they were the first after the Persian
war who fought on behalf of liberty in aid of Hellenes against
Hellenes; they were brave men, and freed those whom they aided,
and were the first too who were honourably interred in this sepulchre by the state. Afterwards there was a mighty war, in which
all the Hellenes joined, and devastated our country, which was very
ungrateful of them; and our countrymen, after defeating them in
Sphac-
teria.
a naval engagement and taking their leaders, the Spartans, at
Sphagia, when they might have destroyed them, spared their lives,
and gave them back, and made peace, considering that they should
war with their fellow-countrymen only until they gained a victory
over them, and not because of the private anger of the state destroy
the common interest of Hellas; but that with barbarians they
should war to the death. Worthy of praise are they also who waged
this war, and are here interred; for they proved, if any one doubted
the superior prowess of the Athenians in the former war with the
barbarians, that their doubts had no foundation—showing by their
victory in the civil war with Hellas, in which they subdued the
other chief state of the Hellenes, that they could conquer singlehanded those with whom they had been allied in the war against the
The
Sicilian
expedi-
tion.

243
barbarians. After the peace there followed a third war, which was
of a terrible and desperate nature, and in this many brave men who
are here interred lost their lives—many of them had won victories
in Sicily, whither they had gone over the seas to fight for the liberties of the Leontines, to whom they were bound by oaths; but,
owing to the distance, the city was unable to help them, and they
lost heart and came to misfortune, their very enemies and opponents winning more renown for valour and temperance than the
friends of others. Many also fell in naval engagements at the Helles-
Cyzicus.
pont, after having in one day taken all the ships of the enemy, and
defeated them in other naval engagements. And what I call the
terrible and desperate nature of the war, is that the other Hellenes,
in their extreme animosity towards the city, should have entered
Hellas
betrayed
to the
Persian.
into negotiations with their bitterest enemy, the king of Persia,
whom they, together with us, had expelled;—him, without us, they
again brought back, barbarian against Hellenes, and all the hosts,
both of Hellenes and barbarians, were united against Athens. And
then shone forth the power and valour of our city. Her enemies had
supposed that she was exhausted by the war, and our ships were
blockaded at Mitylene. But the citizens themselves embarked, and
came to the rescue with sixty other ships, and their valour was con-
fessed of all men, for they conquered their enemies and delivered

their friends. And yet by some evil fortune they were left to perish at sea, and therefore are[1] not interred here. Ever to be remembered and honoured are they, for by their valour not only that sea-fight was won for us, but the entire war was decided by them, and through them the city gained the reputation of being invincible, even though attacked by all mankind. And that reputation was a true one, for the defeat which came upon us was our own doing. We were never conquered by others, and to this day we are still unconquered by them; but we were our own conquerors, and received defeat at our own hands. Afterwards there was quiet and peace abroad, but there sprang up war at home; and, if men are destined to have civil war, no one could have desired that his city should take the disorder in a milder form. How joyful and natural was the reconciliation of those who came from the Piraeus and those who came from the city; with what moderation did they order the war against the tyrants in Eleusis, and in a manner how unlike what the other Hellenes expected! And the reason of this gentleness was the veritable tie of blood, which created among them a friendship as of kinsmen, faithful not in word only, but in deed. And we ought also to remember those who then fell by one another's hands, and on such occasions as these to reconcile them with sacrifices and prayers, praying to those who have power over them, that they may be reconciled even as we are reconciled. For they did not attack one another out of malice or enmity, but they were unfortunate. And that such was the fact we ourselves are witnesses, who are of the same race with them, and have mutually received and granted forgiveness of what we have done and suffered. After this there was perfect peace, and the city had rest; and her feeling was that she forgave the barbarians, who had severely suffered at her hands and severely retaliated, but that she was indignant at the ingratitude of the Hellenes, when she remembered how they had received good from her and returned evil, having made common cause with the barbarians, depriving her of the ships which had once been their salvation, and dismantling our walls, which had preserved their own from falling. She thought that she would no longer defend the Hellenes, when enslaved either by one another or by the barbarians, and did accordingly. This was our feeling, while the Lacedaemonians were thinking that we who were the champions of liberty had fallen, and that their business was to subject the remaining Hellenes. And why should I say more? for the events of which I am speaking happened not long ago and we can all of us remember how the chief peoples of Hellas, Argives and Boeotians and Corinthians,

---

[1] Reading οὐ κεῖνται, or taking οὐκ before ἀναιρεθέντες with κεῖνται.

Menexenus

SOCRATES

Arginusae.

The taking of the city is obscurely intimated

The great reconciliation of kindred.

244

Change in the relation of the Athenians (1) to the other Hellenes; (2) to the Persian king.

came to feel the need of us, and, what is the greatest miracle of all, the Persian king himself was driven to such extremity as to come round to the opinion, that from this city, of which he was the destroyer, and from no other, his salvation would proceed.

And if a person desired to bring a deserved accusation against our city, he would find only one charge which he could justly urge— that she was too compassionate and too favourable to the weaker side. And in this instance she was not able to hold out or keep her resolution of refusing aid to her injurers when they were being enslaved, but she was softened, and did in fact send out aid, and delivered the Hellenes from slavery, and they were free until they afterwards enslaved themselves. Whereas, to the great king she refused to give the assistance of the state, for she could not forget the trophies of Marathon and Salamis and Plataea; but she allowed exiles and volunteers to assist him, and they were his salvation. And she herself, when she was compelled, entered into the war, and built walls and ships, and fought with the Lacedaemonians on behalf of the Parians. Now the king fearing this city and wanting to stand aloof, when he saw the Lacedaemonians growing weary of the war at sea, asked of us, as the price of his alliance with us and the other allies, to give up the Hellenes in Asia, whom the Lacedaemonians had previously handed over to him, he thinking that we should refuse, and that then he might have a pretence for withdrawing from us. About the other allies he was mistaken, for the Corinthians and Argives and Boeotians, and the other states, were quite willing to let them go, and swore and covenanted, that, if he would pay them money, they would make over to him the Hellenes of the continent, and we alone refused to give them up and swear. Such was the natural nobility of this city, so sound and healthy was the spirit of freedom among us, and the instinctive dislike of the barbarian, because we are pure Hellenes, having no admixture of barbarism in us. For we are not like many others, descendants of Pelops or Cadmus or Egyptus or Danaus, who are by nature barbarians, and yet pass for Hellenes, and dwell in the midst of us; but we are pure Hellenes, uncontaminated by any foreign element, and therefore the hatred of the foreigner has passed unadulterated into the life-blood of the city. And so, notwithstanding our noble sentiments, we were again isolated, because we were unwilling to be guilty of the base and unholy act of giving up Hellenes to barbarians. And we were in the same case as when we were subdued before; but, by the favour of Heaven, we managed better, for we ended the war without the loss of our ships or walls or colonies; the enemy was only too glad to be quit of us. Yet in this war we lost many brave men, such as were those who fell owing to the ruggedness of the ground at the battle of Corinth, or by treason at Lechaeum. Brave men, too, were those who delivered the Persian king, and drove the Lacedaemonians from the sea. I remind you of them, and you must celebrate them together with me, and do honour to their memories.

Such were the actions of the men who are here interred, and of others who have died on behalf of their country; many and glorious things I have spoken of them, and there are yet many more and more glorious things remaining to be told—many days and nights would not suffice to tell of them. Let them not be forgotten, and let every man remind their descendants that they also are soldiers who must not desert the ranks of their ancestors, or from cowardice fall behind. Even as I exhort you this day, and in all future time, whenever I meet with any of you, shall continue to remind and exhort you, O ye sons of heroes, that you strive to be the bravest of men. And I think that I ought now to repeat what your fathers desired to have said to you who are their survivors, when they went out to battle, in case anything happened to them. I will tell you what I heard them say, and what, if they had only speech, they would fain be saying, judging from what they then said. And you must imagine that you hear them saying what I now repeat to you:—

'Sons, the event proves that your fathers were brave men; for we might have lived dishonourably, but have preferred to die honourably rather than bring you and your children into disgrace, and rather than dishonour our own fathers and forefathers; considering that life is not life to one who is a dishonour to his race, and that to such a one neither men nor Gods are friendly, either while he is on the earth or after death in the world below. Remember our words, then, and whatever is your aim let virtue be the condition of the attainment of your aim, and know that without this all possessions and pursuits are dishonourable and evil. For neither does wealth bring honour to the owner, if he be a coward; of such a one the wealth belongs to another, and not to himself. Nor does beauty and strength of body, when dwelling in a base and cowardly man, appear comely, but the reverse of comely, making the possessor more conspicuous, and manifesting forth his cowardice. And all knowledge, when separated from justice and virtue, is seen to be cunning and not wisdom; wherefore make this your first and last and constant and all-absorbing aim, to exceed, if possible, not only us but all your ancestors in virtue; and know that to excel you in virtue only brings us shame, but that to be excelled by you is a source of happiness to us. And we shall most likely be defeated, and you will most likely be victors in the contest, if you learn so to order your lives as not to abuse or waste the reputation of your ancestors, knowing that to a man who has any self-respect, nothing is more dishonourable than to be honoured, not for his own sake, but on account of the reputation of his ancestors. The honour of parents is a fair and noble treasure to their posterity, but to have the use of a treasure of wealth and honour, and to leave none to your successors, because you have neither money nor reputation of your own, is alike base and dishonourable. And if you follow our precepts you will be received by us as friends, when the hour of destiny brings you hither; but if you neglect our words and are disgraced in your lives, no one will welcome or receive you. This is the message which is to be delivered to our children.

'Some of us have fathers and mothers still living, and we would urge them, if, as is likely, we shall die, to bear the calamity as lightly as possible, and not to condole with one another; for they have sorrows enough, and will not need any one to stir them up. While we gently heal their wounds, let us remind them that the Gods have heard the chief part of their prayers; for they prayed, not that their children might live for ever, but that they might be brave and renowned. And this, which is the greatest good, they have attained. A mortal man cannot expect to have everything in his own life turning out according to his will; and they, if they bear their misfortunes bravely, will be truly deemed brave fathers of the brave. But if they give way to their sorrows, either they will be suspected of not being our parents, or we of not being such as our panegyrists declare. Let not either of the two alternatives happen, but rather let them be our chief and true panegyrists, who show in their lives that they are true men, and had men for their sons. Of old the saying, "Nothing too much," appeared to be, and really was, well said. For he whose happiness rests with himself, if possible, wholly, and if not, as far as is possible,—who is not hanging in suspense on other men, or changing with the vicissitude of their fortune,—has his life ordered for the best. He is the temperate and valiant and wise; and when his riches come and go, when his children are given and taken away, he will remember the proverb—"Neither rejoicing overmuch nor grieving overmuch," for he relies upon himself. And such we would have our parents to be—that is our word and wish, and as such we now offer ourselves, neither lamenting overmuch, nor fearing overmuch, if we are to die at this time. And we entreat our fathers and mothers to retain these feelings throughout their future life, and to be assured that they will not please us by sorrowing

248

and lamenting over us. But, if the dead have any knowledge of the living, they will displease us most by making themselves miserable and by taking their misfortunes too much to heart, and they will please us best if they bear their loss lightly and temperately. For our life will have the noblest end which is vouchsafed to man, and should be glorified rather than lamented. And if they will direct their minds to the care and nurture of our wives and children, they will soonest forget their misfortunes, and live in a better and nobler way, and be dearer to us.

'This is all that we have to say to our families: and to the state we would say—Take care of our parents and of our sons: let her worthily cherish the old age of our parents, and bring up our sons in the right way. But we know that she will of her own accord take care of them, and does not need any exhortation of ours.'

This, O ye children and parents of the dead, is the message which they bid us deliver to you, and which I do deliver with the utmost seriousness. And in their name I beseech you, the children, to imitate your fathers, and you, parents, to be of good cheer about yourselves; for we will nourish your age, and take care of you both publicly and privately in any place in which one of us may meet one of you who are the parents of the dead. And the care of you which the city shows, you know yourselves; for she has made provision by law concerning the parents and children of those who die in war; the highest authority is specially entrusted with the duty of watching over them above all other citizens, and they will see that your fathers and mothers have no wrong done to them. The city herself shares in the education of the children, desiring as far as it is possible that their orphanhood may not be felt by them; while they are children she is a parent to them, and when they have arrived at man's estate she sends them to their several duties, in full armour clad; and bringing freshly to their minds the ways of their fathers, she places in their hands the instruments of their fathers' virtues; for the sake of the omen, she would have them from the first begin to rule over their own houses arrayed in the strength and arms of their fathers. And as for the dead, she never ceases honouring them, celebrating in common for all rites which become the property of each; and in addition to this, holding gymnastic and equestrian contests, and musical festivals of every sort. She is to the dead in the place of a son and heir, and to their sons in the place of a father, and to their parents and elder kindred in the place of a guardian— ever and always caring for them. Considering this, you ought to bear your calamity the more gently; for thus you will be most endeared to the dead and to the living, and your sorrows will heal and be healed. And now do you and all, having lamented the dead in common according to the law, go your ways.

You have heard, Menexenus, the oration of Aspasia the Milesian.

Men. Truly, Socrates, I marvel that Aspasia, who is only a woman, should be able to compose such a speech; she must be a rare one.

Soc. Well, if you are incredulous, you may come with me and hear her.

Men. I have often met Aspasia, Socrates, and know what she is like.

Soc. Well, and do you not admire her, and are you not grateful for her speech?

Men. Yes, Socrates, I am very grateful to her or to him who told you, and still more to you who have told me.

Soc. Very good. But you must take care not to tell of me, and then at some future time I will repeat to you many other excellent political speeches of hers.

Men. Fear not; only let me hear them, and I will keep the secret.

Soc. Then I will keep my promise.

APPENDIX II

ALCIBIADES II

ERYXIAS

INTRODUCTION

THE two dialogues which are translated in the second appendix are not mentioned by Aristotle, or by any early authority, and have no claim to be ascribed to Plato. They are examples of Platonic dialogues to be assigned probably to the second or third generation after Plato, when his writings were well known at Athens and Alexandria. They exhibit considerable originality, and are remarkable for containing several thoughts of the sort which we suppose to be modern rather than ancient, and which therefore have a peculiar interest for us. The second Alcibiades shows that the difficulties about prayer which have perplexed Christian theologians were not unknown among the followers of Plato. The Eryxias was doubted by the ancients themselves: yet it may claim the distinction of being, among all Greek or Roman writings, the one which anticipates in the most striking manner the modern science of political economy and gives an abstract form to some of its principal doctrines.

For the translation of these two dialogues I am indebted to my friend and secretary, Mr. Knight.

That the Dialogue which goes by the name of the Second Alcibiades is a genuine writing of Plato will not be maintained by any modern critic, and was hardly believed by the ancients themselves. The dialectic is poor and weak. There is no power over language, or beauty of style; and there is a certain abruptness and ἀγροικία in the conversation, which is very un-Platonic. The best passage is probably that about the poets, p. 147:—the remark that the poet, who is of a reserved disposition, is uncommonly difficult to understand, and the ridiculous interpretation of Homer, are entirely in the spirit of Plato (cp. Protag. 339 foll.; Ion 534; Apol. 22 D). The characters are ill-drawn. Socrates assumes the 'superior person' and preaches too much, while Alcibiades is stupid and heavy-in-hand. There are traces of Stoic influence in the general tone and phraseology of the Dialogue (cp. 138 B, ὅπως μὴ λήσει τις . . . κακά: 139 C, ὅτι πᾶς ἄφρων μαίνεται) : and the writer seems to have been acquainted with the 'Laws' of Plato (cp. Laws 3: 687, 688; 7. 801; 11. 931 B). An incident from the Symposium (213 E) is rather clumsily introduced (151 A) and two somewhat hackneyed quotations (Symp. 174 D, Gorg. 484 E) recur at 140 A and 146 A. The reference to the death of Archelaus as having occurred 'quite lately' (141 D) is only a fiction, probably suggested by the Gorgias, 470 D, where the story of Archelaus is told, and a similar phrase occurs,—τὰ γὰρ ἐχθὲς καὶ πρώην γεγονότα ταῦτα, κ.τ.λ. There are several passages which are either corrupt or extremely ill-expressed (see pp. 144, 145, 146, 147, 150). But there is a modern interest in the subject of the dialogue; and it is a good example of a short spurious work, which may be attributed to the second or third century before Christ.

ALCIBIADES II

PERSONS OF THE DIALOGUE

SOCRATES AND ALCIBIADES

Soc. ARE you going, Alcibiades, to offer prayer to Zeus?

Steph.
138
SOCRATES,
ALCIBIA-
DES.

Al. Yes, Socrates, I am.

Soc. You seem to be troubled and to cast your eyes on the ground, as though you were thinking about something.

Al. Of what do you suppose that I am thinking?

Soc. Of the greatest of all things, as I believe. Tell me, do you not suppose that the Gods sometimes partly grant and partly reject the requests which we make in public and private, and favour some persons and not others?

Al. Certainly.

Soc. Do you not imagine, then, that a man ought to be very careful, lest perchance without knowing it he implore great evils for himself, deeming that he is asking for good, especially if the Gods are in the mood to grant whatever he may request? There is the story of Oedipus, for instance, who prayed that his children might divide their inheritance between them by the sword: he did not, as he might have done, beg that his present evils might be averted, but called down new ones. And was not his prayer accomplished, and did not many and terrible evils thence arise, upon which I need not dilate?

The
danger of
a prayer
which is
ill-ad-
vised.

Al. Yes, Socrates, but you are speaking of a madman: surely you do not think that any one in his senses would venture to make such a prayer?

Soc. Madness, then, you consider to be the opposite of discretion?

Al. Of course.

Soc. And some men seem to you to be discreet, and others the contrary?

Al. They do.

Soc. Well, then, let us discuss who these are. We acknowledge that some are discreet, some foolish, and that some are mad?

Al. Yes.

Soc. And again, there are some who are in health?

Al. There are.

Soc. While others are ailing?

Al. Yes.

Soc. And they are not the same?

Al. Certainly not.

Soc. Nor are there any who are in neither state?

Al. No.

Soc. A man must either be sick or be well?

Al. That is my opinion.

Alcibiades first desires and afterwards admits

Soc. Very good: and do you think the same about discretion and want of discretion?

Al. How do you mean?

Soc. Do you believe that a man must be either in or out of his senses; or is there some third or intermediate condition, in which he is neither one nor the other?

Al. Decidedly not.

Soc. He must be either sane or insane?

Al. So I suppose.

Soc. Did you not acknowledge that madness was the opposite of discretion?

Al. Yes.

Soc. And that there is no third or middle term between discretion and indiscretion?

Al. True.

Soc. And there cannot be two opposites to one thing?

Al. There cannot.

Soc. Then madness and want of sense are the same?

Al. That appears to be the case.

Soc. We shall be in the right, therefore, Alcibiades, if we say that all who are senseless are mad. For example, if among persons of your own age or older than yourself there are some who are senseless,— as there certainly are,—they are mad. For tell me, by heaven, do you not think that in the city the wise are few, while the foolish, whom you call mad, are many?

that differences of kind do not exclude differences of degree.

Al. I do.

Soc. But how could we live in safety with so many crazy people? Should we not long since have paid the penalty at their hands, and have been struck and beaten and endured every other form of ill usage which madmen are wont to inflict? Consider, my dear friend: may it not be quite otherwise?

Al. Why, Socrates, how is that possible? I must have been mistaken.

Soc. So it seems to me. But perhaps we may consider the matter thus:—

Al. How?

Soc. I will tell you. We think that some are sick; do we not?

Al. Yes.

Soc. And must every sick person either have the gout, or be in a fever, or suffer from ophthalmia? Or do you believe that a man may labour under some other disease, even although he has none of these complaints? Surely, they are not the only maladies which exist?

Al. Certainly not.

Soc. And is every kind of ophthalmia a disease?

Al. Yes.

Soc. And every disease ophthalmia?

Al. Surely not. But I scarcely understand what I mean myself.

Soc. Perhaps, if you give me your best attention, 'two of us' looking together, we may find what we seek.

Al. I am attending, Socrates, to the best of my power.

Soc. We are agreed, then, that every form of ophthalmia is a disease, but not every disease ophthalmia?

Al. We are.

Soc. And so far we seem to be right. For every one who suffers from a fever is sick; but the sick, I conceive, do not all have fever or gout or ophthalmia, although each of these is a disease, which, according to those whom we call physicians, may require a different treatment. They are not all alike, nor do they produce the same result, but each has its own effect, and yet they are all diseases. May we not take an illustration from the artisans?

Al. Certainly.

Soc. There are cobblers and carpenters and sculptors and others of all sorts and kinds, whom we need not stop to enumerate. All have their distinct employments and all are workmen, although they are not all of them cobblers or carpenters or sculptors.

Al. No, indeed.

Soc. And in like manner men differ in regard to want of sense. Those who are most out of their wits we call 'madmen,' while we term those who are less far gone 'stupid' or 'idiotic,' or, if we prefer gentler language describe them as 'romantic' or 'simple-minded,' or, again, as 'innocent' or 'inexperienced' or 'foolish.' You may even find other names, if you seek for them; but by all of them lack of sense is intended. They only differ as one art appeared to us to differ from another or one disease from another. Or what is your opinion?

Alcibiades II

SOCRATES, ALCIBIADES.

The sick may have many kinds of sickness;

140

so there are different kinds of want of sense.

Al. I agree with you.

Soc. Then let us return to the point at which we digressed. We said at first that we should have to consider who were the wise and who the foolish. For we acknowledged that there are these two classes? Did we not?

Al. To be sure.

Soc. And you regard those as sensible who know what ought to be done or said?

Al. Yes.

Soc. The senseless are those who do not know this?

Al. True.

Soc. The latter will say or do what they ought not without their own knowledge?

Al. Exactly.

141

Men
often, like
Oedipus,
pray un-
advisedly.

Soc. Oedipus, as I was saying, Alcibiades, was a person of this sort. And even now-a-days you will find many who [have offered inauspicious prayers], although, unlike him, they were not in anger nor thought that they were asking evil. He neither sought, nor supposed that he sought for good, but others have had quite the contrary notion. I believe that if the God whom you are about to consult should appear to you, and, in anticipation of your request, enquired whether you would be contented to become tyrant of Athens, and if this seemed in your eyes a small and mean thing, should add to it the dominion of all Hellas; and seeing that even then you would not be satisfied unless you were ruler of the whole of Europe, should promise, not only that, but, if you so desired, should proclaim to all mankind in one and the same day that Alcibiades, son of Cleinias, was tyrant:—in such a case, I imagine, you would depart full of joy, as one who had obtained the greatest of goods.

Al. And not only I, Socrates, but any one else who should meet with such luck.

Soc. Yet you would not accept the dominion and lordship of all the Hellenes and all the barbarians in exchange for your life?

Al. Certainly not: for then what use could I make of them?

Soc. And would you accept them if you were likely to use them to a bad and mischievous end?

Al. I would not.

Soc. You see that it is not safe for a man either rashly to accept whatever is offered him, or himself to request a thing, if he is likely to suffer thereby or immediately to lose his life. And yet we could tell of many who, having long desired and diligently laboured to obtain a tyranny, thinking that thus they would procure an advantage, have nevertheless fallen victims to designing enemies. You

Alcibiades
II

SOCRATES,
ALCIBIA-
DES.

Archelaus
and his
beloved.

142

must have heard of what happened only the other day, how Archelaus of Macedonia was slain by his beloved[1], whose love for the tyranny was not less than that of Archelaus for him. The tyrannicide expected by his crime to become tyrant and afterwards to have a happy life; but when he had held the tyranny three or four days, he was in his turn conspired against and slain. Or look at certain of our own citizens,—and of their actions we have been not hearers, but eyewitnesses,—who have desired to obtain military command: of those who have gained their object, some are even to this day exiles from the city, while others have lost their lives. And even they who seem to have fared best, have not only gone through many perils and terrors during their office, but after their return home they have been beset by informers worse than they once were by their foes, insomuch that several of them have wished that they had remained in a private station rather than have had the glories of command. If, indeed, such perils and terrors were of profit to the commonwealth, there would be reason in undergoing them; but the very contrary is the case. Again, you will find persons who have prayed for offspring, and when their prayers were heard, have fallen into the greatest pains and sufferings. For some have begotten children who were utterly bad, and have therefore passed all their days in misery, while the parents of good children have undergone the misfortune of losing them, and have been so little happier than the others that they would have preferred never to have had children rather than to have had them and lost them. And yet, although these and the like examples are manifest and known of all, it is rare to find any one who has refused what has been offered him, or, if he were likely to gain aught by prayer, has refrained from making his petition. The mass of mankind would not decline to accept a tyranny, or the command of an army, or any of the numerous things which cause more harm than good: but rather, if they had them not, would have prayed to obtain them. And often in a short space of time they change their tone, and wish their old prayers unsaid. Wherefore also I suspect that men are entirely wrong when they blame the gods as the authors of the ills which befall them[2]: 'their own presumption,' or folly (whichever is the right word)—

Men
never re-
fuse the
goods of
fortune,
however
great the
evils
which
may at-
tend
them.

'Has brought these unmeasured woes upon them[3].'

He must have been a wise poet, Alcibiades, who, seeing as I believe, his friends foolishly praying for and doing things which would

---

[1] Cp. Aristotle, Pol. v. 10, § 17.   [2] Cp. Rep. x. 610 C.   [3] Hom. Odyss. i. 32.

not really profit them, offered up a common prayer in behalf of them all:—

'King Zeus, grant us good whether prayed for or unsought by us;
    But that which we ask amiss, do thou avert[1].'

In my opinion, I say, the poet spoke both well and prudently; but if you have anything to say in answer to him, speak out.

Al. It is difficult, Socrates, to oppose what has been well said. And I perceive how many are the ills of which ignorance is the cause, since, as would appear, through ignorance we not only do, but, what is worse, pray for the greatest evils. No man would imagine that he would do so; he would rather suppose that he was quite capable of praying for what was best: to call down evil seems more like a curse than a prayer.

Soc. But perhaps, my good friend, some one who is wiser than either you or I will say that we have no right to blame ignorance thus rashly, unless we can add what ignorance we mean and of what, and also to whom and how it is respectively a good or an evil?

Al. How do you mean? Can ignorance possibly be better than knowledge for any person in any conceivable case?

Soc. So I believe:—you do not think so?

Al. Certainly not.

Soc. And yet surely I may not suppose that you would ever wish to act towards your mother as they say that Orestes and Alcmaeon and others have done towards their parent.

Al. Goods words, Socrates, prithee.

Ignorance
of the
best is
bad: ig-
norance
of the bad
good.

Soc. You ought not to bid him use auspicious words, who says that you would not be willing to commit so horrible a deed, but rather him who affirms the contrary, if the act appear to you unfit even to be mentioned. Or do you think that Orestes, had he been in his senses and knew what was best for him to do, would ever have dared to venture on such a crime?

Al. Certainly not.

Soc. Nor would any one else, I fancy?

Al. No.

Soc. That ignorance is bad then, it would appear, which is of the best and does not know what is best?

Soc. And both to the person who is ignorant and everybody else?

Al. Yes.

Soc. Let us take another case. Suppose that you were suddenly

to get into your head that it would be a good thing to kill Pericles,

---

[1] The author of these lines, which are probably of Pythagorean origin, is unknown. They are found also in the Anthology (Anth. Pal. 10. 108).

your kinsman and guardian, and were to seize a sword and, going to the doors of his house, were to enquire if he were at home, meaning to slay only him and no one else:—the servants reply,'Yes': (Mind, I do not mean that you would really do such a thing; but there is nothing, you think, to prevent a man who is ignorant of the best, having occasionally the whim that what is worst is best?

Al. No.)

Soc. If, then, you went indoors, and seeing him, did not know him, but thought that he was some one else, would you venture to slay him?

Al. Most decidedly not [1][it seems to me][1].

Soc. For you designed to kill, not the first who offered, but Pericles himself?

Al. Certainly.

Soc. And if you made many attempts, and each time failed to recognize Pericles, you would never attack him?

Al. Never.

Soc. Well, but if Orestes in like manner had not known his mother, do you think that he would ever have laid hands upon her?

Al. No.

Soc. He did not intend to slay the first woman he came across, nor any one else's mother, but only his own?

Al. True.

Soc. Ignorance, then, is better for those who are in such a frame of mind, and have such ideas?

Al. Obviously.

Soc. You acknowledge that for some persons in certain cases the ignorance of some things is a good and not an evil, as you formerly supposed?

Al. I do.

Soc. [2]And there is still another case which will also perhaps appear strange to you, if you will consider it?[2]

Al. What is that, Socrates?

Soc. It may be, in short, that the possession of all the sciences, if unaccompanied by the knowledge of the best, will more often than not injure the possessor. Consider the matter thus:—Must we not, when we intend either to do or say anything, suppose that we know or ought to know that which we propose so confidently to do or say?

Al. Yes, in my opinion.

Soc. We may take the orators for an example, who from time to time advise us about war and peace, or the building of walls and

---

[1] These words are omitted in several MSS.   [2] The reading is here uncertain.

A man might be prevented from committing murder by ignorance of the person whom he was going to murder.

All knowledge if unaccompanied by a knowledge of the best is hurtful.

145

the construction of harbours, whether they understand the business in hand, or only think that they do. Whatever the city, in a word, does to another city, or in the management of her own affairs, all happens by the counsel of the orators.

Al. True.

Soc. But now see what follows, if I can [make it clear to you][1]. You would distinguish the wise from the foolish?

Al. Yes.

Soc. The many are foolish, the few wise?

Al. Certainly.

Soc. And you use both the terms, 'wise' and 'foolish,' in reference to something?

Al. I do.

Soc. Would you call a person wise who can give advice, but does not know whether or when it is better to carry out the advice?

Al. Decidedly not.

Soc. Nor again, I suppose, a person who knows the art of war, but does not know whether it is better to go to war or for how long?

Al. No.

Soc. Nor, once more, a person who knows how to kill another or to take away his property or to drive him from his native land, but not when it is better to do so or for whom it is better?

Al. Certainly not.

Soc. But he who understands anything of the kind and has at the same time the knowledge of the best course of action:—and the best and the useful are surely the same?—

Al. Yes.

Soc. Such an one, I say, we should call wise and a useful adviser both of himself and of the city. What do you think?

Al. I agree.

Soc. And if any one knows how to ride or to shoot with the bow or to box or to wrestle, or to engage in any other sort of contest or to do anything whatever which is in the nature of an art,—what do you call him who knows what is best according to that art? Do you not speak of one who knows what is best in riding as a good rider?

Al. Yes.

Soc. And in a similar way you speak of a good boxer or a good flute-player or a good performer in any other art?

Al. True.

Soc. But is it necessary that the man who is clever in any of these arts should be wise also in general? Or is there a difference between the clever artist and the wise man?

[1] Some words appear to have dropped out here.

Al. All the difference in the world.

Soc. And what sort of a state do you think that would be which was composed of good archers and flute-players and athletes and masters in other arts, and besides them of those others about whom we spoke, who knew how to go to war and how to kill, as well as of orators puffed up with political pride, but in which not one of them all had this knowledge of the best, and there was no one who could tell when it was better to apply any of these arts or in regard to whom?

Al. I should call such a state bad, Socrates.

Soc. You certainly would when you saw each of them rivalling the other and esteeming that of the greatest importance in the state,

'Wherein he himself most excelled [1].'

—I mean that which was best in any art, while he was entirely ignorant of what was best for himself and for the state, because, as I think, he trusts to opinion which is devoid of intelligence. In such a case should we not be right if we said that the state would be full of anarchy and lawlessness?

Al. Decidedly.

Soc. But ought we not then, think you, either to fancy that we know or really to know, what we confidently propose to do or say?

Al. Yes.

Soc. And if a person does that which he knows or supposes that he knows, and the result is beneficial, he will act advantageously both for himself and for the state?

Al. True.

Soc. And if he do the contrary, both he and the state will suffer?

Al. Yes.

Soc. Well, and are you of the same mind, as before?

Al. I am.

Soc. But were you not saying that you would call the many unwise and the few wise?

Al. I was.

Soc. And have we not come back to our old assertion that the many fail to obtain the best because they trust to opinion which is devoid of intelligence?

Al. That is the case.

Soc. It is good, then, for the many, if they particularly desire to do that which they know or suppose that they know, neither to know nor to suppose that they know, in cases where if they carry out their ideas in action they will be losers rather than gainers?

A state
would be
bad
[146]
which
was com-
posed
only of
skilful
artists
and clever
politi-
cians, but
where no
one had
the
knowl-
edge of
the best.

The poets
spoke in
riddles a
hidden
truth.

[1] Euripides, Antiope, fr. 20 (Dindorf).

Al. What you say is very true.

Soc. Do you not see that I was really speaking the truth when I affirmed that the possession of any other kind of knowledge was more likely to injure than to benefit the possessor, unless he had also the knowledge of the best?

Al. I do now, if I did not before, Socrates.

The soul
requires
[147]
this
knowl-
edge of
the best
before she
sets sail
on the
voyage of
life.

Soc. The state or the soul, therefore, which wishes to have a right existence must hold firmly to this knowledge, just as the sick man clings to the physician, or the passenger depends for safety on the pilot. And if the soul does not set sail until she have obtained this she will be all the safer in the voyage through life. But when she rushes in pursuit of wealth or bodily strength or anything else, not having the knowledge of the best, so much the more is she likely to meet with misfortune. And he who has the love of learning[1], and is skilful in many arts, and does not possess the knowledge of the best, but is under some other guidance, will make, as he deserves, a sorry voyage:—he will, I believe, hurry through the brief space of human life, pilotless in mid-ocean, and the words will apply to him in which the poet blamed his enemy:—

> '. . . . . Full many a thing he knew;
> But knew them all badly[2].'

Al. How in the world, Socrates, do the words of the poet apply to him? They seem to me to have no bearing on the point whatever.

The poets
spoke in
riddles a
hidden
truth.

Soc. Quite the contrary, my sweet friend: only the poet is talking in riddles after the fashion of his tribe. For all poetry has by nature an enigmatical character, and it is by no means everybody who can interpret it. And if, moreover, the spirit of poetry happen to seize on a man who is of a begrudging temper and does not care to manifest his wisdom but keeps it to himself as far as he can, it does indeed require an almost superhuman wisdom to discover what the poet would be at. You surely do not suppose that Homer, the wisest and most divine of poets, was unaware of the impossibility of knowing a thing badly: for it was no less a person than he who said of Margites that 'he knew many things, but knew them all badly.' The solution of the riddle is this, I imagine: By 'badly' Homer meant 'bad' and 'knew' stands for 'to know.' Put the words together;—the metre will suffer, but the poet's meaning is clear;— 'Margites knew all these things, but it was bad for him to know them.' And obviously, if it was bad for him to know so many things, he must have been a good-for-nothing, unless the argument has played us false.

[1] Or, reading πολυμάθειαν, 'abundant learning.'
[2] A fragment from the pseudo-Homeric poem, 'Margites.'

Al. But I do not think that it has, Socrates: at least, if the argument is fallacious, it would be difficult for me to find another which I could trust.

Soc. And you are right in thinking so.

Al. Well, that is my opinion.

Soc. But tell me, by Heaven:—you must see now the nature and greatness of the difficulty in which you, like others, have your part. For you change about in all directions, and never come to rest anywhere: what you once most strongly inclined to suppose, you put aside again and quite alter your mind. If the God to whose shrine you are going should appear at this moment, and ask before you made your prayer, 'Whether you would desire to have one of the things which we mentioned at first, or whether he should leave you to make your own request:'—what in either case, think you, would be the best way to take advantage of the opportunity?

Al. Indeed, Socrates, I could not answer you without consideration. It seems to me to be a wild thing[1] to make such a request; a man must be very careful lest he pray for evil under the idea that he is asking for good, when shortly after he may have to recall his prayer, and, as you were saying, demand the opposite of what he at first requested.

Soc. And was not the poet whose words I originally quoted wiser than we are, when he bade us [pray God] to defend us from evil even though we asked for it?

Al. I believe that you are right.

Soc. The Lacedaemonians, too, whether from admiration of the poet or because they have discovered the idea for themselves, are wont to offer the prayer alike in public and private, that the Gods will give unto them the beautiful as well as the good:—no one is likely to hear them make any further petition. And yet up to the present time they have not been less fortunate than other men; or if they have sometimes met with misfortune, the fault has not been due to their prayer. For surely, as I conceive, the Gods have power either to grant our requests, or to send us the contrary of what we ask.

And now I will relate to you a story which I have heard from certain of our elders. It chanced that when the Athenians and Lacedaemonians were at war, our city lost every battle by land and sea and never gained a victory. The Athenians being annoyed and perplexed how to find a remedy for their troubles, decided to

148
Alcibiades
is too un-
stable to
be able to
trust his
own
prayers.

---

[1] The Homeric word μάργος is said to be here employed in allusion to the quotation from the 'Margites' which Socrates has just made; but it is not used in the sense which it has in Homer.

send and enquire at the shrine of Ammon. Their envoys were also to ask, 'Why the Gods always granted the victory to the Lacedaemonians?' 'We,' (they were to say,) 'offer them more and finer sacrifices than any other Hellenic state, and adorn their temples with gifts, as nobody else does; moreover, we make the most solemn and costly processions to them every year, and spend more money in their service than all the rest of the Hellenes put together. But the Lacedaemonians take no thought of such matters, and pay so little respect to the Gods that they have a habit of sacrificing blemished animals to them, and in various ways are less zealous than we are, although their wealth is quite equal to ours.' When they had thus spoken, and had made their request to know what remedy they could find against the evils which troubled them, the prophet made no direct answer,—clearly because he was not allowed by the God to do so;—but he summoned them to him and said: 'Thus saith Ammon to the Athenians: "The silent worship of the Lacedaemonians pleaseth me better than all the offerings of the other Hellenes."' Such were the words of the God, and nothing more. He seems to have meant by 'silent worship' the prayer of the Lacedaemonians, which is indeed widely different from the usual requests of the Hellenes. For they either bring to the altar bulls with gilded horns or make offerings to the Gods, and beg at random for what they need, good or bad. When, therefore, the Gods hear them using words of ill omen they reject these costly processions and sacrifices of theirs. And we ought, I think, to be very careful and consider well what we should say and what leave unsaid. Homer, too, will furnish us with similar stories. For he tells us how the Trojans in making their encampment,

'Offered up whole hecatombs to the immortals,'

and how the 'sweet savour' was borne 'to the heavens by the winds';

'But the blessed Gods were averse and received it not.
For exceedingly did they hate the holy Ilium,
Both Priam and the people of the spear-skilled king.'

So that it was in vain for them to sacrifice and offer gifts, seeing that they were hateful to the Gods, who are not, like vile usurers, to be gained over by bribes. And it is foolish for us to boast that we are superior to the Lacedaemonians by reason of our much worship. The idea is inconceivable that the Gods have regard, not to the justice and purity of our souls, but to costly processions and sacrifices, which men may celebrate year after year, although they have committed innumerable crimes against the Gods or against their fellowmen or the state. For the Gods, as Ammon and his prophet

The silent
prayer of
the Lace-
daemon-
ians bet-
ter than
all the
offerings
of the
other
Hellenes.

declare, are no receivers of gifts, and they scorn such unworthy service. Wherefore also it would seem that wisdom and justice are especially honoured both by the Gods and by men of sense; and they are the wisest and most just who know how to speak and act towards Gods and men. But I should like to hear what your opinion is about these matters.

Al. I agree, Socrates, with you and with the God, whom, indeed, it would be unbecoming for me to oppose.

Soc. Do you not remember saying that you were in great perplexity, lest perchance you should ask for evil, supposing that you were asking for good?

Al. I do.

Soc. You see, then, that there is a risk in your approaching the God in prayer, lest haply he should refuse your sacrifice when he hears the blasphemy which you utter, and make you partake of other evils as well. The wisest plan, therefore, seems to me that you should keep silence; for your 'highmindedness'—to use the mildest term which men apply to folly—will most likely prevent you from using the prayer of the Lacedaemonians. You had better wait until we find out how we should behave towards the Gods and towards men.

Alcibiades
cannot
tell
whether
he is ask-
ing for
good or
evil.
'There-
fore let
his words
be few.'

Al. And how long must I wait, Socrates, and who will be my teacher? I should be very glad to see the man.

Soc. It is he who takes an especial interest in you. But first of all, I think, the darkness must be taken away in which your soul is now enveloped, just as Athene in Homer removes the mist from the eyes of Diomede that

'He may distinguish between God and mortal man.'

Afterwards the means may be given to you whereby you may distinguish between good and evil. At present, I fear, this is beyond your power.

Al. Only let my instructor take away the impediment, whether it pleases him to call it mist or anything else! I care not who he is; but I am resolved to disobey none of his commands, if I am likely to be the better for them.

Soc. And surely he has a wondrous care for you.

Al. It seems to be altogether advisable to put off the sacrifice until he is found.

Soc. You are right: that will be safer than running such a tremendous risk.

Al. But how shall we manage, Socrates?—At any rate I will set this crown of mine upon your head, as you have given me such ex-

151

cellent advice, and to the Gods we will offer crowns and perform
the other customary rites when I see that day approaching: nor
will it be long hence, if they so will.

Soc. I accept your gift, and shall be ready and willing to receive
whatever else you may proffer. Euripides makes Creon say in the
play, when he beholds Teiresias with his crown and hears that he
has gained it by his skill as the first-fruits of the spoil:—

> 'An auspicious omen I deem thy victor's wreath:
> For well thou knowest that wave and storm oppress us.'

And so I count your gift to be a token of good-fortune; for I am in
no less stress than Creon, and would fain carry off the victory over
your lovers.

ERYXIAS

PERSONS OF THE DIALOGUE

SOCRATES   ERASISTRATUS

ERYXIAS   CRITIAS

SCENE:—*The portico of a temple of Zeus*

IT happened by chance that Eryxias the Steirian was walking with me in the Portico of Zeus the Deliverer, when there came up to us Critias and Erasistratus, the latter the son of Phaeax, who was the nephew of Erasistratus. Now Erasistratus had just arrived from Sicily and that part of the world. As they approached, he said, Hail, Socrates!

Soc. The same to you, I said; have you any good news from Sicily to tell us?

Eras. Most excellent. But, if you please, let us first sit down; for I am tired with my yesterday's journey from Megara.

Soc. Gladly, if that is your desire.

Eras. What would you wish to hear first? he said. What the Sicilians are doing, or how they are disposed towards our city? To my mind, they are very like wasps: so long as you only cause them a little annoyance they are quite unmanageable; you must destroy their nests if you wish to get the better of them. And in a similar way, the Syracusans, unless we set to work in earnest, and go against them with a great expedition, will never submit to our rule. The petty injuries which we at present inflict merely irritate them enough to make them utterly intractable. And now they have sent ambassadors to Athens, and intend, I suspect, to play us some trick.—While we were talking, the Syracusan envoys chanced to go by, and Erasistratus, pointing to one of them, said to me, That, Socrates, is the richest man in all Italy and Sicily. For who has larger estates or more land at his disposal to cultivate if he please? And they are of a quality, too, finer than any other land in Hellas. Moreover, he has all the things which go to make up wealth, slaves and horses innumerable, gold and silver without end.

Steph.
392

SOCRATES,
ERASI-
STRATUS.

The
trouble-
some
Sicilians.

Eryxias
SOCRATES,
ERASI-
STRATUS.
393
The
wicked
million-
aire.

I saw that he was inclined to expatiate on the riches of the man; so I asked him, Well, Erasistratus, and what sort of character does he bear in Sicily?

Eras. He is esteemed to be, and really is, the wickedest of all the Sicilians and Italians, and even more wicked than he is rich; indeed, if you were to ask any Sicilian whom he thought to be the worst and the richest of mankind, you would never hear any one else named.

I reflected that we were speaking, not of trivial matters, but about wealth and virtue, which are deemed to be of the greatest moment, and I asked Erasistratus whom he considered the wealthier,—he who was the possessor of a talent of silver or he who had a field worth two talents?

Eras. The owner of the field.

Soc. And on the same principle he who had robes and bedding and such things which are of greater value to him than to a stranger would be richer than the stranger?

Eras. True.

Soc. And if any one gave you a choice, which of these would you prefer?

Eras. That which was most valuable.

Soc. In which way do you think you would be the richer?

Eras. By choosing as I said.

Soc. And he appears to you to be the richest who has goods of the greatest value?

Eras. He does.

Soc. And are not the healthy richer than the sick, since health is a possession more valuable than riches to the sick? Surely there is no one who would not prefer to be poor and well, rather than to have all the King of Persia's wealth and to be ill. And this proves that men set health above wealth, else they would never choose the one in preference to the other.

Eras. True.

Soc. And if anything appeared to be more valuable than health, he would be the richest who possessed it?

Eras. He would.

Soc. Suppose that some one came to us at this moment and were to ask, Well, Socrates and Eryxias and Erasistratus, can you tell me what is of the greatest value to men? Is it not that of which the possession will best enable a man to advise how his own and his friends' affairs should be administered?—What will be our reply?

Eras. I should say, Socrates, that happiness was the most precious of human possessions.

Soc. Not a bad answer. But do we not deem those men who are most prosperous to be the happiest?

Eras. That is my opinion.

Soc. And are they not most prosperous who commit the fewest errors in respect either of themselves or of other men?

Eras. Certainly.

Soc. And they who know what is evil and what is good; what should be done and what should be left undone;—these behave the most wisely and make the fewest mistakes?

Erasistratus agreed to this.

Soc. Then the wisest and those who do best and the most fortunate and the richest would appear to be all one and the same, if wisdom is really the most valuable of our possessions?

Yes, said Eryxias, interposing, but what use would it be if a man had the wisdom of Nestor and wanted the necessaries of life, food and drink and clothes and the like? Where would be the advantage of wisdom then? Or how could he be the richest of men who might even have to go begging, because he had not wherewithal to live?

I thought that what Eryxias was saying had some weight, and I replied, Would the wise man really suffer in this way, if he were so ill-provided; whereas if he had the house of Polytion, and the house were full of gold and silver, he would lack nothing?

Eryx. Yes; for then he might dispose of his property and obtain in exchange what he needed, or he might sell it for money with which he could supply his wants and in a moment procure abundance of everything.

Soc. True, if he could find some one who preferred such a house to the wisdom of Nestor. But if there are persons who set great store by wisdom like Nestor's and the advantages accruing from it, to sell these, if he were so disposed, would be easier still. Or is a house a most useful and necessary possession, and does it make a great difference in the comfort of life to have a mansion like Polytion's instead of living in a shabby little cottage, whereas wisdom is of small use and it is of no importance whether a man is wise or ignorant about the highest matters? Or is wisdom despised of men and can find no buyers, although cypress wood and marble of Pentelicus are eagerly bought by numerous purchasers? Surely the prudent pilot or the skilful physician, or the artist of any kind who is proficient in his art, is more worth than the things which are especially reckoned among riches; and he who can advise well and prudently for himself and others is able also to sell the product of his art, if he so desire.

Eryxias looked askance, as if he had received some unfair treatment, and said, I believe, Socrates, that if you were forced to speak

---

Eryxias

SOCRATES,
ERASI-
STRATUS,
ERYXIAS.

394

Of what use would wisdom be, if a man had not the necessaries of life?

The wisdom of Nestor better and even more saleable than the house of Polytion.

And in the arts is not wisdom better than riches?

395

Eryxias is
supposed
to reply
that argu-
ments can
prove
anything
and con-
vince no
one.

Eryxias
disclaims
the an-
swer
which is
attributed
to him.

The argu-
ment is
renewed
from a
fresh
point of
view.
Eryxias
declares
riches to
be a
good;
Critias
maintains
that they
are some-
[396]
times an
evil.

the truth, you would declare that you were richer than Callias the son of Hipponicus. And yet, although you claimed to be wiser about things of real importance, you would not any the more be richer than he.

I dare say, Eryxias, I said, that you may regard these arguments of ours as a kind of game; you think that they have no relation to facts, but are like the pieces in the game of draughts which the player can move in such a way that his opponents are unable to make any countermove[1]. And perhaps, too, as regards riches you are of opinion that while facts remain the same, there are arguments, no matter whether true or false, which enable the user of them to prove that the wisest and the richest are one and the same, although he is in the wrong and his opponents are in the right. There would be nothing strange in this; it would be as if two persons were to dispute about letters, one declaring that the word Socrates began with an S, the other that it began with an A, and the latter could gain the victory over the former.

Eryxias glanced at the audience, laughing and blushing at once, as if he had had nothing to do with what had just been said, and replied,—No, indeed, Socrates, I never supposed that our arguments should be of a kind which would never convince any one of those here present or be of advantage to them. For what man of sense could ever be persuaded that the wisest and the richest are the same? The truth is that we are discussing the subject of riches, and my notion is that we should argue respecting the honest and dishonest means of acquiring them, and, generally, whether they are a good thing or a bad.

Very good, I said, and I am obliged to you for the hint: in future we will be more careful. But why do not you yourself, as you introduced the argument, and do not think that the former discussion touched the point at issue, tell us whether you consider riches to be a good or an evil?

I am of opinion, he said, that they are a good. He was about to add something more, when Critias interrupted him:—Do you really suppose so, Eryxias?

Certainly, replied Eryxias; I should be mad if I did not: and I do not fancy that you would find any one else of a contrary opinion.

And I, retorted Critias, should say that there is no one whom I could not compel to admit that riches are bad for some men. But surely, if they were a good, they could not appear bad for any one?

Here I interposed and said to them: If you two were having an argument about equitation and what was the best way of riding,

[1] Cp. Rep. vi. 487.

supposing that I knew the art myself, I should try to bring you to an agreement. For I should be ashamed if I were present and did not do what I could to prevent your difference. And I should do the same if you were quarrelling about any other art and were likely, unless you agreed on the point in dispute, to part as enemies instead of as friends. But now, when we are contending about a thing of which the usefulness continues during the whole of life, and it makes an enormous difference whether we are to regard it as beneficial or not,—a thing, too, which is esteemed of the highest importance by the Hellenes:—(for parents, as soon as their children are, as they think, come to years of discretion, urge them to consider how wealth may be acquired, since by riches the value of a man is judged):— When, I say, we are thus in earnest, and you, who agree in other respects, fall to disputing about a matter of such moment, that is, about wealth, and not merely whether it is black or white, light or heavy, but whether it is a good or an evil, whereby, although you are now the dearest of friends and kinsmen, the most bitter hatred may arise betwixt you, I must hinder your dissension to the best of my power. If I could, I would tell you the truth, and so put an end to the dispute; but as I cannot do this, and each of you supposes that you can bring the other to an agreement, I am prepared, as far as my capacity admits, to help you in solving the question. Please, therefore, Critias, try to make us accept the doctrines which you yourself entertain.

Crit. I should like to follow up the argument, and will ask Eryxias whether he thinks that there are just and unjust men?

Eryx. Most decidedly.

Crit. And does injustice seem to you an evil or a good?

Eryx. An evil.

Crit. Do you consider that he who bribes his neighbour's wife and commits adultery with her, acts justly or unjustly, and this although both the state and the laws forbid?

Eryx. Unjustly.

Crit. And if the wicked man has wealth and is willing to spend it, he will carry out his evil purposes? whereas he who is short of means cannot do what he fain would, and therefore does not sin? In such a case, surely, it is better that a person should not be wealthy, if his poverty prevents the accomplishment of his desires, and his desires are evil? Or, again, should you call sickness a good or an evil?

Eryx. An evil.

Crit. Well, and do you think that some men are intemperate?

Eryx. Yes.

Crit. Then, if it is better for his health that the intemperate man

Eryxias

SOCRATES,
ERYXIAS,
CRITIAS.

Socrates encourages the two disputants to follow up the argument.

397
Wealth may furnish the opportunity of crime.

Eryxias

SOCRATES,
ERYXIAS,
CRITIAS,
ERASI-
STRATUS.

Eryxias
takes
offence at
Critias,
whose
argument,
as So-
crates
pretends,
is only
the repe-
tition of
one which
had been
used by
Prodicus
of Ceos
on the
day
before,

should refrain from meat and drink and other pleasant things, but
he cannot owing to his intemperance, will it not also be better that
he should be too poor to gratify his lust rather than that he should
have a superabundance of means? For thus he will not be able to
sin, although he desire never so much.

Critias appeared to be arguing so admirably that Eryxias, if he
had not been ashamed of the bystanders, would probably have got
up and struck him. For he thought that he had been robbed of a
great possession when it became obvious to him that he had been
wrong in his former opinion about wealth. I observed his vexation,
and feared that they would proceed to abuse and quarrelling: so I
said,—I heard that very argument used in the Lyceum yesterday
by a wise man, Prodicus of Ceos; but the audience thought that he
was talking mere nonsense, and no one could be persuaded that he
was speaking the truth. And when at last a certain talkative young
gentleman came in, and, taking his seat, began to laugh and jeer at
Prodicus, tormenting him and demanding an explanation of his
argument, he gained the ear of the audience far more than Prodicus.

Can you repeat the discourse to us? said Erasistratus.

Soc. If I can only remember it, I will. The youth began by asking
Prodicus, in what way did he think that riches were a good and in
what an evil? Prodicus answered, as you did just now, that they
were a good to good men and to those who knew in what way they
should be employed, while to the bad and the ignorant they were
an evil. The same is true, he went on to say, of all other things; men
make them to be what they are themselves. The saying of Archilo-
chus is true:—

'Men's thoughts correspond to the things which they meet with.'

398

and had
been re-
futed by
an im-
pertinent
youth.

Well, then, replied the youth, if any one makes me wise in that
wisdom whereby good men become wise, he must also make everything else good to me. Not that he concerns himself at all with these
other things, but he has converted my ignorance into wisdom. If,
for example, a person teach me grammar or music, he will at the
same time teach me all that relates to grammar or music, and so
when he makes me good, he makes things good to me.

Prodicus did not altogether agree: still he consented to what was
said.

And do you think, said the youth, that doing good things is like
building a house,—the work of human agency; or do things remain
what they were at first, good or bad, for all time?

Prodicus began to suspect, I fancy, the direction which the argument was likely to take, and did not wish to be put down by a mere

stripling before all those present:—(if they two had been alone, he would not have minded):—so he answered, cleverly enough: I think that doing good things is a work of human agency.

And is virtue in your opinion, Prodicus, innate or acquired by instruction?

The latter, said Prodicus.

Then you would consider him a simpleton who supposed that he could obtain by praying to the Gods the knowledge of grammar or music or any other art, which he must either learn from another or find out for himself?

Prodicus agreed to this also.

And when you pray to the Gods that you may do well and receive good, you mean by your prayer nothing else than that you desire to become good and wise:—if, at least, things are good to the good and wise and evil to the evil. But in that case, if virtue is acquired by instruction, it would appear that you only pray to be taught what you do not know.

Hereupon I said to Prodicus that it was no misfortune to him if he had been proved to be in error in supposing that the Gods immediately granted to us whatever we asked:—if, I added, whenever you go up to the Acropolis you earnestly entreat the Gods to grant you good things, although you know not whether they can yield your request, it is as though you went to the doors of the grammarian and begged him, although you had never made a study of the art, to give you a knowledge of grammar which would enable you forthwith to do the business of a grammarian.

While I was speaking, Prodicus was preparing to retaliate upon his youthful assailant, intending to employ the argument of which you have just made use; for he was annoyed to have it supposed that he offered a vain prayer to the Gods. But the master of the gymnasium came to him and begged him to leave because he was teaching the youths doctrines which were unsuited to them, and therefore bad for them.

I have told you this because I want you to understand how men are circumstanced in regard to philosophy. Had Prodicus been present and said what you have said, the audience would have thought him raving, and he would have been ejected from the gymnasium. But you have argued so excellently well that you have not only persuaded your hearers, but have brought your opponent to an agreement. For just as in the law courts, if two witnesses testify to the same fact, one of whom seems to be an honest fellow and the other a rogue, the testimony of the rogue often has the contrary effect on the judges' minds to what he intended, while the same evidence if

399
Prodicus
is desired
to leave
the gym-
nasium
because
he is dis-
turbing
the minds
of youth.

given by the honest man at once strikes them as perfectly true. And probably the audience have something of the same feeling about yourself and Prodicus; they think him a Sophist and a braggart, and regard you as a gentleman of courtesy and worth. For they do not pay attention to the argument so much as to the character of the speaker.

Socrates
jesting
professes
to be in
earnest.

But truly, Socrates, said Erasistratus, though you may be joking, Critias does seem to me to be saying something which is of weight.

Soc. I am in profound earnest, I assure you. But why, as you have begun your argument so prettily, do you not go on with the rest? There is still something lacking, now you have agreed that [wealth] is a good to some and an evil to others. It remains to enquire what constitutes wealth; for unless you know this, you cannot possibly come to an understanding as to whether it is a good or an evil. I am ready to assist you in the enquiry to the utmost of my power: but first let him who affirms that riches are a good, tell us what, in his opinion, is wealth.

Eras. Indeed, Socrates, I have no notion about wealth beyond that which men commonly have. I suppose that wealth is a quantity of money[1]; and this, I imagine, would also be Critias' definition.

What is
money?

[400]
It is ob-
served
that dif-
ferent
kinds of
money
pass
current in
different
countries
—Car-
thage,
Lacedae-
mon,
Ethiopia,
Scythia.

Soc. Then now we have to consider, What is money? Or else later on we shall be found to differ about the question. For instance, the Carthaginians use money of this sort. Something which is about the size of a stater is tied up in a small piece of leather: what it is, no one knows but the makers. A seal is next set upon the leather, which then passes into circulation, and he who has the largest number of such pieces is esteemed the richest and best off. And yet if any one among us had a mass of such coins he would be no wealthier than if he had so many pebbles from the mountain. At Lacedaemon, again, they use iron by weight which has been rendered useless: and he who has the greatest mass of such iron is thought to be the richest, although elsewhere it has no value. In Ethiopia engraved stones are employed, of which a Lacedaemonian could make no use. Once more, among the Nomad Scythians a man who owned the house of Polytion would not be thought richer than one who possessed Mount Lycabettus among ourselves. And clearly those things cannot all be regarded as possessions; for in some cases the possessors would appear none the richer thereby: but, as I was saying, some one of them is thought in one place to be money, and the possessors of it are the wealthy, whereas in some other place it is not money, and the ownership of it does not confer wealth; just as the standard

[1] Cp. Arist. Pol. i. 9, §§ 10, 14.

of morals varies, and what is honourable to some men is dishonourable to others. And if we wish to enquire why a house is valuable to us but not to the Scythians, or why the Carthaginians value leather which is worthless to us, or the Lacedaemonians find wealth in iron and we do not, can we not get an answer in some such way as this: Would an Athenian, who had a thousand talents weight of the stones which lie about in the Agora and which we do not employ for any purpose, be thought to be any the richer?

Eras. He certainly would not appear so to me.

Soc. But if he possessed a thousand talents weight of some precious stone, we should say that he was very rich?

Eras. Of course.

Soc. The reason is that the one is useless and the other useful?

Eras. Yes.

Soc. And in the same way among the Scythians a house has no value because they have no use for a house, nor would a Scythian set so much store on the finest house in the world as on a leather coat, because he could use the one and not the other. Or again, the Carthaginian coinage is not wealth in our eyes, for we could not employ it, as we can silver, to procure what we need, and therefore it is of no use to us.

Eras. True.

Soc. What is useful to us, then, is wealth, and what is useless to us is not wealth?

But how do you mean, Socrates? said Eryxias, interrupting. Do we not employ in our intercourse with one another speech and violence (?) and various other things? These are useful and yet they are not wealth.

Soc. Clearly we have not yet answered the question, What is wealth? That wealth must be useful, to be wealth at all,—thus much is acknowledged by every one. But what particular thing is wealth, if not all things? Let us pursue the argument in another way; and then we may perhaps find what we are seeking. What is the use of wealth, and for what purpose has the possession of riches been invented,—in the sense, I mean, in which drugs have been discovered for the cure of disease? Perhaps in this way we may throw some light on the question. It appears to be clear that whatever constitutes wealth must be useful, and that wealth is one class of useful things; and now we have to enquire, What is the use of those useful things which constitute wealth? For all things probably may be said to be useful which we use in production, just as all things which have life are animals, but there is a special kind of animal which we call 'man.' Now if any one were to ask us, What is that of

Wealth is
useful,
but other
things are
[401]
useful
besides
wealth.

which, if we were rid, we should not want medicine and the instruments of medicine, we might reply that this would be the case if disease were absent from our bodies and either never came to them at all or went away again as soon as it appeared; and we may therefore conclude that medicine is the science which is useful for getting rid of disease. But if we are further asked, What is that from which, if we were free, we should have no need of wealth? can we give an answer? If we have none, suppose that we restate the question thus:—If a man could live without food or drink, and yet suffer neither hunger nor thirst, would he want either money or anything else in order to supply his needs?

Eryx. He would not.

Soc. And does not this apply in other cases? If we did not want for the service of the body the things of which we now stand in need, and heat and cold and the other bodily sensations were unperceived by us, there would be no use in this so-called wealth, if no one, that is, had any necessity for those things which now make us wish for wealth in order that we may satisfy the desires and needs of the body in respect of our various wants. And therefore if the possession of wealth is useful in ministering to our bodily wants, and bodily wants were unknown to us, we should not need wealth, and possibly there would be no such thing as wealth.

Eryx. Clearly not.

Soc. Then our conclusion is, as would appear, that wealth is what is useful to this end?

Eryxias once more gave his assent, but the small argument considerably troubled him.

402

Soc. And what is your opinion about another question:—Would you say that the same thing can be at one time useful and at another useless for the production of the same result?

Eryx. I cannot say more than that if we require the same thing to produce the same result, then it seems to me to be useful; if not, not.

Soc. Then if without the aid of fire we could make a brazen statue, we should not want fire for that purpose; and if we did not want it, it would be useless to us? And the argument applies equally in other cases.

Eryx. Clearly.

Soc. And therefore conditions which are not required for the existence of a thing are not useful for the production of it?

Eryx. Of course not.

Soc. And if without gold or silver or anything else which we do not use directly for the body in the way that we do food and drink

and bedding and houses,—if without these we could satisfy the
wants of the body, they would be of no use to us for that purpose?

Eryx. They would not.

Soc. They would no longer be regarded as wealth, because they
are useless, whereas that would be wealth which enabled us to obtain what was useful to us?

Eryx. O Socrates, you will never be able to persuade me that gold
and silver and similar things are not wealth. But I am very strongly
of opinion that things which are useless to us are not wealth, and
that the money which is useful for this purpose is of the greatest
use; not that these things are not useful towards life, if by them we
can procure wealth.

Soc. And how would you answer another question? There are persons, are there not, who teach music and grammar and other arts
for pay, and thus procure those things of which they stand in need?

Eryx. There are.

Soc. And these men by the arts which they profess, and in exchange for them, obtain the necessities of life just as we do by means
of gold and silver?

Eryx. True.

Soc. Then if they procure by this means what they want for the
purposes of life, that art will be useful towards life? For do we not
say that silver is useful because it enables us to supply our bodily
needs?

Eryx. We do.

Soc. Then if these arts are reckoned among things useful, the arts
are wealth for the same reason as gold and silver are, for, clearly,
the possession of them gives wealth. Yet a little while ago we found
it difficult to accept the argument which proved that the wisest are
the wealthiest. But now there seems no escape from this conclusion.
Suppose that we are asked, 'Is a horse useful to everybody?' will not
our reply be, 'No, but only to those who know how to use a horse?'

Eryx. Certainly.

Soc. And so, too, physic is not useful to every one, but only to him
who knows how to use it?

Eryx. True.

Soc. And the same is the case with everything else?

Eryx. Yes.

Soc. Then gold and silver and all the other elements which are
supposed to make up wealth are only useful to the person who
knows how to use them?

Eryx. Exactly.

Soc. And were we not saying before that it was the business of a

Eryxias

Socrates,
Eryxias.

The arts
too are
wealth,
for by
them the
needs of
life are
satisfied.

403

Eryxias

SOCRATES,
ERYXIAS,
CRITIAS.

The good
only
know
how to
use
things.

good man and a gentleman to know where and how anything should be used?

Eryx. Yes.

Soc. The good and gentle, therefore, will alone have profit from these things, supposing at least that they know how to use them. But if so, to them only will they seem to be wealth. It appears, however, that where a person is ignorant of riding, and has horses which are useless to him, if some one teaches him that art, he makes him also richer, for what was before useless has now become useful to him, and in giving him knowledge he has also conferred riches upon him.

Eryx. That is the case.

Soc. Yet I dare be sworn that Critias will not be moved a whit by the argument.

Crit. No, by heaven, I should be a madman if I were. But why do you not finish the argument which proves that gold and silver and other things which seem to be wealth are not real wealth? For I have been exceedingly delighted to hear the discourses which you have just been holding.

Soc. My argument, Critias (I said), appears to have given you the same kind of pleasure which you might have derived from some rhapsode's recitation of Homer; for you do not believe a word of what has been said. But come now, give me an answer to this question. Are not certain things useful to the builder when he is building a house?

Crit. They are.

Soc. And would you say that those things are useful which are employed in house building,—stones and bricks and beams and the like, and also the instruments with which the builder built the house, the beams and stones which they provided, and again the instruments by which these were obtained?

Crit. It seems to me that they are all useful for building.

Soc. And is it not true of every art, that not only the materials but the instruments by which we procure them and without which the work could not go on, are useful for that art?

Crit. Certainly.

Soc. And further, the instruments by which the instruments are procured, and so on, going back from stage to stage *ad infinitum,*— are not all these, in your opinion, necessary in order to carry out the work?

Crit. We may fairly suppose such to be the case.

Soc. And if a man has food and drink and clothes and the other things which are useful to the body, would he need gold or silver or

404

any other means by which he could procure that which he now has?

Crit. I do not think so.

Soc. Then you consider that a man never wants any of these things for the use of the body?

Crit. Certainly not.

Soc. And if they appear useless to this end, ought they not always to appear useless? For we have already laid down the principle that things cannot be at one time useful and at another time not, in the same process.

Crit. But in that respect your argument and mine are the same. For you maintain if they are useful to a certain end, they can never become useless; whereas I say that in order to accomplish some results bad things are needed, and good for others.

Soc. But can a bad thing be used to carry out a good purpose?

Crit. I should say not.

Soc. And we call those actions good which a man does for the sake of virtue?

Crit. Yes.

Soc. But can a man learn any kind of knowledge which is imparted by word of mouth if he is wholly deprived of the sense of hearing?

Crit. Certainly not, I think.

Soc. And will not hearing be useful for virtue, if virtue is taught by hearing and we use the sense of hearing in giving instruction?

Crit. Yes.

Soc. And since medicine frees the sick man from his disease, that art too may sometimes appear useful in the acquisition of virtue, e. g. when hearing is procured by the aid of medicine.

Crit. Very likely.

Soc. But if, again, we obtain by wealth the aid of medicine, shall we not regard wealth as useful for virtue?

Crit. True.

Soc. And also the instruments by which wealth is procured?

Crit. Certainly.

Soc. Then you think that a man may gain wealth by bad and disgraceful means, and, having obtained the aid of medicine which enables him to acquire the power of hearing, may use that very faculty for the acquisition of virtue?

Crit. Yes, I do.

Soc. But can that which is evil be useful for virtue?

Crit. No.

Soc. It is not therefore necessary that the means by which we obtain what is useful for a certain object should always be useful for

Eryxias

SOCRATES, CRITIAS.

A sophism. Gold and silver would be useless if they were not needed to obtain food; and things cannot be at one time useless, at another time useful, in the same actions.

There are indirect means towards ends.

Wealth may be gained discreditably, but spent in the acquisition of virtue.

the same object: for it seems that bad actions may sometimes serve good purposes? The matter will be still plainer if we look at it in this way:—If things are useful towards the several ends for which they exist, which ends would not come into existence without them, how would you regard them? Can ignorance, for instance, be useful for knowledge, or disease for health, or vice for virtue?

Crit. Never.

Soc. And yet we have already agreed—have we not?—that there can be no knowledge where there has not previously been ignorance, nor health where there has not been disease, nor virtue where there has not been vice?

Crit. I think that we have.

Soc. But then it would seem that the antecedents without which a thing cannot exist are not necessarily useful to it. Otherwise ignorance would appear useful for knowledge, disease for health, and vice for virtue.

Critias still showed great reluctance to accept any argument which went to prove that all these things were useless. I saw that it was as difficult to persuade him as (according to the proverb) it is to boil a stone, so I said: Let us bid 'good-bye' to the discussion, since we cannot agree whether these things are useful and a part of wealth or not. But what shall we say to another question: Which is the happier and better man,—he who requires the greatest quantity of necessaries for body and diet, or he who requires only the fewest and least? The answer will perhaps become more obvious if we suppose some one, comparing the man himself at different times, to consider whether his condition is better when he is sick or when he is well?

Crit. That is not a question which needs much consideration.

Health is
a better
condition
than dis-
ease; and
it needs
less.

Soc. Probably, I said, every one can understand that health is a better condition than disease. But when have we the greatest and the most various needs, when we are sick or when we are well?

Crit. When we are sick.

Soc. And when we are in the worst state we have the greatest and most especial need and desire of bodily pleasures?

Crit. True.

Soc. And seeing that a man is best off when he is least in need of such things, does not the same reasoning apply to the case of any two persons, of whom one has many and great wants and desires, and the other few and moderate? For instance, some men are gamblers, some drunkards, and some gluttons: and gambling and the love of drink and greediness are all desires?

Crit. Certainly.

Soc. But desires are only the lack of something: and those who

have the greatest desires are in a worse condition than those who
have none or very slight ones?

Crit. Certainly I consider that those who have such wants are
bad, and that the greater their wants the worse they are.

Soc. And do we think it possible that a thing should be useful for
a purpose unless we have need of it for that purpose?

Crit. No.

Soc. Then if these things are useful for supplying the needs of the
body, we must want them for that purpose?

Crit. That is my opinion.

Soc. And he to whom the greatest number of things are useful for
his purpose, will also want the greatest number of means of accomplishing it, supposing that we necessarily feel the want of all useful
things?

Crit. It seems so.

Soc. The argument proves then that he who has great riches has
likewise need of many things for the supply of the wants of the
body; for wealth appears useful towards that end. And the richest
must be in the worst condition, since they seem to be most in want
of such things.

Cri. No.

Cri. That is my opinion.

Cri. It seems so.

INDEX

THE following index refers to the pages of Stephens, which are given in the margin of the translation. The page of Stephens is divided into five parts by the letters A, B, C, D, E, which are retained in the index, though they are not given in the margin. Thus the letter A signifies the first portion of the page, the letter B the second, and so on.

The order in which the dialogues are arranged in the translation is as follows:—

VOL. I.

VOL. II.

APPENDIX I.

APPENDIX II.

INDEX

A.

ABARIS, the Hyperborean, his charms, Charm. 158 B.

Abdera, Protagoras of, Protag. 309 C; Rep. 10. 600 C.

Abolition of debts, proposed by ancient legislators, Laws 5. 736 C (cp. 3. 684 D).

Abortion, allowed in certain cases, Rep. 5. 461 C; practised by midwives, Theaet. 149 D.

Above and below, Tim. 62 D.

Absolute and relative, Phil. 53 E; the absolute unknown, Parm. 133, 134:—absolute beauty, Euthyd. 301 A; Crat. 439 C; Phaedr. 249 E, 254 A; Symp. 211; Rep. 5. 476, 479; 6. 494 A, 501 B, 507 B (cp. Laws 2. 655 C):—absolute equality, Phaedo 74, 75; Parm. 131 D:—absolute essence, Phaedo 65; Parm. 135 A:—absolute existence, Phaedr. 248; 1 Alcib. 130:—absolute greatness and smallness, Parm. 131 D, 132 B, 150:—absolute good, Rep. 6. 507 B; 7. 540 A:—absolute justice, ib. 5. 479 E; 6. 501 B; 7. 517 E:—absolute knowledge, Phaedr. 248; possessed by God, Parm. 134:—absolute like and unlike, ib. 129 B:—absolute same and other, ib. 146 D:—absolute swiftness and slowness, Rep. 7. 529 D:—absolute temperance, ib. 6. 501 B:—absolute truth, Phil. 58 D:—absolute unity, Rep. 7. 524 E, 525 E; Soph. 245 A:—the absolute and the many, Rep. 6. 507.

Absolute power dangerous to the possessor, Laws 3. 691; 4. 711 E, 713 D, 716 A; 9. 875 B; 1 Alcib. 135.

Abstract ideas, origin of, Phaedo 74; Rep. 7. 523;—abstract and concrete in opposition, Phaedo 103. See Ideas.

Abuse, law about, Laws 11. 935.

Academy, The, at Athens, Lysis 203 A.

Acarnanians, the two, Euthyd. 271 C.

Accents, change of, Crat. 399 B.

Accident, the real legislator, Laws 4. 709 A:—accident and essence, Lysis 217; Rep. 5. 454; Soph. 247.

Acesimbrotus, a physician's name, Crat. 394 C.

Achaeans, Rep. 3. 389 E, 390 E, 393 A, D, 394 A; Laws 3. 682 D, E, 685 E, 706 D, E; 1 Alcib. 112 B.

Achaemenes, 1 Alcib. 120 E.

Acharnian, Callicles the, Gorg. 495 D.

Achelous, Phaedr. 230 B, 263 D.

Acheron, Phaedo 112 E, 113 D.

Acherusian lake, Phaedo 113 A, B, C, 114 A.

Achilles, attacks Scamander, Protag. 340 A; his speech to Ajax (Il. 9. 644), Crat. 428 C; fights with Hector, Ion 535 B; sent by the Gods to the Islands of the Blest, Symp. 179 E, 180 A, B; erroneously called by Aeschylus the lover of Patroclus, ib. 179 E; dies for Patroclus, ib. 208 D; Brasidas compared to, ib. 221 D; the son of Peleus and Thetis, Apol. 28 C; Rep. 3. 391 C; Hipp. Min. 371 D; his grief, Rep. 3. 388 A; his avarice, cruelty, and insolence, ib. 390 E, 391 A, B; his master Phoenix, ib. 390 E; better than Odysseus, Hipp. Min. 363 B, 364 B, C, D, 365 A, 369 B, C, 371 D; taught by Cheiron, ib. 371 D.

Acid, vegetable (ὀπός), Tim. 60 B.

Acquaintance, importance of friendship and, Laws 6. 771 E.

Acropolis, the, Euthyph. 6 B; Eryx. 398 E;—in ancient Athens, Crit. 112 A; in Atlantis, ib. 115 D foll.; of the Model City, Laws 5. 745 (cp. 6. 778 C).

Act, the, distinguished from the state, Euthyph. 10.

Actions, a class of being, Crat. 386 E; not good or bad in themselves, Symp. 181 A; voluntary and involuntary, Laws 9. 860; Hipp. Min. 373, 374; kinds of, Laws 9. 864; have life, ib. 10. 904 A.

Active and passive states, Laws 9. 859 E; 10. 903 B.

Active life, age for, Rep. 7. 539, 540.

Actors cannot perform both tragic and comic parts, Rep. 3. 395 A.

Acumenus, father of Eryximachus, Protag. 315 C; Phaedr. 268 A; Symp. 176 B; a physician, Phaedr. 227 A, 269 A; a companion of Socrates, ib. 227 A.

Acusilaus, the poet, Symp. 178 C.

Adamant, Tim. 59 B.

Adeimantus, son of Ariston, brother of Plato, Apol. 34 A;—a person in the dialogue Republic, Rep. 1. 327 C; his genius, ib. 2. 368 A; distinguished at the battle of Megara, ibid.; takes up the discourse, ib. 362 D, 368 E, 376 D; 4. 419 A; 6. 487 A; 8. 548 E;

Autumn, the gifts of, Laws 8. 844 E.

Auxiliaries, the young warriors of the state, Rep. 3. 414; compared to dogs, *ib.* 2. 376; 4. 440 D; 5. 451 D; have silver mingled in their veins, *ib.* 3. 415 A. Cp. Guardians.

Avarice, disgraceful, Rep. 1. 347 B; forbidden in the guardians, *ib.* 3. 390 E; falsely imputed to Achilles and Asclepius by the poets, *ib.* 391 B, 408 C; characteristic of timocracy and oligarchy, *ib.* 8. 548 A, 553; in despotic rulers, Laws 3. 697 E; a cause of murder, *ib.* 9. 870.

Aviary in the mind, Theaet. 197 C foll.

Axiochus, father of Cleinias, Euthyd. 271 B, 275 A.

Azaes, son of Poseidon, Crit. 114 C.

B.

Bacchic dances, Laws 7. 815 C;—women, Ion 534 A; Laws 7. 790 E (cp. Phaedr. 253 A).

Bad, *see* Evil, Unjust.

Balance required in the state and in the individual, Laws 3. 691, 693 B; 4. 716 A.

Ball, the earth compared to a parti-coloured leathern, Phaedo 110 B. Cp. Games.

Banditti, in Italy, Laws 6. 777 C.

Barbarian words, Crat. 409 E (cp. 417 C, 421 D, 425 E); barbarian forms of government, Rep. 8. 544 D:—barbarians older than Greeks, Crat. 425 E; regard nakedness as improper, Rep. 5. 452 D; the natural enemies of the Hellenes, *ib.* 470 (cp. Statesm. 262 D); admire wealth, Laws 9. 870 A.

Baths, at the Lyceum, Symp. 223 D; in the island of Atlantis, Crit. 117 A; warm baths to be provided for the aged, Laws 6. 761 C;—Socrates takes the bath before his death, Phaedo 115 A, 116 A.

Batiea, name of a hill near Troy (Hom. Il. 2. 813 foll.), Crat. 392 A.

Beast, the great, Rep. 6. 493; the many-headed, *ib.* 9. 588, 589:—'the wild beast within us,' *ib.* 571, 572:—'the fatted beast,' Laws 7. 807 A:—the beast which has killed a man, to be tried for murder, *ib.* 9. 873 E.

Beautiful, the, and the good are one, Lysis 216; Symp. 201 B, 204 E foll.; Rep. 5. 452 (cp. Euthyd. 301 A; Crat. 439; Phaedo 100); the many beautiful contrasted with absolute beauty, Rep. 6. 507 B; he is beautiful who utters the beautiful, Theaet. 185 E; the beautiful and the not-beautiful, Soph. 257.

Beauty, 'a slippery thing,' Lysis 216 C (cp. 1 Alcib. 131); nature of, Lysis 216; Phaedr. 250 foll.; beauty and goodness, Symp. 201; beauty and love, *ib.* 206; gradations of beauty, *ib.* 210; universal science of, *ibid.*;

standard of, Gorg. 474; a means of education, Rep. 3. 401 foll.; pleasure of, Phil. 51; allied to measure, *ib.* 64 E; to mind, *ib.* 65 E; in the scale of goods, *ib.* 65, 66; inferior to virtue, Laws 5. 727 E (cp. Symp. 218 D, E); the desire of beauty in the soul, Laws 8. 841 C;—absolute, Euthyd. 301 A; Crat. 439 C; Phaedr. 249 E, 254 A; Symp. 211; Rep. 5. 476, 479; 6. 494 A, 501 B, 507 B (cp. Laws 2. 655 C);—beauty of Alcibiades, Symp. 217 A, 219 B; 1 Alcib. 104 A; of Charmides, Charm. 154.

Becoming and being, Rep. 7. 518 D, 521 D, 525 D; Tim. 27 E foll.; Theaet. 152, 157 (cp. Protag. 340).

Beds, the figure of the three, Rep. 10. 596 foll.

Bee,—'like the bee, leave my sting in you before I die,' Phaedo 91 C;—laws concerning bees, Laws 8. 843 E; poisoning of bees, *ib.* 11. 933 D:—bee-masters, Rep. 8. 564 C.

Beggars, to be banished from the state, Laws 11. 936 B.

Beginning, the, unbegotten and indestructible, Phaedr. 245 C.

Being, concerned with the invariable, Rep. 9. 585; nature of, Tim. 51 E; perceived by the soul, Theaet. 185 C; being in early Greek philosophy, Soph. 243, 244; (existence) defined as power, *ib.* 247, 248; as a genus, *ib.* 254 foll.; as expressed by language, *ib.* 261: —being, and becoming, Rep. 7. 518 D, 521 D, 525 D; Tim. 27 E foll.; Theaet. 152, 157 (cp. Protag. 340):—being and the many, Parm. 127 E:—being and motion, Theaet. 153 A, 180 E; Soph. 249; movable and immovable in being, Soph. 249; being neither in motion nor rest, *ib.* 250:—being and not-being, Rep. 5. 477; Theaet. 188; Soph. 257 foll.:—being and number, Parm. 144:— being and the one, *ib.* 142 foll.; Theaet. 180 E (cp. One):—being and other, Soph. 259: —being and unity, *ib.* 245:—true being beheld by the soul which follows God, Phaedr. 249, 250; the object of the philosopher's desire, Rep. 6. 484, 485, 486 E, 490, 500 C, 501 D; 7. 521, 537 D; 9. 581 E, 582 C (cp. Phaedr. 249; Phaedo 65, 82; Rep. 5. 475 E; 7. 520 B, 525; Theaet. 173 E; Soph. 249 D, 254 A); the subject of mind and wisdom, Phil. 59. Cp. Essence.

Belief, distinguished from learning, Gorg. 454. Cp. Faith.

Belief in Gods, not universal, Laws 12. 948. Cp. Atheism, Atheists, God.

Belly, the, Tim. 72 E.

Below and above, Tim. 62 D.

Bendis, a title of Artemis, Rep. 1. 327 A:— Bendidea, a feast of Artemis, *ib.* 1. 354 A (cp. 327 A, B).

A; not always to be regarded, Statesm. 283, 286; Laws 4. 721 E; 10. 887 B.

Briareus, how to be armed, Euthyd. 299 C; fabled to have had a hundred hands, Laws 7. 795 C.

Bribes, taking of, punished by death, Laws 12. 955 C.

Building, Rep. 3. 401 A; 4. 438 C; Soph. 266 D; Eryx. 403 D; an exact art, Phil. 56 B.

Bulls sacrificed in Atlantis, Crit. 119 E; bulls with gilded horns offered to the Gods, 2 Alcib. 149 B.

Burial, of the rulers (in the best state), Rep. 3. 413 E; 5. 465 E, 469 A; 7. 540 B; of parents, Laws 4. 717 E; of a rich wife, how to be described in poetry, *ib.* 719 E; of the suicide, *ib.* 9. 873; of the censors of magistrates, *ib.* 12. 947; regulations for burial, *ib.* 958, 959; burial of the dead in battle at Athens, Menex. 234. Cp. Funeral.

Buying and selling, regulations concerning, Laws, 8. 849; 11. 915, 916.

C.

Cadmus, the story of, Laws 2. 663 E (cp. Rep. 3. 414 C; Soph. 247 C); a barbarian, Menex. 245 C;—Cadmus of Thebes (Cebes), Phaedo 95 A:—'Cadmeian victory,' Laws 1. 641 C:—Cadmeians at war with Argives, Menex. 239 B.

Caeneus the Thessalian, changed from woman to man, Laws 12. 944 D.

Caestus, the, worn by would-be Laconizers, Protag. 342 B.

Calculation, defined, Gorg. 451; corrects the illusions of sight, Rep. 10. 602 D (cp. Protag. 356; Rep. 7. 524); the talent for, accompanied by general quickness, Rep. 7. 526 B; the art of, Theaet. 198; Statesm. 259 D. Cp. Arithmetic.

Callaeschrus, father of Critias, Charm. 153 C, 169 B; Protag. 316 A.

Calliades, father of Callias, 1 Alcib. 119 A.

Callias, son of Calliades, a disciple of Zeno, 1 Alcib. 119 A.

Callias, son of Hipponicus, Protag. 311 A, 314 E, 315 D, 335 D; Protagoras at his house, *ib.* 311 A; half-brother to Paralus, *ib.* 314 E; his house the finest in the city, *ib.* 337 D; 'the noble,' *ib.* 362 A; has spent a 'world of money' on the Sophists, Crat. 391 C; Apol. 20 A; guardian of Protagoras' interests at Athens, Theaet. 165 A; famous for his wealth, Eryx. 395 A; father of Protarchus, Phil. 19 B.

Callicles, a person in the dialogue *Gorgias*, Gorg. 481 B-505 E; loves the son of Pyrilampes, *ib.* 481 D, 513 B; Socrates' account of him, *ib.* 487 A foll.; his view of temper-

ance, *ib.* 491 E foll.; an Acharnian, *ib.* 495 D; unfair in argument, *ib.* 499 C foll.; will not continue the argument, *ib.* 506 C; beginning to be a public character, *ib.* 515 A.

Calliope, eldest of the Muses, Phaedr. 259 D.

Cambyses, the son of Cyrus, nearly ruined the Persian empire, Laws 3. 694 C; his folly, *ib.* 695 B, C; his conquests, Menex. 239 E.

Capital causes, in some states not allowed to be decided in one day, Apol. 37 A:—capital punishment, Statesm. 297 D; Laws 9. 854, 859-863, 880 E; 12. 957 E. Cp. Death.

Captain, parable of the deaf, Rep. 6. 488:—rogueries practised by ship captains, Statesm. 298 B. Cp. Pilot.

Carding, Statesm. 281 A, 282 B.

Carelessness, not to be ascribed to the gods, Laws 10. 900 foll. Cp. God.

Carian (proverbial), Laches 187 B; Euthyd. 285 B; Carian wailers, Laws 7. 800 E.

Carpentry, Ion 537 B; Rep. 4. 428 C; an exact art, Phil. 56 B.

'Cart,' performances on the (at Athens), Laws 1. 637 B.

Carthaginians, given to intoxication, Laws 1. 637 D; restrictions on drinking among, *ib.* 2. 674 B; use pieces of leather for money, Eryx. 400 A.

Carving, an image of the dialectical process, Phaedr. 265 E; Statesm. 287 B. Cp. Dialectic.

Casks, image of the, Gorg. 493.

Caste, in Egypt, Tim. 24; in ancient Athens, *ibid.*; Crit. 110, 112.

Castor and Pollux, Euthyd. 293 A; games in honour of (at Lacedaemon), Laws 7. 796 B.

Causal arts, Statesm. 281, 282, 287 B. Cp. Art.

Cause, the idea of the; cause and effect, Euthyph. 10; Phil. 26, 27; 'the tie of the cause,' Meno 98 A; cause and condition distinguished, Phaedo 99; the good denied by some to be a cause, *ibid.*; a cause necessary to creation, Tim. 28 A; the power of the cause, Phil. 30:—God the best of causes, Tim. 29 A:—final causes, Phaedo 97, 98; argument from, applied to justice, Rep. 1. 352; second causes, Tim. 46 (cp. 76 E); two kinds of causes, *ib.* 68 E; creative causes, Phil. 27; the causes of things, ought to be enquired into by men, Laws 7. 821 A; first causes, *ib.* 10. 891 E:—causes of crimes, Rep. 8. 552 D; 9. 575 A; Laws 8. 831 E, 832 D; 9. 863, 870.

Cavalry, Laches 191;—cavalry officers, election of, Laws 6. 755 E.

Cave, the image of the, Rep. 7. 514 foll., 532 (cp. 539 E).

Cebes of Thebes, willing to provide money

for Socrates' escape, Crito 45 B; present at the death of Socrates, and taking part in the dialogue *Phaedo*, Phaedo 59 B; a friend of Philolaus, *ib.* 61 D; his native speech, *ib.* 62 A; his earnestness, *ib.* 63 A; his incredulity, *ib.* 70 A foll., 77 B; he compares the soul to a weaver's coat, *ib.* 87 B foll.; apt to be disconcerted, *ib.* 103 C.

Cecrops, Crit. 110 A.

Celibacy, fines on, Laws 4. 721 D; 6. 774 A.

Celts given to intoxication, Laws 1. 637 D.

Censors of magistrates, Laws 12. 945 947; creation of censors, *ib.* 946; burial of, *ib.* 947; trial of, *ib.* E.

Censorship of fiction, Rep. 2. 377; 3. 386 foll.; 10. 595 foll.;—of the arts, *ib.* 3. 401;—of poetry, Laws 7. 801, 817 D; 8. 829 D. Cp. Fiction, Poets.

Centaurs, Phaedr. 229 D; chorus of (sophist-politicians), Statesm. 291 A, 303 D.

Ceos, subject to Athens, Laws 1. 638 B;—Prodicus of Ceos, Protag. 314 C; Apol. 19 E; Rep. 10. 600 C; Eryx. 397 C; Pythocleides of, Protag. 316 E:—Cean use of the word χαλεπόν, Protag. 341 A:—character of the Ceans, *ib.* E.

Cephalus of Clazomenae, Rep. 1. 330 B; Parm. 126 A foll.

Cephalus, father of Lysias, Phaedr. 227 A, 263 D; father of Polemarchus, Rep. 1. 327 B; offers sacrifice, *ib.* 328 B, 331 D; his views on old age, *ib.* 328 E; his views on wealth, *ib.* 330 A foll.

Cephisus, Antiphon of, Apol. 33 E.

Cepis, father of Adeimantus, Protag. 315 E.

Cerameis, deme of, Protag. 315 E.

Ceramicus, outside the wall of Athens, Parm. 127 C.

Cerberus, two natures in one, Rep. 9. 588 C.

Cercyon, famous (in mythology) for his skill in wrestling, Laws 7. 796 A.

Chaeredemus, father of Patrocles, half-brother to Socrates, Euthyd. 297 E, 298 A, B.

Chaerephon, a person in the dialogue *Charmides*, Charm. 153 A foll.; a kind of madman, *ib.* B (cp. Apol. 21 A); consulted the oracle at Delphi concerning Socrates, Apol. 20 E; dead at the time of the *Apology*, *ib.* 21 A; goes with Socrates to Gorgias, Gorg. 447 A foll.

Chalcis, name of a bird in Homer, Crat. 392 A.

Χαλεπόν, use of the word, Protag. 341.

Chance in war, Rep. 5. 467 E; blamed by men for their misfortunes, *ib.* 10. 619 C (cp. Laws 5. 727 B); the great legislator, Laws 4. 709; together with God, *ibid.;* and art, *ibid.;* 10. 889; and nature, *ib.* 10. 889.

Change, in music, not to be allowed, Rep.

4. 424; Laws 7. 799; in the laws, Statesm. 295 foll.; evil of, Laws 7. 797, 798; the principles of change, *ib.* 10. 893, 894:—changes of the soul, *ib.* 903 E, 904 D; changes in the character of young men, *ib.* 11. 929 C; changes in body and mind during life, Symp. 207 D.

Chaos, Tim. 53 A, 69 B; Theaet. 153 D; Statesm. 273:—the 'Chaos' of Anaxagoras, Phaedo 72 C; Gorg. 465 D.

Character, differences of, in men, Statesm. 307; Rep. 1. 329 D; in women, Rep. 5. 456; affected by the imitation of unworthy objects, *ib.* 3. 395; Laws 2. 668; 7. 798 E; formed in infancy, Laws 7. 791, 792; character and will, *ib.* 10. 904; character of young men, apt to change, *ib.* 11. 929 C (cp. Symp. 207 D):—national character, Rep. 4. 435; affected by climate and soil, Laws 5. 747:—great characters may be ruined by bad education, Rep. 6. 491 E, 495 B; 7. 519 (cp. Laws 8. 831 E):—faults of character, Theaet. 144 B; Rep. 6. 503.

Chariot driving, Lysis 208 A; Ion 537 A.

Charioteer of the soul, Phaedr. 246, 253, 254.

Chariots, not kept in Crete, Laws 8. 834 B.

Charmantides, the Paeanian, present at the *Republic*, Rep. 1. 328 B.

Charmers, punishment of, Laws 10. 909 (cp. Rep. 2. 364; Laws 11. 933 A).

Charmides, the son of Glaucon, Protag. 315 A; a person in the dialogue *Charmides* (*see* Temperance); the most beautiful youth of his time, Charm. 154 A, C, 157 C, 175 E; his disposition, *ib.* 154 E, 157 C, D; Critias his guardian and cousin, *ib.* 155 A, 156 A, 157 C, 176 C; greatness of his ancestors, *ib.* 157 E (cp. Tim. 20 E); Socrates' influence on him, Symp. 222 B.

Charondas, lawgiver of Italy and Sicily, Rep. 10. 599 E.

Chastisement of the soul, Gorg. 505.

Chastity, Laws 1. 636; 8. 835 foll.

Cheerfulness, usually accompanied by a high spirit, Laws 7. 791 C.

Cheese, Rep. 2. 372 C; 3. 405 E.

Cheiron, teacher of Achilles, Rep. 3. 391 C; Hipp. Min. 371 C.

Chene, Myson of, Protag. 343 A.

Child, the new-born, carried round the hearth, Theaet. 160 E:—'the child within us,' Phaedo 77 E:—Children, the greatest riches of their parents, Laches 185 A (cp. Lysis 219 D); have spirit, but not reason, Rep. 4. 441 A (cp. Laws 12. 963 E); why under authority, Rep. 9. 590 E; instincts of, Laws 2. 653; conceive virtue and vice under the forms of pleasure and pain, *ib.* A; prefer comedy to tragedy, *ib.* 658 (cp. Rep. 3. 397 D); a means of immortality,

zens), not allowed in the Model City, Laws 9. 855 A.

Conflagrations, great periodical, signified by the myth of Phaethon, Tim. 22 C.

Conflict, the, of reason with desire, Phaedr. 253 foll.; Rep. 4. 439-442; 9. 571 D; Tim. 69 E foll.; Laws 3. 687, 689:—the immortal conflict of good and evil, Laws 10. 906.

Connection (in style), Phaedr. 264 B.

Connus, son of Metrobius, music-master of Socrates, a harp-player, Euthyd. 272 C (cp. Menex. 235 E); disliked opposition, Euthyd. 295 D.

Consciousness, Phil. 34, 43.

Consonants, Crat. 424 C; Theaet. 203 B; Soph. 253 A; Phil. 18 C.

Constitution, the aristocratic, is the ideal state sketched in Rep. bk. 4 (cp. 8. 544 E, 545 E; Laws 5. 739);—the 'Laws' the 'second-best' constitution, Laws 5. 739; 7. 807 B;—the 'third-best,' *ib.* 5. 739:—defective forms of constitution, Rep. 4. 445 B; 8. 544; Statesm. 291 foll., 301 foll.; 'timocracy' or Spartan polity, Rep. 8. 545 foll.; aristocracy (in the ordinary sense), *ib.* 1. 338 D; Statesm. 291 E, 301 A, 302 D; Laws 3. 681; Menex. 238 C; oligarchy, Rep. 8. 550 foll., 554 E; Statesm. 291, 301, 302; democracy, Rep. 8. 555 foll., 557 D; Statesm. 291, 301; tyranny, Rep. 8. 544 C, 562; 9. 576; Statesm. 276 E, 291 E, 302;—ordinary constitutions not to be called 'polities,' Laws 4. 713 A, 715 A. Cp. Government (forms of), State.

Constitution, the bodily, different in different individuals, Laws 1. 636 A. Cp. Body.

Contentiousness, a characteristic of timocracy, Rep. 8. 546.

Contest, the, of virtue, Laws 5. 731:—various kinds of contests, *ib.* 2. 658; training for contests, Rep. 3. 404 A; 6. 503 E; 7. 535 B; Laws 1. 646 D; 7. 807 C; 8. 830, 839 E, 840 A (cp. Training);—contests of rhapsodes, Ion 530; Laws 2. 658;—the cithara in contests, Gorg. 501 E;—funeral contests at Athens, Menex. 249 B:—(in the Model City), gymnastic contests, Laws 6. 764 C foll.; 8. 828 C, 830, 834; 12. 947 E;—contests of horses, *ib.* 6. 764 E; 8. 834 B; 12. 947 E;—musical, *ib.* 2. 658 A; 6. 764 D foll.; 8. 828 C, 834 E; 12. 947 E; judges of, *ib.* 2. 659; 6. 764 D; 12. 948 E;—in running, *ib.* 8. 833 D;—in strength, *ib.* C; umpires of, *ib.* E; 12. 949 A;—contests in honour of the dead, *ib.* 12. 947 E;—homicide at contests, *ib.* 8. 831 A; 9. 865 A; no abuse to be allowed at, *ib.* 11. 935; law against the obstruction of competitors, *ib.* 955 A.

Contracts, sometimes not protected by law, Rep. 8. 556 A; are holy, Laws 5. 729 E;

laws concerning, *ib.* 8. 847; 11. 920, 921.

Contradiction, proved impossible, Euthyd. 285 D foll.; nature of, Rep. 4. 436; 10. 602 E; power of, *ib.* 5. 454 A.

Contributions (friendly), collection of, Laws 11. 915 E; (in time of war), *ib.* 12. 949 D.

Controversy, kinds of, Soph. 225.

Convention in morals, Gorg. 482 E; convention and nature, Laws 10. 88 E:—the conventional theory of justice (Glaucon), Rep. 2. 359 A; (Protagoras), Theaet. 172 A, 177 C. Cp. Names.

Conversation, should not be personal, Rep. 6. 500 B (cp. Theaet. 174 C).

Conversion of the soul, Rep. 7. 518, 521, 525 (cp. Laws 12. 957 E).

Convivial meetings, should be under a ruler, Laws 1. 639 foll.; 2. 671 E; a kind of education, *ib.* 1. 641; bring out character, *ib.* 650. For a description of a Greek banquet, cp. the *Symposium*, and references under 'Greek Life.'

Cook and physician, Gorg. 521 E; the cook a better judge than the guest, Theaet. 178 D.

Cookery, how far an art, Gorg. 462 foll.; art of, *ib.* 465, 518; cookery and medicine, *ib.* 501 A;—analogy of, employed in the definition of justice, Rep. 1. 332 D.

Co-operative arts, Statesm. 281, 282, 287 B.

Copper, Tim. 59 C.

Corinth, battle of, Theaet. 142 A; Menex. 245 E:—Corinthian courtezans, Rep. 3. 404 D:—Corinthians, the, ask aid of Athens, Menex. 244 D; willing to betray the Asiatic Greeks, *ib.* 245 C:—ὁ Διὸς Κόρινθος, Euthyd. 292 E.

Coronea, battle of, 1 Alcib. 112 C.

Corpses, not to be spoiled, Rep. 5. 469:—corpses of criminals, outside the north wall of Athens, *ib.* 4. 439 E; to be cast beyond the border, Laws 9. 855 A, 873 B; 10. 909 B.

Correction, art of, Soph. 229 A.

Correlations, Phil. 53 E.

Correlative and relative, qualifications of, Gorg. 476; Rep. 4. 437 foll.; how corrected, Rep. 7. 524.

Corruptio optimi pessima, Rep. 6. 491.

Corruption, the, of youth, laid to Socrates' charge, Euthyph. 2, 3, 5; Apol. 24 foll.; not the work of the Sophists, but of public opinion, Rep. 6. 492 A. Cp. Sophist.

Corruption and generation, Phaedo 96; corruption in pleasures and pains, Phil. 41 A.

Corybantes, Symp. 215 E; at the mysteries, Euthyd. 277 D; not in their right mind, Ion 534 A; remedial effects of their dances, Laws 7. 790 D.

Cos, Hippocrates of, Protag. 311 B.

Cosmos, Statesm. 273 B; meaning of the

Fighting, an art, Soph. 219; subdivisions of, *ib.* 225:—fighting in armour, Laches 178 A, 179 E, 181 D foll.; Euthyd. 272 A, 273 D, E; Gorg. 456 D; Laws 7. 795 B, 813 E; 8. 833 E.

Figs, regulations respecting the gathering of, Laws 8. 844 E.

Figure, a common notion, Meno 74; = that which follows colour, *ib.* 75; = the limit of solid, *ib.* 76:—figures and figure, Phil. 12 E.

Final causes, Phaedo 97, 98; argument from, applied to justice, Rep. 1. 352.

Fines, payment of, Laws 9. 855.

Finite and infinite, Phil. 15, 16, 23, 24 foll., 31, 32; the finite comprises what admits of measure, *ib.* 25.

Fire, Tim. 31 E, 49, 53; form of, *ib.* 53, 56; the most penetrating of the elements, *ib.* 58 B, 62 A, 78 A; the various kinds of, *ib.* C; why hot, *ib.* 61 E; the fire within us, and that contained in the universe, Phil. 29; obtained by friction, Rep. 4. 434 E (cp. Theaet. 153 A).

First principles, importance of, Phaedo 107 B; Crat. 436.

Fish, creation of, Tim. 92:—fish-preserves in the Nile, Statesm. 264 C:—fishing, Soph. 219 foll.; regulations respecting, Laws 7. 823. Cp. Angling.

Flatterers, Phaedr. 240 A; Soph. 222, 223; flatterers and rhetoricians, Gorg. 463, 464.

Flattery, should be avoided by the good man, Gorg. 527 C; of the multitude by their leaders, in ill-ordered states, Rep. 4. 426; 9. 590 B; power of, over the soul, Laws 1. 633 D; 11. 923 A; pernicious effect of, on the young, *ib.* 5. 729 A;—the art of flattery, Gorg. 463 foll., 501, 502 (cp. Soph. 222 E).

Flesh, Tim. 61 D, 73, 74; not eaten or offered in sacrifice in primitive times, Laws 6. 782 C (cp. Rep. 2. 372; Statesm. 272 A).

Flute, the, employed in preludes to Athene, Crat. 417 E; in mystic rites, Crito 52 D; to be rejected, Rep. 3. 399; used for music without words, Laws 2. 669 E; Alcibiades would not learn, 1 Alcib. 106 E:—flute girls, Protag. 347 C; Symp. 176 E, 212 E:—flute music, Phil. 56 A:—flute players and flute makers, Rep. 3. 399 D; 10. 601 D:—flute playing, Protag. 327 B; Meno 90 E; Laws 3. 700 E; an art which seeks pleasure only, Gorg. 501 E.

Flux of being, Crat. 401 D, 402 A, B, 411, 437, 440; Symp. 207 D; Theaet. 152 E, 156 A, 160 D, 177 C, 179 D, 181 D, 182, 183 C; Phil. 43 A. Cp. Heracleitus.

Folly, an inanition (κένωσις) of the soul, Rep. 8. 585 A; = anarchy in the soul, Laws 3. 689 B; the worst of diseases, *ib.*

691 D; names for folly, 2 Alcib. 140, 142 E, 150 C.

Food, the condition of life and existence, Rep. 2. 369 C;—arts concerned with the provision of, Statesm. 288 E;—distribution of food (in the Model City), Laws 8. 847 E.

Foreign origin of words, Crat. 409 D, 416 A, 421 D:—foreigners, reception of, Laws 12. 949 E, 952 E (cp. Strangers).

Forgetfulness, Phil. 33 E; a mark of an unphilosophical nature, Rep. 6. 486 D, 490 E:—the plain of Forgetfulness, *ib.* 10. 621 A.

Form and matter, Crat. 389, 390;—beauty of form, Phil. 51.

Fortune and wisdom identical, Euthyd. 279; good fortune without justice an evil, Laws 2. 661 B.

Fountains, ancient, in Attica, Crit. 111 D; in Atlantis, *ib.* 113 E, 117 A:—to be ornamented, Laws 6. 761; in the Agora, *ib.* 764 A.

Fowling, Soph. 220 B; regulations respecting, Laws 7. 823.

Fox, emblem of subtlety, Rep. 2. 365 C.

Fractions, Rep. 7. 525 E.

Frankincense, not to be imported, Laws 8. 847 C.

Freedmen, regulations respecting, Laws 11. 915.

Freedom, the characteristic of democracy, Rep. 8. 557 B, 561-563 (cp. Laws 12. 962 E; Menex. 238 E); among the ancient Persians, Laws 3. 694 B; necessary in the state, *ibid.*, 697 D; entire freedom not so good as a limited government, *ib.* 698 B; easily passes into anarchy, *ib.* 701 B:—freedom of action acquired by knowledge, Lysis 209:—freedom of bequest, not allowed (in the Model City), Laws 11. 922:—freedom of speech at Athens, Protag. 319 A; Gorg. 461 E; in ancient Persia, Laws 3. 694 A:—freedom of the will, *ib.* 10. 904 C (cp. Rep. 10. 617 E).

Friction, used to obtain fire, Rep. 4. 434 E; Theaet. 153 A.

Friend, the, must be, as well as seem, good, Rep. 1. 334, 335; friends have all things in common, Lysis 207 C; Phaedr. 279 B; Rep. 5. 449 C; Laws 5. 739 C:—the friends of the tyrant, Rep. 8. 567 E; 9. 576 (cp. Gorg. 510).

Friendship, Lysis 212 foll.; Phaedr. 232, 255, 256 (*see* Love); impossible between the evil, Lysis 214 D, 217 B, 218 A; Phaedr. 255 A; like and unlike in, Lysis 214, 215; Laws 8. 837; illustrated by the analogy of medicine, Lysis 217; fostered by equality, Phaedr. 240 B; helps to bind together the universe, Gorg. 508 A; arises out of similarity of character, *ib.* 510 B; implies justice, Rep. 1. 351 foll.; in the state, *ib.* 5. 462, 463; Laws 3. 694 A; 5. 738 D, 743 C; 6. 759 B, 771 E; 1 Alcib. 126; destroyed by despotism, Laws 3. 697 D; injured by the feeling of satiety, *ib.* 6. 776 A; a species of hunting, *ib.* 7. 823 B (cp. Soph. 222 E); friendship and love, Laws 8. 837; friendship and agreement, 1 Alcib. 127.

Frost, Tim. 59 E.

Fruits, laws concerning, Laws 8. 844, 845.

Fulling, Statesm. 281 B, 282 A.

Funeral of the guardians, Rep. 3. 413 E; 5. 465 E, 468 E; 7. 540 B; funeral of a censor of the magistrates, Laws 12. 947:—Funerals, expenditure on, to be moderate, *ib.* 4. 719; 12. 959:—washing of the corpse, Phaedo 115 A:—corpses placed on the pyre on the twelfth day, Rep. 10. 614 B:—lamentations, Laws 12. 959 E (cp. *ib.* 7. 800 E; Menex. 248):—funeral orations, Menex. 235. Cp. Burial.

Future life, Crat. 398, 403; Phaedo 63, 67; Rep. 3. 387; 10. 614 foll.; punishment of the wicked in, Phaedr. 249 A; Phaedo 108 B, 114; Gorg. 523 B, 525; Rep. 2. 363; 10. 614 foll.; Theaet. 177 A; Laws 9. 870 E, 881 B; 10. 904 C; 12. 959; the good happy in, Apol. 41; Phaedo 63, 107, 114; Gorg. 526 C, 527 D; union of friends in, Phaedo 68 A (cp. Apol. 41); mystic view of, Phaedo 69; the dead not pleased by the lamentations of the living, Menex. 248. Cp. Hades, World below.

G.

Gadeirus = Eumelus, Crit. 114 B.

Gades, country of, Crit. 114 B.

Gadfly, Socrates compared to a, Apol. 30 E.

Games of children, a means of education, Rep. 4. 425 A; Laws 1. 643 B (cp. Rep. 7. 536 E); influence of, upon manners and morals, Laws 7. 797 B:—ball (σφαῖρα), Euthyd. 277 B; Phaedo 110 B; Theaet. 146 A:—city (πόλις), Rep. 4. 422 E:—dancing on a leathern bottle (ἀσκωλιάζειν), Symp. 190 D:—dice (ἀστράγαλοι), Lysis 206 E; 1 Alcib. 110 B; (κύβοι), Rep. 2. 374 C; 10. 604 C; Laws 12. 968 E; invented by Theuth, Phaedr. 274 D:—draughts (πεττεία), Charm. 174 B; Gorg. 450 D; Rep. 1. 333 A; 2. 374 C; 6. 487 B; Statesm. 292 E; Laws 5. 739 A; 7. 820 C; 1 Alcib. 110 E; Eryx. 395 A; invented by Theuth, Phaedr. 274 D:—prisoner's base (?) (διὰ γραμμῆς παίζειν), Theaet. 181 A:—puppets, Laws 1. 644 E (cp. Rep. 7. 514):—games to be instituted for both sexes (in the Model City), Laws 6. 771 E; 7. 813

foll.; 8. 828 foll. (cp. Dancing, Festival, Gymnastic):—[the Olympic, &c.], glory gained by success in, Rep. 5. 465 D, 466 A; 10. 618 A; the training for, laborious, Laws 7. 807 C (cp. *ib.* 8. 840 A); the first place at, a reward of honour, *ib.* 9. 881 B; 12. 946 E.

Ganymede, Phaedr. 255 C; story of Ganymede invented by the Cretans, Laws 1. 636 C.

Garments (marriage), price of, given as a dowry, Laws 6. 774 D.

Geese, nurseries of, in Thessaly, Statesm. 264 C.

Gems, in the upper earth, Phaedo 110 E:—gem-engraving, Hipp. Min. 368 C; 1 Alcib. 128 C, E.

Genealogies, Hellenic, Tim. 22, 23.

Genera and species, Euthyph. 12; difficulty in fixing, Soph. 267 (cp. Phil. 18 E); not rightly distinguished by the ancients, Soph. 267 D.

General ideas, Soph. 254; unity and existence of, Phil. 15. *See* Idea.

General, the, why superior to the soothsayer, Laches 198 E; the general and the rhapsode, Ion 541; the general ought to know arithmetic and geometry, Rep. 7. 522 E, 525 B, 526 D, 527 B (cp. Laws 7. 818 C); must himself be brave, Laws 1. 639 B, 640 A; 2. 671 E:—the general's art, a branch of hunting, Euthyd. 290 (cp. Soph. 219); a matter of science, Statesm. 304 E; ministerial, not political, *ib.* 305 A; empirical, Phil. 56 A:—generals and tacticians, 'craftsmen of war,' Laws 11. 921 E:—names for generals, Crat. 394 B:—election of generals (in the Model City), Laws 6. 755.

Generalization (in style), Phaedr. 265 E, 273 E.

Generation (γένεσις), Phaedo 71; Tim. 50, 52; cause of, Phaedo 90 (cp. *ib.* 101; Phil. 27); the 'nurse of generation,' Tim. 49-52: —generation and corruption, Phaedo 96:—generation and essence, Soph. 248, 249; Phil. 54:—generation and motion, Tim. 38 A; Laws 10. 893, 894; 12. 966 E:—generation and pleasure, Phil. 53, 55 foll.:—the generation of animals, Tim. 90, 91.

Genesis, of animals, Protag. 321; of man, Symp. 189 E foll.; Statesm. 271 foll.

Gentleness of the just, Gorg. 516 C; characteristic of the philosopher, Rep. 2. 375, 376; 3. 410; 6. 486 C; ought to be found in every man, Laws 5. 731 B.

Geographers, mistaken in their notions about the earth, Phaedo 108 C.

Geometry, invented by Theuth, Phaedr. 274 C; must be learnt by the rulers in the best

element, *i.e. the soul, and combine it in due proportion with the material and perishable. Thus man, 'the most religious of animals,' comes into being, but evil is born within him by reason of his composite nature. Yet with the aid of education he can struggle against his passions and desires, and pass through the pilgrimage of life unharmed. If he yields to temptation, he himself and not his Creator is responsible for his evil state* (cp. Rep. 10. 617 E).—*In the Statesman the riddle of the universe receives a somewhat different solution. There was a time when the Creator Himself presided over the revolutions of the world. This was the so-called 'age of Cronos,' during which men lived the life of nature in peace and innocence. But in the fulness of time He withdrew His hand from the helm, and the world turned back in its course with a mighty shock which caused the destruction of all living creatures. A new race then succeeded, and at first things went fairly well. But gradually the evil which was inherent in matter reasserted itself, and the world was ready to fall into chaos again. The Creator once more took the helm and restored order to creation. At the same time He made the world immortal and self-creating: men and animals no longer grew out of the earth, but reproduced their species, each after their kind. In the beginning the human race was poor and helpless, but gradually by the aid of the gods they acquired the arts of life and learnt to form social communities* (cp. Laws 3. 677 foll.). *In this manner Plato sets forth under a mythical disguise both the origin of evil and the growth of civilization among men.*]

Goddess of ways, Laws 11. 914 B.

Gold (and silver), not allowed to the guardians, Rep. 3. 416 E; 4. 419, 422 D; 5. 464 C; Tim. 18 B; mingled by the God in those who are to rule, Rep. 3. 415 A (cp. 8. 546 E); nature of, Tim. 59; not used in ancient Attica, Crit. 112 C; unknown to primitive society, Laws 3. 679 B; not to be possessed in the Model City, *ib.* 5. 742 A, 743 D, 746 A; not to be offered to the gods, *ib.* 12. 955 E:—refining of gold, Statesm. 303 D.

Golden age, Statesm. 271, 272; Laws 4. 713 (cp. Cronos):—the golden race, Crat. 398 A.

Good, the saving element, Rep. 10. 609:—the good = the beautiful, Lysis 216; Symp. 201 B, 204 E foll.; Rep. 5. 452 (cp. Euthyd. 301 A; Crat. 439; Phaedo 100); how far identical with the expedient, Protag. 333 E foll. (cp. Theaet. 177 D); hard to know, Crat. 384 B; confers happiness on the possessor, Symp. 204 E; the object of desire in love, *ib.* 206; the end of action, Gorg.

468, 499; the cause of the good, *ib.* 497 E; Phil. 22; the good and pleasure, Gorg. 497; Rep. 6. 505, 509 A; Phil. 11, 22 E, 60 A (cp. Protag. 358); the good superior to essence, Rep. 6. 509; the brightest and best of being, *ib.* 7. 518 E; neither wisdom nor pleasure, Phil. 20 B foll., 60 (cp. Rep. 6. 505 B); universally desired, Phil. 20 D; sufficient, *ib.* 20, 60; needs no addition, *ib.* 21; in the mixed life, *ib.* 61, 65; mixture of, *ib.* 62 foll., 64; measure an ingredient in, *ib.* 64; the cause of, is in mind only, *ib.* 65 foll.:—absolute good, Rep. 6. 507 B; 7. 540 A:—the idea of good, *ib.* 6. 505, 508; 7. 517, 534; is the highest knowledge, *ib.* 6. 505; 7. 526 E; nature of, *ib.* 6. 505, 506:—the 'child of the good,' *ib.* 506 E:—good in relation to pleasure, Protag. 354, 356; Phil. 11, 20 foll., 55, 60, 63 foll.; Laws 2. 662, 663, 667; '*corruptio optimi pessima*,' Euthyd. 281; good and honourable, Gorg. 474; Laws 12. 966 A; 1 Alcib. 116; good and order, Gorg. 504; meaning of 'good' as applied to law, Theaet. 177 D; good and false, Hipp. Min. 367:—good and evil alike originate in the soul, Charm. 156 E; explained by the hypothesis of a twofold nature of the soul, Laws 10. 896 E (*v. s. v.* Soul):—good fortune = wisdom, Euthyd. 279:—good things least liable to change, Rep. 2. 381; doing good things a work of human agency, Eryx. 398:—Goods classified, Protag. 334; Gorg. 451 E; Rep. 2. 357, 367 D; Phil. 66; Laws 1. 631; 2. 661 A; 3. 697 (cp. Laws 9. 870 A); enumerated, Euthyd. 279; Meno 78; remedial goods, Protag. 354 A; goods an object of desire to all, Euthyd. 279; use of, depends on knowledge, *ib.* 287; Meno 88; goods of the soul, Meno 88; the goods of life often a temptation, Rep. 6. 491 E, 495 A (cp. Laws 5. 729 A); goods not to be over-estimated, Crit. 120; wrongly judged by the many, Laws 2. 661 A; 5. 742 E; an evil to the evil, *ib.* 2. 661 (cp. Eryx. 396 E foll.).

Good man, the, no evil can happen to, Apol. 30 D, 41 (cp. Rep. 3. 387 C); like the good artist, has a view to the best, Gorg. 503 E; will disdain to imitate ignoble actions, Rep. 3. 396:—Good men are like and friends to one another, Lysis 214 C (cp. Phaedr. 255 A); self-sufficient, Lysis 215 A; Rep. 3. 387 (cp. Menex. 247 E); not good by nature, Meno 89; hated by the world, Apol. 28 A; enjoy happiness in the life to come, *ib.* 41; Phaedo 63, 107, 114; Gorg. 526 C, 527 D; why they take office, Rep. 1. 347; = the wise, *ib.* 350; 1 Alcib. 124, 125; unfortunate (Adeimantus), Rep. 2. 364; will not give way to sorrow, *ib.* 3. 387; 10. 603 E (cp.

Laws 5. 732 B; 7. 792 B, 800 D; Menex. 247 D); appear simple from their inexperience of evil, Rep. 3. 409 A; hate the tyrant, *ib.* 8. 568 A; able to rule themselves, Laws 1. 626, 627, 644 B; the friends of God, and like Him, *ib.* 4. 716 D (cp. Symp. 212 A; Rep. 2. 383 C; 10. 613 A; Theaet. 176 B; Phil. 30 E); ought to impart their virtue, Laws 5. 730 E; ought to be both gentle and passionate, *ib.* 731 D (cp. Rep. 3. 410); will prefer exile to an unjust form of government, Laws 6. 770 E; are the enemies of the evil, *ib.* 10. 908 B; are found even in ill-ordered states, *ib.* 12. 951 B (cp. Phaedo 78 A); best able to tell a falsehood, Hipp. Min. 367 foll.:—sons of good men not good, Laches 179, 180; Protag. 320, 324, 325; Meno 93 (cp. Laws 3. 694 D; 1 Alcib. 118 E).

Goods, community of, Rep. 3. 416; 5. 464; 8. 543 A; Laws 5. 739; 7. 807 B; in ancient Attica, Crit. 110 D; in the days of Cronos, Statesm. 272 A. Cp. Community.

Gorgias, a great master of rhetoric, Phaedr. 261 C; Symp. 198 C; well aware that probability is superior to truth, Phaedr. 267 A; his influence at Larisa, Meno 70; his style of answer, *ibid.* (cp. 76 C); his influence on Meno, *ib.* 71 E; his definition of virtue, *ib.* 73 D; does not profess to teach virtue, *ib.* 95 C; has failed to educate Meno, *ib.* 96 E; goes the round of the cities, Apol. 19 E; the guest of Callicles, Gorg. 447 B; converses with Socrates, *ib.* 449 A-461 A; accustomed to go with his brother Herodicus to persuade patients to take medicine, *ib.* 456 B; his deference to opinion, *ib.* 482 D, 487 A, 494 D; used to maintain that the art of persuasion was superior to every other art, Phil. 58 B foll. Cp. Rhetoric.

Gorgons, Phaedr. 229 E.

Gortys, in Crete, colonized from Gortys in Peloponnesus, Laws 4. 708 A.

Gout, 2 Alcib. 139 E, 140 A.

Government, the art of, slowly grew up among mankind, Protag. 322 B; a science, Statesm. 292, 293; good government possible without laws, *ib.* 294; science of government attained by few, *ib.* 292, 300; government without knowledge, a source of misery, *ib.* 301 E; origin of government, Laws 3. 676 foll.

Government, forms of, should they be administered in the interest of the rulers? Rep. 1. 338 D, 343, 346 (cp. Statesm. 295 E); have undergone many changes in the course of ages, Laws 3. 676 B (cp. 6. 782 A); no form can be destroyed except by the fault of the rulers, *ib.* 3. 683 C;—the patriarchal form the oldest of all, *ib.* 680;

gradual development of the earlier forms, *ib.* 680, 681;—the two mother forms, democracy and monarchy, *ib.* 693 C;—the five [or four] imperfect forms, Rep. 4. 445 B; 8. 544; Statesm. 291 foll., 301 foll. (cp. Laws 4. 712 B, C); arise from unwillingness to accept the rule of the one best man, Statesm. 301 D; their order in capacity for improvement, Laws 4. 711;—succession of changes in states, Rep. 8. 545 foll.;—present forms of government in an evil condition, *ib.* 6. 492 E, 496; none of them adapted to philosophy, *ib.* 497; are 'states of discord,' Laws 8. 832 C; all depend upon a principle of justice, *ib.* 12. 945 D (cp. Rep. 1. 338 E); based on the supremacy of certain classes, Laws 12. 962 E (cp. 4. 714): — peculiar barbarian forms, Rep. 8. 544 D;—the Persian Government in the days of Cyrus, Laws 3. 694 foll.;—the ancient Athenian constitution, *ib.* 698 foll. (cp. Menex. 238 C);—the elements of all forms combined in the Lacedaemonian and Cretan governments, Laws 4. 712:—the first, second, and third forms of the ideal state, *ib.* 5. 739; 7. 807 B. Cp. Constitution, Model City, State.

Government, forms of. [*The three dialogues of Plato which more especially deal with political science,—the Republic, the Statesman, and the Laws,—all contain discussions of the different forms of government and the manner in which they should be classified; and in each of them somewhat different conclusions are reached.—In the Republic the series commences with the perfect state which may be either monarchy or aristocracy, accordingly as 'the one best man' bears rule or many who are all 'perfect in virtue'* [cp. Arist. Pol. iv. 2, § 1]. *The further succession is then somewhat fancifully connected with the divisions of the soul. The rule of reason* [i.e. the perfect state] *passes into timocracy, in which the 'spirited element' is predominant; timocracy into three governments in turn, which represent the 'appetitive principle,'—first oligarchy, in which the desire of wealth is supreme; secondly, democracy, characterized by an unbounded lust for freedom; thirdly, tyranny, in which all evil desires grow unchecked, and the tyrant becomes 'the waking reality of what he once was in his dreams only.' Each of these inferior forms is illustrated in the individual who corresponds to the state and is 'set over against it.'—In the Statesman, after the government of the one or many good has been separated, the remaining forms are classified accordingly as the government has or has not regard to law, and democracy is said to be 'the worst of lawful*

Heracleitus, his thesis that 'all things are in a flux,' Crat. 401 D, 402 A, B, 411, 440 (cp. 437 foll.; Symp. 207 D; Theaet. 160 D, 177 C, 179 D, 182, 183; Phil. 43 A); his reconciliation of opposites, Symp. 187 A; the 'sun of Heracleitus,' Rep. 6. 498 A; his sect, Theaet. 179 D foll.:—Heraclitean philosophy, in regard to names, Crat. 411 B foll., 416 B, 437 A, B, 440 A foll.; applied to sensation and perception, Theaet. 152 E, 156 A foll., 160 D, 181 D foll.

Heracles, connected with the family of Lysis, Lysis 205 C; could not fight against the Hydra, Euthyd. 297 C; his brother and nephew, *ib.* D, E; 'Bravo! Heracles,' *ib.* 303 A; Prodicus on his virtues, Symp. 177 B; 'not a match for two,' Phaedo 89 C; Heracles and Geryon, Gorg. 484 B; genealogies traced to Heracles, Theaet. 175 A; sons of, Laws 3. 685 D; ancestor of the kings of Lacedaemon, 1 Alcib. 120 E:—a Heracles of argument, Theaet. 169 B.

Heracles, columns of, Phaedo 109 B; Tim. 24 E, 25 B; Crit. 108 E, 114 B.

Heralds, Statesm. 260 D, 290 B; Laws 1. 626 A; 11. 928 D; laws concerning, Laws 12. 941.

Herds divided, Statesm. 264, 265; art of managing herds, *ib.* 261 foll., 275 D foll.

Herè, meaning of the name (ἐρατή τις), Crat. 404 B, C; followers of, seek a royal love, Phaedr. 253 B; bound by Hephaestus, Rep. 2. 378 D (cp. Euthyph. 8 B); Herè and Zeus, Rep. 2. 378 D; 3. 390 B; begged alms for the daughters of Inachus, *ib.* 2. 381 D; daughter of Cronos and Rhea, Tim. 41 A; said to have deprived Dionysus of his wits, Laws 2. 672 B; fines on celibacy, &c. to be paid to, *ib.* 6. 774 A foll.

Hereditary tendencies; sons of good men not good, Laches 179, 180; Protag. 320, 324, 325; Meno 93 (cp. Laws 3. 694 D; 1 Alcib. 118 E); reason of this, Protag. 327:—hereditary tendency to crime, Laws 9. 856 D. Cp. Good men, Great men.

Hermaea, Lysis 206 D, E, 223.

Hermes, messenger of Zeus, Protag. 322 C; meaning of the name, Crat. 408 A, 429 C; father of Pan, Crat. 408 B; Phaedr. 263 E; the star sacred to, (Mercury), Rep. 10. 617 A; Tim. 38 D; the god of heralds, Laws 12. 941 A.

Hermocrates, Tim. 20 B; his promised speech, Crit. 108 A.

Hermogenes, son of Hipponicus, a person in the dialogue *Cratylus*, Crat. 383 foll.; meaning of his name, *ib.* B, 384 C, 408 B, 429 C; with Socrates at the last, Phaedo 59 B.

Hermus, Rep. 8. 566 C.

Hero, derivation of the word, Crat. 398;—heroes ought not to lament, Rep. 3. 387, 388; 10. 603-606; to be rewarded, *ib.* 5. 468; to receive divine honours after death, *ibid.* (cp. Laws 12. 947 E);—heroes associated, in worship, with gods and demigods, Rep. 4. 427 B; Laws 4. 717 A; 5. 727 A, 738 D; 7. 801 E; 9. 853 C; 10. 910 A.

Heroic rhythm, Rep. 3. 400 C; heroic verses, Laws 12. 958 E.

Herodicus, brother of Gorgias, a physician, Gorg. 448 B, 456 A.

Herodicus of Selymbria, a first-rate sophist, Protag. 316 E; recommends the walk to Megara and back, Phaedr. 227 D; the inventor of valetudinarianism, Rep. 3. 406 A foll.

Hesiod, a sophist, Protag. 316 D; his works recited by rhapsodes, Ion 531 A, B; Laws 2. 658 D; pleasure of conversing with, in the world below, Apol. 41 A; his genealogy of the Gods, Ion 531 C; Crat. 396 C; Tim. 40 E; his use of the word 'demons,' Crat. 397 E; his children (poems), Symp. 209 D; his rewards of justice, Rep. 2. 363 B; 10. 612 A; his stories improper for youth, *ib.* 2. 377 D, E, 378 A (cp. Euthyph. 6 A; Symp. 195 C); his classification of the races, Rep. 8. 547 A; a wandering rhapsode, *ib.* 10. 600 D; his fame, Tim. 21 C; Hesiod and Epimenides, Laws 3. 677 E. Quoted:—

Theogony.

l. 116, foll., Symp. 178 B.
l. 154, 459, Rep. 2. 377 E.
l. 195, Crat. 406 C.
l. 203, *ib.* 398 A.
l. 780, Theaet. 155 D.

Works and Days.

l. 25, Lysis 215 C.
l. 40, Rep. 5. 466 B; Laws 3. 690 E.
l. 41, Laws 3. 677 E.
l. 109, Rep. 8. 546 E.
l. 120 foll., Crat. 398 A; Rep. 5. 468 E.
l. 233, Rep. 2. 363 B.
l. 256 foll., Laws 12. 943 E.
l. 264, Protag. 340 C; Rep. 2. 364 D; Laws 4. 718 E.
l. 305 foll., Laws 10. 901 A.
l. 309, Charm. 163 B.
l. 359, Crat. 428 A.
l. 454, Theaet. 207 A.

Frag. 117, Rep. 3. 390 E; *incert.* Crat. 402 B.

Hestia, meaning of the name, Crat. 401 D; remains at home while the other gods go in procession, Phaedr. 247 A;—a temple dedicated to, [in the Model City], Laws 5. 745 B; to have temples everywhere, *ib.* 8. 848 D; evidence in trials with the seals of the

Idea. [*The Idea of Good is an abstraction, which, under that name at least, does not occur in any other of Plato's writings except the Republic. But it is probably not essentially different from another abstraction, 'the true being of things,' which is mentioned in many of his dialogues. He has nowhere given an explanation of his meaning, not because he was 'regardless whether we understood him or not,' but, rather, perhaps, because he was himself unable to state in precise terms the ideal which floated before his mind. He belonged to an age in which men felt too strongly the first pleasure of metaphysical speculation to be able to estimate the true value of the ideas which they conceived (cp. his own picture of the effect of dialectic on the youthful intellect,* Rep. 7. 539). *To him, as to the Schoolmen of the Middle Ages, an abstraction seemed truer than a fact: he was impatient to shake off the shackles of sense and rise into the purer atmosphere of ideas. Yet in the allegory of the cave (Republic vii), whose inhabitants must go up to the light of perfect knowledge, but descend again into the obscurity of opinion, he has shown that he was not unaware of the necessity of finding a firm starting-point for these flights of metaphysical imagination (cp.* Rep. 6. 510). *A passage in the Philebus (65 A) will give the best insight into his meaning: 'If we are not able to hunt the good with one idea only, with three we may take our prey,—Beauty, Symmetry, Truth.' The three were inseparable to the Greek mind, and no conception of perfection could be formed in which they did not unite.*

Ideas. [*No part of Plato's philosophy has been more commonly associated with his name than 'the doctrine of ideas.' But his meaning has been often misunderstood, or he*

has been supposed to be formulating a system when he is only 'guessing at truth.' His opinions did not always remain the same, and in his later works the ideas are not so prominent as in the Phaedo or Phaedrus. He is his own best critic in the Parmenides and the Sophist, and has there shown how fully he appreciates the difficulties of the argument.— The ideas are one phase of a conception which he has expressed in many forms in his various writings:—That there is a truth which is beyond sense, and which is perceived by the mind alone when freed from the 'disturbing element' of the body (Phaedo 65; Tim. 51; and cp. Theaet. 185 foll.). In this spirit the subjects of the higher education are discussed in the Republic (Book vii), and the sciences are declared to be valuable only in proportion as they enable us to attain true being. The ideas may be gained by association, which Plato calls 'the reminiscence of knowledge acquired in a previous state,' when we beheld them 'shining in brightness' (Phaedr. 250), and makes a proof of immortality (Phaedo 73, 76): or they may be reached by the 'gracious aid' of dialectic, which uses the objects of sense as steps by which we are able to mount to the sphere of the absolute (Symp. 211, and cp. Rep. 5. 476; 6. 510). They are unchangeable and invisible, and therefore akin to the divine elements in us, that is, the soul (Phaedo 78 E). By participation in them things are what they are: the beautiful is beautiful because it shares in the idea of beauty, that which is just is just because it partakes of the nature of justice (Phaedo 100-105; Parm. 130). Nor could names ever have been found for things, unless the legislator, who was the original name giver, had been acquainted with the ideas which they represent (Crat. 389). Again, the ideas afford an argument against the Heraclitean doctrine of flux: for that which is absolute and true cannot change, but must always abide and exist (ib. 439, 440). The ideas are the work of God, and the artist only imitates them at second- or even third-hand: for there cannot be two or more ideas of the same thing (Rep. 10. 596 foll.; Tim. 28). The Creator when the worlds were made had such a single, perfect idea of the universe, in accordance with which He contrived all His work (Tim. 31). They are almost unintelligible to human apprehension, unless they are expressed by examples, or translated into the language of facts (Statesm. 277).—In the Philebus Plato begins to discuss the 'troublesome questions' which are raised by the doctrine of ideas. How can the one be predicated of the many? Have the ideas real existence? His

J.

Justice. [*The happiness which is conferred by justice is one of the main theses of the Gorgias. The young Sophist, Polus, and Callicles, the man of the world, agree in thinking that the unjust is happy so long as he is able to escape punishment. But Socrates maintains a higher view, which he sets forth under a paradoxical form. The wicked man is unhappy because he is wicked, and still more unhappy when he is not punished for his evil deeds. On the other hand the just and innocent are happy even on earth and amidst the greatest sufferings; and in the world to come all the advantages are on their side. The argument is confirmed in Plato's fashion by a myth. Once upon a time the judgment of souls took place upon the day of death while both the judges and the judged were alive. The result was unsatisfactory: the veil of the body hid the soul from the glance of the judge, who was himself hindered by a like impediment. In order to remedy this evil Zeus made his sons judges in the world below, and the souls were tried after death. There was no more escape for the wicked: the judges beheld his soul stained and corrupted by lust and wickedness and pronounced the fitting penalty.— The argument of the Gorgias is in a manner resumed and completed in the Republic. In the first Book several definitions of justice are attempted, all of which fall before the dialectic of Socrates. Glaucon and Adeimantus then intervene:—mankind regard justice as a necessity, not as a good in itself, or at best as only to be practised because of the temporal benefits which flow from it: can Socrates prove that it belongs to a higher class of goods? Socrates in reply proposes to construct an ideal state in which justice will be more easily recognized than in the individual. Justice is thus discovered to be the essential virtue of the state (a thesis afterwards enlarged upon by Aristotle [Pol. i. 2. 16; iii. 13, § 3]), the bond of the social organization, and, like temperance in the Laws (3. 696, 697; 4. 709 E), rather the accompaniment or condition of the virtues than a virtue in itself. Expressed in an outward or political form it becomes the great principle which has been already enunciated (Rep. 1. 332), 'that every man shall do his own work'; on this Plato bases the necessity of the division into classes which underlies the whole fabric of the ideal state (Rep. 4. 433 foll.; Tim. 17 C). Thus we are led to acknowledge the happiness of the just; for he alone reflects in himself this vital principle of the state (Rep. 4. 445). The final proof is supplied by a comparison of the perfect state with actual forms of government. These, like the individuals who correspond to them, become more and more miserable as they recede further from the ideal, and the climax is reached (Rep. 9. 587) when the tyrant is shown by the aid of arithmetic to have '729 times less pleasure than the king' [i.e. the perfectly just ruler]. Lastly, the happiness of the just is proved to extend also into the next world, where men appear before the judgment-seat of heaven and receive the due reward of their deeds in this life.—In the Laws, no less than in the Republic, justice is assigned a high place among the virtues. Every constitution, however imperfect, must share in justice to some degree; for no association, even of the bad, can be formed unless regard is had to justice (cp. Lysis 214). It is the virtue which makes men civilized, and fits them to dwell together in the state. But injustice is the disease of cities and governments, corre-*

sponding to sickness in the bodily frame. Again, the just man shows his justice especially in his dealings with slaves and inferiors, whom he endeavours to train in virtue (cp. Arist. Pol. i. 13, § 14]. He alone enjoys true happiness; for to him the good and the pleasant are one and the same. He has God always as his friend and guide, whereas the unjust passes through life in wild confusion and soon comes to the end of his seeming prosperity.]

Justice, courts of: see Law Courts.

K.

Kindred, honour of, Laws 5. 729;—marriages of kindred, ib. 11. 924 E.

King, the, pleasures of, compared with those of the tyrant, Rep. 9. 587 foll.; art of, Statesm. 260, 276, 289, 290, 291, 292, 293, 295 B, 300 E, 305 A, 308, 311 (cp. Protag. 321, 322);—king and statesman, Statesm. 259;—king and shepherd, ib. 261, 276 (cp. Theaet. 174 D; Laws 5. 735);—king and tyrant, Statesm. 301, 302:—Kings and philosophers, Rep. 5. 473 (cp. 6. 487 E, 498 foll., 501 E foll.; 7. 540; 8. 543; 9. 592);—ignorance common among kings, Laws 3. 691;—kings of ancient Attica, Menex. 238 C; of Egypt, always priests, Statesm. 290 E; of Persia, Laws 3. 694; 1 Alcib. 121, 122; of Sparta, Laws 3. 691, 696 A; 1 Alcib. 121; of Thrace, Charm. 156 C.

King, the Great, Lysis 209 C; Euthyd. 274 A; Meno 78 D; Gorg. 470 E; Rep. 8. 553 D; Soph. 230 E; Statesm. 264 C; 1 Alcib. 120.

King Archon; see Archon.

Kingship, in primitive society, Laws 3. 681.

Kinsmen, to prosecute for murder, Laws 9. 866, 868, 871, 873 E; not to be judges, ib. 879 A; duties of, towards orphans, ib. 6. 766 D; 11. 923-925; to decide whether a son may be disinherited, ib. 929.

Kisses, the reward of the brave warrior, Rep. 5. 468 C.

Knots, magical, Laws 11. 933 B, D.

Knowledge (ἐπιστήμη, γιγνώσκειν); 'know thyself' at Delphi, Charm. 164 D foll.; Protag. 343 B; Phaedr. 229 E; Phil. 48 C; Laws 11. 923 A; 1 Alcib. 124 A, 129 A, 132 C; knowledge of self, not = knowing what you know and what you do not know, Charm. 169; the proper study of mankind, Phaedr. 230 A:—knowing and not knowing, Theaet. 197; knowing and possessing knowledge, ibid.; knowing and being known, Soph. 248 E; knowing and communicating knowledge, 1 Alcib. 118:—knowledge=knowledge of ideas, Rep. 6. 484; = the sciences, Theaet, 146; = percep-

make the citizens equally brave against pleasure and pain, *ib.* 634; not allowed to be criticized by the young, *ib.* D; laws concerning paederastia, Symp. 182 A; Laws 8. 836 B:—the double monarchy intended to be a check on the state, Laws 3. 691 E; the most ancient of monarchies, *ib.* 4. 712 E; the kings descended from Zeus, 1 Alcib. 120 E foll.; their wives, *ib.* 121 B; compared to the Persian kings, *ibid.;* their wealth, *ibid.*, 122 D foll.:—the Gerousia, Laws 3. 691 E:—the Ephors, *ib.* 692 A; 4. 712 D; watch over the queens, 1 Alcib. 121 C:— Crypteia, Laws 1. 633 B:—Games in honour of the Dioscori, *ib.* 7. 796 B:—Gymnasia; Lacedaemonians first after the Cretans to strip in, Rep. 5. 452 D (cp. Theaet. 162 B, 169 B); moral effect of, Laws 1. 636 B. foll.; virgins take part in gymnastic exercises, *ib.* 7. 806 A; spectators bidden to take part or go, Theaet. 162 B, 169 B:—syssitia, Laws 1. 633 A; 6. 780 C foll.; 8. 842 B:— training, *ib.* 1. 633 foll.:—Lacedaemonians at Plataea, Laches 191 C; came to Marathon a day too late, Laws 3. 698 E; Menex. 240 C; at Tanagra, 1 Alcib. 112 C; Menex. 242 A; at Coronea, 1 Alcib. 112 C; obliged to surrender to the Athenians at Sphagia, Menex. 242 C; driven by the Athenians from the sea, *ib.* 246 A; their conquest and division of Arcadia, Symp. 193 A;—take the greatest interest in war of all Hellenes, Laches 183 A; fond of the poems of Tyrtaeus, Laws 1. 629; consider hunting a training for war, *ib.* 633 B; their endurance of pain, *ibid.;* 1 Alcib. 122 D; restraint laid upon, Laws 1. 635 B, 636 E; absence of intoxication among, *ib.* 637 A foll.; licence of women among, *ib.* B; 6. 781 foll.; superior to all other men in war, *ib.* 1. 638 A; conservative in music, *ib.* 2. 660 B; their education that of a camp, *ib.* 666 E; better at gymnastic than music, *ib.* 673 C; well acquainted with Homer, *ib.* 3. 680 D; have preserved the ancient institutions of the Heracleidae, *ib.* 685 A; constantly at war with the sister states, *ib.* 686 B; defenders of Hellas, *ib.* 692 D; equality of society among, *ib.* 696 A; their treatment of the Helots, *ib.* 6. 776 C; think that a brave city has no need of walls, *ib.* 778 D; mode of life among their women, *ib.* 7. 806 D; their temperance and discipline, 1 Alcib. 122 D; their ambitious character, *ibid.* (cp. Rep. 8. 545 A, 548 C); use pieces of iron instead of coined money, Eryx. 400 A:— the prayer of the Lacedaemonians, 2 Alcib. 148; offer blemished animals to the Gods, *ib.* 149 A.

Laches, a person in the dialogue *Laches*, Laches 180 A foll.; a public man, *ib.* 180 B, 187 A; was with Socrates at Delium, *ib.* 181 B (cp. 188 E; Symp. 221 A); his view of fighting in armour, Laches 182 D foll.; his wealth, *ib.* 186 C; his feeling about an argument, *ib.* 188 C foll.; discusses courage with Socrates and Nicias, *ib.* 190 B foll.

Lachesis, eldest of the fates, Laws 12. 960 C; turns the spindle of Necessity together with Clotho and Atropos, Rep. 10. 617 C; daughter of Necessity, her speech, *ib.* D; apportions a genius to each soul, *ib.* 620 D.

Laconizers, 'who go about with their ears bruised,' Protag. 342 B; Gorg. 515 E.

Laius, Laws 8. 836 D.

Lamachus, the Athenian general, Laches 197 C.

Lamentation, to be checked, Rep. 3. 387; 10. 603 E (cp. Laws 7. 792 B; 12. 949 B);—at sacrifices, Laws 7. 800;—over the dead, Rep. 3. 387 D; Laws 12. 959 E:—Lamentations (Θρῆνοι), a division of music, Laws 3. 700 A.

Lampido, mother, daughter, and wife of a king, 1 Alcib. 124 A.

Lamprus, a musician, Menex. 236 A.

Lampsacus, Metrodorus of, Ion 530 D.

Land, division of, proclaimed by the would-be tyrant, Rep. 8. 565 E, 566 D; difficulty of legislating about, Laws 3. 684; 5. 736 D;—(in the Model City), distribution of, *ib.* 5. 737-740, 745; not to be sold or bought, *ib.* 741. Cp. Model City.

Landmarks, not to be moved, Laws 8. 843 A.

Language, invention of, Protag. 322 A; analysis of, Crat. 421, 422; of the deaf and dumb, *ib.* 422 E; origin of, *ib.* 425, 426; scientific construction of, *ib.* 425; ancient framers of, *ibid.;* complete analysis of, impossible, *ibid.;* greatness of, *ib.* 427 E; pliability or plastic power of, Rep. 9. 588 D (cp. Statesm. 277 B; Laws 4. 712 B; 5. 746 A); proper use of, Theaet. 165 A, 168 B, 184 C, 196 E; analysis of, Soph. 261 foll.;—distinctions of language, Laws 12. 944 B; invented by Prodicus, Charm. 163 D; Laches 197 D; Protag. 337 A, 340 A, 358 A, D; Euthyd. 277 E; Meno 75 E;— languages altered by time, Crat. 418, 421: —'the long and difficult language of facts,' Statesm. 278 D.

Larisa, Meno 97 A:—Larisaeans given to philosophy, *ib.* 70 B.

Laughter, not to be allowed in the guardians, Rep. 3. 388 E (cp. Laws 5. 732 B; 11. 935 B); nor represented in the Gods, Rep. 3. 389 A.

Laurel, wreath of, to be worn by the censors of magistrates, Laws 12. 947 A.

Lavation, ceremonies of, Laws 9. 871 B.

E; a god to the animals, Statesm. 271 E; has two counsellors, pleasure and pain, Laws 1. 644 C; the puppet and plaything of the Gods, *ib.* E; 7. 803; the only animal who has attained to a perception of order, *ib.* 2. 653, 664 E; must obey and follow God, *ib.* 4. 716 A; a partaker of immortality and coeval with time, *ib.* 721 C (cp. Symp. 208 E); must honour his own soul next to the Gods, Laws 5. 727 A; without education the most savage of creatures, *ib.* 6. 766 A (cp. 11. 935 A); has a divinity dwelling within him, which preserves all things, *ib.* 6. 775 E; a troublesome piece of goods, *ib.* 777 C; more inclined to weep than any other animal, *ib.* 791 E; said to be the most cowardly of animals, *ib.* 7. 814 B; 'every man his own best friend,' *ib.* 9. 873 B; man without law would be worse than the beasts, *ib.* 875 A (cp. Protag. 322 D); the most religious of animals, Laws 10. 902 (cp. Tim. 41 E; Menex. 237 E); created for the sake of the world, Laws 10. 903:—the best man a law to himself, *ib.* 9. 875 C; the one best man, Crito 47; Gorg. 490 A; Rep. 6. 502; Statesm. 301; Laws 2. 659 A:—Men always look at their neighbours and not at themselves, Laches 200 A; have a mutual interest in each other's virtue, Protag. 327 B; ignorant about the Gods, Crat. 400 E, 425 C (cp. Rep. 2. 365 E; Crit. 107; Parm. 134 E); better teachers than nature, Phaedr. 230 E; are not generally very good or very bad, Phaedo 90 A (cp. Crat. 386); have a community of feeling, Gorg. 481 D; are not just of their own will, Rep. 2. 366 C; unite in the state in order to supply each other's wants, *ib.* 369; cannot follow two occupations, *ib.* 370; Laws 8. 846 D; are always full of hope, Phil. 39 E; ever at war with one another, Laws 1. 625 E; have in themselves a conflict of good and evil, *ib.* 626 E; are slow to believe the truth, *ib.* 2. 663 E; desire to have their wishes fulfilled, whether wise or foolish, *ib.* 3. 687 (cp. 2 Alcib. 138, 141 foll.); cannot be entrusted with arbitrary power, Laws 3. 691; 4. 713 D; have no particular desire for virtue, *ib.* 4. 718 E; always think others to blame and not themselves, *ib.* 5. 727 B (cp. Rep. 10. 619 C; 2 Alcib. 142 E); must neither joy nor sorrow overmuch, Laws 5. 732 C; are not voluntarily intemperate, *ib.* 734 B; not willing to receive laws at their first imposition, *ib.* 6. 752; will commit any meanness in order to gain wealth, *ib.* 8. 831 D; do evil involuntarily, *ib.* 9. 860 D (cp. Evil); the kindred of the Gods, *ib.* 10. 899 E; saved by virtue, *ib.* 906 B; unbounded in their desires, *ib.* 11. 918 D; are all a little out of their minds, *ib.* 929 D.

Man-haters, chorus of, in Pherecrates' play, Protag. 327 D.

Man-hunting, Soph. 222 C (cp. Laws 7. 823 B).

Man-slaughter, Laws 9. 864-874. (Cp. Homicide.)

Management, voluntary and compulsory, Statesm. 276.

Manners, attended to in schools, Protag. 325 E; influenced by education, Rep. 4. 424, 425; cannot be made the subject of legislation, *ib.* 425 B; freedom of, in democracies, *ib.* 8. 563 A; never to be changed, Laws 7. 797, 798.

Μαντική (μανική), Phaedr. 244 C.

Mantinea, Diotima of, Symp. 201.

Many, the, their opinion not to be regarded, Laches 184; Protag. 353 A; Crito 44, 47, 48 (cp. Phaedr. 260 A); cannot make a man wise or foolish, Crito 44; their morality, *ib.* 49 C; opinion of = opinion of the stronger, Gorg. 488; flatter their leaders into thinking themselves statesmen, Rep. 4. 426; would lose their harsh feeling toward philosophy if they could see the true philosopher, *ib.* 6. 500; their pleasures and pains, *ib.* 9. 586; suppose that the object of music is pleasure, Tim. 47 E; Laws 2. 655, 658 E, 700 E; their mode of argument, Theaet. 168 B; used to be the judges in the theatre, Laws 2. 659 B; form a wrong estimate of goods, *ib.* 661 A; 5. 742 E (cp. Rep. 6. 493 E; Phil. 67; Laws 4. 707 D); ignorant about music, Laws 2. 670 B; 3. 700 E; in old days were the servants of the laws, *ib.* 3. 700 A; wrong in their notions about the honourable and the just, *ib.* 9. 859, 860; think adulteration justifiable, *ib.* 11. 916 E; good judges of virtue though not virtuous themselves, *ib.* 12. 950 B; wrongly suppose that astronomy leads to atheism, *ib.* 967 A; as teachers, 1 Alcib. 110, 111;—'the great beast,' Rep. 6. 493. Cp. Multitude.

Many, the, as applied to the beautiful, the good, etc., Rep. 6. 507; Zeno's argument concerning the many, Parm. 127; the many can coexist with the one, *ib.* 129; the many and the one, Phil. 14-16; Soph. 251. *See* One.

Marathon, Miltiades the hero of, Gorg. 516 D; battle of, Laws 3. 699 A; 4. 707 C; Menex. 240 C-241 B; 'the Lacedaemonians a day too late for,' Laws 3. 698 E; Menex. 240 D; trophies of, Menex. 245 A.

Margites, [the Pseudo-Homeric poem], 2 Alcib. 147.

Mariandynians, Laws 6. 776 D.

Marionette players, Rep. 7. 514 B; Soph. 224 A.

Melesias, son of Thucydides, a person in the *Laches*, Laches 178 A foll.; lives with Lysimachus, *ib.* 179 B; not equal to his father, *ib.* C; Meno 94 C; joins in the conversation, Laches 184 E; one of the best wrestlers in Athens, Meno 94 C.

Meletus, of the deme of Pitthis, Euthyph. 2 B; his appearance, *ibid.;* his impeachment, *ib.* 2 A, 3 B, 5, 12 E, 15 E (cp. Apol. 19 B; Theaet. 210); defender of the poets, Apol. 23 E; questioned by Socrates, *ib.* 24-28; could not have obtained a conviction alone, *ib.* 36 A.

Melissus, the philosopher, Theaet. 180 E, 183 E.

Melita, a deme of Attica, Parm. 126 C.

Melody, in education, Rep. 3. 398 foll.; Laws 2. 654, 655, 670; its influence, Rep. 10. 601; expressive of virtue and vice, Laws 2. 654, 655;—melodies and rhythms should be accommodated to each other, *ib.* 665 A, 669, 670; 7. 802 E; should be consecrated, as in Egypt, *ib.* 7. 799:—the melodies of Marsyas and Olympus, Symp. 215 C. Cp. Rhythm.

Memoria technica, of Evenus, Phaedr. 267 A.

Memory, distinguished from reminiscence, Phaedr. 275 A; Phil. 34; injured by the invention of writing, Phaedr. 274 E; active in childhood, Tim. 26; the memory of perception, Theaet. 163, 166; nature of, *ib.* 191, 193-196; an element in pleasure, Phil. 21; unites with perception to form opinion, *ib.* 38, 39;—art of, Hipp. Min. 368 E, 369 A;—the philosopher should have a good memory, Rep. 6. 486 D, 490 E, 494 B; 7. 535 B.

Memory, the mother of the Muses, Theaet. 191 D.

Mendè, Antimoerus of, Protag. 315 A.

Mendicant prophets, Rep. 2. 364 C;—Mendicants, Laws 11. 936 C.

Menelaus and Proteus, Euthyd. 288 B; a 'faint-hearted warrior,' Symp. 174 C; treatment of, when wounded, Rep. 3. 408 A.

Menexenus, the friend of Lysis, Lysis 206 D; pugnacious, *ib.* 211 B; converses with Socrates, *ib.* 212 A foll., 216 A foll.; present at the death of Socrates, Phaedo 59 B; a person in the dialogue *Menexenus*, Menex. 234 A foll.

Meno, a person in the dialogue *Meno*, Meno 70 A, etc.; 'a fair creature,' *ib.* 76 B, 80 C; son of Alexidemus, *ib.* 76 E; beloved by Aristippus, *ib.* 70; his imperious nature, *ib.* 76 B, 86 E; the hereditary friend of the Great King, *ib.* 78 D; torpified by Socrates, *ib.* 80 A; examination of his slave by Socrates, *ib.* 82 A foll.

Menoetius, father of Patroclus, Rep. 3. 388 C; Laws 12. 944 A.

Mensuration in the arts, Phil. 55 E; twofold, *ib.* 57 A.

Mental blindness, causes of, Rep. 7. 518:—mental states, Phil. 33 D.

Mercenary soldiers, violent and unjust men, Laws 1. 630 B; the resource of the despot, *ib.* 3. 697 E (cp. Rep. 8. 566 foll.):—the guardians compared to a garrison of mercenaries, Rep. 4. 419 (cp. 8. 543).

Merchandise of the soul, Soph. 224.

Merchants, Soph. 223, 224; necessary in the state, Rep. 2. 371 (*but* cp. Laws 4. 705 A).

Messene, early history of, Laws 3. 683 D foll.; —war of, against Lacedaemon *ib.* 692 E, 698 E;—richness of, 1 Alcib. 122 D:—Messenians always in revolt, Laws 6. 777 C.

Mestor, Crit. 114 C.

Metaphysics; analysis of knowledge, Rep. 6. 510;—being and becoming, Tim. 27, 28; Theaet. 152, 157 (cp. Protag. 340: *and see* Being);—cause and effect distinguished, Euthyph. 10; Phil. 26, 27;—essence and attribute distinguished, Euthyph. 12 (*see* Essence);—existence revealed by thought, Phaedo 65;—genera and species distinguished, Euthyph. 12 (*see* Genera);—absolute ideas, Phaedo 65, 74; Rep. 5. 476; Parm. 133; knowledge of, must precede particular knowledge, Phaedo 75; unchangeable, *ib.* 78; origin of abstract ideas, Rep. 7. 523 (*see* Idea);—intuition, Phaedo 66, 79;—recollection and generalization, Phaedr. 249;—relation, difficulty of, Charm. 168; Phaedo 96, 97, 101; axioms of, Theaet. 155 (cp. Relation); relative and correlative, qualification of, Gorg. 476; Rep. 4. 437 foll.; 7. 524;—thought at its best, Phaedo 65; thought attains the idea of the absolute, *ib.* 65, 66; the conversation of the soul with herself, Soph. 264 A:—Eleatic metaphysics, Parm. 137 foll. Cp. Logic, One.

Metempsychosis, Rep. 10. 617 D foll.; Tim. 42, 91, 92. Cp. Soul.

Metics (in the Model City), rules concerning, Laws 8. 850; duration of their stay, *ibid.;* murders of, *ib.* 9. 866; metics who are murderers, *ibid.;* metics, not citizens, to be the retail traders, *ib.* 11. 920.

Metion, father of Daedalus, Ion 533 A.

Metis (Discretion), mother of Poros (Plenty), Symp. 203 B.

Metrobius, father of Connus, Euthyd. 272 C; Menex. 235 E.

Metrodorus, of Lampsacus, a famous rhapsode, Ion 530 C.

Miccus, palaestra of, Lysis 204 A, 206 E.

Mourners, Laws 7. 800 D (cp. 12. 960 A):—
hair cut in mourning, Phaedo 89.
Mouth, Tim. 75 D.
'Move not the immovable,' Laws 11. 913.
Multitude, the, the great Sophist, Rep. 6.
492; their madness, *ib*. 496 C; used to be
the judges in the theatre, Laws 2. 659 B;
obliged to keep silence in ancient Athens,
ib. 3. 700; not able to manage a state, *ib*. 6.
758 A (cp. Statesm. 292 E, 297 B). *See*
Many.
Murder, Euthyph. 4, 8; Laws 9. 869 E-874.
Cp. Homicide.
Murderers, Euthyph. 4; punishment of, in a
future existence, Laws 9. 870 E, 872 D.
Cp. Homicide.
Musaeus, a sophist, Protag. 316 D; a source
of inspiration, Ion 536 B; in the other
world, Apol. 41 A; his pictures of a future
life, Rep. 2. 363 D, E, 364 E.
Muses, invocation to the, Euthyd. 275 D;
Phaedr. 237 A; Crit. 108 C; the name (ἀπὸ
τοῦ μῶσθαι), Crat. 406 A; inspire madness
in the poet, Phaedr. 245 A, 265 B; Ion 534;
Laws 3. 682 A; 4. 719 B (cp. Apol. 22 A);
the Muses and the grasshoppers, Phaedr.
259 A; names and attributes of the Muses,
ib. D; the Muses compared to a magnet,
Ion 533 E, 536 A; their melody due to love,
Symp. 197 B; Musaeus and Orpheus,
children of the Muses, Rep. 2. 364 E; use of
the Muses, Tim. 47 E; Laws 2. 670 A; the
Muses, the daughters of Memory, Theaet.
191 D; partners in our revels, Laws 2. 653
D, 665 A, 672 C; give education, *ib*. 654 A;
source of the sense of harmony, *ib*. 672 D
(cp. Tim. 47 E); aid men to control their
desires, Laws 6. 783 A; their gifts, *ib*. 7. 796
E; patronesses of art, 1 Alcib. 108 C;—
'the hymeneal Muses,' Laws 6. 775 B.
Music, Socrates recommended in a dream to
compose, Phaedo 60 E;—music an art of
imitation, Crat. 423; Laws 2. 655, 668; 7.
798 E, 812 C (cp. Rep. 3. 397; Laws 10. 889
D); music and love, Symp. 187, 197 A; the
end of music the love of beauty, Rep. 3. 403
C; the simpler kinds of, foster temperance
in the soul, *ib*. 404 E, 410 A (cp. Laws 7.
802 E); effect of excessive, Rep. 3. 410,
411; license in, leads to anarchy in the
state, *ib*. 4. 424 E; Laws 3. 701 B (cp. Laws
7. 798 E); not intended to give pleasure,
Tim. 47 E; Laws 2. 655 D, 668 A; 3. 700 E
(*but* cp. Laws 2. 658 E; 7. 802 D); corre-
spondence of strings and notes in, Theaet.
206 B (cp. Laws 7. 812); music and predication, Soph. 253 B; sounds and tones in,
ibid.; Phil. 17; empirical, Phil. 56, 62 C;
origin of, Laws 2. 653, 654, 672 (cp. Tim. 47
E); figures and gestures in, Laws 2. 655;

'colours' in, *ibid.*; right and wrong use of,
ib. 655, 656; importance and difficulty of
forming a correct judgment about, *ib*. 669;
music corrupted by the poets, *ibid.*; 3. 700;
the three kinds of music, *ib*. 3. 700 A; the
excellence of music, 1 Alcib. 108 D:—
Music in education, Protag. 326 B; Crito
50 D; Rep. 2. 398 foll.; 7. 522 A; Laws 2.
654, 660 (cp. Poetry, Poets); includes
literature (λόγοι): Rep. 2. 376 E; to be
taught before gymnastic, *ibid.* (cp. 3. 403
B); like gymnastic, should be studied
throughout life, *ib*. 3. 403 C; ancient forms
of, not to be altered, *ib*. 4. 424; Laws 2.
657; 7. 799, 801 (cp. Laws 7. 816 C); must
be taught to women, Rep. 5. 452 (cp. Laws
7. 804 D); designed to give a wholesome
discipline in a pleasant form, Laws 2. 659
D; the severe and the vulgar sort, *ib*. 7. 802
(cp. Rep. 3. 397); time to be spent in
learning, Laws 7. 810, 812; complex kinds
of, to be rejected, *ib*. 812 D (cp. Rep. 3.
397);—ministers or directors of music,
Laws 6. 764 C; 7. 801 D, 813 A; 12. 949 A;
—solo singing, *ib*. 6. 764 E; choruses,
ibid.;— laws (or types) of music, *ib*. 7. 800;
—songs for men and women, *ib*. 802;—
music in ancient Athens not judged by the
people, *ib*. 3. 700; strictly regulated in
Crete and at Lacedaemon, *ib*. 2. 660; unchangeable in Egypt, *ib*. 657; 7. 799 A.
Music. [*Music to the ancients had a far
wider significance than it has to us. It was opposed to gymnastic as 'mental' to 'bodily'
training, and included equally reading and
writing, mathematics, harmony, poetry, and
music strictly speaking: drawing, as Aristotle tells us* (Pol. viii. 3, § 1), *was sometimes made a separate division. I. Music (in
the wider sense), Plato says, should precede
gymnastic; and, according to a remarkable
passage in the Protagoras* (325 C), *the pupils
in a Greek school were actually instructed in
reading and writing, made to learn poetry by
heart, and taught to play on the lyre before
they went to the gymnasium. In the Republic
Plato does not enter into the details of elementary education, but confines himself to
the discussion of general principles. He is
more explicit in the Laws. The children will
begin to attend school at the age of ten, and
will spend three years in learning to read and
write* (Laws 7. 810 foll.; *and see s. v.* Education). *This seems to us a short time for the
purpose; but Plato expressly says that only a
moderate standard of proficiency will be required. He also wishes the children to commit to memory compositions in prose and
verse; but they are to learn nothing which has
not received the sanction of the Director of*

Patriarchal government, Laws 3. 680, 681.

Patriotism, Crito 51; Menex. 246, 247.

Patrocles, 'the statuary,' half-brother of Socrates, Euthyd. 297 D, E.

Patroclus, Apol. 28 C; Laws 12. 944 A; the horse-race in honour of, Ion 537 A; the lover of Achilles, Symp. 179 E; avenged by Achilles at the price of his life, *ib.* 208 D; cruel vengeance taken by Achilles for, Rep. 3. 391 B; his treatment of the wounded Eurypylus, *ib.* 406 A.

Patrol of the country, Laws 6. 760. *See* Wardens of the Country.

Patronymics used of young children, Lysis 204 E.

Pattern, the heavenly, Rep. 6. 500 E; 7. 540 A; 9. 592 (cp. Laws 5. 739 D);—the patterns of creation, Tim. 38, 48 E;—the two patterns of life, Theaet. 176 E.

Paupers, *see* Poor.

Pausanias, of Cerameis, with Prodicus, Protag. 315 E; wishes to have the drinking easier, Symp. 176 A; his speech in honour of Love, *ib.* 180 C foll.

Payment for teaching, Laches 186 B; Protag. 328 B, 348 E; Crat. 384 B, 391 C; Meno 91 B; Apol. 20 A; Gorg. 519 B, 520 B; Theaet. 167 D; Soph. 223 A, 231 D, 233 B; 1 Alcib. 119 A (cp. Euthyd. 304 A; Rep. 1. 337 D; Laws 7. 804 D);—payment of the Athenian democracy, begun by Pericles, Gorg. 515 E;—the art of payment, Rep. 1. 346;—laws concerning payment, Laws 11. 921.

Peace, too great love of, injurious, Statesm. 307 E; only a name among men, Laws 1. 626 A; better than war, *ib.* 628, 629; 7. 803 E; 8. 829 A; life of peace, *ib.* 7. 803 E; 8. 829 A; dances of peace, *ib.* 7. 815, 816; peace secured by preparation for war, *ib.* 8. 829; not to be made without the authority of the state, *ib.* 12. 955 B; peace and war, the chief subject of the politician's knowledge, 1 Alcib. 107 E foll. (cp. Statesm. 304 E).

Pegasi (winged steeds), Phaedr. 229 D.

Peirithous, son of Zeus, the tale of, not to be repeated, Rep. 3. 391 D.

Peleus, the gentlest of men, Rep. 3. 391 C; nuptial gift of arms to, Laws 12. 944 A.

Pelias, father of Alcestis, Symp. 179 B.

Pelopidae, Rep. 2. 380 A; Menex. 245 D; Pelopidae and Heraclidae, Laws 3. 685 D.

Peloponnesus, Laws 3. 685 B:—Peloponnesians, their jealousy of the Athenians, Menex. 235 D.

Pelops, his name, Crat. 395 C; descendants of, *see* Pelopidae.

Penalties, exaction of, Laws 9. 855.

Penelope's web, Phaedo 84 A; her suitors, 1 Alcib. 112 B (cp. Ion. 535 B).

Penestae, Laws 6. 776 D.

Pentelicus, marble of, Eryx. 394 E.

People, the, in ancient Attica were, not the masters, but the servants of the law, Laws 3. 700 A; ought to have a share in the administration of justice, *ib.* 6. 768 B. Cp. Many, Multitude.

Peparethians, the 'ignoble,' 1 Alcib. 116 D.

Perception (αἴσθησις), Phaedo 65, 79; Rep. 6. 508 foll.; Theaet. 151 foll.; Phil. 33 D, 38, 39; contradictions of, Theaet. 154; theory of motion in relation to, *ib.* 156; may be false, *ib.* 157 E; relativity of, *ib.* 159, 160; perception and understanding, *ib.* 160; perception and the memory of perception, *ib.* 163, 166, 191 B; Heraclitean theory of, *ib.* 182 (cp. 160); perception and knowledge, *ib.* 151 foll., 163 foll., 165, 179, 184, 192 foll.; organs of perception, *ib.* 184, 185; perception of universals, *ib.* 185; medium of, *ibid.* Cp. Pleasure, Sensation.

Perdiccas, father of Archelaus, Gorg. 470 D (cp. 471 A, B); Rep. 1. 336 A.

Perfect state, difficulty of, Rep. 5. 472; 6. 502 E; Laws 4. 711; possible, Rep. 5. 471, 473; 6. 499; 7. 540 (cp. *ib.* 7. 520; Laws 4. 711 E; 5. 739; 12. 968 A); manner of its decline, Rep. 8. 546 (cp. Crit. 120, 121). *See* Ideal state.

Perfection, given partly by nature, partly by art, Phaedr. 269 D, E.

Perfumes, Tim. 65 A; not to be imported, Laws 8. 847 C.

Pergama, the citadel of Troy, Phaedr. 243 B.

Periander, the tyrant, Rep. 1. 336 A.

Pericles, Protag. 329 A: guardian of Alcibiades and Cleinias, *ib.* 320 A; 1 Alcib. 104 B; 2 Alcib. 144 A; what he would have said about rhetoric, Phaedr. 269 A; learned philosophy from Anaxagoras, *ib.* 270 cp. 1 Alcib. 118 C, D); not equal to Socrates as an orator, Symp. 215 E; compared to Nestor and Antenor, *ib.* 221 C; 'magnificent in his wisdom,' Meno 94 A; long walls partly built by his counsel, Gorg. 455 E; his family, *ib.* 472 B; mentioned as 'lately dead,' *ib.* 503 C; a good man in common estimation, *ibid.*; first to give the people pay, *ib.* 515 D, E; effect of his administration, *ibid.*; convicted of theft, *ib.* 516 A; his badness, *ibid.*; one of the real authors of the calamities of Athens, *ib.* 519 A; Pericles and Aspasia, Menex. 235 E; his funeral oration, *ib.* 236 B;—the sons of, Protag. 314 E; inferior to their father, *ib.* 320 A, 328 C; Meno 94 B; 1 Alcib. 118 E.

Perjury, Laws 11. 916 E, 937; 12. 943 E, 948,

949; perjuries of lovers, Symp. 183 A; Phil. 65 C.

Persephone, sends souls back to the light in the ninth year, Meno 81 C; meaning of the name, Crat. 404 C; daughter of Demeter, Laws 6. 782 B.

Perseus, ancestor of the Achaemenids, 1 Alcib. 120 E.

Persia, a rugged land, Laws 3. 695 A:— Persian fabrics, Hipp. Min. 368 D;—Persian government, Laws 3. 694 A foll., 697 C;—Persian kings, *ib.* 694; represent the highest form of monarchy, *ib.* 693 D; their education, *ib.* 694 foll.; 1 Alcib. 121 D foll.; Persian invasion, Laws 3. 692 C foll., 698 B foll.; 4. 707 B, C; Menex. 239; prophecies concerning, Laws 1. 642 D, E;—history of the Persians, Menex. 239 D foll. (cp. Laws 3. 694 A foll.);—Persians at the battle of Plataea, Laches 191 C; their reputation as sailors destroyed by the battle of Salamis, Menex. 241 B; their policy towards subject nations, Laws 3. 693 A;—moderate drinkers, *ib.* 1. 637 D; their luxury, *ib.* E; 1 Alcib. 122 C; are shepherds, Laws 3. 695 A.

Personal identity, Symp. 207 D; Theaet. 154.

Personalities, avoided by the philosopher, Rep. 6. 500 B; Theaet. 174 C.

Personification: the argument, like a bird which slips from our grasp, Euthyd. 291 B; like a horse, must be given the rein, Protag. 338 A; must be pulled up, Laws 3. 701 C:—compared to a troublesome road, Lysis 213 E; to an ocean of words, Protag. 338 A; Parm. 137 A (cp. Phaedr. 264 A; Rep. 4. 441 B; 5. 453 D); to a physician, Gorg. 475 D; to a search or chase, Rep. 2. 368 C; 4. 427 C, 432 (cp. Lysis 218 C; Laches 194 B; Tim. 64 B; Soph. 235; Phil. 65 A; Laws 2. 654 E); to a game of draughts, Rep. 6. 487 B (cp. Laws 7. 820 C; Eryx. 395 A); to a journey, Rep. 7. 532 E; to a charm, *ib.* 10. 608 A; to a river which has to be forded, Laws 10. 892 E, 900 B; to a vesture, 1 Alcib. 113 E:—says 'No' to us, Charm. 175 C; supposed to take a human voice, Protag. 361 A (cp. Phaedr. 274 A; Phaedo 87 A); addresses an oration to us, Laws 5. 741 A:—like to die, Phaedo 89 B; gives way to an attack, *ib.* 95 B; must not wander about without a head, Gorg. 505 D (cp. Laws 6. 752 A); 'has travelled a long way,' Rep. 6. 484 A; veils her face, *ib.* 503 A; a servant who waits our leisure, Theaet. 173 C (cp. Laws 6. 781 E); in danger of being drowned by digressions, Theaet. 177 C; should not be allowed to trample us under foot, *ib.* 191 A; likely to

be blown away, Phil. 13 C; to suffer shipwreck, *ib.* 14 A; strikes a deadly blow, *ib.* 23 A (cp. Euthyd. 303 A; Phaedo 89 A); has to be wrestled with, Phil. 41 B (cp. Soph. 241 D); is in play, Phil. 53 E:—'we are tossing on the waves of the argument,' Laches 194 C; the three waves, Rep. 5. 457 C, 472 A, 473 C (cp. Euthyd. 293 A):— 'following the footsteps of the argument,' Rep. 2. 365 C:—'whither the argument may blow, thither we go,' *ib.* 3. 394 D (cp. Laws 2. 667 A):—'a swarm of words,' Rep. 5. 450 B:—the argument presents to us another handle, Laws 3. 682 E:—the taste of the argument, 1 Alcib. 114 B:—new arguments appear as witnesses, Phaedr. 260 E; come crowding in like unbidden guests, Theaet. 184 A:—arguments from probabilities, apt to be impostors, Phaedo 92 D.

Persuasion, comes from opinion, not truth, Phaedr. 260; produced by the art of rhetoric, Gorg. 453 E; Theaet. 201 A; Statesm. 304 C; two kinds of, Gorg. 454; the art of, Soph. 222 C; Phil. 58 A; persuasion and force, the two instruments of the legislator, Laws 4. 719 E, 722 (cp. 10. 885 D); the power of persuasion given by knowledge, 1 Alcib. 114:—persuasion [or faith] one of the faculties of the soul, Rep. 6. 511 D; 7. 533 E.

Pestilence, a cause of revolution, Laws 4. 709 A.

Phaedo, narrates the *Phaedo* to Echecrates of Phlius, Phaedo 57 A foll.; present at Socrates' death, *ib.* 57 A, 117 D; Socrates plays with his hair, *ib.* 89 B; Phaedo and Simmias, *ib.* 102 B.

Phaedondes, present at the death of Socrates, Phaedo 59 C.

Phaedrus, the Myrrhinusian, Protag. 315 C; Symp. 176 D; Phaedr. 244 A; with Hippias, Protag. 315 C; his eagerness, Phaedr. 228 A, B, 236 D, E; a lover of discourse, *ib.* 228, 242 A, 243 D, 258 E, 276 E; son of Vain Man, *ib.* 244 A; a 'weak head,' Symp. 176 D; complains that love has no encomiast, *ib.* 177 A; his speech in honour of love, *ib.* 178 A foll.

Phaenaretè, mother of Socrates, 1 Alcib. 131 E; a midwife, Theaet. 149 A.

Phaethon, story of, Tim. 22 C.

Phalerum, Apollodorus of, Symp. 172 A.

Phanosthenes of Andros, a foreigner, chosen general by the Athenians, Ion 541 C.

Phantastic art, Soph. 236, 260 E, 265; divisions of, *ib.* 266, 267.

Pharmacia and Orithyia, Phaedr. 229 C.

Phasis, eastern extremity of the Hellenic world, Phaedo 109 B.

us to understand. *A large part of elementary education consisted in learning poetry by heart* (Protag. 326 A; Laws 7. 810 C); *the rhapsode moved the crowds to laughter and tears at the festivals* (Ion 535); *the theatres were free, or almost free, to all, 'costing but a drachma at the most'* (Apol. 26 D); *the intervals at a banquet were filled up by conversation about the poets* (Protag. 347 C). *The ancient philosopher, therefore, who proposed to construct an ideal state was obliged to consider whether the poet could be allowed to practise his art without any restrictions in a city which was designed to be 'an imitation of the best and noblest life'* (Laws 7. 817 A). *But there was 'an ancient quarrel between philosophy and poetry,' which had found its first expression in the attacks of Xenophanes* (538 B.C.) *and Heracleitus* (508 B.C.) *upon the popular mythology. And Plato, though he had himself a double portion of the poetic spirit, fully shares in this hostile feeling. Even in the earlier dialogues there is often an antagonism to the poets which is only slightly veiled by the ironical courtesy of the language. They are 'winged and holy beings'* (Ion 534 B), *who sing by inspiration without knowing the meaning of what they utter, 'for not by art can a man enter into the temple of the Muses'* (Phaedr. 245 A); *but at the same time they are the worst possible critics of their own writings and the most self-conceited of mortals* (Apol. 22 D).—*In the Republic* (II. and III.) *Plato grows more in earnest and brings poetry to a formal trial. Are the tales and legends, he asks, which the tragic and epic poets relate, either true in themselves or likely to furnish good examples to the citizens of the model state? They cannot be true for they are contrary to the nature of God* (see s. v. God), *and they are certainly not proper lessons for youth. There must be a censorship of poetry, and all objectionable passages expunged; suitable rules and regulations will be laid down, and to these the poets must conform. In the Tenth Book the argument takes a still deeper tone. The poet is proved to be an impostor thrice removed from the truth; a wizard who steals the hearts of the unwary by his spells and enchantments. Men easily fall into the habit of imitating what they admire, and the lamentations and woes of the tragic hero and the unseemly buffoonery of the comedian are equally bad models for the citizens of a free and noble state. The poets must therefore be banished, unless, Plato adds, the lovers of poetry can persuade us of her innocence of the charges laid against her.—In the Laws the subject is treated more shortly, but a similar conclusion is reached. The poet is the rival of the legislator, who is striving to set the noblest of dramas in action* (cp. Tim. 19 A); *and he cannot be allowed to address the citizens in a manner which is not in accord with the institutions of the state. The magistrates must maintain a censorship of poetry, and see that the injunctions of the legislator are obeyed. Nor must any poet be licensed by them unless he be a man of years and good repute, and he must only sing of noble thoughts and deeds: it will not matter if his strains are a little inharmonious. (The expulsion of the poets from Plato's commonwealth is not mentioned by Aristotle in the Politics. He may have thought that such a topic was one of the 'digressions' of which he complains* (ii. 6, § 3); *or the omission may be due to the fragmentary nature of his observations on education.*)]

Poets, the, quoted on friendship, Lysis 212; fathers and authors of wisdom, *ib.* 214 A; their works learnt in schools, Protag. 326 A; Laws 7. 810 C, 811 A; talk about, commonplace, Protag. 347 C; sing by inspiration, Phaedr. 245 A, 265 B; Ion 534; Apol. 22 A; Laws 3. 682 A; 4. 719 B (cp. Meno 81 A, 99 D); first in the chain of persons who derive inspiration from the Muses, Ion 533 E, 535 E; winged and holy, *ib.* 534; various kinds of, *ibid.*; each good in his own kind only, *ibid.*; how distinguished from other makers, Symp. 205; create conceptions of wisdom and virtue, *ib.* 209 A; their children (i.e. works), *ib.* C (cp. Rep. 1. 330 C); bear witness to the immortality of the soul, Meno 81; not wise, Apol. 22; speak in parables, Rep. 1. 332 B (cp. 3. 413 B; 2 Alcib. 147 C); on justice, Rep. 2. 363, 364, 365 E; bad teachers of youth, *ib.* 377; 3. 391, 392, 408 C; 10. 600, 606 E, 607 B; Laws 10. 886 C, 890 A; 12. 941 B; must be restrained by certain rules, Rep. 2. 379 foll.; 3. 398 A (cp. Laws 2. 656, 660 A; 4. 719; 7. 817 D; 8. 829 D; 11. 936 A); banished from the state, Rep. 3. 398 A; 8. 568 B; 10. 595 foll., 605 A, 607 A (cp. Laws 7. 817); poets and tyrants, Rep. 8. 568; thrice removed from the truth, *ib.* 10. 596, 597, 598 E, 602 B, 605 C; imitators only, *ib.* 600 E; Tim. 19 (cp. Rep. 3. 393; Laws 4. 719 C); poets and painters, Rep. 10. 601, 603, 605; ought to be controlled by law, Laws 2. 656, 660, 661 C, 662 B; 4. 719 A; 7. 801, 802, 811, 817; 8. 829 D; degraded by the applause of the theatre, *ib.* 2. 659; their corrupt use of music, *ib.* 669, 670 E; 3. 700; need not know whether their imitations are good or not, *ib.* 2. 670 E; 4. 719 C; often attain truth, *ib.* 3. 682 A; when they make prayer for the state, must be careful that

Soul. [*The psychology of Plato, like the rest of his philosophical teaching, is not to be regarded as a formal system to which he always adhered. The progress of thought in his mind is reflected in the Dialogues, while their dramatic form and tentative character cause some difficulty in distinguishing the opinions which he himself would have maintained. Allowing for this element of uncertainty, his conclusions may be summed up as follows:— (1) The soul is prior to the body, both in creation and in order of thought, although in our 'random way of talking' we sometimes invert the relation between them* (Tim. 34 E). *The body is intended by nature to be its servant, and to listen to its commands and admonitions. It is immaterial, not made, 'as the physical philosophers say,' after the four elements and by their aid* (Laws 10. 891); *and, being akin to the divine, it is ever desirous to escape from the body in which it is 'encaged' or 'entombed,' and to go to its home with God.*—(2) *'There are two souls,' Plato says in the Laws, 'a good and an evil.' Such a dualism is not found elsewhere in his writings, and it is not easy to apprehend his precise meaning. But he probably wishes in this manner to account for the existence of evil in the world, just as in the Timaeus he explains the wickedness of man by the hypothesis of a 'mortal soul' which is the work of*

*the inferior Gods, and in which the passions
and desires have their seat* (see s. v. God).—
(3) The division of the soul into three elements, reason, spirit, appetite, is first clearly
stated in the Republic, where it is made the
means of classifying the different forms of
government. Virtue is the harmony or accord
of these elements, when the dictates of reason
are enforced by passion against the appetites,
while vice is the anarchy or discord of the soul
when passion and appetite join in rebellion
against reason.—(4) Regarded from the intellectual side the soul may be analyzed into
four faculties, reason, understanding, faith,
knowledge of shadows. They correspond to
the four divisions of knowledge, two for intellect and two for opinion; and thus arises
the Platonic 'proportion,' being : becoming : :
intellect : opinion, and science : belief : : understanding : knowledge of shadows. These
divisions are partly real, partly formed by
a logical process, which, as in so many distinctions of ancient philosophers, has outrun
fact, and are further explained by the allegory
of the cave (Rep. Book vii).—(5) The pre-
existence of the soul is especially dwelt upon
in the Meno, Phaedo, and Phaedrus, in the
two former of which the 'remembrance of a
previous existence' (ἀνάμνησις) is made a
proof of immortality (Meno 86; Phaedo 73).
It is apparently alluded to in the myth of Er
(Rep. 10. 621 A), where we are told that 'the
pilgrims drank the waters of Unmindfulness;
the foolish took too deep a draught, but the
wise were more moderate.' In the later dialogues it is nowhere mentioned.—(6) The immortality of the soul is chiefly discussed in
the Phaedo and the Republic, but it occupies
a considerable place in many of Plato's other
writings. In the Phaedo the two Thebans,
Simmias and Cebes, admit that the soul has
pre-existence, but doubt that it is immortal.
Simmias affirms that the soul and the body
are related as the harmony is to the lyre: the
harmony is invisible and incorporeal, yet it
does not survive the lyre, which is visible and
corporeal. Cebes fears that the soul, although
she may outlive many bodies, may be worn
out in the end, like a garment, which, after
belonging to many owners, at last perishes
and decays. Socrates denies the assumption
that the soul is a harmony: for (1) it is a
cause, not an effect: (2) it leads the body, but
harmony follows the instrument: (3) it does
not admit of degrees: (4) it allows of discord,
as when reason is arrayed against passion.
Against Cebes he urges the doctrine of the
exclusion of opposites. Life, which is the
essential attribute of the soul, excludes death,
and therefore death cannot be predicated of*

*the soul.—In the Republic (10. 608), Glaucon
hears with amazement Socrates' confident
belief in immortality, although a previous
allusion to another state of existence has
fallen unheeded (6. 498 D); and in earlier
parts of the discussion (e.g. 2. 362; 3. 386)
the censure which is passed on the common
representations of Hades implies in itself
some belief in a future life. The argument by
which Socrates seeks to prove the immortality
of the soul is of a purely verbal character:—
All things which perish are destroyed by some
inherent evil, but the soul is not destroyed by
sin, which is the evil proper to her, and must
therefore be immortal.—In the Phaedrus and
the Laws the soul is said to be self-moved and
a cause of motion; and upon this assertion
the proof of immortality is made to rest. But
there is a curious passage in the Laws (10.
904 B), which is not apparently in accord
with the opinions which Plato elsewhere
maintains. 'The King [i.e. the Creator] . . .
saw that the soul and body, although not, like
the Gods whom the laws recognize, eternal,
were indestructible; for if either of them had
been destroyed, there would have been no generation of living beings.'—(7) The condition
of the soul after death is described by Plato
in several dialogues under the form of myths,
for which he is careful not to demand entire
credence. These representations agree in their
main features. The soul on her release from
the body goes to give account of herself before
the judgment seat. The righteous are sent to
the Isles of the Blessed; the wicked go to
Tartarus, and there suffer punishment, not
hopeless or eternal, but duly proportioned to
their offences. (In the Phaedo (113 E) and
the Gorgias (525), however, a few great sinners, chiefly kings and potentates, are kept
in Hades as a salutary terror to others.)
When the penalty has been paid, the soul
must choose a new life: the responsibility of
choice rests on herself, and if she has learnt
wisdom in her travail she secures a better lot;
but if she persists in folly and chooses un-
wisely, she takes an inferior life or even assumes the form of some lower animal. There
is also a limit to the blessedness of the righteous, and when the appointed time comes,
they too must make a new choice. This at
least is Plato's usual statement (cp. Phaedr.
249; Rep. 10. 619 C); but in the Phaedo,
Socrates, who is so soon to die, consoles himself with the thought that the soul of the philosopher will live after death 'altogether without the body' (114 C).—(8) The doctrine of
the transmigration of souls was probably
adopted by Plato because it agreed, or could
be made to agree, with the conviction which*

State. [*Plato has left us in the Republic and the Laws two companion pictures of the 'best' and the 'second-best' state. The one is confessedly an ideal, which will only be accepted, if ever, when men see the true philosopher ruling the state in righteousness and justice: the other is supposed to be more adapted to ordinary circumstances, and might be set up without any considerable difficulty by a benevolent tyrant or a legislator who had despotic power.—*[I.]* The polity of which Plato 'sketches the outline' in the Republic may be analyzed into two principal elements:—*(i) an Hellenic state of the older or Spartan type, with some traits borrowed from Athens; (ii) an ideal city in which the citizens have all things in common, and the government is carried on by a class of philosopher rulers who are selected by merit. These two elements are not perfectly combined; and, as Aristotle complains (Pol. ii. 5, § 18), very much is left ill-defined and uncertain.—(i) Like Hellenic cities in general, the number of the citizens is not to be great. The size of the state is limited by the requirement that 'it shall not be larger or smaller than is consistent with unity.' Again, the individual is subordinate to the state. When Adeimantus complains of the hard life which the citizens will lead, 'like mercenaries in a garrison' (4. 419), he is answered by Socrates that if the happiness of the whole is secured, the happiness of the parts will inevitably follow. Once more, war is conceived to be the normal condition of the state, and military service is imposed upon all. Trade is regarded as dishonourable;—'those who are good for nothing else sit in the Agora buying and selling' (2. 371 D): the warrior can spare no time for such an employment.—In these respects, as well as in the introduction of common meals,*

Plato was probably influenced by the traditional ideal of Sparta. The Athenian element appears in the intellectual training of the citizens, and generally in the atmosphere of grace and refinement which they are to breathe (see s. v. Art). The restless energy of the Athenian character is perhaps reflected in the discipline imposed upon the ruling class, who when they have reached fifty are dispensed from continual public service, but must then devote themselves to abstract study, and also be willing to take their turn when necessary at the helm of state [*cp.* Thucyd. i. 70; ii. 40].—(ii.) The most peculiar features of Plato's state are (1) the community of property, (2) the position of women, (3) the government of philosophers. The first (see s. v.), though suggested in some measure by the example of Sparta or Crete [*cp.* Arist. Pol. ii. 5, § 6], is not known to have been actually practised anywhere in Hellas, unless possibly among such a body as the Pythagorean brotherhood. (2) Nothing in all the Republic was probably stranger to the contemporaries of Plato than the place assigned by him to women in the state. The community of wives and children, though carefully guarded by him from the charge of licentiousness, would appear worse in Athenian eyes than the traditional 'licence' of the Spartan women [*cp.* Arist. Pol. ii. 9, § 5]. Again, the equal share in education, in war, and in administration which is enjoyed by the women in Plato's state was, if not so revolting, quite as contrary to common Hellenic sentiment [*cp.* Thucyd. ii. 45]. The Spartan women exercised a great influence on public affairs, but this was mainly indirect [*cp.* Laws 7. 806; Arist. Pol. ii. 9, § 8]: they did not hold office or learn the use of arms. At Athens the women, of the upper classes at least, lived in an almost Oriental seclusion, and were wholly absorbed in household duties. (3) Finally, the government of philosophers had no analogy in the Hellenic world of Plato's time. The suggestion may have been taken from the stories of the Pythagorean rule in Magna Graecia; but we cannot doubt that Plato was chiefly indebted to his own imagination for his kingdom of philosophers, or that it remained to himself an ideal, rather than a state which would ever 'play her part in actual life' (Tim. 19, 20). It is at least significant that he never finished the Critias, as though he were unable to embody, even in a mythical form, the 'city of which the pattern is laid up in heaven.'—[II.] The state which is portrayed in the Laws is said by Aristotle to be 'a mixture of oligarchy and democracy, leaning rather to oligarchy' (Pol. ii. 6, § 18).

The description is an inaccurate one; for the only democratic characteristic which Aristotle mentions is the use of the lot in elections, and this, he himself admits, is neutralized by other regulations. Plato's 'second-best state' is in fact an aristocratical government of a narrow and exclusive type, in which wealth plays an important part. The administration is in the hands of the higher classes, and the mode of election is so contrived that they always have a preponderance. The chief magistrates are the thirty-seven guardians of the law, who combine executive and judicial functions in the manner common to Hellenic states. There is also a nocturnal council, composed of the ten oldest guardians, of all those who have gained the prize of virtue, of the Director and the ex-Directors of Education, and of those who have travelled to see the institutions of other countries, besides an equal number of younger colleagues between thirty and forty, appointed, one by each of the seniors. This council seems only to exercise powers of advice and revision, and not to have the initiative in legislation, which was probably intended to be restricted to the guardians. Further, there is a Senate of 360 members, of which a twelfth part sits each month in succession, and a General Assembly. Of the latter very little is said, but we cannot suppose that Plato intended it to have much authority.—The greatest departure from the ideal state is the abandonment of communism, which, as Plato reluctantly confesses, will hardly be accepted by mankind in general (see s. v. Community). On the other hand, the common meals are extended to women, who are thus brought from the retirement of domestic life into the organization of the state.—In two points there is an advance on the Republic:—(i) Plato has discovered that peace is nobler thån war, and passes a severe censure on the military states of which Sparta is the typical example. Yet he has himself given a warlike character to the whole commonwealth, and the 5040 citizens would have formed with their wives an armed force such as was hardly possessed by Sparta at the time of her greatest power. (ii) Although in an earlier part of the work (4. 705 A) Plato repeats the old idea that trade exerts a corrupting influence on men and cities, he exhibits towards the end a more liberal spirit (11. 918). He recognizes the necessity of commerce, and even speculates on the possibility of redeeming trade from reproach by compelling some of the best citizens to open a shop or keep a tavern. [*Cp.* the discussion of the question by Aristotle, Pol. vii. 6.]— In most respects, however, Plato's political

and speech, Soph. 263; the only expression of immaterial things, Statesm. 286 A.

Thracians, their procession in honour of Bendis, Rep. 1. 327 A; characterized by spirit or passion, *ib*. 4. 435 E; drink unmixed wine, Laws 1. 637 D, E; employ their women to till the ground, etc., *ib*. 7. 805 D;—the Thracian Zamolxis, Charm. 156 D, E (cp. 175 E);—the Thracian handmaid and Thales, Theaet. 174 A, C, 175 D;—Zopyrus the Thracian, tutor of Alcibiades, 1 Alcib. 122 B;—the Thracian Boreas, Laws 2. 661 A (cp. Phaedr. 229).

Thrasymachus, the Chalcedonian, Phaedr. 267 E; a person in the *Republic*, Rep. 1. 328 B; breaks in on the discussion, *ib*. 336 B; will be paid, *ib*. 337 D; defines justice, *ib*. 338 C foll.; his rudeness, *ib*. 343 A; his views of government, *ibid*. (cp. 9. 590 D); his encomium on injustice, *ib*. 1. 343 A; his manner of speech, *ib*. 345 B; his paradox about justice and injustice, *ib*. 348 B foll.; he blushes, *ib*. 350 D; is pacified and retires from the argument, *ib*. 354 (cp. 6. 498 C); would have Socrates discuss the subject of women and children, *ib*. 5. 450 A;—his rhetoric, Phaedr. 261 C, 269 E, 271 A.

Thucydides, the Athenian statesman, Laches 178; Meno 94 C; his sons, Laches 179; Meno 94 C.

Thucydides, the younger, Laches 179 A.

Thunderbolts, Tim. 80 C; Laws 9. 873 E.

Thurii, Euthyd. 271 C, 283 E, 288 A;—Thurian youth degrade love, Laws 1. 636 B.

Thyestes, cruelty of Atreus to, Crat. 395 B; Thyestes and the golden lamb, Statesm. 268 E; Thyestes on the stage, Laws 8. 838 C.

Timaeus, the principal speaker in the dialogue *Timaeus*, 17 A foll.; begins his discourse, 27 C; prayer of, Crit. 106 A, B.

Timber, formerly abundant in Attica, Crit. 111 C; required in shipbuilding, Laws 4. 705 C.

Time, created, Tim. 37-39; expressions of time, Parm. 141, 152 B; time and the one, *ibid*., *ibid*. (*see* One); changes brought about by time, Laws 3. 676;—prescription of time (legal), *ib*. 12. 954 C.

Timocracy, Rep. 8. 545 foll.; origin of, *ib*. 547:—the timocratical man described, *ib*. 549; his origin, *ibid*.

Tinker, the prosperous, Rep. 6. 495, 496.

Tiring, art of, Gorg. 463 B.

Tisander, of Aphidnae, a student of philosophy, Gorg. 487 C.

Tisias, aware that probability is superior to truth, Phaedr. 267 A; his definition of probability, *ib*. 273 A foll.

Titanic nature, the old, Laws 3. 701 C.

Tityus, suffers punishment in Tartarus, Gorg. 525 E.

Topography of Athens, Charm. 153; Lysis 203; Phaedr. 227, 229. Cp. Athens.

Tops, Rep. 4. 436

Torch race, an equestrian, Rep. 1. 328 A.

Torpedo fish, Socrates compared to a, Meno 80 A.

Touch, Rep. 7. 523 E.

Touchstones, Gorg. 486 E.

Tournaments, Laws 8. 829 B.

Trade, one of the acquisitive arts, Soph. 219; divisions of, Statesm. 260 C:—injurious effects of, Laws 4. 705 A; 5. 741 E, 743 D; no one to profess two trades, *ib*. 8. 846 D.

Traders, praise their goods in order to deceive customers, Protag. 313 D; necessary in the state, Rep. 2. 371; Laws 11. 918 (*but* cp. Laws 4. 705 A).

Tradition, power of, Laws 8. 838; 11. 913; the ancient tradition about the slayer of kindred, *ib*. 9. 870 D, 872 E; tradition of deluges, *ib*. 3. 677, 702 A (cp. Tim. 22; Crit. 109, 111 B, 112 A);—traditions of ancient times, their truth not certainly known to us, Phaedr. 274 C; Rep. 2. 382 C; 3. 414 C; Tim. 40 D; Crit. 107; Statesm. 271 A; Laws 4. 713 E; 6. 782 D; 11. 927 A; ancient traditions about the world below despised by the wicked, Laws 10. 881 A.

Tragedy, = the goat song, Crat. 408 C; seeks pleasure only, Gorg. 502 A; produces a mingled feeling of pleasure and pain, Phil. 48 A; the favourite entertainment of most persons, Laws 2. 658:—tragedy and comedy the same as to genius, Symp. 223 (*but* cp. Ion 534);—tragedy and comedy in the state, Rep. 3. 394 (cp. Laws 7. 817).

Tragic poets, the, fond of having recourse to a 'Deus ex Machinâ,' Crat. 425 E; eulogizers of tyranny, Rep. 8. 568 A; imitators, *ib*. 10. 597, 598; their representations of Oedipus, etc., Laws 8. 838 D. Cp. Poets.

Training, of body and soul, Gorg. 513 D;—dangers of training, Rep. 3. 404 A; not so severe a test as intense study, *ib*. 7. 535 B; the same amount prescribed for all the pupils in the gymnasia, Statesm. 294 D; at first injurious, Laws 1. 646 D; conducive to temperance, *ib*. 8. 839 E;—training of boxers, *ib*. 830;—training for the games, Rep. 6. 504 A; Laws 7. 807 C; 8. 840 A.

Transfer of children from one class in the state to another, Rep. 3. 415; 4. 423 D.

Transmigration of souls, Phaedr. 248, 249; Meno 81 foll.; Phaedo 70, 81; Rep. 10. 617; Tim. 42, 91 D foll.; Laws 10. 903 E, 904 E. *See* Soul.

Travel, value of, Laws 12. 950, 951.